Western Civilization

Western Civilization

THE CONTINUING EXPERIMENT

THIRD EDITION

Thomas F. X. Noble
University of Notre Dame

Barry S. Strauss
Cornell University

Duane J. Osheim
University of Virginia

Kristen B. Neuschel
Duke University

William B. Cohen
Indiana University

David D. Roberts
University of Georgia

Houghton Mifflin Company   Boston   New York

Editor-in-Chief: Jean L. Woy
Sponsoring Editor: Nancy Blaine
Senior Development Editor: Jennifer E. Sutherland
Editorial Associate: Gillie Jones
Senior Project Editor: Christina M. Horn
Editorial Assistant: Marie Bernard-Jackson
Senior Designer: Henry Rachlin
Senior Production/Design Coordinator: Sarah Ambrose
Senior Manufacturing Coordinator: Sally Culler
Senior Marketing Manager: Sandra McGuire

Cover image: Meeting between King Frederick III, Holy Roman emperor, and Eleanor of Aragon with the pope. Fresco by Bernardino Pinturicchio (1454–1513). Photograph: Pinacoteca Piccolomini, Siena/Dagli Orti/The Art Archive, London.

Text credits begin on page A-17, which constitutes an extension of the copyright page.

Printed in the U.S.A.

Library of Congress Control Number: 2002100808

ISBN: 0-618-24731-9

1 2 3 4 5 6 7 8 9-WEB-05 04 03 02

BRIEF CONTENTS

CONTENTS

CHAPTER 4

Alexander the Great and the Spread of Greek Civilization, ca. 350–30 B.C.   105

CHAPTER 5

Rome: From Republic to Empire, ca. 509–31 B.C.   137

CHAPTER **9**

The Expansion of Europe in the High Middle Ages, 900–1300   275

CHAPTER **10**

Medieval Civilization at Its Height, 900–1300   317

CHAPTER **11**

Crisis and Recovery in Late Medieval Europe, 1300–1500   355

CHAPTER 12
The Renaissance   393

CHAPTER 13
European Overseas Expansion to 1600   429

CHAPTER 14
The Age of the Reformation   461

CHAPTER 15

Europe in the Age of Religious Wars, 1560–1648   499

CHAPTER 16

Europe in the Age of Louis XIV, ca. 1640–1715   539

CHAPTER 28

The Era of the Second World War, 1939–1949   947

CHAPTER 29

An Anxious Stability: The Age of the Cold War, 1949–1989   985

CHAPTER 30

The West and the World Since 1989   1023

MAPS

DOCUMENTS

WEIGHING THE EVIDENCE

INFORMATION TECHNOLOGY

PREFACE

In the days devoted to writing this preface in February 2001, the British prime minister visited the president of the United States, and the American secretary of state visited the Middle East. American and British aircraft bombed Iraq, and U.S. officials made vigorous representation to the Chinese government about reports that they had furnished the Iraqis with radar technology and components. An American submarine on maneuvers in the Pacific surfaced without due caution and sank a Japanese fishing boat. Taliban militants in Afghanistan destroyed ancient Buddhist statues on the grounds that they offended Islam's strict prohibition of idolatry. The pope named forty-four cardinals from all over the world. With these kinds of subjects in the news in the dawning third millennium, one might well ask: Why study Western Civilization any longer?

For some five thousand years, a Western civilization has been growing, changing, reflecting on itself, and sharing ideas with its neighbors. The West alone is not civilized, of course, for there were ancient civilizations in China, India, and Africa. But the West is uniquely civilized in the sense that its ideas and institutions are distinctive. This is not to imply that the West is better or worse than the other civilizations with which it shares the earth. It is simply to emphasize the persistence of one ancient tradition alongside others. But does antiquity alone constitute a claim on the efforts of teachers and students?

We begin to answer that question by pointing out that everyone alive today has been influenced by Western Civilization. The West deserves to be studied because its tale is old and compelling but *demands* to be studied because its story has been central to the development of the world in which we live. Western institutions—most notably representative democracy and commercial capitalism—have spread to every corner of the world. Even capitalism's greatest rival, communism, is fundamentally Western. Western styles in architecture dominate the skylines of every major city in the world. Western popular culture, from movies and music to fast food, are found absolutely everywhere. Communications technologies, from cell phones to e-mail, are as global in spread as they are Western in origin.

Some people, inside and outside the West, have grave reservations about the extent of Western influence in the modern world. Some critics challenge Western religious, philosophical, political, and economic ideas at their core.

Others have no quarrel with Western ideas but regret that local cultures all over the globe are vanishing before a relentless Western onslaught. Still others wonder why Western achievements in political stability and economic prosperity cannot be more widely shared. In other words, to say that the West is dominant is only to state the obvious, not to insist that such domination is inevitable or desirable. But the sheer, unassailable fact of that domination makes the careful study of the West essential for informed, responsible participation in the modern world.

However ancient Western Civilization may be, and however pervasive its influence, the definition of the term itself is controversial. The "West" is sometimes understood in terms of geography and sometimes in terms of culture. Each understanding invites misunderstanding. For most people today, the "West" means western Europe. And yet western Europe was the heir of the peoples and cultures of antiquity. These included Mesopotamians and Egyptians, who were the ancestors of the West, as well as Greeks, Romans, Jews, and Christians, who were the founders of the West. These peoples all lived around the Mediterranean world, and it was those who came after them, who lived in Europe proper, who built the West. Within Europe, some might take the West to mean Paris, London, Vienna, Berlin, and Rome. Others would include Madrid, Dublin, St. Petersburg, Stockholm, Warsaw, and Budapest. Moreover, through exploration, war, and commerce, the "West" gradually imposed its influence on the whole globe. One thinks immediately of the Westernization of the North and South American continents, but Tokyo and Hong Kong, although undeniably Eastern, are strongly marked by Western influences. In short, the West has never been, and is not now, neatly confined to one area or people.

As a cultural phenomenon, "Western" implies many things: freedom and free, participatory political institutions; economic initiative and opportunity; monotheistic religious faiths; rationalism and ordered thought in the social, political, and philosophical realms; an aesthetic sensibility that aspires to a universal sense of truth and beauty. But westerners have felt free to evoke tradition as their guiding light and also to innovate brilliantly; to accommodate slavery and freedom simultaneously; to esteem original thought and to persecute people who deviate from the norm. "Western" indeed has meant many things in various places at different times.

More than a decade ago, the six authors of *Western Civilization: The Continuing Experiment* set out to create a textbook for a course that informs students about a tradition that has powerfully, although not always positively, affected everyone in the contemporary world. Although each of us found something to admire in all of the existing textbooks, none of us was fully happy with any of them. Convinced of both the inherent interest of Western Civilization and the importance of teaching the subject, we were nevertheless disconcerted by the celebratory tone of some books, which portrayed the West as resting on its laurels instead of creatively facing its future. We were disappointed with books that claimed "balance" but actually stressed a single kind of history. We regretted that so many texts were uneven in their command of recent scholarship. We aimed to address the full range of subjects that a Western Civilization book needs to address and to provide the student reader with interesting, timely material in a book that is handsome to look at—in short, a book that helps the instructor to teach and the student to learn.

In preparing the Third Edition, we profited from the experience of using the book, the advice and criticism of dozens of colleagues, and the reactions of thousands of students. We are pleased that fellow teachers have found our vision and approach to be sound and that students have found our material accessible. In this new edition we have incorporated many changes, but we have not abandoned our approach to the subject, our commitment to its importance (and interest!), and our dedication to the students and teachers who share the adventure of learning the subject.

BASIC APPROACH

Western Civilization is a story. Therefore, we aimed for a strong chronological narrative line. Our experience as teachers tells us that students appreciate this clear but gentle orientation. Our experience tells us, too, that an approach that is broadly chronological will leave instructors plenty of room to adapt our narrative to their preferred organization, or to supplement our narrative with one of their own.

Although we maintain the familiar, large-scale divisions of a Western Civilization book, we also present some innovative adjustments in arrangement. For instance, Chapter 2 treats early Greece together with the whole eastern Mediterranean region in the period from about 1500 to 750 B.C. This approach links kindred cultures and respects chronological flow better than customary treatments, which take western Asia to a certain point and then backtrack to deal with early Greece. We present a single chapter on Late Antiquity, the tumultuous and fascinating period from A.D. 284 to 600 that witnessed the transformation of the Roman Empire into three successors: Byzantine, Islamic, and European. One chapter studies those three successors, thereby permitting careful comparisons. But we do assign chapters to some of the greatest issues in Western Civilization, such as the Renaissance, the age of European exploration and conquest, the Scientific Revolution, and the industrial transformation. Our twentieth-century chapters reflect an understanding of the last century formed in its closing years rather than in its middle decades. What is new in our organization represents adjustments grounded in the best scholarship, and what is old represents time-tested approaches.

In fashioning our picture of the West, we take two unusual steps. First, our West is bigger than the one found in most textbooks. We treat the Celtic world, Scandinavia, and the Slavic world as integral parts of the story. We look often at the lands that border the West—Anatolia/Turkey, western Asia, North Africa, the Eurasian steppes—in order to show the to-and-fro of peoples, ideas, technologies, and products.

Second, we continually situate the West in its global context. This is not a world history book. But just as we recognize that the West has influenced the rest of the world, so too we carefully acknowledge how the rest of the world has influenced the West. Silks and spices, algebra and pointed arches, poetic forms and religious ideas have all entered the West from Asia and Africa and left deep marks. We begin this story of mutual interaction with the Greeks and Romans, carry it through the European Middle Ages, focus on it in the age of European exploration and conquest, and analyze it closely in the modern world of industry, diplomacy, empire, and immigration.

Another approach that runs like a ribbon throughout this textbook involves balance and integration. Teachers and students, just like the authors of this book, have their particular interests and emphases. In the large and diverse American academy, that is as it should be. But a textbook, if it is to be helpful and useful, should incorporate as many interests and emphases as possible. For a long time, some said, Western Civilization books devoted excessive coverage to high politics—"the public deeds of great men," as an ancient Greek writer defined the historian's subject. Others felt that high culture—all the Aristotles and Mozarts—were included to the exclusion of supposedly lesser figures and ordinary men and women. In the 1970s books began to emphasize social history. Many applauded this new emphasis even as they debated fiercely what to include under this heading. We capture the Western tradition in its full contours, listening to the voices of all of those who have made durable contributions. Naturally, we have had to make choices about how and where to array key topics within our narrative. We have used two basic rules to guide our writing.

First, we deal with topics when they were historically significant, when they commanded a great deal of attention in the historical past, or when modern historians have been able to discover a lot of information about them. Our approach to the history of women is an instructive example. A glance at this book's table of contents and then at its index is revealing. The former reveals very few sections devoted explicitly and exclusively to women. The latter shows that women appear constantly in every section of this book. Is there a contradiction here? Not at all. Women have not experienced history in complete separation from men. We do not assume that Western Civilization is a male or a female story. But we do recognize that men have been seen as the dominant historical actors, and so, again and again, we turn to *gender* as a tool of historical analysis. This permits us to ask why, in certain political, economic, or social circumstances, either men or women were assigned or denied roles or opportunities.

Second, we have tried to be integrative. For example, when we talk about power we present the institutional structures through which power was exercised, the people who possessed power as well as the people who did not, the ideological foundations for the use of power, and the material conditions that fostered or hindered the truly or the would-be powerful. Similarly, when we talk of great ideas we describe the antecedent ideas from which seemingly new ones were built up, and we ask about the consequences of those ideas. We explore the social position of the authors of those ideas to see if this helps explain the ideas themselves or to gauge their influence. We try to understand how ideas in one field of human endeavor proved to be influential in other fields.

We invite the reader to look at our narrative as if it were a mosaic. Taken as a whole, our narrative, like a mosaic, contains a coherent picture. Viewed more closely, our narrative, like a mosaic, is made up of countless tiny bits that may have their individual interest but that do not even hint at the larger picture. Finally, just as the viewer of a mosaic may find his or her eye drawn especially to one area, feature, color, or style, so too the reader of this book will find some parts more engaging or

compelling than others. But it is only because there is, in this book as in a mosaic, a complete picture that the individual sections make sense, command our attention, excite our interest.

We ask, finally, that you note the subtitle of the book: "The Continuing Experiment." It was carefully chosen to convey our resolve to avoid a deterministic approach. For students and teachers, an appreciation of continuity and change, of unity and diversity, can foster sympathetic participation in our often bewildering world. We try to give individual actors, moments, and movements the sense of drama, possibility, and contingency that they actually possessed. We, with faultless hindsight, always know how things came out. Contemporaries often hadn't a clue. We respect them. Much of the fascination, and the reward, of studying Western Civilization lies precisely in its richness, diversity, changeability, and unpredictability. Moreover, and just as important, the experiment continues.

CHANGES IN THE THIRD EDITION

In preparing our Third Edition, we thought hard about our own experiences in using the book and we paid close attention to the advice given us by many instructors, both those who had used the book and those who had not. The authors of this book have always been attentive to how we organized its contents. But just as our understanding of great historical issues is not static, so too our thinking on the matter of how to present this history undergoes constant revision.

■ New Organization and Content

For this edition the most dramatic organizational changes will be found in the sections dealing with the Middle Ages, the nineteenth century, and the twentieth century. Chapters 9 and 10, on the period from 900 to 1300, have been completely reorganized and heavily rewritten. In the first two editions, each of these chapters was comprehensive in thematic coverage, and they split the period at the year 1150. In the Third Edition, each chapter treats the whole period from 900 to 1300. Chapter 9 covers economic and political history and includes the Crusades. Chapter 10 covers social, religious, and cultural developments.

Chapters 20 and 21 have been reversed. By presenting "The Industrial Transformation of Europe, 1750–1850" (formerly 21 and now 20) before "Restoration, Reform, and Revolution, 1814–1848," it has been possible to resolve some tensions that persisted through the first two editions. As but one example, our former discussion of workers and the working class in Chapter 20 suffered from a lack of economic, industrial background. Chapters 29 and 30 have been reorganized to accommodate both the inclusion of recent events and the altered perspectives that inevitably attend the unpredictable course of history's march. Chapter 29 now covers the years from 1949 to 1989, and Chapter 30 treats the years from 1989 to the present.

Chapters 1–6 contain new discussions of archaeological evidence, revised treatment of Judaism, expanded material on Spartan and Roman women, and new coverage of Roman law. Discussions of the social, political, and military struggles of late medieval Europe in Chapter 11 have been reorganized. There is new material on humanism in Chapter 12. Chapter 14 has a revised treatment of John Calvin and of the Reformation in Scandinavia and eastern Europe. Seventeenth-century Europe's complicated political history has been streamlined. Several aspects of the Scientific Revolution in Chapter 17 have been revised, and there is new material on Galileo and Newton. The treatment of France in Chapters 18 and 19 has been revised, with new material added on eastern Europe. The discussions of socialism and Marxism in Chapter 21 have been reorganized. Chapter 22 has a new treatment of the Canadian Confederation. All of the chapters on the twentieth century contain new material. Chapter 30 incorporates contemporary coverage, for instance on the Russian regime of Vladimir Putin, the new parity laws for elections in France, and the end of the Milosevic regime in Yugoslavia. The chapter concludes with an assessment of the West's relations with the non-Western world in light of the terrorist attacks on the United States on September 11, 2001. In highlighting these changes, it is important to add that *every single chapter* finds new material inserted, old material deleted, and existing material reorganized.

■ New Approaches to Teaching and Learning

To make this book as accessible as possible to students, we have constantly been aware of its place in a program of teaching and learning. Each chapter begins with a vignette that is directly tied to an accompanying picture. The vignettes introduce the reader to one or more of the key aspects of the chapter. Then the reader encounters a thematic introduction that points clearly and in some detail to what will follow.

To make our chapter introductions even more effective, which means to give students greater confidence as they proceed through the book, we took four steps. First we placed on the first page of each chapter a succinct outline that immediately and dramatically tells the student reader what he or she is going to encounter in the following pages. Second, we put at the end of each chapter's introduction a list of three or four Questions to Consider designed to work with the introduction and outline to give the student a clear orientation to what will follow. Third, we added a list of Terms to Know—generally ten or twelve—that alert the student to people, events, or developments demanding special attention. As a complement to text coverage, a ready reference, and a potential study guide, all of the Terms to Know are defined in a Glossary at the back of the book. Fourth, as the reader begins to read the chapter proper, he or she will meet a general chapter chronology that serves as yet another orientation to the material contained in the chapter.

In addition to this fundamental attention to the opening of each chapter, we also sought to improve the book's teachability by adding a pronunciation guide. Whenever we use an unfamiliar name or term, we show the reader how to pronounce it. Instead of using the intricate rules of phonetics, we provided commonsense guides to pronunciation at the foot of the page.

Careful chapter summaries draw together major topics and themes and link the present chapter to the one that follows. To encourage students to strike out on their own historical discoveries, each chapter offers a few carefully selected suggestions for further reading. This book's website (discussed later) contains a lengthy, searchable list of additional readings.

■ New and Revised Features

In preparing this Third Edition, we paid particular attention to the book's features. Beginning with its first edition, this book has presented the two-page feature Weighing the Evidence at the end of each chapter. These features introduce students to the fascinating array of sources that historians use and invite them to think critically about the nature of historical information and inquiry. Each opens with a description of the evidence presented in the feature—sources such as images of Cleopatra, the Ravenna mosaics, a Renaissance painting, eighteenth-century political symbols, the layout of the British Museum, and pop art—and then permits the students to look over the shoulder of the historian to become active participants in the interpretive process. The sources examined are interesting and instructive in their own right, but the Weighing the Evidence features also contribute to the teaching program of the book. There are references to the features at appropriate points in the narrative, they contain cross-references to other sections or illustrations, and they support ongoing discussions.

Our Weighing the Evidence essays have been both distinctive and well received since the First Edition. Feeling no complacency about them, however, the authors prepared eight new ones, including "Gladiators," "Stained Glass," "The Modern City and Photography," and "Advertising."

Many textbooks have boxed documents. In four different respects we have taken special care with our documents for this edition. First, we have added forty-seven new documents. Second, we have included in every chapter at least one document that permits a gendered analysis of a key historical person or problem. Third, each chapter also includes a Global Encounters box, quoting either a Western person commenting on the non-Western world, or vice versa. These boxes further our intention to situate our story in its global context. Fourth, and finally, because some documents cry out for more discussion or context, the website for the book provides exercises to help students analyze one key document per chapter, as well as twelve of the Weighing the Evidence features.

To this edition we have added a distinctive new feature: an Information Technology box with an accompanying image. The book has six of these, detailing papyrus, paper, printing, newspapers, the telegraph, and the Internet. These boxes provide readers with interesting examples of how communication technology affected people's lives. For example, the box on printing discusses how the new technology dramatically reduced the price of books and helped promote literacy across Europe.

We have been conscious of how the book *looks* to the reader from the very beginning. In keeping with our desire to integrate the components of the book into a coherent whole, we carefully anchor the maps and photographs. The authors developed the maps in this book and wrote their captions. Moreover, for this edition there are eight new maps, including European Resources and Trade Routes, ca. 1100; Dominion of Canada, 1873; GDP per Capita in Europe, 2000; and Foreign-Born Population in Western Europe. In addition, nearly twenty of the carry-over maps have been significantly revised. The same is true of the pictures: the authors selected them and wrote all the captions. As part of our continuing quest to make all of the elements of the book work together, the authors replaced about one-third of the photos for the Third Edition and revised the captions of

many others. All of the maps in the book are cross-referenced in the text, some several times, and many of the photos are also referred to directly. Our diverse array of boxed documents—five per chapter—are referred to and tightly anchored in the text, and they support their surrounding discussion. As with the maps, familiar documents are blended with pleasing newcomers.

■ Formats

This book is flexible in format as well as substantive organization. Because schools use different academic calendars, organize Western Civilization courses according to different chronologies, and require or recommend different parts of the course, we issue this book in three formats:

- **One-volume hardcover edition** (Chapters 1–30)
- **Two-volume paperback:** Volume I: To 1715 (Chapters 1–17); Volume II: Since 1560 (Chapters 15–30)
- **Three-volume paperback:** Volume A: To 1500 (Chapters 1–12); Volume B: 1300–1815 (Chapters 11–19); Volume C: Since 1789 (Chapters 19–30)

Volume II begins with a comprehensive Introduction designed for students who did not take the first semester of the course or who are new to this book. It provides a survey of the course of Western Civilization from ancient times to the early centuries of the modern era. This Introduction has been streamlined, organized along more strictly chronological lines, and illustrated for the Third Edition.

SUPPLEMENTS

We have assembled with care an array of text supplements to aid students in learning and instructors in teaching. These supplements, including the website and *Test Items,* are tied closely to the text to provide a tightly integrated and comprehensive program.

The text-specific website contains a wealth of resources for students and instructors. For students, there are over forty web exercises, written by Christopher Carlsmith of Stanford University, relating to the boxed documents and Weighing the Evidence features in the text. Icons in the textbook direct students to the corresponding activities on the Houghton Mifflin website. Students can also test their knowledge of chapter content using

ACE self tests and a comprehensive on-line study guide. To visit the site, begin at the Houghton Mifflin Company home page (**college.hmco.com**) and select the text and/or discipline.

Instructors will find a complete *Instructor's Resource Manual*, written by Sharon Arnoult of Midwestern State University, on the website, including learning objectives, annotated outlines, suggested lecture topics, discussion questions, classroom activities, and paper topics for each chapter of the text. The *Instructor's Resource Manual* also features suggestions for integrating the web exercises into your teaching.

Other website features include an extensive searchable bibliography to aid in student and instructor research, primary source selections, web links, and class presentation maps.

Each chapter of the *Test Items*, prepared by Diane Moczar of Northern Virginia Community College, offers a list of 10 to 20 key terms, 5 to 10 short-answer and essay questions, 2 or 3 map questions, and 40 to 50 multiple-choice questions. Answers to the multiple-choice questions are located at the end of the *Test Items*. We also offer a computerized version of the *Test Items*, enabling instructors to alter, replace, or add questions.

The full package of instructor materials is also available on an *HM ClassPrep* CD-ROM. The *Instructor's Resource Manual* and *Test Items* appear on the CD-ROM in their entirety, in addition to Powerpoint slides of the textbook maps and selected art images. The CD-ROM will function on either a PC or Macintosh platform. In addition, a set of overhead map *Transparencies* for the Western Civilization course is available on adoption.

The *GeoQuest* CD-ROM features thirty interactive maps and thirty presentation maps that illuminate the history of Western Civilization from ancient times to the present. Each of the interactive maps is accompanied by exercises with answers and essay questions. Different types of interactivity allow students to move at their own pace through each section. Four sample maps can be viewed on the Houghton Mifflin history website.

A correlation from the text to the Advanced Placement course description ("acorn book") is available from your McDougal Littell representative.

ACKNOWLEDGMENTS

The authors have benefited throughout the process of revision from the acute and helpful criticisms of numerous colleagues. We thank in particular: **Sharon L. Arnoult,** Midwestern State University; **Pierre Cagniart,** Southwest Texas State University; **Eleanor A. Congdon,** Plymouth State College; **David Dean,** Carleton University; **Maribel Dietz,** Louisiana State University; **George Drake,** Grinnell College; **Janusz Duzinkiewicz,** Purdue University North Central; **Alan Fisher,** Michigan State University; **Peter A. Goddard,** University of Guelph; **Aaron Goldman,** San Jose State University; **Robert W. Hayman,** Providence College; **Charles J. Herber,** Emeritus, George Washington University; **W. Robert Houston,** University of South Alabama; **Gerald E. Kadish,** Binghamton University (SUNY); **Laurie Koloski,** College of William and Mary; **Lawrence N. Langer,** University of Connecticut; **Thomas F. Madden,** Saint Louis University; **Donald M. McKale,** Clemson University; **Shannon McSheffrey,** Concordia University; **Isabel Moreira,** University of Utah; **Mark Munn,** The Pennsylvania State University; **Christopher Oldstone-Moore,** Wittenberg University; **Mary R. O'Neil,** University of Washington; **Ron Palmer,** Jefferson Community College; **Joseph F. Patrouch,** Florida International University; **Craig Pepin,** Western Carolina University; **Thomas Lynwood Powers,** University of South Carolina, Sumter; **Carole Putko,** San Diego State University; **Paul Lawrence Rose,** The Pennsylvania State University; **John Rosser,** Boston College; **Raffael Scheck,** Colby College; **Bernard Schlager,** University of New Hampshire; **Thomas P. Schlunz,** University of New Orleans; **Eileen Soldwedel,** Edmonds Community College; **Alan E. Steinweis,** University of Nebraska, Lincoln; **Charles R. Sullivan,** University of Dallas; **Timothy M. Thibodeau,** Nazareth College of Rochester; **Kevin Uhalde,** Northern Illinois University; and **Leigh Whaley,** Acadia University.

Each of us has also benefited from the close readings and careful criticisms of our coauthors, although we all assume responsibility for our own chapters. Barry Strauss has written Chapters 1–6; Thomas Noble, 7–10; Duane Osheim, 11–14; Kristen Neuschel, 15–19; William Cohen, 20–24; and David Roberts, 25–30.

Many colleagues, friends, and family members have helped us develop this work as well. Thomas Noble wishes to thank Linda Noble for her patience and good humor. He is also grateful to John Contreni, Wendy

The Authors: Duane Osheim, Tom Noble, Kristen Neuschel, Bill Cohen, David Roberts, Barry Strauss

Davies, Thomas Head, Elizabeth Meyer, Julia Smith, Richard Sullivan, John Van Engen, Robert Wilken, and Ian Wood.

Barry Strauss is grateful to colleagues at Cornell and at other universities who offered advice and encouragement and responded to scholarly questions. He would also like to thank the people at Cornell who provided technical assistance and support. Most important have been the support and forbearance of his family. His daughter Sylvie, his son Michael, and, above all, his wife, Marcia, have truly been sources of inspiration.

Duane Osheim wishes to thank his family for support during the writing and revising of this book. He is also grateful to colleagues at the University of Virginia, who helped to clarify the many connections between Western Civilization and the wider world. He would specifically like to thank Erik Midelfort, Arthur Field, Janis Gibbs, and Beth Plummer for comments and advice.

Kristen Neuschel thanks her colleagues at Duke University for sharing their expertise. She is especially grateful to Sy Mauskopf, Bill Reddy, John Richards, Tom Robisheaux, and Alex Roland. She also thanks her husband and fellow historian, Alan Williams, for his wisdom about Western Civilization and his support throughout the project, and her children, Jesse and Rachel, for their patience, joy, and curiosity.

William Cohen thanks his wife, Christine Matheu, and his daughters Natalie, Leslie, and Laurel for their support and encouragement over the many years that this project has matured.

David Roberts wishes to thank Bonnie Cary, Linda Green, and Nancy Heaton for their able assistance and Joshua Cole, Karl Friday, Thomas Ganschow, John Haag,

Michael Kwass, John Morrow, Douglas Northrup, Miranda Pollard, William Stueck, Eve Trout Powell, and Kirk Willis, colleagues at the University of Georgia, for sharing their expertise in response to questions. He also thanks Beth Roberts for her constant support and interest and her exceedingly critical eye, and Ellen, Trina, and Anthony for their college-age perspective and advice.

The first plans for this book were laid in 1988, and over the course of thirteen years there has been remarkable stability in the core group of people who have been responsible for its growth and development. The author team remains intact. Our original Sponsoring Editor, Jean Woy, has become Editor-in-Chief for History, Political Science, and Economics but has never missed a meeting with us or weakened in her interest in and commitment to this book. Christina Horn, our Senior Project Editor, has been the wizard behind the curtain for all three editions. She understood from the beginning our desire to have maps, pictures, and boxes closely integrated with their pertinent text and she has never let us down. Our photo researcher, Carole Frolich, has been with us from the start, and she has always understood the spirit of this book and the wishes of its authors. When the Second Edition was in preparation, a Brief Edition was planned and produced. Our work on that version introduced us to Jennifer Sutherland, who then served as Senior Development Editor for the Third Edition. She

entered quickly into the spirit of our book, but by casting a fresh eye on it she helped us see it again as if for the first time. Elizabeth Welch, our Senior Basic Book Editor for the first two editions, helped us to turn six voices into one and taught us how to write a textbook. We have now worked for several years with Nancy Blaine, our Sponsoring Editor, and we are most appreciative of her tireless energy and her faith in this book and its authors.

Although stability has been the hallmark of this project for years now, we are nevertheless delighted to acknowledge some people who came on board with the Third Edition. Sandra McGuire, Senior Marketing Manager, helped us to understand the many audiences for which we were writing. Gillie Jones, Editorial Associate, was masterful in managing the flow of manuscripts, disks, and e-mail attachments. Penny Peters designed the page layouts and created a pleasing visual effect. Henry Rachlin, Senior Designer, assembled diverse components into a book whose beauty truly facilitates its academic purpose.

Producing a successful textbook is hard work that makes high demands in terms of confidence, good humor, honesty, respect, and understanding. The authors of this book have been fortunate in their long and maturing relationship with their publishers.

Thomas F. X. Noble

ABOUT THE AUTHORS

Thomas F. X. Noble   After receiving his Ph.D. from Michigan State University, Thomas Noble taught at Albion College, Michigan State University, Texas Tech University, and the University of Virginia. In 1999 he received the University of Virginia's highest award for teaching excellence. In 2001 he became Robert M. Conway Director of the Medieval Institute at the University of Notre Dame. He is the author of *The Republic of St. Peter: The Birth of the Papal State, 680–825; Religion, Culture and Society in the Early Middle Ages; Soldiers of Christ: Saints and Saints' Lives from Late Antiquity and the Early Middle Ages;* and *Images and the Carolingians: Tradition, Order, and Worship.* Noble's articles and reviews have appeared in many leading journals, including the *American Historical Review, Byzantinische Zeitschrift, Catholic Historical Review, Revue d'histoire ecclésiastique, Speculum,* and *Studi medievali.* He has also contributed chapters to several books and articles to three encyclopedias. He was a member of the Institute for Advanced Study in 1994 and the Netherlands Institute for Advanced Study in 1999–2000. He has been awarded fellowships by the National Endowment for the Humanities (twice) and the American Philosophical Society.

Barry S. Strauss   Professor of history and Classics at Cornell University, where he is also Director of the Peace Studies Program, Barry Strauss holds a Ph.D. from Yale in history. He has been awarded fellowships by the National Endowment for the Humanities, the American School of Classical Studies at Athens, and the Killam Foundation of Canada. He is the recipient of the Clark Award for excellence in teaching from Cornell. His many publications include *Athens After the Peloponnesian War: Class, Faction, and Policy, 403–386 B.C.; Fathers and Sons in Athens: Ideology and Society in the Era of the Peloponnesian War; The Anatomy of Error: Ancient Military Disasters and Their Lessons for Modern Strategists* (with Josiah Ober); *Hegemonic Rivalry from Thucydides to the Nuclear Age* (co-edited with R. Ned Lebow); *War and Democracy: A Comparative Study of the Korean War and the Peloponnesian War* (co-edited with David R. McCann); and *Rowing Against the Current: On Learning to Scull at Forty.*

Duane J. Osheim   A Fellow of the American Academy in Rome with a Ph.D. in history from the University of California, Davis, Duane Osheim is a professor of history at the University of Virginia. A specialist in late medieval and Renaissance social and institutional history, he is the author of *A Tuscan Monastery and Its Social World* and *An Italian Lordship: The Bishopric of Lucca in the Late Middle Ages,* as well as numerous studies of religious values and rural life in late medieval Italy.

Kristen B. Neuschel   Associate professor of history at Duke University, Kristen Neuschel received her Ph.D. from Brown University. She is a specialist in early modern French history and is the author of *Word of Honor: Interpreting Noble Culture in Sixteenth-Century France* and articles on French social history and European women's history. She has received grants from the National Endowment for the Humanities and the American Council of Learned Societies. In 1988 she received the Alumni Distinguished Undergraduate Teaching Award, which is awarded annually on the basis of student nominations for excellence in teaching at Duke.

William B. Cohen   After receiving his Ph.D. at Stanford University, William Cohen taught at Northwestern University and Indiana University, where he is now professor of history. At Indiana, he served as chairman of the West European Studies and History Departments; he is currently Director of Graduate Studies for the History Department. A previous president of the Society of French Historical Studies, Cohen has received several academic fellowships, including a National Endowment for the Humanities and a Fulbright fellowship. Among his many publications are *Rulers of Empire; The French Encounter with Africans; European Empire Building; Robert Delavignette and the French Empire; The Transformation of Modern France;* and *Urban Government and the Rise of the City.* His current research is on the Algerian war and French memory.

David D. Roberts   After taking his Ph.D. in modern European history at the University of California, Berkeley, David Roberts taught at the Universities of Virginia and Rochester before becoming professor of history at the University of Georgia in 1988. At Rochester he chaired the Humanities Department of the Eastman School of Music, and he chaired the History Department at Georgia from 1993 to 1998. A recipient of Woodrow Wilson and Rockefeller Foundation fellowships, he is the author of *The Syndicalist Tradition and Italian Fascism; Benedetto Croce and the Uses of Historicism;* and *Nothing but History: Reconstruction and Extremity After Metaphysics,* as well as numerous articles and reviews.

Western Civilization

CHAPTER 1

The Ancestors of the West

OUTSIDE the city of Thebes in ancient Egypt, the kings maintained a village of workers to build and decorate royal tombs. Sennejdem°, a high-ranking Theban worker, was himself buried in a splendidly decorated tomb along with his wife Iynefert. In a scene from the tomb depicted to the left, Sennejdem is cutting wheat in the fields of the afterlife, where it grew higher than on earth. The painting illustrates many of humanity's early achievements: settled life, agriculture, technological innovation, representational art, writing (notice the symbols in the upper left corner of the painting), weaving (notice Sennejdem's pleated kilt), and religion.

Those achievements, which Sennejdem and Iynefert probably took for granted, were the most momentous inventions in human history. Approximately 100,000 years ago, the first modern humans evolved from humanlike ancestors. Human beings wrestled with an often-hostile environment, engaging in a continuing series of experiments, until beginning about 10,000 B.C. they learned how to plant crops and tame animals. The shift from a food-collecting to a food-producing economy dramatically increased the amount of human life that the earth could support. Between 3500 and 3000 B.C., human society became well organized in urban centers, supported by farmers in the surrounding territories, and able to keep written records: it had, in short, achieved civilization.

What we call Western civilization, however, was still more than two thousand years away. As a term *Western civilization* is imprecise, inviting disagreement about its definition and about the lands, peoples, and cultures that it embraces at any given time. In this book we give

---

Sennejdem (sen-NEJ-em)

Origins, to ca. 3000 B.C.

Mesopotamia, to ca. 1600 B.C.

Egypt, to ca. 1100 B.C.

Widening Horizons: The Levant and Anatolia, 2500–1150 B.C.

Man harvesting wheat, Egyptian tomb painting.
(Erich Lessing/Art Resource, NY)

Western civilization an evolving definition that permits comparison and reflection over time and space. In the strictest sense, Western civilization means the "West," and that, in turn, has traditionally meant the lands and peoples of western Europe.

Initially, however, the West embraced the Greek and Roman peoples, plus the foundational monotheistic religions of Judaism and Christianity. These first westerners in turn borrowed many ideas and institutions from the earlier civilizations of western Asia and Egypt. (These civilizations are sometimes referred to as the Ancient Near East.) Indeed, civilization began in those lands and came only relatively late to Europe.

Western Asia and Egypt contributed greatly to the cultures of Greece and Rome and to the religious visions of the Jews and Christians. Yet those earlier civilizations are sufficiently different from the West and its society, politics, and religion that they are better considered as ancestors or forerunners of the West rather than as its founders. (For a longer discussion of the definition of Western civilization, see the Preface.)

So, after briefly surveying the origins of the human species, the historian of the West must begin with the emergence of civilizations after 3500 B.C. in two great river valleys: the valley of the Tigris° and Euphrates° in Mesopotamia (today, Iraq and Syria), and the valley of the Nile in Egypt. Impressive in

their own right, Mesopotamia and Egypt influenced a wide range of other early civilizations in western Asia and northern Africa. Among them were the Hittites and the Syro-Palestinian city-states, whose own cultural contributions make them ancestors of the West as well. They are studied in this chapter. The Hebrews and the Greeks were also influenced by Mesopotamia and Egypt, but with the Hebrews and the Greeks, Western civilization begins, and so they are covered in Chapter 2.

QUESTIONS TO CONSIDER

- When, where, and how did modern humans evolve?
- How did people shift from a food-collecting to a food-producing economy?
- What is civilization? When, where, and why did it begin? What is Western civilization or the West?
- What did the civilizations of Egypt and western Asia contribute to the West between about 3500 and 1200 B.C.?

TERMS TO KNOW

hominids	Sumerians
hunter-gatherers	pharaoh
Neolithic Revolution	papyrus
cuneiform	Amarna reform
city-state	Ugarit

ORIGINS, TO CA. 3000 B.C.

 HE earth is old; modern human beings are young; and civilization is a very recent innovation. Physical anthropologists, archaeologists, geneticists, and biochemists have made great strides in explaining human origins. Great disagreement still reigns nonetheless. Each decade seems to bring an

exciting new discovery that calls for the reassessment of previous theories.

We can be more certain about the series of processes, beginning around 10,000 B.C., that led to the emergence of civilization by 3500–3000 B.C. The period studied in this chapter includes both prehistory—the term often used for time before the invention of writing—and recorded history. Writing appeared last among the complex of characteristics that marks the emergence of civilization. Over a period of several thousand years, many humans abandoned a mobile existence for a sedentary one. They learned to domesticate animals and

---

Tigris (TY-gris)   **Euphrates** (yoo-FRAY-tees)

to cultivate plants. They shifted from a food-collecting economy to a predominantly food-producing economy. They developed the first towns, from which, over several millennia, the first urban societies slowly evolved. The result—the first civilizations, found in western Asia and Egypt—laid the groundwork on which later would be built the founding civilizations of the West: Greece, Rome, and ancient Israel.

■ The First Human Beings

Modern human beings, *Homo sapiens sapiens*—genus *Homo*, species *sapiens*, subspecies *sapiens*—first appeared within about 100,000 years ago (scholarly estimates vary). The human family, or hominids, are much older, however. The hominids include many ancient and extinct species, some of which are thought to be our evolutionary ancestors.

Africa, as current research argues, is the cradle of humanity. The first hominids appeared in Africa's tropics and subtropics over 4 million years ago. By 2.5 million years ago they had evolved into creatures who invented the first technology, simple stone tools. Prehistory is traditionally referred to as the Stone Age because stone was the primary medium from which hominids made tools. The hominids were migratory: not less than 1.6 million years ago and perhaps much earlier, they appeared in East Asia and the eastern edge of Europe.

The next important stage in human evolution is *Homo erectus* ("upright person"), a hominid with a large brain who used more complex stone tools and may have acquired language. The appearance of *Homo erectus* is usually dated to 1.8 million years ago, but a recent discovery in China may date *Homo erectus* as early as 2.25 million years ago. Slowly, separate *Homo erectus* populations in different places gave way to the gradual emergence of various archaic forms of *Homo sapiens*.

For many millennia humans struggled with the ebb and flow of glaciers. Their home was the Ice Age, as scholars refer to the period of fluctuating cycles of warm and cold, beginning about 730,000 years ago and ending only about 10,000 years ago. Early humans lived amid great contrasts in temperature, seasons, and landscapes, requiring considerable adaptation—but adapt they did.

Humans came late to Europe, though not as late as scholars once thought. Indeed, recent finds in Spain show the presence of archaic humans in Europe about 800,000 years ago. Beginning about 400,000 years ago, Europe was home to the ancestors of the best-known archaic people, the Neandertals. Fully evolved by 130,000 years ago, Neandertal people lived in Europe and western Asia for the following 100,000 years, to about 30,000

CHRONOLOGY	
ca. 4.4 million years ago	Earliest hominids
800,000 years ago	First humans in Europe
ca. 100,000 years ago	*Homo sapiens sapiens*
40,000–10,000 B.C.	Upper Paleolithic era
10,000–2500 B.C.	Neolithic era
3500–3000 B.C.	First civilizations
3500–3100 B.C.	First writing in Mesopotamia
3300–3200 B.C.	First writing in Egypt
ca. 3200 B.C.	Unification of Nile Valley
2800–2350 B.C.	Early Dynastic Period
2695–2160 B.C.	Egyptian Old Kingdom
2500–2350 B.C.	Cuneiform texts from Ebla
2025–1786 B.C.	Egyptian Middle Kingdom
1650–1180 B.C.	Hittite Old, Middle, and New Kingdoms
1550–1075 B.C.	Egyptian New Kingdom
1450–1300 B.C.	First international system
1400–1200 B.C.	Height of prosperity at Ugarit
1250–1150 B.C.	Sea Peoples invade

(All dates in this chapter are approximate.)

years ago. Their strong and stocky physiques were perhaps an adaptation to the rugged climate of the Ice Age. The Neandertals were far from being the brutes they are usually imagined to be. They were, for example, among the first people to bury their dead, often with grave offerings—for example, flint, animal bones, or flowers—a practice that suggests they were sensitive enough to mourn their losses.

Neandertals, however, were not modern humans. Modern humans entered Europe about 40,000 years ago, having originated in Africa. Within 10,000 years, Neandertals had disappeared; whether through war or through disease or through intermarriage with modern humans, we do not know. The first modern humans tended to be taller and less muscular than Neandertals and other archaic people. They also used their hands more precisely and walked more efficiently, and they lived longer. With its high forehead and tucked-in face, the modern human skull is distinctive, but differences between the modern and archaic human brain are a matter of scholarly debate. Some archaeologists believe that Neandertals were capable of the same level of technology that modern humans achieved. What no one debates, however, is that, with the disappearance of Neandertals, it was modern humans who put into effect a revolution in culture.

■ The Revolution in Human Culture, ca. 70,000–10,000 B.C.

Before the emergence of modern humans and perhaps before Neandertals, people had relatively little ability to change the natural environment. Modern humans changed that. They exploited natural resources largely by means of technology and organization. Thus they began the process of human manipulation of the environment that—sometimes brilliantly, sometimes disastrously—has remained a leading theme of the human experience ever since. The key to this change was a dramatic increase in the amount and complexity of information being communicated—what might be called the first information revolution. The twin symbols of the revolution are cave paintings and notations made on bone, signs that humans were thinking about their environment and their experiences.

It was long thought that these dramatic changes began in Europe about 40,000 B.C.* Recently, however, they have been traced to southern Africa, probably more than 70,000 years ago. The discovery there of carefully worked bone tools and stone spearheads pinpoints the dawn of modern human technology. Still, it is not in Africa but elsewhere that we can best trace the early evolution of the modern human mind. Europe from about 40,000 to about 10,000 B.C. provides reliable evidence of the way of life and the culture of early human hunter-gatherer societies, complex organizations that survived by a food-collecting economy of hunting, fishing, and gathering fruits and

nuts. This period is sometimes called the Upper Paleolithic (Greek for "Old Stone") era. Then, around 10,000 B.C., western Asia offers evidence of a second revolution: the invention of a food-producing economy, consisting of the domestication of animals and the cultivation of crops. The period from about 10,000 to 3000 B.C. is sometimes called the Neolithic (Greek for "New Stone") era.

Archaeology tells us something about early people's way of life. So do analogies from contemporary anthropology, for even today a tiny number of people still exist in hunter-gatherer societies in isolated corners of the globe, for example, in the Kalahari Desert of Africa and in the Arctic. It is reasonable to speculate that early humans lived in small groups, numbering perhaps twenty-five to fifty persons, related by kinship or marriage. Early hunter-gatherers moved from place to place, following the seasonal migration of game, but by the eve of the invention of agriculture, some hunter-gatherers had settled down in villages. Hunting was largely a male preserve, while gathering nuts and berries fell into the female domain. Perhaps women brought their children with them as they worked or relied on kin or friends for childcare.

It was probably common for men and women to pair off, have children, and establish a family, much as marriage is a near-universal practice among humans today. Compared with other animals, humans produce extremely dependent infants requiring years of attention. In order to ensure the survival of the young to adulthood, men as well as women need to play a role in child rearing.

Early people found shelter by building huts or, frequently, by living in caves or rock shelters—hence our notion of the "caveman." Caves offered shelter, could be heated, and made a naturally good vantage point for observing prey and hostile humans. In the Upper Paleolithic era, about 30,000 years ago, caves were the site of the earliest representational art. The most spectacular Upper Paleolithic paintings discovered so far have been found in caves in southern France (for example, at Lascaux° and at Chauvet° Cave) and in Spain (at Altamira). European cave paintings of such animals as the bison, horse, reindeer, and woolly mammoth (a huge, extinct member of the elephant family with hairy skin and long, upward-curving tusks) attest to early human artistic skill. The presence of abstract shapes attests to an interest in symbols. The purpose of cave paintings is unknown, but perhaps they served as illustrations of myths or as attempts to control the environment through magic.

---

* We follow the traditional practice in the West of expressing historical dates in relation to the birth of Jesus Christ (actually, to a now discredited calculation of his birth date because in fact Jesus was not born in A.D. 1; see page 191). Dates before his birth are labeled B.C. (which stands for "before Christ") and dates after his birth are labeled A.D. (*anno Domini*, Latin for "in the year of the Lord"). A widely used alternate refers to these dates as B.C.E. ("before the common era") and C.E. ("of the common era").

Lascaux (lass-CO)   **Chauvet** (show-VAY)

Other early representational art includes engravings on stone of animals, birds, and stylized human females, as well as female figurines carved from ivory or bone. Usually represented with exaggerated breasts or buttocks, the carvings are called Venus figurines, after Venus, the Roman goddess of love. They may represent an attempt to control fertility through magic.

Upper Paleolithic craftsmanship is as impressive as the art. The early human tool kit included the first utensils in such easily worked materials as antler and ivory. Stone tools became longer and the first polished bone tools appeared, as did the first stone and bone spear points and the first bows and arrows. The presence of bone needles and awls (pointed tools for punching holes) implies sewing, probably of animal skins.

The existence of Upper Paleolithic artists and skilled craftspeople demonstrates at least a limited specialization of skills and division of labor: society required organization, albeit on a limited scale. Hunting was a communal enterprise. Related families are likely to have joined together in clans, which in turn may have formed tribes. It is often thought that each of these groups was patriarchal (literally, "ruled by the father"); that is, the family was governed by the father, the tribe by a male headman or chief. To be sure, some later myths (for example, among the ancient Greeks) argue that women were the rulers of prehistoric society. Today some historians see the possibility of matriarchy (literally, "rule by the mother") in the Venus figurines. There is, however, no firm evidence of matriarchy. Male chiefs probably did exist, as in later periods, but some tribes may have had no chief at all, following the decision of the community rather than an individual leader.

Chauvet Cave Art　This black-painted panel shows horses, rhinoceros, and wild oxen. This painting and others in the cave, discovered in 1994 in southern France, are over 30,000 years old, making them perhaps the oldest known paintings in the world.　*(Jean Cottes/Ministère de la Culture/Corbis Sygma)*

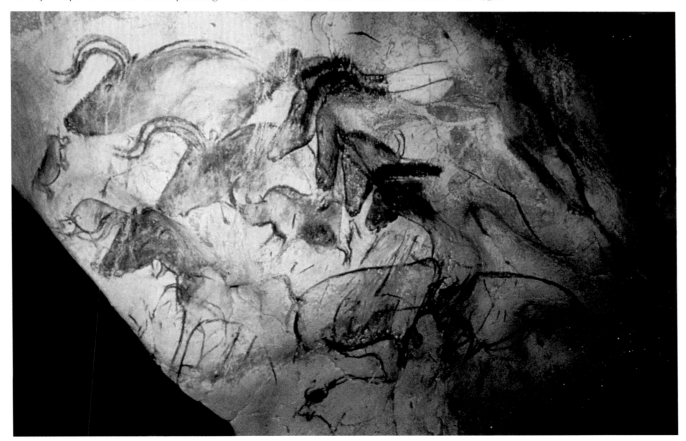

■ The Coming of Agriculture, ca. 10,000–5000 B.C.

The human discovery of agriculture was dramatic, meriting the name "Neolithic Revolution" that scholars sometimes give it. Yet if dramatic, the discovery spread slowly and unevenly. In most areas, hunting and fishing continued to be a major source of food, even though agriculture fed more people. Agriculture was first discovered sometime after 10,000 B.C. in western Asia, then discovered again independently in other parts of the world. By 5000 B.C. information about the new practices had spread so widely that farming could be found in many places around the world.

The story begins about 13,000 B.C., when humans began to specialize in the wild plants they collected and the animals they hunted. They had good reason to do so because hunter-gatherer society had become increasingly

complex, and in some places permanent settlements had appeared. A settled existence probably produced more mouths to feed, stimulating the need for more food. The next step is not surprising: learning how to domesticate plants and animals.

People seem to have begun by domesticating dogs, which were useful in hunting. Then they learned to keep sheep, goats, and cattle. Next came farming. Humans learned first how to grow wheat and barley, then legumes (beans). With males occupied in hunting, it may well have been females who first unraveled the secrets of agriculture.

The earliest area of domestication is a zone of land stretching in a crescent shape west to east from what is today southern Jordan to southern Iran. Scholars call this region of dependable annual rainfall the Fertile Crescent (see Map 1.1). With domestication came small agricultural settlements, which were increasingly com-

Map 1.1   Western Asia   The Neolithic Revolution began after 10,000 B.C. in the Fertile Crescent, an arc-shaped region of dependable annual rainfall. In this area between the Tigris and Euphrates Rivers known as Mesopotamia, the world's first urban civilization took root about 3500–3000 B.C.

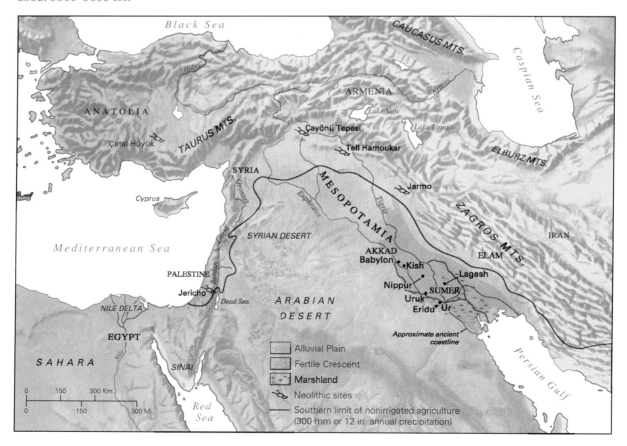

mon after 7000 B.C. Thus was born the farming village, probably the place that most people have called home since the spread of agriculture around the world.

Scholars once thought of Neolithic villages as simple places devoted to subsistence agriculture, with no craft specialization, and as egalitarian societies lacking social hierarchies. In recent years, new evidence and a rethinking of older information have altered this picture considerably. The Neolithic village site of Çayönü Tepesi° in eastern Anatolia, for example, provides evidence of metalworking (of copper) and specialization of labor (in bead making) from approximately 7000 to 6000 B.C. The site also contains the world's earliest known example of cloth, probably linen, woven around 7000 B.C. Other contemporaneous village sites reveal experiments in ironworking and craft specialization. Evidence points to long-distance trade between villages in pottery and in obsidian (a sharp volcanic glass used in tools). Artwork shows men wearing loincloths and headdresses, women wearing pants and halter tops, and both sexes wearing jewelry.

Consider the case of Jericho°, in Palestine near the Dead Sea (see Map 1.1), perhaps the oldest settled community on earth. A small village around 9000 B.C., by about 7000 Jericho had become a town surrounded by massive walls 10 feet thick and 13 or more feet high. The walls, about 765 yards long, probably enclosed an area of about 10 acres. The most prominent feature of the walls was a great tower 33 feet in diameter and 28 feet high with an interior stairway. Inside the walls lived a densely packed population of about two thousand people.

An even larger Neolithic town was Çatal Hüyük° in south central Anatolia (see Map 1.1). Its population of six thousand people in 6000 B.C. made it by far the largest settlement of the era. It was probably a trading center and perhaps a religious shrine. Carbonization from fire has preserved a wealth of artifacts attesting to Çatal Hüyük's sophistication, including woven fabrics, obsidian mirrors, wooden vessels, and makeup applicators.

Agriculture made human populations richer and more numerous, but the resulting concentrations of population bred disease and probably increased the scale of war. More men than ever before were available to fight because agriculture proved to be so efficient a source of food that it freed people for specialized labor. Some became craftsmen, some artists, some priests—and some warriors.

This is not to say that war in Neolithic times was sophisticated. Indeed, the phenomenon perhaps consisted of group skirmishes and sporadic raids rather than systematic warfare. People added new weapons to the spear and the bow: the sling, the dagger, and the mace (a heavy war club). Spanish rock art shows a confrontation between two groups of archers, one following what seems to be a leader. The scene may be a ritual rather than a violent conflict, but we have physical cases of actual bloodshed. The earliest known evidence of organized warfare comes from a cemetery along the Nile River in the Sudan dating from 12,000 to 4500 B.C. The cemetery contains fifty-nine human skeletons, nearly half of whom died violently. Some were speared, some clubbed, and some killed by arrowheads. Some suffered multiple wounds. The victims include women and children.

■ **Neolithic and Copper Age Europe, 7000–2500 B.C.**

Europe was one day to become the center of Western civilization, but the region lagged behind its neighbors at first. Innovations from the east reached Europe after 7000 B.C. and slowly transformed it. Europe was no empty vessel to be filled by eastern technologies, however: Europeans developed their own unique culture.

The term *Europe* refers to a vast peninsula of the Eurasian continent with several very distinct regions. Southern Europe is made up of a rugged and hilly Mediterranean coastal strip, linked to northern Africa and western Asia by the sea and by similarities in climate and landscape. High mountains are found in the Alps of south central Europe, from which chains of lower mountains radiate toward the southwest and southeast. Northern Europe, by contrast, consists in large part of forested plain, indented here and there by great rivers. In the southeast the plain, or steppe, becomes open and mostly treeless. The eastern boundaries of Europe are, in the north, the Ural Mountains and, in the south, the Caucasus Mountains. Georgia, Armenia, and Azerbaijan are all considered parts of Europe.

Before 7000 B.C., Europeans lived a traditional hunter-gatherer existence. Farming began in southeastern Europe around 7000 B.C., when migrants from western Asia introduced the settled way of life of the Neolithic village. That food-producing economy spread across Europe between about 6000 and 4500 B.C., borne alternately by colonization and by native adaptation of new technologies.

The farmers of Early Neolithic Europe (ca. 7000–ca. 4500 B.C.) were pioneers, living in hamlets or villages surrounded by larger hunter-gatherer populations. Not until 2500 B.C. did the majority of Europeans adopt a

---

Çayönü Tepesi (CHAH-yer-ner TEH-peh-see)
Jericho (JEH-rih-co)   **Çatal Hüyük** (CHAH-tal Her-yerk)

food-producing way of life. Between 4500 and 2500 B.C., a give-and-take between pioneers and natives led to the development of regional cultures. This era of European prehistory is known as the Late Neolithic, or the Copper Age, because copper came into use on the Continent during this time, as did gold. Both metals were used primarily as status symbols: the most dramatic example is a Bulgarian burial site dating from about 4000 B.C. in which a 45-year-old man is buried with 990 gold objects as well as copper and flint weapons.

Between about 4500 and about 3500 B.C., Copper Age Europeans developed their own cultures in relative isolation from the more advanced East. For example, European metallurgy probably developed independently. On Europe's northern and western edges people began to set up megaliths—stone tombs and monuments—often of huge blocks. Such monuments may illustrate an awareness of time created by the spread of agriculture, with its seasonal rhythms.

Between about 3500 and 2500 B.C., Copper Age Europe grew in sophistication. The urbanization of Mesopotamia (in modern-day Iraq; see Map 1.1) had an impact on southeastern Europe, which supplied raw materials for western Asia. Greece underwent the greatest transformation, to the extent that it developed its own urban civilization by about 2000 B.C. (see Chapter 2). Elsewhere, especially in the Balkans, technological innovations came into use, from the wheel, to complex metal-casting, to wine cups (evidence of a new taste). The recent discovery of a Copper Age corpse preserved in the ice of the Italian Alps opens a window into northern Italian society of about 3200 B.C. (See the feature "Weighing the Evidence: The Iceman and His World" on pages 36–37.)

In western Europe stone monuments are the most dramatic cultural achievements. On the Mediterranean island of Malta, for example, people built elaborate temple complexes constructed of massive limestone blocks. In Britain, megalithic architecture reached its peak with Stonehenge, built in stages from about 2800 to 1500 B.C. This famous monument consists of a circle of stones oriented precisely on the rising sun of midsummer—a sign both of early Europeans' interest in the calendar and of their skill in technology.

Neolithic and Copper Age sculpture consists of many representations of females but few of males. Consider, for example, the ample, sculpted female figures found in Malta's temples. The enlarged buttocks and thighs of these statues might be symbols of fertility. Some scholars speculate that early Europeans wor-

The Maltese Female   This "Sleeping Lady," a terra-cotta statuette of the late fourth millennium B.C. from Malta, shows a reclining woman, perhaps a goddess or priestess. Her double-egg shaped buttocks are thought to symbolize fertility or regeneration.   *(Erich Lessing/Art Resource, NY)*

shiped goddesses until warlike invaders after 2000 B.C. brought male deities with them. The theory is, however, controversial.

■ The Emergence of Civilization, 3500–3000 B.C.

Civilization is derived from the Latin word *civitas*, meaning "commonwealth," or "city." The first civilizations, beginning in Mesopotamia and Egypt between 3500 and 3000 B.C., probably contained the first cities. What differentiated them from their predecessors, however, was not so much size (a city versus a town) as complexity. Civilization allowed human beings to think big. A large and specialized labor force, organized by a sufficiently strong government, made it possible to expand control over nature, pursue advances in technology, and trade and compete over ever widening areas. An elite class emerged that was able to pursue ever more ambitious projects in art and thought and to invent systems of writing. In short, the advent of civilization in the fourth millennium B.C. marked a major turning point. Thereafter, the human horizon expanded forever.

Civilization arose in Iraq, in the valley between the Tigris and Euphrates Rivers (see Map 1.1), a region that the Greeks named Mesopotamia (literally, "between the rivers"). At around the same time or shortly afterward, civilization also began in the valley of the Nile River in Egypt. Although these civilizations each developed largely independently, some borrowing between the two nonetheless took place.

Both Mesopotamia and Egypt are home to valleys containing alluvial land—that is, a relatively flat tract where fertile soil is deposited by a river. Otherwise, the two regions are quite different. Although the Nile Valley was easy to farm, much of the Tigris-Euphrates plain had to be tamed by would-be farmers. Every summer the Nile flooded in a relatively regular and predictable manner, bringing north to Egypt the waters of the monsoon rains of the Ethiopian highlands, where one of the river's sources—the Blue Nile—rises. The spring deluges of the Tigris and Euphrates were more sudden and less predictable. Moreover, the Nile's waters spread so broadly that it took less human effort than in Mesopotamia to irrigate most of the available farmland. In southern Mesopotamia, by contrast, most of the soil was alternately so dry or so marshy that agriculture would not have been possible without considerable irrigation and drainage—that is, the use of channels, dikes, or dams to control floodwaters and improve the fertility of the land. One Mesopotamian text describes a farmer as "the man of dike, ditch, and plow." Making matters worse, Mesopotamia was given to extreme heat and scorching winds.

Eye Idol   This tiny figurine, made from bone and named for its prominent eyes, may represent a person rather than a god. It comes from Tell Hamoukar in northeastern Syria (ca. 3500 B.C.), which is one of history's earliest cities.   *(Oriental Institute Hamoukar Expedition)*

Some scholars argue that the very hostility of Mesopotamia's environment generated the cooperation and control that civilization requires.

It has long been thought that the first cities developed in southern Mesopotamia. A recent discovery, however, suggests that cities were found in northern Mesopotamia too around the same time, that is, during the Uruk° Period (3800–3200 B.C.). An excavation at Tell Hamoukar° in northeastern Syria, near the Iraqi border, uncovered what appears to be a city of around 3500 B.C. The excavators found ovens and pottery, apparently used for large-scale food production, and they unearthed stamp seals and clay seal impressions, which may indicate a bureaucracy. A mud-brick fortification wall has tentatively been indentified. In short, several signs point to a city.

If cities developed simultaneously in northern and southern Mesopotamia in the mid-fourth millennium

---

Uruk (OO-rook)   **Tell Hamoukar** (tell ha-moo-CAR)

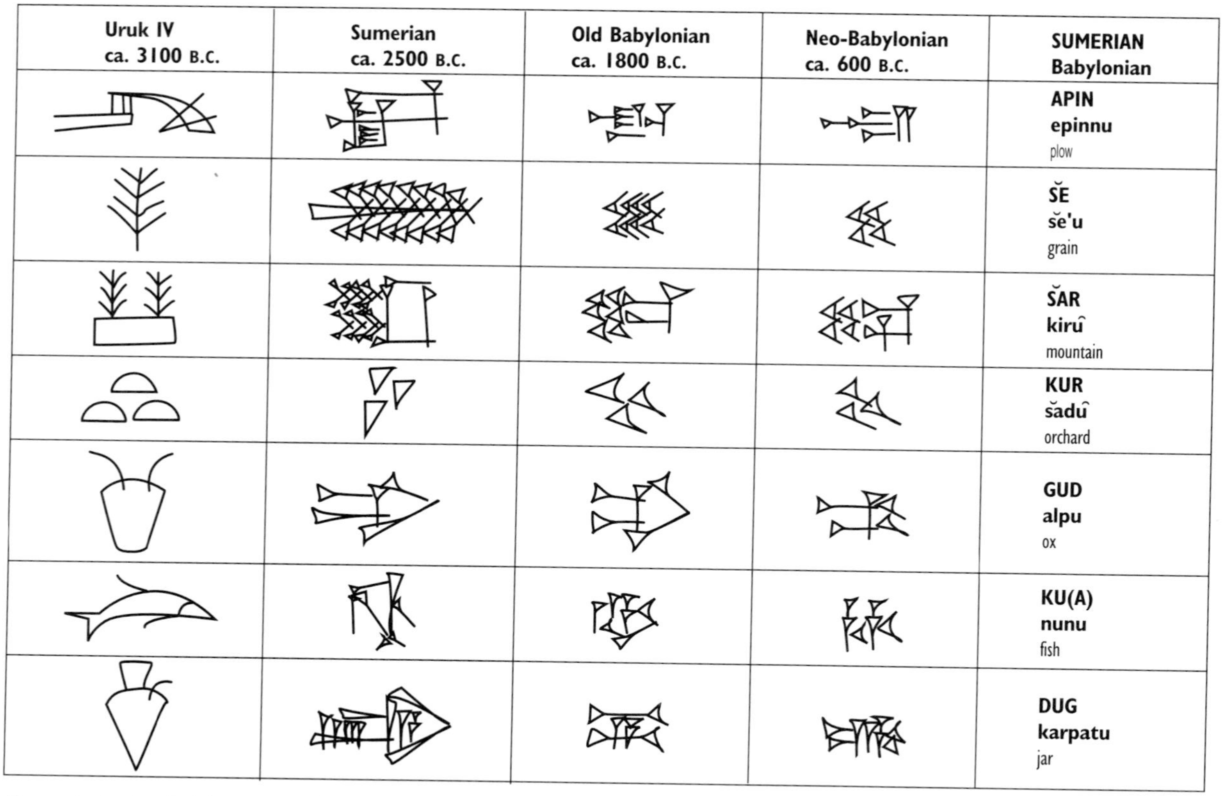

Uruk IV ca. 3100 B.C.	Sumerian ca. 2500 B.C.	Old Babylonian ca. 1800 B.C.	Neo-Babylonian ca. 600 B.C.	SUMERIAN Babylonian
				APIN epinnu plow
				ŠE še'u grain
				ŠAR kirû mountain
				KUR šadû orchard
				GUD alpu ox
				KU(A) nunu fish
				DUG karpatu jar

Figure 1.1 Early Mesopotamian Writing The pictographs of early writing evolved into a system of phonetic syllables and abstract symbols. Simplified and standardized, this writing was *cuneiform,* or "wedge-shaped." Over time, it was adapted from Sumerian to Babylonian and other languages throughout western Asia. *(Source: From* Babylon, *by Joan Oates. Published by Thames and Hudson Ltd., 1978. Used by permission.)*

B.C. they may share a common, earlier source: the Ubaid° culture of mid-fifth-millennium B.C. Mesopotamia. Many questions arise, among them whether Ubaid cities existed as early as 4500 B.C., a thousand years earlier than cities were thought to have first appeared. We will have to wait for future excavation and study to answer such questions.

The first cities emerged through a slow, incremental process of action and reaction. Labor became more specialized and agricultural production was maximized. When part of the population moves to a city, those who remain on the land must work harder or use better farming techniques or increase the amount of land under cultivation. In fourth- and third-millennium B.C. Mesopotamia, farmers did all three. Meanwhile, both the number and variety of settlements increased. Urban populations required the support of people in smaller units—towns, villages, and hamlets—clustered around a city.

Along with the growth of cities came the development of writing, about 3500–3100 B.C. in Mesopotamia. The development of writing from simple recordkeeping can be traced step by step. Before writing, Mesopotamian people used tiny clay or stone tokens to represent objects being counted or traded. By 3500 B.C., with 250 different types of tokens in play, the system had grown unwieldy enough for people to start using signs to indicate tokens. It was a short step to dispensing with the tokens and placing the signs on a clay tablet by making indentations in the clay with a reed stylus: writing. New words were soon added through pictographs (pictures that stand for particular objects). In time the pictographs evolved into ideograms—that is, abstract symbols that are no longer recognizable as specific objects and thus can be used to denote ideas as well as things.

In the centuries following its introduction, Mesopotamian writing became standardized. Scholars call the signs *cuneiform* from the Latin for "wedge-shaped," a good description of what early writing looks like (see Figure 1.1). In its first centuries, cuneiform was used almost entirely for economic records or commercial transac-

Ubaid (oo-BA-id)

12

tions. Then it was adapted to make brief records of offerings to the gods. By 2350 B.C. cuneiform had evolved into a mixed system of about six hundred signs, most of them phonetic (syllabic), with relatively few ideograms.

Experts used to think that writing began in Mesopotamia and spread to Egypt. Recent excavations, however, have found examples of early Egyptian writing securely dated to 3300–3200 B.C. In other words, Egyptian writing was independent: it was not derived from or related to cuneiform. Whether writing began in Egypt or Mesopotamia, therefore, is now an open question. What is clear, however, is that writing was invented to meet economic rather than creative needs. In Egypt the earliest writing includes records of the delivery of linen and oil as taxes to King Scorpion I. The writing consists of early *hieroglyphs* (literally, "sacred carvings"), a system of pictures and abstract signs that represent sounds or ideas, later to become more formal and standardized.

As we shall see, incising cuneiform on clay was much clumsier than writing with pen and ink on papyrus, as became possible in Egypt (see the feature "Information Technology: Papyrus"). Nonetheless, cuneiform was flexible enough to record the spoken language and to be used for poetry as well as for bookkeeping. Moreover, cuneiform became the standard script of various languages of western Asia for several thousand years. Clumsy it may have been, but cuneiform was writing, and writing is both a catalyst for change and the historian's best friend. Mesopotamia after 3000 B.C. was dynamic, sophisticated, and, best of all, intelligible to us.

MESOPOTAMIA, TO CA. 1600 B.C.

A FTER 3000 B.C. the people of Mesopotamia flourished. They experimented in government, in cooperation and conflict among different ethnic groups, in law, and in the working out of class and gender relations. Keenly aware of human limitations and vanity, they sought divine justice, as their literary and religious texts show. Their engineering skill, mathematics, and astronomy set ancient science on an upward path. In later centuries, Western civilization would build on these foundations, and then take off in new directions.

Archaeologists sometimes refer to the third and second millennia in the eastern Mediterranean and western Asia as the Bronze Age. In this period people mastered the technology of making bronze, an alloy of copper and tin, and bronze frequently replaced stone as a primary material for everyday use.

■ The City-States of Sumer

Though their culture is long dead, the Sumerians live on. Whenever someone today counts the minutes, debates politics, or quotes the law, the Sumerians live, for these are all legacies of that ingenious society.

The dominant inhabitants of Mesopotamian civilization in its first flowering are named Sumerians. Present in southern Mesopotamia by 3200 B.C. and probably earlier, the Sumerians entered their great age in the third millennium B.C., when their city-states enjoyed a proud independence (see Map 1.1).

The formative era of Mesopotamian civilization is known as the Uruk Period (ca. 3800–3200 B.C.) after one of its major archaeological sites. During the Uruk Period the Sumerians invented the wheel and the plow, planted the first orchards—of dates, figs, or olives—and developed the first sophisticated metal-casting processes. They built some of the first cities, for example, Uruk. They expanded the size of territories and populations, the scale of war, the complexity of society, and the power of government. Finally, as if to cap a period of remarkable change, at the end of the Uruk Period the Sumerians invented cuneiform writing.

Mesopotamian cities flourished in this era. By the period that scholars have named the Early Dynastic Period (2800–2350 B.C.), named for the first royal dynasties (ruling families), a large Mesopotamian city had grown to the point where it might cover 1,000 acres surrounded by more than 5 miles of walls, within which lived about fifty thousand people. Such a city was part of a network of thirty such city-states with a common culture, commerce, and propensity to make war on one another. Hence the city-states of Mesopotamia may be called the first civilization.

It was a land of cooperation and conflict. The Sumerian cities had much in common: language, literature, arts and sciences, and religion. Yet the cities often quarreled. In some cases conflict erupted over the boundaries of adjacent farmlands. The scarcity of fresh water also led to disputes among cities over water rights.

Each city had its own small urbanized area and a larger agricultural hinterland irrigated by canals. Cities traded with one another and with the outside world. The primary political units of southern Mesopotamia for most of the third millennium B.C., Sumerian city-states were an incubator of civilization.

How were the Sumerian city-states governed? A Sumerian might have responded that they were governed by the gods, for the Sumerians believed that the gods had created, and thus owned, everything on earth. Historians study human government, but the lack of

Papyrus

It grew in the marshes of the Nile River valley, a tall and graceful plant. Once it was picked, it might be eaten, woven into baskets or rope, used as construction material for lightweight boats or shelters, or burned for fuel or as incense. But, most important, this versatile vegetation generated a paperlike writing material that had a huge impact on ancient civilization. Today most paper comes from wood, following a technology developed in China. In the ancient West, however, people wrote on rolled sheets produced from an Egyptian plant. In fact, we derive our word *paper* from the name of the plant, *papyrus*. The Greeks called it *byblos*, from which came the Greek word for book and, eventually, our word *bible*.

Harvested papyrus was transformed into writing material by cutting the stalks into thin strips and laying them in a cross-hatched fashion to form sheets, which were then glued together into rolls, in which form it was sold. The roll was the standard form of both writing paper and books in ancient times. Although sizes varied, a typical roll was about 8 or 9 inches high by about 15 feet long (when unrolled). A sheet of paper was white, shiny, and smooth.

Rolls manufactured from papyrus became the primary writing material of the ancient world, outstripping all competing media. Papyrus was durable and easy to write on, which facilitated all written communication, from paying taxes to reading Plato. Even if they had had only stone or bone or animal skin to write on, humans would have made progress, but papyrus-making technology made things simpler. Progress requires a process of trial and error, which is easier to carry out on paper than in any other nonelectronic medium.

Unlike people in western Asia, where clay tablets were the standard writing medium, Egyptians wrote on papyrus, beginning around 3000 B.C. Carving cuneiform in clay with a reed stylus was cumbersome, but writing on paper with brush and ink was easy, flexible, and even elegant (see the photograph of the Egyptian *Book of the Dead* on page 26). Not only did papyrus allow Egyptians to develop several different written scripts, but it may also have helped stimulate the development of the alphabet. The first alphabet appeared in Egypt in the second millennium B.C., in a Semitic script with Egyptian influences. Although written on stone, that alphabet was probably developed through experimentation more easily done on papyrus.

People wrote everything on papyrus, from contracts to curses, from public documents to poetry, from trivial jottings to holy books. Highly prized because it was durable and flexible, papyrus grew more common than other writing materials available in antiquity, such as parchment (manufactured from animal skins), potsherds, stone, bone, or tablets of wood, wax, or clay. Although expensive for ordinary people, papyrus was cheap for the elites, who had a near-monopoly on literacy.

The papyrus plant has a tall triangular stem and a fluffy crown. It was often the subject of pharaonic art. Look, for example, at this painting from an Egyptian tomb of the fifteenth century B.C. The man on the right has poled the boat into a grove of papyrus plants. The man on the left is pulling a plant out by the stalk, while his coworker in the center is tying stalks into a sheaf.

Papyrus grew in several places around the Mediterranean, but in ancient times its main habitat was Egypt. The

---

evidence makes it difficult to say much with assurance about Sumerian government before the Early Dynastic Period.

Certainly in early times Sumerian temples were wealthy and powerful. A simple structure around 5000 B.C., the temple had become by 4000 B.C. an elaborate, monumental work of architecture built on a raised platform. Each city had at least one temple, the house of its patron god and the common symbol of the community. There is no evidence, though, for the once-prominent theory that the early Sumerian cities were temple-states, governed by priests.

By the beginning of the Early Dynastic Period around 2800 B.C., political power in a Sumerian city rested largely in the hands of its Council of Elders, whose members were probably wealthy landowners. Some scholars argue that the council shared power with a popular assembly, creating, in effect, a bicameral legislature and perhaps even a primitive democracy. The evidence is ambiguous, however, leaving it highly debatable whether ordinary people took part in Sumerian government.

In Sumer, as elsewhere in western Asia and Egypt throughout ancient times, ordinary people often faced

Nile Valley, particularly the delta, became the center of a vast international trade in papyrus in Greek and Roman times, from around 600 B.C. on. Yet the trade began much earlier, at least by around 1100 B.C., when it is known that paper was brought from Egypt to Phoenicia. In pharaonic times the manufacture of papyrus in Egypt may have been under royal supervision. The word *papyrus* itself may mean "that of the pharaoh."

The Classical Greeks got their papyrus from Egypt, at first possibly via the Phoenician port city of Byblos. The Romans considered papyrus to be "an indispensable necessity of public and private business," as one Roman writer put it. From Britain to Iraq, papyrus was in almost universal use during Greek and Roman times for more than a thousand years after 600 B.C.

Harvesting Papyrus   This Egyptian wall-painting, from a tomb of about 1450 B.C., shows boatmen gathering papyrus plants.   *(The Metropolitan Museum of Art [30.4.11])*

limits on their freedom. True, there seem to have been many free peasants. Yet these small "free" farmers often had to provide forced labor for the state as a kind of taxation—maintaining the vast Mesopotamian irrigation system, for example. There also seems to have been a large group of people who were only semi-free because they owned no land of their own but worked others' land. Finally, there were slaves, that is, people who could be bought and sold. Slaves were never very numerous in these societies because no large policing system existed yet to keep them from running away. Still, wealthy people usually had a few slaves to help in the household.

Slaves were usually brought from abroad as war booty or merchandise, although some slaves were local people who had been sold into slavery to pay off a debt; often they were children (especially daughters) sold by their parents.

By about 2700 B.C., political power shifted. It was a time of chronic intercity warfare, and the times demanded a strong hand. The new ruler was not a Council of Elders but rather a "big man" (*lugal*) or, less often, a "governor" (*ensi*)—that is, a king or, occasionally, a queen. The monarch was first and foremost a warrior. He claimed to be the earthly representative of the gods, a position that gave him general responsibility for his subjects' welfare. Accordingly, kings sponsored irrigation works, raised fortification walls, restored temples, and built palaces.

The earliest Sumerian kings, dating from the period 2700 to 2600 B.C., are Enmebaragesi of the city of Kish, his son and successor, Agga, and Gilgamesh° of Uruk, a hero of epic poetry whom many scholars consider a genuine historical personage. In the cities of Ur and Lagash, the king's wife was often a power in her own right. Kish was ruled by Ku-baba (r. ca. 2450 B.C.), the first reigning queen of recorded history.

Though warriors, Sumerian monarchs also recognized a responsibility for promoting justice. History's earliest known reformer of law and society was Uru-inim-gina, king of Lagash around 2400 B.C. Surviving documents describe Lagash as a society in which wealthy landowners encroached on the temples and oppressed the poor, and royal administrators mistreated ordinary people. The king's aims seem to have been both to correct abuses and to weaken independent sources of power threatening royal authority. Uru-inim-gina attempted to manage the bureaucracy, protect the property of humble people, and guard the temples. He also put into effect the first known wage and price controls. Uru-inim-gina's proclaimed intention was to promote impartial justice, a goal that he expressed in the formula "[the king] will protect the mother that is in distress, the mighty man shall not oppress the naked and the widow." If at the same time he also managed to increase his own power, then so much the better. As it turned out, Lagash was conquered only a few years after Uru-inim-gina's reign. His reforms nonetheless survived as the precedent for a long Mesopotamian tradition of royal lawgiving.

■ Conquest and Assimilation, ca. 2350–1900 B.C.

Mesopotamian cities faced competition from the surrounding peoples of the desert and the mountains. Poor and tough, these people coveted Mesopotamia's wealth. Some conquerors came directly from the hinterland to the walls of the city they were attacking; others climbed to power from within the Sumerian city-states. Both groups were sufficiently impressed by Sumerian culture to adopt a great many Sumerian customs and ideas. The most successful warrior-king was Sargon (r. 2371–2316 B.C.), an unusual figure who rose from obscurity to a high position under the king of Kish before founding his own capital city, Agade°. Even more important, Sargon was a native speaker not of Sumerian but of Akkadian.

The Akkadians were originally a seminomadic people who lived on the edge of the desert. Shepherds, they moved their flocks with the seasons. Their language, Akkadian, belongs to the Semitic group of languages, which also includes Arabic and Hebrew. Scholars formerly believed that the Akkadians came directly from the desert to conquer Sumer, but it is now known that they had begun settling in the northern cities of southern Mesopotamia by the end of the Uruk Period. This northern part of southern Mesopotamia was known as Akkad.

As commander of one of history's first professional armies, Sargon conquered all Mesopotamia, and his power extended westward along the Euphrates and eastward into the Iranian Plateau. Rather than rule conquered peoples directly, the Akkadians generally were satisfied with loose control, as long as they could monopolize trade. They adopted Sumerian religion and wrote Akkadian in cuneiform.

Sargon's son inherited his throne. His dynasty boasted that it reigned over "the peoples of all lands" or "the four quarters of the earth." The Akkadian empire reached its greatest height in the reign of Sargon's grandson, Naram-sin (r. ca. 2250–2220 B.C.), but it did not survive the next reign. Sargon nonetheless proved to be one of western Asia's most influential figures. His dynasty's ideal of universal empire was one to which future conquerors would lay claim.

Sargon proved adept at using religion to legitimize his rule. A self-made monarch, he was sensitive to the charge of having stolen power. Indeed, he chose the throne name Sargon (Sharrum-ken in Akkadian) because it means "the king is legitimate." By claiming the status of the gods' representative on earth, Sargon strengthened his authority. He once paraded a defeated enemy in a halter before the temple and priests of Enlil, the chief Sumerian god, confidently proclaiming that Enlil was on his side.

Assimilation was another lasting Akkadian legacy. Although Sargon made Akkadian the official language of administration, he made politic concessions to Sumerian sensibilities. For instance, his daughter Enkheduanna°, whom he appointed high priestess at Ur and Uruk, wrote poetry in Sumerian, poetry powerful enough to be quoted often in later Sumerian texts. The first known woman poet, Enkheduanna described the union of Sumerians and Akkadians.

Gilgamesh (GIL-ga-mesh)

Agade (ah-GAH-day)   **Enkheduanna** (en-khe-du-AN-na)

Around 2200 B.C. the Akkadian empire broke up into a series of smaller successor states. Then, after a century of rule by invaders from the Zagros Mountains on the eastern border of Mesopotamia, the Sumerians returned to power under the Third Dynasty of Ur (2112–2004 B.C.). Far from stripping away all Akkadian influence, the revived Sumerian rulers spoke of themselves as "kings of Sumer and Akkad." It was a title that would have a long and potent history: for the next fifteen hundred years, many of the great kings of western Asia would label themselves, among other honorifics, "king of Sumer and Akkad." By using this title, the Sumerian kings of Ur showed that they recognized the existence of a composite, common Mesopotamian society.

This society survived renewed political turmoil around 2000 B.C. A new kingdom, under the rule of the Amorites, one of several raiding peoples, emerged around 1900 B.C. in southern Mesopotamia. The kingdom of the Amorites, Semitic-speakers, shared Mesopotamian culture and traditions. Babylon, northwest of Ur in the central part of Mesopotamia, became the Amorite capital. From Babylon, Amorite kings issued cuneiform decrees that, although written in a Semitic language, drew heavily on Sumerian material.

Akkadian Bronze   This stern-faced, life-size cast-bronze head, with its stylized ringleted beard and carefully arranged hair, shows Mesopotamian craftsmanship at its finest. Thought by some to be Sargon (r. 2371–2316 B.C.) or Naram-sin (r. ca. 2250–2220 B.C.), it was deliberately mutilated in ancient times.   *(Claus Hansmann, München)*

Plaque of Enkheduanna   This limestone disk depicts a procession of women, including Enkheduanna, daughter of King Sargon (r. 2371–2316 B.C.), a priestess and the first known woman poet.   *(University of Pennsylvania Museum, Philadelphia [neg. #S4-1399330, object #B16665])*

■ Hammurabi's Code

The most famous Amorite king, Hammurabi (r. 1792–1750 B.C.) ruled in Babylon about six hundred years after Sargon. Much of his forty-two-year reign was devoted to creating a Mesopotamian empire. A careful administrator who ushered in an era of prosperity and cultural flowering, Hammurabi is most famous for the text known as Hammurabi's Code. Although the work was less a "code" than a collection listing various crimes and their punishments—a kind of treatise on justice glorifying Hammurabi's qualities as a judge—we shall use the familiar name. Hammurabi's Code became both a legal and a literary classic, much copied in later times.

Hammurabi's Code offers a remarkable portrait of Mesopotamian society. The document contains nearly three hundred rulings in cases ranging from family to commercial law, from wage rates to murder. The administration of justice in Mesopotamia was entirely practical: we find no notion of abstract absolutes or universal principles, not even a word for "law."

Though occasionally less harsh than earlier law codes, which date as far back as around 2100 B.C., Hammurabi's Code was by no means lenient. Whereas earlier codes were satisfied with payment in silver as recompense for crime, Hammurabi's Code was the first to stipulate such ruthless penalties as mutilation, drowning, and impaling. It also introduced the law of retaliation for wounds: "If a man has destroyed the eye of a member of the aristocracy: they shall destroy his eye. If he has broken his limb: they shall break the (same) limb." Moreover, children could be punished for the crimes of their fathers. (See the box "Reading Sources: King Hammurabi Dispenses Justice.")

Inscribed in forty-nine vertical columns on a stone stele about 7½ feet high, and displayed in a prominent public place, Hammurabi's Code symbolized the notion that the law belonged to everyone. Although ordinary people could not read, it was possible for them to find a patron who could. Yet the societies of western Asia and Egypt were anything but egalitarian, and Hammurabi's society was no exception. Punishments there, as elsewhere, were class-based: crimes against a free person, for example, received harsher punishment than crimes against a slave or a semi-free person. Debt seems to have been a serious and widespread problem, frequently leading to debt slavery. Women could own and inherit property and testify in court. The overall direction of the code, however, was patriarchal: it enshrined the power of the male head of the family. For example, a son who struck his father had his hand cut off, while a woman who brought about the death of her husband "because of another man" was impaled on stakes.

■ Divine Masters

The Sumerians were polytheists—that is, they had many gods—and their gods (like the later gods of Greece) were anthropomorphic, or human in form. Indeed, Sumerian (and Greek) gods were thought to be much like human beings, by turns wise and foolish, except that they were immortal and superpowerful. Many Sumerian gods arose out of the forces of nature: An, the sky-god; Enki, the earth-god and freshwater-god; Enlil, the air-god; Nanna, the moon-god; and Utu (Semitic, Shamash), the sun-god. Other Sumerian gods embodied human passions or notions about the afterlife: Inanna (Semitic, Ishtar), goddess of love and war; and Ereshkigal, goddess of the underworld.

The Sumerians sometimes envisioned their gods holding an assembly, much like a boisterous Sumerian prototype. The Sumerians and Akkadians considered Enlil, city-god of Nippur, to be the chief god. The Babylonians replaced him with Marduk, city-god of Babylon.

Every Mesopotamian city had its main temple complex, the most striking feature of which was a *ziggurat*, or stepped tower. Constructed originally as simple raised terraces, ziggurats eventually became seven-stage structures. Unlike the pyramids of Egypt, ziggurats were not tombs but "stairways" connecting humans and the gods.

The keynote of Mesopotamian religion was a certain pessimism about the human condition. It is not surprising that the Mesopotamians, living in a difficult natural environment, regarded the gods with fear and awe. Although the gods communicated with humans, their language was mysterious. To understand the divine will, the Mesopotamians engaged in various kinds of divination: the interpretation of dreams, the examination of the entrails of slaughtered animals, the study of the stars (which stimulated great advances in astronomy, as we will see). By building temples, offering prayers and animal sacrifices, and participating in public rituals and processions, Mesopotamians hoped to appease their gods and discern their wishes.

Most people expected nothing glorious in the afterlife, merely a shadowy existence. It was thought that with a person's last breath, his or her spirit embarked on a long journey to the Netherworld, a place under the earth. More than one Mesopotamian text describes the Netherworld as the "Land-of-no-return" and "the house wherein the dwellers are bereft of light, / Where dust is their fare and clay their food, / Where they see no light,

❧ READING SOURCES

King Hammurabi Dispenses Justice

The Code of Hammurabi, king of Babylon (r. 1792–1750 B.C.), is one of the best-known documents of antiquity. Less a code than a treatise on justice, the text illustrates both the image of himself that the king wished to promote and the class and gender hierarchies of Mesopotamia in the second millennium B.C. The following excerpts are from the preface and body of the text.

[The gods] named me to promote the welfare of the people, me, Hammurabi, the devout, god-fearing prince, to cause justice to prevail in the land, to destroy the wicked and the evil, that the strong might not oppress the weak, to rise like the sun over the black-headed (people), and to light up the land. . . . I established law and justice in the language of the land, thereby promoting the welfare of the people. At that time (I decreed):

128: If a free man acquired a wife but did not draw up the contracts for her, that woman is no wife.

129: If the wife of a free man has been caught while lying with another man, they shall bind them and throw them into the water [that is, submit to the water ordeal, with the river as divine judge]. If the husband of the woman wishes to spare his wife, then the king in turn may spare his subject. . . .

170: When a free man's first wife bore him children and his female slave also bore him children, if the father during this lifetime has ever said "My children!" to the children whom the slave bore him, thus having counted them with the children of his first wife, after the father has gone to (his) fate, the children of the first wife and the children of the slave shall share equally in the goods of the paternal estate, with the first-born, the son of the first wife, receiving a preferential share. . . .

196: If a free man has destroyed the eye of a member of the aristocracy, they shall destroy his eye. . . .

198: If he has destroyed the eye of a commoner or broken the bone of a commoner, he shall pay one mina [approximately one pound] of silver. . . .

202: If a free man has struck the cheek of an aristocrat who is superior to him, he shall be beaten sixty (times) with an oxtail whip in the assembly. . . .

237: When a free man hired a boatman and a boat and loaded it with grain, wool, oil, dates, or any kind of freight, if that boatman was so careless that he has sunk the boat and lost what was in it as well, the boatman shall make good the boat which he sank and whatever he lost that was in it.

Source: Adapted from James B. Pritchard, ed., *Ancient Near Eastern Texts Relating to the Old Testament,* 3d ed., with Supplement (Princeton, N.J.: Princeton University Press, 1969), pp. 164, 171, 173, 175–176.

residing in darkness."[1] The dead resided there permanently, though in some texts their spirits return to earth, often with hostile intent toward the living.

Archaeological evidence indicates a possible shift in such attitudes toward death, at least on the part of the Mesopotamian upper classes, by the late third millennium B.C. The kings and nobles of the Third Dynasty of Ur were buried with rich grave goods and with their servants, who were apparently the victims of human sacrifice following the master's death. Perhaps the rulers now expected to have the opportunity to use their wealth again in a comfortable immortality, possibly influenced by Egyptian ideas (see pages 26–27).

■ Arts and Sciences

The people of Mesopotamia were deeply inquisitive. They focused on the beginning and the end of things. "How did the world come into being?" and "What happens to us when we die?" are perhaps the two fundamental questions of their rich literature. Consider, for example, the Babylonian creation epic known from its

&. READING SOURCES

Heroism and Death in Mesopotamia

The Epic of Gilgamesh *sheds light on categories of gender and power in Mesopotamia. Men such as King Gilgamesh and his friend Enkidu have heroic adventures and risk death. Women lead quieter lives but are wiser and more realistic, as the following excerpts show.*

[Gilgamesh mourns the death of Enkidu.]
"Hear me, O elders and give ear unto me! It is for Enkidu, my friend, that I weep, Moaning bitterly like a wailing woman. The axe at my side, my hand's trust, The dirk in my belt, the shield in front of me, My festal robe, my richest trimming—An evil demon rose up and robbed me! O my younger friend, thou chasedst the wild ass of the hills, the panther of the steppe! We who have conquered all things, scaled the mountains, who seized the Bull and slew him, brought affliction on Hubaba, who dwelled in the Cedar Forest! What, now, is this sleep that has laid hold on thee? Thou art benighted and canst not hear me!" But he lifts not up his head; he touched his heart but it does not beat."

[Beginning lost. Gilgamesh is addressing Siduri, the ale-wife.]
"He who with me underwent all hardships—Enkidu, whom I loved dearly, who with me underwent all hardships—has now gone to the fate of mankind! Day and night I have wept over him. I would not give him up for burial—in case my friend should rise at my plaint—seven days and seven nights, until a worm fell out of his nose. Since his passing I have not found life, I have roamed like a hunter in the midst of the steppe. O ale-wife, now that I have seen thy face, let me not see the death which I ever dread."

The ale-wife said to him, to Gilgamesh: "Gilgamesh, whither rovest thou? The life thou pursuest thou shalt not find. When the gods created mankind, death for mankind they set aside, life in their own hands retaining. Thou, Gilgamesh, let full be thy belly, make thou merry by day and by night. Of each day make thou a feast of rejoicing, day and night dance thou and play! Let thy garments be sparkling fresh, thy head be washed; bathe thou in water. Pay heed to the little one that holds on to thy hand, let thy spouse delight in thy bosom! For this is the task of mankind!"

Source: James B. Pritchard, ed., *Ancient Near Eastern Texts Relating to the Old Testament,* 3d ed., with Supplement (Princeton, N.J.: Princeton University Press, 1969), pp. 89–90.

 For additional information on this topic, go to http://college.hmco.com.

first line as *Enuma Elish*° ("When on high"). An epic poem is the story of heroic deeds, in this case the deeds of the gods of order, who triumphed over the forces of chaos. This poem also commemorates the political ascendancy of Babylon. The poem was recited annually during the New Year's festival by Babylonian priests. Another important Babylonian literary genre, known as wisdom literature, responded to life's vicissitudes with precepts that are sometimes simple, sometimes sophisticated. It proved eventually to influence the wisdom literature of the Hebrew Bible.

The best-known example of Mesopotamian literature is the *Epic of Gilgamesh.* Frequently translated and adapted by various western Asian peoples, *Gilgamesh* may be a Sumerian work dating to about 2500 B.C. Gilgamesh, king of Uruk, was probably a real historical personage, but the poem primarily concerns his fictionalized personal life, in particular his painful pilgrimage from arrogant youth to wise maturity. The main themes

Enuma Elish (eh-noo-MAH EH-lish)

are friendship, loss, and the inevitability of death. Much of the poem discusses Gilgamesh's close relationship with Enkidu, who is first his rival, then his friend, and finally his educator. Enkidu's untimely death makes Gilgamesh aware of his own mortality. Distraught by his friend's passing, Gilgamesh goes on a vain quest for immortality. The *Epic of Gilgamesh* contains stories that presage the later biblical Eden and Flood narratives; there is little doubt but that those narratives found their way from Mesopotamia to the Hebrew Bible. (See the box "Reading Sources: Heroism and Death in Mesopotamia.")

The Mesopotamians made advances in mathematics, astronomy, medicine, and engineering. The Sumerians had two systems of numbers: a decimal system (powers of ten) for administration and business and a sexagesimal system (powers of sixty) for weights and mathematical or astronomical calculations. Like the Babylonians, we still divide hours by sixty today. Furthermore, our modern system of numerical place-value notation—for example, the difference between 42 and 24—is derived, through Hindu-Arabic intermediaries, from the Babylonian system. The Babylonians were adept at arithmetic and could solve problems for which we would use algebra. A millennium before the Greek mathematician Pythagoras (who claimed to have studied the Mesopotamian tradition) proved the validity of the theorem that bears his name, they were familiar with the proposition that in a right triangle the square of the longest side is equal to the sum of the squares of the other two sides. In the first millennium B.C. the Babylonians developed a sophisticated mathematical astronomy (see page 44). As early as the seventeenth century B.C., they made systematic, if not always accurate, recordings of the movements of the planet Venus.

In medical matters they demonstrated considerable critical ability. Physicians made advances in the use of plant products for medicines and in very rudimentary surgery. The Babylonians had a simple pregnancy test of moderate accuracy, for example, and their surgeons were experienced at setting broken bones. When they became ill, however, most people in Mesopotamia set more store by magic and incantations than by surgery or herbal medicine.

Mesopotamian sculptors, particularly the Sumerians, were adept and sophisticated. They did not produce realistic representations of reality—that was not their purpose. Rather, they aimed at creating symbols of religious piety or political or military power. Sumerian statues tend to be stiff and solemn. The head and face are carved in detail, and the body is neglected, sometimes little more than a geometrical form.

The most common type of Mesopotamian sculpture is relief sculpture, in which figures or forms are projected from a flat surface. Steles (upright stone slabs or pillars), plaques, and cylinder seals (small, carved stone or metal cylinders rolled over wet clay to make a stamp, indicating ownership) are all found.

EGYPT, TO CA. 1100 B.C.

FROM Babylon to the valley of the Nile River was about 750 miles by way of the caravan routes through Syria and Palestine—close enough to exchange goods and customs but far enough for a distinct Egyptian civilization to emerge. As in Sumer, civilization in Egypt arose in a river valley, but Egypt was much earlier than Mesopotamia in becoming a unified kingdom under one ruler. Moreover, ancient Egypt survived as a united and independent kingdom for over two thousand years (to be sure, with some periods of civil war and foreign rule). Egypt made great strides in a variety of areas of human achievement, from the arts to warfare. Western civilization borrowed much from Egypt, especially in technology and religion.

■ Geography as Destiny

Ancient Egypt is a product of the unique characteristics of the Nile River (see Map 1.2). Egypt was "the gift of the Nile," to use the well-known phrase of Herodotus, a Greek historian who visited Egypt in the fifth century B.C.

Yet most of present-day Egypt is desert. Only about 5 percent is habitable by humans, including a few oases, the Nile Delta, and the Nile Valley itself, which extends about 760 miles from Cairo to Egypt's modern southern border: Upper Egypt, a long and narrow valley never more than about 14 miles wide. North of Cairo, in Lower Egypt, the Nile branches out into the wide, low-lying delta before flowing into the Mediterranean Sea.

The fertility of the Nile River gave ancient Egypt a prosperous economy and optimistic culture. The river's annual floods, which took place during late summer and autumn, were generally benign. With less human effort than was required in Mesopotamia, the floodwaters could be used to irrigate most of the farmland in the Nile Valley. As a result, Egyptian agriculture was one of the wealthiest in the ancient world. Bread and beer were the national staples.

Egyptian culture celebrated the Nile's bounty. "Hail to Thee, O Nile, that gushest forth from the earth and comest

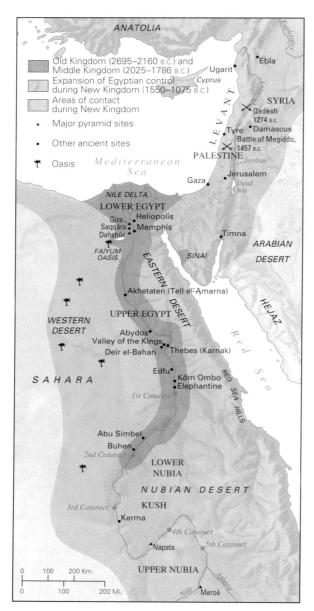

Map 1.2   Ancient Egypt and the Levant   The unique geography of the Nile Valley and its fertile soil left a stamp on ancient Egypt. Egypt enjoyed trade and cultural contact—and sometimes went to war— with nearby lands such as Nubia and the Levant.

to nourish Egypt!" So proclaims an ancient hymn that indicates the Egyptians' confidence in their natural environment. With its plentiful water and fertile land, Egypt suffered far less of the warfare that damaging floods and relative economic scarcity provoked in Mesopotamia.

Egyptian art and literature betray little of the despair over the unpredictability of the universe that developed in the harsher climatic conditions of Mesopotamia. The behavior of the Nile, furthermore, encouraged a static quality in Egyptian ideology. Change seemed undesirable. Even death appeared to be a minor event compared with the eternal regularity of the Nile, which may help explain the prominence in Egyptian religion of belief in the afterlife. In addition, the static outlook helped promote the idea of an absolute, all-powerful, and all-providing king—namely, pharaoh.

Early Egypt developed a distinctive civilization, with no major invasion for nearly 1,500 years after the beginning of the historical period around 3100 B.C. Just how isolated was early Egypt, however, and just how distinctive was its civilization? Debate has arisen in recent years about the relationship of Egypt with western Asia, Europe, and the rest of Africa. Before World War II, most Egyptologists tended to think of Egypt more as part of the Near East (that is, of the culture of western Asia) than as part of Africa. Many imagined that ancient Egyptians looked much like modern Europeans: part of "the Great White Race."[2] More recently, with the liberation after World War II of Europe's former African colonies and with the awakening of a growing interest in Africa by African Americans, some people have argued that Egypt was primarily African in character and that the ancient Egyptians were black.

The truth lies in between these two positions. Much of Egypt's earliest culture is African, as evidenced by both artifacts, such as Neolithic artwork and pottery, and ideas, such as the notion that the ruler represents the ancestors and guarantees the fertility of the soil. Yet in its late Neolithic era (ca. 3400–3050 B.C.), Egypt imported new styles and techniques in art, architecture, ceramics, and metallurgy from western Asia. As for the population, it seems from the fourth millennium B.C., if not earlier, to have consisted of Africans mixed with immigrants from western Asia. The Egyptians considered themselves a distinct ethnic and racial group, unlike their neighbors in Africa or elsewhere. Egyptians were generally darker skinned than the ancient peoples of Europe or western Asia but often lighter skinned than the peoples of Africa south of the Sahara. They included a considerable variety of skin colors and body types. The Egyptians of the southerly Upper Nile were more likely to have the dark skin and facial features characteristic of sub-Saharan Africans.

Egypt was in continual contact with other regions of Africa, particularly the neighboring areas of ancient Libya and Nubia (roughly, modern Sudan). The people of

Nubia, who were black Africans, borrowed from Egypt and were perhaps borrowed from in turn. Some scholars believe, for example, that the early Egyptian notion of monarchy originated in Nubia. In West Africa certain important institutions—including sacred royalty, the cult of the ram, and belief in the afterlife existence of a double of one's physical person—may possibly be of Egyptian origin.

■ Divine Kingship

Agriculture and settled village life emerged in Egypt around 5000 B.C. By 4000, villages had grown into towns, each controlling a strip of territory. About a thousand years later, around 3100 B.C., the Nile Valley had become one unified kingdom of Egypt, with a capital city perhaps at Memphis. We do not know precisely how this process unfolded. Egyptians writing after 3000 B.C. assumed that the Nile Valley had originally been home to two kingdoms roughly corresponding to Upper and Lower Egypt. Then, around 3100, Menes, king of Upper Egypt, is said to have conquered Lower Egypt and united the two into a single realm.

We do not know how much (if any) of this tradition is true. We *do* know that between about 5000 and 3100 B.C., Egyptian communities up and down the Nile Valley succeeded in clearing marshes and expanding the amount of land under cultivation, which in turn could support a larger population. By 3200 B.C., monumental architecture, writing, and kingship appeared. For several centuries Egyptians consolidated their institutions. Although few specifics are known about this Archaic Period (3200–2695 B.C.), it clearly laid the groundwork for the next era. Around 2700 B.C., a remarkable, distinctive, and relatively well-documented period of creativity began, the Third (2695–2600) and Fourth (2600–2500) Dynasties (that is, ruling families) of the Old Kingdom.

The history of third- and second-millennium B.C. Egypt is usually divided into three distinct eras of great prosperity: the Old Kingdom (2695–2160 B.C.), the Middle Kingdom (2025–1786 B.C.), and the New Kingdom (1550–1075 B.C.). Between the kingdoms, central authority broke down in the Intermediate Periods. Broadly speaking, the Old Kingdom was an era of spectacular creativity and originality, symbolized by the building of the Great Pyramids; the Middle Kingdom, an era of introspection and literary production; and the New Kingdom, an era in which Egypt's traditional isolation gave way to international diplomacy and expansion.

The early Egyptian government was the first government in recorded history to govern a large territory. In-deed, a chart of Egypt's power structure would be strictly hierarchical, resembling a pyramid, with a broad base of laborers and artisans supporting a small commanding elite. The occupant of the highest point of power was considered so important that for centuries Egyptians referred to the office rather than to the person, calling it "the Great House": in Egyptian, *per-aa,* or "pharaoh," as the ruler himself (or occasionally herself) was eventually called.

Egyptian kingship was sacred monarchy. In Mesopotamia, the king generally claimed to have been appointed by the gods. In Egypt, pharaoh was deemed to *be* a god. He was referred to as the "good god" in his lifetime and the "great god" after death. Considered the physical child of the sun-god Re, he was also equated with the sky-god Horus, and after dying he became Osiris, god of the underworld. Just as Egyptian myth recounted how the world was created when a god, sitting on a hill, made the waters recede, so pharaoh was thought to make the Nile rise and fall each year. (See the box "Reading Sources: Pharaoh the Divine and Invincible.")

A wall of language and ceremony separated kings from ordinary human beings. Egyptians did not speak "to" the king but rather "in his presence." He was outfitted with a variety of crowns, headdresses, and scepters. Pharaoh's exalted status was apparent on the occasion of a "glorious appearance" before his subjects, especially at the Sed festival or jubilee, a ceremony designed to rejuvenate the king's divine powers.

The most dramatic symbol of the king's divinity, however, was not a festival but a building—or, rather, a series of buildings—the pyramids. The ancients built thirty-five major and many smaller pyramids, of which the best known are the Great Pyramids of Giza—three gigantic, perfectly symmetrical limestone tombs constructed during the Fourth Dynasty. Nearly five thousand years after its construction, the pyramid of King Khufu (r. 2589–2566 B.C., better known by his Greek name, Cheops) is still the largest all-stone building in human history. Near the Great Pyramids stands the Great Sphinx, a human-headed lion carved out of a huge rock outcropping, perhaps representing Khufu's son, King Khafre (r. 2558–2532 B.C., Greek name, Chephren), for whom the second pyramid at Giza was built.

The pyramids were not just monuments to an ego, but temples where the king would continue to be worshiped and served in the afterlife. The structures served a political purpose as well. When the Great Pyramids were constructed, the kingdom of Egypt was still young and fragile. By carrying out an astonishingly large project focused on his person, the king made a statement of his

❧ READING SOURCES

Pharaoh the Divine and Invincible

Egypt's rulers presented themselves as god-kings. Excerpt (a), a selection from the grave stele of a high official of the Twelfth Dynasty of the Middle Kingdom (ca. 1850 B.C.), states pharaoh's divinity unhesitatingly. Excerpt (b), from an inscription about Amenhotep II (r. 1427–1400 B.C.), shows the emphasis that the warrior-pharaohs of the New Kingdom placed on their invincibility in combat—in sport as well as in battle.

(a)

Now, further, his majesty appeared as king as a goodly youth. When he had matured and completed eighteen years on his thighs in valor, he was one who knew every task of Montu [the war-god]; there was no one like him on the field of battle. He was one who knew horses: there was not his like in this numerous army. There was not one therein who could draw his bow. He could not be approached in running.

Worship King Nimaatre, living forever, within your bodies and associate with his majesty in your hearts. He is Perception which is in men's hearts, and his eyes search out every body. He is Re, by whose beams one sees. He is one who illumines the Two Lands more than the sun disc.

He is one who makes the land greener than does a high Nile, for he has filled the Two Lands with strength and life. The nostrils are chilled when he inclines toward rage, but when he is merciful, they will breathe the air. He gives food to them who are in his service, and he supplies them who tread his path.

(b)

Strong of arms, one who did not weary when he took the oar, he [Amenhotep II] rowed at the stern of his falcon-boat as the stroke [the rower who sets the pace] for two hundred men. When there was a pause, after they had attained half an iter's course [about two-thirds of a mile], they were weak, their bodies were limp, they could not draw a breath, while his majesty was (still) strong under his oar of twenty cubits [about 34 feet] in its length. He left off and moored his falcon-boat only after he had attained three iters [about 4 miles] in rowing without letting down in pulling. Faces were bright at the sight of him, when he did this.

Source: James B. Pritchard, ed., *Ancient Near Eastern Texts Relating to the Old Testament*, 3d ed., with Supplement (Princeton, N.J.: Princeton University Press, 1969), pp. 244, 431.

---

power: an eloquent, simple, and irrefutable statement. The sheer size of the Great Pyramids demonstrated the king's ability to organize a vast labor force. Indeed, it has plausibly been suggested that the encampment of workers at Giza represented the largest gathering of human beings to that date. Moreover, the pyramids and the rows of tombs surrounding them reinforced the hierarchical structure of Egyptian society, of which the king was the capstone. Only princes and select officials were given the privilege of erecting a tomb beside the royal pyramids, a privilege that Fourth Dynasty Egyptians viewed as a prerequisite to gaining access to eternal life. The principal

royal wives were permitted to be buried in small pyramids of their own.

In theory the king owned all the land, but in practice Egypt's economy was a mixture of private enterprise and centralized control. The king was thought to watch over Egypt carefully. In the Middle Kingdom, for example, he was represented as a good shepherd, appointed by the sun-god, Re, as one text says, "to keep alive the people and the folk, not sleeping by night as well as by day in seeking out every beneficial act, in looking for possibilities of usefulness." Even sleepless pharaohs needed help, however, and they delegated authority to a large group of

Great Pyramids of Giza   Royal funerary monuments of three Egyptian kings of the twenty-sixth century B.C., the pyramids symbolize the power and ambition of the Old Kingdom. The pyramid of King Khufu (or Cheops, rearmost in the photo) is still the largest all-stone building in human history.   *(Michael Holford)*

officials. Indeed, Old Kingdom Egypt was one of the earliest great bureaucracies. The country was supervised by governors, mayors, military commanders, judges, treasurers, engineers, agricultural overseers, scribes, and others. The highest official was the vizier, a sort of prime minister who had more day-to-day power than pharaoh himself.

The essence of good government was what the Egyptians called *ma'at,* whose basic meaning is "order"—in government, society, or the universe. *Ma'at* can also mean "truth" or "justice." The god-king embodied what we would call law, but the administration of justice rested mainly on others' shoulders. Egypt had a well-functioning system of judges who heard lawsuits, and it probably also had a detailed law code, although few written laws survive.

■ Life and Afterlife

Later peoples, beginning with the Greeks, have assumed that the ordinary Egyptian chafed under royal power. It is true that Egyptians were burdened with a variety of taxes (paid in agricultural produce) and that free people, both men and women, had an obligation of forced labor service on public works, from irrigation projects to the pyramids. Sometimes this service caused resentment. We hear of worker discipline maintained by beatings, of desperate fugitives, of the pious hope that there would be no forced labor in the afterlife, and even, in one unusual case, of a workers' strike.

Both piety and practicality, however, dictated that most people make peace with their public burdens. Far from resenting the king's claim to divinity, ordinary people may have been reassured to be ruled by a god. Nor were the pyramid-builders slaves laboring under a tyrant, as Greek writers assumed. In fact, they might have given their labor gladly to raising the man-god's tomb, as an act of faith, just as people centuries later donated time and money to build medieval cathedrals. The workers reaped material compensations, too: ration supplements for ordinary laborers, steady employment for specialized craftsmen.

Egyptian life was suffused with religious practices, from daily rituals and seasonal festivals to ethical teachings and magic. Egyptian religion tended toward *syncretism*—that is, the blending of mutually opposed beliefs, principles, or practices. For example, Egyptian mythology taught variously that the sky was a cow *or* was held up by a god *or* by a post *or* that it was a goddess stretched over the earth. No one was troubled by such inconsistencies, as a modern worshiper might be, because Egyptians believed that a fundamental unity underlay the varieties of nature. Another example of syncretism is the most important Egyptian god, Re, the sun, often called "universal lord." From time to time, Re was syncretized with other gods to create a powerful new god: for example, Re-Atum, a combination of Re and a creator-god.

But Egypt's religion had an abundance of greater and lesser deities, including human, animal, and composite gods. Various animals, from cats and dogs to crocodiles and serpents, were thought to represent the divine. Innumerable local deities and demons, as well as gods and goddesses of all Egypt, peopled the spirit world. Important deities included Thoth, the moon-god and god of wisdom; Nut, goddess of the sky; Ptah, a creator-god; Osiris, who invented agriculture and became lord of the dead; Horus, son of Osiris, a sky-god imagined as a giant falcon; and Isis, wife of Osiris and mother of Horus, a mother-goddess. Temples were numerous and lavish.

Probably the most striking feature of Egyptian religion was its focus on the afterlife. Unlike the Mesopotamians, the Egyptians believed that death could be an extremely pleasant continuation of life on earth. Hence, they actively sought immortality. The wealthy placed great emphasis on building tombs, decorating them with paintings and inscriptions, and stocking them with cherished possessions for use in the world beyond. The most cherished possession of all, of course, was the body itself, and the Egyptians provided for its preservation through their mastery of the science of embalming— hence the Egyptian mummies. The Egyptians believed that a person's spirit could live on after death, but unlike later civilizations, they were not prepared to jettison the body altogether, believing instead that from time to time a person desired to return to the body after death. That belief made mummification necessary.

Reserved for the king and his officials in the Old Kingdom, by the Middle Kingdom the afterlife became, as it were, democratized. The Middle Kingdom and the First and Second Intermediate Periods were in many ways an inward-looking and reflective era, one in which materialism was de-emphasized and a sense of common humanity appears.

Egyptian Book of the Dead   This scene from a lavishly illustrated papyrus shows a dead person's appearance before a divine court of judgment. His heart is being weighed in the balance to determine his fate in the afterlife.   *(Courtesy of the Trustees of the British Museum)*

By the Middle Kingdom, even ordinary Egyptians believed they could enjoy immortality after death, as gods, as long as they could purchase for their graves funerary texts containing the relevant litanies. The texts emphasize ritual—incantations, magic spells, prayers—as the key to eternal life. Yet from time to time we find other texts, especially from the Middle Kingdom, that say that ritual is not enough: ethical behavior too is required. New Kingdom texts describe the details of a dead person's appearance before a divine court for judgment. Before forty-two judges of the underworld, the dead person declares his or her innocence of a variety of sins. A god then weighs the dead person's heart in the balance against a feather, symbol of *ma'at*, or truth. The sinless are admitted into eternal life in the kingdom of the blessed. The guilty, their heavy hearts devoured by a beast, suffer a second, final death.

Such absolute judgments were not found in daily life. Consider relations between the sexes. Egyptian women did not enjoy equal status with men, but they had a considerably greater measure of equality than women in other ancient societies, particularly in legal matters. As in Mesopotamia, so in Egypt a woman could buy or sell, bequeath or inherit, sue or testify in court, but a married Egyptian woman, unlike her eastern sisters, could do so without a male guardian's approval. A married woman in Egypt retained the status of complete legal independence. She could even own property without her husband's involvement. But how often did women exercise such privileges? Relatively little evidence of female property owners survives from Egypt. Although Egyptian women could work outside the home in a variety of enterprises, they were rarely managers. Women worked in agriculture and trade, in the textile and perfume industries, in dining halls, and in entertainment, and women served as priestesses of various kinds. Yet in Egypt, as elsewhere, women were expected to make the home the focus of their activities. So, although Egyptian women had more freedom outside the home than most ancient women, they exercised nothing like the freedom enjoyed by women in North America today.

■ Expansion, Reform, and Power Shifts, 1786–1075 B.C.

The humane attitudes of the Middle Kingdom were swept away after about 1700 B.C., when Semitic-speaking immigrants from Palestine—the Hyksos°, to employ the commonly used Greek term—conquered much of Egypt.

In many ways gentle conquerors, the Hyksos worshiped Egyptian gods, built and restored Egyptian temples, and intermarried with natives. As foreigners, however, the Hyksos were unpopular. Eventually a war launched from Upper Egypt, which had retained a loose independence, drove the Hyksos out.

The first restored Egyptian ruler of the New Kingdom was Ahmose° I (r. 1550–1525 B.C.). His proved to be a new Egypt indeed. The Hyksos had brought advanced military technology to Egypt, including the horse-drawn war chariot, new kinds of daggers and swords, and the composite bow. Made of laminated materials including wood, leather, and horn, the composite bow could hit a target at 600 yards. Having tasted foreign occupation, Egypt's new rulers determined to use such weapons in aggressive military campaigns abroad.

Warlike, expansionist, and marked by a daring attempt at religious reform, the New Kingdom's Eighteenth Dynasty (1540–1293 B.C.) has long held a special fascination for historians. One of the dynasty's memorable names is that of Queen Hatshepsut°. Widow of Thutmose II (r. 1491–1479 B.C.), Hatshepsut first served as regent for her young stepson and then assumed the kingship herself (r. 1479–1457 B.C.). Other Egyptian queens had exercised royal power before, but Hatshepsut was the first to call herself king. Some statues show her wearing a false beard, and some of her inscriptions refer to Hatshepsut as "he" not "she." Although Hatshepsut dispatched Egyptian armies to fight, her reign is best known for peaceful activities: at home, public works and temple rebuilding; abroad, a commercial expedition over the Red Sea to the "Land of Punt" (perhaps modern Somalia, in eastern Africa).

After her death, Hatshepsut was succeeded by her stepson, Thutmose° III (r. 1479–1425 B.C.). Late in his reign, he tried to erase his stepmother's memory by having Hatshepsut's statues destroyed and her name expunged from records—an attempt, perhaps, to cut off a claim to the throne by her supporters. A warrior-pharaoh, Thutmose III led his dynasty's armed expansion in western Asia and northern Africa. Thutmose won his greatest victory during his first campaign, at the Battle of Megiddo in Palestine in 1457 B.C. (see Map 1.2), where Egypt's triumph prevented the kingdom of Mitanni from expanding southward. Egypt now ruled an empire with territory in Nubia, Palestine, and Syria.

Empire brings power and power often causes conflict. So in imperial Egypt of the fourteenth century B.C., kings and priests struggled over authority. Consider the

---

Hyksos (HICK-sos)

Ahmose (AKH-mose)   **Hatshepsut** (HAT-shep-soot)
Thutmose (THUT-mose)

Egyptian Queen This elegant, red granite statue of the pharaoh Hatshepsut (r. 1479–1457 B.C.) is one of the few to depict her as a woman. She is usually shown as a man, complete with beard, to symbolize her royal power. Centuries later the proportions and carving techniques of Egyptian stone sculpture would influence the Greeks, although Greek artists chose less to copy the Egyptians than to try to outdo them (see the photo on page 82). *(Brian Brake/Photo Researchers, Inc.)*

Amarna° reform, named for a major archaeological site at the modern town of Tell el-Amarna.

The Amarna reform was carried out by Thutmose III's great-great-grandson, King Amenhotep IV (r. 1352–1336 B.C.). Earlier, the god Amun-Re had become the chief deity of the New Kingdom. As supporters of the ideology of imperialism, his temple priests had been so richly rewarded with land and wealth that their power now rivaled pharaoh's own. Amenhotep IV's dramatic response was to forbid the worship of Amun-Re and replace him with the god Aten, the solar disk. Changing his own name to Akhenaten ("pleasing to Aten"), the king ordered the erasure of Amun-Re's name from monuments throughout Egypt. As a further step, Akhenaten created a new capital city in central Egypt at an uninhabited site at the desert's edge: Akhetaten (modern Amarna). The new town had a distinctive culture. Akhenaten's wife, Nefertiti, figures prominently in Amarna art, and she too may have played an important role in the reform.

The reform shifted power away from the priests and toward the king, but we need not doubt the reformers' sincerity. Contemporary literature suggests intense religious conviction in Aten as a benevolent god and one who nurtured not only Egypt but all countries. Although the Aten cult focuses on one god, only Akhenaten and his family were permitted to worship Aten directly; the rest of the Egyptian population was expected to worship the god through pharaoh.

Bold as the reform was, sustaining so dramatic a break with tradition proved impossible. After Akhenaten's death his son-in-law and successor, Tutankhaten (r. 1336–1327 B.C.) restored good relations with the priests of Amun-Re, which he signaled by changing his name to Tutankhamun. The Amun-Re cult was revived, the Aten cult was abolished, and the city of Akhetaten was abandoned. After Tutankhamun's death, the military exercised great influence over the remaining pharaohs of the Eighteenth Dynasty. Then, in 1291, a military officer founded a new dynasty as Ramesses° I (r. 1291–1289).

The Nineteenth (ca. 1291–1185 B.C.) and Twentieth (ca. 1185–1075) Dynasties are known as the Ramesside Era, from the most common name of the pharaohs. Though the era witnessed great warrior-pharaohs and builder-pharaohs, over time the kings lost power to the priests of Amun. Abroad, Egypt remained a formidable power, but it faced armed invasions, some of which required major efforts to repel (see page 34). In any case, many foreigners settled peacefully in the rich farmland of the Nile Delta, giving Egypt a more cosmopolitan character. Both their presence and the building of a great new city in the delta by the Ramesside kings led to a

---

Amarna (a-MAR-na)

Ramesses (RAM-zeez)

power shift within Egypt. When the Twentieth Dynasty ended in 1075, the New Kingdom ended with it, and regional conflict between the Nile Delta and Upper Egypt broke out.

■ Arts and Sciences in the New Kingdom

The Egyptians were superb builders, architects, and engineers. In addition to pyramids and irrigation works, they constructed monumental royal tombs, palaces, forts, and temples, and they erected looming obelisks. At their best, Egyptian architects designed buildings in harmony with the unique landscape—one of the reasons for the structures' lasting appeal. Their most original and enduring work was done in stone. Stone temples, for example, culminated in the imposing pillared structures of the New Kingdom. That period also saw the construction of rock-cut temples, the most famous of which is Ramesses II's (r. 1279–1213 B.C.) project at Abu Simbel (see Map 1.2). In front of the temples sit four colossal statues of Ramesses, also carved out of rock. Obelisks were slender, tapering pillars carved of a single piece of stone. Inscribed with figures and hieroglyphs, and usually erected in pairs in front of a temple, obelisks were meant to glorify the sun-god.

Throughout history, royal courts have excelled as patrons of the arts; the Egyptian court was one of the first and greatest. Egyptian craftsmen were master goldsmiths, glassmakers, and woodworkers. The major arts are well represented in tombs, which were decorated with rich, multicolored wall paintings, the first narrative depictions. Scenes of the gods, court ceremony, ordinary life, war, and recreation amid the crocodiles and hippopotamuses of the Nile Valley adorn subterranean walls. Like so much else in Egypt, painting had a religious purpose. Representations of living people were meant to perpetuate them in the afterlife.

Sculpture was another art form in which Egyptians excelled. Carved in stone, wood, or metal, Egyptian sculpture is a study in contrasts. The body posture is usually rigid and stiff, the musculature only sketchy; the face, in contrast, is often individualistic, the expression full of character and drawn from life. Statues represent kings and queens, gods and goddesses, husbands and wives, adults and children, officials, priests, scribes, animals. Mirroring broader cultural trends, statues of pharaohs underwent stylistic changes through the centuries. In the Old Kingdom, the royal expression was usually one of majesty and power, but in the Middle Kingdom, the king's face often appeared more human and weak. Statues of New Kingdom pharaohs often sug-

gested imperial power, whereas Amarna sculptors emphasized introspective gazes and experimented with the grotesque. Eighteenth Dynasty sculpture often shows a striking interest in feminine beauty and grace.

Ancient Egyptian literature is notable for its variety. Religious subjects, historical and commemorative records, technical treatises in mathematics and medicine, and secular stories survive alongside business contracts and royal proclamations. A good example of Egyptian writing is the *Story of Sinuhe*, a Middle Kingdom prose tale. Sinuhe reveals both the charm of ancient Egyptian literature and its cultural chauvinism. (See the box "Global Encounters: Egyptian Attitudes Toward Foreigners.")

The vastness and variety of ancient Egyptian literature were made possible by the invention of a far more convenient medium for writing than the clunky clay tablets of Mesopotamia—papyrus. (See the feature "Information Technology: Papyrus" on pages 14–15.) Egyptian writing is best known for hieroglyphs. Elaborate and formal, hieroglyphs were generally used after the Archaic Period only for monuments and ornamentation. Two simplified scripts served for everyday use.

The people who built the pyramids had to be skilled at arithmetic and geometry. Egyptians were able to approximate pi (the ratio of the circumference of a circle to its diameter) and to solve equations containing one or two unknowns. Mathematical astronomy never reached the heights in Egypt that it reached in Babylon (see page 44), but the Egyptian calendar was a remarkable achievement. Based on observation of the star Sirius, the Egyptian calendar, with its 365-day year, approximates the solar calendar. Corrected to 365¼ days, it survives to this day as the calendar of Europe, the Americas, and much of the rest of the world.

Egyptian medical doctors were admired in antiquity and in demand abroad. They knew how to set a dislocated shoulder and used a full battery of splints, sutures, adhesive plasters, elementary disinfectants (from tree leaves), and burn treatments (fatty substances). A brilliant treatise, the Edwin Smith Papyrus, demonstrates their sophistication and rationalism. Dating from around 1750 B.C., the document claims to be a copy of an original from 2700 B.C. (the veracity of that claim is uncertain). Possibly a manual for the treatment of battlefield wounds, it is an ancient prototype of modern triage, dividing diseases into three categories: treatable, possibly treatable, and untreatable. In addition to signs of careful observation is tantalizing evidence that Egyptian doctors undertook postmortem dissection in order to understand the human body better.

Egyptian Attitudes Toward Foreigners

The story of Sinuhe is a well-known piece of Middle Kingdom prose literature. A court official, Sinuhe fled Egypt for Syria-Palestine after the assassination of the king. There he married the daughter of a tribal chief and became a successful chief himself. In his old age he received permission to return home. The tale demonstrates Egyptian curiosity about Palestine and Syria, at the same time revealing Egyptian cultural snobbery toward what another Egyptian text calls "the miserable Asiatic."

This decree of the King: . . . Come back to Egypt! See the residence in which you lived! Kiss the ground at the great portals, mingle with the courtiers! For today you have begun to age. You have lost a man's strength. Think of the day of burial, the passing into reveredness.

A night is made for you with ointments and wrappings from the hand of Tait [goddess of weaving]. A funeral procession is made for you on the day of burial; the mummy case is of gold, its head of lapis luzuli. . . . You shall not die abroad! Nor shall Asiatics inter you. You shall not be wrapped in the skin of a ram to serve as your coffin. Too long a roaming of the earth! Think of your corpse, come back! . . .

Copy of the reply to this decree:

The servant of the Palace, Sinuhe, says: In very good peace! . . . May the fear of you resound in lowlands and highlands, for you have subdued all that the sun encircles! . . .

Re [the sun-god] has set the fear of you throughout the land, the dread of you in every foreign country. Whether I am at the residence, whether I am in this place, it is you who cover this horizon. The sun rises at your pleasure. The water in the river is drunk when you wish. The air of heaven is breathed at your bidding. . . . This servant has been sent for! Your Majesty will do as he wishes! One lives by the breath which you give.

[Sinuhe returns to Egypt and is brought into the king's presence.]

Then the royal daughters were brought in, and his majesty said to the queen: "Here is Sinuhe, come as an Asiatic, a product of nomads!" She uttered a very great cry, and the royal daughters shrieked all together. They said to his majesty: "Is it really he, O kings, our lord?" Said his majesty: "It is really he!" . . .

His majesty said: "He shall not fear, he shall not dread! He shall be a Companion among the nobles. He shall be among the courtiers. Proceed to the robing-room to wait on him!"

I left the audience-hall, the royal daughters giving me their hands. We went through the great portals, and I was put in the house of a prince. In it were luxuries: a bathroom and mirrors. . . . Every servant was at his task. Years were removed from my body. I was shaved; my hair was combed. Thus was my squalor returned to the foreign land, my dress to the Sand-farers. I was clothed in fine linen; I was anointed with fine oil. I slept on a bed. I had returned the sand to those who dwell in it, the tree-oil to those who grease themselves with it.

Source: Miriam Lichtheim, *Ancient Egyptian Literature, Volume 1: The Old and Middle Kingdoms* (Berkeley: University of California Press, 1973), pp. 229–233.

WIDENING HORIZONS: THE LEVANT AND ANATOLIA, 2500–1150 B.C.

 EGYPT and Mesopotamia tend to capture our attention, but other early, nearby civilizations are, if less important, also significant contributors to the West. Not only were they the cradle of Western languages and writing systems, but they took part in the first international system of states, a forerunner of later international relations between the West and its neighbors. Let us look in particular at the city-states of the Levant°—that is, the geographic region known today as Syria and Palestine or Israel—and at a kingdom in Anatolia, today's Turkey.

Levant (le-VANT)

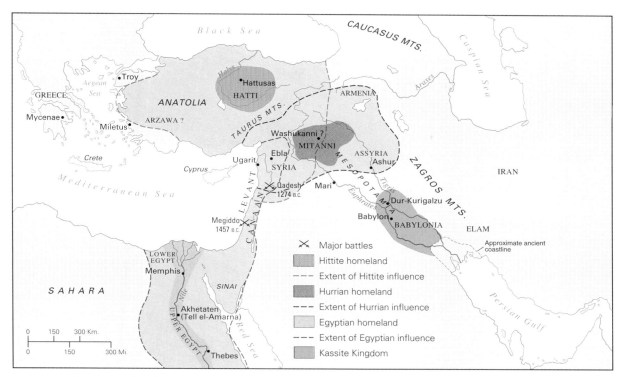

Map 1.3   The International System, ca. 1500–1250 B.C.   This era of competing kingdoms and city-states witnessed considerable war, especially between Egypt and the Hittites for control of Syria and Palestine. Yet it was also a period of international trade, diplomacy, and, from 1450 to 1300 B.C., peace.

■ The City-States of Syria-Palestine, ca. 2500–1200 B.C.

The discovery in 1974 of a huge cuneiform archive at Ebla° (modern Tell Mardikh) in northern Syria revolutionized our knowledge of one such city-state in the mid-third millennium B.C. Another Levantine city-state, Ugarit° (modern Ras Shamra), a cosmopolitan port, flourished in the second millennium B.C.

A prosperous city, Ebla was known for commerce and artisanry as well as scholarship. Its extensive cuneiform archives include the world's earliest known dictionaries. Sometime between 2500 and 2300 B.C., Ebla ruled a large kingdom, extending over much of Syria, and possibly containing as many as 250,000 people, of whom perhaps 30,000 lived in the city (see Map 1.3). Ebla's government fostered trade by negotiating commercial treaties and arranging dynastic marriages. The treaty between Ebla and Ashur, a city about 435 miles to the east, is the earliest known agreement between two states.

When diplomacy failed, Ebla resorted to war, with great success. Ebla's most notable conquest was Mari, a commercial competitor 300 miles downstream on the Euphrates.

Ebla was ruled by an oligarchy (a small, elite group) headed by fourteen regional governors who were probably also clan elders. The king, a sort of first among equals, was chosen by election rather than inheritance; his power was limited by the oligarchic council. Eblaites seem to have conceived of the state as a large family, the "children of Ebla." The queen and queen mother had significant government authority. The queen had her own properties, administered by officials who answered to her. If she was still alive, the queen mother, officially addressed as "the honored mother of the king," had considerable say in the succession.

Ebla fell to the Amorites around 2000 B.C. It remained a wealthy city, though much diminished in power. To find a much more vibrant city in Syria after 2000 B.C., we need only look at the coast and the city of Ugarit (see Map 1.3). Ugarit was a thriving Mediterranean port, especially around 1400–1200 B.C. Its cosmopolitanism made Ugarit

Ebla (EH-bla)   **Ugarit** (OO-ga-rit)

A Hittite Warrior This 6½-foot-tall figure was carved on the wall of an entry gate to the city of Hattusas, the Hittite capital, during the New Kingdom Period (1380–1180 B.C.). Fierce-looking, vigorous, and outfitted with battle ax, sword, kilt, and possibly mail shirt, he is designed to frighten away both human and supernatural enemies. *(Ankara National Museum)*

distinctive among western Asian city-states. As a trading center it linked ships coming from the eastern Mediterranean island of Cyprus or the Anatolian ports with land caravans heading to Babylonia. The native inhabitants of Ugarit spoke a Semitic language. Their culture and that of large numbers of people in southern Syria and Palestine

is called Canaanite (from the Hebrew Bible, which calls Palestine "the land of Canaan"). The merchants of Ugarit, however, were often foreigners, and the bazaars echoed with a multitude of languages.

Ugarit played an important role in the spread of one of history's most important writing systems: the alphabet. Unlike the pictographic or syllabic systems of Mesopotamia, Egypt, and China, each sign in an alphabet stands for one and only one sound. In the 1300s B.C., scribes in Ugarit developed an alphabet. It was not the first alphabet, however. In Egypt, in the desert west of the Nile, limestone inscriptions have recently been found in a Semitic script with Egyptian influences. Dated to about 1900–1800 B.C., during the Middle Kingdom, the writing is now recognized as the earliest known example of an alphabet.

We do not know whether that alphabet was invented by Egyptians or by speakers of a Semitic language who were visiting Egypt. Nor do we know if that alphabet influenced Ugarit. What is clear is that Ugaritic scribes invented thirty cuneiform signs as an alphabet to write their Semitic language. Later adapted by the Phoenicians and, through them, the Greeks, the Ugaritic alphabet is the source of the Roman alphabet, used today by English and many other languages around the world.

■ The Hittites, 1650–1180 B.C.

Almost all the peoples of western Asia and Egypt whom we have discussed so far spoke a language belonging to the large Afro-Asiatic language family. But none of these languages survived antiquity in Europe. Instead, virtually every modern European language—as well as the dominant languages of Iran and India—are descendants of the long-lost proto–Indo-European language. These languages, from English and Russian to Iranian and Hindi, are said to belong to the Indo-European language family.

Indo-European speakers probably originated between 4500 and 2500 B.C. in southern Russia, in the region of the Dnieper and Volga Rivers. A warlike, mobile people, they emigrated east and west. The first speakers of an Indo-European language to establish a civilization in western Asia were the Hittites, who came to Anatolia some time before 1800 B.C. The Hittites were masters of the horse, which their warriors rode into battle. They ruled Anatolia from their city of Hattusas (modern Boghazköy). Rich in minerals and farmland, Anatolia provided a solid foundation for empire.

Hittite history is divided into several periods. The Old Kingdom (ca. 1650–1450 B.C.) was marked by the

Prayers of a Hittite Queen

Puduhepa, wife of Hittite king Hattusilis III (r. 1278–1250 B.C.), played an important role in state religious ritual and propaganda. The following selections from her recorded prayers show Puduhepa's official devotion to her royal husband as well as a belief, common in ancient religion, that women had a special closeness to the gods.

Prayer to the Sun-Goddess Herself

To the Sun-goddess of Arinna, my lady, the mistress of the Hatti lands, the queen of heaven and earth. . . . I, Puduhepa, am a servant of thine from of old, a heifer from thy stable, a foundation stone upon which thou canst rest. Thou, my lady, rearedst me and Hattusilis, thy servant, to whom thou espousedst me, was closely associated with the Storm-god of Nerik, thy beloved son. The place in which thou, Sun-goddess of Arinna, my lady, didst establish us was the residence of the Storm-god of Nerik, thy beloved son. How the earlier kings had neglected it, that thou knowest, Sun-goddess of Arinna, my lady. The earlier kings let fall into ruins even those countries which thou, Sun-goddess of Arinna, my lady, hadst given them. . . .

Sun-goddess of Arinna, my lady, yield to me, hearken to me! Among men there is a saying: "To a woman in travail the god yields her wish." Since I, Puduhepa, am a woman in travail and since I have devoted myself to thy son, yield to me, Sun-goddess of Arinna, my lady! Grant to me what I ask. Grant life to Hattusilis, thy servant [who was ill]! Through the Good-women and the Mother-goddess long and enduring years and days shall be given to him. Since thou, an exalted deity, holdest a place set apart from the gods, all the gods are subservient to thee, and no one appeals to thee in vain. In the assembly of the gods request thou the life of Hattusilis! May thy request be received with favor! Because thou, Sun-goddess of Arinna, my lady, hast shown favor to me and because the good of the land of its realm is close to thy heart, thou shalt enjoy the reverent worship of my family.

Prayer to Lelwanis [probably Ishtar]

. . . Hattusilis, that servant of thine, who is ill. In the presence of Sum. . . , the physician, they spoke charms over him. . . . If Hattusilis is accursed, and if Hattusilis, my husband, has become hateful in the eyes of you, the gods; or if anyone of the gods above or below has taken offence at him; or if anyone has made an offering to the gods to bring evil upon Hattusilis—accept not those evil words, O goddess, my lady! Let evil not touch Hattusilis, thy servant! O gods, prefer not our adversaries, our enviers, . . . to us!

Prayer to the Storm-God of Zippalanda

. . . This word, which I, Puduhepa, thy handmaid, have spoken in prayer, announce and relay thou to thy parents, Storm-god of Zippalanda, my lord! O god, my lord, yield to this word of mine! Because as a woman in travail I have in my own person made reparation to the god, my lord, intercede for me, god, my lord, with the Storm-god, thy father, and the Sun-goddess of Arinna, thy mother! Hattusilis, thy servant, wore himself out in the god's service; he gave himself body and soul to the restoration of Nerik, the beloved city of the god, my lord. So be thou, O god, my lord, favorably inclined toward Hattusilis, thy servant!

Adapted from James B. Pritchard, ed. *Ancient Near Eastern Texts Relating to the Old Testament,* 3d ed., with Supplement (Princeton, N.J.: Princeton University Press, 1969), pp. 393–394.

conquest and consolidation of Anatolia. The Middle Kingdom (ca. 1450–1380 B.C.) was a period of retrenchment and loss of territory. During the New Kingdom (ca. 1380–1180 B.C.) the Hittites first played an active role in international politics and then suffered a collapse in power. The Hittite empire reached its zenith in the New Kingdom, when it extended into Syria and northern Mesopotamia (see Map 1.3). Afterward came the Neo-Hittite era (ca. 1180–700 B.C.), when the Hittite empire had disintegrated into small successor states.

Old Kingdom Hittites could be characterized as a warrior society. A strong and boisterous nobility cultivated military virtues and kept the king weak. Ironically, queens were sometimes forceful and even enjoyed a measure of equality. The monarch was neither a god nor god's representative but rather first among equals. He was supported by an armed and mounted nobility who, in return for land, supplied him with troops and horses. The rising power of the nobility spelled trouble for central authority in the sixteenth century B.C., when conspiracy, feud, and assassination came close to destroying the Hittite kingdom. The powerful King Telepinu finally established himself and his family securely on the throne around 1500 B.C. In the Hittite New Kingdom the balance of power swung further in favor of the king, who was now addressed as "my Sun" during his lifetime and was deified after death.

Hittite queens and queen mothers had strong and independent positions, as at Ebla. Puduhepa°, wife of King Hattusilis° III (r. 1278–1250 B.C.), played a memorable role in state affairs. Puduhepa seems to have been the prime mover in the movement that made the Hurrian sun-goddess of Arinna (a shrine near Hattusas) the chief deity of the Hittite state. (See the box "Reading Sources: Prayers of a Hittite Queen.") Hattusilis publicly declared that he would not have rebelled against the previous king had Puduhepa not first dreamed of divine support for the coup.

Although the Hittites borrowed much of their religion from earlier civilizations, they developed political thought whose sophistication is quite original. Earlier peoples had kept lists and chronicles; Hittite annals are livelier, better argued, and more conscious of cause and effect. The royal annals of King Hattusilis III, for example, read in parts like a lawsuit, carefully pleading a justification of the king's actions. Hattusilis excused his usurpation of the throne by stating that the former king had unjustly stripped him of territory; furthermore, Hattusilis rebelled openly. Hittite treaties with subordinate states similarly argue their cases: each begins with an introduction providing historical background and justifying the relationship sworn to in the body of the text.

■ The First International System and Its Collapse, ca. 1500–1150 B.C.

The Hittites and New Kingdom Egyptians exercised great military power, yet what is even more remarkable about these states and others is their ability to make and

maintain peace. The years from about 1450 to about 1300 B.C. marked a period of peace among the great powers from Egypt to Anatolia and Mesopotamia—what historians call the first international system. The arts of peace are illustrated in surviving treaties and letters between monarchs, the most important of which comes from Amarna. The Amarna Archives (mid-fourteenth century), written in Akkadian cuneiform, illustrate formal communication among states. Rulers of great powers addressed each other as "brother," while Canaanite princes called pharaoh "my lord and my Sungod" and assured him that they were "thy servant and the dirt on which thou dost tread." The texts reveal a system of gift exchange and commerce, politeness and formality, alliance and dynastic marriage, subjects and governors, rebels and garrisons. Two factors seem to have supported peace. First, shared values among kings created mutual respect and a willingness to compromise. Second, although no such concept as our balance of power existed then, a rough equality of power did prevail. Since no great power was likely to defeat the others, the parties avoided all-out war, preferring instead to compete by jockeying for allies among the small border states of Syria and Palestine.

But peace was not to last. By the late fourteenth century, Egypt and the Hittites were back at war. At the Battle of Qadesh in northern Syria in 1274 B.C., twenty thousand Egyptian troops faced seventeen thousand Hittites. Predictably, neither of the two evenly matched powers managed to conquer the other. Instead, they used resources that would soon be dearly needed for defense.

Between about 1250 and 1150 B.C., the international system came to a crashing end. From Mesopotamia to Greece, from Anatolia to Egypt, one state after another collapsed between about 1250 and 1150 B.C. Surviving evidence is fragmentary, but it suggests that both foreign and domestic problems led to the collapse. Raiders and invaders beset the eastern Mediterranean in this period. Called "Sea Peoples" by the Egyptians, they attacked both on land and at sea. We do not know precisely who they were. In addition, some evidence of regional famine and climatic change indicates that natural causes may have led to disruption and rebellion.

Whatever the cause, what followed would prove to be a different world. Yet the end of the international system did not result in the disappearance of ancient cultures. Although new peoples appeared and old peoples changed, both continued to borrow from the cultures that had flowered before 1250 B.C.

Puduhepa (pu-du-HE-pa)   **Hattusilis** (hat-tu-SIL-is)

SUMMARY

THIS chapter covers not just the history of the ancestors of Western civilization but the very origins of civilization itself. Yet that milestone is only a small part of the vast era that ranges from the first hominids to the heirs of the great kingdoms of Egypt and western Asia after the collapse of the thirteenth century B.C. The achievements of this period may make it the most creative epoch in human history. First, probably beginning before 70,000 B.C., came the invention of human culture—that is, the development of communications to the degree that humans could cooperate to exploit their natural environment by means of technology and social organization. Next came the move from a food-collecting to a food-producing economy. After a series of independent discoveries beginning in the Fertile Crescent region of western Asia shortly after 10,000 B.C., food production spread to many places around the globe by 5000 B.C.

Over the thousands of years following the emergence of agriculture, we can trace the development of ever more complex organizations of human beings and ever increasing control of the natural environment, culminating in the emergence of civilization in Egypt and Mesopotamia after 3500 B.C. Elaborate though such large Neolithic towns as Çatal Hüyük or Jericho were, civilization marked a major step forward in sophistication. Civilization brought cities commanding the manpower, technology, and degree of labor specialization needed to build a monumental urban architecture and reshape the agricultural hinterland; civilization brought governments and armies controlling wide areas; civilization brought, finally, writing. By 3000 B.C. civilization was present in the Levant as well. Through trade networks, civilization affected a vast hinterland, including Europe. European societies, especially in southeastern Europe, were reshaped by trade with more advanced neighbors. European civilization emerged in the Aegean around 2000 B.C.

Mesopotamia and Egypt are the first and best remembered of the early civilizations. Their extraordinary achievements, later built on by the Greeks and Hebrews, laid the foundation for important Western concepts in government, religion, technology, art, and literature. It is hard to avoid the appearance of exaggeration when listing the inventions of Mesopotamia and Egypt, among them the first cities, kingdoms, and multi-ethnic empires; the first monumental architecture; the first advances in agriculture sweeping enough to support a large urban population; the first writing, and with it the first written attempts to explore the most profound subjects of life and death.

The years from 2000 to 1000 B.C. were a period of competition, exchange, and warfare among the various civilizations of the eastern Mediterranean region. They were also an era of further advance in literature and science. Then, the great kingdoms of the period collapsed, one after another, around 1250 to 1150 B.C.

It was not long before new states arose in Egypt and western Asia to replace those destroyed in the era of the Sea Peoples. In the first half of the first millennium B.C., new regions joined southern Mesopotamia, Egypt, the Levant, and Anatolia in making lasting contributions to the West: among them, Assyria (northern Mesopotamia), Persia, ancient Israel, and Greece. We turn to those regions in the next chapter.

■ Notes

1. James B. Pritchard, ed., *Ancient Near Eastern Texts Relating to the Old Testament,* 3d ed. (Princeton, N.J.: Princeton University Press, 1969), p. 107.
2. James H. Breasted, *The Conquest of Civilization* (New York: Harper & Bros., 1926), p. 112. Quoted in Brian Tierney, Donald Kagan, and L. Pearce Williams, eds., *Great Issues in Western Civilization from Ancient Egypt Through Louis XIV* (New York: McGraw-Hill, 1992), pp. 68–69.

■ Suggested Reading

Cunliffe, Barry, ed. *The Oxford Illustrated Prehistory of Europe.* 1994. An introduction to European material culture from the Paleolithic era to the early medieval period, with chapters written by a dozen archaeologists. Especially valuable for its treatment of the early period and for its integration of Greco-Roman civilization and the wider continental context.

Gurney, O. R. *The Hittites.* 3d ed. 1975. A sound introductory survey that pays close attention to the sources of evidence.

Hallo, William W., and William Kelly Simpson. *The Ancient Near East. A History.* 2d ed. 1998. A reliable and relatively up-to-date scholarly survey from the Paleolithic Age to the fourth century B.C., covering western Asia and Egypt.

Johanson, D. C. and Edgar B. *From Lucy to Language.* 1996. Excellent and relatively up-to-date introduction to human evolution, with outstanding photographs.

Murnane, William J. *The Penguin Guide to Ancient Egypt.* 1983. Both a well-illustrated travel guide and a scholarly, basic introduction.

Oates, Joan. *Babylon.* Rev. ed. 1986. A well-illustrated historical and archaeological introduction, from Sargon of Agade to the Greeks.

 For a searchable list of additional readings for this chapter, go to http://college.hmco.com.

The Iceman and His World

On September 19, 1991, a German couple went hiking in the Italian Alps. At 10,530 feet above sea level, they thought they had left civilization and its problems behind until they stumbled on an unexpected sight: the body of a dead man lying in the melting ice. Nor was that their only surprise. At first they thought the corpse was the victim of a recent accident. When the authorities arrived, however, the body was discovered to be very old. A helicopter was ordered, and the body was brought to a research institute in Innsbruck, Austria. When the investigators were through, it was clear that the hikers had chanced upon one of the most remarkable archaeological discoveries of the century.*

He was 5,300 years old. The Iceman—as the corpse has become known—is a natural mummy, preserved under the snow: the oldest known remains of human flesh. If that weren't striking enough, consider the clothes and extensive gear that survived with him—they are a window into the European world of about 3200 B.C. The most difficult and most fascinating question is this: Who was the Iceman?

His body offers an introduction. Genetic testing shows that he was a European, a close relative of modern northern and alpine Europeans. Other tests indicate a difficult life. His growth was arrested by periods of illness, grave hunger, or metal poisoning. His teeth are badly worn, the result perhaps of chewing dried meat or, alternatively, of working leather. He may have undergone a kind of acupuncture; at any rate, he is tattooed, which in some cultures is a medical treatment rather than a form of decoration. He has several broken ribs, which indicates either damage under the ice, mishandling when the body was discovered, or an ancient accident or fight.

To get to know the Iceman better, however, we must go beyond his body to the artifacts found with it, which provide tantalizing clues to his social status. Look at the artist's drawing. A woven grass or reed cape lies over the Iceman's deerskin coat, which in turn covers a leather loincloth and garter, held in place by a leather belt. A fur hat, skin leggings, and calfskin shoes, stuffed with grass for insulation, complete his wardrobe. The Iceman and his contemporaries knew how to dress for the cold weather of the mountains.

The Iceman carries a rich tool kit. Notice his copper ax and 6-foot-long bow. A quiver (arrow case), two birch bark containers, a waist pouch, and—probably part of a backpack—a frame hang from his body. Among his items of equipment are flint tools (including a knife, a retouching tool, and a scraper); a piece of net; two birch-fungus-like "polypores" threaded on a leather thong, probably used as a natural antibiotic; and fourteen arrows, all, oddly, broken. In short, it appears that the Iceman was equipped with a state-of-the-art mountain survival kit of his day.

What, however, was he doing on the mountain when he died? Scholars disagree. They all acknowledge that the Iceman probably reached the spot where he died from the south, since it is only from there—northern Italy—that the site was accessible in antiquity. What scholars differ about is the Iceman's occupation. Guesses range from a trader to hunter to metal prospector to shaman (a priest who uses magic).

Some argue that the Iceman was a refugee. His weapons point to violence, and so may his broken ribs. Perhaps he had retreated to the mountains from a fight. If so, it is not clear why he brought broken arrows or how he had time to pack his goods so carefully before fleeing; nor could it have been a small feat to climb mountains with broken ribs.

Perhaps the most convincing theory is that the Iceman was a shepherd. Since ancient times it has been

---

* The best brief introduction to the Iceman is Lawrence Barfield's "The Iceman Reviewed," *Antiquity* 68 (1994): 10–26, on which this discussion relies. See also Konrad Spindler, *The Man in the Ice* (New York: Harmony Books, 1994).

Artist's Rendition of the Ice Man *(New York Times Photo Sales)*

common for shepherds to move their flocks during the summer from the lowlands to greener pastures in the mountains, a pattern of migration known as *transhumance*. It has been suggested that the Iceman brought broken arrows with him to repair during his spare time. Perhaps he encountered a sudden snowstorm and died of exposure, perhaps after having broken his ribs in an accident.

If he was a shepherd, then the Iceman offers a rare illustration of the life of the kind of person who is not represented in most archaelogical sites: a person at the margins of society. Tombs usually yield the skeletons and grave goods of the elite, especially the urban elite: they rarely illustrate the lives of ordinary countryfolk. The Iceman's equipment suggests that he was not poor, but only his copper ax might indicate unusual status—and it is not a decisive index. Were the copper ax a show item, it might imply high status, but observe the Iceman's ax. It was set in a wooden handle and bound with leather, leaving little of the metal visible; it is, in short, a utensil rather than an ornament.

The copper ax is also the key to the Iceman's culture and its relationship with the wider world. Similar axes have been found in northern Italian tombs in Remedello, about 240 miles south of the Alps. Before the discovery of the Iceman, archaeologists believed that Italians learned the metalwork technology needed for such an ax from Anatolia, where similar pieces of metalwork are dated to approximately 2700–2400 B.C. Hence, the Remedello culture was usually also dated about 2700–2400 B.C. The discovery of the Iceman means that Remedello must be backdated by about five hundred years. It is clear, then, that by about 3200 B.C. northern Italians not only borrowed from the more advanced eastern Mediterranean areas but also created their own original technology and culture. So a small object (a copper ax), placed within a larger body of evidence (Italian and Anatolian metalwork), permits broad generalization about the interaction and independence of ancient cultures.

 For additional information on this topic, go to http://college.hmco.com.

CHAPTER 2

The Sword, the Book, and the Myths: Western Asia and Early Greece

THE bull in brick relief shown on the left symbolizes power even today, twenty-six hundred years after it was molded and glazed. About 4 feet high, this bull was one of several dozen figures of bulls and dragons that decorated the massive Ishtar Gate, which led through the inner town wall of Babylon° into the palace. The gate represents only a small part of a magnificent reconstruction of the city by the Neo-Babylonian° kings who ruled western Asia around 600–539 B.C.

Imagine the king's surprise had he known that under his nose an obscure prophet—we know him only as "Second Isaiah°"—was preaching a bold message to his compatriots, a conquered people living in exile in Babylon. Isaiah reminded them that Yahweh°, their god, was a god of justice and mercy—the one and only true god of the entire world—and that Yahweh had chosen the king of mountainous, backward Persia to conquer western Asia and redeem Yahweh's people. The Neo-Babylonian king might have laughed at the idea. Yet the Persians under Cyrus the Great conquered Babylon in 539 B.C. and proclaimed the freedom of Yahweh's people—the Jews—to return to Palestine and re-establish the Temple to their god in the city of Jerusalem°. They did so, and around this time they wrote down their religious and historical traditions in large sections of what would become the Hebrew Bible, or Old Testament.

Also in the sixth century B.C., Peisistratus°, the ambitious ruler of Athens, a tiny city-state a thousand miles northwest of Babylon, sponsored a literary project to preserve the religious and historical traditions of his people. The literary works whose texts were standardized under his patronage are the *Iliad* and *Odyssey*, the epic poems of

---

Babylon (BAB-eh-lon)   **Neo-Babylonian** (NEE-oh bab-eh-LONE-ee-an)
Isaiah (eye-ZAY-ah)   **Yahweh** (YAH-way)   **Jerusalem** (juh-ROO-suh-lem)
Peisistratus (pie-SIS-tra-tus)

Bull from Ishtar Gate, Babylon.   (Staatliche Museen zu Berlin, Museum für Vor- und Frühgeschichte/Bildarchiv Preussischer Kulturbesitz. Photo: Reinhard Saczewski)

Assyrians, Neo-Babylonians, and Persians, ca. 1200–330 B.C.

Israel, ca. 1500–400 B.C.

Early Greece, to ca. 725 B.C.

Homer, who had composed them about two centuries before.

Both the Hebrew Bible and the Homeric poems are deeply religious in outlook, but there the similarities end. The Hebrew Bible is monotheistic and focuses on the individual's subordination to God. Homer is polytheistic and glorifies the hero, who, though doomed to fail, aspires to godlike achievement. For most scholars the Bible and Homer represent two poles of Western civilization: the sacred and the worldly, the reverent and the heroic, holy writ and poetic craftsmanship.

Israel and Greece are, along with Rome, the founders of the West. Israel's holy book, the Hebrew Bible, founded the Western religious tradition. Greece, which founded the Western tradition of philosophy and politics, had its first great literary flowering in the works of Homer, whose epic poems are based on Greek myths.

The Neo-Babylonians, along with the other great empires of the era, the Assyrians and Persians, are ancestors of the West. Conquerors, they came to power by the sword, but once in power they spread civilization, serving as conduits through which the achievements of Mesopotamia were transmitted. They built great empires whose institutions were eventually transformed into notions of mass citizenship under law and justice in a universal empire by the third founder of the West, Rome.

The first half of the first millennium B.C., therefore, left a divergent legacy to the West. On the one hand, new empires arose that were more systematically organized, farther-flung, and more diverse ethnically than those created before. On the other hand, prophets, philosophers, and poets looked in new and deeper ways into the human soul.

In this chapter we look at the deeply influential developments in empire, religion, and thought forged in the first half of the first millennium B.C. At the same time, we consider the peaceful expansion in this era, through trade and colonization, particularly under the Phoenicians. Finally, we examine the material innovation that has earned the period the title "Iron Age."

QUESTIONS TO CONSIDER

■ **What made the first-millennium B.C. empires of the Assyrians, Neo-Babylonians, and Persians so much more effective than earlier empires?**

■ **How did monotheism develop in ancient Israel, and what is its legacy today?**

■ **What are the Homeric poems, and what light do they shed on the culture of early Greece?**

TERMS TO KNOW

Assyrians	Israel
Neo-Babylonians	Torah
Persian Empire	covenant
monotheism	Minoans
Zoroastrianism	Mycenaeans
Phoenicians	Homer

ASSYRIANS, NEO-BABYLONIANS, AND PERSIANS, CA. 1200–330 B.C.

ANCESTORS of the West, three great multiethnic empires emerged between the 800s and 500s B.C. Ruthless soldiers, brutal conquerors, and innovative administrators, the Assyrians established an empire in western Asia and Egypt during the ninth through seventh centuries B.C. They were followed in turn by a Neo-Babylonian empire in the late seventh and sixth centuries. However, neither of these was as successful or as durable as the empire of the Persians (ca. 550–330 B.C.). At its height the Persian Empire stretched from central Asia and northwest India in the east to Macedonia and Libya in the west (see Map 2.1). Persia's vast empire was loosely governed by a Persian ruling elite and its native helpers. Unlike the iron-fisted

Assyrians, the Persians were relatively tolerant and respectful of their subjects' customs. Many of Persia's kings were followers of Zoroastrianism, an ethical and forceful religion. A period of relative peace in most of Persia's domains from the 530s to the 330s B.C. fostered widespread economic prosperity.

Borrowing the administrative methods of the Assyrians and Medes° and the long-established officialdom of Babylon, the Persians built a new and durable imperial government. Their official art stressed the unity of the peoples of the empire under Persian leadership. Persian rule represented the greatest success yet in implementing the notions of universal kingship that dated back to Sargon of Agade (r. 2371–2316 B.C.; see page 16). In turn, Persia transmitted the trappings of absolute kingship to later ambitious rulers, from Alexander the Great to the caesars of Rome and from the Byzantine emperors to the Muslim caliphs.

■ Assyrians and Neo-Babylonians

The Assyrians, whose homeland was in what is today northern Iraq, spoke a Semitic language. For most of the second millennium B.C., they were a military and commercial power. Around 1200 B.C., the Assyrians' state collapsed during that era of international crisis (see page 34), but they held on to a small homeland of about 5,000 square miles, roughly the size of Connecticut. The toughened survivors emerged with an aggressive, expansionist ideology.

Assyria's greatest successes came in the eighth and seventh centuries. One by one, states large and small fell—Babylonia, Syria, the kingdom of Israel, Cilicia in southern Anatolia, even Egypt (though Assyrian rule there lasted only a generation). Assyria became the first state to rule the two great river valleys of the ancient Near East, the Nile and the Tigris-Euphrates (see Map 2.1).

The Assyrians were warriors. Ashur, their main deity, was a war-god. Theirs was an ideology of power, conquest, and control (see the box "Reading Sources: The Banquet of Ashurnasirpal II"). The key to Assyria's success was its army—from 100,000 to 200,000 men strong—which made an unforgettable impression on observers and foes. The Israelite prophet Isaiah of Jerusalem ("First Isaiah") said of Assyrian soldiers: "[Their] arrows are sharpened, and all their bows bent, their horses' hoofs are like flint, their chariot wheels like the whirlwind. Their growling is like that of a lion" (Isaiah 5:28–29). He might have added that Assyrian spearmen,

Medes (meedz)

CHRONOLOGY	
2000 B.C.	First Minoan palaces on Crete
1800–1550 B.C.	Height of Minoan civilization
1626 B.C.	Eruption of Thera volcano
1550 B.C.	Mycenaeans conquer Crete
1375 B.C.	Palace at Knossos destroyed
1400–1200 B.C.	Height of Mycenaean civilization
1250–1150 B.C.	Sea Peoples invade Palestine
1200 B.C.	Mycenaean palaces destroyed
ca. 1200–1000 B.C.	Israelites settle Palestinian hill country
ca. 1050–750 B.C.	Height of Phoenician city-states
1004–928 B.C.	Reigns of David and Solomon
ca. 725 B.C.	Homer
722 B.C.	Assyrians conquer kingdom of Israel
612 B.C.	Conquest of Nineveh ends Assyrian power
598 B.C.	Neo-Babylonians conquer kingdom of Judah
559–530 B.C.	Reign of Cyrus the Great
550–331 B.C.	Achaemenid Persian Empire
539 B.C.	Cyrus conquers Babylon; permits Jews to return to Palestine
ca. 425 B.C.	Judean assembly accepts the Torah

archers, and cavalrymen were equipped with weapons and armor of iron.

Thanks to new heating and cooling techniques, metal smiths in the ancient world produced an alloy of carbon and iron that was harder and more durable than bronze. It was also easier to obtain since iron ore is widespread—unlike tin, an essential element of bronze. Iron tools and weapons were often stronger and cheaper than their bronze predecessors, which opened up new technical and military possibilities.

Adding to its might, Assyria was the first major state to employ regular cavalry units (rather than charioteers)

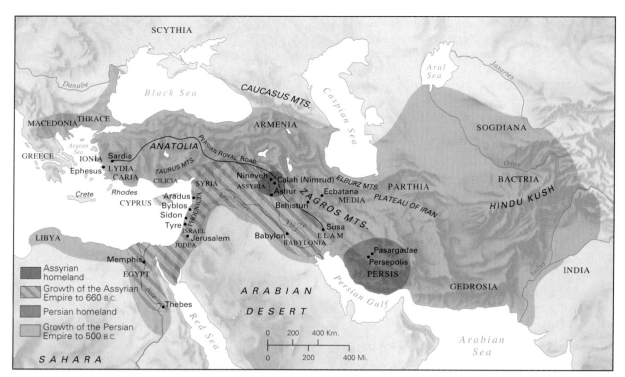

Map 2.1   The Assyrian and Persian Empires   In the 660s B.C. the Assyrians ruled the largest empire the ancient world had seen yet, extending from the Tigris to the Nile. The Persian Empire was even greater. Around 500 B.C. it reached from its heartland in southwestern Iran westward to Macedonia and eastward to India.

as the main strike force. The Assyrians were also excellent engineers, adept at taking walled cities by siege.

In addition, the Assyrians displayed superb organizational skills. The central standing army was supplemented with draftees conscripted from around the empire. Provinces were kept small to prevent the emergence of separate power bases, and independent-minded nobles were regularly checked by the kings.

To control the restive subjects of their far-flung empire, the Assyrians met rebellion with ferocious reprisals. Disloyal cities were attacked and, if need be, destroyed. Sculptured reliefs and inscriptions were set up to show, often in gruesome detail, the fate awaiting Assyria's enemies. We see or read of cities burned to the ground; of men flayed alive, even though they had surrendered, and walls covered with their skin; and of piles of human skulls. (See the feature "Weighing the Evidence: The Siege of Lachish" on pages 66–67.)

The Assyrians also engaged in mass deportation. They uprooted the people of a conquered country, resettled them far away—often in Assyria itself—and colonized their land with Assyrian loyalists. The so-called Ten

Lost Tribes of Israel—the people of the northern Israelite kingdom (see page 53)—were conquered by Assyria in 722 B.C., and many of them were transported to Mesopotamia, where they disappeared from history. (Those who remained in Israel mixed with colonists, and the new group became known, and scorned, as Samaritans.)

Assyrian policy was the result of careful calculation. The political goal was to punish rebellion, the economic goal to create a varied labor force. For example, although it is estimated that the Assyrians deported several million people, they deported not whole populations but a carefully chosen cross section of professions. They also deported entire families together, to weaken deportees' emotional ties to their former homes.

Another reason accounts for Assyria's success: the relative weakness of other powers. Egypt had been at the mercy of factions and invaders for much of the Third Intermediate Period (1075–656 B.C.). Around 950, for example, the kingship came into the hands of Libyan mercenaries. From the eighth century on, their rule was challenged in turn by invaders from the south, rulers of a new Nubian kingdom called Kush (see Map 1.2 on

📎 READING SOURCES

The Banquet of Ashurnasirpal II

This inscription comes from the palace of the Assyrian king Ashurnasirpal II (r. 883–859 B.C.) at his new capital city of Calah (Nimrud). The first two paragraphs illustrate the expansive claims to power of the Assyrian kings. The third shows the effort made to bringing in subjects from far and wide to the inaugural festival of the palace in order to awe them.

This is the palace of Ashurnasirpal, the high priest of Ashur, chosen by Enlil and Ninurta, the favorite of Anu and of Dagan who is destruction personified among the great gods—the legitimate king, the king of the world, the king of Assyria, son of Tukulti-Ninurta, great king, legitimate king, king of the world and king of Assyria—the heroic warrior who always acts upon trust-inspiring signs given by his lord Ashur and therefore has no rival among the rulers of the four quarters of the world; the shepherd of all mortals, not afraid of battle but an onrushing flood which brooks no resistance; the king who subdues the un-submissive and rules over all mankind; the king who always acts upon the trust-inspiring signs given by his lords, the great gods, and therefore has personally conquered all countries; who has acquired dominion over the mountain regions and received their tribute; he takes hostages, triumphs over all countries from beyond the Tigris to the Lebanon and the Great Sea, he has brought into submission the entire country of Laqe and the region of Suhu as far as the town of Rapiqu; personally he conquered the region from the source of the Subnat River to Urartu. . . .

Ashur, the Great Lord, has chosen me and made a pronouncement concerning my world rule with his own holy mouth (as follows): Ashurnasirpal is the king whose fame is power! . . .

When I inaugurated the palace at Calah I treated for ten days with food and drink 47,074 persons, men and women, who were bid to come from across my entire country, also 5,000 important persons, delegates from the country Suhu, from Hindana, Hattina, Hatti, Tyre, and Musasir, also 16,000 inhabitants of Calah from all ways of life, 1,500 officials of all my palaces, altogether 69,574 invited guests from all the mentioned countries including the people of Calah; I furthermore provided them with the means to clean and anoint themselves. I did them due honors and sent them back, healthy and happy, to their own countries.

Source: Adapted from James B. Pritchard, ed., *Ancient Near Eastern Texts Relating to the Old Testament,* 3d ed., with Supplement (Princeton, N.J.: Princeton University Press, 1969), pp. 558–560.

---

page 22). Kushite pharaohs governed Egypt from around 719 until 656, when they withdrew back south. It was they who faced the Assyrian attacks in 671 and 667.

The conquest of Egypt marked imperial Assyria's greatest extent—and its overextension (see Map 2.1). A coalition army consisting of soldiers from a revived Babylonian kingdom and of Medes (who had formed a powerful state in Iran; see page 45) conquered Nineveh°, the Assyrian capital, in 612 B.C. and defeated the remnants of

the Assyrian army in battles in 609 and 605. Few of its subjects mourned the empire's passing.

The destruction of Assyria led to revival for Babylon, whose rulers attempted to revive the glories of Hammurabi's day (see page 18). For a short period, until the Persian conquest in 539 B.C., the Neo-Babylonian dynasty (founded in 626) and the Medes of Iran were the dominant military forces in western Asia. The Neo-Babylonian king Nebuchadrezzar° II (Nebuchadnezzar

---

Nineveh (NIN-eh-veh)

Nebuchadrezzar (neh-boo-khad-REZ-zar)

Assyrian King   This stern-faced, stone statue of Ashurnasirpal II (r. 883–859 B.C.) comes from a temple in his new capital city of Calah (Nimrud). He holds a scepter and flail (a tool for beating out grain from its husk), symbols of power. *(Courtesy of the Trustees of the British Museum)*

in the Hebrew Bible; r. 605–562 B.C.) conquered the kingdom of Judah (in southern Palestine) in 598 and destroyed Jerusalem, its capital, in 586. He deported many thousands of Judeans° to Babylon, an event remembered by Christians and Jews as the Babylonian Captivity. Most of the rest of western Asia also fell to Nebuchadrezzar's troops. His most enduring achieve-

ment was rebuilding Babylon on a grand scale. In addition to the city's numerous temples, shrines, and altars, he created the so-called Hanging Gardens celebrated by later Greek writers. They describe the structure as a large terraced complex that Nebuchadrezzar built for his queen, though it may have been a plant-covered ziggurat.

Neo-Babylonians and Assyrians both made great strides in astronomy. Their prime motive was not scientific but religious—that is, a belief in astrology (the study of the movements of heavenly bodies in the belief that they influence human affairs). Astrology led to advances in the scientific observation of the heavens. Assyrian priests had produced relatively accurate circular diagrams (astrolabes) that showed the positions of the major constellations, stars, and planets over the course of the year. By 600 B.C., Assyrian and Neo-Babylonian astronomers could predict solstices, equinoxes, and lunar eclipses.

Astronomy in Mesopotamia reached its heights in the centuries after 500 B.C. The zodiac, a diagram showing the movement of the sun and planets relative to the constellations, was invented in Persian-ruled Babylon in the fourth century B.C. In the third and second centuries B.C., when Babylonia was under Hellenistic Greek rule, native scientists made impressive advances in mathematical astronomy, composing tables that could be used to calculate movements of the moon and planets. More sophisticated mathematical astronomy would not be produced in the West until the Scientific Revolution of the sixteenth century A.D.

Another western Asian society during this period was created by trade, not war. In both the Hebrew Bible and Homer, the Phoenicians° loom large as merchants and seamen, as "traders the world honored" (Isaiah 23:8). Phoenicians were Canaanites°, speakers of a Semitic language and heirs to the civilization that had prospered in Ugarit around 1400 B.C. (see page 32). After the invasions of the Sea Peoples and others around 1200 B.C., the Canaanites' once large territory was reduced to a narrow strip along the Mediterranean in the area of modern Lebanon and northern Israel (see Map 2.1). Between 1050 and 750 B.C., the inhabitants of the area flourished; historians call them, as did the ancient Greeks, "Phoenicians." Their purple-dyed textiles gave the Greeks their word for the color purple: *Phoenician.*

The Phoenicians were master shipbuilders and sailors. Around 600 B.C., their ships accomplished the first known circumnavigation of Africa. Around 450 B.C., they made the first known commercial sailing trip to the

---

Judeans (joo-DEE-unz)

Phoenicians (fuh-NEESH-anz)   **Canaanites** (CAY-nan-ites)

British Isles. Some scholars think they even reached Brazil. The most lasting Phoenician achievement at sea, however, was the planting of colonies in the Mediterranean, probably beginning in the ninth century B.C. Many of their colonies eventually became independent states. The greatest Phoenician colony was Carthage°, founded by the city of Tyre around 750 B.C. It was the major port city of the western Mediterranean for much of the next thousand years.

Phoenician traders introduced advanced material goods, slaves, and possibly law codes to the Greeks. It was probably from the Phoenicians, whose alphabet derived from Ugarit, that the Greeks adapted their alphabet.

Around 750 B.C., the Phoenician city-states lost their independence to the Assyrians, and in later years Neo-Babylonians, Persians, and other foreign conquerors followed. But Phoenician culture survived—at home, in the colonies, and among the many Mediterranean peoples influenced by it. The result, though unintended, was that Phoenician colonists exported the civilization of western Asia to the western Mediterranean.

■ Building the Persian Empire

A thousand miles east of Phoenicia, a great empire took root. Indo-European-speaking peoples, the Medes and the Persians arrived in western Iran probably around 1500 B.C. but perhaps not until 900 B.C. The two peoples were closely related in language and customs. The Medes lived in the central Zagros Mountains. The Persians made their homeland farther south in Anshan (modern Fars). At first the Medes ruled the Persians, but in 550 B.C., the tables were turned when the Medes were suddenly conquered by the young Persian king Cyrus the Great (r. 559–530 B.C.).

It took Cyrus only twenty years to conquer most of western Asia and much of central Asia. Within five years of his death in 530 B.C., his son and successor, Cambyses° (r. 530–525 B.C.), added Egypt and Libya. Cambyses' successor, Darius° (r. 521–486 B.C.), corraled northwestern India and Thrace. The frontier regions, especially Egypt, were often in revolt, and the attempt of Darius and his successor, Xerxes° (r. 486–465 B.C.), to extend Persian rule to Greece ended in failure (see pages 89–91). The Achaemenid° Persian Empire (named after a legendary founder, Achaemenes), nonetheless, survived for two hundred years, until a Greco-Macedonian army under

Carthage (CAR-thidge)   Cambyses (kam-BYE-seez)
Darius (dah-RYE-us)   Xerxes (ZURK-seez)
Achaemenid (ah-KEE-men-id)

Phoenician Ivory   This delicately carved plaque of a cow and calf, just 3 inches high, illustrates the wealth of artistic talent at the disposal of the Phoenicians, whose civilization reached its peak between 1050 and 750 B.C.   *(Iraq Antiquities Department)*

Alexander the Great, king of Macedon (r. 336–323 B.C.), destroyed it.

Let us consider several reasons for the success of Achaemenid Persia. The first was military prowess. Persia was ruled by a warrior aristocracy whose traditional values, according to the Greek historian Herodotus, were "riding, hunting, and telling the truth." The state was able to field a huge army of about 300,000 men, conscripted from the various subject peoples. Although the resultant hodgepodge of soldiers from across the empire did not always fight as a unit, a crack infantry group, the 10,000 Immortals, provided a solid core. The Persians excelled as bowmen and cavalrymen. Following the Assyrians, they made cavalry into the decisive strike force of the battlefield, assigning a more minor role to chariotry. Persia was even more innovative at sea, where it had its subjects build the first great navy. Although Persians served as marines and sometimes as commanders, the rowers and seamen were usually Phoenicians or Greeks.

The second reason for Persia's success was political. Unlike the Assyrians, the Persians considered generosity and tolerance to be more effective than terrorism and brutality. As Cyrus prepared to attack Babylon, he

❧ READING SOURCES

Cyrus and His Subjects' Gods

Although the Persians sometimes used brutal tactics, they preferred to gain their subjects' loyalty by gestures of goodwill, such as winning the favor of the religious leaders. Excerpt (a), a Babylonian inscription, demonstrates the political skill by which Cyrus the Great secured the surrender of Babylon in 539 B.C. without a battle. Excerpt (b), from the Hebrew Bible, records the favor that Cyrus showed to the Jewish exiles in Babylon.

(a)

He [Marduk] scanned and looked (through) all the countries, searching for a righteous ruler willing to lead him [i.e., Marduk] (in the annual procession). (Then) he pronounced the name of Cyrus, king of Anshan, declared him to be(come) the ruler of all the world. . . . And he [Cyrus] did always endeavor to treat according to justice the black-headed whom he [Marduk] has made him conquer. Marduk, the great lord, a protector of his people/worshipers, beheld with pleasure his [i.e., Cyrus's] good deeds and his upright mind (and therefore) ordered him to march against his city Babylon. . . .

I am Cyrus, king of the world, great king, legitimate king, king of Babylon, king of Sumer and Akkad, king of the four rims (of the earth), son of Cambyses. . . .

When I entered Babylon as a friend and (when) I established the seat of the government in the palace of the ruler under jubilation and rejoicing, Marduk, the great lord, [induced] the magnanimous inhabitants of Babylon [to love me], and I was daily endeavoring to worship him. My numerous troops walked around in Babylon in peace, I did not allow anybody to terrorize (any place) of the [country of Sumer] and Akkad. I strove for peace in Babylon and in all his other sacred cities.

(b)

In the first year of King Cyrus of Persia [539 B.C.] the Lord, to fulfill his word spoken through Jeremiah, inspired the king to issue throughout his kingdom the following proclamation, which he also put in writing: The decree of King Cyrus of Persia. The Lord the God of the heavens has given me all the kingdoms of the earth, and he himself has charged me to build him a house at Jerusalem in Judah. Whoever among you belongs to his people, may his God be with him; and let him go up to Jerusalem in Judah, and build the house of the Lord the God of Israel, the God who is in Jerusalem. Let every Jew left among us, wherever he is settled throughout the country, be helped by his neighbours with silver and gold, goods and livestock, in addition to the voluntary offerings for the house of God in Jerusalem.

Sources: Excerpt (a): Adapted from James B. Pritchard, ed., *Ancient Near Eastern Texts Relating to the Old Testament,* 3d ed., with Supplement (Princeton, N.J.: Princeton University Press, 1969), pp. 315–316. Excerpt (b): Ezra 1:1–3, in *The Oxford Study Bible: Revised English Bible with the Apocrypha* (New York: Oxford University Press, 1992).

portrayed himself as the champion of the traditional Babylonian deity Marduk, whose priests had been challenged as too powerful by the Neo-Babylonian kings. As a result, the Babylonians opened the city gates to the Persian army, allowing Cyrus to achieve that greatest measure of military success: victory without a battle. He also emphasized a sense of continuity with earlier Mesopotamian history in his adoption of the traditional title of "King of Sumer and Akkad." Nor did Cyrus hesitate to break with Assyrian and Neo-Babylonian population transfers, as witnessed in his edict permitting the Jewish exiles in Babylon to return to Judea. (See the box "Reading Sources: Cyrus and His Subjects' Gods.")

The third reason for Persia's success was its skill at administration and organization. Darius played a crucial role in reorganizing the imperial administration and finances (military-minded Persians sneered at him as a "shopkeeper"). Like the Assyrian Empire, the Persian domain was divided into provinces, called *satrapies°*. Each of the twenty satrapies was a unit of administration and tax collection. For the first time, taxes could be paid with a stable, official coinage: the gold daric (named after Darius) and the silver shekel. Coins had been invented in the kingdom of Lydia in western Asia Minor in the seventh century B.C. Croesus (r. 560–547 B.C.), Lydia's king, was known for his wealth—hence the expression "rich as Croesus"—before Cyrus conquered him in 547 B.C.

The provincial governors, or *satraps*, were powerful, often quasi-independent figures. The empire had many centralizing forces to offset their autonomy, however. Each province had a royal secretary and was visited regularly by traveling inspectors known as "the king's eyes." A network of good roads radiated from the capital cities of Susa and Persepolis. The most famous road, the so-called Royal Road, stretched 1,600 miles from western Iran to western Anatolia (see Map 2.1). Covering the whole distance took most travelers three months, but the king's relay messenger corps could make the trip in a week, thanks to a series of staging posts furnished with fresh horses.

Another unifying element was a society that was law-abiding and prosperous. Darius proclaimed in an inscription that he had fostered the rule of law: "These countries [of the empire] showed respect toward my law; as was said to them by me, thus it was done." Although some scholars suggest that Darius turned the great body of traditional Babylonian case law into a new Persian code for the whole empire, evidence survives only for Egypt, where Darius ordered a codification of Egyptian law. Darius and other Persian kings helped create the conditions for compliance and security by taking an interest in the economy. For example, they opened to commercial traffic Persian roads and a canal connecting the Red Sea and the Nile.

Language, too, built unity. Not Persian, which relatively few people spoke, but Aramaic, the most widespread language of western Asia, became the empire's basic language of commerce and administration. A Semitic language related to Hebrew, Aramaic was first used by the Aramaeans°, a nomadic people who settled in northern Syria about 1100 B.C. and ruled an area extending into Mesopotamia before succumbing to Assyrian conquest about 725 B.C. The Aramaeans dominated the overland trade routes, which, combined with the simple and easily learned Aramaic alphabet, contributed to the spread of their language. Aramaic facilitated the devel-

Achaemenid Persian Silver   This silver rhyton (drinking vessel) is in the shape of a griffin, a mythological animal that is part lion and part eagle. Persian rulers commanded the talents of western Asia's best artists and craftsmen, silversmiths among them.   *(Courtesy of the Trustees of the British Museum)*

opment of literacy and recordkeeping. Aramaic would become the common language of western Asia for over a thousand years, until Arabic replaced it; Jesus Christ was to be its most famous native speaker.

■ The King of Kings

Despite its success, Persia's empire was fraught with several weaknesses. First, Cyrus had bequeathed a legacy as a charismatic war leader. Feeling the need to live up to his example, his successors sometimes undertook ambitious and expensive expeditions that failed, such as wars with the Scythians (a tough nomadic people in Ukraine) and the Greeks. Second, however mild Persian rule, however peaceful and prosperous, it was still rule by foreigners and it still involved taxation. Persian officials, military garrisons, and colonists were found—and were resented—in every corner of the empire. Native

---

satrapies (SAY-truh-peez)   **Aramaeans** (air-uh-MAY-unz) resentment, particularly in Egypt, and the independence of certain satraps led to intermittent provincial revolts.

The exaltation of the Persian king served as a counterweight to rebellious tendencies. From Darius on, the Persian monarch tried to overawe his officials with his majesty and might. The "King of Kings," as the monarch called himself, sat on a high, gold and blue throne, dressed in purple, decked out in gold jewelry, wearing fragrant oils and cosmetics, and attended by corps of slaves and eunuchs (castrated men employed in high positions). Although he was not considered a god, he had to be treated with reverence. Persians spoke of the king's *khvarna*, his "kingly glory," a mysterious aura of power. Anyone who came into the royal presence had to approach him with a bow to the ground, face down. Even when entertaining dinner guests, the king normally ate alone in a separate room, looking at the guests through a curtain. If, after dinner, the king wished to drink with his guests, he would sit on a golden-footed couch while they

sat on the floor, and he and they would drink wine from separate casks.

Impressive as the court ceremonial was, Persian kings were not all-powerful. They were bound by the rule of law and by the considerable power of Persia's proud nobility, on whom they relied to fill the top administrative positions. Competing factions of ministers, wives, concubines, eunuchs, and sons often brought intrigue and discord to court, especially in the fourth century B.C., a time of frequent rebellion.

Royal authority was symbolized in the decoration of the great palaces at Susa and Persepolis, a project begun by Darius I and completed by his son and successor, Xerxes. The Susa palace, the larger of the two, reflected the universality of the empire in the variety of hands that built it. In an inscription, Darius points out that the cedar for the palace came from Lebanon, brought by Assyrians to Babylon and from there by Carians and Ionians (two peoples inhabiting western Anatolia; Ionians

Frieze at Persepolis   This sculptured relief lines the stairway to the audience hall of King Darius (r. 521–486 B.C.). It depicts Persian nobles, well groomed and formally dressed, carrying flowers for the New Year's feast.   *(Rony Jaques/Photo Researchers)*

were Greek) to Susa; the gold came from Sardis (western Anatolia) and Bactria; the silver and ebony from Egypt; the ivory from Ethiopia, India, and central Asia. Craftsmen from east and west took part in the construction. The Persepolis palace, too, displayed the heterogeneity of the empire in its architecture. The palace was placed on a terrace, as in Mesopotamia, but contained columned halls as in Egypt, with Assyrian-style column capitals or tops. In Persepolis, a frieze of sculpted relief panels lining a monumental stairway leading to the palace emphasized the king's vast power. The panels depict an endless procession of the peoples of the world paying homage to the King of Kings: from the nobility to the Immortals, to Median and Persian soldiers, to tribute-bearing subjects from the ends of the earth. The overall feeling of the scene is static, as if the Persian Empire would last forever.

■ Zoroastrianism

Like ancient Israel, Persia developed a highly ethical religion in the first millennium B.C. From obscure beginnings, Zoroastrianism° became the religion of Persia that persisted until the Muslim conquest in the seventh century A.D. Although largely extinct in today's Iran, an Islamic country, Zoroastrianism still survives in small communities elsewhere, primarily in India. Some scholars argue that Zoroastrian beliefs eventually influenced Judaism and Christianity, as well as Roman paganism and Indian Buddhism.

It is easier to describe ancient Zoroastrianism in broad strokes than in detail, partly because the religion changed radically over the course of its ancient history, and partly because relatively little information survives before A.D. 300. This much is clear: The religion was founded by a great reformer and prophet named Zarathustra° (Zoroaster in Greek). Zarathustra lived in eastern Iran. His teachings survive in the *Gathas* ("Songs"), a portion of the Zoroastrian holy book called the *Avesta*. Some scholars date Zarathustra as late as 550 B.C.; others prefer an earlier date, 750 or even 1000 B.C.

Zarathustra's society was dominated by warriors whose religion consisted of blood cults, violent gods, animal sacrifice, and ecstatic rituals in which hallucinogens were eaten. Zarathustra rejected such violent practices in favor of an inward-looking, intellectual, and ethical religion. He favored ceremonies involving fire, considered a symbol of purity. Zarathustra was not a strict monotheist like the Jews, but he did emphasize the power of one god over all people, the supremely good and wise creator of the universe, whom he called Ahura Mazda ("Wise Lord"). Unlike the Jews, Zarathustra considered the problem of evil to be virtually the central question of religion. If god was one, good, and omnipotent, how could evil exist?

Zarathustra's answer might be called *ethical dualism* (dualism is the notion of a grand conflict between good and evil). Ahura Mazda had twin children: the Beneficent Spirit and the Hostile Spirit. Each spirit had made a free choice: one for the "truth" and the other for the "lie"—that is, one for good and the other for evil. Every human being faces a similar choice between good and evil. "Reflect with a clear mind—man by man for himself—upon the two choices of decision, being aware to declare yourselves to Him before the great retribution," says Zarathustra.[1] Indeed, humanity is caught in a great cosmic struggle in which individuals are free to make a momentous choice. Zarathustra thus endowed humanity with great freedom and dignity. He distinguished between two states of being: the spiritual and the material. The more a person pursued spiritual purity, the greater was the person's ability to choose good rather than evil.

Zarathustra held a linear conception of history, similar to that in the Hebrew Bible. His religion is marked by a strong *eschatology* (interest in the end of the world) as well as *soteriology* (belief in a savior). He believed that one day, through an ordeal by fire, Ahura Mazda would judge all the people who had ever lived. Those who had chosen good would be rewarded, and those who had chosen evil would be punished. Then would follow a Last Judgment in which the dead would be transfigured and restored to a glorious bodily existence. There would be, Zarathustra promised, "long destruction for the deceitful but salvation for the truthful." The notion of a savior who would initiate the Last Judgment is an early Zoroastrian belief, if perhaps not a doctrine of Zarathustra himself.

In later centuries, Zarathustra's followers eased his uncompromising rejection of Iranian paganism. Under the leadership of priests, known as *magi*° in western Iran, the religion evolved and changed considerably. Lesser deities beneath Ahura Mazda were added to the Zoroastrian pantheon, in part to suit the religion to the needs of the huge, multicultural Persian Empire.

It is tempting to attribute Cyrus's policy of toleration to the ethical teachings of Zarathustra, but it is uncertain whether Cyrus was Zoroastrian. We are on firmer ground with later Persian kings, particularly Darius I, who had an image of himself alongside Ahura Mazda carved on

Zoroastrianism (zoh-roh-AS-tree-un-izm)
Zarathustra (zah-ruh-THOOS-truh)

magi (MAY-jye)

the face of an Iranian cliff. In an accompanying inscription Darius announces: "For this reason Ahura Mazda bore aid, and the other gods who . . . [exist], because I was not hostile, I was not a Lie-follower, I was not a doer of wrong—neither I nor my family. According to righteousness I conducted myself."[2]

ISRAEL, CA. 1500–400 B.C.

N the first millennium B.C. a small, often-conquered people turned imperialism on its head. Human achievement is meaningless, they argued; only the power of divinity matters. There is only one god, they said; all other gods are false. The one true god had revealed himself not to the awesome, imperialistic Assyrians but to the less powerful Hebrews—ancient Jews. They founded the Western tradition of religion. The God of ancient Israel eventually gave rise to the God of Christianity and of Islam as well as of modern Judaism.

The Hebrews, also known as Israelites, had existed as a people since about 1200 B.C. and perhaps for centuries earlier. They spoke a Semitic language.

■ The Hebrew Bible

As literature and as religious teaching, the Bible is unquestionably the most important book in Western civilization. As a source of history, however, it presents difficulties. Much of the Hebrew Bible (called the Old Testament by Christians) is based on written sources that probably date back at least as far as the early Israelite monarchy of about 1000 B.C. Other parts of the Hebrew Bible are probably the product of an oral tradition, and the nature, antiquity, and reliability of that tradition are the subject of much scholarly debate.

Archaeological evidence from the area of ancient Israel, a small number of inscriptions (almost all after 800 B.C.), and some information in Greek and Roman writings provides an alternative source of information. Yet little of that alternative evidence sheds light on the period before about 1200 B.C., and it offers only partial insight into the later period. The historian needs both to pay attention to the Bible and to consider its nature.

The Hebrew Bible reached something close to its current form a century or two before the birth of Christ. It consists of three main sections: (1) the Torah° (literally, "teaching"), also known as the Pentateuch, or five

---

Torah (TOE-rah)

books of Moses (that is, the first five books of the Bible); (2) the Prophets, that is, the "historical" books of the early prophets (Joshua, Judges, Kings, and Chronicles) and the books of the later prophets (Isaiah, Jeremiah, Ezekiel, and the twelve "minor prophets"); and (3) the Writings, various books of poetry, proverbs, and wisdom literature.

The books of the Hebrew (and Christian) Bible are canonical: one by one, each was accepted by established authority as sacred. Two key dates stand out in the canonization of the Hebrew Bible: 622 B.C. and about 425 B.C. On the first date, Josiah, king of Judah (see page 53), assembled "the entire population, high and low" to swear to obey "the scroll of the covenant which had been discovered in the house of the Lord" (the scroll probably was Deuteronomy, now the fifth book of the Torah). On the second date, a similar assembly of the people, called by the religious leader Ezra, swore to accept the five books of the Torah that had by then been assembled. The introduction of the Torah made its worshipers into what they have been ever since, "a people of the Book," as the Muslims would put it many years later. The written tradition and literacy became central to the Hebrews.

The Hebrews are the first people we know of to have a single national history book. That book was written not as secular history but as sacred history. It is the story of the working out of God's pact, or covenant, with the Hebrews, his chosen people. All ancient peoples told stories of their semidivine foundation. Only the Hebrews imagined the nation created by an actual treaty between the people and their God.

The central fact of human existence in the Hebrew Bible is God's covenant with the Hebrews. Because of the covenant, history has meaning. History is the story of the success or failure of the Hebrew people in carrying out God's commandments. The emphatic focus is on the individual: on individual people taking actions that have not just moral but military and political consequences that unfold over time.

Many of the themes, narrative details, and styles of writing in the Hebrew Bible derive from earlier cultures. The biblical Flood story, for example, seems to have been modeled on a similar flood in the *Epic of Gilgamesh* (see page 20). Biblical poems in praise of God are often similar to Egyptian poems in praise of pagan gods, and biblical wisdom literature (that is, works containing proverbs and rules of conduct) often recalls Egyptian or Babylonian parallels. In spite of such borrowings, the Hebrew Bible is dramatically different from its predecessors because it subordinates everything to one central theme: God's plan for humanity and, in particular, for his chosen people—the Hebrews.

Statuette of Bull   This bronze statuette of a Canaanite deity (ca. 1200–1100 B.C.) comes from a sanctuary in the hills of Samaria. At this time, most Israelites still worshiped pagan gods.   *(The Israel Museum, Jerusalem)*

■ The Emergence of Hebrew Monotheism, ca. 1500–600 B.C.

The earliest nonbiblical evidence of the Hebrews is an inscribed monument of the New Kingdom Egyptian pharaoh Merneptah (r. 1224–1214 B.C.). After a military expedition into Canaan° (that is, roughly, Palestine), the pharaoh declared triumphantly that "Israel is laid waste." Most scholars accept this as evidence of an Israelite presence in Canaan, but the question is, how did they get there? The Bible says that the Israelites settled Palestine by conquering its earlier inhabitants. Most scholars now reject that account. Archaeological evidence suggests, rather, a more complex process. Perhaps the Israelites were a combination of three groups: armed conquerors, shepherds who gradually entered the country and later settled down to farming, and dispossessed and oppressed Canaanites who rebelled against their masters.

From such sources the Israelites may have emerged. The Bible, however, tells a different story of Israelite origins. Although much of it is credible, none of it is confirmed by nonbiblical sources. Still, the biblical story of Israelite origins has been so influential in later Western culture that we must examine it. If one follows the Bible, Hebrew history began sometime during the period 2000 to 1500 B.C. with the patriarchs, or founding fathers. Abraham, the first patriarch, migrated to Canaan from the city of Haran in northern Mesopotamia. A seminomadic chieftain, Abraham settled on territory north and west of the Dead Sea, where he grazed his herds. Seminomadic clans in the region frequently made long migrations in antiquity, so the biblical account of Abraham and his descendants, Isaac and Jacob, is plausible.

The Bible, however, emphasizes the implausible: Abraham's extraordinary decision to give up Mesopotamian polytheism for belief in one god. This god commanded Abraham to leave Haran; indeed, he made a treaty, or covenant, with Abraham. In return for Abraham's faith, said the god, "As a possession for all time I shall give you and your descendants after you the land in which you are now aliens, the whole of Canaan, and I shall be their God" (Genesis 17:8). Abraham was not a strict monotheist: Although he worshiped only one god, he did not deny the existence of other gods (see, for a comparison, the discussion of Akhenaten on page 28). Nevertheless, he took a giant step on the road to pure monotheism by coming to believe that only one god rules *all* peoples.

According to the Bible the next important step took place several hundred years later. In a time of famine in Canaan, many of Abraham's descendants left for prosperous Egypt. At first they thrived there, but in time they were enslaved and forced to build cities in the Nile Delta. Eventually, Moses, a divinely appointed leader, released the Hebrews from bondage in Egypt and led them back toward Canaan and freedom.

The Exodus ("journey out," in Greek), as this movement has been called, is a rare example of a successful national liberation movement in antiquity. Among those who accept its historicity, a date in the thirteenth century B.C. is frequently assigned to the Exodus. According to the Bible, the Exodus marked the key moment of another covenant, this time between the god of Abraham and the entire Israelite people. At Mount Sinai°, traditionally located on the rugged Sinai Peninsula between Egypt and Palestine, the Israelites are said to have first accepted as their one god a deity whose name is represented in Hebrew by the letters corresponding to YHWH. YHWH is traditionally rendered in English as "Jehovah," but "Yahweh" is more likely to be accurate. The Israelites accepted Yahweh's laws, summarized by the Ten Commandments. In return for obedience to Yahweh's commandments, they would be God's chosen people, his

---

Canaan (KAY-nan)

Sinai (SYE-nye)

❧ READING SOURCES

The Covenant

The central event in the history of ancient Israel was the establishment, during the Exodus, of the covenant, or treaty, at Sinai (see Map 2.2) between God and his chosen people. Forty years later, just before his death, Moses addresses the Israelites and reminds them of their obligations and God's promise to bless their obedience.

Moses summoned all Israel and said to them: Israel, listen to the statutes and the laws which I proclaim to you this day. Learn them, and be careful to observe them. The Lord our God made a covenant with us at Horeb [Sinai]. . . .

These are the commandments, statutes, and laws which the Lord your God commanded me to teach you to observe in the land to which you are crossing to occupy it, a land flowing with milk and honey, so that you may fear the Lord your God and keep all his statutes and commandments which I am giving to you, both you, your children, and your descendants all your days, that you may enjoy long life. If you listen, Israel, and are careful to observe them, you will prosper and increase greatly as the Lord the God of your forefathers promised you. . . .

What then, Israel, does the Lord your God ask of you? Only this: to fear the Lord your God, to conform to all his ways, to love him, and to serve him with all your heart and soul. This you will do by observing the commandments of the Lord and his statutes which I give you this day for your good. To the Lord your God belong heaven itself, the highest heaven, the earth and everything in it; yet the Lord was attached to your forefathers by his love for them, and he chose their descendants after them. Out of all nations you were his chosen people, as you are this day. So now you must circumcise your hearts and not be stubborn any more, for the Lord your God is God of gods and Lord of lords, the great, mighty, and terrible God. He is no respecter of persons; he is not to be bribed; he secures justice for the fatherless and the widow, and he shows love towards the alien who lives among you, giving him food and clothing. You too must show love towards the alien, for you once lived as aliens in Egypt.

Source: Deuteronomy 5:1–2, 6:1–3, 10:12–19, in *The Oxford Study Bible: Revised English Bible with the Apocrypha* (New York: Oxford University Press, 1992).

"special possession; . . . a kingdom of priests, . . . [his] holy nation." (See the box "Reading Sources: The Covenant.")

The Ten Commandments are both more general and more personal than the laws of Hammurabi's Code. They are addressed to the individual, whom they commit to a universal standard. They emphasize prohibitions, saying more about what one should *not* do than about what one should do. The first three commandments establish Yahweh as the sole god of Israel, prohibit any sculpture or image of God, and forbid misuse of the divine name. The next two commandments are injunctions to observe the seventh day of the week (the Sabbath) as a day free of work and to honor one's parents. The sixth and seventh prohibit destructive or violent acts against neighbors, in particular adultery and killing. The final three command-ments regulate community life by prohibiting stealing, testifying falsely, and coveting another man's wife or goods. In contrast to the starkness of the Ten Commandments, an enormous amount of detailed legal material is also found in the Hebrew Bible.

Many scholars doubt whether Hebrew monotheism emerged as early as the thirteenth century. In any case, the Bible makes clear that many ordinary Hebrews remained unconvinced. For centuries afterward, many Israelite worshipers deemed Yahweh their greatest god but not their only god. Unready for the radical innovation that monotheism represented, they carried out the rituals of various Canaanite deities, whom they worshiped on hilltop altars. Forging a national consensus for monotheism took centuries.

Map 2.2   Ancient Israel   The Israelites settled in the Canaanite hill country west of the Jordan River and the Dead Sea after 1200 B.C. (*top map*). Control of Israelite territory after 928 B.C. was shared between two monarchies (*bottom map*): the kingdoms of Israel (conquered by the Assyrians in 722 B.C.) and Judah (conquered by the Babylonians in 598 B.C.).

From the thirteenth to the late eleventh century B.C., the Hebrews were governed by a series of tribal leaders, referred to as "judges" in the Bible, but eventually the military threat posed by the Philistines° persuaded the tribes to accept a centralized monarchy. The Philistines, one of the Sea Peoples, had captured the Palestinian coast in the twelfth and eleventh centuries and seriously endangered Israel. The first Israelite king, Saul (r. ca. 1020–1004 B.C.), had some success against them but eventually fell in battle along with his son, Jonathan. The next king, David (r. 1004–965 B.C.), a former mercenary captain for the Philistines, defeated them decisively.

David was Israel's greatest king. He extended the kingdom into parts of modern Jordan, Lebanon, and Syria and conquered the Canaanite city of Jerusalem, which he made Israel's capital. David's son and successor, Solomon (r. 965–928 B.C.), was also a great king, a centralizer who moved from a loose kingship toward a tightly organized monarchy. His most famous accomplishment was the construction of a magnificent Temple in Jerusalem. The Temple priesthood and sacrifices became the focus of the national cult of Yahweh. Previously, that focus had been a humble, movable wooden chest known as the Ark of the Covenant.

Solomon's reign represented the high-water mark of the power of the Israelite monarchy. Under his successors the monarchy was split into a large northern kingdom of Israel with a capital at Samaria and a smaller southern kingdom of Judah° centered on Jerusalem (see Map 2.2). In 722 B.C., the Assyrians conquered the kingdom of Israel and deported its inhabitants. Judah survived, first as a state controlled by Assyria and then as an independent power.

The religious history of the period of the two kingdoms (928–722 B.C.) and the Judean survivor-state (722–587 B.C.) is marked by an intense drive toward monotheism. The kings of Judah in the seventh century B.C., especially Hezekiah (r. 715–686 B.C.) and Josiah (r. 640–609 B.C.), aggressively attacked the worship of all gods other than Yahweh and all centers of Yahweh worship

Philistines (FILL-uh-steenz)   **Judah** (JOO-duh)

other than the Temple in Jerusalem. The kings also began the process of canonizing the Hebrew Bible. Ambitious and independent, Hezekiah joined in a revolt against Assyria that was brutally suppressed in 701 B.C. and almost cost him his kingdom (see the feature "Weighing the Evidence: The Siege of Lachish" on pages 66–67).

The Judean kings could not have succeeded without the help of the prophets, who were prominent from approximately 900 to 500 B.C. Seers uttering divinely inspired predictions were universal figures in ancient religion. No other culture of antiquity, however, has anything like the Hebrew prophets: charismatic, uncompromising, terrible figures who announced God's anger and ultimate forgiveness. The prophets remind us of the most radical spiritual teachings of Israel: absolute monotheism, an insistence on righteousness, contempt for materialism and worldly power, love of the powerless. They often supported the kings but did not shrink from confronting authority and insisting on uncompromising justice. Among them were Amos, a humble shepherd who preached the superiority of righteousness to ritual; Jeremiah, who prophesied the destruction of Jerusalem as punishment for the people's idolatry; and Isaiah, who predicted the coming of a savior who would inaugurate a new day of universal peace and justice.

A characteristic story of the prophets is the confrontation between Elijah, perhaps the most famous prophet, and Ahab, king of Israel (r. 871–852 B.C.). Ahab coveted the vineyard of one Naboth, but Naboth refused Ahab's offer to buy it. Spurred on by his wife, Jezebel, Ahab trumped up charges against Naboth, who was unjustly stoned to death. Ahab then confiscated the vineyard. God sent Elijah to declare to Ahab that, as punishment for committing murder, "dogs will lick [Ahab's] blood" and that of his family (1 Kings 21:19). In a remarkable scene, we witness not only Elijah's courage in confronting the king but also the king's surrender and repentance before Elijah's spiritual authority. Ahab (though not Jezebel) humbles himself and is spared, but his son and successor, King Ahaziah, who is equally wicked, is punished with a fatal injury. The Western tradition of civil disobedience owes much to the courage of the Hebrew prophets.

■ Exile and Return, 598–ca. 400 B.C.

The prophets prepared the people of Judah for survival by correctly predicting ruin and exile and promising that divine providence would guarantee return. The tenacity of the Judeans in clinging to this message was remarkable. Indeed, it needed to be, for between 598 and 586 B.C., the Neo-Babylonians conquered Judah, destroying

Jerusalem and the Temple. The cultural, political, and economic elite were deported to Babylon. Those who could, fled for Egypt. The dispirited remnant in Palestine shared their land with colonists from neighboring regions, with whom they intermarried and among whom their religion all but disappeared.

And that, given the usual fate of exiled and uprooted peoples in antiquity, should have been that. Yet not only did the Judeans in the Babylonian Captivity persevere in their religious loyalty; they actually returned to Palestine in large numbers.

The Neo-Babylonian rulers allowed Jewish deportees to continue to practice their religion. Jews* in Babylon were not slaves; rather they rented land on royal estates, and some became prosperous. Although some Babylonian Jews assimilated to local ways, many continued a Jewish religious life. Communal worship was observed in open places, perhaps with associated buildings. Some scholars argue that synagogues ("gatherings" in Greek), modest centers of prayer and study that have been the focus of Jewish worship ever since, first emerged in Babylon. It is also possible that the exiles put together the Torah in something like its current form. Elders led the community while prophets continued to speak out: two examples are Ezekiel, who preached the restoration of the Temple, and the man known to us only as "Second Isaiah" (Isaiah 40–66). Second Isaiah emphasized the universal aspect of the god of Israel, who made empires rise and fall and would bring the exiles home from far-off Babylon.

The Temple in Jerusalem was rebuilt around 515 B.C., only seventy years after its destruction. This remarkable turn of events was possible partly because of the Persians, who conquered Babylon in 539 B.C. and proclaimed the freedom of the Jews to rebuild their Temple in Jerusalem. Still, Persian benevolence would not have been enough if the Judean elite had not kept the faith burning among the exiles.

Second Isaiah's message points to a second important development among the exiles of Judah. As striking as the return to Palestine was the survival of large numbers of Judeans as an unassimilated people outside of Judah—in other words, as Jews. For the first time, membership in a community of worship was divorced from residence. Jewish communities flourished in Babylon, Persia, and Egypt, but the members often chose not to become Babylonians, Persians, or Egyptians. From the sixth century B.C. on, a majority of Jews were living outside Palestine, and the Jewish Diaspora ("dispersion") became a permanent fact of history.

---

*Strictly speaking, the terms *Jew* and *Jewish* are anachronistic before the fifth century B.C.

The People of the Covenant

A rough equality among the people of Israel, limited government, and the rule of law under God were all fundamental Israelite political notions. Eventually, they would become fundamental political ideals for many in the West, and they would be applied not only to Israelites but to all people.

According to Israelite belief, God made humans in his own image. Thus, all individuals were equal in a fundamental sense; all were bound by God's law. A king who disobeyed this law was illegitimate. Indeed, Israel was ambivalent at best about the institution of kingship, which was tolerated as an evil made necessary only by the country's many armed enemies. God's covenant with the Hebrews was a religious contract with political consequences, rendering God the only true king of Israel. Far from being gods themselves or even God's representatives, Israel's kings were merely God's humble servants.

Israelite egalitarianism was restricted to men. Israelite women usually could not own or inherit property, as women could in Hammurabi's Babylon; or sue in court, as women could in pharaonic Egypt; or initiate a divorce, as women could in Classical Athens (see page 88). The powerful goddesses of other ancient cultures were absent in Israel. Women participated in the rituals of early Israelite religion and the original Temple (ca. 940–586 B.C.) but were segregated in a separate women's courtyard in the rebuilt Temple (ca. 515 B.C.–A.D. 79) and absent from Temple ritual. Indeed, the perspective of the Hebrew Bible is predominantly male. Consider just two examples. First, of the 1,426 names in the Hebrew Bible, 1,315 are male; only 111 women's names appear, about 9 percent of the total.[3] Second, only men and boys can bear the sign of the Lord's covenant with Israel—that is, circumcision.

Nevertheless, Israelite women enjoyed honor as mothers and partners in running the household. The Hebrew Bible states that woman (as exemplified by Eve, the first woman) was created as "a suitable partner" for man (Genesis 2:18, 20). Reproduction and hence motherhood assume great importance in the Hebrew Bible; the Lord enjoins humans to "be fruitful and multiply" (Genesis 1:28). The Bible also commands that children honor both their father and their mother: the two parents are equal in parental authority (Exodus 20:12).

The Hebrew Bible sometimes displays sympathy for and insights into the strategies that women used to counter the abuses of male power. Rebecca, for instance, thwarts her husband Isaac's plan to give his blessing to their son Esau. As the eldest, Esau was entitled to this honor, but Rebecca preferred her younger son Jacob, and she saw to it that he and not Esau obtained her husband's blessing.

Only about a half-dozen women in the Hebrew Bible served as leaders of Israel, but that is more than in the literature of most other ancient cultures. Deborah (ca. 1125 B.C.), for example, a charismatic Israelite prophet, organizes an army that destroys the forces of a Canaanite commander. In a later book Esther, a Hebrew woman, becomes the wife of a Persian king whom the Bible calls Ahasuerus (probably Xerxes, r. 485–465 B.C.). Esther works ferociously at the Persian court to defeat a conspiracy to wipe out her people, and she saves them. The Book of Ruth (date uncertain) tells the story of a selfless and loyal woman, Ruth, who rescues her mother-in-law, Naomi, from ruin and poverty. The Bible celebrates Ruth as Naomi's "devoted daughter-in-law, who has proved better to you [Naomi] than seven sons." (See the box "Reading Sources: Ruth.")

Israelite culture prized women for their cunning, courage, and perseverance—qualities that allowed the people to survive. Military prowess was highly valued in men, but their inner qualities were appreciated as well. Schooled in defeat and exile, many Israelites came to the conclusion that "wisdom is better than weapons of war" (Ecclesiastes 9:18). Thus, the Hebrew Bible stresses God's primary interest in goodness of soul: "The Lord does not see as man sees; men judge by appearances, but the Lord judges by the heart" (1 Samuel 16:7). The God of Israel

Israelite Seal This seal stone, which shows a roaring lion, was used by a man named Shema, an official of King Jeroboam of Israel. The stone was used to make an impression in hot wax, creating a seal on a document. *(Reuben and Edith Hecht Collection, University of Haifa, Israel/Erich Lessing/Art Resource, NY)*

❧ READING SOURCES

Ruth

Some parts of the Hebrew Bible prohibit intermarriage. The Book of Ruth, however, praises marriage between Judean men and women from neighboring Moab (modern Jordan; see Map 2.2). This excerpt illustrates such unions, as it does the problem of food shortages, which were a special burden for widows.

Once, in the time of the Judges when there was a famine in the land, a man [Elimelech] from Bethlehem in Judah went with his wife [Naomi] to live in Moabite territory. . . .

Elimelech died, and Naomi was left a widow with her two sons. The sons married Moabite women, one of whom was called Orpah and the other Ruth. [After ten years the sons died.] . . . Then Naomi, bereaved of her two sons as well as of her husband, got ready to return to her own country with her daughters-in-law, because she had heard in Moab that the Lord had shown his care for his people by giving them food. . . .

Naomi said to her daughters-in-law, "Go back, both of you, home to your own mothers. May the Lord keep faith with you, as you have kept faith with the dead and with me; and may he grant each of you the security of a home with a new husband.". . . Then Orpah kissed her mother-in-law and took her leave, but Ruth clung to her.

"Look," said Naomi, "your sister-in-law has gone back to her people and her God. Go, follow her." Ruth answered, "Do not urge me to go back and desert you. Where you go, I shall go, and where you stay, I shall stay. Your people will be my people, and your God my God. Where you die, I shall die, and there be buried. I solemnly declare before the Lord that nothing but death will part me from you." When Naomi saw that Ruth was determined to go with her, she said no more.

[They returned to Naomi's hometown, Bethlehem, in Judah.]

Naomi had a relative on her husband's side, a prominent and well-to-do . . . [man named] Boaz. One day Ruth the Moabite asked Naomi, "May I go to the harvest fields and glean [collect excess grain] behind anyone who will allow me?" "Yes, go my daughter," she replied. So Ruth went gleaning in the fields behind the reapers. [She met Boaz in his fields.] . . .

Boaz said to Ruth, "Listen, my daughter: do not go to glean in any other field. Do not look any farther, but stay close to my servant-girls. Watch where the men reap, and follow the gleaners; I have told the men not to molest you. Any time you are thirsty, go and drink from the jars they have filled." She bowed to the ground and said, "Why are you so kind as to take notice of me, when I am just a foreigner?" Boaz answered, "I have been told the whole story of what you have done for your mother-in-law since the death of your husband, how you left father and mother and homeland and came among a people you didn't know before. The Lord reward you for what you have done. . . ."

[Eventually, Boaz marries Ruth; their great-grandson would be Israel's greatest king, David.]

Source: Ruth 1:1, 3–6, 8–9, 14–18; 2:1–3, 8–12, in *The Oxford Study Bible: Revised English Bible with the Apocrypha* (New York: Oxford University Press, 1992).

prized righteousness above wealth, might, sacrifice, or ritual.

One might say that Israelite law reflected a similar tension between power and righteousness. On the one hand, just as the God of Israel was omnipotent and jealous, so the law of Israel was meant to be comprehensive and forceful. Capital punishment existed for murder, rape, incorrigible rebelliousness of a son against his parents, adultery by a married woman (both she and her lover were to be executed), a woman's loss of her virginity before marriage, and other offenses. Harsh punishment was mandated for Canaanite towns taken by siege: the entire population was to be killed so as not to corrupt Israel with their religious practices.

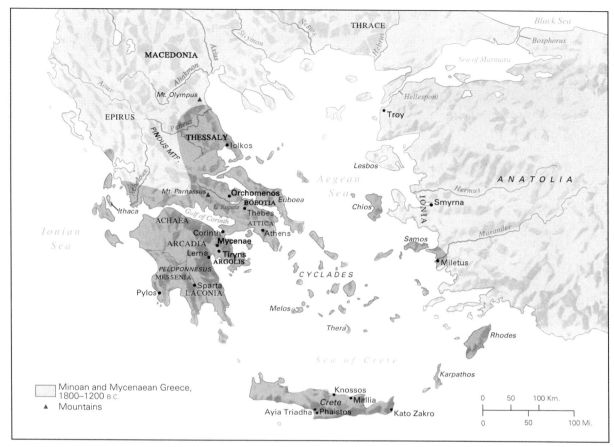

Map 2.3 Aegean Greece The Minoan civilization (height: ca. 1800–1550 B.C.) and the Mycenaean civilization (height: ca. 1400–1200 B.C.) flourished in turn in the second millennium B.C. Aegean region. The center of Minoan civilization was the island of Crete. A mainland people, the Mycenaeans conquered Minoan Crete around 1550 B.C.

On the other hand, by taking intention into account, Israelite law echoed a note already present in Mesopotamia. The so-called Law of the Goring Ox, for instance, allowed a person to go unpunished for owning an ox that gores a person to death, unless the owner knew beforehand that the animal was dangerous. If the owner did know, however, then the owner had to be put to death. Israelite law, moreover, demonstrated a belief in the sanctity of human life by prohibiting human sacrifice. An Israelite had to be ready in his or her heart (but *only* in his or her heart) to sacrifice his or her child to Yahweh, as Abraham was willing to sacrifice Isaac when Yahweh so commanded. After ascertaining Abraham's willingness to obey even to the point of sacrificing his son, Yahweh freed Isaac from the altar and supplied a ram as a substitute offering. Israelite monotheism thus rejected human sacrifice, as did the religions later derived from it.

EARLY GREECE, TO CA. 725 B.C.

THE Greeks founded the Western tradition in politics and philosophy. The ancient Greek genius was at its height in the era of the Greek city-states (ca. 700–300 B.C.), but it is already visible in the *Iliad*° and the *Odyssey*°, the epic poems of Homer (ca. 725 B.C.). Both are products of the first millennium B.C. Civilization, however, flourished in Greece a thousand years earlier, and Homer's works have roots in this earlier era. Most of what we know of this earlier period, called "Aegean° Greece" by scholars, is based on the discoveries of archaeologists. In particular, archaeology provides the evidence for the rise and fall of two monument-building, literate civilizations: the Minoans on the island of Crete and the Mycenaeans on the Greek mainland (see Map 2.3).

Iliad (IL-ee-ud) **Odyssey** (ODD-uh-see) **Aegean** (ih-JEE-un)

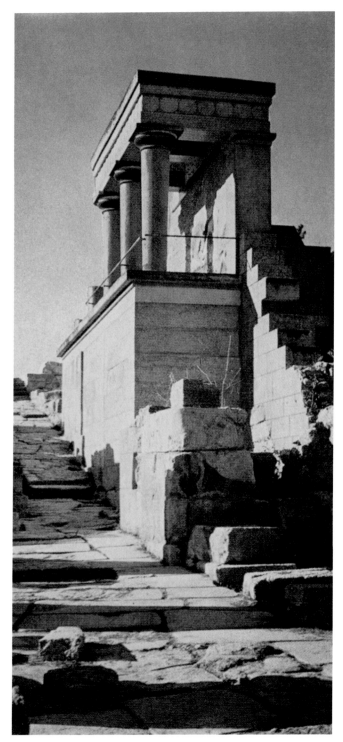

Palace of Knossos A paved ramp and (partially restored) portico are part of an entranceway to the palace. The tapered columns and combination of stone and timber are characteristic features of Minoan architecture. *(Dmitrios Harissiadis/Benaki Museum)*

■ The Minoans and Early Greece, 3000–1375 B.C.

Europe's first civilization appeared in Greece, on the Aegean island of Crete° around 2000 B.C. From there, civilization spread to the Greek mainland.

Civilization came relatively late to Greece, but in comparison with Egypt and even western Asia, Greece is not a hospitable land. Mountainous, and watered by few rivers, it contains little cultivable farmland. Although pastureland and forest are more abundant, one-third of the country is entirely unproductive. Most of the farmland, moreover, is to be found in upland plains, which are divided by mountains, making it difficult to concentrate a large labor force to work the land efficiently. The south enjoys a mild, Mediterranean climate but is quite dry. The north has a Balkan climate of hot summers and cold winters. The indented seacoast provides Greece with many harbors. Greece's geography influenced several recurring features of its history: contrasts between seafarers and mountaineers and between north and south, and the challenge of unifying so mountainous a terrain.

Agriculture preceded civilization in Greece. The first agricultural villages appeared shortly after 7000 B.C., bronze-making skills after 3000. After 3500 B.C., Greece became a supplier of raw materials for the new cities of western Asia. Both on the islands and the mainland, small towns appeared, sometimes fortified with stone walls, occasionally containing substantial stone and mud-brick structures. Between 3000 and 2400 B.C., people living on the Cycladic islands of the Aegean Sea produced exquisite marble sculptures and incised terra-cotta dishes.

Around 2000 B.C. civilization appears on Crete. Its origins are hotly debated, but we know that it was literate because Cretan writing has survived. It consists of a syllabary, or system of simple syllables that form words, known as "Linear A," and though we know its language is not Greek, we do not know what it is. The island of Crete is located on the sea routes between the Greek mainland, Egypt, and Anatolia. The archaeological record contains many signs of trade and cultural contact between Cretans and nearby peoples, from one of whom, perhaps, the Minoans were descended. The evidence for Minoan civilization is concentrated in Crete's palaces—monumental structures that first appeared at various locations on the island around 2000 B.C. After destruction by earthquake, the palaces were rebuilt on an even grander scale, to flourish especially during the period from 1800 to 1550 B.C. Scholars call the palace-builders

---

Crete (KREET)

and their civilization "Minoan°," after King Minos of later Greek myth. He was supposed to have ruled a great sea empire from his palace at Knossos (see Map 2.3). What the Minoans called themselves remains a mystery.

The Minoan palaces were not merely royal residences but centers of administration, religion, politics, and economics. Minoan palace bureaucrats supervised a large sector of the economy, just as their counterparts did in Ugarit, Egypt, the Hittite kingdom, and other ancient societies. The largest Cretan palace, as well as the first to be excavated, Knossos offers a striking example of Minoan civilization. The main building at Knossos covers 3 acres, the associated structures an additional 2 acres. The palace was built around a large central court, 180 feet long by 82 feet wide, probably used for public ceremonies. A mazelike structure surrounded the court. The palace had enormous staterooms, residence quarters, storage rooms, artisans' workshops, and bathrooms, interconnected by corridors, ramps, and stairways. Light wells admitted daylight, and brightly colored frescoes decorated the walls. Cretan architects were aware of palace architecture elsewhere in the eastern Mediterranean and may have borrowed from it, but precisely who influenced whom remains an open question.

The palaces make clear that the Minoans exploited Crete's considerable natural wealth in agriculture and timber. Archaeological and linguistic evidence indicates a widespread Minoan trading network from the Levant to Sicily. A Minoan settlement flourished on the Aegean island of Thera, 70 miles north of Crete (see Map 2.3). This settlement was destroyed in 1626 (or possibly 1628) B.C. by one of the most violent volcanic eruptions in history. So huge a catastrophe produced climate changes for several years, evident in the pattern of tree rings in ancient wood. That is why scholars can offer so specific a date for Thera's eruption.

From the lack of fortifications around Cretan palaces and the small amount of arms and armor found in burial sites, it appears that the Minoans lived in relative peace. Minoan frescoes show that women as well as men played important roles in cult and ritual. The women portrayed by Cretan artists are often beautiful, bejeweled, and elegant, the men often graceful and athletic. We see, for example, acrobats practicing the sport of bull jumping. Landscapes and animals are frequently illustrated. A statuette of a priestess holding a snake in either hand depicts Minoan interest in the relationship between humans and the natural world. In short, Minoan civilization gives an impression of peace, prosperity, and happiness. No wonder we sense a somewhat lost-Eden quality

Minoan (mih-NO-un)

Fresco at Thera   This detail of the so-called Fresco of the Ladies shows one of a pair of murals from a shrine. This festively costumed woman carries clothes and ornaments to a seated woman (not shown), perhaps a goddess.   *(The Ancient Art & Architecture Collection)*

about the violent and relatively sudden destruction of Minoan civilization. All of the palaces except Knossos were destroyed around 1550 B.C.; Knossos fell around 1375 B.C.

No shortage of theories has surfaced about the cause of the destruction, but the archaeological evidence strongly supports the notion of an invasion. But by whom? To find the answer, let us look to the Greek mainland.

■ The Mycenaeans, to ca. 1200 B.C.

A wave of destruction put an end to the Greek mainland's vigorous Copper Age (see page 10) around 2300 B.C. Centuries of relative poverty followed until, around 1700 B.C., signs of power and prosperity appear at a series of burial sites in central Greece and the Peloponnesus. The most dramatic are at Mycenae° (see Map 2.3), where the royal burials contain a treasure house of objects in gold and other precious metals. Many of the other cities in Greece that would later become famous, such as Athens and Thebes, were also thriving cities in this period.

The inhabitants of Mycenae, unlike the earlier inhabitants of the Greek peninsula, were Greek-speakers. They and the wider civilization they represent are called Mycenaean°. Just when and how the Mycenaeans got to Greece are tangled questions. Some scholars imagine migration, others invasion. Some believe the Mycenaeans' ancestors arrived as early as 2300 B.C., whereas others think it was not until 1700, more than a half-millennium later.

The Mycenaeans adopted and adapted technology, ideas, and art from their advanced neighbors in Crete, Egypt, Anatolia, and Syria-Palestine. The Mycenaeans traded with these neighbors. They also fought with them, for Mycenaean society was dominated by warrior-kings, raiders who exchanged booty to show off their wealth.

Around 1550 B.C. the mainland warriors achieved their greatest feat: the conquest of Crete. They destroyed most of the palaces but spared Knossos, which did not fall until about 1375 B.C. (we do not know the cause of that destruction). The warlike Mycenaeans had conquered the sophisticated Minoans. In turn, the Mycenaeans learned from their subjects and adopted a Minoan-style palace economy.

Mycenaean civilization was at its height between about 1400 and 1200 B.C. Kings lived in palaces whose storerooms were crammed with treasures. They traveled through their kingdoms on a network of good roads and could muster rowers and ships. Mycenaean artists excelled at potterymaking and fresco painting, gold inlay work and ivory carving. Mycenaean builders constructed palaces, fortifications, bridges, huge vaulted tombs, and sophisticated drainage works.

Palace officials supervised considerable economic activity, often in minute detail, including agriculture, pasturage, and artisanry. Women and children as well as men were included in the labor force. Our knowledge of the palace economy comes primarily from thousands of clay tablets inscribed by palace scribes around 1200 B.C. They are written in a script scholars call Linear B, mostly an early form of Greek consisting of a combination of syllabary and ideograms (a system of symbols that stand for words or ideas).

Mycenaean merchants replaced Minoans in trade in the central and eastern Mediterranean. From Sicily to the Levant, they exported wine and scented oils and imported metals, ivory, and perhaps slaves. Mycenaean warriors engaged in activities ranging from raids and skirmishes to formal battles.

In the thirteenth century B.C., at the height of Mycenaean power, some unknown threat prompted the Mycenaean kings to fortify the palaces at Mycenae and elsewhere with stone walls. By 1200 B.C. most of the fortified sites had been destroyed. Afterward, only a few people continued to live in the old towns. It appears likely that Mycenaean Greece suffered from a combination of internal weakness and foreign invasion similar to that experienced by most of the eastern Mediterranean around 1250–1150 B.C., the era of the Sea Peoples (see page 34).

■ Between Mycenae and the City-States, ca. 1100–725 B.C.

The era from the fall of Mycenae to the rise of the Greek city-states was long referred to as the Greek Dark Ages. But that gloomy term is used less often as archaeology increases our knowledge of the period from roughly 1100 to 800 B.C. The evidence does, however, suggest a considerable depopulation in Greece from the twelfth through the ninth centuries B.C. It seems that rich and poor alike were worse off than in Mycenaean times.

After the destruction of the palaces around 1200 B.C., Mycenaean culture continued to flicker before finally fading in the early eleventh century. New peoples began to move into central and southern Greece around this time. They probably were the Dorians°, speakers of a Greek dialect who came from northern Greece. Their

---

Mycenae (my-SEE-nee)   **Mycenaean** (my-suh-NEE-un)   **Dorians** (DOOR-ee-unz)

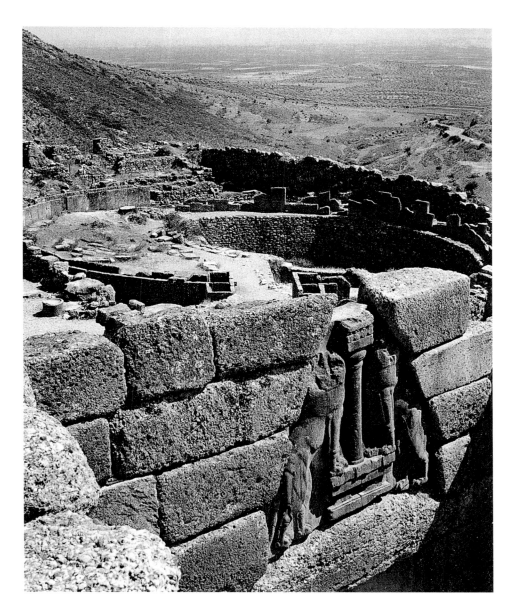

Lion Gate at Mycenae Carved about 1250 B.C. above the main gate of the citadel's massive walls, the lions—flanking a column, their front paws resting on altars—probably represent royal authority. Inside the walls is Grave Circle B, a royal burial site.
(Dmitrios Harissiadis/Benaki Museum)

material culture was rougher and ruder than that of Mycenae's descendants; it boasts few distinctions besides the iron slashing sword and the long bronze fastener. The Dorians drove out or dominated the Mycenaean Greeks, turning much of central and southern Greece, including Crete, into Dorian centers. Among major settlements, only Athens maintained its independence. The city served as an asylum for Mycenaean refugees, many of whom migrated eastward around 1000 B.C. to the Aegean coast of Anatolia, which was destined to become an important center of Greek culture.

Greece from roughly 1100 to 800 B.C. was largely a poor and illiterate society of small towns and low-level agriculture and trade. Nevertheless, it produced notable painted pottery and preserved an oral tradition of poetry handed down from the Mycenaean era. After 800 B.C. a huge change came over Greece.

First of all, peace contributed to a sharp population rise, and the economy shifted from herding to farming, a more efficient source of food. Greek commerce, too, expanded, thanks in part to the impact of Phoenician traders.

Under pressure from rising population, Greeks founded colonies around the Mediterranean and the Black Sea beginning around 750 B.C. Meanwhile, trade and colonization inspired change at home. Dramatic new experiments in politics, warfare, and culture were attempted. It was the dawn of the era of the Greek city-state. We look at these changes in detail in Chapter 3. Here we focus on a milestone in literary artistry that heralded a new age: the epic poetry of Homer.

■ Homer and History

Had ancient Greece produced a Bible, the *Iliad* and *Odyssey* of Homer would have been its two Testaments. Only Hesiod°, a poet who lived around 700 B.C., enjoyed a comparable influence on later generations, but his poems (*Theogony* and *Works and Days*), though composed in the epic tradition, were shorter than Homer's and arguably less dramatic. But Greece did not have a Bible. Homer and Hesiod were poets, not priests. (As far as we know, the Greek world never had a priestly class comparable to that of Egypt or western Asia.) Although their poems inspired, moved, and educated the Greeks—a large part of a Greek boy's education consisted of learning to recite Homer from memory—they were not divine writ.

Homer was not a historian. He was a bard, a professional singer of heroic poetry—of songs praising the deeds of the great. Heroic poetry consciously glorifies and magnifies the actions of its subjects. In all likelihood, a great deal of tall tale colors Homer's stories of Achilles and Odysseus, of Helen and Penelope. We cannot even be sure that these men and women ever really existed.

Indeed, Homer lived neither in the age his poems are set in nor, for that matter, on the Greek mainland. Homer lived in Ionia, a region of the central western coast of Anatolia, perhaps in the city of Smyrna. Although we do not know just when he lived, it was not until centuries after the Trojan War, the pivotal event of his works. Most scholars today would date Homer to about 725 B.C. or later, a period of increasing change, growth, and ferment in Greece. Some scholars question whether there was just *one* Homer and argue that the *Iliad* and *Odyssey* are the works of two different poets.

The author of the poems worked in a continuous poetic tradition going back to the Mycenaean Age, from which he took stories, details, and language. Most scholars accept the theory that this tradition was oral, not written. Like oral poets elsewhere, Homer and his predecessors composed their poems as they sang them, making use of a stock of stories and formulaic expressions (such as the Greek equivalents of "swift-footed Achilles" and "grey-eyed goddess Athena"). In fact, Homer may have been illiterate.

Oral tradition gave Homer knowledge of a society that was long gone by his day. Although Homer studs his poems with accurate details of Mycenaean palace life, the ideology of his characters generally reflects the beliefs of his own, post-Mycenaean society.

Both in Mycenaean times and in Homer's day, the Greeks were polytheists. The gods of Greece are similar in many ways to the gods of Sumer. They share the foibles and foolishness of humanity but are immortal and far more powerful than humans. The gods figure prominently in early Greek poetry, but they are less powerful than Yahweh, less immediate, and less interested in the inner life of men and women. Already emerging at the beginning of the Greek cultural tradition was the belief that became the hallmark of ancient Greece: that "man is the measure of all things," as the thinker Protagoras would declare in the fifth century B.C.

The Greek gods of the first millennium B.C. were worshiped in Mycenaean times—offerings to them are recorded on Linear B tablets. Because they were thought to live on Mount Olympus, a 9,500-foot-high peak in northern Greece (see Map 2.3), the gods were called the Olympians. Hesiod's *Theogony* tells the story of the Olympians' birth and their triumph over an older generation of deities. The "household" of the Olympians—the early Greek pantheon was conceived of as a noble's household—included Zeus°, a sky-god and the "father of gods and men," and his consort, Hera; Zeus's brother, Poseidon, god of the sea, earthquakes, and horses; Ares, god of war; and Aphrodite, goddess of love. Also in the "household" were Zeus's children: Athena, goddess of wisdom and cunning; Hephaestus, god of craftsmen; Hermes, god of travelers and thieves; Apollo, god of disease and healing; and Artemis, goddess of the hunt, of maidens, and of childbirth.

Flawed and sometimes unpredictable, the Greek gods often seem childish, but the natural world they symbolized seemed equally inconstant to the ancients. The gods embody the values of a warrior society that put a premium on *aretê°*, or excellence, especially excellence in battle. The heroes in the *Iliad* and the *Odyssey* seek glory through military exploits. Homer's gods reward great warriors, but the gods insist on justice as well. Zeus punishes those who do evil—those who, for example, break oaths or give false judgments or violate the laws of hospitality. In the *Iliad*, the Trojan prince Paris sparks the Trojan War by abducting the beautiful Helen from her husband, the Greek king Menelaus, while he is a guest in Menelaus's household. In return, the Greeks attack Troy, a wealthy city in northwestern Anatolia. The gods destroy Troy as punishment for Paris's crime.

The *Iliad* and the *Odyssey* focus on the Trojan War and its aftermath. The *Iliad* is set in the tenth year of the conflict. The strain of fighting leads to a quarrel between Greek chieftains: Agamemnon, king of Mycenae and the leader of the expedition, and Achilles°, the greatest Greek warrior. The most prominent Trojans, King Priam

---

Hesiod (HEE-see-ud)   **Zeus** (ZOOS)   **aretê** (ah-reh-TAY)   **Achilles** (uh-KIL-eez)

and his eldest son, Hector, are less petty but will suffer the greater ruin. The *Odyssey* tells the story of the struggle of the Greek hero Odysseus° to return to Ithaca and to regain his kingship after a twenty-year absence, ten years in the war at Troy and ten years wandering homeward. It also focuses on the loyalty and ingenuity of Odysseus's wife, Penelope, who saves the household in her husband's absence, and the maturation of their son, Telemachus°, who helps his father regain his kingdom.

Homer puts as much emphasis on brains as on brawn; Odysseus, for example, is a man of intelligence and cunning, as well as strength. Homer argues, moreover, that the gods hold human beings to a code of justice, hospitality, and respect for parents. Finally, although the Homeric poems focus on the upper classes—and primarily on men—the poems have a strain of sympathy for ordinary people and for women. Indeed, they have a general sympathy for failure. Homer's heroes court death and often obtain it. Unlike the psalmist of the Hebrew Bible, a Homeric hero walks alone "through the valley of the shadow of death" (Psalm 23:4); he has no god to comfort, rescue, or redeem him. He knows that the gods ordain human life to be difficult and full of suffering. Human frailty, however, ennobles Homer's heroes.

Homer's princes are proud and jealous. In the *Iliad*, when Agamemnon is forced by divine command to return his "prize"—a girl captured in a raid—he demands that he take the "prize" of Achilles, his greatest warrior—that is, Achilles' girl. Achilles' response is to sulk in his tent while the Trojans drive his fellow Greeks to near-defeat. In the *Odyssey,* a group of nobles lives off the absent Odysseus's estate, waiting to see which of them Odysseus's wife (and ostensible widow) might marry. Odysseus's honor demands that he punish them by killing every last one. In both cases, Homer recognizes that the hero goes too far: Achilles' inaction leads to the death of his best friend, and ultimately to his own death; Odysseus's thirst for revenge leads to civil war.

■ **World of the Heroes**

Historians must distinguish between ideology and reality in Homer's poems. Homer focuses on the elite. Homeric warriors and their women hold aristocratic values and tend to look down on ordinary people. Scholarship shows, however, that society in Homer's day was more level and egalitarian. Except for a small number of traders and craft specialists who lived in towns, most people in the Greece of 725 B.C. lived in villages and hamlets. Most farmed or herded pigs, goats, or sheep, and most were free. The people of each community were called the *demos*°; the leading men, *basileis*°. *Basileis* means "kings," but it is more accurate to understand them as chiefs. No great difference of wealth existed between the basileis and ordinary free farmers.

Although the basileis took the lead in both government and war, the demos played a crucial role. Homer emphasizes contests between aristocratic champions, but his vivid battle scenes also include large companies of ordinary men fighting in mass combat in close formation. And if the basileis dominated Homeric government, the demos had at least a small say.[4]

The basic instruments of government that would exist for centuries in Greece appear in the *Iliad* and the *Odyssey*: generals, orators, judges, a council, and an assembly. When making decisions about war and peace, a council of elder basileis consults an assembly of the warriors. In this arrangement we see a fundamental principle of Greek government: the political community should be composed of the warriors.

Let us turn now to the ideology of Homer's basileis, which would greatly influence later generations in antiquity. In the epics, the chiefs make friendships and exchange goods across international boundaries. Greek and Trojan chiefs kill each other on the battlefield but rarely hate each other. Indeed, some are bound by hereditary ties of guest-friendship and so decline to fight each other. (See the box "Global Encounters: Greeks and Trojans.")

The main activity of Homer's basileis is warfare. The *Iliad* consists largely of a series of battlefield contests. Since women did not take part in battle, they are not presented on an equal footing with men. Yet Homer rarely criticizes women in general, as some ancient Greek writers would in later centuries. He shows considerable compassion for women, particularly in the *Odyssey*. Homer's women are weaker than men, but they are neither timid nor helpless. Penelope, for example, personifies female resourcefulness: by refusing to marry until she has finished weaving a shroud for Odysseus's elderly father, and then by unraveling every night what she has woven during the day, she puts the noble suitors off for years. She is as concerned with honor as any Homeric man. By refusing to accept an offer of marriage while Odysseus might still be alive, Penelope does honor to her own good name and to her husband's.

Homeric women play important roles in encouraging men or, in a more complex psychological process, in

---

Odysseus (oh-DIS-ee-us)
Telemachus (te-LEH-muh-kus)

demos (DEE-mus)   **basileis** (bah-see-LAYS)

Greeks and Trojans

For Homer's aristocratic heroes, war was a struggle not of nations but of individual loyalties. Friendship and family ties mattered more than patriotism. As these excerpts from the Iliad *show, individual Greeks sometimes considered their enemies, the Trojans (and Trojan allies), to be respected rivals or even honored friends.*

Then looking darkly at [his commander, Agamemnon,] Achilles of the swift feet spoke:

"O wrapped in shamelessness, with your mind forever on profit, how shall any one of the Achaians [Greeks] readily obey you either to go on a journey or to fight men strongly in battle? I for my part did not come here for the sake of the Trojan spearmen to fight against them, since to me they have done nothing.

"Never yet have they driven away my cattle or my horses, never in Phthia where the soil is rich and men grow great did they spoil my harvest, since indeed there is much that lies between us, the shadowy mountains and the echoing sea; but for your sake, o great shamelessness, we followed, to do you favour, you with the dog's eyes, to win your honour and Menalos' from the Trojans.

"Now Glaukos, sprung of Hippolochos, and [Diomedes,] the son of Tydeus came together in the space between the two armies, battle-bent. Now as these advancing came to one place and encountered, first to speak was Diomedes of the great war cry: "Who among mortal men are you, good friend? . . . unhappy are those whose sons match warcraft against me."

Then in turn the shining son of Hippolochos answered: ". . . Hippolochos begot me, and I claim that he is my father; he sent me to Troy, and urged upon me repeated injunctions, to be always among the bravest, and hold my head above others, not shaming the generation of my fathers, who were the greatest men in Ephyre and again in wide Lykia. Such is my generation and the blood I claim to be born from."

He spoke, and Diomedes of the great war cry was gladdened. He drove his spear deep into the prospering earth, and in winning words of friendliness he spoke to the shepherd of the people [Glaukos]: "See now, you are my guest friend from far in the time of our fathers. . . . Let us avoid each other's spears, even in the close fighting. There are plenty of Trojans and famed companions in battle for me to kill, whom the god sends me, or those I run down with my swift feet, many Achaians for you to slaughter, if you can do it. But let us exchange our armour, so that these others may know how we claim to be guests and friends from the days of our fathers."

So they spoke, and both springing down from behind their horses gripped each other's hands and exchanged the promise of friendship; but Zeus the son of Kronos stole away the wits of Glaukos who exchanged with Diomedes the son of Tydeus armour of gold for bronze, for nine oxen's worth the worth of a hundred.

Source: The Iliad of Homer, trans. Richmond Lattimore (Chicago: University of Chicago Press, 1951), pp. 63, 156–159.

 For additional information on this topic, go to http://college.hmco.com.

---

bolstering a man's courage by playing the foil to his doubts and dreads. In the *Iliad*, Hector overcomes his own fears of battle by hearing his wife, Andromache°, express *her* terror at the thought of his dying and leaving her a widow and their infant son an orphan. Moreover, by taking the burden of hearth and home on herself, Andromache allows Hector to define masculinity as making war.

Loyalty to the family played an important role in social relations. A person's obligations to kin included the duty to avenge crime or murder. Friendship, cemented by an exchange of gifts, was another important social institution. Even humble peasants prided themselves on hospitality.

Such values served Homeric society well. Although they would survive in later centuries, they would be challenged after 700 B.C. by the increasing emphasis on public life as the Greek city-state evolved.

Andromache (an-DROM-eh-kee)

SUMMARY

HE first half of the first millennium B.C. witnessed dramatic developments among both the ancestors of the West and its founders. A new form of empire appeared. Multi-ethnic, far-flung, and claiming to be universal, such an empire would one day be brought into the Western tradition by Rome. The process began, however, among the West's ancestors in western Asia.

New military technology, the frank adoption of brutal and inhumane methods, and improvements in administration led to the creation of the Assyrian Empire, stretching from western Iran to Palestine and briefly even to Egypt. After short-lived hegemonies by Neo-Babylonians and Medes, the Persians established an empire that was larger, better organized, and more tolerant than the empire of the Assyrians. Heirs to Canaanite civilization of the second millennium B.C., the Phoenician city-states expanded across the Mediterranean Sea, less by military conquest than by trade and colonization.

The most important developments of the era, however, were not in commerce, weaponry, or imperialism but in new conceptions of the nature and meaning of human life. The Persians developed a new religion, Zoroastrianism, which emphasized ethics, dualism—that is, the conflict of good over evil with the eventual triumph of good—and redemption through a divine savior. The Israelites conquered Palestine and, even after losing it, held on to their identity by means of a tenacious belief in one god. They broke with tradition by insisting that their god was one, merciful, and just. Omnipotent, God gave history meaning and direction. The purpose of life, in the Israelite view, was to serve God by acting righteously. The new religion laid the foundation for Judaism as well as Christianity and Islam. The Jews wrote down their religious and historical traditions in a book that, along with the Christian New Testament, proved to be the most influential single text in the history of the West: the Hebrew Bible.

We know little of the ideologies of the Minoan and Mycenaean civilizations of the second millennium B.C., but their economies and governments seem to have been similar to those of the other palace-run states of the eastern Mediterranean. Yet by the first millennium B.C., the Greeks, like the Persians and the Hebrews, had broken with tradition, but with a greater emphasis on the human than on the divine. Homer's epic poems, which took shape approximately 725 B.C., focus on the fragile dignity of heroic human actions. Homer idealizes a society of aristocratic warriors seeking honor and glory. Although the Greek gods show favor to heroes, they display no transcendent interest in redeeming human souls. Men and women were doomed to die. Homer's legacy, therefore, was to glorify human heroism while recognizing the fleeting frailty of life. It was a legacy that raised as many questions as answers. In the middle centuries of the first millennium B.C., the Greeks would attempt to provide new solutions to Homer's problems. As we will see in the next chapter, their successes and failures in such diverse activities as politics and philosophy, war and art, literature and history, founded much of Western civilization.

■ Notes

1. S. Insler, *The Gāthās of Zarathustra: Acta Iranica*, 8 (Leiden, The Netherlands: E. J. Brill, 1975), p. 33.
2. Roland G. Kent, *Old Persian: Grammar, Texts, Lexicon* (New Haven, Conn.: American Oriental Society, 1950), p. 132.
3. Carol L. Meyers, "Everyday Life: Women in the Period of the Hebrew Bible," in Carol A. Newsom and Sharon H. Ringe, eds., *The Women's Bible Commentary* (Louisville, Ky.: Westminster/John Knox Press, 1992), p. 245.
4. Kurt A. Raaflaub, "Homer to Solon. The Rise of the *Polis*: The Written Sources," in Mogens Herman Hansen, ed., *The Ancient Greek City-State. Symposium on the Occasion of the 250th Anniversary of the Royal Danish Academy of Science and Letters, July 1–4, 1992, Historisk-filosofiske Meddelelser* 67, The Royal Danish Academy of Sciences and Letters (Copenhagen: Munksgaard, 1993), pp. 41–105.

■ Suggested Reading

Cook, J. M. *The Persian Empire.* 1983. A clear and readable introduction, updating earlier conclusions in the light of recent archaeological discoveries, particularly inscriptions.

Dickinson, Oliver. *The Aegean Bronze Age.* 1994. Perhaps the best single introduction to a vast and fascinating subject.

Finley, M. I. *The World of Odysseus.* Rev. ed. 1978. Essential introductory reading on the historicity, society, and ideology of the Homeric poems.

Moscati, Sabatino. *The World of the Phoenicians.* Translated by Alastair Hamilton. 1968. A general survey of politics, society, and culture, with more emphasis on the western than on the eastern Mediterranean.

Oates, J. *Babylon.* Rev. ed. 1986. A well-illustrated survey, from the period of Sargon to the Hellenistic Greeks, with a section on Babylon's cultural legacy.

Saggs, H. W. F. *The Might That Was Assyria.* 1984. A readable introductory history celebrating the Assyrians' achievements.

Shanks, H., ed. *Ancient Israel. A Short History from Abraham to the Roman Destruction of the Temple.* 1988. Short, readable essays by scholars offering up-to-date introductions to the subject.

 For a searchable list of additional readings for this chapter, go to http://college.hmco.com.

The Siege of Lachish

From the distance, it looks like one of the foothills that surround it. Up close, though, it can be clearly seen for what it is: Tel Lachish, the mound of the biblical city of Lachish. It is a link in the chain of evidence that tells one of the most remarkable stories in biblical history.*

Lachish was a great city, a royal fortress, and second only to Jerusalem in its importance to the kingdom of Judah (928–587 B.C.). In 701 B.C. the Assyrians under King Sennacherib (r. 704–681 B.C.) besieged Lachish and took it by force. The siege of Lachish is unique in early biblical history for the wealth of independent corroborating sources. In addition to reports in the Hebrew Bible are many Assyrian written documents. Furthermore, Sennacherib commemorated his victory by depicting the siege and recording the spoils in carved reliefs that he erected in his royal palace at Nineveh. Finally, the mound itself has been excavated, allowing a striking comparison of the archaeological and pictorial evidence of a siege in the biblical period.

Originally a Canaanite town, Lachish was fortified by the Israelite kings because of its strategic location. It sits southwest of Jerusalem in the Judean foothills, dominating the road between the Judean hills to the east and the Philistine coast to the west (see Map 2.2). By the reign of King Hezekiah of Judah (r. 715–686 B.C.), one of the most prominent kings of the House of David, Lachish was a large garrison city constructed on a monumental scale. It included inner and outer rings of thick walls, a massive gate complex, many houses and shops, and, in the center, a palace-fort surrounded by earthen ramps.

Having seen Assyria turn the kingdom of Israel into an occupied province, Hezekiah knew that he was facing the greatest power of the region. Nevertheless, he joined Egypt and the Philistine cities in a revolt soon after Sennacherib came to the throne in 704 B.C. Sennacherib responded by attacking the rebels in 701. The Hebrew Bible states: "In the fourteenth year of the reign of Hezekiah, Sennacherib king of Assyria attacked and took all the fortified cities of Judah" (2 Kings 18:13). We can read the results of the campaign in one of Sennacherib's inscriptions:

"As to Hezekiah, the Jew, he did not submit to my yoke. I laid siege to 46 of his strong cities, walled forts and to the countless small villages in their vicinity, and conquered (them) by means of well-stamped (earth-) ramps, and battering-rams brought (thus) near (to the walls) (combined with) the attack by foot-soldiers, (using) mines, breeches as well as sapper work [that is, digging away foundations]." Hezekiah bowed to Assyrian power. He gave up territory (though not Jerusalem) and agreed to an increase in tribute, which now amounted to "30 talents of gold, 800 talents of silver, precious stones, antimony, large cuts of red stone, couches inlaid with ivory, elephant-hides, ebony-wood, boxwood and all kinds of valuable treasures, his own daughters, concubines, male and female musicians." So the Assyrian inscription records.

The Lachish reliefs (in Sennacherib's palace) offer a vivid picture of the attack on the city. Lachish was well fortified and well defended, but the Assyrians were experts in taking cities by storm. The reliefs show the camp of the attackers, Assyrian archers and slingers advancing on the city, battering rams and siege engines in action against the walls, flaming chariots thrown down by the defenders, and, after the city was taken, captives impaled on sharp stakes.

Look at the artist's reconstruction of an Assyrian assault on the city, based on the archaeological evidence. The soldiers are climbing a massive siege ramp that the Assyrians built against a "vulnerable" point in the city walls. The excavators of Lachish found the ramp, consisting of a level of stones cemented together over a core of boulders. It is the oldest siege ramp so far discovered in the ancient world. In and around the city the excavators found other evidence of the battle: hundreds of arrowheads, many slingstones, a number of pieces of bronze sheet mail used in armor, and what may be the crest of a helmet worn by one of the Assyrian spearmen shown attacking the city walls in the Lachish reliefs. Most dramatic, the excavators discovered about seven hundred skeletons, evidently civilians killed during the Assyrian attack and then buried in mass graves outside the city. Three of the individuals were trepanned; that is, they were operated on before death by removing a portion of their skulls. Perhaps this represents a last attempt, evidently futile, to save the lives of the wounded.

---

* In much of what follows about Lachish (LAH-kish), I rely on the discussion in David Ussishkin, *The Conquest of Lachish by Sennacherib* (Tel-Aviv: Tel-Aviv University, Institute of Archaeology, 1982).

Artist's Reconstruction of an Assyrian Assault on Lachish *(Drawing by Gert le Grange, from David Ussishkin,* The Conquest of Lachish by Sennacherib *[Tel Aviv: Tel Aviv University, Institute of Archaeology, 1982], p. 123. Reproduced with permission.)*

Detail of the Assyrian Conquest of Lachish, a Relief from the Palace of Sennacherib *(British Museum/ Erich Lessing/Art Resource, NY)*

The Lachish reliefs also depict rows of captives and deportees marching toward Sennacherib on his throne. Look at this detail of the relief, showing a large Judean family leaving Lachish for exile. They are allowed to bring cattle with them, and a woman and child are permitted to ride on a wagon. The Assyrians claimed to have deported 200,150 people from Judah, of whom many men ended up as slave laborers working on Sennacherib's palace.

As for Lachish, it was burned to the ground, as the excavations confirm. Sometime in the seventh century the city was restored and refortified. Lachish was destroyed again, however, in 598 B.C., during the first of two military campaigns in Judah by Nebuchadrezzar, the Neo-Babylonian king. The excavators found a group of pottery sherds with ink inscriptions (called *ostraca*) in old Hebrew script, dating to just before that destruction. This unique set of documents in classical Hebrew writing consists of letters to a man named Yaush, the military governor of Lachish. They testify, among other things, to the worship of Yahweh, to the signal system linking the fortresses of Judah, and to the practices of the scribal profession. Once again, the city's misfortune has proved illuminating to students of the past.

CHAPTER 3

The Age of the Polis: Greece, ca. 750-350 B.C.

I T is dawn. The light reveals a hillside in the city of Athens, a natural auditorium. Its rocky slopes, visible in the photograph opposite, would have been covered, beginning about 500 B.C., with wooden benches facing a platform cut into the rock. The six thousand men gathered there constitute a diverse group, ranging from farmers to philosophers, from dockyard workers to aristocrats. As they take their seats, these, the citizens of Athens, watch priests conducting prayers and offering a sacrifice. Then, all eyes turn to the individual who mounts the platform—a herald. His booming voice asks the question that marks the start of business: "Who wishes to speak?" Someone rises to address the assembly. It is the first democracy in history—and the central laboratory in this great experiment in participation.

The assembly meeting recalls the defining features of what was, in its era, the characteristic political institution in much of Greece: the *polis* (plural, *poleis*). Usually translated as "city-state," the polis is better understood as "citizen-state." The polis was the product of communal activities, whether in the assembly or the military or the theater, undertaken by its members—its citizens. Not every polis was a democracy, but every polis emphasized cooperative activities whose participants enjoyed at least a measure of equality. Every polis also sought a balance between the group and the individual, be that person the speaker or a military hero or a freethinker.

Balance is a difficult state to achieve, however, and the equilibrium of the polis was frequently disturbed by tension and exclusion. Paradox marked the polis. Greek democracy failed to grant equal rights to women or immigrants, and it depended on slave labor. Relations among poleis were less often a matter of cooperation than of war. Although the Greeks created magnificent religious architecture, a portion of their intellectual elite came to the conclusion that the gods were of little importance in explaining the universe. Although

Athenian Acropolis, with Pnyx Hill in foreground.
(Photo: Julia M. Fair)

one leading polis, Sparta, was a paragon of militarism, obedience, and austerity, scorning the life of the mind, another, Athens, prided itself on freedom and cultural attainments. Yet the Greeks made the most even of such tensions, exploring them in literary genres—tragedy, comedy, history, and philosophy—that focused on the polis as a central theme. Creative tensions also marked Greek achievements in sculpture, painting, and architecture.

The era of the polis proved to be a defining moment in Western history. Although the Greeks of this era borrowed much from neighboring cultures, they were remarkably original. In the mid-first millennium B.C., the monotheistic religious heritage of the West first emerged among the Jews. During that same era, the Greeks founded the Western tradition in a broad range of culture, including politics; philosophy; literary genres such as comedy, tragedy, and history; and the visual and plastic arts of painting, sculpture, and architecture.

QUESTIONS TO CONSIDER

- What was the Greek polis, and why was its development a defining moment in Western civilization?

- What was the nature of ancient Greek democracy?

- What were the differences between Athens and Sparta, and what did each contribute to the Western experiment?

- What were the limits of freedom and equality in the polis, and how did ancient Greek thinkers and writers explore those limits?

TERMS TO KNOW

polis	Pericles
Archaic Greece	Socrates
hoplite phalanx	Plato
Solon	Aristotle
Sappho	tragedy
Classical Greece	Herodotus
demokratia	Thucydides

SOCIETY AND POLITICS IN ARCHAIC GREECE, CA. 750–500 B.C.

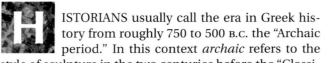

ISTORIANS usually call the era in Greek history from roughly 750 to 500 B.C. the "Archaic period." In this context *archaic* refers to the style of sculpture in the two centuries before the "Classical period" (480–323 B.C.). Archaic Greece was a patchwork of hundreds of separate city-states, tribal leagues, and monarchies (see Map 3.1). Nevertheless, it displayed a distinctive style and outlook not only in art but also in politics, military arrangements, technology, economics, literature, and religion.

Although it was a period of paradox, the Archaic era laid the groundwork for much of lasting importance in Western civilization. Archaic Greece witnessed the simultaneous growth of individualism and a tight community spirit, the emergence of social cohesion despite a continual state of war, the coexistence of deep religious piety and the West's first nontheistic philosophy. The Archaic period also saw the origin of characteristic Western

types of governmental regimes—tyranny, oligarchy, and the first steps toward democracy—and of fundamental Western notions of citizenship and the rule of law.

■ Agriculture, Trade, Colonization, and Warfare

An observer of ninth-century B.C. Greece would hardly have predicted greatness of that poor, illiterate society of small settlements and low-level trade. Yet, as we saw in the discussion of Homer in Chapter 2, everything began to change in Greece in the eighth century. It was out of these changes that a new communal institution emerged: the polis°.

Change was a product of peace, which stimulated a sharp population rise. In response, the economy shifted from herding to farming, a more efficient source of food. Seeking new agricultural land in the rocky Greek peninsula, farmers terraced hillsides and drained marshes. The typical agricultural unit was the family farm. Most

---

polis (PO-liss)

farms were small and roughly equal in size, apparently a stimulus of social and political equality in Greece.

Greek commerce, too, was expanding. Shortly before 800 B.C., Greeks from the island of Euboea, perhaps following the example of Phoenician merchants and seafarers who had been casual traders in Greece for a century (see pages 44–45), established a trading post in Syria at Al-Mina on the mouth of the Orontes River, at the terminus of the chief caravan route from Mesopotamia (see Map 3.2). Shortly afterward, Euboeans established another trading post in the west, at Neapolis (now, the Bay of Naples) in Italy. In both east and west, Greek merchants sought iron and luxury goods. What they offered in return was probably silver, of which ancient Greece had rich deposits, and slaves.

From commerce it was but a short step to colonization in order to siphon off the extra mouths created by population growth. In colonization as in trade, the Greeks may have followed the example of the Phoenicians, who had begun establishing colonies probably in the ninth century B.C. Between about 750 and 500 B.C., the Greeks founded colonies throughout the Mediterranean and the Black Sea, planting nearly as many cities as already existed in Greece (see Map 3.2). Colonization in Italy and Sicily began in earnest around 750 B.C.; in the Chalcidice° in the northeast Aegean perhaps a generation later; in the Sea of Marmara about 680; in North Africa around 630; and in the Black Sea about 610. In the far west, Massalia (modern Marseilles) was established about 600. Southern Italy and Sicily, whose climate and landscape recalled the Aegean, were especially intense areas of Greek settlement, so much so that the Romans later called the region *Magna Graecia* ("Great Greece"). In the long run, Greek colonization proved to be of great importance for the spread of urban civilization westward, especially into Italy.

One important consequence of foreign contact was the introduction to Greece of the alphabet, borrowed from the Phoenicians. The first datable examples of the Greek alphabet were inscribed on pots in about 750 B.C. The alphabet spread rapidly and widely in the next century. Literacy underlay the achievements in poetry, philosophy, and the law that Archaic Greece has left behind. However, so few people at the time could read and write well that ancient Greek culture remained primarily oral culture.

Another consequence of foreign contact was the introduction of new military technology, which the

CHRONOLOGY

ca. 750 B.C.	Greek colonization of Magna Graecia begins
ca. 725 B.C.	Sparta conquers Messenia
ca. 675 B.C.	Pheidon becomes tyrant of Argos
ca. 625 B.C.	Sappho active as poet
594 B.C.	Solon is archon in Athens
ca. 560 B.C.	Pisistratus becomes tyrant of Athens
508 B.C.	Cleisthenes begins reforms in Athens
499 B.C.	Ionians revolt against Persia
490 B.C.	Battle of Marathon
480–479 B.C.	Persia invades Greece
477 B.C.	Delian League founded
460–429 B.C.	Pericles at peak of power
458 B.C.	Aeschylus's *Oresteia* first performed in Athens
431–404 B.C.	Peloponnesian War
395–386 B.C.	Corinthian War
399 B.C.	Trial of Socrates
371 B.C.	Battle of Leuctra

increase in wealth allowed Greeks to adopt. Social changes, furthermore, fostered new tactics on the battlefield. The result was the hoplite phalanx°, a tightly ordered unit of heavily armed, pike-bearing infantrymen. The phalanx not only became the dominant military force in Archaic Greece, but, with relatively few changes in equipment and tactics, it remained supreme on land in Greece, western Asia, and other Mediterranean regions for centuries, until its defeat by a Roman army in 197 B.C.

The phalanx emerged through a process of evolution rather than in a revolutionary leap. Before 800 B.C., single combat among the basileis appears to have decided battles. Around 800–750 B.C., armies began to include more men, fighting in close formation. Around

---

Chalcidice (kal-SID-uh-see)

hoplite phalanx (HOP-lite FAY-lanks)

72

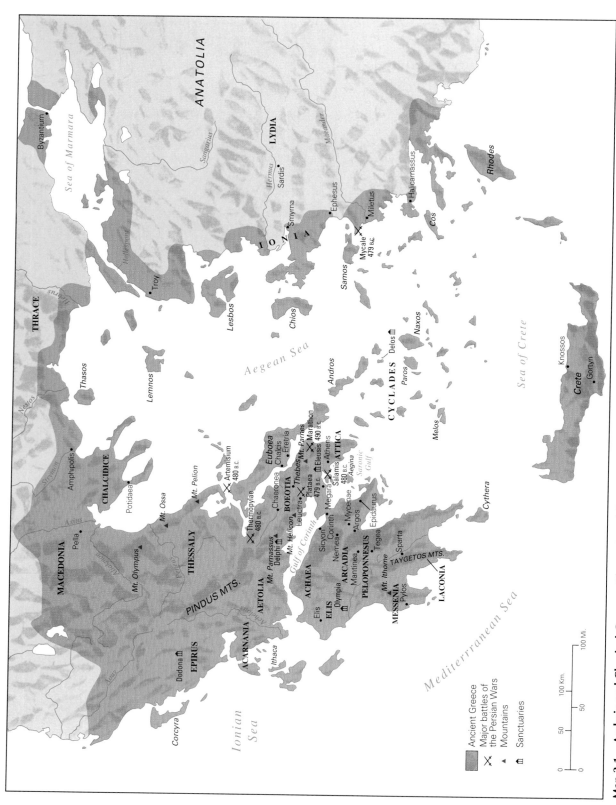

Map 3.1 Archaic and Classical Greece The region of the Aegean Sea was the heartland of Greek civilization around 750–350 B.C. The mountainous terrain, rugged coastline, and numerous islands encouraged political fragmentation.

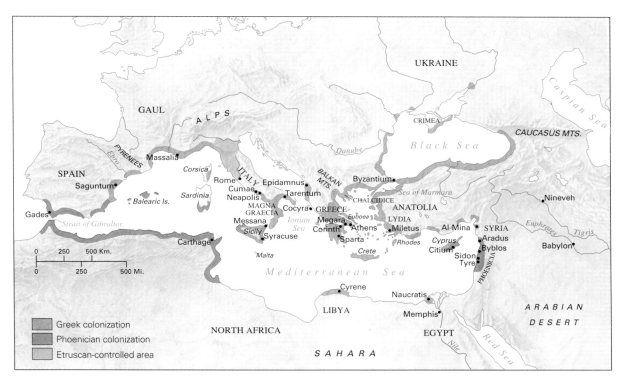

Map 3.2   Phoenician and Greek Colonization   Both the Phoenicians (beginning perhaps after 900 B.C.) and the Greeks (beginning around 750 B.C.) established numerous colonies on the coasts of the Mediterranean and Black Seas.

700 B.C. came new armaments. The result was the phalanx. The heavily armed infantryman (hoplite) of the fighting unit (phalanx) wore bronze armor on his shins and chest and a bronze helmet slit with a narrow opening for eyes and mouth. He carried a heavy wooden shield in his left hand. His weapons were a pike—a heavy wooden, iron-tipped thrusting spear at least 9 feet long—and a short, iron stabbing sword.

The men of the phalanx were arranged in close ranks, normally four to eight deep. Soldiers stood together in line, each man's shield overlapping his neighbor's. Hoplite combat involved set battles: head-to-head, army against army, all-or-nothing affairs, rather than individual skirmishes or guerrilla raids. Too unwieldy for Greece's mountains, the phalanx fought only in the plains. Battle usually consisted of an initial charge, followed by a grueling contest. The men in the front line pounded the enemy with their pikes while the men in the rear pushed forward. Finally one side would give way. The defeated ran away, if they could, while the victors staked their claim to the bloody field by erecting a trophy.

Greek hoplite warfare built on deep societal roots. Only independent men of means could afford hoplite armor. Thanks to the spread of the family farm, such men were common in Greece by around 700 B.C. Hoplites were amateur soldiers. Most were full-time farmers outside the fighting season, which lasted only for the summer months. The notion of the farmer-soldier, independent and free, would have a lasting impact in Western political thought. So would the warrior values of what became a way of life in Greece.

Aretê°, now translated as "excellence" or "virtue" but originally meaning "warrior prowess," was a central concept for the Greeks. In Homer, a warrior fought mainly for personal and familial honor (see page 63). By around 650 B.C., aretê referred also to the community. According to the poet Tyrtaeus (ca. 650 B.C.), the ideal soldier not only fights bravely but "heartens his neighbor by his words." Should he die, his death brings glory not only to

aretê (ah-reh-TAY)

Hoplites   A detail from a Corinthian vase of 625–600 B.C. shows pike-wielding hoplites closed in battle over a fallen comrade. In this image as elsewhere, Greek artists rendered warriors seminude and fighting in small groups, but in reality hoplites went into battle wearing heavy armor and fought in large units.   *(Louvre © R.M.N.)*

his father but also to his city and his countrymen. Although the battlefield remained the favored arena for displays of aretê, the assembly or the council house became increasingly acceptable as an alternative.

■ Emergence of the Polis

Paradoxes abound in the origins of the polis. The polis was both a product of the changes of the eighth century B.C. and itself a stimulus for change. As an urban settlement, the polis existed as early as the ninth or even the tenth century B.C. but its intense communal spirit did not emerge until around 700 B.C. In agriculture, the most important single profession, the prevalence of the family farm created a kind of rough social equality, which was reflected in a cultural emphasis on equality. Yet the polis rankled with social inequality as some grew rich on the profits of trade.

Polis came to denote not just a city but the community as a whole, corresponding roughly to a country or nation. One crude gauge of the centrality of the polis is the number, not to mention significance, of words the Greeks derived from it: among them, *polites* (citizen), *politeia* (constitution), *politeô* (to govern), *ta politika* (politics), and *politikos* (politician).

Most poleis° were small, many less than 100 square miles in size. Athens was one of the largest. Its territory, known as Attica (see Map 3.3), covered 1,000 square

poleis (PO-lays)

miles (approximately the size of Rhode Island). At its height (ca. 430 B.C.) the population of Athens was about 400,000, but a typical polis contained only between 5000 and 10,000 people. The philosopher Aristotle° (384–322 B.C.) wrote that an ideal polis should be small enough that the citizens know one another personally.

The polis consisted of two parts: the urban area, which usually was tiny, and the surrounding country-side, where most people lived. From the earliest times, the urban public space included both a defensible hill (preferably with a water supply), called a "high city" (*acropolis*°), and a "gathering place" (*agora*°) used as a marketplace and meeting place. At least one temple usually served as a focal point. After around 500 B.C. stone buildings, including council houses, theaters, covered porticoes, gymnasia, and baths, became increasingly common.

What distinguished the early polis, however, was not its buildings but its spirit. As the poet Alcaeus (b. ca. 630 B.C.) puts it, "Not houses finely roofed or the stones of walls well-built, nay nor canals and dockyards, make the polis, but men able to use their opportunity."

The Greeks came to call the polis a "common thing" (*koinon*). It was a shared commonwealth. It belonged to its people, not to a few nobles or to a king or a god. As early as about 700 B.C., important public documents were inscribed on stone. Acts of state were attributed not to a personified polis but to the community—for example, not to Thera but to "the Thereans," not to Sybaris but to "the Sybarites." The emphasis is on the plurality.

The emphasis was on equality as well. The early polis developed an ethos of measure and moderation. The ideal citizen was thought to be neither rich nor poor but of moderate means. All citizens should be roughly similar. Practice, however, proved different from theory, as the politics of the early polis makes clear.

■ Tyranny

Trade and colonization inspired change at home, for one thing, making increasing numbers of Greeks into seafar-ers. This was a critical development, for as the historian Thucydides (ca. 455–397 B.C.) argues, a sea power tends to be more dynamic and innovative than a land power. Seafarers are likely to come into contact with new ideas and institutions. In antiquity, ships moved more quickly and cheaply than land transport; thus, seafaring usually accelerated the rate of change.

One such change was Greece's growing wealth. To some extent, this wealth was general. The poet Hesiod, for example, records the increasing size and prosperity of the class of free farmers. Some individuals, however, grew far wealthier than others. Yet many of these newly rich lacked the status of the *basileis,* the elite of land-owning families who monopolized political power and honor. In order to claim a share, the newly rich seem to have made common cause with the independent farm-ers who staffed the hoplite phalanx. The result was tyranny.

Tyrant, a term borrowed from the East, possibly from Lydia (a wealthy kingdom in Anatolia), originally referred not to an arbitrary and oppressive ruler but rather to a champion of the people. Having overthrown a narrow and entrenched aristocracy, tyrants were popu-lar at first. *Tyrant* did not become a pejorative word be-fore roughly 550 B.C., when the people soured on the second and third generation of tyrants.

Greek tyranny began in Argos, a polis in the north-eastern Peloponnesus°, around 675 B.C. (see Map 3.1). The first tyrant was an Argive named Pheidon. By 660 tyranny had spread to nearby Corinth. Over the course of the seventh and sixth centuries B.C., all the major Greek poleis except Sparta became tyrannies.

Sources of evidence for the first tyrannies are poor, and much about the tyrants is debated by scholars. Yet it does seem that, in the seventh century B.C., wealthy men who had been denied political power rose on the shoul-ders of the hoplites and overthrew a narrow elite. They set up one-man rule, not in the name of the basileis, but on behalf of a much broader group: the prosperous farmers who fought in the phalanx.

Much of what the tyrants did, especially in the first generation, was popular and progressive. They stimu-lated the economy by founding colonies on trade routes, standardizing weights and measures, and encouraging the immigration of skilled craftsmen from other poleis. Corinth under the tyrant Cypselus (r. ca. 657–625 B.C.), for example, became the wealthiest city in Greece by ex-porting agricultural produce. Tyrants built temples and instituted festivals, providing both jobs and leisure-time activities.

When tyrants passed power on to their sons, how-ever, the second generation tended to rule oppressively. Buoyed by the discontent of the demos, the basileis re-grouped and tried to take back power. Thraysbulus of Miletus (ca. 600 B.C.), one second-generation tyrant, ad-vised accordingly: To maintain power, a tyrant should

---

Aristotle (AR-is-tot-il)   acropolis (uh-CROP-uh-liss)
agora (AH-go-rah)

Peloponnesus (pel-uh-puh-NEE-suss)

"lop off the tallest ears of grain"—that is, execute or exile aristocrats in order to deny leaders to the opposition. But the tide of discontent was not to be stopped. Few tyrannies lasted beyond the third generation, when they were overthrown and replaced by oligarchy (literally, "rule by the few") or, less often, by democracy (literally, "power of the people"). By 500 B.C. tyranny had disappeared from most of Greece.

■ Sparta

Located in Laconia, a fertile valley in the south-central Peloponnesus, in the southern part of mainland Greece, Sparta seemed destined by geography for prosperity but not for glory. It was situated not at a crossroads or beside a great harbor but rather by rugged mountains that might have left it isolated (see Map 3.1). Yet Sparta proved to be an influential model of citizenship and constitutionalism, virtue and community, austerity and militarism.

The history of Sparta is not easy to write. Sparta was a closed military society, contemptuous of book learning, suspicious of foreigners, and secretive toward the outside world. Scholarship has lifted the veil a little, however. For example, Spartans believed that their unique system had been created at a stroke by the legendary lawgiver Lycurgus, who is supposed to have lived (according to the most common version) in the eighth century B.C. and whose charter for Sparta was a divine command. Nowadays, scholars argue for gradual innovations in Sparta rather than revolutionary change, for a process beginning around 650 B.C. and continuing for generations. And it is by no means clear that there ever was a Lycurgus. Let us consider the question of origins.

The foundations of Spartan society were laid around 650 B.C., when a three-part class system emerged. Helots°, unfree laborers who worked the land for their masters, were at the lowest level. In the middle ranks were *perioikoi* (roughly, "neighbors"), who were free but subordinate to the highest class. At the top stood Similars, who were the only full citizens. We do not know the number of helots, but we do know that they vastly outnumbered the other two classes.

Compared with individuals of the other classes, a Similar had a good life. If male and over 30, he had the right to attend the assembly and to hold public office. Each male Similar, moreover, was given a similar land allotment that was worked by helots, thereby freeing him to fight. As the name implies, Similars were alike but not equal. Wealthy Similars owned more land than the basic allotment.

Although Sparta is remembered as a conservative society, the idea of a large group of men sharing power was radical in its day. When the system began around 650 B.C., Similars numbered about nine thousand. What gave them their clout and prestige? The Similars were probably hoplites, the backbone of Sparta's army.

In the mid-seventh century B.C., Sparta was even more dependent on its army than was the average polis; the reason is the helots. Most helots were Messenians, whose fertile territory had been conquered by Sparta in about 725 B.C. Although the Messenians were Greeks, they were forced to labor for the conquerors. Sparta profited, but it now faced a security problem. The restive Messenian helots had to be policed, and a dramatic revolt sometime between 675 and 650 B.C. almost succeeded in expelling the Spartans. To keep Messenia, Sparta needed a crack army; to get that, Sparta needed to train, nourish, and glorify its soldiers. The political and economic result was to make all Spartan hoplites into Similars.

Sparta was no democracy, however. The ancients classified the Spartan government as "mixed" because it distributed power among the Similars through a combination of monarchy, oligarchy (that is, rule by an elite few), and popular government. The assembly of Similars constituted the popular element in the regime, but its powers were limited. Real power was shared among those Similars who were kings, elders, and *ephors* (overseers), men generally belonging to a few wealthy families.

The elite did not lead lives of luxury, however, at least not after around 550 B.C., when austerity became the order of the day. Society was re-ordered to promote the discipline and preparedness needed to maintain control of the helots. For example, Spartans' diet was famous for its simplicity. The preferred food was a black broth of pork cooked in its own blood and spiced with salt and vinegar. To discourage consumption, Sparta issued no coins; the official "currency" consisted of heavy and unwieldy iron skewers. Since the outside world was considered corrupt, Sparta engaged in little trade and admitted few foreigners to its territory—and they were subject to periodic expulsion.

Whereas other poleis offered little or no formal public education, Sparta schooled its sons from childhood to be soldiers—a system known as the *agoge*° ("upbringing"). Limited to male Similars, the agoge created a life cycle unique in Greece. At birth, babies were examined by public inspectors. Those who were considered deformed or unfit were "exposed"; that is, they were abandoned without food or shelter. The victims might die, but

---

helot (HEL-ut)

agoge (ah-go-GAY)

they might also be sold into slavery or even secretly adopted. (Other Greeks also practiced exposure of infants but the choice was a family matter, not public policy.) Surviving children were raised at home up to the age of 7, at which point boys left the family to be boarded with a "herd" of their age mates. For the eleven years from age 7 to age 18, a boy went through the rigorous training of the agoge. On the theory that good soldiers should be strong and silent, boys learned only enough reading and writing for practical ends—for example, for messages to and from military headquarters.

Many boys between the ages of 18 and 20 served in the *krypteia* (secret service), living covertly in the hills of Messenia, where they survived by hunting, foraging, and stealing. They spied on the ever-rebellious Messenian helots, whom they could kill with impunity because every year Sparta declared war on them. By age 20, all Similars had become hoplites, and they continued to serve in the army until age 60. Supported by helot labor, they devoted all their time to fighting and training the next generation.

Anything but democratic, Sparta ironically offered more opportunities outside the home to elite women than did other Greek states. For example, unlike most Greek girls, Spartan girls received a public education—limited, however, to physical training, which was thought to strengthen females for childbearing. Still, the sight of girls running, wrestling, and throwing the discus and javelin, which was common in Sparta, was unthinkable elsewhere in Greece. So was Sparta's unique recognition of the risks of maternity. Like Spartan men who died in battle, Spartan women who died in childbirth were allowed to have their names inscribed on their tombstones. All other Spartan burials were anonymous.

Spartan women were relatively more independent than women elsewhere in Greece. With the men consumed by military training or warfare, women ran the day-to-day operations of life, controlling the helot farm workers and servants, and raising the girls and the very small boys. Women married around age 20, men around 30. Newlyweds were supposed to spend only enough time together to produce offspring. Often neglected by their husbands, and having been schooled to assertiveness by youthful physical training outdoors, Spartan women also had the advantage of being able to inherit property, unlike Athenian women. (See the box "Reading Sources: Spartan Women.")

Beginning around 550 B.C., Sparta used its military might to build up a network of alliances (dubbed the "Peloponnesian° League" by scholars) in the Pelopon-

Spartan Woman   This bronze statuette (4¾ inches tall) from Laconia (ca. 530 B.C.) shows a woman running. Unlike other Greek women, elite Spartan women underwent physical education. Although their personal freedom was limited in Sparta, women suffered fewer restrictions than their counterparts in democratic Athens did.   *(National Archaeological Museum, Athens/Archaeological Receipts Fund)*

nesus and central Greece. It may seem paradoxical that a society that feared foreigners, as Sparta did, became the *hegemon*° (literally, "leader") of an extensive alliance system, but Sparta's fear made its leadership careful and deliberate. Sparta intervened in the wider world only to prevent threats from arising on the horizon. It used its power abroad when need be, but usually only after exhaustive debate and with utmost caution.

By around 500 B.C., all of the Peloponnesian poleis except Argos had alliances with Sparta, and in central Greece, Thebes came aboard shortly afterward. Allies swore "to follow Sparta wherever it may lead and to have the same friends and enemies." Until its breakup in the aftermath of the Peloponnesian War (431–404 B.C.; see page 91), the Peloponnesian League was the dominant

---

Peloponnesian (pell-uh-puh-NEE-shun)

hegemon (HEJ-uh-mahn)

Spartan Women

Spartan women were famous in antiquity for their remarkable freedom, but male observers differed as to whether the results were good or bad. In the following excerpts, Aristotle (384–322 B.C.) criticizes Spartan women, whereas Plutarch (ca. A.D. 50–120), a Greek scholar living in the Roman Empire, praises them.

Aristotle Complains

. . . the legislator [Lycurgus] wished the city as a whole to be hardy, and this is manifest in terms of the men; but he thoroughly neglected it in the case of the women, who live licentiously in every respect and in luxury. Wealth will necessarily be honored in a regime of this sort, particularly if they are dominated by women, as is the case of most stocks that are fond of soldiering and war. . . . This was the case with the Spartans, and many matters were administered by the women during the period of their [imperial] rule [405–371 B.C.]. And yet what difference is there between women ruling and rulers who are ruled by women? For the result is the same. . . .

Now this laxness concerning women appears to have arisen among the Spartans in a way that is quite reasonable. They spent much time away from their own land when they were at war. . . . As for the women, they say Lycurgus attempted to lead them toward the laws, but they were resistant, and he gave it up. . . . That what is connected with the women is not finely handled would seem not only to create an inappropriateness in the regime in its own terms, as was said earlier, but to contribute to their greed. For next to what has just been said, one must censure what pertains to the disparity in possessions. For it has happened that some of them possess too much property, and others very little; hence the territory has come into the hands of a few. . . . Indeed, nearly two-fifths of the entire territory belongs to women, both because many have become heiresses and because large dowries are given.

Plutarch Counters

Aristotle claims wrongly that he [Lycurgus] tried to discipline the women but gave up when he could not control the considerable degree of license and power attained by women because of their husbands' frequent campaigning. . . . Lycurgus rather showed all possible concern for . . . [women] too. First he toughened the girls physically by making them run and wrestle and throw the discus and javelin. Thereby their children in embryo would make a strong start in strong bodies and would develop better, while the women themselves would also bear their pregnancies with vigour and would meet the challenge of childbirth in a successful, relaxed way. He did away with prudery, sheltered upbringing and effeminacy of any kind. He made young girls no less than young men grow used to walking nude in processions, as well as to dancing and singing at certain festivals with the young men present and looking on. . . .

There was nothing disreputable about the girls' nudity. It was altogether modest, and there was no hint of immorality. Instead it encouraged simple habits and an enthusiasm for physical fitness, as well as giving the female sex a taste of masculine gallantry, since it too was granted equal participation in both excellence and ambition.

Sources: Aristotle, *The Politics*, trans. Carnes Lord (Chicago: University of Chicago Press, 1984), pp. 74–75; Plutarch, "Life of Lycurgus," in Richard J. A. Talbert, trans., *Plutarch on Sparta* (Harmondsworth, U.K.: Penguin, 1988), p. 24.

 For additional information on this topic, go to http://college.hmco.com.

land power in Greece and, after the defeat of Persia in 480 B.C., in the entire eastern Mediterranean.

Sparta exemplified community spirit and respect for law. The people of Sparta, as the historian Herodotus°

Herodotus (he-ROD-uh-tus)

(ca. 485–425 B.C.) quotes a Spartan king, "are free . . . , but not entirely free; for they have a master, and that master is Law, which they fear." Sparta was also an exemplar of equality—limited equality, to be sure, but equality extended to a wider group than ever before in Greece. The notion of the Similars, moreover, contains the germ of

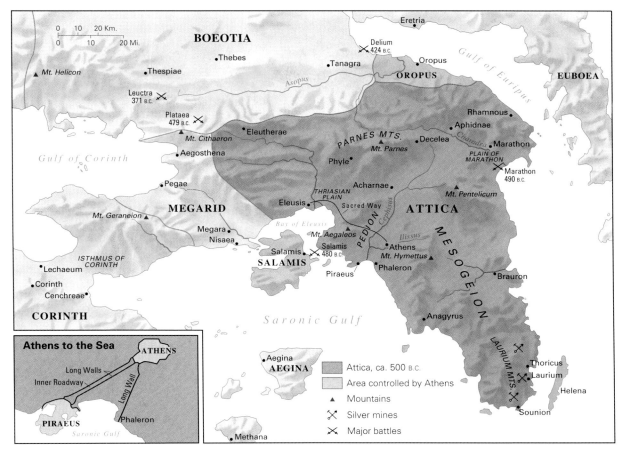

Map 3.3   Attica   Mountains and plains alternate in the 1,000-square-mile area of ancient Attica. The Long Walls connecting Athens with the port city of Piraeus were built around 450 B.C.

the idea of the citizen: a free member of the political community who, unlike a subject, has rights as well as duties. Few other poleis could match the stability and sense of civic duty fostered by Sparta. In the realms of equality and citizenship, however, Sparta was eventually outstripped by Athens. In the realm of liberty, Athens wrote a new chapter in Western history.

■ Early Athens

Around 650 B.C. the basileis of the Pedion, or Attic, Plain (see Map 3.3), who proudly called themselves the Eupatrids° ("well-fathered men"), ruled Athens. They served in one-year magistracies and afterward became life members of the Areopagus°, a council of elders named for its meeting place on the "hill of Ares." By its prestige,

this aristocratic council held the lion's share of power, both in politics and in justice, for it also served as a court. The demos° (the people) met in an assembly. Probably from early times on, the assembly had, in theory, supreme lawmaking power as well as authority over war and peace, but voting was by shouting, and few people challenged Eupatrid wishes.

By 632 B.C. the aristocrats faced trouble in Athens as elsewhere because of corruption, economic change, and assertive hoplites. A failed attempt that year to establish a tyranny left the forces for change eager. In 621 B.C. a loose coalition opposed to Eupatrid rule forced a codification of the laws, which were then issued in writing. This Code of Draco°, named for its main drafter, was infamous for its harsh provisions (hence the adjective *draconian*); it was written, a later commentator suggested,

---

Eupatrid (YOO-pat-rid)   **Areopagus** (ar-ee-OP-uh-gus)

demos (DEE-mus)   **Draco** (DRAY-co)

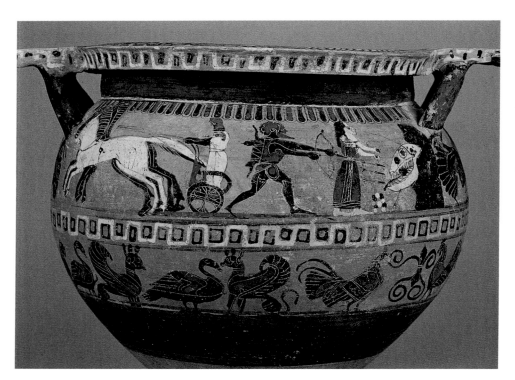

Myth or Memory?
The Monster of Troy vase pits
Heracles and Hesione against a
legendary monster whose skull
(*upper right*) has recently been
identified as a fossil giraffe.
The scene, therefore, illustrates
how the ancient Greeks used
myth to recall prehistory.
(Helen and Alice Colburn Fund, 63.420.
Courtesy, Museum of Fine Arts, Boston)

"not in ink but blood." Yet Draco's Code seems only to have whetted an appetite for change. A wealthy non-Eupatrid elite of hoplites was emerging, grown rich exporting olive oil. Some were merchants; most were prosperous farmers. They now wanted political power. As for ordinary Athenians, they typically worked small family farms. Over the years, bad harvests and soil exhaustion had sent many into debt. Those who had pledged their land as collateral became known as *hektemoroi* ("sixth-parters"), probably because they owed one-sixth of their crops to their creditors. Other farmers sank even further into debt and had only themselves or their children as collateral. Some ended up as slaves, sometimes sold abroad. Because both rich and poor Athenians had grievances against the Eupatrids, revolution was in the air. Enter Solon° (ca. 630–560 B.C.), who was appointed to the emergency position of sole *archon* (chief officer) for one year, probably 594 B.C. A Eupatrid who had become a merchant, Solon understood both the old and the new elite, and he was sympathetic to ordinary Athenians as well. As his surviving writings show, Solon was a moderate. He could have become tyrant, but he preferred to be a mediator; as such, he said, he "stood

with a strong shield before both parties [the common people and the powerful] and allowed neither one to win an unfair victory."[1]

Solon's reforms were comprehensive, spanning both economics and politics. He helped ordinary people by the "shaking off of burdens," measures that abolished the institution of hektemorage and probably canceled some debts. He also abolished the practice of making loans on personal surety and set up a fund to redeem Athenians who had been sold into slavery abroad. By freeing the hektemoroi, Solon ensured Athens a large class of independent small farmers.

Solon's other economic reforms were aimed at encouraging Athenian trade. To foster production of olive oil, a cash crop, he restricted all other agricultural exports. He changed Athenian weights, measures, and perhaps coins to conform to the most common Greek standard. The result was a commercial boom.

Solon made fundamental changes in Athenian government, too. He changed qualifications for office from birth to wealth, a boon to the non-Eupatrid elite. He established four census classes based on agricultural production. Most offices were reserved for men of property, but the poorest class, known as *thetes,* could participate in the assembly and courts. Solon probably established a Council of 400, which prepared the assembly's agenda.

Solon (SO-lun)

He is probably also responsible for regularizing council and assembly meetings and replacing the assembly's voice votes with the counting of hands.

Solon's moderation, respect for law, and liberation of the poor and downtrodden are milestones in Greek history. Yet, ironically, Solon's reforms had an unexpected byproduct—the growth of slavery in Athens. Though booming, the Athenian economy lost its cheap labor when Solon freed debt slaves and hektemoroi. The solution was to buy slaves abroad and import them to Athens. At the time, the island city-state of Chios was the center of the slave trade in Greece (see Map 3.2). After Solon, Athens along with Chios developed one of history's first large-scale slave systems. Slaves worked in agriculture, crafts, trade, and elsewhere in the economy. Unlike helots, slaves could be bought and sold and were often uprooted, and the system was better policed than in earlier societies.

If free Athenians had any moral doubts about slavery, they went unrecorded. Yet there was much dissatisfaction with Solon's reforms since his middle way satisfied neither Eupatrids nor champions of the free poor. After years of conflict, around 560 B.C. advocates of radical reform established a tyranny under Pisistratus° (ca. 600–528 B.C.). He and his sons held power for forty of the next fifty years.

Supported by the thetes, the Pisistratids exiled many Eupatrids and confiscated and redistributed their land. Pisistratus kept the façade of Solon's reforms while ensuring that loyal supporters held all key offices.

A stable regime, the tyranny witnessed prosperity at home and the expansion of Athenian influence abroad. Yet Pisistratus's dynasty lasted only two generations. A steadfast opponent of tyrants, Sparta deposed his son, Hippias, in 510 B.C. Athens's elites by birth and wealth were ready to establish an oligarchy, but the way was open for an unexpected development: the emergence of popular government.

THE CULTURE OF ARCHAIC GREECE

HILE one trend in Archaic culture was communal solidarity, as reflected in the hoplite phalanx, another was quite the opposite: a growing elevation of individualism. Increased prosperity and mobility (social, geographic, and political) during the Archaic period encouraged the breakdown of old ties

and left some people with a sense of their uniqueness. Archaic poetry and sculpture both demonstrate this new consciousness of the self.

Meanwhile, although most Archaic Greeks celebrated religion, a small group of thinkers expressed religious doubts. While monumental stone temples and international centers for divination were being erected to honor the pantheon of gods, Greek thinkers began to move away from divine and toward abstract and mechanistic explanations of the universe. Their defection marked the start of the Western philosophical tradition.

■ Revealing the Self: Lyric Poetry and Sculpture

Between approximately 675 and 500 B.C., the dominant Greek literary form was lyric poetry. This genre consisted of short poems written in a variety of styles but sharing a willingness to experiment, sometimes by revealing private feelings, sometimes by commenting on contemporary politics (as in the poetry of Tyrtaeus). Epic poetry, by contrast, was longer, grander in theme and tone, and less personal.

Homer never speaks directly about himself, and Hesiod reveals only a few personal details. In contrast, Archilochus° of Paros (ca. 700–650 B.C.), the earliest known of the lyric poets, flaunts the self. Born on the Cycladic island of Paros, Archilochus was the son, perhaps the illegitimate son, of a noble. He was a mercenary soldier (that is, he fought for pay for a foreign country) and a colonist before returning home and dying in a hoplite battle against a neighboring island. The varied subjects of Archilochus's poetry include love, travels, and war. Much of his poetry is satire, sometimes mocking and ironic, sometimes vicious and abusive. Archilochus takes a cynical and detached view of hoplite ideals, freely admitting that he once tossed away his shield to escape the battlefield: "And that shield, to hell with it! Tomorrow I'll get me another one no worse."[2]

Sappho° of Lesbos (ca. 625 B.C.) is also famous as a private poet, one who composed unmatched descriptions of intimate feelings, among them love for other women. Sappho is one of the few women poets of antiquity whose work has survived—very little, unfortunately, but enough to show that she was educated, worldly, and versed in politics. Like a modern experimental poet, she uses language self-consciously. Sappho's sensuality comes through in a description of her feelings at seeing a woman whose company she wants talking with a man: her heart shakes, her tongue is stuck, her eyes cannot

---

Pisistratus (pie-SIS-trah-tus)

Archilochus (ar-KIL-uh-kus)   **Sappho** (SAF-oh)

see, her skin is on fire. "I am greener than grass," Sappho writes, "I feel nearly as if I could die."[3]

Sappho discusses female sexuality, a subject that Greek elite culture, dominated by males, tended to ignore. We know little about the sexuality of Greek women or of nonelite males. Among the male elite, romantic love in Archaic and Classical Greece was homosexual love or, to be precise, pederasty ("boy love"). The ideal relationship was supposed to involve a man in his twenties and a boy in his teens. The male elite was, strictly speaking, bisexual. By age 30, a man was expected to marry and raise a family. Perhaps bisexuality prevailed among elite females as well; Sappho, for example, eventually married and had a child.

Athenian Kore   This statue of a young woman (*kore*) exemplifies Archaic Greek sculpture's interest in the idealized human form. Note the slight smile, the carefully coiffed hair, and the elaborate clothes. Influenced by contemporary Egyptian statues, the Greek sculptors nonetheless created a new and original style.   *(Robert Frerck/Odyssey Productions)*

Another sign of Archaic Greece's interest in the personal is the growing attention paid to the depiction of the human body, both in painting (most of the surviving examples are painted pottery) and in sculpture. Archaic artists displayed increasing skill and sensitivity in depicting the human form. The rich marble deposits in Greek soil gave sculptors promising material; baked clay (terra cotta) and bronze were other common sculptural media.

Early Archaic marble sculpture (seventh century B.C.) was strongly influenced by the way Egyptian sculpture represented the human body. Like Egyptian statuary, early Greek sculpture tended to be formal and frontal. But over the course of the seventh and sixth centuries B.C., Greek sculptors experimented with a greater variety of poses and with increasing realism in showing musculature and motion. This realism, however, was expressed within limits, for the favorite subject of Archaic sculptors was not ordinary people but idealized, beautiful youth. Typical sculptural forms were the naked young man (*kouros*) and clothed young woman (*kore*), which often served as grave markers or monuments. The goal was to show people not as they were but as they might be.

■ Religious Faith and Practice

The Olympian gods who had been worshiped in the Mycenaean era survived in later ages, suitably adapted to fit new political and social conditions. In the Archaic period, accordingly, the Olympian gods became gods of the polis.

Although the Olympians were revered throughout Greece, each polis had its patron deity: Apollo at Corinth, Hera at Argos and Samos, Athena at Athens and Sparta. Each polis also had its favorite heroes or demigods—for example, Theseus, the legendary founder of Athens, and Heracles (Hercules), a favorite of Dorian cities such as Sparta and Thebes. Devotees considered it important to build a "house"—that is, a temple—for the local patron god or at least for his or her statue. The first temples were built of wood; the earliest stone temple, a temple of Apollo at Corinth, was built around 550 B.C.

Temples were rectangular structures with long sides on the north and south, short sides on the east and west, a colonnade around all four sides, and a pitched roof. The columns were based loosely on those of Egyptian architecture. Greek temples faced east so sunlight would illuminate the interior, which consisted of two rooms: a small treasury, open to the west, and a larger main chamber, in which a statue of the deity stood. The interior decoration of the temple was simple. Outside, however, brownish-red roof tiles, painted sculpture above the colonnade and in the pediments (the area between the gables and the front and rear doorways), and terra-cotta roof ornaments created a festive and lively effect. The bare white ruins seen today are misleading.

The emphasis on exterior rather than interior decoration in a Greek temple reflects the way the building was used. The main ceremony took place outside. A long altar stood in front of the temple and parallel to it. On feast days—and under the tyrants the number of such days was increased greatly, as a concession to the common people—temple priests would sacrifice animals (pigs, goats, lambs, and, less often, bulls) on the altar. Only the thighs would be burned for the gods. The rest of the meat would be boiled and distributed to worshipers.

As in other ancient cultures, so in Greece divination was an important element of religion. Divination was institutionalized in *oracles*, places where, it was believed, a god or hero might be consulted for advice. Of the various Greek oracles, that of Apollo at Delphi° (in central Greece) became the most prestigious and respected. At Delphi, Apollo spoke through the Pythia, a priestess who went into a trance. The utterances of Apollo of Delphi were famous among the Greeks for being ambiguous. Because different people might interpret them in different ways, Apollo could always be absolved after the fact if things did not turn out as the listener expected.

The oracle of Delphi was regularly consulted by poleis wishing to establish colonies. The oracle gave advice about the choice of location and the appropriate patron god or goddess, and it helped settlers draft new law codes. Delphi was also active in the search for new constitutions in the old poleis of Greece. Tradition says that Sparta based its government on a pronouncement of the Delphic oracle.

Archaic thinkers pondered the theme of divine justice. In Archaic literature we see less of the petty squabblings among the gods than in Homer and more of Zeus's majesty and justice. Although the wicked might seem to prosper, Zeus eventually punishes them or their descendants. "It never escapes him all the way when a man has a sinful spirit; and always, in the end, his judgment is plain," says Solon.[4]

Archaic writers delighted in portraying human emotions, but they had no confidence about the human ability to master emotions. In Archaic literature, people are weak and insignificant; their fortune is uncertain and mutable. Further, the gods are jealous of human success. People who aim too high are guilty of *hubris*—that is, arrogance with overtones of violence and transgression.

Hubris inevitably brings *nemesis,* "punishment" or "allotment." The safest course is for a person to be pious and humble.

So Archaic religion taught a humbling, even pessimistic, lesson. Yet religious teachings were not always heeded. The pages of Archaic history are full of examples of politicians, generals, athletes, merchants, and artists who aimed high and sought success with seemingly little worry, and no dire consequences. In Ionia° (the territory of the Greek cities along the central western Anatolian coast; see Map 3.2), one group of Greek thinkers made a radical break with Archaic religion and invented speculative philosophy.

■ The Origins of Western Philosophy

Abstract, rationalistic, speculative thinking emerged in Greece during the sixth century B.C. The first developments took place in Miletus, an Ionian city. It is often said that the thinkers of Miletus (the Milesians°) and their followers in other parts of Ionia invented philosophy. So they did, but we must be precise about what this means.

The Ionians were not the first to ask questions or tell stories about the nature and origins of the universe; virtually every ancient people did so. Nor did the Ionians invent science. They themselves conducted no experiments. By 600 B.C., moreover, science—including mathematics, astronomy, medicine, and engineering—had been thriving for over two thousand years in Egypt and Mesopotamia, a heritage with which the Ionians were familiar and from which they borrowed.

The real importance of the Ionians is as pioneers of rationalism. They began the movement away from anthropomorphic or divine explanations and toward an abstract and mechanistic explanation of the universe. They themselves did not make a clear distinction between reason and revelation, but they made it possible for later Greek thinkers to do so. Later Greek philosophers were rarely (if ever) atheists, but they took for granted what the Ionians labored to establish: the primacy of human reason.

The Ionians saw themselves as students of nature—*physis* (from which the word *physics* is derived). Although they also commented on morality and politics, their interest in natural phenomena is what makes the Ionians significant. In their own day, the Ionians were called "wise men" (*sophoi*); to a later generation, they were

---

Delphi (DEL-fye)

Ionia, Ionian (eye-OH-nee-uh, eye-OH-nee-un)
Miletus, Milesian (my-LEE-tus, my-LEE-zhen)

"lovers of wisdom," *philosophoi* (from which *philosopher* comes).

Thales°, the first Milesian thinker, made a name for himself by successfully predicting a solar eclipse in 585 B.C. He is credited with founding Greek geometry and astronomy. Little survives of his writings or those of the other Milesians, but it is clear that he created the first general and systematic theory about the nature of the universe. According to Thales, the primary substance, the element from which all of nature was created, was water. He emphasized the mobility of water and its ability to nourish life.

A reply was not long in coming. Around 550 B.C., Anaximander of Miletus wrote the first known book of prose in Greek, expounding his own philosophy of nature. He attacked Thales for oversimplifying and for failing to do justice to the dynamism of nature. Anaximander accepted Thales' monist assumption°—that all matter originated from one primary substance—but he called the substance "the unlimited" or "the undefined" rather than water. A third Milesian, Anaximenes, replied that the primary substance might be unlimited but it was not undefined. It was air, whose properties of condensation and rarefaction symbolized the dynamic and changing nature of things.

Humble as these theories might seem today, they represent a dramatic development: an open and critical debate among thinkers, each of whom was proposing an abstract and rational model of the universe. Many scholars have speculated about the origins of this development. Why Miletus? Why the sixth century B.C.? There are no sure answers, although certain influences have been suggested. Among them are Miletus's contacts on the trade routes with sophisticated Babylon, the proximity of Ionia to non-Greek peoples and the resulting Milesian appreciation of variety and complexity, and the search for law and order in contemporary Greek political life and its extension to the philosophical plane.

In its second generation early Greek philosophy moved to other Ionian cities and then migrated westward across the Mediterranean. Heracleitus° of Ephesus (ca. 500 B.C.) proposed fire as the primary substance. Although fire was ever changing, it had an underlying coherence. According to Heracleitus, this paradox nicely symbolized the nature of the universe. He summed up the importance of change by the aphorisms "All things flow" and "You cannot step into the same river twice." The universe witnessed a constant struggle of opposites,

yet an essential unity and order prevailed. To describe this order, Heracleitus used the term *logos*. This key concept of Greek philosophy is difficult to translate: among other definitions, *logos* can mean "word," "thought," "reason," "story," or "calculation."

Heracleitus's contemporary, Pythagoras° of Samos, was both a rationalist and a religious thinker. On the one hand, Pythagoras was a mathematician who discovered the numerical ratios determining the major intervals of the musical scale, that is, the range of sound between high and low. It is less certain if, as tradition has it, he discovered the so-called Pythagorean theorem—that in a right triangle the hypotenuse squared is equal to the sum of the squares of the other two sides.

On the other hand, Pythagoras believed that the purity of mathematics would improve the human soul. Just as he had imposed numerical order on the musical scale, so could philosophers understand the entire universe through number and proportion. The resulting knowledge was no mere academic exercise but a way of life. He devoted himself to "observation" or "contemplation"—to *theoria* (from which *theory* comes).

In Croton in Magna Graecia (southern Italy), Pythagoras founded a religious community. Its members observed strict secrecy, but it appears that they abstained from meat because they believed in the kinship of all living things. They also believed in the reincarnation of the human soul, though not necessarily into a human body. Pythagoras is said to have stopped a man from beating a dog because he recognized from the barking that the dog was the reincarnation of a friend who had died.

The early Greek philosopher whose work is most fully preserved is Parmenides° of Elea in Magna Graecia. Parmenides (b. ca. 515 B.C.) completely distrusted the senses. He believed that reality was a world of pure being: eternal, unchanging, and indivisible, comparable to a sphere. To Parmenides, change was a mere illusion. Parmenides, therefore, is the first Western philosopher to propose a radical difference between the world of the senses and reality. This fundamental strain of Western thought would be taken up by Plato and his followers and then passed to Christianity.

To sum up, in philosophy as in so many other endeavors, the Archaic Greeks were great borrowers and even greater innovators who left a profound mark on later ages. By the late sixth century B.C., Archaic Greece was poised on the brink of a revolution that would give birth to the Classical period of Greek civilization.

Thales (THAY-leez)
Heracleitus (her-uh-CLY-tus)

Pythagoras (py-THAG-uh-russ)
Parmenides (par-MEN-uh-deez)

CLASSICAL GREECE

 HE word *democracy* comes from the Greek word *demokratia°*, coined in Athens early in the fifth century B.C. *Demokratia* literally means "the power *(kratos)* of the people *(demos)*." A modern democracy is characterized by mass citizenship, elections, and representative government. Athenian demokratia, in contrast, was a direct democracy in which elections mattered less than direct participation; citizenship was narrowly restricted; women were excluded from politics; resident aliens could almost never become citizens; and citizens owned slaves and ruled an empire. Modern democracies may cover a huge territory, but Athens encompassed only 1,000 square miles. Modern democracies tend to emphasize individual rights. Athens, in contrast, often placed the community first. In spite of these differences, Athenian demokratia established principles that are enshrined in democracy today: freedom, equality, citizenship without property qualifications, the right of most citizens to hold public office, and the rule of law.

The young democracy's greatest achievement was to spearhead Greece's victory over the Persian invaders in 480 B.C. After that victory, Athens became Greece's leading sea power. Yet Sparta remained the superior land power, and the two poleis were soon locked in a cycle of competition and war. The result nearly destroyed Athenian democracy while, even more serious, it undermined Greece's very independence.

■ The Development of Demokratia, 508–322 B.C.

Tyranny often gave way to oligarchy—to government by wealthy men, both Eupatrids and non-Eupatrids. In Athens after Pisistratid rule, however, conditions were ripe for revolution. Solon had left a society of independent small farmers, while the Pisistratids had strengthened the ranks of immigrants and weakened the Eupatrids. Elite leaders nonetheless tried to establish an Athenian oligarchy. We may imagine strong popular opposition.

Ironically, a Eupatrid, a member of the Alcmeonid clan by the name of Cleisthenes° (d. ca. 500 B.C.), led the revolution. Originally Cleisthenes aimed to head the oligarchy, but his rivals shut him out of power. He turned then to the demos, whose leader he became. The watchwords of the day were *equality* and *mixing*.

demokratia (deh-mo-kra-TEE-uh)
Cleisthenes (KLICE-the-neez)

Frightened by the assertive populace, the oligarchs called for Spartan military assistance, but to no avail: Cleisthenes rallied the people to victory. The Athenian triumph proved, in Herodotus's opinion, "that equality is an excellent thing, not in one way only but in many. For while they were under a tyranny, [Athenians] were no better at fighting than any of their neighbors, but once they were rid of tyrants they became by far the best."[5]

Cleisthenes extinguished Eupatrid power once and for all by attacking its local bases of support. For example, he abolished the four traditional tribes and apportioned the people among ten new tribes. Immigrants and their descendants, who had been excluded from the old tribes, now joined natives in the new tribes. The tribes formed the basis of a new Council of 500 to replace Solon's Council of 400. The council was divided into ten tribal units, each serving as a kind of executive committee for one of the ten months of the civic year.

The centerpiece of the government was the assembly, some of whose members, emboldened by the new spirit of equality, now spoke up for the first time. The new Council of 500, like its predecessor, prepared the assembly's agenda, but assemblymen felt free to amend it. Only the Areopagus council remained a privileged preserve.

The last and most unusual part of the Cleisthenic system was ostracism, a sort of annual *un*popularity contest that received its name from the pieces of broken pottery *(ostraka)* on which the names of victims were chiseled. The "winner" was forced into ten years of exile, although his property would not be confiscated. Ostracism was meant to protect the regime by defusing factionalism and discouraging tyrants. Judging by Athens's consequent political stability, it worked.

In 508 B.C. the poorest Athenians had relatively little power in Cleisthenic government. They lacked the financial means, the political consciousness, and the self-confidence needed to engage in politics. Changing conditions by the 450s rendered Athens even more democratic. During that period, the oldest principle of Greek politics came to the fore: Whoever fights for the state governs it. To counter the Persian threat against Greece in the 480s (see page 91), Athens built a great navy. The standard ship was a trireme°, an oared warship rowed by 170 men on three decks. The core of the rowers consisted of Athenian thetes. Just as hoplites supported new regimes in Greece after 700 B.C., so rowers supported new regimes in Greece after 500 B.C.

trireme (TRY-reem)

Greek Trireme   The *Olympias* is a hypothetical reconstruction of an Athenian war galley of about 400 B.C. Rowed by 170 oarsmen arranged on three decks, the trireme fought by ramming an enemy ship with the bronze ram attached to its bow.   *(Courtesy of the Trireme Trust)*

A second revolution occurred around 461 B.C., when Ephialtes (d. ca. 460 B.C.) and his young associate, Pericles° (ca. 495–429 B.C.), targeted the last bulwark of privilege, the Areopagus. They stripped away the council's long-standing supervisory powers over the regime and redistributed those powers to the Council of 500 and the people's court. The decade of the 450s saw another innovation: payment for public service, specifically for jurors, who received a half-drachma (perhaps a half-day's wages) for a day of jury duty. Eventually other public servants also received pay. Conservatives complained bitterly because they perceived, rightly, that state pay made political activity by poor people possible. State pay was, an Athenian said, "the glue of demokratia."

Demokratia became closely connected with Pericles, who inherited the constituency of Ephialtes after his assassination around 460 B.C. For much of the next thirty years, Pericles dominated Athenian politics. An aristocrat who respected the common people, an excellent orator who benefited from an education in philosophy, an honest and tireless worker, a general who led in peace as well as war, Pericles was a political giant. Under

his leadership, demokratia became firmly entrenched as the government and way of life in Athens.

Athenian democracy survived, with occasional oligarchic intrusions, for 150 years after Pericles' death. During those years it became more institutionalized and cautious, but it also became more thoroughly egalitarian.

■ How Demokratia Worked

Unlike most modern democracies, Athenian demokratia was direct and participatory. Pericles once claimed that in Athens "people pay attention both to their own household and to politics. Even those occupied with other activities are no less knowledgeable about politics."[6] This is part boast, but only part. Large numbers of ordinary citizens attended the assembly from time to time and held public office or served on the Council of 500 for a year or two. (See the box "Reading Sources: The Debate on Democracy.")

The instruments of government are easily sketched. The central institution was the assembly. Open to all male citizens over age 20, assembly meetings were held in the open air, on a hillside seating several thousand on benches (see the photograph on page 68). In the fourth century B.C. the assembly gathered a minimum of forty times per year, about once every ten days.

Pericles (PAIR-ih-kleez)

The Debate on Democracy

Characters in Greek drama often discuss general principles. In this excerpt from Euripides' tragedy The Suppliant Women *(ca. 420 B.C.), Theseus, legendary king of Athens, and a herald from Creon, tyrant of Thebes, debate the merits of democracy.*

Herald

What man is tyrant in this land? To whom / Must I give the word I bring from Creon, ruler / In Cadmus' country [Thebes] . . . ?

Theseus

One moment, stranger. / Your start was wrong, seeking a tyrant here. / This city is free, and ruled by no one man. / The people reign, in annual succession. / They do not yield the power to the rich; / The poor man has an equal share in it.

Herald

That one point gives the better of the game / To me. The town I come from is controlled / By one man, not a mob. And there is no one / To puff it up with words, for private gain, / Swaying it this way, that way. . . . / The people is no right judge of arguments. / Then how can it give right guidance to a city? / A poor man, working hard, could not attend / To public matters, even if ignorance / Were not his birthright. When a wretch, a nothing, / Obtains respect and power from the people / By talk, his betters sicken at the sight.

Theseus

. . . Nothing / Is worse for a city than a tyrant. / In earliest days, before the laws are common, / One man has power and makes the law his own: / Equality is not yet. With written laws, / People of small resources and the rich / Both have the same recourse to justice. Now / A man of means, if badly spoken of, / Will have no better standing than the weak; / And if the little man is right, he wins / Against the great. This is the call of freedom: / "What man has good advice to give the city, / And wishes to make it known?" He who responds / Gains glory; the reluctant hold their peace. / For the city, what can be more fair than that?

Source: Adapted from Euripides, *The Suppliant Women*, trans. Frank Jones, in *Euripides IV: The Complete Greek Tragedies*, ed. David Grene and Richmond Lattimore (Chicago: University of Chicago Press, 1958), pp. 73–74.

The assembly heard the great debates of the day. It made decisions about war and peace, alliance and friendship; it conferred honors and issued condemnations; it passed decrees relating to current issues and set up commissions to revise fundamental laws. In the assembly great orators addressed the people, but everyone, however humble, was theoretically entitled to speak.

The judicial branch consisted of courts, which, with a few exceptions, were open to all citizens, no matter how poor. Aristotle or a member of his school comments that "when the people have the right to vote in the courts, they control the constitution." Juries were large, commonly consisting of several hundred men chosen by lottery; small juries, it was felt, were easily bribed. After a preliminary hearing, cases were decided in a single day.

The executive consisted of the Council of 500 and some seven hundred public officials (also, under Athens's empire in the fifth century B.C., several hundred others living abroad). All male citizens over age 30 were eligible to serve. Most public officials were chosen by lottery, which put rich and poor, talented and untalented, on an equal footing. To guard against installing incompetents or criminals, all officials had to undergo a scrutiny by the council before taking office and an audit after the term. Most magistracies, moreover, were boards, usually of ten men, so even if a bad man managed to pass this scrutiny, he would be counterbalanced by his colleagues. Only generals and treasurers were chosen by election.

Athens had a relatively weak executive, and no chief executive such as a president or prime minister.

Generals and orators led assembly debates, and sometimes exercised great influence, but ordinary people set the agenda and made the decisions by taking votes at each assembly meeting. On the local level, every deme (county) had an annually chosen executive and a deme assembly of all citizens.

So novel and populist a system of government has not been without critics, either in antiquity or today. Some have charged that the Athenian people were uneducated, emotional, and easily swayed by oratorical tricks. Others say that demokratia degenerated into mob rule after the death of Pericles. Still others complain about the lack of a system of formal public education, which denied many citizens equality of opportunity.

The copybook of Athenian democracy does have some blots in its history, particularly in the heat of wartime. The Peloponnesian War (431–404 B.C.) witnessed several Athenian atrocities and judicial murders. Yet these were exceptions: In its roughly two hundred years of existence, Athenian demokratia was generally stable, law-abiding, and fair-minded.

■ Metics, Women, and Slaves

Another serious charge against Athenian demokratia is that it was democracy for a small elite only. Adult male citizens never accounted for more than one-tenth of the population, approximately 40,000 out of a total population—men, women and children, resident aliens, and slaves—of about 400,000. To become a citizen, at age 18 a boy had to prove that he was the legitimate son of a citizen father and a citizen maternal grandfather. Girls were never officially registered as citizens. Although the term *citizeness* existed, Athenian citizen women were usually referred to as "city women." As for resident aliens, whether male or female, they rarely attained citizenship.

In the fifth and fourth centuries B.C., Athens had a large population of foreigners. Some were transient. Others were officially registered resident aliens, or *metics°*. Metics came by the thousands from all over the Greek world and beyond. Some, like Aristotle (a native of a Greek colony in Macedonia°), were attracted by the city's schools of philosophy, but most came because of its unparalleled economic opportunities. Metics could not own land in Athens, and they had to pay extra taxes and serve in the Athenian military. Nevertheless, they prospered in Athenian commerce and crafts.

Athenian women generally led restricted lives. They were excluded from politics and played only a modest role in commerce as small retailers. They rarely received an education, not even in physical fitness as at Sparta. In legal and contractual matters Athenian women were almost always required to be represented by a male guardian.

Yet perhaps Athenian women led less restricted lives than it might seem. Let us distinguish between theory and practice. Paradoxically, the more power was distributed among the male citizenry, the more hostile to women's freedom did Athens's citizen ideology become. Greek males believed that the more honor a woman brought the man who won her, the more danger she might bring by tempting outsiders to seduce her. Hence demokratia promulgated an ideal of seclusion for women.

Practice, however, was another matter. As Aristotle asks rhetorically, "How is it possible to prevent the wives of the poor from going out?" *Poor* is a synonym for *ordinary* in ancient Greek. Ordinary women could not stay at home because they had to run errands, draw water, and sometimes even help make ends meet. Ordinary houses, moreover, were small and cramped, and in the Mediterranean heat women could not stay inside all the time.

Women played a major role in Athenian religion. They were priestesses in more than forty major cults. They participated each year in many festivals, including several reserved for women only. One such festival, the Thesmophoria, a celebration of fertility held each autumn, featured a three-day encampment of women on a hillside in the city, right beside the Athenian assembly amphitheater. Women attended public funeral orations in honor of soldiers who had died fighting for Athens, and probably attended plays.

We occasionally get glimpses, sometimes more, of Athenian women resisting or working behind the scenes to correct male mistakes. An inheritance case reveals a woman go-between interceding among her quarreling male relations. Greek comedy shows women mocking male pretensions and establishing sisterly friendships. A woman who brought a large dowry into a marriage could use it and the threat of divorce to influence her husband (the dowry had to be returned to the woman's father or guardian if there was a divorce). In short, Athenian women had some access to the world outside the household and some influence within the household. There existed, nonetheless, a real disparity in power between men and women.

One small group of noncitizen women, *hetairai* or courtesans (that is, prostitutes patronized by men of

---

metic (MEH-tik) **Macedonia** (mah-suh-DOE-nee-uh)

wealth and status) sometimes had unusual access to power. The most famous example is Aspasia°, an educated woman from Miletus, who for many years was the mistress of Pericles, to whom she bore a son. Aspasia and Pericles gathered around them a glittering circle of thinkers and artists. Some say that Aspasia even influenced Pericles' political decisions.

Turning to slavery, that institution was widespread in democratic Athens. Some slaves served in agriculture, some labored under miserable conditions in Athenian silver mines, and some were engaged in commerce or the military (where some rowers were slaves). Most, however, worked as domestics or in small workshops as, for example, metalworkers or furniture makers. The vast majority of slaves were non-Greek. Most were prisoners of war; some were victims of pirates or debtors from states where, unlike Athens, citizens might still end up in debt-slavery. Thrace (roughly, modern Bulgaria) and Anatolia were the main sources of slaves, but some slaves came from North Africa and other Mediterranean regions.

The living conditions of slaves were usually poor and in the silver mines abysmal. Emancipation, however, was more common in Athens than in the American South before 1865. A few ex-slaves even rose to positions of wealth and power in Athens. A striking and unusual case is that of Pasion (d. 370 B.C.). Originally a slave employee of a banking firm, he bought his freedom and became the wealthiest Athenian banker of his day, as well as an Athenian citizen.

Athenian demokratia lacked many features of modern democracy: among them, a notion of universal human rights, the possibility for immigrants to become citizens, gender equality, the abolition of slavery, and public education. To its small citizen body, however, Athenian demokratia offered extraordinary freedom, equality, and responsibility, and a degree of participation in public life seldom equaled. Demokratia was a model of what democracy could be, but not of who could take part.

■ The Persian Wars, 499–479 B.C.

In 500 B.C. Sparta, hegemon of the Peloponnesian League, was the most prominent power of the Greek mainland. Across the Aegean Sea in Anatolia, the Greek city-states had been under Persian rule for two generations, since Cyrus the Great's conquest in the 540s. In 499 B.C., however, events began to unfold that not only would revo-

Women at Work   This Classical vase painting shows women filling jugs with water at a fountain and carrying the jugs back home. Fetching water was daily work for women, often slaves, which the women in this scene may well be.
(Louvre © R.M.N.)

lutionize that balance of power but would throw the entire eastern Mediterranean into two hundred years of turmoil.

Led by Miletus, the Ionian Greek city-states rose in revolt against Persia in 499 B.C. Athens sent troops to help, but despite initial successes Athens reconsidered the alliance and withdrew its forces. The Ionian coalition broke down thereafter and was crushed by Persia. Miletus was besieged and destroyed, but otherwise Persia was relatively lenient in Ionia.

Upstart Athens, however, could not go unpunished. In 490 B.C., Darius I sent a large naval expedition to Athens carrying about 25,000 infantrymen and 1,200 cavalrymen (with horses). They landed at Marathon, some 24 miles from the city of Athens (see Map 3.3). Athens sent 10,000 men (including 1,000 allies) to defend Marathon. A great battle ensued.

Persian overconfidence and the superiority of the Greek phalanx over Persia's loosely organized infantrymen won Athens a smashing victory: Persia suffered 6,400 casualties, Athens only 192. (The story, unconfirmed, that a messenger ran from the battlefield to the city of Athens with the news, "Rejoice, we conquer!" is the inspiration for the modern marathon race, a slightly

---

Aspasia (uh-SPAY-see-uh)

The Enemy as Barbarian

Classical Greeks no longer regarded the enemy as honored rivals, as Homer's heroes had regarded Trojans. Rather, they looked down on the enemy as a barbarian. Greece's archenemies, the Persians, were portrayed as indulgent, effeminate, emotional, slavish, cruel, and dangerous. Consider the contrasting portraits of Persians and Greeks in these excerpts from the historian Herodotus's account of Persia's invasion of Greece in 480 B.C.

The Persians

He [King Xerxes of Persia] then prepared to move forward to Abydos, where a bridge had already been constructed across the Hellespont from Europe to Asia. . . . It was here not long afterwards that the Greeks under Xanthippus the son of Ariphron took Artayctes the Persian governor of Sestos, and nailed him alive to a plank—he was the man who collected women in the temple of Protesilaus at Elaeus and committed various acts of sacrilege. This headland was the point to which Xerxes' engineers carried their two bridges from Abydos—a distance of seven furlongs. . . . The work was successfully completed, but a subsequent storm of great violence smashed it up and carried everything away. Xerxes was very angry when he learned of the disaster, and gave orders that the Hellespont should receive three hundred lashes and have a pair of fetters thrown into it. And I have heard before now that he also sent people to brand it with hot irons. He certainly instructed the men with the whips to utter, as they wielded them, the following words: "You salt and bitter stream, your master lays this punishment upon you for injuring him, who never injured you. But Xerxes the King will cross you, with or without your permission. No man sacrifices to you, and you deserve the neglect by your acrid and muddy waters"—a highly presumptuous way of addressing the Hellespont, and typical of a barbarous nation. In addition to punishing the Hellespont Xerxes gave orders that the men responsible for building the bridge should have their heads cut off. This unseemly order was duly carried out. . . .

The Greeks

To the Spartan envoys . . . [the Athenians] said: "No doubt it was natural that the Lacedaemonians [Spartans] should dread the possibility of our making terms with Persia; nonetheless it shows a poor estimate of the spirit of Athens. Were we offered all the gold in the world, and the fairest and richest country the earth contains, we should never consent to join the common enemy and bring Greece into submission. There are many compelling reasons to prevent our taking such a course, even if we wish to do so: the first and greatest is the burning of the temples and images of our gods—now mere heaps of rubble. It is our bounden duty to avenge this desecration with all the power we possess—not to clasp in friendship the hand that wrought it. Again, there is the Greek nation—the common blood, the common language; the temples and religious ritual; the whole way of life we understand and share together—indeed, if Athens were to betray all this it would not be well done. We would have you know, therefore, if you did not already know it, that we will never make peace with Xerxes so long as a single Athenian remains alive."

Source: Herodotus, *The Histories,* trans. Aubrey de Sélincourt (Baltimore: Penguin, 1954), pp. 429, 550.

longer distance of about 26 miles.) After the battle, Athens experienced a burst of confidence that propelled it to power and glory.

Meanwhile, Persia sought a rematch. After Darius's death in 486, his son and successor, Xerxes, amassed a huge force of about a thousand ships and several hundred thousand soldiers and rowers, vastly outnumbering potential Greek opposition. Athens, under the leadership of Themistocles (ca. 525–460 B.C.), prepared by building a fleet of two hundred ships. Athens joined

Sparta and twenty-nine other Peloponnesian poleis in a Hellenic League of defense, with Sparta in overall command. Most poleis either stayed neutral or, like Thebes and Argos, collaborated with Persia. The Greeks had over three hundred ships and about fifty thousand infantrymen.

Persia invaded Greece in 480 B.C. and won the opening moves. At the narrow pass of Thermopylae in central Greece (see Map 3.1), the Persians outflanked and crushed a small Spartan army, who died fighting to the last man, including their king Leonidas. This sacrifice added to the Spartan reputation for courage but left the road south open. Abandoned by its defenders, Athens was sacked.

The tide then turned. The Greeks lured the Persian fleet into the narrow straits between Athens and Salamis. The Persians could not use their numerical superiority in this confined space, and the Greeks had the home-base advantage. The result was a crushing Persian defeat under the eyes of Xerxes himself, who watched the battle from a throne on a hillside near the shore.

Because their sea links to the Levant had been cut, Xerxes and the remainder of the Persian fleet left for home. Soon afterward the united Greek army under Spartan leadership defeated Persian forces on land at Plataea (just north of Attica; see Map 3.1) in 479 B.C. At about the same time, the Greek fleet defeated a reorganized Persian fleet off the Anatolian coast near Mycale. The victorious Greeks sailed the coast and liberated the Ionians. Not only did Persia fail to conquer the Greek mainland, but it also lost its eastern Aegean empire.

Greeks did not remember the invader fondly. After 480 they thought of Persians not merely as enemies but as barbarians—that is, cultural inferiors. (See the box "Global Encounters: The Enemy as Barbarian.") At the same time, Greeks became more conscious of their own common culture.

■ Struggles for Hegemony, 478–362 B.C.

The Greek unity forged by the struggle against Persia was fragile and short-lived. What followed was a constant struggle in diplomacy and war among city-states, usually arranged in leagues under hegemons.

Following the Greek victory over Persia, Athens expanded its power as hegemon of a new security organization. Founded on the island of Delos in the Aegean Sea, the so-called Delian League aimed both at protecting Greek lands and at plundering Persian territory. The number of allies grew from about 150 in 477 B.C. to about 250 in 431 B.C. at the height of the league.

Fearful as ever of entanglements outside the Peloponnesus, Sparta preferred to leave the Aegean to Athens. Many Spartans nonetheless watched with unease and jealousy as Athenian power boomed.

Afraid of the new titan, the major allied states rebelled, one by one, beginning with Thasos in 465 B.C., but Athens crushed each rebellion. Sometimes after surrender, rebels were executed and their wives and children were sold into slavery. Allied complaints began to stir Sparta. A conflict between Greece's greatest land power, Sparta, and Greece's greatest sea power, Athens, started to look all but inevitable.

The Peloponnesian War, as this conflict is known today, came in 431 B.C. and lasted intermittently until 404. The war proved bloody and bitter. Battles between huge fleets, economic warfare, protracted sieges, epidemic disease, and ideological struggle produced a devastating war. It was clear that the Greeks could not maintain their unity against Persia; indeed, they appeared to be destroying themselves. (See the box "Reading Sources: Pericles' Funeral Oration.")

In this era both democratic Athens and oligarchic Sparta sought to promote their respective ideologies. Some unfortunate states became ideological battlegrounds, often at great cost of life. In Corcyra (modern Corfu; see Map 3.4), for example, bloody civil war marked a series of coups and countercoups in the 420s B.C.

Given Spartan supremacy on land and Athenian mastery of the sea, it is not surprising that the Peloponnesian War remained undecided for a decade and a half. The balance of power shifted only after an Athenian blunder, an expedition to conquer Sicily (415–413 B.C.) that became a quagmire and then a disaster, leading to total defeat and thousands of Athenian casualties. In the aftermath most of the Athenian empire rose in revolt. Persia re-emerged and intervened on Sparta's side—in return for Sparta's restoration of Ionia to Persia, an ironic counterpoint to Sparta's role in driving Persia from Greece in 479. Athens, nevertheless, was sufficiently wealthy and plucky to hold out until 404 B.C.

Sparta won the Peloponnesian War, but establishing a new Greek order proved beyond its grasp. Trained as soldiers not as diplomats, never fully reconciled to using sea power, lacking the oratorical skills valued by other Greeks, sure of themselves and contemptuous of others, Spartans made poor leaders. Sparta took over Athens's former empire and quickly had a falling-out with its allies, Persia, Corinth, and the Boeotian° city-states, especially Thebes.

Boeotia, Boeotian (bee-O-shuh, bee-O-shun)

≈ READING SOURCES

Pericles' Funeral Oration

The historian Thucydides reports that in winter 431–430 B.C., at the end of the first year of the Peloponnesian War (431–404 B.C.), Athens's leading politician, Pericles (ca. 495–429 B.C.), gave a speech at the public funeral of the Athenians who had died fighting that year. Pericles used the occasion to celebrate Athens's way of life.

Our constitution does not copy the laws of neighboring states; we are rather a pattern to others than imitators ourselves. Its administration favors the many instead of the few; this is why it is called a democracy. . . .

Further, we provide plenty of means for the mind to refresh itself from business. We celebrate games and sacrifices all the year round, and the elegance of our private establishments forms a daily source of pleasure and helps to distract us from what causes us distress; while the magnitude of our city draws the produce of our world into our harbor, so that to the Athenian the fruits of other countries are as familiar a luxury as those of his own.

If we turn to our military policy, there also we differ from our antagonists. We throw open our city to the world, and never by alien acts exclude foreigners from any opportunity of learning or observing, although the eyes of an enemy may occasionally profit by our liberality; trusting less in system and policy than to the native spirit of our citizens; while in education, where our rivals from their very cradles by a painful discipline seek after manliness, at Athens we live exactly as we please, and yet are just as ready to encounter every legitimate danger. . . .

We cultivate refinement without extravagance and knowledge without effeminacy; wealth we employ more for use than for show, and place the real disgrace of poverty not in owning to the fact but in declining the struggle against it. . . .

In short, I say that as a city we are the school of Hellas; while I doubt if the world can produce a man, who where he has only himself to depend upon, is equal to so many emergencies, and graced by so happy a versatility as the Athenian.

Source: Robert B. Strassler, ed., *The Landmark Thucydides, A Comprehensive Guide to the Peloponnesian War* (New York: Touchstone, 1996), pp. 112–114.

In addition, Sparta suffered a vast decline in the number of citizens. The original nine thousand Similars of the seventh century B.C. had dropped to about only fifteen hundred in 371 B.C. The main problem seems to have been greed. Rich Spartans preferred to get richer by concentrating wealth in fewer hands rather than open the elite to new blood. Thousands of men could no longer afford to live as elite soldiers.

The result was military disaster. In 371 B.C. the Boeotian army crushed the Spartans at the Battle of Leuctra, killing a thousand men (including four hundred Similars) and a Spartan king. In the next few years Boeotia in-vaded the Peloponnesus, freed the Messenian helots, and restored Messenia to independence, after some 350 years of bondage. It was a fatal blow to Spartan power, but Boeotia, too, was exhausted and its main leaders, Epaminondas (d. 362 B.C.) and Pelopidas (403–364 B.C.), were dead. None of the Greek city-states had been able to maintain hegemony.

Nothing better demonstrates the fatal excess of individualism in classical Greece and the absence of cooperative virtues than the wars of the city-states in the fourth century B.C. They accomplished nothing but leaving a weakened Greece prey to outsiders.

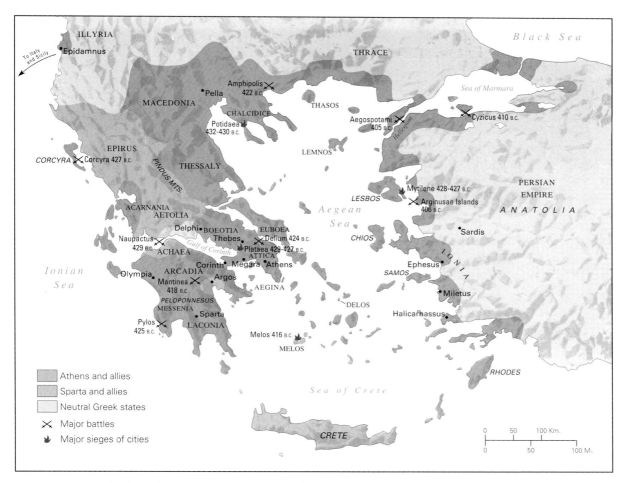

Map 3.4   Greece in the Peloponnesian War   During the long and bloody Peloponnesian War
(431–404 B.C.), much of the Greek world was divided in two camps: one led by Sparta, the
other by Athens.

THE PUBLIC CULTURE OF CLASSICAL GREECE

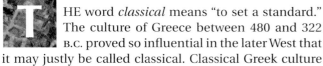

THE word *classical* means "to set a standard." The culture of Greece between 480 and 322 B.C. proved so influential in the later West that it may justly be called classical. Classical Greek culture was public culture. Poets were not inward-looking or alienated figures. Rather, to quote the Athenian playwright Aristophanes° (ca. 455–385 B.C.), they were "the teachers of men" who commented on contemporary public debate. (As the quotation might also suggest, men, especially citizens, dominated public life.) Dramas were performed in a state theater at state religious festivals. The philosopher Socrates° (469–399 B.C.) discussed philosophy in marketplaces and gymnasia. It was not private individuals but the public that was the major patron of sculpture and architecture.

Public life, accordingly, is the central theme of Classical Greek art and literature. In tragedy, for example, regardless of the particular hero or plot, the same character always looms in the background: the polis. The Classical historians Herodotus, Xenophon, and especially Thucydides focus on public affairs rather than private life. Classical philosophy ranged from biology to metaphysics; however, politics was undoubtedly its central focus.

Aristophanes (air-ih-STOF-uh-neez)

Socrates, Socratic (sock-ruh-TEEZ, suh-KRAT-ik)

The Parthenon   The temple of Athena Parthenos ("the Maiden") on the Athenian Acropolis, the Parthenon was dedicated in 438 B.C. One of the largest and most complex Greek temples, it was built of fine marble. The partially restored ruins symbolize the wealth, power, and greatness of classical Greece.   *(William Katz/Photo Researchers)*

■ Religion and Art

A hallmark of Classical culture is the tension between the religious heritage of the Archaic period and the worldly spirit of the Classical age. The Classical period was a time of prosperity, political debate, and military conflict. "Wonders are many on earth, and none more wondrous than man," said the Athenian tragedian Sophocles° (ca. 495–406 B.C.). Yet Sophocles was a deeply religious man who also believed that people were doomed to disaster unless they obeyed the laws of the gods. Sophocles mirrored a widespread debate, for he knew his countrymen well. He was not only a popular playwright but also a general, state treasurer, priest, and friend of Pericles.

Classical religion was less sure of itself than its Archaic predecessor. A few people even questioned the very existence of the gods, although most Greeks wanted religion to be adapted to the new age, not discarded altogether. Thus, Athenian religion was tailored to the needs of a democratic and imperial city. In the 440s B.C., under Pericles' leadership, Athens embarked on a vast, ambitious, and expensive temple-building project, using Delian League funds and serving as a large public employment program. Temples were built in and around the city, most notably on the Athenian Acropolis. (See the feature "Weighing the Evidence: The Parthenon" on pages 102–103.)

Classical sculptors completed the process begun by their Archaic forebears of mastering the accurate representation of the human body. In anatomical precision, Classical Greek sculpture was the most technically proficient sculpture the world had seen. Like Archaic sculpture, it was not, however, an attempt to portray humans "warts and all," but an idealization of the human form.

To adapt religion to a new age, new cults were introduced. The most popular was the worship of Asclipius, god of healing. Traditionally a minor figure and considered a son of Apollo, Asclipius became enormously popular in his own right beginning in the late fifth century B.C., perhaps in response to the high mortality of the Peloponnesian War. Outside Athens, large shrines to

---

Sophocles (sof-uh-KLEEZ)

Asclipius at Epidauros (in the Peloponnesus) and Cos (an island off the Anatolian coast) became pilgrimage centers in the fourth century B.C. for ailing people in search of a cure.

■ The Sophists and Socrates

Success in democratic politics required a knowledge of oratory. This demand was met in the late fifth century B.C. by the arrival in Athens of itinerant professional teachers of *rhetoric*, the art of speaking. They were known as Sophists° (from a word meaning "to instruct" or "make wise"). Sicilian Greeks invented rhetoric around 465 B.C. by drawing up the rules of argument. For a fee— rarely small and sometimes astronomical—Sophists taught young Athenians the art of speaking. Their curriculum consisted not only of rhetoric but also of the rudiments of linguistics, ethics, psychology, history, and anthropology—in other words, any aspect of "human nature" that might help an aspiring politician. Within a few years most ambitious young Athenians of prosperous families were studying with Sophists.

At their best, Sophists sharpened young minds. Athenian tragedians, historians, and philosophers all benefited from sophistic teaching. Protagoras (b. ca. 485 B.C.), perhaps the best-known Sophist, summed up the spirit of the age in his famous dictum "Man is the measure of all things"—an appropriate credo for the interest in all things human that is apparent in Classical literature and art. There is, however, a more troubling side to the Sophists. As teachers of rhetoric, they taught respect for success, not for truth. Thus, they acquired a reputation as word-twisters who taught men how to make "the weaker argument defeat the stronger."

Much to the distress of conservatives, Sophists drew a distinction between *nomos,* a word that means "law" or "convention," and *physis,* which means "nature." The distinction had revolutionary potential. In general, Sophists had little respect for the established order, or nomos. They considered it mere convention. A great man trained by a Sophist might rise above convention to realize the limitless potentialities of his nature, or physis: If he used his skill to overturn democracy and establish a tyranny, so much the worse for democracy. Indeed, the Sophists trained both unscrupulous democratic politicians and many of the oligarchs who launched coups d'état against Athenian democracy at the end of the fifth century B.C. As a result, *sophist* became a term of abuse in Athens and remains so to this day.

Classical Greek advances in rhetoric, therefore, were as problematic as they were brilliant. The Sophists had a wide-ranging effect on many different branches of thought. Consider, for example, the work of the philosopher Democritus° (b. ca. 460 B.C.), a native of the northern Greek polis of Abdera but a visitor to Athens. Democritus was not a Sophist, but he shared the common Sophistic notion that the reality of nature was far more radical than conventionally thought. He concluded that all things consisted of tiny, indivisible particles, which could be arranged and rearranged in an infinite variety of configurations. He called these particles *atoma,* "the uncuttable" (from which the word *atom* is derived).

The physicians of the Aegean island of Cos are known as Hippocratics, from Hippocrates° (b. ca. 460 B.C.), the first great thinker of their school. If they were not directly influenced by the Sophists, they shared similar habits of thought. Like the Sophists, the Hippocratics were religious skeptics. They considered disease to be strictly a natural phenomenon in which the gods played no part. Hippocratic medicine was noteworthy for its methodology, which emphasized observation and prognosis (the reasoned prediction of future developments). The Hippocratics were the most rigorously naturalistic physicians to date, although no more successful in healing illness than earlier practitioners.

In the fifth century B.C. not all thinkers welcomed the conclusions of the Sophists. Perhaps their most notable critic, and the greatest of all fifth-century philosophers, was Socrates (469–399 B.C.). Unlike the Sophists, he charged no fees, had no formal students, and did not claim to teach any positive body of knowledge. In fact, his basic thesis was negative: the radical ignorance of most people, including himself. His only superiority, he believed, was his awareness of his ignorance. Unlike the Sophists, most of whom were metics, Socrates was an Athenian citizen.

Socrates, however, resembled the Sophists in his intense interest in political theory. Like any good Athenian citizen, Socrates served in the military—as a hoplite during the Peloponnesian War. He had his doubts about democracy, which he criticized for inefficiency and for giving an equal voice to the uneducated. He preferred rule by a wise elite. Nonetheless, Socrates was too loyal an Athenian to advocate revolution.

Yet Socrates made many enemies because of his role as a self-styled "gadfly": Socrates stung the pride of

---

Sophist (SOF-ist)

Democritus (dee-MOCK-ruh-tus)
Hippocrates, Hippocratics (hih-POK-ruh-teez, hih-puh-KRAT-iks)

Athens's leaders by demonstrating their ignorance. Mistakenly considered a Sophist by the public because of his unconventional opinions, in 399 Socrates was tried, convicted, and executed by an Athenian court for alleged atheism and "corrupting the young." The Athenian public soon had second thoughts, and the trial of Socrates is usually considered one of history's great miscarriages of justice, as well as one of Athenian democracy's greatest blunders.

Socrates was trained in the Ionian natural philosophy tradition. He went beyond it, as the Roman thinker Cicero later said, by bringing philosophy "down from the heavens into the streets"; he changed the emphasis from the natural world to human ethics. Like most Greeks, Socrates believed that the purpose of life was the pursuit of aretê. Unlike his contemporaries, however, he did not consider aretê to be primarily excellence in battle or in public life but, rather, excellence in philosophy. One became good by studying the truth, which is part of what Socrates meant by his saying "Virtue (aretê) is knowledge." He also meant that no one who truly understood goodness would ever choose to do evil.

Such an outlook downgrades the importance of willpower or the emotions in shaping action, but it makes education into the cornerstone of society. Teach people well, according to Socrates, and they will behave morally. Socrates has gone down in history as an inspiring teacher despite his protestations of not teaching anything. His emphasis was not on research or writing—Socrates refused to write anything down. He believed that truth could be found only in persons, not through books—that philosophy requires a thoughtful verbal exchange. His favorite technique was to ask people difficult questions. Pedagogy that relies on inquiry is still called the "Socratic method."

■ Plato and Aristotle

Because Socrates never wrote anything down, we are dependent on others for our knowledge of him. Fortunately for us, he inspired students who committed his words and ideas to paper. Socrates' most distinguished student, and our most important source for his thought, was Plato° (427–348 B.C.), who in turn was the teacher of Aristotle (384–322 B.C.). Together, these three men laid the foundations of the Western philosophical tradition. They were thinkers for the ages, but each was also a man of his times.

Socrates grew up in confident Periclean days. Plato came of age during the Peloponnesian War, a period culminating in the execution of Socrates. Shocked and disillusioned, Plato turned his back on public life, although he was an Athenian citizen. Instead of discussing philosophy in public, Plato founded a private school in an Athenian suburb, the Academy. Plato held a low opinion of democracy, and when he did intervene in politics, it was not in Athens but in far-off Syracuse (in Sicily). Syracuse was governed by a tyranny, and Plato hoped to educate the tyrant's heir in philosophy—a vain hope, as it turned out.

In an attempt to recapture the stimulating give-and-take of a conversation with Socrates, Plato did not write straightforward philosophical treatises but, rather, dialogues or speeches. All of Plato's dialogues have more than one speaker, and in most the main speaker is named "Socrates": Sometimes this figure is the historical Socrates, sometimes merely a mouthpiece for ideas Plato wished to explore.

A voluminous writer, Plato is not easily summarized. The word that best characterizes his legacy, though, is *idealism,* of which Plato is one of Western philosophy's greatest exponents. Like Parmenides, Plato believed that the senses are misleading. Truth exists but is attained only by training the mind to overcome common-sense evidence. The model for Plato's philosophical method is geometry. Just as geometry deals not with this or that triangle or rectangle but with ideal forms—with a pure triangle, a pure rectangle—so the philosopher could learn to recognize purity. A philosopher would not be misled by, for example, comparing aretê in Athens, Sparta, and Persia; a philosopher would understand the meaning of pure, ideal aretê. No relativist, Plato believed in absolute good and evil.

Philosophy is not for everyone, according to Plato. Only a few people have the requisite intelligence and discipline. In the *Republic,* a dialogue that is perhaps his best-known work, Plato demonstrates the nature of his idealism and its political consequences. He envisioned a society whose elite would study philosophy and attain enlightenment. They would understand the vanity of political ambition but would nonetheless accept the responsibility of governing the masses. Plato never makes clear precisely why they should assume this burden. It is possible he was enough of a traditionalist, in spite of himself, to consider a citizen's responsibility to the polis to be obvious. In any case, Plato's ideal state was one in which philosophers would rule as kings, benevolently and unselfishly. (See the box "Reading Sources: Plato on Philosopher-Kings.")

Plato explored the details of such a state in the *Republic* and in other dialogues, particularly the *Laws.* It is not clear how wedded he was to specific details; indeed, some of them may have been meant merely to shock or

---

Plato (PLAY-toe)

Plato on Philosopher-Kings

Plato (427–348 B.C.) in his masterpiece, The Republic, *argues that the ideals of justice can never be reached until philosophers put aside their books and run the government—and until politicians step aside to let them do so. The following fictional discussion between Socrates and Glaucon (Plato's brother) shows just how unusual such an ideal community would be and just how hard it would be to establish.*

And I said: Cities will have no respite from evil, my dear Glaucon, nor will the human race, I think, unless philosophers rule as kings in the cities, or those whom we now call kings and rulers genuinely and adequately study philosophy, until, that is, political power and philosophy coalesce, and the various natures of those who now pursue the one to the exclusion of the other are forcibly debarred from doing so. . . .

. . . The uneducated who have no experience of truth would never govern a city satisfactorily, nor would those who are allowed to spend their whole life in the process of educating themselves; the former would fail because they do not have a single goal at which all their actions, public and private, must aim; the latter because they would refuse to act, thinking that they have settled, while still alive, in the faraway islands of the blessed.—*True.*

It is then our task as founders, I said, to compel the best natures to reach the study which we have previously said to be the most important, to see the Good and to follow that journey upward. When they [the best natures] have accomplished their journey and seen it sufficiently, we must not allow them to do what they are allowed to do today. —*What is that?*

To stay there, I said, and to refuse to go down again to the prisoners in the cave [that is, ordinary people who live unenlightened lives], there to share both their labours and their honours, whether these be of little or of greater worth.

Are we then, he said, *to do them an injustice by making them live a worse life when they could live a better one?*

You are again forgetting my friend, I said, that it is not the law's concern to make some one group in the city outstandingly happy but to contrive to spread happiness throughout the city, by bringing the citizens into harmony with each other by persuasion or compulsion, and to make them share with each other the benefits which each group can confer upon the community. The law has not made men of this kind in the city in order to allow them to turn in any direction they wish but to make use of them to bind the city together. —*You are right, I had forgotten.*

Source: G. M. A. Grube, trans., *Plato's Republic* (Indianapolis: Hackett Publishing Company, 1974), pp. 133, 171–172.

---

to satirize. An overall picture emerges, however. The ideal state would be like a small polis: self-sufficient and closed to outside corrupt influences like Sparta, but committed to the pursuit of things intellectual like Athens. Society would be sharply divided into three classes—philosophers, soldiers, and farmers—with admission to each class based on merit rather than heredity. Poetry and drama would be strictly censored. Plato advocated public education and toyed with more radical notions: not only gender equality but the abolition of the family and private property, institutions that he felt led to disunity and dissension.

Plato's ideas have always been controversial but almost never ignored. Even in his own day, most people considered Plato far too radical. The writings of his great student Aristotle were more to contemporary tastes. Originally from Macedonia, Aristotle spent most of his life in Athens, first as a student at the Academy, then as the founder of his own school, the Lyceum°. Like Plato, Aristotle wrote dialogues, but none has survived. His main extant works are treatises, largely compilations by students of his lecture notes. One of the most wide ranging of intellectuals, Aristotle had a voracious appetite for knowledge and for writing. His treatises embrace politics, ethics, poetry, botany, physics, metaphysics, astronomy, rhetoric, zoology, logic, and psychology.

Although influenced by Plato's idealism, Aristotle was a far more practical, down-to-earth thinker. His

---

Lyceum (lie-SEE-um)

Aristotle This bronze bust, found in a Roman-era villa in the Italian city of Herculaneum, is said to represent the great Classical philosopher. The statue has the dignified and pensive look betokening one of the giants of ancient Greek thought. *(Alinari/Art Resource, NY)*

father had been a doctor, which may account for Aristotle's interest in applied science and in biology and the biological method. Unlike Plato, Aristotle placed great emphasis on observation and fieldwork and on classification and systemization.

Aristotle agreed with Plato about the existence of absolute standards of good and evil, but he emphasized the relevance of such standards to everyday life. Unlike Plato, Aristotle considered the senses important guides; change, he believed, was not an illusion but rather an important phenomenon. Aristotle's view of change was teleological—that is, he emphasized the goal (*telos* in Greek) of change. According to Aristotle, every organism changes and grows toward a particular end and is an integral and harmonious part of a larger whole. The entire cosmos is teleological, and each and every one of its parts has a purpose. Behind the cosmos was a principle that Aristotle called "the unmoved mover," the supreme cause of existence.

Aristotle defined an object's aretê as the fulfillment of its inherent function in the cosmos. The aretê of a horse, for example, was to be strong, fast, and obedient; the aretê of a rose was to look beautiful and smell sweet. As for the aretê of a human being, Aristotle agreed with Plato: Only the philosopher achieved true aretê. As a

pragmatist, however, Aristotle did not imagine philosophers becoming kings. Not that he advocated democracy, which he considered mob rule. Instead, Aristotle advocated a government of wealthy gentlemen who had been trained by philosophers—not the best regime imaginable but, in Aristotle's opinion, the best one possible.

Aristotle believed that men had stronger capacities to make judgments than women and so should rule over them. He condemned states like Sparta that accorded power to women. (See the box "Reading Sources: Spartan Women" on page 78.) Hence, Aristotle would be cited in later centuries to justify male dominance. Ironically, however, Aristotle was more enlightened on gender issues than most contemporaries. For example, he believed that since women played a crucial role in the family, they should receive education in morality.

Aristotle may be the single most influential thinker in Western history. His scientific writings not only were the most influential philosophical classics of Greek civilization, and of Roman civilization as well, but remained so during the Middle Ages in the Arabic and Latin worlds. It took nearly two thousand years before serious rivals challenged Aristotle's intellectual supremacy.

■ Athenian Drama

Perhaps the greatest art form that emerged in the polis was drama. Modern comedy and tragedy find distant ancestors in the productions of Athens's theater of Dionysus, named for the god of unrestraint, liberation, and wine. Comedy and tragedy began in religious festivals honoring Dionysus (also known as Bacchus) but quickly became an independent forum for comment on public life. Ancient drama was poetry, not prose. Because it highlighted the relation of the individual to the community, drama proved to be the most suitable poetic medium for the ideology of the polis.

According to ancient tradition, tragedy was first presented at the Dionysian festival in Athens by one Thespis in the 530s B.C. (hence the word *thespian* for "actor"). The first surviving tragedy dates from the 470s, the first surviving comedy from the 420s. A play in the fifth century B.C. consisted of a chorus (a group of performers working in unison) and three individual actors who played all the various individual speaking parts. Plays were performed in an open-air theater on the south hillside of the Acropolis. Enormously popular, drama spread all over Greece, and eventually most poleis had a theater.

Classical Athenian tragedy was performed at the annual Dionysia in March. Each playwright would submit a trilogy of plays on a central theme, plus a raucous farce to break the tension afterward. Comedies, which were

Theater at Delphi Open to the air, an ancient Greek theater contained tiers of stone benches above a circular area where the action took place, behind which backdrops could be erected. The audience often had a view of stirring scenery that, at Delphi, included the temple of Apollo and the valley below. *(Vanni/Art Resource, NY)*

independent plays rather than trilogies, were performed both at the Dionysia and at a separate festival held in winter. Wealthy producers competed to outfit the most lavish and impressive productions. Judges would award prizes for the best plays—a typical reflection of Greek competitiveness.

Tragedy is not easy to define, except generally: a serious play with an unhappy ending. Perhaps a short tag from the playwright Aeschylus° can be said to sum up tragedy if anything can: *pathos mathei,* "suffering teaches." The essence of tragedy is what has been called the tragic sense of life: the nobility in the spectacle of a great man or woman failing but learning from failure. In *Oedipus the Tyrant* (ca. 428 B.C.) by Sophocles, for example, the hero unknowingly kills his father and unknowingly marries his mother. Oedipus cannot escape the consequences of his deeds, but he can react to his fate with dignity and heroism; he can try to understand it. Oedipus loses his power as tyrant and goes into exile, but he retains a degree of honor. He executes his own punishment by blinding himself. As Aristotle observed, tragedy derives its emotional power from the fear and pity that it evokes and from the purification of the senses *(katharsis)* that it leaves in its aftermath.

The great period of Attic tragedy began and ended in the fifth century B.C. Aeschylus (525–456 B.C.), Sophocles (ca. 495–406 B.C.), and Euripides° (ca. 485–406 B.C.) were and are considered the three giant playwrights. Although other tragedians wrote plays, only the works of these three men (or, rather, a small fraction of their works) have survived. Aeschylus was perhaps the most pious of the three. His plays—notably the trilogy of the *Oresteia* (the *Agamemnon,* the *Libation Bearers,* and the *Eumenides*), the only surviving tragic trilogy, dating from 458 B.C.—take as their central question the justice of Zeus. The subject is the myth of the house of Atreus—in particular, the murder of King Agamemnon by his much-wronged wife, Clytemnestra, and her murder in turn by their son, Orestes, avenging his father. Aeschylus casts this primitive saga into an epic of the discovery of justice. In fulfillment of the will of Zeus, Athena puts an end to vengeance killings and institutes the supposed first court of law: the court of the Areopagus in Athens.

Sophocles, too, was interested in divine justice. His tragedies focus on the relationship between the individual and the community. Heroic individuals have a spark of the divine in them, but their towering virtues are threats to ordinary people. In *Antigone* (ca. 442 B.C.), for example, the heroine refuses to compromise with injustice. Her late brother had committed treason, for which his corpse is denied burial—the standard Greek punishment. Antigone, however, insists on following a higher law, Zeus's law, which demands that all bodies be buried. Turmoil, disorder, and death ensue, but Antigone stays true to principle.

Of the three tragedians, Euripides is the least traditional and the most influenced by the Sophists. His plays reflect the disillusionment of the Peloponnesian War era. Euripides was more impressed by divine power than by divine justice. The central gods of Aeschylean drama are Zeus the father and Apollo the lawgiver, while Sophocles

---

Aeschylus (ESS-kih-luhs)   **Euripides** (yoo-RIP-uh-deez)

focuses on semidivine heroes, but Euripides' major deities are Dionysus and Aphrodite, goddess of erotic passion. In *Medea* (431 B.C.), for example, Euripides dissects the feelings of love, jealousy, and revenge that drive a woman to murder her own children in order to take revenge on her faithless husband (the children's father). In the *Bacchae* (406 B.C.), an arrogant young king named Pentheus is punished for refusing to recognize the power of Dionysus (Bacchus). When he goes to the hills to spy on drunken women called Bacchae who are worshiping the god, he ends up as their prisoner. Driven to frenzy by Dionysus, the women do not recognize the king; Pentheus's own mother, one of the Bacchae, mistakes him for an animal and kills him.

The changes in tragedy from Aeschylus to Euripides reflect the changes in Athens as first imperial arrogance and then the Peloponnesian War took their moral toll. Aeschylus's confidence in the goodness of the community gives way first to a focus on the individual struggling to be good and then to a fundamental doubt about the possibility of goodness. The civic order, celebrated so confidently at the end of the *Oresteia* (458 B.C.), looks less certain in Sophocles' *Oedipus* (ca. 428 B.C.) and by the time of Euripides' *Bacchae* (406 B.C.) seems terrifyingly weak.

Comedy, too, was invented in Athens in the Classical period. Like tragedy, comedy offers a moral commentary on contemporary Athenian life. Unlike tragedy, which is usually set in the past and takes its characters from mythology, Athenian comedy (the so-called Old Comedy) is set in the present and pokes fun at politicians and public figures. Whereas tragedy is generally serious and sad, comedy is light, biting, and humorous.

The greatest writer of comedy in the fifth century B.C. was Aristophanes (ca. 455–385 B.C.). His extant plays are lively, ribald, even scatological, and full of allusions to contemporary politics. Aristophanes loved to show the "little guy" getting the better of the powerful and women deflating the pretensions of men. In *Lysistrata* (411 B.C.), his best-known play, he imagines the women of Greece stopping the Peloponnesian War by going on a sex strike, which forces the men to make peace.

■ Historical Thought and Writing

Like drama, history flourished in the exciting intellectual atmosphere of classical Athens. Indeed, its two greatest historians, Herodotus (ca. 485–425 B.C.) and Thucydides° (ca. 455–397 B.C.), are among the founders of history-

writing in the West. This judgment is not meant to discount the contributions of, for example, the Hittites or Hebrews, or the chronicles, inventories, and genealogies of early Greece. Herodotus and Thucydides, however, are more rationalistic than their predecessors, and their subject matter was war, politics, peoples, and customs—what we think of as the stuff of history-writing today. Indeed, the word *history* comes from a word used by Herodotus, *historiai*, meaning "inquiries" or "research."

The works of Herodotus (*The Histories*) and Thucydides (*The Peloponnesian War*) have unifying themes. The thread through *The Histories* is the cyclical rise and fall of empires. Herodotus sees the Persian Wars as merely one episode in a vast historical drama. Again and again, hardy, disciplined peoples conquered their neighbors, grew wealthy, were corrupted by a life of luxury, and were eventually conquered in turn. Success made people arrogant, driving them to commit injustices, which were eventually punished by Zeus. The breadth of Herodotus's vision is noteworthy. A native of Halicarnassus (a polis on the southwestern coast of Anatolia; see Map 3.4), Herodotus traveled widely, eventually settling in Athens. He wrote not only about Greeks but also about Persians, Egyptians, and a host of other peoples in Europe, Asia, and Africa. (See the box "Global Encounters: The Enemy as Barbarian" on page 90.)

Only a child at the time of the Persian Wars, Herodotus gathered information by interviewing older people in various countries as well as by checking what limited written public records existed. Herodotus also wrote about previous centuries and places he had not visited, but with uneven accuracy. He could rarely resist a good story, and alongside solid research are tall tales, unconfirmed accounts, and myths.

Thucydides, however, by contrast, prided himself on accuracy. He confined himself mainly to writing about an event that he had lived through and participated in: the Peloponnesian War. A failed Athenian general, Thucydides spent most of the Peloponnesian War in exile, carefully observing, taking notes, and writing.

Like Herodotus, Thucydides was influenced by the grandeur of Classical tragedy. He also shows the signs of the sophistic movement, especially in the finely crafted speeches he includes. Thucydides' great theme is the disastrous effect of war on the human soul. His case study, the Peloponnesian War, proved that war is a harsh teacher: It strips away the veneer of civilization and reveals the savagery of human nature. In Thucydides' opinion, Periclean Athens had been a high point in the history of civilization. The strain of prolonged war, however, destroyed Athens's moral fiber as well as its empire.

Thucydides (thoo-SID-uh-deez)

Summary

WESTERN philosophy, science, politics, sculpture, painting, and literary genres such as comedy, tragedy, and history all emerged in Archaic and Classical Greece. The focus of ancient Greek life was the city-state, or polis. Though small, exclusive, often factionalized, and rarely capable of achieving unity in a large area, the polis may be unparalleled in its ability to foster individual creative genius. At the same time, the polis promoted the idea that public duty is more important than private advantage.

Paradox was the hallmark of the polis. The Greeks invented democracy while at the same time limiting the freedom of women and immigrants, oppressing slaves, and engaging in imperialism. Although the Greeks originated the concept that natural phenomena have natural causes, they nonetheless recognized the power of the irrational—be it divine whims or human emotions. With its democracy, freedom, and high culture, Athens stands for one aspect of the achievement of the polis; with its hierarchy, militarism, and austerity, Sparta stands for another.

Athens reached its peak under Pericles, whose leadership in the mid-fifth century B.C. ushered in a time of empire, prosperity, and cultural greatness. The major tragedians were all active, and the sophistic movement was at its most optimistic and progressive. Periclean Athens was unique, not only for the sheer concentration of talent, but also for the sense that the state, the cultural elite, and the people were united in a common purpose.

Although later times witnessed a fall from that state of grace, they did not suffer any decline in creative achievement. The outbreak of the Peloponnesian War in 431 B.C. marked the beginning of a century in which Greek warfare was more brutal than before. Yet this century also delighted in the comedies of Aristophanes, devoured the history-writing of Herodotus and Thucydides, and debated the philosophy of Socrates, Plato, and Aristotle.

By the end of the fourth century, as we shall see in Chapter 4, the polis was to lose its independence to a powerful monarchy. In succeeding years, new cities in western Asia and Egypt would amass the wealth and power to challenge such old centers as Athens as cultural capitals. Yet the culture that flourished in the new sites was Greek culture. The polis lost its freedom but gained a central place in the legacy of the West.

■ Notes

1. Excerpt from a poem by Solon, quoted in Aristotle, *Constitution of Athens,* trans. Barry S. Strauss.
2. Charles Rowan Beye, *Ancient Greek Literature and Society,* 2d ed., rev. (Ithaca, N.Y.: Cornell University Press, 1987), p. 78.
3. Ibid., p. 79.
4. Adapted from Richmond Lattimore, trans., *Greek Lyrics,* 2d ed. (Chicago: University of Chicago Press, 1960), p. 19.
5. Herodotus, *The Histories,* trans. Barry S. Strauss.
6. Thucydides, *The Peloponnesian War,* trans. Barry S. Strauss.

■ Suggested Reading

Beye, C. R. *Ancient Greek Literature and Society.* 2d ed. 1987. A witty and readable analysis from Homer to the Hellenistic era.

Biers, W. *The Archaeology of Ancient Greece: An Introduction.* Rev. ed. 1987. A clear presentation of the achievements and variety of archaeological excavation in Greece.

Boardman, John. *The Greeks Overseas: Their Early Colonies and Trade.* 4th ed. 1999. The standard introduction, authoritative, vivid, updated, and beautifully illustrated.

Cartledge, Paul, ed. *The Cambridge Illustrated History of Ancient Greece.* 1998. Twelve fine essays by leading scholars on subjects ranging from the natural environment to the status of women to philosophy, featuring lively writing and excellent photos.

Connolly, Peter, and Hazel Dodge. *The Ancient City: Life in Classical Athens and Rome.* 1998. Connolly's gorgeous illustrations and outstanding reconstructions distinguish this introduction to daily life in the two cities.

Hansen, Mogens Herman. *Athenian Democracy in the Age of Demosthenes.* 1991. An authoritative introduction to Athenian democracy that places the political system in its social context.

Martin, Thomas. *Ancient Greece from Prehistoric to Hellenistic Times.* 2000. A readable and scholarly introduction, emphasizing politics and war.

Osborne, Robin. *Greece in the Making, 1200–479 B.C.* 1996. Excellent, detailed, scholarly, up-to-date, and very stimulating history of Greece from the end of the Mycenaean world to the end of the Archaic period.

Pomeroy, Sarah B. *Goddesses, Whores, Wives, and Slaves: Women in Classical Antiquity.* 1975. An overview of women in politics and society in Greece, the Hellenistic world, and Rome, and still the best introduction to the subject.

Pomeroy, Sarah B., Stanley M. Burstein, Walter Donlan, and Jennifer Tolbert Roberts. *Ancient Greece: A Political, Social, and Cultural History.* 1999. A balanced introduction from the prehistoric to Hellenistic periods, with special emphasis on classical Greece.

 For a searchable list of additional readings for this chapter, go to http://college.hmco.com.

The Parthenon

The Parthenon, completed in 432 B.C., dominates both the skyline of Athens and the historical imagination of the West. The building's fine marble and classical proportions symbolize the free, confident, and united society that one might expect of Periclean Athens, the world's first democracy (see the photograph on page 94). A close look, however, suggests a more complex story. The Parthenon's sculpture offers glimpses of the tensions behind the classical façade.

The temple of Athena Parthenos ("the Maiden"), as the Parthenon is formally known, was a public project of Greece's wealthiest city-state, leading naval power, and premier democracy. Athenians spared no expense on its construction. Sculpture included a gold and ivory statue of the goddess Athena inside the temple and, on the outside, statuary in each pediment (the triangular space under the eaves) and sculptured reliefs running around the building above the exterior and interior colonnades.

So lavish a program of art demonstrated Athenian wealth but also served an educational purpose: to illustrate basic Athenian values. Because every Athenian male was expected to fight for the city when called on, militant competition is a central theme. Above the exterior colonnade, for example, ninety-two separate panels of relief sculpture depict gods and heroes fighting such foes as giants and centaurs. The sculpture above the interior colonnade is not so easily characterized, however.

The interior sculpture forms a continuous band, or frieze, around the four sides of the building. Warriors aplenty, primarily cavalrymen but also hoplites and charioteers, compose the line-up. See the detail from the west wall. Two riders are illustrated here: one turning and signaling, the other taking control of a rearing horse. Naked youths, they embody the ideal of strong bodies in the service of the polis. The long hair worn by the first rider, popular among the upper classes, was a reminder that Athenian cavalrymen were aristocrats.

The Parthenon Frieze, Detail from the West Wall   *(Courtesy of the Trustees of the British Museum)*

The Parthenon Frieze, Detail from the East Wall *(The Louvre)*

Not all of the men in the interior frieze are warriors, though, and women, too, are depicted. See the detail from the east wall. Look at the four women shown here. Like the riders, they are young and in pairs, but there the similarity ends. The women are on foot, clothed, and in solemn procession. The heavy folds of their robes, the hands held at the side, and the expression on the one visible face all suggest calm and decorum.

From both of these pieces we may detect Athenian commonplaces about gender. Young women were expected to be maidenly, reserved, and modest. Their bodies were to be kept private. Young men were expected to be outgoing and assertive. Although men wore clothes in public, they exercised naked in gymnasia, wrestling grounds, and stadiums, competing in a healthy activity considered to be effective preparation for war.

The historian finds subtler messages in the two scenes. For example, however constrained the role of women, their very presence in the frieze is significant. Women were not permitted to attend the Athenian assembly, but they participated in the rituals and festivals that played so large a role in Athenian public life. Notice, for instance, the two girls shown in the back who are carrying ritual vessels.

One group of people is notably absent from the frieze: Athenian rowers. The oarsmen who manned Athens's warships, though poor, were the city's most loyal supporters of democracy. Why are they not depicted on a temple built by vote of Athens's popular assembly, the disbursements for whose construction were inscribed in stone and posted nearby so that any citizen could inspect the handling of public funds?

The answer depends on knowing precisely what the frieze as a whole depicts, but that knowledge—despite the fame of the Parthenon and the relative wealth of documentation from Periclean Athens—is embarrassingly shaky. Most scholars argue that the subject is the Pan-Athenaic procession, held once every four years to honor Athena. The people depicted are said to be the people of Athens—a daring novelty, considering that all previous Greek temple sculpture was restricted to gods, heroes, and mythological figures.

Yet if the scene is the Pan-Athenaic procession, how are we to explain the absence of certain well-known features of that procession—for instance, a large ship model? Some scholars prefer to view the scene as an illustration of a legend from the early history of Athens, a period in which rowers played little role in the Athenian military. Still, there are many nautical motifs in Athenian myth, motifs the Athenians could have chosen to illustrate if they had wished to celebrate the rowers.

Clearly, the Athenians preferred to depict hoplites and horsemen. Some might conclude that Athens was not as democratic as it claimed to be. Another explanation is that Athenian rowers, despite all their political assertiveness, admired the ideal of the hoplite and appreciated good horsemanship, and that conservative traditions died hard even in democratic Athens.

Alexander the Great and the Spread of Greek Civilization ca. 350–30 B.C.

AROUND 275 B.C. a grand procession made its way through the stadium and along the broad avenues of Alexandria, the capital city of Egypt. The attractions included exotic animals from Ethiopia, Arabia, India, and Greece; floats carrying statues of gods, kings, and personifications of cities; soldiers in armor and women in finery; and gold and silver everywhere, in crowns, cups, and jewelry. At the center of the parade was the likeness of the man who had founded Alexandria, Alexander the Great himself. He was shown much as we see him on the silver coin shown on the left, which was minted in Alexandria: a young man in classical profile and wearing an elephant skin on his head, symbol of a career of conquest that had taken Greek-speakers into Egypt and across western and central Asia as far as India. To the kings of Egypt, the dynasty of the Ptolemies, Alexander was a symbol of power and authority, so it is no wonder that they featured him in the parade that they sponsored.

Alexander had created new realities of power in barely a dozen years (336–323 B.C.) as king of Macedon°. A northeastern Greek kingdom that had previously been only a fringe power, Macedon rose meteorically under King Philip II (r. 359–336 B.C.) to become the leading military power in Greece. Philip was a brilliant and ambitious general, but his son and successor, Alexander the Great, outstripped him.

Alexander laid the foundations of a new Greek world: the world of the Hellenistic° period (323–30 B.C.), in which Hellenic, or Greek, language and civilization spread and were transformed. This era was distinct in many ways from the preceding Hellenic period (ca. 750–323 B.C.). In Hellenistic times, Macedonians and Greeks replaced Persians

---

Macedon, Macedonian (MAH-seh-don, mah-seh-DOE-nee-un)
Hellenistic (hel-len-IS-tik)

Alexander the Great, silver coin from Alexandria.
(Fitzwilliam Museum, Cambridge/Dagli Orti/The Art Archive)

Philip and Alexander

The Hellenistic Kingdoms, 323–30 B.C.

The Alexandrian Moment

The Turn Inward: New Philosophies, New Faiths

as the ruling people of Egypt and western Asia. Large numbers of Greek-speaking colonists moved south and east. Governed by Macedonian dynasties, Egypt and the Levant became integral parts of the Greek world and remained so until the Arab conquest in the seventh century A.D. Greek-speaking kingdoms thrived briefly as far east as modern Afghanistan and Pakistan. At times the new ruling elite was open to natives who learned Greek and adopted Greek ways, but more often the natives were excluded and exploited.

Conquest put huge amounts of wealth into Greek hands. Alexander and his successors built great new cities: Antioch° in Syria, Pergamum° in Anatolia, Seleucia° in Mesopotamia, and, greatest of all, Alexandria in Egypt. Trade increased and expanded southward and eastward. In political life, individual cities continued to be important, but federal leagues (that is, unions of city-states) and monarchies ruled most of the Greek-speaking world.

Material and political expansion led to unanticipated cultural changes, which may be summarized as a turn inward. Frequently finding themselves among strange peoples, the Greeks sought comfort in new philosophies, religions, and modes of literary and artistic expression. Many of these new cultural forms emphasized people's emotions and intentions, not simply their actions. Science, meanwhile, flourished under royal patronage, as did the emerging discipline of literary criticism. The prestige of royal women tended to promote improvements in the overall status of Greek women.

Hellenistic Greeks boasted of having created one world, a common or ecumenical region (from the Greek *oikoumene*°, "inhabited [area]"). In truth, that world was complex. Native cultures flourished, while Greeks adapted and Hellenized a number of Egyptian and Asian deities.

Hellenistic Greek contact with one native culture in particular—Judaism—proved to have a lasting impact on the West. Under the impact of the Greeks, Judaism became more self-conscious and placed a greater emphasis on salvation, martyrdom, and individual study and prayer. Some Jews resisted Greek culture, others adopted it, and still others resolved to convert Greeks to Judaism. Reshaped by its contacts with the Greeks, Hellenistic Judaism was poised to transform Western religion.

QUESTIONS TO CONSIDER

■ How did Macedon conquer both the Greek city-states and the Persian Empire, and what new states emerged as a result?

■ How did Greek civilization spread during the Hellenistic era, and what distinguished it from the civilization of the preceding Classical period?

■ What power did women, slaves, and native peoples have in Hellenistic society?

■ What new philosophies, religions, and modes of literary and artistic expression were developed in the Hellenistic period?

TERMS TO KNOW

Macedon	Stoics
Philip II	Epicureans
Alexander the Great	Maccabees
Hellenism	mystery religions
Alexandria	
Antioch	
Ptolemies	
Seleucids	
Antigonids	

Antioch (AN-tee-ock)   **Pergamum** (PUR-guh-mum)
Seleucia (seh-LOO-she-uh)
oikoumene (oy-koo-men-AY)

PHILIP AND ALEXANDER

THE Hellenistic world was founded by two conquerors: Philip II of Macedon (382–336 B.C.) and his son, Alexander III, known as Alexander the Great (356–323 B.C.). After a century of indecisive warfare among the Greek city-states, Philip swept south and conquered them in twenty years; in even less time Alexander conquered Egypt and all of western Asia as far east as modern Pakistan. The legacy of these impressive conquests was to spread Greek civilization and to change it, both of which consequences were revolutionary developments.

■ The Rise of Macedon

Macedon was a border state, long weaker than its more advanced neighbors but capable of learning from them and ultimately of conquering them. Though rich in resources and manpower, Macedon lacked the relatively efficient organization of the polis. It included both tribal groups and scattered cities. Several dialects of Greek were spoken, some unintelligible to southern Greeks, who considered Macedonians "barbarians" (from the Greek *barbaros,* meaning "a person who does not speak Greek"). Ordinary Macedonians lived rough, sturdy lives, while the king and the royal court inhabited a sophisticated capital city: at Pella they sponsored visits by leading Greek artists and writers. Philip confounded Greek stereotypes of Macedonian barbarism by turning out to be a brilliant soldier and statesman—a man of vast ambition, appetite, and energy. A hard drinker, vain, and a man with numerous wives and lovers, he was also an excellent orator and general. Philip's goals were to make himself dominant in Macedon and then, after neutralizing opposition in Greece, to conquer the Persian Empire, or at least its holdings in Anatolia. He accomplished all but the last.

The instrument of Philip's success was his army, a well-trained, professional year-round force. Macedon, with its plains and horses, was cavalry country, and Philip raised cavalry to a new level of importance. In battle, the Macedonian phalanx would first hold the enemy phalanx until the cavalry could find a weak spot and break the enemy line. Then the phalanx would attack and finish the job. Macedonian hoplites carried extra-long pikes to keep the enemy at a distance. Philip also mastered the technology of siegecraft, raising it to a level unseen since Assyrian days (see page 42).

Philip used his army effectively. After capturing the lucrative gold mine of Mount Pangaeum in Thrace (the

CHRONOLOGY

359–336 B.C.	Reign of Philip II of Macedon
ca. 342–292 B.C.	Life of playwright Menander
338 B.C.	Greece falls to Philip at Battle of Chaeronea
336–323 B.C.	Reign of Alexander the Great
331 B.C.	Battle of Gaugamela completes Persian defeat
322–275 B.C.	Wars of the Successors
313 B.C.	Zeno founds Stoic philosophy in Athens
312 B.C.	Seleucus I conquers Babylon
304 B.C.	Ptolemy I king of Egypt
294 B.C.	Museum founded in Alexandria
276 B.C.	Antigonus Gonatas king of Macedon
263 B.C.	Kingdom of Pergamum founded
ca. 246 B.C.	Parthia revolts from Seleucids
ca. 245 B.C.	Bactria gains independence
244–222 B.C.	Reforms of Agis and Cleomenes in Sparta
ca. 225 B.C.	Eratosthenes of Cyrene calculates earth's circumference
217 B.C.	Battle of Raphia brings Palestine under Ptolemies
167–142 B.C.	Maccabean revolt in Judea
146 B.C.	Antigonid Macedonia becomes a Roman province
64 B.C.	Seleucid Syria becomes a Roman province
30 B.C.	Ptolemaic Egypt becomes a Roman province

region east of Macedon), he turned to the Greek city-states nearby. Olynthus, the most important, fell in 348 B.C. Led by the Athenian Demosthenes° (ca. 385–322 B.C.), the main Greek city-states prepared to make a stand.

Demosthenes (de-MOSS-thuh-neez)

Demosthenes was a superb orator, but his attempts to forge a unified force came too late. By 338 B.C., when an Atheno-Theban army met the Macedonians, Philip had already won over much of the Greek world through diplomacy, bribes, and threats. His complete military victory at Chaeronea in Boeotia was followed up with a lenient settlement in which all the Greeks except Sparta acknowledged Philip's hegemony (see Map 4.1). The Greeks would rebel against Macedon more than once, but always in vain, until they fell under the even greater power of Rome. The day was over when the polis could decide the fate of the eastern Mediterranean.

In 336 B.C. Philip was murdered by a disgruntled courtier, and the invasion of the Persian Empire fell to his 20-year-old son, Alexander, the new king.

■ Alexander the Conqueror

Alexander III of Macedon (r. 336–323 B.C.) is as famous in art as in literature, in romance as in history, in Iran or India as in Europe or America. Yet the evidence for the historical Alexander is almost as problematic as that for the historical Socrates or Jesus. After Alexander's untimely death at age 32, contemporaries wrote histories and memoirs, but none has survived. Several good historical accounts, based on earlier texts, are extant, but none was written less than three hundred years after Alexander's day. (See the box "Reading Sources: Virtues and Vices of Alexander the Great.") Alexander, moreover, was not only a legend in his own time but a master propagandist. Many of the incidents of his life took place in remote regions or among a few individuals, and they tended to grow with the telling.

Still, Alexander's virtues are clear. He was charismatic, handsome, intelligent, and well educated; as a teenager he had Aristotle himself as a private tutor. Alexander was ruthless as well as cultured. He began his reign with a massacre of his male relatives, but he brought a team of Greek scientists along with him on his expedition through the Persian Empire. Although he destroyed peoples and places, Alexander founded twenty cities. One of those cities was born in 331 B.C., at the site of a fishing village in the northwestern part of Egypt's delta. Alexander and his advisers planned a great trad-

Alexander Mosaic   This detail of a Roman-era mosaic from Pompeii shows Alexander the Great in battle, probably at Issus. Shining in his battle armor, Alexander is bareheaded, with a wide-eyed, intense gaze betokening his power. The larger scene includes the Persian king Darius, fleeing in his chariot.   *(Scala/Art Resource, NY)*

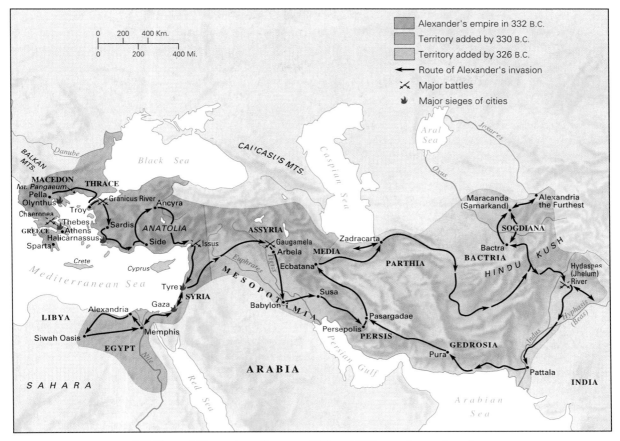

Map 4.1   Conquests of Philip and Alexander   Between 359 and 323 B.C., the armies of Macedon conquered first the Greek city-states and then the Persian Empire. Macedonian power extended from Greece and Egypt eastward to modern Pakistan.

ing center to replace Tyre, whose inhabitants had been killed or enslaved by the Macedonians who stormed the town in 332 B.C. The new city, called Alexandria, later grew into the largest city in the Mediterranean.

For all his varied interests, however, Alexander was first and foremost a warrior. Battlefield commander of the Macedonian cavalry at age 18, he devoted most of the rest of his life to warfare. As a leader of men, Alexander was popular and inspiring, and he shared risks with his troops. He knew the value of propaganda and took pains to depict his expedition to the Greek city-states as a war of revenge for Persia's invasion of Greece in 480 B.C. instead of what it actually was: the onslaught of Macedonian imperialism. He loved the colorful gesture. He began his expedition to conquer Persia in 334 B.C. by sacrificing animals to the gods at Troy, a site evoking Homer's heroes.

On the eve of invasion, Persia vastly outnumbered Macedon on both land and sea. Darius III of Persia was rich; Alexander's treasury was virtually empty. The Macedonian expeditionary force was short on supplies. The peoples in Persia's multi-ethnic empire were restive, but so too were Alexander's Greek allies, the mainstay of his fleet. One of Darius's advisers proposed a naval campaign to raise a revolt in Greece and force the Macedonians home. How then did Alexander propose to conquer Persia?

The answer was the Macedonian army. Although Alexander invaded Anatolia with only about thirty-five thousand men, they were the fastest marching, most experienced, and most skilled army in the eastern Mediterranean. If Persia would fight the Macedonians in a set battle, Alexander might be confident of victory—and it appeared that Persia would indeed fight. Persian elite

❧ READING SOURCES

Virtues and Vices of Alexander the Great

Writing in the second century A.D., *four centuries after Alexander's death, the historian Arrian composed from earlier accounts what is now the best surviving history of Alexander. A military man himself, Arrian appreciated Alexander's skills but was not blind to his flaws.*

Alexander died in the 114th Olympiad, in the archonship of Hegesias at Athens [June 323 B.C.]. . . . He had great personal beauty, invincible power of endurance, and a keen intellect; he was brave and adventurous, strict in the observance of his religious duties, and hungry for fame. Most temperate in the pleasures of the body, his passion was for glory only, and in that he was insatiable. He had an uncanny instinct for the right course in a difficult and complex situation, and was most happy in his deductions from observed facts. In arming and equipping troops and in his military dispositions he was always masterly. Noble indeed was his power of inspiring his men, of filling them with confidence, and, in the moment of danger, of sweeping away their fear by the spectacle of his own fearlessness. When risks had to be taken, he took them with the utmost boldness, and his ability to seize the moment for a swift blow, before the enemy had any suspicion of what was coming, was beyond praise.

Doubtless, in the passion of the moment Alexander sometimes erred; it is true he took some steps towards the pomp and arrogance of the Asiatic kings: but I, at least, cannot feel that such errors were very heinous, if the circumstances are taken fairly into consideration. For, after all, he was young; the chain of his successes was unbroken, and, like all kings, past, present, and to come, he was surrounded by courtiers who spoke to please, regardless of what evil their word might do. On the other hand, I do indeed know that Alexander, of all the monarchs of old, was the only one who had the nobility of heart to be sorry for his mistakes.

Source: Arrian, *The Campaigns of Alexander,* trans. Aubrey de Sélincourt. Rev. J. R. Hamilton (Harmondsworth, England: Penguin, 1971), pp. 395–396.

 For additional information on this topic, go to http://college.hmco.com.

---

ideology impelled the army to face the enemy head-on. Darius, moreover, was a new monarch and a usurper and so under pressure to prove himself in the field. As expected, Macedon crushed the enemy. The war was decided in three great battles (see Map 4.1): at the Granicus River in Anatolia (334 B.C.), at Issus in Syria (333 B.C.), and at Gaugamela in Mesopotamia (331 B.C.). Darius fled into Iran and was deposed, assassinated, and replaced by a man whom Alexander captured and executed. By 328, Alexander's claim to be king of Persia was sealed with blood and iron.

Having conquered the Persian heartland, Alexander turned eastward. The last seven years of his career are marked by three themes. First is the continuing and, in Alexander's mind, apparently open-ended military campaign. He pushed his army not only into the eastern parts of the Persian Empire but beyond, into modern Pakistan, which had not been controlled by Persia since the early fifth century B.C. The Macedonians won a major

victory there in 326 B.C. near the Hydaspes River (modern Jhelum River) over the army of King Porus, a force employing as many as two hundred elephants (see Map 4.1). Alexander's infantry suffered considerable casualties before inflicting enough wounds on the elephants to make them uncontrollable. Alexander prepared to continue eastward, perhaps as far as the Bay of Bengal, but his exhausted and homesick men had other plans. They mutinied beside the Hyphasis River (modern Beas River, near the modern Indo-Pakistani border) and forced Alexander finally to turn back. He reached Persia in late 325 B.C.

The second theme of Alexander's later career is his increasing despotism. After conquering Persia, Alexander turned on the Macedonian nobility, among whom he feared potential rivals, for Macedonian nobles had a tradition of rebelling against strong kings. The years after 330 B.C. are marked by conspiracy trials, purges, and assassinations. The most spectacular took place in 328 in

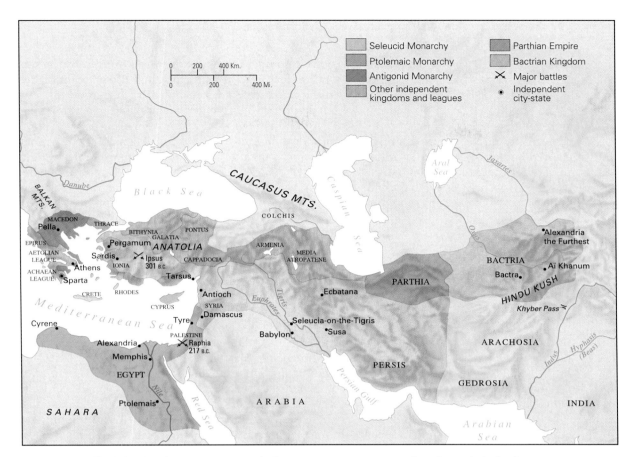

Map 4.2   Hellenistic Kingdoms, Leagues, and City-States, ca. 240 B.C.   After Alexander's death, his empire lost its political unity. Great new cities and kingdoms arose in the lands he had conquered.

Maracanda (modern Samarkand, located in Uzbekistan) when, after a drunken quarrel, Alexander himself murdered Cleitus, one of his senior commanders.

Another sign of Alexander's growing despotism was his demand for the trappings of Persian kingship. After conquering Persia, for example, he made independent-minded Greeks and Macedonians bow down before him. He required that the Greek city-states deify him. "If Alexander wishes to be a god, let him be," was the concise reply of the Spartans, but Alexander had now set a precedent for both Hellenistic monarchs and Roman emperors.

The third theme of Alexander's later career is his novel policy of fusion. After returning from the Indian subcontinent, Alexander began training an army of thirty thousand Iranians and dismissed a large number of Macedonian troops. He forced his main commanders to marry Iranian women, just as he did himself. In 324 B.C. Alexander staged a grand banquet in Mesopotamia for nine thousand, at which he prayed for "concord and a partnership in rule between Greeks and Persians." Such actions were a sharp break with the traditional Greek belief in their national superiority. Aristotle, for example,

had referred to the peoples of western Asia as fit only to be slaves. Alexander's policy probably owed less to idealism than to a desire for a new power base independent of the Macedonian nobility.

Alexander died in Babylon in June of 323 B.C., a month before he turned 33, probably of malarial fever, although some contemporaries suspected poison and some historians have suggested drunkenness. Alexander did not designate a successor. His wife, pregnant at his death, would give birth to a son and heir, but he was shunted aside by the Macedonian generals, who began a long and bloody round of wars over the spoils of empire. It took approximately fifty years of fighting, from 322 to 275 B.C., to make clear that three large kingdoms—Macedon (under the Antigonid dynasty), Ptolemaic° Egypt, and the Seleucid° realm—would inherit most of Alexander's empire. The rest was divided among small kingdoms, federal leagues, and independent city-states (see Map 4.2).

Ptolemaic (tol-eh-MAY-ik)   **Seleucid** (seh-LOO-sid)

In the long run, Alexander's life was far more influential than his death. His conquests did nothing less than lay the foundations of the Hellenistic world. It is ironic to measure in such impersonal terms the achievements of one who, more than most people in history, exemplifies individual success. Whether it was exalting a savior or debunking a hero, much of Hellenistic culture centered on the myth of heroism that Alexander had engendered. Historians who insist the individual is insignificant will rarely have a more challenging refutation than Alexander.

THE HELLENISTIC KINGDOMS, 323–30 B.C.

ARIETY, flexibility, and the creation of a new elite to transmit Greek culture compose the Hellenistic political legacy. Hellenistic political units ranged from multi-ethnic kingdoms to small, ethnically homogeneous city-states (see Map 4.2). The Greek peninsula saw both a monarchy with republican pretensions and experiments in federalism and in social revolution. In Asia and Egypt, a new ruling elite emerged consisting both of Greeks and Macedonians and of natives. Although the first group tended to dominate high office, natives were by no means excluded. The immigrants wanted land, wealth, or adventure. Their paths were smoothed by a new ideology that identified being Greek less with loyalty to an individual city than with participation in a common Greek civilization.

Although the Hellenistic world became relatively peaceful after 275 B.C., conflict among the kingdoms continued. Generally waged at a low level of intensity, with bribes and diplomacy as weapons, the conflict nonetheless sometimes broke out into major battles. A number of small states emerged in Anatolia, notably Pergamum, whose wealthy rulers were patrons of literature and art, and Galatia°, carved out by Celtic invaders from Europe.

■ Colonialism, Greek Style

Many Greeks and Macedonians emigrated from home during the fourth and third centuries B.C., but we do not know how many. The few available statistics indicate a significant migration but not a mass exodus. By the second century B.C., the colonizing impulse had diminished in Greece and Macedon, but a large number of Jews left war-torn Palestine, particularly for Egypt. Ptolemaic Egypt and the Seleucid realm were also the most common destinations for Greek and Macedonian migrants.

Greek migrants could take advantage of a new definition of being Greek that had begun to emerge even before Alexander's conquests. Disappointed by the narrow and self-destructive localism of the Greek city-states, Isocrates° (428–338 B.C.), an Athenian teacher of rhetoric, sought a wider horizon. Isocrates redefined the meaning of Greek identity. He promoted the idea that Greece was not a collection of city-states but, rather, a civilization. "The people we call Hellenes," that is, Greeks, he wrote, "are those who have the same culture as us, not the same blood."[1]

The ideal of Greek culture made it easier for the migrants to maintain a Greek identity. For that matter, it was now possible for foreigners to become Greek by learning the Greek language and literature. The number of Hellenized foreigners was relatively small, yet their very existence marked a break from the Classical polis, where even a resident genius such as Aristotle could not obtain Athenian citizenship because he was not of Athenian descent.

The Greek language also served as a common denominator, along with Aramaic, both of which became the languages of trade in the eastern Mediterranean. To get a sense of the importance of Isocrates' redefinition of Hellenism, consider that one of the most famous Greek-speakers of all antiquity was Paul, the Christian apostle who was born a Jew in Tarsus, a city in southern Anatolia.

Immigrants sought to realize dreams of prosperity or adventure. Although agriculture was the main economic pursuit, trade, industry, finance, administration, and military service also offered opportunities. The large Ptolemaic bureaucracy needed administrators and tax collectors.

In the Ptolemaic and Seleucid realms, administration was a joint effort of both immigrants and natives. The Macedonian conquerors might have preferred to rely on Macedonians and Greeks, but their territories never attracted enough immigrants from "home" to make that possible. Besides the new rulers needed both the goodwill and the local knowledge of the people whom they had conquered. Thus, the upper echelons of government were dominated by Greek and Macedonian

---

Galatia (guh-LAY-shuh)

Isocrates (eye-SOCK-rah-teez)

immigrants and their descendants, but native elites held governmental positions as well. Especially after about 200 B.C., some natives served the new rulers as administrators or soldiers, usually in low- or mid-level positions but sometimes in high office. Others worked in the traditional native administrative structures that survived largely intact in the new kingdoms, for example, as judges or village headmen or priests.

Consider, for example, soldiers. To create a permanent, hereditary military group living in the countryside, Ptolemy° I settled his soldiers on land allotments. Native Egyptians were excluded from the army at first but served as policemen. By the second century B.C., however, the dynasty turned to native Egyptians as a new source of soldiers. In return for military service, natives now received land, tax breaks, and the right to call themselves Hellenes. Their Hellenism sometimes merely scratched the surface, but sometimes it went deeper.

An Egyptian named Plenis, a villager in middle Egypt in the late second century B.C., is a good example of this cultural cross-fertilization. Plenis was a tenant farmer on a royal estate and a priest in a local Egyptian cult. His horizon was not narrow, however; like his father before him, Plenis served as a soldier in the Ptolemaic army. Plenis, moreover, could write Greek as well as Egyptian, and he even used a Greek name: Dionysius, son of Kephalas.

Temples, which often administered large estates, represented important sources of native power. Priests shaped local opinion and were in a position, therefore, both to enjoy considerable independence and to demand royal patronage. Both Ptolemies and Seleucids complied: from Babylon to Edfu, money poured into temple-building and renovation.

The Seleucids addressed the security needs of their far-flung realms by establishing over seventy colonies extending to central Asia. Some colonies were civilian, but most were military, composed of retired or reserve soldiers, mostly Greeks or Macedonians, but also including Jews and other non-Greek peoples. Colonists received land allotments. Greek-style public buildings were erected, and some cities were laid out according to a rectilinear grid plan reminiscent of the Classical polis. The gymnasium attained a great practical and symbolic importance as both the center of Greek culture and the preparatory school for entry into the elite. The Hellenistic gymnasium offered education in literature, philosophy, and oratory as well as athletics.

***

Ptolemy (TOL-eh-mee)

Singing African   This Hellenistic bronze figurine shows a black African, perhaps an Ethiopian, playing a musical instrument (now missing). The lithe body and emotionalism of the work are typically Hellenistic. Africans were a common subject for the sculptors of Alexandria, whence this piece may have come.   *(Bibliothèque Nationale de France)*

Some Seleucid colonies developed into flourishing cities. For example, Greek cities dominated the Syrian coastline and much of Anatolia until the coming of Islam in the seventh century A.D. Greek urbanization should not create the false impression, however, that the Seleucids were motivated by some civilizing mission. They were not. They established colonies to increase their power.

Tanagra Figurine   A terra-cotta (baked clay) statuette of around 320 B.C. shows a modestly dressed woman, wearing a hat and carrying a fan. Named for its place of manufacture in Greece, this popular style of figurine demonstrates the Hellenistic taste for ordinary, household themes.   *(Staatliche Museen zu Berlin, Antikensammlung/Bildarchiv Preussischer Kulturbesitz)*

■ Economic Expansion

Immigration and colonization were not the only sources of new economic opportunities. At the beginning of the Hellenistic era, Alexander turned the huge gold and silver reserves of Persia into coinage and released it onto the market virtually all at once. Although Alexander's action stimulated a rapid inflation lasting about seventy-five years, it also had the positive effect of greatly stimulating commerce. In particular the economy of Hellenistic Egypt became highly monetarized, even on the village level. Barter continued to exist in Egypt, but the widespread presence of money served to increase the production and circulation of goods, helping to render Egypt an economic powerhouse. Another stimulus to trade was the creation of thriving new Hellenistic cities, especially Alexandria with its great harbors, canals, marketplaces, and infrastructure of banks, inns, courts, and shipbuilding facilities.

During Hellenistic times, trade and commerce tended to shift from Greece proper to Anatolia and Egypt (see Map 4.3). The island of Rhodes, located off the southwest tip of Anatolia, grew into a major trading center, especially for grain. This development was the result of excellent harbors; a location on the merchant routes between Asia, Africa, and southeastern Europe; and a superb fleet. The Rhodian aristocracy grew rich off taxes and duties, wisely reinvesting a portion of the profits in naval infrastructure (such as arsenals and dockyards) and in campaigns against pirates. Egypt too had many products to trade. Grain was the most important, but textiles, glass, papyrus (from which a kind of paper was produced; see the feature "Information Technology: Papyrus" on page 14), and luxury goods were also significant. Egyptian goods were sold throughout the Mediterranean. A network of canals connecting Alexandria to the Nile and the Red Sea beyond also made possible active trading with Sudan, Arabia, and India.

The Seleucid kingdoms controlled rich trade routes to Arabia, India, and central Asia. Commerce was facilitated by good roads, safe sea travel between the Persian Gulf and India, and a unified royal coinage. The Seleucids traded agricultural goods and manufactured products such as textiles, glassware, and metalwork for spices from India and Arabia. In the first century B.C. they even had trade contacts with China, whose silk garments reached the Mediterranean. The kingdom of Pergamum, which stretched inland from Anatolia's northwest coast, exported the agricultural products of the rich hinterland it controlled, as well as the local gray-blue building stone and, as an alternative to Egyptian papyrus, parchment.

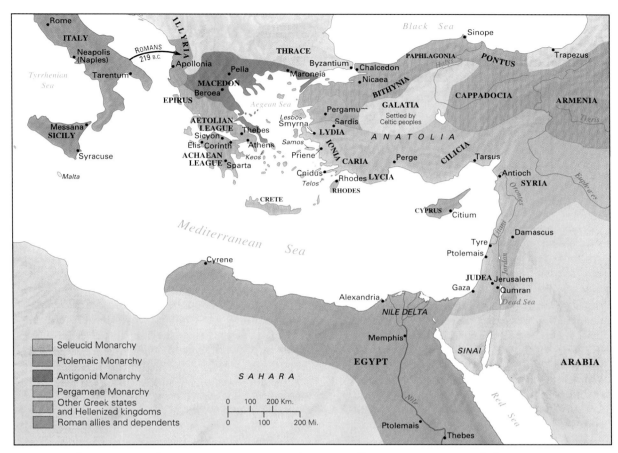

Map 4.3   The Eastern Mediterranean, ca. 200 B.C.   The great Hellenistic powers contended for control of this vibrant, turbulent, and prosperous region. Conflict centered on Palestine and the Aegean islands, the rulership of which frequently changed hands.

Slavery was an important part of the Hellenistic social and economic scene. Although war and piracy were the main sources of enslavement, some people were born into slavery. In Sicily and southern Italy, slaves worked huge plantations, but eastern Mediterranean slaves were commonly found in the household or in administration, and in cities rather than in the countryside. Many unfree laborers worked on farms in Egypt and western Asia. Following the pre-Greek traditions of those regions, they were generally tenant farmers tied to kings or potentates rather than outright slaves.

On some plantations, conditions for slaves were harsh enough to lead to mass uprisings. It was not unusual, however, for domestic or administrative slaves to buy their freedom, sometimes using savings they were allowed to keep, sometimes borrowing money from the master or from friends (see the box "Reading Sources: Macedonian Slaves Buy Their Freedom"). Greeks enslaved fellow Greeks, but often, it seems, with guilty consciences; they frequently made special efforts to help Greek slaves win their freedom. Even in bondage, therefore, Greeks had special privileges.

■ Macedon and Greece

Macedon was the last of the three great Hellenistic kingdoms to emerge from civil war after Alexander's death. Not until 276 B.C. was Antigonus Gonatas, grandson of Alexander's general Antigonus the One-Eyed, established firmly on the throne. His Antigonid° dynasty

---

Antigonid (an-TIG-on-id)

❧ READING SOURCES

Macedonian Slaves Buy Their Freedom

This marble inscription of either 280 or 235 B.C., from the city of Beroia in Macedonia, records the manumission of about a dozen slaves. Note that the slaves had to pay for their freedom, that they had to continue to serve their mistress, Attinas, for the rest of her life, and that they ran the risk of re-enslavement.

In the reign of King Demetrios, seventh and twentieth year, month Peritios, in the priesthood of Apollonides the son of Glaukios. Payment for their freedom was made by Kosmas, Marsyas, Ortyx to Attinas, daughter of Alketas, for themselves and their wives, Arnion, Glauka, Chlidane, and for their children, both those now alive and any that may later be born, and for all their possessions, each fifty gold *staters* [coins]; and Spazatis for herself and her possessions paid gold *staters,* twenty-five of them. And for them if they remain with Attinas while Attinas lives and do whatever Attinas orders, and Attinas dies, they may depart to wherever they wish. And it shall not be possible for Alketas nor Alketas' wife nor the descendants of Alketas nor Lareta to seize them or their wives or their children or Spazatis or to reduce

[them] to slavery or to take away anything of their possessions on any pretext nor by another on their behalf. But if not, they shall be free and the one attempting to reduce them to slavery shall pay for each person one hundred gold *staters* and to the king another hundred for each person. And if anyone from their possessions takes [something], he shall pay double the value of that which he took from them. [But if] they do not remain and do not do whatever Attinas orders, they and [their] wives and their [children], while Attinas [lives, for the] one not doing [thus], his freedom shall be invalid. . . .

Source: Adapted from Stanley M. Burstein, *The Hellenistic Age from the Battle of Ipsos to the Death of Cleopatra VII* (Cambridge: Cambridge University Press, 1985), pp. 73–74.

---

lasted about a century, when the conquering Romans made Macedon first a republic and then a Roman province.

True to the traditions of Macedon, the Antigonids projected an image of simplicity and toughness. Like Philip II and Alexander the Great, Antigonus immersed himself in the culture of the Greek city-states, partly because he admired it, partly because it brought him prestige. As a young man, Antigonus had studied the new school of Stoic philosophy in Athens (see page 128). As king, he devoted himself to the Stoic dictates of duty, describing his office as "noble servitude" and his diadem as a mere "rag." Antigonus shared the traditional Macedonian ambition to dominate the Greek city-states, but he faced rival powers. Besides Ptolemaic Egypt, there was the kingdom of Epirus in northwestern Greece and two new federal leagues in the south, the Aetolians° (north of

the Corinthian Gulf) and the Achaeans° (in the Peloponnesus; see Map 4.3).

The federal leagues were more tightly organized than Classical Greek military leagues (such as the Peloponnesian League) and larger than the Boeotian League, a fourth-century B.C. federal alliance that had covered a relatively small territory. The new leagues permitted some participation by ordinary men but were dominated by the wealthy; they were not democracies.

Yet the leagues interest us as models of federalism that would one day influence the founders of the United States. The Aetolians, for example, practiced proportional representation by population in a federal council for constituent cities. The Achaeans successfully balanced local and federal authorities. Constituent cities kept their own constitutions while recognizing federal jurisdiction. The federal government consisted of a

---

Aetolians (ay-TOL-ee-unz)

Achaeans (uh-KEE-unz)

governing general (both president and commander-in-chief) and ten subordinate magistrates, an executive council, and a general assembly.

Athens, less successful than Sparta in maintaining independence, repeatedly experienced Macedonian rule. Through a combination of war and diplomacy, however, Athens won periods of freedom from the late fourth to the mid-second century B.C., when Rome held sway over Greece. Athens remained a vibrant democracy until the late third century B.C., when the oligarchic upper classes finally won the upper hand for good.

Extremes of wealth and poverty, problems of debt, and class conflict challenged Hellenistic Greece. The decline of democracy enabled the wealthy to contribute less to the public good in taxes and to amass private fortunes. The result was sometimes class conflict, but the elite usually made just enough concessions to avoid full-scale revolution.

Sparta was an exception. In the late third century B.C. a social revolution was launched from above by Agis and Cleomenes, two Spartan kings working together. After defeat in the fourth century B.C., Sparta had become impoverished (see page 92). The reformers now offered debt relief, a redistribution of land, and a restoration of Classical Spartan austerity and equality. Popular in Sparta, the revolution threatened to spread elsewhere. Peloponnesian oligarchs called in Macedonian forces, which crushed Sparta in 222 B.C. and ended the revolution.

■ Ptolemaic Egypt

The wealthiest, the most sophisticated, and the longest lasting of the Hellenistic kingdoms was Ptolemaic Egypt. One of Alexander's great generals, Ptolemy (d. 283 B.C.), became governor of Egypt in 323 B.C. and proclaimed himself king in 304. His dynasty lasted until Rome annexed Egypt in 30 B.C., after the suicide of the last of the line, Queen Cleopatra (see page 126). By contrast, Macedon was absorbed by Rome a century earlier, in 146; Pergamum was annexed in 133; the Seleucid kingdom succumbed to Rome in 64.

Unlike the Antigonids, the Ptolemies did not pursue the simple virtues but rather gloried in wealth and grandeur. Ptolemy I showed the way to his successors when he had Alexander's funeral procession hijacked on its way to Macedonia and established a tomb and then a cult in the capital city, Alexandria—a Greek hero-shrine in the land of the pyramids. Ptolemy I made arrangements to have himself proclaimed "Savior God" after his death; his successors, less reticent, took divine honors while still alive.

The most important Ptolemaic borrowing, however, was the pharaonic tradition of royal intervention in the economy, which the Ptolemies combined with Greek customs of literacy and the use of money rather than barter. The result was a highly complex and profitable economy. Putting to use the science of the Museum, the great institute in Alexandria (see page 121), the Ptolemies sponsored irrigation and land reclamation projects, the introduction of new crops (for example, new varieties of wheat), and the greatly expanded cultivation of old ones (such as grapes for wine).

Most of the people of Egypt made their living in agriculture, either as independent small farmers or as tenants on large estates. Government enriched itself through taxes, rents, demands for compulsory labor, state monopolies (on such diverse items as oils, textiles, and beer), and various internal tolls and customs duties. The result was boom times under strong kings and queens in the third century B.C. Egypt became the most prosperous part of the Hellenistic world, and Alexandria became the wealthiest, most populous city in the Mediterranean, as well as its literary capital (see Map 4.3). In the second century B.C., however, continued economic prosperity was derailed by decline. Weak kings, bureaucratic corruption, inflation of the currency, and the end of Greek immigration created conditions for revolt.

Since pharaonic times, tendencies toward regional independence had bedeviled Egypt's government. The Ptolemaic period was no exception. Regional unrest stirred in the 240s and then mushroomed after the Battle of Raphia in 217 B.C., a struggle in Gaza between the Ptolemies and Seleucids for control of Palestine. The Ptolemies won, but only by enrolling thousands of Egyptians in the Macedonian phalanx, responding to a shortage of Greek mercenaries. Emboldened by their new military power, people in Upper Egypt soon broke into armed revolt against the government in far-off Alexandria. Rival kings appeared in the south, and unrest continued for about a century.

To advance their cause, the rebels inflamed anti-Greek sentiment. High taxes and regional rivalries, however, probably carried more weight than nationalism in the minds of most people. Although friction between immigrants and natives sparked from time to time, most Egyptians accepted the Ptolemies as pharaohs as long as they brought peace and prosperity. (See the box "Global Encounters: Egyptians versus Greeks in a Temple.")

Nor did the Ptolemies allow national sentiment to stand in the way of reasserting their power. In 196 B.C., for example, Ptolemy V Epiphanes celebrated his coronation in full pharaonic ceremonial in Memphis. Egyp-

⊕ GLOBAL ENCOUNTERS

Egyptians versus Greeks in a Temple

*This second-century B.C. papyrus, a petition to the authorities from a Greek wor-
shiper of Serapis, provides insight into relations between Greeks and Egyptians in
Hellenistic Egypt. It shows how Greeks lived in the temple at Memphis in order to
worship Serapis, a Hellenized Egyptian god (see page 129). It also depicts violence
and hostility across ethnic lines.*

To Dionysius, general and one of the "friends" [of the king], from Ptolemy son of Glaucias, a Macedonian, one of those "held in detention" [that is, on a voluntary, religious retreat] for twelve years in the great Temple of Serapis in Memphis. As I have suffered grave injustice and my life has been frequently endangered by the temple cleaners whose names are listed below, I am taking refuge with you in the belief that in this way I would best secure justice. For on . . . [November 9, 161 B.C.] they came to the temple of Astarte, which is in the sanctuary, and in which I have been living "in detention" for the number of years mentioned above; some of them had stones in their hand and others sticks, and they tried to force their way in, in order to seize the opportunity to plunder the temple and to put me to death because I am a Greek, like men laying a plot against my life. But when I anticipated them and shut the door of the temple, and shouted to them to withdraw in peace, they did not go away even so. When Diphilus, one of the worshipers held "in detention" by Serapis besides me, expressed indignation at their conduct in such a temple, they pushed him back, handled him very roughly and beat him up, so that their lawless brutality was clear for all to see. When these same men treated me in the same way in . . . [November 163], I immediately addressed a petition to you, but as I had no one to look after the matter further, they were let off scot-free and became even more arrogant. I therefore ask you, if you please, to order them to be brought before you, so that they may receive the punishment they deserve for all these misdeeds. Farewell.

[There follows a list of seven non-Greek names, of which six are Egyptian and one possibly Anatolian.]

Source: Adapted from M. M. Austin, *The Hellenistic World from Alexander to the Roman Conquest: A Selection of Ancient Sources in Translation* (Cambridge: Cambridge University Press, 1981), pp. 434–435.

tian priests commemorated the occasion in a decree written in Egypt's traditional language of kingship in a trilingual inscription (Greek, hieroglyphic, and demotic—ordinary—Egyptian). This inscription, discovered by French soldiers in 1798 and dubbed the Rosetta Stone (named for the place where it was found), led to the modern European deciphering of hieroglyphics.

Despite the frictions, evidence points to native-settler cooperation, especially in the countryside, where intermarriage and bilingualism became common. Many an ordinary Greek became fully assimilated to Egyptian ways, and even wealthy, sophisticated, urban Greeks adopted a smattering of Egyptian customs. The Egyptian calendar, Egyptian names, and mummification were all in use. By 98 B.C., assimilation was evident in the cultural

hybrid of a group of 18- and 19-year-old male youths who received traditional Greek military and literary training but prayed to Egypt's crocodile-god.

■ Seleucids and Attalids

The kingdom founded by Alexander's general Seleucus° (ca. 358–281 B.C.) experienced shifting borders and inhabitants. The Seleucid kingdom began when Seleucus took Babylon in 312 B.C. and ended in 64 B.C. when Syria became a Roman province. Many territorial changes occurred in between. The first three kings ruled a domain stretching from the Aegean to Bactria° (modern

Seleucus (suh-LOO-kus)   **Bactria** (BACK-tree-uh)

Afghanistan), but by the early second century B.C., most of the Iranian Plateau and lands eastward had been lost. At its height, in the third century B.C., the Seleucid kingdom had three nerve centers: Ionia (in western Anatolia), with a capital at Sardis; Syria, with a capital at Antioch; and Babylonia, whose capital was Seleucia-on-the-Tigris (near modern Baghdad; see Map 4.2).

Unlike the compact Nile Valley with its relatively homogeneous population, the far-flung and multi-ethnic Seleucid lands presented an enormous administrative challenge. To govern such a conglomerate, the kings took over the Persian system of satraps (provincial governors), taxes, and royal roads and post (see page 47), to which they added an excellent army trained according to Macedonian traditions, a common coinage, and a Hellenistic ruler cult. The chief Seleucid innovation was the establishment of colonies. Greek and Macedonian

soldiers and administrators dominated, but natives also filled bureaucratic slots.

The greatest Seleucid city was Antioch, which became one of the wealthiest and most luxurious of all eastern Mediterranean cities; only Ptolemaic Alexandria outstripped it. The intellectual and artistic capital of Greek Asia in Hellenistic times, however, was not Antioch but Pergamum, in northwestern Anatolia (see Map 4.3).

The rulers of Pergamum, the Attalid dynasty of kings, carved out a small kingdom that became independent of the Seleucids in 263 B.C. and fell into Roman hands in 133 B.C. The Attalids made Pergamum into a showplace of Greek civilization, a would-be second Athens. As in Athens, public building was focused on a steep acropolis. The upper city of Pergamum was laid out on hillside terraces rising to a palace and fortified citadel. One of the terraces housed the famous Pergamum Altar, a huge

Panel from Pergamum Altar   This frieze (ca. 180–150 B.C.) decorating the podium of the altar of Zeus illustrates the war of the gods and the giants, imparting a heroic dimension to the battles of the Attalid kings and the Celts. The theme of Greeks versus barbarians recalls the sculpture of Athens's Parthenon, suggesting that Pergamum was the successor to Athens as the champion of Greek civilization.   *(Art Resource, NY)*

A Greek-Influenced Indian Statue This figure of a *bod-hisattva* ("enlightened one") belongs to the Gandharan school, which was heavily influenced by Hellenistic sculpture. The statue's proportions, facial features, and draped clothing particularly recall Hellenistic motifs, suggesting that it may be the work of a Greek sculptor. *(Royal Ontario Museum)*

monument to an Attalid victory over the Celts, who first invaded Anatolia in 278 B.C. and whose advance the Attalids checked. They could not, however, stop the Celts from settling in central Anatolia, where they created their kingdom of Galatia.

Pergamum was famous for its sculptors and for a library second only to Alexandria's. Pergamene writers focused on scholarship to the exclusion of poetry, perhaps as a result of the influence of Stoic philosophers, who disapproved of poetry's emotionalism.

■ The Greco-Indian Interaction

The Seleucids' hold on Alexander's vast eastern domains turned out to be temporary. A new Persian dynasty, the Parthians°, achieved independence in the mid-third century B.C. and over the next century carved out an empire extending westward into Mesopotamia. But to the east, Bactria remained Greek, if not Seleucid. From the mid-third century B.C., an independent Greek Bactria prospered (see Map 4.2).

Vivid evidence of Greek colonization in Bactria comes from the site of Aï Khanum (its ancient name is unknown) in northern Afghanistan. This prosperous and populous city contained many reminders of Greece, among them a gymnasium, theater, and library. A pillar in the gymnasium was inscribed in the mid-third century B.C. with 140 moral maxims from Delphi in Greece, over 3,000 miles away.

In the second century B.C., Bactrian kings extended their rule into the Indus River valley and the Punjab, a region with a modest Greek presence since the fifth century B.C., when the Persians settled Greek mercenaries there. Virtually no literary evidence survives, but monuments and, particularly, coins demonstrate Greco-Indian cultural interaction. For example, some coins from the second century B.C. show bilingual inscriptions in Greek and Indian languages. Their designs include a variety of Indian religious motifs, such as the lotus plant, symbol of Lakshmi, goddess of wealth and good fortune. Indians admired Hellenistic astronomy; one text goes so far as to say that Greek scientists should be "reverenced like gods."

The Hellenistic world seems to have intrigued King Asoka° (r. ca. 270–230 B.C.), who ruled almost the entire subcontinent, the largest empire in India to date. Asoka is best remembered as a religious reformer. A convert to Buddhism, he played a major role in its spread, which proceeded under the slogan of *dhamma*, that is, morality or righteousness. One of his inscriptions records "victory" by dhamma, "where reigns the Greek king named Antiochus, and beyond the realm of Antiochus in the lands of the four kings named Ptolemy, Antigonus, Magas, and Alexander," which is generally thought to refer to embassies to the Hellenistic kingdoms.[2]

The envoys apparently found few converts, for it is difficult to find any trace of Buddhism in Hellenistic Greek culture, at least outside the Greco-Indian kingdoms. There, one of the most powerful Greek rulers, Menander Soter Dikaios (r. ca. 155–130 B.C.), may have converted to Buddhism in the mid-second century B.C.

Parthians (PAR-thee-unz)   **Asoka** (uh-SO-kuh)

But certain aspects of Indian religion *did* interest Greek intellectuals around the Mediterranean in Hellenistic and Roman times, especially India's powerful currents of asceticism, mysticism, and monasticism. Observers on Alexander's expedition, Hellenistic envoys, merchants, and philosophers in search of Eastern wisdom—all served as conduits between East and West. One of the most influential was Megasthenes, a Seleucid ambassador to the court of Asoka's grandfather, who published his *Indika*, a description of India, around 300 B.C.

Yet the degree to which this interest influenced Greek and Roman culture is debatable. Although ancient writers mention Greek or Roman philosophers who were attracted by Indian culture, modern scholars tend to be cautious. The ancients had a weakness for tall tales and stories of exotic inspiration. Consider, for example, the following reports. Pyrrho of Elis, founder of the Hellenistic philosophical school of skepticism (see page 128), supposedly based his notion of the imperturbable sage on one Calanos, an Indian whom Pyrrho saw step calmly on a funeral pyre when Pyrrho was part of Alexander's expedition. Around A.D. 40, one Apollonius of Tyana, a pagan religious thinker, is supposed to have traveled to India to study with its sages. Two centuries later the great Neo-Platonic philosopher Plotinus (A.D. 235–270) is reported to have traveled with the Roman emperor Gordian's army eastward, hoping in vain to reach India. Some scholars see Indian influence in Plotinus's mysticism and pantheism, but others dismiss these various reports.

Central Asian nomads overran Bactria in the late second century B.C. The Hellenistic kingdoms of India and Pakistan, however, survived until about the time of Christ, and some Greek communities lasted until the fifth century A.D. The Gandharan sculptors who flourished in a formerly Greek-ruled region in about A.D. 200 used Greek artistic techniques to depict Buddhist subjects, which might suggest the impact of Indian culture on the remaining Greek population.

THE ALEXANDRIAN MOMENT

BY the first century B.C., Alexandria was a city of a half-million or more inhabitants. It was one of the largest, wealthiest, and most important cities in the world. The bulk of the population were Egyptian, but Greeks and Jews made up large minorities, and no one would have been surprised, in this cosmopolitan center, to see an Indian or a Celt, an Italian or a Persian.

The capital of Egypt, Alexandria was also perhaps the most important place where Greek culture was spread and transformed in the Hellenistic era. At the same time, it was a mix of ethnic cooperation and conflict. Underwater archaeologists, for example, looking for submerged parts of the city in Alexandria harbor, have found Egyptian sphinxes and obelisks as well as Greek statues. Written sources portray a picture of social change in the elite, an increase in leisure time, a growth in educational opportunities for both sexes, royal patronage of culture, and the value of even a limited knowledge of Greek literature as the ticket to advancement.

■ The Anti-Epic Temperament

In 294 B.C. King Ptolemy I invited the deposed tyrant of Athens, Demetrius of Phalerum, to found an institution of culture in Alexandria. A writer himself, Ptolemy was no less sincere because the new foundation would bring him prestige and keep his engineers up to date on new technology for warfare and agriculture. Demetrius had studied with Aristotle's successor at the Lyceum, Theophrastus° (ca. 370–288 B.C.), a practical man interested in compiling and cataloging knowledge.

The new institution was called the Museum (literally, "House of the Muses," or the home of the female deities who inspired creativity). The Museum was a residence, study, and lecture hall for scholars, scientists, and poets. One of its key components was the Library, in its day the largest repository of Greek writing in the world. In the third century B.C.—at the height of the Ptolemaic kingdom—the Library contained 700,000 papyrus rolls, the equivalent of roughly 50,000 modern books. Its nearest competitor, at Pergamum, contained less than a third as many rolls.

The Library reflects an increase in the size of the Hellenistic reading and writing public. As independence vanished, city-states converted their military training programs for 18- and 19-year-old men into educational programs in literature and philosophy. The names of over a thousand writers of the Hellenistic era survive, and after 300 B.C., anthologies, abridgments, and school texts proliferated.

Although modeled on Athens's Lyceum, the Museum represented a departure from the public culture of the Classical period. The denizens of the Museum were an elite, dependent on royal patronage and self-consciously Greek, as if to set up a barrier against Egyptians. At the Museum, culture was an object of study, not a part of

Theophrastus (the-uh-FRAS-tus)

civic life as it had been in Classical Athens. A witticism of Timon, a philosopher from the Peloponnesus who lived in the third century B.C., rings true: "In Egypt, land of diverse tribes, graze many pedants, fatted fowls that quarrel without end in the hen coop of the Muses."

Before we examine Alexandrian literature further, it is worth noting how greatly Hellenistic Athenian literature diverged from Classical culture. The greatest Hellenistic Athenian writer, and a figure of international renown, was Menander° (ca. 342–292 B.C.). He was the master of a style of comedy called "New Comedy," as distinguished from the "Old Comedy" of Aristophanes, which had flourished a century earlier (see page 100). Where Old Comedy was raucous and ribald, New Comedy was restrained; where Old Comedy focused on public matters such as war and politics, New Comedy was domestic and private. New Comedy epitomized the turn away from public life in Hellenistic times.

Menander wrote over seventy plays, but only one complete work has survived, *Dyskolos* (*The Grouch*). There are also substantial excerpts from several other comedies as well as Roman imitations. The elements of Menander's skill and popularity shine through. Witty and fluent, he favored stock plots and stock characters: the boastful soldier, the clever slave, the dashing but inept young man, the sweet maiden, and the old miser. Within those limitations, Menander created realistic and idiosyncratic characters. As a Hellenistic critic asked rhetorically: "O Menander and Life, which of you imitated the other?"

Like Menander, Alexandrian writers spurned public themes, but in Alexandria the characteristic literary figure was not the playwright but the critic. He was a professional man of letters, as likely to write literary history as poetry. His works tended to be scholarly, even pedantic; they were refined, erudite, subtle—in a word, courtly. Prime concerns of the critics were establishing a literary canon and standardizing the texts of the canonical authors. Adopted by the Romans, Alexandrian critical standards have influenced the West to this day.

Of the three greatest Alexandrian writers, two— Callimachus° (305–240 B.C.) and Apollonius° of Rhodes (b. ca. 295 B.C.)—worked at the Library; the third, Theocritus° (ca. 300–260 B.C.), probably lived on a stipend from the Ptolemies. Popular for centuries, Callimachus was probably the most influential, the complete Hellenistic poet. A native of Cyrene (see Map 4.2) who came to Alexandria as a schoolteacher, Callimachus found a position in the Library. There he composed a virtually universal history of all recorded Greek (and much non-Greek) knowledge.

A prolific writer, Callimachus generally preferred short to long poems: "Big book, big evil," was his maxim. Earlier Greek poets were usually austere and public minded; Callimachus preferred the private, the light, and the exotic. "Don't expect from me a big-sounding poem," he writes; "Zeus thunders, not I."[3] Callimachus was expert at the pithy statement in verse, the epigram.

The Causes, Callimachus's masterwork (of which little survives), is at seven thousand lines his one long poem, but it is a collection of brief vignettes rather than a unified narrative. The central theme is the origins of festivals, customs, institutions, and names, many of them obscure. Arcane diction and complex allusions abound. Only an elite could understand such writing, but Callimachus was an elitist. "I detest all common things," he states.

Another major Alexandrian writer was Callimachus's student, Apollonius of Rhodes. Tradition claims that Apollonius retired to Rhodes after his epic poem *Argonautica*° (*Voyage of the Argo*) was poorly received. The subject is the legend of Jason and the heroes who travel on the ship *Argo* to Colchis, at the far end of the Black Sea, in pursuit of the Golden Fleece (the skin of a winged ram). With the help of the Colchian princess Medea, who falls in love with Jason, the heroes succeed and return home safely after numerous adventures.

Apollonius devotes much of the poem to a discussion of the roots of various names, cults, and customs. The main novelty, however, is a fundamental and pervading doubt about the very possibility of heroism. Apollonius's Jason is no Achilles, no Odysseus. Homer describes Odysseus as "never at a loss"; Apollonius describes Jason as "helpless." Men move the action in the *Iliad* and the *Odyssey*; Jason depends on a woman, Medea, for his success. Indeed, much of the *Argonautica* focuses on Medea and in particular on her love for Jason. With the exception of the works of Sappho, previous Greek poetry generally either ignored female eroticism or presented it in a hostile light. Apollonius's work illustrates both the improved status of women in Hellenistic ideology and the great interest of the age in the inner life of the emotions. All in all, the *Argonautica* is less a traditional epic than an anti-epic.

Like Callimachus, Theocritus, a native of Syracuse, wrote short, polished poetry. He composed thirty-one subtle and refined poems, conventionally known as idylls. The best-known of the poems focus on country life. They are the first known pastoral poems; indeed,

---

Menander (meh-NAN-der)   **Callimachus** (kah-LIH-muh-kus)
Apollonius (ap-uh-LO-nee-us)   **Theocritus** (the-OCK-rih-tus)

Argonautica (ar-go-NAW-tih-kuh)

Street Musicians   The lively scene of a mixed group of young and old, male and female,
recalls the jaunty mimes popular with the Hellenistic public. A mosaic of about 100 B.C., the
artwork comes from a private villa in the Greco-Italian city of Pompeii.   *(Museo Nazionale, Naples)*

Theocritus probably invented the genre. Theocritus's pastorals explore nature, but always self-consciously, always with the city in mind. His peasants and shepherds are marvelously cultured, more like townspeople on an excursion than true rustics. Through his Roman admirers, Theocritus's love of nature has exerted a powerful hold on the Western literary imagination.

Outside the Museum, Alexandria had a lively popular culture, much of it Egyptian or influenced by Egyptian models. A glimpse of it is afforded in the seven surviving mimes, or farces, of an obscure writer named Herondas or Herodas. Although written in literary Greek, they discuss commonplace subjects—shopping for shoes, tourism, lawsuits, and beatings at school—and titillating themes such as adultery and prostitution. Lively, bawdy, and funny, filled with the grit of everyday life in the third century B.C., they are a reminder of just how specialized the culture of the Museum was.

■ Advances in Science and Medicine

The Ptolemies not only reaped practical benefits in military and agricultural technology from their Museum, but they became the patrons of a flourishing period in the history of pure scientific inquiry. They also unwittingly promoted a split between philosophy and science that has characterized much of Western culture since. Antigonid patronage of ethical and political philosophy helped keep Athens pre-eminent in those fields. The study of science, in contrast, tended to shift to Alexandria. The rulers of Pergamum and, far to the west, Syracuse, a flourishing Hellenistic city in Sicily, were great patrons of science as well. Wealth, improved communications and literacy, continued warfare, and cross-fertilization between Greek and non-Greek traditions, especially Greek and Babylonian astronomy, were all catalysts of Hellenistic science.

Some of the best-known figures of Hellenistic science were mathematicians. In his *Elements,* the Alexandrian Euclid (active ca. 300 B.C.) produced a systematic exposition of geometry, hugely influential in both Western and Islamic civilizations. A Sicilian Greek, Archimedes° of Syracuse (287–212 B.C.), did original work on the geometry of spheres and cylinders, calculated the approximate value of pi (the ratio of a circle's circumference to its diameter), and made important discoveries in astronomy, engineering, optics, and other fields. Archimedes was as great an inventor as he was a theoretician. One of the most important of his innovations was the water snail, also known as Archimedes' screw: a device to raise water for irrigation. Invented by Archimedes during a stay in Egypt, the screw made it possible to irrigate previously barren land, as did the ox-driven water wheel, another Ptolemaic invention.

Advances in mathematics promoted advances in astronomy. Aristarchus of Samos (active ca. 275 B.C.) is known for his heliocentric hypothesis, which confounded tradition by having the earth revolve around the sun, instead of the sun around the earth. He was right, but Hellenistic astronomy lacked the data to prove his theory, so its rejection was not unreasonable at the time. Eratosthenes° of Cyrene (active ca. 225 B.C.) was saddled with the frustrating nickname of "Beta" (the second letter of the Greek alphabet) because he was considered second best in every branch of study. This "second best" nonetheless calculated through simple geometry an extraordinarily accurate measurement of the earth's circumference.

Hellenistic medicine thrived in Alexandria. Both Greece and Egypt had long-established medical traditions. Egyptian drugs, and possibly Egyptian doctors' knowledge of the eye as well as their emphasis on measurement, helped stimulate Alexandrian medical progress, as no doubt did the mere fact of cross-fertilization. The key to medical advance, however, was the dissection of human cadavers in Alexandria, a first in the history of science. In Greece, as in many ancient societies, religious tradition demanded that dead bodies not be mutilated. But in the frontier atmosphere of early Alexandria, this traditional taboo lost much of its force. Although Egyptians did not practice dissection, they did practice embalming, which may have helped Alexandrian Greeks overcome the prohibition against cutting open the human body. Ever supportive of research, the Ptolemies provided corpses to Greek scientists for dissection. Indeed, they had condemned criminals sent from prison for live dissection by scientists. The practice, only a short-lived experiment in the early third century B.C., outraged many writers in antiquity, just as today it would be considered an atrocity.

The leading scientific beneficiary was Herophilus° of Chalcedon (ca. 320–250 B.C.), a practicing physician in Alexandria. Among his achievements was the recognition (against Aristotle) that the brain is the center of the nervous system, a careful dissection of the eye, the discovery of the ovaries, and the description of the duodenum, which he named (*duodenum* is a Latin translation of a Greek word meaning "twelve fingers," describing the organ's length). In addition, Herophilus developed a detailed theory of the diagnostic value of measuring pulse rates.

Hellenistic technology has long fascinated and frustrated scholars. The great engineers invented both numerous engines of war and various "wonderworks" to amuse the royal court. Among the latter were mechanical puppets and steam-run toys. Given these advances, why did the Greeks achieve neither a scientific revolution along the lines of the one begun in the early modern era by such thinkers as Copernicus and Galileo, nor an industrial transformation, such as was ushered in by the steam engine around A.D. 1800? Historians are not entirely sure but can venture a guess. Greek machine-making technology was not as sophisticated as that of eighteenth-century Europe. The prevalence of slavery in antiquity, moreover, discouraged the invention of labor-saving machines; steam was used only for playthings and gadgets. A related point is the elitist bias of Greek intellectual life. After Archimedes' death, for example, it was claimed that although he had written copiously on theoretical matters, he never bothered to write about his mechanical inventions because he considered them "ignoble and vulgar."

Perhaps the most important point is the Greek attitude toward nature. Whereas Jews and Christians learned from the Bible that human beings have dominion over nature, thereby making possible the conclusion that it is appropriate to conquer nature, the Greeks thought in more restricted terms. They believed that nature set limits, that a virtuous person tried to follow nature, not subdue it. Thus, Greek engineers were not inclined to make the revolutionary changes that their modern counterparts have promoted.

Archimedes (ar-kuh-MEE-deez)
Eratosthenes (er-uh-TOSS-the-neez)

Herophilus (her-AH-fih-lus)

■ Men and Women in Art and Society

Like Hellenistic literature, Hellenistic art attests to changing male attitudes toward women and toward gender issues. The portrait of Jason and Medea in Apollonius's *Argonautica* makes fun of masculine pretensions and celebrates the triumph of female intelligence. It also presents a sympathetic portrait of a woman's romantic desire for a man, as does Theocritus's work. In the Classical period, depictions of romantic love were generally restricted to male homoeroticism. Accordingly, statues of naked males were common, but women were almost always depicted clothed. Hellenistic sculpture, by contrast, affords many erotic examples of the female nude.

There are indications that the Hellenistic Greek male of the elite was much more willing than his Classical predecessor to see lovemaking as a matter of mutuality and respect. Classical vase-painting often depicts heterosexual lovemaking with the mood lusty and explicit. In Hellenistic vase-painting, in contrast, the emphasis is more often on tenderness and domesticity. Hellenistic men wrote with sensitivity about satisfying a woman's needs and desires. The vogue in Hellenistic art for representations of Hermaphrodite°, the mythical creature who was half female and half male, may suggest a belief that the feminine was as important a part of human nature as the masculine.

Many a Hellenistic artist or writer seems to be as interested in emotion as in action and to focus on the inner as much as on the outer life. Hellenistic art often depicts women, children, and domestic scenes. Representations of warriors are as likely to focus on their unrestrained emotions as on their soldierly self-control.

Hellenistic women enjoyed small improvements in political and legal status and considerable improvements in economic and ideological status. A number of reasons explain these advances. First, Greek women, particularly in the elite, benefited from the spread of monarchy. For one thing, queens and princesses in royal courts had power and prestige that had been denied women in city-states. For another, under monarchy the notion of the loyal and prosperous subject replaced that of the independent citizen-warrior. Citizens in the Classical polis had been encouraged to be aggressive and exaggeratedly masculine to the point of hostility to women. Subjects in Hellenistic monarchies were meant to cultivate the more passive and reflective virtues of legalism, obedience, and economic enterprise. Because

Hermaphrodite (her-MAF-ro-dyte)

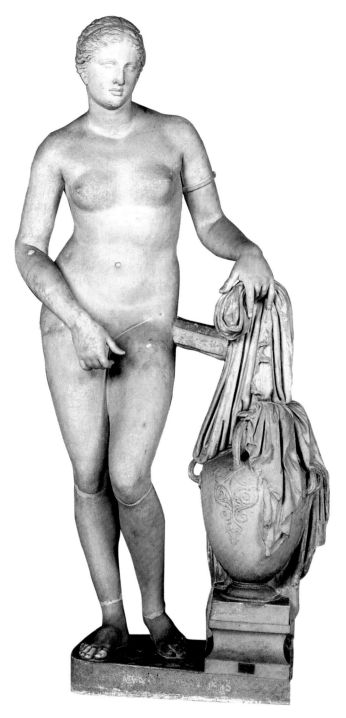

Aphrodite of Cnidos   This 7½-foot-tall marble statue is a Roman copy of an original by Praxiteles (ca. 350–330 B.C.). Perhaps the most famous of Hellenistic female nudes, the statue was housed in a special shrine where it could be viewed in the round to accommodate all the interest it generated.   *(Vatican Museums)*

❧ READING SOURCES

The Power of Hellenistic Women—and Its Limits

These two inscriptions commemorate prominent women. The first, written about 218 B.C. in the city of Lamia, honors Aristodama of Smyrna. Note that although Aristodama is free to perform in public, her brother Dionysios probably traveled with her as her official guardian. The second inscription, from the city of Priene, perhaps in the first century B.C., recalls Phile, who funded an aqueduct and was rewarded with public office.

Aristodama

. . . With good fortune. Resolved [by the city] of the Lamians. Since Aristo[d]ama, daughter of Amyntas, a citizen of Smyrna in Io[nia], epic poetess, while she was in our city, gave several [public recitations] of her poems in which the nation of the Aetolians [and] the People's ancestors were worthily commemorated and since the performance was done with great enthusiasm, she shall be a proxenos [diplomatic representative] of the city and a benefactress, and she shall be given citizenship and the right to possess land and [a house] and the right of pasture and inviolability and security on land and sea in war and peace for herself and her descendants and their property for all time together with all other privileges that are given to other proxenoi and benefactors. And Diony[sios], her brother, and his descendants shall have the rights of a proxenos, citizenship, [inviolability]. . . .

Phile

[Phil]e, daughter of Apollonios and wife of Thessalos, the son of Polydektes, having held the office of stephanephoros [magistrate], the first woman [to do so], constructed at her own expense the reservoir for water and the city aqueduct.

Source: Adapted from Stanley M. Burstein, *The Hellenistic Age from the Battle of Ipsos to the Death of Cleopatra VII* (Cambridge: Cambridge University Press, 1985), pp. 59, 86–87.

Greek men associated these virtues with women, their respect for female qualities tended to increase. Also, in the new cities, as in many a frontier society, women more often were permitted to inherit and use property than in old Greece.

It was an era of powerful queens: Olympias, Alexander the Great's mother, played kingmaker after her son's death. Arsinoe II Philadelphus was co-ruler of Egypt with her husband (who was also her brother) for five years at the height of Ptolemaic prosperity around 275 B.C. The most famous Hellenistic woman, Cleopatra VII, was queen of Egypt from 51 to 30 B.C. Although she was the lover of two of the most powerful men in the world, the Romans Julius Caesar and Mark Antony, Cleopatra was no exotic plaything. Rather, she was a brilliant and ambitious strategist who nearly succeeded in winning a world empire for her family. (See the feature "Weighing the Evidence: Images of Cleopatra" on pages 134–135.)

Writers in the new Hellenistic cities often described freedom of movement for women. Theocritus and Herondas, for example, show women visiting a temple or a show. Nor did Hellenistic men, even in Athens, obey Pericles' injunction not to speak of women, even good women. In Hellenistic Athens, aristocratic fathers put up inscriptions in honor of their daughters who had participated in the cult of Athena. Although women generally continued to need a male guardian to represent them in public, in some situations, at least in Egypt (where the evidence is most plentiful), a woman could represent herself. A woman could petition the government on her own behalf. Widows and mothers of illegitimate children could give their daughters in marriage or apprentice their sons. A few cities granted women citizenship or even permitted them to hold public office.

Some Hellenistic cities admitted women to the gymnasium, previously a male preserve. Heretofore only

Sparta had promoted physical education for women, but by the first century A.D., women were even competing in the great Pan-Hellenic games. Gymnasia were also centers of education in music and reading. One consequence of growing literacy was the re-emergence of women poets and the first appearance of women philosophers in the West. Before dying at age 19, Erinna, who lived on the Aegean island of Telos during the late fourth century B.C., wrote the *Distaff*, a poem in memory of her childhood friend Baucis. This three-hundred-line poem, famous in antiquity, described the shared experiences of girlhood. Hipparchia° of Maroneia (b. ca. 350 B.C.), like her husband Crates of Thebes, studied Cynic philosophy. The Cynics, like another philosophical school, the Epicureans, supported a measure of equality between women and men. Hipparchia and Crates led an itinerant life as popular teachers and the Hellenistic equivalent of counselors or psychologists.

Much of the explanation for the relative freedom of elite women lies in the new economic power of this group. The new cities generally imposed fewer restrictions on women's economic roles than had Classical poleis such as Athens. In many cities women could sell land, borrow money, and decide whether their husbands could make loans or contracts on the strength of their dowries. Free women could manumit slaves as well. (See the box "Reading Sources: The Power of Hellenistic Women—and Its Limits.")

The role reversals of male and female in Hellenistic art and literature, therefore, are indicators of genuine social change. Hellenistic women never attained the equality that sometimes exists between men and women today, but they did enjoy genuine though limited improvements in status. Men and women played new roles in a changed, complex world. The new Hellenistic philosophies and religions attempted to address that complexity.

THE TURN INWARD: NEW PHILOSOPHIES, NEW FAITHS

THE events of the Hellenistic era—emigration, a trend from independent city-states to monarchies and federal leagues, new extremes of wealth and poverty, and contact with foreign peoples and customs—all these generated uncertainty. In response, Greek culture was spread and transformed. As literacy expanded, more Greeks than ever before could participate in cultural debate. New philosophies and religions arose to meet new spiritual concerns, generating ideas that would be influential for centuries.

The meeting of Jews and Greeks proved to be just as significant. Challenged by Greek conquest, Greek colonization, and their own migration to Greek lands, Jews alternately embraced Hellenism and engaged in resistance, both cultural and armed. In the process, first Judaism and then Hellenism were changed forever.

■ Cynics, Stoics, Epicureans, and Skeptics

Although the polis lost its military and political preeminence in the fourth century B.C., philosophy continued to thrive. It was, however, much changed. With the city-state losing significance as a focus of loyalty, and with the Greek-reading public growing in size and geographic extent, Hellenistic philosophy paid less and less attention to politics. Moreover, as we have seen, Hellenistic science tended to become a separate discipline from philosophy. What was left as the prime subject of philosophy was ethics, the discovery of the best way to live. The essence of the good life, most philosophers agreed, was finding peace of mind, or freedom from troubles. Hellenistic philosophers won wide followings; indeed, for many people, primarily in the elite, philosophy became a way of life, even a religion.

Several competing philosophical schools emerged. The first to attract attention was Cynicism°. Never a widespread philosophy, Cynicism is nonetheless important as a precursor of the two most popular doctrines, Stoicism and Epicureanism. Finally, Skepticism rejected the main philosophies as mere dogmatism and proposed instead a commonsense attitude toward ethics.

The first Cynic was Diogenes° of Sinope (ca. 400–325 B.C.). An exile in Athens, Diogenes developed a philosophy that rejected all conventions. People find happiness, he decided, by satisfying their natural needs with simplicity. Accordingly, Diogenes chose a life of poverty. A beggar in rags, he delighted in shocking conventional morality. Famous for wit and shamelessness, he was nicknamed "Dog" (*kuon*) because the Greeks considered dogs to be shameless animals; his followers were called "Doglike" (*kunikoi*, whence the name *Cynic*).

Although he founded no school, Diogenes cast a wide shadow. Among those whom he indirectly influenced was Zeno (335–263 B.C.), who began one of the

---

Hipparchia (hih-PAR-kee-uh)

most important philosophical systems of antiquity: Stoicism°. Zeno came to Athens in 313 B.C. from Citium in Cyprus, a multi-ethnic city; he was possibly of Phoenician origin. Influenced by both Cynicism and Socratic philosophy, Zeno developed his own doctrines, which he taught in the *Stoa Poikile* ("Painted Porch," whence the name *Stoic*), a public building.

Like Plato and Aristotle, Zeno sought an absolute standard of good on which to base philosophical decisions. He found it in the divine reason (*logos*), which he considered the organizing principle of the universe and the guide to human behavior. The best life was a life in pursuit of wisdom—that is, a life of philosophy. Only that rare and forbidding figure, the Sage, could truly attain wisdom; ordinary people could merely progress toward it. What was required was study and the attempt to be free from all passion.

Stoicism may seem harsh. It is not surprising that *stoical* has come to describe austere indifference to pain. In some ways, however, Stoicism was comforting. First, freedom from passion was meant to bring peace of mind and happiness. Second, unlike Plato, the Stoics were empiricists—that is, they trusted the evidence of the senses, an attitude that they thought would inspire confidence and security. Third, the common share in divine logos entailed a common human brotherhood—led, to be sure, by a Greek-speaking elite. Fourth, because brothers have a duty to one another, the Stoics argued that a good person should play an active role in public life.

Like Hellenistic poets or portraitists, the Stoics emphasized the inner life. They believed that intentions matter. This Stoic belief was an important departure from Greek tradition, which tended to emphasize the outcome of an action, not its motivation. Stoicism also departed from traditional Greek localism, embracing a more cosmopolitan outlook. "This world is a great city, [and] has one constitution and one law," wrote Philo of Alexandria (30 B.C.–A.D. 45), a Stoic and a Jew. Many Stoics believed in a natural law or law of nations—that is, that overarching and common principles governed international relations.

With its emphasis on duty and order, Stoicism became popular with Greek ruling elites, both Macedonian kings and their opponents in city-states and leagues. Stoicism would enjoy even greater success with the Romans, who found its strictures congenial to their own stern morality and who used its concept of a universal state to justify their empire. A great deal of Stoicism was later embraced by early Christian writers.

Epicurus (341–270 B.C.), an Athenian citizen, founded his philosophical school at around the same time as Zeno founded Stoicism. There were other similarities: Both schools were empiricist and materialist (that is, they tended to trust the evidence of the senses), both sought peace of mind, and both inspired widespread followings. Epicurus, however, taught not in a public place but in a private garden. Whereas the Stoics encouraged political participation, Epicureans counseled withdrawal from the rough and tumble of public life. "Calm" and "Live in hiding" are famous Epicurean° maxims.

Epicurus's materialism is based on the atomic theory of Democritus (see page 95). It envisions a thoroughly mechanistic universe in which the gods exist but play no active role in events. Individuals need fear neither fickle deities nor an unhappy afterlife because the soul is merely a combination of atoms that ceases to exist after death. What might be the purpose of life in such an unheroic universe? The answer was the avoidance of pain and pursuit of pleasure. The latter component of Epicureanism was called hedonism (from *hedone,* Greek for "pleasure"), but not, as the word has come to mean today, indulgence in food, drink, or sex. Instead, Epicureans meant intellectual pleasure. Friendship and fraternity were Epicurean ideals—the private analogs, as it were, of Stoic brotherhood.

The Epicureans raised eyebrows and sometimes ire, occasionally suffering persecution by the state. They were accused of atheism and sensuality; to this day, *epicurean* connotes a fondness for luxury and pleasure. Classical Greek philosophy defined virtue as the highest good. The Epicurean emphasis on pleasure, even spiritual pleasure, seemed perverse to some. Yet Epicureanism was simple, sure of itself, practical, and offered both friendship and a sense of community. It became a popular philosophy, especially among the wealthy.

Skepticism° was founded by Pyrrho of Elis (ca. 360–270 B.C.), a Greek who traveled with Alexander to India. Like Stoics and Epicureans, Skeptics sought peace of mind. They rejected those thinkers' conclusions, however, on the grounds that they were dogmatic—that is, based not on positive proof but merely on opinion (*doxa*). Considering the senses unreliable, Skeptics rejected the commonsense approach of Stoics and Epicureans. They preferred to suspend judgment on the great philosophical questions (hence our term *skepticism* for a doubting state of mind). Whoever was able to do so could accept the customs of the community, avoid politics, and thereby obtain peace of mind.

Stoicism (STO-ih-sizm)

Epicurean (eh-pi-kyuh-REE-un)   **Skepticism** (SKEP-tih-sizm)

■ The Mystery Religions

The traditional Greek religion of the Olympian gods came under attack on every front in the Hellenistic era. First, the newly divinized kings stole the spotlight. Second, Hellenistic philosophers, like their Archaic and Classical predecessors, criticized the Olympians as primitive, unsophisticated, and immoral; their critique reached an ever widening audience. A third attack came from science and scholarship. Around 300 B.C., Euhemerus of Messene wrote in his *Sacred Scripture* that Zeus, Ouranos, and Kronos were not divine beings but merely great kings of the past who were rewarded with deification, much as a Hellenistic monarch might be. Debunking the Olympians became a popular literary pastime. For instance, Poseidon was said to be worshiped as the sea-god because he had been the first shipbuilder, and Hades, god of the dead, was said to have invented burial rites.

The Olympians retained their temples, but the rituals seemed hollow and antiquarian. What was to replace them? Of the several new religious movements that marked the age, three stand out: the divinization of kings, the cult of Tyche (Fortune), and the mystery religions.

Under the Ptolemies and Seleucids, the ruler-worship that Alexander had demanded became standard procedure. Many subjects no doubt considered the divinity of their king or queen merely a patriotic formality. Others treated the divinized monarch as something like a patron saint who could intercede in heaven. The old Greek city-states, especially the democracies, bristled at ruler-worship. "To transfer to men the honor due to the gods," the Athenian playwright Philippides (active ca. 300 B.C.) wrote, "is to dissolve the democracy."

He might have said much the same about the Hellenistic cult of Tyche° (Fortune or Luck), often worshiped as a goddess, sometimes as the protector of a particular city. The most famous example was the Tyche of Antioch, personified as a statue of a woman wearing the battlements of the city on her head as a kind of crown—a very popular statue, to judge by the many copies found around the Hellenistic world.

The third major Hellenistic trend, the mystery religions, offered similar solace to that of the philosophical schools: ethical guidance, comfort, release from worries, reassurance about death, and a sense of unity. Unlike philosophies, however, they achieved their goals through the revelation of secret doctrines, or "mysteries," into which worshipers were initiated. Long a feature of Greek religion, mystery cults grew in popularity during Hel-

A Cretan Dream Interpreter in Egypt   A painted stele (ca. 200 B.C.) advertises the services of a Greek in Memphis near the temple of Serapis, a Greco-Egyptian god. The inscription and pediment are Greek, while the pilasters, women, and sacred bull (facing an altar) are Egyptian. *(Egyptian Museum, Cairo)*

lenistic times. Consider the cult of Demeter at Eleusis, a town just outside the city of Athens. Demeter was the goddess of fertility. Her daughter, Persephone, supposedly spent half the year in the underworld, among the dead, but came back to earth each spring. As told to initiates, the myth symbolized the promise of a blessed afterlife. The precise details of the ritual remain unknown to this day. What is clear is that they included fasting, ritual bathing in the sea, a procession, and a torch-lit ceremony in the great hall at Eleusis.

Various new mystery religions from outside Greece became more popular, particularly the Hellenized Egyptian cults of Serapis and of Isis. Created under Ptolemy I, Serapis° was meant to combine Osiris, the Egyptian god of the afterlife, with Apis, the god of the Nile flood. Serapis also suggested Pluto, the Greek god of the underworld.

Tyche (TOO-kay)

Serapis (SEH-ruh-pis)

Bronze Coin with Menorah   This issue of Mattathias Antigone (r. 40–37 B.C.), the last Hasmonean king, is an early example of the use of the seven-branched candelabrum as the symbol of the Jewish people. A similar candelabrum was used in the Temple of Jerusalem.   *(Erich Lessing/Art Resource, NY)*

Hence, it is an early example of the common Hellenistic practice of religious syncretism, or fusion. Despite its roots, Serapis-worship had little appeal to native Egyptians, but the god became popular in the Greek world as patron of healing and sailing.

Another traditional Egyptian deity, Osiris's wife, Isis°, also became a popular Greek and, later, Roman goddess. Called the Goddess of Ten Thousand Names, Isis was said to symbolize all the female deities of antiquity. Hers was a cult of the afterlife and of the suffering but tender and loving mother; she was particularly popular among women. Thus, under Ptolemaic sponsorship, ancient Egyptian cults were recast and spread throughout the Greek-speaking world, circulating such notions as the suffering mother, the Last Judgment, and blessed eternal life after death. Early Christianity was much influenced by such Greco-Egyptian religious notions, but it was more directly the product of debate and ferment within Hellenistic Judaism.

Isis (EYE-sis)

■ Hellenistic Judaism

Few consequences of Alexander's conquests had so lasting an impact as the mixing of Greeks and Jews. Even before Alexander took Judea from the Persians in 332 B.C., the two peoples were in occasional contact, but in the Hellenistic era, their fates became intertwined. The Greeks governed Judea and then lost it to a Jewish independence movement. Meanwhile millions of Jews settled in Egypt, Syria, Anatolia, and Greece.

Changed by its contact with Greek culture, Hellenistic Judaism placed a greater emphasis on salvation, martyrdom, and individual study and prayer. Jewish responses to Greek culture varied: they ranged from admiration to resistance to outreach—that is, the desire to convert Greeks to Judaism. In its creative ferment, Hellenistic Judaism proved to have a long-lasting impact on the West.

Hellenistic Judea was governed first by the Ptolemies until 200 B.C., afterward by the Seleucids, until the establishment of an independent Jewish state in 142 B.C., which came under Roman suzerainty in 63 B.C. The Greeks were not absentee rulers. Rather, they estab-

∾ READING SOURCES

The Jews Struggle over Hellenism

Greek colonists introduced Hellenic customs to Palestine in the second century B.C. The Jewish response varied greatly, from eager assimilation to violent resistance, as is demonstrated by the following selections from the First Book of Maccabees, written around 100 B.C. The book is considered part of the Bible by some Christians but not by Jews.

At that time, lawless men arose in Israel and seduced many with their plea, "Come, let us make a covenant with the gentiles around us, because ever since we have kept ourselves separated from them we have suffered many evils." The plea got so favorable a reception that some of the people took it upon themselves to apply to the king, who granted them liberty to follow the practices of the gentiles. Thereupon they built a gymnasium in Jerusalem according to the customs of the gentiles. . . . They joined themselves to the gentiles and became willing slaves to evil-doing. . . .

The king [Antiochus IV] wrote to all his kingdom, for all to become one people and for each to abandon his own customs. All the gentiles agreed to the terms of the king's proclamation. Many Israelites, too, accepted his religion and sacrificed to idols and violated the Sabbath. . . .

Many Israelites strongly and steadfastly refused to eat forbidden food. They chose death in order to escape defilement by foods and in order to keep from violating the Holy Covenant, and they were put to death. Indeed, very great wrath had struck Israel. . . .

[An Israelite sacrifices to Zeus.] When [the Jewish priest] Mattathias saw this, he was filled with zeal and trembled with rage and let his anger rise, as was fitting; he ran and slew him upon the altar. At the same time he also killed the king's official in charge of enforcing sacrifices, and he destroyed the altar.

Source: The First Book of Maccabees 1:11–15, 41–43, 62–64; 2:24–25, in *The Anchor Bible,* vol. 41 (New York: Doubleday, 1976).

---

lished a large number of Greek colonies in and around Judea, especially under the Seleucids. Many Jews, especially wealthy ones, adopted some degree of Greek culture. Not all of these so-called Hellenizers abandoned Judaism. Indeed, some reshaped Jewish traditions to appeal to a Greek audience. Yet some Hellenizers abandoned Jewish customs altogether for the Greek gymnasium, theater, and political institutions. With the help of the Seleucid king Antiochus IV Epiphanes (r. 175–163 B.C.), Jewish Hellenizers in 175 B.C. had Jerusalem proclaimed a Greek polis, renamed Antioch, like many a Seleucid city; they even built a gymnasium at the foot of the Temple Mount. In 167 B.C. they went further by outlawing Sabbath observance, prohibiting circumcision, and rededicating the Temple to Olympian Zeus.

The traditionalists, however, resisted. Aided by the political ineptitude of their opponents, who raised taxes, they rallied the Jewish masses into opposition. Soon a guerrilla revolt began in the countryside, led by the Hasmonean family, also known as the Maccabees, whose successes are celebrated today by Jews during the religious holiday of Hanukkah. (See the box "Reading Sources: The Jews Struggle over Hellenism.")

The guerrilla movement developed into a disciplined armed uprising, which forced the Seleucids to tolerate an independent state under the Hasmonean dynasty. Religiously conservative at home, the state was expansionist abroad, conquering nearby territories such as the Galilee and forcing their inhabitants to convert to Judaism.

During the struggle over Hellenism, new elements of lasting significance became part of Judaism. First, the Jews developed a literature of spiritual resistance to the foreigner. This literature was apocalyptic—that is, it claimed to reveal dramatic, heretofore secret truths. Drawing on both biblical and Mesopotamian traditions, Jewish apocalyptic writing predicted a future cataclysm, when a royal redeemer would evict the foreigner and establish a new kingdom of Israel. The redeemer was often identified with another notion that first became popular in this era: the Messiah (literally, "anointed one"), someone anointed with oil signifying his election as king, a descendant of King David, who would save Israel. Another new aspect of Hellenistic Judaism was martyrdom, the notion of the holy sacrifice of one's life for a religious cause. There was also a growing belief in a final judgment day and resurrection, when God would raise the meritorious dead to live again on earth in their own bodies.

Hellenistic Judaism was far from monolithic. Various sects each proposed its own version of Judaism. Among these sects were the Sadducees° ("righteous ones"), a wealthy establishment group for whom the rituals of the Jerusalem Temple were the heart of Judaism. Their opponents, the Pharisees° ("those who separated themselves"), insisted on the validity of the oral tradition of interpretation alongside the written law of the Hebrew Bible and the Temple rituals. The Pharisees proposed a kind of democratization of Judaism, emphasizing study and prayer in small groups. A third group was the Essenes°, generally identified with the Qumran° community in the Judean desert (see page 192). As for the Hellenizers, although some were merely status seekers, others sincerely wished to combine Jewish ethical monotheism with the cosmopolitan spirit of Hellenistic civilization. They wanted, in short, to bring Jewish teachings to non-Jews, or Gentiles ("the nations").

Most Jews of the Hellenistic era lived outside Judea. The Diaspora had spread into (among other places) Syria, Anatolia, the Greek mainland, and Egypt, where a strong Jewish presence during the Persian period grew even stronger, particularly in Alexandria. Jews served the Ptolemies as soldiers, generals, bureaucrats, and tax collectors. They also prospered in private enterprise. Jewish success, as well as their maintenance of a separate culture, led to hostility among ordinary Greeks and Egyptians. Such attitudes spawned the first anti-Semitic

literature as well as sporadic violence that at times broke into riots and persecution. Yet there was also considerable admiration among Greek intellectuals for what they saw as Jewish virtue and antiquity.

Greek was the common tongue of Diaspora Jews. Between around 300 and 100 B.C. in Alexandria the Hebrew Bible was translated into Greek. Known as the Septuagint, or Seventy, from the number of translators who, legend has it, labored on the project, this text made the Bible accessible to a Jewish community increasingly unable to understand Hebrew or Aramaic. In later centuries, the Septuagint became the Old Testament of Greek-speaking Christians.

Foreign conversions and immigration into the Diaspora began to change the meaning of the word *Jew*. The word came to mean less "inhabitant of Judea" than "practitioner of Judaism." In short, *Jew* came to denote as much a religion as a nation.

SUMMARY

 HE major legacy of the Hellenistic age was its culture. This Greek-speaking culture—which now extended across the Persian Empire and encompassed Egypt—was dominated by inhabitants of or immigrants from old Greece and their descendants. The broad-minded ideas of Isocrates smoothed the way for the Greeks of different city-states to unite in kingdoms but offered less hope to others. We must not lose sight, however, of the continued flourishing of native cultures in the multi-ethnic kingdoms of the Ptolemies and Seleucids. Although Greeks and Macedonians dominated these regimes, they never imposed homogeneity, either in politics or in culture.

The most important Greek cultural development of the age was a retreat from a complex of values associated with the citizen-warrior ideal of the Classical city-state. The polis came under the shadow of federal leagues and kingdoms; philosophers questioned the very point of political activity. The hero gave way to the antihero, often a man whose success was dependent on the kindness and love of a woman. The female nude became as important a subject for sculptors as the male nude. Hellenistic women were freer than their predecessors in their movement and their ability to hold property and have some say in public life.

Stoic philosophers were far more interested in intention (versus action) than were their Classical predecessors. Yet their interest in the subject pales before that

---

Sadducees (SAJ-oo-seez)   **Pharisees** (FAIR-ih-seez)
Essenes (EH-seenz)   **Qumran** (koom-RAHN)

of the Jews, new actors on the Greek stage. Judaism placed an emphasis on the interior dialogue between humans and the divine that was more radical than anything in the Greek tradition. Some Greeks admired Jewish ethics, but few were willing to accept Jewish laws and rituals. Greeks did, however, borrow from other native religions. Hellenistic religion, therefore, was an exception to the general Greek indifference to native culture. The common denominator of the new religious teachings was a close, personal relationship with a savior-god who would guarantee comfort, peace, and eternal life after death.

Ironically, these very doctrines brought their Greek adherents closer to Hellenistic Judaism, which preached righteousness and justice in this life and the hereafter through subordination to the truth of the one and only God. The Jewish doctrine of messianic kingship might even have reminded Greeks of their own ruler cults. Imperceptibly, Hellenic and Hebraic were drawing closer. Under the Roman successor state, which we examine in Chapters 5 through 7, Hellenism and Judaism would be combined in a new and powerful form: Christianity.

■ Notes

1. Isocrates, "Panegyricus," trans. H. I. Marrou, in *A History of Education in Antiquity*, trans. George Lamb (New York: Mentor Books/New American Library, 1956), p. 130.
2. Romila Thapar, *Aśoka and the Decline of the Mauryas* (Oxford: Oxford University Press, 1961), p. 256.
3. Quoted in Charles Rowan Beye, *Ancient Greek Literature and Society*, 2d ed., rev. (Ithaca, N.Y.: Cornell University Press, 1987), p. 265.

■ Suggested Reading

Bowman, Alan K. *Egypt After the Pharaohs*. 1986. An excellent and highly readable introduction to the social history of the Ptolemaic and later periods.

Cohen, Shaye. *From the Maccabees to the Mishnah*. 1987. An excellent introduction by a distinguished scholar of Second Temple Judaism.

Grant, Michael. *From Alexander to Cleopatra: The Hellenistic World*. 1982. A lively and readable introduction, at its best on cultural history.

Green, P. *Alexander to Actium: An Essay in the Historical Evolution of the Hellenistic Age*. 1989. A collection of elegant essays synthesizing scholarship on a wide variety of topics in political, cultural, and social history.

Long, A. A. *Hellenistic Philosophy: Stoics, Epicureans, Sceptics*. 2d ed. 1986. A concise critical analysis of the main ideas and methods of thought of the major Hellenistic philosophers.

Walbank, F. W. *The Hellenistic World*. Rev. ed. 1993. A fine introduction, especially to political history, by a leading scholar of Polybius.

Wood, Michael. *In the Footsteps of Alexander the Great*. 1997. An engaging story that retraces Alexander's path today while it narrates his history; magnificent color photos of seldom-seen sites.

 For a searchable list of additional readings for this chapter, go to http://college.hmco.com.

Images of Cleopatra

"Cleopatra's nose: if it had been shorter, the whole face of the earth would have changed," wrote the French philosopher Blaise Pascal (1623–1662). He does Cleopatra an injustice. It was not a pretty face and classical features that enabled her to win the throne of Egypt (r. 51–30 B.C.), to obtain first Julius Caesar and then Mark Antony as ally and lover, and finally to come close to gaining control of the Roman Empire. Intelligence, daring, charm, and extraordinary diplomatic skill account for Cleopatra's success.

Let us consider the queen's manipulation of her public image—no mean task, given the fragility of Ptolemaic power in the first century B.C. Within Egypt, the monarch had to satisfy several different ethnic groups. Most important were the Greeks and Macedonians—who dominated government, the military, and the economy—and the native Egyptian majority. Daughter of Ptolemy XII (r. 80–51 B.C.), Cleopatra was supposed to rule jointly with her brother, but they had a falling-out. She wrested the throne from him and then from another brother and thus had to assert her legitimacy. Also, Ptolemaic Egypt had to project an image of unity to the Romans, who were threatening to annex it as they had the other Hellenistic monarchies.

Cleopatra, like earlier Ptolemaic monarchs, met these challenges by presenting two faces to the world. To the Greeks and Romans she was a Hellenistic monarch; to the Egyptians she was an ancient pharaonic queen. Look first at the bronze coin of Cleopatra issued at Alexandria probably in the 30s B.C. The queen is shown as a young woman. Her hair, tied in a bun at the nape of her neck, is in the so-called melon style often seen in Hellenistic female portraits. She wears a diadem (royal headband), its ends hanging behind her neck. More commonly worn by Hellenistic kings than by queens, the diadem signifies Cleopatra's claim to authority.

So does the queen's profile. She is portrayed with a prominent chin, a large mouth, and a rugged nose. These features may not be the standard attributes of beauty, but they are precisely the features that mark coin portraits of Cleopatra's father. By emphasizing Cleopatra's physical similarity to her father, the portrait artist perhaps subtly suggests her right to sit on his throne.

The side of the coin not shown here is far from subtle: its legend states clearly in Greek, "Queen Cleopatra."

The illustration is of an eagle and thunderbolt and a double cornucopia (horn of plenty) entwined with a diadem. The eagle and thunderbolt recall the Greek god Zeus, and the two cornucopias suggest fertility and prosperity. All are recurrent symbols of Ptolemaic royalty. The coin thus portrays Cleopatra as a Greek monarch, the worthy heir of her father. It would have been an effective image in Alexandria, a city dominated by Greeks and visited by Romans, but not in the countryside, especially south of the Nile Delta, in Upper Egypt, an area that was primarily Egyptian. Following dynastic custom, Cleopatra changed her image there.

In Upper Egypt, earlier Ptolemies frequently had been represented in stone in traditional pharaonic style, and they were great restorers of ancient Egyptian temples and builders of new ones. Look at the sculptural relief from the temple of the Egyptian cow-goddess Hathor at Dendera in Upper Egypt. The temple was a monumental structure initiated and underwritten by Ptolemy XII. Cleopatra, his daughter, added an enormous relief on the outside of the rear wall. Carved into the stone are two persons carrying offerings for Egyptian deities. The persons are Cleopatra (*left*) and her son Ptolemy XV Caesar, who ruled with his mother from 44 to 30 B.C. Alleged

Bronze Coin of Cleopatra *(Courtesy of the Trustees of the British Museum)*

to be the illegitimate son of Julius Caesar, Ptolemy XV was commonly known as Caesarion or "little Caesar." At Dendera, however, he and his mother are shown neither as Romans nor as Greeks but as Egyptians.

Look closely at Cleopatra. She wears a long body-hugging robe. On her head is a royal headdress with symbols of the Egyptian gods: the lyre-shaped cow horns and sun-disk of Hathor, the tall plumes of Isis, and the ram's horn of Amon. Caesarion is shown as a pharaoh, wearing the double crown of Upper and Lower Egypt. Mother and son offer incense to the local deities. The small figure between Caesarion and Cleopatra is his *ka*, or soul.

Cleopatra's face is in profile but otherwise has very little in common with her portrait on the Alexandrian coin. Although the features are stylized pharaonic commonplaces, the shape of her head perhaps echoes the elegant and graceful relief portraits of Hatshepsut (r. 1479–1457 B.C.), the most famous female pharaoh before Cleopatra.

Cleopatra commissioned other artworks and monuments in the native style in the Nile Valley. This was the custom of her dynasty, and Cleopatra had absorbed its traditions, but she stands second to none of the Ptolemies in shrewdness and subtlety. She was the only Ptolemaic monarch to learn to speak Egyptian, and she was the only one to come even close to gaining the upper hand over Rome. As the artifacts shown here indicate, she was able to put on an Egyptian face as easily as a Greek one, but she never lost sight of her true interests.

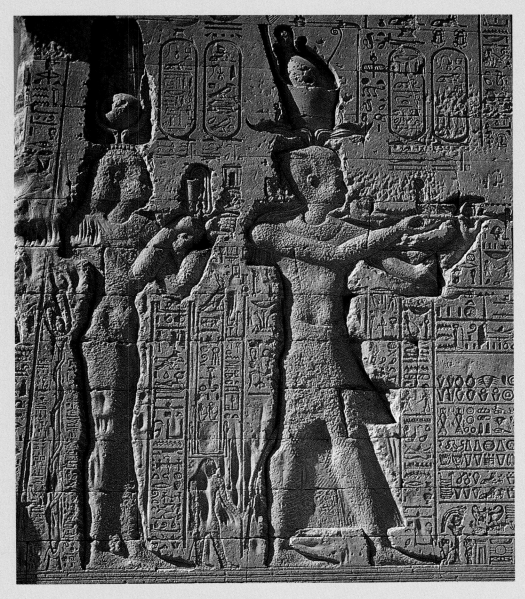

Relief of Cleopatra and Caesarion *(Erich Lessing/ Art Resource, NY)*

CHAPTER 5

Rome: From Republic to Empire ca. 509–31 B.C.

ERE is the Roman Forum. The photograph takes us from an arch celebrating military triumph to the ruins of, first, a public hall; then, behind it, a temple; and, in the rear, the remains of buildings on the Palatine Hill. On this hill, shepherds founded the city of Rome, and on this hill, centuries later, emperors lived. We see, in short, the civic center of the city destined to give the Western world many of its fundamental ideas about government and empire.

The ancient Romans were a practical people. Virgil (70–19 B.C.), for example, the greatest Roman poet (see pages 179–180), celebrates not his countrymen's artistry or cultivation but rather their pragmatic accomplishments:

> For other peoples will, I do not doubt,
> still cast their bronze to breathe with softer features,
> or draw out of the marble living lines,
> plead causes better, trace the ways of heaven
> with wands and tell the rising constellations;
> but yours will be the rulership of nations,
> remember, Romans, these will be your arts:
> to teach the ways of peace to those you conquer,
> to spare defeated peoples, tame the proud.[1]

The Romans turned an Italian city-state into one of the largest empires in history, including all the countries of the Mediterranean as well as large parts of western Asia and of northern and central Europe. By holding this empire for centuries and by promoting prosperity in every corner, Rome planted in what would become Britain, France, Germany, and Spain (among other places) the seeds of the advanced civilizations of the Mediterranean.

The Forum, Rome.
(Mike Yamshita/Woodfin Camp & Associates)

Rome is no less important for its influence on the Western civic tradition. Much of the modern vocabulary of politics, from *president* to *inauguration* to *forum*, can be traced back to Rome. After an early period of monarchy, Rome was for centuries a republic (Latin, *res publica*, literally "public thing") before becoming essentially a monarchy again under the Caesars. The Roman Republic mixed popular power with government controlled by wealthy landowners. The government was divided into three branches, which created a system of checks and balances that tended toward consensus. The result was efficiency and, for centuries, stability.

Roman politicians sought to control ordinary citizens but in some ways were more flexible than Greek democrats: unlike Greece, Rome extended its citizenship to a large population, first throughout Italy and then across its entire empire. The modern nation-state with its mass citizenship owes much to Rome. Indeed, although Rome was not democratic, modern democracy—that is, popular government with a large population, whose officials are elected by the people—has roots in the Roman Republic as well as in the Greek city-state.

Fueled by fear, ambition, and greed, Roman expansion generated its own momentum. Rome's arrogance matched its success: in consolidating power over huge territories, the Romans committed atrocities, enslaved whole peoples, and destroyed cities with little provocation. Ironically, military success slowly undermined both Rome's political stability at home and the socioeconomic basis of its army. Meanwhile, the Romans showed great open-mindedness in borrowing from other societies, in particular from the Greeks, to whom the Republic owed great cultural debts. Also fascinating is the shrewdness and generosity with which the Romans shared their citizenship with the elites whom they had conquered, thereby winning their loyalty and strengthening Rome's grip on their territories.

Historians conventionally divide the Republic into three periods: Early (509–287 B.C.), Middle (287–133 B.C.), and Late (133–31 B.C.). This chapter begins with the origins of the city of Rome in the early first millennium B.C. and then traces the Republic from its foundation to its imperial conquests to its collapse under their weight. Success spoiled Rome. The unintended consequences of conquest on Rome's society, politics, and culture led to a revolution that, in the century beginning in 133 B.C., saw the Republic's downfall.

QUESTIONS TO CONSIDER

- How was the Roman Republic governed, and to what degree did that government shape the later political tradition of the West?
- How much access to power did women, conquered peoples, and slaves have in Roman society?
- How did Rome acquire an empire that stretched from Britain to Iraq?
- What were the unintended consequences of conquest on Rome, and how did they lead to revolution that destroyed the Republic?

TERMS TO KNOW

Latin	triumph
res publica	legion
Etruscans	Gracchi
senate	Caesar
paterfamilias	Cicero
Punic Wars	Cato the Elder

Before the Republic, 753–509 B.C.

HE ancient Romans believed that their city was founded on April 21, 753 B.C., by Romulus, a descendant of refugees from the Trojan War. Although the name "Romulus" supplies a convenient etymology for "Rome," little stock can be placed in this story. Nevertheless, archaeology provides a kind of confirmation. The first evidence of buildings in Rome comes from the eighth century B.C. A simple village of farmers and shepherds—a collection of huts—was established then on the Palatine Hill, one of the seven hills on which Rome would cluster and the place where tradition puts the settlement of 753 (see inset, Map 5.2, on page 150).

Archaeological evidence does not mean that we have to accept mythology as history, but it does revive basic questions: What were Rome's origins, and how did it grow? Are seeds of Roman greatness visible in its early history? By examining the data of archaeology and of those elements in ancient historiography that seem to be based on accurate tradition, we can answer these questions, at least in outline.

■ Archaic Rome and Its Neighbors

Italy is a long peninsula, shaped roughly like a boot, extending about 750 miles from the Alps into the Mediterranean (see Map 5.1). In the far north, the high Alps provide a barrier to the rest of Europe. To the east, the Adriatic Sea separates Italy from modern Slovenia and Croatia; to the west, the Tyrrhenian Sea faces the large islands of Sardinia and Corsica (and the smaller but iron-rich island of Elba) and, beyond, the coasts of France and Spain. Off the "toe" of the Italian boot, and separated from the mainland by a narrow, 3-mile strait of water, is the large island of Sicily, rich farm country in ancient times. Sicily is only 90 miles from North Africa. In short, Italy is centrally located in the Mediterranean. It was both a target for conquerors and a springboard for conquest.

Italy contained some of the ancient Mediterranean's most fertile and metal-rich land. From the alluvial watershed of the Po and Adige Rivers in the north, the agriculturally rich plains of Etruria° (modern Tuscany), Latium° (the region of Rome), and Campania (the region of Naples) unfold southward down Italy's west coast. Although the Apennine° Mountains run north–south along most of the Italian peninsula, they are low com-

---

Etruria (ee-TROO-ree-uh)   **Latium** (LAY-shum)
Apennine (AP-puh-nine)

CHRONOLOGY	
753–509 B.C.	Monarchy (traditional dates)
509–287 B.C.	Early Republic
449 B.C.	Law of the Twelve Tables
338 B.C.	Latin League dissolved; Roman citizenship extended
289 B.C.	First Roman coinage (traditional date)
287–133 B.C.	Middle Republic
264–146 B.C.	Punic Wars
240 B.C.	First play produced at Rome
197 B.C.	Rome defeats Macedonian phalanx
146 B.C.	Rome destroys Carthage and Corinth
133–31 B.C.	Late Republic
133–121 B.C.	The Gracchi
107–78 B.C.	Marius and Sulla
66–62 B.C.	Pompey's eastern campaigns
63 B.C.	Consulship of Cicero
58–51 B.C.	Caesar conquers Gaul
44 B.C.	Caesar assassinated
31 B.C.	Antony defeated at Actium; Octavian in power

pared with the Alps and contain many passes, permitting the movement of armies.

In the first millennium B.C., Italy was a hodgepodge of peoples and languages. They included the Etruscans in the north, Greek colonists in southern Italy and in Sicily, and such mountain peoples as the Sabines and the Samnites. Latium was home to a number of small Latin-speaking towns, one of them Rome. In the fifth century B.C. another important people arrived on the Italian scene: Celts (called Gauls by the Romans), large numbers of whom crossed the Alps and settled in northern Italy after roughly 500 B.C. Most of these various peoples spoke Indo-European languages, of which Latin, the language of the Romans (as well as other peoples of Latium), was one.

Rome's location in Italy was central and protected. Rome is located in Latium, which is about half-way

Latium

0 15 Km.
0 15 Mi.

Lake Sabatinus
Veii
Tibur
AEQUI
Rome
Gabii
L A T I N S
Tusculum
Praeneste
HERNICI
Ostia
Lake Albanus
Mt. Albanus
Anagnia
Lavinium
Lake Nemorensis
Cora
Ardea
Norba
V O L S C I
Satricum
Privernum
Antium
Tyrrhenian Sea

Roman territory, ca. 500 B.C.

ALPS

VENETI

Adige
Po
Mantua
LIGURES
Felsina (Bologna)
ETRUSCANS
Spina
Ravenna

Ligurian Sea
Arno
Faesulae
Volaterrae
Arretium
UMBRI
PICENTES
Populonia
ETRURIA
Perusia
Clusium
Vetulonia
Elba
Volsinii
APENNINES
SABINES
Vulci
ETRUSCANS
Tiber
Tarquinii
Veii
SAMNITES
Caere
Rome
APULI
LATIUM
LATINS

Adriatic Sea

ILLYRIA

Alalia
LIGURES
Corsica

Capua
CAMPANIA
Cumae
Neapolis (Naples)
Puteoli
Herculaneum
Pithecusae
Pompeii
Bay of Naples
OSCI
MESSAPII
Tarentum

Sardinia
SARDI
LUCANI
Gulf of Tarentum

Tharros

BRUTTII
Sybaris

Tyrrhenian Sea
MAGNA GRAECIA

Carales
Croton

Mediterranean Sea

Messana
Panormus
SICANI
SICULI
Sicily

Utica
Cape Bon
Acragas (Agrigentum)
Syracuse
Hippo Regius
Carthage

NORTH AFRICA

Malta

0 50 100 Km.
0 50 100 Mi.

Etruscans of Etruria
Expansion of Etruscans
Greeks
Carthaginians
OSCI Other peoples

Etruscan Tomb Painting
This wall painting from Tarquinia shows a married aristocratic couple at a banquet. The style of the figures is derived from Greek art, but the depiction of husband and wife dining on the same couch is characteristically Etruscan. *(National Museum, Tarquinia/Scala/Art Resource, NY)*

down the Italian peninsula. Located 15 miles inland on the Tiber°, the largest river on Italy's west coast, Rome had access to the sea. A midstream island makes Rome the first crossing place upstream from the Tiber's mouth, offering the Romans freedom of movement north and south. Yet strategically, Rome was protected. It was far enough from the sea to be safe from raiders and pirates. And its seven hills offered a natural defense.

In the seventh century B.C., Archaic Rome (as the pre-Republican period is called) began to change from a large village into a city. In this era Rome saw its first stone houses, its first public building, and its first forum or civic center. In the sixth century, streets, walls, drains, temples, and a racetrack followed. What caused the transformation? Probably the key factor was contact with

Magna Graecia°, the Greek colonies to the south (see Map 5.1). Established in the eighth and seventh centuries B.C., the colonies transported westward the sophisticated urban civilization of the eastern Mediterranean.

More controversial is the impact of Rome on its neighbors to the north, the Etruscans°. The twelve Etruscan city-states were organized in a loose confederation centered in Etruria. They grew wealthy from the mining of iron, copper, and silver, from piracy, from trade, and from a network of influential Etruscan emigrants throughout central Italy, possibly including Rome's last three kings (traditionally dated 616–509 B.C.).

Most scholars argue that the Etruscans conquered pre-Republican Rome and left a significant cultural and material legacy. Recent research, however, suggests a pattern of cross-fertilization and emigration rather than conquest; it further argues that the Etruscan legacy in Rome was superficial. According to this new view, to the extent that any outside culture influenced Archaic Rome, it was the Greeks—who also influenced the Etruscans and other central Italian peoples, for that matter. The Etruscan city-states were similar to Rome; they were its peer, not its elder sibling.

Tiber (TY-ber)

Map 5.1 Early Italy and Region of City of Rome
Early Italy comprised a variety of terrain and peoples. Rome was located in the central Italian region of Latium. The Alps separate Italy from northern Europe. The Apennine mountain range runs almost the entire length of the Italian peninsula. Much of the rest of Italy is fertile plain.

Magna Graecia (MAG-nuh GREE-shuh)
Etruscans (ee-TRUS-kunz)

Since most societies resist outside influence, it makes sense to downplay the Etruscan impact on Rome, as the new theory argues. Yet too little evidence survives from Archaic Rome to allow a firm conclusion. Likewise, our inability to decipher the Etruscan language (which is neither Indo-European nor Semitic) also dictates caution. At least we can be certain of some things about the Etruscans: They were great artists, for example, and Etruscan elite women had high status compared with their Greek or Roman counterparts. Etruscan women kept their own names, and Etruscan children bore the names of both parents. In addition, Etruscan elite women were permitted to attend athletic contests in spite of the presence of naked male athletes.

■ The Roman Monarchy

Tradition says that Rome was ruled by seven kings before the foundation of the Republic. Although the number of kings may be a later invention, their existence is undoubted. In addition to traces of the monarchy in Republican institutions, there is archaeological proof: a form of the Latin word *rex* ("king"), for example, has been found inscribed on a Roman monument from the early sixth century B.C. The king's power, called *imperium* (from *imperare*, "to command"), was very great, embracing religious, military, and judicial affairs.

The king was advised by a council of elders, called the "fathers" (*patres* in Latin) or the "senate" (*senatus,* from *senex,* "old man"). In theory the senate was primarily an advisory body, but in practice it was very powerful. Senators were the heads of the most important families in Rome, so the king rejected their advice at his peril. Romans spoke of the senate's *auctoritas,* a quasi-religious prestige.

Most senators were patricians°, as early Rome's hereditary aristocracy was known. The rest of the people, the bulk of Roman society, were called plebeians°. Plebeians were free; most were ordinary people, though some were wealthy. Patricians monopolized the senate and priesthoods, and they did not intermarry with plebeians.

The whole people, probably both patricians and plebeians, met in an assembly organized in thirty local units, or *curiae,* hence the name *curiate assembly.* Though the assembly's numbers were large, its powers were limited. Before becoming law, resolutions of the assembly required approval by the senate.

Early Rome was a class-based society, but it was open to foreigners. Among others, Etruscans, Sabines, and Latins—as the inhabitants of other Latin-speaking towns are called—came to settle in Rome. The Tarquins, whose family is traditionally said to have provided two kings of Rome, including the last, may have originally come from Corinth. Unlike Athenians, who tried to hide the presence of immigrants in their country by a myth of indigenous origins, Romans openly discussed their mixed roots. Foreigners at first had low status, but they gained equality around 550 B.C., for pragmatic purposes. Rome needed soldiers to fight its wars; in order to expand the body of loyal infantrymen, the immigrants were granted citizenship—a reform traditionally associated with King Servius Tullius (578–535 B.C.).

Servius probably introduced to Rome the hoplite phalanx (see page 71), with immigrants included in its ranks. The changes in the army contributed to the process that, within several generations of Servius's reform, took Rome from monarchy to republic.

GOVERNMENT AND SOCIETY IN THE EARLY AND MIDDLE REPUBLICS, CA. 509–133 B.C.

TRADITION says that the Roman Republic was established in 509 B.C., when the kings were overthrown. Nowadays, scholars envision a long process rather than a single, dramatic upheaval. In either case, the new Republic was destined to have a unique influence on Western political institutions, so it is worth a close look.

The Republic differed from the monarchy in two basic ways. First, the Republic stood for liberty, which for the Romans meant both freedom from the arbitrary power of a king and freedom to participate in public affairs. Second, the Republic was a commonwealth, in Latin, *res publica°,* literally "public thing," as opposed to *res privata,* "private thing," as the Romans characterized monarchy. As a kingdom Rome belonged to the royal family, but as a republic it belonged to the Roman people. In theory, the Roman people was sovereign—that is, the people ruled the state.

But which people? This is a key question because the Romans did *not* embrace another principle that might seem to follow from liberty: equality. Rather, they believed in order, balance, and competition, all of which are central themes of Roman Republican history. Roman

---

patricians (puh-TRIH-shunz)   **plebeians** (pleh-BEE-unz)   **res publica** (rays POO-blee-kuh)

society and culture, moreover, were conservative. Once the young Republic had its new values in place, it tried to maintain those values over the centuries with little change. Nor did the Republic give up entirely on the old values of the monarchy. Rather, it continued some of those values.

■ What Kind of Republic?

The Early Republic (509–287 B.C.) witnessed centuries of social and political conflict. The Middle Republic (287–133 B.C.) was a shorter period of relative stability and consensus. Then social and political conflict broke out again with a vengeance in the Late Republic (133–31 B.C.), ultimately rendering the Republic a terminal blow.

The best and most even-handed ancient analyst of Roman politics is the historian Polybius° (ca. 200–118 B.C.). A Greek and former hostage who lived in Rome, Polybius observed his adopted city with an outsider's discerning eye. Polybius argued that in the Middle Republic of his day, Rome was a "mixed constitution," balancing the power of the masses with the authority of the elite. The fortunate result was a strong and stable state.

Underlying Polybius's appraisal is a division of Roman political institutions into three branches: executive, deliberative, and legislative. Influenced by the Romans, the American founders adopted a similar division, but with the legislative and deliberative functions combined and a judicial branch added. In Rome, various magistrates of the executive branch administered justice, in addition to their other responsibilities. The Roman senate, which made up the deliberative branch, was far more influential than the U.S. Senate, although during the Republic the Roman senate could not make law. The Roman legislative branch consisted of several popular assemblies.

The three parts of the Roman constitution, then, were the magistrates, the senate, and the people. For Polybius, the assemblies were a democratic element in Rome's constitution; the senate, an oligarchic element; and the magistrates, a royal element.

Not all historians agree with Polybius. His critics argue that he was misled by the democratic façade of Rome's several popular assemblies. In the last analysis, they maintain, the Roman oligarchy controlled the state. The oligarchs monopolized high office, both civil and military; rigged elections; dominated proceedings in the senate; set the course of cultural life; and controlled religion in a society that knew no separation of church and state.

Polybius (po-LIH-bee-us)

Although these criticisms contain some truth, they overstate the case. Rome experienced real political competition and a real need to court the voters; all laws were debated in public meetings, often fiercely debated; candidates for office ran ambitious campaigns, which suggests that the results were not rigged; the people's representatives could veto any action taken by public officials; and freed slaves became citizens, which was rarely true in a democratic Greek state such as Athens. Of course the wealthy elite had considerable power, but that power was limited, which means that, as Polybius writes, the Roman political system was balanced and competitive.

In short, Rome was a mixed constitution. It was not always a stable society, however. Let us survey Rome's political institutions and then examine the conflicts of the Early Republic and the compromises that resolved them in the middle era. We will turn to the revolution that destroyed the Late Republic at the end of this chapter.

■ Political Institutions

Executive power lay in the hands of Rome's magistrates. They were more powerful and more elite figures than their counterparts in Greek democracies. Magistrates were elected to office by the Roman people rather than chosen by lottery, as in Greek democracy. Election required extensive campaigning, which in turn necessitated money and connections, but also an ability to persuade the people. Magistracies were time-consuming jobs, but offered no salary, unlike public office in Greek democracy. Thus, only a wealthy elite few could afford to be magistrates.

Eager for strong, effective magistrates but ever fearful that power might lead to corruption, Rome imposed the principles of *collegiality* and *annuality* on its officials. Every magistrate was accountable to one or more colleagues, and the tenure of office was only one year. The chief magistrates were eventually called consuls, of which there were two. Each consul had the power to veto the other's actions. Like the former king, each consul had *imperium*, the power to issue commands and order punishments, including execution.

From about 500 B.C. to about 300 B.C., other magistracies emerged to assist the consul as administration grew more complex. In addition to those annual magistrates were two censors, older men elected once every few years for eighteen-month terms. At first their job was to supervise the census, the military register of citizens that recorded each man's property class. Later, the censors

A Clear Sign of Power   The lictor, or official, depicted in this bronze statuette (ca. first century A.D.) accompanied Roman magistrates, who had *imperium,* the power to issue punishments resulting in execution. That power is visible in the fasces he holds—an ax in a bundle of wooden rods bound with straps.   *(Courtesy of the Trustees of the British Museum)*

became, as it were, supervisors of public morals, since they could punish "bad" citizens.

The Republic's government adapted flexibly to trying circumstances. In times of emergency, for example, the Republic turned power over to a single magistrate. The dictator, as he was called, made decisions that were beyond appeal, but he held office for only six months.

The deliberative branch of the Roman constitution consisted of the senate, which guided and advised the magistrates. During most of the Republic, the senate consisted of three hundred men, each of whom served for life. In the third century B.C. and later, every senator was a former magistrate. Senators possessed great authority. They supervised public expenditures and were for all practical purposes in charge of foreign policy.

The legislative branch of the constitution consisted of four popular assemblies: the curiate assembly, the centuriate assembly, the council of the plebs, and the tribal assembly. Like the political system as a whole, Roman assemblies combined democratic and nondemocratic features. On the one hand, all decisions were made by majority vote, and only after speeches had been heard or campaigns conducted. Assembly meetings were often preceded by public meetings, typically in the forum, in which issues were debated in lively discussion. Women, free noncitizens, and even slaves could attend. On the other hand, voting took place by groups and those groups were unrepresentative. Furthermore, in contrast to Greece, in Rome assembly participants stood rather than sat down and received no salary for attendance.

Although the curiate assembly of the monarchy survived, in the Republic it was relegated to a largely ceremonial role. The centuriate assembly held real power: it elected magistrates, voted on laws and treaties, accepted declarations of war and peace, and acted as a court in cases of treason, homicide, and appeals from the magistrates' decisions. This assembly offered popular participation but under strict control. The assembly was divided according to wealth into census classes of fighting men. The classes voted in order of wealth. First came the equestrians, or cavalrymen, then five classes of infantrymen, and finally the *proletarii* ("breeders"), men too poor to provide their own arms. Because the equestrians and the first class of infantry—the wealthiest men—constituted a majority, in many elections the four remaining classes of infantry and the proletarii did not vote at all.

The two other assemblies were the council of the plebs and the tribal assembly. The latter supplanted the former; in fact it became Rome's main legislative body in the third century B.C., outstripping the centuriate assembly in making laws. To understand the evolution and workings of the tribal assembly, we turn now to the class conflicts in Rome during the fifth through third centuries B.C.

■ Conflict of the Orders

The Early Republic was a crucible. Social and political conflict, usually considered a struggle between the patrician and plebeian orders, severely tested the Roman state between 494 and 287 B.C. A relatively stable state emerged, one that assigned the leading role to a widened elite (though still a relatively narrow one) while offering a measure of popular power. As Rome reached a domestic political consensus, it presented an ever stronger military front to its external opponents. By 300 B.C., Rome was ready to grow from local power to dominance in Italy and then the Mediterranean.

Tradition gives Rome only 136 patrician families in 509 B.C., but they dominated the Early Republic. The plebs, in contrast, comprised masses of poor peasants and a tiny number of men who, though wealthy, were not patricians; there were plebeian artisans, traders, and shopkeepers, but they composed only a small part of the population. In their own ways, the various plebeian groups each wanted to break patrician power. Wealthy plebeians wanted unrestricted access to high office, from which they had been largely excluded. Ordinary plebeians demanded relief from debt, redistribution of land, and codification and publication of the law. For a century and a half, the two groups of plebeians made common cause, writing an important chapter in the history of political resistance.

Debt and hunger loomed large in the Early Republic. A form of debt-bondage called nexum° forced a free man who defaulted on a loan to work off what he owed, often for the rest of his life. Plebeians wanted nexum abolished. The average peasant farm was too small to feed a family, rendering most peasants dependent on public land for farming and grazing. Time and again throughout Republican history, however, public land was occupied by the wealthy, who denied or restricted access to the poor. The only plebeian hope was to change the system.

The story of the plebs in the fifth century B.C. was one of solidarity. They organized themselves as kind of a state within the state, complete with their own assembly (the council of the plebs) and officials (the tribunes of the plebs). The decisions of the council of the plebs, called *plebiscita* (from which *plebiscite* comes), were

binding only on the plebs; they did not receive the full force of law for over two hundred years. Yet the plebs did not retreat. On several occasions during the Early Republic they resorted to secession: the plebs as a whole left the city, often for the Aventine Hill, where they stayed until their grievances were addressed (see inset, Map 5.2).

The ten tribunes°, elected annually by the plebs, were the people's champions. A tribune's house stood always open to any plebeian who needed him, and he could not leave the city limits. Inside the city of Rome, a tribune also had the right to veto any act of the magistrates, assembly, or senate that harmed plebeians. In return, the plebs swore to treat the tribunes as sacrosanct and to lynch anyone who harmed them.

Impressive as plebeian activity was, the patricians had formidable resources with which to oppose them. They controlled important priesthoods and had many supporters in the military. Furthermore, the new tribal assembly, created around the same time as the council of the plebs, used a system of representation that heavily favored landowners such as patricians. The tribal assembly elected lower magistrates and, like the centuriate assembly, voted on laws and acted as a court of appeals.

Nevertheless, the plebeians pressed onward, wringing concession after concession from the patricians, until finally the patricians retreated: they decided to neutralize the opposition by meeting the main demands of the plebeian elite. The outcome was a new, combined patrician-plebeian nobility. The patricians had wisely decided to compromise to preserve most of their privileges. The personnel changed, but the elite continued to have great power in Rome.

The specific events in the patrician-plebeian conflict follow two lines of development: concessions to wealthy plebeians and concessions to poor ones. A key moment came in 449 B.C. with publication of the law code known as the "Twelve Tables," eventually, if not at first, on twelve bronze tablets in the Forum. By modern standards, the code was primitive and severe, but its very existence was a plebeian victory because published law became accessible and dependable. Unfortunately, the complex legal procedure remained a secret of the priests for another 150 years, which ensured that no poor man could go to court without the help of a patron.

Continued plebeian pressure slowly yielded other gains through the fourth century B.C. Around 445 B.C., the patricians accepted patrician-plebeian intermarriage, but it took nearly another eighty years, until 367 B.C., until they agreed to plebeian consuls. That same

---

nexum (NEKS-em)

tribunes (TRIB-yoonz)

Shrine of a Wealthy Household This painting from Pompeii shows the spirit of the paterfamilias in a toga, which is wrapped around his head in keeping with Roman procedures of sacrifice. He is flanked by the spirits of departed ancestors. A snake symbolizes fertility. *(Alinari/Art Resource, NY)*

year saw a debt-relief law, and nexum was finally abolished in 326 B.C.

Finally, in 287 B.C., the merging of patrician and plebeian orders culminated in a law that made decisions of the council of the plebs and the tribal assembly binding on the whole community. Rome's new, combined patrician-plebeian elite was based on wealth, not heredity. The overwhelming majority of Romans remained excluded, but they had won important concessions too: freedom from nexum, access to the published laws, increased power for their assembly, and, most important, protection from arbitrary power via the tribunes.

The problems of poverty continued, but during these same Early Republican years the poor began to find another form of relief in the new land that Rome acquired through conquest.

■ The Roman Household

The Latin word *familia* is broader than the English word *family.* Better translated as "household," it connotes slaves, animals, and property, as well as the members of a nuclear family and their ancestors or descendants. The familia was the basic unit of Roman society. A center of both production and consumption, it was also a model

of political authority. In theory, though not always in practice, the Roman household was an authoritarian institution governed by a male; thus, the familia is an example of patriarchy.

The legal head of the familia was the *paterfamilias*°, the oldest living male—usually the father in a nuclear family, though occasionally the grandfather or, in cases of unusual longevity, the great-grandfather. According to Roman law, the paterfamilias had supreme power within the household. Although he was supposed to call a council of senior male relatives to consult on major decisions, he was not required to follow their advice. He had the right to sell family members into slavery and the rarely used power to kill an errant wife or child. A son, no matter how old, was always legally subject to the authority of a living paterfamilias. Only the paterfamilias, moreover, could own property free and clear. Thus, a 30-year-old man might be under the authority of his paterfamilias and dependent on him for an allowance.

Roman respect for the paterfamilias stemmed from Roman esteem for ancestors, who were more important than in Greek culture. All patricians and some plebeians belonged to a *gens*° (plural, *gentes*), a kinship group that traced its ancestry back to a purported common ancestor. All Roman males had a personal and family name, and patricians and elite plebeians also had a third (middle) name, indicating their gens: for example, Gaius Julius Caesar, whose personal name Gaius was followed by the gens name Julius and the familia name Caesar.

In theory, the paterfamilias was the focus of power in the household, but practice was more complex. The sources are full of fathers who showed affection, love, and even indulgence toward their children. Moreover, Roman women usually married in their late teens and men in their late twenties. Given the low life expectancies, it was common for a man of 25 to have already buried his father. Many, perhaps even most, adult males were independent of a paterfamilias.

Unlike men, Roman women never became legally independent, even on the death of a paterfamilias. Instead of receiving a personal name, a daughter was called by the name of her father's gens. For example, Gaius Julius Caesar's daughter was called Julia; if Caesar had had a second daughter, she would have been Julia Secunda ("Julia the Second"). Although fathers were expected to support all male children, they had to support only the first of their daughters. In other words, they were free to "expose" additional daughters—that is, leave them in the open to die or, as was perhaps more likely, to

---

paterfamilias (PAH-ter-fah-MIL-ee-us) **gens** (jenz)

The Rape of Lucretia

The historian Livy attributes the founding of the Roman Republic to outrage over the rape of the aristocratic woman Lucretia by Sextus Tarquinius, son of King Tarquinius Superbus. Though of dubious historicity, the story reveals a great deal about Roman attitudes toward gender, honor, and their political implications.

[A guest in Lucretia's house in her husband's absence, Sextus Tarquinius demands that she sleep with him.] But all in vain; not even the fear of death could bend her will. "If death will not move you," Sextus cried, "dishonor shall. I will kiss you first, then cut the throat of a slave and lay his naked body by your side. Will they not believe that you have been caught in adultery with a servant—and paid the price?" Even the most resolute chastity could not have stood against this dreadful threat.

[After being violated by Sextus Tarquinius, Lucretia summons her husband and father.] "In your bed, Collatinus, is the impress of another man. My body only has been violated. My heart is innocent, and death will be my witness. Give me your solemn promise that the adulterer shall be punished—he is Sextus Tarquinius. He it was who last night came as my enemy disguised as my guest, and took his pleasure of me. . .

"What is due to him," Lucretia said, "is for you to decide. As for me, I am innocent of fault, but I will take my punishment. Never shall Lucretia provide a precedent for unchaste women to escape what they deserve." With these words she drew a knife from under her robe, drove it into her heart, and fell forward, dead.

Her father and husband were overwhelmed with grief. While they stood weeping helplessly, Brutus [aristocrat and family friend] drew the bloody knife from Lucretia's body, and holding it before him cried: "By this girl's blood—none more chaste till a tyrant wronged her—and by the gods, I swear that with sword and fire, and whatever else can lend strength to my arm, I will pursue Lucius Tarquinius Superbus, his wicked wife, and all his children, and never again will I let them or any other man be King in Rome."

Source: Livy, *The Early History of Rome*, trans. Aubrey de Sélincourt (Harmondsworth, England: Penguin, 1971), pp. 98–99.

---

be adopted or raised as a slave. A father also arranged a daughter's marriage and provided her with a dowry. In theory, again, the customs suggest a most severe relationship, but the evidence shows considerable father-daughter affection, including married daughters who sought advice or aid from their fathers.

Most women in early Rome married *cum manu*° (literally, "with hand")—that is, they were "handed over" to their husbands, who became their new paterfamilias. Even so, Roman wives and mothers had more prestige and freedom than their counterparts in Classical Greece. Legends of early Rome mention some who were peacemakers, negotiators, or catalysts of quarrels among men. (See the box "Reading Sources: The Rape of Lucretia.") Roman women regularly shared meals and social activities with their parents and were expected to take an interest in their husbands' political lives.

---

cum manu (kum MAN-oo)

■ Patrons and Clients

Patron (derived from *pater,* "father") means "defender" or "protector." *Client* means "dependent." Roman society consisted of pyramidal patron-client networks. Most patrons were in turn clients of someone more powerful; only a very few men stood at the top of the pyramid. To the Romans, justice meant not that patron and client treated each other as equals but rather that they showed each other respect and fulfilled mutual obligations.

Various paths led to the status of client. A peasant in need of help on his farm might ask a wealthy neighbor to become his patron. A manumitted slave became the client of his former owner. A conquered foe became the client of the victorious general. The status of client or patron was hereditary.

Patron and client might help each other in various ways. A patron might provide a client with food or with property for a dowry. He might settle disputes or provide legal assistance. In return, a client owed his patron respect and service. He escorted his patron in public on important occasions—possession of a large clientele signified prestige and power. If his patron sought political office, the client voted for him and urged others to do so. If his patron needed money, the client was obligated to contribute, perhaps to an election campaign or to pay fines or ransoms.

Cloaked in an elaborate language of goodwill, the patron-client relationship was considered a matter of *fides*° ("good faith" or "trustworthiness"). Romans spoke not of a client submitting to a patron's power but rather of a client "commending himself" to the patron's fides. A patron spoke not of his clients but of his "friends," especially if they were men of standing or substance.

A patron was supposed to put his clients before his kin by marriage; only blood or adoptive relations were to take precedence. According to the Twelve Tables, a patron who defrauded his client was accursed and subject to death with impunity.

Patronage played an important role in Roman domestic politics, but it was not decisive. For example, a wealthy patron expected his humble clients to vote as he wished, but he abused them at his peril. If a man's clients grew discontented, they might find a new patron. Patronage was relatively more important in foreign affairs. Experience as patrons schooled Roman leaders in treating the peoples they conquered as clients, often as personal clients. Moreover, the Roman state sometimes took foreign countries into its collective fides— much as a patron did a client—thus allowing Rome to extend its influence without the constraints of a formal alliance.

■ Religion and World-View

If we knew nothing about early Roman religion, we could deduce much about it from the familia and patronage. We could expect to find an emphasis on powerful fathers and binding agreements, and both are indeed present. The task of a Roman priest, whether an official of the state or an individual paterfamilias, was to establish what the Romans called the "peace of the gods." Roman cults aimed at obtaining the gods' agreement to human requests, at "binding" the gods—the Latin term for which is *religio*.

The earliest Roman religion was animistic; that is, it centered on the spirits that, the Romans believed, haunted the household and the fields and forests and determined the weather. The Lares, the spirits of departed ancestors, guarded the house, and the Penates watched over stored grain. The spirit of the hearth was Vesta; of the door, Janus; of the rain and sun, Jupiter (later identified with the Greek sky-god and the father-god Zeus); of the crops and vegetation, Mars (later identified with the Greek war-god Ares). The Romans believed that these spirits needed to be appeased—hence the contractual nature of their prayers and offerings. Over the years, as a result of Greek influence, anthropomorphism (that is, the worship of humanlike gods and goddesses) supplanted Roman animism.

Roman state religion grew out of house religion. Vesta, the hearth-goddess, became goddess of the civic hearth; Janus, the door-god, became god of the city's gates; Jupiter became the general overseer of the gods; and Mars became the god of war. When trade and conquest brought the Romans into contact with foreign religions, the Romans tended to absorb them. The senate screened and sometimes rejected new gods, but by and large Roman polytheism was tolerant and inclusive.

The Republic sponsored numerous priestly committees, or colleges, to secure the peace of the gods. Originally restricted to patricians, most of the highest priesthoods were opened to plebeians by law in 300 B.C. Although some priesthoods were full-time jobs, most left the officeholder free to pursue a concurrent career as a magistrate or a senator. The two most important priestly colleges were the augurs°, who were in charge of foretelling the future from omens and other signs, and the pontiffs, who exercised a general supervisory function over Rome's numerous rituals, sacrifices, offerings, prayers, temples, and festivals. The chief pontiff, the *pontifex maximus*°, was the head of the state clergy. He was chosen by election. The pontiffs alone controlled the interpretation of the law until the fourth century B.C. The Romans allowed priests to interpret the law on the theory that an offense against humans was also an offense against the gods.

The system provided for only two colleges of priestesses: those of Ceres, goddess of fertility and death, and those of the Vestal Virgins. The six Vestals tended the civic hearth and made sure that its fire never went out. They served, as it were, as wives of the whole community, as guardians of the civil household. The Vestals were the only Roman women not under the authority of a paterfamilias. Chosen between the ages of 6 and 10 by the pontifex maximus, they had to remain virgins for thirty years or face death. The Vestals' chastity was considered an index of male honor and so was watched closely.

---

fides (FEE-days)

augur (AW-ger)
pontifex maximus (PON-tih-fex MAX-ih-mus)

Roman ideology promoted simple and austere farmers' virtues—discipline, hard work, frugality, temperance, and the avoidance of public displays of affection even between spouses. Such virtues underlined the difference between the Republic and the kings with their luxury and sophistication. At the same time, these virtues papered over class distinctions between rich and poor and so promoted stability.

Other Roman ideals included the supreme virtue of the household, *pietas*—devotion and loyalty to the familia, the gods, and the state. Household duties and gender obligations were defined clearly. Women were to be modest, upright, and practical. Men were to project *gravitas* (weight, seriousness), never lightness or levity. A serious man would display self-control and constancy, the ability to persevere against difficult odds. The masculine ideal was *virtus* (literally, "manliness"), which indicated excellence in war and government.

Roman men who attained virtus considered themselves entitled to the reward of *dignitas,* meaning not only public esteem but the tangible possession of a dignified position and official rank—in short, public office. The ultimate test of virtus, however, was in battle. Rome's wars supplied ample occasion to display it.

FROM ITALIAN CITY-STATE TO WORLD EMPIRE, CA. 509–133 B.C.

 T the beginning of the Republic (ca. 509 B.C.), Roman territory comprised about 500 square miles. By 338 B.C., Rome controlled the 2,000 square miles of Latium and was moving north into Etruria and south into Samnite country. Three-quarters of a century later, in 265 B.C., Rome controlled all of the Italian peninsula south of an imaginary line from Pisae (modern Pisa) to Ariminum (modern Rimini), an area of about 50,000 square miles (see Map 5.2). By 146 B.C., Roman provinces included Sicily, Cisalpine Gaul (northernmost Italy), Sardinia, Corsica, and Spain (divided into two provinces). Once-great Carthage was the Roman province of Africa (roughly, modern Tunisia), and once-mighty Macedon was the province of Macedonia, whose governor was also effectively in charge of Greece. The Seleucid kingdom was free but fatally weakened. Rome was the supreme power between Gibraltar and the Levant. It was the greatest empire of the ancient West. How and why had Rome, from its humble beginnings as a local power, reached this breathtaking height?

■ Republican Expansion: The Conquest of Italy, ca. 509–265 B.C.

Romans maintain that they conquered an empire without ever committing an act of aggression. When war was declared, a special college of priests informed the gods that Rome was merely retaliating for foreign injury. True, the Romans were frequently attacked by others, but often only after provocative behavior by Rome had left its rivals little choice.

Rome's early conquests reveal many of its lasting motives for expansion. No doubt lust for conquest played a part, as did fear and hatred of outsiders, but self-control and shrewdness were stronger Roman characteristics. Greed, particularly land-hunger, was a perennial theme. Sometimes a domestic political motive was at work, for foreign adventure was a convenient way of deflecting plebeian energies. Perhaps the most significant factors, however, were the personal ambitions of a warrior elite and the presence of conflict in early Italy.

Victory in battle promised both prestige and booty and the political success that might follow. Military achievement brought unique acclaim. For example, certain victorious generals were allowed to celebrate a triumph; no such ceremony rewarded the feats of peacemakers or distinguished judges or other public benefactors. The triumphant general rode a chariot through the city to the temple of Jupiter on the Capitoline Hill. He was accompanied by his troops, by the spoils of victory including famous captives, and by the magistrates and senators. (See the box "Reading Sources: A Roman Triumph.")

The harsh reality of Italian politics also ruled against pacifism. Without the willingness to fight, Rome could never have maintained its freedom. Yet what began as a pragmatic response to present dangers hardened into a habit of meeting even remote threats with force. In the fourth century B.C., having gained control of Latium, Rome considered the Samnites of central and southern Italy to be a potential threat. In the third century B.C., once Rome controlled Italy, it felt threatened by the powerful Carthage. After Carthage, the threat of Macedon was squelched, and after Macedon, Seleucid Syria, and so on.

Though flexible and far-reaching, Roman diplomacy sometimes ended up in war. Rome made formal alliances with some states, granting protection in return for obedience and troops or ships when needed by Rome. Short of a formal commitment, however, Rome might accept a state "into its fides"—that is, treat the state as a client. The result was only a moral, and not a legal, commitment, which sometimes sufficed to frighten

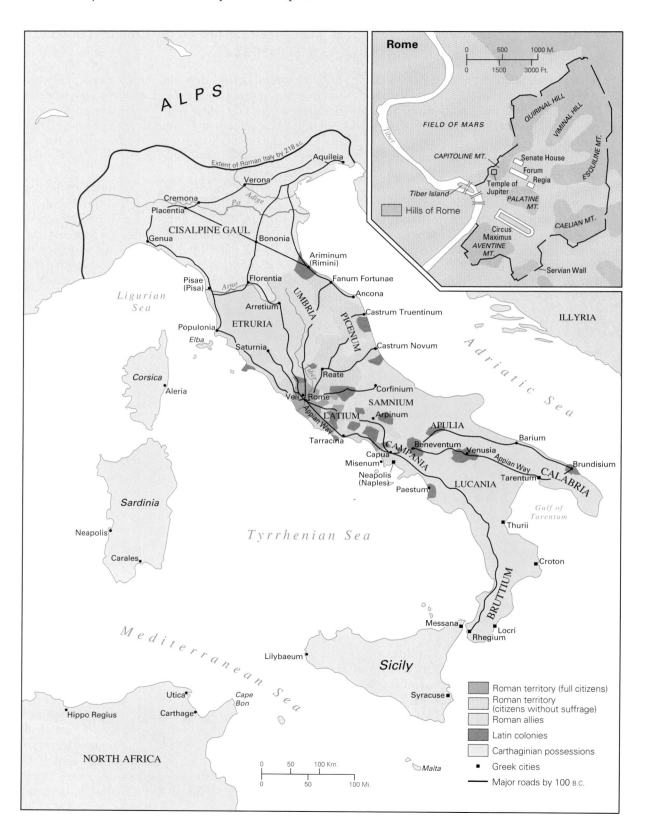

🐚 READING SOURCES

A Roman Triumph

The Roman triumph symbolizes the prestige flowing from military success in Rome; it also demonstrates the senate's attempt to control victorious generals. This description is drawn from the Epitome of Zonaras, *a Byzantine historian of the twelfth century* A.D. *Zonaras drew his material on Rome from Plutarch (ca.* A.D. *50–120) and Dio Cassius (second–third century* A.D.*).*

When any great success worthy of a triumph had been gained, the general was immediately saluted as imperator by the soldiers, and he would bind sprigs of laurel upon the *fasces* [bladed axes bundled in rods, carried as a symbol of authority] and deliver them to the messengers who announced the victory to the city. On arriving home he would assemble the senate and ask to have the triumph voted him. And if he obtained a vote from the senate and from the people, his title of *imperator* was confirmed. . . .

Arrayed in the triumphal dress and wearing armlets, with a laurel crown upon his head, and holding a branch in his right hand, he called together the people. After praising collectively the troops who had served with him, and some of them individually, he presented them with money and honored them also with decorations. . . . A large part of the spoils also was assigned to the soldiers who had taken part in the campaign. . . .

After these ceremonies the triumphant general would mount his chariot [with his children and rela-

tives]. . . . A public slave . . . rode with the victor in the chariot itself, holding over him the crown of precious stones set in gold, and kept saying to him, "Look behind!" . . . Thus arrayed, they entered the city, having at the head of the procession the spoils and trophies and figures representing the captured forts, cities, mountains, rivers, lakes, and seas—everything, in fact, that they had taken. . . . When these adjuncts had gone on their way, the victorious general arrived at the Roman Forum, and after commanding that some of the captives be led to prison and put to death, he rode up to the Capitol. There he performed certain rites and made offerings and dined in the porticoes up there, after which he departed homewards towards evening, accompanied by flutes and pipes.

Source: From Naphtali Lewis and Meyer Reinhold, eds., *Roman Civilization: Selected Readings,* vol. 1: *The Republic and the Augustan Age,* 3d ed. (New York: Columbia University Press, 1990), pp. 230–231.

any would-be aggressor from harassing Rome's new friend. If not, Rome had to go into battle to prove its trustworthiness as a patron.

Military success requires tenacity, discipline, and flexibility—all qualities that Rome cultivated. Roman organizational ability and love of order made the Roman military camp a much more regular and systematic place than anything seen since Assyrian days. Beginning in the

Map 5.2 Roman Italy, ca. 265 B.C. Rome controlled a patchwork of conquered territory, colonies, and allied states in Italy, held together by a network of treaties and of roads. The city of Rome (*inset*) was built on seven hills beside the Tiber River.

fourth century B.C., Rome began to reward its soldiers with regular pay; this and the distribution of conquered land improved morale. Two other points are even more significant: the willingness to utilize foreign military technology and the combination of generosity and firmness with which Rome treated its allies.

Borrowed from the Greeks in the sixth century B.C., the hoplite phalanx suited Rome on the relatively level ground of Latium but fared poorly in the rugged Apennines against the Samnites. Following a major defeat in 321 B.C., the Romans adopted with great success the Samnites' equipment and tactics.

Unlike the phalanx, which overpowered the enemy by fighting as one thickly massed unit, a Roman legion was flexible and adaptable. Legions were drawn up into three lines, thirty maniples ("handfuls"), and sixty centuries (literally "hundreds," although the number of men per century varied); and each century was commanded by a centurion. A legion marched in a checkerboard pattern, leaving gaps in the lines. In battle each line closed its gaps as it attacked in turn. Unlike hoplites, who engaged the enemy at short range, legionnaires first threw their javelins at long range. Then, having broken the enemy's order, they charged and fought with sword and shield. The semi-independence of the maniples, each with its own commander and banner, created a more maneuverable army than that of the phalanx and one better suited for mountain fighting. When Rome's

legions beat the Macedonian phalanx decisively in 197 B.C., military history entered a new era.

Rome was the leading power among the Latins, whom it led in an alliance known as the Latin League. Rome was first among equals, but the citizens of even the humblest Latin state had reciprocal rights of intermarriage and commerce with Romans and the right to become a citizen of another state by migrating there. Under Roman leadership the Latin League successfully defended Latium's borders against a series of enemies during the fourth and fifth centuries B.C. But eventually Rome had to confront a bitter two-year-long Latin revolt (340–338 B.C.).

The year 338 B.C. marked a turning point. Defeated peoples in the ancient world were often executed, deported, or enslaved. Victorious against the Latins, Rome, by contrast, pursued generosity. The Latin League was dissolved. Some of its member states were annexed, and their inhabitants became Roman citizens; others retained independence and alliance with Rome though no longer with one another. The non-Latin allies of the former rebels were also annexed by Rome, but they received the unique halfway status of "citizenship without suffrage." They shared the burdens of Roman citizenship but also all the rights except the vote; they also retained the right of local self-government. The settlement of 338 B.C. broke new ground by making it possible for Rome and its former allies and enemies to live together on the basis of relative equality.

The settlement also set a precedent for future Roman expansion. As Rome conquered Italy, a number of privileged Italian cities (called *municipia*) received the status of citizenship without suffrage. Others remained independent but were tied to Rome by perpetual alliance. Romans often annexed a portion of the land of these states.

If municipia were the carrots of Roman imperialism, the stick was a network of military roads and colonies crisscrossing Italy, allowing Rome to keep an eye on

Bronze War God This elegant, fourth-century B.C. Etruscan bronze, thought to represent Mars, the god of war, shows the metal breastplate worn by a warrior of that era. *(Scala/Art Resource, NY)*

The Appian Way   Named for the censor Appius Claudius Caecus, who proposed its construction, Rome's first great road was built in 312 B.C. during the Samnite Wars. It originally ran 132 miles from Rome to Capua and was extended an additional 234 miles, probably by 244 B.C., to Brundisium, on Italy's southern Adriatic coast.   *(F. H. C. Birch/Sonia Halliday Photographs)*

potential rebels. Roman roads allowed the swift movement of troops and linked the growing network of colonies. Colonies were established in strategically vital areas. The inhabitants, Roman and Latin, owed military service to Rome.

In later years, Italians would complain about treatment by Rome, but compared with inhabitants of Roman provinces outside Italy, they had a privileged status. Romans too would complain about allied demands for equality, but Rome received from its allies a huge and seemingly inexhaustible pool of military manpower. The allies staffed the Roman armies that conquered Samnites, Etruscans, and Gauls, all of whom came into the Roman orbit by the early third century B.C. Manpower abundance won Rome's war (280–276 B.C.) against the Greek general

Pyrrhus° of Epirus (319–272 B.C.), an adventurer who intervened in southern Italy. Although Pyrrhus won battle after battle, he was unable to match Roman willingness to sustain thousands of casualties time and again. Pyrrhus's seeming victories, therefore, turned out to be defeats, which sent him home to Greece disappointed and left us with the expression "Pyrrhic victory."

As for Rome, by 265 B.C. it emerged as the ruler of all of Italy south of the Pisae-Ariminum line (see Map 5.2). One might say that Rome unified Italy, although Italy was less a unity than a patchwork of Roman territory and colonies and of diverse cities, states, and peoples each allied to Rome by separate treaties.

Pyrrhus (PIR-us)

■ Rome Versus Carthage: The Punic Wars, 264–146 B.C.

The conquest of Italy made Rome one of two great powers in the central Mediterranean. The other was Carthage°. Founded around 750 B.C. by Phoenicians from Tyre, Carthage controlled an empire in North Africa, Sicily, Corsica, Sardinia, Malta, the Balearic Islands, and southern Spain. (The adjective *Phoenician* is *Punicus* in Latin, hence the term *Punic*° for Carthaginian.) Like Rome, Carthage was guided by a wealthy elite, but it was mercantile in character rather than agrarian. Rome was a land power, Carthage a sea power. Rome had virtually no navy. Carthage, on the other hand, commanded a great war fleet, and its merchant ships dominated the western Mediterranean and played a major role in the East.

Carthage was an economic powerhouse. The Carthaginians exploited the mineral-rich mines of Spain. They were the first Mediterranean people to organize large-scale plantations of slaves for the production of single crops. Even though the Romans zealously wiped out most of Carthaginian elite culture, they did make sure to preserve one Carthaginian classic: a multivolume work on agriculture by Mago. Translated from Punic into Latin by order of the senate, Mago's treatise had enormous impact on Roman landowners, who, with the importation of massive numbers of slaves, adopted the plantation system in Italy (see page 157).

Carthage boasted brilliant generals, especially in the Barca family, whose most famous member was Hannibal° (247–183 B.C.). Carthage might have been a handicapper's favorite at the outbreak of its long wars with Rome in 264 B.C., yet the end result was disaster for Carthage. A combination of Carthaginian weaknesses and Roman strengths accounts for the outcome.

Unlike Rome, Carthage did not have a citizen army. The commanders were Carthaginian, but most of the soldiers were mercenaries and so of questionable loyalty. A second difference in the two states lay in the treatment of allies. Rome treated the Italians with considerable respect and tolerance. Carthage showed contempt for its allies, who repaid the favor by revolting whenever they had the chance. Third, although Carthage's military manpower resources were considerable, they were not as great as Rome's.

At the start of the Punic Wars, Rome had no navy or commanders to match the Barca family, but it proved

---

Carthage (CAR-thidge)   **Punic** (PYOO-nik)
Hannibal (HAN-uh-bull)

Punic Mask   This grey terra-cotta mask comes from Carthage and dates to the third or second century B.C. Masks like these were placed in tombs to keep evil spirits away.   *(Bardo Museum/The Ancient Art & Architecture Collection)*

adaptable, tenacious, and ruthless. To win the First Punic War (264–241 B.C.), for example, Rome not only built a navy but outlasted the enemy in a long, bloody, and exhausting conflict. After initially granting a mild peace treaty, Rome took advantage of later Carthaginian weakness to seize Sardinia and Corsica and to demand an additional indemnity.

Forced to give in to these treacherous exactions, Carthage decided to build a new and bigger empire in Spain, beginning in 237 B.C., under Barca family leadership. Hannibal's father, the general Hamilcar Barca (d. 229 B.C.), had gone undefeated in the First Punic War, and is said to have raised his son to seek a rematch. With Spain's rich deposits of silver and copper at its disposal, Carthage once again posed a credible threat to Rome. In the mid-220s, an ever watchful Rome challenged Carthaginian power in Spain through a Roman client there. The new Carthaginian commander, 27-year-old Hannibal Barca, was not to be cowed, however, and the Second Punic War ensued (218–201 B.C.).

Carthage was willing to risk war because Hannibal promised a quick, cheap, and easy victory. Because Carthage no longer had a fleet, the Romans felt secure in Italy; Hannibal surprised them by marching overland to Italy, making a dangerous passage across the Alps. A tactical genius, Hannibal reckoned that with his superior generalship he could defeat the Romans in battle and cause them enormous casualties, and he was right. Hannibal's forces dominated the battlefield. Among his victories was the Battle of Cannae in Apulia (southeastern Italy) where, in 216 B.C., Carthage gave Rome the bloodiest defeat in its history, killing perhaps thirty thousand Romans.

A crushing Barca success, but huge casualties alone could not bring Rome to its knees. Nor did Rome's allies revolt en masse, as Hannibal had hoped. Most stood by Rome, which had treated them relatively benignly in the past and which now threatened rebels with terrible reprisals. Roman pragmatism, moreover, showed itself able to deal with crisis. After Cannae, Rome's leadership accepted a cautious strategy of harassment, delay, refusal to fight, and attrition. Hannibal was stymied by an enemy who lost battles but refused to surrender. Nor did Hannibal have the power to take the city of Rome.

In the meantime, Rome had bought valuable time to regroup. A new military star emerged: Publius Cornelius Scipio° (236–183 B.C.), a Roman who finally understood Hannibal's tactics and matched them. First Scipio conquered Carthage's Spanish dominions, and then he forced Hannibal back to North Africa for a final battle in 202 B.C. near Zama (in modern Tunisia). Scipio won the battle and gained the surname Africanus ("the African"). As for Hannibal, he played a prominent role in Carthaginian politics for about a decade, until Rome forced him into exile in Syria. In about 183 B.C., after taking part in the Seleucids' unsuccessful war against Rome, he committed suicide rather than face extradition to Rome.

The peace settlement of 201 B.C. stripped Carthage of its empire. Yet soon its economy rebounded, reviving old Roman fears of Carthage's political ambitions. In the Third Punic War (149–146 B.C.), Rome mounted a three-year siege under the leadership of Scipio Aemilianus (185–129 B.C.), finally destroying the city of Carthage in 146 B.C. Approximately a century later, Carthage was resurrected as a Roman colony and became one of the empire's greatest cities. In the meantime, it was left desolate, its people killed or enslaved.

Rome emerged from the Punic Wars as the greatest power in the Mediterranean. It had acquired new provinces in Sicily, Sardinia, Corsica, Spain, and North Africa (where Carthage's former territory was annexed as the province of Africa). The road to further conquest seemed to lead in all directions.

Scipio (SIP-ee-o)

■ Victories in the Hellenistic East, ca. 200–133 B.C.

Most countries would have savored peace after such an ordeal as the Punic Wars, but Rome immediately leaped into a long conflict in Greece and Anatolia. Its aims were to weaken the power of Macedon, which it feared might threaten Rome one day, especially since the Macedonian king Philip V (r. 221–179 B.C.) had made an alliance with Hannibal after Cannae. Rome won a relatively quick and easy victory when in 197 B.C. the legions crushed the Macedonian phalanx at Cynoscephalae in central Greece (see Map 5.3).

Rome had hoped to impose a patron-client relationship on Greece and Macedon, thereby avoiding having to sustain a permanent military presence, but that hope failed. The independent-minded Greeks chafed at Roman domination. Several years of miscommunication and intrigue followed, only to lead to renewed wars. First the Seleucids, under the ambitious king Antiochus III (r. 223–187 B.C.), challenged Rome for hegemony on the Greek peninsula. It was in this war that Hannibal took a small, doomed part. Roman forces made short work of the enemy. Driven out not only from Greece but from Anatolia as well, the Seleucids in effect recognized Roman supremacy in the Mediterranean (188 B.C.).

Then came another two rounds of war that pitted Rome against Macedon and various Greek states (171–167 and 150–146 B.C.). Victorious in both wars, Rome deprived the Greeks and Macedonians of their independence. Wherever democracy had survived in Greece, it was replaced with oligarchy. In 146 B.C., Rome destroyed Corinth, one of Greece's wealthiest cities, as a warning against further rebellion. Greece then suffered Roman neglect and taxation for nearly two hundred years.

By annexing Carthage, Macedon, and Greece in the mid-second century B.C., Rome created a dynamic for expansion around the entire Mediterranean. Before the century was over, southern Gaul was annexed, and Rome had gained a foothold in Asia. The kingdom of Pergamum (northwestern Anatolia) had supported Rome throughout Rome's wars in the east. When Attalus III of Pergamum died without an heir in 133 B.C., he surrendered his kingdom to the Roman people, who made it into a province of Asia.

Two great Hellenistic states remained independent: the Seleucid kingdom and Ptolemaic Egypt (see Map 5.3). Roman ambassadors and generals frequently interfered in their affairs, however, and no one was surprised when, in the first century B.C., they too were annexed by Rome.

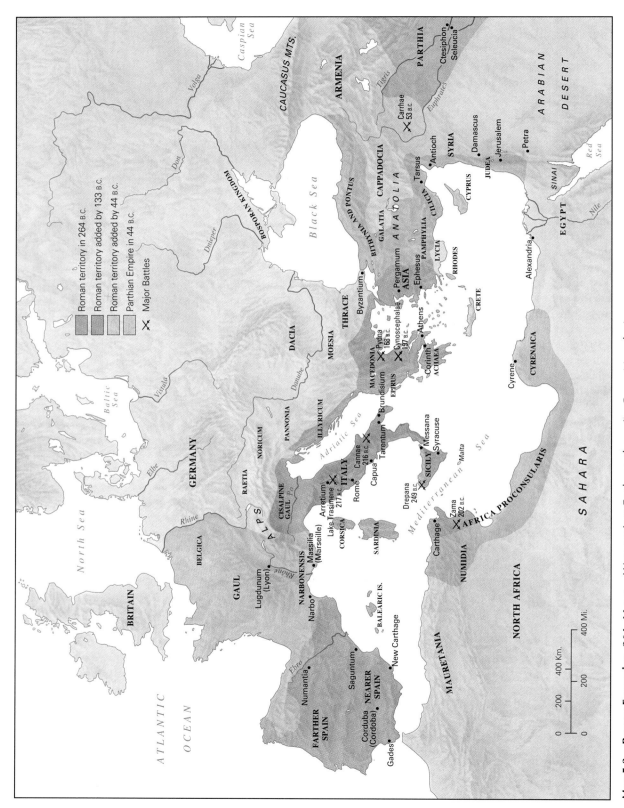

Map 5.3 Roman Expansion, 264–44 B.C. Wars against Carthage, the major Greco-Macedonian powers, Gauls, Germans, North Africans, and other peoples brought Rome an empire on three continents.

■ The Socioeconomic Consequences of Expansion

Expansion led to enormous and unintended changes in Rome's society, economy, and culture. Already wealthy, the Roman elite now came into fabulous riches. Huge profits awaited the generals, patrons, diplomats, magistrates, tax collectors, and businessmen who followed Rome's armies. In Italy, most profits were in the form of land; in the provinces, not only in land, but in slaves, booty, and graft. One of the worst grafters, Gaius Verres, governor of Sicily from 73 to 71 B.C., was prosecuted by Cicero (see page 166), then beginning his oratorical career, for allegedly extorting tens of thousands of pounds of silver from his province. But even Cicero skimmed off several thousand pounds of silver as governor of the province of Cilicia (southern Anatolia) from 51 to 50 B.C.

The first Roman coinage, traditionally dated to 289 B.C., facilitated commercial transactions. Previously, the Romans had made do with barter, uncoined bronze, and cast bronze bars, but now they imitated the workmanship and style of Greek coins. Equally prominent in the homes of wealthy Romans were Greek metalwork, jewelry, art objects, and other luxury goods. Conservatives bemoaned the decline of traditional Roman austerity, but they fought a hopeless rear-guard action. (See the feature "Weighing the Evidence: Luxury Goods and Gender Wars in Rome" on pages 170–171.)

Ordinary Romans needed no reminder of the virtues of austerity, for they did not share in the elite's profit from Roman expansion. Indeed, a century of intensive warfare—from the outbreak of the Punic Wars in 264 B.C. to the destruction of Carthage and Corinth in 146 B.C.—strained the lot of the Roman people to the breaking point. Hannibal's invasion left much of the farmland of southern Italy devastated and Italian manpower considerably reduced. Yet most people might have rebounded from these problems within a generation or two, if they had not faced other serious troubles.

Conscription had become the norm. The average term of military service between ages 17 and 46 was six years; the maximum term was twenty years. Because experienced legionnaires were at a premium, commanders were loath to release them from service. But the longer a man was away in the army, the harder it was for his wife and children to keep the family farm running. With help from a patron, they might be able to make do, though most patrons in fact added to the problem through the introduction to Italy of large-scale agricultural entrepreneurship. Those who sought wealth monopolized Italian farmland, imported huge numbers of slaves, and brought ruin on the free peasantry of Italy.

The last two centuries B.C. witnessed the transformation of Roman rural society from a society of independent farmers to one in which slave labor played a major role. By the end of the first century B.C. Italy's slave population was estimated at 2 to 3 million, about a third of the peninsula's total. Prisoners of war and conquered civilians provided a ready supply of slaves. Most worked in agriculture or mining, and their treatment was often abominable; the fewer house slaves were usually better off.

Wealthy Romans wanted to invest in large landed estates, or *latifundia*°, worked by slaves. These estates were either mixed farms (most often devoted to cultivating vines, olives, and grain) or ranches (establishments where animals were raised for meat, milk, and wool). One devotee of the latter was the prominent conservative Marcus Porcius Cato° (234–149 B.C.), known as Cato the Censor. Cato argued that there were only three ways to get rich: "pasturage, pasturage, and pasturage." All a would-be entrepreneur needed was land. Conquests had gained Rome a plenitude of land in Italy. Called public land, it belonged to the Roman people, but an individual was legally entitled to claim about 320 acres as his own. Many entrepreneurs flouted the law, however, and grabbed large chunks of public land for pasturage. They often forced families of absent soldiers off private land, either by debt foreclosure or by outright violence. Sometimes families would leave the land for the city, but usually they stayed as tenants.

Before about 170 B.C., poor Romans were sometimes able to find land in colonies. By 170 B.C., however, Rome had established all the colonies in Italy that its security demanded, so this avenue of escape from poverty was closed. A displaced farmer who wanted to compete in the labor market would have found it difficult to underbid cheap slave labor; in any case, Roman ideology frowned on wage labor by citizens. Nor was it practical for a poor farmer to sue a wealthy patron who seized his land, because a plaintiff himself had to bring the accused into court.

The situation of the Italian peasantry was becoming increasingly miserable by the mid-second century B.C. As one modern scholar has put it, "In conquering what they were pleased to call the world, the Romans ruined a great part of the Italian people."[2]

---

latifundia (lat-uh-FUN-dee-uh)
Cato (KAY-toe)

The Round Temple   This elegant, circular, Corinthian-columned structure in the Forum Boarium in Rome, built around 150–100 B.C., is the oldest surviving marble temple in the city. Greek in style, it is an example of Roman borrowing from sophisticated Hellenistic culture. *(Scala/Art Resource, NY)*

■ The Impact of Greece on Rome and Its Empire

Rome learned much from its new encounters with foreign peoples—and from none more than the Greeks. Wealthy Romans cultivated interests in Greek art, literature, rhetoric, and speculative thought; poor and rich alike enjoyed Greek drama. Before the mid-third century B.C., Roman literature was virtually nonexistent. An oral tradition of songs, ballads, and funeral oratory kept alive the deeds of the famous, for writing was generally restricted to commercial and government records and inscriptions. In short, the Romans conquered Italy without writing about it.

Contact with the Greek cities brought changes. Large numbers of Roman soldiers in Magna Graecia (southern Italy and Sicily) were introduced to comedy, tragedy, mimes, and sophisticated song lyrics, and many developed a permanent taste for them. It is no accident that the first production of a drama at Rome took place in 240 B.C., the year after the end of the First Punic War. Afterward, the annual production of such dramas became standard procedure.

No one could accuse the Romans of rushing headlong into a new age, however. The authorities continued to have their doubts about theater, which seemed excessively emotional and probably corrupt. They did not allow the building of a permanent theater in Rome until 55 B.C., insisting that the wealthiest city in the Mediterranean make do with makeshift wooden structures. Nor did the Roman elite readily become playwrights or poets. The first gentleman-poet in Rome, Lucilius (180–102 B.C.), did not arrive until the second century B.C., and he was a Latin, not a Roman. His predecessors, the founders of Latin literature, were all of low social status; little of their work survives.

The two great early Latin playwrights are Titus Maccius Plautus (ca. 254–184 B.C.) and Publius Terentius Afer, today known as Terence (ca. 195–159 B.C.). Both of them wrote comedies on the model of the great Greek comic playwright Menander (see page 122). Plautus was an Umbrian and a poor man who learned his Latin in Rome; Terence was a North African slave, educated and freed in Rome. Twenty-one plays by Plautus and six by Terence survive. Plautus's plays are generally earthy slapstick farces. They are invariably set in Greece, not Rome, in part out of escapism (many were written during the Second Punic War), in part out of the censorial demands of the Roman authorities. They nonetheless reveal much about Roman society. Terence's plays are more subtle than Plautus's, indicating the growing sophistication of Roman theatergoers.

Latin prose developed more slowly than did poetry and drama. The first histories by Romans, composed after the Second Punic War, were written in Greek, for Latin lacked the vocabulary or the audience for history. Cato the Censor was the first historian of Rome to write in Latin. His *Origines,* of which we have only remnants, recounted Roman history from the origin of the city to about 150 B.C. The earliest surviving Latin prose work is Cato's *On Agriculture.*

In the traditional education of a Roman aristocrat, parents and close family friends played the primary role. Although this practice continued, in the second century B.C., wealthy Romans began acquiring Greek slaves to educate their sons in Greek language and literature. Soon Greek freedmen began setting up schools offering the same subjects. Before long, similar Latin grammar schools also opened.

One of the forms of Greek literature that appealed most to the practical-minded Romans was rhetoric. Roman orators studied Greek models, and many would say that they eventually outdid the Greeks. Cato was the first Roman to publish his speeches, and he also wrote a book on rhetoric. Both gave impetus to the spread of sophisticated rhetoric in Rome.

Scipio Aemilianus, conqueror of Carthage in 146 B.C., had a distinguished political and military career. He was also patron of a group of prominent statesmen and soldiers who shared his love of Hellenism. Among the writers whom they supported were the playwright Terence, the poet Lucilius, the historian Polybius, and the Stoic philosopher Panaetius (ca. 185–109 B.C.). The Stoic emphases on duty, wisdom, and world brotherhood appealed both to Rome's traditional ideology and to its more recent acquisition of empire. Yet not all Romans shared Scipio's admiration of Greek culture: Cato, for example, was famously ambivalent.

Cornelia, Scipio Aemilianus's mother-in-law, was an educated lover of Hellenism who wrote letters that existed several hundred years later as examples of elegant Latin prose. Her villa in the resort of Misenum on the bay of Naples was well known for the distinguished guests whom she received there. When her husband, an outstanding statesman and general, died, Cornelia chose to remain a widow. One of the men who tried to change her mind was no less a figure than the king of Egypt. The widow spent her time managing her own estate and supervising the education of her two sons, the future tribunes Tiberius and Gaius Gracchus (see page 161).

Although Cornelia's privileges were extraordinary, she is nonetheless a reminder of the opportunities that imperial expansion offered to wealthy Roman women. Marriage practices are one example of change. Few women were married *cum manu* anymore, that is, handed over by their fathers to their husbands. A woman's father or nearest male relative, not her husband, was most likely to be her paterfamilias, which meant that a husband's control over his wife's dowry was limited. The result was more freedom, at least for wealthy women.

Cornelia is also a reminder of the fundamental conservatism of Roman society. Although we know the years of birth and death of numerous elite Roman males of the second century B.C., we do not know Cornelia's. Nor did her literary interests entail any neglect of home and family. Cornelia bore twelve children, though only three of them lived to adulthood (such was the reality of infant mortality even for the wealthiest Romans).

THE REVOLUTION FROM THE GRACCHI TO THE CAESARS, 133–31 B.C.

CITIZEN of the Roman Republic in the mid-second century B.C. might have looked forward to a long and happy future for his country, unaware that the Republic—after 350 years of expansion—was about to begin a century of domestic and foreign unrest that would bring down the whole system. Why and how did the Republic collapse? More than a century of warfare weighed heavily on the ordinary people of Italy—the Romans and allied peasants whose farms were ruined while they were off fighting. The Roman elite was bitterly divided over what to do about the problems of the peasants. One group wanted to redistribute land on behalf of the poor; another group had no sympathy for them.

By the Late Republic the city of Rome was crowded and populous: scholars estimate the number of inhabitants to have reached 1 million by the end of the first century B.C. The government had to take charge of the grain supply. But elite politicians exploited the issue for partisan purposes. Once before, during the struggle between the patrician and plebeian orders in the Early Republic, the elite had been similarly divided and had resolved its differences through compromise (see page 145). The Late Republic, however, was an age of individualism, sophistication, and cynicism. Ambitious nobles were no longer willing to subordinate themselves to the community. Thwarted from above, it was not long before competing armies of land-hungry peasants were marching across Italy.

■ The Gracchi

Many Romans fretted over the military dimension of the agrarian crisis. In modern societies, draftees are often the poorest people. In Rome, military service was a prestigious activity, so a property qualification was imposed and the poor were not drafted. As fewer and fewer potential soldiers could afford to own property, however, during the second century it became necessary to reduce the property qualification several times. By 150 B.C., a conscript had to own property worth only 400 denarii—roughly a small house, a garden, and some personal belongings. If the peasantry continued its decline, Rome would either have to drop the property qualification for the military altogether or stop fielding armies. Clearly, something had to be done.

Into the breach stepped Tiberius Sempronius Gracchus° (d. 133 B.C.), one of the ten tribunes for the year 133 B.C. (See the box "Reading Sources: Tiberius Gracchus on Rome's Plight.") The son of Cornelia and a distinguished general and ambassador (whose name Tiberius shared), Tiberius belonged to the eminent Gracchi° family. He seemed an excellent spokesperson for a group of prominent senators who backed land reform. He proved, however, to be arrogant and overly ambitious. In pursuit of his goals he deposed one of his fellow tribunes, Octavius, an opponent of reform, and thereby shocked and angered conservatives.

Tiberius's proposed law restored the roughly 320-acre limit to the amount of public land a person could own (plus an exception for a man with two sons, who was allowed to hold about 667 acres). A commission was to be set up to repossess excess land and redistribute it to the poor, in small lots that were to be inalienable—that is, the wealthy could not buy them back. The former landowners would be reimbursed for improvements they had made, such as buildings or plantings.

The proposal was moderate, but wealthy landowners repudiated it outright. Many senators suspected that Tiberius wanted to set himself up as a kind of superpatron, buoyed by peasant supporters. The senate was in fact more disturbed by Tiberius's methods than by the substance of his proposed law because those methods threatened the senate's power. In addition to deposing Octavius, Tiberius, when the bill became law, intervened in the senate's bailiwicks of foreign affairs and finances by earmarking tax receipts from the new province of Asia to finance land purchases. Finally, Tiberius broke with custom by running for a second consecutive term as tribune. While the tribal assembly prepared to vote on the new tribunes, some senators led a mob to the Forum and had Tiberius and three hundred of his followers clubbed to death.

This shocking event marked the first time in the Republic that a political debate was settled by bloodshed in Rome itself. The ancient sources agree that it was the beginning of a century of revolution. Tiberius's killers had not merely committed murder, but had attacked the traditional inviolability of the tribunes. Yet over the next century public violence grew as a weapon of politics in the Republic. The land commission went ahead with its work, even without Tiberius. His younger brother, Gaius°

Tiberius Gracchus (ty-BEER-ee-us GRAK-us)
Gracchi (GRAK-eye)   **Gaius** (GUY-us)

ぶ READING SOURCES

Tiberius Gracchus on Rome's Plight

In 133 B.C. Tiberius Gracchus proposed to confiscate from wealthy landowners public land possessed in excess of the legal limit and to redistribute it to poor Roman citizens. The proposal, and Tiberius's unorthodox methods of getting it passed into law, sparked a controversy that led to his murder. Plutarch (ca. A.D. 50–120) discusses Tiberius's motives and paraphrases one of his speeches.

His brother Gaius recorded in one of his writings that when Tiberius on his way to Numantia [in Spain] passed through Etruria and found the country almost depopulated and its husbandmen and shepherds imported barbarian slaves, he [Tiberius] first conceived the policy which was to be the source of countless ills to himself and to his brother. But it was the people themselves who chiefly excited his zeal and determination with writings on the porticoes, walls, and monuments, calling on him to retrieve the public land for the poor.

. . . Tiberius, fighting for an honorable and just cause with an eloquence that would have dignified even a meaner cause, was formidable and invincible whenever, with the people crowding around . . . , he took his place and spoke in behalf of the poor. "The wild beasts that roam over Italy," he said, "have their dens, each has a place of repose and refuge. But the men who fight and die for Italy enjoy nothing but the air and light; without house or home they wander about with their wives and children. Their commanders lie when they exhort the soldiers in battle to defend sepulchers and shrines from the enemy, for not one of these many Romans has either hereditary altar or ancestral tomb; they fight and die to protect the wealth and luxury of others; they are styled masters of the world, and have not a clod of earth they can call their own."

Source: Plutarch, *Life of Tiberius Gracchus,* in Naphtali Lewis and Meyer Reinhold, eds., *Roman Civilization: Selected Readings,* vol. 1: *The Republic and the Augustan Age,* 3d ed. (New York: Columbia University Press, 1990), pp. 251–252.

(d. 121 B.C.), ready to continue Tiberius's work, became tribune himself in 123 B.C. Gaius expanded Tiberius's coalition, adding to it supporters from the equestrian order and the urban populace, mainly composed of slaves and freedmen. He gave the plebs cheap grain at subsidized prices. The equestrians were wealthy, landed gentry, similar to senators in most respects except for their failure to have reached the senate; they yearned for political power. A small but important group of equestrians was engaged in commerce and tax collection in the provinces. The senate regulated their activities through the so-called extortion courts, which tried corruption cases. Gaius staffed those courts with equestrians. Alluding to the new equestrian power, Gaius remarked, "I have left a sword in the ribs of the senate."

Gaius's ultimate aims are unclear, but one thing is certain: he posed a dangerous threat to the senate's power. He sponsored an extension of his brother's agrarian law, new colonies, public works, and relief for poor soldiers. Eventually Gaius ran aground on a plan to include the Italian allies as beneficiaries of agrarian reform—a farsighted notion but one unpopular with the Roman people, who were jealous of their privileges. Gaius was denied a third term as tribune in 121 B.C. (he had won a second the previous year). Soon his supporters engaged in violent scuffling with their opponents. The senate responded to his action by passing a declaration of public emergency, empowering the magistrates to use any means necessary to protect the state.

One of the consuls had Gaius and 250 of his followers killed. Another 3,000 Gracchans were executed soon thereafter. Within a few years, the Gracchan land commission was abolished. It is estimated that approximately 75,000 citizens had been given land. The law, however, was amended to permit the resale of redistributed land, and with the wealthy poised to buy land back, the settlers' future was uncertain. The senatorial oligarchy was back in control.

Or so it seemed. In fact, Roman politics had become an unstable brew. In time, it became clear that the Gracchi had divided the political community into two loose groupings. On one side were the *optimates*° ("the best people"), conservatives who asserted the rule of the senate against popular tribunes and the maintenance of the estates of the wealthy in spite of the agrarian crisis. On the other side were the *populares*° ("men of the people"), who challenged the rule of the senate in the name of relief of the poor. The populares were not democrats. Like the optimates, they were Roman nobles who believed in hierarchy, but they advocated the redistribution of wealth and power as a way of restoring stability and strengthening the military.

■ Marius and Sulla

By 100 B.C., Rome's agrarian crisis had become a full-scale military crisis, too. Roman armies under senatorial commanders fared poorly, both in Numidia (modern Algeria) and in southern Gaul against Germanic invaders (see Map 5.3). The situation was saved by an outsider to established privilege, an equestrian named Gaius Marius° (157–86 B.C.), the first member of his family to be elected consul, for 107 B.C. This "new man" proved to be a military reformer and a popularis. Marius made several moves to streamline and strengthen the Roman army: Camp followers were reduced in number, and individual soldiers were made to carry their own equipment. To meet the Germans, who attacked in overwhelming waves, maniples—the tactical subunits of a legion—were reorganized and combined into larger units called cohorts, rendering the army firmer and more cohesive. Most important, Marius abandoned altogether the property qualification for the military. As a result, Roman soldiers were no longer peasants doing part-time military service but rather were landless men making a profession of the military.

Politically they became a force to be reckoned with. As an indispensable general, Marius demanded and won six elections to the consulship, unconstitutional though that was. Furthermore, after winning the wars in North Africa and Gaul, Marius championed his soldiers. In 100 B.C. he asked that land be distributed to them. The senate refused but its victory was temporary. The poor recognized that only military leaders such as Marius desired to meet their need for land. As a result, ordinary Romans, who were all now eligible for the army, transferred their loyalty from the senate to their commander.

The Republic was weak, and it became weaker still as a result of two new wars. First, its Italian allies rose against Rome in a bloody and bitter struggle from 91 to 89 B.C. known as the "Social War"—that is, war with the *socii* ("allies"). The allies fought hard, and Rome, in order to prevail, had to concede to them what they had demanded at the outset: full Roman citizenship. The war wrought devastation in the countryside, further destabilizing the Republic. The other conflict of this period pitted Rome against Mithridates (120–63 B.C.), a rebellious king in northern Anatolia. Mithridates conquered Roman territory in western Anatolia and slaughtered the numerous Italian businessmen and tax collectors there. Once again a military man rose to save the day for Rome: Marius's rival and former lieutenant, Lucius Cornelius Sulla° Felix (ca. 138–78 B.C.), consul for the year 88 B.C., patrician and optimas.

Yet Marius was jealous, and his troops and Sulla's fought a civil war over the issue of the command against Mithridates. Sulla's forces won the first round by marching on Rome, but after they departed for the East, Marius's men retook the city and settled scores. Victorious over Mithridates, Sulla returned to Italy in 83 B.C. for a final reckoning. Sulla defeated Marius's men (minus Marius himself, who had died in 86), then sealed his victory with proscription: that is, he had posted the names of his political opponents, as many as two thousand men. Their land was confiscated, their sons disenfranchised, and they were executed. Sulla settled his veterans, about eighty thousand men, on land in Italy from which he had expelled entire communities that had opposed him.

Having assumed the long-dormant office of dictatorship—now, unconstitutionally, for life—Sulla attempted to restore the senatorial rule of pre-Gracchan days. To this end, he greatly weakened the tribunate and strengthened the senate, whose size he doubled, from about three hundred to about six hundred members.

optimates (op-tee-MAH-tayz)
populares (pah-poo-LAH-rayz)   **Marius** (MARRY-us)

Sulla (SUL-luh)

Bust of Julius Caesar This marble sculpture accurately conveys the conqueror's firmness of expression and perhaps his intelligence— but not his looks, since Caesar was bald.
(Vatican Museums/Scala/Art Resource, NY)

The most long-lasting of Sulla's measures was his reform of the courts. He abolished trials before popular assemblies and equestrian-staffed courts. Criminal cases were now heard before one of seven standing courts, whose juries were composed of senators. Although later Roman criminal law evolved considerably, it was founded on Sulla's actions. Generally only wealthy people had access to the standing courts; alleged crimes involving ordinary people were heard before lesser magistrates.

Sulla retired in 79 B.C. and died a year later. His hope of restoring law and order under the senate died with him. Within ten years, the old powers of the tribunes had been restored. Discontent smoldered among the men whose land Sulla had confiscated. Equally serious, many senators, aspiring to what Sulla had done and not to what he had said, pursued personal power, not the collective interests of the senate.

■ Pompey and Caesar

New would-be Mariuses or Sullas now arose. The dominant leader of the seventies and sixties B.C. was the optimas Pompey° the Great (106–48 B.C.), a brilliant general and a supporter of Sulla. Young Pompey went from command to command: he put down an agrarian rebellion in Italy and a rebellion in Spain, cleared the Mediterranean of pirates, defeated Mithridates again, and added rich conquests to the empire in Anatolia, Syria, Phoenicia, and Palestine. In the fifties B.C. the tide began turning in favor of Gaius Julius Caesar° (100–44 B.C.), an even more gifted general and politician—indeed, perhaps one of history's greatest. A popularis, Caesar had family connections to Marius and his supporters. Caesar's career depended on his dazzling oratory, his boldness, and his

Pompey (POM-pee)   **Caesar** (SEE-zer)

sheer talent at war and politics. Caesar conquered Gaul, gained a foothold in Britain, and laid the foundations of Roman rule in Egypt (see Map 5.3).

While the elite of the Late Republic struggled to maintain order and secure power, ordinary people struggled for survival itself. Violence had become a way of life in rural Italy. Many once-prosperous farmers, dispossessed peasants, and runaway slaves ended up as robbers or bandits. It was also an era of slave revolts, the most serious of which lasted from 73 to 71 B.C. under the leadership of Spartacus, a Thracian slave who had been a gladiator. An able commander, Spartacus beat nine separate Roman armies in two years before finally suffering defeat. At the same time, Rome also faced major wars in Spain and Anatolia.

Roman women were sometimes pawns, sometimes partners in the political careers of Pompey and Caesar. In 80 B.C., for example, Pompey divorced his first wife to advance his career by marrying Aemilia, Sulla's stepdaughter. Aemilia was not only married at the time but pregnant by her first husband. Soon after her divorce and remarriage, she died in childbirth. Caesar took many mistresses, among whom was the queen of Egypt, Cleopatra (see pages 134–135). Caesar had a penchant for certain Egyptian institutions, such as the Egyptian calendar, and he toyed with becoming a monarch himself, an inclination that Cleopatra perhaps encouraged. Another of Caesar's mistresses was Servilia, stepsister of Marcus Porcius Cato (Cato the Younger, 95–46 B.C.), great-grandson of the famous censor (see page 157). She was also mother of Brutus, the man who would eventually help murder Caesar.

Pompey was an *optimas*, Caesar a *popularis*, but the two of them agreed that they, not the senate or the assemblies, should dominate Rome. Each man's ambition was more important to him than any political principles. In 60 B.C. they entered into a pact with a third ambitious noble, Marcus Licinius Crassus (d. 53 B.C.). Known today as the "First Triumvirate," this coalition amounted to a conspiracy to run the state. Their individual ambitions rebuffed by the senate, each man had an agenda that could be achieved by pooling resources in the triumvirate: for Pompey, ratification of his acts in the East and land for his veterans; for Caesar, who became consul for 59 B.C., a long period of command in Gaul and a free hand in his behavior there; for Crassus, a rebate for the tax collectors of Roman Asia, whom he championed, and eventually a command in Syria to make war on Parthia (the revived Persian Empire).

Having achieved its goal, the triumvirate did not long survive, but its very existence shows how little the Republic now meant. Crassus died in an inglorious defeat at Carrhae in Syria in 53 B.C., tarnished further by the Parthians' successful capture of Roman legionary standards (see Map 5.3). Frightened by Caesar's stunning victories in Gaul, Pompey returned to the senatorial fold, now led by Cato the Younger. Cato and his supporters stood for the traditional rule of the senatorial oligarchy. In 49 B.C. they ordered Caesar to give up his command in Gaul, but instead Caesar marched on Italy with his army. Italy's northern boundary was marked by a tiny stream called Rubicon; when Caesar defiantly crossed it, he declared, "The die is cast." Indeed it was, for civil war. Caesar swept to victory against the senate's army, led by Pompey, at Pharsalus in Greece in 48 B.C. Pompey fled but was assassinated. The complete destruction of the senate's forces took until 45 B.C.

The years of civil war took Caesar from Spain to Anatolia. During the fighting he showed the qualities that made him great: he was fast, tough, smart, adaptable, and a risk-taker. He was a diplomat too, offering mercy to any of his enemies who joined him. A talented writer, Caesar published two books about his military campaigns: *On the Gallic War* and *On the Civil War,* the latter appearing after his death. These works glorified Caesar's conquests and defended his decision to wage civil war. (See the box "Global Encounters: Caesar on the Gauls.")

Back in Rome, Caesar sponsored a huge number of reforms. His political goal was to elevate Italians and others at the expense of old Roman families. To achieve this, Caesar conferred Roman citizenship liberally, on all of Cisalpine Gaul (northernmost Italy) as well as on certain provincial towns. He enlarged the senate from six hundred to nine hundred, adding his supporters, including some Gauls, to the membership. Caesar sponsored social and economic reforms too, including reducing debt and founding the first colonies outside Italy, where veterans and poor citizens were settled. He undertook a grand public building program in the city of Rome. Caesar's most long-lasting act was to introduce the calendar of 365¼ days, on January 1, 45 B.C. Derived from the calendar of Egypt, it is known as the Julian calendar.

Caesar did not hide his contempt for Republican constitutional formalities. By accepting a dictatorship for life he offended the old guard; by flirting with the title of king he infuriated them. With one eye toward avenging Crassus and another toward equaling the achievements of Alexander the Great, Caesar made preparations for a war against Parthia, but in vain. His career ended abruptly on March 15, 44 B.C. (the Ides of March by the Roman calendar), when sixty senators stabbed him to death. The assassination took place in the portico attached to the Theater of

Caesar on the Gauls

Julius Caesar (ca. 100–44 B.C.) advertised his achievements in conquering Gaul (58–51 B.C.) in his Commentaries on the Gallic War. *The book focuses on battles and negotiations, but here Caesar discusses the society of the Gauls (also known as Celts). He depicts the inhabitants as superstitious and belligerent.*

In the whole of Gaul two types of men are counted as being of worth and distinction. The ordinary people are considered almost as slaves: they dare do nothing on their own account and are not called to counsels. When the majority are oppressed by debt or heavy tribute, or harmed by powerful men, they swear themselves away into slavery to the aristocracy, who then have the same rights over them as masters do over their slaves. Of the two types of men of distinction, however, the first is made up of the druids (priests), and the other of the knights.

The druids are involved in matters of religion. They manage public and private sacrifices and interpret religious customs and ceremonies. Young men flock to them in large numbers to gain instruction, and they hold the druids in great esteem. For they decide almost all disputes, both public and private: if some crime has been committed, if there has been murder done, if there is a dispute over an inheritance or over territory, they decide the issue and settle the rewards and penalties. If any individual or group of people does not abide by their decision, the druids ban them from sacrifices. This is their most severe punishment. Those who are banned in this way are counted among the wicked and criminal: everyone shuns them and avoids approaching or talking to them, so as not to suffer any harm from contact with them. . . .

Druids are not accustomed to take part in war, nor do they pay taxes like the rest of the people. . . . The principal doctrine they attempt to impart is that souls do not die but after death cross from one person to another. Because the fear of death is thereby set aside, they consider this a strong inducement to physical courage. Besides this, they debate many subjects and teach them to their young men—for example, the stars and their movements, the size of the universe and the earth, the nature of things, and the strength and power of the immortal gods.

The second class is that composed of the knights. When necessity arises and some war flares up—which before Caesar's arrival used to happen almost every year, so that they were either on the offensive themselves or fending off attacks—they are all involved in the campaign. Each man has as many retainers and dependents about him as is appropriate to his status in terms of his birth and resources. This is the sole form of power and influence they know.

The whole of the Gallic nation is much given to religious practices. For this reason those who are afflicted with serious illnesses and those who are involved in battles and danger either offer human sacrifice or vow that they will do so, and employ the druids to manage these sacrifices. For they believe that unless one human life is offered for another, the power and presence of the immortal gods cannot be propitiated.

Sources: Julius Caesar, *Seven Commentaries on the Gallic War with an Eighth Commentary by Aulus Hirtius,* trans. Carolyn Hammond (New York: Oxford University Press, 1996), pp. 126–128.

For additional information on this topic, go to http://college.hmco.com.

Pompey, in front of a statue of Pompey himself, where the senate was meeting that day. It had been eighty-nine years since the murder of Tiberius Gracchus.

The assassins called themselves Liberators, believing that they were freeing themselves from tyranny just as the founders of the Republic had done centuries before. Indeed, one of the chief conspirators, Marcus Junius Brutus (ca. 85–42 B.C.), claimed descent from Lucius Junius Brutus, traditional leader of the revolt against the Tarquins that was thought to have established the Republic. Like his co-conspirator Gaius Longinus Cassius (d. 42 B.C.), Brutus had been a magistrate, military officer, and provincial administrator.

The assassination of Caesar threw Rome back into turmoil. Civil war followed for the next thirteen years, first between the Liberators and Caesar's partisans and then between the two leading Caesarians. The final struggle pitted Mark Antony (Marcus Antonius, ca. 83–30 B.C.), Caesar's chief lieutenant and the man who inherited his love affair with Cleopatra, against Octavian (Gaius Julius Caesar Octavianus, 63 B.C.–A.D. 14), Caesar's grandnephew and adopted son and heir to Caesar's name and his huge fortune. At first it looked as if Antony had the upper hand because Octavian was young and inexperienced, was not a general, and was cursed with poor health. Octavian was, however, a man of unusual cunning and prudence. His forces defeated Antony and Cleopatra at the naval battle of Actium (off northwestern Greece) in 31 B.C.; their suicides followed shortly. The Roman world held its breath to see how Octavian would govern it.

■ The World of Cicero

Marcus Tullius Cicero° (106–43 B.C.) is one of the best-known figures of all antiquity. Like Marius, he was a wealthy equestrian from the central Italian town of Arpinum who, as consul (in 63 B.C.), became a "new man." Cicero was an optimas and defender of the senate, though ready for compromise with the equestrians, from whose ranks he himself had arisen. He made his name by successfully leading the opposition to Lucius Sergius Catilina, a down-and-out patrician who organized a debtors' revolt in Etruria; the army smashed the rebellion.

Cicero was intelligent, ambitious, and talented. As a young man he studied philosophy and oratory in Greece. As a result, he produced elevated and serious writings. Never as original as Plato or Aristotle, Cicero

---

Cicero (SIS-er-o)

nonetheless was crucial in making the Latin language a vessel for the heritage of Greek thought. A prolific writer, Cicero produced over a hundred orations, of which about sixty survive; several treatises on oratory; philosophical writings on politics, ethics, epistemology (the study of the nature of knowledge), and theology; poetry, of which little survives; and numerous letters. After his death in 43 B.C., his immense correspondence was published with little censored. The letters and speeches provide a vivid, detailed, and sometimes damning picture of politics.

Politics in the Late Republic was loud and boisterous. The elite prided itself on free speech and open debate. In senate deliberations, court cases, and public meetings in the Forum that preceded assembly votes, oratory—sometimes great oratory—was common. Few orators in history, though, have matched Cicero's ability to lead and mislead an audience by playing on its feelings. He knew every rhetorical trick and precisely when each was appropriate.

Because of increased freedom and greater educational opportunities, during the Late Republic it was possible for elite women as well as men to study oratory. Private tutors were common among the aristocracy, and girls often received lessons alongside their brothers. Girls sometimes also profited from a father's expertise. A particularly dramatic case is that of Hortensia, daughter of Quintus Hortensius Hortalus (114–50 B.C.), a famous orator and rival of Cicero. An excellent speaker herself, Hortensia defied tradition by arguing successfully in the Roman Forum in 42 B.C. against a proposed war tax on wealthy women.

Cicero pilloried one elite woman who enjoyed considerable freedom: Clodia (b. ca. 95 B.C.). Sister of the notorious populist gang leader Clodius and wife of optimas politician Metellus Celer (d. 59 B.C.), Clodia moved in Rome's highest circles. Cicero accused her of poisoning her husband (the charge was unprovable). She is better remembered from the poems of Catullus (ca. 85–54 B.C.), where she is called Lesbia. In passionate and psychologically complex verse, Catullus describes the ups and downs of their affair, which Clodia eventually ended.

Ordinary people lacked the education and freedom to express themselves in the manner of a Catullus or Hortensia, but a less civilized means of expression was open to them: the political gang. Brawls and violence between the rival groups of Clodius, a supporter of Caesar, and Milo, a supporter of the senate, became increasingly common in the fifties B.C. As dictator, Caesar abolished the gangs. (See the box "Reading Sources: Cicero in Defense of Milo.")

❧ READING SOURCES

Cicero in Defense of Milo

On January 18, 52 B.C., a brawl between the rival gangs of Clodius and Milo on the Appian Way left Clodius dead. Cicero himself defended Milo, a fellow optimas, but Milo was convicted and exiled. As this excerpt shows, Cicero's speech to the jury reveals both the violence of Late Republican life and the elegance of his rhetoric.

As subsequent events demonstrated, his [Clodius's] plan was to take up a position in front of his own country manor, and set an ambush for Milo on the spot. . . .

Meanwhile, Milo . . . attended the Senate on that day, until the meeting was concluded. Then he proceeded to his home, changed his shoes and his clothes, waited for the usual period when his wife got ready, and then started off at just about the time when Clodius could have got back to Rome if it had been his intention to return at all on the day in question. But instead he encountered Clodius in the country. . . .

And so at about five in the afternoon, or thereabouts, he found himself confronted by Clodius before the gates of the latter's house. Milo was instantly set upon by a crowd of armed men who charged down from the higher ground; while, simultaneously, others rushed up from in front and killed the driver of the coach. Milo flung back his cloak, leapt out of the vehicle, and defended himself with energy. But meanwhile the people with Clodius were brandishing their drawn swords, and while some of them ran towards the coach in order to fall upon Milo from the rear, others believed he was already slain and began to attack his slaves who had been following behind him. A number of those slaves of Milo's lost their lives defending their master with loyal determination. Others, however, who could see the fight round the coach but were unable to get to their mas-

ter's help, heard from Clodius' own lips that Milo was slain, and believed the report. And so these slaves, without the orders or knowledge or presence of their master—and I am going to speak quite frankly, and not with any aim of denying the charge but just exactly as the situation developed—did what every man would have wished his own slaves to do in similar circumstances.

The incident, gentlemen, took place exactly as I have described it. The attacker was defeated. Force was frustrated by force; or, to put the matter more accurately, evil was overcome by good. Of the gain to our country and yourselves and all loyal citizens, I say nothing. It is not my intention to urge that the deed be counted in favor of Milo—the man whose self-preservation was destined to mean the preservation of the Republic and yourselves. No, my defense is that he was justified in acting to save his life. Civilized people are taught this by logic, barbarians by necessity, communities by tradition; and the lesson is inculcated even in wild beasts by nature itself. . . . That being so, if you come to the conclusion that this particular action was criminal, you are in the same breath deciding that every other man in the history of the world who has ever fought back against a robber deserves nothing better than death. . . .

Source: Cicero, "In Defense of Titus Annius Milo," in *Selected Political Speeches of Cicero,* trans. Michael Grant (Harmondsworth, England: Penguin, 1969), pp. 232–234.

Cicero's works provide evidence of a crucial development in the practice of Roman law. Often unheralded, what Cicero's contemporaries did was invent the notion of the legal expert, a person devoted to explaining and interpreting the law. Roman law needed interpretation because it was complex and intricate. Much of it was the work not of legislators but of magistrates, who issued annual statements setting forth how their courts would work. The result was unsystematic and sometimes contradictory and cried out for someone to make sense of it.

Enter the jurisconsults, legal interpreters who emerged in the third and second centuries B.C. At first they had no special standing, but in the first century they became true jurists; their interpretations began to be considered authoritative. No earlier Mediterranean society had a professional class of legal experts, but no earlier society had faced issues as complicated and turbulent, or had grown to 3 million citizens, as the Roman Republic did in the mid-first century B.C. The Western tradition of legal science has its roots in Rome.

Rome's political system, unlike its legal system, did not adapt flexibly to changing circumstances. The disenfranchised of the Late Republic had reasonable goals: land for those who had fought for their country and admission to the senate of a wider group. Yet the old elite resisted both. Cicero's solution was to build on Sulla's reforms by uniting the senatorial and equestrian orders and by widening the Roman ruling class to include the elite of all Italy. The expanded ruling class could close ranks and establish *otium cum dignitate,* "peace with respect for rank." Cicero's proposed new order was distinctly hierarchical.

In the turbulent times of the Late Republic, the Roman elite often turned to the Hellenistic philosophers. The poet Lucretius° (ca. 94–55 B.C.) describes the Epicurean ideal of withdrawal into the contemplative life in a long didactic epic called *On the Nature of Things.* Most elite Romans, however, including Cicero, preferred the activist philosophy of Stoicism (see page 128). Cicero put forth a generous view of human brotherhood. He argued that all people share a spark of divinity and are protected by natural law. Consequently, all persons have value and importance and should treat others generously. Such ideas would be influential in the new Roman Empire when, under the leadership of Augustus, fair treatment of provincials was a major theme. For Cicero, however, these ideas existed more as theory than as practice.

Cicero did not hide his lack of sympathy for his fellow citizens who were poor. In one speech he castigated "artisans and shopkeepers and all that kind of scum"; in a letter he complained about "the wretched half-starved populace, which attends mass meetings and sucks the blood of the treasury." Cicero also made his disdain for democracy clear: "The greatest number," he said, "should not have the greatest power."

Elitist as Cicero's views were, they were by no means extremist. Cassius, Brutus, and the other Liberators had little interest in even Cicero's limited compromises.

Their stubbornness proved to be their downfall, for dispossessed peasants and ambitious equestrians transferred their loyalties to Julius Caesar and, later, to Augustus. One of Caesar's supporters, Sallust (86–ca. 34 B.C.), wrote biting and bitter works of history that indicted the greed and corruption of the optimates, whom he blamed for the decline of the Republic. In any case, peace was not restored, for the generation of Liberators was wiped out in renewed civil war and a new generation emerged, weary for peace.

SUMMARY

 ROME was destined to provide Western civilization with many basic notions about government and empire, but Rome sprang from humble origins. A central Italian village at first, Rome was urbanized after contact with more sophisticated neighbors. Rome became a monarchy and then a republic. It practiced imperialism with almost unlimited success, but ultimately the weight of empire brought down first the social system and then the political regime.

The Republic was a mixed constitution. It combined popular power with control by an oligarchy. In its first centuries, the oligarchy displayed flexibility and wisdom. It proved able to accommodate not only the competitive instincts of the aristocracy and the recently rich but also the land-hunger of the common people. The old aristocracy of the patricians opened its ranks to the newly ambitious leaders of the plebeians and also made room in the government for popular representation. The engrained hierarchy of the Roman social and cultural system helped keep politics stable.

The elite channeled popular energies into protecting the young Republic from its numerous rivals in central Italy. Rome consolidated its control of that region by wisely treating its allies with a mixture of firmness and generosity. By extending Roman citizenship, Rome gave them a stake in continued Roman hegemony. Having disposed of its nearest enemies, Rome mounted a quest for absolute security, a quest that led to conquest in Italy and the rest of the Mediterranean. Greed and ambition, as well as fear, were powerful motives of expansion.

Having defeated all opponents near and far, Rome seemed to have won absolute security by the mid-second century B.C. Yet its strength was deceptive. Contact with Greek culture liberated the Romans from ruder, peasant ways but also loosened previous restraints. A

Lucretius (loo-CREE-shus)

huge influx of slaves made acquisition of large estates profitable. The Italian peasantry was already weakened by conscription and the devastation of farmland, and the elite was arrogant from its military success. Thus, it became easy for the strong to confiscate the land of the weak. The result was a growing and dangerous social instability with military and political ramifications. At the very moment of triumph, the Republic was in grave danger.

Members of the Roman elite, rather than displaying that talent for compromise that had made the Republic great, refused to share their wealth with the poor. The poor, however, got their revenge by throwing their support to new patrons, military leaders who raised private armies to win land for their followers and glory for themselves. By the first century B.C., the Republic had collapsed under the weight of political maneuvering, judicial murders, gang warfare, and civil war. The time was right for the last of the private commanders—Octavian—to recreate the Roman state under his leadership as Augustus, first of the emperors. In the next chapter we examine the world that he remade.

■ Notes

1. *The Aeneid of Virgil*, trans. Allen Mandelbaum (Berkeley: University of California Press, 1971), pp. 160–161.
2. P. A. Brunt, *Social Conflicts in the Roman Republic* (New York: Norton, 1971), p. 17.

■ Suggested Reading

Barker, H., and T. Rasmussen. *The Etruscans*. 1997. Excellent historical introduction and guidebook, written with gusto.

Beard, Mary, and Michael Crawford. *Rome in the Late Republic: Problems and Interpretations*. 2d ed. 1999. An unusual and innovative approach to the subject, emphasizing sociocultural and institutional analysis more than narrative.

Brunt, P. A. *Social Conflicts in the Roman Republic*. 1971. A fine, non-Marxist view of the importance of class conflict throughout Republican history.

Cornell, T. J. *The Beginnings of Rome: Italy and Rome from the Bronze Age to the Punic Wars (c. 1000–264 B.C.)*. 1995. A readable and ambitious survey combining archaeological and literary evidence, often in support of iconoclastic conclusions.

———, and J. Matthews. *Atlas of the Roman World*. 1982. A readable introduction to Roman history written by two scholars; the maps and photos are beautiful, among the best available.

Crawford, Michael. *The Roman Republic*. 2d ed. 1993. The best short introduction, sophisticated, lively, and concise.

Dixon, Suzanne. *The Roman Family*. 1992. A good historical study in complexity, strongly aware of the difference between the myth and reality of the Roman family, and nicely written.

Ward, A. M., F. M. Heichelheim, and C. A. Yeo. *A History of the Roman People*. 3d ed. 1998. The best introductory textbook, scholarly and readable.

 For a searchable list of additional readings for this chapter, go to http://college.hmco.com.

Luxury Goods and Gender Wars in Rome

The carefully wrought gold earrings shown here represent the height of fashion in the central Mediterranean around 200 B.C. Hellenistic taste favored such gold hoop earrings embellished with inlaid colored glass. This set, moreover, displays one of the favorite decorative motifs of the goldsmiths of Magna Graecia in southern Italy during this period: the dove. The artist has crafted the doves as pendants: note how each dove hangs from the earring and stands on a small base trimmed with a garland. Two inches tall, the earrings are miniature sculptures. A Roman woman might wear such jewelry proudly, certain that it bespoke not only good taste and wealth but also the power of her city to command the best artistry of the Greek world.

Not all Romans, however, looked with favor on such finery. Some said it represented not Roman success but decadence. While some observers saw, reflected in the gold, the sight of Greek craftsmen dancing to Roman tunes, others perceived a scene of corruption and wastefulness. Both men and women in the Roman elite began to indulge a taste for luxury in the third century B.C., but women came in for special criticism.

Conservatives considered women's luxuries to pose a special threat to society because they represented not only foreign influence but a threat to right order in the household. If women controlled the economic power to purchase luxury goods, where, then, was the authority of the paterfamilias? More open-minded Romans defended women's contributions to society and their right to the recognition that luxury goods betokened. A debate on women's luxuries raged in Rome around 200 B.C. Let us examine both its historical background and the position of its most famous participant, the conservative champion Marcus Porcius Cato (234–149 B.C.), known as Cato the Censor.

From their first conquest in Magna Graecia in the third century B.C., Romans began to bring home Greek artists and craftsmen and their works. The trickle of art flowing toward Rome is said to have become a flood when Roman armies entered Greece and Anatolia. The simple and frugal elite of traditional Roman ideology began to give way in the third century B.C. to lovers of the good life.

The new wealth and new tastes created a luxury goods industry in Rome. Traditionalist opinion was shocked. Not that Rome lacked wealthy households before 300 B.C. Rather, before then Republican ideology had successfully frowned on conspicuous consumption and display. Now it became common for elite men to wear rings and their wives and daughters to don jewelry as well as fine clothes and cosmetics and—a particular sign of wealth and honor—to ride in carriages. Hannibal's invasion of Italy put the brakes on luxury, however, because it forced Romans to adopt austerity for the duration of the war. In 215 B.C. the Oppian Law put limits on the gold and fine clothing women could own and on their privilege of riding in carriages.

Twenty years later, in 195 B.C., when the emergency had passed, a proposal was made to repeal the law. Elite women demonstrated in favor of repeal. According to the historian Livy, Valerius (one of the consuls for 195) supported their position:

> Women cannot claim magistracies or priesthoods or triumphs or military decorations or awards or the spoils of war. Cosmetics and adornments are women's decorations. They delight and boast of them and this is what our ancestors called women's estate.[*]

Enter Cato, the other consul for 195 and an advocate of traditional Roman values of austerity. Livy reports that Cato denounced luxury goods as signs of Greek corruption and women's license, even perhaps of women's eventual equality. Although some scholars doubt whether Cato ever so criticized the Greeks, there

---

[*]Trans. E. Fantham in Elaine Fantham, Helene Peet Foley, Natalie Boymel Kampen, Sarah B. Pomeroy, and H. A. Shapiro, *Women in the Classical World: Image and Text* (New York: Oxford University Press, 1994), p. 261.

Hellenistic Earrings, Gold and Inlaid Glass
(Harriet Otis Cruft Fund. Courtesy of the Museum of Fine Arts, Boston)

is no doubt about his hostility to luxury. As censor in 184 B.C., he assessed taxes on luxury goods and slaves at ten times their market value in order to discourage their use.

Nor is there any doubt about the degree of male worry about women's wealth in Cato's Rome—even though the repeal of the Oppian Law eventually passed in 195 B.C., over Cato's opposition. For example, a character in the play *Pot of Gold,* by Cato's contemporary Plautus, condemns wealthy wives with their "fine clothes and jewelry . . . and maids and mules and coachmen and footmen and pages and private carriages."** In 186 B.C., nine years after the repeal of the Oppian Law, some elite women were found guilty of participation in alleged orgies of the god Bacchus (the Greek Dionysus). Seventeen years later, in 169 B.C., a law was passed forbidding the wealthiest Roman men from leaving more than half of their property to a daughter, in order to prevent the loss through marriage of most of a family's wealth.

How can we explain such attention by the government to the behavior of elite women? The answer in large part is that war and empire had brought such women new power, power that elite men feared. While those men had often spent years abroad fighting Rome's wars, their wives had learned how to run households. The enormous wealth brought home from those wars often ended up as dowries. Women had the right to retain control of part of their dowries, which sometimes made them wealthier than their husbands. Cato complained that some wives went so far as to lend money to their husbands and then send slaves to reclaim the interest.

So the museum-piece earrings that now win our admiration as works of art once stirred up gender wars that rocked the Roman elite. They remind us how rich in unanticipated consequences was Rome's imperial success. Nonetheless, they must not blind us to the imbalance of wealth in Rome. As the carriages of wealthy women rolled by, the vast majority of Roman women could only stand and watch, hoping to catch a glimpse of gold.

**Ibid.

CHAPTER **6**

THE imperial family of Rome walks in stately procession to a sacrifice: Livia, wife of Augustus, first of the emperors; his daughter, Julia; Julia's husband, Agrippa; and various cousins and in-laws and their children. They are formally dressed in togas and gowns, heads wreathed. The men and women gaze seriously; the boys and girls have impish looks, betraying thoughts of mischief as they hold their parents' hands. They are all carved in stone, one of several sculptured reliefs decorating the walls of a public monument in Rome. Dedicated on Livia's birthday in 9 B.C., the monument shown here illustrates the propaganda themes of the new regime, among them the happy family as symbol of peace after generations of civil war. The senate, which had commissioned the monument, called it the *Ara Pacis Augustae,* or Altar of Augustan Peace.

Having made peace was no idle boast on Augustus's part. Not only did he end the Roman revolution, but he began a period of two hundred years of prosperity and stability in the Roman Empire. Augustus took advantage of Rome's war-weariness to create a new government out of the ruins of the Republic. Like the builders of the Early Republic's constitution, Augustus displayed the Roman genius for compromise. He had superb political instincts. Although Augustus retained the final say, he shared a degree of power with the senate. He made financial sacrifices to feed the urban poor and distribute farms to landless peasants. He ended Rome's seemingly limitless expansion and stabilized the borders of the empire. He began to raise the provinces to a status of equality with Italy.

Imperial Rome
31 B.C.–A.D. 284

Augustus and the Principate,
31 B.C.–A.D. 68

The Roman Peace and Its Collapse,
A.D. 69–284

Early Christianity

Ara Pacis (detail), Rome.
(Scala/Art Resource, NY)

The *pax Romana*° ("Roman peace"), at its height between A.D. 96 and 180, was an era of enlightened emperors, thriving cities, intellectual vitality, and artistic and architectural achievement in an empire of 50–100 million people. Yet it was also an era of slavery. More positively, the Roman peace was a period of heightened spirituality. In the peaceful and diverse empire, ideas traveled from people to people, and the religious beliefs of an obscure sect from western Asia began to spread around the Mediterranean and into northern Europe. The new religion was Christianity.

After 180, Rome slowly passed into a grim period marked in turn by bad emperors, civil war, inflation, plague, invasion, and defeat. After reaching a nadir around 235–253, Rome's fortunes began to improve under a series of reforming emperors who would forge a stronger and vastly different empire.

QUESTIONS TO CONSIDER

- How did Augustus lay the foundations of the new, imperial government that would replace the Roman Republic? Why was he so successful?

- What was life like in the era of the Roman peace?

- How was the Roman Empire shaken by the crisis of the third century A.D., and how did it survive?

- What were the origins of Christianity in Palestine, and how did the new religion spread around the Roman world?

TERMS TO KNOW

Augustus	Virgil
Principate	Tacitus
Livia	Jesus of Nazareth
pax Romana	Paul of Tarsus
Flavians	Christianity
Julio-Claudians	rabbinic Judaism
third-century crisis	

AUGUSTUS AND THE PRINCIPATE, 31 B.C.–A.D. 68

 N 31 B.C. Gaius Julius Caesar Octavianus (63 B.C.–A.D. 14), or Octavian, as Augustus was then known, stood at the top of the Roman world. His forces had defeated those of Mark Antony and Cleopatra at the Battle of Actium in northwestern Greece, whereupon his two chief enemies committed suicide. Few could have predicted the vision and statesmanship that Octavian now displayed. He spent the next forty-five years healing the wounds of a century of revolution. He did nothing less than lay the foundations of the prosperous two centuries enjoyed by the empire under the Roman peace (see Map 6.1).

■ The Political Settlement

Octavian was both an astute politician and a lucky one. He was lucky in the length and violence of the civil wars. After Actium, most of his enemies were dead, so establishing the one-man rule that he claimed was necessary to restore stability was relatively easy. He was also lucky to live to be nearly 80—he had plenty of time to consolidate his rule. He was a cagey man and a sharp judge of others. A careful planner who loved to gamble with dice, Octavian never took chances in the game of power. Octavian learned the lesson of Caesar's greatest mistake. He understood that the Roman elite, however weakened, was still strong enough to oppose a ruler who flaunted monarchial power. To avoid a second Ides of March, therefore, Octavian was infinitely diplomatic.

Rather than call himself Dictator, Octavian took the title of *Princeps*° ("First Citizen"), an old title of respect in the senate. From *princeps* comes *Principate*,° a term often used to describe the constitutional monarchy of the "Early Empire," the name that historians have given to the period from 31 B.C. to A.D. 192. Four years after Actium, in 27 B.C. the senate granted Octavian the honorific title *augustus*, symbolizing the augmentation, or increase, of Octavian's authority. He was also known as *Caesar* and *divi filius* ("son of a god"), which tied him to Julius Caesar. Another name, *imperator* ("commander" and, later, "emperor"), recalled the military might that Augustus (as we shall henceforth call him) could call on if needed.

---

pax Romana (PAHKS ro-MAHN-uh)

princeps (PRIN-keps)   Principate (PRIN-sih-pate)

In 27 B.C. Augustus proclaimed "the transfer of the state to the free disposal of the senate and the people"—that is, the restoration of the Republic. Remembering similar claims by Sulla and Caesar, few Romans were likely to believe this, and few would have wanted the Republic restored in any case. They no doubt appreciated their ruler's tact, however. (See the box "Reading Sources: Augustus: The Official Story.")

Two strokes of genius marked the new regime. First, Augustus held power without monopolizing public offices. He held the civil authority of the tribunate without being a tribune and the military authority of provincial generals without holding a specific command. Ambitious Romans could still attain public office while deferring to Augustus's power. Second, the new government divided the provinces between Augustus and the senate. To check any new would-be Caesar, Augustus kept for himself the frontier provinces, with the main concentration of armies, as well as grain-rich Egypt (which had been annexed as a Roman province after Actium). The local commanders were loyal equestrians who owed their success to Augustus. Most of the other provinces continued to be ruled as before by senators serving as governors.

Augustus wanted advice without dissent. He used the senate, or rather a committee of senators and magistrates, as a sounding board; the group evolved into a permanent advisory body. Ordinary senate meetings, however, what with informers and secret agents, lost their old freedom of speech. The popular assemblies fared even worse, as their powers were limited and eventually transferred to the senate. Nor would unruly crowds be tolerated. Augustus established the city of Rome's first police force and also stationed there his own personal guard. Called the praetorians°, or Praetorian Guard, the name used for a Roman general's bodyguard, the guard would play a crucial role in future imperial politics.

More important for the public good, Augustus established the first civil service, consisting of a series of prefectures—or departments—supervising, for example, the city watch, the grain supply, the water supply, the building of roads and bridges, tax collection, and the provisioning of the armies. Equestrians and freedmen were prominent in these prefectures and in provincial government, so they enthusiastically supported the Principate.

Although one may speak loosely of "imperial bureaucracy," neither Augustus nor his successors ever established a tight administrative grip on their far-flung empire. As in all ancient empires, Roman government tended to be decentralized and limited. In an age in which few public officials received a salary, bribes were winked at.

CHRONOLOGY

31 B.C.	Octavian defeats Antony and Cleopatra at Actium
27 B.C.	Augustus establishes Principate
27 B.C.–A.D. 68	Julio-Claudian dynasty
19 B.C.	Death of Virgil
ca. A.D. 27–30	Ministry of Jesus
ca. 67	Death of Paul of Tarsus
69–96	Flavian dynasty
70	Temple in Jerusalem destroyed
79	Eruption of Vesuvius
96–180	The "Five Good Emperors"
ca. 117	Death of Tacitus
193–235	Severan dynasty
ca. 200	Mishnah and New Testament each completed
212	Almost all free inhabitants of empire awarded Roman citizenship
235–284	Period of military anarchy

■ The Economic and Social Settlement

The old Roman ruling class made its peace with Augustus, but some never forgave him for ending their ancient privileges. The conservative historian Tacitus° (ca. A.D. 55–117) looked back wistfully to the Late Republic as a golden era of freedom, eloquence, and "the old sound morality." (See the box "Reading Sources: Augustus: A Skeptical View.") Even Tacitus, however, was forced to admit that most people in the Roman world welcomed and admired the Principate. The reason is simple: Augustus and his successors brought peace and prosperity after a century of disasters under the Late Republic.

The Augustan period enjoyed affluence, especially in Italy; the other provinces caught up with Italy by the second century A.D. Agriculture flourished with the end of civil war. Italian industries became leaders in exports. Italian glass bowls and windowpanes, iron arms and tools, fancy silver eating utensils and candlesticks, and

---

praetorians (pre-TOR-ee-unz)

Tacitus (TASS-ih-tus)

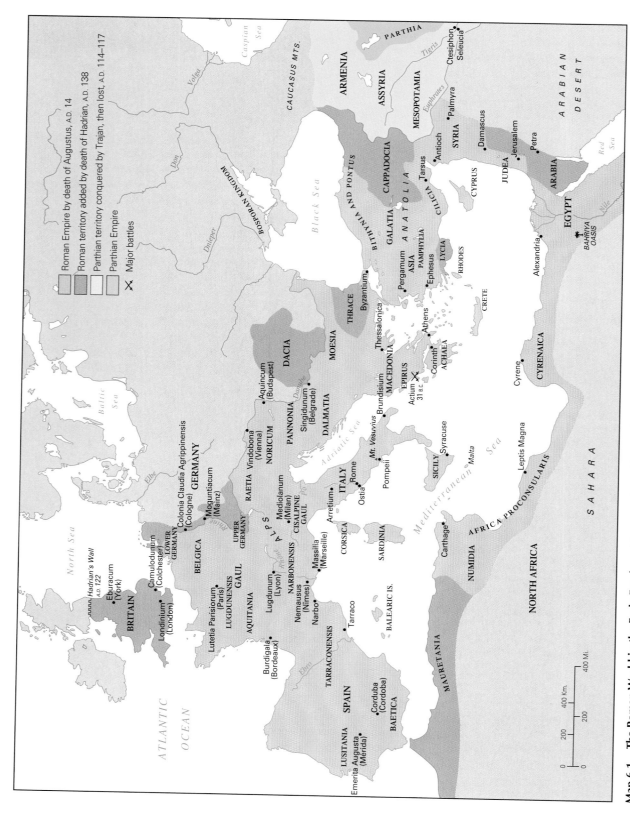

Map 6.1 **The Roman World in the Early Empire** Many modern cities are built on the sites of Roman foundations, evidence of the immense extent of the Roman Empire at its height.

Roman Empire by death of Augustus, A.D. 14

Roman territory added by death of Hadrian, A.D. 138

Parthian territory conquered by Trajan, then lost, A.D. 114–117

Parthian Empire

X Major battles

❧ READING SOURCES

Augustus: The Official Story

Not long before his death in A.D. 14, the emperor Augustus arranged for the display in Rome of two bronze tablets containing a record of his achievements. Copies of "the achievements of the Divine Augustus, by which he brought the world under the empire of the Roman people, and of the expenses which he bore for the state and people of Rome" were displayed around the empire. A complete copy survived in the Roman city of Ancyra in Anatolia (modern Ankara, Turkey).

1. At the age of nineteen on my own responsibility and at my own expense I raised an army, with which I successfully championed the liberty of the republic when it was oppressed by the tyranny of a faction. . . .

3. I undertook many civil and foreign wars by land and sea throughout the world, and as victor I spared the lives of all citizens who asked for mercy. 2. [*sic*] When foreign peoples could safely be pardoned I preferred to preserve rather than eliminate them. 3. The Roman citizens who took the soldier's oath of obedience to me numbered about 500,000. I settled rather more than 300,000 of these in colonies or sent them back to their home towns after a period of service; to all these I assigned lands or gave money as rewards for their military service. . . .

20. I restored the Capitol and the theatre of Pompey, both works at great expense without inscribing my name on either. 2. I restored the channels of the aqueducts, which in several places were falling into disrepair through age, and I brought water from a new spring into the aqueduct called Marcia, doubling the supply. . . . 4. In my sixth consulship I restored eighty-two temples of the gods in the city on the authority of the senate, neglecting none that required restoration at the time. . . .

26. I extended the territory of all those provinces of the Roman people on whose borders lay peoples not subject to our government. . . .

27. I added Egypt to the empire of the Roman people. . . .

28. . . . I compelled the Parthians to restore to me the spoils and standards of three Roman armies and to ask as suppliants for the friendship of the Roman people. Those standards I deposited in the innermost shrine of the temple of Mars the Avenger. . . .

35. In my thirteenth consulship the senate, the equestrian order and the whole people of Rome gave me the title of Father of my Country, and resolved that this should be inscribed in the porch of my house and in the Curia Julia and in the Forum Augustum below the chariot which had been set there in my honor by decree of the senate. 2. At the time of writing I am in my seventy-sixth year.

Source: P. A. Brunt and J. M. Moore, eds., *Res Gestae Divi Augusti: The Achievements of the Divine Augustus* (New York: Oxford University Press, 1967), pp. 19–37.

bronze statues and pots circulated from Britain to central Asia.

The perennial problem of the Late Republic had been land-hunger, which drove peasants into the arms of ambitious generals. Augustus kept his troops happy by compensating 300,000 loyal veterans with land, money, or both, often in new overseas colonies. At first he paid out these rewards from his own private sources; after A.D. 6, he made the rich pay via new taxes. In other words, Augustus made the elite part of a property transfer that they had resisted since the time of the Gracchi. Yet it was only a partial transfer, limited to soldiers and their families. The result kept the peace, but many non-soldiers in Italy remained poor, as of course did the huge numbers of slaves.

As for the renegade commanders who had bedeviled the Late Republic, Augustus cut their potential power base by reducing the size of the army, gradually cutting

❧ READING SOURCES

Augustus: A Skeptical View

Tacitus, a member of the senatorial elite of the Early Empire, looked back longingly to the freedom of the Roman Republic. His Annals *offer a scathing view of the early emperors, beginning with Augustus, whose reign he discusses briefly.*

Famous writers have recorded Rome's early glories and disasters. The Augustan Age, too, had its distinguished historians. But then the rising tide of flattery exercised a deterrent effect. The reigns of Tiberius, Gaius, Claudius, and Nero were described during their lifetimes in fictitious terms, for fear of the consequences; whereas the accounts written after their deaths were influenced by still raging animosities. So I have decided to say a little about Augustus, with special attention to his last period, and then go on to the reign of Tiberius and what followed. I shall write without indignation or partisanship: in my case the customary incentives to these are lacking.

The violent deaths of Brutus and Cassius left no Republican forces in the field. Defeat came to Sextus Pompeius in Sicily, Lepidus was dropped, Antony killed. So even the Caesarian party had no leader left except the "Caesar" himself, Octavian. He gave up the title of Triumvir emphasizing instead his position as consul; and the powers of a tribune, he proclaimed, were good enough for him—powers for the protection of ordinary people.

He seduced the army with bonuses, and his cheap food policy was successful bait for civilians. Indeed, he attracted everybody's goodwill by the enjoyable gift of peace. Then he gradually pushed ahead and absorbed the functions of the senate, the officials, and even the law. Opposition did not exist. War or judicial murder had disposed of all men of spirit. Upper-class survivors found that slavish obedience was the way to succeed, both politically and financially. They had profited from revolution, and so now they liked the security of the existing arrangement better than the dangerous uncertainties of the old regime. Besides, the new order was popular in the provinces. There, government by Senate and People was looked upon skeptically as a matter of sparring dignitaries and extortionate officials. The legal system had provided no remedy against these, since it was wholly incapacitated by violence, favoritism, and—most of all—bribery.

Source: Tacitus, *The Annals of Imperial Rome,* rev. ed., trans. Michael Grant (Harmondsworth, England: Penguin, 1988), p. 32.

---

the number of legions from over sixty to twenty-eight. The total size of the army, including light infantry and cavalry, was about 300,000. This reduction lightened Rome's tax burden but left Augustus with little room to expand the empire. In A.D. 9 Rome lost three legions to a native revolt against Rome's plan to extend its rule in Germany as far east as the Elbe River. Short of manpower, Augustus had to accept the Rhine River as Rome's new German frontier (see Map 6.1).

Imperial defense remained a major issue. Strong Roman armies were a necessity along the hostile European frontier. On the friendlier border in western Asia and northern Africa, Augustus and his immediate successors set up client kingdoms, such as Judea and Armenia, to protect Roman territory. As for Parthia, Augustus compromised. He won no new territory but did achieve the symbolic victory of a return of the legionary standards lost by Crassus at Carrhae in 53 B.C.

Back in Rome the urban poor, many of them freedmen, enjoyed a more efficient system of free grain distribution under Augustus and a large increase in games and public entertainment—the imperial policy of "bread and circuses" designed to content the masses. Augustus also set up a major public works program, which provided jobs for the poor. He prided himself on having found Rome "a city of brick" and having left it "a city of marble."

To promote his ideology of renewal, Augustus sponsored social legislation embodying the old Republican virtues. He passed a series of laws encouraging marriage and childbearing and discouraging promiscuity and adultery. Such legislation was so flagrantly disobeyed that in 2 B.C. Augustus felt compelled to make an example of his own daughter, Julia (39 B.C.–A.D. 14), his only child, whose adulteries were the talk of Rome. As punishment she was banished to a barren islet.

Augustus's era marks the beginning of the classical period of Roman jurisprudence, during which the professionalism that had begun to mark Roman law in the Late Republic became a permanent fact. It was probably Augustus who established the practice, followed by later

Augustus of Prima Porta   Named for the place where it was found, this statue (early first century A.D.) depicts an idealized and heroic Augustus. Scenes of victory, peace, and prosperity—symbols of the Principate—decorate his breastplate. Riding a dolphin, the Cupid at Augustus's feet recalls the Julian family's claim of descent from the goddess Venus. *(Alinari/Art Resource, NY)*

emperors, of granting a few distinguished jurists the exclusive right to issue legal opinions "on behalf of the princeps." He ensured, therefore, that experts guided the administration of justice. The first law school was opened in Rome under Augustus. Roman jurists, many of them provincials, adapted Roman law to the practices of the provinces. Although various provincial legal systems remained in use, the international system of Roman law was also used widely in the provinces.

In religion, too, Augustus was a legislator and reformer. He restored once-neglected cults and temples in order to appear as Rome's savior. He would probably have approved when, after his death, he was deified, just as Julius Caesar had been. Even while he was still alive, Augustus was worshiped in the provinces as a god— in both the East, where the cult of Roma and Augustus grew in popularity, and the West, where centers of emperor-worship were established at the sites of Lyon and Cologne (see Map 6.1). The imperial cult, an important part of state propaganda until the empire became Christian in the fourth century A.D., was well underway.

Deification, whether formal or informal, was a heady brew, but Augustus deserved it more than most. He not only ended the Late Republican era of civil wars but established the Roman Empire on a completely new footing. Republican freedom was gone, but the emperor and bureaucrats brought stability. The peace of the Augustan Principate would last, with few interruptions, for two hundred years. Few people in history have created order so successfully.

■ The Culture of the Augustan Age

Like *Periclean,* the adjective *Augustan°* has come to signify an era of literary and artistic flowering. In both periods strong elements of classicism shaped the arts—that is, an attempt to project fundamental, heroic, and idealized values, the values that the self-confident rulers of each epoch wished to promote. Both prose and poetry flourished in Augustus's empire. The emperor and his close adviser Maecenas° (d. 8 B.C.) were patrons of a number of important poets, chief among them Virgil° (70–19 B.C.) and Horace (65–8 B.C.). The historian Livy° (59 B.C.–A.D. 17), who wrote his history of Rome from the founding of the city to 9 B.C. under Augustus, also elicited the princeps's interest in his work. All three men contributed in their writings to the Augustan renewal and rededication of Rome.

Augustan (aw-GUS-tin)   **Maecenas** (my-SEE-nus)
Virgil (VER-jill)   **Livy** (LIV-ee)

Virgil Writing the Aeneid   This Roman mosaic from second- or third-century A.D. Tunisia shows Virgil seated, holding a copy of the *Aeneid*. He is flanked by two Muses, mythical sources of inspiration.   *(C. M. Dixon)*

In many ways, Virgil speaks for his contemporaries. In the *Eclogues*, poems that, following an Alexandrian model (see page 122), have rustic settings, Virgil describes the miseries of the civil wars and the blessings of peace under Augustus. "A god created this peace for us; for he will always be a god to me," as one character says. In the Fourth Eclogue, Virgil speaks of the birth of a child to usher in a restored Golden Age. At the church Council of Nicaea in A.D. 325 (see page 213), and later, this poem was given a Christian interpretation. In the *Georgics*, Virgil describes the glories of Italian agriculture, which, thanks to Augustus, could be practiced peacefully again.

Virgil's masterpiece is an epic poem, the *Aeneid*°, "the story of Aeneas," the legendary Trojan founder of Rome, or at least of the Latin town from which Rome's founders eventually came. Legend also makes Aeneas the ancestor of Augustus. Thus the *Aeneid* indirectly celebrates Augustus, often considered Rome's second founder. The poem explores the pain and burden as well as the glory of empire.

If Virgil's work has the grandeur of marble, Horace's poems—*Odes, Epodes, Satires, Epistles*, and *Ars Poetica* (*Art of Poetry*)—are more like finely cut gems. They tend to be polished, complex, and detached. Like Virgil, Horace explores the themes of war and peace and praises Augustus. "With Caesar [Augustus] holding the lands, I shall fear neither turmoil nor violent death," declares one of the *Odes*. Both Horace and Virgil successfully adapted Greek models and, in the process, created something new. Few writers have had a greater influence on the later Western literary tradition.

Only 35 of the original 142 books of Livy's ambitious history have survived. Livy is both a master storyteller and a superb ironist. His anecdotes of Roman history are vivid and told in a grand rhetorical style. Livy is our major source for the Roman monarchy and Early Republic, although his account of early Rome is long on myth and short on fact. Nevertheless, Livy is not merely an entertaining stylist but a profound thinker on the meaning of history. He embroiders the facts and engages in frank, subjective judgments intended to inspire both patriotism and reflection on the ironies of history.

Another patron of writers in Augustus's circle was Messalla, himself an orator as well as a statesman. Love poetry was his special interest. Among the poets Messalla supported were Ovid, best known for works on love and mythology; Tibullus, an eligist; and his ward, Sulpicia. Although little survives of Sulpicia's work, more of her work exists than of any other Roman woman. She describes her passion for one Cerinthus: "a worthy man . . . at last a love . . . of such a kind that my shame, Gossip, would be greater if I kept it covered than if I laid it bare."[1]

Augustus and his entourage were also great patrons of the arts and of architecture, which they considered propaganda tools. They sponsored many major building projects throughout the empire, especially in Rome, which gained temples, a new Forum of Augustus, the Theater of Marcellus, the Baths of Agrippa, the Pantheon, and the Mausoleum of Augustus.

■ The Julio-Claudians

Augustus and his successors presented the imperial household to the world as the ideal family, the very model of social order. Behind the walls of the palace, however, dwelt a troubled and sordid reality.

Augustus had only one child, Julia, from his first marriage, which ended in divorce. In 38 B.C. Augustus took as his second wife Livia° (58 B.C.–A.D. 29), who divorced her husband to marry Augustus even though she was pregnant with their second son. She did not bear Augustus children. Seeking a male successor, Augustus used Julia as a pawn in a game of dynastic marriage, divorce, and re-

---

Aeneid (ee-NEE-id)

Livia (LIV-ee-uh)

Julio-Claudian Cameo Known as the Grand Camée de France, this superb gem depicts the imperial family in its glory. The central scene shows Tiberius, Livia, and, among others, the child Caligula (extreme left). The deified Augustus hovers above them while barbarian captives are below. *(Giraudon/Art Resource, NY)*

marriage, but to no avail. Julia's first two husbands both predeceased her, as did two sons, each of whom Augustus had adopted. (In Rome it was common for a man without a birth son to adopt a son.) In the end, Augustus was forced to choose as successor, and adopt, a man he disliked, Tiberius° (42 B.C.– A.D. 37), Livia's elder son.

Livia was among the most powerful women of Roman history. One of Augustus's main advisers, she developed a reputation for intrigue, aimed, so gossip had it, at securing the succession for Tiberius. Livia's enemies accused her of poisoning many people, including Julia's husbands and sons; her own grandson, Germanicus (a brilliant general whose popularity threatened Tiberius's); and even Augustus himself, who died in bed after a short illness in A.D. 14.

From A.D. 14 to 68, Rome was ruled by other emperors from Augustus's family. The dynasty, known as the Julio-Claudians, consisted of Augustus's stepson Tiberius, great-grandson Caligula, grandnephew Claudius, and great-great-grandson Nero. For many elite Romans, this era was one of decadence and scandal and oppression of the old nobility. Ordinary people, however, generally enjoyed the benefits of stable, effective, and peaceful government.

The reign of Tiberius (r. 14–37) was remembered with trepidation by the elite for its treason trials and murders. The senate chafed as it steadily lost power to the princeps. The Roman masses grumbled because Tiberius cut back on games and building projects. But despite his shortcomings, Tiberius was a skilled and prudent administrator. He wisely drew back from war on the borders, reduced taxes and spending, and promoted honesty among provincial governors.

His successor, his nephew Gaius (r. 37–41), nicknamed Caligula° ("Baby Boots," after the boots he had worn as a little boy in his father's army camp), humiliated the senate and tried to have himself declared a living god. He made scandal into an art form. For example,

---

Tiberius (ty-BEER-ee-us)

Caligula (ca-LIG-yoo-luh)

he appointed his favorite horse not only high priest of a new cult in honor of Caligula the god but also a member of the senate. Caligula raised taxes and trumped up charges of treason in order to confiscate property. He wanted to have his statue erected in the Temple at Jerusalem. He would have had his way, but he was assassinated first, the victim of a high-level Roman conspiracy. After his death the senate debated restoring the Republic, but it was not to be.

Caligula's uncle, Claudius, was proclaimed emperor by the Praetorian Guard, which left the senate little choice but to support him. Physically handicapped, Claudius (r. 41–54) was often the butt of jokes, but he was a man of substance: a historian, politician, and priest and someone fully versed in the cunning ways of his family. An activist emperor, he expanded the imperial offices with their powerful freedmen; oversaw the construction of an artificial harbor at Rome's silt-clogged port of Ostia; and conquered Britain, where Roman arms had not intervened since Julius Caesar's forays in 55–54 B.C.

Claudius's death may have been the result of poisoning by his wife, who was also his niece, Agrippina° the Younger (A.D. 15–59); in any case, her son by a previous marriage, Nero, became emperor (r. 54–68). As princeps, Nero's scandalous behavior rivaled Caligula's, and his treason trials outdid Tiberius's. A great fire in 64 destroyed half of Rome. Nero mounted an extravagant rebuilding program afterward, although he was accused of having started the fire so that he could become famous as a builder. Nero found a scapegoat for the fire in the members of a small and relatively new religious sect, the Christians, whom he persecuted. Yet most ordinary Romans received good government from Nero, and they rewarded him with support. He was unpopular with the senatorial elite, however, and more serious, he failed to pay all his troops promptly. Confronted with a major revolt in 68, Nero committed suicide.

The next year, 69, witnessed Rome's first civil war in about a century. Three men each claimed the imperial purple after Nero. Finally, a fourth, Vespasian° (Titus Flavius Vespasianus, r. 69–79), commander of the army quelling revolt in the province of Judea, was able to make his claim stick. Peace was restored, but not the rule of Augustus's family. Vespasian founded a new dynasty, the Flavians° (r. 69–96), which was followed in turn by the Nervo-Trajanic (r. 96–138) and Antonine° (r. 138–192) dynasties. The ultimate tribute to Augustus may be that his regime was stable enough to survive the extinction of his family.

THE ROMAN PEACE AND ITS COLLAPSE, A.D. 69–284

MUCH about Rome in the second century A.D. appears attractive today. Within the multiethnic empire, opportunities for inhabitants to become part of the elite were increasing. The central government was on its way to granting Roman citizenship to nearly every free person in the empire, a process completed in the year 212. The emperors emphasized sharing prosperity and spreading it through the provinces. Italy was no longer the tyrant of the Mediterranean, but merely first among equals. To be sure, rebellions were crushed, but few people rebelled. This period, known as *pax Romana* or "the Roman peace," seems particularly golden in contrast with what followed: the disastrous and disordered third century A.D., in which the empire came close to collapse but survived because of a radical and rigid transformation.

■ The Flavians and the "Good Emperors"

The Flavian dynasty of Vespasian (r. 69–79) and his sons Titus (r. 79–81) and Domitian (r. 81–96) provided good government, and their successors built on their achievements. Unlike the Julio-Claudians, Vespasian hailed not from the old Roman nobility but from an Italian propertied family. A man of rough-and-ready character, Vespasian is supposed to have replied when Titus complained that a new latrine tax was beneath the dignity of the Roman government, "Son, money has no smell." Unlike his father and brother, Domitian reverted to frequent treason trials and persecution of the aristocracy, which earned him assassination in 96, although the empire as a whole enjoyed peace and sound administration under his reign.

The so-called Five Good Emperors are Nerva (r. 96–98), Trajan° (r. 98–117), Hadrian° (r. 117–138), and the first two Antonines, Antoninus Pius (r. 138–161) and Marcus Aurelius° (r. 161–180). They are in several ways examples of the principle of merit. Trajan, a Roman citizen born in Spain, was Rome's first emperor from outside Italy. Hadrian and Marcus Aurelius also came from Spain, and Antoninus Pius from Gaul. Each of the Five Good Emperors except Marcus Aurelius adopted the most competent person, rather than the closest blood relative, as his son and successor, thus elevating duty over sentiment. Marcus Aurelius, a deeply committed

---

Agrippina (a-grip-PIE-nuh)   **Vespasian** (ves-PAY-zhun)
Flavians (FLAY-vee-unz)   **Antonine** (AN-toe-nine)

Trajan (TRAY-jun)   **Hadrian** (HAY-dree-un)
Marcus Aurelius (MAR-kus o-REEL-ee-us)

Stoic, gave full vent to his sense of duty in his *Meditations,* which he wrote in Greek while living in a tent on the Danube frontier, where he fought long and hard against German raids. Antoninus was surnamed "Pius" (Dutiful) because he was devoted to his country, the gods, and his adoptive father, Hadrian.

The Five Good Emperors made humaneness and generosity the themes of their reigns. Trajan, for example, founded a program of financial aid for the poor children of Italy. They also went to great lengths to care for the provinces. These emperors not only commonly received petitions from cities, associations, and individuals in far-off provinces but answered them. Yet humaneness does not mean softness. Hadrian, for instance, ordered a revolt in Judea (A.D. 132–135) suppressed with great brutality.

Like the Julio-Claudians, the Five Good Emperors advertised their wives to the world as exemplars of traditional modesty, self-effacement, and domesticity. In fact, they were often worldly, educated, and influential. Trajan's wife, Plotina, for example (d. A.D. 121 or 123), acted as patron of the Epicurean school at Athens, whose philosophy she claimed to follow. She advised her husband on provincial administration as well as dynastic matchmaking. Hadrian's wife, Sabina, traveled in her husband's entourage to Egypt (A.D. 130), where her aristocratic Greek friend, Julia Balbilla, commemorated the trip by writing Greek poetry, which she had inscribed alongside other tourists' writings on the leg of one of two statues of Amenhotep III at Thebes, referred to in classical times as the "colossi of Memnon."

A darker side of the second-century empire was the problem of border defense. Augustus and the Julio-Claudians had established client kingdoms where possible, to avoid the expense and political dangers of raising armies. The emperors of the day tended to be more aggressive on the borders than were Augustus and the Julio-Claudians. They moved from client kingdoms to a new border policy of stationary frontier defense. Expensive fortification systems of walls, watchtowers, and trenches were built along the perimeter of the empire's border and manned with guards. A prominent example is Hadrian's Wall, which separated Roman Britain from the enemy tribes to the north. Stretching 80 miles, the wall required fifteen thousand defense troops.

The most ambitious frontier policy was that of Trajan, who crossed the Danube to carve out the new province of Dacia (modern Romania) and who used an excuse to invade Parthian Mesopotamia. He won battles as far away as the Persian Gulf, but he lost the war. As soon as his army left, Mesopotamia rose in revolt, followed by Germany. Trajan's reign marked the empire's greatest geographic extent, but Trajan had overextended Rome's resources. When he died, his successor, Hadrian, had to abandon Trajan's province of Mesopotamia (see Map 6.1).

■ Prosperity and Romanization in the Provinces

Compared with a modern economy, the Roman economy was underdeveloped. Most people worked in agriculture, employed primitive technology, and lived at a subsistence level. Even so, the Roman Empire experienced modest economic growth during the first two centuries A.D. The chief beneficiaries were the wealthy few, but ordinary people shared in the economic expansion as well. In addition to stability and peace, several other factors encouraged economic development. The western provinces witnessed the opening of new lands to agriculture, where improved techniques were applied. The growth of cities increased agricultural demand. Changes in Roman law aided commerce by making it easier to employ middlemen in business transactions. Travel and communications were relatively easy and inexpensive.

Trade boomed, as a recent archaeological discovery in the Italian city of Pisa° recalls. Nine Roman ships were found in the site of the ancient harbor here in 1999: they are merchant ships, both coastal freighters and small harbor craft. One of the ships was filled with amphoras (storage jars), still stacked in neat rows and filled with wine and sand. Both come from the region of the Bay of Naples, whose sand was used for concrete that could set under water. The finds, which seem to date from the mid-second century A.D., offer a vivid picture of trade up and down the west coast of Italy. When the cargo was unloaded at Pisa, the ships probably picked up the local grain and marble, which was shipped in turn to Rome.

Rome was an economic magnet, but so, to a lesser extent, were all cities, and the second century A.D. was a great age of city life. New cities were founded far from the Mediterranean. They began as veterans' colonies, market towns, and even army camps, and some grew into cities of permanent importance in European history: Cologne (Colonia Claudia Agrippinensis), Paris (Lutetia Parisiorum), Lyon (Lugdunum), London (Londinium), Mérida (Emerita Augusta), Vienna (Vindobona), and Budapest (Aquincum).

Whether old or new, cities attracted a large elite population. The Principate was not a domain of country gentry, but rather one in which ambitious people wanted to live in great cities, in emulation of the greatest

Pisa (PEE-zuh)

Double Portrait, Pompeii   This wall painting from a house joined to a bakery depicts a married couple, possibly the wealthy baker P. Paquius Proculus and his wife. The portraiture is realistic. The couple carry symbols of education: she holds wax tablets and a stylus (pen), while he grasps a sealed scroll. *(Scala/Art Resource, NY)*

city of the empire, Rome, which was by Augustus's day a city of perhaps a million people. In cities men competed for positions as magistrates, in imitation of the two consuls, or for seats on the local town council, often called a *curia°*, like the senate in Rome; town councilors were called *decurions°* and known collectively as the *curial order*. Decurions further played one-upmanship in sponsoring public buildings in the Roman style, one man endowing a new forum, another a triumphal arch, a third a library, a fourth an amphitheater, and so on. From Ephesus in Anatolia to Colchester in Britain, from Mainz in Germany to Leptis Magna in Libya, a Roman could find familiar government institutions, architecture, and street plans. At Zeugma on the Euphrates River, for example, a city of seventy thousand people, aristocrats on Rome's eastern frontier lived in Italian-style villas, decorated with classical frescoes and mosaics and adorned with bronze statues of the Greco-Roman gods.

---

curia (KYOO-ree-uh)   **decurion** (day-KYOO-ree-un)

Unlike men, women did not usually hold magistracies, but wealthy women of the empire could and did lavish money on public benefactions. Women endowed temples and synagogues, amphitheaters and monumental gateways, games and ceremonies. They were rewarded with wreaths, front-row seats, statues, priesthoods, and inscriptions honoring them as "most distinguished lady," "patron," and even as "father of the city," to cite an extraordinary case from Roman Egypt.

The buildings were visible examples of Romanization, although the Romans did not use the term. If they had, it would have had a limited meaning because the emperors neither would nor could impose a lock-step cultural uniformity on their subjects. The empire was too big and ancient technology too primitive for that. The total population of the empire consisted of between 50 and 100 million people, most of whom lived in the countryside. The small and largely urbanized Roman administration had little direct contact with most people. So, for example, only a minority of the inhabitants of the empire spoke Latin; in the East, Greek was the more common language of administration. Millions of people spoke neither Greek nor Latin. Celtic, Germanic, Punic, Berber, Coptic, Aramaic, and Syriac were other common languages in Roman domains. In short, the empire lacked the unity of a modern nation-state.

What, then, besides buildings and language might Romanization entail? One index has already been suggested: the participation of provincials in the central government, even as emperor. By around A.D. 200, for example, about 15 percent of the known Roman equestrians and senators came from North Africa. By this time, the senate was no longer dominated by Italians but was representative of the empire as a whole.

Participation in government implies another index of Romanization, the extension of Roman citizenship, outside Italy, to magistrates, decurions, or even whole cities. Citizens took Roman names reflecting the emperor or promagistrate who had enfranchised them. Thus the provinces were full of Julii, Claudii, and Flavii, among others.

The spread of Roman customs is another measure of Romanization. For example, the gladiatorial shows that Romans loved became popular from Antioch to England. These combats advertised both Roman culture and Roman brutality. (See the feature "Weighing the Evidence: Gladiators" on pages 200–201.)

By the same token, native customs might be adopted by Romans. Consider the case of Egypt where, in the late 1990s, archaeologists discovered a vast Roman-era cemetery about 230 miles southwest of Cairo, in the Bahriya Oasis, Roman Egypt's wine country. The population was Romanized here. Yet the cemetery, with its dozens of gilded mummies from the first and second centuries A.D., shows the persistence of mummification processes of the pharaohs.

Another ambiguous symbol of Romanization is found in A.D. 212. In a law known as the *Constitutio Antoniana*, the emperor Caracalla (r. 211–217) rendered nearly all of the free inhabitants of the empire Roman citizens. On the one hand, the law is a historical landmark. Near-universal Roman citizenship was a kind of halfway point between ancient empire and modern mass democracy. On the other hand, the *Constitutio Antoniana* was something of a gimmick. It was probably less an instrument of unification than of taxation, for citizens had a heavier tax burden than noncitizens.

The Roman army, by contrast, did promote Romanization. In antiquity as today, military service offered education and social mobility. Only citizens could join the legions; non-Romans served as auxiliaries. They received Roman citizenship after completing their regular term of service, twenty-five years. And with good reason because, for example, a Syrian or Gallic peasant who served in the Roman military would experience a way of life with old and deep roots in central Italy.

Non-Italians had, and took, the opportunity to rise high in the army or government. This was all to Rome's credit. Yet as Italians became a minority in the Roman army, and as ever larger numbers of frontier peoples were recruited, it became conceivable that someday the army might abandon its loyalty to Rome.

■ Roman Law on Class and Marriage

Roman law is one of the ancient world's most influential and enduring legacies. Logical, practical, orderly, and—within the limits of a society of slaves and masters—relatively fair, Roman law influences today the legal system in most Western countries and in many non-Western countries. The law governing Roman citizens was called *ius civile,* or "civil law." Originally this term covered a very broad range of legal matters, but in the empire its meaning was narrowed to private matters. Criminal law became a separate category.

Theater in Roman Spain   This splendid structure at Mérida (ancient Augusta Emerita) was originally built in 24 B.C. and later reconstructed.   *(Vanni/Art Resource, NY)*

The law helped Rome administer its empire. Roman law was not universal, and noncitizens continued to use their own laws for local matters, but the governors used Roman law to run their provinces, so local elites had to become familiar with it. Like so many Roman customs, the law was both hierarchical and flexible. Let us consider two areas in which the law affected daily life: class and marriage.

The law reflected Roman society's ingrained social inequality. Traditional special classes such as senators and equestrians survived, to be joined by the new distinction between citizens and noncitizens. Another important division cut across the citizen-alien distinction, that between *honestiores* (in general, the curial order) and *humiliores* (everyone else). Privileges previously inherent in citizenship, such as exemption from flogging by officials, now tended to be based on this new distinction, enshrined in private and criminal law.

The most basic legal distinction was that between free and slave—and the empire contained millions of slaves. A third category, ex-slaves or freedmen, also became increasingly important. Freedmen technically owed service to their former masters, who became their patrons, and most freedmen were humble. A few, however, grew rich in commerce or wielded enough power in imperial administration to lord it over even Roman aristocrats. The result was strong elite hostility to freedmen, which is often reflected in Roman literature. Witness the stereotype of the vulgar freedman, embodied in Trimalchio in the *Satyricon*°, a novel by Petronius (first century A.D.). Trimalchio had more estates than he could remember and so much money that his wife counted it by the bushel-load.

As regards marriage, in principle, Roman family law was strict and severe. In practice, it often proved pragmatic and even humane. Consider three cases: elite marriages, slave marriages, and soldiers' marriages.

As in the Late Republic, so in the Early Empire most Roman women married without legally becoming members of their husband's family—or their children's. This gave women a degree of freedom from their husbands but it left elite women, who owned property, with a problem: technically that property was controlled by their fathers or brothers. Yet society recognized a woman's wish to leave her property to her children, and imperial law increasingly made it possible for her to do so—although the conservative Romans waited until the sixth century A.D. before abolishing completely the rights of greedy uncles. Another case is a mother's right to have a say in

her children's choice of marriage partner. This maternal prerogative became accepted social practice even though Roman law gives women no such right.

Roman slaves married and had children, but they had to do so in the face of both legal and practical obstacles. Roman law gave slaves no right to marry, and it made slave children the property of the owner of the slave mother. Owners could and did break up slave families by sale. Even if a slave was freed, the law expressed far more concern with the continuing obligations of freedmen to their former masters than with the rights of slave families. Yet during the Early Empire cracks appeared in the wall of law that allowed slave families to slip through. (See the box "Reading Sources: Slaves with the Right Stuff.")

For example, although the law insisted a slave be age 30 before being freed, it made an exception for an owner who wished to free a female slave younger than 30 in order to marry her. To take another example, the law conceded that slave children owed devotion and loyalty (*pietas*) to their slave parents.

Career soldiers from at least the time of Augustus on could not marry, probably on the grounds of military discipline. Yet soldiers often cohabited anyhow, often with noncitizen women in the area where they served, and frequently children were the result. Not until the reign of Septimius Severus° (r. 193–211) were soldiers permitted to marry formally, and that only after twenty-five years of service. Yet not only had commanders permitted cohabitation for two centuries, but the law made concessions now and then. For example, the Flavians gave soldiers a degree of freedom to make wills, which could allow them to leave property to illegitimate children. Various emperors gave groups of soldiers the privilege, on discharge, to legalize a marriage with a noncitizen, which was not permitted ordinary Romans.[2]

■ The Culture of the Roman Peace

In Latin poetry the century or so after the death of Augustus is often referred to as the "Silver Age," a term sometimes applied to prose as well. The implication is that this period, though productive, fell short of the golden Augustan era. It might be fairer to say that the self-confidence of the Augustan writers did not last. As the permanence of monarchy became clear, many in the elite looked back to the Republic with nostalgia and bitterness. Silver Age writing often takes refuge in satire or

---

Satyricon (suh-TEER-uh-con)

Severus (SEH-ver-us)

Slaves with the Right Stuff

In his book On Agriculture, *Columella (first century A.D.) reveals Roman attitudes toward slaves, who he suggests need to be hardened for farmwork after the corruption of city life. He thinks of female slaves as breeding machines and as a restraining influence on male slaves. He opposes cruelty but not chains, if needed.*

A landowner must be concerned about what responsibility it is best to give each slave and what sort of work to assign to each. I advise that you not appoint a foreman from that type of slave who is physically attractive, and certainly not from the type who has been employed in the city, where all skills are directed toward increasing pleasure. This lazy and sleepy type of slave is accustomed to having a lot of time on his hands, to lounging around [waiting for his master at] the Campus Martius [playing fields], the Circus Maximus [race track], the theaters, the gambling dens, the snack bars, and the brothels, and he is always dreaming of these same foolish pleasures. If a city slave continues to daydream when he has been transferred to a farm, the landowner suffers the loss not just of the slave but actually of his whole estate. You should therefore choose someone who has been hardened to farm work from infancy, and who has been tested by experience. . . .

The foreman should be given a female companion both to keep him in bounds and also to assist him in certain matters. . . . He should not be acquainted with the city or the weekly market, except in regard to matters of buying and selling produce, which is his duty. . . .

. . . The foreman should not only be skilled in agricultural operations, but also be endowed with such strength and virtue of mind (at least as far as his slave's personality permits) that he may oversee men neither with laxity nor with cruelty. . . . There is no better method of maintaining control over even the most worthless of men than demanding hard labor. . . . After their exhausting toil, they will turn their attention to rest and sleep rather than fun and games. . . .

It should be an established custom for the landowner to inspect the slaves chained in the prison, to examine whether they are securely chained, whether their quarters are safe and well guarded, whether the foreman has put anyone in chains or released anyone from chains without his master's knowledge. . . .

A diligent master investigates the quality of his slaves' food and drink by tasting it himself. He examines their clothing, hand-coverings, and foot-coverings. He should even grant them the opportunity of registering complaints against those who have harmed them either through cruelty or dishonesty. . . . I have given exemption from work and sometimes even freedom to very fertile female slaves when they have borne many children, since bearing a certain number of offspring ought to be rewarded. For a woman who has three sons, exemption from work is the reward; for a woman who has more, freedom.

Source: Jo-Ann Shelton, *As the Romans Did: A Sourcebook in Social History,* 2d ed. (New York: Oxford University Press, 1998), p. 169.

 For additional information on this topic, go to http://college.hmco.com.

rhetorical flourish. Writing under Trajan, for example, the historian Tacitus pours scorn on the Julio-Claudians and Flavians. Other Silver Age writers indulged in flattery and obsequiousness toward the emperor.

The Silver Age was an era of interest in antiquities and in compiling handbooks and encyclopedias, an era of self-consciousness and literary criticism. In the first two centuries A.D., Roman writers came from an ever greater diversity of backgrounds and wrote for an ever wider audience, as prosperity and educational opportunities increased. Consider Lucian (ca. A.D. 115–185), an essayist and satirist. A native of Syria who probably spoke Aramaic before learning Greek, he served as an administrator in Roman Egypt.

Many writers of the era pursued public careers, which offered access to patronage. Tacitus, for instance, rose as high as proconsul of the province of Asia. Prominent literary families emerged, such as that of Pliny° the Elder (A.D. 23–79), an encyclopedic author on natural science, geography, history, and art; and his nephew, Pliny the Younger (ca. A.D. 62–ca. 113), orator and letter writer. The most notable literary family is that of Seneca° the Elder (ca. 55 B.C.–A.D. 40), a historian and scholar of rhetoric; his son, Seneca the Younger (ca. 4 B.C.– A.D. 65); and Seneca the Younger's nephew, the epic poet Lucan (A.D. 39–65).

The family came from Cordoba in Spain. The younger Seneca moved at an early age to Rome, where he became a successful lawyer and wealthy investor. He was well connected enough to be banished in A.D. 41 for alleged adultery with a sister of Caligula. Recalled in 49, he became tutor to the young Nero. When Nero became emperor in 54, Seneca became one of his chief advisers and helped bring good government to the empire. Seneca eventually fell out of favor, however, and was forced first into retirement and then, in A.D. 65, into suicide. He had been the major literary figure of his age, a jack-of-all-trades: playwright, essayist, pamphleteer, student of science, and noted Stoic philosopher.

A literary career was safer under the Five Good Emperors. Consider Tacitus and his contemporary, the poet Juvenal° (ca. A.D. 55–130). Juvenal's *Satires* are bitter and brilliant poems offering social commentary. He lamented the past, when poverty and war had supposedly kept Romans chaste and virtuous. Amid "the woes of long peace," luxury and foreign ways had corrupted Rome, in his opinion. Critics often blame society's troubles on marginal groups. Juvenal, for example, launches harsh attacks on women and foreigners. Tacitus, too, is sometimes scornful of women.

Yet if he is biased on matters of gender, Tacitus was far from ethnocentric. Few historians have expressed graver doubts about the value of their country's alleged success. For example, Tacitus highlighted the simple virtues of the German tribes, so different from the sophisticated decadence of contemporary Rome. Nostalgia for the Republic pervades his two greatest works, *The Histories,* which covers the civil wars of A.D. 69, and *The Annals* (only parts of which survive), chronicling the emperors from Tiberius through Nero. A masterpiece of irony and pithiness, Tacitus's style makes an unforgettable impression on the reader. (See the box on page 178.)

Plutarch° (ca. A.D. 50–120), whose *Parallel Lives of Noble Greeks and Romans* later captured the imagination of Shakespeare, is probably the best-known pagan Greek writer of the first two centuries A.D. Like Livy, Plutarch emphasized the moral and political lessons of history. A careful scholar, Plutarch found his true calling in rhetorical craftsmanship—polished speeches and carefully chosen anecdotes. As in Rome, rhetoric was the basis of much of Greek literary culture in this period.

Another star of Greek culture in this period was the physician Galen° of Pergamum (A.D. 129–?199). In his many writings, Galen was to medicine what Aristotle had been to philosophy: a brilliant systematizer and an original thinker. He excelled in anatomy and physiology, and proved that the arteries as well as the veins carry blood. He was destined to have a dominant influence on European medicine in the Middle Ages.

■ The Crisis of the Third Century, A.D. 235–284

Leaving the relative calm of the second century A.D. behind, the third-century Roman Empire descended into an ever widening spiral of crisis. Barbarian invasions, domestic economic woes, plague, assassinations, brigandage, urban decline: the list of Rome's problems is dramatic. The empire went "from a kingdom of gold to one of iron and rust," as Dio Cassius put it, summing up Roman history after the death of Marcus Aurelius in A.D. 180, when the seeds of crisis were sown.

Stability first began to slip away during the reign of the last of the Antonines, Marcus Aurelius's birth-son, Commodus° (r. 180–192), a man with Nero's taste for decadence and penchant for terrorizing the senatorial elite. His predictable assassination led to civil war, after which Septimius Severus, commander of the Danube armies, emerged as the unchallenged emperor (r. 193–211); he founded the Severan dynasty, which survived until 235.

Severan reformers attempted to re-establish the empire on a firmer footing, but they only brought the day of crisis nearer. The main theme of Septimius's reign was the transfer of power—from the senate to the army and from Italy to the provinces. To extend the Roman frontier in North Africa and western Asia, Septimius expanded the army and improved the pay and conditions of service. These measures might have been necessary, but Septimius went too far by indulging in war with Parthia (197–199)—unnecessary war, because the crumbling Parthian kingdom was too weak to threaten Rome. What

---

Pliny (PLIH-nee)   **Seneca** (SEH-neh-kuh)
Juvenal (JOO-veh-nal)

Plutarch (PLOO-tark)   **Galen** (GAY-len)
Commodus (KOM-uh-dus)

Hadrian's Wall   Built in A.D. 122–126, this extensive structure protected Roman England from raids by the tribes of Scotland. It represents the strategy of stationary frontier defense.
(Roy Rainford/Robert Harding Picture Library)

the war *did* accomplish, however, was to inspire the enemy's rejuvenation under a new Eastern dynasty, the Sassanids°.

The Sassanid Persians spearheaded increased pressure on Rome's frontiers. The Sassanids overran Rome's eastern provinces and captured the emperor Valerian himself in 260. (See the box "Global Encounters: Syria Between Rome and Persia.") The caravan city of Palmyra (in Syria) took advantage of Rome's weakness to establish independence; its most famous leader was the queen Zenobia. Meanwhile, two Germanic tribes, the Franks and the Goths, hammered the empire from the northwest and northeast.

Fending off invasions at opposite fronts stretched Rome to the breaking point. To pay for defense, the emperors devalued the currency, but the result was massive inflation. As if this were not bad enough, a plague broke out in Egypt in midcentury and raged through the empire for fifteen years, compounding Rome's military manpower problems.

Assassinations and civil wars shook the stability of the government. Between 235—when the last Severan emperor, Severus Alexander, was murdered—and 284, twenty men were emperor, however briefly in some cases. Civilians suffered in the resulting disorder.

Yet the empire rebounded, which is a tribute to Roman resilience as well as a sign of the disunity and lack of staying power among the empire's enemies. Recovery began during the reign of Gallienus (r. 253–268), who ended the Frankish threat and nearly polished off the Goths. By 275, Aurelian (r. 270–275) had defeated the Goths and reconquered the eastern provinces, including Palmyra. Gallienus excluded senators from high military commands and replaced them with professionals. Moreover, he began a new, more modest policy of border defense. The Romans now conceded much of the frontier to the enemy and shifted to a defensive mode: fortified cities near the frontier served as bases from which to prevent deeper enemy penetration into Roman territory.

Sassanid (SASS-uh-nid)

⊕ GLOBAL ENCOUNTERS

Syria Between Rome and Persia

Rome and Persia fought three great battles in western Asia in A.D. 244, 252, and 260, all resounding victories for Persia under King Shapur I (r. ca. 241–272). In the first selection Shapur celebrates his success in an inscription carved in rock near Persepolis. The second selection provides a Greek view of what Syria's inhabitants endured when Shapur "burned, ruined and pillaged" in A.D. 252. It comes from the Thirteenth Sibylline Oracle, *a verse commentary on contemporary events, purporting to be ancient prophecy.*

The Persian Inscription

I, the Mazda worshipping lord Shapur, king of kings of Iran and non-Iran, whose lineage is from the Gods. . . .

When at first we had become established in the empire, Gordian Caesar raised in all of the Roman Empire a force from the Goth and German realms and marched on Babylonia against the Empire of Iran and against us. On the border of Babylonia at Misikhe, a great "frontal" battle occurred. Gordian Caesar was killed and the Roman force was destroyed. And the Romans made Philip Caesar. Then Philip Caesar came to us for terms, and to ransom their lives, gave us 500,000 denars, and became tributary to us. . . .

And Caesar lied again and did wrong to Armenia. Then we attacked the Roman Empire and annihilated at Barbalissos a Roman force of 60,000 and Syria and the environs of Syria we burned, ruined and pillaged all. In this one campaign we conquered of the Roman Empire fortresses and towns . . . a total of 37 towns with surroundings.

In the third campaign when we attacked Carrhae and Urhai [Edessa] and were besieging Carrhae and Edessa Valerian Caesar marched against us. He had with him a force of 70,000. . . .

And beyond Carrhae and Edessa we had a great battle with Valerian Caesar. We made prisoner ourselves with our own hands Valerian Caesar and the others, chiefs of that army, the praetorian prefect, senators; we made all prisoners and deported them to Persis.

And Syria, Cilicia and Cappadocia we burned, ruined and pillaged. . . .

And men of the Roman Empire, of non-Iranians, we deported. We settled them in the Empire of Iran. . . .

We searched out for conquest many other lands, and we acquired fame for heroism, which we have not engraved here, except for the preceding. We ordered it written so that whoever comes after us may know this fame, heroism, and power of us.

The Sibylline Oracle

. . . the evil Persians . . .

. . . the Persians, arrogant men . . .

. . . the arrow-shooting Persians . . .

Now for you, wretched Syria, I have lately been piteously lamenting; a blow will befall you from the arrow-shooting men, terrible, which you never thought would come to you. The fugitive of Rome will come, waving a great spear; crossing the Euphrates with many myriads, he will burn you, he will dispose all things evilly. Alas, Antioch, they will never call you a city when you have fallen under the spear in your folly; he will leave you entirely ruined and naked, houseless, uninhabited; anyone seeing you will suddenly break out weeping. . . .

Alas . . . they will leave ruin as far as the borders of Asia, stripping the cities, taking the statues of all and razing the temples down to the all-nourishing earth.

Sources: Inscription: Richard N. Frye, trans., in his *History of Ancient Iran* (Munich: C. H. Beck'sche Verlagsbuchhandlung, 1984), pp. 371–372. Oracle: D. S. Potter, trans., in his *Prophecy and History in the Crisis of the Roman Empire* (Oxford: Clarendon Press, 1990), p. 175.

They also concentrated mobile armies at strategic points in the rear, moving them where needed.

Gallienus's reforms pointed the way to imperial reorganization, but they remained to be completed by the two great reforming emperors at the end of the third century and the beginning of the fourth: Diocletian (r. 284–305) and Constantine (r. 306–337), subjects of the next chapter. When their work was done, the new Roman Empire of Late Antiquity might have been barely recognizable to a citizen of the Principate.

EARLY CHRISTIANITY

NCREASING contact between Rome and its western provinces served to plant Roman cities, Roman law, and the Latin language (or its derivatives) in western Europe. As Rome in turn owed much to other Mediterranean peoples, it may be said that the Roman Empire was a vessel that transported ancient Mediterranean civilization to northern and western Europe. No feature of that civilization was to have a greater historical impact than the religion born in Tiberius's reign: Christianity.

Christianity began in the provincial backwater of Palestine among the Jews, whose language, Aramaic, was understood by few in Rome. It immediately spread to speakers of the two main languages of the empire, Greek and Latin, and the new movement addressed the common spiritual needs of the Roman world. By the reign of Diocletian, Christians had grown from Jesus's twelve original followers to perhaps millions, despite government persecution (see Map 6.2). In the fourth century A.D., Christianity unexpectedly became the official religion of the entire Roman Empire, replacing polytheism—one of the most momentous changes in Mediterranean history. We turn to that change in the next chapter; here we consider the career of Jesus and the early spread of the Christian Gospel (literally, "Good Tidings").

■ Jesus of Nazareth

Christianity begins with Jesus. For all its historical importance, Jesus's life is poorly documented. The main source of information about it is the New Testament books of Matthew, Mark, Luke, and John. Jesus left no writings of his own. Early Christians, however, wrote a great deal. Between the second and fourth centuries A.D., Christians settled on a holy book consisting of both the Hebrew Bible, called the "Old Testament" by Christians, and a collection of writings about Jesus and his followers, called the "New Testament." The account of the Gospel According to Mark, probably the earliest Gospel, was most likely written about forty years after Jesus's crucifixion; several of the letters written by Paul of Tarsus (see page 194) date from the 40s A.D.; the earliest non-Christian sources are later in date and are scanty.

No personality has generated as much discussion among Western scholars as has Jesus. Many would distinguish the Jesus of theology, the object of faith, from the Jesus of history, the figure who really lived in first-century Palestine. Recent work argues that the historical Jesus must be understood within the Judaism of his day. He was a product of the popular culture of the Palestinian countryside, a culture that was peasant and oral. Much of what the Gospels have to say about Jesus, some argue, must be rejected as later invention. These are controversial points, but many scholars would agree with one thing: we must be careful to avoid anachronism. By A.D. 200, two new religions had emerged, orthodox Christianity and rabbinic Judaism. Both groups claimed to be the rightful heir of the biblical covenant. They engendered new perspectives that have colored the way Christians and Jews envisage the past before 200. The following account of Jesus seeks a middle ground among today's schools of interpretation.

Jesus was born a Jew. A speaker of Aramaic, he may have also known at least some Greek, widely spoken by both Jews and non-Jews in the several Hellenized cities of Palestine. To his followers, Jesus was Christ—"the anointed one" (from Greek *Christos*), the man anointed with oil and thus marked as the king of Israel. They considered him, that is, the Messiah (from the Hebrew for "anointed one") foretold in the Hebrew Bible who would redeem the children of Israel and initiate the kingdom of heaven. The dynamism and popularity of his teachings led to a clash with Jewish and Roman authorities in Jerusalem, the capital city of Judea, and to his crucifixion. His mission began, however, in a corner of the Jewish world, in the northern region of Galilee°, where he lived in the town of Nazareth° (see inset, Map 6.2).

Jesus was probably born not long before the death in 4 B.C. of Herod, the Roman-installed client-king of Judea. (The date of 1 A.D. for Jesus's birth, a mistaken calculation of Late Antiquity, does not accord with the data of the New Testament.) At around age 30, Jesus was baptized by the mysterious preacher John the Baptist; soon afterward Herod Antipas, the Romans' client-king of

---

Galilee (GAL-uh-lee)   **Nazareth** (NAZ-uh-reth)

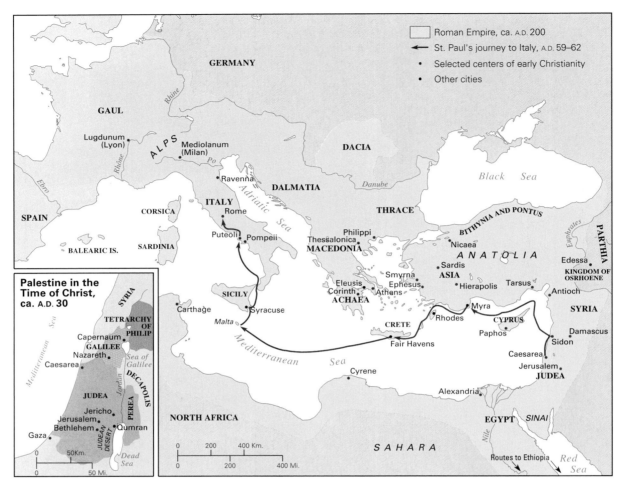

Map 6.2 The Expansion of Christianity to A.D. 200 After its origin in Palestine, early Christianity found its main centers in the Greek-speaking cities of the Roman East. Missionaries such as Paul also brought the new faith to the Latin-speaking West, as well as to Ethiopia and Mesopotamia.

Galilee, ordered the execution of John. John had preached that God's kingdom was about to arrive, a time of universal perfection and an end of misery. In preparation, sinful humankind needed to repent. Just how much influence John had on Jesus is a matter of debate, as is the question of John's relationship to the religious community of the Essenes°. Debate may be appropriate, for Judaism in the first century A.D. was in a state of creative disagreement. This era endorsed no one normative Judaism, but rather a variety of Judaisms.

The Essenes lived apart from society in pursuit of a new covenant with God. The community at Qumran° in the Judean desert, whose history is documented in the

Dead Sea Scrolls, ancient texts discovered in 1947, was probably Essene. The tenets of Qumran included frugality, sharing, participating in a sacred communal meal, and avoiding oath-taking. Adherents anticipated the coming of the Messiah and an end of days in which God would punish the wicked. Although Essene doctrine has much in common with early Christianity, early Christians did not withdraw from the world as the Essenes did, but faced it.

There are both similarities and differences between Jesus's teaching and contemporary doctrines of Palestinian Judaism. The most popular group among Palestinian Jews, the Pharisees°, focused on the spiritual needs of

---

Essenes (ES-seenz) **Qumran** (koom-RAHN)

Pharisees (FAIR-uh-seez)

The Good Shepherd   This ceiling painting comes from a Christian catacomb in Rome dating before A.D. 284. The pastoral image, common in the early church, recalls Christ's ministry. It symbolizes both his beneficence and his sacrifice, as well as his closeness to ordinary people. *(Scala/Art Resource, NY)*

ordinary folk (see page 132). Pharisees believed that law was central to Judaism but argued that it could be interpreted flexibly, in light of the oral tradition that had grown up alongside the written text of the Hebrew Bible. The Pharisees emphasized charity toward the poor. They spoke in parables, vivid allegories that made their teaching accessible.

Jesus argued similarly. Like the Pharisees, moreover, he strongly criticized the pillar of the Jewish establishment, the Sadducees°, the priests and wealthy men who saw the Jerusalem Temple and its rites as the heart of Judaism. Like the Pharisees, Jesus rejected the growing movement of the Zealots°, advocates of revolt against Roman rule, although there were Zealots among his followers. Yet Jesus was neither a Pharisee nor an Essene.

His teaching went further than the Pharisees in rejecting the need to follow the letter of biblical law. Inward purity became the key principle, as reflected in Jesus's statement to his disciples (that is, close followers): "Whoever does not accept the kingdom of God like a child will never enter it" (Mark 10:15). Only an adult could become expert in biblical law, but it is probably easier for a child than for an adult to attain spiritual innocence.

Jesus argued that the kingdom of God, which John the Baptist had said was coming soon, was actually already beginning to arrive. Jesus, moreover, said that he himself, acting through the direct order of God, could forgive sins. He emphasized the notion of God as a loving and forgiving father. Jesus often spoke in parables and announced himself through miracles, particularly faith healing. He welcomed marginalized groups, including prostitutes and lepers.

Sadducees (SAD-yoo-seez)   **Zealot** (ZELL-ot)

Jesus's teaching is typified in the Sermon on the Mount, addressed to his many followers in Galilee. He praised the poor and the humble and scorned the pursuit of wealth instead of righteousness. He called for generosity and forgiveness, recalling the traditional Jewish Golden Rule—to treat others as one would like to be treated. He said that prayer, fasting, and acts of charity should be conducted in private, not in public, in order to emphasize purity of motive. He called on his followers to endure persecution in order to spread his teachings: "You are light for all the world," he told them.

Jesus spoke with conviction and persuasiveness—with "authority," as his followers said. In Galilee they greeted him as king. For some this was a purely spiritual designation; others planned an overthrow of Roman rule, although Jesus rejected that course of action. In any case, his teachings won him hostility from some Pharisees, who considered blasphemous his claim to be able to forgive sins, and from Sadducees stung by his criticisms. Neither group accepted Jesus as the Messiah. It should be emphasized, nevertheless, that most of Jesus's followers were Jewish.

Jesus challenged central authority by going to Jerusalem and teaching and healing in the Temple under the eyes of the priests whom he criticized. Nor did he confine his opposition to words: he drove merchants and money-changers away from the Temple precincts by overturning their tables and perhaps even threatening them with a whip. Jesus attracted large crowds of followers, at least some of whom were armed. Sadducee authorities feared trouble, and so did the overlords of Judea, the Romans. The governor, Pilate (Pontius Pilatus), had already endured vehement Jewish objections to the display in Jerusalem of an imperial medallion and of an inscription that seems to have asserted Augustus's divinity. Pilate had no need of further uproar. Temple police and Roman soldiers were called on to arrest Jesus quietly.

Jesus's subsequent trial and execution have always been controversial. The New Testament emphasizes the role of the Jewish leadership and the Jerusalem mob in Jesus's death. Written after the First Jewish Revolt (A.D. 66–77), however, the Gospels may reflect anti-Jewish sentiment in the empire. Crucifixion, the method used to execute Jesus, was a Roman penalty (the traditional Jewish method was stoning), and Jesus was executed by Romans, not Jews. Jesus probably appeared in informal and hurried proceedings before both the Jewish Council and Pilate. He suffered slow death by crucifixion on Golgotha (Calvary) Hill just outside the city. It was a spring Friday, on the eve of the Passover festival, around A.D. 30.

■ Paul of Tarsus

According to the Gospel writers, Jesus died on a Friday and rose from the dead on Sunday, an event commemorated by Christians at Easter. He is said to have then spent forty days on earth, cheering and commissioning his disciples in Galilee and working miracles, before finally ascending to heaven. Heartened, the disciples returned to Jerusalem and spread Jesus's teachings. They preached in synagogues, private households, and even the Temple, and to Greek-speaking as well as Palestinian Jews. Their movement spread in the thirties and forties A.D. throughout Palestine and into Syria. In Jerusalem Christians were known as Nazarenes—that is, followers of Jesus of Nazareth; it was at Antioch that they were first called "men of Christ" (*christianoi*).

The leaders of the movement were known as apostles, from the Greek *apostolos*, "one who is sent" and who enjoys the authority of the sender. The apostles, that is, believed that Jesus had sent them and given them authority. The apostles included Jesus's twelve original followers or disciples. The most prominent disciple was Peter, a Galilean fisherman whom Jesus endowed with particular authority. After the crucifixion, Peter became a miracle-worker and leading apostle. According to a reliable tradition, he went to Rome, whose church he headed and where he died as a martyr in A.D. 64.

It was not clear at first that Christians would form a new religion separate from Judaism. Although Sadducees and Jewish civil officials were hostile, Christians found much support among Pharisees. Some Christians, however, contemplated a radical break; among them no one was more important than Paul of Tarsus (d. A.D. 67?).

Only Jesus himself played a greater role than Paul in the foundation of Christianity. A remarkable figure, Paul embodied three different and interlocking worlds. Born with the name of Saul, he was a Jew of the Diaspora from the southern Anatolian city of Tarsus. A learned Pharisee, Paul was a native speaker of Aramaic and knew Hebrew and Greek. His father was one of the few Jews to attain Roman citizenship, a privilege that Paul inherited. Paul's heritage speaks volumes about the variety of the Roman peace, and his religious odyssey speaks volumes more (see Map 6.2).

At first Paul joined in the persecution of the Christians, whom he considered blasphemous. Around A.D. 36, however, he claimed to see a blinding light on the road to Damascus, a vision of Jesus that convinced him to change from persecutor to believer. It was a complete turnaround, a *conversio* ("conversion"), to use the

Latin word that would grow so important in years to come. Saul changed his name to Paul and became a Christian.

He also changed what being a Christian meant. The key to Paul's faith was not so much Jesus's life, although that was a model for Christian ethics, as it was Jesus's death and resurrection. Jesus's fate, Paul wrote, offered all humanity the hope of resurrection, redemption, and salvation. Paul retained his belief in Jewish morality and ethics but not in the rules of Jewish law. Following the law, no matter how carefully, would not lead to salvation; only faith in Jesus as Messiah would.

Such doctrines bespoke a break with Judaism, as did Paul's attitudes toward converts. Hellenistic Judaism had long reached out to Gentiles. Some became Jews. Others, scattered throughout the cities of the Roman Empire, were known as "God-fearers"—that is, they accepted the moral teachings of Judaism but refrained from following strict dietary laws, circumcision, and other Jewish rituals. Seneca the Younger, writing in the sixties, complains about the spread of Judaism: "The customs of this accursed race have gained such influence that they are now received throughout the world."[3]

The Jerusalem church baptized converts and considered them Jews, but Paul considered them not Jews but converts in Christ. For Pauline Christians, circumcision, dietary laws, and strict observance of the Sabbath were irrelevant. From the late forties to the early sixties A.D., Paul tirelessly undertook missionary journeys through the cities of the Roman East and to Rome itself. He aimed to convert Gentiles, and so he did; but many of his followers were Hellenized Jews and "God-fearers." (See the box "Reading Sources: Christian Community and Christian Relationships.")

Paul started Christianity on the road to complete separation from Judaism. Events over the next century widened the division. First, while Pauline churches prospered, departing ever more from Jewish customs, the Jerusalem church was decimated. Jewish authorities persecuted its leaders, and after Rome's suppression of the First Jewish Revolt and destruction of the Jerusalem Temple in A.D. 70, the rank and file of Palestinian Jews rallied to the Pharisees. Second, Jews and Christians competing for converts emphasized their respective differences. Third, although many Jews made their peace with Rome in A.D. 70, enough Jewish-Roman hostility remained to lead to uprisings in the Diaspora in 115 and to the Second Jewish Revolt in 132–135. Both were suppressed mercilessly by Rome, and Judaism became ever more stigmatized among Gentiles.

Bereft of the Temple at Jerusalem, Judaism nonetheless continued to prosper as a religion. Indeed, Jewish missionary activities continued, although they did not keep pace with the number of converts gained by Christianity. More striking is the emergence of the rabbis (the religious leaders of the Pharisees) as the mentors of Judaism. Popular among Jews, the rabbis also attracted the Romans because most rabbis opposed revolt. After both A.D. 70 and 135, the Romans made the rabbis responsible for Jewish self-government in Palestine. The rabbis left their mark on history, however, not in administration but in an intellectual movement. Continuing in the tradition of the Pharisees, the rabbis amplified the oral law; that is, they wrote interpretations of the Hebrew Bible that clarified the practice of Judaism. They developed the notion of the "dual Torah," elevating the oral law to equal authority with the written law of the Hebrew Bible. The notion legitimized the rabbis' enterprise, which made it possible for Judaism to evolve flexibly. The basic text of rabbinic Judaism is the Mishnah° (ca. A.D. 200), a study of Jewish law. In rabbinic Judaism lies the basis of the medieval and modern forms of the Jewish religion.[4]

■ Expansion, Divergence, Persecution

Although Jesus's mission was mainly in the countryside, early Christianity quickly became primarily an urban movement. Through missionary activity and word of mouth, the religion slowly spread. It was concentrated in the Greek-speaking East, but by the second century A.D. Christian communities dotted North Africa and Gaul and, beyond Roman boundaries, appeared in Parthian Iraq and in Ethiopia (see Map 6.2).

By around A.D. 200, an orthodox (Greek for "right-thinking") Christianity had emerged. Rooted in Judaism, it was nonetheless a distinct and separate religion that found most of its supporters among Gentiles. A simple "rule of faith," emphasizing belief in one God and the mission of his son, Jesus, as savior, united Christians from one end of the empire to the other. Christianity attracted both rich and poor, male and female; its primary appeal was to ordinary, moderately prosperous city folk. Believers could take comfort from the prospect of salvation in the next world and in a caring community in the here-and-now. Christians emphasized charity and help for the needy, qualities all too often absent in Greco-Roman society. A Christian writer justly described a

Mishnah (MISH-nuh)

❧ READING SOURCES

Christian Community and Christian Relationships

Traditionally considered a letter of Paul to the church of Ephesus, the New Testament book of Ephesians is perhaps rather the work of a Pauline Christian in about A.D. 100. As in undisputed letters of Paul, the text emphasizes the union of Jew and Gentile in the new Christian community: a community of spiritual equality but physical hierarchy by age, class, and gender.

Remember then your former condition, Gentiles as you are by birth, "the uncircumcised" as you are called by those who call themselves "the circumcised" because of a physical rite. You were at that time separate from Christ, excluded from the community of Israel, strangers to God's covenants and the promise that goes with them. Yours was a world without hope and without God. Once you were far off, but now in union with Christ Jesus you have been brought near through the shedding of Christ's blood. For he is himself our peace. Gentiles and Jews, he has made the two one, and in his own body of flesh and blood has broken down the barrier of enmity which separated them; for he annulled the law with its rules and regulations, so as to create out of the two a single new humanity in himself, thereby making peace. This was his purpose, to reconcile the two in a single body to God through the cross, by which he killed the enmity. So he came and proclaimed the good news: peace to you who were far off, and peace to those who were near; for through him we both alike have access to the Father in the one Spirit. Be subject to one another out of reverence for Christ.

Wives, be subject to your husband as though to the Lord; for the man is the head of the woman, just as Christ is the head of the church. Christ is, indeed, the saviour of the body; but just as the church is subject to Christ, so must women be subject to their husbands in everything.

Husbands, love your wives, as Christ loved the church and gave himself up for it, to consecrate and cleanse it by water and word, so that he might present the church to himself all glorious, with no stain or wrinkle or anything of the sort, but holy and without blemish. In the same way men ought to love their wives, as they love their own bodies. In loving his wife a man loves himself. For no one ever hated his own body . . . the husband must love his wife as his very self, and the wife must show reverence for her husband.

Children, obey your parents; for it is only right that you should. . . .

Fathers, do not goad your children to resentment, but bring them up in the discipline and instruction of the Lord.

Slaves, give single-minded obedience to your earthly masters with fear and trembling, as if to Christ. Give cheerful service, as slaves of the Lord rather than of men. You know that whatever good anyone may do, slave or free, will be repaid by the Lord.

Masters, treat your slaves in the same spirit: give up using threats, and remember that you both have the same Master in heaven; there is no favouritism with him.

Source: The Letter of Paul to the Ephesians 2:11–17, 5:21–6:9, in *The Oxford Study Bible: Revised English Bible with the Apocrypha* (New York: Oxford University Press, 1992).

pagan's amazed comment on Christian behavior: "Look how they love each other." Most early Christians expected Christ's return—and the inauguration of the heavenly kingdom—to be imminent.

Early churches were simple and relatively informal congregations that gathered for regular meetings. The liturgy, or service, consisted of readings from the Scriptures (the Old and New Testaments), teaching, praying, and singing hymns. Baptism was used to initiate converts. The Lord's Supper, a communal meal in memory of Jesus, was a major ritual. The most important parts of the meal were the breaking and distribution of bread at the beginning and the passing of a cup of wine at the end; these recalled the body and blood of Christ. As organizational structures emerged (see pages 212–213), churches in different cities were in frequent contact with one another, discussing common concerns and coordinating doctrine and practice.

Just as Jewish women were not rabbis, so early Christian women did not hold the priesthood. Jewish women, however, did hold office in the synagogue, and Christian women likewise served as deaconesses. Both endowed buildings and institutions. For example, consider the Italian Jewish woman Caelia Paterna, an officeholder honored by her congregation as "mother of the synagogue of the people of Brescia." Or the two Christian deaconesses, both slaves, whom Pliny the Younger had tortured during his governorship of the Anatolian province of Bithynia (ca. A.D. 110) in an attempt to extract information about the worrisome new cult. Deaconesses played an active part in church charities and counseling and now and then preached sermons.

As Christianity spread, its troubles with the authorities deepened. For one thing, Christians met in small groups, a kind of assembly that conservative Romans had long suspected as a potential source of sedition. More troubling, however, was Christians' refusal to make sacrifices to the emperor. The Romans expected all subjects to make such sacrifices as a sign of patriotism. The only exception was the Jews, who were permitted to forgo the imperial cult because their ancestral religion prohibited them from worshiping idols. The Christians, however, were a new group, and Romans distrusted novelty.

As a result, the emperors considered Christianity at best a nuisance and at worst a threat. Christians were tested from time to time by being asked to sacrifice to the emperor; those who failed to do so might be executed, sometimes in the arena. More often, however, Romans tacitly tolerated Christians as long as they kept their religion private. Christians could not proselytize in public places, put up inscriptions or monuments, or build churches. Christianity thus spread under severe restrictions, but spread it did, particularly in the cities of the East. The willingness of martyrs to die for the faith made a strong impression on potential converts. Although the number of Christians in the empire is not known, it is clear that by the late third century they were, although a minority, a significant and growing one.

■ Mystery Religions

Roman policy toward Christianity by no means reflected an attempt to impose a single, unified religion on the empire. As polytheists, Romans were usually willing to admit new gods to their pantheon, as long as their worshipers took part in the patriotic emperor cult. Roman conservatism, moreover, engendered respect for other peoples' traditional faiths. Although from time to time during Roman history the authorities had tried to expel these faiths from the city of Rome itself, the spread of new religions during the first three centuries A.D. proved irresistible. Besides Christianity and Judaism, the most important were Greek mystery cults, the cults of Isis and Mithras, and Manichaeism. These religions displayed a tendency toward syncretism, often borrowing rites, doctrines, and symbols from one another.

Greek mystery cults included cults of Dionysus, the god of wine, and of Demeter, goddess of grain, who was worshiped at annual ceremonies at Eleusis, a town outside Athens. The "mystery" consisted of secret rites revealed only to initiates. In the case of Demeter, the rites apparently had something to do with the promise of eternal life.

The cult of Isis° derived from the ancient Egyptian cult of Isis (see page 26), her brother and husband, Osiris, and their son, Horus. Its central theme, too, was eternal life, through the promise of resurrection achieved by moral behavior in this life. Isis, the "Goddess of Ten Thousand Names," was portrayed as a loving mother caring for her son; elements of Isis were later syncretized in the cult of the Virgin Mary. Followers of Isis marched in colorful and at times terrifying parades through the streets of Roman cities, flagellating themselves as a sign of penitence.

Although men joined in the worship of Isis, the cult appealed particularly to women. The goddess's popularity crossed class lines; devotees ranged from slaves to one Julia Felix, whose estate at Pompeii included a garden shrine to Isis and Egyptian statuettes. By contrast with the followers of Isis, men, especially soldiers, dominated the worship of Mithras°. Mithras, a heroic Persian god of light and truth, also promised eternal life. His worshipers believed that Mithras had captured and killed a sacred bull whose blood and body were the source of life. Accordingly, Mithraism focused on bull sacrifice carried out in a vaulted, cavelike temple called a *Mithraeum*. Initiates were baptized with bull blood and participated in various other rituals, among them a

---

Isis (EYE-sis)   **Mithras** (MYTH-rus)

Mithraeum This sculpted relief comes from an underground sanctuary along the Rhine frontier. It shows the hero-god Mithras sacrificing a bull, the central symbol of Mithraism. Actual bull sacrifices were carried out in temples known as Mithraea. *(Hildesheim Museum/Richard Erdoes)*

sacramental meal. Their moral code advised imitating the life of their hero.

Manichaeism° also originated in Persia, but later, in the third century A.D. The founder, the Persian priest Mani, was martyred by conservative religious authorities. Mani is said to have traveled to India. His cult recognized not only Jesus but Zoroaster and Buddha as

prophets. The main tenet of Manichaeism was philosophical dualism, which emphasized the universal struggle between good (Light) and evil (Darkness). According to believers, the world had been corrupted by Darkness, but eventually the Light would return. In the meantime, good Manichaeans were to attempt to lead pure lives. Manichaeism was a powerful religious force for two centuries; the great theologian Augustine flirted with it before becoming a Christian.

Manichaeism (MAN-ih-kee-izm)

SUMMARY

BETWEEN the first century B.C. and the third century A.D., the Romans changed from a people who had come to destroy into a people who had come to fulfill. At the beginning of this period, the conquered provinces were oppressed by greedy bureaucrats and tax collectors, and Rome's imperial victories had nearly ruined the Italian peasantry. The Republic had collapsed under the weight of political maneuvering, judicial murders, gang skirmishes, and civil war.

A shrewd and sickly outsider, Octavian, confounded expectations by creating a new empire that would enjoy two centuries of stability; as Augustus, he served as its first emperor. Augustus reconciled the senatorial class by sharing a degree of power, but he guaranteed peace by keeping most of the armies in his own hand. He wisely reduced military spending and compromised with Rome's enemies to stabilize the frontiers. He solved the problem of rebellious soldiers by raising taxes to provide farms for veterans. Perhaps most important, he began a new policy toward the provinces, which were slowly raised to equality with Italy. In short, Augustus initiated the prosperous Roman peace, an era lasting until the third century A.D. To survive the crises of that century, it was necessary for Rome to maintain a bigger army supported by higher taxes collected by a larger bureaucracy, requirements that would shake the social, political, and cultural foundations of the empire, as Chapter 7 discusses.

Literature and the arts flourished in the peaceful period of the Early Empire. In the provinces, the Roman peace made possible an era of architectural and literary flowering. It was a prosperous era but not for everyone, as slavery remained widespread. Rome was a multi-ethnic empire whose inhabitants increasingly mixed with one another and exchanged ideas. None of these exchanges was more momentous than the emergence of several new religions, one of which would become in Late Antiquity the main religion of the Roman world: Christianity. Without the pax Romana of the Caesars, the Christian Gospel could not have been spread.

■ Notes

1. Mary R. Lefkowitz and Maureen B. Fant, trans., in their *Women's Life in Greece & Rome: A Source Book in Translation*, 2d ed. (Baltimore: Johns Hopkins University Press, 1992), p. 9.
2. This discussion of marriage and law owes much to Susanne Dixon, *The Roman Family* (Baltimore: Johns Hopkins University Press, 1992), pp. 36–60.
3. Seneca, *De Superstitione*, trans. Menachem Stern, in *Greek and Latin Authors on Jews and Judaism*, vol. 1 (Jerusalem: Israel Academy of Sciences and Humanities, 1976), p. 431.
4. On these points, see Lawrence H. Schiffman, *From Text to Tradition: A History of Second Temple and Rabbinic Judaism* (Hoboken, N.J.: Ktav Publishing House, 1991), pp. 1–16.

■ Suggested Reading

Cohen, Shaye J. D. *From the Maccabees to the Mishnah.* 1987. An excellent synthesis of work that sites the origins of both Christianity and rabbinic Judaism in the turbulent Jewish history of this era.

Earl, D. C. *The Age of Augustus.* 1968. A beautifully illustrated introduction to government, society, and religion.

Fantham, Elaine, Helene Peet Foley, Natalie Boymel Kampen, Sarah B. Pomeroy, and H. A. Shapiro. *Women in the Classical World: Image and Text.* 1994. Chapters 10–13 provide an excellent introduction to the social and cultural history of women in the Roman Empire.

Frend, W. H. C. *The Rise of Christianity.* 1984. A thorough and detailed account from the first century B.C. to the sixth century A.D., emphasizing religion in its social context.

Garnsey, Peter, and Richard Saller. *The Roman Empire: Economy, Society, and Culture.* 1987. A thematic rather than chronological introduction by two distinguished social historians.

Luttwak, E. N. *The Grand Strategy of the Roman Empire from the First Century A.D. to the Third.* 1976. A perceptive overview by a nonspecialist of the evolution of strategies of imperial defense from Augustus to the Late Empire.

Wells, Colin. *The Roman Empire.* 2d ed. 1995. A sweeping, lively, and thoughtful overview of the subject from 44 B.C. to A.D. 235.

For a searchable list of additional readings for this chapter, go to http://college.hmco.com.

Gladiators

Historians and novelists write about them, film makers portray them, revolutionaries salute them, and a few years ago television athletes claimed to be American updates of them. They are gladiators, literally men who carried a *gladius,* or sword. They fought to the death as entertainment, and they enraptured the Roman Empire.

Gladiators took part in so-called games or combat before large crowds. Armed with various specialized weapons, they fought each other and sometimes wild animals. Some unfortunates were thrust into fights with no weapons at all. The audience, seated in rank order, ranged from slaves to senators to the emperor himself. There was nothing tame about what they had come to see. Consider the word *arena,* referring to the site of the games. It literally means "sand," which is what covered the floor, and soaked up the blood.

Our fascination with the gladiator is nothing compared to the Romans'. Everybody in Rome talked about gladiators. At Pompeii, graffiti celebrated a star of the arena whom "all the girls sigh for." Jokes poked fun at gladiators, philosophers pondered their meaning, and literature is full of references.

Gladiatorial images decorated art around the empire, from mosaics to household lamps. Look at this mosaic from a Roman villa in Germany, one of several mosaic panels on the floor of the building's entrance hall, depicting scenes from the arena. The illustration shows a *retiarius,* or net-and-trident bearer, fighting a better-armed *secutor,* literally "pursuer," under the watchful eyes of a *lanista,* or trainer. As was typical, the retiarius wears no armor except for a shoulder-piece protecting his left side. To defend himself against the dagger wielded by the secutor (in the mosaic, hidden behind the shield), the retiarius had to be fit enough to be able to keep moving. The difference between various types of gladiators would have been as obvious to a Roman as the difference between a catcher and a pitcher is to a baseball fan today.

As for the amphitheaters where gladiatorial combats took place, they were as common in Italy and the Roman Empire as skyscrapers are in a modern city. Look, for example, at this photograph of the amphitheater in the city of El Djem in modern Tunisia (the Roman province of Africa). Built of high-quality local stone in the third century A.D., the structure was meant to have sixty-four arches but it was never completed. The openings in the floor permitted animals to be released into the arena. A large amphitheater like this one held at least thirty thousand spectators and the largest amphitheater of all, the Flavian Amphitheater—or Colosseum—at Rome, seated around fifty thousand. Amphitheaters were less common in the East, but the fans there too were loyal so the games went on—in theaters.

Most gladiators were condemned criminals, prisoners of war, or slaves bought for the purpose. The most famous slave gladiator was Spartacus, a Thracian. Along with seventy-seven other gladiators in the Italian city of Capua, Spartacus instigated a slave rebellion that attracted thousands and shook Italy for two years (73–71 B.C.).

Yet some gladiators were free men who volunteered for a limited term of service. Once even the emperor Commodus (r. 180–192) served, to the disgust of other Roman nobles, who found the arena fascinating but low-class. The gladiator was part warrior, part athlete, part showman, and part butcher. Yet there was something of the pagan priest in the gladiator too, for his was a solemn profession. Every gladiator took an oath to endure being burned, bound, beaten, and killed by the sword. They began each combat by greeting the official in charge (in Rome, the emperor): "We who are about to die salute you."

Students of the Romans find it hard to believe that they adored such a murderous sport, in which dozens and occasionally hundreds of men might die in a single day, to the roar of the crowds. Yet perhaps the arena makes us uncomfortable not so much because it is foreign but because it is familiar. Although we no longer flock to games in which men kill each other, we do go in droves to blood sports such as boxing, and we pack hockey rinks to watch men regularly give each other concussions. Modern people no longer kill animals in the arena for sport, but we hunt, fish, go on big-game safaris, watch cock-fights, and, in Spain, kill bulls and occasionally get killed by them.

Besides, perhaps our discomfort reflects our instinctive understanding of the symbolism of the arena. The games were brutal, but so was the empire. Rome had brought peace to three continents, but it had done so by

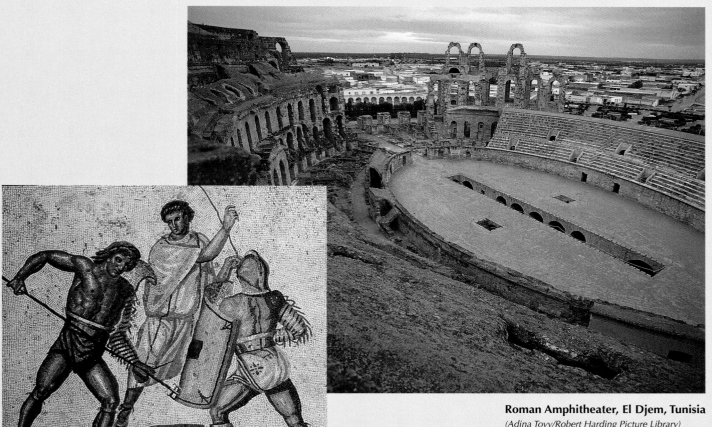

Roman Amphitheater, El Djem, Tunisia
(Adina Tovy/Robert Harding Picture Library)

Gladiator Mosaic, Nennig, Germany
(Bildarchiv Preussischer Kulturbesitz)

brandishing a sword, and it kept the peace by its readiness to fight. The arena kept Romans tough and warlike, or so an intellectual could argue, as does Pliny the Younger, who says that gladiatorial games

> inspired a glory in wounds and a contempt of death, since the love of praise and desire for victory could be seen, even in the bodies of slaves and criminals. (*Panegyric* 33)

Arguably the arena also contributed to public order. This was no small achievement since the imperial army could not police a population of 50–100 million, and few places had even the elementary police force that the city of Rome did. The violence that bloodied the amphitheater stepped into the breach by reminding criminals—or those defined as criminals—what punishment awaited them. Rob or kill and you might end up in the arena. Refuse to worship the emperor and you might be fed to the lions, as Christians were from time to time. Rebel against Rome and you might find yourself on a chain-gang building a new amphitheater, as tradition says thirty thousand prisoners of the Jewish Revolt (A.D. 66–70) did. The result was the Colosseum.*

Occasionally pagan as well as Christian writers condemned gladiatorial games. Seneca the Younger (ca. 4 B.C.–A.D. 65), for example, criticized them for inciting greed, aggression, and cruelty. Yet gladiators and their games were not abolished until around A.D. 400. And not until A.D. 681 did the Byzantines abolish the feeding of criminals to wild beasts. So popular was Rome's theater of power.

 For additional information on this topic, go to http://college.hmco.com.

---

*The preceding two paragraphs lean heavily on the fine discussion in Colin Wells, *The Roman Empire*, 2d ed. (Cambridge, Mass.: Harvard University Press, 1995), pp. 248–255.

CHAPTER 7

The World of Late Antiquity 284–ca. 600

C ONSTANTINE the Great (r. 306–337) erected a huge basilica in Rome that featured his own monumental statue. The surviving head from this statue, itself more than 8 feet tall, is depicted on the left. Statues of earlier Roman emperors tended to be life-size or a bit larger, but Constantine's statue defies all human scale. His expressionless face did not meet the gaze of his subjects. He cared, it seems, nothing for them. His immense size proclaims imperial majesty in the abstract, not the visible presence of a human ruler.

The scale of Constantine's statue is proportionate to this emperor's place in Roman history. Calling himself "the restorer of the Roman Empire," Constantine struggled to solve some of the pressing problems that, as we saw in Chapter 6, were afflicting the empire. He instituted military reforms that paved the way for a massive militarization of public life in the Roman world. He contracted treaties with various barbarian peoples that, in the long run, allowed them to incorporate themselves into, and finally radically transform, the Roman Empire itself. He ended the persecution of Christianity and became a Christian himself, the first emperor to do so. But in granting privileges to the Christian church, he intertwined the Roman regime and the emerging Catholic Church. When Constantine died, the Roman Empire was stronger than it had been for generations. But it was also very different.

The reigns of Constantine and his immediate predecessor, Diocletian (r. 284–305), inaugurate a period that scholars now label "Late Antiquity." For many years educated people, often taking their lead from the elegant and influential *Decline and Fall of the Roman Empire* by the British historian Edward Gibbon (1737–1794), believed

Colossal statue of Constantine.
(Scala/Art Resource, NY)

203

that, beset by insurmountable problems, the Roman Empire "fell" in the fifth century. With that fall, such a view insisted, the glories of classical civilization gave way to the gloom of the "Dark Ages." Today, on the contrary, specialists in the period from roughly 300 to 600 see vigor and achievement. They emphasize continuity and coherence over calamity and collapse. No one denies that the Roman world in 600 was different from the Roman world of 300. But recent scholarship stresses how the Romans themselves created a stable framework for change. No catastrophic time, place, or event marked the "fall of Rome."

From the time of its founding, the Roman Empire had suffered from various structural problems. In particular, the Roman world was vast geographically and diverse in its human and material resources. Changes were inevitable in such a world. This chapter identifies the most important changes that took place while the Roman Empire was evolving into its medieval European, Byzantine, and Muslim successors.

QUESTIONS TO CONSIDER

■ What were the most important reforms of Diocletian, Constantine, and their successors, and what roles did those reforms play in saving and in transforming the empire?

■ Who were the "barbarians," and what kinds of relations did Romans and barbarians have in Late Antiquity?

■ How and why did a Catholic Church emerge in Late Antiquity?

■ How did women and men, elites and ordinary people, urban dwellers and farmers, experience continuity and change in Late Antiquity?

TERMS TO KNOW

tetrarchy	barbarian kingship
Edict of Milan	Visigoths
Arianism	Justinian
Council of Nicaea	Hagia Sophia
papacy	Saint Augustine
Monophysitism	Vulgate Bible
monasticism	

REBUILDING THE ROMAN EMPIRE, 284–395

HE third-century Roman Empire had lurched from crisis to crisis. Decisive action was needed if Rome were to survive. The chronic civil wars had to be brought to an end. The army needed to be reformed and expanded to meet new threats on the frontiers. And the economy had to be stabilized to bring in the revenue the government needed for administrative and military reforms. Rome was fortunate in raising up two rulers, Diocletian° and Constantine, with more than fifty years of rule between them, who understood the empire's problems and legislated energetically to address them. Although these rulers thought of themselves as traditional Romans, they actually initiated a far-reaching transformation of the Roman Empire.

■ The Reforms of Diocletian (r. 284–305)

The son of a poor Dalmatian farmer, Diocletian rose through the ranks of the army until he attained a key position in the emperor's elite guards. When the emperor was murdered, the soldiers elevated Diocletian to the imperial office.

In about 293 Diocletian devised a regime that historians call the "tetrarchy°," or rule by four (see Map 7.1). He intended to address both the political instability of the Roman regime and the awesome size and complexity of the empire. First Diocletian decided to divide the empire into eastern and western halves and then selected an imperial colleague for himself. Ruling from Nicomedia, and retaining the position of senior emperor, Diocletian took charge of the wealthy and militarily threatened eastern half of the empire. Diocletian and his colleague each selected a subordinate official who would eventually succeed to the imperial office. The ad-

---

Diocletian (dy-oh-KLEE-shun)

tetrarchy (teh-TRAR-kee)

vantage of the tetrarchy was that it yielded four men of imperial rank who could lead armies and make decisions in political and administrative matters. Diocletian hoped that the tetrarchy would provide orderly succession to the imperial office and promote experienced, respected men.

Historians call the regime instituted by Augustus the "Principate" because the emperors pretended to be the "first citizen" and heir of the republican magistrates even though their real power depended on control of the army. Diocletian abandoned all pretense of being a magistrate. Scholars call his regime the "Dominate" from the Latin *Dominus,* meaning "lord and master." Diocletian adopted Eastern, especially Persian, habits, such as wearing gorgeous clothes and a jeweled diadem, sitting on an elevated throne, rarely appearing in public and then only amid awe-inspiring ceremony, and requiring those who approached to prostrate themselves before him. Diocletian succeeded in enhancing the prestige of the imperial office but did so at the price of making the emperor more remote from his subjects.

Given its size and problems, the Roman Empire was dramatically *under*governed. The empire had some fifty provinces, which varied greatly in size, population, wealth, strategic importance, and degree of Romanization, but the imperial administration was made up largely of aristocratic amateurs and numbered only a few hundred men when Diocletian ascended the throne. Rome had traditionally asked for relatively little from its empire—primarily taxes, military recruits, and loyalty. Local authorities generally did the tax collecting and military recruiting, with little interference from imperial agents.

Diocletian increased the number of officials and doubled the number of provinces by dividing old, large provinces into smaller ones. He then organized groups of provinces into thirteen dioceses and joined the dioceses into four prefectures. Diocletian subordinated each prefecture to a tetrarch and equipped each prefecture with a force of military, legal, financial, and secretarial officials headed by a praetorian prefect. By 350 the number of officers from the provincial to the prefectorial level had risen from a few hundred to thirty-five or forty thousand. Diocletian wished to fill the bureaucracy with trained administrators instead of with wealthy senators and equestrians who viewed government service as a means of enriching themselves and advancing the interests of their families.

Diocletian also attended to Rome's military problems. His major initiative was an attempt to double the size of the army from about 300,000 to 600,000 men, although the final total ended up being only around 450,000. Diocletian also built new forts along the fron-

CHRONOLOGY

284–337	Reforms of Diocletian and Constantine
300–400	Origins and spread of Christian monasticism
325–553	First five ecumenical councils of the Christian church
325–360	Foundation and development of Constantinople
379–395	Reign of Theodosius I, last emperor of a united empire
350s–ca. 600	Age of the Church Fathers
370s–530s	Beginnings of the Germanic kingdoms inside the Roman Empire
410	Visigoths sack Rome
412–418	Visigoths settle in Gaul
430	Vandals begin conquest of North Africa
450–600	Anglo-Saxons settle in Britain
476	Last Roman emperor in the West deposed
481–511	Clovis founds Frankish kingdom
493	Beginning of Ostrogothic kingdom in Italy
408–450	Reign of Theodosius II; consolidation of eastern Roman Empire
440–604	Development of the Roman papacy
527–565	Reign of Justinian I

tiers and improved the roads that supplied frontier defenders. He began the systematic incorporation of barbarians into the army, a step that led to a blurring of the distinction between Romans and barbarians. Military service had long been attractive to people in the empire because it provided Roman citizenship as well as a secure income. After 212, almost every free man in the empire enjoyed automatic citizenship. As a result, mainly noncitizen barbarians living along the frontiers, whose only hope of citizenship was military service, found the army attractive. For a while the army tended to Romanize the barbarians, but as the proportion of barbarian soldiers and officers grew, the culture and ethos of the army began to change.

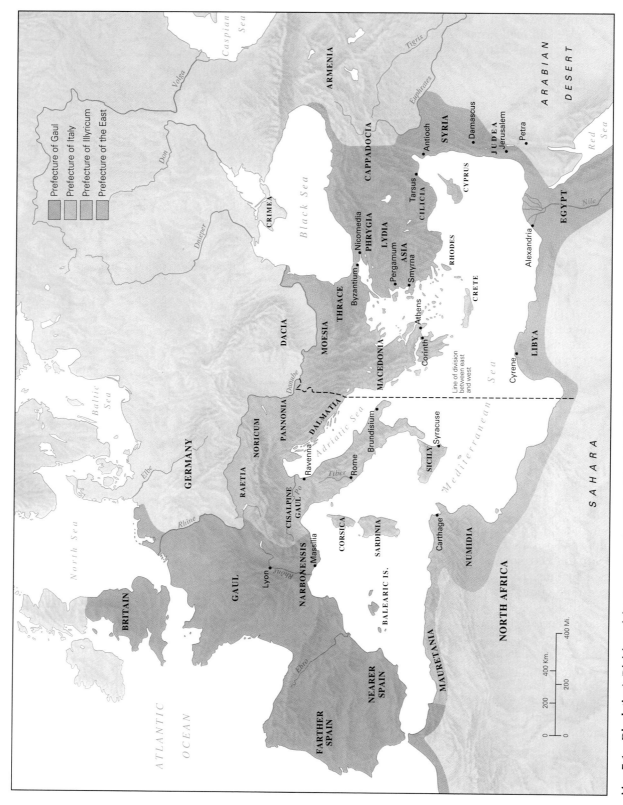

Map 7.1 Diocletian's Division of the Roman Empire, 286 Diocletian divided the empire into eastern and western halves; each half was divided into two prefectures. Thus, four regions, rulers, and bureaucratic administrations replaced the ineffective rule of one man.

Diocletian's reforms were expensive and required a predictable income. Thus, Diocletian attempted to regularize the tax system in the empire. The government conducted a census to identify all taxpayers and assessed the productive value of land. To address the mounting inflation of the third century, Diocletian issued in 302 the Edict of Maximum Prices, which froze the costs of goods. Since senators successfully defended their long-standing exemptions from taxes, and the taxation of business ventures remained low, virtually the whole cost of the Roman system continued to fall on agriculture, in particular on small farmers. Diocletian's reform of the tax structure brought in more revenue, but it also caused hardships. A rising tax burden threatened those who were most vulnerable. And with more officials handling vastly greater sums of money, corruption ran rampant. Most people never saw the emperor, but they saw too much of his tax-gouging local minions. (See the box "Reading Sources: A Contemporary View of Diocletian's Reforms.")

The rationale behind Diocletian's reforms is easy to understand; their results were less easy to anticipate. The actions were costly in three unintended respects: moral, social, and economic. The emperors had always been military dictators, but Diocletian removed all pretense that they served at the behest of the Roman people. His frankness may have enhanced the aura of the imperial office, but it also loosened the ties between

Tetrarchy   Ideal and reality are both evident in this sculpture of the tetrarchy. The rulers, depicted equal in size, embrace one another but also bare their weapons—to one another and to the world.

(Scala/Art Resource, NY)

⊱ READING SOURCES

A Contemporary View of Diocletian's Reforms

Historians usually praise Diocletian's reforms, but this passage, from a bitterly hostile Christian writer who hated Diocletian as a persecutor, may actually give the view of the ordinary person.

While Diocletian, who was the inventor of wicked deeds and the contriver of evil, was ruining everything, he could not keep his hands even from God. This man, through both avarice and cowardice, overturned the whole world. For he made three men sharers in his rule; the world was divided into four parts, and armies were multiplied, each of the rulers striving to have a far larger number of soldiers than the emperors had had when the state was ruled by single emperors. The number of those receiving pay from the state was so much larger than the number of those paying taxes that, because of the enormous size of the assessments, the resources of the tenant farmers were exhausted, fields were abandoned, and cultivated areas were transformed into wildernesses. And to fill everything with fear, provinces were cut into bits; many governors and more minor offices lay like incubi [evil spirits] over each region and every municipality, likewise many procurators of revenues, administrators, and deputy prefects. Very few civil cases came before all of these, but only condemnations and frequent confiscations, and there were not merely frequent but perpetual exactions of innumer-

able things, and in the process of exaction intolerable wrongs.

Whatever was imposed to maintain the soldiery might have endured, but Diocletian, with insatiable avarice, would never permit the treasury to be diminished. . . . When by various iniquities he brought about enormously high prices, he attempted to legislate the price of commodities. Thus much blood was spilled, and nothing appeared on the market, and prices soared still higher. . . . In addition he had a certain endless passion for building, and made no small exactions from the provinces for maintaining laborers and artisans and for supplying wagons and whatever else was necessary for the construction of public works. Here basilicas, there a circus, here a mint, there a shop for making weapons, here a house for his wife, there one for his daughter.

Source: Lactantius, *On the Deaths of the Persecutors,* vii, in *Roman Civilization. Sourcebook II: The Empire,* Naphtali Lewis and Meyer Reinhold, ed. and trans. (New York: Harper and Row, 1966), pp. 458–459.

the ruler and his subjects. By reducing the official duties of the senatorial order, Diocletian alienated an influential group of about two thousand leading citizens. The enlarged imperial administration necessarily impinged on the autonomy of cities and their local leaders, for three centuries the key components of the imperial system. Finally, the expanded administration and army cost dearly in real cash. That cash had to be extracted from an empire that was in serious economic distress.

■ The Reforms of Constantine (r. 306–337)

Diocletian's careful plans for the imperial succession collapsed almost immediately after his voluntary retirement in 305. When Diocletian's western colleague (Constantius

I) died in 306, his troops reverted to the hereditary principle and declared his son, Constantine, emperor. From 306 to 313 as many as six men claimed to be emperor somewhere in the empire. From 313 to 324, Constantine shared rule with one man, and from 324 to 337 he ruled alone over a reunited empire, although he made his sons subordinates in various parts of the empire. This compromise between the hereditary and tetrarchal systems persisted for the next two centuries.

Constantine had entered the imperial court as a young man in 293, when his father was made co-emperor, and he later served with him in Britain and Gaul. He knew the system well and maintained the administrative structure that Diocletian had introduced. Constantine continued the eastward shift of power by creating a second imperial capital in the east. He selected an old Greek city, Byzantium°, and renamed it after himself, "Constantine's polis" or Constantinople (modern Istanbul). Byzantium's location more than its size, wealth, or fame recommended it. The city straddled military roads between the eastern and western halves of the empire, overlooked crucial trade lanes to and from the Black Sea region, and was well sited to respond to threats along both the Balkan and the eastern frontiers (see Map 7.1).

In financial affairs, too, Constantine's work echoed his predecessor's. He issued a new gold *solidus,* the principal money of account in the Roman Empire. This coin promoted monetary stability in the Mediterranean world for nearly a thousand years. Unfortunately, both a stable currency and Diocletian's price controls braked but could not stop the headlong rush of inflation.

In military affairs, Constantine believed that Rome's frontiers stretched too far to be held securely by garrisons so he expanded the use of mobile field armies. These armies, recruited largely (as under Diocletian) from barbarians living along or beyond the frontiers, were stationed well inside the borderlands so that they could be mobilized and moved quickly to any threatened point. They were given their own command structures, under officers whom the Romans called "Masters of the Soldiers." The praetorian prefects were deprived of their military responsibilities and became exclusively civilian officials. The separation of civilian and military command made sense administratively and politically because it meant that no individual could combine the command of an army with the authority of a government post.

Scholars have long debated the strategic and political wisdom of Constantine's arrangements. Moving experienced troops away from the frontiers may have invited rather than deterred attacks. Recruiting barbarians into the field armies and leaving frontier defenses to barbarian auxiliaries may have created divided loyalties and conflicts of interest. Most Roman provincials had not lived near soldiers. Now the soldiers and the veterans of the field armies became daily companions. One certain result of the reforms of Diocletian and Constantine was the militarization of Roman society—the transformation of the Roman Empire into a vast armed camp. The financial resources of that empire were now largely devoted to maintaining an expensive military establishment that was socially diverse and potentially politically volatile.

Diocletian and Constantine responded with imagination to the third-century crisis. They created a new kind of rulership. The statue of Constantine with which this chapter begins is an indicator of the late antique imperial ideology. Constantine's size in stone serves to emphasize a distance that the viewer cannot articulate but cannot help feeling. The huge statue does not so much depict Constantine as proclaim emperorship. The majesty of Constantine and his long, productive reign, in conjunction with Diocletian's success and longevity, stands in stark contrast to the troubles of the third century. But we may ask, as contemporaries did, whether order was purchased at too high a price in terms of personal freedom.

◼ The Fourth-Century Empire: A Fragile Stability

Diocletian and Constantine considered themselves to be Roman traditionalists, but their wide-ranging reforms had actually introduced deep changes in the Roman system. When Constantine died in 337, the Roman Empire was more peaceful and stable than it had been throughout the crisis-ridden third century. But Rome's rulers were now more despotic; Rome's government was bigger, more intrusive, and more expensive; and Rome's military was larger and increasingly barbarian in composition. The open question in 337 was whether Rome would revert to the chaos of the third century or continue along the path marked out by the reforms of Diocletian and Constantine.

Succession to the imperial office remained a troubling issue despite the introduction of the tetrarchy. Constantine had employed a combination of the tetrarchal and dynastic systems. He had three subordinates, all of them his sons. They did not base their activities in the four prefectures, and they succeeded him jointly when he died. Constantine's sons had no heirs of their own, and when the last of them died in 361, the army turned to Julian (331–363), a nephew of Constantine. Julian was a great leader and a man who looked out for his troops. Nevertheless, people were trying to find a legitimate heir to Constantine, not merely a general who would reward the army. (See Table 7.1 for the succession of emperors in the eastern and western empires.)

Julian ruled for only two years before he was killed fighting in Mesopotamia. Because Julian had no heirs, the army controlled the succession. The choice fell on Valentinian (r. 364–375) and his brother, Valens (r. 364–378). Valentinian ruled in the west, his brother in the east. Valentinian established a dynasty that ruled the Roman world for ninety-one years (364–455). In 378, when

---

Byzantium (bizz-AN-tee-um)

Table 7.1
Roman Emperors from Diocletian to Justinian, 284–565

East	West
Diocletian (284–305)	Maximian (285–305, 307–310)
	Constantius I (293–306)
Galerius (293–311)	
	Constantine I (306–337)
Maximinus (305–313)	Severus (306–307)
	Maxentius (307–312)
Licinius (308–324)	
Licincianus (317–323)	
	Crispus (317–325)
Constantius II (324–361)	Constantine II (317–340)
	Constans (333–350)
	Dalmatius (335–337)
Gallus (350–354)	
	Julian (355–363)
Julian (361–363)	Jovian (363–364)
Valens (364–378)	Valentinian I (364–375)
	Gratian (375–383)
	Maximus (383–387)
Theodosius I (379–395)	Valentinian II (383–392)
	Theodosius I (392–395)
Arcadius (395–408)	Honorius (395–423)
Theodosius II (408–450)	John (423–425)
Marcian (450–457)	Valentinian III (425–455)
Leo I (457–474)	Petronius Maximus (455)
	Avitus (455–456)
	Majorian (457–461)
	Libius Severus (461–465)
	Anthemius (465–472)
	Olybrius (472)
	Glycerius (473)
Leo II (474)	Julius Nepos (473–480)
Zeno (474–491)	Romulus Augustulus (475–476)
Anastasius (491–518)	
Justin I (518–527)	
Justinian I (527–565)	

Valens was killed in battle, Valentinian's sons sent their brother-in-law, Theodosius° I (r. 379–395), who had risen through the military ranks in Spain, to the east to restore order.

Until his own death in 395, Theodosius was the most powerful man in the Roman world, and, after his last brother-in-law died in 392, sole ruler. He enjoyed the confidence of the people and the army—the former because he was exceptionally competent and honest and the latter because he was an old military man and a superb general. He divided the empire between his two sons without dynastic or military challenge. His branch of the family lived on until the deaths of Theodosius II in the east in 450 and of Valentinian III in the west in 455. Later rulers of the dynasty sometimes ruled alone, sometimes with chosen colleagues or subordinates. Dynastic and tetrarchal systems were thus blended effectively.

Following the reforms of Diocletian and Constantine, the army was supposed to protect the empire, not play a role in Roman politics. Events proved otherwise. In the 340s the Romans faced a renewed threat in the east from Persia, where an ambitious king sought to revive the glories of his ancestors. The Romans did not take this Persian threat lightly, for they knew that in the Persians they faced an old and formidable foe. In the west, Rome faced one serious challenge from the Visigoths (discussed below). These military provocations inevitably enhanced the role of the army in public life and elevated military concerns over civilian ones. The presence of new threats contributed to the army's prominence in selecting emperors.

The fourth century did not witness the kind of intensive and sustained administrative reforms that characterized the reigns of Diocletian and Constantine. But emperors did introduce many modest measures, some of which had outcomes very different from those intended by their implementers. One example may stand for many.

During his reign, Valentinian I, a soldier raised to the imperial office by the army, wanted to make military careers more attractive and soldiers' lives more comfortable. To achieve these ends, Valentinian proposed to provide soldiers with plots of land and seed grain. He aimed to supplement soldiers' pay, to tie them more securely to a particular region, and to make them more loyal to him. This creative idea complemented earlier military reforms.

Nonetheless, Valentinian's program angered the senators, who were still rich and influential. They agitated

Theodosius (thee-oh-DOE-zhus)

Missorium of Theodosius I   Dating from 388, this commemorative plate depicts Theodosius investing an official (the figure just below and to the left of the emperor) with his office. Pictured, too, are Theodosius's imperial colleagues and his Germanic retainers. The overall scene is Classical but the figures are expressionless and eternal (compare Constantine on page 202).   *(Scala/Art Resource, NY)*

against the reform because, they said, the emperor was spending too much time worrying about the army, and he was depriving them of lands they desired. The senators also complained that the new program was expensive, and they were absolutely right. To pay for land and seed, Valentinian had to raise taxes.

Higher taxes were especially unpopular in the cities, where the burden of collecting them fell on the *decurions,* the main local officials who composed the town councils. From the time of Valentinian in the late fourth century, evidence points to a steady decline in loyalty to Rome among these provincial urban elites. Part of Rome's success under the Principate had been directly tied to the regime's ability to win over local elites all over the empire. Now, a military reform whose rationale was clear and defensible actually provoked suspicion and disloyalty among senators and decurions.

When Theodosius died in 395, the Roman world still seemed reasonably secure. The families of Constantine and Valentinian had produced effective rulers. Scattered threats clouded the frontiers, but for the moment conditions appeared stable. Programs of institutional and economic reform continued apace, generally along the lines marked out by Diocletian and Constantine.

In the late fourth century, the empire may have numbered some 50 or 60 million inhabitants. Of these, not more than 5 to 10 million lived in towns. Because Roman government was based on towns, the actual capacity of the Roman administration to keep track of, tax, coerce, and Romanize the population as a whole was limited. Nevertheless, as the Roman Empire became an increasingly militarized state, its towns were being dominated by central authorities as never before, and its rural population was being pressed hard by tax policies necessitated by larger civil and military structures. The reforms of Diocletian and Constantine continued to provide the framework within which these changes took place.

THE CATHOLIC CHURCH AND THE ROMAN EMPIRE, 313–604

WHILE Rome's rulers were trying to stabilize the state during the fourth century, the empire was experiencing a dynamic process of religious change. The formerly small and persecuted communities of Christians were achieving majority status in the Roman world and building an impressive organizational structure. The Christianization of the empire's population (see Map 7.2), first in towns and then in the countryside, along with the emergence of the Catholic Church were two of the greatest transformations of the ancient world. Still, these changes took place slowly, and with different results in different areas.

■ The Legalization of Christianity

Since the first century, Christianity had been making steady progress throughout the Roman world, and by 300, Christians were living in every province. The Roman Empire was rich in varieties of religious experience, but no pagan cult combined compelling teachings with a sophisticated institutional foundation.

The earliest Christian communities were urban and had three kinds of officials, whose customary titles in English are *bishop, priest,* and *deacon.* Deacons were clearly subordinate to the other two. They were responsible for charitable works and for arranging meetings. Bishops and priests presided at celebrations—most prominently the Eucharist (or Holy Communion as it came to be called)—preached, and taught. Distinctions between bishops and priests developed over time. Depending on

Map 7.2   The Spread of Christianity to A.D. 600   From its beginnings in Palestine (see Map 6.2 on page 192), Christianity, while still illegal, spread mainly in heavily urbanized regions. After Constantine legalized Christianity, the faith spread into every corner of the Roman world.

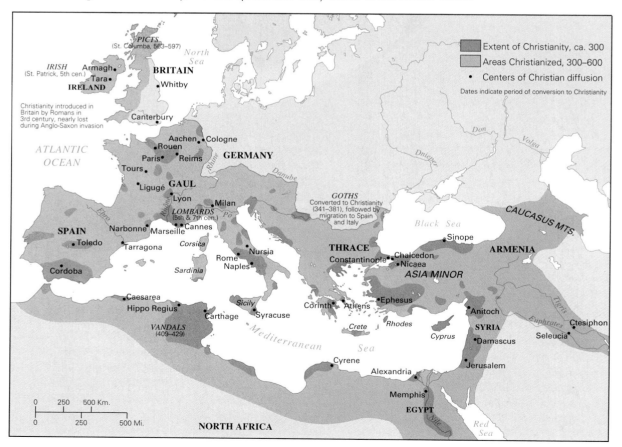

their relative size, towns would have many independent Christian groups, each headed by a priest. By about 200, as a sign of unity and authority, the eldest priest came to be called "overseer," the literal meaning of *bishop.* As more people converted, as the church acquired property, and as doctrinal quarrels began to cause divisions among the faithful, bishops began to be influential local officials. By the late fourth century, the bishops in the major cities of the empire were called *metropolitan bishops,* or sometimes *archbishops,* and they had responsibility for territories often called *dioceses.* In essence, the church was adapting to its own purposes the administrative geography of the Roman Empire.

Diocletian will always be remembered for undertaking the last persecution of Christianity, between 303 and 305. Why did he do it? He was a man of conventional Roman piety, and he was truly convinced that the presence of Christians in the army offended his ancestral gods. The persecution was harsh and well planned. Diocletian ordered churches to be closed and the Scriptures seized. His decrees demanded the arrest of the clergy and required citizens to make sacrifices at a temple. Since Diocletian's agents had trouble enforcing his decrees, it is difficult to gauge the effect of the persecution. It certainly did not eradicate Christianity, and it may even have strengthened the faith by making heroes of its victims, the martyrs whose blood, according to a contemporary, was "the seed of the church."

Unlike Diocletian, Constantine sought to promote the unity of the empire by embracing, not attacking, Christianity. No full explanation has ever been found for the source or depth of Constantine's Christianity. Constantine's mother, Helena, was a Christian. She surely exposed her son to the new faith, but the young Constantine was raised at the court of Diocletian, where he received a traditional pagan upbringing. In 312, while marching toward Rome to fight one of his rivals for the imperial office, Constantine believed that he saw in the sky a cross accompanied by the words, "In this sign you shall conquer." Persuaded, Constantine put chi-rho monograms (the first two letters of *Christos,* "Christ" in Greek) on his soldiers' uniforms and defeated his rival Maxentius at the Milvian Bridge near Rome. Constantine attributed his victory to the God of the Christians. In 313 Constantine and his eastern colleague issued the Edict of Milan, which made Christianity a legal religion in the empire. In the years ahead, Constantine did more than just treat Christianity as the equal of all other religions. He promoted the Christian church, granting it tax immunities and relieving the clergy of military service. He

chi-rho

provided money to replace the books and buildings that had been destroyed in persecutions. He and his mother sponsored vast church-building projects in Rome, Constantinople, and Jerusalem.

Constantine soon discovered that his support of the church drew him into heated disputes over doctrine and heresy. *Heresy* comes from a Greek word meaning "to choose." Heretics are persons who choose teachings or practices that religious or state authorities deem wrong. The first and most widespread heresy arose over the central mystery of Christianity itself: the deity (or "godness") of Jesus Christ.

Christian belief holds that there is one God who exists as three distinct but equal persons: Father, Son, and Holy Spirit. But around 320 a priest of Alexandria, Arius° (ca. 250–336), began teaching that Jesus was the "first born of all creation." Christians had long been stung by the charge that their monotheism was a sham, that they really worshiped three gods. Arianism, as the faith of Arius and his followers is called, preserved monotheism by making Jesus slightly subordinate to the Father. Arianism won many adherents.

Constantine was scandalized by disagreements over Christian teachings and distressed by riotous quarrels among competing Christian factions. Constantine dealt with religious controversies by summoning individual theologians to guide him and by assembling church councils to debate controversies and reach solutions. In 325 at Nicaea°, near Constantinople (see Map 7.2), the emperor convened a council of more than three hundred bishops, the largest council by far that had met up to that date. This was the first of many "ecumenical"—or all-world—councils in church history. The Council of Nicaea condemned Arius and his teaching. The bishops issued a creed, a statement of beliefs, one of whose central tenets maintained that Christ was "one in being with the Father," co-equal, and co-eternal.

By the middle of the fifth century that creed took definitive shape as the "Nicene Creed," which is still recited regularly in many Christian churches. With the Council of Nicaea we can see the first clear evidence that people were striving for a *catholic* form of Christianity. This Greek word means "universal." Strictly speaking, catholic Christianity would be the one form professed by all believers. A fifth-century writer said the catholic faith was the one believed "everywhere, all the time, by everyone."

Religious unity remained elusive, however. The Council of Nicaea's attempt to eliminate Arianism was

---

Arius (AIR-ee-us)   Nicaea (ny-SEE-uh)

unsuccessful in the short term. Constantius II (r. 337–361), Constantine's son and successor in the eastern half of the empire, was an avowed Arian, as were some later emperors. For more than forty years, Rome's rulers occasionally embraced a faith that had been declared heretical. It was during this time that the Visigothic priest Ulfilas entered the empire, was converted to Arian Christianity, and returned to spread this faith among his people. Arian Christianity spread widely among the barbarian peoples living along the empire's frontiers. By the time those people began to enter the empire in significant numbers (see pages 219–224), catholic Christianity had triumphed over Arianism, leaving the barbarians as heretics.

One emperor, Constantine's nephew, Julian, called "the Apostate" by his Christian opponents, made a last-ditch attempt to restore paganism during his short reign (361–363). He did not resort to persecution but forbade Christians to hold most government or military positions or to teach in any school. Christianity had only been legalized in 313 but by the 360s it was too well entrenched to be barred from the public sphere, and Julian's pagan revival died with him.

■ The Institutional Development of the Catholic Church, ca. 300–600

The Catholic Church was hierarchically organized under bishops and usually aligned with the imperial government. Whereas individual Christian communities had developed hierarchical structures under their own bishops in the second and third centuries, the growing authority of the bishops of Rome within the church as a whole is the most striking organizational process of the fourth and fifth centuries. But the steadily growing importance of bishops everywhere was a marked feature of the age. Beginning when Constantine called the Council of Nicaea and granted privileges to the church, the Catholic Church's entanglement with the Roman state grew more intense, just as its involvement with the lives of ordinary people expanded dramatically.

From its earliest days the Christian community had espoused the doctrine of *apostolic succession*. In other words, just as Jesus had charged his apostles with continuing his earthly ministry, that ministry was passed on to succeeding generations of Christian bishops and priests through the ceremony of ordination. When one or more bishops laid their hands on the head of a new priest or bishop, they were continuing an unbroken line of clerics that reached back through the apostles to Jesus himself. The bishops of Rome coupled this general notion of apostolic succession with a particular emphasis on the original primacy of Peter, in tradition the leader of the apostles and the first bishop of Rome. The theory of "Petrine Primacy" held that just as Peter had been the leader of the apostles so the successors to Peter, the bishops of Rome, continued to be the leaders of the church as a whole. By the late fourth century the bishop of Rome was usually addressed as "papa," or *pope* in English.

The Roman world continued to experience religious controversies in the years after Nicaea. Attempts to resolve these controversies strengthened the ecumenical council as a regular organ of church government, increased the power of the papacy, and drew emperors more deeply into the public life of the church. What were the religious controversies? We have already met Arianism, and we have seen that despite its condemnation at Nicaea, this heresy persisted. Arianism was the major "Trinitarian" heresy of Late Antiquity. Trinitarian theology tries to explain the relationships among the Father, Son, and Holy Spirit, the three persons of the Trinity. In the fourth century these disputes gave way to "Christological" controversies. Christology is the branch of theology that addresses itself to the relationship between the divine and human natures in Jesus Christ.

In 380 Emperor Theodosius I (r. 379–395), in the hope of imposing religious unity on the battling groups of Christians, issued a decree requiring all Christians to believe as the bishops of Rome. This was essential, Theodosius said, because Peter had transmitted the unblemished faith directly to Rome and Peter's successors had preserved it there. The bishops of Rome took an ambivalent view of Theodosius's actions. On the one hand, they were glad to have the emperor's support. On the other hand, they did not wish for their authority or teaching to rest on imperial decrees. Theodosius's decree reflects the growing power of the bishops of Rome and demonstrates the degree to which the state and the church were becoming intertwined.

The decree itself failed to achieve the unity Theodosius desired. Accordingly in 381 he summoned another ecumenical council in Constantinople. This council again condemned Arianism, which thereafter declined in significance within the empire although it remained vigorous among the barbarian peoples living along Rome's frontiers.

In the fifth century Monophysitism—literally "one-nature-ism"—emerged. Theologians were struggling to find a way to talk about the divine and human natures in Christ. Some emphasized one nature, some the other. Logically either proponent could have been called a

Santa Maria Maggiore   Imagine away the altar canopy and some of the decoration, and this church in Rome is a splendid example of a fifth-century basilica. Note its elegant, harmonious design. Secular buildings of the same time were no longer being built on this scale.   *(Alinari/Art Resource, NY)*

Monophysite°, but true Monophysites stressed the divine over the human nature of Christ. In 451 the eastern emperor Marcian called a new council at Chalcedon° to deal with the issue of Monophysitism. Like his predecessors, the emperor sought unity, and he was willing to let the theologians define the doctrines. At Chalcedon the theologians condemned the Monophysites and pronounced that Jesus Christ was true God and true man— that he had two authentic natures.

Pope Leo I (440–461) had sent representatives to the council bearing his doctrinal formulation. Leo insisted that as the bishop of Rome he had full authority to make decisions in doctrinal controversies. Marcian skillfully

steered Leo's "Tome" to acceptance by the council, but to appease many eastern bishops, who felt that too much authority was being claimed by the pope, the emperor also encouraged the council to assert that the bishop of Constantinople (or patriarch, as he was often called) was second in eminence and power to the bishop of Rome. Leo, the greatest exponent, although not the originator, of the "Petrine theory" of papal primacy, objected strenuously to Chalcedon's procedures. He disliked the prominent role of the emperor, complained that eastern bishops had no right to challenge his doctrinal authority, and particularly opposed the elevation of Constantinople's status. Indeed, Leo said, Rome's position derived from its Petrine succession and not from imperial or conciliar decrees.

Monophysite (muh-NAH-fizz-ite)   **Chalcedon** (KAL-seh-dun)

A generation later Pope Gelasius° I (r. 492–496) sent a sharply worded letter to Emperor Anastasius (r. 491–518), who had intervened in a quarrel between the Catholics and the still numerous monophysites. Gelasius protested the emperor's intervention. He told the emperor that the world was governed by the "power" of kings and by the "authority" of priests. Ordinarily, the pope said, the jurisdictions of kings and priests are distinct. In a controversy between them, however, priestly authority must have precedence because priests are concerned with the salvation of immortal souls whereas kings rule only mortal bodies. Gelasius was telling the emperor to stay out of theology, but he was implying much more. His opposition of the words *power*—meaning mere police power, the application of brute force—and *authority*—legitimacy, superior right—was of great importance. Gelasius elevated the church, with the pope at its head, above the whole secular regime with the emperor at its head. Despite his lofty claims, Gelasius had no means of coercing emperors. Moreover, many clergy in the eastern Mediterranean refused to accept the idea that the pope had supreme authority in either doctrine or church government.

The pontificate of Pope Gregory I "the Great" (r. 590–604) exemplifies the position of the papacy as Late Antiquity drew to a close. Gregory was the scion of an old senatorial family. He had risen through several important positions in the Roman administration but then decided to abandon public life, sell off his family's property, and pursue a life of spiritual retreat. Soon, however, the Roman people elected him pope. His reputation for holiness was important to his election but so too were his impeccable social credentials and wide political connections. Rome was threatened by the Lombards (a barbarian group who had entered Italy in the 560s), the local economy was in a shambles, and relations with the imperial government had been strained. Gregory did not wish to be elected pope, but given his conventional Roman sense of duty and obligation, he had little choice but to accept the office. Immediately he undertook dangerous diplomatic measures to ward off the Lombard threat. He also tried hard to improve relations with the emperor. And he put the local economy on reasonably sound footing. He reorganized the vast patrimonies of the church to place their products and revenues at the disposal of the Romans. In the absence of effective imperial administration in and around Rome, Gregory also began to attend to urban services and amenities: streets, aqueducts, baths.

By 600, then, the bishops of Rome—the popes—viewed themselves as the heads of a universal, a catholic, church. Many members of the clergy disputed that view. Some simply disagreed with specific papal teachings. Others claimed that Jesus had given his authority equally to all the apostles and not uniquely to Peter, and thus to Peter's successors. Emperors, too, rejected papal overreaching. After all, they had always claimed for themselves authority in all aspects of their subjects' lives, religious affairs included. By 600, however, there were no longer emperors in the West and the eastern rulers had few means of controlling the bishops of Rome. For their part, the bishops of Rome were gradually focusing their efforts on the western regions of the old Roman world.

The rise of the pope in the church as a whole was paralleled by the rise of bishops throughout the empire. By the last years of the fourth century, various ranking members of the social elite were everywhere entering the clergy and rising to its highest offices. This capture of the elite was the final, decisive factor in the triumph of Christianity.

The clergy was an outlet for the talents and ambitions of the elite. For some time, senators had been excluded from military offices and reduced in civilian influence, and decurions were growing dissatisfied with public service. The *episcopal* office (that is, the office of bishop) was desirable to prominent men for many reasons. It was prestigious. Bishops wore distinctive clothing when officiating and were addressed by special titles—traditional Roman marks of respect. They had opportunities to control patronage in the way that prominent Romans always had done. They could intervene on behalf of individuals at the imperial court. They came to control vast wealth, as the generosity of pious Christians put more resources at their disposal. Communities elected their own bishops, and by the middle of the fifth century the dominant person in most towns was the bishop, not a civilian official. The bishops, however, were the same persons, from the same families, who had once dominated local society through civic service. The overall affect of these social changes was dramatic in the long run, but it happened very gradually.

The change from a secular to an ecclesiastical elite in Roman cities even led to alterations of the topography of the cities themselves. The elite usually financed local building projects, such as temples, basilicas, forums, and amphitheaters. Such benefactions declined sharply during the third century because of the uncertainty of the times. The fourth century at first saw little building on private initiative, but then came the construction of Christian cathedrals (a bishop's church, from *cathedra*,

Gelasius (jul-LAY-zee-us)

the chair or seat of the bishop's authority), episcopal residences, baptisteries, and local parish churches. Such buildings as a rule were not placed in the old city centers, which had associations with the pagan past. Instead, they were placed away from town centers and on the edges of populated districts. In the future, these Christian centers served as poles around which ancient towns were reconfigured. The Roman elites built to show pride in their cities and to promote themselves. This did not change in Late Antiquity, but this time the elites were bishops or rich Christians, and the buildings were religious.

■ The Rise of Christian Monasticism

For some men and women the call of the Gospel was radical. They yearned to escape the world and everything that might come between them and God. To do so, many of them embraced a new way of life—monasticism. Christian monks and nuns developed a theology and an institution that were among the most creative and long-lived achievements of Late Antiquity.

The practice of rigorous self-denial (*askesis*) was common to several religious and philosophical sects in antiquity—for example, the Pythagoreans and the Stoics—and was well known among the Jews in the time of Christ, as the Essenes show (see page 192). Ascetics believed that if they could conquer the desires of the body, they could commune with the supernatural beings who were greater and purer than humans encumbered by lust for food, drink, knowledge, sex, and adventure. Sometimes ascetic practices were adopted by tightly knit groups, sometimes by heroic solitaries.

The founder of Christian monasticism was a young Egyptian layman, Anthony (d. 356). At 19, Anthony gave away all his possessions and took up in the Egyptian desert a life of prayer and renunciation. His spiritual quest became famous, and many disciples flocked to him. Finally, he decided to organize these seekers into a very loose community: the followers remained in solitude except for worship and meals. Anthony's form of monasticism is called *eremitic,* from the Greek *heremos* for "desert," hence the word *hermit.*

Pachomius° (290–346) created a more communal form of monastic life. A former Roman soldier, he was baptized a Christian in 313 and retired to the Egyptian desert, where he studied with a hermit. Eventually Pachomius founded a community of ascetics, which before long had grown to thousands of members. Perhaps because of his military background, or because his religious instincts favored order and unity, Pachomius wrote the first Rule, or code for daily living, for a monastic community. He organized most aspects of his community by designing a common life based on routines of private prayer, group worship, and work. By the time of his death Pachomius led nine male and two female communities. Pachomius's pattern of monasticism is called *cenobitic°*, from the Greek for "common life." People living this common life were called *monks,* and the place where they lived this orderly life was called a *monastery.* The head of the community was designated *abbot,* a word meaning "father." In later times the term *abbess,* meaning "mother," was coined for the woman who led a female community, and those communities of nuns came to be called convents.

Monasticism spread from Egypt by means of texts such as the *Life of Anthony* (a late antique "best-seller"), collections of the wise sayings of famous desert abbots, and books written by persons who went to Egypt seeking a more perfect life—among whom were several prominent women. (See the box "Reading Sources: Melania the Younger: The Appeal of Monasticism to Women.") One attraction of monasticism among the devout was that it seemed to be a purer form of Christian life, uncorrupted by the wealth, power, and controversy of the hierarchical church. Many pious women embraced monasticism at least partly because they could not be ordained priests. Positions in monasteries, including that of abbess, provided responsible roles for talented women. Monasticism gave women a chance to choose a kind of family life different from the one available in households dominated by fathers and husbands.

Eremitic monasticism was prominent in Palestine and Syria and eventually throughout the Greek-speaking world. Eastern monasticism produced a great legislator in Basil (330–379), whose Rule was the most influential in the Orthodox Church (for this term, see page 231). Generally these monks assembled only for weekly worship and otherwise ate, prayed, and worked alone.

Eremitic monasticism arrived in the West in the person of Martin of Tours (336–397). Like Pachomius, Martin was a pagan Roman soldier who, after his military service, embraced both Christianity and asceticism. Even though he was elected bishop of Tours, Martin kept to his rigid life of denial. Martin's form of monasticism influenced many in the western regions of the Roman world but struck especially deep roots in Ireland. There

---

Pachomius (pack-OH-mee-us)

cenobitic (sen-oh-BIT-ik)

෨ R E A D I N G   S O U R C E S

Melania the Younger: The Appeal of Monasticism to Women

The appeal of monasticism was great for men and women, rich and poor, as the career of Melania (383–438) shows. She came from a wealthy Roman family but renounced her possessions and traveled widely in Italy, North Africa, Egypt, and Palestine, visiting holy men and women. These selected passages from her biography provide glimpses of her life.

Melania was foremost among the Romans of senatorial rank. Wounded by divine love, she had from earliest youth yearned for Christ, and longed for bodily chastity. Her parents, because they were illustrious members of the Roman senate and expected that through her they would have a succession of the family line, forcibly united her in marriage . . . when she was fourteen and her husband, seventeen. [After having two children, Melania persuaded her husband to join her in renouncing the world.] She bridled nature and delivered herself to death daily, demonstrating to everyone that woman is not surpassed by man in anything that pertains to virtue, if her decision is strong. She was by nature a gifted writer and wrote without mistakes in notebooks. She decided for herself how much she should write every day, and how much she should read in the canonical books and in the collections of homilies. Then she would go through the Lives of the fathers as if she were eating dessert. The blessed woman read the Old and New Testaments three or four times a year. The most holy fathers [Egyptian abbots] received her as if she were a man. In truth, she had been detached from the female nature, and had acquired a masculine disposition, or rather, a heavenly one.

Source: Elizabeth A. Clark, ed. and trans., *The Life of Melania the Younger,* cc. 1, 12, 23, 26, 39, *Studies in Women and Religion,* vol. 14 (New York: Edwin Mellen Press, 1984), pp. 27–28, 35, 46, 53–54.

---

the whole organization of the church was based on monasteries. At Kildare the abbess Brigid (d. 523) had more authority than the local bishop.

In the West cenobitic monasticism became the dominant pattern. Benedict of Nursia (480–545) abandoned his legal studies and a potential government career to pursue a life of solitary prayer in a mountain cave east of Rome. Benedict's piety attracted a crowd of followers, and in about 520 he established a monastery at Monte Cassino, 80 miles south of Rome. The Rule he drafted for his new community is marked by shrewd insights into the human personality. It emphasizes the bond of mutual love among the monks and obedience to the abbot. The Rule assigns the abbot wide powers but exhorts him to exercise them gently. The Rule allows monks a reasonable diet and decent, though modest, clothing. Although providing for discipline and punishment, the Rule prefers loving correction. In later centuries Benedict's Rule dominated monastic life.

Eremitic or cenobitic, East or West, monasticism was a conscious alternative and an explicit challenge to the civic world of classical antiquity. Monks and nuns did not seek to give their lives meaning by serving the state or urban communities. They went into remote places to serve God and one another. They sought not to acquire but to abandon. Spiritual wisdom was more important to them than secular learning, and they yearned for acknowledgment of their holiness not recognition of their social status.

At the dawn of Late Antiquity, the church was persecuted and struggling. By the end of the period, the church was rich and powerful, its leaders were prominent and prestigious, and in the monasteries at least, its spiritual fervor deep. This change was gradual but fundamental.

THE RISE OF GERMANIC KINGDOMS IN THE WEST, CA. 370–530

T HE years from the 370s to the 530s were decisive in the history of the Roman Empire in the west. When this period opened, the dynasty of Valentinian was firmly in control. When it closed, the western provinces of the empire had become a number of Germanic kingdoms, most of which maintained some formal relationship with the eastern Roman Empire. Roman encounters with the barbarians took many different forms ranging from violent conflict to peaceful accommodation. The key point to understand is that although the barbarians supplanted Roman rule in the West, they did so slowly and often with Roman permission and assistance.

■ Invasions and Migrations

Few images of the ancient world are more fixed in the popular imagination than the overrunning of the Roman Empire by hordes of barbarians who ushered in a dark age. The Romans inherited the word *barbarian* from the Greeks, who had divided the world between those who spoke Greek and those who did not. Barbarians were literally babblers, foreigners who spoke an unknown language. After the Romans granted citizenship to virtually everyone in the empire in 212, they adopted a Greek-style differentiation between Romans and barbarians. Technically, the latter were merely foreigners, but in practice Romans thought barbarians inferior to themselves.

Individual groups of barbarians did invade the empire in various places at different times, but there was never a single, coordinated barbarian invasion of the Roman world that had well-formulated objectives. The Romans and barbarians did not face one another as declared enemies. Indeed, peaceful encounters outnumbered violent confrontations in the history of Romanobarbarian relations. The Romans had long traded with the barbarian peoples, carried out complicated diplomacy with them, and recruited them into their armies. Barbarian veterans were settled in most provinces of the empire.

If we cannot label one grand movement as "the barbarian invasions," we must also avoid the idea that the barbarians were naturally nomadic and migratory. Holding this view would tempt us to see the entry of the barbarians into the empire as one stage in a long process of human movement. Archaeological evidence collected to date makes it clear that the barbarians were settled agriculturalists. They lived in villages, farmed the surrounding country, and raised livestock. If barbarians moved

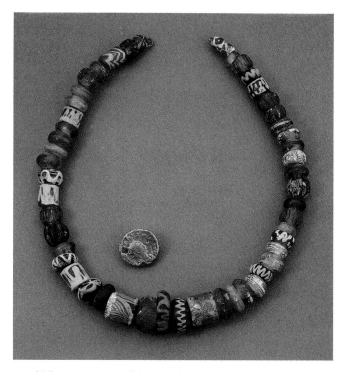

Frankish Woman's Necklace   This sixth-century "choker" necklace consists of brightly colored beads of glass, amber, amethyst, and rock crystal. The Franks were accomplished glassmakers, and this necklace provides some insight into women's taste.   *(Staatliche Museen zu Berlin, Museum für Vor- und Frühgeschichte/Bildarchiv Preussischer Kulturbesitz. Photo: Klaus Goken)*

from one place to another, their movement must be explained with reference to specific developments and cannot be attributed to migratory habits.

Who were the barbarians? Linguists classify them as belonging to the Germanic branches of the Indo-European family of languages. The Germanic peoples can be differentiated from the Celts and Slavs with whom they shared much of central and eastern Europe, but apart from some minor linguistic variations, it is difficult to distinguish one Germanic group from another. What are we to make of the profusion of names offered to us by our sources: Franks, Saxons, Vandals, Visigoths, Ostrogoths, Lombards, Burgundians? The Romans referred to the Germanic peoples as tribes, but that does not mean that they were actually groups of related people. Every Germanic "tribe" was a confederation, and these confederations formed, dissolved, and re-formed many times. For example, the Visigoths who crossed the Danube in 376 included Visigoths proper and more than a half-dozen other peoples. The confederations were formed either by powerful leaders who coerced less powerful people to join them or by groups of villages that banded together to protect themselves from aggressive neighbors. As a tribe was forming, its constituent peoples would intermarry and adopt the language, law, and lifestyle of the dominant group.

■ Incorporating the Barbarians

The transformation of the western Roman Empire began as a result of an unexpected set of events involving the Huns, nomadic warriors from the central Asian steppes. After plundering the frontiers of Persia and China for centuries, they turned west in search of booty and tribute. In 374 or 375 they fell on the Ostrogoths, who lived near the Black Sea, and frightened the Visigoths, who requested permission to cross the Danube and enter the empire.

Recent years had been difficult for the empire. Julian had fallen in battle with the Persians in 363, and dynastic quarrels were disturbing the West. The Romans thus delayed responding to the Visigoth request. Fearful of the Huns, the Visigoths crossed the Danube on their own and then asked if they might settle in the Balkans. Reluctantly, Valens° (r. 364–378) acceded but postponed permanent arrangements. While the central government considered how to deal with the Visigoths, local authorities sold them food at exorbitant prices and even traded dog meat for Gothic children, who were then enslaved. When the Visigoths revolted, Valens foolishly marched north to meet them with a small force. The Visigoths defeated his army and killed him at Adrianople in 378.

The history of the Visigoths thus presents an instructive example of Romano-Germanic relations. They had served as auxiliary troops entrusted with defending a stretch of the Danube frontier for a long time when they requested permission to enter the empire in 376. They did not cross the border as part of a massive invasion but because they were themselves sorely threatened. In 382 Theodosius, whom we have met several times already, marched east to pacify the situation. He agreed to grant the Visigoths what they had been demanding: land to settle on and a Roman military title—that is, official status—for their king. A spokesman for Theodosius explained the emperor's motives: "Which is better: To fill Thrace with corpses or with farmers? To fill it with graves or with people? To travel through wilderness or cultivated land? To count those who have perished or those who are ploughing?" For decades, barbarians had been settling inside the Roman frontiers, and they had served loyally in the army. Beginning in the fourth century, most

high military officers in the Roman world were barbarians. The only peculiarity about the Visigoths' situation was that never before had the Romans admitted a whole people.

For about thirty years the Visigoths struggled to improve the terms of their settlements in the Balkans. Alaric°, the Visigothic king after 395, grew tired of unfulfilled promises and forced matters by attacking Italy. In 410 the Visigoths sacked Rome. The taking of the city for the first time in eight hundred years shocked the entire Roman world, and has loomed large for centuries in people's ideas about the "fall" of the Roman Empire. Actually, it was a ploy by Alaric to improve the terms of his already official status. Alaric died in 410 and his brother led the Visigoths north into southern Gaul. For good measure, the new Visigothic king captured the western emperor's sister, Galla Placidia, and forced her to marry him. However objectionable this act must seem, the Visigoths viewed it as a further demonstration of their loyalty to Rome and their determination to effect a satisfactory new treaty.

In 418 the Roman government gave in. A new treaty permitted the Visigoths to settle in southern Gaul, with Toulouse as their base of operations. They were assigned the task of protecting the area from marauding bands of brigands. In return for their service, the Visigoths were given land allotments and a portion of Roman tax receipts as pay.

The Visigoths' treaty with Rome made theirs the first Germanic kingdom on Roman soil. From 418 to 451 the Visigoths' king, Theodoric I, served Rome loyally and earned the respect of the Gallo-Roman aristocrats among whom he ruled. Between 466 and 484, the Visigothic kingdom in Gaul reached its high point and continued to receive official recognition from Roman rulers. Southern Gaul, one of Rome's oldest provinces, gradually passed from the hands of the Roman bureaucracy and the local nobility into the control of the Visigoths. Nevertheless, from Constantine's first treaty with the Visigoths through the continuing recognition by the Romans of Visigothic kings, it was Roman policy more than Visigothic policy that determined the accommodation of this first Germanic kingdom within the framework of the western Roman Empire.

While they were dealing with the Visigoths, the Roman authorities realized that the Huns, who had settled in the Danube basin after driving the Visigoths into the empire, were a serious menace. They raided the Balkans, preyed on trade routes that crossed the region, and demanded tribute from the eastern emperor. In 434 the

---

Valens (VAY-lenz)

Alaric (AL-uh-rik)

Two Views of the Huns

The dread and disgust inspired by the Huns is well captured in the first passage, from the Roman historian Ammianus Marcellinus, while the second passage, from a surviving fragment of the history of Priscus, shows the Huns in quite a different light.

(a)

From the moment of their birth they make deep gashes in their children's cheeks, so that when in due course hair appears its growth is checked by the wrinkled scars; as they grow older this gives them the unlovely appearance of beardless eunuchs. They have squat bodies, strong limbs, and thick necks, and are so prodigiously ugly and bent that they might be two-legged animals. Their shape, however disagreeable, is human. They have no use for seasoned food, but live on the roots of wild plants and the half-raw flesh of any animal, which they warm a little by placing it between their thighs and the backs of their horses. They have no buildings to shelter them. They wear garments of linen or of the skins of field-mice stitched together. Once they have put their necks into some dingy shirt they never take it off or change it until it rots and falls to pieces. They have round caps of fur on their heads, and protect their hairy legs with goatskins. They are ill-fitted to fight on foot, and remain glued to their horses, hardy but ugly beasts, on which they sometimes sit like women to perform their everyday business and they even bow forward over their beasts' narrow necks to enjoy a deep and dreamy sleep.

(b)

[The Roman ambassadors] came upon a very large village in which the dwelling of Attila was said to be more notable than those elsewhere. It had been fitted together with highly polished timbers and encircled with a wooden palisade, conceived not for safety but for beauty. Next to the king's dwelling that of Onegisus [chief minister to Attila] was outstanding, and it also had a circuit of timbers but was not embellished with towers in the same way as Attila's. Not far from the enclosure was a large bath. . . . Maidens came to meet Attila as he entered this village, advancing before him in rows under fine white linen cloths stretched out to such a length that under each cloth, which was held up by the hands of the women along either side, seven or even more girls walked. There were many such formations of women under the linen cloths, and they sang Scythian songs. When he [Attila] came near the house of Onegisus, the wife of Onegisus came out with a host of servants, some bearing dainties and others wine, greeted him and asked him to partake of the food which she had brought for him with friendly hospitality. To gratify the wife of his intimate friend, he ate sitting on his horse, the barbarians accompanying him having raised the silver platter up to him. Having also tasted the wine, he went on to the palace, which was higher than the other houses and situated on a high place.

Sources: Excerpt (a): Ammianus Marcellinus, *The Later Roman Empire (A.D. 354–378)*, ed. and trans. Walter Hamilton (Harmondsworth, England: Penguin, 1986), 31.2, pp. 411–412. Excerpt (b): Priscus, Fragment 8, in C. D. Gordon, *The Age of Attila: Fifth-Century Byzantium and the Barbarians* (Ann Arbor: University of Michigan Press, 1961), pp. 84–85.

fearsome warrior Attila murdered his brother and became sole ruler of the Huns. In return for a huge imperial subsidy, he agreed to cease raiding in the Balkans. At the same time, a Roman general in Gaul concluded an alliance with the Huns in an attempt to use them to check the expansion of the Burgundians, an allied people who lived in the central Rhineland.

Together Attila and the Romans routed the Burgundians, but Attila realized the weakness of the Roman position in the west. He attacked Gaul in 451 and was stopped only by a combined effort of Romans, Visigoths, Burgundians, and Franks. Attila turned to Italy in 452, even approaching Rome, where Pope Leo I, not the emperor, convinced, or bribed, him to withdraw. Attila died in 454, and before another year was out, the short-lived Hunnic kingdom, largely Attila's personal creation, had vanished. (See the box "Global Encounters: Two Views of the Huns.")

■ More Kingdoms: The End of Direct Roman Rule in the West

To meet threats in Gaul and elsewhere, the Romans had begun pulling troops out of Britain in the fourth century and abandoned the island to its own defense in 410. Thereafter, raiding parties from Scotland and Ireland, as well as seaborne attackers—called "Saxons" by contemporaries because some of them came from Saxony in northern Germany—ravaged Britain. The British continually appealed to the military authorities in Gaul for aid, but to no avail. Between 450 and 600, much of southern and eastern Britain was taken over by diverse peoples whom we call the "Anglo-Saxons." The newcomers jostled for position with the Celtic Britons, who were increasingly confined to the north and west of the island. Gradually several small kingdoms emerged. Although Britain retained contacts with Gaul, the island had virtually no Roman political or institutional inheritance.

Valentinian III (r. 425–455) was born in 419 and became emperor of the West as a 6-year-old. Even when he came of age, his court was weakened by factional strife, and his regime was dominated by military men. After Valentinian the western empire saw a succession of nonentities, the last of whom was deposed by Odoacer°, a Germanic general, in 476. Ruling in Italy, Odoacer simply sent the imperial regalia to Constantinople and declared that the West no longer needed an emperor. This is all that happened in 476, the traditional date for the "fall" of the Roman Empire.

After the vast coalition defeated the Huns in Gaul in 451, the remaining Roman authorities in the Paris region discovered that the Visigoths were expanding north of the Loire River into central Gaul. To check this advance, the Roman commander in Paris forged an alliance with the Franks. The Franks, long Roman allies, had been expanding their settlements from the mouth of the Rhine southward across modern Holland and Belgium since the third century.

The fortunes of the Frankish kingdom, indeed of all of Gaul, rested with Clovis. He became king of one group of Franks in 481 and spent the years until his death in 511 subjecting all the other bands of Franks to his rule. He gained the allegiance of the Frankish people by leading them to constant military victories that brought territorial gains, plunder, and tribute. The greatest of Clovis's successes came in 507, when he defeated the Visigoths and drove them over the Pyrenees into Spain.

Clovis was popular, not only with the Franks but also with the Gallo-Roman population, for three reasons. First, Clovis and the Romans had common enemies: Germanic tribes still living beyond the Rhine and pirates who raided the coast of Gaul. Second, whereas most of the Germanic peoples were Arian Christians, the majority of the Franks passed directly from paganism to Catholicism. Thus, Clovis and the Gallo-Romans had a shared faith that permitted Clovis to portray his war against the Visigoths as a kind of crusade against heresy. Third, Clovis eagerly sought from Constantinople formal recognition and titles, appeared publicly in the dress of a Roman official, and practiced such imperial rituals as distributing gold coins while riding through crowds. The Frankish kingdom under Clovis's family—called "Merovingian°" from the name of one of his semilegendary ancestors—became the most successful of all the Germanic realms.

Several early Germanic kingdoms were short-lived. The Burgundian kingdom that had once prompted the Romans to ally with the Huns was swallowed up by the Franks in the 530s. The Vandals, who crossed the Rhine in 406 and headed for Spain, crossed to North Africa in 429 (see Map 7.3). They were ardent Arians who persecuted the Catholic population. They refused imperial offers of a treaty on terms similar to those accepted by other Germanic peoples. And they constantly plundered the islands of the western Mediterranean and the Italian coast, even sacking Rome in 455. Roman forces from Constantinople eliminated the Vandals in 534.

The Ostrogoths, allies who had been living in Pannonia since the 370s as subjects of the Huns, began to pose a threat to the eastern empire after Attila's death. In 493 the emperor decided to send them to Italy to remove Odoacer, who had earned the displeasure of the Roman administration by laying hands on the sentimentally significant land of Italy—and doing so on his own initiative instead of the emperor's directive. The government at Constantinople was familiar with the Ostrogoths' king, Theodoric, because he had been a hostage there for several years. The emperor also wished to remove the Ostrogoths from the Danube basin. Sending Theodoric to Italy seemed like a way to solve two problems simultaneously.

Theodoric ousted Odoacer quickly enough and set up his capital in Ravenna°, the swamp-surrounded and virtually impregnable city that had sheltered the imperial administration for much of the fifth century after the

---

Odoacer (OH-doe-ace-er)

Merovingian (mehr-oh-VIN-jun)   **Ravenna** (rah-VEN-nuh)

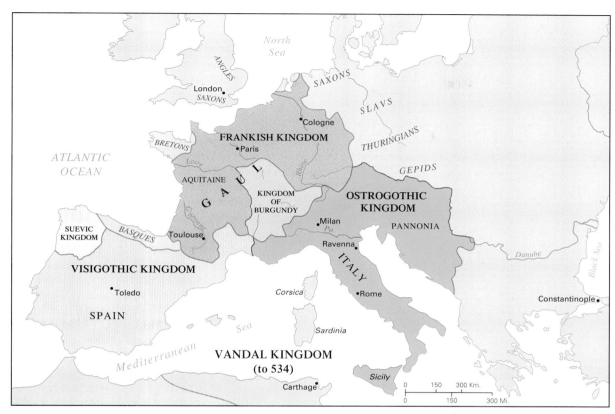

Map 7.3   The Germanic Kingdoms, ca. 530   By 530 the western provinces of the Roman Empire (compare Map 6.1 on page 176) had evolved into Germanic kingdoms. Just as Roman provincial boundaries had changed numerous times, the existence and extent of Germanic kingdoms were also impermanent.

Visigothic attack had exposed the weakness of Rome's defenses. Through the force of his personality, and by a series of marriage alliances, Theodoric became the dominant ruler in western Europe. In Italy he promoted peace, stability, and good government. Still, Theodoric had two strikes against him. One, he and his people were Arians. Two, although the population of Italy was accustomed to having an imperial court dominated by barbarians and to having Germanic military men in Gaul as the real powers in the state, they had never been directly ruled by a barbarian, and some of them could not accept Theodoric. By the 520s Theodoric grew increasingly suspicious and dictatorial. After he died in 526, the government in Constantinople launched an attack on Italy that put an end to the Ostrogothic kingdom but also devastated Italy in twenty years of brutal warfare.

By the 530s the western Roman Empire had vanished, the conclusion of a process initiated by the entry of the Visigoths into the Balkans in 376. Of all the peoples who had contested for a share of Rome's legacy, only the Franks in Gaul, the Visigoths in Spain, and the Anglo-Saxons in Britain had created durable political entities. Most of two prefectures with their several dozen provinces had turned into a small number of kingdoms (see Map 7.3).

Why did the Roman government perish in the West? Beginning with Diocletian, Rome's best rulers were resident in and concerned mainly about the East. The Visigoths and other peoples were settled in their own kingdoms on Roman soil instead of being enrolled in and dispersed among Roman army units. Also during Diocletian's rule, the army was increasingly Germanized, and Germanic military men gained high offices in the state. Those leaders often dominated imperial courts and negotiated the series of treaties that submitted former provinces to barbarian peoples. Provincial elites had long

Amalasuntha, Daughter of Theodoric   This ivory plaque (ca. 530) depicts Amalasuntha in the way that Roman consuls and emperors had long been depicted on their assumption of office. Since the late fifth century, empresses had been depicted this way, too. Amalasuntha projects an image of legitimacy. Compare her appearance with that of Theodora on page 227.   *(Kunsthistorisches Museum, Vienna)*

been accustomed to having prominent Germans in their midst. The new situation was not unusual to them. Churchmen readily embraced the Catholic Franks and tolerated Arians, such as the Visigoths, when they promoted peace and good government without abusing the Catholic population.

■ Old and New in the West

The Germanic kingdoms had a great deal in common with one another and very much resembled the late Roman Empire, which had been their common tutor. Each realm was led by a king who usually appeared in two distinct guises. To his people, the king was the military leader. The essential bond of unity among each Germanic people was loyalty to the leader, who repaid his followers in booty, tribute, land, legal protection, and military security. To the Romans, the king appeared as an ally and magistrate. Almost all Germanic kings bore Roman titles such as *consul* or *patrician,* and in these officially conferred titles resided the authority necessary to govern Roman populations. The kings also succeeded to a long line of Germanic Masters of the Soldiers, the title of the highest military officers in a prefecture. Each monarchy was led by a dynasty—for example, the Merovingians among the Franks—that was pre-eminent in wealth and possessed a sacral aura not unlike that of the Roman emperors.

The most common local officials were counts, a combined civilian-military position that made its first appearance in the fifth century. Initially a direct representative of the emperor, a count had financial, judicial, and military responsibilities. Local notables, usually great landowners, initially resented counts but gradually aspired to the office. Kings were careful to promote important locals, both Romans and their own people, to the office of count.

Local administration remained based in cities and towns. Taxes continued to be paid to royal governments throughout the sixth century. Provincial populations did not find this policy odd or unjust. Their taxes had always gone primarily to pay for the Roman military establishment, and the monarchies were the heirs of that establishment. Latin persisted as the language of administration. Until the end of Late Antiquity, notaries continued to draw up wills, records of land transactions, and legal documents of all kinds. Law codes issued by the Germanic kingdoms were largely adaptations of Roman provincial law. In other words, the legal conditions under which most people lived changed little. In sum, people's daily lives changed surprisingly little as a result of the replacement of Roman provinces by Germanic kingdoms.

THE ROMAN EMPIRE IN THE EAST, 395–565

HE creation of the tetrarchy at the end of the third century had separated the eastern and western halves of the Roman Empire administratively. In theory there was only one empire, ruled by one senior emperor, but in practice the eastern and western courts followed different policies in many areas, notably in their relations with the Germanic peoples. Fundamental cultural differences also distinguished East from West. The East was more populous, more heavily urbanized, and more prosperous. The eastern Mediterranean was Greek in culture and livelier intellectually than the West. From Diocletian in the third century to Justinian in the sixth, the eastern Roman Empire evolved slowly along the path marked out by its first great reformers. Moreover, the eastern empire survived as the western empire was being parceled out into kingdoms.

■ Constantinople and Its Rulers

Constantius II (r. 337–361), Constantine's son and his successor in the East, began making Constantinople a truly imperial city. He gave "New Rome" its own senate and urban magistrates, placing the city on an equal constitutional footing with Rome. Constantinople did not have an ancient aristocracy, so Constantius had to create a senatorial order. This he did by recruiting some Romans and promoting prominent and cultivated persons from cities in the eastern half of the empire, thereby forging bonds between the capital and its hinterland. Constantius and his successors also built palaces, public buildings, and churches to give the city a truly imperial character (see Map 7.4).

With the exception of the founder, the ablest members of the dynasty of Valentinian ruled in the East. The greatest of these was Theodosius II (r. 408–450), who enjoyed the longest imperial reign in Roman history. Through skillful diplomacy and the occasional application of force, he managed to keep the eastern empire free of serious Germanic incursions and the Persians at bay in Mesopotamia. To protect his capital on the landward side, he built massive walls whose ruins are impressive even today. Along with his wife and his sister, he promoted learning in the city and both added and beautified important buildings. Theodosius and his family made the new capital a real intellectual center.

Theodosius's greatest achievement was his law code of 438. The most comprehensive collection of Roman law yet produced, this code brought together all Roman laws issued since Constantine and arranged them in systematic fashion. The principal Germanic kingdoms were established just after the Theodosian code was issued. From this text, and from the Roman institutional structures that employed it, the barbarians were taught the rule of law and regulations for the conduct of daily affairs.

■ Emperor Justinian (r. 527–565)

After Theodosius II died in 450, the eastern empire endured seventy-seven years of rule by military men who lacked the culture, vision, or administrative capacity of their predecessors. But they preserved the empire and kept its government functioning. It was from these rough soldiers that Justinian emerged to become the greatest ruler of Late Antiquity, one of the greatest of all Rome's emperors. (See the feature "Weighing the Evidence: The Ravenna Mosaics" on pages 236–237.)

Justinian was born in an Illyrian village (Croatia, today), entered the army, and secured high office under his illiterate uncle Justin, who had likewise risen from the peasantry to the imperial office (518–527). Despite growing up in rural military camps, Justinian showed a wide range of interests and abilities. He surrounded himself with remarkable people and gave them considerable latitude. He flouted convention by marrying the actress Theodora (d. 548). A woman of intelligence, imagination, and great courage, Theodora was one of Justinian's key advisers. Justinian identified and promoted such previously obscure figures as the gifted general Belisarius°, the administrative genius John the Cappadocian, and the greatest legal mind of the age, Tribonian°. He entrusted two mathematicians, Anthemius° of Tralles and Isidore of Miletus, with the task of designing the church of Hagia Sophia, which remains his principal monument.

Almost immediately on assuming the throne, Justinian put John the Cappadocian to work reforming an administration that had been little altered in two centuries despite vast changes in the scope of the empire. John worked particularly to secure tighter control of provincial administrators, to ensure a steady flow of tax revenue, and to eliminate official corruption. Tribonian and

---

Belisarius (bel-uh–SAR-ee-us)   **Tribonian** (tree-BONE-ee-un)
Anthemius (an-THEE-mee-us)

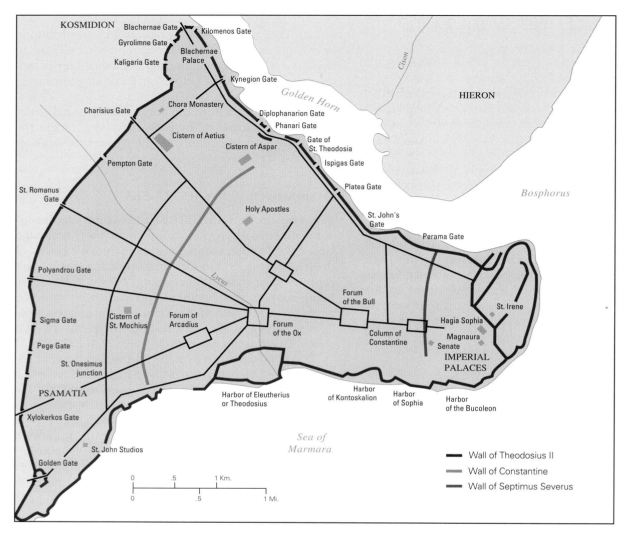

Map 7.4 Constantinople in Late Antiquity Protected by the sea, the Golden Horn, and its massive landward walls, Constantine's new city was an impregnable fortress for a thousand years. Note how the city was equipped with palaces, forums, wide thoroughfares, and other urban amenities. *(Source:* The Cambridge Illustrated History of THE MIDDLE AGES, *edited by Robert Fossier, translated by Janet Sondheimer. Copyright © 1989. Used by permission of Cambridge University Press.)*

a commission were assigned the task of producing the first comprehensive collection of Roman law since that of Theodosius II in 438. Between 529 and 533, Justinian's code was issued in three parts. The *Code* was a systematically organized collection of all imperial legislation. The *Digest* was a collection of the writings of the classical Roman jurists, the legal philosophers of the Early Empire. The *Institutes* was a textbook for law students. (See the box "Reading Sources: Basic Principles of Roman Law.") Justinian's code is the most influential legal collection in human history. It summarized a thousand years of legal

work, remained valid in the eastern empire until 1453, and has subsequently influenced almost every legal system in the modern world.

Not long after undertaking his legal and administrative reforms, Justinian launched an ambitious attempt to reunite the empire by reconquering its lost western provinces. Belisarius retook Africa from the Vandals and Italy from the Ostrogoths. Justinian also landed an army in Spain to attempt to wrest Iberia from the Visigoths. However, he never had the resources to carry out this daunting task successfully.

Justinian's ability to sustain major campaigns in the west was limited by the need to ward off constant threats in the east. The empire faced new enemies—Bulgars and Slavs—in the Balkans and a resurgent old foe—the Persians in Mesopotamia. Costly treaties and humiliating subsidies bought a string of cease-fires but no definitive settlements in these areas. The emperor's campaigns were so expensive that his administrative reforms wound up looking like contrivances to make more money for the emperor to waste. In 532 violent mobs coursed through the streets of Constantinople demanding the dismissal of John the Cappadocian and other imperial agents. Justinian almost fled but Theodora persuaded him to put down the riot. In 542 the Mediterranean world was visited by the most devastating plague in centuries, one more blow to the empire.

Justinian's religious policy also met with sharp opposition. A genuinely pious man, Justinian legislated frequently on behalf of the church and, along with Theodora, practiced generous charitable benefactions. Still, by both personal conviction and a sense of official duty, Justinian desired religious unity. Justinian was mildly Monophysite, and his wife was enthusiastically so. Justinian tried again and again to find a compromise that would bring all parties together. His church council of 553 assembled amid high hopes, but his proposed doctrinal compromises alienated the clergy in Syria, Egypt, and Rome.

To create a monument equal to his lofty vision of the empire, Justinian sought out Anthemius and Isidore. He charged the two great mathematicians to design a church that would represent the place where heaven and earth touched. Regular meetings in this place of the emperor, the patriarch, and the people gave repeated symbolic confirmation of the proper ordering of the state. There is no evidence that Justinian dictated the form of

Theodora   This magnificent sixth-century mosaic from Ravenna (it is one of a pair; see page 237) depicts Empress Theodora in all her power and majesty.   *(Scala/Art Resource, NY)*

Basic Principles of Roman Law

Roman law is distinguished not only by its particular rules but also by its approach to the subject of law as a whole. These words are from the beginning of Justinian's Institutes, *his lawbook for students.*

Justice is an unswerving and perpetual determination to acknowledge all men's rights. Learning in the law entails knowledge of God and man, and mastery of the difference between justice and injustice. . . . The commandments of the law are these: live honorably; harm nobody; give everyone his due. There are two aspects to the subject: public and private. Public law is concerned with the organization of the Roman state, while private is about the well-being of individuals. [Private law] has three parts, in that it is derived from the law of nature, of all peoples, or of the state. The law of nature is the law instilled by nature in all creatures. It is not merely for mankind but for all creatures of the sky, earth and sea. From it comes intercourse between male and female, which we call marriage; also the bearing and bringing up of children. Observation shows that other animals also acknowledge its force. The law of all peoples and the law of the state are distinguished as follows. All peoples with laws and customs apply law which is partly theirs alone and partly shared by all mankind. The law which each people makes for itself is special to its own state. It is called "state law," the law peculiar to that state. But the law which natural reason makes for all mankind is applied the same everywhere. It is called the "law of all peoples" because it is common to every nation. The law of the Roman people is also partly its own and partly common to all mankind. . . . The name of a particular state, Athens for example, is used to identify its state law. Similarly we refer to the law of the Roman people as the Roman state law. By contrast, the law of all peoples is common to all mankind. The reality of the human condition led the peoples of the world to introduce certain institutions. Wars broke out. People were captured and made slaves contrary to the law of nature. By the law of nature all men were initially born free. Nearly all the contracts come from this law of all peoples: sale, hire, partnership, deposit, loan, and many others. Next, our law is either written or unwritten. . . . Written law includes acts, plebeian statutes, resolutions of the senate, imperial pronouncements, magistrates' edicts, and answers given by jurists. . . . Law comes into being without writing when a rule is approved by use. Long-standing custom founded on the consent of those who follow it is just like legislation. . . . The law of nature, which is observed uniformly by all peoples, is sanctioned by divine providence and lasts forever, strong and unchangeable. The law which each state establishes for itself is often changed either by tacit consent of the people or by later legislation.

Source: Peter Birks and Grant McLeod, ed. and trans., *Justinian's Institutes*, 1.1–2 (Ithaca, N.Y.: Cornell University Press, 1987), pp. 37–39.

 For additional information on this topic, go to http://college.hmco.com.

his church—the church of Hagia Sophia° ("Holy Wisdom")—but the fact that he did not turn to any of the city's regular builders suggests that he was not looking for a traditional basilica.

Hagia Sophia was the largest Christian church ever built. The building begins with a square just over 100 feet on a side, 70 feet above which are four great arches. Two of the arches are solid and form the nave walls of the church; the other two give way to semicircular continuations of the nave. Above the main square is a dome that seems to float on the blaze of light that pours through its windows. The inside is a riot of color achieved by marble fittings in almost every imaginable hue and by the mysterious play of light and shadow. The effect of the whole is disorienting. Space in most basilicas is ordered, controlled, elegant. Space in Hagia Sophia is horizontal and vertical, straight and curved, square and round. The inside is by turns dark and light, purple and green, red and

Hagia Sophia (AYE-yuh so-FEE-yuh)

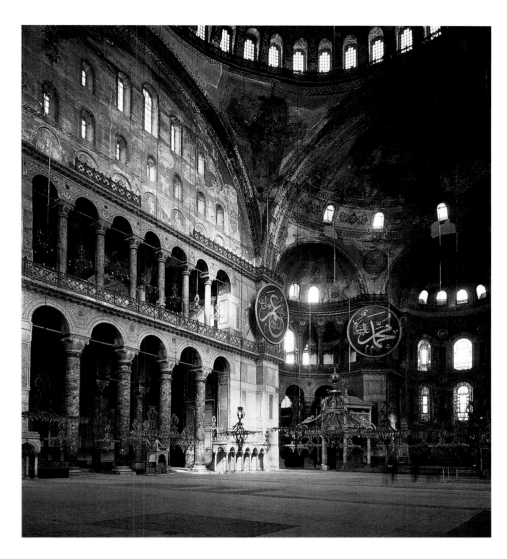

Hagia Sophia This interior view of Hagia Sophia conveys some sense of the dazzling complexity of this greatest of all late antique buildings. Compare it to Santa Maria Maggiore (page 215). *(Giraudon/Art Resource, NY)*

blue. It is indeed as if one has entered a realm that is anchored to this world but that gives access to another one. When Justinian first saw his church in its completed state, he said, "Solomon, I have outdone thee."

It is appropriate that in assessing his great church Justinian should have looked backward to Solomon, the Hebrew king who built Jerusalem's Temple. In almost all respects Justinian was a traditional, backward-looking ruler. His concern for the administrative minutiae of his empire would have made perfect sense to Diocletian. His combination of military and diplomatic initiatives would have been appreciated by Theodosius I, whose namesake, Theodosius II, would have admired Justinian's legal code. In his religious policies, especially in his quest for unity, Justinian drew from a deep well of imperial precedent. Even in his attempt to restore direct rule in Rome's former western provinces, Justinian showed himself a traditionalist.

SOCIETY AND CULTURE IN LATE ANTIQUITY

DURING these centuries of the ascendancy of the eastern Roman Empire, and the splintering of the western, the daily lives of men and women of every social class changed relatively little in terms of power relationships and economic opportunities. Nevertheless, provincial elites, members of the clergy, and barbarians gained unprecedented influence. Ordinary farmers, the overwhelming majority of the population, experienced changes in their legal status but not in their material well-being. Secular intellectual life lost most of its vitality, but a vibrant Christian culture flourished in the writings of the Church Fathers. Christianity added yet another element to the diversity that always characterized the Roman world.

■ Social Hierarchies and Realities

Roman society had long been hierarchical, and from Republican times Rome had been governed by a hereditary class. Although the members of this class affected a style of life that set them apart, they were never a closed caste. First, they did not reproduce themselves very effectively. About two-thirds of the Roman aristocracy was replaced every century—a typical pattern in premodern societies. This turnover created significant opportunities for social mobility. Second, just as the empire had been born in a social transformation that brought the Italian aristocracy into the Roman governing class, so Late Antiquity was characterized by a transformation that brought provincial elites and barbarians into the framework of power. Paradoxically, social change was always masked as social continuity because when new men reached the top, they tried to embrace the culture and values of those whom they had replaced.

Three ideals guided the lives of elite men: *otium, amicitia,* and *officium. Otium,* leisure, meant that the only life worth living was one of withdrawal in which the finer things of life—literature, especially—could be cultivated. *Amicitia,* friendship, implied several things. It could mean the kinds of literary contacts that the thousands of surviving letters from Late Antiquity reveal. Friendship could also mean patronage. The doorstep of every noble household was crowded every morning with hangers-on who awaited their small offerings and any commands as to how they might do their patron's will. *Officium,* duty, was the sense of civic obligation that Roman rulers communicated to the provincial upper classes.

Aristocrats governed in both public and private ways, which are almost impossible to differentiate. Though gradually excluded from key military and administrative posts, nobles did not lose their influence. They used their wealth to win or reward followers, bribe officials, and buy verdicts. In towns decurions controlled local market privileges, building trades, police forces, fire brigades, and charitable associations. Their public and private means of persuasion and intimidation were immense. In the West, in the growing absence of an imperial administration, Roman public power did not so much "decline and fall" as find itself privatized and localized. Patronage and clientage in Roman society had a benevolent dimension, but they also revealed the raw realities of power.

In Roman society power was everything and those who lacked power were considered "poor," regardless of their financial status. On this reckoning, much of the urban population was poor because they lacked access to the official means of coercion and security that the notables enjoyed. Merchants, artisans, teachers, and others were always vulnerable because their social, political, or economic positions could change at a moment's notice. They lacked the influence to protect themselves.

Most citizens of the late antique world can be classed as farmers, but this categorization is misleading because it lumps together the greatest landowners and the poorest peasants. Late Antiquity saw a trend in the countryside that continued into the Middle Ages: freedom and slavery declined simultaneously. Many small, independent farmers, probably people who had long been the clients of local grandees, handed over their possessions—*commended* them is the technical term—and received back the use of them in return for annual rents in money or in kind. They became *coloni,* tenants. Their patrons promised to protect them from lawsuits or from severe economic hardship. More and more, these coloni were bound to their places of residence and forced to perform services or pay fees that marked their status as less than fully free. At the same time, many landlords who could no longer afford to house, feed, and equip slaves gave them their freedom and elevated them to the status of coloni. Probably the day-to-day lives of the great mass of the rural population changed very little, and their position at the bottom of the social hierarchy did not alter.

Women's lives are not as well known to us as men's. "Nature produced women for this very purpose," says a Roman legal text, "that they might bear children and this is their greatest desire." Ancient philosophy held that women were intellectually inferior to men; science said they were physically weaker; and law maintained that they were naturally dependent. In the Roman world women could not enter professions, and they had limited rights in legal matters. Christianity offered women opposing models. There was Eve, the eternal temptress through whom sin had fallen on humanity, and then there was Mary, the virginal Mother of God. The Bible also presented readers with powerful, active women, such as Deborah and Ruth, and loyal, steadfast ones, such as Jesus's female disciples. Amid this varied popular and learned opinion, we can still detect some possibilities for independent and influential activity on the part of women.

Girls usually did not choose their marriage partners. Betrothals could take place as early as age 7 and lawful marriages at 12. Most marriages took place when the girl was around 16; husbands were several years older. A daughter could reject her father's choice only if the intended man was unworthy in status and behavior. Women could inherit property from their fathers and retained some control over their marital dowries. Divorce was possible but only in restricted cases. A divorced woman who had lost the financial security provided by her husband and father was at a distinct disadvantage legally and economically unless she had great wealth.

Christianity brought some interesting changes in marriage practices. Since the new faith prized virginity and celibacy, women now had the option of declining marriage. The church at Antioch supported three thousand virgins and widows. Christian writers tried to attract women to the celibate life by emphasizing that housework was drudgery. Christianity required both men and women to be faithful in marriage, whereas Roman custom had permitted men, but not women, to have lovers, prostitutes, and concubines. Christianity increased the number of days when men and women had to abstain from sex. Ancient cultures often prohibited sexual intercourse during menstruation and pregnancy but Christianity added Sundays and many feast days as forbidden times. Further, Christianity disapproved of divorce, which may have accorded women greater financial and social security, although at the cost of staying with abusive or unloved husbands.

Traditionally, women were not permitted to teach in the ancient world, though we do hear of women teachers such as Hypatia of Alexandria (355–415), renowned for her knowledge of philosophy and mathematics. Some Christian women, such as Melania (see page 218), were formidably learned. Until at least the sixth century the Christian church had deaconesses who had important responsibilities in the instruction of women and girls. Medical knowledge was often the preserve of women, particularly in areas such as childbirth, sexual problems, and "female complaints."

Christianity also affected daily life. Churchmen were concerned that women not be seen as sex objects. They told women to clothe their flesh, veil their hair, and use jewelry and cosmetics in moderation. Pious women no longer used public baths and latrines. Male or female, Christians thought and lived in distinctive new ways. All Christians were sinners, and so all were equal in God's eyes and equally in need of God's grace. Neither birth nor wealth nor status was supposed to matter in this democracy of sin. Theological equality did not, however, translate into social equality.

The church also introduced some new status distinctions. Holiness became a badge of honor, and holy men and women became Late Antiquity's greatest celebrities. After their death they were venerated as saints. Sanctuaries were dedicated to them, and people made pilgrimages to their tombs to pray and seek healing from physical and spiritual ailments. Miracle stories became popular. Thus, in some ways Christianity produced a society the likes of which the ancient world had never known, a society in which the living and the dead jockeyed for a place in a hierarchy that was at once earthly and celestial. But in other ways, Christianity reoriented traditional Roman patron-client relations so that client sinners in this world were linked to sanctified patrons in heaven.

■ The Quest for a Catholic Tradition

As a practical matter, the Catholic Church had been striving for doctrinal universality since the Council of Nicaea. It is no accident that the Catholic Church grew up in a Roman world steeped in ideas of universality. The most deeply held tenet of Roman ideology was that Rome's mission was to civilize the world and bend it to Roman ways.

One intriguing development in Late Antiquity is the emergence of several Christian communities claiming fidelity to a universal—a catholic—tradition. The Latin Christian church in the West was staunchly Nicene and Chalcedonian and took its bearings from Latin church writers. In the eastern Mediterranean, writers tended to use the word *Orthodox,* which means "right believing" but also carries clear implications of catholicism, that is, of universality. The Orthodox Church centered primarily on the emperors and patriarchs, used Greek, and followed Greek Christian writers. The Coptic Church in Egypt was Monophysite, followed the teachings of the patriarchs of Alexandria, and used the Coptic language. The Jacobite Church, a mildly Monophysite, Syriac-speaking group, was originally strong in Syria, from where it spread to Mesopotamia and beyond. Each of these churches produced a literature, an art, and a way of life that marked its members as a distinct community. These traditions did not reflect the emergence of something new in Late Antiquity so much as a Christian reinterpretation of very old cultures and ideals. Each of these traditions exists today.

Christianity drew much from the pagan and Jewish environments within which it grew, but its fundamental inspiration was the collection of writings called in modern times the Bible. In antiquity this material was called *ta hagia biblia* or *sacra biblia,* meaning "the holy books." It was understood to be a collection of sacred writings, and the individual items in that collection had different meanings. From the second century, Christian writers began trying to define a canon, a definitive list of genuine Old and New Testament scriptures. It was widely recognized that without an official, standardized set of Christian writings, there could be no uniformity of Christian belief. This process of determining authentic

Sarcophagus of Junius Bassus Junius Bassus, prefect of Rome, died in 359 and was laid to rest in this splendid sarcophagus (from the Greek "body eater"!). Three points are important: First, as members of the Roman elite became Christian, they could afford to employ the finest craftsmen. Second, as Christianity became legal, it could search for artistic expression. Third, these Old and New Testament scenes proclaim Christ's divinity but, in an age of intense theological quarrels, glide over his humanity. *(Hirmer Verlag Munchen)*

Scripture was not completed until the middle of the fifth century.

While the search was underway for an authoritative list of books, it was also necessary to try to get uniform versions of the books that were being pronounced canonical. The Greek East used the Greek version of the Old Testament and the Greek New Testament. But that version was unsuitable in the West, where Latin was the principal tongue. Late in the fourth century, Pope Damasus° commissioned Jerome (331–420), a man who had renounced his wealth for a life of monasticism and scholarship, to prepare a Latin version based on a new translation of the Hebrew Scriptures and Greek New Testament. Jerome's version was called the "Vulgate" because it was the Bible for the "people" (*vulgus*) who knew Latin.

Once a scriptural canon had been identified, there was also a need for a creedal statement that would set down precisely what Christians believed. The councils of Nicaea and Constantinople defined the nature of the Trinity, and Chalcedon formulated the relationship between the human and divine natures of Christ. There were also debates about the nature of the priesthood, the structure and authority of the church, and the problem of human free will. Practical questions came up, too. How could Christians fulfill the moral demands of their faith while living in a world whose values were often at odds with church teachings?

Answers to these kinds of questions were provided by a group of Greek and Latin writers who are called the "Church Fathers" and whose era is called "patristic" (from *patres*, the Latin word for "fathers"). In versatility and sheer output they have few rivals at any time. Their intellectual breadth was matched by their elegant style and trenchant reasoning.

Many Christian writers addressed the problems of moral living in the world. In his treatise *On Duties*, Ambrose of Milan (339–397) attempted to Christianize the public ethos that Cicero had spelled out many years before in his book of the same name. Cicero talked of citizens' obligations to one another and to the law and the need for those in power to be above reproach in the conduct of their personal lives. Ambrose reinterpreted these obligations as duties that Christians owed to one another because of their common worship of God.

Pope Gregory I wrote *The Pastoral Rule* to reformulate Cicero's and Ambrose's ideas in ways that made them relevant to society's Christian leaders, the clergy. John Chrysostom° (347–407), a patriarch of Constantinople and one of the most popular and gifted preachers of Late Antiquity (his name means "golden tongued"), bitterly castigated the immorality of the imperial court and aristocracy: by setting a bad example, they endangered the souls of their subjects.

Damasus (DAM-uh-sus)

Chrysostom (KRIH-sus-tum)

■ Saint Augustine and the Christian Tradition

The most influential Christian thinker after Saint Paul was Augustine of Hippo (354–430). Augustine was born in North Africa to a pagan father and a Christian mother. His family was of modest means but, at great sacrifice, they arranged for him to receive the best education available. He embarked on a career as a professor of rhetoric. Once he had established himself, he moved on to Rome and then to Milan, which in the fourth century was the unofficial western capital. Augustine fell under the spell of Ambrose and embraced the Christianity that his mother, Monica, had been urging on him throughout his life. Later Augustine chronicled his quest for truth and spiritual fulfillment in his *Confessions,* a classic of Western literature. (See the box "Reading Sources: The Moment of Augustine's Spiritual Awakening.") In 395 Augustine became a bishop and until his death served the North African community at Hippo, and the wider Christian world, with a torrent of writings.

Not a systematic thinker, Augustine never set out to provide a comprehensive exposition of the whole of Christian doctrine. Instead he responded to problems as they arose, crucial among which were the relationship between God and humans, the nature of the church, and the overall plan of God's creation.

In the early fifth century some people believed that they could achieve salvation by the unaided operation of their own will. Augustine responded that although God did indeed endow humankind with free will, Adam and Eve had abused their will to rebel against God. Ever since that first act of rebellion, a taint, called by theologians "original sin," predisposed all humans to continual rebellion, or sin, against God. Only divine grace can overcome sin, and only by calling on God can people receive grace. Here was a decisive break with the classical idea of humanity as good in itself and capable of self-improvement, perhaps even perfection, in this world. According to Augustine, all people were sinners, in need of God's redemption.

Some North African heretics taught that sacraments celebrated by unworthy priests were invalid. Augustine believed that the efficacy of the church's sacraments—those ritual celebrations that were considered to be channels for the communication of grace, of God's special aid and comfort to the faithful—did not depend on the personal merit of the minister. A priest or a bishop acted in God's place and through divine grace. Therefore, faith in God was paramount. The church was thus a community of acknowledged sinners led by the clergy in a quest for eternal salvation. To Augustine, God alone was perfect. Clergy, rulers, churches: these were all human institutions, all more or less good in particular circumstances.

To many adherents of the traditional Roman religion, the sack of Rome by the Visigoths in 410 was repayment for Rome's abandonment of its traditional gods. To refute them, Augustine wrote the most brilliant and difficult of all his works, *The City of God.* This book is a theology of history. Augustine sees time not as cyclical, the traditional classical view, but as linear. Since the creation of the world, a plan has been in operation—God's plan—and that plan will govern all human activity until the end of time. History is the struggle between those who call on divine grace, who are redeemed, who are citizens of the City of God, and those who keep to the ways of the world, who persist in sin, who live in the earthly city. One may observe the unfolding of the divine plan by seeing how much of the earthly city has been redeemed at any given time.

Even though the Roman Empire was officially Christian, Augustine refused to identify his City of God with it. Nor would he say that the church and the City of God were identical. What he did say was that the sack of Rome was a great irrelevance because many kingdoms and empires had come and gone and would continue to do so, but only the kingdom of God was eternal and, in the long run, important. To a Roman people whose most cherished belief held that the world would last exactly as long as Rome's dominion, Augustine's dismissal of Rome's destiny sounded the death knell of the classical world-view.

Augustine also addressed the problem of education. He regarded salvation as the goal of life but realized that people had to carry on with their ordinary occupations. He also knew that almost the entire educational establishment was pagan in design and content. Education was confined mainly to the elite, who sought schooling partly to orient themselves within their cultural tradition and partly to gain employment, often in the imperial or urban service. This education had three mainstays. Latin or Greek grammar—rarely both—was the first. Augustine, for instance, knew little Greek, and by the sixth century few people in the East knew Latin. The second was rhetoric, once the art of public speaking but now, increasingly, literary criticism. The third was dialectic, or the art of right reasoning. In Late Antiquity public schools were fast disappearing as the need for them slipped away. But the church still needed educated persons, so it provided schools in cathedrals and monasteries.

In a treatise entitled *On Christian Doctrine,* Augustine expressed some ideas about education that proved influential for a millennium. He argued that everything a person needs to know to achieve salvation is contained

The Moment of Augustine's Spiritual Awakening

In this passage Augustine relates the moment of his conversion and abandonment of his former life. Notice the roles of God, books, his old friend Alypius, and his devoted mother, Monica.

So that I might pour out all these tears and speak the words that came with them I rose up from Alypius and went further away that I might not be embarrassed even by his presence. This was how I felt and he realized it. No doubt I had said something or other, and he could feel the weight of my tears in the sound of my voice. And so I rose to my feet, and he, in a state of utter amazement, remained in the place where we had been sitting. I flung myself down on the ground somehow under a fig tree and gave free rein to my tears; they streamed and flooded from my eyes. . . . And in my misery I would exclaim: "How long, how long this 'tomorrow and tomorrow'? Why not now? Why not finish this very hour with my uncleanness?"

So I spoke, weeping in the bitter contrition of my heart. Suddenly a voice reaches my ears from a nearby house. It is the voice of a boy or a girl (I don't know which) and in a kind of singsong the words are constantly repeated: "Take it and read it. Take it and read it." At once my face changed and I began to think carefully of whether the singing of words like these came into any kind of game which children play, and I could not remember that I had ever heard anything like it before. I checked the force of my tears and rose to my feet, being quite certain that I must interpret this as a divine command to me to open the book and to read the first passage which I should come upon. For I had heard this about Anthony: He had happened to come in when the Gospel was being read, and as though the words read were spoken directly to himself, he had received the admonition: "Go, sell your possessions, and give to the poor. You will then have treasure in heaven. After-

ward, come back and follow me" [Matthew 19:21]. And by such an oracle he had been converted to you.

So I went eagerly back to the place where Alypius was sitting, since it was there that I had left the book of the Apostle [Paul] when I rose to my feet. I snatched up the book, opened it, and read in silence the passage on which my eyes first fell: "Not in carousing and drunkenness, not in sexual excess and lust, not in quarreling and jealousy. Rather, put on the Lord Jesus Christ and make no provisions for the desires of the flesh" [Romans 13:13–14]. I had no wish to read further; there was no need to. For immediately I had reached the end of this sentence, it was as though my heart was filled with a light of confidence and all the shadows of my doubt were swept away.

Before shutting the book I put my finger or some other marker in the place and told Alypius what had happened. By now my face was perfectly calm. Alypius in his turn told me what had been going on in himself. He asked me to see that passage which I had read. . . . He was strengthened by the admonition. . . . The next thing we do is go inside and tell my mother. How happy she is! We describe to her how it all took place, and there is no limit to her joy and triumph . . . for she saw that with regard to me you had given her so much more than she used to ask for when she wept so pitifully before you. . . . I was now standing on that rule of faith just as you had shown me to her in a vision so many years before.

Source: St. Augustine, *The Confessions of St. Augustine,* trans. Rex Warner (New York: Mentor, 1963), pp. 182–183.

in the Bible. But the Bible, written in learned language, is full of difficult images and allusions. How is an ordinary person to learn what he or she needs to know in order to master this great book of life? Only by getting some schooling, and that education would inevitably be in the classical languages and literatures. To express his attitude toward that schooling, Augustine used the image of "spoiling the Egyptians," borrowed from the account of

the Hebrews' Exodus from Egypt, when they took with them whatever they could use. Augustine's attitude toward classical learning was that it was useful only to the extent that it equipped individuals to read the Bible, to understand it, and to seek salvation. Classical culture had no intrinsic merit. It might give pleasure, but it was equally likely to be a distraction or a temptation to immorality.

The Italian writer Cassiodorus° (ca. 485–580) gave this Augustinian interpretation of the classical heritage its definitive statement in his treatise *On Divine and Human Readings*. After the fall of the Ostrogothic kingdom, whose king Theodoric he had served loyally, Cassiodorus retired and set up a school of Christian studies. His treatise served as a kind of annotated bibliography and curriculum of the major writings on school subjects such as grammar, rhetoric, and dialectic, and on biblical commentary. For centuries, schools organized on Augustine's and Cassiodorus's model did an estimable job of preparing the clergy to carry out their functions.

SUMMARY

 HEN the late antique period opened, Rome's vast and diverse empire was beset with innumerable political, military, and economic problems. The classical culture that had evolved over centuries in the Mediterranean, world seemed to have lost much of its vigor and appeal. But energetic rulers such as Diocletian and Constantine undertook a half-century of intense military, economic, and administrative reform that put the empire on firm footings while simultaneously changing forever the basic nature of the Roman state.

By 600 a Roman Empire still survived, but it was confined to the eastern Mediterranean, where it would persist for another millennium. In the West, Rome's former provinces had evolved into a series of barbarian kingdoms. Each of those kingdoms retained significant features of the governmental systems of the provinces in which they arose. Whether in the East or in the West, military men led a world whose culture was less civilian than in early imperial times. But the militarization of public life in Late Antiquity preserved the eastern empire and created a stable framework for the transition from empire to kingdoms in the West.

In 300, barbarians were a worrisome threat along the northern frontiers of the empire. By 600, barbarians had created, from Britain to Spain, a succession of kingdoms the most successful of which owed great debts to Rome. The barbarians did not appear suddenly in Late Antiquity. Rome knew these people, had traded, fought, and allied with them for centuries. The barbarians did not come to destroy Rome but to join it, to benefit from it, to learn its ways. The creation of the barbarian kingdoms was in many ways one of Rome's most creative political acts.

In 300 the Christian church was suffering persecution. By 600 the church spanned the old Roman world. A hierarchy of sophisticated leaders ably governed the church. Christianity had absorbed what it could of ancient culture, and the church had adapted Roman institutions. Prominent families had once governed Roman towns and provinces through urban institutions. The bishops and patriarchs who governed late antique towns via their church offices often came from those same families, or families just like them. The Church Fathers addressed some of the most fundamental problems of human existence in correct, sometimes elegant and moving, Greek and Latin.

The late antique world was fully embroiled in a process of evolution. That evolution would go on. In the West, kingdoms would appear and disappear, but the basic political structure of the European Middle Ages would be the kingdom. The eastern Roman Empire would shed more and more of its Roman heritage and turn into a regime we call "Byzantine." But the Byzantines themselves always insisted that they were Romans. The lands of North Africa and the Middle East that had long but tenuous relations with Rome would produce a new political order under the followers of the prophet Muhammad. But that world too would owe much to its Roman predecessor while also inheriting some of that world's old and deep divisions. In 600 the basic building blocks of the West were in place: Greco-Roman culture and institutions, Judeo-Christian religious beliefs, and barbarian peoples. In the world we call "medieval" those building blocks would be assembled in new configurations.

■ Suggested Reading

Bowersock, G. W., P. Brown, and O. Grabar, eds., *Late Antiquity: A Guide to the Post-Classical World.* 1999. Although basically an encyclopedia, this masterful volume contains long entries on all the major topics and up-to-date essays on big themes.

Brown, Peter. *The World of Late Antiquity.* 1971. A sprightly and beautifully illustrated interpretation of cultural crosscurrents by the most gifted interpreter of Late Antiquity.

Cameron, Averil. *The Mediterranean World in Late Antiquity, A.D. 395–600.* 1993. A superb and readable survey of all the major problems and interpretations.

Clark, Gillian. *Women in Late Antiquity: Pagan and Christian Lifestyles.* 1993. A first-ever attempt to capture the lives of late antique women in all respects.

Markus, Robert. *The End of Ancient Christianity.* 1990. This stimulating and beautifully written book explores the changing meanings of sacred and secular in the period from 400 to 600.

 For a searchable list of additional readings for this chapter, go to http://college.hmco.com.

Cassiodorus (cass-ee-oh-DOR-us)

The Ravenna Mosaics

Propaganda. The word has unsavory connotations. It suggests that someone is trying to convince someone else to do or to believe what is wrong. Actually, the word means only "things to be propagated," a message to be gotten out. The message itself may be good or bad, true or false.

When we think of propaganda, we must consider both the message and the medium in which it is conveyed. In antiquity, governments had several means of getting their messages out. Almost all the means were public, visible, striking.

Mosaics are among the most spectacular art forms of Late Antiquity, and in the churches of Ravenna they attained the summit of their propagandistic power. A mosaic is a picture formed by the intricate arrangement of thousands of tiny bits (called *tesserae*) of glass, stone, or metal. An artist created a rough sketch of the intended picture and then laid out the tesserae to conform to the sketch. Next the artist applied wet plaster to a small section of the surface, usually a wall or a floor, that was to receive the picture and then embedded that section's tesserae into the plaster. This process was repeated until the whole mosaic was completed. The result was a durable art form of great beauty and visual interest. In the picture on the opposite page you can see the tesserae and even some of the sparkle produced by the effect of sunlight and candlelight reflecting off the mosaic.

Mosaics were sometimes placed in private homes by the very wealthy, but more often they were put in conspicuous public places. Churches commonly received them in Late Antiquity. As more of society became Christian, aristocrats in particular were happy to spend lavishly to adorn their places of worship with beautiful decorations. Masses of people saw those decorations, reflected on who had financed them, and pondered the meaning of the image itself.

The greatest patron of all was the emperor. By putting up any work of art, the emperor proclaimed his power and influence. His reach was vast even if he never left Constantinople. Nothing shows this better than the Ravenna mosaics erected by Justinian.

Let us recall the situation. The Arian Ostrogoths had taken over Italy in 493. Ruling from Ravenna, they claimed to be imperial allies and representatives. Down to 535 there were always strains between Ravenna and Constantinople, and in that year Justinian launched the twenty-year-long Gothic War. During and after the war churches were erected as symbols of the imperial restoration.

The mosaic pictured here is located on the left-hand side of the apse, above and behind the altar, in the church of San Vitale in Ravenna. Its central figure is the emperor Justinian. Immediately opposite it is another mosaic (partially reproduced on page 227) focusing on Empress Theodora. San Vitale was a monument to the defeat of the Arian Goths. Any worshiper who raised his or her eyes from the altar saw immediately both Justinian and Theodora. These images made a powerful statement in a city that had been ruled by a Gothic king for thirty-three years. Justinian was leaving no doubt about who was now in charge. Consider, too, the prominence accorded to Theodora. Justinian really did view her as a partner in his rule.

That the emperor and empress were in charge is indicated in several distinct ways. They are slightly larger and are standing in front of their attendants. They are not quite like the other humans shown in the mosaic. They wear crowns and rich purple—that is to say, imperial—garments. They present gifts: he a gold paten holding the eucharistic bread and she a golden chalice containing the eucharistic wine. Thus the emperor and empress are represented as the donors of the church and as the guarantors of authentic worship.

Justinian tried throughout his reign to promote *homonoia* ("concord"). He tried to reconcile many political and religious factions. Notice the figure to Justinian's left (your right), over whose bald head you can read "MAXIMIANUS." This man was the archbishop of Ravenna, a close ally of the emperor and the person responsible both for eradicating Arianism and for reconciling Arians. His prominent position next to the emperor, and the fact that he alone is named, assured everyone of the correct doctrinal position. And in case anyone needed a further reminder, Maximianus holds in his hand the cross of Christ: there would be no more Arian subordination of the second person of the Trinity to the first.

We may note one more piece of propaganda. Look at the man standing to the left of Justinian and slightly behind him—between Justinian and Maximianus. This is Julianus Argentarius, a wealthy layman who was in all things the emperor's agent in Ravenna. He helped to finance and oversaw the construction of not only San Vitale but also several other churches in Ravenna. His presence signifies *homonoia*, the traditional concord between the emperor and the elite throughout the empire. Relations between the court and the Italian elite had been very strained under the Ostrogoths. Julianus's presence signaled that all was well once again. Vanity played a role too. Julianus paid for the art, so he had himself included in it.

The church of San Vitale was itself a propaganda statement. Theodoric was buried in a grand octagonal tomb. Justinian's builders chose an octagonal form for San Vitale. This church, too, is a sepulchre—a shrine for the remains of Saint Vitalis, an early Ravenna Christian who was martyred for the true faith.

In a world without the modern mass media, the media of antiquity served well to broadcast messages to people who understood their real and symbolic language. Recall the image on a Hellenistic coin (page 134). Look again at the statue of the tetrarchs (page 207) and the massive statue of Constantine (page 202). Cassiodorus once said that Rome was "a forest of statues." Every one of them was a propaganda statement.

 For additional information on this topic, go to http://college.hmco.com.

Justinian and His Courtiers, Apse Mosaic, San Vitale, Ravenna *(Scala/Art Resource, NY)*

CHAPTER 8

Early Medieval Civilizations 600–900

A

N empty throne: grand, majestic, imperial perhaps, and a little mysterious. The photo to the left is of Charlemagne's throne, modeled on that of King Solomon and placed in a setting rich with Roman architectural reminiscences. The West had known no emperors since 476, but on Christmas Day in 800, Pope Leo III placed a crown on the head of Charles, the king of the Franks. A contemporary called Charles "the Father of Europe," and in truth the last decades of the eighth century and the first decades of the ninth witnessed the birth of something new in the lands that had once been Rome's western provinces. Charles did not rule from Rome, however. After his coronation he trekked far to the north to his palace and chapel, where this throne sits—to Aachen°, a small town near the modern border between Holland and Germany.

A time traveler transported to the Mediterranean world of 600 would almost certainly have predicted only two heirs to Rome: the eastern empire and the kingdoms of the barbarian West. It is extremely unlikely that our intrepid wanderer would have foreseen one of the most dramatic developments in the history of Western civilization: the rise of the Arabs and their Islamic faith. In this chapter, three areas and histories, not just two, engage our attention: the Islamic East, the Byzantine Empire, and the Latin West. For each, the seventh century was an era of dramatic change, the eighth century an era of reform and consolidation, and the ninth century a time of upheaval. A new imperial tradition developed in all three areas. Muslims, Orthodox, and Catholics all believed themselves to be chosen by God, and their rulers defined themselves as God's earthly agents. In all

The Islamic East

The Byzantine Empire

Catholic Kingdoms in the West

The Carolingian Empire

Early Medieval Economies and Societies

Aachen (AH-ken)

The throne of Charlemagne, Aachen Palace chapel.
(Erich Lessing/Art Resource, NY)

three realms the interaction of local traditions with the Roman past produced new forms of central government that would prove influential for centuries. Commercial ties began to transform the Mediterranean world into a community of peoples who needed to balance mutual interests with bitter rivalries.

The period from 600 to 900 is commonly called the "early Middle Ages." What does this term mean? In the seventeenth century a Dutch scholar wrote of the *Medii Aevi*, the "Middle Times" that lay between antiquity and the dawning modern world. The name stuck. As a label for the post-Roman world, "Middle Ages" (whose adjectival form is "medieval") has become traditional. The fact that we no longer talk of an abrupt and catastrophic "fall" of the Roman Empire means that we no longer use the word *medieval* in negative ways.

QUESTIONS TO CONSIDER

■ **What were the most important factors in the rise of the Arab peoples and of the Islamic faith?**

■ **Why did a distinctive civilization that can be called "Byzantine" emerge?**

■ **In what ways were the Frankish and Anglo-Saxon kingdoms successful?**

■ **What were the chief similarities among the early medieval civilizations? the chief differences?**

TERMS TO KNOW

Muhammad	Papal States
Five Pillars of Islam	Charlemagne
Quran	vassal
caliphate	Carolingian Renaissance
Orthodoxy	manor
iconoclasm	

THE ISLAMIC EAST

A NCIENT writers took little notice of the Arabs, who inhabited much of the area from the Arabian peninsula to the Euphrates River. Around 600 the prophet Muhammad (570–632) appeared among them preaching a faith old in its basic elements but new in its formulation. With unprecedented spiritual and military fervor, converts to that new faith conquered territories from Spain to the frontiers of China. Slowly, they built an imperial system with a coherent government and ideology. At the same time, cultural elites began forging a new civilization out of the ethnic, religious, and historical diversity of that vast realm.

■ Arabia Before Muhammad

The Arab world in the early seventh century was large and turbulent. Long dominated by the Roman and Persian Empires, the region had no stable, large-scale political entities. People belonged to close-knit clans, or extended families, that in varying associations formed tribes. In theory, tribes were groups of people tracing descent from a known ancestor; in reality—and in this

Arab and Germanic peoples were alike—tribes were complex groups of relatives, allies, and political or economic clients.

As complex as its political situation was the region's ethnic and religious composition. The Roman world was overwhelmingly Christian, though there were many kinds of Christians. The Persian realm was officially Zoroastrian, but it had Jewish, Christian, Manichaean, and Buddhist minorities. The Arabs themselves were generally pagans, but Arabia had Jewish and Christian minorities.

The Arab East was also economically intricate and fragile. Bedouins° (Arabs who were nomadic pastoralists) provided for their own needs from their herds of sheep and goats, from small-scale trading in towns, and from regular raids on one another and on caravans. Some farmers worked the land, but in many areas soils were too poor and rain was too infrequent to support agriculture. Cities supported traders who carried luxury goods, such as spices, incense, and perfumes, from the Indian Ocean region and southern Arabia along caravan routes to the cities of the eastern Mediterranean. These traders formed the economic and political elite of Arabia, and they led the tribes. Mecca, dominated by the

bedouins (BED-oo-inz)

powerful tribe of the Quraysh°, was the foremost city of Arabia, but competition among cities and tribes was fierce.

A solution to the competition among tribes and towns for control of trade routes was the institution of *harams*°, or sanctuaries—places where contending parties could settle disputes peacefully. Mecca was one of the chief harams in Arabia, and its founding was attributed to the Israelite patriarch Abraham and one of his sons, Ishmael. The focus of the sanctuary was the black stone shrine known as the Kaaba°, founded by Abraham, according to Arab tradition. For centuries people from all over Arabia had made pilgrimages to Mecca, to the Kaaba, supposedly following Abraham's example.

■ The Prophet and His Faith

Muhammad was born in 570 to a respectable though not wealthy or powerful clan of the Quraysh tribe. His father died before he was born, his mother shortly afterward, leaving Muhammad under the care of his grandparents and an uncle. Like many young Meccans, he entered the caravan trade. By the time he was 20, Muhammad held such a reputation for competence and moral uprightness that he became financial adviser to a wealthy Quraysh widow, Khadija° (555–619). Although older than Muhammad, she became his wife in 595, and they had a loving marriage until her death.

From his youth Muhammad was a man of spiritual insight. In 610 he received the first of many revelations that commanded him to teach all people a new faith that called for an unquestioned belief in one god, Allah, and a deep commitment to social justice for believers. Muhammad began teaching in Mecca, but he converted few people outside his own circle—his wife was his first convert. Some Meccans were envious of Muhammad. Others feared that his new faith and new god might call into question the legitimacy of the shrines in Mecca and jeopardize the traditional pilgrimages to the Kaaba and the trade that accompanied them. By 619, Muhammad's well-connected wife and uncle were dead, and his position was precarious.

At this juncture citizens from Medina, a smaller trading community wracked by dissension among pagan Arabs, Jews, and followers of Muhammad, asked Muhammad to establish a haram there. In the summer of 622, small groups of Muhammad's disciples made their way to Medina, and in September Muhammad joined them. His journey from Mecca to Medina, the

CHRONOLOGY	
570–632	Life of Muhammad
597	Pope Gregory I sends missionaries to England
610–641	Reign of Heraclius in Byzantium
622	Hijra
632–733	Muslim conquests
661–750	Umayyad caliphate
664	Council of Whitby
711–716	Muslim conquest of Spain
750	Founding of Abbasid caliphate
751	Lombard conquest of Ravenna
755–774	Frankish conquest of Lombards
755–756	Foundation of Papal States
717–802	Isaurian dynasty at Byzantium
726–787, 815–842	Byzantine iconoclasm
757–796	Reign of Offa of Mercia
768–814	Reign of Charlemagne
786–809	Reign of Harun al-Rashid
800	Imperial coronation of Charlemagne
780s–860s	Carolingian Renaissance
843	Treaty of Verdun creates three Frankish kingdoms
867–886	Reign of Basil I

hijra°, marks the beginning of a new era, symbolized to this day in the Arab world by a calendar that dates "In the year of the Hijra."

Although Muhammad was fully in control in Medina, Mecca remained the focus of his attention. In addition to his sentimental attachment to Mecca, its political and economic importance were critical to his emerging desire to convert all of Arabia. His followers began attacking Meccan caravans and battled with the Meccans several times in the 620s. In 630 Muhammad and many

---

Quraysh (KOOR-aysh)   **harams** (HAR-ahmz)
Kaaba (KAH-bah)   **Khadija** (KAH-dee-ah)

hijra (HEEZH-rah)

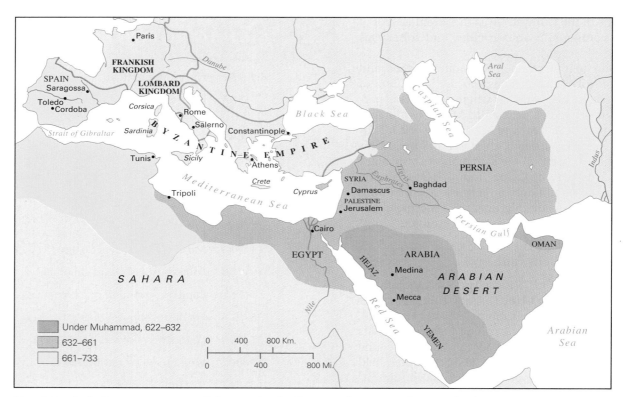

Map 8.1   Arab Conquests to 733   This map vividly illustrates the spectacular gains by the Arabs in the time of Muhammad, under the first caliphs, and under the Umayyads. Later, slow, steady gains in Africa, central Asia, and India expanded the empire even farther. Muslim conquest did not at first mean widespread conversion to Islam; Egypt, for example, was not majority Muslim before the tenth century.

of his followers returned to Mecca in triumph. Muhammad left the Quraysh in control, and he retained the Kaaba as a focus of piety. After making local arrangements, he returned to Medina and set about winning over the bedouins of the Arabian desert. When Muhammad died in 632, he had converted most of Arabia (see Map 8.1).

To what, exactly, had Muhammad and his followers converted? At the most basic level, people were asked to surrender completely to Allah, the one true God—that is, they were asked to make *al-Islam*, "the surrender." Those who surrendered became *Muslims* and joined the *umma muslima°*, a completely new kind of community in which membership depended only on belief in Allah and acceptance of Muhammad as Allah's prophet. No longer were one's duties confined to a particular clan, tribe, or town. All members of the umma were understood to have personal and communal responsibility for all other

members. Because of the experience of the hijra, Islam was a religion of exile, of separation from the ordinary world, and of reliance on God.

The basic teachings of Islam are traditionally described as "Five Pillars": (1) the profession of faith, "There is no God but Allah and Muhammad is His Prophet"; (2) individual prayer five times daily, plus group prayers at noon on Friday in a *mosque*, a Muslim house of prayer; (3) the sunup-to-sundown fast for one month per year; (4) the donation of generous alms to the poor; and (5) pilgrimage to Mecca at least once in a person's lifetime. These pillars are still the central requirements of Islam.

In the early decades the pillars sustained a faith that stressed strict monotheism and practices that affirmed Islam and built up a sense of community. At certain times of the day all Muslims everywhere bowed in prayer, with their heads facing toward Mecca. Everyone paid alms, creating thereby a feeling of solidarity among all members of the umma. Mecca itself and the experi-

umma muslima (OO-mah MOOSE-lee-mah)

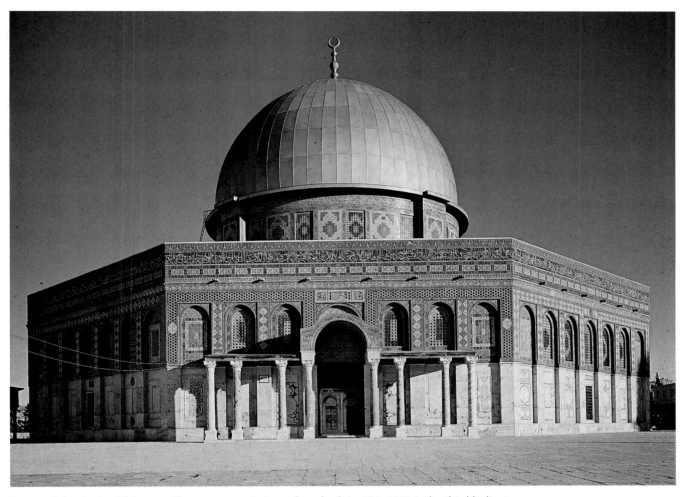

Dome of the Rock This magnificent mosque in Jerusalem (built in 691–692) is the third holiest shrine of Islam—after the Kaaba in Mecca and the prophet's mosque in Medina. Muslims believe that Muhammad ascended to heaven from this spot. *(Michael Holford)*

ence of pilgrimage were central to all Muslims. Originally there was no elaborate theology, intricate doctrinal mysteries, creed, or clergy. Men called *imams* led the Friday prayers in the mosque and usually offered sermons that applied Muslim teaching to the issues of the day, but Islam involved no ordained priesthood as in Judaism or Christianity and no hierarchy as in the Christian churches.

Muhammad communicated God's teaching to his followers, always insisting that he was transmitting a direct, verbal revelation and not offering his own interpretations. That revelation came in the form of "recitations" that make up the *Quran°*, the scriptures of Islam. Not

Quran (koo-RAHN)

long after Muhammad's death his closest followers arranged the recitations into 114 *Suras*, or chapters. The Quran contains legal and wisdom literature like the Hebrew Scriptures and moral teaching like the Christian New Testament. It also prescribes regulations for diet and for personal conduct. For example, the Quran forbids alcohol and gambling, censures luxury and ostentation, and imposes strict sexual restraints on both men and women. (See the box "Reading Sources: The Message of the Quran.")

Initially the Quran was interpreted rather freely within the umma, doubtless because there was no clergy to impose a uniform interpretation. After the prophet's death, some people felt the need for an authoritative teaching—as early Christians had felt the need for a

⮞ READING SOURCES

The Message of the Quran

The Quran consists of 114 Suras, literally the "steps" by which one rises to knowledge of Allah; we might say chapters. The Quran in its earliest versions was also equipped with a running commentary. The first four extracts below illustrate the simplicity and elegance of Muslim prayer and the absolute transcendence of Allah. The last two extracts demonstrate the profound sense of religious continuity that marked Muhammad's teaching.

Sura 1

In the name of Allah, Most Gracious, Most Merciful. / Praise be to Allah, the Cherisher and Sustainer of worlds; / Most Gracious, Most Merciful. / Master of the Day of Judgment. / Thee do we worship and Thine aid we seek. Show us the straight way, the way of those on whom Thou hast bestowed Thy grace, Thou whose portion is not wrath, and who do not go astray.

Sura 4.171

O People of the Book! Commit no excesses in your religion, nor say of Allah anything but truth. Christ Jesus the son of Mary was a messenger of Allah . . . so believe in Allah and in his messengers. Say not "Trinity" . . . for Allah is One God. Glory be to Him for He is exalted above having a son. To him belong all things in the heavens and on earth.

Sura 3.84

Say ye: We believe in Allah, and the revelation given to us, and to Abraham, Ismail, Isaac, Jacob and the descendants (children of Jacob), and that given to Moses and to Jesus and that given to all prophets from their Lord, but we make no difference between one and another of them, and we bow to Allah.

Sura 2.87

We gave Moses the book and followed him up with a succession of messengers; We gave Jesus the son of Mary clear signs and strengthened him with the Holy Spirit.

Sura 48

If the People of the Book rely upon Abraham, let them study his history. His posterity included both Israel and Ismail. Abraham was a righteous man of Allah, a Muslim, and so were his children. Abraham and Ismail built the Kaaba as the house of Allah and purified it, to be a centre of worship for all the world: For Allah is the God of all peoples.

Sura 56

God's truth is continuous, and His prophets from Adam, through Noah and Abraham, down to the last of the prophets, Muhammad, form one brotherhood. Of Imran father of Moses and Aaron sprang a woman, who devoted her unborn offspring to Allah. That child was Mary the mother of Jesus. Her cousin was the wife of the priest Zakariya, who took charge of Mary. To Zakariya, in his old age, was born a son Yahya, amid prodigies: Yahya was the herald of Jesus the son of Mary and was known as John the Baptist.

Source: The Meaning of the Holy Qur'an, New edition with revised translation, commentary, and newly compiled comprehensive index by Abdullah Yusuf Ali (Beltsville, Md.: Amana Publications, 1998), pp.14, 40, 51, 55–56, 134–35.

canon of Christian scripture and teaching—and their efforts resulted in the collections called the *sunna*, which means roughly the "good practice"—that is, the words and customs of Muhammad himself. Crucial in the development of the sunna were the *hadith*, the "sayings" of the prophet, the comments he sometimes made about how God's revelation was to be understood and applied. Extant compilations of the sunna date from the ninth century, and scholars are not sure what portion of them derives authentically from the age of the prophet.

■ The Arab Conquests

Muhammad's death brought a crisis. Who or what was to succeed him? In 632 the Meccan elite chose Abu Bakr as *caliph*°, or "successor to the prophet." Abu Bakr was elderly, an early convert to Islam, and a former secretary to Muhammad. He and his three successors down to 661 (Umar, Uthman, and Ali) were all Meccans, relatives of the prophet by marriage, and early converts. Islamic tradition calls them the "Rightly Guided Caliphs."

Abu Bakr left his successor, Umar, a united Arabia (see Map 8.1), no small feat in that fractious world. Umar began the lightning conquests by the Arabs of much of the Roman and Persian Empires. He initiated the policy of granting choice positions in the expanding caliphate, the Arab empire, to old converts and of ranking them according to precedence in conversion. As the old elite divided up the new provinces of the caliphate, some of them became *emirs* (governors), and others became lower administrators. Arab administrators then collected from all conquered people personal taxes and land taxes. Converts to Islam paid only land taxes. Arab settlers paid no taxes and received salaries from the taxes paid by others.

Umar was murdered by a slave in 644, leaving his successor, Uthman, a huge empire to administer. A great centralizer, Uthman chose emirs, regulated the finances of the provinces, and authorized the preparation of the definitive text of the Quran. In attempting to preserve the advantages of the old Meccan elite, Uthman alienated many people, particularly in Egypt, Syria, and Iraq, who had benefited from conquest and who guarded jealously their newfound local wealth and power. Uthman was murdered in 656 and replaced by Ali, Muhammad's son-in-law, whose goal was to create a truly Islamic government by emphasizing the religious side of the caliph's office as the leader of the umma. Ali was in turn killed by a disillusioned follower in 661. Years later some Muslims looked back to Ali as the true model for the caliph. These Muslims formed the *Shi'a*, the "Party of Ali."

When Ali was killed, the caliphate passed to Mu'awiya°, a Meccan who was the governor of Syria and commander of the finest army in the Arab world. That army ensured Mu'awiya's position. From 661 to 750 the Umayyads°, as Mu'awiya's family is called, built many of the caliphate's institutions.

Umayyads instituted greater centralization. This involved the introduction of a unified coinage, the Arabization of the administration—granting all key positions to Arabs—and taking tight control of provincial government and taxation. The Umayyads moved the capital of the caliphate to Damascus in their own power base of Syria, more centrally located than the old towns of Mecca and Medina and closer to the militarily active zones in eastern Iran and along the Byzantine frontier in Syria. In addition, the Umayyads presided over the final territorial expansion of the caliphate (see Map 8.1). To the west, the caliph's forces took North Africa and Spain and conducted raids deep into Gaul. In the east, though stymied by unsuccessful sieges against Constantinople, campaigns moved the frontier against the Byzantine Empire into the mountains of southern Anatolia and, farther east, established nominal authority as far as the Indus River valley.

Rome's empire expanded for 350 years, but the caliphate reached its zenith in scarcely 100. How can we account for the astonishingly rapid creation of such a vast empire? External factors were important. Byzantium and Persia had financially and militarily weakened themselves in a series of wars that ended just as the caliphate of Umar commenced. Moreover, the Byzantine and Persian states were exceedingly diverse, and the Arab armies dismantled them piecemeal. Both old empires, but especially the Byzantine, had deep religious divisions. Coptic Egypt and Jacobite Syria, for example, willingly yielded to the Arabs, who demanded taxes and submission but otherwise left them alone. The Byzantines and Persians tended to depend on static frontier garrisons and large armies that could not be quickly mobilized and moved long distances. The Arabs rarely risked great pitched battles. They preferred a gradually expanding military frontier gained by numerous lightning strikes.

Internal factors were more significant, however. For centuries, raiding and plundering had been a way of life in Arabia, but because Islam forbade Muslims from raiding other Muslims, a new outlet for traditional violence was needed. The prophet himself had believed firmly in the need to expand the faith, and his successors shared that belief. Muslim ideology divided the world into the "House of Islam" and the "House of War." In the House of Islam, the justice of Allah reigned supreme. In the House of War, *jihad,* holy war, was the rule. Christians and Jews, as fellow "Peoples of the Book"—sharers in a scriptural tradition reaching back to Abraham—were spared the choice of conversion or death, but "infidels" were expected to submit and convert. The Arab conquests were carefully planned and directed to channel violence out of Arabia, to populate much of western Asia with loyal Muslims, and to reward members of the umma.

---

caliph (KAY-lif)   **Mu'awiya** (MOO-ah-wee-uh)
Umayyads (OO-my-ahdz)

■ The Abbasid Revolution

Despite their military and administrative successes, the Umayyads were not popular. Many resented their bureaucratic centralization. Such resentment was acute in areas heavily populated by recent converts, who had always disliked the old Arabian elites, and in frontier provinces, where Arab immigrants along with local converts desired autonomy. The secular nature of Umayyad rule also offended those pious Muslims who expected a high standard of personal morality from their rulers. The opposition came to a head in a series of rebellions that culminated in the naming of a rival caliph, Abu'l Abbas, in 749. In 750 he defeated his Umayyad opponent.

The Abbasids° reigned until the thirteenth century. Initially, especially in the caliphate of Harun al-Rashid° (r. 786–809), they brought the Islamic world its first golden age. Harun's reign was marked by political stability, economic prosperity, and cultural achievements. Abbasid successes are attributable to political acumen and ideological restructuring.

With their frontier origins, the Abbasids were sympathetic to the caliphate's provincial populations. Thus, they created a more international regime. Non-Arabs and recent converts felt toward Islam, the prophet, and the prophet's family a loyalty that they would not grant to the old Arabian potentates who had led and initially benefited from the Arab conquests. The Abbasid polity was based on the idea of the fundamental equality of all believers, old or new, Arab or not.

Members of the Abbasid family received some key government posts, as did Iranians and other non-Arabs. Most importantly, however, local persons got more choice positions than Meccan or Syrian aristocrats. The capital of the caliphate was moved from Syria to Iraq, but to avoid favoring any existing group or region, the Abbasids built a new city, Baghdad, which they called "the navel of the universe." By addressing regional and ethnic sensitivities in an effective way, they were able to maintain, even extend, the centralized state of the Umayyad period.

The daily business of governing was usually in the hands of the *wazir*, who headed the administration, advised the caliph, and often exercised a powerful formative influence on the caliph's children and heirs. The first caliphs chose administrators from loyal Arabs and from experienced Christian subjects. Under the Umayyads the regime was Arabized. Then under Harun al-Rashid the government became international, professional, and hereditary. The chief agency of government was the treasury, which had separate branches dealing with the Muslim alms, with the land and poll taxes paid by subjects, and with the land taxes paid by converts. Alone among early medieval governments, the caliphate could draw up annual budgets. Alongside the treasury in exerting power was a prestigious group of palace servants. They did not hold major offices, but their informal influence on the caliph and his family was great. The army was another prominent body within the state.

The central government had several links to the provinces. In addition to controlling the army and provincial governorships, the caliph employed a network of regular envoys and spies. The court, especially under the Abbasids, drew able young men from all over into the service of the caliph and created hopes among provincial elites that they too might be chosen. In every district and city there were judges, *qadi*°, to oversee the application of Islamic law. Qadi were under the authority of the caliph.

The death of Harun in 809 sparked a century of problems. Intense family rivalries touched both the succession to the caliphate and the possession of key provincial positions. The bureaucracy became an increasingly influential pressure group, and the palace servants began to foment intrigues. The army became more and more a professional body comprising non-Arabs, especially Turks, hired from the frontiers and beyond because Arabs, enjoying their salaries, declined to serve. The parallel with the Germanization of the late Roman army is striking. The army, the bureaucracy, and the courtiers all had different and conflicting interests and did not hesitate to press their own advantages. Religious divisions persisted, even intensified. Many felt the Abbasids had not gone far enough in erecting a truly Islamic regime, but some felt that the caliphs had gone too far in claiming both the political and religious authority of the prophet. Whole regions took advantage of Abbasid leniency in granting local autonomy and began to fall away. After the early tenth century the Abbasid caliphs had little effective power.

■ The Emergence of Islamic Culture

Two currents are apparent in the culture of the Islamic East. One is the elaboration of religious thought; the other is the assimilation of multiple cultural heritages. Both were influenced by the spread of Islam that mixed Greek, North African, Iranian, Turkish, and even Hindu elements into a culture already rich with Arab, Christian, and Jewish ingredients.

Abbasids (uh-BASS-idz)
Harun al-Rashid (hah-ROON al-rah-SHEED)

qadi (KAH-dee)

Muslims assembled for prayer in mosques, the often beautiful buildings usually modeled on the original mosque in Medina. The worshipers—with men and women in separate areas—arrayed themselves in parallel rows and were led in prayer by an imam. In time the imams started offering interpretations of the Quran, and collections of these interpretations began to circulate. Similarly, Muslim judges began to issue opinions on how the Quran and sunna might be applied to the daily lives of believers. Teachers in mosque schools were also influential. Together these authority figures, collectively the *ulama*, developed a body of religious thought. Lacking elaborate theology and creeds, Islamic religious thought pertains to practice and allegiance more than ideas. The point is less to *know* Islam than to *live* it.

The late ninth and early tenth centuries saw the emergence of a religious split in the Islamic world that persists to this day. The opposing groups were Shi'ite and Sunni Muslims. Shi'ites believed that caliphs should be chosen only according to strict standards of moral and spiritual worthiness. Further, they insisted that the only way to ensure such worthiness was to choose caliphs from the line of Ali, the fifth caliph, husband of Muhammad's daughter Fatima and, in 661, a victim of assassination. Moreover, they believed that the whole ulama should measure up to Shi'ite standards. Sunni Muslims, always the vast majority, proclaimed that only they adhered to the sunna, the "good practice" of Muhammad himself. Sunnis accept the legitimacy of the whole line of Umayyad and Abbasid caliphs and the teachings of the ulama.

In 832 an Abbasid caliph endowed the "House of Wisdom," an academy for scholars in Baghdad (compare Charlemagne's palace school, pages 262–264), and from this point on Muslim scholars had the leisure and wherewithal to begin tackling the corpus of Greek thought, especially the scientific writers. The earliest Arab scholars sought mainly to master the learning of the past. Greek, Persian, and Indian works were collected and translated, manuscripts were copied, and libraries were built. Muslims showed little interest in the *literary* heritage of antiquity, the ancient legacy that was so important and controversial to Christian scholars.

So we may ask: Was the Islamic caliphate part of the West or not? Was it brother, or cousin, to the emerging Byzantine and Latin worlds? From the vantage point of 900, the answer we might give to those questions— "largely Western"—differs from the answer we might give today—"largely Eastern." In later chapters we will see how the Islamic world became less western and more eastern.

THE BYZANTINE EMPIRE

THE century after Justinian's death in 565 was difficult for the eastern Roman Empire. Attacks by Persians, Bulgars, and Muslims, riots and rebellions, plagues and famines, and some weak rulers put the empire in a perilous position. Two fundamental changes transformed the eastern Roman Empire into a new civilization that we call "Byzantine°," from Byzantium, the ancient Greek name for the capital city, Constantinople. In external affairs, the empire experienced a sharp geographic contraction until it stabilized into the shape it would hold into the thirteenth century. In internal affairs, the empire changed both its basic administrative structures and its cultural orientation.

■ External Changes

In 600 the empire still laid claim, along the southern and eastern shores of the Mediterranean, to most of the lands that Rome had ruled for centuries. But in the east the empire had been suffering recurrent losses to Persia. In 610 Heraclius°, a gifted ruler, ascended the throne. Between 622 and 629 Heraclius campaigned brilliantly and recovered almost everything that had been lost. But he faced a cruel irony. When the Arab expansion began under Umar, Heraclius's empire was militarily and financially exhausted. As the seventh century wore on, Arabs captured Syria and Palestine, Mesopotamia, and began a centuries-long push into Anatolia. Eventually they even threatened the capital, Constantinople.

In the Balkans Heraclius and his successors fought constant battles, with mixed results. They checked the advance of the Slavic peoples, who had been expanding southward for some years. The Slavic advance was partly generated by social and political forces among the Slavs themselves and partly a result of pressure from the Avars and Bulgars. These peoples, who were related to the Huns, had begun penetrating into the Danube basin in the late sixth century. The empire tried hard, with varying success, to check their forward march.

Where the West was concerned, Heraclius and his successors were powerless to stop the Arab advance in North Africa and Spain. In Italy, imperial control was confined to a few outposts around Rome, Ravenna, and Sicily. Generally, Italy was too far away and strategically insignificant to attract much attention from the imperial government.

Byzantine (BIZZ-un-teen)   **Heraclius** (her-ACK-lee-us)

Greek Fire   Invented in the seventh century by Callimachus, a Syrian engineer, Greek fire was a mixture formed from petroleum, sulfur, saltpeter, and lime that ignited on contact with water. It was first used to repel the Muslim siege of Constantinople in 678.   *(Institut Amatller d'Art Hispanic)*

By around 700 the empire was assuming the basic geographic shape it would hold for centuries. In contrast to the vast lands once ruled by Rome, the empire was now confined to the eastern Balkans and to western Anatolia. Then in 717 Leo III "the Isaurian°" (Leo was actually Syrian but later legends made him a resident of Isauria in Anatolia) became emperor in a moment of acute crisis. Arab armies had seized much of Anatolia and had laid siege to Constantinople itself. The city would surely have fallen had it not been for the "Greek fire" that made it impossible for the attacking navy to operate beneath the seaward walls. Leo repulsed the attack and then ruled successfully until 741. He was followed by his able and charismatic son, Constantine V (r. 741–775). Constantine held the line in Anatolia and enjoyed decades of military success along the Balkan frontier.

In Italy alone Isaurian policy was unsuccessful. When Justinian reconquered Italy from the Ostrogoths (see page 226), his armies devastated the region and left it poor and weak. Into the gap stepped the Lombards, who gradually built a kingdom in the north of Italy— Lombardy still bears their name—and set up a series of duchies in the center and south of Italy. The Byzantines prudently dedicated their resources to holding their

Balkan and Anatolian frontiers, but this strategy left their subjects in Italy clamoring for aid. Eventually the popes put themselves at the head of a movement in Italy that turned to the Franks for protection. In 755 and 756 the Frankish king marched to Italy, defeated the Lombards, and donated the territories he seized from them to the pope. On the one hand, this inaugurated the "Papal States," the ever-changing set of lands in Italy whose current remnant is Vatican City. On the other hand, this military encounter put an end to effective Byzantine control in Italy, except for the areas around Naples and Sicily. In 827 Muslims seized Sicily, and in the ensuing decades they subjected southern Italy to continuous raids and occasional conquests.

Constantine V's promising son, Leo IV (r. 775–780), survived him only briefly. He left a 6-year-old heir, Constantine VI, and a remarkable widow, Irene, as regent for her son. Irene was a skilled politician, but under her the army grew restive because she preferred to make treaties, sometimes on unfavorable terms, than to send troops into the field. She did not trust the military's loyalty. Moreover, Irene had to contend with a foolish son who spent his time trysting with ladies of the court rather than attending to his official duties. In 797 Irene had him blinded, ironically in the very palace chamber where she had given birth to him. This was not a barbaric

Isaurian (eye-SOAR-ee-un)

Muslim and Byzantine "Diplomacy"?

This excerpt from an Arabic chronicle reveals something of the attitudes of Muslims and Byzantines toward each other and of their frontier relations. Notice the mistakes and misunderstandings.

A woman [Irene] came to rule over the Romans because at that time she was the only one of their royal house who remained. She wrote to the Caliphs with respect and deference and showered them with gifts. When her son [Constantine VI] grew up and came to the throne in her place, he brought trouble and disorder and provoked [Harun] al-Rashid. The empress, who knew al-Rashid and feared his power, was afraid lest the kingdom of the Romans pass away and their country be ruined. She therefore overcame her son by cunning and put out his eyes so that the kingdom was taken from him and returned to her. But the people disapproved of this and hated her for it. Therefore Nicephorus [emperor, 802–811] rose against her. . . . He wrote to al-Rashid, "From Nicephorus, the king of the Romans, to al-Rashid,

the king of the Arabs" as follows: "That woman put you in the place of kings and put herself in the place of a commoner. I put you in a different place and am preparing to invade your lands and attack your cities unless you repay me what that woman paid you. Farewell." Al-Rashid replied, "In the name of God, the Merciful, the Compassionate, from the servant of God, Harun, Commander of the faithful, to Nicephorus, dog of the Romans" as follows: "I have understood your letter, and I have your answer. You will see it with your eye, not hear it." Then he sent an army against the land of the Romans.

Source: Abu'l-Faraj al-Isfahani, *Al-Aghani,* in Bernard Lewis, ed., *Islam from the Prophet Muhammad to the Conquest of Constantinople,* vol. 1 (New York: Harper & Row, 1974), pp. 27–28.

---

act in the Byzantine way of thinking. By mutilating Constantine VI, she merely rendered him unfit to rule—Roman ideology held that only a physically perfect person could reign; the alternative would have been to murder him. In any case, Irene's credibility sank to nothing, and in 802 she was deposed by a wily old soldier, Nicephorus° (r. 802–811).

Whether in some ideal situation Nicephorus might have been successful is impossible to say. His problems came from two fearsome foes. In Anatolia he faced the redoubtable and aggressive Harun al-Rashid, and in the Balkans he contended with the clever Bulgarian Khan Krum° (r. ca. 803–814). Nicephorus got a break when Harun died in 809, but he fell in battle with Krum, who gruesomely made a drinking cup out of his skull. The Isaurian reputation for invincibility died on that battlefield. (See the box "Global Encounters: Muslim and Byzantine 'Diplomacy'?")

For two generations Byzantium suffered through short reigns, usurpations, political unrest, and military reverses. In 867 a rough soldier, Basil I (r. 867–886), seized the throne and, like Heraclius and Leo III before him, reversed the fortunes of the state. He established a new dynasty, the "Macedonian," and for the first time in years won important military victories. Faced as they were by worthy foes in both Anatolia and the Balkans, the Byzantines, the heirs of the Romans, might have vanished from history. But capable leaders emerged just often enough, especially in the eighth century, to preserve a state that, even in a vastly reduced shape, carried the Roman legacy into the future.

■ Internal Changes

Even as its territory was shrinking, Byzantium undertook military and administrative reforms, revised its laws, and refocused its culture, particularly its religious practices. In the early Middle Ages a distinctive "Byzantium" emerged in place of Rome.

Nicephorus (nye-SEFF-for-us)
Krum (KROOM)

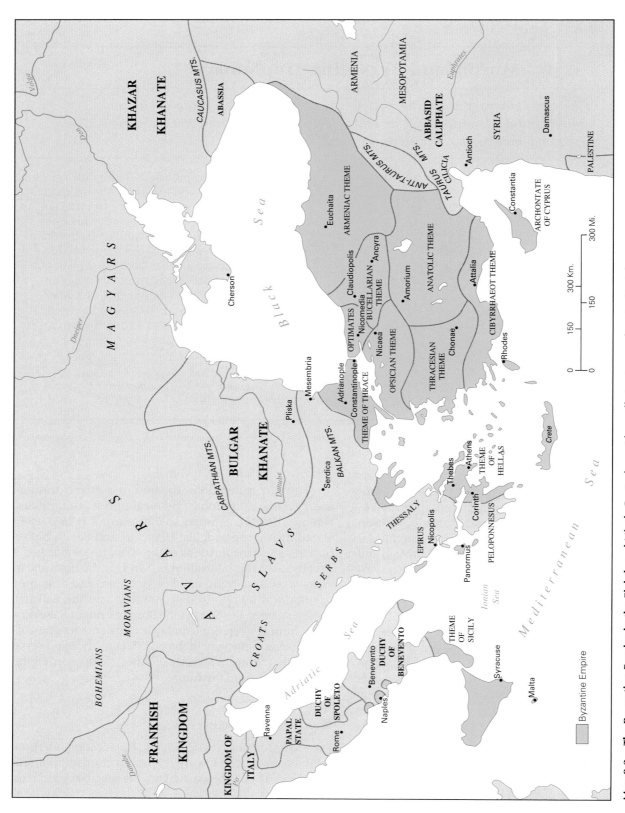

Map 8.2 The Byzantine Empire in the Eighth and Ninth Centuries After suffering tremendous territorial losses to the barbarians and Arabs, the Byzantine Empire transformed its military, institutional, and cultural structures to create a regime that lasted until it was conquered by Crusaders in 1204. This map shows the *themes,* Byzantium's major institutional innovation.

Leo and Constantine, the Isaurians, are reminiscent of Diocletian and Constantine, or of Justinian. They energetically brought to completion military reforms that had been pursued half-heartedly since the late sixth century. These reforms amounted to a major administrative change. For centuries, Rome had recruited, trained, and paid professional troops out of tax revenues; they even used tax revenues to settle barbarian soldiers in their midst. Leo and Constantine put the finishing touches on a new "theme" system.

Men from frontier regions were now recruited and settled on farms in military districts called *themes*. All themes, whether land-based army ones or sea-based naval ones, were under the command of a leader who was simultaneously the civil and military chief of his theme. The farmer-soldiers did not pay tax on their farms but discharged their obligation to the state by personal service. Some standing troops were retained, mainly around the capital, but henceforth the thematic armies (see Map 8.2) formed the backbone of the Roman system.

The new system was less of a drain on the state treasury than the old one. Lower tax revenues were needed and, correspondingly, fewer bureaucrats to collect the money. The empire was smaller than in the past and needed a different kind of army: smaller squadrons concentrated near the threatened frontier regions in Anatolia and the Balkans rather than large armies that were expensive to maintain and cumbersome to transport over long distances.

The Isaurians undertook other reforms too. Leo issued the *Ecloga*°, the first major revision and updating of Roman law since Justinian's. Issuing a law code was a matter of pride and a clear representation of power and authority. But the *Ecloga* was "a selection of laws," an abridgment whose purpose was to provide a simplified code adapted to the empire's new circumstances.

Leo and Constantine also instituted far-reaching reforms in imperial administration, which had changed little in centuries. Roman bureaucracy had consisted of a few large departments headed by officials with immense responsibilities and power. The revised Byzantine system was characterized by a profusion of departments under officers who had little real power or sway. The emperor neutralized the bureaucrats by drawing them from all social classes, paying them well, giving them pompous titles and lots of public recognition, all the while dividing their responsibilities, curbing their influence, and making them dependent on himself. The

Byzantine government was never a breeding ground for factional squabbles as in the caliphate.

Byzantine culture came to be increasingly defined by the church. The massive Arab conquests that stripped Byzantium of so much territory also removed the ancient patriarchates of Alexandria, Jerusalem, and Antioch from effective contact with Constantinople. Often in the past the empire had been disturbed by severe theological quarrels generated by the differing views held in the several patriarchates. These disputes had been disruptive, but they had also prompted a great deal of learned religious writing. Now, deprived of this stimulus, Byzantium turned inward.

Inside the smaller Byzantine Empire, monasticism gradually assumed a more prominent place in religious life. So many members of elite families sought to become monks that the Isaurians actually tried to limit entry into the religious life. Byzantine monks tended to be deeply learned, intensely critical of the patriarchs of Constantinople—whom they regarded as worldly and political—and opposed to imperial interference in the church. In Theodore of Studion (759–826) Byzantine monasticism found its greatest reformer and legislator since Basil, four centuries earlier.

In 726 Emperor Leo III embarked on a bold new religious policy: iconoclasm. For centuries a beautiful and inspiring religious art had been emerging that troubled the emperor. Leo, a man of simple but fervent piety, believed that the presence of religious images, called "icons," in churches and public places was offensive to God. Moreover, Leo was convinced that the military disasters suffered by the empire in recent years were attributable to divine displeasure at the violation of the Mosaic prohibition of "graven images." Accordingly, he and his son banned religious images. They and some of their more enthusiastic followers even destroyed a few of them. Hence they were called "iconoclasts," which means "image breakers." Iconoclasm was officially proclaimed by a church council in 754, repudiated by another council in 787, proclaimed again in 815, and then definitively rejected in 843.

Although it might seem like an odd and local dispute, iconoclasm had several important consequences in its own time and reveals important aspects of emerging Byzantium to the modern observer. Iconoclasm was categorically rejected as heretical by the popes. This difference drove a sharp wedge between Eastern and Western Catholics. The debates over iconoclasm finally sharpened Byzantine thinking on the role and function of art in religious life. To this day, the icon plays a more prominent role in religious devotion in the East than in the West.

Ecloga (ECK-low-guh)

Moreover, the battle over iconoclasm evoked some of the most sophisticated Greek religious writing since Late Antiquity. Writers such as John of Damascus (675–749) and Theodore of Studion wrote learned treatises in defense of religious art that drew on Greek patristic writing and on ancient Greek philosophy in ways that sharply differentiated Byzantine and Western religious thought.

Saint Peter   A rare pre-iconoclastic icon from Mt. Sinai: Peter is depicted as a late antique magistrate—wise and distinguished—not as a simple fisherman. The medallions depict Christ in the center, Mary on the right, and John the Evangelist on the left. In a late antique depiction of a consul, the images would have had the emperor in the center, the empress on the right, and the co-consul on the left. *(Alexandria-Michigan-Princeton Archeological Expedition to Mount Sinai/Roger Wood/Corbis)*

As the Byzantines turned more and more deeply into their own traditions, they exposed other differences between themselves and the West. Some of these were important such as the dispute over the so-called *filioque.* In the East, people taught and believed that the Holy Spirit proceeded "from the Father." In the West, people said that the Holy Spirit proceeded "from the Father *and from the Son*" (*filioque* in Latin). Greek monks shaved the front of their heads whereas Western monks shaved a circlet on the top. The Greek Church used leavened (with yeast) bread in worship whereas the Western church used unleavened bread. Taken together these differences amounted to a sharpening of the divide between Christian groups whom we may now label "Orthodox" and "Roman Catholic." Neither group wished to see a division in the Christian world, but physical separation and independent cultural evolution were producing two different traditions based, paradoxically, on a single late antique Christianity.

With its new geographic shape and its Orthodox faith, Byzantium was at once something old and something new. In official Byzantine ideology, the Roman Empire had always been one and inseparable. It is interesting to ask how familiar Augustus Caesar would have found the empire of Constantine V. With its indebtedness to classical and Christian traditions, there can be no question that Byzantium was a part of the West. But in its comparatively modest size, its constantly threatened frontiers, and its Orthodox traditions, Byzantium was going to have a somewhat different future than the portions of the West situated inside Rome's former western provinces. It is worth noting too that, as in the Muslim world, so also in Byzantium, the seventh and ninth centuries were acutely tumultuous whereas the eighth was marked by consolidation and achievement.

CATHOLIC KINGDOMS IN THE WEST

IN the Latin West, too, the seventh century was marked by challenges, the eighth century by innovation and accomplishment, and the ninth century by new threats and in some areas near collapse. The social and political heritages of both the Germanic and the Roman past interacted with Christianity and the church to produce the third early medieval civilization: Catholic Europe. Crucial to these developments were the evangelization of the countryside, the growth of an ecclesiastical hierarchy, the shift of papal interests away from the Mediterranean world toward western Europe, and the evolving relationship between royal governments and the Catholic Church.

■ The Struggles of Visigothic Spain

After their defeat at Clovis's hand in 507, the Visigoths were never able to re-establish dynastic continuity. As a result, Spain witnessed rebellions and usurpations more frequently than any other area in the West. In addition to internal struggles, Spain faced external threats from the Franks, the Ostrogoths in Italy, the Byzantines, and finally the Muslims.

The accomplishments of the Visigothic king Leovigild° (r. 568–586) seem remarkable given the state of Spain on his accession. He nearly unified the country, and he established a capital (Toledo) and a seat of government—which the Visigoths had been lacking since they lost Toulouse in 507. Leovigild was a good general and a charismatic leader who understood the value of enhancing the royal office. He wore royal vestments, sat on a throne, and issued coins with his own image and name. Leovigild's greatest problem was the Arianism of the Visigothic minority in the midst of the Catholic population. An Arian himself, he tried hard to convert Catholics to Arianism but failed. In 589, under King Reccared (r. 586–601), the Visigoths officially embraced Roman Catholicism.

The conversion of the Visigoths permitted close cooperation between the church and the monarchy and placed the resources of the church at the disposal of the king as he attempted to unite and govern the country. The career of Archbishop Isidore of Seville (560–636) is a prime indicator of those resources. He came from an old Hispano-Roman family, received a fine education, and wrote histories, biblical commentaries, and a learned encyclopedia. By the mid-seventh century, economic prosperity, a high degree of assimilation between Goths and Hispano-Romans, and a brilliant culture marked the high point of Visigothic Spain. The succession problem, however, was never overcome, and a stable central government was beyond reach.

In 711, Muslims from North Africa invaded Spain. Within five years Berbers (native North Africans and recent converts to Islam who were led by Arabs) completed the conquest of much of the Iberian Peninsula, except for the northwest. In 716 the caliph at Damascus introduced an emir who ruled from Cordoba. The emirate of Cordoba struggled to make good its authority over all of Spain but failed to do so. Christians in the rugged mountains of the northwest—the region called Asturias°—could not be dislodged, and the Muslims' part of Spain—known as al-Andalus°—was plagued by the same divisions as the Islamic East: Arab factions against other Arab factions, Arabs against non-Arab Muslims, and Muslims against non-Muslims. Secure in mountainous Asturias (see Map 8.3 on page 259), Christian kings built a capital at Oviedo and, in the ninth century, launched attacks against al-Andalus. For six hundred years this conflict between Christians and Muslims was the chief dynamic of Spanish history.

■ Italy and the Papal States

In 600 the Italian political scene was crowded. Several Germanic groups, several Byzantine outposts, and the popes were all contending for power. By the late eighth century, the Franks dominated northern Italy, the popes had created a state in the center, and the Byzantines clung to Naples and Sicily, much of which they lost to Muslims in the ninth century.

As we have seen, the Lombards conquered most of the Italian peninsula after the Gothic Wars. Neither numerous nor united, the Lombards were also Arians. Although the Lombard kings converted to Catholicism by 680, formed a strong government, and issued the most sophisticated Germanic law code, they always faced a dilemma. The kings had not systematically organized the conquest of Italy. From their capital at Pavia, they dominated the Po Valley, but other Lombards settled elsewhere and created independent duchies. Kings were weakened because they did not control the duchies and because between Lombardy and the duchies lay Rome and Ravenna, which were nominally Byzantine.

The strongest Lombard king of the eighth century, Aistulf° (r. 749–757), decided to risk the consequences of attacking Ravenna and Rome. He conquered the former but caused the pope to turn to Pippin III, the king of the Franks, for aid and protection. Pippin came to Italy, defeated Aistulf, and forced him to give to the pope all the lands he had taken from Rome and from Ravenna. A few years later Aistulf's successor reopened hostilities in central Italy. In 774 Charlemagne, Pippin's son and successor, defeated the Lombards, deposed their king, and took the Lombard crown for himself.

The Franks guaranteed to the popes undisputed possession of a substantial territory in central Italy. This first papal state was the culmination of three processes. First, as Roman imperial power declined in Late Antiquity, bishops often became the effective leaders of their towns. This position brought them power and prestige but also burdens. The popes found themselves responsible for

---

Leovigild (lee-OH-vuh-gild) **Asturias** (ahs-TOUR-ee-ahs)
al-Andalus (al-AHN-dah-loose)

Aistulf (ICE-tulf)

A Mother Hen and Seven Chicks   This delightfully frivolous object may have been a gift from Pope Gregory I to the Lombard queen Theudelinda. It helps us to appreciate the aesthetic tastes of the barbarians. *(Cathedral Treasure, Monza/Scala/Art Resource, NY)*

Rome's food and water supply, the upkeep of its public buildings, and local charitable services. To pay for these functions, the popes began to organize the efficient bureaucratic administration of the patrimonies, the lands of the Roman church.

Second, the popes took the lead in protecting many people in central Italy, whether they lived on the patrimonies or not: preserving their purses from Byzantine taxes and their souls from heresy. This effort, too, forged bonds between the popes and the Italians. Third, eighth-century Rome spawned a justification for papal temporal rule. According to the *Donation of Constantine,* a document written in Rome (probably in the 760s), when Constantine departed Rome for the East in the 320s, he allegedly gave to the pope the authority to rule Rome and the whole West. In reality, no pope ever made such grandiose claims, and no concrete claims were ever based on the *Donation.* But the existence of the document signals a crucial progression from protection to direct rule. From the beginning, however, the Papal States were vulnerable and required a protector.

■ The Fate of the British Isles

Britain was less thoroughly Romanized, more quickly abandoned by the Romans, and more deeply influenced by Germanic peoples than any other locality in the West. Around 600 the small Anglo-Saxon kingdoms created in the sixth century took the first steps toward converting to Christianity, transforming Britain into England, and joining England inseparably to the European world (see Map 8.3). And another history was unfolding in the

British Isles, that of the Celtic peoples in the north and west of Britain itself and in Ireland.

The Celts—Britain's inhabitants before the Romans invaded in the first century—were related to peoples who lived in a broad band from Anatolia to Ireland and Spain. The Anglo-Saxons confined the British Celts to the western regions of Cornwall and Wales and to the northern area of Scotland. Ireland, seemingly beyond reach, had almost no Roman or Anglo-Saxon imprint.

The period between 600 and 900 saw only the faint beginnings of consolidation in the Celtic realms where the development of the Catholic Church preceded large-scale political organization. Each Celtic region produced an elaborate mythology connected with heroic missionaries who supposedly brought the Christian faith in Late Antiquity. The best-known stories swirl around Ireland's Saint Patrick (390?–461?). The son of a Roman official in the north of Britain, Patrick was captured by pirates, enslaved in Ireland, freed, and eventually made a priest; he then returned to Ireland as a missionary. From his base at Armagh°, Ireland's first bishopric, Patrick and his successors spread Christianity, and a vigorous monasticism, throughout the island. Historical too is the Irish aristocrat Columba (521–597) who, after his family lost a great battle, migrated in 563 to the isle of Iona off the coast of Scotland. From his monastery on Iona, Columba and his successors began the evangelization of the native Picts in Scotland.

Among the most successful Anglo-Saxon kingdoms were Wessex, Northumbria, and Mercia. Each had a rea-

---

Armagh (ARR-mah)

The Prophet Ezra from the Codex Amiatinus
This huge manuscript (13.3 inches by 19.7 inches; 1,033 folios) was written at Wearmouth, England, and shows an adaptation of Mediterranean styles. In tradition Ezra was the prophet who helped the Jews recover their law and heritage after the exile. The seventh- or eighth-century manuscript, or codex, makes the point that biblical law had come to England. *(Scala/Art Resource, NY)*

sonably large population and territory and opportunities for expansion. Wessex, for example, spread south and west into Devon, Cornwall, and Wales; Northumbria, which stretched along the North Sea coast, spread west to the Irish Sea and north into lowland Scotland (see Map 8.3). These kingdoms had ambitious rulers whose wars provided booty, land, and glory for old followers and new recruits. English kings quickly adopted symbolic aspects of rule to legitimize their authority and enhance their prestige. Archaeologists have found fine scepters and coins bearing early kings' names. The kings of Northumbria presided in a magnificent wooden hall and their movements were preceded and announced by banners.

Relations with the church were important also. Two issues proved crucial: the conversion to Christianity and the development of an ecclesiastical hierarchy. In 597 Pope Gregory I sent a small band of missionaries under a Roman monk named Augustine (d. 604) to King Aethelbert of Kent, whose Christian wife, Bertha, had prepared the ground for the newcomers. From their base of operations at Canterbury in southeastern England, Augustine and his successors had limited success spreading Christianity, but a new field of influence was opened to them when Aethelbert's daughter married a king of Northumbria and took missionaries to her new home. Monks from Iona, as noted, were already introducing Christianity into central and lowland Scotland. When later Northumbrian kings turned to Iona for missionaries and bishops, Roman and Celtic Christianity came face to face in Northumbria.

Two English Holy Women: Hilda and Leoba

These passages reveal some of the opportunities available to high-born women who embraced the religious life. Hilda, abbess of Whitby, was of royal descent and involved herself in many of the great events of her day. Leoba, of noble birth, joined a significant monastery in Wessex but later, and quite unusually, migrated to the continent where she joined forces with the famous missionary Boniface.

[Hilda] led her life in two equal parts, the first thirty-three years devoted to secular occupations and the second even more nobly devoted to the Lord in monastic life. She was indeed nobly born, the daughter of Hereric, a nephew of King Edwin. . . . When, having abandoned her secular garb, she decided to serve God alone, she went away to the land of the East Angles, whose king was a relative, from where she aimed to travel to Gaul and live as an exile for the Lord's sake where her sister Hereswith, mother of king Aldwith of the East Angles, was already living. But Bishop Aidan called her home and gave her land for a monastery. . . . Later she undertook to found a monastery at Whitby . . . and there she taught righteousness, mercy, purity, and other virtues, but above all peace and charity. . . . So great was her discretion that not only common people but even kings and princes used to come and ask her advice. . . . Those who submitted to her leadership had to study the scriptures . . . and five men from this monastery became bishops.

[Leoba's] mother consecrated her and handed her to Mother Tetta (abbess of Wimbourne and sister of an English king) to be taught the sacred sciences. . . . The girl, therefore, grew up and was taught with such care by the abbess and all the nuns that she had no interests other than the monastery and the pursuit of sacred knowledge. She took no pleasure in aimless jests and wasted no time on girlish romances but, fired by the love of Christ, fixed her mind always on reading or hearing the Word of God. Whatever she heard or read she committed to memory, and put all that she learned into practice. . . . Boniface sent messengers to Tetta asking him to send Leoba . . . for Leoba's reputation for learning and holiness had spread far and wide and her praise was on everyone's lips. . . . When she came, the man of God [Boniface] received her with the deepest reverence, holding her in great affection, not so much because she was related to him on his mother's side as because he knew that by her holiness and wisdom she would confer many benefits by her word and example. . . . He gave her the monastery at a place called Bischofsheim, where there was a large community of nuns. These were trained according to her principles in the discipline of monastic life and made such progress in her teaching that many of them became superiors of others, so that there was hardly a convent of nuns in that part that did not have one of her disciples as abbess.

Sources: (Hilda): Venerabilis Baedae, *Historiam Ecclesiasticam Gentis Anglorum,* 4.21, ed. Charles Plummer (Oxford: Oxford University Press, 1896), pp. 252–254 (translated and adapted by T. Noble); (Leoba): Thomas F. X. Noble and Thomas Head, eds., *Soldiers of Christ: Saints and Saints' Lives from Late Antiquity and the Early Middle Ages* (University Park: Pennsylvania State University Press, 1995), pp. 264–266.

The Christianity brought from Ireland did not differ in fundamental ways from the Roman Christianity imported at Canterbury. Indeed, the Irish were Roman Catholics. But Ireland had been isolated from the centers of Christian life since Late Antiquity, and its church had developed a number of distinctive local customs. For example, the two traditions used different calendars and thus celebrated Easter—the commemoration of the resurrection of Jesus Christ and the central celebration of the Christian year—on different days. In 664 a Northumbrian king called a church council at the monastery of Whitby, whose abbess was the former royal princess Hilda (614–680), a champion of Celtic customs. (See the box "Reading Sources: Two English Holy Women: Hilda and Leoba.") At Whitby, Roman and Irish representatives debated their positions. The king, choosing the universal over the particular, decided for Rome.

In 668 the pope sent to England a new archbishop of Canterbury, Theodore (r. 668–690). He was a Syrian monk who had traveled widely in the East, lived for a time in Rome, gained great experience in church administration, and acquired a reputation for both learning and discretion. The church in England was in an administrative shambles. Working tirelessly, Theodore built up a typical Roman ecclesiastical structure, introduced authoritative Roman canon law for the church, and promoted Christian education. Theodore laid the foundations for a unified English church that contributed to the eventual political unification of England.

Ecclesiastical peace led to the flourishing of monastic life. Monasteries played two important roles in this period. First, they led the way in bringing Christianity to ordinary people. Despite early gains among kings and nobles, Christianity had barely begun to penetrate the countryside. Second, monks maintained international connections, ranging from Ireland to Rome, that attached England to the major intellectual currents of the day and enabled the English to make their own contributions.

After Theodore's school at Canterbury, the most important early center of learning was in Northumbria. There English, Irish, Frankish, and Roman currents flowed together in the monasteries of Lindisfarne, Wearmouth, and Jarrow, and in the cathedral school of York. British schools produced some of the most beautiful illuminated manuscripts—books whose texts are adorned with gorgeous paintings—of the early Middle Ages.

The greatest product of this intellectual tradition was Bede (673–735). When he was 7, his parents placed him in the monastery at Wearmouth. He soon transferred to neighboring Jarrow and spent the rest of his life there. Bede was a teacher of genius, an erudite scholar, and a superb Latin stylist. His *Ecclesiastical History of the English People,* the most important source for English history from the fifth century to the eighth, did much to identify the Anglo-Saxons as a single English people. His biblical commentaries remained influential all over Europe for centuries. His studies of temporal reckoning popularized the use of A.D. dating, which replaced a bewildering array of local systems.

The career of King Offa of Mercia° (r. 757–796) shows the trends in early Britain. His ancestors were pagans, but he was a patron of the church, convener of councils, and recipient of papal envoys. He dominated all of Britain and was the first to call himself "King of the English." He issued a law code, reformed Mercia's institutions, and signed England's first international trade agreement—with Charlemagne.

After Offa's death, Viking raiders (see page 265) destroyed whatever unity had been achieved. For two

Mercia (MUR-sha)

generations, local rulers struggled just to survive, and in 865 a Viking army launched a conquest of the whole country. In 871 Alfred the Great (r. 871–899) ascended the throne of Wessex, won a series of military victories, rallied the English, and began the slow reconquest of northern and eastern England from the Vikings. Alfred promoted intellectual recovery, church reform, and political stability. After a half-century of chaos, Alfred revived the centralizing and unifying work of his eighth-century predecessors and laid the foundations for the English state of the tenth and eleventh centuries.

Britain's integration into the wider world is revealed by a seventh-century ship burial unearthed near Sutton Hoo (in East Anglia) in 1939. The ship, either a grave for or a memorial to an unknown king, had been hauled up onto the land, filled with treasures, and buried. The array of goods found at Sutton Hoo is astonishing. The hull contained Byzantine silver, represented by spoons and a large dish; Frankish gold, in the form of dozens of coins, jewelry, and personal adornments from many places; and pots, beakers, and other domestic items of varied provenance. The artistic decorations on these items demonstrate influences ranging from the Mediterranean to the Rhineland, Scandinavia, and Ireland.

THE CAROLINGIAN EMPIRE

 LOVIS and the Franks created the most effective of the early Germanic kingdoms. During the seventh century that kingdom, too, experienced difficulties but did not disappear. Just as Roman aristocrats had borne the ancient heritage into the Middle Ages, so now a Frankish family, called "Carolingian" from the name of its greatest member, Charlemagne, assembled the talent and resources of the Frankish realm in a new way. Charlemagne reformed his government and church, patronized learning, and resurrected the western empire. Early medieval civilization reached its culmination in the work of Charlemagne and his dynasty.

■ The Rise of the Carolingian Family, 600–768

When Clovis died in 511, he divided his realm among his sons, and thereafter several kingdoms coexisted. The Merovingian royal families feuded constantly, sought to expand at one another's expense, and drew local aristocracies into their battles. Trade and intellectual life declined, and some regions that had been conquered in the sixth century slipped away.

Nevertheless, the *idea* of a single kingdom of the Franks persisted. Kings and aristocrats in the small kingdoms competed for leadership of the realm as a whole. The flourishing culture of late antique Gaul was largely gone, but a creative Christian monastic culture was growing up in all parts of the Frankish kingdom. Monks began accomplishing the difficult task of converting the countryside to Christianity. The seventh century, in other words, was a time when the late antique regime was slowly changing into the medieval regime.

Central to this development was the rise to prominence of the Carolingians. The family appeared in history just after 600 and thereafter monopolized the office of mayor of the palace (sort of a prime minister) to the king in Austrasia° (the easternmost kingdom; see Map 8.3). The Carolingians were the boldest and wealthiest family in Austrasia, perhaps in the Frankish world. Within two generations they unified the Frankish realm and increased their own power.

The Carolingians used several methods to accomplish their ends. They formed alliances with powerful noble families in many regions. They waged war against the enemies of the Franks to restore the territorial integrity of the kingdom. Charles Martel (d. 741), Charlemagne's grandfather, led the Frankish forces that put an end to Arab raiding in Gaul, defeating a large force near Poitiers in 733. With booty from their wars, tribute from conquered peoples, spoils taken from recalcitrant opponents, and even lands seized from the church, the Carolingians attracted and rewarded more and more followers until no one was a match for them. The Carolingians also allied themselves very early with leading churchmen, both episcopal and monastic. They aided missionaries in the work of converting central Germany, thereby expanding Frankish influence in that area.

For years the Carolingians were content with the office of mayor of the palace. Then in 749, Pippin III (son of Charles Martel) decided to send envoys to the pope to ask whether it was right that the person who had all the power in the land of the Franks was not the king. The pope responded that this situation ran counter to the divine plan. Accordingly, in 751, the last Merovingian king was deposed, and Pippin was elected in his place (r. 751–768). Pippin had prepared his usurpation very carefully with his Frankish supporters, but he appealed to the pope to make it appear that he had become king with divine approval and not by crude seizure. Hard-pressed by the Lombards in Italy, the pope probably gave Pippin the answer he wanted primarily to enlist him as an ally.

Map 8.3   The Carolingian World   The territory over which Charlemagne exerted direct or indirect control was vast. The areas beyond the Rhine and Danube, never part of the Roman Empire, became under the Carolingians a permanent part of Western civilization. The Treaty of Verdun (see inset), signed by Charlemagne's grandsons in 843, was the first and most important of many divisions of the Carolingian Empire that eventually led to the emergence of France and Germany.

Three years later the pope visited the Frankish kingdom, where he crowned and anointed Pippin and his sons, including Charlemagne. (The practice of anointing the head of a ruler with holy oil, which renders the recipient sacred, dates back to the kings of Israel. The head and hands of Catholic bishops were also anointed. The anointing of rulers and churchmen persisted throughout the Middle Ages and into the modern world.) The pope also forbade the Franks ever to choose a king from a family other than the Carolingians and received from their new favorites a promise of aid in Italy.

■ The Empire of Charlemagne, 768–814

Charlemagne (Carolus Magnus, "Charles the Great" in Latin) was a huge man, and his stature has grown in European history and legend. (See the box "Reading Sources: A Contemporary Portrait of Charlemagne.") Like all great leaders, Charlemagne (r. 768–814) was complex. He spoke and read Frankish, Latin, and some Greek but never learned to write. He promoted Christian morality but perpetrated unspeakable brutalities on his enemies and enjoyed several concubines. Many battles were fought in his name, but he rarely accompanied his armies and fought no campaigns that are remembered for strategic brilliance. Determination and organization were the hallmarks of his forty-six-year reign.

It took until the mid-780s for Charlemagne to assess and understand his world (see Map 8.3). His first major achievement was the articulation of a new ruling ideology in the Latin West. In capitularies°—royal executive orders—of 789, Charlemagne required all males to swear an oath of allegiance to him, and he compared himself to a biblical king in his responsibility to admonish, to teach, and to set an example for his people. He referred to the people of his realm as a "New Israel," a new chosen people. Interestingly, this chosen people was not exclusively Frankish. No distinctions were to be made among Franks or Bavarians or Saxons. Everyone was to be equal

---

Austrasia (aw-STRAY-zhuh)

capitularies (kuh-PITCH-u-lar-eez)

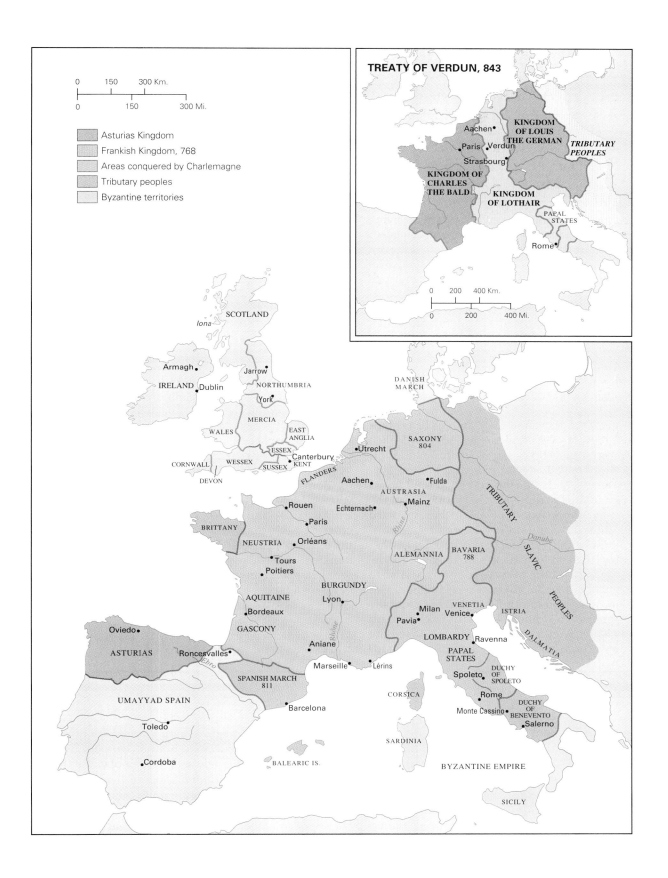

TREATY OF VERDUN, 843

KINGDOM OF LOUIS THE GERMAN

TRIBUTARY PEOPLES

Aachen • • Verdun
Paris •
Strasbourg

KINGDOM OF CHARLES THE BALD

KINGDOM OF LOTHAIR

PAPAL STATES

Rome •

0 200 400 Km.
0 200 400 Mi.

Asturias Kingdom
Frankish Kingdom, 768
Areas conquered by Charlemagne
Tributary peoples
Byzantine territories

0 150 300 Km.
0 150 300 Mi.

SCOTLAND
Iona
Armagh •
IRELAND Dublin •
Jarrow •
NORTHUMBRIA
York •
MERCIA
WALES
EAST ANGLIA
ESSEX
CORNWALL WESSEX Canterbury
SUSSEX KENT
DEVON

DANISH MARCH

SAXONY 804

FLANDERS
Utrecht •
Aachen • • Fulda
AUSTRASIA
Rouen • Echternach • Mainz •
BRITTANY
Paris •
NEUSTRIA Orléans •
ALEMANNIA
Tours •
Poitiers •
BURGUNDY
AQUITAINE Lyon •
Bordeaux •
GASCONY
Oviedo •
ASTURIAS Roncesvalles •
Ebro
Aniane •
SPANISH MARCH 811
UMAYYAD SPAIN
Marseille • Lérins •
Barcelona •
Toledo •
Cordoba •
BALEARIC IS.
CORSICA
SARDINIA

Rhine
Rhine
Danube
TRIBUTARY
SLAVIC
PEOPLES
ISTRIA
DALMATIA
BAVARIA 788
VENETIA
Milan • Venice •
Pavia •
LOMBARDY Ravenna •
PAPAL STATES
Spoleto • DUCHY OF SPOLETO
Rome •
Monte Cassino • DUCHY OF BENEVENTO
Salerno •
BYZANTINE EMPIRE
SICILY

❧ READING SOURCES

A Contemporary Portrait of Charlemagne

Here is Einhard's description of Charlemagne. Einhard selected suitable passages from Lives of the Caesars, *by the first-century Roman historian Suetonius, to build up a picture of Charlemagne that accords well with what is otherwise known about him.*

He loved foreigners and took great pains in receiving them, so much so that their vast numbers seemed an unwelcome burden not only for his palace but even for his kingdom. On account of his magnanimity he was scarcely troubled by this burden for the praise of his liberality and of his good name more than compensated for this considerable inconvenience. His body was full and strong, very tall but not more than was fitting, for his height was seven times the length of his feet. His head was round and his eyes, large and piercing. His nose was longer than normal, his white hair was beautiful, and his expression was happy, even joyful. The power and dignity of his form were very great when he was sitting or standing. His neck was short and thick and his belly stuck out a bit, but the overall fineness of his form veiled these features, indeed his step was firm and all his bearing was manly. His voice was clear but too high for so great a body. His health was good until fevers struck him in the last four years of his life, and at the end he was lame in one foot. Even then he acted more on his own than on the advice of his doctors, whom he practically considered to be enemies because they tried to convince him to give up the roasted foods to which he was accustomed and to live on boiled dishes. He always exerted himself vigorously in riding and hunting which came naturally to him—indeed you cannot find any race on earth that equals the Franks in this activity. He loved the hot-steam baths at Aachen (they were his reason for

his constructing his palace there) and he exercised in the water when he could. No one could beat him in swimming. . . . Sometimes he invited his sons, nobles, and as many as a hundred men into the baths with him. . . . He dressed in the Frankish style. Next to his body he put on a linen shirt and drawers, then hose and a tunic with a silk border. He wore shoes and strips of cloth wound around his legs. In winter he protected his chest and shoulders with a jacket of otter or ermine. He wrapped himself in a blue cloak and wore a sword with hilt and belt of gold and silver. On festive days or to receive ambassadors, he wore a jeweled sword. The clothes of other peoples, however beautiful, he hated and would never endure to put them on except at Rome, once when Pope Hadrian asked him to and again when his successor Leo requested it at Rome. Then he dressed in a long tunic and a heavy cloak and wore shoes made in the Roman style. On feast days he wore clothing woven with gold, jeweled shoes, a golden brooch to fasten his cloak, and crown with gold and gems. On other days his clothing hardly differed from that of the ordinary people. He was temperate in eating and drinking, particularly in drinking, for he hated drunkenness in anyone and especially in himself or in his own men.

Source: Eginhard [Einhard], *Vie de Charlemagne,* 4th ed., ed. Louis Halphen (Paris: Société d'Edition [Les Belles Lettres], 1967), cc. 21–23, pp. 64–70 (translated and adapted by T. Noble).

---

in allegiance to the king and in membership in a sort of Augustinian City of God.

Einhard (ca. 770–840), Charlemagne's friend and biographer, reports that Augustine's *City of God* (see page 233) was the king's favorite book. The king understood it to mean that two opposing domains contended for power on earth: a City of God consisting of all right-thinking Christians—the "New Israel"—and a City of

Man consisting of pagans, heretics, and infidels. This idea is similar to the Islamic umma (see page 242). To Charlemagne and his advisers, it was obvious that as God was the sole legitimate ruler in heaven, Charlemagne was the sole legitimate and divinely appointed ruler on earth.

Modern readers may think that Charlemagne had crossed a boundary between church and state. It is crucial to understand that to Charlemagne, as to his Muslim and Byzantine contemporaries, no such boundary existed. Church (or religion) and state were complementary attributes of a polity whose end was personal salvation, not military security or personal fulfillment. Charlemagne's ideological legacy was twofold. On the one hand, it created possibilities for bitter struggles later in the Middle Ages between secular rulers and ecclesiastical powers about the leadership of Christian society. On the other hand, it made it hard to define the state and its essential purposes in other than religious terms.

The most disputed event in the reign of Charlemagne was his imperial coronation in Rome on Christmas in 800. It is important to separate how this event happened from what it meant to the participants. In April 799, some disgruntled papal bureaucrats and their supporters attacked Pope Leo III (r. 795–816) in an attempt to depose him. Leo was saved by an ally of Charlemagne and then traveled all the way to Saxony, where the king was camped with his army. Charlemagne agreed to restore the pope to Rome and, as his ally and protector, to investigate those who had attacked him. No real offenses could be proved against the pope, who appeared publicly in Rome to swear that he had done nothing wrong. Everything was handled to avoid any hint that the pope had been put on trial. When Charlemagne went to Saint Peter's Basilica on Christmas Day, he prayed before the main altar. As he rose from prayer, Pope Leo placed a crown on his head, and the assembled Romans acclaimed him as emperor.

Debate over this coronation arises from a remark of Einhard, who said that if Charlemagne had known what was going to happen, he would not have gone to church that day, even though it was Christmas. Einhard's point was not that Charlemagne did not wish to be emperor. For at least fifteen years, prominent people at the Carolingian court had been addressing Charlemagne in imperial terms in letters, treatises, and poems. Moreover, some were saying that because of Irene's usurpation, the imperial throne was vacant—implying that a woman could not truly rule. What Einhard did mean was that Charlemagne saw himself as a Frankish and Christian emperor, not as a *Roman* emperor. The imperial office dignified his position as leader of the Frankish "Israel." Charlemagne did not wish to be beholden to the pope or to the Romans.

Charlemagne's policies did not change after his coronation. He continued his program of legal and ecclesiastical reform and put the finishing touches on some military and diplomatic campaigns. In 806 he divided his empire among his three legitimate sons; but then two of them died, so in 813 he made Louis his sole heir and successor. Charlemagne outlived most of the friends and companions of his youth and middle age. He outlived four wives and many of his children. Old and alone, ill and lame, he died in early 814.

Charlemagne's legacy was great. He brought together the lands that would become France, Germany, the Low Countries, and northern Italy and endowed them with a common ideology, government, and culture. He provided a model that Europeans would look back to for centuries as a kind of golden age. His vast supra-regional and supra-ethnic entity, gradually called "Christendom," drew deeply on the universalizing ideals of its Roman, Christian, and Jewish antecedents but was, nevertheless, original. With its Roman, Germanic, and Christian foundations, the Carolingian Empire represented the final stage in the evolution of the Roman Empire in the West.

■ Carolingian Government

Charlemagne accomplished much through the sheer force of his personality and his boundless energy. But he also reformed and created institutional structures. These helped him to carry out his tasks, guaranteed a measure of permanence to his reforms, and created government patterns that lasted in many parts of Europe until the twelfth century.

The king (or emperor—the offices differed little in practical importance) was the heart of the system. In theory, the king ruled by God's grace and did not have to answer for his conduct to any person. In reality, the king necessarily sought consensus through a variety of means. The king controlled vast lands, which gave him great wealth of his own and also the means to reward loyal followers. By controlling appointments to key positions, the king required men to come to him for power, wealth, and prestige.

The Eastern contemporaries of the Carolingians relied on large numbers of carefully trained, paid civil servants. In contrast, the Carolingians employed a limited number of men who were tied to them by bonds of familial and personal allegiance. The Carolingian court included several ceremonial officers and a domestic staff, all desirable positions. For example, the constable, an officer in charge of transporting the royal entourage, was usually a great aristocrat; the real work of the office was carried out by underlings. The treasurer was the keeper of the king's bedchamber, where the royal treasure chest was kept. Several chaplains, whose primary duty was to see to the spiritual needs of the court, kept official records. The queen controlled the domestic staff and the stewards who managed the royal estates.

Local government was mainly entrusted to counts. About six hundred counts, and several times that number of minor officials, managed the empire. As in Merovingian times, the counts were administrative, judicial, and military officials. Most came from prominent families, and the office increased the wealth and importance of its holders. Counts had to promulgate and enforce royal orders and preside in regular sessions of local courts. They got one-third of the fines, so the zealous pursuit of justice was in their interest.

The royal court and the localities were linked in several ways. Under Charlemagne and his successors it became usual for all major officers, whether secular (counts and their subordinates) or ecclesiastical (bishops, abbots), to be *vassals* of the king. Vassals solemnly pledged loyalty and service to the king. Vassalage drew on both Roman and Germanic customs. Patron-client ties had always been socially and politically important among the Romans, and the allegiance of warriors to a chief was a key Germanic bond. But by connecting personal loyalty with public office, Charlemagne created something essentially new. Only a few thousand men, a tiny fraction of the total population, were vassals at any time. They constituted the political and social elite.

Another connection between the king and his local agents was the assembly that met in various places once or twice a year. In theory, all free men could attend these gatherings, which sometimes had separate secular and ecclesiastical sessions, to advise the king on matters of great importance, such as war and peace or legal reforms. In practice only the vassals had the means or the interest to ensure their presence. Most of the great Carolingian reforms were formulated in these assemblies by cooperation between the king and his most important subjects. The assemblies served to defuse dissension, but the king also brought his power to bear locally by traveling widely. The monarchy possessed estates all over the heartlands of the kingdom, and the royal entourage often moved from one place to another. Monasteries and cathedrals provided hospitality to the king. As the royal party traveled about the realm, they were able to check on local conditions and to compel local officials to comply with royal wishes.

In 788 Charlemagne began to build a palace at Aachen, and in the last twenty years of his life he usually resided there (see Map 8.3). The later Carolingian rulers all tended to have fixed residences, as did the Byzantines and the Abbasids. In adopting fixed residences and elaborate court rituals, the Carolingians may have been returning to Roman precedents or copying their contemporaries to appear as sophisticated as they. Elegant courts and intricate rituals project an aura of grandeur that enhances people's respect for their rulers. It is no accident that a key innovation of Charlemagne's reign coincided with his permanent residence in Aachen. In the late 780s he began to send out pairs of roving inspectors, *missi dominici°*, envoys of the lord king. Their function was to see that royal orders were being observed, that counts were dispensing justice honestly, and that persons of power were not oppressing the powerless.

■ The Carolingian Renaissance

Charlemagne's reforms culminated in a revival of learning that scholars have named the "Carolingian Renaissance" (from *renaissance*, French for "rebirth"). Charlemagne's fundamental ideas are revealed by the constant use in contemporary sources of words such as *rebirth, renewal, reform,* and *restoration*. Charlemagne, his advisers, and his successors looked back for inspiration to Christian and papal Rome, to Saint Peter and Constantine, and to the Church Fathers. To them, the rebirth of Western society as a "New Israel" was equivalent to the theological rebirth of an individual in baptism. The Carolingians were the driving force behind intellectual growth in their era, and in all areas they subordinated learning to their ideological program.

To accomplish his objectives, Charlemagne required every cathedral and monastery to establish a school. To set up and run those schools, he summoned to his court many of the most able and influential intellectual figures of the day, among them Franks, such as his biographer Einhard, grammar teachers from Italy, and Visigothic theologians from the Spanish border. His most famous recruit was the Anglo-Saxon Alcuin° (735–804), the most learned man of his day and the heir of Bede and of the brilliant culture of Northumbria.

Much of the work of Alcuin and his associates was devoted to producing textbooks and to teaching elementary knowledge. Charlemagne was convinced that people needed to be taught the basic truths of Christianity if he were to accomplish his task of leading them to salvation. A massive effort was thus undertaken to copy manuscripts of the Bible and the writings of the Latin Church Fathers. These books, the essential resources for the whole program, needed to be disseminated as widely as possible. The process of copying was facilitated by a new script, Caroline minuscule. (See the feature "Weighing the Evidence: The Manuscript Book" on pages 272–273.)

---

missi dominici (MISS-ee doe-MEE-nee-kee)
Alcuin (AL-kwin)

Model of Charlemagne's Palace at Aachen   In the foreground is the octagonal chapel and throne room of Charlemagne's palace at Aachen. It is joined by galleries to the residential quarters in the background. Construction was begun in 788. The models for these buildings were found in Rome and Ravenna.   *(Römische-Germanisches Zentralmuseum)*

It is significant that Charlemagne could attract Alcuin from York, the most renowned school in the West, to head his palace school, just then forming. Alcuin recognized that Charlemagne could place more resources at his disposal than anyone else, and had the will to do so. Alcuin also saw the long-term benefits that would come from his work. Alcuin's pupils spread out in the next generation to create a network of schools that went right on multiplying across the ninth century. That is a powerful legacy. And Alcuin did more than just teach. He wrote learned works and poetry and was for twenty years Charlemagne's most trusted adviser.

With his plan, personnel, and schools in place, Charlemagne took many concrete steps. He secured from Rome a copy of the then-authoritative canon law of the church. In 789, after some years of study by his court scholars, this law was issued for his whole kingdom. In about 786, Charlemagne got from the pope a sacramentary, a service book for worship in cathedral churches, and, again after a period of examination, this was imposed throughout the kingdom. Charlemagne sought an authoritative copy of the *Rule of St. Benedict,* and after study and commentary, this Rule was imposed on all monasteries in the kingdom.

Secular reforms mirrored religious ones. Orders regularized the management of all royal estates. Charlemagne attempted to update local law codes and to make them as uniform as possible. Not since Rome had governments possessed either the interest in or the means to promote such centralization. It is striking that in the eighth century the caliphate, the Byzantine Empire, and the Carolingian Empire were engaged in similar centralizing activities.

Maiestas Domini (The Lord in Majesty) An ivory book cover from Charlemagne's court or a closely associated workshop, this image shows the enthroned Christ trampling beasts and encircled by scenes from his life. The image is an excellent Carolingian adaption of late antique themes and styles. *(Stiftsbibliothek, St. Gallen)*

the only one who knew Hebrew. He wrote the official Frankish response to Byzantine iconoclasm. He also composed theological treatises, many letters, and dozens of poems. At Germigny° he designed a church that is a masterpiece of early Carolingian architecture.

Carolingian art is a crowning glory of the age. The manuscripts decorated under Charlemagne's patronage and then, for three generations, under the patronage of his descendants and of prominent churchmen show versatility, respect but not awe for the past, and innovation. Several distinct currents inspired and informed Carolingian art. Most prominent were the animal and geometric decorative motifs of Irish and Anglo-Saxon art; the elegance, formality, and sense of composition of classical art; basic elements of style from Byzantine painting; actual scenes from papal Rome; and the mysteries of Christian theology. Every element was borrowed, but the finished product was new.

Architecture shows the same trends. Charlemagne's palace complex at Aachen has parallels in imperial Constantinople, papal Rome, and Ostrogothic Ravenna. Workers and building materials were fetched from all over the empire. From 768 to 855, 27 cathedrals were built along with 417 monasteries and 100 royal residences. For basic buildings the Carolingians adapted the basilica. The classical basilica was a horizontal building, but the Carolingians, by altering the western end and façade, added the dimension of verticality. In Romanesque and Gothic architecture this innovation would have a long career (see pages 346–349).

■ The Fragmentation of Charlemagne's Empire, 814–887

The Carolingian Empire itself did not outlive the ninth century. Rome's empire lasted much longer, as did Byzantium's and Islam's. All of these realms were fatally weakened by similar problems, but those problems arose more quickly and acutely in the Carolingian world than elsewhere. By the end of the ninth century small political entities had replaced the unified Carolingian Empire.

Size and ethnic complexity contributed to the disintegration of the Carolingian Empire. The empire included many small regions—Saxony, Bavaria, Brittany, and Lombardy, for example—that had their own resident elites, linguistic traditions, and distinctive cultures, which had existed before the Carolingians came on the scene and persist to this day. The Merovingian and Carolingian periods were basically a unifying intrusion into a history characterized by regional diversity. The Carolingians

Versatility was a hallmark of Carolingian learning. Various scholars excelled at poetry, history, and biography. Biblical studies and theology attracted a lot of attention. One figure who personifies the Carolingian Renaissance is the Visigoth Theodulf°. He came to court in about 790 and served thereafter as a missus, royal adviser, abbot of several monasteries, and bishop of Orléans. He issued important legislation for his diocese. He was the foremost Old Testament expert of his day and

Theodulf (THEE-oh-dulf)

Germigny (JHER-mee-nee)

made heroic efforts to build a common culture and to forge bonds of unity, but the obstacles were insuperable.

Another key issue in the breakup of the Carolingian Empire was political and dynastic. The Carolingians regularly tried to create subkingdoms for all their legitimate sons while preserving the imperial title for one of them. This was a creative attempt to concede limited autonomy to particular regions by means of local kingships—for instance in Bavaria, Italy, and Aquitaine—while preserving the "Augustinian" unity of the empire as a whole. Unfortunately, younger sons rarely yielded to their older brothers, and the bonds of loyalty among cousins, nephews, and grandchildren grew slender. Frequent divisions of the empire, or of segments of it, placed local nobilities in the difficult position of changing their allegiance frequently and of jeopardizing their offices and landholdings.

In the Treaty of Verdun in 843 (see the Map 8.3 inset) the three grandsons of Charlemagne—Charles the Bald, Louis the German, and Lothair—divided the empire into three realms: the West Frankish, the East Frankish, and the Middle Kingdoms. After fierce battles among the brothers, each appointed forty members to a study commission that traversed the whole empire to identify royal properties, fortifications, monasteries, and cathedrals so that an equitable division could be made of these valuable resources. Each brother needed adequate resources to solidify his rule and to attract or hold followers. The lines drawn on the map at Verdun did not last even for a generation.

Slowly large West Frankish and East Frankish Kingdoms emerged, swallowing the Middle Kingdom, and created a framework for the future France and Germany. But they had to compete with many smaller entities. Some of these, in Italy, in the Rhineland, and in southern France, were old and distinctive regions that recaptured their former independence. Other areas were essentially new creations, born in the absence of firm Carolingian control. Newcomers also appeared on the scene, most prominently Scandinavian and Slavic principalities.

Before the ninth century, Scandinavia had known only small-scale political units under local chieftains and their trusted followers. Economic and political pressure from the Carolingians gradually began to push both Denmark and Norway in the direction of greater political consolidation. A single Danish monarchy has a continuous history from the late ninth century, and Norway's monarchy dates from the early tenth.

To the east of the Carolingian Empire lay a vast swath of Slavic lands. The Carolingians fought, allied, and traded with these peoples for decades. Charlemagne destroyed the Avar khanate in the Danube basin in campaigns between 788 and 804. By the middle of the ninth century, the princes of Great Moravia dominated the region and played a complicated diplomatic game between the East Frankish rulers and the Byzantine emperors. To the east of the Moravians, the Bulgarians profited from the Avar and then the Carolingian collapse to expand their kingdom. For two centuries the Bulgarians dominated eastern Europe and threatened Byzantium.

The most durable consequence of this political restructuring along the eastern frontier of the Frankish world was religious. In 863, on an invitation from Moravia and in hopes of countering the Franks, the Byzantine emperor sent the missionaries Cyril° (826–869) and Methodius° (805–884) into eastern Europe. The emperor hoped to erect an Orthodox union of his own realm, the southern Slavs, and the newly converted Bulgarians. Likewise he was seeking a diplomatic bulwark between the Bulgarians in the east and the Franks in the west. Unfortunately for Byzantium, Cyril and Methodius agreed with the pope to introduce Roman Catholic Christianity in return for the pope's permission to use the Slavonic language in worship. Cyril and Methodius were formidable linguists who created a religious literature in "Church Slavonic" that went far toward creating a new cultural realm in central Europe.

Finally, a new wave of attacks and invasions contributed decisively to the fragmentation of the Carolingian Empire. In the middle decades of the ninth century, Muslims, Vikings, and Magyars wreaked havoc on the Franks.

Based in North Africa and the islands of the western Mediterranean, Muslims attacked Italy and southern France. The Byzantines lost Sicily to raiders from North Africa in 827 and found themselves seriously challenged in southern Italy. In the 840s, Muslims raided the city of Rome. These same brigands preyed on trade in the western Mediterranean and even set up camps in the Alps to rob traders passing back and forth over the mountains.

"From the fury of the Northmen, O Lord, deliver us," was a plaintive cry heard often in ninth-century Europe. Those Northmen were Vikings, mainly Danes and Norwegians, seeking booty, glory, and political opportunity. Most Viking bands were formed by leaders who had lost out in the dawning institutional consolidation of the northern world. Some were opportunists who sought to profit from the weakness of Carolingian, Anglo-Saxon, and Irish rule. In the mid-ninth century, Vikings began settling and initiated their own state-building activities in Ireland, England, northwestern France ("Normandy"— the region of the Northmen), and Rus (early "Russia").

Cyril (SEER-ul)   **Methodius** (meth-oh-DEE-us)

Oseberg Ship Discovered in 1880, the Oseberg ship was buried in Norway in (probably) the tenth century. The ship may have belonged to a king, and contained the remains of Queen Asa. It is 21.6 meters long and 5 meters wide. Its crew would have been thirty to forty men. *(University Museum of National Antiquities, Oslo)*

Magyars, relatives of the Huns and Avars who had preceded them into eastern Europe, were accomplished horsemen whose lightning raids, beginning in 889, hit Italy, Germany, and even France. East Frankish Carolingians tried to use the Magyars as mercenaries against the troublesome Moravians. In the end, the Magyars destroyed the incipient Moravian state and raided with impunity.

All of these attacks were unpredictable and caused local regions to fall back on their own resources rather than look to the central government. Commerce was disrupted everywhere. Schools, based in ecclesiastical institutions, suffered severe decline. The raids represented a thousand pinpricks, not a single, deadly sword stroke. Yet their collective effect amounted to despair and disruption on a massive scale.

Even though the Carolingian Empire itself disintegrated, the idea of Europe as "Christendom," as a single political-cultural entity, persisted. The Latin Christian culture promoted by Carolingian schools and rulers set the tone for intellectual life until the twelfth century. Likewise, Carolingian governing structures were inherited and adapted by all of the successor states that emerged in the ninth and tenth centuries. In these respects the Carolingian experience paralleled the Roman, and the Islamic and Byzantine, too: A potent, centralizing regime disappeared but left a profound imprint on its heirs. For hundreds of years, Western civilization would be played out inside the lands that had been Charlemagne's empire and between those lands and their Byzantine and Muslim neighbors.

EARLY MEDIEVAL ECONOMIES AND SOCIETIES

HE economic and social history of the early Middle Ages provides additional evidence of the similarities among the three early medieval civilizations, while also revealing differences. Overall, the world remained rural, society was hierarchical, and women were excluded from public power. Although broad political frameworks changed, the lives of most people changed rather little.

Trade and Commerce

In the simplest terms, trade is a mechanism for exchanging goods from one person or group to another. There are many such exchange mechanisms. The Roman government, for example, moved large amounts of goods from the center of the empire to the frontiers to supply its armies. Roman, Byzantine, and Islamic governments raised taxes in one place, bought goods in another, and then consumed their purchases someplace else. Tribute and plunder were also effective exchange mechanisms, as were diplomatic gifts: a caliph, for example, sent Charlemagne an elephant.

The commonest exchanges were intensely local, but several major trading networks operated during the early Middle Ages. In the East, Mesopotamia was linked by rivers to the Persian Gulf, East Africa, and southern Asia, by land and sea to Byzantium, and by land and rivers to the Black Sea region, Slavic Europe, and the Baltic. Byzantines traded mainly by sea. The whole Mediterranean was open to them, and from the Black Sea they received the products of the Danube basin. The Muslim world was fundamentally a land empire that had relatively poor roads and primitive wheeled vehicles, so transport considerations were crucial: a caravan of some five hundred camels could move only one-fourth to one-half the cargo of a normal Byzantine ship.

The West had many trade routes. The Rhône-Saône river system carried goods, as did the land routes through the Alpine passes. The North and Baltic Seas were the hubs of a network that linked the British Isles, the whole of the Frankish north—by means of its rivers—the Rhineland, Slavic Europe, Byzantium, and the Muslim world. The Danube was also a major highway. The major trade networks intersected at many points. Despite religious and ideological differences, Rome's three heirs regularly traded with one another.

Food and other bulk goods never traveled very far because the cost was prohibitive. Most towns were supplied with foodstuffs by their immediate hinterlands, so the goods that traveled long distances were portable and valuable. Cotton and raw silk were transported to the Mediterranean, where they were made into cloth in, respectively, Egypt and Byzantium. Paper and pottery were transported around the caliphate. Asian spices and perfumes were avidly sought everywhere. The Byzantines traded in silk cloth, fine ivories, delicate products of the gold- and silversmiths' art, slaves, and naval stores. Byzantium, with its large fleet, usually controlled the Black and Mediterranean Seas. Reduced in prosperity, the empire could no longer dictate trade terms to subject peoples and competed badly with the Muslims. Trade in the west was partly in high-value luxury goods but mainly in ordinary items such as plain pottery, raw wool, wool cloth, millstones, weapons, and slaves.

Town and Countryside

To think of the ancient world is to think of cities. But to think of the medieval world is to envision forests and fields. Actually, from 80 to 90 percent of people in antiquity lived in rural settings, and in the early Middle Ages the percentage was not much higher. What changed was the place occupied by towns in the totality of human life. Fewer government functions were based in towns, cultural life was less bound to the urban environment, and trade in luxuries, which depended on towns, declined.

Towns in the West lost Roman governmental significance but often survived as focal points of royal or, more often, ecclesiastical administration. A cathedral church required a large corps of administrators. Western towns were everywhere attracting *burgs,* new settlements of merchants, just outside their centers. Because Vikings frequently raided these burgs, their existence was precarious. Few Western towns were impressive in size or population. Rome may have numbered a million people in the time of Augustus, but only about 30,000 lived there in 800. Paris had perhaps 20,000 inhabitants at that time. These were the largest cities by far in Catholic Europe.

In the Byzantine East, apart from Constantinople, the empire had a more rural aspect after the Muslims took control of the heavily urbanized regions of Syria, Egypt, and parts of Anatolia in the seventh century. The weakening of the caliphate in the second half of the ninth century was a spur to renewed urban growth in the Byzantine Empire. In provincial cities, population growth and urban reconstruction depended heavily on military conditions: cities threatened by Arabs or Bulgarians declined.

The Arabs were great city-builders. Baghdad—four times larger in area than Constantinople, with a million residents to the latter's 400,000—was created from scratch. The most magnificent city in the West was Cordoba, the capital of Muslim Spain. Its population may have reached 400,000, and its great mosque, begun in 785, held 5,500 worshipers, more than any Latin church except Saint Peter's. The city had 900 baths, 1,600 mosques (Rome had about 200 churches), 60,000 mansions, and perhaps 100,000 shops. Its libraries held thousands of books when the largest Carolingian book collections numbered a few hundred.

Agriculture nevertheless remained the most important element in the economy and in the daily lives of most people in all three realms. Farming meant primarily the production of cereal grains, which provided diet

Labors of the Months From a ninth-century West Frankish manuscript, this picture illustrates the labors of the various months of the year. How many of them can you figure out? How do these compare with farm labors where you live? (*Österreichische Nationalbibliothek*)

staples such as bread, porridge, and beer. Regions tended to specialize in the crops that grew most abundantly in local circumstances. For example, olives and grapes were common in the Mediterranean area whereas cereals predominated around the Black Sea and in central Gaul. Animal husbandry was always a major part of the rural regime. English sheep provided wool and meat. In Frankish and Byzantine regions pigs, which were cheap to raise, supplied meat, but for religious reasons pork was almost absent in the Muslim East—Islam adopted the Jewish prohibition against it.

A key development in the Frankish West was the appearance of a bipartite estate, sometimes called a "manor." On a bipartite estate, one part of the land was set aside as a reserve (or *demesne°*), and the rest was di-

vided into tenancies. The reserve, consuming from one quarter to one half of the total territory of the estate, was exploited directly for the benefit of the landlord. The tenancies were generally worked by the peasants for their own support. The bipartite estate provided the aristocrats with a livelihood while freeing them for military and government service.

Estates were run in different ways. A landlord might hire laborers to farm his reserve, paying them with money exacted as fees from his tenants. Or he might require the tenants to work a certain number of days per week or weeks per year in his fields. The produce of the estate might be gathered into barns and consumed locally or hauled to local markets. The reserve might be a separate part of the estate, a proportion of common fields, or a percentage of the harvest. The tenants might have individual farms or work in common fields. Al-

demesne (duh-MEEN)

though the manor is one of the most familiar aspects of European life throughout the Middle Ages, large estates with dependent tenants were also evolving in the Byzantine and Islamic worlds.

■ Social Patterns

Most of the surviving medieval records were written by elite members of society and reveal little about the middle and lower orders of society. Nevertheless, certain similarities are evident in the social structures of all levels in all three societies. The elites tended to be large landholders, to control dependent populations, and to have access to government offices. There were regional differences, too. Scholars ranked higher in Byzantium and the caliphate than in the West; and churchmen, especially bishops, were powerful in Christian societies but had no counterparts in Muslim ones. Literature, surely reflecting social realities, portrays the cultivated Muslim gentleman in the Abbasid period. This social type, marked by learning, good manners, and a taste for finery, does not appear in Byzantium or in the West until the twelfth century.

The middling classes show some disparities among the regions. Merchants, for example, often rose through the social ranks to become great aristocrats in Muslim societies. Islamic society often evinced great mobility, because of its restless, expanding nature and because Islamic ideology rejected distinctions in the umma. In Byzantium, traditional Roman prejudices against merchants and moneymaking activities persisted. Thus, rich merchants whose wealth gave them private influence frequently lacked public power and recognition. In the West, merchants were neither numerous nor powerful in the Carolingian period. In some towns, moreover, commerce was in the hands of Jews, always outsiders in a militantly Christian society. (See the box "Reading Sources: The Status of Carolingian Jews.")

Merchants were not the only people occupying the middle rungs of the social ladder. All three societies, in fact, possessed both central elites and provincial elites. Service at the Carolingian, Byzantine, or Abbasid court counted for more than service in a provincial outpost. It was one thing to be abbot of a great monastery and quite a different thing to preside over a poor, tiny house. The thematic generals in Byzantium were lofty personages; their subordinates held inferior positions. The vassals of a Carolingian king formed a real aristocracy; but vassals' vassals were of decidedly lower rank.

Degrees of freedom and local economic and political conditions shaped the lives of peasants. In all three societies some farmers were personally free and owed no

cash or labor services to anyone but the central government. In areas such as Abbasid Iraq, ordinary free farmers led a comfortable life. In the Frankish world, most peasants existed outside the dawning manorial system. They were free, and if they lived in areas of good land and political security, such as the Paris basin, their lives most likely were congenial. Byzantine peasants, though free, often lived in areas of military danger, and in some parts of the Balkans they eked a living from poor soils. Highly taxed and perpetually endangered, their freedom may have been small compensation for their economic and personal insecurity. All peasants were alike in their subjection to political forces over which they had no control.

At the bottom of the social scale everywhere were slaves. Christianity did not object to slavery itself but forbade the enslavement of Christians. Islam likewise prohibited Muslims from enslaving other Muslims. Slaves therefore tended to be commonest in still-pagan societies—Scandinavia, for example—or in frontier regions where neighboring pagans could be captured and sold. There were more slaves in the Muslim world than in Byzantium, which had, in turn, more than the West.

Women were bound to the same social hierarchies as men. Predictably enough, women had few formal, public roles to play. Their influence, however great, tended to function in the private sphere, rarely revealed to us by sources that stem from the public realm of powerful men. Aristocratic women had opportunities and power that were denied ordinary women. Irene ruled at Byzantium as empress. Frankish and Anglo-Saxon queens were formidable figures in the life of their realms. Carolingian queens managed the landed patrimony of the dynasty, dozens of huge estates with tens of thousands of dependents. A lack of evidence and the rigorous exclusion of women from public life in the Islamic world means that virtually no Muslim women emerge as distinct personalities in the early Middle Ages.

The conversion of England to Christianity was fostered by women. Most convents of nuns had aristocratic abbesses who presided over complex enterprises and, often, schools. In the Frankish world aristocratic women secured some learning, and one, Dhuoda, wrote in 841 a manual of advice for her son that conveys biblical and patristic teachings as well as practical wisdom. The Frankish convent at Chelles was a renowned center for the copying of manuscripts. Some Anglo-Saxon nuns owned ships and invested in commercial activities to support their convents. Almost all aspects of the cloth industry were in women's hands.

One example of the problems in the evidence concerning women relates to church roles. Women could not hold priestly office; and although deaconesses

The Status of Carolingian Jews

In 826 or 827 Archbishop Agobard of Lyon wrote this protest to Emperor Louis the Pious because the emperor had issued legislation favorable to the Jewish minority in general and to Jewish merchants in particular. Agobard's anti-Semitism is probably typical for the period and serves to indicate the precarious position of the Jews in the militantly Christian Frankish empire.

I commit myself to your goodness and patience as I inform you of what is ruinous to pass over in silence. There came Gerric and Frederick who were preceded by Evrard, your missi [envoys] in fact, yet not doing your will completely but rather acting on behalf of another. They showed themselves to be terrible to the Christians and mild to the Jews, especially in Lyon, where they set up a persecuting faction against the Church and they goaded the church to many groans, sighs, and tears.

When the Jews first arrived, they gave me a message in your name and another one to the man who rules the district of Lyon in place of the count; [this message] ordered him to offer aid to the Jews against me. We absolutely did not believe that such messages as these issued from your judgment, although they were read out in your sacred name and sealed with your ring. The Jews began to rage with a certain odious insolence, threatening that we would be afflicted with every sort of injury by the agents whom they had obtained to take vengeance upon Christians. After them, Evrard arrived and repeated the same thing and said that your majesty was truly angry with me because of the Jews. Then the aforementioned agents arrived, holding in their hands a tax code and a capitulary of sanctions which we do not believe exists by your command. Consequently, certain of our priests whom they threatened by name, did not dare to show their faces. We suffered these things from the Jews' supporters and for no other reason but that we preached to Christians that they should not sell Christian slaves to them; that they should not allow these Jews to sell Christians to Spain nor to possess them as paid domestics lest Christian women celebrate the Sabbath with them, work on Sundays, eat with them during Lent, and their paid servants eat meat on these days; and that no Christian should buy meats sacrificed and butchered by Jews and sell them to other Christians; and that they should not drink their wine or other things like this. . . .

. . . It is absolutely necessary that your pious solicitude know how the Christian faith is being harmed by the Jews in certain ways. For when they lie to simple Christians and boast that they are dear to you because of the patriarchs; that they enter and leave your sight with honor; that most excellent people desire their prayers and blessings and confess that they wished they had the same author of the law as the Jews; when they say that your counselors are aroused against us for their sake, because we forbid Christians from drinking their wine; when, in trying to claim this, they boast that they have received from Christians many, many pounds of silver from the sale of wine and cannot find out, after running through the canons, why Christians should abstain from their food and drink; when they produce commands signed with golden seals in your name and containing words which, in our opinion, are not true; when they show people women's clothes as if they were sent to their wives by your kinsmen or matrons of the palaces; when they expound upon the glory of their forefathers; when they are permitted, contrary to the law, to build new synagogues—[when all this occurs] it even reaches the point when naive Christians say that the Jews preach to them better than our priests. And this was particularly true when the aforementioned agents ordered that the markets that usually occur on Saturdays should be moved lest [the Jews'] Sabbatism be impeded, and they let [the Jews] choose on which days they had to go to market from then on, claiming that this suited the utility of the Christians because of the Sunday vacation.

Source: Translated by W. L. North from *Agobardi Lugdunensis Opera Omnia*, Opusculum XI, ed. L. Van Acker, Corpus Christianorum. *Continuatio Mediaevalis* 52 (Turnholt: Brepols, 1981), pp. 191–195.

 For additional information on this topic, go to http://college.hmco.com.

served at Hagia Sophia in the sixth century, they disappeared soon after and had long before vanished in the West. Religious power could come from personal sanctity as well as holding office. One study of some 2,200 saints from the early Middle Ages finds only about 300 females. It was hard for women to gain recognition as saints. And if a woman became a saint, her holiness was inevitably described either as "manly"—an extreme ascetic was praised for having the strength and courage of a man—or as beautiful, virginal, and domestic, in other words, with female stereotypes.

The domestic sphere is another difficult realm to enter. The Quran permitted a man up to four wives, if he could care for them and would treat them equitably. A Muslim woman, however, was given her dowry outright, and multiple marriages may have meant that relatively more Muslim women could gain a measure of security. In Byzantium and the West, families rarely arranged marriages for more than one or two daughters. Others remained single or entered convents. Women at all social levels tended to pass from the tutelage of their fathers to that of their husbands. In antiquity a suitor usually paid a fee, a "bride price," to his prospective wife's father and then endowed his wife with "bridewealth," money or possessions of her own. Gradually this practice changed to a system whereby a bride's father paid a dowry to her future husband. Thus, a wife who was cast aside could be left impoverished, for in most places the law did not permit her to inherit land if she had brothers. Females were such valuable property in the marriage market that rape was an offense not against a girl but against her father. A man could divorce, even kill, his wife for adultery, witchcraft, or grave robbing, and then marry again. A woman could usually gain a divorce only for adultery, and she could not remarry. For the vast majority of women, daily life was hedged about with legal limitations and personal indignities.

SUMMARY

 E have traced three parallel histories in the development of early medieval civilizations. The first one is chronological. In the Arab, Byzantine, and Latin worlds, the seventh century was an age of rapid, dynamic change, the eighth century a time of consolidation and reform, and the ninth century a period of renewed challenges.

The second history is political, religious, and ideological. Three different peoples built large imperial states. Each state fashioned a central government that focused on a powerful leader who was seen as a specially

chosen agent of God. Each state erected a system of rule that tied a government capital to its outlying regions. In the Muslim and Byzantine worlds, that system was highly bureaucratic; in the Carolingian Empire, the system was more amateur and personal. A religion—Islam, Orthodoxy, or Roman Catholicism—provided the glue that held each society together and defined the mission of its government. The cultural life of each area was inspired mainly by an attempt to integrate a powerful religious message with older intellectual traditions.

The third history concerns the fate of these imperial realms. In the Islamic and Latin worlds, large states broke down to leave many smaller heirs. In each instance, changes in the caliber of leadership, unpredictable foreign attacks, and the sheer diversity of the polity pulled the large state apart. The Byzantine Empire, much smaller than the Roman Empire had been, managed to defend its territory, but that territory was greatly reduced from former times.

We began this chapter by imagining what Rome's legacy might be. Islam and the caliphate emerged as surprising elements, while Byzantium and the Carolingian worlds followed more predictable courses. In the next chapter, we ask what happened after about 900. This time the surprising element will be found in the West. Although battered in 900, western Europe was on the verge of an astonishing period of growth and development.

■ Suggested Reading

Brown, Peter. *The Rise of Western Christendom.* 2d ed. 2000. A verbal feast, this book presents a stimulating assessment of the place of Christianity in the rise of Western culture.

Collins, Roger. *Charlemagne.* 1997. The first new biography of Charlemagne in a generation, this one is brief and readable.

Denny, Frederick M. *An Introduction to Islam.* 2d ed. 1994. By far the most accessible, readable account of the Islamic faith; the book covers all periods but is helpful for the early centuries.

Kennedy, Hugh. *The Prophet and the Age of the Caliphates: The Islamic Near East from the Sixth to the Eleventh Century.* 1986. Detailed but readable, this is the best modern introduction to the emergence and spread of Islam.

Riché, Pierre. *Daily Life in the World of Charlemagne.* Translated by Jo Ann McNamara. 1978. A highly readable account of how people lived—from diet, wardrobe, and dwellings, to their customary beliefs and superstitions.

Whittow, Mark. *The Making of Orthodox Byzantium, 600–1025.* 1996. Lively, readable, controversial, engaging, this book challenges standard views.

 For a searchable list of additional readings for this chapter, go to http://college.hmco.com.

The Manuscript Book

How long do you think it would take you to copy this whole textbook by hand? We know that it took about a year for two skilled monastic scribes to copy a Bible. Every medieval book was literally a manuscript (from *manuscriptum*, "written by hand"). Manuscripts contain important texts but are also revealing artifacts in their own right.

Codicology and paleography are the primary manuscript sciences. Codicology, the study of books as physical objects, investigates the materials and techniques used to make them. Paleography, the study of handwriting, seeks to read texts and to date and localize surviving books.

Depicted here is a folio (a page) of the Dagulf Psalter, named for the Carolingian scribe who wrote it in 795 on Charlemagne's orders as a gift for Pope Hadrian I (r. 772–795). The rich and powerful often used books as gifts. A psalter is a collection of the 150 biblical psalms and other canticles (songs or prayers derived from the Bible and used for worship). Can you make out the Latin words INCIPIUNT CANTICI, at the very top of the page? They mean "Here begin the canticles." The text is the Canticle of the Prophet Isaiah (Isaiah 12:1–6). Its title is CANTICUM ESAIE PROP[H].

Cathedrals and monasteries usually had *scriptoria*, "writing offices," where scribes and illuminators worked with bookmakers to produce manuscripts. Manuscripts were made from parchment, animal skin. According to an old legend, in the second century B.C. the Egyptians cut off the supply of papyrus to the kingdom of Pergamum forcing the Pergamenes to use animal hides to make writing material. Be that as it may, the English word *parchment* derives from the Latin name for this writing material: *pergamenum*. By the sixth century A.D., parchment had supplanted papyrus as the primary writing material in most of Europe.

Parchment was made by soaking an animal's hide in a caustic lye solution for three to six weeks to remove fat, hair, and blemishes. The hide was then scraped vigorously, washed, rubbed smooth with ashes or pumice, and then stretched on a frame to dry. The finest parchments, called *vellum*, were made from the hides of calves, lambs, or kids. It was almost white in color and nearly translucent. Most parchments were not so fine.

When the parchment was dry, the bookmaker cut and lined it—notice how straight and even the lines are in the picture. Then he took four sheets, or folios, of parchment, laid them down together, and folded them, placing the fold at the left, to form a booklet of sixteen pages called a quire (see the drawing). Because the two sides of a piece of parchment differ in color (the "hair side," or outside, is usually darker than the "flesh side," or inside) the quires were arranged so that hair sides faced hair sides and flesh sides faced flesh sides. A manuscript consisted of many quires sewn together. The smallest surviving manuscript is 2 inches by 3 inches; the largest is about 36 by 19. The larger the pages, the more costly was the book. One huge Bible produced in Bede's Northumbria required the hides of five hundred sheep.

The first page of the first quire was numbered 1[r] and 1[v], or 1 recto and 1 verso, meaning 1 "right side" and 1 "turned side." The second sheet was numbered 2[r] and 2[v]. Today, book pages are numbered 1, 2, 3, and so on, and books always start with an odd-numbered page on the right side—an inheritance from medieval manuscripts.

Scribes and illuminators received the prepared quires. Scribes wrote text onto the parchment. Illuminators added beautiful pictures or designs. You have on pages 248, 255, 268, 278, 287, 300, 303, and 329 examples of the magnificent illuminations that were painted into medieval books. Most books, however, had no such images at all.

Now you are ready to learn some paleography. We have already deciphered the first two lines of the folio shown here. These lines are written in a "display script." For visual appeal and to facilitate reference, scribes often used different handwritings, colors, or both to highlight first letters, first words, or first lines. Books, including the one you are reading, maintain this tradition. The huge writing—can you make out CONFITE?—marks the beginning of Isaiah's text. It continues, on line four, with *bor tibi dne qnm ira*. Line five carries on with *tus es mihi.conversus*. Look at line six: *est furor tuus&consolatusesme*. Can you make out the letters yourself? These words mean, "I will confess to you, O Lord, for you were angry with me but you turned your anger away and brought me consolation."

Several things bear notice here. First, the main script is Caroline minuscule, the new script that accompanied

The Dagulf Psalter *(Österreichische Nationalbibliothek)*

A Quire

Charlemagne's educational reforms. Because of its clarity, it is the basis for many modern typefaces. Compare the letters in the picture with the ones you are reading.

Second, notice the frequent recourse to abbreviation. Writing was time- and space-consuming, prompting the development of elaborate systems of abbreviation. Can you see, in line four, the letters *dne* with a strike over them, and then the letters *qnm,* also with a strike? In this case the words expand to *domine* and *quoniam.* Look at line two, where you see *prop^h,* shorthand for *Prophetae,* ("Prophet"). Also notice the ampersands in lines six, eight, nine, and ten. They stand for *et,* Latin for "and." Note too how the last words in line six run together.

Third, in antiquity, texts had neither breaks between words nor punctuation. As non–Latin-speakers learned to write the language, however, they usually put breaks between the words to facilitate understanding. You can see that most of this text has breaks, except in line six. In lines one, eight, and ten, you can also see a rather curious symbol: ⁖. It is a full stop, or period.

What else might you learn from a manuscript? Handwriting and systems of abbreviation are distinctive, and specialists use them to date and localize manuscripts. Because parchment was prepared in different ways, some manuscripts can be dated or placed by an analysis of their parchment. Inks differed in chemistry and in appearance and thus help to date and localize books as well. Styles of illumination and forms of images can also be localized or traced from one scriptorium to another. By knowing when, where, and by whom books were written or illuminated, historians can reconstruct the life and work of intellectual centers that were scattered long ago.

It is estimated that a medieval manuscript without illuminations was worth one year's wages for an ordinary working person. Would you spend a year's wages on a book?

MARE

CHAPTER 9

The Expansion of Europe in the High Middle Ages 900–1300

THE picture to the left represents one small section of the Bayeux Tapestry, a narrative account—in words and illustrations—of the conquest of England in 1066 by Duke William of Normandy. This scene is an apt introduction to the central theme of this chapter: expansion.

This section of the 230-foot-long tapestry depicts William setting sail for England. William had already gained greater authority in the duchy of Normandy than any duke before him. Now he was about to press his claim to the throne of England. He gathered soldiers from all over western France and boldly crossed the English Channel. Leaving nothing to chance, he transported horses too, as you can see in the picture.

One group of Normans conquered England while another seized control of southern Italy. Still other Normans played a decisive role in the period's most prominent manifestation of expansion: the Crusades. Meanwhile, certain Scandinavians settled Iceland and Greenland to the west while others founded the first state on Russian soil. Spanish Christians pushed back the Muslims in Iberia. From the Baltic to the Balkans, Slavic rulers founded new states and pressed hard against their neighbors. German rulers crossed the Alps into Italy, French kings reached the Pyrenees, and English monarchs pushed into Wales, Scotland, and Ireland. Seldom has Europe's political geography expanded so dramatically as during the High Middle Ages.

Between 900 and 1300, Europe's population began one of its longest periods of sustained growth. People brought more land under cultivation, introduced new crops, and made agriculture more efficient. Villages, towns, and cities grew in number and size. Trade expanded in every material and in every direction.

Economic Expansion

The Heirs of the Carolingian Empire: Germany, Italy, and France

The British Isles

The Growth of New States

The Crusades, 1095–1291

Bayeux Tapestry (ca. 1077), depicting the fleet of William the Conqueror of Normandy sailing to England in 1066.   (Michael Holford)

Europe witnessed the re-emergence of centralizing monarchies in France, England, and Spain. Some new realms, for example, Denmark and Hungary, built strong central governments. And an explosion of new states occurred along the frontiers of the old Carolingian Empire.

The "West" began taking on a more *western European* character. The Crusades complicated relations between Christian Europeans and Muslims, and both the Crusades and increasing religious differences alienated western Europe from Byzantium, and Roman Catholics from Orthodox believers. The center of Western civilization became more and more anchored to northwestern Europe. And that same western Europe was expanding to influence lands in Scandinavia and the Slavic world that had played no role at all in the West's classical, Mediterranean phase. The High Middle Ages repeatedly posed the question: Where is the West?

QUESTIONS TO CONSIDER

- **What were the main causes of the economic, political, and military expansion of Europe during the High Middle Ages?**
- **What basic problems confronted rulers who wished to expand the power and influence of central governments?**
- **How did the Catholic Church both help and hinder political development?**
- **What basic factors contributed to the rise, persistence, and eventual decline of the crusading movement?**

TERMS TO KNOW

guilds	Magna Carta
lay investiture	Parliament
communes	Reconquista
Papal Monarchy	Crusades
feudal revolution	

ECONOMIC EXPANSION

 HE economic expansion of Europe is manifest in many kinds of evidence that are more often qualitative than quantitative. Medieval people did not keep the kinds of records of births, deaths, population, or business activity that modern states routinely accumulate. Literary anecdotes can be revealing of course, but they are no substitute for hard data. After about 1000, every available indicator points to a growing population and an expanding scale and sophistication of economic activity.

■ The Growing Population

The population of Europe began rising slowly in the Carolingian period and may have doubled between 1000 and 1200. Scattered bits of evidence suggest that the total population of western Europe grew from around 30 million in 1000 to 55 or 60 million in 1200. In the thirteenth century, population growth gradually slowed.

In a few regions where family size can be estimated, fertile marriages were producing on the average 3.5 children in the tenth century and from 6 to 7 in the twelfth. All families continued to experience the loss of children. Three queens—those of William "the Conqueror," John of England, and Louis VIII of France—lost, respectively, 4 of 10, 6 of 14, and 7 of 12 children. The key change is that more babies were being born. People were also living longer than their forebears. Studies of aristocrats, high clergy, and soldiers show that a surprising 40 percent of them were over 40 years old. Male life expectancy was surely longer than female because of the dangers of childbirth, always the great killer of women in the premodern world. The general trend is clear: more babies being born, more infants living into adulthood, more adults living longer.

Everywhere in Europe, new land was brought into cultivation. More than half of the French documents relating to land in the twelfth century mention *assarting,* the bringing of previously untilled land under the plow. Literary texts often tell about knights wandering in a dense forest and suddenly entering a meadow. Those meadows did not get there by nature or accident. Thousands of acres of forest were felled. Marshes were reclaimed from the sea. Some 380,000 acres were drained along the western coast of France and probably twice that amount in both Flanders and England. This activity is inexplicable without assuming a growing number of mouths to feed.

Agriculture benefited from a warmer and drier climate through this whole period. Not a single vegetable blight was recorded. Food was more abundant and also more nutritious. Animals were increasingly reared for their meat, and higher meat consumption meant more protein in the diet. Beans and other legumes, also rich in protein, were more widely cultivated. Fine grains such as wheat replaced poorer cereals, ryes and spelts, in many areas. People of every class and region were almost certainly eating better and living longer and healthier lives.

■ Technological Gains

The eleventh century was a decisive period in the spread of new technologies in Europe. Innovations occurred in agriculture, transportation, mining, and manufacturing. Agricultural changes came first as a rising population created an increased demand for food that could be met only by new practices. In the Carolingian period, the return on seed—the amount of seed realized for each seed sown—is estimated at about 3 or 4 to 1. By the late twelfth century, this ratio had risen in many areas to 8 or 10 to 1. Given the combination of more land under cultivation and more yield per acre, the overall gains in the food supply were enormous.

The increases can be accounted for in several ways. Horses were more frequently used as draft animals. They were more expensive to acquire than oxen but no more costly to feed, and they did, in a day, a third or half again as much work. For much less "fuel," horses could haul loads farther and faster than oxen. Thus, fewer people could, with horses, cultivate more land than their predecessors managed with oxen. In addition, they could cultivate the land more frequently and increase yields because more seed would fall on more finely plowed soil. The dissemination of the horse collar made possible the expanded use of horses—older forms of harness suitable for the low-slung, broad-shouldered ox would have choked a horse.

Plows too were improved. The light wooden scratch plow used by the Romans was satisfactory for the thin soils of the Mediterranean region but barely disturbed the heavy soils of northern Europe. The invention of a heavy wheeled plow with an iron coulter (or plowshare)

CHRONOLOGY	
862	Founding of Kiev
870–930	Settlement of Iceland
962	Imperial coronation of Otto I
987	Accession of Hugh Capet in France
988	Kievan Rus accept Orthodox Christianity
1016	Conquest of England by Cnut
1066	Norman Conquest of England
1072–1085	Pontificate of Gregory VII
1077	Henry IV at Canossa
1078	Decree against lay investiture
1085	Spanish reconquest of Toledo
1086	*Domesday Book*
1095–1099	First Crusade
1122	Concordat of Worms
1171	Henry II of England invades Ireland
1176	Battle of Legnano
1198–1216	Pontificate of Innocent III
1202–1204	French drive English out of Normandy
1203	Fourth Crusade
1212	Battles of Bouvines and Las Navas de Tolosa
1215	Magna Carta
1250–1272	Germany's "Great Interregnum"
1265	First Parliament in England
1295	Model Parliament
1294–1303	Quarrel between Boniface VIII and Philip IV

and a moldboard was a real breakthrough. The iron plowshare cut deep furrows, and then the moldboard turned and aerated the soil. This heavy plow allowed farmers to exploit good soils more fully without exhausting the ground too rapidly. This plow seems to have been introduced into Carolingian Europe from the Slavic world, but it was not widely adopted before the eleventh century.

Wider adoption of nitrogen-fixing crops, such as peas and some kinds of beans, retarded soil exhaustion and also put more protein in the diet. Leaving land fallow was another means of avoiding soil exhaustion. In the early Middle Ages this meant setting aside about half of the arable land every year (the two-field system) or working the land intensively for a few years and then moving on. By the twelfth century three-field schemes of crop rotation were common.

Under the three-field system, two-thirds of the arable land saw nearly constant use. The amount of an estate under cultivation rose from 50 to 67 percent. Crop rotation brought other benefits as well. Horses ate oats, but (except in a few places such as Scotland) medieval

Heavy Wheeled Plow   The improved plow, the horse collar, and the cooperative labors of many peasants in preparing the fields led to an agricultural boom in the European countryside. *(Bibliothèque Nationale de France)*

people generally did not. If farmers wished to use horses, they had to dedicate some of their land to growing oats. A three-field rotation allowed some flexibility. Finally, the alternation of winter crops (wheat and rye), spring crops (oats, barley, and legumes), and fallow ensured against a single season of unusually harsh weather.

Surplus produce was intended mainly for the growing towns. To supply that market, improvements in transportation were necessary. Kings often passed laws to secure the safety of highways, and popes three times (in 1097, 1132, and 1179) threatened highwaymen—robbers who preyed on travelers—with excommunication. Landlords required their dependents to maintain roads and bridges. Many stone bridges were constructed in France between 1130 and 1170 because wooden bridges were so vulnerable to fire. Indeed, fire destroyed the bridge at Angers (in western France) five times between 1032 and 1167.

Transport improved not only because of safer roads but also thanks to better vehicles. Documents and pictures in manuscripts agree that the old two-wheeled cart, drawn by oxen, began giving way to the sturdy four-wheeled, horse-drawn wagon. Because greater quantities of foodstuffs could be moved farther and faster, urban communities could be supplied from larger areas. This was a crucial factor in enabling cities to grow and in providing urban residents with a predictable and diverse range of foods.

Evidence from several parts of Europe points to the years after 925 as the beginning of real growth in the mining industry. Notable improvements occurred in both the quarrying of stone and the extraction of metals. Mines were not deep because people lacked the means to keep the shafts and galleries free of water. Still, the exploitation of surface and near-surface veins of ore—principally iron but also tin and silver—intensified, to supply the increased demand for plowshares, tools, weapons, construction fittings, and coins. Stone quarrying, the commonest form of mining in the Middle Ages, benefited directly from more efficient stone saws and indirectly from improvements in transport. Better techniques in stone cutting, construction, and conveyance help to explain, for example, the increase in the number of England's stone religious buildings from sixty to nearly five hundred in the century after 1050.

■ Forms of Enterprise

Agricultural specialization became common. People began to cultivate intensively those crops that were best suited to local conditions. The area around Toulouse, for example, concentrated on herbs from which blue and yellow dyes were made. The central regions of France focused on cereal grains, while the Bordeaux and Burgundy regions emphasized the grapes that produced wine. Northern Germany specialized in cattle raising; northern England favored sheep.

Agricultural specialization helps to explain the growth in trade that is discernible everywhere (see Map 9.1). For certain commodities, local trade continued to flourish. Italian wines and olive oil, for example, were not produced for far-off markets; they tended to move from countryside to town within a region. The same was true of French or English grains. However, French wines were much prized throughout Europe, especially in England; and certain products, such as English wool and Flemish cloth, were carried far and wide. Salt fish from the Baltic found its way all over the continent. Lumber was routinely traded across the Mediterranean to the wood-poor Muslim world. Spain was a source of warhorses. Southern Europe supplied the northern demand for spices, oranges, raisins, figs, almonds, and other exotic foodstuffs. Caen, in Normandy, sent shiploads of its beautifully colored and textured stone to England for the construction of churches and monasteries. Rising population, higher productivity, and greater prosperity added up to a larger volume of goods moving farther and more frequently.

The lumber industry reveals many facets of medieval economic activity. Before the twelfth century, wood was the main building material, and even later it yielded to stone mainly for the church and aristocracy. But wood could be used for more than construction. For example, the Venetian shipyards needed about twenty oaks, twenty towering pines, and fifty or so beeches to make a ship. In the early twelfth century the Venetians were making about ten vessels a year, twice the number they had been building two centuries earlier. Whether for ships or for homes, the demand for wood grew steadily. In England, to take another example, about 500 cords (a cord is a stack measuring 128 cubic feet) of wood, nearly ten acres' worth, were needed to smelt one ton of silver. Under King Ethelred II (r. 978–1016), moneyers coined thirty tons of silver, consuming in the process some 15,000 cords of wood.

Wood exemplifies the expansion and interconnectedness of the medieval economy and society. Forests were essential to daily life, providing the wood for houses, fences, and fuel in villages and towns. Animals, especially pigs, were grazed at the edges of the forest to permit as much land as possible to be dedicated to food crops. Wild animals were hunted in the forest. For aristocrats hunting was as much for sport as for food. For poorer rural people, however, wild game made up a significant part of

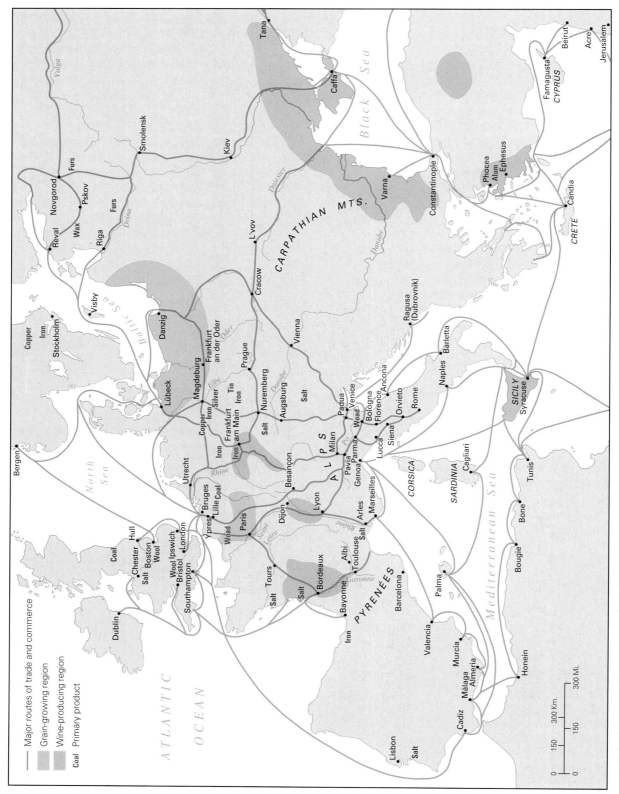

Map 9.1   European Resources and Trade Routes, ca. 1100   In an age of expansion, some products were consumed locally, but many others were transported over longer and longer distances. Commercial connections expanded too, creating several interlocking networks.

Twelfth-Century Timbered House, Rouen, France The house at the center of this picture was destroyed in World War II after holding its place for nearly eight hundred years. It shows one of the many uses of timber, and its narrow street gives an authentic feel of a medieval town. *(Roger-Viollet)*

the regular diet. The forest was also a plentiful source of fruits, nuts, and honey. If the peasants in a given place decided to cut a stand of timber to process the king's silver, or to build a wooden stockade around their village, or to dispatch masts to Venice, they had to wrestle with serious consequences. After the trees were gone, where would they hunt, or graze their animals, or gather their berries?

■ The Roles of Cities and Towns

All over Europe, towns grew impressively in size and importance. Table 9.1 shows the growth of three Italian cities. Such growth also occurred in cities in Flanders, such as Bruges and Ghent, and in Paris, London, and other cities that were becoming national capitals. Ghent expanded its city walls five times between 1160 and 1300, a sure sign of growth even in the absence of population figures. Similar forces were operating in the countryside, too. In 1100 about 11 fortified villages surrounded Florence, but by 1200 the city was ringed by 205.

Table 9.1
Population Increases in Italian Cities, 1200–1300

City	1200	1300	Percentage of increase
Florence	15,000	96,000	+640%
Siena	19,000	52,000	+274%
Pisa	20,000	38,000	+190%

Source: Adapted from Malcolm Barber, *The Two Cities: Medieval Europe,* 1050–1320 (London: Routledge, 1992), p. 270.

For the first time since late antiquity, cities were becoming centers for many activities. Governments, which required larger staffs of trained personnel, settled in towns. The towns of Italy and Flanders, though not national capitals, ruled over extensive hinterlands. Schools and eventually universities (see pages 341–342) were urban institutions. Mercantile, industrial, and legal organizations were located in towns. Ecclesiastical organization was always urban based. Towns began to compete with royal and aristocratic courts as literary centers, and cathedrals, the great buildings of the age, were exclusively urban.

One distinctive urban phenomenon was the rise of guilds. In 1200, for example, Paris had one guild of merchants and four or five craft or trade associations. By 1270 the city had 101 craft or trade guilds, and by 1292 the number had risen to 130.

The guilds had many functions. Their main purpose was economic: to regulate standards of production, to fix prices, and to control membership in their respective trades. But as towns grew larger and more impersonal, these associations of people engaged in similar occupations fostered a sense of belonging, a feeling of community. Members tended to live in the same areas and to worship together in a parish church. Growing wealth in general, coupled with fierce local pride, produced building competitions whose results are still visible in the huge neighborhood churches that survive in most European towns. The guilds indulged in elaborate festivals and celebrations, which sometimes turned into drunken debauches despite being held to honor saints. The guilds were also mutual assurance societies. That is, they assisted colleagues who fell on hard times, saw to the funeral expenses of members, and provided for widows and orphans.

The guilds had a damaging impact on women. As more economic activity came under the umbrella of the guild structures, women were more systematically excluded from guild membership. Usually women could become guild members only as wives or widows. They could not open economic enterprises of their own, although they were workers in many trades. Despite a growing, diversifying economy, women were increasingly denied opportunities, although later centuries would find women establishing their own guilds.

■ **Commercial Growth and Innovation**

Towns were focal points in commercial networks. The basic trade routes and networks had existed since Carolingian times, but a novelty of the twelfth century was the emergence of the Champagne fairs as a meeting point for the commerce of north and south. Since the early Middle Ages, a few locations hosted permanent fairs, and many places sponsored occasional fairs. By the middle of the twelfth century, however, the spices, silks, and dyes of the Mediterranean, the wool of England, the furs and linens of Germany, and the leather products of

Spain began to be sold in a series of six fairs held in the Champagne region of France from spring to autumn.

At any time of year, travel was difficult and costly. Few dared to venture across the Alps in the winter, and the northern seas, especially the passage around Denmark, were treacherous in cold weather. Even in the relatively calm Mediterranean, the Venetians refused to send out their trading fleet between November and March. Overland trade was impeded by snow, rain, mud, and highwaymen. Governments tried to restrain robbers, but no one could change the weather. After the road between Pisa and Florence was paved in 1286, it was passable most of the time, but paved roads were few. All these hazards made overland trade extraordinarily expensive, often multiplying the cost of goods tenfold. No wonder transport by water was preferred wherever possible.

Seaborne trade expanded. The stern rudder, better sails, the compass (in use by 1180), and better navigational charts facilitated sea travel, as did the growing use of larger ships. An Italian fleet sailed to Flanders in 1277, and within a few years the old overland trade routes, and with them the Champagne fairs, began a decline that was not reversed until the invention of the railroad in the nineteenth century. (See the box "Reading Sources: Two Views of Medieval Markets.")

■ **Changing Economic Attitudes**

As medieval society generated more wealth and populations concentrated in cities, people who were relatively well-off became more conscious of those who were less fortunate. Moralists began to argue that the poor were a special gift of God to the rich, who could redeem their own souls by generous charitable benefactions. Most towns established schemes of poor relief. But the numbers of poor people grew so rapidly, particularly in large towns, that helping seemed hopeless, and some gave up trying. Hospitals, for example, began to refuse abandoned babies for fear that they would be deluged with them.

Efforts to alleviate the condition of the poor constituted one ethical concern of medieval thinkers, but two issues attracted even more attention. First, theologians and lawyers alike discussed the "just price," the price at which goods should be bought and sold. Christian teaching had long held that it was immoral to hoard food during a famine or knowingly to sell a damaged item. But what was the correct price in ordinary circumstances? A theological view, often dismissed as unrealistic, held that items could be sold for only the cost of the materials in

⬥ READING SOURCES

Two Views of Medieval Markets

Europe's expanding commerce induced rulers to foster conditions favorable to trade but provoked serious concerns in the minds of moralists. In the first of these documents Germany's emperor Frederick Barbarossa (1152–1190) takes steps to promote a fair at Aachen; in the second, the distinguished theologian Humbert of Romans (1194–1277) criticizes and satirizes the new economy.

Frederick Promotes

Since the royal palace of Aachen excels all provinces and cities in dignity and honor . . . it is fitting and reasonable that we . . . should fortify that same place with lavish gifts of liberty and privileges as if with walls and towers. We have therefore decreed that there should be held twice a year the solemn and universal fairs of Aachen. And this we have done on the advice of the merchants. . . . We have given this liberty to all merchants, that they may be quit and free of toll throughout the year at these fairs in this royal place, and they may buy and sell goods freely just as they wish. No merchant nor any other person may take a merchant to court for payment of debt during these fairs, nor take him there for any business that was conducted before the fairs began. . . . And all people coming to, or staying at, or going from the fairs shall have peace for their persons and goods. And lest the frequent changing of coins, which are sometimes light and sometimes heavy, redound to the hurt of so glorious a place . . . we have ordered money to be struck there of the same purity, weight, and form, and in the same quantity, and to be kept to the same standard. . . . Whoever out of boldness decides to oppose our decree, or by temerity to break it, shall be in our mercy and will pay a hundred pounds of gold to our court.

Humbert Protests

Though markets and fairs are terms often used indiscriminately, there is a difference between them, for fairs deal with larger things, occasionally, and to them come men from afar. But markets are for lesser things, the daily necessities of life, and they are held weekly and only people near at hand come. Hence markets are usually morally worse than fairs. They are held on feast days and men thereby miss the divine office and sermon . . . sometimes too they are held in graveyards and other holy places. Frequently you will hear men swearing there "By God I will not give you so much for it," or "By God I will not take a smaller price." . . . Sometimes the lord is defrauded of market dues, which is perfidy and disloyalty . . . sometimes quarrels happen and violent disputes . . . drinking is occasioned. . . . Thus the legend runs of a man who, entering an abbey, found many devils in the cloister but in the market place found only one. This filled him with wonder. But it was told to him that in the cloister all is arranged to help souls to God, so many devils are required to lead monks astray, but in the market place, since each man is a devil to himself, only one other demon suffices.

Source: Roy C. Cave and Herbert H. Coulson, *A Source Book for Medieval Economic History* (New York: Bruce, 1936), pp. 120–121, 113 (slightly adapted).

them and the labor absolutely necessary to produce them. A commercial view, often dismissed as immoral, insisted that a fair price was whatever the market would bear, regardless of costs or consequences. A working consensus held that a just price was one arrived at by bargaining between free and knowledgeable parties.

The other ethical issue concerned usury, the lending of money at interest. Christian writers were always hostile to commercial enterprise, and they had plenty of biblical warrant for their view. Psalm 15 warned that no one can be blameless "who lends his money at usury." Luke's Gospel admonished Christians to "give without expecting to be repaid in full." Luke actually forbade the profit that makes most commercial enterprises possible. In the twelfth century, churchmen began to be much more assiduous in their condemnations of usury, a practice that had been winked at for centuries.

Prohibitions against usury in twelfth-century Europe (a society in full economic expansion) produced some remarkably inventive ways to get around the prohibitions. One person might agree to sell another person an item at a certain price and then buy it back on a fixed date at a higher price. Exchange rates between currencies could be manipulated to mask usurious transactions. Gradually thinkers began to defend usury on the grounds that a person who lent money incurred a risk and deserved to be compensated for that risk.

Investment demands credit, and credit requires some payback for the lender. Even in the face of deep hostility, credit mechanisms spread in thirteenth-century Europe. They were held up to minute scrutiny by theologians and popular preachers and were found to be evidence of man's sinfulness, acquisitiveness, greed. But all these practices persisted, fueled by the expansion of the European economy, and began putting individual profit alongside community interest at the heart of social and economic thought.

THE HEIRS OF THE CAROLINGIAN EMPIRE: GERMANY, ITALY, AND FRANCE

THE scope of political and institutional life expanded everywhere between 900 and 1300. In 900 the Carolingian Empire was collapsing. By 1300 France had emerged as a large, stable kingdom, and Italy had turned into several reasonably coherent regional entities. One might have predicted these post-Carolingian outcomes from the pre-Carolingian experience of these two areas. The most surprising political development within the old Carolingian lands, indeed within Europe as a whole, was Germany's rise to a premier position in the tenth century and then its long, slow decline. The states that evolved out of the Carolingian Empire faced common challenges: the achievement of territorial integrity; the growing responsibility of the central government; complicated political relations among kings, aristocrats, and churchmen; and the elaboration of new ideas about the state and its responsibilities.

■ Germany and the Empire, 911–1272

From the ninth century to the present, no state in Europe has been less stable territorially and politically than Germany and the German Empire. Time after time the Germans confronted new possibilities and challenges. An investigation of four questions in particular will help us comprehend German history after the Carolingians. First, what role did dynastic instability play in German history? Second, exactly where and what is Germany, and what constituted its empire? Third, what rules governed political development in the German lands? Fourth, how did the German rulers regulate relations with the leaders of the church?

When the Treaty of Verdun (see page 265) assigned an East Frankish kingdom to Louis the German in 843, it created something essentially new. Frankish rulers had long claimed authority over some of the lands that eventually became Germany, but before 843 no kingdom had ever existed in the territories east of the Rhine River (see Map 9.2). The Carolingians tried hard to impose common institutions on the diverse regions running from Saxony in the north to Bavaria in the south but they faced immense difficulties in doing so. The lands had no tradition of common or unified rule. There was no single "German" people; Saxons thought of themselves as Saxon, for example, not as German. Roman culture had barely penetrated into German lands, and Christian culture was recent and fragile. "Germany" had—has—no natural frontiers. Germany was, finally, the most thoroughly rural area of the Carolingian world.

After the last East Frankish Carolingian died in 911, the dukes—or leaders—of Germany's major regions chose one of their number as king. In 919 they did so again, their choice this time falling on Duke Henry of Saxony. Henry and his successors, each of whom was named Otto, ruled capably until 1002 when Otto III died without an heir. This time the German dukes turned to a distantly related family, the Salians. The Salian family died out in the middle of the twelfth century and was replaced by the Staufer, who ruled until 1250. Then, after twenty-two years without a recognized ruler, the Germans elected a member of the Habsburg family. Although not always Germany's rulers, this family was a powerful force in German politics until the twentieth century. This record of frequent dynastic change might be compared with the situation in France, where one family reigned from 987 to 1328, followed by another branch of the same family until 1598.

Who were these dukes, and why were they so influential? German romantic tradition regarded them as the

Map 9.2   Germany and Its Duchies, ca. 1000–1200
The chief political dynamic in Germany was a contest for power between the kings and the dukes. The duchies emerged in the ninth and tenth centuries and outlived one dynasty of kings after another.

heroic leaders of distinct ethnic communities, the so-called Tribal Duchies. In fact, the dukes were the descendants of local potentates introduced by the Carolingians. Between about 750 and 900, many dukes held authority over large territories that were often threatened militarily by neighboring Slavic peoples. By the middle of the tenth century five main duchies constituted the basis for German political life: Saxony, Franconia, Lorraine, Swabia, and Bavaria. The dukes were wealthy and powerful. They often controlled the bishops and abbots in their duchies. In most cases, they had managed to make vassals out of the lower ranks of the aristocracy in their territories. Although their ancestors had owed their offices to the Carolingians and were usually their vassals, the dukes of the tenth and later centuries rarely were beholden to the currently reigning dynasty. And they were extremely jealous of their independence.

Rulers of Medieval Germany

Saxons
 Henry I (919–936)
 Otto I (936–973)
 Otto II (973–983)
 Otto III (983–1002)
 Henry II (1002–1024)
Salians
 Conrad II (1024–1039)
 Henry III (1039–1056)
 Henry IV (1056–1106)
 Henry V (1106–1125)
Staufer
 Conrad III (1138–1152)
 Frederick Barbarossa (1152–1190)
 Henry VI (1190–1197)
 Frederick II (1212–1250)

One royal dynasty after another devised various stratagems to control the dukes. Kings sometimes married into ducal families, or tried to introduce their own relatives into a duchy if the reigning ducal family died out. Force and intimidation were not unusual. Frederick Barbarossa (1152–1190), the first great Staufer, patiently worked to get the dukes to recognize his overlordship even though he was powerless to demand payments or services from them. His plan was slowly to build up the idea that the king was the highest lord in the land (a plan that his French and English contemporaries used effectively). In the thirteenth century Frederick II (1212–1250) so despaired of governing Germany that he conceded the "Statute in Favor of the Princes," which lodged royal power in ducal hands in return for a vague acknowledgment of his overlordship. The kings themselves were dukes and their areas of truly effective control were usually limited to one duchy. The Saxons were based in the north, the Salians in the center, and the Staufer and Habsburgs in the south. The German monarchy thus had a very limited territorial base and, compared with their Carolingian predecessors or their French and English contemporaries, they possessed unimpressive governmental institutions.

If Germany was a collection of duchies over which the kings had little control, Germany's kings were not without means of enhancing their authority. The Saxons were especially capable military leaders. They fended off the Vikings, pressed deep into the Slavic lands lying to the east, and won a great victory over the Magyars at the

Battle of Lechfeld in 955. The Saxons had been elected at a time of acute military crisis and knew how to take advantage of the honor afforded by constant victories. But after the tenth century military successes were few.

In 962 Otto I was crowned emperor in Rome by the pope, thus reviving the Carolingian imperial office. The imperial title conferred two benefits on the German kings. It gave them immense prestige and power that owed nothing to the dukes, and it raised the possibility of securing huge material resources in Italy where, as emperors, they did not have to share power the way they did in Germany. In 1158 Frederick Barbarossa summoned representatives of the major northern and central Italian cities to demand full recognition of his regalian, or ruler's, rights. These included military service; control of roads, ports, and waterways, tolls, minting, fines, vacant fiefs, and confiscated properties; appointment of magistrates; construction of palaces; and control of mines, fisheries, and saltworks. No king had these kinds of rights inside Germany.

Germany's involvement with Italy and the imperial title has occasioned no end of controversy. To some, royal involvement in Italy signals a failure to deal imaginatively with Germany itself. To others, the quest for prestige, power, and money in Italy was actually a creative solution to the monarchy's relative impotence in Germany. Nevertheless, the struggle for control of Italy brought Germany's rulers two unforeseen consequences. First, since the imperial title had to be obtained in Rome from the pope, the papacy was handed an unprecedented opportunity to meddle in German politics. That opportunity evolved from an initial request for protection, through periodic demands for political concessions, to a claim that the pope actually had the right to decide whether a particular individual was morally fit to be crowned emperor.

Second, some feared that Italy itself would become the prime object of the German ruler's attention. This actually happened with the Staufer. Frederick I (Barbarossa, or "Red Beard"), who had negotiated for regalian rights south of the Alps, tried hard to impose his will on Italy only to have a group of Italian cities ally against him in the Lombard League and then inflict a humiliating defeat on him at Legnano° in 1176. Shortly thereafter, his grandson Frederick II was born in Sicily. His father had married a Sicilian heiress and then died suddenly leaving a widow who knew nothing of Germany and an infant son who grew up in the sunny south and neither liked nor knew much about Germany itself. Frederick tried creatively to build effective institutions in

Legnano (len-YAN-oh)

Italy but incurred the wrath of the Italians and of the popes, neither of whom wanted a powerful rival in their own back yard.

The Italian entanglement was not the only reason for German rulers' struggles with the church. The Saxon dynasty inherited from the Carolingians the idea that the king was God's specially chosen agent on earth and that the higher clergy were the king's natural helpers in governing the realm. Even though the kings could not control the dukes they could sometimes wrest the naming of bishops and abbots all over Germany from ducal hands. Control of the church was partly a matter of practical politics and partly a matter of royal ideology.

In the middle of the eleventh century, a group of ardent church reformers appeared in Rome. Committed to improving the moral and intellectual caliber of the clergy all over Europe, they targeted the chief impediment to reform: the control of church appointments by laymen—"lay investiture," as they called it. German kings,

or emperors, of course regarded themselves as much more than mere laymen. Just as Charlemagne had reigned supreme in the Carolingian "City of God," so these German rulers stood, in their own view, nearest to God in a great hierarchy; the clergy occupied the rungs beneath them in human society. To the reformers, the proper organization of society was just the opposite: the clergy, with the pope at its head, stood nearest to God, with secular monarchs subordinate to the church. In the eleventh century, these reformers challenged royal supremacy.

When Henry III died in 1056, he left a 6-year-old heir, and in the next decade Germany collapsed into anarchy. When Henry IV (1066–1106) came of age, he faced opposition on all sides, controlled no duchies, was not yet emperor, and had lost much of his father's control of the church. When he tried to make church appointments in the traditional way, he encountered the fierce opposition of the new reformers in the person of Pope Gregory

Henry IV, Duchess Matilda of Tuscany, and Abbot Hugh of Cluny   The embattled Henry IV here implores Matilda, a tremendously wealthy landowner and ally of Pope Gregory VII, to intercede with the pope. The powerful abbot of Cluny looks over the scene protectively. Written documents do not portray women's power as vividly as this image does.   *(Vatican Library, Rome)*

≈ READING SOURCES

The Issues in the Investiture Controversy

These two documents illustrate the range of issues involved in the conflict between the emperor Henry IV and Pope Gregory VII. The first excerpt is from a long letter written by Henry in 1076. The second is a decree issued by Gregory in 1078.

Henry Denounces the Pope

Henry, king not by usurpation but by the holy ordination of God, to Hildebrand, not now pope but false monk:

Such greeting as this you have merited through your disturbances, for there is no rank in the church on which you have brought, not honor but disgrace, not blessing but curse. To mention only a few notable cases, you have dared to assail the holy rulers of the church, archbishops, bishops, and priests, and you have trodden them underfoot like slaves ignorant of what their master is doing; . . . you have regarded them as knowing nothing, yourself as knowing all things. . . .

We have endured all this in our anxiety to save the honor of the apostolic see, but you have mistaken our humility for fear and have ventured to attack the royal power conferred on us by God, and threatened to divest us of it. As if we had received our kingdom from you! As if the kingdom and empire were in your hands, not God's! For our Lord Jesus Christ did call us to the kingdom. . . . You have assailed me who, though unworthy of anointing, have nevertheless been anointed to the kingdom and who, according to the traditions of the holy fathers, are subject to the judgment of God alone. . . . The true pope Peter exclaims "Fear God, honor the king."

But you, who do not fear God, dishonor me, His appointed one. . . .

You, therefore, damned by this curse and by the judgment of all our bishops and ourselves, come down and relinquish the apostolic chair which you have usurped. I, Henry, king by the grace of God, together with all our bishops, say to you: "Come down, come down, to be damned throughout all eternity."

Gregory Strikes Back

[Gregory VII] Inasmuch as we have learned that, contrary to the ordinances of the holy fathers, the investiture of churches is, in many places, performed by lay persons, and that from this cause many disturbances arise in the church by which the Christian religion is degraded, we decree that no one of the clergy shall receive the investiture of a bishopric, abbey, or church from the hand of an emperor, or king, or of any layperson, male or female. If anyone shall presume to do so, let him know that such investiture is void by apostolic authority, and that he himself shall lie under excommunication until fitting satisfaction shall have been made.

Source: James Harvey Robinson, *Readings in European History,* vol. 1 (Boston: Ginn, 1904), pp. 279–281, 275 (slightly adapted).

VII (1073–1085). Gregory was brilliant, proud, and inflexible—and determined to bend Henry to his will. Their battles inaugurated the so-called investiture controversy, which lingered on until 1122 when both of the original foes were long dead. (See the box "Reading Sources: The Issues in the Investiture Controversy.") Control of church offices was one key issue, but just as important was a contest over authority in the Christian world. Everyone agreed that all legitimate authority came from God. They disagreed, however, over who on

earth was primarily responsible for exercising authority in God's name. Finally the Concordat of Worms° stipulated that episcopal (bishopric) elections should be free and conducted according to church law. Only after a man had been duly elected bishop could a king, or emperor, invest him with the symbols and offices of secular authority. The Concordat was a blow to the German political system as it had existed for centuries and yet

---

Worms (VORM)

another destabilizing factor in medieval Germany. In the middle of the twelfth century, Frederick Barbarossa spoke of his "Holy Roman Empire." He meant that his power came, on the one hand, from God himself and, on the other, from the Romans via Charlemagne. Theory and reality did not match, however, and the papacy was able to thwart virtually every political initiative by the German rulers.

Even so, Germany was not without great rulers. Otto III was universally acclaimed as "the Great." Barbarossa was intelligent, handsome, athletic, chivalrous. Frederick II maintained a brilliant court and instituted governmental reforms in Italy that were ahead of their time. Yet rulership itself failed in Germany. One wonders: Might a long-lived dynasty have made a difference? Was the Italian venture a mistake? Given that France, England, and other states had difficult but not disastrous relations with the papacy, might Germany's have been handled differently? With its promise, undoubted achievements, yet ultimate failure, Germany is the political mystery of medieval Europe.

■ The Varying Fortunes of Italy

The history of Italy has always been played out in three regions: north, central, and south. The Carolingians and the Germans after them laid a heavy hand on northern Italy. In the center of the peninsula the Papal States was the key player. Outsiders always dominated the south, but their identities changed often.

As we have seen, German attempts to impose their authority on northern Italy met with limited success. One key obstacle to German rule was the communal movement (see Map 9.3), the most dynamic element on the Italian scene. Two conditions help to explain the rise of communes. The first relates to economic expansion. In the early eleventh century Italian towns began to rid the Mediterranean of Muslim pirates. By 1100 Italian merchants could trade anywhere in the Mediterranean world with confidence.

The second contributing factor relates to political developments in Italian towns. The Carolingians governed towns through resident counts, and German emperors tried to maintain this system. The powers of the counts tended to be weak, however, so the Germans also relied on bishops, who were, in Italy as in Germany, key props to the system of imperial rule. But bishops and counts were not alone in holding urban power. Since the late tenth century both bishops and counts had been granting fiefs to local men in order to strengthen their own authority and to procure defenses for the towns.

Gradually these men, whose lands made them wealthy in the expanding economy, moved into the towns and, in turn, gave fiefs to other men in the countryside. These lords were wealthy and jealous of their power.

Communes were sworn associations of the local nobility—these landed lords—and their vassals. Commune members swore to uphold one another's rights and called themselves the *popolo,* the "people," although the people as a whole had nothing to do with the early communes. The commune accorded a high degree of participation to its members in choosing leaders and in coming together in an assembly that voted on matters of common concern. The leaders of the early communes were usually called *consuls*—a deliberate attempt to evoke the Roman past. Usually elected for a single year, the consuls varied in number from four to twenty in different cities. The consuls proposed matters to an assembly for ratification. By the 1140s every significant city in northern and central Italy had a commune.

The communes did not necessarily originate as attempts to make cities independent. Frequently, however, as communal governments became more established and confident, that is what they did. One by one, cities either refused to recognize papal or imperial overlordship or else renegotiated the terms under which they would acknowledge the rule of their historic masters. The working out of this ongoing relationship was a major development in the history of the Italian cities in the twelfth century.

Although each Italian commune constituted an entity unto itself, a fairly coherent evolution is evident. By the late twelfth century, the consular communes were still governed by oligarchies of men whose wealth and power came from land, trade, and industry. Guild interests, however, gained in prominence at the expense of the landed groups among whom the communal movement had arisen, and ordinary workers began to clamor for participation. The communes were becoming increasingly volatile and violent.

One solution to this potential crisis was the introduction of the *podestà*°, a sort of city manager chosen by the local oligarchy. The podestà often came from the outside, served for a set period (usually six months or a year), and underwent a careful scrutiny at the conclusion of his term. He was expected to be competent not only at ordinary administration but also at military leadership, so that he could police the city as well as defend it. He brought with him a group of seasoned officials as subordinates. Normally, he could not be a property

---

podestà (poe-des-TAH)

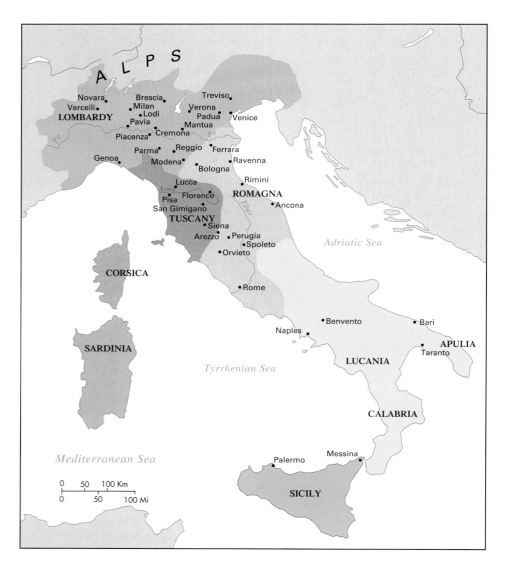

Map 9.3   The Communal Movement in Italy   Beginning in the late eleventh century, many towns in northern Italy, some in the central regions, and a very few in the south erected communal forms of government. This distribution reflects the relative wealth of north and south and the power of the popes in the center. North of the Alps only Flanders and northern France experienced comparable communal movements.

owner in the town, marry into local society, or dine privately with any citizen. By the middle of the thirteenth century, some podestàs were becoming virtual professional administrators. One man, for example, was elected sixteen times in nine cities over a period of thirty-four years, four times in Bologna alone.

The Italian commune was a radical political experiment. Everywhere else in medieval Europe, power was thought to radiate downward—from God, the clergy, the emperor, the king. In a commune, power radiated upward from the popolo to its leaders. For several centuries, the Italian city was arguably the most creative institution in the Western world. When Frederick Barbarossa tried to introduce tight imperial control, the future of northern and central Italy hung in the balance. But his defeat at the hands of the Lombard League at

Legnano in 1176 left the Italian cities free to continue their distinctive political evolution.

Although some communes emerged in central Italy—even, briefly, in Rome in the 1150s—the key power in this region was the papacy, and the main political entity the Papal States. In the political turmoil of the tenth and eleventh centuries, the papacy lost a great deal of territory. Throughout the twelfth and thirteenth centuries, therefore, a basic objective of papal policy was to recover lost lands and rights. This quest to restore the territorial basis for its power and income helps explain why the popes so resolutely opposed German imperial influence in Italy.

The most striking development pertaining to the papacy is the expansion of its institutions. Gradually there emerged what historians have long called the "Papal Monarchy." This term is meant to characterize a church whose power was increasingly centralized in the hands of the popes. In Rome, the pope presided over the *curia,* the papal court. The College of Cardinals, potentially fifty-three in number, formed a kind of senate for the church. They elected the popes (by majority after 1059 and by a two-thirds majority after 1179), served as key advisers, headed the growing financial and judicial branches of the papal government, and often served as legates. Legates were papal envoys, some of whom were sent to particular people or places provisionally, to communicate a message or to conduct an investigation, and some of whom were more like resident ambassadors who represented the pope on a continuing basis. Lateran Councils met often and gathered the clergy from all over Europe to legislate for the church as a whole. The hierarchical structure of the church became more visible as ecclesiastical business tended to accumulate in Rome.

High medieval popes also reserved to themselves certain jurisdictional and coercive prerogatives. Only popes could officially canonize a saint, a powerful reservation of rights against local communities. Popes could excommunicate persons, that is, exclude them from the sacraments of the church and the community of Christians. This was a form of social death in that excommunicated persons could not eat, converse, or socialize with others. Popes could lay a territory under interdict. This decree forbade all religious services except baptisms and burials and was designed to bring maximum pressure to bear on a particular individual. Finally, popes could invoke the inquisition. Despite horror stories about the inquisition, this was a judicial mechanism fully rooted in Roman law and widely used in the medieval West. Basically, an inquisition involved churchmen taking sworn testimony in an attempt to discover heresy.

Important Popes During the High Middle Ages
Gregory VII (1073–1085)
Urban II (1088–1099)
Innocent III (1198–1216)
Boniface VIII (1294–1303)

Who were the popes? What were they like? Most of them had been cardinals with years, if not decades, of experience in the government of the church. Many of the twelfth- and thirteenth-century popes were lawyers, which may explain, in part, their dedication to institutional and legal reforms. Not a single pope from this period has been canonized as a saint. One Englishman was elected; the rest were Roman, Italian, or French. Most were noblemen.

Institutions were important, but personalities mattered, too. Innocent III (r. 1198–1216), for example, was the most powerful man ever to hold the papal office. He came from a minor Italian noble family, received early training in theology and law, and entered the papal administration while in his twenties. His entire life was dedicated to promoting the legal prerogatives of the papacy and the moral improvement of Christian society. As a young man Innocent wrote *On the Contempt of the World,* in which he expressed his hope for a life of peace and contemplation. As an older man he hurled legal thunderbolts at the greatest public figures of the day.

Finally, the south: From the ninth century, the region south of Rome was contested among Byzantines, North African Muslims, and local potentates. In 1026 Norman pilgrims bound for the Holy Land landed in southern Italy, where local people invited them to enlist in the fight against the Muslims. By the 1040s the original Normans had been joined by many more who were seeking land and adventure. Initially opposed to the Normans, the papacy later allied with their leader as a counterweight against the Germans.

From his capital at Palermo, Roger II "the Great" (r. 1130–1154) ruled a complex state that blended Byzantine, Lombard, and Norman structures. In Italy, as in England (see page 297), the Normans showed a genius for adaptation. Perched advantageously at the juncture of the Latin, Greek, and Arab worlds, the Norman court was more advanced in finance and bureaucratic administration than any of its European contemporaries. No one forgot for a moment, however, that the Normans were primarily great warriors. A chronicler said of the Normans, "They delight in arms and horses."

Coronation of Roger II of Sicily, 1130 Roger's coronation by Jesus Christ makes a powerful ideological statement: he owes his office to no earthly power. The cultural crosscurrents of Sicily are visible: Roger is depicted more like a Byzantine emperor than a Western king, and the inscriptions above his head ("Rogerios Rex") and above Christ's ("JesuS CHristos") are in Greek, not Latin. *(Scala/Art Resource, NY)*

When the male Norman line died out, its heiress, Constance, married Henry VI of Germany (Barbarossa's son) and gave birth to Frederick II. For two generations the papacy struggled to break German control of southern Italy. Once the popes had defeated Frederick II, they decided to look for more pliant allies in the south. They invited a succession of French and Spanish princes to assume the crown thus touching off long-standing rivalries in the area. A profusion of outsiders always dominated southern Italy.

■ Capetian France, 987–1314

When the Treaty of Verdun created the West Frankish Kingdom, no one knew what the future France might be like. The twentieth-century French leader Charles de Gaulle once quipped, "It is impossible to govern a country with 325 kinds of cheese." He was referring to France's tremendous diversity, not its dairy industry. During the late ninth century and much of the tenth, the area suffered cruelly from constant waves of Viking attacks and from repeated failures of the Carolingian family to produce adult heirs to the throne. Chroniclers often quoted the lament of King Solomon: "Woe to thee, O land, whose king is a child." At the end of the tenth century, however, the Carolingians were replaced by the Capetians°, the family of Hugh Capet (r. 987–996). Thereafter the French monarchy steadily enhanced its position. That is the first issue we address. Then, bearing in mind de Gaulle's joke, we explore how a large—France is today about the size of Texas—but very complex group of territories was assembled into a kingdom. Finally we look at the nature of government in medieval France.

The Capetian kings of France were remarkably successful in capitalizing on their resources and opportunities. Of utmost significance is the fact that one family ruled for over three centuries. Contrast this with Germany's experience. Very early, the reigning Capetian kings began during their own lifetimes to have their sons crowned as successors. This meant that when the old king died, a new king was already in place and the nobility could not meddle in the succession. Robert I (r. 996–1030) displayed the "royal touch," a ceremony in which the king was believed to be able to cure people of scrofula (a common respiratory ailment) by touching them. No French nobleman, no matter how powerful, ever laid claim to such miraculous powers. Capetian kings had an elevated sense of the grandeur of the royal office. Louis VII (r. 1137–1180) began to make elegant tours of the country to put himself, his office, and his sparkling entourage on display. In Louis IX (r. 1226–1270) the Capetian family produced a saint of the Catholic Church—Saint Louis.

In addition to its religious and ideological resources, Capetian kingship also had some valuable practical bases. If the kings did not control directly much of France in the tenth and eleventh centuries, they nevertheless controlled the old, rich, prestigious, and centrally located city of Paris. The kings promoted the shrine of St.

Capetians (kuh-PEE-shunz)

The Capetian Kings of France
Hugh Capet (987–996)
Robert II (996–1031)
Henry I (1031–1060)
Philip I (1060–1108)
Louis VI (1108–1137)
Louis VII (1137–1180)
Philip II (1180–1223)
Louis VIII (1223–1226)
Louis IX (1226–1270)
Philip III (1270–1285)
Philip IV (1285–1314)

Denis, the legendary first bishop of Paris, as a kind of "national" shrine for France. The kings were also keen to attract to their court the most powerful men of the realm and to get those men to swear oaths of allegiance to the Crown. Slowly but surely the Capetians turned this ceremonial obedience into effective subjection. This is certainly what Frederick Barbarossa was aiming at in Germany. The kings also controlled about two dozen bishoprics and some fifty monasteries in northern France. This power base gave the king unrivaled opportunities to extend his influence and, in turn, to build up a cadre of loyal and articulate supporters. Although French kings provoked a few battles with the papacy, France experienced no investiture controversy.

The French kingdom, understood as the territory ruled more or less directly and effectively by the king, expanded dramatically from 900 to 1300. Internal politics and foreign wars contributed to this result. The Capetian family were heirs of the dukes of Paris. This meant that they controlled no more than Paris and its immediate region. In reality they contested for control of this region with a number of ambitious and aggressive families. In the early twelfth century Louis VI (r. 1108–1137) systematically ground down all his local opponents and made his area—the Ile de France—one of the best-governed regions in all of France.

But military successes were even more important than local political ones. The background to French military success is complicated. In the late eleventh and early twelfth centuries, one family of French magnates, the counts of Anjou° (see Map 9.4), acquired control over

a good deal of western France by marriage, diplomacy, and intimidation. Then Geoffrey of Anjou married the heiress of the duchy of Normandy whose father, William the Conqueror, we will meet later. A bit later Geoffrey's son and heir married Duchess Eleanor of Aquitaine, the recently divorced wife of Louis VII of France. In 1154 Henry of Anjou, as a result of incredibly complicated political and matrimonial alliances, became King Henry II of England. But he still retained control of about 60 percent of France.

For several generations the kings of France hammered away at this "Angevin° Empire." Henry of Anjou's four sons were viciously jealous of one another, and French kings exploited their rivalries to weaken Angevin authority in western and southwestern France. When one of Henry's sons, King John of England, absconded with the fiancée of a vassal of Philip II, the king of France, Philip summoned him to court to answer for his conduct. Of course, John refused to appear, and war ensued between 1202 and 1204. Philip won a resounding victory and a substantial portion of western France fell into his hands. Several times in the thirteenth century the kings of England and France came to blows over their competing claims to French territory. Each time the French won, including a major victory over an allied English and German army at Bouvines° in 1214.

Southeastern France was gained by wars of a different kind. In the last decades of the twelfth century, several cities in the southeast became hotbeds of the Albigensian° heresy—an important religious movement (see Chapter 10). Some Catholic locals and many churchmen urged the kings to undertake military action against the heretics. The French kings were prudent and bided their time until they had the resources to deal with this turbulent region. Under Louis VIII and Louis IX, the French monarchy finally extended its authority to France's Mediterranean coast.

The chief political dynamic in France was the contest for power between the kings and the territorial princes (see Map 9.4). Who were the territorial princes? In fact, they were rather like the German dukes. That is, they were locally powerful magnates, most of whose ancestors had been officials appointed by the Carolingians. But whereas Germany comprised five major duchies, France had a dozen or more territorial principalities. Obviously the Carolingians had elevated more than just a dozen local officers. In the tumultuous

---

Anjou (ahn-JHOU)

Angevin (AN-juh-vin)   **Bouvines** (BOO-veen)
Albigensian (al-buh-JEN-see-un)

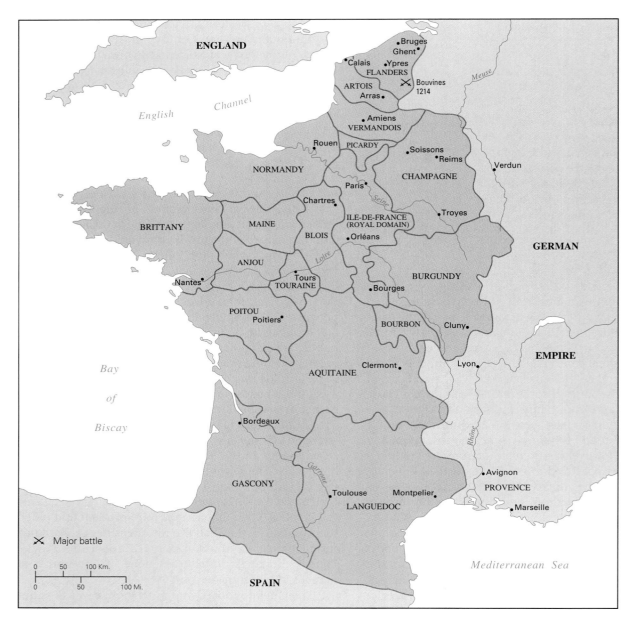

Map 9.4 French Territorial Principalities, ca. 1200 As the Carolingian West Frankish Kingdom (see Map 8.3, page 259) broke down and feudal bonds proliferated, many territories arose under counts and dukes. Their struggles to impose control locally and to fight off royal supervision animated French history.

circumstances of the tenth and eleventh centuries, some individuals and families had been remarkably successful in building castles, reducing the local population to subjection, and gathering into their own hands the powers that the Carolingian kings had once exercised in their localities. (See the feature "Weighing the Evidence: The Medieval Castle" on pages 314–315.) The fate of the French monarchy depended on the ability of the kings to cooperate with and finally to supersede these potentates.

Ironically, the territorial princes also faced localized rivalries for power and influence. Countless individuals also built castles, brutally subjected local peasants, and became lords. Sometimes these individuals were the vassals of the territorial princes—say the dukes of Normandy or the counts of Anjou—and sometimes they had vassals of their own. In the increasing absence of effective royal public authority, these lords wielded power for which they rarely answered to anyone. In the Carolingian world the number of vassals was small, their fidelity reasonably solid, and their services reliable. By 1100 the number of vassals was immense, their fidelity was constantly shifting, and they tended to provide only local military service. Scholars call this shift from effective Carolingian government to myriad local lordships a "feudal revolution."

For the kings of France to recreate central government, they had to overcome the disruptive tendencies of this revolution and then rebuild consolidated institutions. In the twelfth and thirteenth centuries the Capetians patiently and consistently followed a few basic policies to increase their ability to govern. They circumvented the local lords as much as possible. When they won military victories, the kings did not dole out the seized lands to lords as new fiefs but instead kept them in their own hands, or in the hands of family members as *appanages*. What is more, the kings introduced into these lands local officials, called bailiffs or provosts, who were of modest social background, had no personal ties to their assigned regions, often had some schooling in law, and were intensely loyal to the kings. By the time of Saint Louis, officials called *enqueteurs*° were sent around the country to inspect the work of bailiffs and provosts. Such roles had been unheard of since the Carolingian *missi dominici*. Louis also began to issue *ordonnances*, what we might call executive orders, that were binding on all the land under the king's control. These precepts are reminiscent of Carolingian capitularies.

If in 1000 France was a land of innumerable tiny lordships, then by 1300 it was the best-governed kingdom in Europe. Indicative of France's position is the outcome of two battles between King Philip IV (r. 1285–1314) and Pope Boniface VIII (r. 1294–1303). First Philip attempted to tax the French clergy, and then he sought to bring a bishop before his court. Boniface angrily objected to Philip's intervention in ecclesiastical affairs. But things had changed drastically since the fateful con-

frontation between Henry IV and Gregory VII. Boniface had to back down.

Welsh humorist Walter Map (1140–1209) provides this assessment of France in his day:

> The emperor of Byzantium and the king of Sicily may boast about their gold and silken cloth, but they have no men who can do more than talk, men incapable of war. The Roman emperor or, as they say, the emperor of the Germans, has men apt in arms and warlike horses, but no gold, silk or any other wealth. . . . The king of England lacks nothing and possesses everything, men, horses, gold, silk, jewels, fruits and wild beasts. And we in France have nothing except bread, wine and joy.[1]

Walter comically underestimates the resources of the French. In 1300 theirs was the largest, richest, and best-governed kingdom in Europe. French culture and language were increasingly dominant. Considering France's situation in 900, and compared with Germany's in 1300, these were impressive achievements.

THE BRITISH ISLES

N the British Isles, expansion had three dimensions: the tremendous growth of the English government; England's relentless push into the Celtic world; and the emergence of states in the Celtic world itself. England, about the size of Alabama, is smaller than France or Germany and more homogeneous in population, culture, and language than either of them, or than Italy. Building effective governance in England was therefore a somewhat easier task than it was elsewhere. Nevertheless, England faced some acute dynastic, military, and political crises. Moreover, England shared an island with two Celtic neighbors, Wales and Scotland, whose inhabitants were close kin to the people of England's neighboring island, Ireland (see Map 9.5). For better or worse, the fates of the English and Celtic inhabitants of the British Isles are inseparable.

■ England: Wars and Families, 871–1307

Ironies abound in England. Dynastic instability was as prevalent in England as in Germany but without the disastrous consequences. Military victories helped the French to grow, and most of those victories came at the

---

enqueteurs (on-KEH-turs)

expense of the English. But losses did not severely weaken England or its kings.

Alfred (see page 257) rallied the English against the Vikings, and his descendants ruled England for more than a century. They gradually rolled back the frontier of the "Danelaw," the areas of eastern and northern England controlled by Viking settlers (mainly Danes, hence the name). Late in the tenth century, however, English leadership failed in the face of a severe threat from a new generation of Vikings. These were powerful, ambitious men who had contested unsuccessfully for the kingship in Denmark and Norway. One of them, Swein Forkbeard, conquered England in 1014, but he survived his conquest by only two years. He was replaced by his son Cnut, who ruled from 1016 to 1035, and then by Cnut's sons, who ruled until 1042.

Cnut was no wild and woolly barbarian. He was simultaneously king of Denmark and England, and for a time of Norway too. He was a gifted ruler who maintained what was best in English institutions. He wed his daughter to Emperor Henry III and himself married Emma, the widow of the last English king. He was cultured, Christian, and an acquaintance of the pope.

When Cnut's sons died without heirs, the English nobles called over from Normandy Edward, called "the Confessor," the son of the last English king. Edward had grown up in Normandy, was unusually pious, and had taken a vow of chastity. Because he was not going to have an heir, claimants to the English throne began jockeying for position. Edward seems to have promised his throne to William, the duke of Normandy. Most of the English nobles preferred Harold of Wessex, one of their number. In Norway, Harald Hardrada prepared to make a claim as Cnut's rightful heir.

When Edward died, the English elected Harold, and immediately he learned that Hardrada had invaded. He marched to meet the Norse challenger and won an impressive victory at Stamford Bridge only to learn that William had meanwhile landed in the south. Foolishly, Harold rushed south to meet William without resting or

Map 9.5 Northern and Eastern Europe, ca. 1200 Apart from Germany, the core states of Europe emerged inside the former Roman frontiers or right alongside them. After 900 an arc of new states emerged from the Celtic realms and Iceland in the west, to Scandinavia in the north, to the western, southern, and eastern Slavs in eastern Europe.

Important Kings of England
Alfred (871–899)
Ethelred II (978–1016)
Cnut (1016–1035)
Edward the Confessor (1042–1066)
Harold of Wessex (1066)
William I (the Conquerer) (1066–1089)
William II (1089–1100)
Henry I (1100–1135)
Stephen I (1135–1154)
Henry II (1154–1189)
Richard I (1189–1199)
John (1199–1216)
Henry III (1216–1272)
Edward I (1272–1307)

reinforcing his troops. At Hastings, William defeated Harold and England was his for the taking.

With a brutal pacification campaign from 1066 to 1071, William assured himself control of most of the country. William was succeeded by two of his sons in turn, William II (1089–1100) and Henry I (1100–1135). Henry's only son drowned in a shipwreck, and the English nobles would accept neither his daughter Matilda as their queen nor her husband Geoffrey of Anjou as their king. Owing to William's conquest and settlement, most of the English elite were in fact Normans, and the Normans and Angevins were old, bitter foes. Consequently, the English turned in 1135 to a French prince, Stephen of Blois, who was a grandson of William the Conqueror through a daughter.

Stephen then died childless in 1154 and bequeathed his kingdom to Henry of Anjou—Henry II of England, the son of Geoffrey and Matilda. Henry's family, the Angevins, ruled England for centuries. But Henry was as much a French prince as an English king. From his father, mother, and wife (Eleanor of Aquitaine; see page 293), he had inherited a large part of France and was much preoccupied with his continental realm. He constantly battled with his sons for control of these vast French holdings without ever imposing on them common law or institutions. One of Henry's sons, John, was defeated by Philip II, inducing contemporaries to mock him as John "Lackland" and John "Softsword." Gradually the Angevins learned to focus their attention on England, although they never gave up their interests in France.

■ The Government of England

Alfred and his successors built strong central, and centralizing, institutions. All free men in the realm owed allegiance to the king and could in principle be called to the militia, the *fyrd°*. The great men of the realm attended meetings of the royal council, the *witan°*, which was partly a court of law and partly a deliberative, consultative body. The king could issue writs, executive orders rather like Carolingian capitularies. Danegeld—literally "money for the Danes"—was originally collected solely in times of danger and then slowly transformed into a regular tax. All of England was divided into shires, and each shire had a royally appointed officer the shire-reeve (or sheriff).

No other rulers in Europe had so effective a system so early, and it is no surprise that neither Cnut nor William the Conqueror desired to dismantle or replace the old English institutions. But William had won England by conquest, and he did introduce some changes. He turned most of the estates in England into fiefs and distributed them among some 180 of his most loyal followers. Each of these vassals held his fief in return for a fixed quota of soldiers for the royal army. To raise the approximately five thousand soldiers required by William, each of his vassals had to create vassals of his own. The technical name for this process of vassals creating vassals is *subinfeudation*. In 1087 William exacted the Salisbury Oath, which established the principle of liege homage°, according to which the king was the final lord of all vassals. To avoid creating compact territorial principalities on the French model, William scattered his vassals' holdings around the kingdom. Finally, to learn as much as he could about his new kingdom, and about the fiefs he had assigned to his followers, William conducted a massive survey of England that resulted in 1086 in the *Domesday Book,* named for the day of judgment against which there was no appeal. No comparable survey of any state was accomplished until the American census of 1790.

In the twelfth century English kings pursued four broad policies. They refined the financial machinery of the English government, the Exchequer, named for the checkerboard table on which the accounts were reckoned. They vastly improved the judicial institutions. Henry I began to send itinerant justices around the realm. He brought the royal court with its swift, fair, and competent justice within the reach of most people, and

fyrd (FEERD)   **witan** (WHIT-un)
liege homage (LEEGE AHM-idge)

he made royal justice more attractive than the justice available in local lords' courts. Henry II expanded the work of the courts and created an extensive system of writs. These documents, available to almost anyone, had the effect of transferring cases into the royal courts. This expansion of the work of the royal courts led to the emergence of a common law in England—a law common to all people, courts, and cases.

Henry II used the sworn inquest to learn about his realm. He conducted an inquest of knights' service to find out what service vassals owed to which people. He conducted an inquest of sheriffs to learn how the sheriffs were performing their jobs. On discovering that some were shirking their responsibilities, Henry replaced them. This action is the context for the Robin Hood stories about the cruel sheriff of Nottingham and the kind king who looks out for the people. Finally, the Norman and Angevin kings employed in their government "men raised from the dust," as one aristocratic contemporary contemptuously called them. These were men from the middling ranks of society, perhaps with some training in law, who were loyal to the king and advanced his interests against the aristocrats who were intensely jealous of their own rights and privileges.

The rising power of the king and his agents provoked the struggles of thirteenth-century England. Barons, a general name for the upper ranks of English society, were increasingly upset that an expanding royal government limited their influence. In 1215 a large group of disgruntled barons forced King John to sign the Magna Carta, the "Great Charter" (so called because it was written on an unusually large sheet of parchment). This document was a pact between the king and his social elite requiring the king to respect the rights of feudal lords, not abuse his judicial powers, and consult his "natural" advisers, that is, the barons. (See the box "Reading Sources: Selections from Magna Carta.")

John tried to wiggle out of the Magna Carta provisions, but he died in 1216 leaving only a minor heir, and the barons exacted many concessions from the regency government. When Henry III came of age, he struggled to win a limited application of Magna Carta. The barons, on the contrary, wanted a voice in devising royal policy, especially military policy in light of recent defeats (that is, Normandy and Bouvines). They also wished to have some say in naming the king's closest advisers and in controlling the work of the king's agents, especially judges.

Several times in the thirteenth century contemporaries called meetings of the royal court *parliaments.* This was a French word meaning, roughly, "talking together." The genuine ancestors of England's historic Par-

liament met in 1265 and 1295. Initially these meetings had no fixed rights or procedures, no set group of attendees, and no defined role. The kings viewed them as rubber stamps, clever political devices to win support for royal policies. The barons viewed them as opportunities to play a real role in a government that had been marginalizing them. In retrospect we can see that the English were groping to find a way to build consultation into their system.

England's relations with the church fell somewhere between Germany's and France's in both intensity and outcome. Anglo-Saxon kings generally enjoyed cordial relations with the church on a traditional Carolingian model. William the Conqueror controlled the church with an iron hand but introduced reforms and reformers who were acceptable to Rome. Perhaps Gregory VII left William alone because he did not wish to fight on too many fronts simultaneously. Archbishop Anselm of Canterbury and Henry I had a quarrel that lasted several years but finally mended their differences in a settlement that anticipated the terms of the Concordat of Worms.

England's most famous clashes with the church came in the reigns of Henry II and John. Henry was always anxious to extend the influence of his courts. In 1164 he decided that "criminous clerks," or members of the clergy who had committed a crime, should be judged in royal courts. The archbishop of Canterbury, Thomas Becket (ca. 1118–1170), protested that clerics could be tried only in church courts. He fled the country and Henry suffered widespread criticism, so a reconciliation was patched together and Becket returned to England. Unfortunately a band of overly zealous knights murdered Becket, believing that they were doing the king's bidding. In fact, the crime so outraged the church and the public that Henry had to back down on criminous clerks.

John's case was a little different. He had run afoul of the church several times for illegally seizing church revenues. Then he got into a row with Pope Innocent III because he refused to admit to England the pope's candidate for the archbishopric of Canterbury. Finally, however, John submitted because Innocent had laid England under interdict, and the king needed the pope's support for his planned war against Philip II of France. True to his nickname "Softsword," John lost at Bouvines and thus ended his quarrel with Rome. If no English king ever cowed a pope into submission, at least no English king suffered the humiliations of an investiture controversy. English government did not depend so heavily on the church that it was vulnerable to a challenge to its authority in ecclesiastical affairs.

❧ READING SOURCES

Selections from Magna Carta

When the English barons forced King John to sign the Magna Carta in 1215, they had very practical grievances and concrete priorities. The following selections from the charter's sixty-three articles are representative of the kinds of issues involved in the barons' dispute with the king. Note the absence of flowery rhetoric and grandiose statements of philosophical principles.

1. Know that we in the first place have granted to God and by this our present charter have confirmed, for us and for our heirs in perpetuity, that the English church shall be free, and shall have its rights undiminished and its liberties unimpaired.

2. If any of our earls or barons, or others holding of us in chief by knight service shall die, and at his death his heir be of full age and owe relief [a payment for an heir to succeed to a fief], he shall have his inheritance on payment of the ancient relief. . . .

4. The guardian of the land of such an heir who is under age shall not take from the land more than the reasonable revenues, customary dues and services, and that without destruction or waste of men or goods.

7. After her husband's death, a widow shall have her marriage portion and her inheritance at once and without any hindrance; nor shall she pay anything for her dower, her marriage portion, or her inheritance which she and her husband held on the day of her husband's death; and she may stay in her husband's house forty days after his death, within which period her dower shall be assigned to her.

8. No widow shall be compelled to marry so long as she wishes to live without a husband, provided that she gives security that she will not marry without our consent if she holds of us, or without the consent of the lord of whom she holds, if she holds of another.

12. No scutage [tax] or aid is to be levied in our realm except by the common counsel of our realm, unless it is for the ransom of our person, the knighting of our eldest son, or the first marriage of our eldest daughter.

16. No man shall be compelled to perform more service for a knight's fee or any other free tenement than is due from it.

38. Henceforth no bailiff shall put anyone on trial by his own unsupported allegation, without bringing credible witnesses to the charge.

39. No free man shall be taken or imprisoned or disseised [dispossessed] or outlawed or exiled or in any way ruined, nor will we go or send against him, except by the lawful judgment of his peers or by the law of the land.

Source: J. C. Holt, *Magna Carta* (Cambridge: Cambridge University Press, 1969), pp. 317, 319, 321, 323, 327.

 For additional information on this topic, go to http://college.hmco.com.

■ The Celtic Realms

When the Romans appeared on the scene, Celtic peoples could be found in virtually every region from Ireland to Anatolia. Most Celts were absorbed by more numerous and powerful Germanic and Slavic peoples. It was in the British Isles that the most durable and distinctive Celtic regions evolved into Ireland, Wales, and Scotland. Two essential dynamics characterized each of these regions. First, tiny political entities gradually turned into larger kingdoms. Second, relations between England and the Celtic realms were everywhere decisive in the historical development of the latter (see Map 9.5).

In each of the Celtic realms the movement toward greater unity was opened by the efforts of powerful, ambitious leaders to subjugate numerous well-entrenched

Howell the Good This picture of Howell, from a manuscript of his laws, depicts him wearing a crown, holding a scepter, and sitting on a tufted throne that looks like a palace. These are key symbols of rule. *(The National Library of Wales)*

local potentates, many of whom had expanded their power during the period of Viking invasions. In Ireland, Brian Boru (r. 976–1014) became the first ruler to exercise real authority over most of the island. In Wales, Rhodri the Great (d. 898) and Howell the Good (d. 950) were the first rulers to gain at least nominal authority over the whole of the land. Although disunity is a continuous theme of Scottish history, the centuries after the reign of Kenneth MacAlpin (r. 843–858) give evidence for the slow creation of a national tradition.

The course of development in the Celtic lands was disrupted by the English in the eleventh and especially in the twelfth century. The Norman Conquest of England brought adventurers to the frontiers of Wales and Scot-

land. Sometimes these continental knights advanced with the support of William the Conqueror and his sons, but more often they looked to wild frontier regions for opportunities to escape tight control. In Wales some Normans allied with various local princes who resented the growing power of the Welsh kings. Prince Grufydd ap Cynan° (d. 1137) then turned to King Henry I in 1114 and promised allegiance if Henry would aid him in his quest to establish his authority throughout Wales. From that time forward the actual power of Welsh rulers varied greatly, and English kings usually claimed some author-

---

Grufydd ap Cynan (GRIFF-ith op KY-nun)

ity over the region. Scottish kings managed to enlist a good many Norman knights into their service, but this recruitment effort angered the English kings and clouded the lines of allegiance in Northumbria, where many of those knights had been sent in the first place. Civil disturbances in Ireland induced King Rory O'Connor to turn to King Henry II of England for mercenaries to help him establish his power. But by 1171 Henry had invaded Ireland himself and inaugurated the complicated English involvement in the affairs of Ireland that persists to this day.

Edward I of England intervened repeatedly in the Celtic world. In 1277 he invaded Wales with the intention of totally subduing the Welsh. He built immense castles whose ruins are impressive today. Edward also made his son the Prince of Wales—still the title of the heir to the British throne. Between 1100 and 1260, England and Scotland went to war four times, and Edward resolved to put an end to this struggle by annexing Scotland. The Scots, however, rallied to the standard of Robert Bruce (r. 1306–1328), a dashing knight who was, ironically, of Norman extraction. Robert managed to free Scotland for centuries.

THE GROWTH OF NEW STATES

THE proliferation of new states constitutes one of the most remarkable examples of expansion in high medieval Europe. In Spain, Christian rulers waged a steady war of reconquest against the Islamic caliphate of Cordoba that led to the emergence of the kingdoms of Portugal, Castile, and Aragon. In Scandinavia, mighty leaders built durable kingdoms in Denmark, Norway, and Sweden. Local potentates created a band of new Slavic states running from the Baltic to the Balkans, from Poland to Bulgaria. To the east of those Slavic realms, around the city of Kiev, the Scandinavian Rus founded the first state on Russian soil. Between 900 and 1300, the geographic range of Europe's political entities more than doubled.

■ Reconquista and Kingdom Building in Spain

Historians perceive two driving forces in the rich and colorful history of medieval Spain. One is the bloody experience of several centuries of war along an expanding frontier. The other is the constant interplay within the Iberian Peninsula of three vibrant cultures: Christian,

Jewish, and Muslim. We describe the first of these forces in this chapter and the second in the next.

The emirate of Cordoba (see page 253) began breaking up after 1002, and the weakness of the tiny successor realms afforded an unprecedented opportunity to the Christians living in the north of the peninsula. King Sancho I (r. 1000–1035) of Navarre launched an offensive against the Muslims. This war, carried on intermittently until the fifteenth century, came to be called the *Reconquista*°, the Reconquest.

Before he died, Sancho divided his realm among his sons; thus, the kingdoms of Aragon and Castile arose alongside Navarre. Alfonso I (r. 1065–1109) of Castile really advanced the Reconquista. In 1085 his forces captured the Muslim stronghold and old Visigothic capital of Toledo, an important moral and strategic victory. Alfonso's military successes owed much to the dashing warrior Rodrigo Díaz de Vivar, known as "El Cid" ("the Lord," from the Arabic *sayyid*). Rodrigo, a gifted but slightly unscrupulous mercenary, fought for both Muslims and Christians. The Reconquista was moving on three fronts (see Map 9.6). In the east, the emerging kingdom of Aragon-Catalonia advanced along the Mediterranean coast. In the center, León-Castile pressed hard against al-Andalus. In the west, the nascent kingdom of Portugal became a factor in Iberian politics. Rodrigo's successes, and the reconquest of Toledo, led the retreating Muslims to summon aid in the 1150s from militant North African Muslims. The Christian advance temporarily stopped.

In the early thirteenth century Pope Innocent III stirred up crusading zeal and lent encouragement to clerics and nobles in Spain who wished to reopen hostilities against the Muslims. In 1212 a combined Castilian-Aragonese army won a decisive victory at Las Navas de Tolosa, south of Toledo. The victory of Las Navas de Tolosa was a great turning point in Spanish history. The outcome of the Reconquista, which did not conclude until the fifteenth century, was never again in doubt.

Twelfth-century Spanish kings, especially in Castile, imposed hereditary rule and exacted oaths of allegiance from their free subjects. The kings tried to force powerful nobles to become their vassals. They were more successful on the military frontier than back in their homelands because in the war zones nobles could be assigned new fiefs carved out of recent conquests. Kings

Reconquista (ray-con-KEE-stuh)

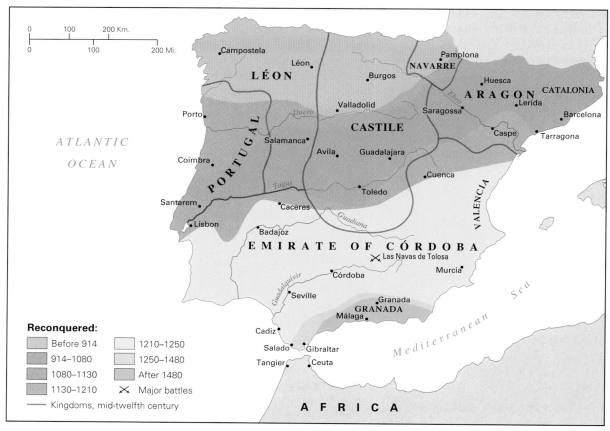

Map 9.6   The Christian Reconquista of Muslim Spain   From slow beginnings in the ninth century to the epochal Battle of Las Navas de Tolosa (1212), the Christians in Spain pushed back the Muslim frontier and built durable states behind it. (*Source: David Nicholas,* The Evolution of the Medieval World. *Copyright © 1992. Used by permission of Longman Group UK.*)

profited from the Reconquista to enhance their status and power.

In the thirteenth century Spain produced kings of genius, especially James I of Aragon (r. 1213–1276) and Ferdinand III (r. 1217–1252) and Alfonso X (r. 1252–1284) of Castile. These rulers were pious men, genuinely inspired by the ideal of the Crusades (discussed below), zealous in the promotion of the church. They were also hard-headed rulers. James turned Aragon-Catalonia into the greatest naval power of the western Mediterranean and a formidable economic power, too. Ferdinand and Alfonso derived great prestige from their successful wars. Those wars also provided a flow of booty and a supply of lands to reward the Castilian nobles who spent

their energy on the frontier rather than on attacking the king. These kings built strong central governments. Increasingly they used professional officers in key government posts and dispatched roving officials from the court to check on local rulers. Alfonso issued a major law book for the whole of Castile. These laws were based on Roman law and emphasized royal power. The Cortes, a representative assembly made up primarily of urban notables, began forging an alliance between the king and the towns. Iberia was not united in the thirteenth century, but it had evolved into four coherent blocks: a small and impotent Muslim region in Valencia and Granada, and three vibrant kingdoms centered on Portugal, Castile, and Aragon.

Alfonso X "the Wise"   The Spanish king, depicted here in a thirteenth-century manuscript from Spain, is judging his Muslim and Christian subjects. Alfonso's reputation for impartiality was important in his culturally diverse realm.   *(Biblioteca Nacional, Madrid)*

■ Scandinavia

Europe's expanding map saw new states in Scandinavia, the Roman name for the lands that became Denmark, Norway, and Sweden. Although the faint beginnings of political consolidation in Denmark can be traced to the Carolingian period, actual development of the states of Scandinavia dates from the tenth and eleventh centuries. Overseas expansion played one key role in northern political development. Another was the slow achievement of political unity by kings who had to overcome powerful local interests (see Map 9.5).

The sea, not the land, is the great fact of Scandinavian history. Norway has more than 1,000 miles of coastline, and no point in Denmark is more than 35 miles from the sea. Scandinavia did not offer opportunities for large, land-based kingdoms or empires, but the sea provided Scandinavians with a wide scope for activities.

More than any other people of the north, the Vikings capitalized on the sea as a highway. Vikings were raiders, of course, but also settlers. Much of northeastern England, the Danelaw, was settled by Northmen. In 911 the Norwegian Rollo and his followers settled what became Normandy in northern France. Between 870 and 930 many Norwegians and some Danes settled Iceland and a little later established bases in Greenland. In 862 a Swedish force, accustomed to raiding and trading along

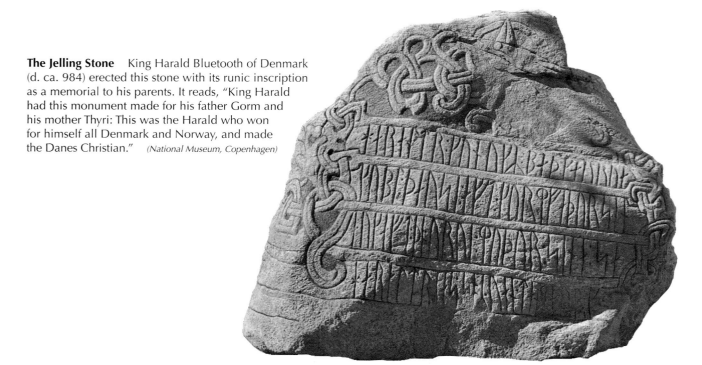

The Jelling Stone   King Harald Bluetooth of Denmark (d. ca. 984) erected this stone with its runic inscription as a memorial to his parents. It reads, "King Harald had this monument made for his father Gorm and his mother Thyri: This was the Harald who won for himself all Denmark and Norway, and made the Danes Christian." *(National Museum, Copenhagen)*

the rivers of later Russia, established a base at Novgorod. Raiders, traders, and settlers, the Scandinavians fostered the expansion of Europe.

Because the sea made exit from Scandinavia so easy, and because the whole region had absolutely no tradition of unified government, kings had a hard time establishing their power. Essentially kings were war-leaders with loyal bands of followers. Territorial states were thus built up as powerful leaders persuaded or forced more and more men to join them. Denmark's was the first of the northern monarchies to emerge in the early tenth century. Norway's monarchy arose a little later in the tenth century, but for much of the eleventh century Norway was under Danish control. As the Danes fell more and more under German influence in the eleventh century, Norway managed to break free. Sweden's monarchy was the last to emerge in the northern world; it was not fully stable until the twelfth century, but by 1300, it had become the most powerful.

Christianity came rather late to Scandinavia, with the first missionaries entering the region in the ninth century and widespread conversion ensuing in the eleventh. Norway's King Olaf (r. 1016–1028), affectionately remembered as Saint Olaf, was the first northern king who actively promoted Christianization. Scandinavian kings viewed the church as a useful adjunct to their power. They cooperated in creating bishoprics on the assumption that members of the high clergy would be educated, talented allies in the process of building central governments. Ironically, the church was a stabilizing force in Scandinavia during the very years when the investiture controversy wreaked havoc in Germany.

■ The Slavic World

In eastern Europe, between the rivers Elbe and Dnieper° lived numerous peoples customarily called Slavs. Their languages were once much alike but differentiated over time. Partly because of language differences and partly because of the areas in which these people settled, scholars divide them into western, southern, and eastern Slavs. These peoples were never conquered by the Romans, assimilated few influences from the classical world, and received Christianity later than western Europe. Still, as states began emerging in eastern Europe, they exhibited many of the same problems that older and more westerly states had encountered: shifting frontiers, clashes between ambitious rulers and powerful nobles, and outside military and cultural influences (see Map 9.5).

Dnieper (NEE-per)

Twelfth-Century Polish Castle This reconstruction of a castle shows it to have been a combination of earthworks and wooden stockades. Such castles, common in western Europe in the tenth and eleventh centuries, afforded protection to people from a wide area and permanent dwellings to a few. *(CAF Warsaw/Sovfoto)*

The first west Slavic state was Great Moravia, created in the 830s by capable dukes while the Carolingian Empire was experiencing civil wars. As we saw in Chapter 8 (page 265), the Moravian leaders invited the missionaries Cyril and Methodius to their realm, thereby beginning the establishment of Christianity in eastern Europe. Moravia's early promise was cut short in 906 by the Magyars. Also in the late ninth century the Přemysl° dynasty forged a kingdom in Bohemia that lasted through the Middle Ages although for long periods it was under German domination.

The greatest of the west Slavic states was Poland. In the 960s and 970s Duke Mieszko° (d. 992) unified a substantial territory and received Christianity from Rome. The first action created the Polish state, and the second anchored Poland firmly within the orbit of the Latin West. Mieszko's descendants, the Piast dynasty of kings, ruled until Boleslav III divided the kingdom among his three sons in 1138. For more than two centuries Polish development was retarded as weak rulers contested for power with local magnates, who themselves were successfully subordinating both peasants and men of middling status.

Přemysl (PURR-em-ih-sill)

Mieszko (mee-ESH-koe)

The creation of a Hungarian state played a decisive role in dividing the western and southern Slavs. The Magyars were disruptive raiders from the 880s until their defeat by Otto I in 955. After that disaster, the Magyars concentrated on building a state within the Danube basin, the home base from which they had launched their raids. Magyars, who were related to the Huns and Avars, blended with local Slavs. King, later Saint, Stephen (r. 997–1038), who received Christianity from Rome, was the real founder of Hungary. Like Poland, then, Hungary was attached to the Latin West. Stephen's family, the Arpads, ruled in Hungary for centuries. They built ruling centers at Buda and Esztergom, created an impressive

Virgin of Vladimir   The holiest icon of Russia, once the miraculous protector of the city of Vladimir and later of Moscow, this image was painted in Constantinople in 1131. Rus, and later Russian, icons tended to follow Byzantine traditions very closely.   *(Scala/Art Resource, NY)*

territorial organization, and promoted the growth of the church. They also expanded in almost every direction.

The southern Slavs built a band of states that extended across the Balkans. The first, reaching back to the seventh century, was Bulgaria. The Bulgars were a Turkic people who first led and then merged into the local Slavic population. The first Bulgarian state lasted until the early eleventh century when the Byzantines, who had suffered many defeats at Bulgarian hands, destroyed it. By the late twelfth century, when Byzantium itself had weakened, a new Bulgarian state emerged, but its rulers never had the firm control that their predecessors had wielded. Under Khan Boris (r. 852–879), Bulgaria made the momentous decision to accept Orthodox Christianity from Constantinople instead of Roman Catholicism, despite the pope's best efforts.

To the west of Bulgaria lay Serbia, a region dominated until the fourteenth century by Bulgaria and Byzantium. Perhaps because of constant outside threats, Serbia made little progress toward internal unity. The region accepted Orthodox Christianity. To the west of Serbia lay Croatia, a land formed when two originally independent areas, Dalmatia on the Adriatic coast and Croatia itself, were joined together in the early tenth century. Through much of the tenth and eleventh centuries, Croatia managed to preserve itself and evade the clutches of Hungary, Byzantium, and Venice. By 1107, however, Croatia was incorporated by Hungary as a more or less autonomous region. Croatia, owing to Italian and Hungarian influence, became Roman Catholic.

The creation of the major east Slavic state is shrouded in mystery and legend. It seems that in 862 a Swedish Viking named Rurik and his followers, called Varangians, established or seized a trading camp at Novgorod. A few years later Oleg (r. 879–912) took over Kiev and made it his base of operations. Thus was founded Kievan Rus, a state that, like Hungary and Bulgaria, began with an outside, elite leadership over a local Slavic majority. Kievan Rus lasted until the Mongols destroyed it in 1240.

Kiev was ruled by grand dukes who pursued four basic policies. They created a vast trading network that linked Germany, Scandinavia, Byzantium, and the caliphate. They shared power with regional nobles who built up several important towns of their own. They received Orthodox Christianity from Constantinople in 988. And, finally, they struggled to defend Kiev, indeed the Rus territory as a whole, from wave after wave of invaders from the eastern steppes.

Eventually, Kievan Rus was destroyed by the Mongols. These were a loose coalition of pastoral nomads

William of Rubruck Reports on the Mongols

Mongol attacks deep into eastern Europe prompted the papacy to send missionaries to convert the Mongols to Catholicism, in hopes of using them in a grand crusade against the Muslims. Here are extracts from the report of William of Rubruck, who visited the khan Baatu, the grandson of Jenghiz Khan and the founder of the Golden Horde, between 1253 and 1255. Rubruck was particularly struck by domestic arrangements.

The dwelling in which they sleep has as its base a circle of interlaced sticks, and is made of the same material; these sticks converge into a little circle at the top and from this a neck juts up like a chimney; they cover it with white felt . . . the felt around the top they decorate with lovely and varied paintings. Before the doorway they also hang felt worked in multicolored designs. . . . The married women make for themselves really beautiful carts. . . . A wealthy Mongol may well have a hundred such carts with chests. Baatu has twenty-six wives and each of these has a large house . . . belonging to each house a good two hundred carts. When they pitch their houses the wife places her dwelling at the extreme west end and after her the others according to their rank, so that the last wife will be at the far east end, and there will be the space of a stone's throw between the establishment of one wife and another. . . . The camp of a rich Mongol will look like a large town and yet there will be very few men in it. One woman will drive twenty or thirty carts, for the country is flat. They tie together the carts, which are drawn by oxen or camels, one after the other, and the woman will sit on the front one driving the ox. . . . When they have pitched their houses with the door facing south, they arrange the master's couch at the northern end. The women's place is always on the east side . . . and the men's place is on the west side. On entering the house the men would by no means hang up their quivers in the women's section. Over the head of the master there is always an idol like a doll or little image of felt which they call the master's brother, and a similar one over the head of the mistress, and this they call the mistress's brother. . . . In the winter they make an excellent drink from rice, millet, wheat, and honey . . . in the summer they do not bother about anything but *cosmos* [fermented mare's milk]. *Cosmos* is always to be found inside the house before the entrance door, and near it stands a musician with his instruments. Our lutes and viols I did not see but many other instruments that are not known among us. When the master begins to drink, then one of his attendants cries out in a loud voice "Ha!" and the musician strikes his instrument. When it is a big feast they are holding they all clap their hands and also dance to the sound of the instrument, the men before the master and the women before the mistress. . . . Then they drink all around, the men and the women, and sometimes they vie with each other in drinking in a really disgusting and gluttonous manner. . . .

Source: Christopher Dawson, ed., *The Mongol Mission* (New York: Sheed and Ward, 1953), pp. 93–98, 103–104, passim.

from Mongolia (lands lying east of the Caspian Sea and north of China) and Turkic soldiers. The charismatic leader Jenghiz Khan (1154–1227) turned the Mongols into an invincible fighting force. He and his successors built an empire stretching from China to eastern Europe. In 1221 the Mongols began their attacks on the Rus and in 1240 Kiev fell.

Jenghiz Khan's empire was divided into several khanates on his death, with the Rus dominated by the Golden Horde, so called because of the splendid golden tent from which they ruled. The Mongols accorded subject people considerable autonomy, but they demanded heavy taxes and occasionally carried out brutal raids to remind everyone who was in control. Through their domination of trade, the Mongols weakened the urbanization and commerce built up by the Kievan Rus. (See the box "Global Encounters: William of Rubruck Reports on the Mongols.")

When Charlemagne was crowned emperor in 800, only Bulgaria existed as a state in the vast lands of eastern Europe. But the overriding trends of the era inexorably swept into that region. Three centuries later those lands were home to several small states and also to some impressively large and successful ones. The Slavic world was thoroughly pagan in 800 and largely Christian by 1200. State building and Christianization in eastern Europe represent two significant examples of European expansion in the High Middle Ages.

THE CRUSADES, 1095–1291

N 1096 an army of Christian knights who called themselves pilgrims left Europe to liberate the Holy Land from the Muslim "infidel." (This was the first of many Crusades, so called because the warriors were *crucesignati,* "signed by the cross.") By the late eleventh century, Europe was a fortress that had marshaled its resources for an attack on the world around it. Europe's expanding population, economic dynamism, political consolidation, and buoyant optimism made possible not only the First Crusade, but many more over two centuries.

■ The Background: East and West

With the accession in 867 of the Macedonian dynasty in the person of Basil I, the Byzantine Empire experienced a period of vigorous, successful rule that lasted until 1025. Although the Macedonians fostered striking cultural achievements, carried out significant administrative reforms, and established the kind of tight control of the church that had been so elusive in the iconoclastic era (see page 251), they were primarily great soldiers. Along the Balkan frontier the Macedonian rulers kept both the Bulgarians and Kievan Rus at bay while also neutralizing many smaller Slavic principalities. Basil II (r. 976–1025), called "the Bulgar Slayer," wore down Bulgaria in a series of relentless campaigns. In the west, the Macedonians maintained an effective diplomacy with Venice that permitted lucrative commercial opportunities in the Adriatic. In the east, the Macedonian rulers profited from the gradual dissolution of the Abbasid caliphate by expanding their frontier in Anatolia.

By contrast, throughout the ninth and tenth centuries the ability of the caliphs in Baghdad to control their vast empire declined precipitously. Egypt and North Africa escaped Baghdad's control almost completely, and religious strife between Sunni and Shi'ite Muslims further destabilized the Islamic state.

After Basil II's death in 1025, Byzantium suffered a long period of short reigns and abrupt changes in policy. Great aristocratic families in Anatolia slipped from imperial control. In the capital, factional squabbling swirled around the imperial court, and in the person of Patriarch Michael Cerularius (r. 1043–1058) the church sought to break out from two centuries of domination. When in 1054 Cerularius and Pope Leo IX quarreled so bitterly over ecclesiastical customs that they excommunicated each other, the traditionally cooperative papal-Byzantine religious diplomacy gave way to a deep schism between the Roman and Orthodox Churches that still exists. Religious tensions were complicated when the staunchly anti-Byzantine Normans began creating their kingdom in southern Italy.

It was in these divisive circumstances that the Seljuk Turks appeared on the eastern frontier of Anatolia. Bands of Turks, peoples from central Asia, had been serving the caliphs as mercenaries since the ninth century. With new leaders at their head, and with both the caliphate and the empire distracted, the Turks broke into Anatolia with a vengeance. In 1071 at Manzikert a skirmish between Byzantine and Turkish soldiers turned into a rout in which Byzantium lost an army, an emperor, and the Macedonian reputation for military prowess.

Ever since the emergence of the Turkish threat in the early eleventh century, the Byzantines had been seeking mercenary help. The imperial defeat at Manzikert made their search more urgent and led to appeals to the West. Some troops were rounded up but not enough, so in 1095 Emperor Alexius Comnenus (r. 1081–1118) sent envoys to ask Pope Urban II to support a plea for mercenary help against the Turks.

To most in western Europe, the Turkish threat to Byzantium mattered little. What *did* alarm Westerners was Turkish attacks on pilgrims to Jerusalem. The popes saw in the plight of the Byzantines and of Western pilgrims some opportunities to manifest their leadership of the church. The papacy also wanted very much to heal the Roman-Orthodox rift. The popes therefore placed a high value on aiding the Byzantines.

Moreover, a crusade was perfectly consonant with the ethos of the knights of western Europe. Knights were born and trained to fight. The literature of the age glorified war and warriors. But churchmen had for some years been advancing an ideal of Christian knighthood that stressed fighting God's enemies. In the late tenth century there arose, first in France and then in many other places, peace movements called the "Peace of

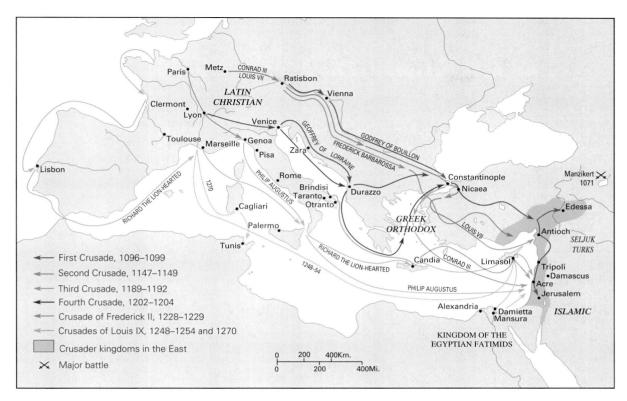

Map 9.7   The Crusades, 1095–1270   The long-standing Western interest in the Holy Land is vividly illustrated by the Crusades. Note the numerous routes taken, lands traversed, destinations attained, and points of cultural encounter.

God" or the "Truce of God." These movements sought to prevent war in certain seasons, such as around Christmas and Easter, and on certain days of the week, chiefly Sundays. Peace movements also attempted to outlaw fighting near churches, protect noncombatants, and soften the treatment of enemies and captives. Together the movements induced knights to fight non-Christians outside Europe.

■ The "Pilgrimage" to Jerusalem

Pope Urban II received Alexius's envoys in 1095 and then left Italy for France. He was actually a fugitive because Henry IV controlled Rome. In November at Clermont, Urban delivered a rousing speech to a vast Christian assembly. He ignored the eastern emperor's appeal for aid and instead promised salvation to soldiers who would enlist in a great struggle to free the Holy Land. The crowd acclaimed his words with a shout of "God wills it!"

By 1096 four large armies, which eventually swelled to perhaps a hundred thousand men—mostly French

knights with a smattering of troops from other parts of Europe—assembled under the leadership of the pope's legate. The forces were to rendezvous at Constantinople, where they seem to have expected a cordial imperial welcome and all necessary assistance. Alexius, however, took a rather different view. A ragtag band of ordinary people preceding the Crusaders had torn through the Balkans like a plague of locusts. Then, the crusading armies themselves sorely taxed the imperial authorities, who spent a lot of time and money arranging their passage from the frontier of Hungary to the gates of Constantinople. Finally, Alexius wanted mercenaries to fend off Turks in Anatolia, not armed pilgrims intent on liberating Palestine (see Map 9.7).

After receiving nominal promises of loyalty and the return or donation of any lands captured, Alexius moved the Crusaders into Anatolia. Almost immediately the Latin army defeated a Turkish force, thus earning a valuable, though short-lived, reputation for invincibility. The troops then entered Syria and laid siege to Antioch, which did not fall until 1098. At this point, rivalries

❧ READING SOURCES

An Arab Perspective on the First Crusade

The Muslim historian Ibn al-Athir (1160–1233) provides several interesting perspectives on the First Crusade in his work The Perfect History. *The Baldwin with whom this account opens is not historical; or perhaps he is a composite of the many Baldwins then active in the West. Nevertheless, al-Athir's depiction of the crudeness of Roger of Sicily is interesting as are his incidental revelations of Christian-Muslim cooperation and of divisions in the Islamic world.*

Baldwin, their king, assembled a great army and sent word to Roger [of Sicily] saying: "I have assembled a great army and now I am on my way to you, to use your bases for my conquest of the African coast. Thus you and I shall become neighbors." Roger called together his companions and consulted them about these proposals. "This will be a fine thing for them and for us!" they declared, "for by this means these lands will be converted to the Faith." At this Roger raised one leg and farted loudly, and swore that it was of more use than their advice. "Why?" "Because if this army comes here it will need quantities of provisions and fleets of ships to transport it to Africa, as well as reinforcements from my own troops. Then, if the Franks succeed in conquering this territory they will take it over and will need provisioning from Sicily. This will cost me my annual profit from the harvest. If they fail they will return here and be an embarrassment to me here in my own domain. As well as this Tamim [the emir of Tunisia in North Africa] will say that I have broken faith with him and violated our treaty, and friendly relations and com-

munications between us will be disrupted. As far as we are concerned, Africa is always there. When we are strong enough we will take it."

He summoned Baldwin's messenger and said to him: "If you have decided to make war on the Muslims your best course will be to free Jerusalem from their rule and thereby win great honour. I am bound by certain treaties and promises of allegiance with the rulers of Africa." So the Franks made ready to attack Syria.

Another story is that the Fatimids [local rulers] of Egypt were afraid when they saw the Seljuqids extending their empire through Syria as far as Gaza, until they reached the Egyptian border and Atziz [a general] invaded Egypt itself. They therefore sent to invite the Franks to invade Syria and so to protect Egypt from the Muslims [the Fatimids, although militantly Muslim, were regarded as heretics by other Muslims]. But God knows best.

Source: Francesco Gabrieli, *Arab Historians of the Crusades* (Berkeley: University of California Press, 1969), pp. 3–4.

among the Crusaders came into the open. One force went to the frontier of Armenia and carved out a principality. One of the ubiquitous Normans kept Antioch for himself. The main army pressed on to Jerusalem and, after a short but fierce siege, conquered it in July 1099. A Muslim historian described the scene:

> In the Masjid [Mosque] al-Aqsa the Franks slaughtered more than 70,000 people, among them a large number of Imams and Muslim scholars, devout and ascetic men who had left their homelands to live lives of pious

seclusion in the Holy Place. The Franks stripped the Dome of the Rock [the Mosque of Umar, near the al-Aqsa mosque, pictured on page 243] of more than forty silver candelabra, each of them weighing 3,600 drams [almost 40 pounds], and a great silver lamp weighing forty-four Syrian pounds, as well as a hundred and fifty smaller candelabra and more than twenty gold ones, and a great deal more booty.[2]

Godfrey of Bouillon, leader of the troops that had "liberated" Jerusalem, was named "Advocate of the Holy Sepulcher" and became ruler of the Christians in the East. He lived only a short time, however, and was replaced by his brother, Baldwin, as king of Jerusalem in 1100.

Judged on its own terms, the First Crusade was a success. The Holy Land was retaken from the infidel, and the pilgrim routes were passable once more. Entirely uncertain, however, were the prospects of the crusader states, the future course of Western relations with Byzantium, and the reaction of the Islamic world once it recovered from its initial shock. (See the box "Reading Sources: An Arab Perspective on the First Crusade.")

■ **The Later Crusades**

Crusading was intended to protect the Holy Land and keep open the pilgrim routes to Jerusalem. The creation of the small crusader states in the hostile environment of Syria and Palestine made continued crusading almost inevitable. In 1144 the tiny crusader state at Edessa on the Armenian frontier fell to a Muslim army. Although the news saddened Europeans, it took immense efforts by the papacy and other religious leaders to launch another crusade. Finally Conrad III of Germany and Louis VII of France agreed to lead it, but because neither would willingly submit to the other's authority, the Second Crusade accomplished little. Its one achievement was an accident. In 1147 an army of English, French, and Flemish soldiers who were proceeding to the Holy Land by sea put in on the Iberian coast and captured Lisbon. This opened a new front in the Reconquista and laid the foundations for the later kingdom of Portugal (see Map 9.7).

The papacy called for the Third Crusade when Saladin° (1138–1193), a powerful local leader typical of the disintegrating Abbasid caliphate, recaptured Jerusalem in 1187. It is a measure of the force of the crusading ideal that the greatest crowned heads of the day—Frederick Barbarossa, Philip II, and Richard the Lionheart—answered the call. It must be said, however, that only Frederick did so enthusiastically. Frederick died en route in 1190, while Philip returned home in 1191 and Richard in 1192. Because neither Richard nor Philip would stay in Palestine to fight Saladin, this crusade merely won access to Jerusalem for pilgrims.

Disappointed with the results of the Third Crusade, Innocent III began calling for another crusade immediately on his election in 1198. Popular preachers summoned an army, once again largely French, and the pope and the Fourth Crusade's military leaders engaged the

Venetians to construct a fleet of war and transport ships. In less than eighteen months they produced 50 galleys and 450 transports, a tribute to the awesome capabilities of the Venetian shipyards.

Ships, however, were expensive, and the Venetians drove hard bargains. When too few Crusaders and too little money appeared, the Venetians suggested that the Crusaders could discharge some of their debt by recapturing from the Hungarians the formerly Venetian port of Zara on the Dalmatian coast. This idea outraged the pope, but he could do little about it. Then into the camp of the Crusaders came a pretender to the Byzantine throne, who promised that if the Crusaders would help him to claim his patrimony, he would contribute to the cost of the Crusade. The Venetians urged the indebted Crusaders to accept this offer, and, to the horror of Innocent III, the Fourth Crusade turned to Constantinople.

Once in Constantinople, the Crusaders learned that their new ally had few friends in the Byzantine capital, but the venture hardly collapsed. The Venetians saw an opportunity to expand business opportunities in the East, and the soldiers welcomed a chance to plunder the Mediterranean's greatest city and to avenge what they regarded as a century of Byzantine perfidy. Thus, the Fourth Crusade captured not Jerusalem but Constantinople. Until 1261, the Eastern and Western churches were reunited under papal leadership, and substantial tracts of the Balkans fell to Western knights under a "Latin emperor" of Constantinople.

In later decades, popes began to take a more active role in planning crusades. No pope wanted to lose control of a crusade as Innocent had done, and all popes saw that the liberation of Jerusalem required a solid base of operations in the eastern Mediterranean. Egypt was the objective of the Fifth Crusade (1218–1221) and of the Sixth (1248–1250). Despite a few victories, the Crusaders could not win a secure base. No further crusades to the East were organized in the thirteenth century. In 1291 Acre, the last Crusader stronghold, fell and the original crusading era ended.

During the crusading period, the Holy Land was not the sole object of Crusaders' attentions. In about 1140 the pope preached a crusade against the Normans in southern Italy, and several popes in the thirteenth century, fearful of imperial encroachment, preached crusades against the Staufer dynasty in Italy. In 1147 the papacy authorized a crusade in the Baltic that opened nearly four centuries of German expansion into the pagan Slavic lands to the east of Saxony. In 1208 Innocent III proclaimed a crusade against the Albigensians in southwestern France.

Saladin (sah-lah-DEEN)

Why did the Crusades end? There are several reasons. By the late thirteenth century, more violence was being directed inward against heretics and political foes of the papacy than outward against the alleged enemies of Christendom itself. As rulers became more sophisticated and controlled more territory, they had less interest in the intangible benefits of crusading such as prestige. Whereas the cities of Italy once needed to open up Mediterranean ports, now they wished to secure comparative advantage over one another. The Christian ideals of poverty, charity, and service were incompatible with warfare. Literary images provide another insight into the decline of the Crusades. After 1300, we are less likely to read about a Christian knight fighting honorably for God and king than about a gentleman of manners seeking the favor of a fair lady.

A balance sheet for the crusading movement as a whole reveals more losses than gains. The Crusades exported many violent men from Europe, but it is not clear that Europe became a less violent place. As might be expected, the Crusades devastated relations between Christian Europe and the Muslim world. The Fourth Crusade mortally wounded Byzantium and worsened the already tense standoff between the Catholic and Orthodox Churches. Crusading zeal was directed deliberately against heretics and coincidentally against Jews. The Crusades did not create anti-Semitism, but they aggravated it. Some women, particularly in France, from which the majority of all Crusaders came, may have enjoyed momentary benefits in terms of control of land, wealth, and people while their husbands were away. But the long-term trend in feudal society was disadvantageous to women, and the Crusades did not change that. Finally, the Crusades may have done as much to disrupt Mediterranean trade as to promote it. Italian urban rivalries took the place of Latin-Muslim-Byzantine ones. That a single new product, the apricot, entered Europe in the crusading era seems small reward for such huge effort.

SUMMARY

 ETWEEN 900 and 1300 Western civilization experienced a long period of dramatic, sustained expansion. In the early Middle Ages, Rome's three heirs—western Europe, Byzantium, and the Islamic caliphate—were poised in a rough equilibrium. By the High Middle Ages, western Europe had seized the upper hand thanks to a strong economy, polit-

ical centralization, and Europe's first concerted attempt to reverse the tide of Islamic conquests.

Several factors contributed to Europe's economic growth. The population rose steadily. People everywhere brought new land under cultivation, adopted better agricultural techniques, and improved transportation systems. Greater efficiencies in agriculture promoted urban growth, as some people were freed from farming to undertake commercial and artisanal pursuits. Never before had Europe's economy grown so rapidly.

Governments expanded their power in most parts of Europe. Rulers in England, France, and Spain drew on both precedent and the innovative spirit of the present to create effective centralized institutions. In the Celtic, Scandinavian, and Slavic worlds, dynamic new states emerged. In Italy, durable urban governments dotted the landscape while the Roman church expanded its governing structures and the popes assumed a leading position in European society. A German kingdom arose where none had existed before, became briefly the greatest state in Europe, and then collapsed under the weight of innumerable problems.

European rulers faced a variety of problems in enlarging or consolidating their states. England, Spain, and Hungary all expanded at the expense of their neighbors. England, again, as well as France, Denmark, and Norway, expanded by extending control over local magnates. England, France, Hungary, and Spain developed the strongest governmental institutions.

Several states failed to consolidate their power. The German emperors were challenged by local rulers and buffeted by the investiture controversy. Their dream of a unified German state faded away. Poland could not survive dynastic divisions and a Mongol attack. The largest European state, Kievan Rus, was wiped from the map by an expansionary power from the East, the Mongols.

Europe's economic dynamism, increasing political stability, military might, and militant Christianity came together to produce the Crusades. Around 900, Europe was suffering attacks from Vikings, Muslims, and Magyars. Vikings and Magyars were incorporated into Europe, but from 1100 to 1300 Europe retaliated against the Muslim world. The Crusades embittered relations between Latin Christians, on the one hand, and Orthodox Christians and Muslims, on the other. But the crusading movement stands for the history student as perhaps the key indicator of the expansive nature of late medieval Europe.

Europeans of the High Middle Ages did more than just plant fields, pass laws, and fight wars. They lived in increasingly complex social structures, broadened their range of religious experiences, invented two new architectural styles, created a novel intellectual institution (the university), and wrote literary masterpieces. To all these creative—and expanding—realms of human endeavor we will turn in the next chapter.

■ Notes

1. Walter Map, *De nugis curialum*, 5.5, in John H. Mundy, *Europe in the High Middle Ages* (London: Longman, 1973), p. 387.
2. From the *Gesta Francorum,* trans. August C. Krey, in *The First Crusade* (Princeton, N.J.: Princeton University Press, 1921), p. 257 (slightly adapted).

■ Suggested Reading

Bartlett, Robert. *The Making of Europe: Conquest, Colonization and Cultural Change, 950–1350.* 1993. An engaging account of the expansion and "Europeanization" of Europe.

Bisson, Thomas, ed. *Cultures of Power: Lordship, Status, and Process in Twelfth-Century Europe.* 1995. The thirteen sparkling essays in this book cover much of Europe and attempt to explain how power was actually wielded in a society in which states were just emerging.

Bloch, Marc. *Feudal Society.* Translated by L. A. Manyon. 2 vols. 1964. This best-known book by one of this century's greatest historians seeks to explain the total history of the post-Carolingian world in terms of the ideals and practices of feudalism.

Reynolds, Susan. *Fiefs and Vassals.* 1994. Brilliant, controversial, and difficult, this massive book challenges many long-standing ideas about feudalism.

———. *Kingdoms and Communities in Western Europe, 900–1300.* 2d ed. 1997. After exploring the kinds of legal notions that guided medieval community building, this lively book turns to communities themselves, ranging from the parish to the kingdoms.

Riley-Smith, Jonathan, ed. *The Oxford Illustrated History of the Crusades.* 1997. A set of essays with lavish illustrations that explores almost every aspect of the Crusades and the world that produced them.

 For a searchable list of additional readings for this chapter, go to http://college.hmco.com.

The Medieval Castle

Storybook castles, in the manner of Disneyland, figure prominently in almost everyone's idea of the Middle Ages. The reality was different. Medieval castles were generally small, stark, and uncomfortable, not beautiful and romantic.

Castles represent a stage in the history of both dwellings and fortifications. Initially, castles were private, residential, and military. A consideration of these three elements will place the castle in historical context and illustrate what historians learn from the impressive ruins that dot the landscape of Europe and the crusader states.

The first medieval castles were constructed in the tenth century. The French word *château* (from the Latin *castellum*) means "great house," signifying the castle's residential purpose. Powerful aristocrats erected castles not just as their principal dwellings but also as a base for securing and extending their social and political influence. From his castle a lord could dominate the surrounding region. The castle also sheltered the lord's immediate dependents temporarily in the event of an attack and his military retainers more or less permanently.

A few castles were built exclusively for military purposes. In 1110 Crusaders captured a strategic plateau rising 2,000 feet above the main road from inner Syria to the Mediterranean. Between 1142 and 1205 Crusaders continually expanded the fortifications of the castle pictured here, the "Krak des Chevaliers" (from Syriac *karka*, meaning "fortress," and the Old French word for "horsemen"). This castle fell to Muslim attackers in 1271. The techniques of fortification developed in the crusader East influenced castle building in Europe.

The privately built castles of the tenth, eleventh, and twelfth centuries reflected the extreme localization of power in Europe at that time. As European governments grew stronger in the twelfth century, they began to monopolize the construction of castles and suppressed private castles as military entities. For example, Cerreg Cennen°, on the opposite page, was built by a Welsh prince, Lord Rhys° (d. 1197), and then seized from his descendants by Edward I around 1300. From the fourteenth century on, as in Roman times, fortresses served

---

Cerreg Cennen (CARE-reg KEN-nen) **Rhys** (REES)

essentially public and military purposes, and resident garrisons were their primary occupants.

Castles took many forms. From 900 to 1200 the "motte and bailey" castle was the most common. A lord commanded his dependents to dig a circular ditch and heap the dirt into a mound (the motte). The ditch, together with a wooden palisade—a fencelike wall—was the bailey. A wooden tower was often built atop the mound. Some castles included an elaborate series of mounds, ditches, and wooden walls—look at the picture of the Polish motte and bailey castle on page 305—but usually these structures were quite simple.

As siege techniques improved (catapults could hurl projectiles weighing 600 pounds), the wooden building of the bailey began to be replaced by stone. By 1150 or 1200, stone towers (*donjons*, from the Latin *dominium* for "lordship") were only the inner portion—the "keep"— of a more complicated structure of walls, towers, and gates. It was not unusual for walls to be 75 or 100 feet high. Because of the growing power of bombarding engines, castle walls often had to be made thicker. Towers built at 40- or 50-foot intervals projected beyond the walls so that defenders armed with bows and arrows could fire at attackers along the length of a castle wall. Look at the spacing of the towers in the castles pictured here. At Krak des Chevaliers we see one of the earliest examples of a double ring of walls. Two walls made it more difficult for attackers to take the keep and permitted defenders to battle invaders from inside both the inner and the outer walls.

To allow people to enter and leave, castles had gate towers, usually with two gates, one on the outside and one on the inside. Intricate systems of winches, cranks, and counterweights regulated the raising and lowering of the gates. Speedy operation was essential. Some castles had small "sally-ports" from which soldiers could make a rapid dash to attack a besieging enemy.

When possible, lords sited their castles on the edges of cliffs because fewer sides were open to assault and a garrison of modest size could defend the remaining walls. Cerreg Cennen stands 300 feet above a gorge, as you can see from the left side of the picture. Krak too sits on an impressive natural site. To walls and natural defenses were sometimes added ditches, as at Krak.

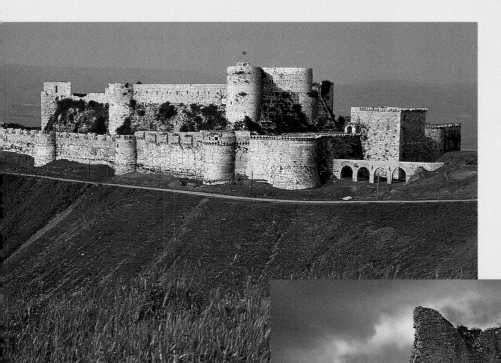

Krak des Chevaliers, Syria, ca. 1200
(Michael Jenner/Robert Harding Picture Library)

Cerreg Cennen Castle, Wales, Late Twelfth Century
(Michael Holford)

Much can be learned from the number of castles in a particular area. The presence of numerous small castles across the countryside suggests an extreme decentralization of power in that place and time. Remains of several hundred castles have been found in France alone; and England in 1100 boasted a castle every 10 miles. Conversely, areas with only a few large, strategically sited castles were likely subject to greater central control. Careful mapping of the known locations of castles can tell historians a great deal about the structure of social and political relationships.

Castles both contributed and responded to developments in military technology, such as more powerful catapults. Stone castles proliferated as Europe grew wealthier and as quarrying technology improved. Castles grew larger as monarchies rather than private individuals built them. Like cathedrals, massive state-funded castles tended to be built by professionals rather than by local laborers.

Both fortifications and magnificent dwellings have existed in Western civilization for millennia. From about 900 to 1200 the castle met the needs of a politically dominant warrior aristocracy for a private residence with military significance. In later centuries, the castle, as a château, retained its private and residential nature but lost much of its military character to garrisoned fortresses in the service of kings and princes.

 For additional information on this topic, go to http://college.hmco.com.

315

CHAPTER 10

Medieval Civilization at Its Height 900–1300

LOOKING down the nave of Chartres Cathedral, built between 1192 and 1220, produces a number of somewhat contradictory sensations. The size and verticality, the play of light and dark, the amazing array of shapes, corners, and angles, all are a bit mysterious. They were meant to be. At the same time, there is a logically ordered geometric elegance to the building that is plain to see. And this was intended too.

The cathedral at Chartres aptly symbolizes the range of historical currents dominant in high medieval Europe. We saw in Chapter 9 that Europe was expanding economically, politically, and militarily. Like its greater context, this building is very large; the cathedrals built in the burgeoning cities of the twelfth and thirteenth centuries were larger than any that had been built since Justinian erected Hagia Sophia. The bishops of Chartres expended most of their considerable income—Chartres lies in France's richest grain-growing region—for some twenty years to build this church. Literally dozens of these great buildings were going up at the same time all over Europe, providing employment for thousands of ordinary workers and numerous master craftsmen. Nobles and townsfolk donated windows and other fixtures to the building, making the building itself an expression of the period's more complex society.

Chartres Cathedral is an excellent example of the Gothic style in architecture, medieval Europe's supreme architectural achievement, Gothic being one of two major stylistic innovations in this period. The other was Romanesque, a style that had reached the summit of its beauty and power in the early twelfth century just as Gothic was about to appear. This change in architectural styles parallels others in the High Middle Ages. The Carolingian focus on grammar, on the

The Traditional Orders of Society

Social and Religious Movements, ca. 1100–1300

Latin Culture: From Schools to Universities

The Vernacular Achievement

Nave of Chartres Cathedral, looking east.
(Éditions Gaud)

most basic literary skills, gave way to an interest in logic. Intellectual problems that had in the past been solved by appeals to scriptural or patristic authority were now addressed by human reason. This produced a new style of intellectual endeavor called "Scholasticism." Monasteries and cathedrals housed schools in the Carolingian world, but by the thirteenth century the university had emerged as a higher kind of cultural institution.

Latin remained the dominant language of scholars, but almost everywhere the vernacular spoken languages were becoming graceful and effective tools for written communication. Religious themes were still foremost in writings of all kinds, but adventures, romances, and other works dedicated to secular themes were gaining in prominence. The Christian tradition still undergirded intellectual life, but that tradition was now spurred on to new heights of insight and expression by encounters with long-lost Greek texts and with the writings of Jewish and Muslim intellectuals. Look where you will, cultural life was richer and more complex than ever before.

The previous chapter concentrated on the economic foundations of society and on the ways in which people organized themselves politically. This chapter begins by introducing the increasingly complex social structures within which people lived and then turns to a study of what those people thought, said, and built.

QUESTIONS TO CONSIDER

- Into what principal social groups were the people of high medieval Europe organized?

- What role did logic play in spurring intellectual development and in contributing to the growth of Scholasticism?

- Why did some spiritual movements result in heresy while others ended in new religious orders?

- What cultural achievements mark the High Middle Ages as a period of crowning achievement?

TERMS TO KNOW

Cluny (Cluniacs)	canon law
Bernard of Clairvaux	Thomas Aquinas
Hildegard of Bingen	summa
chivalry	Romanesque
Dominic	Gothic
Francis of Assisi	

THE TRADITIONAL ORDERS OF SOCIETY

AFTER centuries of various experiments with ordering social relations after the end of the Roman Empire in the West, a new social order had evolved by 900 that was distinctively medieval. Alfred the Great (r. 871–899) of England once said that a kingdom needed "men of prayer, men of war, and men of work." In the tenth century two French bishops wrote lengthy works exploring this same theme. This three-way division reveals the way the elite looked at the world. It provided neat places for the clergy, warrior-aristocrats, and peasants. The clergy and the nobil-

ity agreed that they were superior to the "workers," but fierce controversies raged over whether ultimate leadership in society belonged to the "pray-ers" or to the "fighters."

By the time this tripartite view of society was fully established in the West, it had begun to fit social realities less well. It excluded townspeople, who were becoming ever more important. Town residents worked for a living, of course, but only farmers were considered "workers." Alfred and the bishops did not speak about women, and they consciously excluded minorities, chiefly Jews. To form a full picture of Europe's increasingly intricate social relations, we begin with contemporary theoretical pronouncements and then look for the people whom the theoreticians neglected.

■ Those Who Pray: The Clergy

As the church promoted its own vision of the tripartite ordering of society, it assigned primacy to the "pray-ers," to its own leaders. Within the clergy, however, sharp disagreements arose over whether the leading "pray-ers" were the monks in the monasteries or the bishops in their cathedrals. Whereas in the Carolingian world, the clergy served occasionally as an avenue of upward social mobility for talented outsiders, in the High Middle Ages church offices were usually reserved to the younger sons of the nobility. The church was always hierarchical in organization and outlook so the increasingly aristocratic character of the church's leadership tended to reinforce those old tendencies.

In the aftermath of the Carolingian collapse, a great spiritual reform swept Europe. It began in 910 when Duke William of Aquitaine founded the monastery of Cluny° in Burgundy on lands that he donated (see Map 9.4, page 294). At a time when powerful local families dominated almost all monasteries, Cluny was a rarity because it was free of all lay and episcopal control and because it was under the direct authority of the pope. Cluny's abbots were among the greatest European statesmen of their day and became influential advisers to popes, French kings, German emperors, and aristocratic families.

In the tradition of the Carolingian monastic reforms, Cluny placed great emphasis on liturgical prayer. The monks spent long hours in solemn devotions and did little manual work. Because Cluniac prayer was thought to be especially efficacious, nobles all over Europe donated land to Cluny and placed local monasteries under Cluniac control. Many independent monasteries also appealed to Cluny for spiritual reform. By the twelfth century, hundreds of monasteries had joined in a Cluniac order. Individual houses were under the authority of the abbot of Cluny, and their priors had to attend an annual assembly. Although the majority of houses reformed by Cluny were male, many convents of nuns also adopted Cluniac practices.

Cluny promoted two powerful ideas. One was that the role of the church was to pray for the world, not to be implicated deeply in it. The other was that freedom from lay control was essential if churches were to concentrate on their spiritual tasks.

The same spiritual forces that motivated the Cluniacs inspired Bishop Adalbero of Metz in 933 to promote the restoration of Benedictine practices in the dilapi-

CHRONOLOGY	
ca. 900	*Beowulf*
910	Foundation of Cluny
940–1003	Gerbert of Aurillac
960–1028	Fulbert of Chartres
d. 970	Roswitha of Gandersheim
1000–1088	Berengar of Tours
ca. 1033–1109	Anselm of Canterbury
ca. 1050–1150	Emergence of the Romanesque
1079–1142	Peter Abelard
1184	Waldensians declared heretics
1090–1153	Bernard of Clairvaux
1098	Foundation of Cîteaux
1098–1179	Hildegard of Bingen
ca. 1100	*Song of Roland*
1135–1183	Chrétien de Troyes
1170–1221	Dominic
ca. 1177–1213	Mary of Oignies
1181–1226	Francis of Assisi
1194–1253	Clare of Assisi
1208	Albigensian Crusade launched
1210–1280	Mechtild of Magdeburg
1225–1274	Thomas Aquinas
1265–1321	Dante Alighieri

dated Lorraine monastery of Gorze°. Customs at Gorze resembled those at Cluny, and they spread widely in Lorraine, Germany, and England. The Gorze reform was well received by kings and nobles; its aim was not so much to withdraw from the world as to improve it. Monks from the Gorze and Cluniac traditions bitterly condemned clerical immorality and inappropriate lay interference in the church. They preached against clerical marriage and simony, the buying and selling of church offices.

Cluny (CLUE-nee)

Gorze (GORTZ-eh)

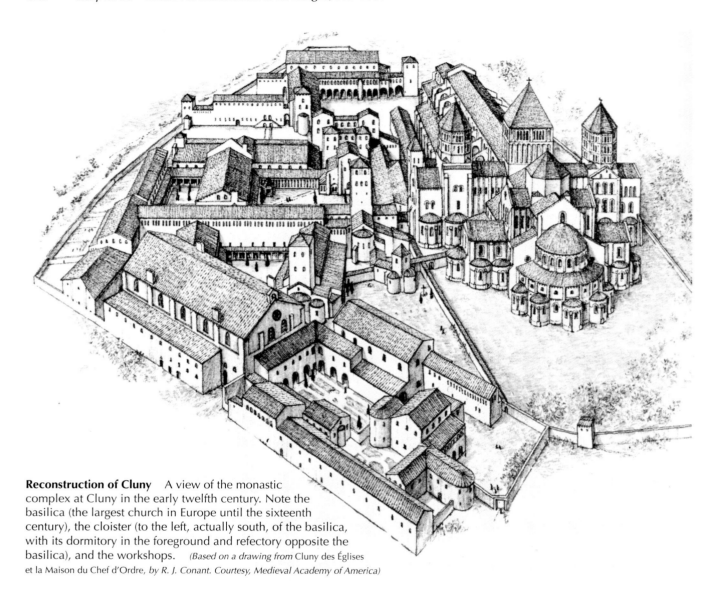

Reconstruction of Cluny A view of the monastic complex at Cluny in the early twelfth century. Note the basilica (the largest church in Europe until the sixteenth century), the cloister (to the left, actually south, of the basilica, with its dormitory in the foreground and refectory opposite the basilica), and the workshops. *(Based on a drawing from* Cluny des Églises et la Maison du Chef d'Ordre, *by R. J. Conant. Courtesy, Medieval Academy of America)*

Reformers in the more ascetic eremitic tradition (see page 217) desired more profound changes. They criticized the monastery at Cluny, saying that it had become too opulent and successful, and the monastery at Gorze because it seemed too immersed in worldly affairs. A desire to build new communities according to their vision of the apostolic church, featuring a life of poverty, self-denial, and seclusion, captivated the ascetics. Thus, the eleventh and early twelfth centuries saw a proliferation of both male and female experiments in eremitic monasticism. Other Europeans believed that the apostolic calling demanded not only an austere regimen of

personal renunciation but also an active life of Christian ministry. Cathedral clergy, called canons, in particular, adapted the rule of Saint Augustine so that they could live a communal life and also carry out priestly duties.

The greatest critics of the Cluniac tradition, and the real monastic elite of the early twelfth century, were the Cistercians. In 1098 Abbot Robert left his Burgundian monastery of Molesme° because he believed it had abandoned the strict teachings of Saint Benedict. He founded a new monastery at Cîteaux° in Burgundy. This

---

Molesme (MOE-lem)   **Cîteaux** (SEE-toe)

house was to follow the Benedictine Rule literally and to refuse all secular entanglements: lands, rents, and servile dependents. So rigorous and poor was the community that it struggled until a charismatic young Burgundian nobleman named Bernard (1090–1153) joined in 1112. Three years later Bernard left to found a daughter house at Clairvaux, of which he remained abbot for the rest of his life. Through his writing, preaching, and personal example, Bernard dominated the religious life of Europe in his lifetime. By the end of the twelfth century there were about 500 Cistercian (from the Latin for *Cîteaux*) monasteries in Europe, and Bernard's own Clairvaux had 700 monks. Initially the Cistercians wished to be an order of adult men. They successfully avoided admitting young boys, but by 1200 they had authorized about 100 convents of Cistercian nuns.

And it was not just the Cistercians and the traditional Benedictines who attracted women. The twelfth century saw many new communities of women from England to eastern Europe. The age's growing prosperity and population contributed both potential nuns and healthy endowments, but the key factor was that women were responding to the spiritual forces of the age in the same way men were.

With the monastic clergy gaining so much in prestige and visibility, the episcopal clergy countered with its own view of society. Surely, the bishops agreed, spiritual, moral, and intellectual improvement were desirable. Likewise, it was time to end the grossest examples of lay interference in the church. But precisely because so many bishops came from great families and were so well connected, they were less inclined to be rigid about the line of demarcation between lay and clerical responsibilities. In Germany, for example, the king's chapel recruited young noblemen to train them as clerics and to inculcate in them the policies and ethos of the court. Many of these chaplains were appointed to bishoprics and then advanced the king's interests in their new ecclesiastical areas of authority. They were often men of spiritual depth and resented what they regarded as monastic carping about their worldliness. By the middle of the twelfth century, bishops, and finally popes, too, had imposed on the church a view that monks belonged in their monasteries and that bishops should lead society.

It was always the special responsibility of the clergy to look after the moral order of society. In the turbulent world of gentlemen-warriors, the church had its own ideas about what a perfect "fighter" should do. The English bishop and scholar John of Salisbury (d. 1180), reflecting on knighthood in the twelfth century, concluded that it existed "to protect the church, to attack infidelity, to reverence the priesthood, to protect the poor, to keep the peace, to shed one's blood and, if necessary, to lay down one's life for one's brethren."

Turning large numbers of violent young men into servants of the church was a tall order for the clergy, and they had only limited success. One strategy that worked was the creation of military orders. The Palestine-based Knights of St. John, or Hospitallers, and Knights of the Temple, or Templars, are the major examples, but others existed in Spain and Germany. The Hospitallers started near Jerusalem as a foundation under Benedictine auspices dedicated to charitable works and care of the sick. They evolved into a monastic order using a version of the Rule of Saint Benedict and devoted themselves to the defense of pilgrims to the Holy Land. The Templars were men living under religious rule and sworn to protect the small states created by the Crusaders (see pages 309–311). These military orders measured up very well to the clergy's idea of what a perfect knight should be.

The clergy could also regulate disputes in society. For example, when a community was divided by a difficult conflict that demanded resolution, it might turn to the *ordeal*—a judicial procedure that sought divine judgment by subjecting the accused to a physically painful or dangerous test. An accused person might walk a certain distance carrying hot iron or plunge a hand into a boiling cauldron to pluck out a pebble. The resulting wounds would be bandaged for a set time and then examined. If they were healing, the person was considered innocent; if festering, guilty. The clergy officiated at ordeals until the papacy forbade their participation in 1215.

Clergymen were also the conservators of the shrines where people gained special access to the holiness of the saints. The clergy wrote and preached about the miracles of the saints, and stories circulated through the church about relics, or artifacts associated with these martyrs. The shrines where relics were preserved attracted pilgrims seeking healing from illness, injury, or misfortune. The clergy thus played unique roles in forming and nurturing communities in the world and in interceding for this world with God in the next.

■ Those Who Fight: The Nobility

In recent years scholars have spilled a sea of ink trying to define the medieval nobility. The matter is important because even though the nobility constituted only a small minority of the total population, nobles were and expected to be the ruling class. To appreciate their crucial role, we need to consider the shape of the nobility and the nobles' lifestyle and ethos.

The Knight at Prayer   This stained glass window from Chartres depicts the church's idealized conception of one of God's warriors: his sword and pious disposition combat the enemies of religion.
(Sonia Halliday Photographs)

In English the word *noble* can be either an adjective or a noun. More commonly, it is an adjective, as in a "noble sentiment" or a "noble deed." Before the twelfth century, the Latin *nobilis* was almost exclusively an adjective. The word pertained to certain desirable personal qualities. Then, gradually, the word became a noun and pertained to a certain kind of person.

What kind of a person? In the ideal case, a noble was a well-born, cultivated, office-holding soldier. In the earlier Middle Ages, many men held offices without necessarily being considered noble. Virtually all free men were expected to be soldiers, but few of them ranked as nobles. It was in the century or so following the feudal revolution (see page 295) that these distinct elements were fused into a single social order.

In a world in which lords were everywhere extending their power, military prowess became more valuable. At the same time, the need for horses and for more expensive arms and armor made it almost impossible for ordinary freemen to be soldiers. Likewise, ambitious lords who wished to expand their influence, and who were often, in an expanding economy, more prosperous than their forebears, were looking for ways to use their resources to gain followers. These trends came together as lords granted to their followers either military gear or lands, which would generate the income necessary to obtain arms and horses. We call those followers "vassals" and the lands they obtained "fiefs°." Vassalage became a widespread institution all over Europe and fief-holding became a normal accompaniment to vassalage. By contrast vassalage was unusual in the Carolingian world and rarely connected with fief-holding (see page 262).

These vassals, often called knights by contemporary sources, obviously could not claim high birth or venerable ancestry. Nor were they initially officeholders appointed by kings or emperors. Moreover, they were not wealthy and could not sustain the kind of lavish lifestyle that one might expect from nobles. Across the eleventh and twelfth centuries, knights saw their status change, in part because they aped the behavior of the nobles who themselves accepted the necessity of military ability.

All over Europe, especially where royal power was ineffective, both knights and nobles secured tighter control of peasant labor. This process provided knights and nobles with the money to build castles and to acquire fine possessions. As governments expanded their competence, these nobles and knights often held high offices, or if they did not, they pressured kings to concede such offices to them. Lords also tended to gather their lands into coherent blocks and to name themselves after the castles they built on their lands. Families also began to produce genealogies tracing their ancestry to relatives in the distant past, and to kings if at all possible. At the same time, families began to practice primogeniture— that is, reserving their lands, castles, and titles to the *primus genitus*, or "first-born" son.

This allotment of the choicest inheritances to a shrinking group turned loose a large number of younger sons. Many of them entered the clergy, a tendency that helps to explain the rising aristocratic character of the church. It should be emphasized right away, however, that this was not a punishment. Sons were not "dumped" on the church. Clerical careers were prestigious and relatively comfortable. But more numerous than clerics were the young men who were without an estate and who lacked the means to secure a bride and to form a family of their own. It was from these men that vast crusading armies were recruited. These were also the men who traipsed about Europe looking for fame and fortune, or failing that, a lord to serve. Many of these "young" men were 30 or 40 years old. They were called young because they had not yet established themselves.

So, by 1200 the nobility was a group identified by the profession of arms, the holding of office, a consciousness of family traditions, and an elevated lifestyle. A spe-cific ethos—chivalry—belonged to the nobility. Today, chivalry is often thought of as either an elaborate code of conduct regulating relations between the sexes or the value system behind the literary image of dashing knights in shining armor saving damsels in distress from fire-breathing dragons. Actually, its very name derives from *cheval,* French for "horse," the classic conveyance of a knight, a *caballarius* in Latin. Chivalry began as the code of conduct for mounted warriors.

Chivalry highly esteemed certain masculine, militant qualities. Military prowess was the greatest of chivalric virtues. A knight who was not a great warrior was useless. Literature of the time exalts the knight who slays fearsome beasts or the hero who single-handedly overwhelms impossible numbers of the enemy. Open-handed generosity was another key virtue. The truly noble person engaged in sumptuous display to manifest his power, to show concern for his dependents, and to enlarge his entourage. Medieval literature is full of rich banquets and stunning presents. In Anglo-Saxon England the king was called "the giver of rings." Knights were obsessed with their honor, their reputations. They sought glory, the better to win a lord or a bride or, if a lord already, to attract followers.

Chivalry also involved loyalty, the glue that held feudal society together. But we must take into account statements such as the following one by a twelfth-century English historian, William of Malmesbury: "They [knights] are faithful to their lords, but swift to break faith. A breath of ill fortune and they are plotting treachery, a bag of money and their mind is changed." Knights, especially the "young," were loyal to their lords when they could be, but fundamentally they were loyal to themselves.

What role was left to noblewomen in a world of chivalry and lordship? By the late eleventh century three developments adversely affected the position of aristocratic women. First, the elaboration of the chivalric ethos defined most key social and political roles as military and "manly" and thereby excluded women. By the middle of the twelfth century it was rare for a woman to hold a castle and unheard-of for one to ride to arms. Second, the consolidation of lineages by aristocratic families accompanied a moral campaign by the church to promote monogamous, unbreakable marriages. This situation subordinated women's freedom in the marriage market to the dynastic and patrimonial demands of great families. Third, the spread of lordship, with its intricate network of personal and proprietary relationships based on military service, tended to deprive women of independent rights over land.

But every rule has its exceptions. As noble families married off fewer of their daughters to noblemen, "extra"

fiefs (FEEFS)

daughters account in part for the dramatic increase in the number and size of convents. Convents of aristocratic nuns were places where women could be highly educated and almost entirely in control of their own affairs. Matilda, daughter of the German empress Adelaide, was abbess of Quedlinburg, mistress of vast estates in northern Germany, and a dominant figure in German politics. But knights looking for brides would often marry the younger daughters of noblemen because, if they could establish a household, then any children born of that marriage could lay claim to the noble lineage of their maternal grandfathers.

Less predictably, Gaita, wife of a Norman prince in Italy, fought in helmet and armor alongside her husband, as did Duchess Agnes of Burgundy. And let us reflect on the career of Adela of Blois (ca. 1067–1137). She was a daughter of William the Conqueror, the wife of a powerful French count, and the mother of King Stephen I of England (see page 297). In addition to regularly accompanying her husband as he administered his county, Adela founded monasteries, promoted religious reform, hosted Pope Paschal II, helped to reconcile her brother Henry I with the archbishop of Canterbury (thus averting an English investiture controversy), issued formal legal judgments, held fairs, and skillfully negotiated the aristocratic politics of western France after her husband's death. Adela may be unusual because we know so much about her. In other words, noblewomen in high medieval society may often have led interesting, active lives.

■ Those Who Work: The Peasants

The peasants were the "workers" in the tripartite model. An extremely diverse segment of society, "peasants" ranged from slaves to free persons of some means. Except in frontier zones, where victims were available and religious scruples diminished, slaves declined dramatically in numbers during the tenth and eleventh centuries (as illustrated by the shift in meaning of the classical Latin *servus* from "slave" to "serf"). Serfs, persons bound to the soil, everywhere constituted the majority of the peasants, although their legal and social statuses differed considerably from place to place. In the twelfth century serfdom was disappearing in France even as its terms were hardening in central and eastern Europe. Serfdom was a mixture of economic, legal, and personal statuses. The serf could be flogged in public, could be set upon by dogs, was excluded from many judicial proceedings, required approval to contract a marriage, and was denied the right to bear arms.

The tenth and eleventh centuries were decisive in the reshaping of rural society. As lordships of all kinds and sizes formed in the countryside, they drew communities of people. Castles were critical. Powerful men generally sited their castles in close proximity to wood, water, and iron. Sometimes a monastery, rural church, or graveyard also attracted a castle or else grew up near one and helped to anchor a site. (See the feature "Weighing the Evidence: The Medieval Castle" in Chapter 9 on pages 314–315.)

People from a fairly wide area settled in the vicinity of the castle. Many, originally free, commended themselves to the local lord by handing over their properties and receiving them back in return for rents or personal services. Other people fell into dependent status through military or economic misfortune. What eventually emerged was the manor, an institution best described as a powerful lord controlling the lives of an often large number of dependents. He required payments and services from them and regulated their ordinary disputes. His control was simultaneously public and private.

A minor castellan, or lord of a castle, might control only a small manor and would probably be the vassal of a great lord. A powerful landed lord, on the other hand, would generally control many manors and would often give some of them to retainers as fiefs. In other words, the reorganization of the countryside affected the nobility and the peasantry and created parallel sets of vertical bonds of association: Feudal lords and vassals entered into political bonds; lords and peasants entered into economic bonds.

The structure of individual manors, and the dues owed by peasants, varied tremendously across Europe. Certain trends were fairly consistent, however. As the economy expanded, as trade brought more and different products into Europe, and as a more consciously aristocratic lifestyle spread, the nobility began to want disposable cash. Thus, in many places corvées° (labor services) were commuted into cash payments. Peasants were required to pay rent from their own holdings instead of working on the lord's lands. But lords still needed provisions, so they sometimes split peasant payments into cash and kind. Old forms of service could be wholly retained, involving many days per year of work on the lord's demesne, the portion of the manor the lord reserved for his own benefit. In such cases, the lord could still extract money from his peasants by requiring them to use his mill and oven and then charging them gristing and kilning fees.

---

corvées (KOR-vays)

The Furnishings of a Welsh Household

This passage from the laws of Howell the Good concerns the distribution of household property in case of divorce. The aim was to achieve a nearly even split. Notice the kinds of objects a house might hold and who got what.

The husband shall have all the pigs, the wife the sheep. The husband shall have all the horses and mares, the oxen and cows, bullocks and heifers; the wife shall have the goats. . . . All the vessels for milk, except one pail, are the wife's; all the dishes, except one meat dish, are the husband's. One cart and yoke are the wife's. All the jars and drinking vessels are the husband's. Of the bedding, the husband shall have all the bedclothes which are beneath, the wife those which are above. The husband shall have the cauldron, the pillow, the winnowing sheet, the coulter, the wood axe, the gimlet [hole-borer], the flog, all the sickles except one, and the gridiron. The wife shall have the pan and the tripod, the broadaxe and the sieve, the ploughshare, the flax and the seed of the flax, and the precious things except gold and sil-ver. If there are any of these (gold or silver) they are to be divided in two equal parts. The products of the loom shall be divided in two equal parts, both linens and woolens. The husband shall have the barn and the grain and whatever is above or in the ground, and the hens and the geese and one cat. The wife shall have the meat that is salted and the cheese that is fresh . . . and the vessel of butter . . . and the ham . . . and as much of the flour as she can carry. Each of them shall have his or her personal clothing, except the cloaks, which shall be divided.

Source: Ian F. Fletcher, ed. and trans., *Latin Redaction A of the Law of Hywel* (Aberystwyth, Wales: Center for Advanced Welsh and Celtic Studies, 1986), pp. 58–59.

The trend everywhere, however, was for labor services to diminish. In one region in northern France, twelfth-century peasants owed only three corvées of two days' each per year for harvesting and haymaking. Elsewhere, peasants might still be required to haul crops to market or to keep roads, bridges, and buildings in repair. On many estates where the menfolk had been largely freed from corvées, the women might still have to work in the lord's house washing laundry, sewing, plucking fowl, cooking, minding dogs, and tending to other household chores.

In the expanding economy of the eleventh and twelfth centuries, the peasants grew more prosperous, and their lords constantly sought new ways to extract the fruits of that prosperity. Peasants thus began to band together to demand that "customs" be observed. These customs were more-or-less formal agreements spelling out the terms under which work and fees would be arranged. In general, life improved for the peasants in terms of both legal status and living conditions.

The European village was a key product of the tenth and eleventh centuries. People who originally gathered together around a castle for security and livelihood began to form a durable human community. Their church and graveyard helped to reinforce the community by tying together the living and the dead and by giving the village a sense of memory and continuity. Peasants generally worked only 250 to 270 days per year so they had a good deal of time for festivals and celebrations. Births, baptisms, betrothals, and deaths provided opportunities for the community to come together and affirm its mutual ties. Market days and sessions of the lord's court also assembled the village. Villagers needed to cooperate in many of the operations of daily life. They shared tools, plow teams, and wagons. They performed their corvées together. The peasants experienced much less social differentiation than the nobility, and so less tension.

The status of women in peasant society tended to be, in legal theory and in daily reality, the same as that of men at a time when the status of aristocratic women was fragile. Marriage contracts from northern Italy show that brides often entered marriages with a complement of valuable tools. This suggests that peasant women retained some control over their own personal property and also reminds us that the huge gains in rural productivity are almost certainly attributable in part to the work and ingenuity of women. (See the box "Reading Sources: The Furnishings of a Welsh Household.")

■ Those Left Out: Townspeople and Jews

The tripartite model excluded two important groups of people. The first neglected group consisted of the increasingly numerous citizens of Europe's growing towns. Obviously people in towns worked; but the prejudices of the aristocracy were rural, so the only "workers" deemed necessary to the smooth functioning of the social order were farmers. In the second group were Europe's principal religious minority, the Jews. Jews could be found almost everywhere although they constituted only about 1 percent of the population as a whole and, outside of Rome and parts of Spain, formed no single community numbering more than 1,500 to 2,000.

The central factor in the growth of towns was the rise in the productivity and profitability of medieval agriculture. For the first time in history, a regular and substantial farm surplus could support an urban population that did not produce its own food. Increased local exchange, coupled with the relentless growth of a money economy, meant there were fortunes to be made and cash to be spent. Some of that cash was spent on luxury and exotic products that increasingly became the objects of far-flung commercial networks. A good part of the cash was spent by rural nobles, who earned it from rents, booty, and the profits of the private exercise of public power. When those nobles moved into towns, they created opportunities for merchants, craftsmen, day laborers, domestic servants, and professional people such as notaries and lawyers. This was particularly true in Europe's most heavily urbanized regions: Flanders, southern France, and northern Italy. The key point is that the growth of the medieval city and of its human community began in the medieval countryside.

Town society was hierarchical, but its structures were new, ill defined, and flexible. Rich men built up bands of followers who supported them in urban politics, protected their neighborhoods, and occasionally

San Gimignano The towers of this Tuscan city reveal the concentrated and competitive nature of power in the Italian communes. Most of these towers date from around 1300. *(Scala/Art Resource, NY)*

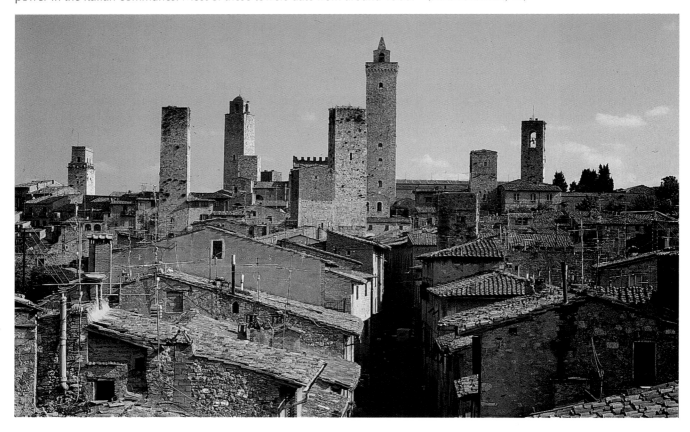

raided the houses of their enemies in the next neighbor-hood. Relatives, friends, neighbors, people from a common rural district, or those engaged in similar trades tended to worship together in particular churches, observe certain festivals, and look after one another's families.

In the rapidly changing world of the tenth and eleventh centuries, towns provided numerous opportunities for women. In urban industries such as cloth making, tanning, laundering, and brewing, women sometimes managed and even owned enterprises. Apart, perhaps, from finance and the law, distinctions between male and female roles were not as sharp in towns as in rural areas.

If urban men and all women stood in an ambiguous relationship to the ideals of the male, rural, aristocratic elite, we can hardly imagine what it must have been like for Jews. Jewish communities had existed in most European towns since antiquity. Then, because the Byzantine and Islamic worlds vacillated between persecution and toleration, many Jews migrated to western Europe, with the largest numbers settling in northern France and the German Rhineland. The Jewish community in England formed only around 1100. Paris had northern Europe's largest Jewish community, perhaps 2,000 people in the twelfth century. Many cities had Jewish populations numbering 200 to 300, but groups of 40 or 50 were common. Although some Jews in Italy, Spain, and Germany owned farms and vineyards, most Jews settled in cities, where they could live and worship in community with other Jews. Urban clusters also provided strength in numbers for people who could at any moment fall victim to persecution and whose power was not based on landholding.

Three of the most important developments in high medieval Europe were disastrous for the Jews. First, the growth of the European economy with its attendant urban and commercial expansion brought countless Christians into the practice of trade, an occupation dominated by Jews since Late Antiquity. As Jews were excluded from commercial opportunities, they were more and more confined to moneylending. Jews had been moneylenders before the economic surge of the High Middle Ages, and they were never alone in this practice. But the expanding economy made financial operations more widespread than ever before. Given that, as we saw in Chapter 9, Christian moralists considered handling money to be the devil's own work, the visibility of Jews as moneylenders brought them much criticism.

The second phenomenon that adversely affected Jews was the reform of the church. With so much attention being paid to the proper Christian life and the cor-rect organization of the church, it was inevitable that more attention would be directed to the one prominent group in Western society that was not Christian.

Third, the Crusades unleashed vicious attacks on the Jews. As crusading armies headed east in 1096, they visited unspeakable massacres on the Jewish communities of several German towns. This awful process was repeated on the eve of the Second Crusade in 1146–1147 and again just before the third in 1190. Popular frenzy identified the Jews as Christ-killers and equated them with Muslims as the enemies of Christianity. In fact, and despite grotesque and groundless stories about Jews kidnapping and ritually killing Christian children, Jews everywhere wished to live in peace with their Christian neighbors and to be left alone to observe their distinctive religious, dietary, and social customs.

The Jews were not without sympathetic champions, however. From the time of Gregory I (r. 590–604), the papacy urged peaceful coexistence and prayers for Jewish conversion. In the twelfth and thirteenth centuries, popes forcefully reminded Christians that while converting Jews was highly desirable, Jews were to be tolerated and left in peace. The Carolingians had protected the Jews, and some kings in succeeding centuries repeated or even expanded upon Carolingian legislation. Spanish Jews were taken under royal protection in reconquered areas in 1053, and Henry IV took German Jews under his protection in 1084. In England and France Jews enjoyed royal protection until the late twelfth century. Jews frequently served as royal advisers in Spain and were often entrusted with sensitive diplomatic missions elsewhere.

Despite such policies, Jews were vulnerable to attack at almost any time from people who simply disliked them or who owed them money. But in 1181 Philip II of France, always on the lookout for income, had his henchmen arrest Jews and confiscate their possessions. In 1182 he expelled them from the royal demesne. Across the thirteenth century French kings accorded the Jews less and less protection and often abused them financially. In 1306 Philip IV expelled the Jews from France after confiscating their goods. In England the story is much the same. The impecunious Henry II laid crushing taxes on the Jews in 1171. In 1189 in London and in 1190 in York, massive riots stirred by false rumors raged against the Jewish populations. In 1290 Edward I seized Jewish possessions and expelled them from the country. Royal protection of German Jews was reasonably effective until the death of Frederick II in 1250, after which time local princes often repudiated debts to Jewish lenders and appropriated Jewish property.

Social and Religious Movements, ca. 1100–1300

WELFTH- and thirteenth-century Europe witnessed several social movements unlike any that had occurred before. Spurred by increasingly intrusive governments, economic dislocation, and spiritual turmoil, they involved large numbers of people; cut across lines of gender, wealth, status, and occupation; and appeared in many places. Most of these movements had cohesive beliefs, even ideologies, and well-determined goals. They are the first large-scale social movements in European history.

◼ Heretics and Dissidents

The canon lawyer Gratian (see page 335) defined *heresy* as a situation in which "each man chooses for himself the teaching he believes to be the better one"; that is, he ignores official doctrines. For Gratian and his like-minded contemporaries, faith was not an individual matter. Unity of belief was crucial in a Catholic ("universal") Christian Europe. In the twelfth century, the church reacted ever more strictly to challenges to its teachings or to its exclusive right to teach. The effort by the church to define its law, theology, and bureaucratic procedures with greater precision drew lines more sharply than ever before between what was and was not acceptable.

Heretics did not see themselves as secessionists from the true church. Quite the contrary, they saw themselves as its only representatives. Church teachings always encountered a degree of popular skepticism. Not everyone believed, for example, that Jesus was born of a virgin or that he was true God and true man. But such doubts had not previously led to mass defections. Before the middle of the twelfth century, challenges to the church came from men—as far as we can tell the ringleaders were all men—who saw themselves as inspired reformers.

Tanchelm° of Antwerp preached between 1100 and 1115 in the Netherlands. He scandalized the mainstream by calling churches brothels and clerics whores. He rejected the sacraments and the payment of tithes. Although Tanchelm was radical and pugnacious, his ideas constituted a fairly coherent program of criticism. Like many others, he was concerned about the immorality and wealth of the church. But Tanchelm and his follow-

ers went even further. The heretic distributed his nail and hair clippings as relics of a sort, and in a bizarre public ceremony he "married" a statue of the Virgin Mary. Across the twelfth century church orthodoxy was challenged by others whose influence seems to have been local. What is interesting is how numerous, and similar, they all were.

Coherent movements of much larger proportions emerged later in the century. In 1173 Waldo, a rich merchant of Lyon, decided to sell all his property, give the proceeds to the poor, and embrace a life of poverty and preaching. Waldo was motivated by the same quest for the apostolic life that had animated the eremitical movement of the eleventh century. But there was a difference: he was a layman. Waldo attracted many followers (known as Waldensians), and in 1179 Pope Alexander III (r. 1159–1181) scrutinized him closely, found his beliefs to be essentially correct, and approved his vow of poverty. But the pope commanded Waldo to preach only when invited to do so by bishops. The bishops, jealous about their own power, extended no such invitations.

Waldo and his "Poor Men of Lyon" went right on preaching and in 1184 were formally declared heretics. Until this point it was not their ideas so much as their appropriation of a clerical duty, preaching, that had set the church against them. From this time on, however, the Waldensians became more radical in their attacks. In about 1204 one group of Waldensians was reconciled to the Catholic Church; but the majority, who had spread all over southern France and Italy, into Germany, and as far away as Poland, remained estranged. Waldensian communities exist to this day.

The most serious of the popular heretical movements was Catharism (from the Greek *katharos,* meaning "pure"). Because there were numerous Cathars near the southern French town of Albi, the whole movement is sometimes called "Albigensian." In fact, Cathars could be found all over Europe, although they did cluster in northern Italy and southern France. Cathars were the religious descendants of Mani (see page 198), a third-century Persian who taught an extreme dualism that featured polarities in almost all things: good-evil, love-hate, flesh-spirit. Extreme Cathars abstained from flesh in all ways: they were vegetarians and renounced sexual intercourse so as not to produce offspring—that is, more flesh. Probably radiating from Bulgaria, Cathar ideas had spread widely in the West by the 1140s. Catharism attracted many converts when Nicetas, the Cathar bishop of Constantinople, visited northern Italy and southern France between 1166 and 1176. People of every station joined the new church, which, in its own view, was the only true church.

Tanchelm (TANK-elm)

The Expulsion of the Albigensians from Carcassone in 1209
This picture from a fourteenth-century manuscript depicts the grim realities of the Albigensian Crusade launched in 1208. But the Cathars of Carcassone fared less badly than those of Beziers, who were massacred.
(British Library)

The Catholic Church sent isolated preachers against the Cathars, but with little success. In 1198 and 1203, Pope Innocent III organized systematic preaching tours in southern France, but these too lacked solid results, and in 1208 the pope's legate was murdered by a supporter of the count of Toulouse, who was sympathetic to the Cathars. The killing led to the launching of the Albigensian Crusade, a loosely structured military action that lasted into the 1260s. Although the crusade itself was largely over by the 1220s, violence against Albigensians sputtered for decades: a massacre in 1244, and inquisitorial campaigns in 1246 and again in 1256–1257. Isolated resisters struggled on into the fourteenth century.

Albigensians denounced the clergy of their day as rich and corrupt. These teachings attracted urban dwellers who resented the wealth and pretensions of the clergy—the same people who followed Waldo. Nobles may have been drawn to the movement because it gave them opportunities to take possession of extensive tracts of church lands, something the investiture controversy had denied them. In addition, embracing Catharism may have been a way for nobles to resist the increasing encroachment of the government of far-off Paris. The Albigensians also attracted many women. Unlike the Catholic Church, which denied clerical, preaching, and teaching offices to women, the heretical sects tended to permit women to hold leading roles.

The Albigensians, like the Waldensians, were driven by the same spiritual zeal and desire for ecclesiastical reform that moved many of their contemporaries. They differed from other would-be reformers in that they did not seek to reform the Catholic Church from within but departed from it or insisted that they alone represented it. Thus these heretical movements marked the first serious challenge to the ideology of a uniformly Catholic Christendom since Late Antiquity. (See the box "Reading Sources: Pronouncements of the Fourth Lateran Council on Heresy.")

Pronouncements of the Fourth Lateran Council on Heresy

By 1215 the papacy had become alarmed at the number and strength of the heretical movements in Europe, and it began to take strong measures to counter the dissidents.

3. Convicted heretics shall be handed over for due punishment to their secular superiors, or the latter's agents. If they are clerks [members of the clergy], they shall first be degraded [lose their clerical rank]. The goods of the layman thus convicted shall be confiscated; those of the clergy shall be applied to the churches from which they drew their stipends. . . . If a temporal lord neglects to fulfil the demand of the church that he purge his land of the contamination of heresy, he shall be excommunicated by the metropolitan and other bishops of the province. If he fails to make amends within a year, it shall be reported to the Supreme Pontiff, who shall pronounce his vassals absolved from fealty to him and offer his land to Catholics. . . . Catholics who assume the cross and devote themselves to the extermination of heretics shall enjoy the same indulgence and privilege as those who go to the Holy Land. . . .

7. Further we add that every archbishop and bishop, in person or by his archdeacon or other suitable and trustworthy persons, shall visit each of his parishes, in which there are said to be heretics, at least once a year. And he shall compel three or more men of good reputation, or even, if need be, the whole neighborhood, to swear that, if any of them knows of any heretics or of any who frequent secret conventicles or who practise manners and customs different from those common amongst Christians, he will report them to the bishop; and, unless they clear themselves of the accusation, or if they relapse into their former mischief, they shall receive the canonical punishment.

Source: Henry Bettenson, *Documents of the Christian Church*, 2d ed. (London: Oxford University Press, 1963), p. 133.

■ Reform from Within: The Mendicant Orders

Traditional monastic orders continued to win adherents, but their interpretation of the apostolic life meant ascetic withdrawal from the world, not pastoral work and preaching. Laymen who wished both to embrace poverty and to preach fell under the suspicion of the ecclesiastical authorities. Early in the thirteenth century a new movement arose, the mendicants (literally, beggars). Mendicants were men who aimed to preach, to be poor, and to create formal but noncloistered religious orders. Though similar to the heretics in many ways, they submitted willingly to ecclesiastical authority.

The mendicant phenomenon began when Francis of Assisi° (1181–1226), the son of a rich Italian merchant, decided to renounce the wealth and status that were his

Assisi (uh-SEE-zee)

birthright. He carried out his renunciation in a most public display before the bishop of Assisi in 1206. Francis had gradually grown tired of a life of ease and luxury, but he also experienced a blinding moment of spiritual insight when, by chance, his eyes fell on the passage in the Scriptures in which Christ commanded the rich young ruler, "Go, sell all you have, and follow me." Francis stripped himself naked so "that naked he might follow the naked Christ."

For a few years Francis wandered about Italy begging for his meager sustenance, repairing churches, caring for the sick, and preaching repentance to all who would listen. By 1210 he had attracted many followers, and together they set out to see Innocent III to win approval. After considering the matter for a while, Innocent decided to approve the new order of friars (that is "brothers," from the Latin *fratres*) as long as they would accept monastic tonsure—a ritual haircut signifying

The Confirmation of the Rule of Saint Francis, 1223   This painting by Giotto di Bondone (1265–1337) depicts Pope Honorius III confirming the much-revised version of Francis's rule, first approved by Innocent III in 1210. Giotto, one of the greatest medieval painters, pioneered the use of geometric perspective.   *(Scala/Art Resource, NY)*

submission—profess obedience to the pope, and swear obedience to Francis. The pope was genuinely won over by Francis himself, but he also sensed that by permitting the formation of the Franciscan order, he could create a legitimate and controllable repository for the explosive spiritual forces of the age.

Francis prepared a simple Rule based on his understanding of the scriptural ideals of poverty, preaching, and service. Alarmed by the vagueness of the first Rule and by the extraordinary influx of new members, the papal curia in 1223 prevailed on Francis to submit a revision that stressed order, a hierarchy of officials, and a novitiate—a regularized period of training for new members. Somewhat disappointed by this regulated formality, Francis withdrew more and more from the world and lived reclusively in the hills near Assisi.

After Francis died, the issues of property, power, education, and ordination provoked deep controversies within his order. Usually called "Franciscan," Francis's order is technically the "Friars Minor." The movement had begun among laymen, but over time more Franciscan brothers became ordained priests. Franciscans established schools in most great cities, and by the middle of the thirteenth century some of Europe's greatest intellects were Franciscans. This prominence, like the sacramental power of ordination, was a kind of wealth that Francis had wished to avoid. The real issue of wealth, however, turned on the possession of property. Francis had aimed for both personal and corporate poverty. In the 1230s papal legislation had alleviated strict poverty by permitting the order to acquire property to support its work. Nevertheless, the issue of property continued to spark controversy among the Franciscans.

Of the nine or ten mendicant orders that developed, the other major one was the Dominican, a product of very different experiences than the Franciscan. Its founder, Dominic de Guzman (1170–1221), was the son of a Spanish nobleman. He became a priest and later a cathedral canon. While traveling, he saw firsthand the Albigensian heresy in southern France, and in 1206 he went to Rome to seek permission to preach against the heretics. The Albigensian Crusade began in 1208, but Dominic's methods were those of persuasion, not coercion.

Albigensian criticisms of the ignorance, indifference, and personal failings of the clergy could never be applied to Dominic and his fellow preachers. Dominic and his followers were supported enthusiastically by the bishop of Toulouse, who saw how useful these zealous preachers of unblemished lives could be. In 1215 Dominic, with his bishop's assistance, attempted to form a new order, but by that time Rome had forbidden the creation of new orders for fear of heresy or uncontrollable diversity. Thus, Dominic's "Order of Preachers" (the proper name for the "Dominicans") adopted the Rule of Saint Augustine, which many communities of cathedral canons had been using since the eleventh century.

In 1217 Dominic presided at the first general meeting of the order. The Dominicans decided to disperse, some going to Paris, some (including Dominic) to Rome, some to other cities in Europe. Henceforth, the order saw its mission as serving the whole church. Dominican schools were set up all over Europe, and the order acquired a reputation for learning and scholarship. The

Dominicans were voluntarily poor, but the order was never rent by a controversy over property as the Franciscans were. Dominic's was a vision of personal, not corporate, poverty. Likewise, as a preaching order, the Dominicans had to be learned and ordained. Franciscan misgivings on these issues did not touch them.

Both the Franciscan and Dominican orders reflected a widespread desire to emulate the apostolic life of the early church by poverty and preaching. Both submitted to legitimate authority. Francis's religious vision of charity and service was the product of a heartfelt need for repentance and renewal. This concern for the soul caused Franciscans often to serve as missionaries. Dominic set out to save the church from its enemies. He desired preachers who were sufficiently learned that they could combat the errors of heretics. Both men saw the need for exemplary lives. Francis was a more charismatic figure than Dominic, and his apostolate to the urban poor was more compelling. By 1300 Franciscan houses outnumbered Dominican by 3 to 1. The mendicants were the greatest spiritual force in high medieval Europe.

■ Communities of Women

The religious forces that attracted men drew women as well. Traditional orders, however, tended to be hostile to women. Cluniacs and Cistercians struggled to keep women out of their ranks. The wandering preachers of the twelfth century, without exception, acquired women as followers, but the usual results were either segregation of the women in cloisters or condemnation of the whole movement.

In 1212 Francis attracted the aristocrat Clare of Assisi (1194–1253), who was fleeing from an arranged marriage. She wanted to live the friars' life of poverty and preaching, and Francis wanted to assist her. Aware that the sight of women begging or preaching would be shocking, in 1215 he gave Clare and his other female followers their own rule. Clare became abbess of the first community of the "Poor Clares." Although cloistered and forbidden to preach, the Clares lived lives of exemplary austerity and attracted many adherents.

Beguines° were communities of women who lived together, devoted themselves to charitable works, but did not take vows as nuns. The Beguine movement grew from the work in Nivelles, near Liège°, of Mary of Oignies° (ca. 1177–1213). She was drawn to the ideals of voluntary

---

Beguines (BAY-geenz)   **Liège** (lee-EZHE)
Oignies (OWN-yeese)

poverty and service to others. So strong was the pull that she renounced her marriage, gave away all her goods, worked for a while in a leper colony, and thought of preaching against the Cathars. Instead she formed a community.

Groups of Beguines appeared all over the Low Countries, western Germany, and northern France. This was the first exclusively women's movement in the history of Christianity. Beguines sometimes vowed poverty and sometimes did not. They sometimes cloistered themselves into communities and sometimes taught and served the poor and outcast. They neither challenged the officials and teachings of the church nor demanded a right to preach. As laywomen, they did not give rise to scandal as noncloistered nuns would have. They were content to have power over their own lives and communities but not seek a voice in the wider world around them. (See the box "Reading Sources: New Orders for Women: Clares and Beguines.")

Thirteenth-century Europe knew more female than male mystics, and female mysticism tended to focus on Jesus, especially on His presence in the Eucharist. This is

The Parting of Mary from the Apostles   Duccio di Buoninsegna lived from the middle of the thirteenth century to 1318 or 1319. He did his finest work in Siena, including a huge altarpiece, one of whose panels depicts the touching scene of Mary taking leave of the apostles just before her death. Note the clever way Duccio has arranged the figures, and how he balances Saint Paul, standing in the doorway, with Mary, reclining on the bed.   *(Scala/Art Resource, NY)*

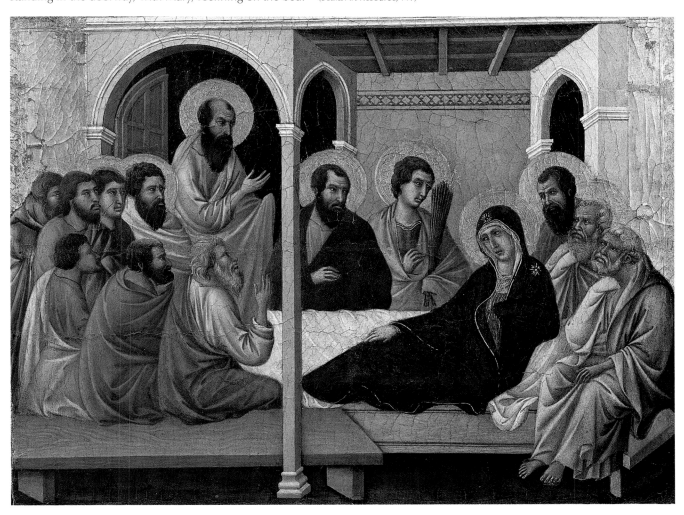

✦ READING SOURCES

New Orders for Women: Clares and Beguines

These excerpts, from the prologue to Clare's Rule and from a document detailing the origins of the Beguines, illustrate the initiative of women in the new religious orders. Observe too how the women's submission to authority relieved them from suspicion of heresy or insubordination.

Clare's Rule

Clare, the unworthy servant of Christ and the little plant of the most blessed Francis, promises obedience and reverence to the Lord Pope Innocent [III] and his canonically elected successors, and to the Roman Church. And, just as at the beginning of her conversion, together with her sisters she promised obedience to the Blessed Francis, so now she promises his successors to observe that same obedience inviolably, and the other sisters shall always be obliged to obey the successors of Blessed Francis and Sister Clare and other canonically elected abbesses who succeed her.

The Beguines

Those ladies of good memory, Joanna and her sister Margaret, successive countesses of Flanders and Hainault, noticed that the region was greatly abounding in women for whom, because of their own position or that of their friends, suitable marriages were not possible, and they saw that the daughters of re-

spectable men, both nobles and commoners, wished to live chastely, but could not easily enter a monastery because of the great number of these girls and the poverty of their parents, and that respectable and noble but impoverished damsels had to go begging or shamefully support themselves or seek support from their friends, unless some solution could be found. Then by divine inspiration, as it is piously believed, having first obtained the advice and consent of respectable men of the diocese and elsewhere, in various parts of Flanders they set up certain spacious places which are called Beguinages, in which the aforesaid women, girls, and damsels were received, so that living in common therein, they might preserve their chastity, with or without taking vows, and where they might support and clothe themselves by suitable work, without shaming themselves or their friends.

Source: Emilie Amt, *Women's Lives in Medieval Europe* (New York: Routledge, 1993), pp. 236, 264.

---

the first religious devotion that can be shown to have been more common to women than to men. Most of the mystics were either nuns or Beguines. As the clergy was defining its own prerogatives more tightly, and excluding women more absolutely from the exercise of formal public power, female communities provided a different locus for women's activity.

Women who spent their lives in community with other women reveal, in their writings, none of the sense of moral and intellectual inferiority that was routinely attributed to women by men and often by women themselves. Women who were in direct spiritual communion with God acquired, as teachers, mediators, and counselors in their communities, power that they simply could not have had outside those settings.

LATIN CULTURE: FROM SCHOOLS TO UNIVERSITIES

HE dynamism so evident in the economic, social, and political life of Europe is just as apparent in cultural life. As in the late antique and Carolingian periods, courts and churches were the greatest patrons of artists and authors. But in this age of expansion the number and geographic spread of such patrons increased dramatically. By 1150 the church comprised 50 percent more bishoprics and about three times as many monasteries as it had in 900. In 1300 monarchies reigned in many places—Scandinavia and the Slavic world, for example—where none had existed in

900. In addition to an increase in the sheer amount of cultural activity, the years between 900 and 1300 also witnessed innovations. Logic replaced grammar at the heart of the school curriculum. Latin letters remained ascendant, but literature in many vernacular (native) languages began to appear in quantity and quality. Romanesque art and architecture were fresh and original interpretations of their Carolingian ancestors. Europe's incipient urbanization produced the first stirrings of a distinctively urban culture. In one of those cities, Paris, a new kind of academic institution emerged—the university—which was arguably the period's greatest legacy to the modern world.

■ The Carolingian Legacy

Cultural life depends on both creative geniuses and generous patrons. Political dislocation and constant attacks in the ninth and tenth centuries initially deprived schools and masters of the Carolingian patronage that they had enjoyed for a century or more. The Carolingians left firm enough foundations in a few centers for intellectual life to continue, but the scale of activity between 900 and 1050 was smaller than before. Three examples serve to capture the spirit of the age that set the stage for the High Middle Ages.

Gerbert of Aurillac° (940–1003) was the most distinguished intellect of his age. He left his home in Aquitaine to study in Spain and Italy before settling in Reims, in northern France, where he was a teacher and then briefly a bishop. He attracted the attention of the emperor Otto III and spent some time at the German court, earning appointments as abbot of Bobbio, bishop of Ravenna, and, finally, pope. Gerbert followed Carolingian tradition in being a collector of manuscripts and critic of texts, but he departed from older traditions in his interest in mathematics and in his study of logic, the formal rules of reasoning that, in the Western tradition, trace back over many thinkers to Aristotle (see pages 97–98).

Fulbert of Chartres° (960–1028), Gerbert's finest pupil, elevated the cathedral school of Chartres to the paramount place in academic Europe. Fulbert wrote letters in elegant Latin and composed fine poems. He carried on his master's literary interests more than his scientific ones, and well into the twelfth century Chartres remained a major center of literary studies.

Another figure of interest is the aristocratic German nun Roswitha of Gandersheim (d. 970). She wrote poems on saints and martyrs, as well as a story about a priest who sold his soul to the devil. In her mature years, Roswitha wrote Latin plays in rhymed verse based on the Roman writer Terence. In these plays she refashioned tales from Roman and biblical history to convey moral truths.

■ The Study of Law

Law was a field of major innovation. The increasing sophistication of urban life demanded a better understanding of law. The growing responsibilities of the church called for orderly rules, and the church's frequent quarrels with secular rulers demanded careful delineations of rights and responsibilities. Governments issued more laws and regulations than at any time since antiquity.

In about 1012, Burchard, bishop of Worms, produced a collection of canon law that was influential for more than a century and heightened reformers' awareness of the law of the church. By midcentury, scholars studying canon law in Italy and France helped to promote the papal view of reform. In Bologna (see map 10.1), Irnerius° (d. ca. 1130), a transplanted German and protégé of Emperor Henry V, began teaching Roman law from the law code of Justinian (see page 226). This legal work culminated in the publication in 1140 of the *Decretum* of the Bolognese monk Gratian°. The most comprehensive and systematic book of canon law yet written, Gratian's work remained authoritative for centuries.

Throughout the twelfth century, canon lawyers studied and wrote commentaries on Gratian's *Decretum.* These legists are called "decretists." Gratian had systematically collected earlier papal decretals, official pronouncements, but popes continued to issue them. Several collections of these new decretals were prepared in the thirteenth century, and the scholars who studied these later decrees are called "decretalists." The church thus produced a vast corpus of law and of legal commentary.

Law was by no means confined to the church. England was precocious in creating a common law, a single law applied uniformly in its courts. But English law was based on the careful accumulation of legal decisions—or precedents—and not on the routine application of the provisions of a law code. Of law codes elsewhere, there were many. Alfonso X of Castile issued the *Siete Partidas*, a comprehensive law code largely reliant on Roman law. Prince Iaroslav (d. 1054) is reputed to have issued the first version of the laws of the Kievan Rus (see Map 9.5 on page 296). Iaroslav's laws were written in Old Russian but

---

Gerbert of Aurillac (DJAIR-bear of OR-ee-ak)
Fulbert of Chartres (FULL-bear of SHART)

Irnerius (ear-NAIR-ee-us)   **Gratian** (GRAY-shun)

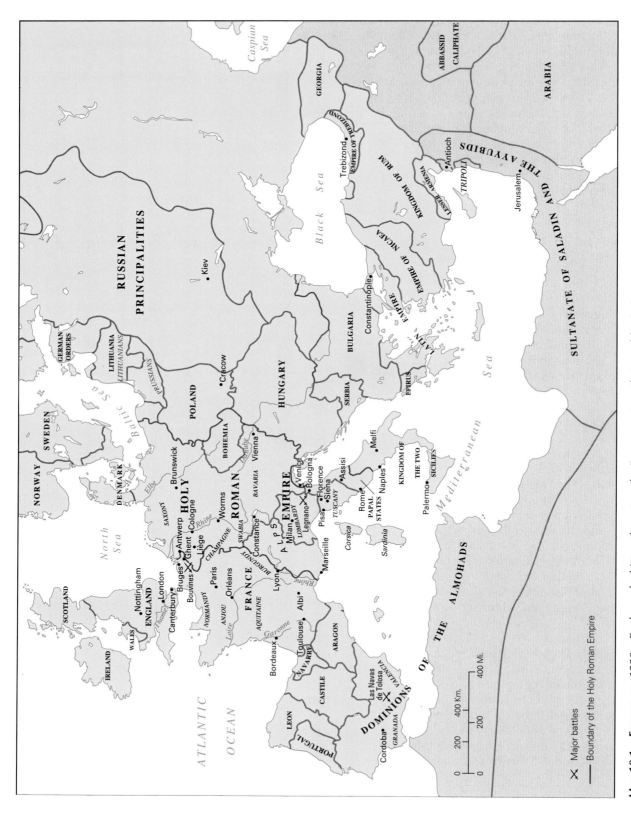

Map 10.1 Europe, ca. 1230 By the early thirteenth century the European states that would exist into modern times were clearly visible, although each would continue to undergo changes. To gain a sense of the evolution of Europe, compare this map with Maps 6.1, 7.3, and 8.3.

they drew heavily on the laws and legal traditions of neighboring peoples. Byzantine law was revised under the Macedonian dynasty.

■ Greek, Arab, and Jewish Contributions

Norman and German settlement in southern Italy and Sicily, the Reconquista in Spain, the Crusades, and the creation of Italian communities in many Mediterranean cities brought European thinkers face to face with the intellectual traditions of classical Greece, Islam, and medieval Judaism. Between 1100 and 1270 almost the whole corpus of Aristotle's writings, virtually unknown in the West for a millennium, became available. Arab commentaries on Aristotle, as well as Jewish philosophical and theological works, began to circulate. The presence of all these texts and currents of thought was decisive in expanding the range and raising the level of Western thought.

Prior to about 1100 only a few of Aristotle's writings had been available in the West, primarily some of his early writings on logic. Gradually scholars recovered Aristotle's full treatment of logic, then his scientific writings, and finally his studies of ethics and politics. Aristotle's books posed a number of problems for Christian scholars. If knowledge is a good thing, and good things are gifts of God, how did a pagan get so smart? Is it possible that faith is unnecessary to knowledge? What relationship exists between faith and reason? Aristotle taught that the universe was eternal and mechanistic. His thought left no room for creation or for the continuing role of a Creator. For Christian thinkers Aristotle asked questions that demanded answers: Were the Scriptures true? Did God create the world as Genesis said? Did God continue to intervene in this world?

Between 750 and 900, mainly in Iran, a group of Arabic-speaking Christians began translating into Arabic the Greek texts of Aristotle as well as the more than fifteen thousand pages of commentary on Aristotle that had been produced between about A.D. 100 and 600. These translators were Monophysite Christians chased out of Syria by Emperor Heraclius when he conquered the area from the Persians (see page 247). This flood of material inspired generations of Arab scholars to tackle the thought of the man often called simply "The Philosopher."

Two major Arab thinkers were particularly influenced by the vast Aristotelian corpus. Ibn-Sina (980–1037), called Avicenna° in the West, was drawn to the fundamental problem of how to understand the relationship between objects that exist in the world and the knowledge of those objects that is formed and held in the human mind. (See the box "Global Encounters: The Making of an Arab Scholar.") Ibn Rushd (1126–1198), called Averroes°, wrote no fewer than thirty-eight commentaries on the works of Aristotle, and at least fifteen of these were translated into Latin in the thirteenth century. Among many contributions, Averroes particularly tried to clarify the relationship between truths acquired through the exercise of reason and truths that depended on divine revelation. Although his exact meaning remains controversial, his contemporaries and many later scholars understood him to teach the "double truth." Truths about the natural world were more or less accessible to everyone depending on a person's intellectual ability. Revealed truths, however, were available only to the most enlightened.

Spain and northern France were both important centers of Jewish thought. In Spain some Jewish thinkers also grappled with Aristotle. Solomon ibn Gebirol (1021–1070), called Avicebron°, wrote *The Fountain of Life,* a treatise that attempted to reconcile Aristotle with the Jewish faith by finding a role for God in communicating knowledge to every human mind. The greatest of all medieval Jewish thinkers, Moses ben Maimon (1135–1204), called Maimonides°, wrote *A Guide for the Perplexed.* The perplexed he had in mind were those who had trouble reconciling the seemingly opposed claims of reason and faith. Maimonides taught a doctrine very close to Averroes's double truth.

Solomon ben Isaac (1040–1105), called Rashi, was educated in Jewish schools in the Rhineland and then set up his own school in Troyes°. He became the most learned biblical and Talmudic scholar of his time, indeed one of the wisest ever. The Talmud was a detailed and erudite commentary on the scriptural studies of the ancient rabbis. It existed in two collections made in the fifth century, one in Palestine and one in Babylon. Later in the twelfth century Rashi's grandsons carried on his work and earned great fame on their own. Christian scholars who wished to know the exact meaning of passages in the Bible sometimes consulted them.

From Persia to Spain to France, then, countless thinkers were engaged in serious reflection on the mechanics of knowing, the nature of reality, the relationship between reason and faith, and the meaning and significance of revelation. In the years just around 1100, Latin Christian scholars began to encounter this torrent of thought and writing.

Avicenna (ah-vih-SENN-uh)

Averroes (uh-VERR-oh-eese)   Avicebron (uh-VIH-sih-bron)
Maimonides (my-MON-uh-deez)   Troyes (TWAH)

⊕ G L O B A L   E N C O U N T E R S

The Making of an Arab Scholar

These excerpts from the engaging life of Avicenna reveal not only his remarkable intellectual attainments but also his ongoing encounter with Greek thought. Avicenna was deeply influenced by Aristotle, and, in turn, his writings influenced Jewish and Christian writers who were also coming to grips with the greatest of Greek philosophers. His writings on medicine were authoritative until the seventeenth century.

My father was from Balkh and moved from there to Bukhārā [now Turkmenistan] . . . where I was given teachers of the Quran and polite letters [literature, especially poetry]. By the time I was ten years old I had mastered the Quran and so much of polite letters as to provoke wonderment. My father decided to send me to a certain grocer who knew Indian arithmetic so that I could learn it from him. Then Abu Abdallah al-Natili, who claimed to be a philosopher, came to Bukhārā. My father lodged him in our house in the hope that I would learn something from him. Before he came I was studying jurisprudence . . . and I was one of the best pupils. Then, under the guidance of al-Natili, I began to study the *Isagogue* [a commentary on some of Aristotle's works]. Thus I learned from him the broad principles of logic, but he knew nothing of the subtleties. Then I began to read books and study commentaries on my own until I mastered logic. I also read the geometry of Euclid. Then I passed on to the *Almagest* [Ptolemy's second-century astronomical treatise]. Eventually I busied myself with the study of the [treatises] and other commentaries on physics and metaphysics [subjects treated at great length by Aristotle and by Avicenna's Arab predecessors, especially al-Farabi], and the doors of knowledge opened before me. Then I took up medicine and began to read books written on this subject. Medicine is not one of the difficult sciences, and in a very short time I undoubtedly excelled in it, so that physicians of merit studied under me. At the same time I carried on debates and controversies in jurisprudence. At this point I was sixteen years old.

I resumed the study of logic and all parts of philosophy. During this time I never slept a whole night through and I did nothing but study all day long.

Whenever I was puzzled by a problem . . . I would go to the mosque, pray, and ask the Creator of All to reveal to me that which was hidden from me and to make easy for me that which was difficult. Then at night I would return home, put a lamp in front of me, and set to work reading and writing.

I returned to the study of divine science. I read the book called *Metaphysics* [by Aristotle], but could not understand it, the aim of its author remaining obscure for me. I read the book forty times, until I knew it by heart, but I still could not understand its meaning or its purpose. Then one afternoon I happened to be in the market of the booksellers, and a crier was holding a volume in his hand and shouting the price. I bought it and found that it was Abu'l Nasr al-Farabi's book explaining the meaning of the *Metaphysics*. I returned to my house and made haste to read it. Immediately the purposes of this book became clear to me because I already knew it by heart. I was very happy at this, and the next day I gave much alms to the poor in thanksgiving to Almighty God.

In my neighborhood there lived a man who asked me to write him an encyclopedic work on all the sciences. I compiled the *Majmū* for him and named it after him. In it I dealt with all sciences other than mathematics. I was then twenty-one years old.

Source: Bernard Lewis, ed., *Islam: From the Prophet Muhammad to the Capture of Constantinople*, 2 vols. (New York: Harper and Row, 1974), vol. 2, pp. 177–181.

 For additional information on this topic, go to http://college.hmco.com.

■ The Development of Western Theology

Carolingian schools had focused on grammar, that is, on the basic foundations of language. Gradually logic supplanted grammar at the center of both intellectual interests and school curricula. Problems inside Europe initiated this shift, but soon the external influences we just described increased its scope. Eventually the wider application of logic produced a new intellectual style and also evoked bitter criticisms.

Berengar (ca. 1000–1088), master of the school of Tours, wrote a treatise that denied Christ's presence in the Eucharist—the communion bread and wine received by Catholics and Orthodox in the celebration of the mass. This position was heretical. Ordinarily, churchmen would have refuted Berengar simply by quoting various passages from the Scriptures or from the writings of the Church Fathers along with conciliar pronouncements about the consecrated elements. The evidence, however, was ambiguous. Berengar's claim was finally proved false, at least to the satisfaction of his opponents, by Lanfranc, archbishop of Canterbury during the reign of William the Conqueror. Lanfranc used Aristotelian logical argumentation to dispose of Berengar's heretical arguments.

Anselm (ca. 1033–1109), Lanfranc's successor as archbishop of Canterbury, developed an ingenious logical proof for the existence of God. The French theologian and philosopher Peter Abelard (1079–1142) used logic to reconcile apparent contradictions in the Scriptures and in the writings of the Church Fathers. We must not suppose that Anselm and Abelard were skeptics. Anselm's motto was "Faith seeking understanding." For him logic was the servant of divine truth. He would have agreed completely with Abelard's assessment that "Faith has no merit with God when it is not the testimony of divine truth that leads us to it, but the evidence of human reason."

For conservatives such as Bernard of Clairvaux (1090–1153) and Hildegard of Bingen (1098–1179), however, faith and immediate divine inspiration were primary. To them, logical approaches to divine truth were the height of arrogance. Hildegard, well educated, gifted musically, knowledgeable in medical matters, was perhaps the most profound psychological thinker of her age. More than anyone before her, Hildegard opened up for discussion the feminine aspects of divinity. She, like Bernard, believed that God was to be found deep within the human spirit, not in books full of academic wrangling. (See the box "Reading Sources: The Making of a Saint and Scholar: Hildegard of Bingen.")

The future lay with Anselm and Abelard, however. Anselm was the most gifted Christian thinker since Augustine. He wrote distinguished works on logic, and his theological treatise *Why God Became Man* (ca. 1100) served for three hundred years as the definitive philosophical and theological explanation of the incarnation of Christ, the central mystery of the Christian faith.

Peter Abelard was a more colorful figure. He argued rudely and violently with all his teachers, though in the end he was probably more intelligent than any of them. He rose to a keener understanding of Aristotle than anyone in centuries, and he developed a sharper sense of both the power and the limitations of language than anyone since the Greeks. He concerned himself with ethics, too, and was one of the first writers to see intention as more important than simple action.

Abelard seduced and then secretly married Heloise, one of his pupils and the daughter of an influential Paris churchman. Heloise's relatives castrated Abelard for his refusal to live openly with his wife. Abelard then arranged for Heloise to enter a convent, and he joined a monastic community, where he continued writing and teaching. The two carried on a voluminous correspondence that reveals Heloise as a first-rate philosophical thinker and one of her age's most knowledgeable connoisseurs of classical literature. Some of Abelard's more imaginative ideas earned him formal ecclesiastical condemnations in 1121 and 1140. He popularized the schools of Paris, however, and attracted to them promising scholars from all over Europe.

Abelard and several of his contemporaries engaged in one of the first widespread intellectual debates in Western history, the quarrel over "universals." *Universal* is the philosophical name for a concept that applies to more than one seemingly related object. The dispute over universals went to the heart of people's understanding of reality, their sense of the limitations of human reason, and their awareness of problems of language.

To illustrate: May we agree that you are reading a book right now? May we further agree that the book you are reading is not identical to any other book on your bookshelf? And may we go one step further and agree that no book on your bookshelf is exactly like any other book on that shelf? So, why do we call all of these objects books? "Book" is here the universal that we are trying to understand.

A medieval "realist," whose thought may be traced back to Plato, would say that there is a concept, let us call it "bookness," that exists in our minds before we ever encounter any particular object that we label a book. Just as no book is ever identical to any other, so too no specific

❧ READING SOURCES

The Making of a Saint and Scholar: Hildegard of Bingen

Although she was a great scholar, Hildegard's biographers stressed her native intelligence and divine inspiration more than her formal education.

When Henry IV was the king of the Holy Roman Empire, there lived in Rhenish Franconia a maiden lady well known because of her aristocratic background as well as her holiness. Her name was Hildegard. Although her parents were involved in the cares of the world and were richly blessed with temporal goods, they were thankful for the gifts of their creator, and they consecrated their daughter to the service of God. Even in her early years the young lady showed signs of virginity since she appeared to withhold consent to desires of the flesh. When she was hardly able to utter her first words, she made those around her understand through her words and signs that she was conscious of an exceptional gift of visions.

When she was eight years old, she entered the monastery on the mountain of St. Disibod in order to be buried with Christ and to rise with him to immortality. She was under the care of the pious, consecrated Jutta. It was this lady who carefully trained her in the virtues of humility and chastity, and superbly trained her in learning and singing the sacred songs of David. Except for simple instruction in the psalms, she received no other schooling, either in reading or in music. Still, she left behind not a small, but rather a significant legacy of writings. It is worthwhile to explain this by using her own words:

"When I was twenty-four years and seven months old, I saw an extremely strong, sparkling, fiery light coming from the open heavens. It pierced my brain, my heart, and my breast through and through like a flame which did not burn; however, it warmed me. It heated me up very much like the sun warms an object on which it is pouring its rays. And suddenly I had an insight into the meaning and interpretation of the psalter, the Gospel, and the other Catholic writings of the Old and New Testaments, but not into the meaning, the sentence structure and the hyphenation; also I had no understanding of events and times."

Source: Gottfried and Theodoric, *The Life of the Holy Hildegard,* 1.1, trans. James McGrath (Collegeville, Minn.: Liturgical Press, 1995), pp. 35–36.

book is a perfect representation of that concept "bookness." The concept is fully real, and all representations of it in the world are mere hints, suggestions of a more perfect reality.

A medieval "nominalist," on the contrary, would say that "book" is merely a name (*nomen* in Latin, whence nominalism) that we apply to objects that we deem to bear sufficient similarity to one another that they can be adequately captured by one name. But only each particular book is fully real.

Problems aplenty surround the quarrel over universals: Is reality purely an intellectual proposition, or is reality a quality of existence in the world? How does the mind acquire knowledge of the universal? How does the mind know to which objects to apply the universal? What specific differences exist between objects to which the same name is applied?

With the emergence of the problem of universals, we enter fully into a new intellectual approach that has long been called "Scholasticism." This word has come to have many different meanings, but at the most basic level it describes a movement that attempted to show that Christian theology is inherently rational, that faith and reason need not be contradictory or antithetical. Scholasticism also implies a certain systematization of thought. Gratian's attempt to organize all of canon law rationally and systematically was a Scholastic exercise. Twelfth-century biblical scholars tried to produce a single, systematic commentary on the Bible. In 1160 Peter Lombard produced the *Four Books of Sentences*, a comprehensive treatment of all of Christian theology.

Thomas Aquinas (1225–1274) was the greatest of the Scholastics, the most sensitive to Greek and Arab thought, and the most prolific of medieval philosophers.

A Dominican friar, Thomas was educated at Naples, Cologne, and Paris. Apart from brief service at the papal court, he spent the years after 1252 teaching and writing in Paris. His two most famous works are the *Summa Contra Gentiles* and the *Summa Theologiae*. A *summa* was an encyclopedic compendium of carefully arrayed knowledge on a particular subject. One might think of Gratian's and Peter Lombard's works as precursors to the great summas of the thirteenth century. Thomas's first summa addressed natural truth—that is, the kinds of things that any person could know through the operation of reason. His second summa was a summation of the revealed truths of the Christian faith.

Thomas's works are distinctive for two reasons. First, no one before him had so rigorously followed the dialectical method of reasoning through a whole field of knowledge, not just a particular problem. For thousands of pages, Thomas poses a question, suggests answers, confronts the answers with objections, refutes the objections, and then draws a conclusion. Then he repeats the process. Second, Thomas carefully distinguished between two kinds of truths. On the one hand were *natural truths,* truths (even theological ones) that anyone can know (or so Thomas thought)—for example, that God exists. On the other hand were *revealed truths,* truths that can be known (if not understood) only through faith in God's revelation—for example, the Trinity or the incarnation of Christ. Thomas maintained that natural and revealed truths simply could not contradict one another because God was ultimately the source of both. If natural truth—for example, Aristotle's contention that the world is eternal—appeared to contradict a revealed truth, then Aristotle was wrong. Thomas was accused by some contemporaries of applying reason too widely, and after his death some of his ideas were condemned by the church. But he actually steered a middle path between intellectual extremes. In this respect Thomas was like Maimonides and Averroes.

■ The University

In the early decades of the twelfth century, students gathered wherever famous teachers might be found. Such teachers—figures like Peter Abelard—clustered in a few centers, and the students congregated there as well. The last decades of the twelfth century saw a swarm of masters and students in Paris. Like members of secular guilds (see page 282), the masters organized. The University of Paris was the result of their efforts. By 1300 universities had formed elsewhere in France, as well as in Italy, England, and western Germany.

Several forces drove masters to organize. They wanted to negotiate with the bishop's chancellor, the traditional head of all schools in an episcopal city. They wanted to regulate the curriculum that students followed and to prescribe the requirements for entry into their own ranks. They also desired to set the fees to be charged for instruction. By 1209 the bishop of Paris, the pope, and the king of France had granted formal recognition to the university.

In Bologna, the university developed a little differently. Here the students came primarily to study law, after already acquiring a basic education. These law students were usually older and more affluent than students elsewhere, and foreign to Bologna. Consequently, in Bologna the university arose from a guild of students who united to set standards in fees and studies and to protect themselves against unscrupulous masters.

Universities were known for certain specializations: Paris for arts and theology, Bologna for law, Salerno in Italy and Montpellier in France for medicine, Oxford for mathematical and scientific subjects. Still, the basic course of study was similar. At Paris, a young scholar came to the city, found lodgings where he could, and attempted to find a master who would guide him through the arts curriculum. These boys might be in their early teens or several years older, depending on their earlier educations and financial resources. The arts course, which was the prerequisite to all higher faculties, usually lasted from four to six years. The bachelor's degree was a license to teach, but a bachelor who wished to teach in a university needed to go on for a master's degree. The master's degree required at least eight years of study (including the baccalaureate years), which culminated in a public oral examination. Some masters went on to become doctors in theology, law, or medicine. A doctorate required ten to fifteen years of study. Medieval academicians were immensely learned.

Student life was difficult. In many ways, students were always foreigners. Although their presence in a town enhanced its prestige, townspeople exploited them by charging exorbitant prices for food and rent. Students' own behavior was not always above reproach. There was surely some truth in the frequently lodged charge that students were noisy, quarrelsome, given to drinking, and excessively fond of prostitutes. England's Oxford and Cambridge were unique in always providing residential colleges for students; Paris got one later and the mendicants often established houses of study. Typically, though, students were on their own.

Students had to work very hard. The arts curriculum demanded a thorough acquaintance with all the famous texts of grammar, logic, and rhetoric. Higher studies added more Aristotle, particularly his philosophical writings. In theology, the students had to master the Scriptures, the principal biblical commentaries from patristic times to the present, and the *Four Books of Sentences.* In medicine, the ancient writings of Galen and Hippocrates were supplemented by Arab texts as well as by observation and experimentation.

The basic method of teaching provides yet another definition of Scholasticism; that is, the method of studying in the schools. The teacher started by reciting a short piece of a set text, carried on with the presentation and discussion of many authoritative commentaries on that text, and concluded with his own explanations. The teacher then presented another passage of the set text and repeated the whole process. This education focused on standard books and accepted opinions and required students to remember large amounts of material. The curriculum nevertheless produced thinkers of prodigious originality.

In principle, universities were open to free men, but in practice they were restricted to those who had the means to attend them. Women were not accepted at universities, either as students or as teachers. It was generally thought, by men, that learning made women insubordinate. Lacking the required education, women were denied entry into the learned professions of theology, law, and medicine, despite the fact that many rural and some urban medical practitioners were women. Nevertheless, women commonly possessed and transmitted knowledge of both folk remedies and scientific medicine. Trotula of Salerno, who probably lived in the twelfth century, wrote a knowledgeable treatise, *On the Diseases of Women.* Documents from medieval Naples record the names of twenty-four women surgeons between 1273 and 1410. How these women were educated is utterly unknown.

THE VERNACULAR ACHIEVEMENT

MAJOR achievement of high medieval civilization, from Iceland to Kievan Rus, was the appearance of rich literatures in native tongues. Vernacular, from the Latin *vernaculus* meaning "home-born" or "domestic," is the name for the languages other than Latin, say, English or French. Although Latin remained the language of the clerical elite, writers of vernacular prose and poetry produced some of the greatest works in Western literature.

■ Literatures and Languages

The number of people who could speak, read, or write Latin was always a minority in western Europe, just as native Greek-speakers were a minority in Byzantium. As Latin, beginning in Late Antiquity, slowly evolved into the Romance (from Roman) languages, people who used what eventually became French, Italian, and Spanish had some advantages over the peoples in Celtic, Germanic, or Slavic lands, where the languages bore no obvious relationship to Latin. Persons who spoke Old French in their towns and villages would have had an easier time learning Latin than people who spoke Irish or Polish. Nevertheless, vernacular literatures began to appear at roughly the same time all over Europe, between about 800 and 1000.

Of course, many writers continued to use Latin for several centuries. University scholars continued to compose their learned treatises in the ancient tongue, but now often in a style that was less ornate than before. Most law books and public documents were still in Latin, but in a "vulgar" Latin that was reasonably close to the vernacular in areas where Romance languages were spoken. Technical manuals, on farming and animal husbandry, on warfare and armaments, or on law and government, were prepared in Latin, too, but again in a style that was far more accessible than that of their ancient models. Popular literature—poetry, history and biography, and romance and adventure—was still often written in Latin. Some of this material was serious, but some breathed a light and carefree spirit. The anonymous German known as the Archpoet (d. 1165) wrote poems about drinking and womanizing. These lines are typical of his work:

> In the public house to die
> Is my resolution;
> Let wine to my lips be nigh
> At life's dissolution:
> That will make the angels cry,
> With glad elocution
> "Grant this drunkard, God on high,
> Grace and Absolution!"[1]

No less insouciant were the authors of biting satires such as the anonymous *The Gospel According to the Silver Marks,* which parodied the wealth and greed of the papal curia. But after 1200 this fresh spirit was largely confined to writings in the vernacular. For after that year Latin was rarely used as the language for serious, original literary compositions. (See the feature "Information Technology: Paper.")

The literary masterpieces of the High Middle Ages are almost entirely written in vernacular languages. The epic poem *Beowulf* is the first classic of English literature. We do not know who wrote it or when it was written. Scholars formerly assigned it to the eighth century, but they now usually place it later, in the ninth or possibly in the tenth century. The story focuses on three great battles fought by the hero, Beowulf°. The first two are against the monster Grendel and Grendel's mother, who have been harrying the kingdom of an old ally of Beowulf's family; the third is against a dragon. *Beowulf* is a poem of adventure and heroism, of loyalty and treachery. It treats lordship, friendship, and kinship. Themes of good and evil resound throughout. The poem is barely Christian but nevertheless deeply moral. It speaks, in a mature, vigorous, and moving language, to and for the heart of a warrior society.

Beowulf is the best-known Anglo-Saxon work but by no means the only one. One of the Viking attacks that led to the undoing of Ethelred II was commemorated in *The Battle of Maldon.* Several volumes of elegiac and lyric poetry, mostly on religious themes, also survive. And Anglo-Saxon writers produced chronicles, legal materials and charters, and at least one large collection of homilies.

Some fragments of poetry in Old French survive from the ninth century, but the great *chansons de gestes* ("songs of deeds," or celebrations of the great) appeared in the eleventh century. Undoubtedly they were transmitted orally for a long time before they were written down. The best is the *Song of Roland,* written around 1100. In 778 as Charlemagne's army was returning from Spain, Basques raided the baggage train and killed Count Roland. By 1100 this obscure event, long kept alive in oral traditions, had been transformed into a heroic struggle between Charlemagne and his retinue and an army of countless thousands of "paynim," who are crude caricatures of Muslims.

Like *Beowulf, Roland* is a story about loyalty and treachery, about bravery in the face of insuperable odds, about the kindness and generosity of leaders. They take us into a man's chivalric world. Females are all but absent. The two works do not show us personal hopes, fears, or motivations. Everything that we think should be private is made public. What pours forth is the communal ethos and the dominant values of the elite, male social group. Although *Beowulf* is lightly clothed in Christianity, *Roland* is thickly vested in the faith.

The heroic epic tradition that *Beowulf* and the *Song of Roland* represent did not disappear as the Middle Ages unfolded, but literary energies were applied in new directions. Southern France, in the middle and last decades of the twelfth century, added something new to Western literature: the love lyrics of the troubadours. This poetry, composed by both men and women, profoundly influenced an age and created the literary movement that has long been called "courtly love." Chivalry was initially a code for men interacting with other men. In the world of courtly love, chivalry became an elaborate set of rules governing relations between men and women.

Courtly love had several sources. The classical poet Ovid (43 B.C.–?A.D. 17), who wrote *The Art of Love,* a manual of seduction, was one. Another was the lyrical poetry of Muslim Spain. Ironically, feudal values such as loyalty and service played a critical role as men became, in effect, love vassals. Platonic ideas made some contribution, too, particularly the notion that any love in this world could be only a pale imitation of real love. The courtly poets sung of *fin'amours,* a pure love in contrast to the mere lust of the masses. A lover cherished an unattainable lady. He would do anything for the merest display of pleasure or gratitude on her part, as we see in these lines from Bernart de Ventadorn, court poet of the counts of Toulouse in the late twelfth century:

> Down there, around Ventadorn, all my friends
> have lost me, because my lady does not love me;
> and so, it is right that I never go back there again,
> because always she is wild and morose with me.
> Now here is why the face she shows me is gloomy and
>   full of anger:
> because my pleasure is in loving her and I have settled
>   down to it.
> She is resentful and complains for no other reason.[2]

Male troubadours placed women on pedestals and, in ballads, worshiped them from afar. Women troubadours took a different line. Women's poems were more realistic, more human, more emotionally satisfying. Castellozza° (b. ca. 1200), the southern French wife of a Crusader, idealized not at all when she wrote these lines:

> Friend, if you had shown consideration,
> meekness, candor and humanity,
> I'd have loved you without hesitation,
> but you were mean and sly and villainous.

Beowulf (BAY-oh-wolf)

Castellozza (KAHS-teh-lohtz-eh)

Paper

Today paper is so common, so plentiful, that we scarcely give it a moment's notice. The words you are reading right now are printed on paper. Chances are, you have paper of several kinds, sizes, thicknesses, and colors around your desk. But paper was not always so familiar. In Europe, paper was not widely used before 1300 and did not supplant parchment as a writing material until about 1600. Where, then, did paper come from? What is it, exactly, and how is it made? Why is it important?

The Chinese invented paper, probably in the second century B.C. For two or three centuries, however, the Chinese did not discern paper's possibilities as a writing material. Instead, they used it as a wrapping material, for personal hygiene—rather like a tissue—and for clothing. By A.D. 100 the Chinese had adopted paper as their preferred writing material. For centuries thereafter they kept the papermaking process a closely guarded secret.

Legend has it that in 751 the Arabs learned the art of papermaking from some Chinese prisoners of war in Samarkand and carried the knowledge westward into the caliphate. Until perhaps 1200 the Arabs kept the secret from contemporary Christians, largely because they were able to sell paper in Mediterranean ports at hugely profitable prices. The oldest surviving Western paper document is the 1102 will of Adelaide of Sicily, the widow of King Roger I. Gradually, Christians in Sicily and Spain, places with intense Muslim-Christian contacts, learned how to make paper. By the thirteenth century there were a number of papermaking centers in Italy, southern France, and Spain. By 1500 the paper industry was flourishing all over Europe.

Paper takes its name from papyrus, the writing material common in antiquity but largely replaced by parchment (see page 272) in the early Middle Ages. Paper and papyrus are, however, utterly different. Papyrus was made from the inner bark of the papyrus plant, whereas the Chinese originally made paper from pulpy plants such as flax or hemp. Gradually the Chinese learned to make paper from rags, discarded textiles. The Arabs learned how to make rag paper and communicated this knowledge, not quite willingly, to the Christian West. Today most paper is made from wood pulp.

A papermaker would put rags and water in a cauldron and repeatedly stir and beat the contents, sometimes over heat, until a thick, gooey film formed on the surface. The papermaker then would take a square or rectangular metal frame with tiny perforations in it and drag it through the thick mixture. When he pulled out the frame, it would have a thin coating of the fluid, known as the "deckel." After the deckel was dry, he peeled it off the frames and placed it on a sheet of felt. Another felt cloth was then placed on top of the deckel, followed by another deckel, another felt, and so forth, until the pile was perhaps a foot high. Using a mechanical press, the papermaker removed excess moisture from the pile of deckels and felts. He then hung up the deckels—now paper—to dry. Finally he "sized" the sheets, coating them with animal glue so that they would accept ink without smudging.

And she did not assign the active role exclusively to the man:

> Handsome friend, as a lover true
> I loved you, for you pleased me,
> But now I see I was a fool,
> for I've barely seen you since.[3]

Count William IX of Poitou° (1071–1127) was among the first of the troubadours, and his daughter, Eleanor of Aquitaine, brought the conventions of this poetry and point of view to the French and Angevin courts. She and her daughters were the greatest literary patrons of the late twelfth century. The wives of kings and nobles who were frequently away from home maintained stunning courts and cultivated vernacular literature.

The courtly literature of northern France owed much to the troubadour tradition of the south but broke new ground in both forms and content. The romance and the lay were the chief new forms. Both drew on classical literature, the heroic Germanic past, and the Arthurian legends of the Celtic world to create stories of love and adventure. The romance usually develops a complex narrative involving several major characters

Poitou (PWAH-too)

Paper's historical importance may be considered from several points of view. Paper provides an exceptionally good example of a technology that the West learned from other people, and it illustrates how technologies can travel long distances. The wider use of paper promoted business firms dedicated to selling notebooks, tablets, and fine single sheets. Written documents ranging from personal letters to public records became more numerous once a cheaper writing material became more readily available. One scholar suggests that alphabetization became widespread only after the existence of paper made the arranging of disposable slips feasible. When printing (about which you will learn in Chapter 12; see page 414) was introduced into Europe, the possibility arose of quickly making multiple copies of a given book or document. Parchment was too expensive for this purpose. Thus the more rapid dissemination of books and ideas that marks the transition from the medieval to the modern world was facilitated by the fortunate conjunction of paper and printing.

Woodcut by Jost Amman, the Oldest Illustration of Papermaking Note the vat, frame, and press. The printer's assistant ("devil") is carrying away deckels to dry. *(From Jules Heller,* Papermaking *[New York: Watson-Guptill Publications, 1978]. Reproduced with permission.)*

over a long time. The lay is brief and focuses on a single incident. The most famous twelfth-century writer of romance was Chrétien de Troyes (1135–1183), the court writer of Marie of Champagne, a daughter of Eleanor of Aquitaine. The greatest writer of lays was Marie de France, who wrote at the Angevin court in the 1170s.

The romances and lays explore the contradictions and tensions in a variety of human relationships. Loyalty and honor make frequent appearances. Lancelot, a paragon of knightly virtue, desperately loves his lord Arthur's wife, Guinevere. What is he to do? How can he be loyal to his lord, to his love, and to himself? What will he do when a single course of action brings both honor and dishonor?

In the epics, speeches are made to swords, to horses, or sometimes to no one in particular; the points being made are universalized. In the romances, credible human beings struggle to resolve powerful and conflicting emotional and moral dilemmas.

Slavic literatures began with the missionaries Cyril and Methodius (page 265), who developed both a language, Church Slavonic, and a script, Glagolitic. The Glagolitic script was modified into the Cyrillic, which was adopted by all the Slavic peoples who embraced Orthodoxy and remains in use today. The earliest writing in the Slavic languages was religious: biblical translations, saints' lives, and selections from the Church Fathers.

Among the Kievan Rus, in the twelfth century, historical writings and imaginative literature, such as the *Tale of Igor*, made their appearance. The latter work, a semilegendary account of Prince Igor and his many battles, is reminiscent of the *chansons des gestes*.

The Scandinavians who settled Iceland produced a diverse literature. They created law books, detailed accounts of their settlements, and a mighty saga tradition. *Saga* means "things said," and it is almost certainly the case that the greatest sagas were oral tales long before they were written down between about 1150 and 1350. Sagas fall into two categories: Historical sagas blend fact and fiction to praise the deeds of the great heroes of the Viking age. Family sagas mix history and myth to relate the stories of the great families who settled Iceland.

France led the way in the production of vernacular literature, but French models did not inspire slavish imitation. This is seen most clearly in the work of the master of all vernacular writers, Dante Alighieri° (1265–1321). Dante began as a poet in *la dolce stil nuova*, "the sweet new style" that came from France and captivated Italians. But he moved beyond it in many ways. Dante was a man of extraordinarily wide learning and reading. He served Florence in public capacities and became an exile amid political strife. He wrote a long treatise in defense of the empire—or, really, against the secular rule of the church. But he is best known for one of the masterpieces of world literature, *The Divine Comedy*.

The secret of the *Comedy*'s success is not easy to grasp. It is a long and difficult poem, but it is also humorous, instructive, and moving. In an exquisitely beautiful Italian, Dante took the most advanced theology and philosophy of his time, the richest poetic traditions, a huge hoard of stories, many contemporary events, and a lot of common sense and wove them into an allegorical presentation of the journey of the whole human race and of the individual lives of all people.

Accompanied by the Roman poet Virgil (see page 180), Dante travels through Hell and Purgatory, commenting along the way on the condition of the people he meets. Then, because Virgil is a pagan and only Dante's true love can accompany Dante into paradise, Beatrice, the love of Dante's youth, joins him for a visit to Heaven. The poet's central metaphor is love; the love he feels for Beatrice symbolizes the love God feels for the world. Dante canvasses humanity from the pits of Hell, which he reserved for traitors, to the summit of Paradise, where a man inspired by pure love might, despite his sinfulness, dare to look into the face of God.

Although the romances and lays were by no means the exclusive preserve of the elite, very little is known about popular literature. Two exceptions are the mystery play and women's devotional writing. Mystery plays made their first appearance in the eleventh century. The liturgy of the church, which formally re-enacted the life of Christ, was confined to the clergy. But this limitation did not prevent troupes of actors from staging, on church porches or village greens, scenes from the life of Christ in simple, direct language. By the twelfth and thirteenth centuries, guilds in many towns sponsored the production of plays commemorating the Christian mysteries. Such plays served as both a form of popular entertainment and a device for teaching elementary Christian ideas. The female religious movements of the age gave rise to prose and verse works in various vernaculars. Mechtild of Magdeburg (1210–1280), a German Beguine, wrote *The Flowering Light of Divinity*, a mystical, allegorical account of the marriage between God and a spiritual woman. The vernaculars opened avenues of expression to women, who were normally denied Latin learning.

■ Innovations in Architecture

Romanesque, "in the Roman style," is a term coined in the nineteenth century to characterize the architecture and, to a lesser extent, the painting of the period between the waning of Carolingian art and the full emergence of Gothic art in the late twelfth century. Today scholars view the Romanesque style as transitional between Carolingian and Gothic.

At several places in Ottonian Germany, a return of political stability led to the construction of churches. Ducal dynasties and women of the imperial family were among the most generous patrons. Pride in their Carolingian inheritance and their new imperial dignity led the Germans to a distinctive architectural style marked by very thick walls, alternating piers and columns in the nave, and galleries. As this architectural style spread all over Europe in the eleventh century, it produced true Romanesque, a style that differed from Roman and Carolingian styles mainly in the greater internal height and space made possible by vaulting (see Figure 10.1). To the rectangular elegance of the classical basilica and the height of the Carolingian westworks (see page 264), Romanesque builders added a refined verticality.

Among the distinctive features of Romanesque churches were their wall paintings and frescoes, their sculpture, reliquaries, pulpits, and baptisteries—in short, their exuberant decoration and ornament. Europe's growing wealth and sophistication, and the pride of the church's aristocratic patrons, are very much in ev-

---

Dante Alighieri (DAHN-tay ah-lih-GYAIR-ee)

idence. Especially in the south of France, the façades of Romanesque churches provided space for sculpture. The tympanum above the doors, a space seen by all who entered, was a favored location. Large-scale sculpture had made a comeback after its almost total absence in the early Middle Ages.

It is surely no coincidence that Gothic art and architecture emerged just as the West was absorbing the rediscovery of Euclid's mathematical writings and applying the intensely ordered logic of Aristotle to everything from legal problems to theological mysteries. One of the most familiar images of the Middle Ages is the inspiringly beautiful Gothic cathedral. It is thus ironic that the word *Gothic* first appeared in the sixteenth century as a term of derision for what was then regarded as an outmoded style so ugly that only the horrible conquerors of Rome, the Goths, could have been responsible for it. The name stuck, but today it simply identifies a period in

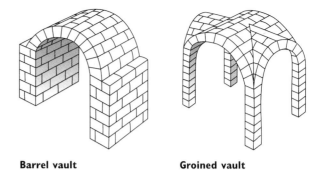

Barrel vault   **Groined vault**

Figure 10.1   The Structure of Romanesque Architecture
The basic structural element of Romanesque architecture was the barrel vault, which, when two were joined at right angles, formed a groin vault. These vaults produced great height and strength but gave buildings a massive, fortresslike appearance. *(Source: Anne Shaver-Crandell, The Middle Ages. Copyright © 1982 Cambridge University Press. Reprinted with permission of Cambridge University Press.)*

Saint Sernin, Toulouse   This fortresslike church (ca. 1080–1120) was paid for by the offerings of pilgrims on their way to shrines in Spain. Its massive walls and numerous colonnades are typical of Romanesque architecture. The form of the building suggests the cross of Christ. For the interior of a Romanesque church (Vezelay) see page 348.   *(Jean Dieuzaid, Toulouse)*

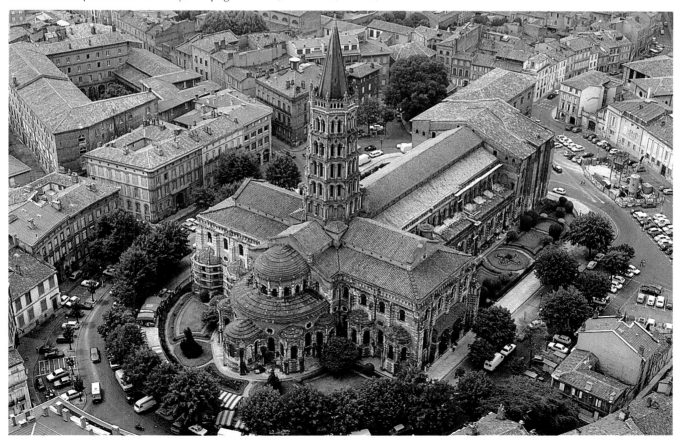

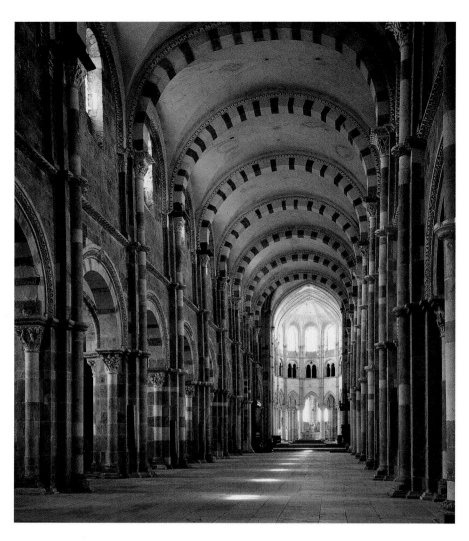

Nave of Vezelay, 1104–1132 The basilica of Sainte-Madeleine is a crowning achievement of French Romanesque architecture, featuring height and a sense of airy spaciousness. Compare this nave with the Gothic nave of Chartres on page 316. *(Éditions Gaud)*

European architecture, sculpture, and painting that began in the middle of the twelfth century and that in some places lasted until the early sixteenth century.

Gothic is a French invention. It was Abbot Suger° (1085–1151) of St.-Denis, a monastery outside Paris, who, in rebuilding his basilica beginning in 1135, consciously sought a new style. He desired to achieve effects of lightness, almost weightlessness, in the stonework of his church and to admit large amounts of light to create a dazzling and mysterious aura on the inside. The Bible often uses images of light to refer to God, and Suger wished to give expression to those images in the house of God for which he was responsible.

Suger produced something startlingly original by combining a number of elements that had long been in use—three in particular: A *pointed arch* is more elegant

than a round one; and it permits the joining of two arches of identical height but different widths, which, in turn, permits complex shapes and sizes. The *ribbed vault* is lighter and more graceful than the barrel and groin vaults characteristic of Romanesque architecture; it also exerts less stress and facilitates experimentation with shapes (see Figure 10.2). Finally, *point support*—basically, the support of structural elements at only certain points—permitted the replacement of heavy, stress-bearing walls with curtains of stained glass. The points of support might be massive internal piers or intricate skeletal frameworks, called *buttresses,* on the outside of the church.

These three elements—pointed arch, ribbed vault, and point support—produce a building that is characterized by verticality and translucency. Everything seems to spring upward, and stone surfaces appear so frequently punctured by light as almost to disappear altogether. The desired, and achieved, effect is one of harmony, order, and mathematical precision.

Suger (SOO-jhay)

The Gothic style soon spread in central and northern France. The cathedral of Notre-Dame of Paris was built beginning in the 1150s, and the royal portal at Chartres Cathedral was reconstructed after 1145. Gothic churches could be huge. The interior of Notre-Dame, for example, is 493 feet long and 107 feet high. To avoid a sense of sheer mass, Gothic builders used triple or quadruple elevations inside the buildings and took advantage of point support to pierce the walls at frequent intervals with stained glass windows. Exterior surfaces were broken up with windows, sculptures, colonnades, and towers. No opportunity was missed to create visual interest and complexity. (See the feature "Weighing the Evidence: Stained Glass" on pages 350–351.)

The thirteenth century was the most mature period for French Gothic architecture and also the time when Gothic spread most widely throughout Europe. Its popularity may be attributed to the superiority of French masons and stonecutters and also to the tremendous prestige of French culture. By 1300 distinctive Gothic traditions shaped the urban landscape in almost all parts of Europe from Iceland to Poland.

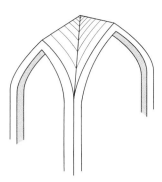

Figure 10.2 The Structure of Gothic Architecture
The adoption of pointed arches, an import from the Islamic world, let Gothic builders join structures of identical heights but different widths (something that barrel and groin vaulting could not do; see Figure 10.1 on page 347). The resulting structures were high, light, airy, and visually interesting.
(Source: Anne Shaver-Crandell, The Middle Ages. Copyright © 1982 Cambridge University Press. Reprinted with permission of Cambridge University Press.)

Exterior of Notre-Dame, Paris This most famous of cathedrals (1163–1220) shows all the classic elements of the Gothic style: highly decorated western end, cross shape formed by the nave and transept, flying buttresses to support the walls and roof, and side walls that seem like curtains of glass. *(Altitude, Paris)*

(continued on page 352)

Stained Glass

To walk into one of Europe's great churches is to enter a realm of mystery and beauty produced by the play of light—the brilliant light of the morning sun, the softer glow of the evening sun, the muted tones of a cloudy day—on thousands of square feet of colored glass. This mystery and beauty were created intentionally in Europe in the High Middle Ages. But the magnificent surviving medieval windows are not important solely for their beauty. Their images provide unique and crucial insights into religious and secular life.

Pictured here are two thirteenth-century cathedral windows. The one from Canterbury depicts that city's great bishop and martyr, Thomas Becket. A large window at Chartres depicts Saint Lubin, a sixth-century bishop of the city who was the patron saint of the town's inn and tavern keepers, and Noah, according to the Bible the first planter of grape vines. Here we see barrels of wine being hauled to market, in a window donated by the vintners guild.

Many of Canterbury's windows represent aspects of the life of the murdered archbishop. The one pictured here shows Thomas as a bishop, not as a martyr. He is wearing a mitre, the traditional headgear of a bishop. He also wears a *pallium*, a white wool band sent to a new archbishop by the pope. Becket's vestments are green, the commonest liturgical color of the religious year (others were white, purple, and red). This window, then, would have served to remind people of their beloved bishop as he was in life, not martyrdom.

In Chartres, wine was important to the church because of its use in Mass, and it was also a staple of the local economy. Accordingly, the vintners are portrayed in twenty-three of this window's forty-one panels. By comparison, most guilds are depicted only once in the windows they donated. These windows remind us, as they reminded contemporaries, of how these magnificent buildings fitted into the daily life of their communities. Religious devotions and secular preoccupations blended in one spot.

Glass is made by heating silica, found naturally in sand, flint, and quartz, to a very high temperature and then fusing the molten silicate with a borate or phosphate often obtained from ashes produced by burning natural substances. Colored glass was made by adding metal oxides to the molten mixture. Iron oxide produced red, copper oxide produced green, and cobalt, blue.

Such glass, called "pot" glass, tended to be opaque, obviously unsuitable for windows. To achieve greater translucency, glassmakers made "flashed" glass by fusing at low temperature a layer of colored liquid to the surface of a panel of clear glass. Although fine glass vessels were made in a number of places, notably in Venice and the Rhineland, the large sheets of colored glass used for church windows were commonly manufactured in Lorraine and Normandy.

To make a stained glass window, a master glazier first drew a cartoon—a sort of rough draft—on a flat board, or perhaps on a piece of parchment. He then cut pieces of colored glass into various irregular shapes according to his design. To produce facial features, folds in garments, or other details, the glazier painted the inner sides of the colored glass pieces with dark-colored paints and then fired them at low temperatures to produce an enamel-like effect. You can see this patina on Thomas's face. Once the glazier had all his pieces cut and placed, he joined them together by means of lead strips that were **H** shaped. If you look closely, you can see the pieces of glass, lead stripping, and painted details in the images on these pages. The whole picture was then fitted into a metal frame and mounted in a window opening.

Documents first mention the use of glass in church windows in the sixth century. The oldest surviving fragments of stained glass date from the ninth century, and the oldest complete windows from around 1100. With large Romanesque, and even more with the huge Gothic churches, came opportunities to use more and more glass. First the greater height of Romanesque buildings meant that tall windows could be placed high up in the nave walls. Then the structural innovations of Gothic architecture that removed stress, and hence stone, from the walls permitted them to become vast expanses of glass. Chartres Cathedral has 176 windows. Many high medieval churches had windows more than 50 feet high.

So far we have looked at *how* medieval Europeans created stained glass and incorporated it into their greatest churches. But *why* did they undertake such time-consuming and costly decoration? Suger, the scholarly twelfth-century abbot of St.-Denis outside Paris who rebuilt his basilica in the Gothic style, spoke of the spiritual force of his new glass windows:

Canterbury, Thirteenth-Century Window:
Thomas Becket   *(Sonia Halliday Photographs)*

Chartres, Thirteenth-Century Window:
Story of Saint Lubin   *(© Clive Hicks)*

When . . . the loveliness of the many-colored gems has called me away from external cares . . . then it seems to me that I see myself dwelling in some strange region of the universe which neither exists entirely in the slime of the earth nor entirely in the purity of heaven; and that, by the grace of God, I can be transported from this inferior to that higher world.*

In the Greek philosophers, the Bible, and the Church Fathers, light always represents one way of imagining the unimaginable reality of God. For Suger and his contemporaries, the luminous effect of stained glass suggested the very presence of God.

Earthquakes, fires, and wars have destroyed most of the glass that was installed in the Middle Ages. Today's

visitor to Europe views more-or-less valid nineteenth-century reconstructions except at Canterbury in England and Chartres in France, where almost all of the original glass survives. Usually, medieval churches were laid out on an east-west axis. The western façade was normally pierced by tall "lancet" windows and by a single "rose" window (look at the front of Notre-Dame on page 349). These typically portrayed scenes from the life of Christ and/or the Virgin Mary. The northern aisle windows usually contained Old Testament scenes, the southern windows New Testament scenes.

Stained glass played a key role, alongside sculpture, preaching, and churchyard dramas, in communicating the faith to ordinary people. Seldom has a teaching tool been so beautiful! Scholars also speak of stained glass as "painting with glass." Indeed, the art form most like stained glass is painting, especially the painting of illuminations on the pages of manuscripts.

---

* Suger, *De rebus in administratione sua gestis*, ed. E. Panofsky, 2d ed. (Princeton, 1979), pp. 63–65.

SUMMARY

COMPARISONS between the Europe of 900 and 1300 are instructive both as reminders of what had happened and as suggestions of what was to come. In 900 Carolingian Europe was being attacked on every side. By 1300 Europe was vastly larger than in Carolingian times; not only was its geography greater, so also had it expanded in economic, political, military, and cultural terms.

Europe's traditional social orders—the "Three Estates" as they would later be called—came fully into view after 900. Described by contemporaries as pray-ers, fighters, and workers, these orders accounted for some but not all of the major groups. The clergy was more numerous and more diverse in structure than ever before. Women played important roles as nuns, writers, and reformers. The nobility was more tightly organized into lineages, and an aristocratic ethos, chivalry, characterized noble lifestyles. Some peasants gained in personal freedom, some lost; some grew more prosperous and comfortable, some lived in want and misery. The townsfolk of an expanding Europe constituted a growing and increasingly important group that was never a part of the society of rural gentlemen-warriors. Minorities, chiefly Jews, enjoyed some new opportunities in the High Middle Ages but also suffered attacks and prejudice.

Large-scale social movements appeared for the first time in Western history. These movements were generally religious. Sometimes they were motivated by desires to reform the church, and sometimes they arose from a longing for the primitive, pristine days of Christianity. A few of the movements, the Waldensians and Albigensians, for example, would end up as heresies. Other groups, the mendicants above all others, managed to accommodate themselves to the church and thus lent it their energy and insight. For the first time, women played important roles in the new religious movements.

As Europe expanded, Latin Christendom encountered long-lost classical learning as well as Arab and Jewish thought. The cultural life of the traditional intellectual centers—monastic and cathedral schools—was immeasurably enriched by these cultural meetings and mixings. Gradually European intellectual life was so stimulated that a new approach to scholarship—Scholasticism—and a new kind of institution—the university—ensued.

But while Latin remained the language of lecture hall and courtroom, vernacular languages took their place alongside the ancient tongue. Impressive literatures arose from Iceland to Rus in prose and verse. Tales of love and adventure predominated in vernacular literature, but inspiring moral and religious works appeared too. Women contributed in many languages. In addition to literature, the high medieval period saw first Romanesque and then Gothic architecture.

As the fourteenth century dawned, people all over Europe had reasons to be both hopeful and anxious. They were, in fact, at the start of one of the most turbulent and creative periods in Western history, a period when crisis after crisis would afflict the expanded Europe and the spectacular achievements of the High Middle Ages.

■ Notes

1. John Addington Symonds, *Wine, Women and Song: Medieval Latin Students' Songs* (reprint, New York: Cooper Square, 1966), p. 69.
2. Frederick Goldin, *Lyrics of the Troubadours and Trouvères: An Anthology and a History* (New York: Doubleday, 1973), p. 135.
3. Meg Bogin, *The Women Troubadours* (New York: Norton, 1976), p. 69.

■ Suggested Reading

Bony, Jean. *French Gothic Architecture of the Twelfth and Thirteenth Centuries.* 1983. Huge, clearly presented, and magnificently illustrated, this is a browser's book as well as a sustained essay by a master of his subject.

Bouchard, Constance B. S*trong of Body, Brave and Noble: Chivalry and Society in Medieval France.* 1998. A superb summation of the social and cultural history of the medieval aristocracy.

Bynum, Caroline Walker. *Jesus as Mother: Studies in the Spirituality of the High Middle Ages.* 1982. A collection of sparkling essays by a major historian that makes the feminine in religious thought accessible, even central, to any discussion of medieval religion.

Colish, Marcia. *Medieval Foundations of the Western Intellectual Tradition.* 1997. The first original and comprehensive history of medieval thought in a generation.

Grundmann, Herbert. *Religious Movements in the Middle Ages.* 1995. Translated into English sixty years after its appearance in German, this book has lost none of its interest or explanatory power.

Jaeger, C. Stephen. *The Envy of Angels: Cathedral Schools and Social Ideals in Medieval Europe, 900–1200.* 1994. A work of vast learning and common sense on controversial topics.

Lambert, Malcolm. *Medieval Heresy: Popular Movements from the Gregorian Reform to the Reformation.* 2d ed. 1992. Brilliant and readable, this book is the best history of medieval heresy ever written and one of the best books on medieval religion generally.

Southern, R. W. *Scholastic Humanism and the Unification of Europe.* 1995. A truly brilliant overview of twelfth-century culture by its greatest twentieth-century student.

 For a searchable list of additional readings for this chapter, go to http://college.hmco.com.

Questa e lentrata et lusciuta della genierale bicchernia delchomio
dusiena fatta altempo de sauii huomini thomme di nofrio di tu
ra chamarlengho per uno anno chomincando adi pmo di gienaio 1436
et finito adi ultimio di dicembre 1437. et dicheche di soggias. misser baldassarre

I N the fourteenth century, Europeans sang an old Franciscan hymn, "Day of Wrath, Day of Burning." Its verses described the fear and disorder that would accompany the end of the world and God's judgment of the saved and the damned. That hymn could well have been in the mind of the painter of the facing illustration. When countless Europeans, such as these poor souls beneath the winged angel of death, fell victim to epidemic disease, many people thought they knew why. The illustrator seems to believe it was God's judgment against sinners, including these gamblers sickened by the angel's plague-tipped arrows. The flood, fire, and pestilence that ravaged late medieval Europe were thought to be premonitions of the breakdown of the world and a time of judgment.

The late Middle Ages (ca. 1300–1500) are often described as a period of continued crisis and decline that put an end to the growth and expansion of the previous three centuries. In truth, however, the years of crisis in the fourteenth and early fifteenth centuries gave way to a dramatic economic, social, and political recovery in the fifteenth century. The cultural and intellectual changes that accompanied the crisis and recovery are the focus of Chapter 12, "The Renaissance."

Military, political, religious, economic, and social crises burdened Europe in the fourteenth and early fifteenth centuries. Between 1337 and 1453, France and England fought a war that touched most of the states of western Europe. The Hundred Years' War, as it has come to be known, was fought primarily over English claims to traditionally French lands. Problems were not confined to England and France. Aristocrats in many parts of Europe challenged the hereditary rights of their rulers. In the towns of Germany and Italy,

Crisis and Recovery in Late Medieval Europe 1300–1500

The Crisis of the Western Christian Church

War, Disorder, and Revolts in Western Europe, 1300–1450

Economy and Society

The Consolidation of the Late Medieval Governments, 1450–1500

Painted cover for a fifteenth-century government account book from Siena, Italy, showing symbols of death—arrows, a scythe, and a horse —to carry the angel of death from place to place. (Staatliche Museen zu Berlin, Preussischer Kulturbesitz Kunstgewerbemuseum. Photo: Mues-Funke)

patrician classes moved to reduce the influence of artisans and laborers in government, instituting oligarchies or even aristocratic dictatorships in place of more democratic governments.

Questions of power and representation also affected the Christian church as ecclesiastical claims to authority came under attack. Secular governments challenged church jurisdictions. Disputed papal elections led to the so-called Great Schism, a split between rival centers of control in Rome and Avignon (a city in what is now the south of France). In the aftermath of the crisis, the papacy was forced to redefine its place in both the religious life and the political life of Europe.

A series of economic and demographic shocks worsened these political and religious difficulties. Part of the problem was structural: the population of Europe had grown too large to be supported by the resources available. Famine and the return of the bubonic plague in 1348 sent the economy into long-term decline. In almost every aspect of political, religious, and social life, then, the fourteenth and early fifteenth centuries marked a pause in the growth and consolidation that had characterized the earlier medieval period.

Yet out of the crises, a number of significant changes would emerge. By 1500 the European population and economy were again climbing. England and France emerged strengthened by military and political conflicts. And the consolidation of the Spanish kingdoms, the Ottoman Empire, and the states of eastern Europe altered the political and social makeup of Europe. None of the transformations could have been predicted in 1300 as Europe entered a religious, political, and social whirlwind.

QUESTIONS TO CONSIDER

- How did the Great Schism change the church and the papacy?

- What forces worked to limit the power of rulers in the fourteenth and early fifteenth centuries?

- What was the impact of the Black Death?

- How did the political makeup of Europe in 1500 differ from that in 1300?

TERMS TO KNOW

Jan Hus	Golden Bull
Council of Constance	Black Death
Great Schism	Hanseatic League
Hundred Years' War	Spanish Inquisition
Joan of Arc	Sultan Mehmed II

THE CRISIS OF THE WESTERN CHRISTIAN CHURCH

 EARLY in the fourteenth century, the Christian church endured a series of crises that instigated a debate about the nature of church government and the role of the church in society. First, the popes and their entourages abandoned their traditional residences in central Italy and moved to Avignon, an imperial enclave in the south of modern France. Then, in the wake of a disputed election, two and later three rivals claimed the papal throne. Simultaneously, the church hierarchy faced challenges from radical reformers who wished to change it. At various times all the European powers became entangled in the problems of the church. By the mid-fifteenth century, the papacy realized that it needed a stronger, independent base. Papal recovery in the fifteenth century was predicated on political power in central Italy.

■ The Babylonian Captivity, 1309–1377

The Christian church was in turmoil as a result of an attack on Pope Boniface VIII (r. 1294–1303) by King Philip IV (r. 1285–1314) of France. The king attempted to kidnap Boniface, intending to try him for heresy because of the pope's challenges to the king's authority within his own kingdom. The outstanding issues revolved around the powers of the pope and the responsibilities of the clergy to political leaders. It was, in fact, largely because of tensions with the northern kingdoms that the French archbishop of Bordeaux° was elected Pope Clement V (r. 1305–1314). Clement chose to remain north of the Alps in order to seek an end to warfare between France and England and to protect, to the extent possible, the wealthy religious order of the Knights Templar (see page 321), which Philip was in the process of suppressing. Clement also hoped to prevent the king from carrying through his threatened posthumous heresy trial of Boniface. After the death of Boniface, it was clear that the governments of Europe had no intention of recognizing papal authority as absolute.

Clement's pontificate marked the beginning of the so-called Babylonian Captivity, a period during which the pope resided almost continuously outside of Italy. In 1309 Clement moved the papal court to Avignon, on the Rhône River in a region that was still part of the Holy Roman Empire—the name that by the fourteenth century was given to the medieval empire whose origin reached back to Charlemagne. His successor, Pope John XXII (r. 1316–1334), set the tone for the brilliant papal court. To celebrate the marriage of his grandniece in 1324, for example, he ordered a wedding feast during which the numerous guests consumed 4,012 loaves of bread, 8¾ oxen, 55¼ sheep, 8 pigs, 4 boars, and vast quantities of fish, capons, chickens, partridges, rabbits, ducks, and chickens. The repast was topped off with 300 pounds of cheese, 3,000 eggs, and assorted fruits. The guests washed down this feast with about 450 liters of wine.

The papacy and its new residence in Avignon became a major religious, diplomatic, and commercial center. The size of the court changed as dramatically as its venue: although the thirteenth-century papal administration required only two hundred or so officials, the bureaucracy in Avignon grew to about six hundred. It was not just the pope's immediate circle that expanded the population of Avignon. Artists, writers, lawyers, and merchants from across Europe were drawn to the new center of administration and hub of patronage. Kings, princes, towns, and ecclesiastical institutions needed representatives at the papal court. Papal administrators continued to intervene actively in local ecclesiastical affairs, and the pope's revenues from annates (generally a portion of the first year's revenues from an ecclesiastical office granted by papal letter), court fees, and provisioning charges continued to grow.

Bordeaux (bor-DOE)

CHRONOLOGY

1303	Pope Boniface VIII attacked at Anagni and dies
1305	Election of Pope Clement V
1309	Clement V moves papal court to Avignon; beginning of Babylonian Captivity
1337	Beginning of Hundred Years' War between England and France
1348–1351	The Black Death
1356	German emperor issues Golden Bull
1378	The Great Schism
1381	The English Rising
1397	Union of Kalmar unites Denmark, Norway, and Sweden
1410	Battle of Tannenberg
1414–1417	Council of Constance
1415	Battle of Agincourt
1420	Treaty of Troyes
1431	Execution of Joan of Arc
1438	Pragmatic Sanction of Bourges
1453	End of the Hundred Years' War Ottoman Turks conquer Constantinople
1469	Marriage of Ferdinand and Isabella unites kingdoms of Aragon and Castile
1480	Ivan III ends Tartar overlordship of Muscovy
1485	Tudor dynasty established in England
1492	Spanish conquest of Granada Jews expelled from Spanish lands Columbus commissioned to discover new lands
1494	Charles VIII invades Italy

❧ READING SOURCES

Saint Catherine of Siena and the Avignon Papacy

Catherine Benincasa (1347–1380) joined the Dominican Order at age 16. Renowned for her piety and spirituality, she used her influence to pressure the popes to return to Rome and reform the church. This letter to Pope Gregory XI was probably dictated (Catherine was illiterate) in 1376.

My soul longs with inestimable love that God in His infinite mercy will take from you each passion and all tepidity of heart and will reform you into another man by rekindling in you an ardent and burning desire, for in no other way can you fulfill the will of God and the desires of all His servants. Alas, my sweetest Babbo [literally "Daddy"], pardon my presumption in what I have said and am saying—the sweet and primal Truth forces me. This is His will, Father; He demands this of you. He demands that you require justice in the multitude of iniquities committed by those nourished and sheltered in the garden of the Holy Church; He declares that beasts should not receive men's food. Because He has given you authority and because you have accepted it, you ought to use your virtue and power. If you do not wish to use it, it might be better for you to resign what you have accepted; it would give more honor to God and health to your soul.

In addition, His will demands that you make peace with all Tuscany where now you have strife. Receive all your wicked and rebellious sons whenever you can peacefully do so—but punish them as a father would an offending son. . . . [T]hat which appears impossible to you is possible to the sweet goodness of God who has ordained and willed that it be so. Beware, as you hold your life dear, that you are not negligent in this nor treat lightly the works of the Holy Spirit. . . . You can have peace by avoiding the perverse pomps and delights of the world and by preserving God's honor and the Holy Church's rights.

Source: Robert Coogan, *Babylon on the Rhone: A Translation of Letters by Dante, Petrarch, and Catherine of Siena on the Avignon Papacy* (Potomac, Md.: Studia Humanitatis, 1983), p. 115.

Not everyone approved of this situation. It was the Italian poet and philosopher Francesco Petrarch (1304–1374) who first referred to the Avignon move as a "Babylonian Captivity of the papacy." Recalling the account in the Hebrew Bible of the exile of the Israelites and New Testament images of Babylon as the center of sin and immorality, he complained of

> [an] unholy Babylon, Hell on Earth, a sink of iniquity, the cesspool of the world. There is neither faith, nor charity, nor religion, nor fear of God, nor shame, nor truth, nor holiness, albeit the residence . . . of the supreme pontiff should have made it a shrine and the very stronghold of religion.[1]

To Petrarch and others, the exile of the papacy epitomized all that was wrong with the church. Many people renowned for their piety, including women such as Saint

Catherine of Siena and Saint Bridget of Sweden, appealed to the pope to return to simpler ways and to Rome, his episcopal city. (See the box "Reading Sources: Saint Catherine of Siena and the Avignon Papacy.")

■ The Great Schism, 1378–1417

In 1377 Pope Gregory XI (r. 1370–1378) bowed to critics' pressure and did return to Rome. He was shocked by what he found: churches and palaces in ruin and the city violent and dangerous. By the end of 1377 he had resolved to retreat to Avignon, but he died a few months later. In a tumultuous election during which the Roman populace entered the Vatican Palace and threatened to break into the conclave itself, the cardinals finally elected a compromise candidate acceptable to both the French cardinals and the Roman mob. Urban VI (r. 1378–1389)

Sixtus IV Appoints a Librarian
The pope's nephew, the future Pope Julius II, stands between the seated pope and a kneeling librarian. The influence of papal families was one of the excesses that reformers of the fifteenth and sixteenth centuries hoped to curb. *(Scala/Art Resource, NY)*

may have been electable, but he was also violent, intemperate, and eager to reduce the privileges of the clerical hierarchy. In response the French cardinals questioned the legitimacy of the election, which they came to believe had been conducted under duress. Within months they deposed Urban and elected in his place a French cardinal who took the name Clement VII (r. 1378–1394). Urban responded by denouncing the cardinals and continuing to rule in Rome. The church now had two popes.

After some hesitation, Western Christians divided into two camps, initiating the Great Schism°, a period of almost forty years during which no one knew for sure who was the true pope. This was a deadly serious issue for all. The true pope had the right to appoint church

officials, decide important moral and legal issues, and allow or forbid taxation of the clergy by the state. Each side found ready supporters among the states of Europe; however, support for one pope or the other often had more to do with political rivalries than with religious convictions. The two sides largely mirrored the political tensions in Europe. France and those governments most closely allied with it tended to support Clement, who eventually resettled in Avignon. These included Burgundy, Savoy, Naples, Scotland, and Castile. The English, together with most Italian governments, the German Empire, Scandinavia, Hungary, Portugal, and Poland supported Urban, the pope in Rome.

The crisis gave impetus to new discussions about church government: Should the pope be considered the sole head of the church? Debates within the church

---

Schism (SKIZ-em)

followed lines of thought already expressed in the towns and kingdoms of Europe. Representative bodies—the English Parliament, the French Estates General, the Swedish Riksdag°—already claimed the right to act for the realm, and in the city-states of Italy ultimate authority was thought to reside in the body of citizens. Canon lawyers and theologians similarly argued that authority resided in the whole church, which had the right and duty to come together in council to correct and reform the church hierarchy. Even the most conservative of these "conciliarists" agreed that the "Universal Church" had the right to respond in periods of heresy or schism. More radical conciliarists argued that the pope as bishop of Rome was merely the first among equals in the church hierarchy and that he, like any other bishop, could be corrected by a gathering of his peers—that is, by an ecumenical council.

The rival popes found themselves under increased pressure to end the schism. The issue seemed on its way to resolution when the two parties agreed to meet in northern Italy in 1408. In the end, though, the meeting never took place, and in retrospect many doubted whether either party had been negotiating in good faith. In exasperation the cardinals, the main ecclesiastical supporters of the rival popes, called a general council in Pisa, which deposed both popes and elected a new one. Since the council lacked the power to force the rivals to accept deposition, the result was that three men now claimed to be the rightful successor of Saint Peter. Conciliarists, by themselves, could not mend the split in the church.

Resolution finally came when the Holy Roman emperor Sigismund (r. 1411–1437) forced the diplomatically isolated third papal claimant, John XXIII (r. 1410–1415), to call a general council of the church. The council, which met from 1414 to 1417 in the German imperial city of Constance, could never have succeeded without Sigismund's support. At one point he forced the council to remain in session even after Pope John had fled the city in an attempt to end deliberations.

■ Heresy and the Council of Constance, 1414–1418

Sigismund hoped a council could help him heal deep religious and civil divisions in Bohemia, the most important part of his family's traditional lands (see Map 11.3). Bohemia and its capital, Prague, were Czech-speaking.

But Prague was also the seat of the Luxemburg dynasty of German emperors and the site of the first university in the German world. Religious and theological questions quickly became embroiled in the competing claims of Czech and German factions. The preaching and teaching of Czech reformer Jan Hus (ca. 1370–1415) were at the center of the debate. As preacher in the Bethlehem Chapel in Prague from 1402 and eventually as rector of the university, Hus was the natural spokesman for the non-German townsmen in Prague and the Czech faction at the university. His criticisms of the church hierarchy, which in Prague was primarily German, fanned into flame the smoldering embers of Czech national feeling. It was Sigismund's hope that a council might clarify the orthodoxy of Hus's teachings and heal the rift within the church of Bohemia.

The council's response to the issue of heresy was based on the church's experience with heresy over the previous forty years, primarily the teachings of John Wyclif (1329–1384). In the 1370s Wyclif, an Oxford theologian and parish priest, began to criticize in increasingly angry terms the state of the clergy and the abuses of the church hierarchy. By 1387 his ideas had been declared heretical and his followers were hunted out. Wyclif's most dangerous criticism was his denial of the priest's indispensable position as an intermediary between God and believers. Wyclif believed that the church could be at once a divine institution and an earthly gathering of individuals. Thus, in his opinion, individual Christians need not unquestioningly obey the pronouncements of the church hierarchy. That special homage was due only to Scripture, insisted Wyclif, who sponsored the first translations of the Bible into English. He gathered about himself followers called Lollards, who emphasized Bible reading and popular piety; some even supported public preaching by women. According to one disciple, "Every true man and woman being in charity is a priest."[2] Because of their attacks on the ecclesiastical hierarchy, Lollards were popular among the nobility of England, and especially at the court of Richard II during the 1390s. In the first two decades of the fifteenth century, however, their influence waned.

Wyclif's influence continued on the Continent, in the circle of Jan Hus and the Czech reformers. While Hus disagreed with some of Wyclif's more radical ideas, he too attacked clerical power and privileges. By 1403 the German majority in the university had condemned Hus's teaching as Wycliffite, thus initiating almost a decade of struggle between Czechs and Germans, Hussites and Catholics. This was the impasse Sigismund hoped the

---

Riksdag (RIX-dog)

Council of Constance could settle. Accordingly he offered a suspicious Hus a safe conduct pass to attend the council. When Hus arrived, it became clear that the councilors and Hus himself were in no mood to compromise. The council reneged on the pledge of safe conduct and ordered Hus to recant his beliefs. He refused. The council condemned him as a heretic and burned him at the stake on July 6, 1415.

Far from ending Sigismund's problems with the Bohemians, the actions of the council provided the Czechs with a martyr and hero. The execution of Hus provoked a firestorm of revolution in Prague. Czech forces roundly defeated an imperial army sent in to restore order in Prague. The Hussite movement gathered strength and spread throughout Bohemia. Moderate Hussites continued Hus's campaign against clerical abuses and claimed the right to receive both the bread and the wine during the sacrament of communion. Radical Hussites argued that the true church was the community of spiritual men and women. They had no use for ecclesiastical hierarchy of any kind. The German emperors were unable to defeat a united Hussite movement. In 1433 a new church council and moderate Hussites negotiated an agreement that allowed the Hussites to continue some of their practices, including receiving both bread and wine at communion, while returning to the church. Radical Hussites refused the compromise, and the war dragged on until 1436. Bohemia remained a center of religious dissent, and the memory of Hus's execution at a church council would have a chilling effect on discussions of church reform during the Reformation in the sixteenth century.

Pope Martin Receiving the Crown from a Council
Delegates to the Council of Constance stated that even the pope had to accept the decrees of a council sitting for the whole church. *(From* Chronik des Konstanzen Konzils, *1414–1418. Courtesy, Rosgartenmuseum, Constance)*

■ The Reunion and Reform of the Papacy, 1415–1513

To most of the delegates at the Council of Constance, the reunion and reform of the papacy were more important than the issue of heresy. And as we will see, the crisis of the schism brought in its aftermath a transformed Christian church.

After initially agreeing to abdicate if his rivals did the same, John changed his mind and fled from Constance. Sigismund recaptured him and returned him to the council, where he was deposed. Pope Gregory XII (r. 1406–1415), the Roman pope, realizing he had lost all his support, resigned—after himself calling the council, as a rightful pope should do. Benedict III (r. 1394–1417), the pope in Avignon, refused to resign and he too was deposed. Finally, in 1417, the council elected a Roman nobleman as Martin V (r. 1417–1431).

The council justified its actions in what was perhaps its most important decree, *Haec sancta synodus* ("This sacred synod"):

> This sacred synod of Constance . . . declares . . . that it has its power immediately from Christ, and that all men, of every rank and position, including even the pope himself are bound to obey it in those matters that pertain to the faith.[3]

Popes could no longer expect to remain unchallenged if they made claims of absolute dominion. And ecclesiastical rights and jurisdictions increasingly were matters for negotiation.

Critics agreed that the pope no longer behaved like the "Servant of the Servants of Christ" but instead acted like the "Lord of Lords." Cardinals claimed to represent the church at large as counterweights to papal abuse, but as the nobility of the church, they and other members of the hierarchy required the income from multiple offices to maintain their presence at the papal court. Both the cardinals and the popes viewed any reforms to the present system as potential threats to their ability to function. The council, however, recognized the need for further reforms. A second reform council met at Basel from 1431 to 1449, but with little success. The council again tried to reduce papal power, but this time it received little support from European governments.

Because of the continuing conciliarist threat, the papacy needed the support of the secular rulers of Europe. Thus the papacy was forced to accept compromises on the issues of reform, on ecclesiastical jurisdictions and immunities, and on papal revenues. Various governments argued that it was they, and not the pope, who should be responsible for ecclesiastical institutions and jurisdictions within their territories.

Lay rulers focused on several issues. They wanted church officials in their territories to belong to local families. They wanted ecclesiastical institutions to be subject to local laws and administration. And by the 1470s, it was clear that they wanted to have local prelates named as cardinal-protectors. These were not churchmen who could serve the church administration in Rome; rather they functioned as mediators between local government and the papacy. The most famous of these new political cardinals was Thomas Wolsey of England (ca. 1470–1530), who was an important supporter of King Henry VII and chancellor of England under Henry VIII.

The reunited papacy had to accept claims it would have staunchly opposed a century earlier. One of the most important of these was the Pragmatic Sanction of Bourges of 1438. The papacy was unable to protest when the French clergy, at the urging of the king, abolished papal rights to annates, limited appeals to the papal court, and reduced papal rights to appoint clergy within France without the approval of the local clergy or the Crown. Similar concessions diminished church authority throughout Europe. Perhaps the most momentous was a bull issued in 1478 by Pope Sixtus IV (r. 1471–1484) that allowed Ferdinand and Isabella of Aragon and Castile to institute a church court, the Spanish Inquisition, under their own auspices (see page 387).

With reduced revenues from legal fees, annates, and appointments, the popes of the fifteenth century were forced to derive more and more of their revenue and influence from the Papal States in central Italy. By 1430, the Papal States accounted for about half of the annual income of the papacy. Papal interests increasingly centered on protecting the papacy's influence as a secular ruler of a large territory. Thus, the papacy had to deal with many of the same jurisdictional, diplomatic, and military challenges that faced other medieval governments.

WAR, DISORDER, AND REVOLTS IN WESTERN EUROPE, 1300–1450

 LAWYER who served King Philip IV of France (r. 1285–1314) observed that "everything within the limits of his kingdom belongs to the lord king, especially protection, high justice and dominion."[4] Royal officials in England and France generally believed that "liberties"—that is, individual rights to local jurisdictions—originated with the king. These ideas were the result of several centuries of centralization of political power in royal hands. At almost the same time, however, an English noble challenged royal claims on his lands, saying, "Here, my lords, is my warrant," as he brandished a rusty longsword. "My ancestors came with William the Bastard [that is, with William the Conqueror in 1066] and conquered their lands with the sword, and by the sword I will defend them against anyone who tries to usurp them."[5] The views of the royal lawyer and the feisty earl exemplify the central tension over power in the late Middle Ages. A series of political, dynastic, and military crises in the fourteenth and early fifteenth centuries made clear that many believed it was time to rein in royal claims.

■ England, France, and the Hundred Years' War, 1337–1453

In the twelfth and thirteenth centuries centralization of royal power in England and France had proceeded almost without interruption. In the fourteenth century, matters changed in both countries. Questions of the nature of royal power, common responsibility, and hereditary rights to rule challenged the power of the English and French monarchs.

In England fears arising from the growing power of the English crown and the weakness of a gullible king brought issues to a head during the reign of Edward II (r. 1307–1327). By the early fourteenth century, resident justices of the peace (JPs) were replacing the expensive and inefficient eyre system of traveling justices. In theory, the JPs were royal officials doing the king's bidding.

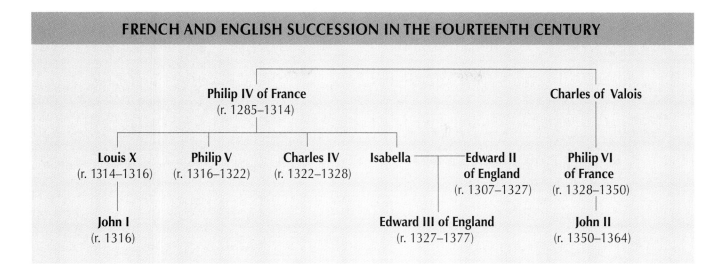

FRENCH AND ENGLISH SUCCESSION IN THE FOURTEENTH CENTURY

Philip IV of France (r. 1285–1314)

Charles of Valois

Louis X (r. 1314–1316)

Philip V (r. 1316–1322)

Charles IV (r. 1322–1328)

Isabella

Edward II of England (r. 1307–1327)

Philip VI of France (r. 1328–1350)

John I (r. 1316)

Edward III of England (r. 1327–1377)

John II (r. 1350–1364)

In reality, these unpaid local officials were modestly well-to-do gentry who were often clients of local magnates. Justices were known to use their offices to carry out local vendettas and feuds and to protect the interests of the wealthy and powerful.

The barons, the titled lords of England, were interested in controlling more than just local justices. Fearing that Edward II would continue many of the centralizing policies of his father, the barons passed reform ordinances in 1311 limiting the king's right to wage war, leave the realm, grant lands or castles, or appoint chief justices and chancellors without the approval of Parliament, which they dominated. Special taxes or subsidies were to be paid to the public Exchequer rather than into the king's private treasury. Some of these ordinances were later voided, but the tradition of parliamentary consent remained a key principle of English constitutional history. In spite of Parliament's potential power to limit royal acts, kings needed Parliament because it alone had the power to vote new taxes and generally did so when funds were necessary for the defense of the realm—a common occurrence during these centuries. Thus, English kings willingly supported the establishment of a parliamentary tradition since Parliament generally gave them the financial support they needed.

The baronial influence grew because Edward II was a weak and naive king, easily influenced by court favorites. After a humiliating defeat at the hands of the Scots at the Battle of Bannockburn (1314), his position steadily deteriorated until he was deposed in 1327 by a coalition of barons led by his wife, Queen Isabella. After a short regency, their son, Edward III (r. 1327–1377), as-

sumed the throne. He was a cautious king, ever aware of the violence and rebelliousness of the baronage.

A continuing succession crisis during the early fourteenth century made clear the limits of French kingship. In 1328 the direct Capetian line, which had sired the kings of France since the election of Hugh Capet in 987, finally died out. The last Capetians did produce daughters, but by the fourteenth century many argued that according to custom the French crown should pass through the male line only. Thus, the French nobility selected as king Philip of Valois (Philip VI; r. 1328–1350), a cousin of the last king through the male line. He was chosen in preference to the daughters of the last kings and, more significantly, in preference to King Edward III of England, whose mother was the daughter of the late king Philip IV.

Controversy over succession was just one of the disputes between the French and English. An even longer-standing issue was the status of lands within France that belonged to the English kings. In 1340, climaxing a century of tensions over English possessions in France, Edward III of England formally claimed the title "King of France."

The Hundred Years' War was a series of short raids and expeditions punctuated by a few major battles and marked off by truces or ineffective treaties. The relative strengths of the two kingdoms dictated the sporadic nature of the struggle. With a population of about 16 million, France was far richer and more populous than England. On at least one occasion the French managed to field an army of over 50,000; at most the English mustered only 32,000. These armies were easily the largest

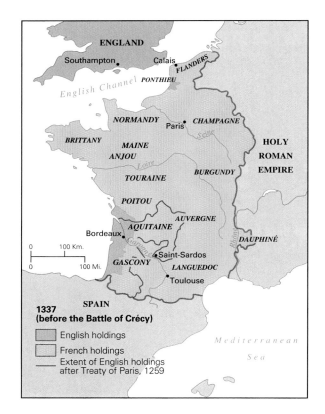

1337
(before the Battle of Crécy)

- English holdings
- French holdings
- Extent of English holdings after Treaty of Paris, 1259

1360
(after the Battle of Poitiers)

- English holdings
- French holdings
- ✕ Major battles

ca. 1429
(after the siege of Orléans)

- English holdings
- French holdings
- Burgundian lands allied with England to 1435
- ✕ Major battle

1453
(end of war)

- English holdings
- French holdings
- Burgundian lands reconciled with France after 1435
- ✕ Last battle

Map 11.1   England and France in the Hundred Years' War
The succession of maps depicts both why hit-and-run tactics worked for the English early in the war and why the English were ultimately unable to defeat the French and take control of all of France.

ever assembled by a medieval European kingdom. In almost every engagement the English were outnumbered. The most successful English strategy was to avoid pitched battles and engage in a series of quick, profitable raids during which they stole what they could, destroyed what they could not steal, and captured enemy knights to hold for ransom.

Initially, the war was characterized by a rapid series of English assaults and victories (see Map 11.1). The few pitched battles, Crécy (1346) and Poitiers (1356), occurred when the English found themselves trapped and unable to avoid the French. In these cases the English gathered their forces in careful defensive positions and took advantage of an individualistic French chivalric ethos according to which, in the words of one knight, "Who does the most is worth the most." The key to the English defensive position was use of longbowmen to attack the French knights as they labored up a hill in a vain attempt to reach the English lines. The longbow was developed in Wales, and the English perfected their use of it in numerous border wars with the Scots. Arrows from the longbow had more penetrating power than a bolt from a crossbow. And as significant, a longbow could be fired much more rapidly.

In the confusion and unrest following the French disaster at Poitiers in 1356, Étienne Marcel, provost (director) of the merchants of Paris, mobilized a protest movement designed to reduce royal and aristocratic power. This revolution seemed too radical to conservative townsmen in the provinces. Marcel's only allies were bands of rebellious countrymen roaming the region around Paris. The rural movement, or *jacquerie°* (the name comes from *jacque*, French for the "jacket" typically worn by peasants), began in response to long-standing economic and political grievances in the countryside that had been worsened by warfare. The rebels and eventually Marcel himself were isolated and then defeated by aristocratic armies.

England was soon rocked by unrest as well. The Rising of 1381 is often called the Peasants' Revolt despite

jacquerie (jack-eh-REE)

the fact that townsfolk as well as peasants participated. Already, England seethed with unrest as a result of plague (see page 371) and landlord claims for traditional dues. But the final straw was a poll tax to pay for the war: commoners responded with violent protests. The heart of the uprising was a revolt by rural peasants and artisans in the southeast, primarily in Kent and Essex. Popular armies led by Wat Tyler (d. 1381), who may have had some military experience, converged on London in June 1381. Tyler was murdered during a dramatic meeting with Richard II outside London, and a reaction against the rebels quickly ensued. (See the box "Reading Sources: The Rising of 1381.")

The rest of Richard's reign was anything but tranquil. Recognizing the dangers of noble influence, Richard II tried to insulate himself from the peers of the realm by choosing advisers from the lesser nobility and the middle classes as well as from the peerage. The result was increasing tensions with the peers and charges that Richard's rule was tyrannical. Simmering discontent boiled over, and leaders of the peers captured and forced Richard to abdicate in 1399. Parliament then elected as king Henry IV (r. 1399–1413), the first ruler from the house of Lancaster. Richard himself died in prison under mysterious circumstances in 1400.

Ever mindful of the situation that brought him to power, Henry IV was quite successful, placating both the masses and the magnates. He avoided war taxes and was careful not to alienate the nobles. The effect was that Lancastrian caution brought a truce to the French and English hostilities.

A fateful shift in relations occurred in the early fifteenth century. King Charles VI (r. 1380–1422) of France suffered bouts of insanity throughout his long reign, which made effective French government almost impossible. With the aid of the dukes of Burgundy, the English king Henry V (r. 1413–1422) renewed his family's claim to the French throne. At Agincourt in 1415, the English (led by Henry himself) again enticed a larger French army into attacking a fortified English position, and again a hail of arrows from English longbows shattered the advance. With Burgundian aid, Henry gained control over Normandy, Paris, and much of northern France. By the terms of the Treaty of Troyes (1420), Charles VI's son (the future Charles VII) was declared illegitimate and disinherited; Henry married Catherine, the daughter of Charles VI; and he was declared the legitimate heir to the French throne. A final English victory seemed assured, but both Charles VI and Henry V died in 1422, leaving Henry's infant son, Henry VI (r. 1422–1461), to inherit both thrones.

READING SOURCES

The Rising of 1381

The author of this chronicle—probably the most complete account of the English peasant revolt of 1381—seems to have been an eyewitness to the dramatic events in London. Like most literate people, the chronicler seems more comfortable with the attitudes and opinions of civil officials and landlords than with the concerns of the "rabble."

Wherefore the commons rose against [the royal] commissioner sent to investigate [rebellious acts in the region] and came before him to tell him that he was a traitor to the king and the kingdom and was maliciously proposing to undo them by the use of false inquests taken before him. Accordingly they made him swear on the Bible that never again would he hold such sessions nor act as a justice in such inquests. They proposed to kill all the lawyers, jurors and royal servants they could find. . . .

[The rebels came to London, where they executed several royal servants. They, and possibly their leader, Wat Tyler, forced the king to agree to allow them to deal "with all the traitors against him."] And they required that henceforth no man should be a serf nor make homage or any type of service to any lord, but should give four pence for an acre of land. They asked also that no one should serve any man except at his own will and by means of a regular covenant. . . .

[In a confused melée during a meeting with King Richard, Tyler was stabbed.] Wat spurred his horse, crying to the commons to avenge him, and the horse carried him some four score [eighty] paces and then he fell to the ground half dead. And when the com-

mons saw him fall, and did not know for certain how it happened, they began to bend their bows and to shoot. Therefore the king himself spurred his horse, and rode out to them, commanding them that they should all come before him at the field of St. John of Clerkenwell [a few hundred yards from where Tyler was wounded].

Afterwards, when the king had reached the open fields, he made the commons array themselves on the west side. . . . [The mayor of London had Wat Tyler] carried out to the middle of Smithfield [a market area on the edge of town]. . . and had him beheaded. . . . And so ended his wretched life. But the mayor had his head set on a pole and carried before him to the king, who still remained on the field. . . . And when the commons saw that their chieftain, Wat Tyler, was dead in such a manner, they fell to the ground there among the corn, like beaten men, imploring the king for mercy for their misdeeds. And the king benevolently granted them mercy.

Source: The Anonimalle Chronicle, in R. B. Dobson, The Peasant's Revolt of 1381 (New York: St. Martin's Press, 1970), pp. 123, 125, 128, 161, 166–167.

The kings' deaths ushered in the final stage of the Hundred Years' War, the French reconquest, from 1422 to 1453. In 1428, military and political power seemed firmly in the hands of the English and the great aristocrats. Yet in a stunning series of events, the French were able to reverse the situation.

In 1429, with the aid of the mysterious Joan of Arc (d. 1431), the French king—Charles VII—was able to raise the English siege of Orléans° and begin the recon-

quest of the north of France. Joan was the daughter of prosperous peasants from an area of Burgundy that had suffered under the English and their Burgundian allies. Like many late medieval mystics, she reported regular visions of divine revelation. Her "voices" told her to go to the king and assist him in driving out the English. Dressed as a man, she was Charles's most charismatic and feared military leader. With Joan's aid, the king was crowned in the cathedral at Reims, the traditional site of French coronations. Joan was captured during an audacious attack on Paris itself and eventually she fell into

Orléans (or-lay-OHN)

The Battle at Agincourt   The English victory at Agincourt marked the high point of English influence in France. Once again, English archers defeated a larger, mounted force.
(The Granger Collection, New York)

English hands. Because of her "unnatural dress" and her claim to divine guidance, she was condemned and burned as a heretic in 1431. A heretic only to the English and their supporters, Joan almost instantly became a symbol of French resistance. Pope Calixtus III reversed the condemnation in 1456, and in 1920 she was canonized. (See the box "Reading Sources: The Inquisition of Joan of Arc.") The heretic became Saint Joan, patron of France.

Despite Joan's capture, the French advance continued. By 1450 the English had lost all their major centers except Calais°. In 1453 the French armies captured the fortress of Castillon-sur-Dordogne° in what was to be the last battle of the war (see Map 11.1). There was no treaty, only a cessation of hostilities.

Calais (Ca-lay)
Castillon-sur-Dordogne (kas-ti-YON sir dor-DON-ya)

The war touched almost every aspect of life in western Europe: political, religious, economic, and social. It ranged beyond the borders of France as Scotland, Castile, Aragon, and German principalities were at various times drawn into the struggle. French and English support for rival popes prevented early settlement of the Great Schism in the papacy (see pages 358–361). Further, the war caused a general rise in the level of violence in society. As Henry V casually observed, "War without fire is as bland as sausages without mustard."[6] And because of the highly profitable lightning raids, the war was never bland. Soldiers regularly stole or ransomed all the booty they could take. What they could not carry, they burned. During periods of truce many soldiers simply ranged through France pillaging small towns and ravaging the countryside. Others went in search of work as mercenaries especially in Germany, Poland, and Italy. Truces in France did not necessarily mean peace in Europe.

❧ READING SOURCES

The Inquisition of Joan of Arc

An important question at the trial of Joan of Arc was whether her acts had any authoritative value: Did the voices she heard originate with God or the Devil? The judges wanted to demonstrate to their own satisfaction that Joan was one of "the sowers of deceitful inventions" of which the Gospels warned. They fully expected that external signs could reveal hidden truths.

The following memorandum is a summation of the commission's case against the maid.

You said that you wore and still wear man's dress at God's command and to His good pleasure, for you had instruction from God to wear this dress, and so you put on a short tunic, jerkin, and hose with many points. You even wear your hair cut above the ears, without keeping about you anything to denote your sex, save what nature has given you. . . . The clergy declare that you blaspheme against God, despising Him and His sacraments, that you transgress divine law, Holy Scripture and the canons of the Church, that you think evil and err from the faith, that you are full of vain boasting, that you are given to idolatry and worship of yourself and your clothes, according to the customs of the heathen.

You have declared that you know well that God loves certain living persons better than you, and that you learned this by revelation from St. Catherine and St. Margaret; also that those saints speak French, not English, as they are not on the side of the English. And since you knew that your voices were for your king, you began to dislike the Burgundians.

Such matters the clergy pronounce to be a rash and presumptuous assertion, a superstitious divination, a blasphemy uttered against St. Catherine and St. Margaret, and a transgression of the commandment to love our neighbors.

And you have said . . . that you know that all the deeds of which you have been accused in your trial were wrought according to the command of God and that it was impossible for you to do otherwise. . . . Wherefore the clergy declare you to be schismatic, an unbeliever in the unity and authority of the Church, apostate and obstinately erring from the faith. . . . [The inquisitor admonished her,] "You have believed in apparitions lightly, instead of turning to God in devout prayer to grant you certainty; and you have not consulted prelates or learned ecclesiastics to enlighten yourself: although, considering your condition and the simplicity of your knowledge, you ought to have done so."

Source: The Trial of Jeanne d'Arc, trans. W. P. Barrett (New York: Gotham House, 1932), pp. 331–338.

 For additional information on this topic, go to http://college.hmco.com.

■ Italy

Compared with France and England, fourteenth- and fifteenth-century Italy was a land of cities. In northern Europe a town of over 20,000 or 30,000 people was unusual; only Paris and London boasted more than 100,000 people in the fourteenth century. Yet at one time or another in the late Middle Ages, Milan, Venice, Florence, and Naples all had populations near or exceeding 100,000, and countless other Italian towns boasted populations of well over 30,000. Unlike northern European states with their kings or emperors, however, the Italian peninsula lacked a unifying force. The centers of power were in Italy's flourishing cities. Political life revolved around the twin issues of who should dominate city governments and how could cities learn to coexist peacefully.

By the late thirteenth century, political power in most Italian towns was divided among three major groups. First was the old urban nobility that could trace its wealth back to grants of property and rights from kings, emperors, and bishops in the tenth and eleventh centuries. A second was made up of merchant families who had grown wealthy in the twelfth and thirteenth centuries as Italians led the European economic expansion into the Mediterranean. Challenging these entrenched urban groups were modest artisans and merchants who had organized trade, neighborhood, or militia groups and referred to themselves as the *popolo*, that is, "the people." Both within these groups and between them, competition for political power and social influence was fierce. "War and hatred have so multiplied among the Italians," observed one Florentine, "that in every town there is a division and enmity between two parties of citizens." Townsmen gathered themselves together in factions based on wealth, family, profession, neighborhood, and even systems of clientage that reached back into the villages from which many of the townsmen had come.

Riven with factions, townsmen would often turn control of their governments over to a *signor°*, that is, a "lord," or "tyrant," often a local noble with a private army. Once firmly in power, a tyrant often allowed the town's government to continue to function as it had, requiring only that *he* now should control all major political appointments. The process might seem democratic, but it represented a profound shift in power. In 1264, for example, Obizzo d'Este° took control of the town of Ferrara when a carefully managed assembly of the people proclaimed him to be "Governor and Ruler and General and Permanent Lord of the City of Ferrara." The rise of the Este lords seemed peaceful, but the transformation was clearer in Mantua. "[Pinamonte Bonacolsi (d. 1293)] usurped the lordship of his city and expelled his fellow-citizens and occupied their property," according to a chronicler. "And he was feared like the devil."[7] In the case of Milan, the noble Visconti° used support from the Emperor Henry VII (r. 1308–1313) to drive their opponents out of the city. Eventually granted Milan and its territories as a duchy, the Viscontis and later their Sforza successors made marriage alliances with the French crown and created a splendid court culture. In a series of wars between the 1370s and 1450s, the dukes of Milan expanded their political control throughout most of Lombardy, Liguria, and, temporarily, Tuscany. The Visconti maintained control of the city and much of the region of Lombardy until the last scion of the family died in 1447.

The great republics of Venice and Florence escaped domination by signori, but only by undertaking significant constitutional change. In both republics political life had been disrupted by the arrival of immigrants and by the demands of recently enriched merchants and speculators for a voice in government. In 1297, reacting to increased competition for influence, the Venetian government enacted what would come to be known as the Closing of the Grand Council. The act enlarged to about eleven hundred the number of families eligible for public office, but its ultimate effect was to freeze out subsequent arrivals from ever rising to elite status. The Venetian patriciate became a closed urban nobility. Political, factional, and economic tensions were hidden beneath a veneer of serenity as Venetians developed a myth of public-spirited patricians who governed in the interests of all the peoples, leaving others free to enrich themselves in trade and manufacture.

In Florence the arguments over citizenship and the right of civic participation disrupted public life. Violent wealthy families, immigrants, and artisans of modest backgrounds were cut off from civic participation. A series of reforms culminating in the Ordinances of Justice of 1293–1295 restricted political participation in Florence to members in good standing of certain merchant and artisan guilds. Members of violence-prone families were defined as "Magnate" (literally, "the powerful") and disqualified from holding public office. The reforms guaranteed that political power remained concentrated in the hands of the great families, whose wealth was based primarily on banking and mercantile investments. These families used their political influence and economic power to dominate Florentine life.

There were short-lived attempts to reform the system and extend the rights of political participation to include the more modest artisans and laborers. The most dramatic was in 1378 when the Ciompi°, unskilled workers in Florence's woolen industry, led a popular revolution hoping to expand participation in government and limit the authority of the guild masters over semiskilled artisans and day laborers. They created new guilds to represent the laborers who previously had had no voice in government. Barely six weeks after the Ciompi insurrection, however, wealthy conservatives began a reaction suppressing, exiling, or executing the leaders of the movement and eventually suppressing the new guilds. Political and economic power was now even more firmly in the grip of the patricians.

Following a crisis in 1434 brought on by war and high taxes, virtual control of Florentine politics fell into the hands of Cosimo de' Medici, the wealthiest banker in the city. From 1434 to 1494, Cosimo; his son, Piero; his grandson, Lorenzo; and Lorenzo's son dominated the government in Florence. Although the Medicis were

---

signor (sin-YOUR)   **Obizzo d'Este** (oh-BITZ-oh duh-ES-tay)
Visconti (vis-KON-tee)

Ciompi (CHOMP-ee)

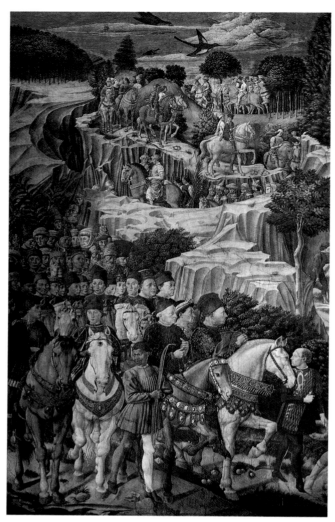

The Journey of the Magi   The story of the journey of the Magi to Bethlehem to find the baby Jesus seemed a perfect image of the power and wisdom of rulers. This painting (a detail) of the Magi was commissioned for the private chapel of Cosimo de' Medici, the de facto ruler of Florence.   *(Palazzo Medici Riccardi, Florence/Scala/Art Resource, NY)*

always careful to pay homage to Florentine republican traditions, their control was virtually as complete as that of the lords of towns such as Ferrara or Milan.

Indeed, by the middle of the fifteenth century, little differentiated the republics—Florence and Venice—from the cities such as Milan or Mantua where lords held sway. Although Florentines maintained that they intervened to protect Florentine and Tuscan "liberty" when the Visconti of Milan threatened Tuscany and central Italy, their interests went beyond simple defense. Rela-

tions among the great cities of Milan, Venice, Florence, Rome, and Naples were stabilized by the Peace of Lodi and the creation of the Italian League in 1454. In response to endemic warfare in Italy and the looming threat of the Ottoman Turks in the eastern Mediterranean (see page 381), the five powers agreed to the creation of spheres of influence that would prevent any one of them from expanding at the expense of the others.

The limits of these territorial states of Italy became clear when King Charles VIII of France invaded Italy in 1494. Ludovico Sforza of Milan enticed the French king to assert his hereditary claim to the kingdom of Naples. The French invasion touched off a devastating series of wars called the Habsburg-Valois Wars. French claims were immediately challenged by the Spanish, who themselves made claims on southern Italy and much of Lombardy. The cost of prolonged warfare kept almost all governments in a state of crisis. Unrest brought on by the invasion even allowed Pope Alexander VI (r. 1492–1503) to attempt to create a state for his son, Cesare Borgia° (1475–1507), in central Italy.

In Florence the wars destroyed the old Medici-dominated regime and brought in a new republican government. Anti-Medici efforts were initially led by the popular Dominican preacher Girolamo Savonarola (1452–1498). In the constitutional debates after 1494, Savonarola argued that true political reform required a sweeping purge of the evils of society. Gangs of youth flocked to his cause, attacking prostitutes and homosexuals. Many of his followers held "bonfires of vanities," burning wigs, silks, and other luxuries. In 1498, when his followers had lost influence in the government, Savonarola himself was arrested, tortured, and executed.

In spite of republican reforms, new fortresses, and a citizen militia, the Florentine government was unable to defend itself from papal and imperial armies. In 1512 the Habsburg emperor restored Medici control of Florence. The Medicis later became dukes and then grand dukes of Tuscany. The grand duchy of Tuscany remained an independent, integrated, and well-governed state until the French Revolution of 1789. Venice also managed to maintain its republican form of government and its territorial state until the French Revolution; but, like the grand dukes of Tuscany, the governors of Venice were no longer able to act independently of the larger European powers.

The Habsburg-Valois Wars continued for over a half-century, ending with the Treaty of Cateau-Cambrésis° in

Borgia (BOR-zheh)
Cateau-Cambrésis (kah-toe kam-bray-SEE)

1559, which left the Spanish kings in control of Milan, Naples, Sardinia, and Sicily. Thus, war and the political integration of the fifteenth century destroyed the tiny city-republics and snuffed out any illusions among the remaining territorial states that they could act independently of foreign powers.

ECONOMY AND SOCIETY

FTER nearly three centuries of dramatic growth, Europe in 1300 was seriously overpopulated, with estimates ranging from about 80 million to as high as 100 million. In some parts of Europe, populations would not again be this dense until the late eighteenth century! Opportunities dwindled because of overpopulation, famine, war, and epidemics. These shocks brought changes in trade and commerce. Lowered population, deflation, and transformed patterns of consumption also affected agriculture, which was still the foundation of the European economy. Recovery from these crises altered the structure and dynamics of families, the organization of work, and the culture in many parts of Europe.

◼ The Plague and Demographic Crisis

People in many parts of Europe were living on the edge of disaster in 1300. Given the low level of agricultural technology and the limited amounts of land available for cultivation, it became increasingly difficult for the towns and countryside to feed and support the growing population. The nature of the problem varied from place to place. Evidence points to a crisis of both births (low birthrates) and deaths (from famine and illness).

Growing numbers of people competed for land to farm and for jobs. Farm sizes declined throughout Europe as parents tended to divide their land among their children. Rents for farmland increased as landlords found they could play one land-hungry farmer against another. Competition for jobs kept wages low, and when taxes were added to high rents and low wages, many peasants and artisans found it difficult to marry and raise families. Thus, because of reduced opportunities brought on by overpopulation, poor townsmen and peasants tended to marry late and have small families.

More dramatic than this crisis of births were the deadly famines that occurred in years of bad harvests. The great famine of 1315–1322 marks a turning point in the economic history of Europe. Wet and cold weather repeat-

edly ruined crops in much of northern Europe. Food stocks were quickly exhausted, and mass starvation followed. People died so quickly, English chroniclers reported, that survivors could not keep up with the burials. At Ypres, in Flanders, 2,800 people (about 10 percent of the population) died in just six months. And shortages continued. Seven other severe famines were reported in the south of France or Italy during the fourteenth century.

If Europe's problem had merely been one of famine brought on by overpopulation, rapid recovery should have been possible. But because of the return of a deadly epidemic disease, the population did not recover. In 1348 the Black Death, or "the great Mortality" as contemporaries called it, struck Europe. The most likely cause is bubonic plague, which returned to western Europe for the first time in six hundred years. Genoese traders contracted the plague in Caffa on the Black Sea coast. Infected sailors carried the disease south into Egypt and west to Sicily and then on to Genoa and Venice. From there it followed established trade routes first into central Italy and later to the south of France, the Low Countries, England, and finally through the North and Baltic Seas into Germany and the Slavic lands to the east (see Map 11.2).

Mortality rates varied, but generally 60 percent or more of those infected died. In the initial infestation of 1348–1351, from 25 to 35 percent of Europe's population may have died. In some of Europe's larger cities, the proportion may have been as high as 60 percent. In Florence, the population probably declined by almost half, from about 90,000 to 50,000 or even less. (See the box "Reading Sources: The Black Death.") And the nearby town of Siena likely fared even worse, with a total mortality of 55 percent in the town and its suburbs.

Just as areas were rebounding from the initial outbreak, the plague returned again in 1363, and then for three centuries thereafter almost no generation could avoid it. Less is known about the plague in Muslim lands and in the eastern Mediterranean, but the situation seems to have been similar to the European experience. Because the plague tended to carry off the young, the almost generational return of the disease accounts for the depressed population levels found in many parts of Europe until the late fifteenth century and in western Asia until the late seventeenth or eighteenth century.

Lacking an understanding of either contagion or infection, fourteenth-century doctors depended on traditional theories inherited from the Greeks, especially the work of Galen°. In Galenic medicine, good health was a

Galen (GAY-len)

condition that depended on the proper balance of bodily and environmental forces; it could be upset by corrupt air, the movements of planets, and even violent shifts in emotions. Blind to the biological nature of the disease and its spread, Europeans were unable to treat the plague effectively. Yet in the fifteenth and sixteenth centuries, as the rhythms of the plague infestations became clearer, towns and, later, territorial governments perceived the contagious nature of the disease. Officials instituted increasingly effective quarantines and embargoes to restrict the movement of goods and people from areas where the plague was raging. This innovative effort at public health regulation that limited the movement of infected products probably explains the disappearance of plague from western Europe by the early eighteenth century.

Alongside medical theory, however, another class of explanations developed. Taking a lead from miracle stories in which Jesus linked illness and sin, many Christians considered "the great Mortality" a signal of the end times, or at least a sign of the severe judgment of God on a sinful world. Given that view, a traditional, and logical, religious response was to urge various moral reforms or penitential acts—charitable gifts, special prayers, holy processions. (See the feature "Weighing the Evidence: A Painting of the Plague" on pages 390–391.) Many Muslim theologians also concluded that "the plague is part of Allah's punishment." Women were often thought to be a source of moral pollution and hence one of the causes of God's wrath. In Muslim Egypt, women were ordered off the streets; in Christian Europe prostitutes were driven out of towns.

Map 11.2   The Progress of the Black Death   The Black Death did not advance evenly across Europe; rather, as is clear from the dates at which it struck various regions, it followed the main lines of trade and communication.

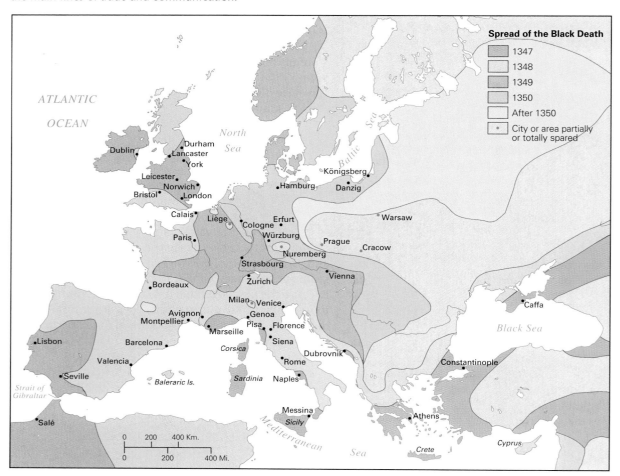

🐾 READING SOURCES

The Black Death

The plague of 1348 in Florence dominates the histories of Florence written in the fourteenth century. Marchione di Coppo Stefani (1336–?) describes the impact of "the great Mortality" on the city of Florence itself as well as on the surrounding countryside.

In the year of the Lord 1348 there was a very great pestilence in the city and district of Florence. It was of such a fury and so tempestuous that in houses in which it took hold previously healthy servants who took care of the ill died of the same illness. Almost none of the ill survived past the fourth day. Neither physicians nor medicines were effective. Whether because these illnesses were previously unknown or because physicians had not previously studied them, there seemed to be no cure. There was such a fear that no one seemed to know what to do. When it took hold in a house it often happened that no one remained who had not died. . . . Child abandoned the father, husband the wife, wife the husband, one brother the other, one sister the other. In all the city there was nothing to do but to carry the dead to a burial. . . .

In the said year, when the mortality stopped, women and men in Florence were unmindful of [traditional modesty concerning] their dress. . . . The workers on the land in the countryside wanted rent contracts such that you could say that all they har-

vested would be theirs. And they learned to demand oxen from the landlord but at the landlord's risk [and liability for any harm done to the animal]. And then they helped others for pay by the job or by the day. And they also learned to deny [liability for] loans and [rental] payments. Concerning this serious ordinances were instituted; and [hiring] laborers became much more expensive. You could say that the farms were theirs; and they wanted the oxen, seed, loans quickly and on good terms. It was necessary to put a brake on weddings as well because when they gathered for the betrothal each party brought too many people in order to increase the pomp. And thus the wedding was made up of so many trappings. How many days were necessary and how many women took part in a woman's wedding. And they passed many other ordinances concerning [these issues].

Source: Marchione di Coppo Stefani, *Cronaca fiorentina, Rerum Italicarum Scriptores,* vol. 30, ed. Niccolo Rodolico (Città di Castello, 1927). Translation by Duane Osheim.

A movement of penitents called "flagellants" arose in Hungary and spread quickly into Germany and across France and the Low Countries. In an imitation of Christ's life and sufferings, they sought to atone in their own bodies for the sins of the world. Following an ancient Christian tradition, they ritually beat (flagellated) themselves between the shoulders with metal-tipped whips. Through their processions and sufferings, these pilgrims hoped to bring about a moral and religious transformation of society. The arrival of flagellants was often an occasion for an end of feuds and political violence within a community. In a quest for a purer, truly Christian society, the flagellants brought suspicion on all those who were not Christian or who were otherwise suspect.

Some parts of Europe witnessed murderous attacks on outsiders, especially lepers and Jews, who were suspected of spreading the contagion in an attempt to bring down Latin Christendom. These attacks probably have more to do with tensions and fears already existing in parts of Europe than with the provocations of the flagellants. Like many other anti-Semitic myths, the rumors of wells poisoned by Jews seemed to arise in the south of France and spread in their most virulent forms to German towns along the Rhine. In Strasbourg, attacks on Jews even preceded the arrival of plague. Except in a few districts, officials opposed attacks on Jews, lepers, and heretics. Doctors and churchmen often observed that Jews were unlikely culprits since plague claimed Jewish as well as Christian victims. After a few months of violence, the flagellants and the leaders of the religious riots were recognized as dangerous and driven from towns.

It was a commonplace among contemporary chroniclers that "so many did die that everyone thought it was the end of the world." Yet it was the very young, the elderly, and the poor—those least likely to pay taxes, own shops, or produce new children—who were the most common victims. Even in towns such as Florence, however, where mortality rates were extraordinarily high, recovery was rapid. Government offices were closed at most for only a few weeks; markets reopened as soon as the death rate began to decline. And within two years tax receipts were back at preplague levels. Below the surface, however, plague and population decline fueled the economic and social transformations of the late Middle Ages.

■ Trade and Agriculture

In the aftermath of plague, the economy of Europe changed in a number of profound ways. Disruptions brought on by population decline were accompanied by changes in the basic structure of economic life. In particular, Italy's domination of the European economy was challenged by the growth of trade and manufacturing in many other parts of Europe. Further, Italian bankers came to face competition from equally astute local bankers.

Discussions of the economy must begin with Italy because it was the key point of contact between Europe and the international economy. In 1300 Italian merchants sold woolens produced in Flanders and Italy to Arab traders in North Africa, who sold them along the African coast and as far south as the Niger Delta. The Italians used the gold that they collected in payment to buy spices and raw materials in Byzantium, Egypt, and even China. They resold these highly prized goods in the cities and at regional fairs of northern Europe. Italian traders also sold spices, silks, and other luxuries throughout Europe, from England to Poland.

Because of their expertise in moving bullion and goods and their ready sources of capital, Italian merchants, such as the Ricciardis of Lucca who flourished in England, were ideal bankers and financial advisers to the popes and European rulers, who appreciated sources of ready capital. In time of war, rulers tended to trade the rights to various revenues to Italian bankers, who had cash at hand. Merchants from Cremona, Genoa, Florence, and Siena forged commercial agreements with the kings of France, Aragon, and Castile, and with the papacy.

The most powerful bank in fifteenth-century Europe was the Medici bank of Florence. Founded in 1397 by Giovanni de' Medici° (1360–1429), the bank grew quickly because of its role as papal banker. Medici agents transferred papal revenues from all parts of Europe to Rome and managed papal alum mines, which provided an essential mineral to the growing cloth industry. Cosimo de' Medici° (1389–1464), Giovanni's son and successor, transformed the enterprise into a series of bilateral partnerships with easily controlled junior partners in other parts of Europe. In this way he avoided the problem of supervision and control that plagued other banks, whose partners were equal and free to speculate and invest as they wished.

The dramatic career of the Frenchman Jacques Coeur (1395?–1456) demonstrates that by the mid-fifteenth century, Italian merchants were not the only Europeans who understood international trade. After making a fortune trading in southern France, Coeur managed the French royal mint and became the financial adviser of King Charles VII (r. 1422–1461). He put the French monarchy back on a solid financial footing after the Hundred Years' War, becoming in the process the wealthiest individual in France. Not surprisingly, his wealth and influence earned him jealous enemies, who tried to bring him down with outrageous claims: he was accused of murdering the king's mistress, trading with Muslims, and stealing royal funds. In 1451 his property was confiscated, and he was jailed for a short time. He later led a papal expedition against the Turks in the Aegean, where he died.

By 1500 Italians faced increased competition from local merchants throughout Europe. From as early as the late thirteenth century, trade along the North and Baltic Seas in northern Europe was dominated by the Hanseatic League, an association of over a hundred trading cities centered on the German city of Lübeck. By the late fourteenth and early fifteenth centuries, the Hansa towns controlled grain shipments from eastern Europe to England and Scandinavia. The league's domination waned in the second half of the fifteenth century, however, as Dutch, English, and even south German merchants gained shares of the wool, grain, and fur trades. Towns in the eastern Baltic found that their interests no longer coincided with those of the towns in western Germany that made up the Hanseatic League. Wroclaw° (in

Giovanni de' Medici (joe-VAHN-nee day-MAY-di-chi)
Cosimo de' Medici (CAW-see-moe day-MAY-di-chi)
Wroclaw (VROT-swav)

The Feast of Saint John the Baptist   John the Baptist was the patron saint of Florence. Each year a procession in his honor included government officials, the great associations and guilds in the city, and representatives from surrounding villages.   *(Scala/Art Resource, NY)*

modern Poland) signaled the nature of the change when it resigned from the league in 1474 to expand trade connections with the south German towns.

In contrast to the Hanseatic League of towns, merchants in south Germany adopted Italian techniques of trade, manufacture, and finance to expand their influence throughout central Europe. German merchants regularly bought spices in the markets of Venice and distributed them in central and eastern Europe. By the fifteenth century, the townsmen of south Germany also produced linen and cotton cloth, which found ready markets in central and eastern Europe.

The Fugger° family of Augsburg in southern Germany, the most prosperous of the German commercial families, exemplifies the variety of activities undertaken by south German merchants. Hans Fugger (1348–1409) moved to Augsburg from a nearby village in the 1360s and quickly established himself as a weaver and wool merchant. By the 1470s, Hans's grandson, Jacob Fugger (1459–1525), was a dominant figure in the spice trade and also participated in a number of unusually large loans to a succession of German princes. The Fuggers

became leaders in the Tyrolean silver-mining industry, which expanded dramatically in the late fifteenth century. And in the early sixteenth century, they handled all transfers of money from Germany to the papacy. Jacob Fugger's wealth increased fourfold between 1470 and 1500. The Fuggers were indispensable allies of the German emperors. Jacob himself ensured the election of Charles V as Holy Roman emperor in 1519, making a series of loans that allowed Charles to buy the influence that he needed to win election.

As wealthy as the great merchants were, in most parts of Europe prosperity was still tied to agriculture and the production of food grains. In northern and western Europe, foodstuffs were produced on the manorial estates of great churchmen and nobles. These estates were worked by a combination of farmers paying rents, serfs who owed a variety of labor services, and day laborers who were hired during planting and harvesting. In the face of a decimated population, landlords and employers found themselves competing for the reduced number of laborers who had survived the plague. In 1351 the English crown issued the Statute of Laborers, which pegged wages and the prices of commodities at pre-plague levels. According to the statute, regulation was necessary because laborers "withdrew themselves from

---

Fugger (FOO-ger)

serving great men and others unless they have living [in food] and wages double or treble of what they were [before the plague]." This statute and similar ones passed in other parts of Europe were dead letters. So long as population levels remained low, landowners were unable to keep wages low and rents high.

Cloth manufacture, not agriculture, was the part of the European economy that changed most dramatically in the late Middle Ages. First in Flanders, then later in England, Germany, and the rest of Europe, production shifted from urban workshops to the countryside. Industries in rural areas tended to be free of controls on quality or techniques. Rural production, whether in Flanders, England, or Lombardy, became the most dynamic part of the industry.

Rural cloth production, especially in southwest Germany and parts of England, was organized through the putting-out system. Merchants who owned the raw wool contracted with various artisans in the city, suburbs, or countryside—wherever the work could be done most cheaply—to process the wool into cloth. Rural manufacture was least expensive because it could be done as occasional or part-time labor by farmers, their wives, or children during slack times of the day or season. Because production was likely to be finished in the countryside (beyond guild supervision), the merchant was free to move the cloth to wherever it could most easily and profitably be sold; guild masters had no control over price or quality.

Two other developments also changed the woolen trade of the fifteenth century: the rise of Spain as an exporter of unprocessed wool and the emergence of England, long recognized as a source of prime wool, as a significant producer of finished cloth. Spain was an ideal region for the pasturing of livestock. By the fifteenth century, highly prized Spanish wool from merino sheep was regularly exported to Italy, Flanders, and England. By 1500 over 3 million sheep grazed in Castile alone, and revenues from duties on wool formed the backbone of royal finance.

In England, in contrast, economic transformation was tied to cloth production. During the fifteenth century England reduced its export of its high-quality raw wool and began instead to export its own finished cloth. In 1350 the English exported just over 5,000 bolts of cloth. By the 1470s exports had risen to 63,000 bolts, and they doubled again by the 1520s. The growth of cloth exports contributed enormously to the expansion of London. During the fourteenth and fifteenth centuries, English commerce became increasingly controlled by London merchant-adventurers. Soon after 1500, over 80

percent of the cloth for export passed through the hands of the Londoners. This development, coupled with the rise of London as a center of administration and consumption, laid the foundation for the economic and demographic growth that would make London the largest and most prosperous city in western Europe by the eighteenth century.

All these patterns of economic change in the fifteenth century challenged customs and institutions by admitting new entrepreneurs into the marketplace. But Europe was still a conservative society in which social and political influence was more prized than economic wealth. Patricians in many European towns acted to dampen competition and preserve traditional values. Great banking families such as the Medicis of Florence tended to avoid competition and concentrations of capital. They did not try to drive their competitors out of business because the leaders of rival banks were their political and social peers. In northern Europe, governments in towns such as Leiden restricted the concentration of resources in the hands of the town's leading cloth merchants. Their aim was to ensure full employment for the town's laborers, political power for the guild masters, and social stability in the town.

Full employment was for men only, however. Opportunities for women declined significantly in the fifteenth century. Although men had controlled the guilds and most crafts in the thirteenth and early fourteenth centuries, women in England and many other parts of northern Europe had been actively involved in the local economy. Unlike southern Europe, where women had no public roles, some northern towns apparently allowed women's guilds to protect their members' activities as artisans and even peddlers. Because they often worked before marriage, townswomen in northern Europe tended to marry at a later age than did women in Italy. Many women earned their own marriage dowries. Since they had their own sources of income and often managed the shop of a deceased husband, women could be surprisingly independent. They were consequently under less pressure to remarry at the death of a spouse. Although their economic circumstances varied considerably, up to a quarter of the households in northern towns—for example, Bern or Zurich—were headed by women, almost all independent widows.

The fifteenth century brought new restrictions into women's lives. In England brewing ale had been a highly profitable part-time activity that women often combined with the running of a household. Ale was usually produced in small batches for household use and whatever went unconsumed would be sold. The introduction

Women at Work   Although guild records tended to ignore the contributions of women, many women worked in their husband's shop. In this miniature, a woman is selling jewelry. Widows often managed the shops they inherited.   *(Bibliothèque Nationale de France)*

of beer changed matters. Because hops were added during brewing as a preservative, beer was easier to produce, store, and transport in large batches. Beer brewing became a lucrative full-time trade, reducing the demand for the alewife's product and providing work for men as brewers. At the same time the rights of women to work in urban crafts and industries were reduced. Wealthy fathers became less inclined to allow wives and daughters to work outside the home. Guilds banned the use of female laborers in many trades and severely limited the rights of widows to supervise their spouses' shops. For reasons that are not entirely clear, journeymen—employees of guild masters who themselves hoped to become masters—objected to working alongside women. Their complaints may have come from workers who realized that their status as employees was permanent instead of a temporary stage before promotion to master. By the early sixteenth century, journeymen in Germany

considered it "dishonorable" for a woman, even the master's wife or daughter, to work in a shop.

Despite the narrowing of economic opportunities for women, the overall economic prospects of peasants and laborers improved. Lowered rents and increased wages in the wake of plague meant a higher standard of living for small farmers and laborers. Before the plague struck in 1348, most poor Europeans had subsisted on bread or grain-based gruel, consuming meat, fish, and cheese only a few times a week. A well-off peasant in England had lived on a daily ration of about two pounds of bread and a cup or two of oatmeal porridge washed down with three or four pints of ale. Poorer peasants generally drank water except on very special occasions. After the plague, laborers were more prosperous. Adults in parts of Germany may have consumed nearly a liter of wine and a third of a pound of meat along with a pound or more of bread each day. Elsewhere people could substitute an equivalent portion of beer, ale, or cider for the wine. Hard times for landlords were good times for peasants and day laborers.

Landlords in England responded to the shortage of labor by converting their lands to grazing in order to produce wool for the growing textile market. In parts of Italy, landlords invested in canals, irrigation, and new crops in order to increase profits. In eastern Germany and Poland, landlords were able to take advantage of political and social unrest to force tenants into semi-free servile status. This so-called second serfdom created an impoverished work force whose primary economic activity was in the lord's fields, establishing commercial grain farming. Increasingly in the second half of the century, grains cultivated in Poland and Prussia found their way to markets in England and the Low Countries. Europe east of the Elbe River became a major producer of grain, but at a heavy social cost.

The loss of perhaps a third of the urban population to the plague had serious consequences in the towns of Europe. Because of lower birthrates and higher death rates, late medieval towns needed a constant influx of immigrants in order to expand or even to maintain their populations. These immigrants did not find life in the cities to be easy, however. Citizenship in most towns was restricted to masters in the most important guilds, and local governments were in their hands, if not under their thumbs. In many towns, citizens constructed a system of taxation that worked to their own economic advantage and fell heavily on artisans and peasants living in territories controlled by the town. Unskilled laborers and members of craft guilds depended for their economic well-being on personal relationships with powerful citizens who controlled the government and the markets. Peace and order in towns and in the countryside required a delicate balance of the interests of the well-to-do and the more humble. When that balance was shattered by war, plague, and economic depression, the result was often a popular revolt, such as the jacquerie of 1356 in France, the Ciompi Revolution of 1378 in Florence, and the Rising of 1381 in England.

THE CONSOLIDATION OF THE LATE MEDIEVAL GOVERNMENTS, 1450–1500

BY 1500 it seemed that the French royal lawyer's claim that all within the kingdom belonged to the king was finally accepted. With the exception of Italy and Germany, strong central governments recovered from the crises of war and civil unrest that

wracked the fourteenth and fifteenth centuries. The Hundred Years' War and the resulting disorganization in France and England seemed to strike at the heart of the monarchies. But through the foundation of standing armies and the careful consolidation of power in the royal court, both countries seemed stronger and more able to defend themselves in the second half of the century. And as the Italians learned in the wars following the French invasion of 1494, small regional powers were no match for the mighty monarchies.

■ France, England, and Scandinavia

In France recovery from a century of war was based on a consolidation of the monarchy's power. A key to French military successes had been the creation of a paid professional army, which replaced the feudal host and mercenary companies of the fourteenth century. Charles VII created Europe's first standing army, a cavalry of about eight thousand nobles under the direct control of royal commanders. Charles also expanded his judicial claims. He and his son, Louis XI (r. 1461–1483), created new provincial *parlements*, or law courts, at Toulouse°, Grenoble°, Bordeaux, and Dijon°. They also required that local laws and customs be registered and approved by the parlements.

A second key to maintaining royal influence was the rise of the French court as a political and financial center. Through careful appointments and judicious offers of annuities and honors, Charles VII and Louis XI drew the nobility to the royal court and made the nobles dependent on it. "The court," complained a frustrated noble, "is an assembly of people who, under the pretense of acting for the good of all, come together to diddle each other; for there's scarcely anyone who isn't engaged in buying and selling and exchanging . . . and sometimes for their money we sell them our . . . humanity."[8] One of Louis XI's advisers noted that Charles VII never had revenues greater than 18,000 francs in a single year but that Louis collected 4.7 million. By 1500 France had fully recovered from the crisis of war and was once again a strong and influential state.

The fate of the English monarchy was quite different. Henry VI (r. 1422–1461) turned out to be weak-willed, immature, and prone to bouts of insanity. The infirmity of Henry VI and the loss of virtually all French territories in 1453 led to factional battles known as the Wars of the Roses—the red rose symbolized Henry's house of Lancaster, the white the rival house of York.

Toulouse (too-LOOZ)   **Grenoble** (greh-NO-bul)
Dijon (dee-ZHON)

Edward of York eventually deposed Henry and claimed the crown for himself as Edward IV (r. 1461–1483). He faced little opposition because few alternatives existed. English public life was again thrown into confusion, however, at the death of Edward IV. The late king's brother, Richard, duke of Gloucester, claimed the protectorship over the 13-year-old king, Edward V (r. April–June 1483), and his younger brother. He seized the boys, who were placed in the Tower of London and never seen again. Richard proclaimed himself king and was crowned Richard III (r. 1483–1485). He withstood early challenges to his authority but in 1485 was killed in the Battle of Bosworth Field, near Coventry, by Henry Tudor, a leader of the Lancastrian faction. Henry married Elizabeth, the surviving child of Edward IV. Symbolically at least, the struggle between the rival claimants to the Crown appeared over.

Like his predecessor Edward IV, Henry VII (r. 1485–1509) recognized the importance of avoiding war and taxation. Like the French kings, he created a patronage network of local officials to secure allies for his dynasty. Royal power, however, was not based on a transformation of the institutions of government. Following Edward IV's example, Henry VII controlled local affairs through the traditional system of royal patronage. He also imitated Edward in emphasizing the dignity of the royal office. Though careful with his funds, he was willing to buy jewels and clothing if they added to the brilliance of his court. As one courtier summed up his reign, "His hospitality was splendidly generous. . . . He knew well how to maintain his majesty and all which pertains to kingship." Henry solidified ties with Scotland and Spain by marrying his daughter, Margaret Tudor, to James IV of Scotland and his sons, Arthur and (after Arthur's death) Henry, to Catherine of Aragon, daughter of the Spanish rulers Ferdinand and Isabella.

The English monarchy of the late fifteenth century departed little from previous governments. The success of Henry VII was based on several factors: the absence of powerful opponents; lowered taxation thanks to twenty-five years of peace; and the desire, shared by ruler and ruled alike, for an orderly realm built on the assured succession of a single dynasty.

In the fourteenth and fifteenth centuries, the Scandinavian kingdoms of Denmark, Sweden, and Norway lay open to economic and political influences from Germany. German merchants traded throughout the area and completely controlled access to the important port of Bergen in Norway. German nobles sought to influence northern political life, especially in Denmark. The Scandinavian aristocracy, however, especially in Denmark,

remained wary of German interests. Alert to outside pressures, Scandinavian elites tended to marry among themselves and forge alliances against the Germans.

Public authority varied greatly across Scandinavia. In Norway, Denmark, and Sweden, the power of the king was always mediated by the influence of the council, made up of the country's leading landowners. Power was based on ownership or control of lands and rents. All the Scandinavian countries were home to a significant class of free peasants, and they were traditionally represented in the Riksdag in Sweden and the Storting in Norway, popular assemblies that had the right to elect kings, authorize taxes, and make laws. Scandinavians spoke similar Germanic languages and were linked by close social and economic ties. Thus, it is not surprising that the crowns of the three kingdoms were joined during periods of crisis. In 1397 the dowager Queen Margaret of Denmark was able to unite the Scandinavian crowns by the Union of Kalmar, which would nominally endure until 1523.

■ Eastern Europe and Russia

Two phenomena had an especially profound effect on the governments of eastern Europe. One was the emergence of a newly important ruling dynasty. The other was the decline of Mongol, or Tartar, influence in the region. Since the thirteenth century, much of eastern Europe had been forced to acknowledge Tartar dominion and pay annual tribute. Now, the Tartar subjugation was challenged and finally ended.

As in much of Europe, political power was segmented and based on personal relationships between family members, communities, clients, and friends. Life in the east was further complicated by the mix of languages, cultures, and religions. In the fourteenth century Ashkenazi Jews migrating from Germany were added to the mix of Catholic and Orthodox Christian and Muslim communities. Like the other groups, the Ashkenazi in Poland, Lithuania, and certain Russian lands lived under their own leaders and followed their own laws.

This mix of cultures and religions played a role in the growth of new states. Under the pretext of converting their pagan neighbors to Christianity, the mostly German Teutonic knights sought to expand eastward against the kingdom of Poland and the Lithuanian state. They were thwarted, however, by a profound dynastic shift. In 1386 Duke Jagiello (r. 1377–1434) of Lithuania converted to Catholic Christianity and married Hedwig, the daughter and heir of King Louis of Poland (r. 1370–1382). The resulting dynastic union created a state with a population of perhaps 6 million that reached from the Baltic nearly to the Black Sea. Polish-Lithuanian power slowed and finally halted the German advance to the east. Most serious for the knights was their defeat in 1410 at Tannenberg in Prussia by a Polish-Lithuanian army led by Jagiello's cousin, Prince Vytautus of Lithuania. The Polish-Lithuanian union was only dynastic. The descendents of Jagiello, called Jagiellonians, had no hereditary right to rule in Poland, and the Lithuanians opposed any Polish administrative influence in their lands. Yet because of Jagiellonian power, the Poles continued to select them as kings. At various times, Jagiellonians also sat on the thrones of Bohemia and Hungary.

The fourteenth and fifteenth centuries represented a high point of Polish culture and influence. Polish nobles managed to win a number of important concessions, the most significant being freedom from arbitrary arrest and confinement. This civil right was secured in Poland well

before the more famous English right of habeas corpus. It was during this period, and under the influence of the Polish kings, that Cracow emerged as the economic and cultural center of Poland. Cracow University was founded in 1364 in response to the foundation of Prague University by Emperor Charles IV in 1348. After the dynastic union of Poland and Lithuania, Polish language and culture increasingly influenced the Lithuanian nobility.

Lithuanian expansion was in part the result of a decline in Tartar power. The rise of Moscow, however, was even more directly related to Tartar decline. Since the Mongol invasions in the thirteenth century, various Russian towns and principalities had been part of a Tartar sphere of influence. This primarily meant payment of an annual tribute.

A key to the emergence of Moscow occurred when Ivan I (r. 1332–1341), Prince of Moscow, was named

Moscow The city's newly constructed walls allowed Muscovites to defeat the invading Lithuanian army in 1368, which was a key event in the growth of Muscovite power. *(Novosti)*

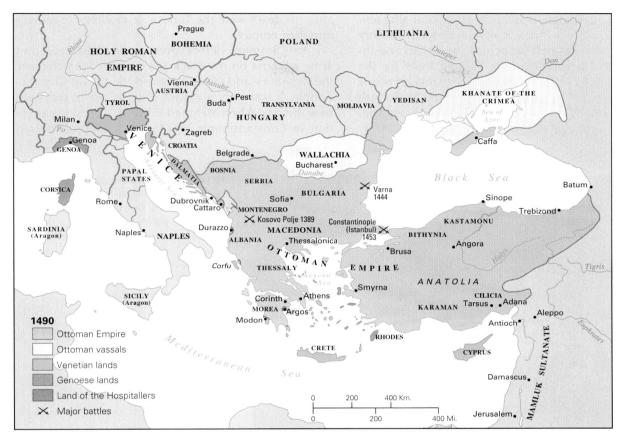

Map 11.3 Turkey and Eastern Europe   With the conquest of Constantinople, Syria, and Palestine, the Ottoman Turks controlled the eastern Mediterranean and dominated Europe below the Danube River. The Holy Roman emperors, rulers of Italy, and kings of Spain had to be concerned about potential invasions by land or by sea.

Grand Prince and collector of tribute from the other Russian princes. Not for nothing was he called "the Money-bag." It was during this same period that the head of the Russian Orthodox Church was persuaded to make his home in Moscow. And in 1367, the princes began to rebuild the Kremlin walls in stone.

The decisive change for Moscow, however, was the reign of Ivan III (r. 1462–1505). By 1478, Ivan III, called "the Great," had seized the famed trading center of Novgorod. Two years later he was powerful enough to renounce Mongol overlordship and refuse further payments of tribute. And after marriage to an émigré Byzantine princess living in Rome, Ivan began to call himself "Tsar" (Russian for "Caesar"), implying that in the wake of the Muslim conquest of Constantinople, Moscow had become the new Rome.

■ The Ottoman Empire

The eastern Mediterranean area was a politically tumultuous area in the fourteenth century when the Ottoman Turks were first invited into the Balkans by the hard-pressed Byzantine emperor. Early in the fifteenth century, the Turks were only one, and perhaps not even the greatest, of the Balkan threats to the Byzantine Empire and the other Balkan states (see Map 11.3). Hungarians, Venetians, and Germans also competed for influence in this volatile area. Individuals and groups added to the turmoil by expediently switching their political allegiances and even their religions. In the 1420s, for example, as the Turks and the Hungarians fought for influence in Serbia, the Serbian king moved easily from alliance with one to alliance with the other. Elites often retained their political and economic influence by changing religion. The Christian aristocracy of late-fifteenth-century Bosnia, for example, was welcomed into Islam and instantly created a cohesive elite fighting force for the Turks. Conversely, as Turkish power in Albania grew, one noble, George Castriota (d. 1467), known by his Turkish name Skanderbeg, reconverted to Christianity and became a leading figure in the resistance to the Turks. Only

after his death were the Turks able to integrate Albania into their empire.

An Ottoman victory over a Christian crusading army at Varna on the Black Sea coast in 1444 changed the dynamics and virtually sealed the fate of Constantinople. It was only a matter of time before the Turks took the city. When Mehmed II finally turned his attention to Constantinople in 1453, the siege of the city

The Siege of Constantinople   The siege of Constantinople by the Turks required the attackers to isolate the city both by sea and by land. This miniature from the fifteenth century shows the Turkish camps, as well as the movements of Turkish boats, completing the isolation of the city. *(Bibliothèque Nationale de France)*

lasted only fifty-three days. Turkish artillery breached the walls before a Venetian navy or a Hungarian army could come to the city's defense. The destruction of the last vestiges of the Roman imperial tradition that reached back to the emperor Augustus sent shock waves through Christian Europe and brought forth calls for new crusades to liberate the East from the evils of Islam. It also stirred anti-Christian feelings among the Turks. The leader of the Ottoman army, Sultan Mehmed° II the Conqueror (r. 1451–1481), was acclaimed the greatest of all *ghazi*—that is, a crusading warrior who was, according to a Turkish poet, "the instrument of Allah, a servant of God, who purifies the earth from the filth of polytheism [i.e., the Christian Trinity]." The rise of the Ottoman Turks transformed eastern Europe and led to a profound clash between Christian and Muslim civilizations.

After the fall of Constantinople, the Turks worked to consolidate their new conquests. Through alliance and conquest, Ottoman hegemony extended through Syria and Palestine and by 1517 to Egypt. Even the Muslim powers of North Africa were nominally under Turkish control. To the west and north of Constantinople, the Ottoman advance was initially thwarted by Matthias Corvinus (r. 1458–1490), Hungary's greatest late medieval king. Matthias reduced the power of the Hungarian nobility, increased state revenues, and built a standing army to oppose the Ottomans. With his death, however, the Hungarian monarchy withered, and the Ottomans resumed their advance. In short order, they dominated Croatia, Bosnia, Dalmatia, Albania, eastern Hungary, Moldavia, Bulgaria, and Greece. Turkish strength was based on a number of factors. The first was the loyalty and efficiency of the sultan's crack troops, the Janissaries. These troops were young boys forcibly taken from the subject Christian populations, trained in Turkish language and customs, and converted to Islam. Although they functioned as special protectors of the Christian community from which they were drawn, they were separated from it by their new faith. Because the Turkish population viewed them as outsiders, they were particularly loyal to the sultan.

The situation of the Janissaries underlines a secondary explanation for Ottoman strength: the unusually tolerant attitudes of Mehmed, who saw himself not only as the greatest of the ghazi but also as emperor, heir to Byzantine and ancient imperial traditions. Immediately after the conquest of Constantinople, he repopulated the city with Greeks, Armenians, Jews, and Muslims.

Mehmed especially welcomed Sephardic Jews from Spain and Portugal to parts of his empire. Religious groups lived in separate districts centered on a church or synagogue, and each religious community retained the right to select its own leaders. (See the box "Global Encounters: A Disputation.") Mehmed made Constantinople the capital of the new Ottoman Empire. And by building mosques, hospitals, hostels, and bridges, he breathed new life into the city, which he referred to as Istanbul—that is, "the city." In the fifty years following the conquest, the population of the city grew an extraordinary 500 percent, from about 40,000 to over 200,000, making it the largest city in Europe, as it had been in Late Antiquity.

At a time when Christian Europe seemed less and less willing to tolerate non-Christian minorities, the Ottoman Empire's liberal attitude toward outsiders seemed striking. By Muslim law, Christians and Jews were supposed to be tolerated, and as long as they paid a special poll tax and accepted some Ottoman supervision, they were. Christian and Jewish leaders supervised the internal affairs of their respective communities. Muslims and non-Muslims belonged to the same trade associations and traveled throughout the empire. Mehmed had no qualms about making trade agreements with the Italian powers in an attempt to consolidate his power. And in Serbia, Bulgaria, Macedonia, and Albania, he left in place previous social and political institutions, requiring only loyalty to his new empire.

Mehmed had to tread carefully, though, because the Turks had a number of powerful enemies. Serious problems, for example, surfaced during the reign of Mehmed's son, Bayazid° (r. 1481–1512). Following Turkish tradition, Mehmed had not chosen a successor but let his sons fight for control. Normally, the successful claimant achieved the throne by doing away with his closest relatives. Bayazid's brother, Jem, however, fled into the protective custody of Christian powers, where he spent the rest of his life. In times of crisis, kings and popes would threaten to foment rebellion in Ottoman lands by releasing him. Bayazid also had to worry about the Mamluk Turks, who controlled Egypt and Syria, and the new Safavid dynasty in Persia. Although both were Muslim, they were willing to join with various Christian states to reduce the power of the Ottomans. Only in the second decade of the sixteenth century, after Bayazid's son, Selim (r. 1512–1520), had defeated the Persians and the Mamluks, were the Ottomans finally safe from attack from the east or south.

Mehmed (MEH-met)

Bayazid (bay-a-ZEED)

⊕ G L O B A L   E N C O U N T E R S

A Disputation

Konstantin Mihailovic, a Serb by birth, was captured by the Turks during the conquest of Constantinople in 1453. He later served with the Turks until he returned to the Christian forces in 1463. His description of a typical Turkish disputation, or debate, taking place in the presence of the sultan or other dignitary is an interesting example of how the Muslim, Jewish, and Christian peoples of the Balkans tried to understand one another.

The masters and scribes have among themselves this custom: they arrange their deliberations before the highest lord after the emperor. . . . And then they begin to argue one against the other, speaking mostly about the prophets. Some [of these Turkish scribes] recognize Our Lord Jesus Christ as a prophet, and others as an archprophet, alongside God the Creator of Heaven and earth. And also the Lord, from the time when the Mohammedan faith began, created eight hundred camels, like invisible spirits, which go around every night and gather evil *Busromane* [i.e., the Muslim, or the Chosen People of God] from our [Muslim] graves and carry them to *kaur* graves [the Kaury are "the Confused People," i.e., the Christians]; and then gather good kaury and carry them to our graves. And now the good kaury will stand with our Busroman council and the evil Busromane will stand with the kaur council on Judgment Day before God. For [a pious one] says . . . , "The Christians have a faith but have no works." Therefore Mohammed will lead the Busromane to Paradise and Jesus will order the Christians to hell. Moses will sorrow for the Jews that they have not been obedient to him. . . . He [one of the scribes] spoke in this way: "Elias and Enoch are both in body and soul in paradise; but before Judgment Day they must die. But Jesus both in body and in soul is in heaven. He is the only one who will not die a death but will be alive forever and ever. Mohammed both in body and soul was in heaven, but remained with us on earth." And then the masters began to dispute, one in one way and one in another, and there were many words among them. And having raised a cry one against another, they began to throw books at one another. [Then the official in charge of the disputation] . . . told them to cease this disputation and he ordered that food be brought them according to their custom and they gave them water to drink, since they do not drink wine. And then, having eaten their fill, they gave thanks to God, praying for the souls of the living and the dead and for those who fight against the kaury or Christians.

Source: Konstantin Mihailovic, *Memoirs of a Janissary,* translated by Benjamin Stolz; commentary and notes by Svat Soucek (Ann Arbor, Mich.: Joint Committee on Eastern Europe, American Council of Learned Societies; and the Department of Slavic Languages and Literatures, University of Michigan, 1975), pp. 25–27.

■ The Union of Crowns in Spain

While expanding across the Mediterranean, the Turks came in contact with the other new state of the fifteenth century, the newly unified kingdom of Spain. As in Poland-Lithuania, the Spanish monarchy was only a dynastic union. In 1469 Ferdinand, heir to the kingdom of Aragon and Catalonia, married Isabella, daughter of the king of Castile. Five years later Isabella became queen of Castile, and in 1479 Ferdinand took control of the kingdom of Aragon. This union of crowns eventually would lead to the creation of a united Spain, but true integration was still a distant dream in 1469.

The permanence of the union was remarkable because the two kingdoms were so different. Castile was a much larger and more populous state. It had taken the lead in the Reconquista, the fight begun in the eleventh century to reclaim Iberia from Muslim rule. As a result, economic power within Castile was divided among those groups most responsible for the Reconquista: military orders and nobles. The military orders of Calatrava, Santiago, and Alcantara were militias formed by men who had taken a religious vow similar to that taken by a monk, with an added commitment to fight against the enemies of Christianity. In the course of the Reconquista, the military orders assumed control of vast districts. Lay nobles who aided in the Reconquista also held large tracts of land, and proudly guarded their independence.

Castile's power stemmed from its agrarian wealth. During the Reconquista, Castilians took control of large regions and turned them into ranges for grazing merino sheep, producers of the prized merino wool exported to the markets of Flanders and Italy. To maximize the profits from wool production, the kings authorized the creation of the Mesta, a brotherhood of sheep producers. The pastoral economy grew to the point that by the early sixteenth century Castilians owned over 3 million sheep. Farmers who lived along the routes by which the vast flocks moved from mountains to the plains often lost their crops to the hungry animals. The agricultural economy was virtually extinguished in some areas.

Economic power in Castile lay with the nobility, but political power rested with the monarch. Because the nobility was largely exempt from taxation, nobles ignored the *cortes*°, the popular assembly, which could do little more than approve royal demands. The towns of Castile were important only as fortresses and staging points for militias rather than as centers of trade and commerce. No force was capable of opposing the will of the monarch. As John II of Castile (r. 1406–1454) explained

> All my vassals, subjects, and people, whatever their estate, . . . are, according to all divine, human, . . . and even natural law, compelled and bound . . . to my word and deed. . . . The king holds this position not from men but from God, whose place he holds in temporal matters.[9]

The kingdom of Aragon was dramatically different. The center of the kingdom was Barcelona, an important trading center in the Mediterranean. In the fourteenth and fifteenth centuries the kings of Aragon concentrated their efforts on expanding their influence in the Mediterranean, especially south of France and Italy. By the middle of the fifteenth century the Aragonese empire included the kingdom of Naples, Sicily, the Balearic° Islands, and Sardinia.

The power of the Aragonese king, in sharp contrast to the Castilian monarchy, was limited because the Crown was not unified. The ruler was king in Aragon and Navarre but only count in Catalonia. Aragon, Catalonia, and Valencia each maintained its own cortes. In each area the traditional nobility and the towns had a great deal more influence than did their counterparts in Castile. The power of the cortes is clear in the coronation oath taken by the Aragonese nobility: "We who are as good as you and together are more powerful than you, make you our king and lord, provided that you observe our laws and liberties, and if not, not."[10] The distinction with Castile could not be stronger.

Initially the union of the crowns of Aragon and Castile did little to unify the two monarchies. Nobles fought over disputed boundaries, and Castilian nobles felt exploited by Aragonese merchants. Trade duties and internal boundaries continued to be disputed. The two realms even lacked a treaty to allow for the extradition of criminals from one kingdom to the other. Castilians never accepted Ferdinand as more than their queen's consort. After the death of Isabella in 1504, he ruled in Castile only as regent for his infant grandson, Charles I (r. 1516–1556). "Spain" would not emerge in an institutional sense until the late sixteenth century.

Nonetheless, the reign of Isabella and Ferdinand marked a profound change in politics and society in the Iberian kingdoms. The monarchs visited all parts of their realm, reorganized municipal governments, took control of the powerful military orders, strengthened the power of royal law courts, and extended the international influence of the monarchies. Many of their actions were designed to advance the interests of Aragon in the Mediterranean. Ferdinand and Isabella married their daughter, Joanna, to Philip of Habsburg in 1496 to draw the Holy Roman Empire into the Italian wars brought on by the French invasion (see page 370). The marriage of their daughter, Catherine of Aragon, to Prince Arthur of England in 1501 was designed to obtain yet another ally against the French. Those two marriages would have momentous consequences for European history in the sixteenth century.

The reign of Ferdinand and Isabella is especially memorable because of the events of 1492. In January of that year, a crusading army conquered Granada, the last Muslim stronghold in Iberia. In March, Ferdinand and Isabella ordered the Jews of Castile and Aragon to convert or leave the kingdom within four months. In April, Isabella issued her commission authorizing Christopher Columbus "to discover and acquire islands and mainland in the Ocean Sea" (see pages 440–441).

---

cortes (cor-TEZ)   **Balearic** (ba-LEER-ik)

Ferdinand and Isabella Interrogating a Jew   Jews in Spain and many other parts of Europe were considered to be under the specific jurisdiction of local rulers. Jews and their converso relatives turned to the king and queen in 1492 when Jews faced the order to convert or leave the kingdom.
(Museo de Zaragoza)

dom. In the fourteenth century, perhaps 2 percent of the population of Iberia was Jewish, and the Muslim population may have been as high as 50 percent. The various groups were inextricably mixed. The statutes of the Jewish community in Barcelona were written in Catalan, a Spanish dialect, rather than in Hebrew. *Maranos,* Jewish converts to Christianity, and *moriscos,* Muslim converts, mixed continuously with Christians and with members of their former religions. It was difficult at times to know which religion these converts, or *conversos,* actually practiced. One surprised northern visitor to Spain remarked that one noble's circle was filled with "Christians, Moors, and Jews and he lets them live in peace in their faith."

This tolerant mingling of Christians, Muslims, and Jews had periodically occasioned violence. All three communities, in fact, preferred clear boundaries between the groups. In 1391, however, a series of violent attacks had long-lasting and unfortunate effects on Iberian society. An attack on the Jews of Seville led to murders, forced conversions, and suppression of synagogues throughout Spain. In the wake of the assault, large portions of the urban Jewish population either converted to Christianity or moved into villages away from the large commercial cities. The Jewish population in Castile may have declined by a fourth. Although the anti-Jewish feelings were expressed in religious terms, the underlying cause was anger over the economic prominence of some Jewish or *converso* (recently converted Jewish-Christian) families. After 1391 anti-Jewish feeling increasingly became racial. As one rebel said, "The converso remains a Jew and therefore should be barred from public office."[11]

Hostility and suspicion toward Jews grew throughout the fifteenth century until Ferdinand and Isabella concluded that the only safe course was to order all Jews to accept baptism. Jews who would not convert would have to leave the kingdom within four months. The order was signed on March 31, 1492, and published in late April after an unsuccessful attempt by converso and Jewish leaders to dissuade the monarchs from implementing it.

Many Jews could not dispose of their possessions in the four months allowed and so chose to convert and remain. But it is estimated that about ten thousand Jews left Aragon and that even more left Castile. Many moved to Portugal and then to North Africa. Some went east to Istanbul or north to the Low Countries. A number of others moved to the colonies being established in the New World in the vain hope of avoiding the Inquisition. In 1504 the expulsion order was extended to include all Muslims.

The conquest of Granada and the expulsion of the Jews represented a radical shift in the Spanish mentality. Until the beginning of the fifteenth century, Spain maintained a level of religious tolerance unusual in Christen-

The economic and social costs of the expulsion were profound. Not every Muslim or Jew was wealthy and cultured, but the exiles did include many doctors, bankers, and merchants. Spanish culture, long open to influences from Muslim and Jewish sources, became narrower and less willing to accept new ideas. After the expulsion, a chasm of distrust opened between the "Old Christians" and the "New," that is, newly converted. As early as the first decades of the fifteenth century, some religious orders had refused to accept "New Christians." They required that their members demonstrate *limpieza de sangre*, a purity of blood. By 1500 the same tests of blood purity became prerequisites for holding most religious and public offices. Thus, by the end of the fifteenth century, the Iberian kingdoms had created more powerful, unified governments, but at a terrible cost to the only portion of Christendom that had ever practiced religious tolerance.

Complaints that led to the expulsion arose from a variety of sources. The fact that many of the most important financiers and courtiers were Jews or conversos bred jealousies and tensions among the communities. The most conservative Christians desired a community free of non-Christian influences. All three religious communities favored distinct dress and identifying behaviors for each group. Christians seemed concerned that many of the conversos were likely to reconvert to Judaism, and the fear of reconversion, or "judaizing," led many to advocate the institution of the Spanish Inquisition.

Inquisitions were well known in many parts of Europe, but the Spanish Inquisition was unique because in 1478 Pope Sixtus IV placed the grand inquisitor under the direct control of the monarchs. Like most Christian rulers, Ferdinand and Isabella believed that uniform Christian orthodoxy was the only firm basis for a strong kingdom. Inquisitors attacked those aspects of converso tradition that seemed to make the conversos less than fully Christian. They were concerned that many conversos and maranos had converted falsely and were secretly continuing to follow Jewish or Muslim ritual. The "New Christians" tended to live near their Muslim or Jewish relatives, eat the foods enjoyed in their former communities, and observe holy days, such as Yom Kippur, the Jewish day of atonement. Over four thousand converso families fled from Andalusia in southern Spain following the arrival of an inquisitor in 1490.

Because its administration, finances, and appointments were in Spanish not papal hands, the Spanish Inquisition quickly became an important instrument for the expansion of state power. Many inquisitors used their offices to attack wealthy or politically important converso families not just to drive them from public life but also to fill the royal treasury, which was where the estates of those judged guilty wound up. "This inquisition is as much to take the conversos' estates as to exalt the faith," was the despairing conclusion of one conversa woman.[12]

■ The Limits of Consolidation: Germany

The issue of central versus local control played a key role in German affairs as well. The Holy Roman Empire of the late Middle Ages was dramatically different from the empire of the early thirteenth century. Emperors generally were unable to claim lands and preside over jurisdictions outside Germany. And within Germany, power shifted eastward. Imperial power had previously rested on lands and castles in southwestern Germany. These strongholds melted away as emperors willingly pawned and sold traditional crown lands in order to build up the holdings of their own families. Emperor Henry VII (r. 1308–1313) and his grandson, Charles IV (r. 1347–1378), for example, liquidated imperial lands west of the Rhine in order to secure the house of Luxemburg's claims to the crown of Bohemia and other lands in the east. The Habsburgs in Austria, the Wittelsbachs in Bavaria, and a host of lesser families staked out power bases in separate parts of the empire. As a result, Germany unraveled into a loose collection of territories. And more seriously, the power of each emperor depended almost entirely on the wealth and power of his dynastic lands.

The power of regional authorities in the empire was further cemented by the so-called Golden Bull of 1356, the most important constitutional document of late medieval German history. In it, Charles IV declared that henceforth the archbishops of Cologne, Mainz, and Trier plus the secular rulers of Bohemia, the Rhenish Palatinate, Saxony, and Brandenburg, would be the seven electors responsible for the choice of a new emperor. He further established that the rulers of these seven principalities should have full jurisdictional rights within their territories. The Golden Bull acknowledged the power of regional princes, but it did nothing to solve the inherent weakness of an electoral monarchy. Between 1273 and 1519, Germany elected fourteen emperors from six different dynasties, and only once, in 1378, did a son follow his father. The contrast between Germany and the monarchies of Iberia, France, and England is striking. By 1350 Germany had no hereditary monarchy, no common legal system, no common coinage, and no representative assembly. Political power rested in the hands of the territorial princes.

Territorial integration was least effective in what is now Switzerland, where a league of towns, provincial knights, and peasant villages successfully resisted a territorial prince. The Swiss Confederation began modestly enough in 1291 as a voluntary association to promote regional peace. By 1410 the confederation had conquered most of the traditionally Habsburg lands in the Swiss areas. By the 1470s the Swiss had invented the myth of William Tell, the fearless woodsman who refused to bow his head to a Habsburg official, as a justification for their independent and anti-aristocratic traditions. Although still citizens of the Holy Roman Empire, the Swiss maintained an independence similar to that of the princes. Their expansion culminated with the Battle of Nancy in Lorraine in 1477, when the Swiss infantry defeated a Burgundian army and killed Charles the Bold, the duke of Burgundy. From then on "Turning Swiss" became a battle cry for German towns and individuals who hoped to slow territorial centralization.

SUMMARY

UROPE in 1500 was profoundly different from the Europe of two centuries earlier. The religious, political, and economic crises of the fourteenth and early fifteenth centuries seemed about to destroy the progress of the previous centuries. But the recovery of the second half of the fifteenth century was nearly as dramatic as the preceding disasters.

In the aftermath of schism and conciliar reform, the church also was transformed. Because of conciliar challenges to papal authority, popes had to deal much more carefully with the governments of Europe. They found themselves vulnerable to pressures from the other European powers. Recognizing that, in the end, popes could count on support only from those areas they controlled politically, the papacy became an Italian regional power.

The economy had grown more complex in the wake of plague and demographic change. New patterns of trade and banking and new manufacturing techniques spread throughout Europe. As important as simple recovery, the new economy was now more firmly rooted in northern Europe. Italian merchants and bankers faced stiff competition from local counterparts throughout Europe.

Recovery was equally dramatic for the kings of France and England, the princes and despots in Germany, and the rulers of eastern Europe. After the Hundred Years' War and challenges from aristocrats, townsmen, and peasants,

governments grew stronger as kings, princes, and town patricians used royal courts and patronage to extend their control. Military advances in the fifteenth century, such as the institution of standing armies, gave advantages to larger governments. This was as true in Hungary as it was in France.

Yet recovery among the traditional Western powers was largely overshadowed by the rise of Muscovite Russia and the Ottoman and Spanish Empires. These three emergent powers upset the political and diplomatic balance in Europe. It was they who would dominate politics and diplomacy in the next century.

In addition to their obvious political power, most of these states—from Spain to Scandinavia to Istanbul—became adept at using art, literature, and history to explain and magnify their courts and confirm their places in history and society. This was certainly true of the papacy and over the course of the fifteenth century; it became true of other governments as well. It is to the role of culture that we turn in the next chapter.

■ Notes

1. Quoted in Guillaume Mollat, *The Popes at Avignon, 1305–1378* (London: Thomas Nelson, 1963), p. 112.
2. Quoted in Mary Aston, *Lollards and Reformers: Images and Literacy in Late Medieval Religion* (Ronceverte, W.V.: Hambledon, 1984), p. 60.
3. Quoted in Francis Oakley, *The Western Church in the Later Middle Ages* (Ithaca, N.Y.: Cornell University Press, 1979), pp. 65–66.
4. Quoted in Charles T. Wood, *Joan of Arc and Richard III* (New York: Oxford University Press, 1988), pp. 56–57.
5. Quoted in Michael T. Clanchy, "Law, Government, and Society in Medieval England," *History* 59 (1974): 75.
6. A. Buchon, *Choix des Chroniques* (Paris, 1875), p. 565, as quoted in John Gillingham and J. C. Holt, eds., *War and Government in the Middle Ages* (Totowa, N.J.: Barnes & Noble, 1984), p. 85.
7. Salimbene de Adam, quoted in John Larner, *Italy in the Age of Dante and Petrarch, 1215–1380* (New York: Longman, 1980), p. 141.
8. Quoted in Peter Shervey Lewis, *Later Medieval France: The Polity* (New York: Macmillan, 1968), p. 15.
9. Quoted in Angus MacKay, *Spain in the Middle Ages: From Frontier to Empire, 1000–1500* (London: Macmillan, 1977), p. 137.
10. Ibid., p. 105.
11. Quoted in Angus MacKay, "Popular Movements and Pogroms, in Fifteenth-Century Spain," *Past & Present* 55 (1972): 52.
12. Haim Beinart, ed., *Records of the Trials of the Spanish Inquisition in Ciudad Real*, vol. 1, trans. Duane Osheim (Jerusalem: Israel Academy of Sciences and Humanities, 1974), p. 391.

■ Suggested Reading

Duffy, E. *Saints & Sinners: A History of the Popes.* 1997. An excellent introduction to the papacy by a leading historian. The sections on the late Middle Ages are clear and balanced.

Dyer, C. *Standards of Living in the Later Middle Ages: Social Change in England, c. 1200–1500.* 1989. An account that includes a sophisticated discussion of dietary changes in the wake of population decline and changed commodity prices in fifteenth-century England.

Guenée, B. *States and Rulers in Later Medieval Europe.* Translated by Juliet Vale. 1985. The best general introduction to the nature of government in the late Middle Ages. It introduces recent trends in historical research.

Herlihy, D. *The Black Death and the Transformation of the West.* 1997. This short, very readable book is an excellent introduction to the plague and its impact on Europe.

Inalcik, H. *The Ottoman Empire: The Classical Age, 1300–1600.* 1973. A general discussion of the growth of the Ottoman state by Turkey's best medieval historian.

Keen, Maurice H. *English Society in the Later Middle Ages, 1348–1500.* 1990. A recent general introduction to late medieval England that covers culture and religion as well as politics.

Nicholas, D. *The Transformation of Europe, 1300–1600.* 1999. A comprehensive survey of politics and society in Europe between 1300 and 1600; includes coverage of Scandinavia and the Slavic lands as well as northwestern Europe.

Oakley, Francis. *The Western Church in the Later Middle Ages.* 1979. The best general history of the church in the late Middle Ages. Oakley gives superior treatments of the Great Schism and conciliarism.

Warner, Marina. *Joan of Arc: The Image of Female Heroism.* 1981. An excellent and quite readable book that emphasizes the conflicting religious and political opinions about "the Maid."

 For a searchable list of additional readings for this chapter, go to http://college.hmco.com.

A Painting of the Plague

Writers who survived the coming of pestilential disease in 1348 described a world of terror in which things seemed changed forever. Look at this painting, *St. Sebastian Interceding for the Plague-Stricken,* created by the Flemish artist Josse Lieferinxe between 1497 and 1499. One dying man seems to be falling terrified to the ground while a female bystander in the background screams in alarm. Images of Christ, Saint Sebastian (pierced by arrows), a devil, and a priest seem to indicate that something terrifying and undreamed-of is happening. But what exactly was the terror, and what had changed?

The art of the later Middle Ages is an extremely valuable source for understanding social and religious values. As you look at *St. Sebastian Interceding for the Plague-Stricken,* the first step is to understand what men and women in the fourteenth and fifteenth centuries thought about death. After 1400, European Christians often depicted the universality of death in paintings showing the Dance of Death. The motif varies, but typically Death grasps the hands of men and women, rich and poor, noble and peasant, and leads them away. Deathbed scenes were another popular motif. In the late Middle Ages most people believed that at death the good and evil acts committed by an individual were tallied in the Book of Life and the person was either granted eternal life, first in Purgatory and then Paradise, or consigned to eternal suffering in Hell. Judgment scenes often depict the Virgin Mary or another saint pleading before God or contending with the Devil or demons over the souls of the dying.

It was essential for people to prepare for a good death. Individuals studied the *artes moriendi,* the arts of dying. A lingering, painful illness was often interpreted as an opportunity for penitential suffering that would benefit the soul. At the point of death, the dying person could confess and receive absolution for sins and the last sacraments of the church. From that moment on, he or she needed to maintain a calm faith, free from fear. Salvation and eternal life depended on avoiding further sin, especially the questioning of God's forgiveness and mercy. Death was a public event. Clergy, family, religious societies, even neighbors helped the dying person to avoid losing faith at the end. The person might pray,

"Virgin Mary, Mother of God, I have placed my hope in you. Free my soul from care, and from Hell, and bitter death."*

The concept of a good death is critical to understanding the European response to bubonic plague. To be sure, individuals rarely look forward to death, then or now. Numerous writers and chroniclers lamented the suddenness of death and the lack of priests to hear confession. (See the box "Reading Sources: The Black Death" on page 373.) Individuals who were healthy in the morning might be dead by nightfall. The suddenness, the lack of time to prepare for a good death, heightened the dread that accompanied the onset of the illness.

Medieval Christians turned to saints to represent them before God at the point of death and to stop the onslaught of the plague. Three patron saints were especially popular. The Virgin Mary was often shown using her cloak to shelter towns and individuals from arrows carrying pestilence. Saint Roch, himself a victim of plague, was thought to intercede and protect those who prayed in his name. And Saint Sebastian, an early Christian martyr slain with arrows (later understood as symbols of death by plague), was thought to be an especially effective patron during epidemics. In times of plague, people went on pilgrimages to local shrines dedicated to these or local saints, carried images of the saints in processions, and built churches and chapels in honor of the saints in thanks for deliverance from plague.

With these issues in mind, what do we see in Lieferinxe's painting? The painting portrays an outbreak of plague. We note first the body of the dead person, carefully shrouded. Ideally, the dead, like the corpse here, were taken to a church and given a Christian burial. But chroniclers often reported that so many died, and died so quickly, that no one could be found to bury them properly. In many towns the dead were gathered on carts and hauled to gaping common graves outside the town. We can see one such cart leaving the castle in the background. In a series of images, then, Lieferinxe shows what mattered most to people. In the foreground is the shrouded body attended by a priest and other clerics

---

*Quoted in Philippe Ariès, *The Hour of Our Death* (New York: Knopf, 1981), p. 108.

Lieferinxe: St. Sebastian Interceding for the Plague-Stricken (The *Walters Art Museum, Baltimore*)

bearing a cross. This person experienced a good death. In contrast, the man who has fallen behind the body is suffering a bad death, one that caught him unaware. He is the object of the concern and grief of those near him. In the sky just above the castle walls, a white-robed angel and a horned, ax-wielding demon contend over the souls of the dead and dying. At the top of the painting, Christ listens to the prayers of Saint Sebastian. The painting thus portrays the impact and horror of plague and also the way Christians were expected to respond to it.

Returning to our original question, we can conclude that the terror of epidemic plague was not entirely like a modern panic. Medieval people saw the Black Death, its ghastly devastation—and its only possible solution or meaning—in terms of traditional religious values: the true terror was to be caught unaware.

 For additional information on this topic, go to http://college.hmco.com.

CHAPTER 12

The Renaissance

THE painting on the left, "The School of Athens" by Raphael, was commissioned for the Stanze°, the papal apartments in the Vatican. At the center Plato and Aristotle advance through a churchlike hall, surrounded by the great thinkers and writers of the ancient world. But Raphael portrayed more than just ancient wisdom. The figure of Plato is, in fact, a portrait of Leonardo da Vinci. A brooding Michelangelo leans on a marble block in the foreground. In a companion painting on the opposite wall, Raphael depicted a gathering of the greatest scholars of Christendom. In this way he brought together Christian and classical, writers and artists, and captured the entire cultural reform plan of the Renaissance.

The revival these paintings celebrate was a response to the religious, social, economic, and political crises discussed in the previous chapter. Italians, and later Europeans generally, found themselves drawn to imitate Roman literature, ethics, and politics. The ideas of the distant past seemed to offer more opportunity for moral and political reform than the theological ideas of the recent past.

Renaissance Italians wrote of themselves and their contemporaries as having "revived" arts, "rescued" painting, and "rediscovered" classical authors. They even coined the phrases "Dark Ages" and "Middle Ages" to describe the period that separated the Roman Empire from their own times. They believed that their society saw a new age, a rebirth of culture. And to this day we use the French translation of "rebirth," *renaissance,* to describe the period of intense creativity and change from 1300 to 1500, not just in Italy, but in all of Europe.

Stanze (STAN-zay)

Humanism and Culture in Italy, 1300–1500

The Arts in Italy, 1250–1550

The Spread of the Renaissance, 1350–1536

The Renaissance and Court Society

Raphael, *School of Athens* (detail). Raphael created this classical ruin by using the technique of linear perspective.
(Scala/Art Resource, NY)

This view comes to us primarily from the work of the nineteenth-century Swiss historian Jacob Burckhardt. In his book *The Civilization of the Renaissance in Italy* (1860), he argued that Italians were the first individuals to recognize the state as a moral structure free from the restraints of religious or philosophical traditions. Burckhardt believed that individuals were entirely free. Their success or failure depended on personal qualities of creative brilliance rather than on family status, religion, or guild membership. What Burckhardt thought he saw in Renaissance Italy were the first signs of the romantic individualism and nationalism that characterized the modern world.

In fact, as brilliant as Renaissance writers and artists were, they do not represent a radical shift from the ideas or values of previous medieval culture. As we have seen, there was no "Dark Age." Although the culture of Renaissance Europe was in many aspects new and innovative, it had close ties both to the ideas of the High Middle Ages and to traditional Christian values.

How, then, should we characterize the Renaissance in Europe? The Renaissance was an important cultural movement that aimed to reform and renew by imitating what the reformers believed were classical and early Christian traditions in art,

education, religion, and political life. Italians, and then other Europeans, came to believe that the social and moral values as well as the literature of classical Greece and Rome offered the best formula for changing their own society for the better. This enthusiasm for a past culture became the vehicle for changes in literature, education, and art that established cultural standards that were to hold for the next five hundred years.

QUESTIONS TO CONSIDER

- How did Europeans try to use classical values to reform their world?

- What was "new" about Renaissance art?

- In what ways did humanism outside Italy differ from Italian humanism?

- How did European rulers use Renaissance art and culture?

TERMS TO KNOW

humanism	linear perspective
civic humanism	Sistine Chapel
Petrarch	Gutenberg
On the Donation	Thomas More
of Constantine	Erasmus
Machiavelli	

HUMANISM AND CULTURE IN ITALY, 1300–1500

 TALIANS turned to models from classical antiquity in their attempts to deal with current issues of cultural, political, and educational reform. A group of scholars who came to be known as humanists began to argue the superiority of the literature, history, and politics of the past. As humanists discovered more about ancient culture, they were able to understand more clearly the historical context in which Roman and Greek writers and thinkers lived. And by the early sixteenth century, their debates on learning, civic

duty, and the classical legacy had led them to a new vision of the past and a new appreciation of the nature of politics.

■ The Emergence of Humanism

Humanism initially held greater appeal in Italy than elsewhere in Europe because the culture in central and northern Italy was significantly more secular and more urban than the culture of much of the rest of Europe. Members of the clergy were not likely to dominate government and education in Italy. Quite the reverse: Boards dominated by laymen had built and were administering the great urban churches of Italy. Religious hospitals and charities were often reorganized and centralized under government control. In 1300 four cities in Italy had populations of about 100,000 (Milan, Venice, Florence, and Naples), and countless others had populations of 40,000 or more. By contrast, London, which may have had a population of 100,000, was the only city in England with more than 40,000 inhabitants. Even the powerful Italian aristocracy tended to live at least part of the year in towns and conform to urban social and legal practices.

Differences between Italy and northern Europe are also apparent in the structure of local education. In northern Europe, education was organized to provide clergy for local churches. In the towns of Italy, education was much more likely to be supervised by town governments to provide training in accounting, arithmetic, and the composition of business letters. Public grammar masters taught these basics, and numerous private masters and individual tutors were prepared to teach all subjects. Giovanni Villani, a fourteenth-century merchant and historian, described Florence in 1338 as a city of about 100,000 people in which perhaps as many as 10,000 young girls and boys were completing elementary education and 1,000 were continuing their studies to prepare for careers in commerce. Compared with education in the towns of northern Europe, education in Villani's Florence seems broad-based and practical.

Logic and Scholastic philosophy (see page 340) dominated university education in northern Europe in the fourteenth and fifteenth centuries but had less influence in Italy, where education focused on the practical issues of town life rather than on theological speculation. Educated Italians of this period were interested in the *studia humanitatis*, which we now call humanism. By *humanism*, Italians meant rhetoric and literature—the arts of persuasion. Poetry, history, letter writing, and oratory based on standardized forms and aesthetic values consciously borrowed from ancient Greece and Rome were the center of intellectual life. In general, fourteenth-century Italians were suspicious of ideological or moral programs based on philosophical arguments or religious assumptions about human nature.

Italian towns were the focus of theorizing about towns as moral, religious, and political communities. Writers wanted to define the nature of the commune—the town government. Moralists often used "the common good" and "the good of the commune" as synonyms. By 1300 it was usual for towns to celebrate the feast days of their patron saints as major political as well as religious festivals. And town governments often supervised the construction and expansion of cathedrals, churches, and hospitals as signs of their wealth and prestige.

CHRONOLOGY

1304–1314	Giotto paints Arena Chapel in Padua
1345	Petrarch discovers Cicero's letters to Atticus
1348–1350	Boccaccio, *The Decameron*
1393–1400	Chaucer, *The Canterbury Tales*
1401	Ghiberti wins competition to cast baptistery doors, Florence
1405	Christine de Pizan, *The Book of the City of the Ladies*
1427	Unveiling of Masaccio's *Trinity*
1434	Van Eyck, *The Arnolfini Wedding*
1440	Valla, *On the Donation of Constantine*
1440s	Da Feltre establishes Villa Giocosa in Mantua
1450s	Gutenberg begins printing with movable metal type
1460	Gonzaga invites Mantegna to Mantua
1475	Pope Sixtus IV orders construction of Sistine Chapel
1494	Dürer begins first trip to Venice
1511	Michelangelo, *David* Erasmus, *The Praise of Folly*
1513	Machiavelli, *The Prince*
1516	More, *Utopia*
1527	Castiglione, *The Book of the Courtier*

Literature of the early fourteenth century tended to emphasize the culture of towns. The most famous and most innovative work of the fourteenth century, *The Decameron* by Giovanni Boccaccio° (1313–1375), pondered moral and ethical issues, but in the lively context of Italian town life. Boccaccio hoped the colorful and irreverent descriptions of contemporary Italians, which make his *Decameron* a classic of European literature, would also lead individuals to understand both the essence of

Giovanni Boccaccio (jo-VAH-nee bo-KAH-chi-o)

human nature and the folly of human desires. The plot involves a group of privileged young people who abandon friends and family during the plague of 1348 to go into the country, where on successive days they mix feasting, dancing, and song with one hundred tales of love, intrigue, and gaiety. With its mix of traditional and contemporary images, Boccaccio's book spawned numerous imitators in Italy and elsewhere. Many credit him with popularizing a new, secular spirit. But the point too often missed by Boccaccio's imitators was, as he himself said, that "to have compassion for those who suffer is a human quality which everyone should possess. . . ."

The majority of educated Italians in the early fourteenth century, such as Boccaccio, were not particularly captivated by thoughts of ancient Rome. Italian historians chose to write the histories of their hometowns. Most, including Giovanni Villani of Florence, were convinced that their towns could rival ancient Rome. Theirs was a practical world in which most intellectuals were men trained in notarial arts—the everyday skills of oratory, letter writing, and the recording of legal documents.

■ Early Humanism

The first Italians who looked back consciously to the literary and historical examples of ancient Rome were a group of northern Italian lawyers and notaries who imitated Roman authors. These practical men found Roman history and literature more stimulating and useful than medieval philosophy. Writers such as Albertino Mussato of Padua (1262–1329) adopted classical styles in their poetry and histories. Mussato used his play *The Ecerinis* (1315) to tell of the fall of Can Grande della Scala, the tyrannical ruler of Verona (d. 1329) and to warn his neighbors of the dangers of tyranny. From its earliest, the classical revival in Italy was tied to issues of moral and political reform.

This largely emotional fascination for the ancient world was transformed into a literary movement for reform by Francesco Petrarch (1304–1374), who popularized the idea of mixing classical moral and literary ideas with the concerns of the fourteenth century. Petrarch was the son of an exiled Florentine notary living at the papal court in Avignon. Repelled by the urban violence and wars he had experienced on his return to Italy, Petrarch was highly critical of his contemporaries: "I never liked this age," he once confessed. He criticized the "Babylonian Captivity" of the papacy in Avignon, as he named it (see page 358); he supported an attempt to resurrect a republican government in Rome; and he believed that imitation of the actions, values, and culture of the ancient Romans was the only way to reform his sorry world.

Petrarch believed that an age of darkness—he coined the expression "Dark Ages"—separated the Roman world from his own time and that the separation could be overcome only through a study and reconstruction of classical values: "Once the darkness has been broken, our descendants will perhaps be able to return to the pure, pristine radiance."[1] Petrarch's program, and in many respects the entire Renaissance, involved first of all a reconstruction of classical culture, then a careful study and imitation of the classical heritage, and finally a series of moral and cultural changes that went beyond the mere copying of ancient values and styles.

Petrarch labored throughout his life to reconstruct the history and literature of Rome. He learned to read and write classical Latin. While still in his twenties, he discovered, reorganized, and annotated fragments of Livy's *Roman History*, an important source for the history of Republican Rome. His work on Livy was merely the first step. In the 1330s he discovered a number of classical works, including orations and letters by Cicero, the great philosopher, statesman, and opponent of Julius Caesar (see page 166). Cicero's letters to his friend Atticus were filled with gossip, questions about politics in Rome, and complaints about his forced withdrawal from public life. They create the portrait of an individual who was much more complex than the austere philosopher of medieval legend.

Despite his role in heralding secular humanism, Petrarch was and remained a committed Christian. He recognized the tension between the Christian present and pagan antiquity. "My wishes fluctuate and my desires conflict, and in their struggle they tear me apart," he said.[2] Yet he prized the beauty and moral value of ancient learning. He wrote *The Lives of Illustrious Men,* biographies of men from antiquity whose thoughts and actions he deemed worthy of emulation. To spread humanistic values, he issued collections of his letters, written in classically inspired Latin, and his Italian poems. He believed that study and memorization of the writings of classical authors could lead to the internalization of the ideas and values expressed in those works, just as a honeybee drinks nectar to create honey. He argued that the ancient moral philosophers were superior to the Scholastic philosophers, whose work ended with the determination of truth, or correct responses. "The true moral philosophers and useful teachers of the virtues," he concluded, "are those whose first and last intention is to make hearer and reader good, those who do not merely teach what virtue and vice are but sow into our hearts love of the best . . . and hatred of the worst."[3] (See the box "Reading Sources: Petrarch Responds to His Critics.")

≈ R E A D I N G   S O U R C E S

Petrarch Responds to His Critics

Many traditional philosophers and theologians criticized humanists as "pagans" because of their lack of interest in logic and theology and their love of non-Christian writers. In this letter defending humanistic studies, Petrarch explains the value of Cicero's work to Christians.

[Cicero] points out the miraculously coherent structure and disposition of the body, sense and limbs, and finally reason and sedulous activity. . . . And all this he does merely to lead us to this conclusion: whatever we behold with our eyes or perceive with our intellect is made by God for the well-being of man and governed by divine providence and counsel. . . . [In response to his critics who argued for the superiority of philosophy he adds:] I have read all of Aristotle's moral books. . . . Sometimes I have become more learned through them when I went home, but not better, not so good as I ought to be; and I often complained to myself, occasionally to others too, that by no facts was the promise fulfilled which the philosopher makes at the beginning of the first book of his Ethics, namely, that "we learn this part of philosophy not with the purpose of gaining knowledge but of becoming better.". . . However, what is the use of knowing what virtue is if it is not loved when known? What is the use of knowing sin if it is not abhorred when it is known? However, everyone who has become thoroughly familiar with our Latin authors knows that they stamp and drive deep into the heart the sharpest and most ardent stings of speech by which those who stick to the

ground [are] lifted up to the highest thoughts and to honest desire. . . .

Cicero, read with a pious and modest attitude, . . . was profitable to everybody, so far as eloquence is concerned, to many others as regards living. This was especially true in [Saint] Augustine's case. . . . I confess, I admire Cicero as much or even more than all whoever wrote a line in any nation. . . . If to admire Cicero means to be a Ciceronian, I am a Ciceronian. I admire him so much that I wonder at people who do not admire him. . . . However, when we come to think or speak of religion, that is, of supreme truth and true happiness, and of eternal salvation, then I am certainly not a Ciceronian, or a Platonist, but a Christian. I even feel sure that Cicero himself would have been a Christian if he had been able to see Christ and to comprehend His doctrine.

Source: Petrarch, "On His Own Ignorance and That of Many Others," in *The Renaissance Philosophy of Man,* ed. Ernst Cassirer, Paul Oskar Kristeller, and John H. Randall (Chicago: University of Chicago Press, 1948), pp. 86, 103, 104, 114, 115.

 For additional information on this topic, go to http://college.hmco.com.

■ Humanistic Studies

Petrarch's articulation of humanism inspired a broad-based transformation of Italian intellectual life that affected discussions of politics, education, literature, and philosophy. His style of historical and literary investigation of the past became the basis for a new appreciation of the present.

Petrarch's program of humanistic studies became especially popular with the wealthy oligarchy who dominated political life in Florence. The Florentine chancellor

Coluccio Salutati° (1331–1406) and a generation of young intellectuals who formed his circle evolved an ideology of civic humanism. Civic humanists wrote letters, orations, and histories praising their city's classical virtues and history. In the process they gave a practical and public meaning to the Petrarchan program. Civic humanists argued, as had Cicero, that there was a moral and ethical value intrinsic to public life. In a letter to a friend, Salutati

---

Coluccio Salutati (ko-LOO-chi-o sal-you-TAH-tee)

Isabella d'Este   As part of the program to revive ancient Roman practices, Italian rulers had medals struck containing their own images. This image of Isabella was meant to celebrate the woman herself and the fact that her husband held the imperial office of duke.   *(Kunsthistorisches Museum, Vienna/ Erich Lessing/Art Resource, NY)*

wrote that public life is "something holy and holier than idleness in [religious] solitude." To another he added, "The active life you flee is to be followed both as an exercise in virtue and because of the necessity of brotherly love."[4]

More than Petrarch himself, civic humanists desired to create and inspire men of virtue who could take the lead in government and protect their fellow citizens from lawlessness and tyranny. In the early years of the fifteenth century, civic humanists applauded Florence for remaining a republic of free citizens rather than falling under the control of a lord, like the people of Milan, whose government was dominated by the Viscontis (see page 369). In his *Panegyric on the City of Florence* (ca. 1400), Leonardo Bruni (ca. 1370–1444) recalled the history of the Roman Republic and suggested that Florence could re-create the best qualities of the Roman state. To civic humanists, the study of Rome and its virtues was the key to the continued prosperity of Florence and similar Italian republics.

One of Petrarch's most enthusiastic followers was Guarino of Verona (1374–1460), who became the leading advocate of educational reform in Renaissance Italy. After spending five years in Constantinople learning Greek and collecting classical manuscripts, he became the most successful teacher and translator of Greek literature in Italy. Greek studies had been advanced by Manuel Chrysoloras (1350–1415), who, after his arrival from Constantinople in 1397, taught Greek for three years in Florence. Chrysoloras was later joined by other Greek intellectuals, especially after the fall of Constantinople to the Turks in 1453. Guarino built on this interest.

Guarino emphasized careful study of grammar and memorization of large bodies of classical history and poetry. He was convinced that through a profound understanding of Greek and Latin literature and a careful imitation of the style of the great authors, a person could come to exhibit the moral and ethical values for which Cicero, Seneca, and Plutarch were justly famous. Although it is unclear whether Guarino's style of education had such results, it did provide a thorough education in literature and oratory. In an age that admired the ability to speak and write persuasively, the new style of humanistic education pioneered by Guarino spread quickly throughout Europe. The elegy spoken at Guarino's funeral sums up Italian views of humanistic education as well as the contribution of Guarino himself: "No one was considered noble, as leading a blameless life, unless he had followed Guarino's courses."

Guarino's authority spread quickly. One of his early students, Vittorino da Feltre (1378–1446), was appointed tutor to the Gonzaga dukes of Mantua. Like Guarino, he emphasized close literary study and careful imitation of classical authors. But the school he founded, the Villa Giocosa°, was innovative because he advocated games and exercises as well as formal study. In addition, Vittorino required that bright young boys from poor families be included among the seventy affluent students normally resident in his school. Vittorino was so renowned that noblemen from across Italy sent their sons to be educated at the Villa Giocosa.

Humanistic education had its limits, however. Leonardo Bruni of Florence once composed a curriculum emphasizing literature and moral philosophy for a young woman to follow. But, he suggested, there was no reason to study rhetoric: "For why should the subtleties of . . . rhetorical conundrums consume the powers of a woman, who never sees the forum? . . . The contests of the forum, like those of warfare and battle, are the sphere of men."[5] To what extent did women participate in the cultural and artistic movements of the fourteenth and fifteenth centuries? Was the position of women better

Giocosa (jo-KO-sa)

than it had been previously? The current of misogyny—the assumption that women were intellectually and morally weaker than men—continued during the Renaissance, but it was not unopposed.

During the fifteenth century many women did learn to read and even to write. Religious women and wives of merchants read educational and spiritual literature. Some women needed to write in order to manage the economic and political interests of their families. Alessandra Macinghi-Strozzi° of Florence (1407–1471), for example, wrote numerous letters to her sons in exile describing her efforts to find spouses for her children and to influence the government to end their banishments.

Yet many men were suspicious of literate women. Just how suspicious is evident in the career of Isotta Nogarola (b. 1418) of Verona, one of a number of fifteenth- and sixteenth-century Italian women whose literary abilities equaled those of male humanists. Isotta quickly became known as a gifted writer, but men's response to her work was mixed. One anonymous critic suggested that it was unnatural for a woman to have such scholarly interests and accused her of equally unnatural sexual interests. Guarino of Verona himself wrote to her warning that if she was truly to be educated, she must put off female sensibilities and find "a man within the woman."[6]

The problem for humanistically educated women was that society provided no acceptable role for them. A noblewoman such as Isabella d'Este° (see page 420), wife of the duke of Mantua, might gather humanists and painters around her at court, but it was not generally believed that women themselves could create literary works of true merit. When women tried, they were usually rebuffed and urged to reject the values of civic humanism and to hold instead to traditional Christian virtues of rejection of the world. In other words, a woman who had literary or cultural interests was expected to enter a convent. That was a friend's advice to Isotta Nogarola. It was wrong, he said, "that a virgin should consider marriage, or even think about that liberty of lascivious morals."[7] Throughout the fifteenth and early sixteenth centuries, some women in Italy and elsewhere in Europe learned classical languages and philosophy, but they became rarer as time passed. The virtues of humanism were public virtues, and Europeans of the Renaissance remained uncomfortable with the idea that women might act directly and publicly. (See the box "Reading Sources: Cassandra Fedele Defends Liberal Arts for Women.")

Macinghi-Strozzi (ma-CHIN-ghee STRO-tzi)
d'Este (duh-ES-tay)

Women and Culture   This painting of Saint Barbara from the early fifteenth century shows a typical Flemish interior with a woman reading. It was not unusual for well-to-do women to read even if they could not write.   *(Museo de Prado/Institut Amatller d'Art Hispanic)*

❧ READING SOURCES

Cassandra Fedele Defends Liberal Arts for Women

Cassandra Fedele (1465–1558) had learned Latin by age 12 and later learned Greek, rhetoric, and history. The Venetian senate praised her as an ornament of learning, but beyond being admired, there was no public role for an educated woman. In this oration delivered at the university, she adds her own plea for education for women.

Aware of the weakness of my sex and the paucity of my talent, blushing, I decided to honor and obey [those who have urged me to consider how women could profit from assiduous study] . . . in order that the common crowd may be ashamed of itself and stop being offensive to me, devoted as I am to the liberal arts. . . . What woman, I ask, has such force and ability of mind and speech that she could adequately meet the standard of the greatness of letters or your learned ears? Thus daunted by the difficulty of the task and conscious of my weakness, I might easily have shirked this opportunity to speak, if your well-known kindness and clemency had not urged me to it. For I am not unaware that you are not in the habit of demanding or expecting from anyone more than the nature of the subject itself allows, or the person's own strength can promise of them.

Even an ignorant man—not only a philosopher—sees and admits that man is rightly distinguished from a beast above all by [the capacity of] reason. For what else so greatly delights, enriches and honors both of them than the teaching and understanding of letters and the liberal arts? Moreover, simple men, ignorant of literature, even if they have by nature this potential seed of genius and reason, leave it alone and uncultivated throughout their whole lives, stifle it with neglect and sloth, and render them-

selves unfit for greatness. But learned men, filled with a rich knowledge of divine and human things, turn all their thoughts and motions of the mind toward the goal of reason and thus free the mind, [otherwise] subject to so many anxieties, from all infirmity. States and princes, moreover, who favor and cultivate these studies become much more humane, pleasing, and noble, and purely [through liberal studies] win for themselves a sweet reputation for humanity. For this reason the ancients rightfully judged all leaders deficient in letters, however skillful in military affairs, to be crude and ignorant. As for the utility of letters, enough said. Of these fruits I myself have tasted a little and [have esteemed myself in that enterprise] more than abject and hopeless; and armed with distaff and needle—woman's weapons—I march forth [to defend] the belief that even though the study of letters promises and offers no reward for women and no dignity, every woman ought to seek and embrace these studies for that pleasure and delight alone that [comes] from them.

Source: M. L. King and A. Rabil, *Her Immaculate Hand: Selected Works by and About the Women Humanists of Quattrocento Italy* (Binghamton, N.Y.: Center for Medieval and Early Renaissance Studies, State University of New York, 1983), pp. 74–77.

■ The Transformation of Humanism

The fascination with education based on ancient authorities was heightened by the discovery in 1416 in the Monastery of Saint Gall in Switzerland of a complete manuscript of Quintilian's *Institutes of Oratory*, a first-century treatise on the proper education for a young Roman patrician. The document was found by Poggio

Bracciolini° (1380–1459), who had been part of the humanist circle in Florence. The discovery was hardly accidental. Like Petrarch himself, the humanists of the fifteenth century scoured Europe for ancient texts to read and study. In searching out the knowledge of the past, these fifteenth-century humanists made a series of

Poggio Bracciolini (PO-joe bra-chi-o-LEE-nee)

discoveries that changed their understanding of language, philosophy, and religion. Their desire to imitate led to a profound transformation of knowledge.

A Florentine antiquary, Niccolò Niccoli, coordinated and paid for much of this pursuit of "lost" manuscripts. A wealthy bachelor, Niccolò (1364–1437) spent the fortune he had inherited from his father by acquiring ancient statuary, reliefs, and, most of all, books. When he died, his collection of more than eight hundred volumes of Latin and Greek texts became the foundation of the humanist library housed in the Monastery of San Marco in Florence. Niccolò had specified that all his books "should be accessible to everyone," and humanists from across Italy and the rest of Europe came to Florence to study his literary treasures. Niccolò's library prompted Pope Nicholas V (r. 1447–1455) to begin the collection that is now the Apostolic Library of the Vatican in Rome. The Vatican library became a lending library, serving the humanist community in Rome. Similar collections were assembled in Venice, Milan, and Urbino. The Greek and Latin sources preserved in these libraries allowed humanists to study classical languages in a way not possible before.

The career of Lorenzo Valla (1407–1457) illustrates the transformation that took place in the fifteenth century as humanism swept Europe. Valla was born near Rome and received a traditional humanistic education in Greek and Latin studies. He spent the rest of his life at universities and courts lecturing on philosophy and literature. Valla's studies had led him to understand that languages change with time—that they, too, have a life and a history. In 1440 he published a work called *On the Donation of Constantine*. The *Donation of Constantine* purported to record the gift by the emperor Constantine (r. 311–337) of jurisdiction over Rome and the western half of the empire to the pope when the imperial capital was moved to Constantinople (see page 209). In the High and late Middle Ages, the papacy used the document to defend its right to political dominion in central Italy. The donation had long been criticized by legal theorists, who argued that Constantine had no right to make it. Valla went further and attacked the legitimacy of the document itself. Because of its language and form, he argued, it could not have been written at the time of Constantine:

> Through his [the writer's] babbling, he reveals his most impudent forgery himself. . . . Where he deals with the gifts he says "a diadem . . . made of pure gold and precious jewels." The ignoramus did not know that the diadem was made of cloth, probably silk. . . . He thinks it had to be made of gold, since nowadays kings usually wear a circle of gold set with jewels.[8]

Valla was correct. The *Donation* was an eighth-century forgery.

Valla later turned his attention to the New Testament. Jerome (331–420) had put together the Vulgate edition of the Bible in an attempt to create a single accepted Latin version of the Old and New Testaments (see page 232). In 1444 Valla published his *Annotations on the New Testament*. In this work he used his training in classical languages to correct Jerome's standard Latin text and to show numerous instances of mistranslations. His annotations on the New Testament were of critical importance to humanists outside Italy and were highly influential during the Protestant Reformation.

The transformation of humanism exemplified by Valla was fully expected by some Florentines. They anticipated that literary studies would lead eventually to philosophy. In 1456 a young Florentine began studying Greek with just such a change in mind. Supported by the Medici rulers of Florence, Marsilio Ficino° (1433–1499) began a daunting project: to translate the works of Plato into Latin and to interpret Plato in light of Christian doctrine and tradition.

Ficino believed that Platonism, like Christianity, demonstrated the dignity of humanity. He wrote that everything in creation was connected along a continuum ranging from the lowliest matter to the person of God. The human soul was located at the midpoint of this hierarchy and was a bridge between matter and God. True wisdom, and especially experience of the divine, could be gained only through contemplation and love. According to Ficino, logic and scientific observation did not lead to true understanding, for humans know logically only what they can define in human language; individuals can, however, love things, such as God, that they are not fully able to comprehend.

Ficino's belief in the dignity of man was shared by Giovanni Pico della Mirandola° (1463–1494), who proposed to debate with other philosophers nine hundred theses dealing with the nature of man, the origins of knowledge, and the uses of philosophy. Pico extended Ficino's idea of the hierarchy of being, arguing that humans surpassed even the angels in dignity. Angels held a fixed position in the hierarchy, just below God. In contrast, humans could move either up or down in the hierarchy, depending on the extent to which they embraced spiritual or worldly interests. Pico further believed that he had proved that all philosophies contain at least some

---

Ficino (fi-CHI-no)   **Giovanni Pico della Mirandola**
(joe-VAH-nee PIH-ko del-ah mi-RAHN-do-la)

truth. He was one of the first humanists to learn Hebrew and to argue that divine wisdom could be found in Jewish mystical literature. Along with others, he studied the Jewish Cabala, a collection of mystical and occult writings that humanists believed dated from the time of Moses. Pico's adoption of the Hebrew mystical writings was often controversial in the Jewish community as well as among Christians.

Pico's ideas were shared by other humanists, who contended that an original divine illumination—a "Pristine Theology," they called it—preceded even Plato and Aristotle. These humanists found theological truth in what they believed was ancient Egyptian, Greek, and Jewish magic. Ficino himself popularized the *Corpus Hermeticum* (the Hermetic collection), an amalgam of magical texts of the first century A.D. that was mistakenly thought to be the work of an Egyptian magician, Hermes Trismagistos. They assumed Hermes wrote during the age of Moses and Pythagoras. Like many neo-Platonic writings of the first century, Hermetic texts explained how the mind could influence and be influenced by the material and celestial worlds.

Along with exploring Hermetic magic, many humanists of the fifteenth and sixteenth centuries investigated astrology and alchemy. All three systems posit the existence of a direct, reciprocal connection between the cosmos and the natural world. In the late medieval and Renaissance world, astrological and alchemical theories seemed reasonable. By the late fifteenth century many humanists assumed that personality was profoundly affected by the stars and that the heavens were not silent regarding human affairs. It was not by accident that for a century or more after 1500, astrologers were official or unofficial members of most European courts.

Interest in alchemy was equally widespread though more controversial. Alchemists believed that everything was made of a primary material and that therefore it was possible to transmute one substance into another. The most popular variation, and the one most exploited by hucksters and frauds, was the belief that base metals could be turned into gold. The hopes of most alchemists, however, were more profound. They were convinced that they could unlock the explanation of the properties of the whole cosmos. On a personal and religious level as well as on a material level, practitioners hoped to make the impure pure. The interest in understanding and manipulating nature that lay at the heart of Hermetic magic, astrology, and alchemy was an important stimulus to scientific investigations and, ultimately, to the rise of modern scientific thought.

■ Humanism and Political Thought

The humanists' plan to rediscover classical sources meshed well with their political interests. "One can say," observed Leonardo Bruni, "that letters and the study of the Latin language went hand in hand with the condition of the Roman republic." Petrarch and the civic humanists believed that rulers, whether in a republic or a principality, should exhibit all the classical and Christian virtues of faith, hope, love, prudence, temperance, fortitude, and justice. A virtuous ruler would be loved as well as obeyed. The civic humanists viewed governments and laws as essentially unchanging and static. They believed that when change did occur, it most likely happened by chance—that is, because of fortune (the Roman goddess Fortuna). Humanists believed that the only protection against chance was true virtue, for the virtuous would never be dominated by fortune. Thus, beginning with Petrarch, humanists advised rulers to love their subjects, to be magnanimous with their possessions, and to maintain the rule of law. Humanistic tracts of the fourteenth and fifteenth centuries were full of classical and Christian examples of virtuous actions by moral rulers.

The French invasions of Italy in 1494 (see page 370) and the warfare that followed called into question many of the humanists' assumptions about the lessons and virtues of classical civilization. Francesco Guicciardini° (1483–1540), a Florentine patrician who had served in papal armies, suggested that, contrary to humanist hopes, history held no clear lessons. Unless the causes of separate events were identical down to the smallest detail, he said, the results could be radically different. An even more thorough critique was offered by Guicciardini's friend and fellow Florentine, Niccolò Machiavelli (1469–1527). In a series of writings Machiavelli developed what he believed was a new science of politics. He wrote *Discourses on Livy*, a treatise on military organization, a history of Florence, and even a Renaissance play entitled *The Mandrake Root*. He is best remembered, however, for *The Prince* (1513), a small tract numbering less than a hundred pages.

Machiavelli felt that his contemporaries paid too little heed to the lessons to be learned from history. Thus, in his discourses on Livy he comments on Roman government, the role of religion, and the nature of political virtue, emphasizing the sophisticated Roman analysis of political and military situations. A shortcoming more serious than ignorance of history, Machiavelli believed, was his contemporaries' ignorance of the true motivations for people's actions. His play *The Mandrake Root* is

---

Francesco Guicciardini (fran-CHES-ko gwih-char-DI-nee)

a comedy about the ruses used to seduce a young woman. In truth, however, none of the characters is fooled. All of them, from the wife to her husband, realize what is happening but use the seduction to their own advantage. In the play Machiavelli implicitly challenges the humanistic assumption that educated individuals will naturally choose virtue over vice. He explicitly criticizes these same assumptions in *The Prince*. Machiavelli holds the contrary view: that individuals are much more likely to respond to fear and that power rather than rhetoric makes for good government.

Machiavelli's use of the Italian word *virtù* led him to be vilified as amoral. Machiavelli deliberately chose a word that meant both "manliness" or "ability" and "virtue as a moral quality." Earlier humanists had restricted *virtù* to the second meaning, using the word to refer to upright qualities such as prudence, generosity, and love. Machiavelli tried to show that in some situations these "virtues" could have violent, even evil, consequences. If, for example, a prince was so magnanimous in giving away his wealth that he was forced to raise taxes, his subjects might come to hate him. Conversely, a prince who, through cruelty to the enemies of his state, brought peace and stability to his subjects might be obeyed and perhaps even loved by them. A virtuous ruler must be mindful of the goals to be achieved—that is what Machiavelli really meant by the phrase often translated as "the ends justify the means."

Machiavelli expected his readers to be aware of the ambiguous nature of virtue—whether understood as ability or as morality. "One will discover," he concludes, "that something which appears to be a virtue, if pursued, will end in his destruction; while some other thing which seems to be a vice, if pursued, will result in his safety and his well-being."[9]

Like Guicciardini, Machiavelli rejected earlier humanistic assumptions that one needed merely to imitate the great leaders of the past. Governing is a process that requires different skills at different times, he warned: "The man who adapts his course of action to the nature of the times will succeed and, likewise, the man who sets his course of action out of tune with the times will come to grief."[10] The abilities that enable a prince to gain power may not be the abilities that will allow him to maintain it.

With the writings of Machiavelli, humanistic ideas of intellectual, moral, and political reform came to maturation. Petrarch and the early humanists believed fully in the powers of classical wisdom to transform society. Machiavelli and his contemporaries admitted the importance of classical wisdom but also recognized the ambiguity of any simplistic application of classical learning to contemporary life.

Machiavelli   In this portrait Machiavelli is dressed as a government official. After being exiled from Florence by the Medici, he wrote to a friend that each night when he returned from the fields he dressed again in his curial robes and pondered the behavior of governments and princes. *(Scala/Art Resource, NY)*

THE ARTS IN ITALY, 1250–1550

TOWNSMEN and artists in Renaissance Italy shared the humanists' perception of the importance of classical antiquity. Filippo Villani (d. 1405), a wealthy Florentine from an important business family, wrote that artists had recently "reawakened a lifeless and almost extinct art." In the middle of the fifteenth century, the sculptor Lorenzo Ghiberti concluded that with the rise of Christianity "not only statues and paintings [were destroyed], but the books and commentaries and handbooks and rules on which men relied for their training." Italian writers and painters themselves believed that the recovery of past literary and artistic practices was essential if society was to recover from the "barbarism" that they believed characterized the recent past.

Giotto's Naturalism Later painters praised the naturalistic emotion of Giotto's painting. In this detail from the Arena Chapel, Giotto portrays the kiss of Judas, one of the most dramatic moments in Christian history. *(Scala/Art Resource, NY)*

The Renaissance of the arts is traditionally divided into three periods. In the early Renaissance, artists imitated nature; in the middle period, they rediscovered classical ideas of proportion; in the High Renaissance, artists were "superior to nature but also to the artists of the ancient world," according to the artist and architect Giorgio Vasari (1511–1574), who wrote a famous history of the eminent artists of his day.

■ The Artistic Renaissance

The first stirrings of the new styles can be found in the late thirteenth century. The greatest innovator of that era was Giotto° di Bondone of Florence (ca. 1266–1337). Although Giotto's background was modest, his fellow citizens, popes, and patrons throughout Italy quickly recognized his skill. He traveled as far south as Rome and

as far north as Padua painting churches and chapels. According to later artists and commentators, Giotto broke with the prevailing stiff, highly symbolic style and introduced lifelike portrayals of living persons. He produced paintings of dramatic situations, showing events located in specific times and places. The frescoes of the Arena Chapel in Padua (1304–1314), for example, recount episodes in the life of Christ. In a series of scenes leading from Christ's birth to his crucifixion, Giotto situates his actors in towns and countryside in what appears to be actual space. Even Michelangelo, the master of the High Renaissance, studied Giotto's painting. Giotto was in such demand throughout Italy that his native Florence gave him a public appointment so that he would be required by law to remain in the city.

Early in the fifteenth century, Florentine artists devised new ways to represent nature that surpassed even the innovations of Giotto. The revolutionary nature of these artistic developments is evident from the careers

---

Giotto (JO-toe)

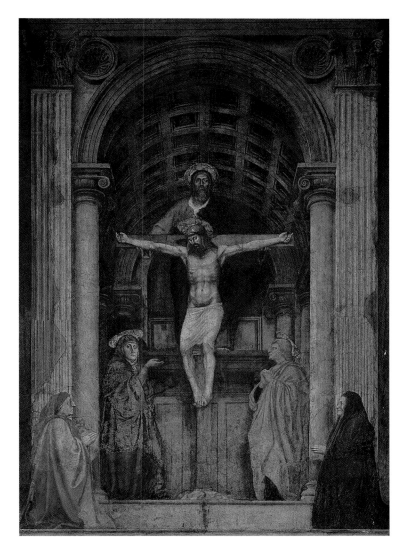

The Doors of Paradise   Ghiberti worked on panels for the baptistery from 1403 to 1453. In his representations of scenes from the Old Testament he combined a love of ancient statuary with the new Florentine interest in linear perspective.
(Alinari/Art Resource, NY)

of Lorenzo Ghiberti (1378–1455), Filippo Brunelleschi° (1377–1446), and Masaccio° (born Tomasso di ser Giovanni di Mone, 1401–ca. 1428). Their sculpture, architecture, and painting began an ongoing series of experiments with the representation of space through linear perspective. Perspective is a system for representing three-dimensional objects on a two-dimensional plane. It is based on two observations: (1) As parallel lines recede into the distance, they seem to converge; and (2) a geometric relationship regulates the relative sizes of objects at various distances from the viewer. Painters of the Renaissance literally found themselves looking at their world from a new perspective.

In 1401 Ghiberti won a commission to design door panels for the baptistery of San Giovanni in Florence. He was to spend the rest of his life working on two sets of

Brunelleschi (broon-eh-LES-key)   **Masaccio** (ma-SAH-cho)

bronze doors on which were recorded the stories of the New Testament (the north doors) and the Old Testament (the east doors). Ghiberti used the new techniques of linear perspective to create a sense of space into which he placed his classically inspired figures. Later in the sixteenth century Michelangelo remarked that the east doors were worthy to be the "Doors of Paradise," and so they have been known ever since.

In the competition for the baptistery commission, Ghiberti had beaten the young Filippo Brunelleschi, who, as a result, gave up sculpture for architecture and later left Florence to study in Rome. While in Rome he is said to have visited and measured surviving examples of classical architecture—the artistic equivalent of humanistic literary research. According to Vasari, he was capable of "visualizing Rome as it was before the fall." Brunelleschi's debt to Rome is evident in his masterpiece, Florence's foundling hospital. Built as a combination of hemispheres and cubes and resembling a Greek stoa or an arcaded Roman basilica, the long, low structure is an example of how profoundly different Renaissance architecture was from the towering Gothic of the Middle Ages.

In the first decade of the fifteenth century, many commentators believed that painting would never be as innovative as either sculpture or architecture. They knew of no classical models that had survived for imitation. Yet the possibilities in painting became apparent in 1427 with the unveiling of Masaccio's *Trinity* in the Florentine church of Santa Maria Novella. Masaccio built on revolutionary experiments in linear perspective to create a painting in which a flat wall seems to become a recessed chapel. The space created is filled with the images of Christ crucified, the Father, and the Holy Spirit.

In the middle years of the fifteenth century, artists came to terms with the innovations of the earlier period. In the second half of the fifteenth century, however, artists such as the Florentine Sandro Botticelli° (1445–1510) added a profound understanding of classical symbolism to the technical innovations of Masaccio and Brunelleschi. Botticelli's famous *Primavera* (*Spring,* 1478), painted for a member of the Medici family, is filled with neo-Platonic symbolism concerning truth, beauty, and the virtues of humanity. (See the feature "Weighing the Evidence: The Art of Renaissance Florence" on pages 426–427.)

The high point in the development of Renaissance art came at the beginning of the sixteenth century in the work of several masters throughout Italy. Artists in Venice learned perspective from the Florentines and added their own tradition of subtle coloring in oils. The works of Italian artists were admired well beyond the borders of Italy. Even Sultan Mehmed II of Constantinople valued Italian painters. (See the box "Global Encounters: Gentile Bellini Travels to Meet the Turkish Sultan.")

The work of two Florentines, Leonardo da Vinci (1452–1519) and Michelangelo Buonarroti (1475–1564),

best exemplifies the sophisticated heights that art achieved early in the sixteenth century. Leonardo, the bastard son of a notary, was raised in the village of Vinci outside of Florence. Cut off from the humanistic milieu of the city, he desired above all else to prove that his artistry was the equal of his formally schooled social superiors. In his notebooks he confessed, "I am fully conscious that, not being a literary man, certain presumptuous persons will think they may reasonably blame me, alleging that I am not a man of letters."[11] But he defended his lack of classical education by arguing that all the best writing, like the best painting and invention, is based on the close observation of nature. Close observation and scientific analysis made Leonardo's work uniquely creative in all these fields. Leonardo is famous for his plans, sometimes prophetic, for bridges, airships, submarines, and fortresses. There seemed to be no branch of learning in which he was not interested. In painting he developed chiaroscuro, a technique for using light and dark in pictorial representation, and showed aerial perspective. He painted horizons as muted, shaded zones rather than with sharp lines. "I know," he said, "that the greater or less quantity of air that lies between the eye and the object makes the outlines of that object more or less distinct."[12] It was his analytical observation that made Leonardo so influential on his contemporaries.

Michelangelo, however, was widely hailed as the capstone of Renaissance art. In the words of a contemporary, "He alone has triumphed over ancient artists, modern artists and over Nature itself." In his career we can follow the rise of Renaissance artists from the ranks of mere craftsmen to honored creators, courtiers who were the equals of the humanists—in fact, Michelangelo shared Petrarch's concern for reform and renewal in Italian society. We can also discern the synthesis of the artistic and intellectual transformations of the Renaissance with a profound religious sensitivity.

The importance of Michelangelo's contribution is obvious in two of his most important works: the statue *David* in Florence and his commissions in the Sistine Chapel of the Vatican in Rome. From his youth Michelangelo had studied and imitated antique sculpture, to the point that some of his creations were thought by many actually to be antiquities. He used his understanding of classical art in *David* (1501). Citizens recalled David's defeat of the giant Goliath, saving Israel from almost certain conquest by the Philistines. *David* thus became a symbol of the youthful Florentine republic struggling to maintain its freedom against great odds. As Vasari noted, "just as David had protected his people and governed

---

Botticelli (bot-ti-CHEL-ee)

Gentile Bellini Travels to Meet the Turkish Sultan

Giovanni and Gentile Bellini were two of the leading Renaissance artists in Venice. Their fame spread throughout the Mediterranean and resulted in this unusual cultural meeting in 1479. A portrait of the emperor Mehmed II by Gentile now hangs in the National Gallery in London.

Some portraits having been taken to Turkey to the Grand Turk [the sultan] by an ambassador, that emperor was so struck with astonishment that, although the Mohammedan laws prohibit pictures, he accepted them with great goodwill, praising the work without end, and what is more, requesting that the master himself be sent to him. But the senate, considering that Giovanni could ill support the hardships, resolved to send Gentile his brother, and he was conveyed safely in their galleys to Constantinople, where being presented to Mehmed [II], he was received with much kindness as an unusual visitor. He presented a beautiful picture to the prince, who admired it much, and could not persuade himself to believe that a mortal man had in him so much of the divinity as to be able to express the things of nature in such a lively manner. Gentile painted the Emperor Mehmed himself from life so well that it was considered a miracle, and the emperor, having seen many specimens of his art, asked Gentile if he had the courage to paint himself; and Gentile having answered "Yes," before many days were over he finished a life-like portrait by means of a mirror, and brought it to the monarch, whose astonishment was so great that he would have it a divine spirit dwelt in him. And had not this art been forbidden by the law of the Turks, the emperor would never have let him go. But either from fear that people would murmur, or from some other cause, he sent for him one day, and having thanked him, and given him great praise, he bade him to ask whatever he would and it should be granted him without fail. Gentile modestly asked for nothing more than that he would graciously give him a letter of recommendation to the Senate and Lords of Venice. His request was granted in as fervent words as possible, and then, loaded with gifts and honors, and with the dignity of a cavalier, he was sent away. Among the other gifts was a chain of gold of two hundred and fifty crowns weight, worked in the Turkish manner. So, leaving Constantinople, he came safely to Venice, where he was received by his brother Giovanni and the whole city with joy, every one rejoicing in the honors which Mehmed had paid him. When the Doge and Lords [of Venice] saw the letters of the emperor, they ordered that a provision of two hundred crowns a year should be paid him all the rest of his life.

Source: Stories of the Italian Renaissance from Vasari, arranged and translated by E. L. Seeley (London and New York, 1908), pp. 135–137.

them justly, so whoever ruled Florence should vigorously defend the city and govern it with justice."[13]

Michelangelo was a committed republican and Florentine, but he spent much of his life working in Rome on a series of papal commissions. In 1508 he was called by Pope Julius II to work on the ceiling of the Sistine Chapel. Michelangelo spent four years decorating the ceiling with hundreds of figures and with nine scenes from the book of Genesis, including the famous *Creation of Adam.* In the late 1530s, at the request of Pope Clement VII, he completed *The Last Judgment,* which covers the wall above the altar. In that painting the techniques of perspective and the conscious recognition of debts to classical culture recede into the background as the artist surrounds Christ in judgment with saints and sinners. In the hollow, hanging skin of flayed Saint Bartholomew we can detect a psychological self-portrait of an artist increasingly concerned with his own spiritual failings.

Michelangelo's self-portrait reminds us that the intellectual content of the artist's work is one of its most

The Sistine Chapel Painted from 1508 to 1512, the ceiling of the Sistine Chapel is Michelangelo's most famous work. Powerfully summarizing Renaissance faith in the unity of Christian truth and pagan wisdom, Michelangelo illustrated God's giving life to Adam (among other biblical scenes), while around the ceiling's border he placed *sibyls,* classical symbols of knowledge.

(Vatican Museums. Photo: A. Bracchetti/P. Zigrossi)

enduring traits. He was a Platonist who believed that the form and beauty of a statue were contained, buried, in the stone itself. The artist's job was to peel away excess material and reveal the beauty within. As he noted in one of his poems, sculpting was a process not unlike religious salvation:

> Just as by carving . . . we set
> Into hard mountain rock
> A living figure
> Which grows most where the stone is most removed;
> In like manner, some good works . . .
> Are concealed by the excess of my very flesh.[14]

■ Art and Patronage

The religious passion of Michelangelo's poetry indicates one of the reasons that art was so popular in Renaissance Italy. Art, like poetry, provided symbols and images through which Italians could reason about the most important issues of their communities. Italians willingly spent vast sums on art because of its ability to communicate social, political, and spiritual values.

Italy in the fourteenth and fifteenth centuries was unusually wealthy relative to the towns and principalities of northern Europe. Despite the population decline caused by plague and the accompanying economic dislocations, per person wealth in Italy remained quite high. Because of banking, international trade, and even service as mercenaries, Italians, and particularly Florentines, had money to spend on arts and luxuries. Thus, the Italians of the Renaissance, whether as public or private patrons, could afford to use consumption of art as a form of competition for social and political status. And it was not just the elite who could afford art. Surprisingly modest families bought small religious paintings, painted storage chests, and decorative arts. Thus the market for art steadily increased in the fourteenth and fifteenth centuries, as did the number of shops and studios in which artists could be trained.

Artists in the modern world are accustomed to standing outside society as critics of conventional ideas. In the late Middle Ages and Renaissance, artists were not alienated commentators. In 1300 most art was religious in subject, and public display was its purpose. Throughout Europe art fulfilled a devotional function. Painted crucifixes, altarpieces, and banners were often endowed as devotional or penitential objects. The Arena Chapel in Padua, with its frescoes by Giotto, was funded by a merchant anxious to pay for some of his sins.

In the late Middle Ages and Renaissance, numerous paintings and statues throughout Italy (and much of the rest of Europe) were revered for their miraculous powers. During plague, drought, and times of war, people had recourse to the sacred power of the saints represented in these works of art. (See the feature "Weighing the Evidence: A Painting of the Plague" in Chapter 11, pages 390–391.) The construction of the great churches of the period was often a community project that lasted for decades, even centuries. The city council of Siena, for example, voted to rebuild its Gothic cathedral of Saint Mary, saying that the blessed Virgin "was, is and will be in the future the head of this city" and that through veneration of her "Siena may be protected from harm." Accordingly, although the subject of art was clearly and primarily religious, the message was bound up in the civic values and ideas of the fourteenth and fifteenth centuries.

The first burst of artistic creativity in the fourteenth century was paid for by public institutions. Communal governments built and redecorated city halls to house government functionaries and to promote civic pride. Most towns placed a remarkable emphasis on the beauty of the work. Civic officials often named special commissions to consult with a variety of artists and architects before approving building projects. Governments, with an eye to the appearance of public areas, legislated the width of streets, height limits, and even the styles of dwelling façades.

The series of paintings called the *Good Government of Siena* illustrates the use of art to communicate political ideas. Painted in the first half of the fourteenth century by Ambrogio Lorenzetti° (ca. 1300–1348), *Good Government* combined allegorical representations of Wisdom and the cardinal virtues on one wall with realistic street scenes of a well-ordered Siena on an adjacent wall. Across from the scenes of good government are its opposite, graphic representations of murder, rape, and general injustice and mayhem. In this ambitious work, with its specific scenes and unmistakable tone, the government broadcast a clear political message in realistic brushstrokes. The popular preacher San Bernardino of Siena (1380–1444) reinforced the point of Lorenzetti's painting: "To see Peace depicted is a delight and so it is a shame to see War painted on the other wall." And Bernardino's sermon reminded listeners of the conclusions they should draw: "Oh my brothers and fathers, love and embrace each other . . . give your aid to this toil which I have undertaken so gladly, to bring about love and peace among you."[15]

Public art in Florence was often organized and supported by various guild organizations. Guild membership was a prerequisite for citizenship, so guildsmen set the tone in politics as well as in the commercial life of the city. Most major guilds commissioned sculpture for the Chapel of Or San Michele, a famous shrine in the grain market (its painting of the Virgin was popularly thought to have wonder-working powers) and seat of the Guelf party, the city's most powerful political organization. Guilds took responsibility for building and maintaining other structures in the city as well. Guildsmen took pride in creating a beautiful environment, but as the cloth makers' decision to supervise the baptistery shows, the work reflected not only on the city and its patron saint but also on the power and influence of the guild itself.

The princes who ruled outside the republics of Italy often had similarly precise messages that they wished to communicate. Renaissance popes embarked on a quite specific ideological program in the late fifteenth century to assert their dual roles as spiritual leaders of Christendom and temporal lords of a central Italian state (see page 422). Rulers such as the Este dukes of Ferrara and the Sforza dukes of Milan constructed castles within their cities or hunting lodges and villas in the countryside and adorned them with pictures of the hunt or murals of knights in combat, scenes that emphasized their noble virtues and their natural right to rule.

By the mid-fifteenth century, patrons of artworks in Florence and most other regions of Italy were more and more likely to be wealthy individuals. Republics, in which all families were in principle equal, initially distrusted the pride and ambition implied by elaborate city palaces and rural villas. By the middle of the fifteenth century, however, such reserve was found in none but the most conservative republics, such as Venice or Lucca.

Ambrogio Lorenzetti (am-BROH-jo loh-ren-ZET-ee)

Palaces, gardens, and villas became the settings in which the wealthy could entertain their peers, receive clients, and debate the political issues of the day. The public rooms of these *palazzos* were decorated with portraits, gem collections, rare books, ceramics, and statuary. Many villas and palaces included private chapels. In the Medici palace in Florence, for example, the chapel is the setting for a painting of the Magi (the three Wise Men who came to worship the infant Jesus) in which the artist, Benozzo Gozzoli (1420–1498), used members of the Medici family as models for the portraits of the Wise Men and their entourage. The Magi, known to be wise and virtuous rulers, were an apt symbol for the family that had come to dominate the city.

Artists at princely courts were expected to work for the glory of their lord. Often the genre of choice was the portrait. One of the most successful portraitists of the sixteenth century was Sofonisba Anguissola° (1532–1625). Anguissola won renown as a prodigy because she was female and from a patrician family; one of her paintings was sent to Michelangelo, who forwarded it to the Medici in Florence. Since women would never be allowed to study anatomy, Anguissola concentrated her talents on portraits and detailed paintings of domestic life. Later she was called to the Spanish court, where the king, queen, and their daughter sat for her. She continued to paint after her marriage and return to Italy. Even in her nineties, she welcomed painters from all parts of Europe to visit and discuss techniques of portraiture.

THE SPREAD OF THE RENAISSANCE, 1350–1536

BY 1500, the Renaissance had spread from Italy to the rest of Europe. Well beyond the borders of the old Roman Empire, in Prague and Cracow, for example, one could find a renewed interest in classical ideas about art and literature. As information about the past and its relevance to contemporary life spread, however, the message was transformed in several important ways. Outside Italy, Rome and its history played a much less pivotal role. Humanists elsewhere in the West were interested more in religious than in political reform, and they responded to a number of important local interests. Yet the Renaissance notion of renewal based on a deep understanding and imitation of the past remained at the center of the movement. The nature of the transformation will be clearer if we begin by considering the nature of vernacular literatures before the emergence of Renaissance humanism.

■ Vernacular Literatures

The humanistic movement was not simply a continuation of practical and literary movements. The extent of its innovation will be clearer if we look briefly at the vernacular literatures (that is, written in native languages, rather than Latin) of the fourteenth and fifteenth centuries.

As in Italy, fourteenth-century writers were not immediately drawn to classical sources. Boccaccio's work, for example, influenced another vernacular writer, Geoffrey Chaucer (ca. 1343–1400), the son of a London burgher, who served as a diplomat, courtier, and Member of Parliament. In addition to the pervasive French influence, Chaucer read and studied Boccaccio. Chaucer's most well-known work, *The Canterbury Tales,* consists of stories told by a group of thirty pilgrims who left the London suburbs on a pilgrimage to the shrine of Saint Thomas Becket at Canterbury Cathedral. The narrators and the stories themselves describe a variety of moral and social types, creating an acute, sometimes bitter, portrait of English life. The Wife of Bath is typical of Chaucer's pilgrims: "She was a worthy woman all her life, husbands at the churchdoor she had five." After describing her own five marriages, she observes that marriage is a proper way to achieve moral perfection, but it can be so only if the woman is master.

Although Chaucer's characters present an ironic view of the good and evil that characterize society, Chaucer's contemporary, William Langland (ca. 1330–1400), takes a decidedly more serious view of the ills of English life. Whereas Boccaccio and Chaucer all told realistic tales about life as it truly seemed to be, Langland used the traditional allegorical language (that is, symbolic language in which a place or person represents an idea) of medieval Europe. In *Piers Plowman* Langland writes of people caught between the "Valley of Death" and the "Tower of Truth." He describes the seven deadly sins that threaten all of society and follows with an exhortation to do better. Both Chaucer and Langland expected that their audiences would immediately recognize commonly held ideas and values.

Despite the persistence of old forms of literature, new vernacular styles arose, although they still dealt

---

Anguissola (an-GWIS-so-lah)

with traditional values and ideas. Throughout Europe many writers directly addressed their cares and concerns. Letters like those of the Paston family in England or Alessandra Macinghi-Strozzi in Italy described day-to-day affairs of business, politics, and family life. Letters dictated and sent by Saint Catherine of Siena and Angela of Foligno offered advice to the troubled. Small books of moral or spiritual writings were especially popular among women readers in the fourteenth and fifteenth centuries, among them *The Mirror for Simple Souls* by Marguerite of Porete (d. 1310). Though Marguerite was ultimately executed as a heretic, her work continued to circulate anonymously. Her frank descriptions of love, including God's love for humans, inspired many other writers in the fourteenth and fifteenth centuries. Less erotic but equally riveting was the memoir of Margery Kempe, an alewife from England, who left her husband and family, dressed in white (symbolic of virginity), and joined other pilgrims on trips to Spain, Italy, and Jerusalem.

One of the most unusual of the new vernacular writers was Christine de Pizan (1369–1430), the daughter of an Italian physician at the court of Charles V of France. When the deaths of her father and husband left her with responsibility for her children and little money, she turned to writing. From 1389 until her death, she lived and wrote at the French court. She is perhaps best known for *The Book of the City of the Ladies* (1405). In it she added her own voice to what is known as the *querelle des femmes,* the "argument over women." Christine wrote to counter the prevalent opinions of women as inherently inferior to men and incapable of moral judgments. She argued that the problem was education: "If it were customary to send daughters to school like sons, and if they were then taught the natural sciences, they would learn as thoroughly and understand the subtleties of all the arts and sciences as well as sons." Christine described in her book an ideal city of ladies in which prudence, justice, and reason would protect women from ignorant male critics.

All these vernacular writings built on popular tales and sayings as well as on traditional moral and religious writings. Unlike the early humanists, the vernacular writers saw little need for new cultural and intellectual models.

■ The Impact of Printing

The spread of humanism beyond Italy was aided greatly by the invention of printing. In the fifteenth century the desire to own and to read complete texts of classical works was widespread, but the number of copies was severely limited by the time and expense of hand copying, collating, and checking manuscripts. Poggio Bracciolini's letters are filled with complaints about the time and expense of reproducing the classical manuscripts he had discovered. One copy he had commissioned was so inaccurate and illegible as to be nearly unusable. Traveling to repositories and libraries was often easier than creating a personal library. It was rarely possible for someone who read a manuscript once to obtain a complete copy to compare with other works.

The invention of printing with movable lead type changed things dramatically. (See the feature "Information Technology: The Print Revolution" on pages 414–415.) Although block printing had long been known in China and was a popular way to produce playing cards and small woodcuts in Europe, only with the creation of movable type by Johann Gutenberg in the 1450s did printing become a practical way to produce books. Between 180 and 200 copies of the so-called Gutenberg Bible were printed in 1452–1453. It was followed shortly by editions of the Psalms. German printers spread their techniques rapidly. By 1470 printing had spread to Italy, the Low Countries, France, and England. It has been estimated that by 1500 a thousand presses were operating in 265 towns (see Map 12.1). The output of the early presses was extremely varied, ranging from small devotional books and other popular and profitable literature to complete editions of classical authors and their humanistic and theological texts.

Printing allowed for the creation of agreed-upon standard editions of works in law, theology, philosophy, and science. Scholars in different parts of the European world could feel fairly confident that they and their colleagues were analyzing identical texts. Similarly, producing accurate medical and herbal diagrams, maps, and even reproductions of art and architecture was easier. Multiple copies of texts also made possible the study of rare and esoteric literary, philosophical, and scientific works. An unexpected result of the print revolution was the rise of the printshop as a center of culture and communication. The printers Aldus Manutius (1450–1515) in Venice and Johannes Froben (d. 1527) in Basel were humanists. Both invited humanists to work in their shops editing their texts and correcting the proofs before printing. Printshops became a natural gathering place for clerics and laymen. Thus, they were natural sources of humanist ideas and later, in the sixteenth century, of Protestant religious programs.

Map 12.1   The Spread of Printing   Printing technology moved rapidly along major trade routes to the most populous and prosperous areas of Europe. The technology was rapidly adopted in peripheral areas as well as in highly literate centers such as the Low Countries, the Rhine Valley, and northern Italy.

■ Humanism Outside Italy

As the influence of the humanist movement extended beyond Italy, the interests of the humanists changed. Although a strong religious strain infused Italian humanism, public life lay at the center of Italian programs of education and reform. Outside Italy, however, moral and religious reform formed the heart of the movement. Northern humanists wanted to renew Christian life and reinvigorate the church. Critics of the church complained that the clergy were wealthy and ignorant and that the laity were uneducated and superstitious. To amend those failings, northern humanists were involved

in building educational institutions, in unearthing and publishing texts by Church Fathers, and in chronicling local customs and history. The works of the two best-known humanists, Thomas More and Desiderius Erasmus, present a sharp critique of contemporary behavior and, in the case of Erasmus, a call to a new sense of piety. The religious views of Erasmus were so influential that northern humanism has generally come to be known as "Christian humanism."

The intellectual environment of centers into which humanism spread from Italy had changed significantly since the thirteenth century. The universities of Paris and Oxford retained the status they had acquired earlier but found themselves competing with a host of new foundations. Like Paris, almost all had theological faculties dominated by Scholastically trained theologians. Nevertheless, the new foundations often had chairs of rhetoric, or "eloquence," which left considerable scope for those who advocated humanistic learning. These new universities, from Cracow (1367) to Uppsala in Sweden (1477), also reflected the increased national feeling in various regions of Europe. The earliest university in the lands of the German empire, the Charles University in Prague (1348), was founded at the request of Emperor Charles IV of Luxemburg, whose court was in Prague. The foundation of a new university at Poszony (1465) by Johannes Vitéz was part of a cultural flowering of the Hungarian court at Buda. A supporter of King Matthias Corvinus, Vitéz corresponded with Italian humanists, collected manuscripts, and tried to recruit humanist teachers to come to Buda. Vienna (1365), Aix (1409), Louvain (1425), and numerous other universities owed their foundations to the pride and ambition of local rulers.

Humanists on faculties of law in French universities used humanistic techniques of historical and linguistic study. Italian-trained French lawyers introduced what came to be called the "Gallican style" of jurisprudence. Because legal ideas, like language, changed over time, they argued that Roman law had to be studied as a historically created system and not as an abstract and unchanging structure. Humanists like Guillaume Budé (1468–1540) moved from the study of law to considerations of Roman coinage, religion, and economic life in order to better understand the formation of Roman law. The desire to understand the law led other humanist-legists to add the study of society in ancient Gaul to their work on Rome, and then to examine the law of other societies as well.

The new universities often became centers of linguistic studies. Humanistic interest in language inspired the foundation of "trilingual" colleges in Spain, France, and the Low Countries to foster serious study of Hebrew, Greek, and Latin. Like Italian humanists, other humanists believed that knowledge of languages would allow students to understand more clearly the truths of Christianity. Typical of this movement was the archbishop of Toledo, Francisco Jiménez de Cisneros (1436–1517), who founded the University of Alcalá in 1508 with chairs of Latin, Greek, and Hebrew. He began the publication of a vast new edition of the Bible, called the "Polyglot Bible" ("many tongue"; 1522) because it had parallel columns in Latin, Greek, and, where appropriate, Hebrew. Unlike Valla, Jiménez did not intend his translations to challenge the Vulgate, but merely clarify its meaning. The university and the Bible were part of an effort to complete the conversion of Muslims and Jews and to reform religious practices among the old Christians.

To these humanists, the discovery and publication of early Christian authors seemed critical to any reform within the church. Jacques Lefèvre d'Étaples° (1455–1536) of France was one of the most famous and influential of these humanistic editors of early Christian texts. After 1500 he concentrated on the edition of texts by the early Church Fathers. The true spirit of Christianity, he believed, would be most clear in the works and lives of those who had lived closest to the age of the apostles. Christian humanists inspired by Lefèvre became key players in the later Reformation movements in France. Lefèvre's faith in the value of classical languages was shared by John Colet (1467–1519) of England, founder of St. Paul's School in London. He instituted a thorough program of teaching Latin and Greek aimed at creating scholars who would have access to the earliest Christian writings.

Tensions between the humanists and the advocates of Scholastic methods broke out over the cultural and linguistic studies that formed the heart of the humanist program. Taking to heart the humanistic belief that all philosophies and religions, not just Christianity, contained universal moral and spiritual truths, Johannes Reuchlin° (1455–1522) of Württemberg embarked on a study of the Cabala. Johannes Pfefferkorn, a Dominican priest and recent convert from Judaism, attacked Reuchlin's use of Jewish traditions in the study of Christian theology. Sides were quickly drawn. The theological faculties of the German universities generally supported the Dominican. The humanists supported Reuchlin. In his own defense Reuchlin issued *The Letters of Illustrious Men*, a volume of correspondence he had received in support of his position. This work gave rise to one of the great satires of the Renaissance, *The Letters of Obscure Men* (1516), written by anonymous authors and purporting to be letters from various narrow-minded Scholastics in defense of the Dominican. Although the debate arose over the validity of Hebraic studies for Christian theology and not over humanistic ideas of reform or wisdom, it indicates the division between the humanists and much of the Scholastic community. Many initially misunderstood the early controversies of the Protestant Reformation as a continuation of the conflicts between humanists and Scholastic theologians over the uses of Hebrew learning.

Lefèvre d'Étaples (le-FEV-ra du-TAHP-le)
Reuchlin (RYE-klin)

The Print Revolution

For more than five thousand years, from the dawn of civilization in Mesopotamia and Egypt, people in the West wrote by hand. Imperial decrees, sacred scriptures, commercial transactions, private letters—all required the skills of a select group of scribes, clerks, or monks. In Korea and China, however, mechanical printing using carved wooden blocks had been introduced by A.D. 750. Moveable type, using characters made of baked clay, was invented in China in the eleventh century. But the Chinese continued to prefer block printing well into the modern period. Written Chinese consists of thousands of ideographic characters. The labor of creating, organizing, and setting so many different bits of type made it much simpler to cut individual pages from a single wooden block. European languages, which can be written with fewer than a hundred characters, were much better adapted to printing with movable, reusable type.

It appears that the Mongol armies brought examples of Chinese printing—the Venetian Marco Polo described seeing paper money during his travels—to western Asia and Europe at the end of the thirteenth century. In the early fourteenth century Europeans began using block printing techniques to produce religious images, short prayers, and even decks of playing cards. As with Chinese printing, European block printing was a slow and expensive process for printing large numbers of varied texts. The print revolution had to wait another century, until the innovations of the German goldsmith Johann Gutenberg (ca. 1399–1468).

Gutenberg drew on his knowledge of metallurgy to devise a lead-tin-copper alloy that could be cast into durable, reusable type. His crucial invention was a type mold consisting of a flat strip of metal—stamped in the same way a coin is minted, leaving the impression of a single letter—inserted in the bottom of a rectangular brass box held together by screws. Molten metal was poured into it, producing a single piece of type. An experienced type founder could produce up to six hundred pieces of type a day. No wooden-block carver could have approached that rate. To solve the remaining problems, Gutenberg adapted the screw press commonly used to produce linen, paper, and wine to make a printing press. He followed the example of Flemish painters by adding linseed oil to the ink to make it thick enough to adhere uniformly to the metal type.

In 1455 the Gutenberg Bible was published in Mainz, Germany—but not by Gutenberg. After years of costly experimentation, Gutenberg was forced to turn over his equipment and newly printed Bibles to his partner and creditor, the wealthy merchant and moneylender Johann Fust.

The new technology, which enabled printers to create a thousand or more copies in a single print run, was highly efficient. Simple printed school texts cost only a quarter of the price of hand-copied texts. The leading bookseller in the university town of Bologna managed to stock ten thousand copies of texts, treatises, and commentaries. By 1500 even street singers sold printed copies of their songs.

Gutenberg's invention was revolutionary because, for the first time, the same information and ideas were avail-

■ Thomas More and Desiderius Erasmus

The careers of two humanists in particular exemplify the strength of the humanistic movement outside Italy, and its limits: Sir Thomas More (1478–1535) of London and Desiderius Erasmus (1466–1536) of Rotterdam. Their careers developed along very different paths. More had been educated at St. Anthony's school in London and became a lawyer. A friend of John Colet, he translated Lucan and wrote a humanistic history of Richard III while pursuing his public career. He is most famous for his work *Utopia* (1516), the description of an ideal society located on the island of Utopia (literally, "nowhere") in the newly explored oceans. This powerful and contradic-

tory work comprises two volumes. Book I is a debate over the moral value of public service between Morus, a well-intentioned but practical politician, and Hythloday, a widely traveled idealist. Morus tries to make the bureaucrat's argument about working for change from within the system. Hythloday rejects the argument out of hand. Thomas More himself seems to have been unsure at that time about the virtues of public service. He was of two minds, and the debate between Morus and Hythloday reflects his indecision. As part of his critique of justice and politics in Europe, Hythloday describes in Book II the commonwealth of Utopia, in which there is no private property but strict equality of possessions, and, as a result, harmony, tolerance, and little or no violence.

able throughout Europe at virtually the same time. The great Venetian printer Aldus Manutius (1450–1515) produced over 120,000 volumes, many in the new, smaller, easily portable "octavo" format—about 6 by 9 inches. Books from the Aldine Press and other humanistic publishers played a decisive role in spreading humanism to parts of Europe where manuscript books were difficult to acquire.

Moreover, book owning was no longer the exclusive preserve of scholars. This was all the more true because printers included on their lists works in vernacular languages, not just the ancient classics. Perhaps one half of the books produced by most publishers were small prayer books and short selections of Bible stories or saints' lives. The very popularity of printed vernacular texts affected language. William Caxton (1422–1492), for example, began printing books in English in 1472. His pioneering work helped standardize modern English, just as the publication of Martin Luther's German translation of the Bible in 1522 would standardize modern German. The advent of printing had other far-reaching consequences: it promoted the increase of literacy throughout Europe, and in the sixteenth century printed books and pamphlets would become a prime vehicle for Protestants and Catholics to spread religious ideas and protests.

By the eighteenth century, printed books had changed the nature of popular culture. Myths, folk songs, and popular histories were traditionally passed by word of mouth, often changing in the telling to fit the time and place. Once they appeared in print, they could no longer be performed and refashioned, only recited. Printing not only changed the way information was transmitted but also changed the information itself.

A French Printshop The production of a book took many skills. This sixteenth-century illumination shows the entire process. On the left, one man works the press while a second prepares to ink a press. On the right we see the scholar with a manuscript (*rear*), a compositor selecting type as he checks the text in a book, and finally a second scholar checking the broadsides produced by the press. *(Giraudon/Art Resource, NY)*

Since the publication of *Utopia*, debates have raged about whether More, or anyone, could ever really hope to live in such a society. Some scholars have questioned how seriously More took this work—he seems to have written the initial sections merely to amuse friends. Yet whatever More's intentions, Utopia's society of equality, cooperation, and acceptance continues to inspire social commentators.

Ironically, More himself, like his creation Morus, soon found himself trying to work for justice within precisely the sort of autocratic court that Hythloday criticized. Not long after the completion of *Utopia*, More entered the service of King Henry VIII (r. 1509–1547), eventually serving as chancellor of England. As a staunch Catholic and royal official, More never acted on utopian principles of peace and toleration. He was, in fact, responsible for the persecution of English Protestants in the years before the king's break with Rome (see page 479). More's opposition to Henry's divorce and repudiation of papal authority, and his refusal to acknowledge Henry as the head of the English church, led him to resign his offices. He was eventually imprisoned and beheaded. More's writing was a stinging critique of political values. He implied that society could be reformed, yet in the period after 1521, his humanism and his vision of Utopia had no influence on his own public life.

Unlike More, who was drawn to the power of king and pope, Erasmus always avoided working for authorities.

ᴤ READING SOURCES

A Pilgrimage for Religion's Sake

Desiderius Erasmus wrote numerous colloquies (short stories) as Latin exercises for young students. In this way, he hoped to reveal, in a humorous fashion, some of the contemporary customs that were long overdue for change. Here he describes a visit to the English pilgrimage shrine of Saint Thomas Becket at Canterbury.

My friend Gratian made a faux pas here. After a short prayer, he asked the keeper, "I say good father, is it true, as I have heard, that in his lifetime Thomas was most generous to the poor?" "Very true," the man replied, and began to rehearse the saint's many acts of kindness to them. Then Gratian: "I don't suppose his disposition changed in this matter, unless perhaps for the better." The custodian agreed. Gratian again: "Since then, the saint was so liberal towards the needy, although he was still poor himself and lacked money to provide for the necessities of life, don't you think he'd gladly consent now that he's so rich and needs nothing if some poor wretched woman with hungry children at home, or daughters in danger of losing their virtue because they have no money for dowries, or a husband sick in bed and penniless—if, after begging the saint's forgiveness, she carried off a bit of all this wealth to rescue her family as though

taking it from someone who wanted her to have it, either as a gift or a loan?" When the gatekeeper in charge of the gilded head made no reply to this, Gratian, who is impulsive, said, "For my part, I'm convinced the saint would even rejoice that in death, too, he would relieve the wants of the poor by his riches." At this the custodian frowned and pursed his lips, looking at us with Gorgon eyes, and I don't doubt he would have driven us from the church with insults and reproaches had he not been aware that we were recommended by the archbishop. I managed to placate the fellow by smooth talk, affirming that Gratian hadn't spoken seriously, but liked to joke, and at the same time I gave him some coins.

Source: Erasmus, *Ten Colloquies*, translated by Craig R. Thompson (London and New York: Macmillan, 1986), pp. 83–84.

Often called the "Prince of Humanists," he was easily the best-known humanist of the early sixteenth century. He was born the illegitimate son of a priest in the Low Countries. Forced by relatives into a monastery, he disliked the conservative piety and authoritarian discipline of traditional monastic life. Once allowed out of the monastery to serve as an episcopal secretary, he never returned. He lived and taught in France, England, Italy, and Switzerland. Of all the humanists, it was Erasmus who most benefited from the printing revolution. The printer Aldus Manutius invited him to live and work in Venice, and he spent the last productive years of his life at Johannes Froben's press in Basel. He left the city only when Protestant reformers took control of the city government.

Over a long career Erasmus brought out repeated editions of works designed to educate Christians. His *Adages*, first published in 1500, was a collection of proverbs from Greek and Roman sources. The work was

immensely popular, and Erasmus repeatedly issued expanded editions. He tried to present Greek and Roman wisdom that would illuminate everyday problems. *The Colloquies* was a collection of popular stories, designed as primers for students, that taught moral lessons even as they served as examples of good language. (See the box "Reading Sources: A Pilgrimage for Religion's Sake.") His ironic *Praise of Folly* (1511) was dedicated to Thomas More. An oration by Folly in praise of folly, it was satire of a type unknown since antiquity. Folly's catalog of vices includes everyone from the ignoramus to the scholar. But more seriously, Erasmus believed, as Saint Paul had said, that Christians must be "fools for Christ." In effect, human existence is folly. Erasmus's Folly first made an observation that Shakespeare would refine and make famous: "Now the whole life of mortal men, what is it but a sort of play in which . . . [each person] plays his own part until the director gives him his cue to leave the stage."[16]

Erasmus's greatest contributions to European intellectual life were his edition of and commentaries on the New Testament. His was a critical edition of the Greek text and a Latin translation independent of the fourth-century Latin Vulgate of Jerome. Unlike Jiménez, Erasmus corrected parts of the Vulgate. He rejected the authority of tradition, saying, "The sin of corruption is greater, and the need for careful revision by scholars is greater also, where the source of corruption was ignorance."[17] What was revolutionary in his edition was his commentary, which emphasized the literal and historical recounting of human experiences. Erasmus's Bible was the basis of later vernacular translations of Scripture during the Reformation.

Underlying Erasmus's scholarly output was what he called his "Philosophy of Christ." Erasmus was convinced that the true essence of Christianity was to be found in the life and actions of Christ. Reasonable, self-reliant, truly Christian people did not need superstitious rituals or magic. In his *Colloquies* he tells of a terrified priest who during a shipwreck promised everything to the Virgin Mary if only she would save him from drowning. But, Erasmus observed, it would have been more practical to start swimming!

Erasmus believed that a humanistic combination of classical and Christian wisdom could wipe away violence, superstition, and ignorance. Unlike More, Erasmus never abandoned the humanistic program. Yet his philosophy of Christ, based on faith in the goodness and educability of the individual, was swamped in the 1520s and 1530s by the sectarian claims of both Protestants and Catholics. Although Erasmus's New Testament was influential in the Reformation, his calls for reforms based on tolerance and reason were not.

■ Renaissance Art in the North

In the early fifteenth century, while Brunelleschi and Masaccio were revolutionizing the ways in which Italian artists viewed their world, artists north of the Alps, especially in Flanders, were making equally striking advances in the way they painted and sculpted. Artistic innovation in the North began with changes tied closely to the world of northern courts; only later did artists take up the styles of the Italian Renaissance. Northerners took Italian Renaissance art and fit it to a new environment.

Northern art of the late fourteenth and fifteenth centuries changed in two significant ways. In sculpture, the long, austere, unbroken vertical lines typical of Gothic sculpture gave way to a much more complex and emotional style. In painting, Flemish artists moved from ornate, vividly colored paintings to experiments with ways to create a sense of depth. Artists strove to paint and sculpt works that more faithfully represented reality. The sculptures of Claus Sluter (1350–1406), carved for a family chapel of the Burgundian dukes at Champmol, captured a lifelike drama unlike the previous Gothic sculpture. Court painters such as Jan van Eyck (ca. 1390–1441) in miniatures, portraits, and altar paintings also moved away from a highly formalized style to a careful representation of specific places. In Van Eyck's portrait of the Italian banker and courtier Giovanni Arnolfini and his bride, the image of the painter is reflected in a small mirror behind the couple, and above the mirror is written, "Jan van Eyck was here, 1434." Whereas Italians of the early fifteenth century tried to recreate space through linear perspective, the Flemish used aerial perspective, softening colors and tones to give the illusion of depth.

Van Eyck: The Arnolfini Wedding   Careful observation of people and places was typical of the new art of both the north and the south. Van Eyck seems to have re-created this scene to the smallest detail. His own image appears in the mirror on the wall.   *(Reproduced by Courtesy of the Trustees, The National Gallery, London)*

Portrait of a Black Man   Albrecht Dürer sketched this portrait in the early sixteenth century, most likely in a commercial center such as Venice or Nuremberg. By that time it was common to show one of the three Wise Men as black, but such depictions, unlike Dürer's drawing here, were rarely based on portrait studies.   *(Graphische Sammlung, Albertina)*

The influence of Renaissance styles in the north of Europe dates from the reign of the French king Francis I (r. 1515–1547), when Italian artists in significant numbers traveled north. Francis invited Italian artists to his court—most notably Leonardo da Vinci, who spent his last years in France. The most influential of the Italian-style creations in France was doubtless Francis's château Fontainebleau, whose decorations contained mythologies, histories, and allegories of the kind found in the Italian courts. Throughout the sixteenth century, Italianate buildings and paintings sprang up throughout Europe.

Perhaps the most famous artist who traveled to Italy, learned Italian techniques, and then transformed them to suit the environment of northern Europe was Albrecht Dürer of Nuremberg (1471–1528). Son of a well-known goldsmith, Dürer became a painter and toured France and Flanders learning the techniques popular in northern Europe. Then in 1494 he left Nuremberg on the first of two trips to Italy, during which he sketched Italian landscapes and studied the work of Italian artists, especially in Venice. What he learned in Italy, combined with the friendship of some of Germany's leading humanists, formed the basis of Dürer's works, which blended northern humanistic interests with the Italian techniques of composition and linear perspective. Dürer worked in charcoal, watercolors, and paints, but his influence was most widely spread through his numerous woodcuts covering classical and contemporary themes. His woodcut *Whore of Babylon*, prepared in the context of the debate over the reform of the church, is based on sketches of Venetian prostitutes completed during his first visit to Italy.

Numerous other artists and engravers traveled south to admire and learn from the great works of Italian artists. The engravings they produced and distributed back home made the southern innovations available to those who would never set foot in Italy. In fact, some now lost or destroyed creations are known only through the copies engraved by northern artists eager to absorb Italian techniques.

THE RENAISSANCE AND COURT SOCIETY

THE educational reforms of the humanists and the innovations in the arts between 1300 and 1550 provided an opportunity for rulers and popes alike to use culture to define and celebrate their authority. Art, literature, and politics merged in the brilliant life of the Renaissance Italian courts, both secular and papal. To understand fully the Renaissance and its importance in the history of Europe, we need to examine the uses of culture by governments, specifically investigating the transformation of European ideas about service at court during the fourteenth and fifteenth centuries. We will take as a model the politics and cultural life at one noble court: the court of the Gonzaga family of Mantua. We will also discuss the development of the idea of the Renaissance gentleman and courtier made famous by Baldassare Castiglione°, who was reared at the

---

Castiglione (ka-stil-ee-OH-nee)

Gonzaga court. Finally, we will see how the Renaissance papacy melded the secular and religious aspects of art, culture, and politics in its glittering court in Rome.

■ The Elaboration of the Court

The courts of northern Italy interested themselves in the cultural and artistic innovations of the Renaissance artists and humanists inspired by classical civilization, and they closely imitated many of the values and new styles that were developing in the courts of northern Europe, such as the court of Burgundy. Throughout Europe, attendance at court became increasingly important to members of the nobility as a source of revenue and influence. Kings and the great territorial lords were equally interested in drawing people to their courts as a way to influence and control the noble and the powerful.

Rulers in most parts of Europe instituted monarchical orders of knighthood to reward allies and followers. The most famous in the English-speaking world was the Order of the Garter, founded in 1349 by King Edward III. The orders were but one of the innovations in the organization of the court during the fourteenth and fifteenth centuries. The numbers of cooks, servants, huntsmen, musicians, and artists employed at court jumped dramatically in the late Middle Ages. In this expansion, the papal court itself was a model for the rest of Europe. The popes at Avignon in the fourteenth century already had households of nearly six hundred persons. If all the bureaucrats, merchants, local officials, and visitors who continually swarmed around the elaborate papal court were also counted, the number grew even larger.

Courts were becoming theaters built around a series of widely understood signs and images that the ruler could manipulate. Culture was meant to reflect the reputation of the ruler. On important political or personal occasions, rulers organized jousts or tournaments around themes drawn from mythology. The dukes of Milan indicated the relative status of courtiers by inviting them to participate in particular hunts or jousts. They similarly organized their courtiers during feasts or elaborate entries into the towns and cities of their realms.

The late fourteenth and fifteenth centuries were periods of growth in the political and bureaucratic power of European rulers. The increasingly elaborate and sumptuous courts were one of the tools that rulers used to create a unified culture and ideology. At the court of the Gonzagas in Mantua, one of the most widely known of the fifteenth-century courts, the manipulation of Renaissance culture for political purposes was most complete.

■ The Court of Mantua

The city of Mantua, with perhaps 25,000 inhabitants in 1500, was small next to Milan or Venice—the two cities with which it was most commonly allied. Located in a rich farming region along the Po River, Mantua did not have a large merchant or manufacturing class. Most Mantuans were involved in agriculture and regional trade in foodstuffs. The town had been a typical medieval Italian city-state until its government was overthrown by the noble Bonacolsi family in the thirteenth century. The Bonacolsis, in turn, were ousted in a palace coup in 1328 by their former comrades, the Gonzagas, who ruled the city until 1627.

The Gonzagas faced problems typical of many of the ruling families in northern Italy. The state they were creating was relatively small, their right to rule was not very widely recognized, and their control over the area was weak. The first step for the Gonzagas was to construct fortresses and fortified towns that could withstand foreign enemies. The second step was to gain recognition of their right to rule. In 1329 they were named imperial vicars, or representatives in the region. Later, in 1432, they bought the title "marquis" from Emperor Sigismund for the relatively low price of £12,000—equivalent to a year's pay for their courtiers. By 1500 they had exchanged that title for the more prestigious "duke."

Presiding over a strategic area between the Milanese and Venetian states, the Gonzagas maintained themselves through astute diplomatic connections with other Italian and European courts and through service as well-paid mercenaries in the Italian wars of the fifteenth and sixteenth centuries. Marquis Lodovico (d. 1478) served the Venetians, the Milanese, the Florentines, and even the far-off Neapolitans. With considerable understatement, Lodovico concluded, "We have worn armor for a long time."

The family's reputation was enhanced by Gianfrancesco° (d. 1444) and Lodovico, who brought the Renaissance and the new court style to Mantua. By 1500 as many as eight hundred or more nobles, cooks, maids, and horsemen may have gathered in the court. Critics called them idlers "who have no other function but to cater to the tastes of the Duke." It was under the tutelage of the Gonzagas that Vittorino da Feltre created his educational experiment in Villa Giocosa, which drew noble pupils from throughout Italy. It would be hard to overestimate the value for the Gonzagas of a school that attracted sons of the dukes of Urbino, Ferrara, and Milan

---

Gianfrancesco (jan-fran-CHES-ko)

and of numerous lesser nobles. The family also called many artists to Mantua. Lodovico invited Antonio Pisano, called Pisanello (ca. 1415–1456), probably the most famous court artist of the fifteenth century. Pisanello created a series of frescoes on Arthurian themes for the Gonzaga palace. In these frescoes Lodovico is portrayed as a hero of King Arthur's round table.

The Gonzagas are best known for their patronage of art with classical themes. Leon Battista Alberti redesigned the façade of the church of Sant'Andrea for the Gonzagas in the form of a Roman triumphal arch. The church, which long had been associated with the family, became a monument to the Gonzaga court just as the Arch of Constantine in Rome had celebrated imperial power a thousand years earlier. In the 1460s Lodovico summoned Andrea Mantegna (1441–1506) to his court. Trained in Padua and Venice, Mantegna was at that time the leading painter in northern Italy. His masterwork is the *Camera degli Sposi* (literally, "the room of the spouses"), completed in 1474. It features family portraits of Lodovico Gonzaga and his family framed in imitations of Roman imperial portrait medallions. One scene shows Lodovico welcoming his son, a newly appointed cardinal, back from Rome—proof to all of the new status of the Gonzagas.

The Gonzaga court, like most others, was both public and private. Finances for the city, appointments to public offices, and important political decisions were made by the men who dominated the court. On the other hand, as the prince's domestic setting, it was a place where women were expected to be seen and could exert their influence. Women were thus actively involved in creating the ideology of the court. Through the patronage of classical paintings, often with moral and political messages, wives of princes helped make the court better known and more widely accepted throughout Italy and Europe.

The arrival of Isabella d'Este (1494–1539) at court as the wife of Franceso Gonzaga marked the high point of the Renaissance in Mantua. Isabella had received a classical education at Ferrara and maintained an interest in art, architecture, and music all her life. As a patron of the arts, she knew what she wanted. (See the box "Reading Sources: Isabella d'Este Orders Art.") Isabella was also an accomplished musician, playing a variety of string and keyboard instruments. She and others of the Gonzaga family recruited Flemish and Italian musicians to their court. By the end of the sixteenth century, Mantua was one of the most important musical centers of Europe. One festival brought twelve thousand visitors to the city. Later, it would be in Mantua that Claudio Monteverdi

(1567–1643) wrote works that established the genre of opera.

In the fourteenth century Petrarch had complained that however enjoyable feasting in Mantua might be, the place was dusty, plagued by mosquitoes, and overrun with frogs. By the end of the fifteenth century, the Gonzagas had secured for themselves and their city a prominent place on the Italian, and the European, stage.

■ Castiglione and the European Gentleman

Renaissance ideas did not just spread in intellectual circles. They also were part of the transformation of the medieval knight into the early modern "gentleman." In 1528 Baldassare Castiglione (1478–1529) published *The Book of the Courtier*, a work in which he distilled what he had learned in his years at the various courts of Italy. Castiglione was born in Mantua, a distant relative to the ruling Gonzaga family. He grew up at court and was sent to the Sforza court in Milan to finish his education. During his career Castiglione met the greatest lights of the Renaissance. While he was in Rome, he became friends with Michelangelo and Raphael as well as with numerous humanistic writers. He died in Spain while on a mission for Pope Clement VII. When informed of his death, the emperor Charles V remarked, "One of the greatest knights in the world has died!" In his life and in his book, Castiglione summed up the great changes that had transformed the nature of late medieval chivalry.

The Book of the Courtier reports a series of fictional discussions at the court of Urbino held over the course of four nights in March 1507. Among the participants are the duchess of Urbino, Elizabeth Gonzaga; her lady-in-waiting; and a group of humanists, men of action, and courtiers. In four evenings, members of the circle try to describe the perfect gentleman of court. In the process they debate the nature of nobility, humor, women, and love.

It was in many respects a typical gathering at court, and its discourses reflect contemporary views of relations between men and women. The wives of princes were expected to be organizers of life at court, but still paragons of domestic virtues. The women organize the discussion, but the men discuss. Women direct and influence the talk by jokes and short interventions but cannot afford to dominate debate. "[Women] must be more circumspect, and more careful not to give occasion for evil being said of them . . . for a woman has not so many ways of defending herself against false calumnies as a man has."[18]

🐚 R E A D I N G   S O U R C E S

Isabella d'Este Orders Art

Isabella d'Este, the marchioness of Mantua, created one of the foremost collections of Renaissance art in sixteenth-century Italy. In her quest to acquire representative works by the leading artists of the period, she has left an unparalleled collection of letters. In the following directive to Pietro Perugino, she describes what she expects from a painting she had commissioned from him.

Master Perugino, painter, [shall] make a painting on canvas 2½ braccia [5 feet] high and 3 braccia [6 feet] wide, and the said Pietro, the contractor, is obliged to paint on it a certain work of Lasciviousness and Modesty (in conflict) with these and many other embellishments, transmitted in this instruction to the said Pietro by the said Marchioness of Mantua, the copy of which is as follows:

Our poetic invention, which we greatly want to see painted by you, is the battle of Chastity against Lasciviousness, that is to say, Pallas [Athena] and Diana fighting vigorously against Venus and Cupid. And Pallas should seem almost to have vanquished Cupid, having broken his golden arrow and cast his silver bow underfoot; with one hand she is holding him by the bandage which the blind boy has before his eyes, and with the other she is lifting her lance and about to kill him. . . . And to give more expression and decoration to the picture, beside Pallas I want to have the olive tree sacred to her, with a shield leaning against it bearing the head of Medusa, and with the owl, the bird peculiar to Pallas, perched among the branches. And beside Venus I want her favorite tree, the myrtle, to be placed, but to enhance the beauty, a fount of water must be included, such as a river or the sea, where fauns, satyrs and more cupids will be seen, hastening to the help of Cupid, some swimming through the river, some flying, and some riding upon white swans, coming to join such an amorous battle. . . .

I am sending you all these details in a small drawing so that with both the written description and the drawing you will be able to consider my wishes in this matter. But if you think that perhaps there are too many figures in this for one picture, it is left to you to reduce them as you please, provided that you do not remove the principal basis, which consists of the four figures of Pallas, Diana, Venus and Cupid. If no inconvenience occurs I shall consider myself well satisfied; you are free to reduce them, but not to add anything else. Please be content with this arrangement.

Source: David S. Chambers, *Patrons and Artists in the Italian Renaissance* (London and New York: Macmillan, 1970), pp. 136–138.

The topics were not randomly chosen. Castiglione explained that he wished "to describe the form of courtiership most appropriate for a gentleman living at the courts of princes." Castiglione's popularity was based on his deliberate joining of humanistic ideas and traditional chivalric values. Although his topic was the court with all its trappings, Castiglione tells his readers that his models for the discussion are Greek and Latin dialogues, especially those of Cicero and Plato. As a Platonist, he believed that all truly noble gentlemen had an inborn quality of "grace." It had to be brought out, however, just as Michelangelo freed his figures from stone. Castiglione held that all moral and courtly virtues existed in tension with their opposites: "no magnanimity without pusillanimity." With numerous examples of good and bad in the world, wisdom could be revealed only through careful imitation, for like the classical authors favored by humanists, Castiglione advises, "He who lacks wisdom and knowledge will have nothing to say or do."[19]

But what struck Castiglione's readers was his advice about behavior. Francesco Guicciardini of

Florence once remarked, "When I was young, I used to scoff at knowing how to play, dance, and sing, and other such frivolities. . . . I have nevertheless seen from experience that these ornaments and accomplishments lend dignity and reputation even to men of good rank."[20] Guicciardini's comment underlines the value that readers found in Castiglione's work. Grace may be inbred, but it needed to be brought to the attention of those who controlled the court. Courtiers should first of all study the military arts. They had to fight, but only on occasions when their prowess would be noticed. Castiglione adds practical advice about how to dress, talk, and participate in music and dancing: never leap about wildly when dancing as peasants might, but dance only with an air of dignity and decorum. Castiglione further urges the courtier to be careful in dress: the French are "overdressed"; the Italians too quickly adopt the most recent and colorful styles. Reflecting political as well as social realities, Castiglione advises black or dark colors, which "reflect the sobriety of the Spaniards, since external appearances often bear witness to what is within."

The courtier always must take pains "to earn that universal regard which everyone covets." Too much imitation and obvious study, however, lead to affectation. Castiglione counseled courtiers to carry themselves with a certain diffidence or unstudied naturalness *(sprezzatura)*° covering their artifice. Accomplished courtiers will exhibit "that graceful and nonchalant spontaneity (as it is often called) . . . so that those who are watching them imagine that they couldn't and wouldn't even know how to make a mistake." Thus, Castiglione's courtier walked a fine line between clearly imitated and apparently natural grace.

Castiglione's book was an immediate success and widely followed even by those who claimed to have rejected it. By 1561 it was available in Spanish, French, and English translations. The reasons are not difficult to guess. It was critical for the courtier "to win for himself the mind and favour of the prince." And even those who disliked music, dancing, and light conversation learned Castiglione's arts "to open the way to the favour of princes." Many of the courtly arts that Castiglione preached had been traditional for centuries. Yet Castiglione's humanistic explanations and emphasis on form, control, and fashion had never seemed so essential as they did to the cultured gentlemen of the courts of the Renaissance and early modern Europe.

---

sprezzatura (spretz-ah-TU-ra)

■ The Renaissance Papacy

The issues of power and how it is displayed had religious as well as secular dimensions. After its fourteenth- and fifteenth-century struggles over jurisdiction, the Renaissance papacy found itself in need of a political and ideological counterweight to the centrifugal forces of conciliarism, reform, and local loyalties. Popes needed to defend their primacy within the church from conciliarists who had argued that all Christians, including the pope, were bound to obey the commands of general councils. The ideological focus of the revived papacy was Rome.

The first step in the creation of a new Rome was taken by Pope Nicholas V (r. 1446–1455), a cleric who had spent many years in the cultural environment of Renaissance Florence. Hoping to restore Rome and its church to their former glory, Nicholas and his successors patronized the arts, established a lively court culture, and sponsored numerous building projects. Nicholas was an avid collector of ancient manuscripts that seemed to demonstrate the intellectual and religious primacy of Rome. He invited numerous artists and intellectuals to the papal court, including the Florentine architect and writer Leon Battista Alberti (1404–1472). On the basis of his research in topography and reading done in Rome, Alberti wrote his treatise *On Architecture* (1452), the most important work on architecture produced during the Renaissance. It was probably under Alberti's influence that Nicholas embarked on a series of ambitious urban renewal projects in Rome, which included bridges, roads, and a rebuilt Saint Peter's Basilica.

The transformation of Rome had an ideological purpose. As one orator proclaimed, "Illuminated by the light of faith and Christian truth, [Rome] is destined to be the firmament of religion . . . , the secure haven for Christians."[21] Thus, the papal response to critics was to note that Rome and its government were central to political and religious life in Christendom. By reviving the style and organization of classical antiquity, the church sought to link papal Rome to a magnificent imperial tradition reaching back to Augustus and even to Alexander the Great. To papal supporters, only one authority could rule the church. Early tradition and the continuity of the city itself, they assumed, demonstrated papal primacy.

One particular monument in Rome captures most vividly the cultural, religious, and ideological program of the papacy: the Sistine Chapel in the Vatican Palace. The chapel is best known for the decoration of the ceiling by the Florentine artist Michelangelo (see page 408) and for the striking images in his painting of the Last Judgment.

Giving of the Keys to Saint Peter   Pietro Perugino's painting of Saint Peter's receiving from Christ the keys to "bind and loose" on earth and in heaven illustrates the basis of papal claims to authority within the Christian church. This is the central message of the decorative plan of the Sistine Chapel. *(Scala/Art Resource, NY)*

The chapel, however, was commissioned by Pope Sixtus IV in 1475. It was to be an audience chamber in which an enthroned pope could meet the representatives of other states. In addition, it was expected that the college of cardinals would gather in the chapel for the election of new popes.

The decorations done before Michelangelo painted the ceiling reflect the intellectual and ideological values that Sixtus hoped to transmit to the churches and governments of Christendom. Along the lower sidewalls are portraits of earlier popes, a feature typical of early Roman churches. More significant are two cycles of paintings of the lives of Moses and Christ, drawing parallels between them. To execute the scenes, Sixtus called to Rome some of the greatest artists of the late fifteenth century: Sandro Botticelli, Domenico Ghirlandaio°, Luca

Signorelli°, and Pietro Perugino°. The works illustrate the continuity of the Old Testament and New Testament and emphasize the importance of obedience to the authority of God. The meaning is most obvious in Perugino's painting of Saint Peter receiving the keys to the Kingdom of Heaven from Christ. The allusion is to Matthew 16:18: "Thou art Peter and upon this rock I shall build my church." The keys are the symbol of the claim of the pope, as successor to Saint Peter, to have the power to bind and loose sinners and their punishments.

Directly across from Perugino's painting is Botticelli's *The Judgment of Corah*, which portrays the story of the opponent who challenged the leadership of Moses and Aaron while the Israelites wandered in the wilderness. Corah and his supporters, according to Numbers 16:33, fell live into Hell. Various popes recalled the fate of

---

Ghirlandaio (gear-lan-DIE-yo)

Signorelli (seen-yor-EL-lee)   **Perugino** (peh-roo-JEE-no)

Corah and the rebels. The pope was bound to oppose the council, Pope Eugenius argued, "to save the people entrusted to his care, lest together with those who hold the power of the council above that of the papacy they suffer a punishment even more dire than that which befell Corah."[22]

The effects of Renaissance revival were profound. Rome grew from a modest population of about 17,000 in 1400 to 35,000 in 1450. By 1517 the city had a population of over 85,000, five times its population at the end of the Great Schism. The papal program was a success. Rome was transformed from a provincial town to a major European capital, perhaps the most important artistic and cultural center of the sixteenth century. Visitors to the Sistine Chapel, like visitors to the papal city itself, were expected to leave with a profound sense of the antiquity of the papal office and of the continuity of papal exercise of religious authority. Because the building and decorating were being completed as the Protestant Reformation was beginning in Germany, some historians have criticized the expense of the political and cultural program undertaken by the Renaissance popes. But to contemporaries on the scene, the work was a logical and necessary attempt to strengthen the church's standing in Christendom.

Summary

HE Renaissance was a broad cultural movement that began in Italy in response to a series of crises in the early fourteenth century. It was a cultural and ideological movement based on the assumption that study and imitation of the past was the best method for reform and innovation in the future. Neither the thoughtful world of Petrarch nor the courtly world of Castiglione, however, sparked the origins of modern individualism or introduced a culture radically different from the medieval past. Between 1300 and 1500, however, Europe experienced profound cultural innovation in literature, political and social thought, and art. The attitudes toward the past and ideas about education formed in this period became the model of European cultural life for the next two hundred years. The cultural values of modern Europe were those inherited from the Renaissance.

The impulse for change arose from the belief, shared by thinkers from Petrarch to Machiavelli, that there was a great deal to be learned from study of the Roman past. This was the basis for humanistic innovations in language, history, and politics. Even revolution-

ary thinkers such as Lorenzo Valla and Niccolò Machiavelli began with the study of classical literature and history. The same transformation is evident among the artists. Early in the fifteenth century, Florentines who experimented with perspective were intent on recovering lost Roman knowledge, and Michelangelo was praised not only for mastering but for surpassing Roman norms.

Issues of reform and renewal were less tied to public life outside of Italy. Moral and spiritual issues were more important. Yet the same movement from imitation to transformation is evident. Erasmus and Dürer assimilated the best of the new art and culture from Italy, but in the *Praise of Folly* and in Dürer's woodcuts, the use of past ideas and models was neither simple nor direct.

The integration of art, literature, and public life was most evident in the ways that art was used by governments. The Gonzaga court and the papacy clearly recognized the value of artistic and literary works as vehicles for explaining and justifying power and influence. The beauty of Mantegna's painting and the power of Michelangelo's frescoes do not obscure their messages about power and authority.

Innovation depended on the study of the past. As humanists came to know more fully the art and history of Greece and Rome, they recognized the extent to which classical culture represented only one source of legal, historical, or moral understanding. Europeans' recognition of other, often competing, traditions would be tested in the sixteenth century, when they came face to face with a previously unknown world.

■ Notes

1. Quoted in J. B. Trapp, ed., *Background to the English Renaissance* (London: Gray-Mills Publishing, 1974), p. 11.
2. Quoted in N. Mann, *Petrarch* (Oxford: Oxford University Press), p. 67.
3. Petrarch, "On His Own Ignorance and That of Many Others," in *The Renaissance Philosophy of Man*, ed. Ernst Cassirer, Paul Oskar Kristeller, and John H. Randall (Chicago: University of Chicago Press, 1948), p. 105.
4. Quoted in Benjamin G. Kohl and Ronald G. Witt, *The Earthly Republic* (Philadelphia: University of Pennsylvania Press, 1978), p. 11.
5. Quoted in M. L. King, *Women of the Renaissance* (Chicago: University of Chicago Press, 1991), p. 194.
6. Quoted ibid., p. 222.
7. Quoted ibid., p. 198.
8. K. R. Bartlett, *The Civilization of the Italian Renaissance* (Lexington, Mass.: D. C. Heath, 1992), p. 314.
9. Quoted in *The Portable Machiavelli*, ed. and trans. Peter Bondanella and Mark Musa (New York: Penguin Books, 1979), p. 128.

10. Quoted ibid., p. 160.
11. Quoted in *The Notebooks of Leonardo da Vinci*, ed. J. P. Richter, vol. 1 (New York: Dover, 1883 and 1970), p. 14.
12. Quoted ibid., p. 129.
13. Giorgio Vasari, *The Lives of the Artists*, trans. George Bull (Baltimore: Penguin, 1965), p. 338.
14. Julia Bondanella and Mark Musa, eds., *The Italian Renaissance Reader* (New York: Meridian Books, 1987), p. 377.
15. I. Origo, *The Merchant of Prato: Francesco di Marco Datini*, 1335–1410 (New York: Knopf, 1957), pp. 155–156.
16. Quoted in A. Rabil, Jr., *Renaissance Humanism: Foundations, Forms, and Legacy*, vol. 2 (Philadelphia: University of Pennsylvania Press, 1988), p. 236.
17. Quoted ibid., p. 229.
18. Quoted in R. M. San Juan, "The Court Lady's Dilemma: Isabella d'Este and Art Collecting in the Renaissance," *Oxford Art Journal* 14 (1991): 71.
19. Unless otherwise noted, quotes of Castiglione are from Baldassare Castiglione, *The Book of the Courtier*, trans. George Bull (Baltimore: Penguin Books, 1967).
20. Quoted in R. W. Hanning and D. Rosand, eds., *Castiglione: The Ideal and the Real in Renaissance Culture* (New Haven, Conn.: Yale University Press, 1983), p. 17.
21. Raffaele Brandolini, as quoted in Charles L. Stinger, *The Renaissance in Rome* (Bloomington: Indiana University Press, 1985), p. 156.
22. Quoted in Leopold D. Ettlinger, *The Sistine Chapel Before Michelangelo* (Oxford: Oxford University Press, 1965), p. 105.

■ Suggested Reading

Brown, Alison. *The Renaissance*. 2d ed. 1999. An excellent short introduction to Renaissance art and culture designed for those with little or no background in the field.

Burke, Peter. *The European Renaissance: Centres and Peripheries*. 1998. A broad account of Renaissance cultural movements in Europe.

———. *The Fortunes of the Courtier: The European Reception of Castiglione's Cortegiano*. 1995. A well-written survey of the influence of Castiglione's ideas.

Goldthwaite, Richard. *Wealth and the Demand for Art in Italy, 1300–1600*. 1993. A thoughtful essay about the social and economic influences on the creation and patronage of art.

Goodman, A., and A. Mackay, eds. *The Impact of Humanism*. 1990. A volume of basic surveys of the arrival of Italian humanistic ideas in the various lands of Europe.

Hale, John R. *The Civilization of Europe in the Renaissance*. 1994. A beautifully written survey of the culture of Europe from the fifteenth to the seventeenth century.

King, M. L. *Women of the Renaissance*. 1991. A survey of the social, economic, and cultural experience of women during the Renaissance.

Stinger, Charles L. *The Renaissance in Rome*. 1985. An engaging survey of the vibrant cultural life at the papal court and in the city during the Renaissance.

Welch, E. S. *Art and Society in Italy, 1350–1500*. 1997. A well-written, well-illustrated discussion of the social context in which artists worked.

Witt, R. G. *"In the Footsteps of the Ancients": The Origins of Humanism from Lovato to Bruni*. 2000. The definitive work on European humanism and the cultural connections between Italy and France.

 For a searchable list of additional readings for this chapter, go to http://college.hmco.com.

The Art of Renaissance Florence

In 1478 or shortly thereafter, Lorenzo di Pierfrancesco de' Medici, a relative of Lorenzo the Magnificent, commissioned Sandro Botticelli to create the painting *Primavera (Spring)*. Since its completion, critics have been fascinated by its composition and lyrical qualities. Notice the figures who make up the picture. At the center is Venus, goddess of love. The group to Venus's left tells the classical myth of the return of spring. Zephyrus, the west wind, who brings the rebirth of springtime, pursues Chloris, a goddess of fertility. Flowers flow from Chloris's mouth as Zephyrus changes her into Flora, the flower-covered goddess of spring, who stands to her right. These figures are balanced by the group to Venus's right—the three Graces, who are dancing beside the figure of Mercury, the messenger and in this context the god of May. We can easily agree with the critics and connoisseurs who praise the grace and enchantment of Botticelli's mysterious grove filled with dark trees laden with oranges and his meadow blanketed with flowers. The work demonstrates Botticelli's great artistic skill and the sophisticated knowledge of classical mythology current in Florence in the last quarter of the fifteenth century. But, you might ask, how much more can it tell us about the culture of Renaissance Florence?

Historians and art historians have struggled to find the best way to use art as a tool in historical studies. In the late nineteenth and early twentieth centuries, art connoisseurs carefully studied brush strokes and coloring so that they could understand and immediately recognize the techniques of the great masters. They believed that knowledge of an artist's technique would allow them to understand why the works of that artist were so widely popular. Modern historians, however, usually approach a work of art in other ways. We can ask, "What did the artist mean to paint?" Or we can ask, "How does Botticelli's *Primavera* compare with other great works of art, such as Pablo Picasso's *Guernica?*" But the most fruitful inquiry is, "What might Botticelli's contemporaries have noticed in the work?"

To answer that last question, it becomes important to know the social and artistic conventions that might illuminate the meanings in the work, where the work was intended to be displayed, and, finally, how the work comments on the social and cultural interests of the people whom the artist expected to view it.

Contemporaries valued Botticelli's brush stroke—that is, his artistic touch. But, surprisingly, they valued just as highly the materials in which he worked. One of the few contracts we have for a work by Botticelli notes carefully the cost and quantities of gold foil and aquamarine blue paint (an expensive and precious color). From this we can see that Botticelli's contemporaries were very aware of color. As Leon Battista Alberti observed critically of fifteenth-century Italians, most people associate gold leaf and deep blue colors with sumptuousness and majesty. Florentines were also very aware of the writings of contemporary humanists—and especially of the humanist belief that classical and Christian wisdom were basically inseparable. Imbuing classical images with contemporary meanings did not seem odd to them. Botticelli's great popularity in Florence actually rested in part on his sophisticated use of classically inspired figures to comment on contemporary issues.

Primavera was meant to decorate the palace of a relative of Lorenzo de' Medici. It was probably designed to be seen by Lorenzo the Magnificent himself, who not only held a position of political and economic importance in the city but was a gifted poet and leader of a *brigata*, or company of poets and humanists. The brigata, in fact, may have been the primary audience for Botticelli's work. Lorenzo and the poets of his circle were actively combining what they believed was the best of their Tuscan culture with the classical philosophy and literature revived by the humanists. Lorenzo once wore on his armor the motto *Le Tems revient*, which loosely translated means "The ages shall be renewed." As we have seen, this renewal was an idea popular among the artists and humanists of Renaissance Italy. In *Primavera* Botticelli uses a number of symbols meant to remind viewers of Lorenzo de' Medici and his cultural interests. Look at the oranges in the trees, for example. They resemble the three balls on the Medici crest. The promising arrival of spring in the person of Flora is precisely the sort of image with which Lorenzo wanted to be associated.

But what of the three Graces? How do they fit into a picture meant to celebrate the merging of old and new in Medicean Florence? For Lorenzo's contemporaries, they may have been the best possible image of the marriage of classical and Tuscan traditions. Lorenzo and his friends knew of the Graces and their association with spring from a variety of classical sources. These particular Graces, however, are Tuscan. The cut of their gowns and their dance would have been recognizable to Lorenzo's friends as typically Florentine. Lorenzo himself had earlier composed a dance, "A Simple Dance Called Venus," which could easily be the dance that they are performing. Next to them stands Venus, the goddess of love. But here she represents spring, flowering (Flora is, after all, the root of the name Florence), and renewal.

Her arm is raised in a gesture of invitation. She is inviting us, or more accurately the Florentines of Lorenzo's time, to join in a dance of celebration and renewal.

What do we finally see in Botticelli's *Primavera*? It is not simply an imitation of either a classical text or any known classical figure. It seems instead that Botticelli created a scene that incorporated numerous themes of classical learning and cultural renewal that were, by the late 1460s and 1470s, widely associated with Lorenzo de' Medici, the cultural and political master of Florentine life. The historian finds in the art of the Renaissance works of great beauty that convey through their materials, composition, and symbols a sense of the values and ideas that animated contemporary politics and culture.

Botticelli: Primavera (*Scala/Art Resource, NY*)

veyotlipan.

onca qr
q maca q

CHAPTER 13

European Overseas Expansion to 1600

HERNÁN Cortés's° march in 1519 through the Valley of Mexico toward Tenochtitlán°, the Aztec capital, was recorded not only in Spaniards' journals but also by local witnesses. In the native portrayal shown here, an elegantly garbed Mexica leader brings food and supplies to Cortés. Behind the adventurer are his own Spanish soldiers as well as his native allies. Many native peoples saw the Spanish as their defenders against the Aztecs, their harsh, recently arrived overlords. The woman standing next to Cortés is Malintzin° (who later adopted the Spanish name Doña Marina). She was an Aztec noblewoman traded by her stepfather to the Mayas and eventually given to Cortés. As a translator and interpreter, she was an essential ally during the conquest of Mexico.

The image itself, with its baskets of bread, meats, and fodder, is part of a pictograph telling the story of Cortés in the Nahuatl° language of the Mexica peoples themselves. The arrival of the Spanish began a cultural exchange between the Spanish and the peoples of the Americas more complex than even they initially imagined. The picture captures the contradictory aspects of European contact with Asia and the Americas. Europeans called it discovery, but they were entering sophisticated, fully functioning political and cultural worlds. Doña Marina's presence also reminds us of a more general truth—that without allies, pilots, and interpreters among the native peoples, Europeans would have been lost both in the New World and in the Old.

Cortés's meeting with the Mexicans was part of a program of European overseas expansion that began in the last decade of the

Cortés (kor-TEZ)   **Tenochtitlán** (teh-NOCK-tit-lan)   **Malintzin** (ma-LIN-tzin)
Nahuatl (na-HWAT-luh)

The European Background, 1250–1492

Portuguese Voyages of Exploration, 1350–1515

Spanish Voyages of Exploration, 1492–1522

Spain's Colonial Empire, 1492–1600

The Columbian Exchange

Cortés—shown with Doña Marina—is greeted by local leaders during the march to Tenochtitlán. (Trans. no. V/C 31[2]. Courtesy Department of Library Sciences, American Museum of Natural History)

fifteenth century and would eventually carry Europeans to every part of the world. It would change how Europeans thought of themselves and how they understood their own connection to the rest of the world. Their expansion unified the "Old World" continents of Asia, Africa, and Europe with a "New World": the Americas and the islands of the Pacific. Accounts of contacts between the Old World and the New are influenced, perhaps more than any other episode of Western history, by the perspectives of the writer and the reader.

Those who focus on the transfer of European religion and culture view exploration and settlement as marking the creation of a new world with new values. However, the descendants of the native peoples who greeted the newly arriving Europeans—the Amerindians and the Aborigines, Maori, and Polynesians of the Pacific islands—remind us that the outsiders brought slavery, modern warfare, and epidemic diseases that virtually destroyed indigenous cultures.

Spain sent its explorers west because the Portuguese already controlled eastern routes to Asia around the African coast and because certain technological innovations made long open-sea voyages possible. Thus, as those who celebrate European expansion have said, the story includes national competition, the development of navigational techniques, and strategic choices.

Finally, the Europeans overthrew the great empires of the Aztecs and Inca, but the transfer of European culture was never as complete as the Europeans thought or expected. As our image suggests, the language and customs of the conquered peoples, blanketed by European language and law, survived, though the lands colonized by the Europeans would never again be as they had been before their encounter with the Old World.

THE EUROPEAN BACKGROUND, 1250–1492

Y 1400 Europeans already had a long history of connections with Africa and Asia. They regularly traded with Arabs in North Africa, traveled through the Muslim lands on the eastern edge of the Mediterranean, and eventually reached India, China, and beyond. After 1400, however, Europeans developed the desire and the ability to travel overseas to distant lands in Africa and Asia. Three critical factors behind the exploratory voyages of the fifteenth and early sixteenth centuries were technology, curiosity and interest, and geographic knowledge. A series of technological innovations made sailing far out into the ocean less risky and more predictable than it had been. The writings of classical geographers, myths and traditional tales, and merchants' accounts of their travels fueled popular interest in the East and made ocean routes to the East seem safe and reasonable alternatives to overland travel.

■ Navigational Innovations

The invention of several navigational aids in the fourteenth and fifteenth centuries made sailing in open waters easier and more predictable. Especially important was the fly compass, consisting of a magnetic needle attached to a paper disk (or "fly"). The simple compass had been invented in China and was known in Europe by the late twelfth century, but because it was not initially marked off in degrees, it was only a rudimentary aid to navigation. By 1500 astrolabes and other devices enabling sailors to use the positions of the sun and stars to assist in navigation had also become available. An astrolabe allowed sailors to measure the altitude of the polestar in the sky and thereby calculate the latitude, or distance north or south of the equator, at which their ship was sailing. Still, until the general adoption of charts marked with degrees of latitude, most navigators relied on the compass, experience, and instinct—dead reckoning.

The most common Mediterranean ship of the late Middle Ages was a galley powered by a combination of sails and oars. Such a vessel was able to travel quickly and easily along the coast, but it was ill-suited for sailing the open seas. Throughout the Mediterranean, shipbuilders experimented with new designs, and during the fifteenth century the Portuguese and Spanish perfected the caravel and adapted the European full-rigged ships. (See the feature "Weighing the Evidence: The Ships of Exploration" on pages 458–459). Large, square sails efficiently caught the wind and propelled these ships forward, and smaller triangular sails (lateens) allowed them to tack diagonally across a headwind, virtually sailing into the wind. The Spanish and Portuguese ships were tiny compared with the huge junks sailed at nearly the same time by the great Chinese admiral Zheng He°. The western ships were more maneuverable, however. And with smaller crews, they were much more efficient as commercial vessels.

By the 1490s the Portuguese and Spanish had developed the ships and techniques that would make long open-sea voyages possible. What remained was for Europeans, especially the Portuguese and Spanish, to conclude that such voyages were both necessary and profitable.

■ Lands Beyond Christendom

The Greeks and Romans had cultivated contacts with the civilizations of Asia and Africa, and despite the nation-building focus of the Middle Ages, interest in the lands beyond Christendom had never been lost. In the thirteenth and fourteenth centuries, European economic and cultural contacts with these lands greatly increased.

Zheng He (JUNG HUH)

CHRONOLOGY

ca. 1400	Portuguese reach Azores
1444	Prince Henry "the Navigator" discovers Cape Verde Islands
1487	Dias becomes first European to sail around Cape of Good Hope
1492	Columbus reaches New World
1494	Treaty of Tordesillas
1497	Da Gama sails to India around Cape of Good Hope
1497	Cabot sights Newfoundland
1501	Vespucci concludes Columbus discovered a new continent
1507	Waldseemüller issues the first map showing "America"
1510	Portuguese capture Goa
1513	Balboa becomes first European to see Pacific Ocean
1519–1522	Magellan's expedition sails around the world
1519–1523	Cortés conquers the Aztecs, destroys Tenochtitlán
1533	Pizarro conquers Cuzco, the Inca capital
1534	Cartier discovers St. Lawrence River
1542	Charles V issues "New Laws"
1545	Spanish discover Potosí silver mines

The rising volume of trade between Europe and North Africa brought with it information about the wealthy African kingdoms of the Niger Delta. The Mongols in the thirteenth century allowed European merchants and missionaries to travel along trade routes extending all the way to China, opening regions formerly closed to them by hostile Muslim governments.

Trade in the Mediterranean also kept Christians and Muslims, Europeans and North Africans in close contact. Europeans sold textiles to Arab traders, who carried them across the Sahara to Timbuktu, where they were sold for gold bullion from the ancient African kingdoms of Ghana and Mali located just above the Niger River.

❧ READING SOURCES

Sir John Mandeville Describes Prester John

The Travels of Sir John Mandeville is said to have been the work of an English cleric. In fact, Travels *was probably written before 1350 in France or the Low Countries. The book, which combines pilgrimage accounts, ancient geographic lore, and contemporary ideas about "marvels," was immediately a "bestseller." It helped to create popular expectations in the minds of travelers to Asia and the New World. His description of Prester John's kingdom typifies knowledge of the wider world in the late Middle Ages.*

This emperor, Prester John, holds a vast, great land, and has many great cities and good towns in his realm, and many large and diverse isles. . . . This Prester John has many kings and many islands and many different peoples of diverse conditions under him. And this land is very good and rich, but not so rich as is the land of the great Khan. For the merchants do not often come there in search of merchandise, as they do in the land of the great Khan, for it is too far to travel. And on the other part, in the Isle of Cathay [China], men find all manner of things that are necessary—cloths of gold and silk, spices and all manner of goods. And therefore although men find greater markets in the land of Prester John, nonetheless men dread the long way and the great peril of the sea in those parts.

For in many places the sea is made up of rocks of adamant that attract iron. Therefore no ships pass that have either bonds or nails in them. . . . And also they dread the long way. And therefore they go to Cathay, for it is nearer. And yet it is not so near for a man must travel eleven or twelve months by sea and land from Genoa or Venice before he comes to Cathay. And yet the land of Prester John is further and requires more perilous journeys. . . . In that desert there are many wild men that are hideous to look at; they are horned and they do not speak but grunt like pigs. And there are also very many wild hounds. And there are many parrots that they call *psittakes* in their language. And they speak without any training and salute men who go through the desert and speak naturally as if they too were men.

Source: The Travels of Sir John Mandeville (London: MacMillan & Co., 1900; reprint, Dover, 1964), pp. 178–181; modernized by Duane J. Osheim.

European chroniclers recorded the pilgrimage to Mecca of Mansa Musa, the fabulously wealthy fourteenth-century emperor of Mali. Italian merchants tried unsuccessfully to trade directly with the African kingdoms, but Muslim merchants prevented any permanent contact.

Europeans enjoyed more successful trade connections farther east. The discovery in London of a brass shard inscribed with a Japanese character attests to the breadth of connections in the early fourteenth century. After the rise of the Mongols, Italian merchants regularly traveled east through Constantinople and on to India and China. By the fourteenth century, they knew how long travel to China might take and the probable expenses along the way. European intellectuals also maintained an interest in the lands beyond Christendom.

They had read the late classical and early medieval authors who described Africa, the Indies, and China.

The work of the greatest of the classical geographers, Ptolemy° of Alexandria (ca. A.D. 127–145), was known only indirectly until the early fifteenth century, but medieval thinkers read avidly and speculated endlessly about the information contained in the works of authors from Late Antiquity, such as Martianus Capella, who lived in the fifth century A.D. Martianus preserved fantastic myths and tales along with astute geographic observations. He reported, for example, that certain snakes in Calabria, in isolated southern Italy, sucked milk from cows and that men in the right circumstances became

Ptolemy (TOL-eh-mee)

The World Beyond Christendom   Medieval Christians believed that wondrous peoples lived beyond the borders of Christendom. Images of headless or one-legged men were usually included in travel accounts. This picture from Marco Polo's *Travels* shows what many Europeans expected to find when they traveled.   *(Bibliothèque Nationale de France)*

wolves—the earliest mention of werewolves. By the twelfth century, fictitious reports circulated widely in the West of a wealthy Christian country in the East or possibly in Africa. Chroniclers since the twelfth century talked of Prester John, who some thought was a wealthy and powerful descendant of the Wise Men from the East who Scripture says visited the baby Jesus. The legend of the kingdom of Prester John probably reflects some knowledge of the Christian groups living near the shrine of Saint Thomas in India or the kingdom of Ethiopia. In the fifteenth century, European Christians looked to Prester John for aid against the rising Turkish empire. (See the box "Reading Sources: Sir John Mandeville Describes Prester John.")

Tales of geographic marvels are epitomized by *The Travels of Sir John Mandeville*, a book probably written in France but purporting to be the observations of a knight from St. Albans, just north of London. Mandeville says that he left England in 1322 or 1323 and traveled to Constantinople, Jerusalem, Egypt, India, China, Persia, and Turkey. In the first half of the book he describes what seems to be a typical pilgrimage to the Holy Land. As the author ventures farther eastward, however, the narrative shifts dramatically. Sir John describes the islands of won-

ders, inhabited by dog-headed humans, one-eyed giants, headless men, and hermaphrodites. Less fantastically, Mandeville reports that the world could be, and in fact has been, circumnavigated. He adds that the lands south of the equator, the Antipodes°, are habitable.

More reliable information became available in the thirteenth century largely because of the arrival of the Mongols. Jenghiz Khan° and his descendants created an empire that reached from eastern Hungary to China (see page 307). This *pax Mongolica*, or area of Mongol-enforced peace, was a region in which striking racial and cultural differences were tolerated. In the 1240s and 1250s a series of papal representatives traveled to the Mongol capital at Karakorum near Lake Baikal in Siberia. The letters of these papal ambassadors, who worked extensively to gain converts and allies for a crusade against the Turks, were widely read and greatly increased accurate knowledge about Asia. Other missionaries and diplomats journeyed to the Mongol court and some continued farther east to India and China. By the early fourteenth century, the church had established a bishop in Beijing°.

Antipodes (an-TIP-o-deez)   **Jenghiz Khan** (JEN-gus KAHN)
Beijing (bay-JING)

Italian merchants followed closely on the heels of the churchmen and diplomats. The pax Mongolica offered the chance to trade directly in Asia and the adventure of visiting lands known only from travel literature. In 1262 Niccolo and Maffeo Polo embarked from Venice on their first trip to China. On a later journey they took Niccolo's son, Marco (1255–1324). In all, they spent twenty-four years in China. Marco dictated an account of his travels to a Pisan as they both languished as prisoners of war in a Genoese jail in 1298. It is difficult to know how much of the text represents Marco's own observations and how much is chivalric invention by the Pisan. Some historians even have speculated that Marco himself never traveled to China. His contemporaries, however, had no doubts. The book was an immediate success even among Venetians who would have exposed a fraud. Columbus himself owned and extensively annotated a copy of Marco Polo's *Travels.*

In his narrative Marco claims to have been an influential official in China, and very likely he was a tax official and functionary of the emperor Kublai Khan°. Marco describes the long, difficult trip to China, his equally arduous return, and the cities and industries he found. He was most impressed by the trade of Ch'nan (modern Hangzhou on the central coast of China)—one hundred times greater, he thought, than the trade of Alexandria in Egypt, a renowned port on the Mediterranean. Marco also visited modern Sri Lanka, Java, and Sumatra. His tales mix a merchant's observations of ports, markets, and trade with an administrator's eye for people and organizations.

By 1300 a modest community of Italians had settled in China. By the late thirteenth and fourteenth centuries, Italian traders were traveling directly to the East in search of Asian silks, spices, pearls, and ivory. They and other European merchants could consult the *Handbook for Merchants* (1340) compiled by the Florentine Francesco Pegalotti°, which described the best roads, the most hospitable stopping points, and the appropriate freight animals for a trip to the East. Fragmentary reports of Europeans in the Spice Islands (also known as the Moluccas), Japan, and India indicate that many Europeans in addition to ambitious merchants traveled simply for the adventure of visiting new lands.

■ The Revolution in Geography

The situation changed significantly over the course of the fourteenth century. With the conversion of the Mongols to Islam, the breakdown of Mongol unity, and the subsequent rise of the Ottoman Turks, the highly integrated and unusually open trade network fell apart. The caravan routes across southern Russia, Persia, and Afghanistan were abruptly closed to Europeans. Western merchants once again became dependent on Muslim middlemen.

The reports of travelers, however, continued to circulate long after the trade routes shut down, contributing to a veritable revolution in geography in the decades before the Portuguese and Spanish voyages.

In 1375 Abraham Cresques°, a Jewish mathematician from the Mediterranean island of Majorca, produced what has come to be known as the *Catalan World Atlas.* He combined the traditional medieval *mappamundi* (or world map) with a Mediterranean portolan. The mappamundi often followed the O-T form—that is, a circle divided into three parts representing Europe, Africa, and Asia, the lands of the descendants of Noah. Jerusalem—the heart of Christendom—was always at the center of the map. What the map lacked in accuracy, it made up in symbolism. The portolan, in contrast, was entirely practical, with sailing instructions and reasonable portrayals of ports, islands, and shallows along with general compass readings. The *Catalan World Atlas* largely holds to the portolan tradition but has more correct representations of the lands surrounding the Mediterranean.

In the fifteenth century, following Ptolemy's suggestions, mapmakers began to divide their maps into squares marking lines of longitude and latitude. This format made it possible to show with some precision the contours of various lands and the relationships between landmasses. Numerous maps of the world were produced in this period. The culmination of this cartography was a globe constructed for the city of Nuremberg in 1492, the very year Columbus set sail. From these increasingly accurate maps, it has become possible to document the first exploration of the Azores, the Cape Verde Islands, and the western coast of Africa.

After his voyages, Columbus observed that maps had been of no use to him. True enough. But without the accumulation of knowledge by travelers and the mingling of that knowledge with classical ideas about geography, it is doubtful whether Columbus or the Portuguese seaman Vasco da Gama would have undertaken—or could have found governments willing to support—the voyages that so dramatically changed the relations between Europe and the rest of the world.

Kublai Khan (KOOB-lie KAHN)
Pegalotti (peg-ah-LOW-tee)

Cresques (KRESK)

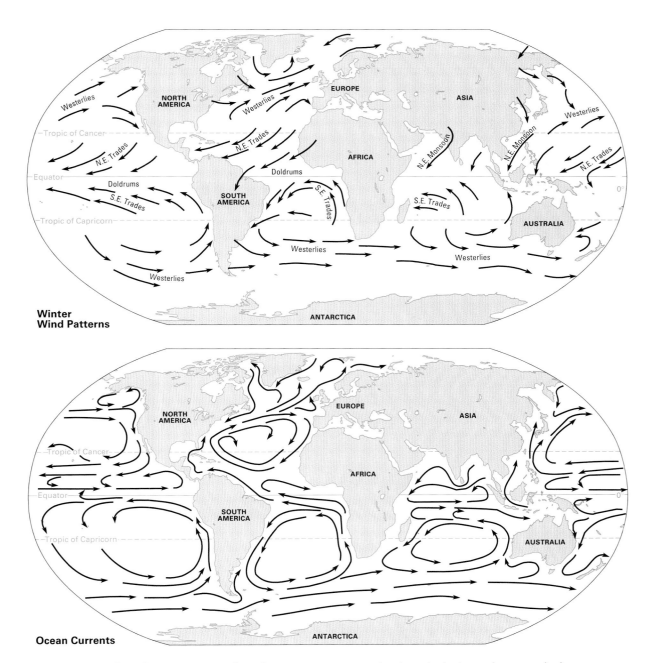

Winter Wind Patterns

Ocean Currents

Map 13.1   Winds and Currents   Winds and ocean currents move in giant clockwise and counterclockwise circles that limit the directions in which ships can sail efficiently. It was impossible, for example, for the explorers to sail directly south along the entire western coast of Africa.

PORTUGUESE VOYAGES OF EXPLORATION, 1350–1515

PORTUGAL, a tiny country on the edge of Europe, for a short time led the European overseas expansion. Portuguese sailors were the first Europeans to perfect the complex techniques of

using the winds and currents of the south Atlantic, especially along the western coast of Africa (see Map 13.1). Portugal's experience reflects the range of options open to Europeans as they extended their influence into new areas. As the Portuguese moved down the African coast and later as they tried to compete commercially in Asia, they adapted traditional Mediterranean cultural and commercial attitudes to fit the new environment in

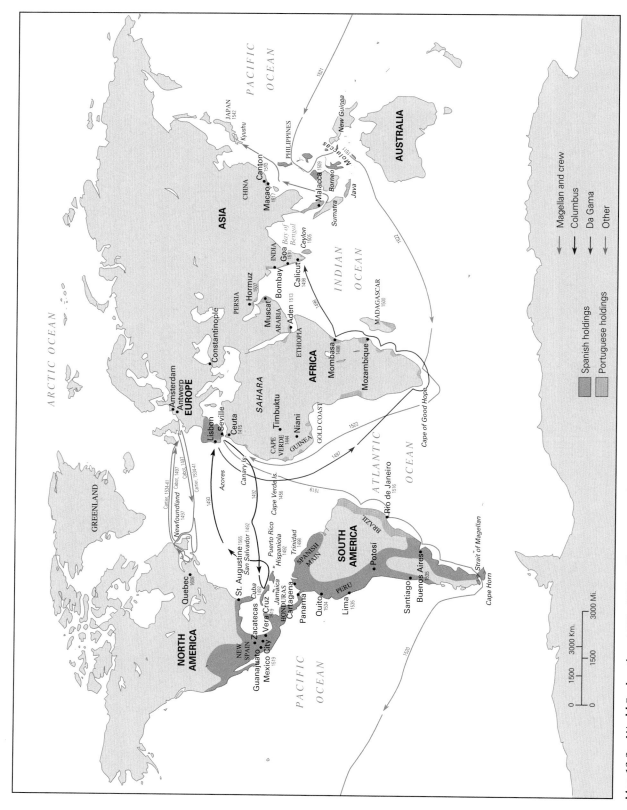

Map 13.2 World Exploration, 1492–1535 The voyages of Columbus, da Gama, and Magellan charted the major sea-lanes that became essential for communication, trade, and warfare for the next three hundred years.

which they found themselves. In some areas the Portuguese created networks of isolated naval and trading stations to control the movement of goods. In other areas they attempted to create substantial colonies, inhabited with Portuguese settlers. In still other areas they introduced plantation slavery to create commercial products for the international market. Spain and the other European states would use these same strategies in Asia and in the New World as they too expanded their economic and political interests overseas.

■ The Early Voyages

Portugal, like other late medieval European states, hoped that exploration and expansion would lead to "gold and Christians." The search for Christians was accelerated in the fifteenth century by the growing power of the Ottoman Turks. Europeans increasingly desired an alliance with the mythical Christian kingdoms of the East to open a second front against the militant Turks. Further, rediscovering the "lost" Christians and reclaiming Jerusalem fed Christian expectations that they were living in the last days before Christ's return.

For the Portuguese, facing the Atlantic and insulated from a direct Turkish threat, the lure of gold was always mixed with their religious motives. The nearest source of gold was well known to late medieval Christians: the African kingdoms of the Niger Delta. The problem for European traders and their governments was that commercial contacts with this wealthy region remained controlled by the Muslim Berber merchants of North Africa. The Portuguese and Spanish hoped to break the monopoly by taking control of the North African coast or by means of a flanking movement along the western coast of Africa.

Actual exploration of the Atlantic had begun long before Europeans recognized the extent of the Turkish threat. By 1350 the Madeiras and the Canaries, groups of islands off the western coast of Africa, regularly were included on European maps. By about 1365, Portuguese, Spanish, and probably French sailors were visiting the Canary Islands. By 1400 the Azores°, a chain of islands one-third of the way across the Atlantic, were known and from early in the fifteenth century were routine ports of call for Portuguese ships (see Map 13.2). These voyages were no mean feat, calling for sophisticated ocean sailing out of sight of land for weeks at a time.

In the second decade of the fifteenth century the Portuguese expansion began in earnest with the capture of the Muslim port of Ceuta° on the coast of Morocco.

From then on, the Portuguese, led by Prince Henry "the Navigator" (1394–1460), younger son of King John I (r. 1385–1433), moved steadily down the western coast of Africa. Contemporaries reported that Prince Henry was intent on reaching the "River of Gold"—that is, the Gold Coast of Africa and the Niger Delta. To accomplish this, he directed efforts to colonize the Canaries (which eventually were lost to the Spanish), the Azores, and Madeira°, the largest of the Madeira Islands. He also sponsored a series of expeditions down the African coast, reaching Senegal and the Cape Verde Islands by 1444. The Portuguese quickly established trading stations in the region and soon were exporting gold and slaves to Lisbon.

The islands off the coast of Africa were uninhabited, except for the Canaries, which the Portuguese tried unsuccessfully to keep from the Spanish. Thus, the Portuguese could not merely plant trading communities within a larger population, for the Azores and Madeira had no native population. As a result, by the early 1440s the Portuguese were bringing sheep, seed, and peasants to these hitherto unoccupied islands, and the Crown was granting extensive lordships to encourage reluctant nobles to relocate to the Azores. The islanders survived largely by exporting sheep and grain to Iberia.

A significant transformation occurred on Madeira in the 1440s, when the Portuguese introduced sugar cane to the island. Within a decade sugar dominated the island's economy. By 1452 entrepreneurs had erected a water mill for processing the cane, and in the 1470s sugar revenues from Madeira constituted nearly 2 percent of the Portuguese crown's total income.

Sugar production was capital- and labor-intensive. A great many workers were needed to cut the cane, and expensive mills and lengthy processing were required to extract and produce sugar. On Madeira most of the work was done by Portuguese peasants. But when the Portuguese extended sugar cultivation to the newly discovered and colonized Cape Verde Islands in the 1460s, they found that Portuguese peasants would not work voluntarily in the sultry equatorial climate. Soon the Portuguese introduced a slave-based plantation system to maximize production and profits.

Slaves imported from the Black Sea areas had been used in agriculture since the introduction of sugar cultivation into the Mediterranean in the thirteenth century. The Portuguese had been trading in slaves along the western coast of Africa since the 1440s—the date from which black slaves appear in Lisbon. African slaves along with slaves

Azores (AY-zorz)   **Ceuta** (say-OO-tuh)   **Madeira** (ma-DEER-uh)

from the North and East could be found in Italy and throughout the Mediterranean in the fifteenth century, most often as domestics or laborers in small enterprises. Not since Roman times, however, had slave-based industries developed on the scale of the Portuguese sugar plantations. Sugar production in the New World would be modeled on the plantation system perfected by the Portuguese on their island colonies in the Atlantic.

■ The Search for a Sea Route to Asia

Until the middle of the fifteenth century, the Niger Delta remained the focus of Portuguese interest. Only after securing control of the western coast of Africa through the expansion of sugar cultivation to Madeira and the Cape Verdes, developing the gold and slave trade in Senegal, and constructing a fortress to control the Volta River (in modern Ghana) and secure access to most gold-producing areas of West Africa did the Portuguese look seriously at sailing around Africa and discovering a sea route to Asia.

The fifteenth-century sailors who first tried to sail down the coast of Africa faced enormous difficulties. Water and wind currents tend to move in clockwise and counterclockwise circles against which it is difficult for a sail-powered ship to make progress (see Map 13.1). Winds near the equator generally blow from the east; farther north and south, the westerlies prevail. Some zones, in certain seasons, are pockets of stillness—called doldrums—with few breezes to propel ships. A navigator had to find winds and currents moving in the direction he wished to travel. Sailing directly from port to port was virtually impossible.

Knowledge of winds and currents allowed Bartholomeu Dias (1450?–1500) in 1487 to explore the coast of southern Africa (see Map 13.2). He followed the traditional Portuguese routes until southeasterly winds forced him to sail south and west, almost to the Brazilian and Argentine coasts. Then he was able to ride the westerlies well past the southern tip of Africa, where he turned north. On his return he sighted what he called "the Cape of Storms," later renamed "the Cape of Good Hope" by the Portuguese king. Dias had perfected the techniques for searching out currents in the Southern Hemisphere and opened the way to India.

A decade after Dias's return from the Cape of Good Hope, Vasco da Gama (1460?–1524) set sail on a voyage that would take him to Calicut on the western coast of India. Using the information gathered from countless navigators, travelers, and even spies sent into East Africa, da Gama set sail in 1497 with four square-rigged, armed caravels and over 170 men. He had been provided with maps and reports that indicated what he might expect to find along the eastern coast of Africa. He also carried textiles and metal utensils, merchandise of the type usually traded along the western coast of Africa. This was a trade mission and in no sense a voyage of discovery.

Da Gama followed established routes beyond the Cape of Good Hope and into the Indian Ocean. He traveled up the coast until he reached Malindi in Mozambique, where he secured an Arab pilot who taught him the route to Calicut. Although the goods the Portuguese traders presented were not appropriate for the sophisticated Asian market, da Gama did manage to collect a cargo of Indian spices, which he brought back to Portugal, arriving in 1499. From that pioneering voyage until the Portuguese lost their last colonies in the twentieth century (Goa, 1961; Mozambique, 1975), Portugal remained a presence in the Indian Ocean.

■ The Portuguese in Asia

Trade in the Indian Ocean was nominally controlled by Muslims, but in fact a mixture of ethnic and religious groups—including Muslims, Hindus, Jains, and Nestorian Christians—participated in the movement of cottons, silks, and spices throughout the region. The hodgepodge of trade reflected the political situation. Vasco da Gama's arrival coincided with the rise of the Moguls, Muslim descendants of Jenghiz Khan. By 1530 they had gained control of most of northern India, and during the sixteenth century Mogul influence increased in the south. The wealth and security of the Moguls depended on landed power. They generally left traders and trading ports to themselves. Throughout the sixteenth century the Moguls remained tolerant of India's religious, cultural, and economic diversity. Neither Muslim nor Hindu powers initially considered the Portuguese an unusual threat.

Asians may not have worried much about the Portuguese because at first there were so few of them. Vasco da Gama arrived with only three ships. And the subsequent fleet of Pedro Alvares Cabral carried only fifteen hundred men. In the 1630s, after more than a century of emigration, probably no more than ten thousand Portuguese were scattered from modern Indonesia to the east coast of Africa. In addition to government officials, Portuguese settlers were likely to be petty traders, local merchants, and poorly paid mercenaries.

The problem for the Portuguese was that their numbers were so few and their trade goods had so little value in sophisticated, highly developed Asian markets. In most cases they bought spices, textiles, and dyes with gold and silver brought from mines in central Europe and the New World. In response to this difficult situation, they created a seaborne "trading-post empire," an empire based on control of trade rather than on colonization. It was, in fact, a model that fit well with their crusading experience in North Africa and their desire to push back Muslim control.

Portugal's commercial empire in the East was based on fortified, strategically placed naval bases. As early as Vasco da Gama's second expedition in 1502, Portuguese bombarded Calicut and defeated an Arab fleet off the coast of India. This encounter set the stage for Portugal's most important strategist of empire, Alfonso d'Albuquerque (1453–1515), governor-general of Portuguese colonies in India. He convinced the monarchy that the key to dominance in the region was the creation of fortified naval bases commanding the Bay of Bengal and thereby controlling access to the coveted Spice Islands. (See the box "Reading Sources: Albuquerque Defends the Portuguese Empire.") By 1600 the Portuguese had built a network of naval bases that reached from Mozambique and Mombasa on the east coast of Africa to Goa on the west coast of India and to the island of Macao off southeastern China (see Map 13.2).

The Portuguese established a royal trading firm, the Casa da India, to manage the booming market in cinnamon, ginger, cloves, mace, and a variety of peppers. Although their control was far from total, the Portuguese did become significant exporters of spices to Europe. More significant was the creation of the Portuguese Estado da India, or India office, to oversee Portuguese naval forces, administer ports, and regulate maritime trade. Under the Portuguese system all merchants were expected to acquire export licenses and to ship products through Portuguese ports.

Both the casa and the estado depended on naval power for their influence. Local boats were no match for the sturdy Portuguese ships armed with cannon. Although the Portuguese navy was too small to enforce a complete blockade of clandestine trade, the Portuguese did manage to change the patterns of commerce in the area. Asians often found it more convenient to cooperate than to resist: most agreed to pay for export licenses and trade through Portuguese ports. They even found it expedient to ship in European-style vessels and to use Portuguese as the language of commerce.

Portuguese in India   This watercolor by a Portuguese traveler shows the varied people and customs and the great wealth to be found in India. Europeans were fascinated by all that seemed different from their own world.   *(Biblioteca Casanatense, Rome. Photo: Humberto Nicoletti Serra)*

❧ R E A D I N G   S O U R C E S

Albuquerque Defends the Portuguese Empire

In this letter of 1512 to the king of Portugal, Alfonso d'Albuquerque, the governor-general of Portugal's colonies in India, informs the king of conditions in the East, explains his strategy, and defends himself against his critics.

The first time the Muslims entered Goa, we killed one of their captains. They were greatly grieved by the [Portuguese] capture of Goa and there is great fear of Your Highness among them. You must reduce the power of [the Muslim] rulers, take their coastal territories from them and build good fortresses in their principal places. Otherwise you will not be able to set India on the right path and you will always have to have a large body of troops there to keep it pacified. Any alliance which you may agree with one or other Indian king or lord must be secured, Sire, because otherwise you may be certain that, the moment your back is turned, they will at once become your enemies.

What I am describing has now become quite usual among them. In India there is not the same punctiliousness as in Portugal about keeping truth, friendship and trust, for nobody here has any of these qualities. Therefore, Sire, put your faith in good fortresses and order them to be built; gain control over India in time and do not place any confidence in the friendship of the kings and lords of this region be-cause you did not arrive here with a just cause to gain domination of their trade with blandishments and peace treaties. Do not let anybody in Portugal make you think that this is a very hard thing to achieve and that, once achieved, it will place you under great obligation. I tell you this, Sire, because I am still in India and I would like people to sell their property and take part in this enterprise that is so much to your advantage, so great, so lucrative and so valuable. . . .

In a place where there is merchandise to be had and the Muslim traders will not let us have precious stones or spices by fair dealing, and we want to take these foods by force, then we must fight the Muslims for them. If, on the other hand, they see us with a large body of troops, they do us honor, and no thought of deceit or trickery enters their heads. They exchange their goods for ours without fighting and they will abandon the delusion that they will expel us from India.

Source: T. F. Earle and J. Villiers, eds., *Albuquerque: Caesar of the East* (Warminster, U.K.: Aris and Phillips, 1990), p. 109.

SPANISH VOYAGES OF EXPLORATION, 1492–1522

SPANISH overseas expansion seems a logical continuation of the centuries-long Reconquista. In 1492 Castile was finally able to conquer the last Muslim kingdom of Granada and unify all of Iberia, with the exception of Portugal, under a single monarchy. Initially in 1479 the Spanish kingdoms had agreed to leave the exploration and colonization of the African coast to the Portuguese, yet they watched nervously as the Portuguese expanded their African contacts. Portuguese successes led Castilians to concentrate their efforts on what came to be called the "Enterprise of the Indies"—that is, the conquest and settlement of Central and South America.

The sailing and exploring necessary to compete with the Portuguese produced critical information about ocean winds and currents and facilitated later voyages. They also established the basic approaches that the Spanish would follow in their exploration, conquest, and colonization of the lands where they dropped anchor.

■ The Role of Columbus

The story of the enterprise begins with Christopher Columbus (1451–1506), a brilliant seaman, courtier, and self-promoter who has become a symbol of European expansion. Columbus, however, was not a bold pioneer who fearlessly did what no others could conceive of doing. He benefited from long-standing interests in the world beyond the European shores.

Columbus was born into a modest family in Genoa and spent his early years in travel and in the service of the Castilian and Portuguese crowns. He apparently first put his plans to sail west to Asia before King John II (r. 1481–1495) of Portugal. Only after Portuguese rejection did he approach the Spanish monarchs, Ferdinand and Isabella. His vision seems to have been thoroughly traditional and medieval. He knew the medieval geographic speculations inherited from Arab and ultimately Classical Greek sources. Medieval seafarers did not fear a flat earth; rather, the concern was whether a ship could cover the vast distances necessary to sail west to Asia. Studying information in *Imago Mundi*° (*Image of the World,* 1410), by the French philosopher Pierre d'Ailly° (1350–1420), Columbus convinced himself that the distance between Europe and Asia was much less than it actually is. Pierre d'Ailly had figured that water covered only about one-quarter of the globe. This estimate put the east coast of Asia within easy reach of the western edge of Europe. "This sea is navigable in a few days if the wind is favorable," was d'Ailly's conclusion.

D'Ailly's theories seemed to be confirmed by the work of the Florentine mathematician Paolo Toscanelli°. Columbus knew of Toscanelli's calculations and even revised them downward. From his own study, he concluded that the distance from the west coast of Europe to the east coast of Asia was about 5,000 miles instead of the actual 12,000. Columbus's reading of traditional sources put Japan in the approximate location of the Virgin Islands. (It is not surprising that Columbus remained convinced that the Bahamas were islands just off the coast of Asia.)

Like Marco Polo before him, Columbus expected to find the marvels reported in the classical sources. Since he and the people he met initially shared no common language, he could only guess at the meanings of their signs and gestures. He interpreted these attempts at communication in the light of the ancient sources he had read and studied. He interpreted what he was told in the context of his assumptions. When Amerindians told him of Cuba, he concluded that it "must be Japan according to the indications that these people give of its size and wealth."[1]

And on the basis of first-century descriptions, he assured Spanish authorities that King Solomon's mines were only a short distance west of his newly discovered islands. In addition to finding the gold of Solomon, Columbus also expected that by sailing farther west he could fulfill a series of medieval prophecies that would lead to the conversion of the whole world to Christianity. This conversion, he believed, would shortly precede the Second Coming of Christ. In Columbus's own view, then, his voyages were epochal not because they were ushering in a newer, more empirical world but because they signaled the fulfillment of history, God's plan for redemption.

Columbus's enthusiasm for the venture was only partially shared by Ferdinand and Isabella. Vasco da Gama had been well supplied with a flotilla of large ships and a crew of over 170 men, but Columbus sailed in 1492 with three small vessels and a crew of 90. Da Gama carried extra supplies and materials for trade and letters for the rulers he knew he would meet. Columbus had nothing similar in his sea chest. His commission did authorize him as "Admiral of Spain" to take possession of all he should find, but royal expectations do not seem to have been great.

Yet on October 12, about ten days later than he had expected, Columbus reached landfall on what he assumed were small islands in the Japanese chain. He had actually landed in the Bahamas (see Map 13.2). Because Columbus announced to the world he had arrived in the Indies, the indigenous populations have since been called "Indians" and the islands are called the "West Indies." (See the box "Reading Sources: Christopher Columbus Describes His Discoveries.")

Columbus returned to the New World three more times—in 1493, 1498, and 1502—exploring extensively in the Bahamas and along the coast of Panama and Venezuela, 800 miles to the south and east of the island of Hispaniola. The enthusiasm his discoveries generated was evident on his second voyage. He oversaw a fleet of seventeen ships with fifteen hundred sailors, churchmen, and adventurers. And Columbus's initial rewards were great. He was granted a hereditary title, a governorship of the new lands, and one-tenth of all the wealth he had discovered.

Columbus reported to the Spanish monarchs that the inhabitants on the islands were friendly and open to the new arrivals. He described primitive, naked people, eager, he believed, to learn of Christianity and European ways. The Tainos, or Arawaks, whom he had misidentified, did live simple, uncomplicated lives. The islands easily produced sweet potatoes, maize, beans, and squash, which along with fish provided an abundant diet. Initially these peoples shared their food and knowledge with the newcomers, who they seem to have thought were sky-visitors.

Imago Mundi (i-MAHG-o MUN-di)   **d'Ailly** (die-YEE)
Toscanelli (toss-ka-NELL-ee)

❧ READING SOURCES

Christopher Columbus Describes His Discoveries

Columbus's hopes for success depended on maintaining the goodwill of Ferdinand and Isabella. Columbus wrote this letter toward the conclusion of his first voyage, which he believed might secure his rights to lordship over all the new territories he found. He took pains to make clear that what he had found was what one would expect to find on the edge of Asia.

In conclusion, to speak only of what has been accomplished on this voyage, which was so hasty, their highnesses can see that I give them as much gold as they may need, if their highnesses will render me very slight assistance; moreover, spice and cotton, as much as their highnesses shall command; and mastic [yellow resin necessary for various adhesives], as much as they shall order to be shipped and which, up to now, has been found only in Greece, in the island of Chios, and the Seignory [of Venice] sells it for what it pleases; and also wood, as much as they shall order to be shipped, and slaves, as many as they shall order to be shipped and who will be from the idolaters. And I believe that I have found rhubarb and cinnamon [essential ingredients for medicines], and I shall find a thousand other things of value, which people I have left here will have discovered, for I have not delayed at any point and in truth I shall have done more, if the ships had served me as reason demanded.

Source: C. Columbus, A. Bernáldez, et al., eds., *The Voyages of Christopher Columbus*, part 1 (London: Argonaut Press, 1930), p. 16.

The Spanish, for their part, praised this smiling and happy people. The visitors generally believed they had discovered a compliant, virtuous people who, if converted, would be exemplars of Christian virtues to the Europeans. Columbus himself observed that

> they are very gentle and do not know what evil is; nor do they kill others, nor steal; and they are without weapons. They say very quickly any prayer that we tell them to say, and they make the sign of the cross, †. So your Highnesses ought to resolve to make them Christians.[2]

The Spanish authorities changed their opinion quickly. The settlers Columbus left at his fortress set an unfortunate example. They seized foodstocks, kidnapped women, and embarked on a frenzied search for gold. Those who did not kill one another were killed by the Tainos.

During succeeding voyages, Columbus struggled to make his discoveries the financial windfall he had promised the monarchs. He was utterly unable to administer this vast new land. He quickly lost control of the colonists and was forced to allow the vicious exploitation of the island population. He and other Spanish settlers claimed larger and larger portions of the land and required the Indians to work it. Islands that easily supported a population of perhaps a million natives could not support those indigenous peoples and the Spanish newcomers and still provide exports to Spain. Largely because of diseases (see pages 453–454), scholars have estimated that the native population of the islands may have fallen to little more than thirty thousand by 1520. By the middle of the sixteenth century, the native population had virtually disappeared.

Columbus remained convinced that he would find vast fortunes just over the horizon. But he found neither the great quantities of gold he promised nor a sea passage to Asia. With the islands in revolt and his explorations seemingly going nowhere, the Spanish monarchs stripped Columbus of his titles and commands. Once he was returned to Spain in chains. Even after his final transatlantic trip, he continued to insist that he had finally found either the Ganges° River of India or one of the rivers that flow out of the earthly paradise. Although

---

Ganges (GAN-jeez)

Vespucci Explores the Coast   Amerigo Vespucci was one of the many Italians who participated in the explorations of the Americas. It was his letters describing what he had found that gave most Europeans their notions of the New World.   *(Courtesy of the James Ford Bell Library, University of Minnesota)*

Columbus died in 1506, rich and honored for his discoveries, he never gained all the power and wealth he had expected. He remained frustrated and embittered by the Crown's refusal to support one more voyage, during which he expected to find the mainland of Asia.

In 1501, after sailing along the coast of Brazil, the Florentine geographer Amerigo Vespucci° (1451–1512) drew the obvious conclusion from the information collected by Columbus's explorations. He argued that Columbus had discovered a new continent unknown to the classical world. These claims were accepted by the German mapmaker Martin Waldseemüller°, who in 1507 honored Amerigo's claim by publishing the first map showing "America."

■ Columbus's Successors

Columbus's explorations set off a debate over which nations had the right to be involved in trade and expansion. Portuguese claims were based on a papal bull of

1481, issued by Pope Sixtus IV (r. 1471–1484), that granted Portugal rights to all lands south of the Canaries and west of Africa. After Columbus's return, the Spaniards lobbied one of Sixtus's successors, Alexander VI (r. 1492–1503), whose family, the Borgias, was from the kingdom of Aragon. In a series of bulls, Pope Alexander allowed the Spanish to claim all lands lying 400 miles or more west of the Azores. Finally, in the Treaty of Tordesillas° (1494), Spain and Portugal agreed that the line of demarcation between their two areas should be drawn 1,480 miles west of the Azores. The treaty was signed just six years before Pedro Alvares Cabral (1467–1520) discovered the coast of Brazil. Thus the Spanish unwittingly granted the Portuguese rights to Brazil.

Adventurers and explorers worried little about the legal niceties of exploration. Even as Columbus lay dying in 1506, others, some without royal permission, sailed up and down the eastern coasts of North and South America. Amerigo Vespucci traveled on Spanish vessels as far as Argentina, while Spanish explorers sailed among the islands of the Caribbean and along the coast

Amerigo Vespucci (ah-MARE-ih-go ves-POO-chi)
Waldseemüller (vald-SAY-mill-er)

Tordesillas (tor-day-SEE-yas)

of the Yucatán Peninsula. Vasco Nuñez de Balboa° crossed the Isthmus of Panama in 1513 and found the Pacific Ocean exactly where the natives living in the region said it would be.

The most important of the explorations that Columbus inspired was the voyage undertaken by Ferdinand Magellan in 1519 (see Map 13.2). Although his motives are unclear, Magellan (1480?–1521) may have planned to complete Columbus's dream of sailing to the Indies. By the 1510s mariners and others understood that the Americas were a new and hitherto unknown land, but they did not know what lay beyond them or what distance separated the Americas from the Spice Islands of Asia. After sailing along the well-known coastal regions of South America, Magellan continued south, charting currents and looking for a passage into the Pacific. Late in 1520 he beat his way through the dangerous straits (now the Strait of Magellan) separating Tierra del Fuego° from the mainland. These turbulent waters marked the boundary of the Atlantic and the Pacific Oceans. It took almost four months to travel from the straits to the Philippines. During that time, a crew member reported, "We ate biscuit, which was no longer biscuit, but powder of biscuit swarming with worms, for they had eaten the good."[3] The crew suffered greatly from scurvy and a shortage of water and at times had to eat the rats aboard ship to survive. Nevertheless, Magellan managed to reach the Philippines by March 1521. A month later, he was killed by natives.

Spanish survivors in two remaining ships continued west, reaching the Moluccas, the Spice Islands, where they traded merchandise that they had carried along for a small cargo of cloves. A single surviving ship continued around Africa and back to Spain, landing with a crew of 15 at Cádiz in September 1522 after a voyage of three years and the loss of four ships and 245 men. Magellan completed and confirmed the knowledge of wind and ocean currents that European sailors had been accumulating. One of his sailors wrote of him: "More accurately than any man in the world did he understand sea charts and navigation."[4] The way was now open for the vast expansion of Europeans and European culture into all parts of the world.

Spanish adventurers were not the only ones to follow in Columbus's wake. The French and the English, however, concentrated their explorations farther north. Building on a tradition of fishing off the coast of Newfoundland, English sailors under the command of John Cabot (1450?–1499?) sighted Newfoundland in 1497, and later voyages explored the coast as far south as New En-

gland. Cabot initiated an intense period of English venturing that would lead to an unsuccessful attempt to found a colony on Roanoke Island in 1587 and eventually to permanent settlement at Jamestown in 1607. French expeditions followed Cabot to the north. In 1534 Jacques Cartier° (1491–1557) received a royal commission to look for a northern passage to the East. He was the first European to sail up the St. Lawrence River and began the process of exploration and trading that would lead to a permanent presence in Canada beginning in the early seventeenth century. But British and French settlements in the New World came later. The sixteenth century belonged to the Spanish.

SPAIN'S COLONIAL EMPIRE, 1492–1600

SPANISH penetration of the New World was a far cry from the model of the Portuguese in Asia. The Spaniards established no complex network of trade and commerce, and no strong states opposed their interests. A "trading-post empire" could not have worked in the New World. To succeed, the Spaniards needed to colonize and reorganize the lands they had found.

Between 1492 and 1600, almost 200,000 Spaniards immigrated to the New World. New Spain, as they called these newly claimed lands, was neither the old society transported across the ocean nor an Amerindian society with a thin veneer of Spanish and European culture. To understand the history of New Spain, it is essential to grasp what it replaced, and how: the Spaniards overthrew two major civilizations and created new institutions in the wake of conquest. The whole story is not conquest and extermination—many of the Spanish attempted to secure fair treatment for the indigenous peoples who were now part of the Spanish Empire.

■ The Americas Before the European Invasion

The Spaniards and later their European peers entered a world vastly different from their own. It was a world formed by two momentous events—one geological, the other anthropological. The first was the creation of the continents of North and South America. The Americas, along with Africa and the Eurasian landmass, were once part of a single supercontinent. The breakup of this supercontinent left the Americas, Africa, and Eurasia free

---

Vasco Nuñez de Balboa (VAS-ko NOON-yez day bal-BO-a)
Tierra del Fuego (ti-AIR-ah del foo-WAY-go)

Cartier (kar-ti-YAY)

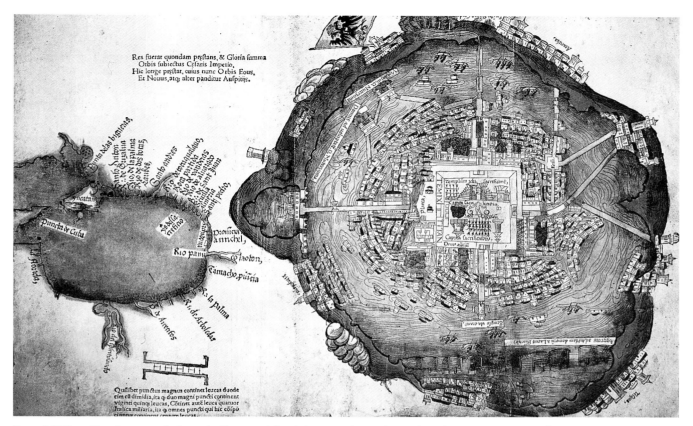

Tenochtitlán   The Aztec capital was built on an island. Its central temples and markets were connected to the rest of the city and the suburbs on the lake shore by numerous canals. The city and its surrounding market gardens seemed to the Spanish to be floating on water.   *(The Newberry Library, Chicago)*

to evolve in dramatically different ways. The continental breakup occurred millions of years ago, long before the appearance of human beings and many other forms of mammalian life.

The second momentous event was the peopling of the Americas. Some migrants may have come over the seas. Most, though, arrived thanks to a temporary rejoining of the Americas to the Eurasian landmass by land and ice bridges that allowed Asians to cross over what is now the Bering Strait to the Americas in the period between 30,000 and 10,000 B.C. Their timing had a great impact. They arrived in the Americas long before the beginnings of the Neolithic agricultural revolution, which involved the domestication of numerous plants and animals. The agricultural revolution in the Americas occurred around 3000 B.C., perhaps six thousand years after similar developments in the Old World. The peoples of the Americas created complex societies, but those societies lacked large domesticated meat or pack animals (the llama was the largest), iron, other hard metals, and the wheel.

Nonetheless, by the time of Columbus's arrival, relatively populous societies were living throughout North and South America. Population estimates for the two continents range from 30 million to 100 million—the lower figure is probably more accurate. North America saw the development of complex mound-builder societies in the East and along the Mississippi River and pueblo societies in the deserts of the American Southwest. But the greatest centers of Amerindian civilization were in central and coastal Mexico and in the mountains of Peru.

In the late fifteenth century, as the cultural collision approached, the two most powerful centers were the empires of the Aztecs and the Inca. When the collection of tribes now known as the "Aztec" (or Mexica) peoples appeared in central Mexico in the early fourteenth century, they found an already-flourishing civilization concentrated around the cities and towns dotting the Valley of Mexico. Through conquest, the Aztecs united the many Nahuatl-speaking groups living in the valley into a confederation centered in Tenochtitlán, a city of perhaps 200,000 people built on an island in Lake Texcoco (see Map 13.3). In early-sixteenth-century Europe, only London, Constantinople, and Naples would have been as large as the Aztec capital. It literally rose out of the water

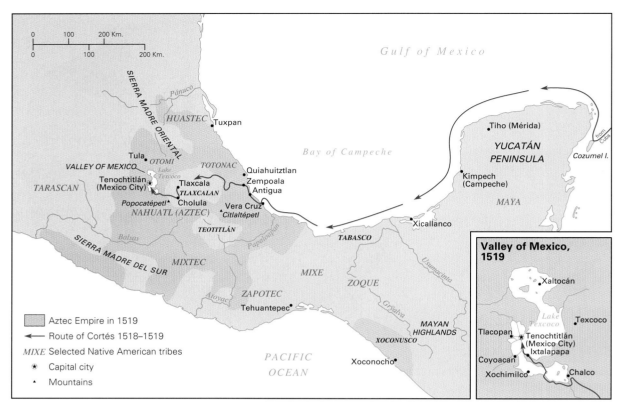

Map 13.3   Mexico and Central America   The Valley of Mexico was a populous region of scattered towns, most of which were part of the Aztec Empire. As Cortés marched inland from Vera Cruz toward the valley, he passed through lands that for generations had been in an almost constant state of war with the Aztecs.

of Lake Texcoco. Only Venice could have equaled the sight. The whole valley supported an unusually high population of about a million. Using canals along the edge of the lake and other canals in Tenochtitlán itself, merchants easily moved food, textiles, gold and silver ornaments, jewels, and ceremonial feathered capes into the city markets. Spaniards later estimated that fifty thousand or more people shopped in the city on market days.

Religion was integral to the Aztecs' understanding of their empire. They believed that the world was finite and that they lived in the last of five empires. It was only regular human sacrifice to Huitzilopochtli° that allowed the world to continue—the hearts of victims were necessary to sustain their god, to ensure that the sun would rise again each morning. Thus, life for the Aztecs required a relentless parade of death.

Tenochtitlán was the center of an imperial culture based on tribute. Towns and villages under Aztec control owed ongoing allotments of food and precious metals. To emphasize that Aztec power and dominance were complete, the Aztecs not only collected vast quantities of maize, beans, squash, and textiles but demanded payment in everything down to centipedes and snakes. The most chilling tribute, however, was in humans for sacrifice. When the wars of expansion that had provided prisoners came to an end, the Aztecs and their neighbors fought "flower wars"—highly ritualized battles to provide prisoners to be sacrificed. Five thousand victims were sacrificed at the coronation of Moctezuma° II (r. 1502–1520) in 1502. Even more, reportedly twenty thousand, were sacrificed at the dedication of the great temple of Huitzilopochtli in Tenochtitlán.

Aztec society maintained a perpetual state of war with the peoples beyond the mountains that ringed the Valley of Mexico—especially the people along the Caribbean coast. Given this constant state of war, plus the

Huitzilopochtli (wheat-zeel-oh-POSHT-lee)

Moctezuma (mok-teh-ZOO-ma)

Aztec Warrior   This watercolor, by a Mexican artist who was trained in European painting, depicts a pre-Aztec ruler. But the dress and the stone-edged sword would have been typical of the Aztecs, too.   *(Bibliothèque Nationale de France)*

heavy burdens in tribute placed on the nearby subject cities, it is no small wonder that the Aztecs were obsessed by the contingencies of life. At the end of each calendar cycle of fifty-two years, all fires in the empire were extinguished until fire-priests ascertained that the world would continue. And the Aztec world did continue until August 1523 (see page 449).

The other great Amerindian empire of the fifteenth century, the empire of the Inca, was also of recent origin. During the fifteenth century the Inca formed efficient armies and expanded their control beyond the central highlands of Peru. Fifteen thousand miles of road and a sophisticated administrative system allowed the Inca to create a state that extended from Ecuador to Chile (see Map 13.4). As they expanded, they demanded political control and tribute but seem to have been tolerant of local traditions and language. The Inca perfected systems of irrigation and bridge-building initiated by earlier in-

habitants of the region. The empire, centered on the city of Cuzco high in the mountains of Peru, was able to sustain a population that may have reached 10 million by the end of the fifteenth century. (See the box "Global Encounters: An Inca Nobleman Defends His Civilization.")

Human sacrifice, though not unknown to the Inca people, was not an essential part of their religious life. Their state was unsettled, however, by increasingly harsh tax exactions. Under the Inca system, the title Paca Inca, or "Great Inca," was inherited by the eldest son of the ruler's principal wife. The ruler's wealth, however, was retained by the rest of his family, who maintained the court as if the ruler still lived. Thus, each new ruler needed money to finance the creation of an entirely new court, and taxes were not only high but continuously climbing.

Both great Amerindian empires, despite their brilliance, rested on uneasy conquests. Subject groups would be willing allies for any invader.

Map 13.4   The Inca Empire   The Inca Empire was accessible from Spanish strongholds in Mexico only by sea. Spanish exploration and domination brought the destruction of Inca mountain citadels and the transfer of administrative power to the new Spanish city of Lima on the coast.

⊕ GLOBAL ENCOUNTERS

An Inca Nobleman Defends His Civilization

Huamán Poma was born into a noble Inca family with a long history of service first to the Inca kings and later to the Spanish administrators. Although Huamán Poma became a Christian and adapted to Spanish rule, he appealed to the king of Spain in 1613 to intervene on behalf of the Inca civilization, which he feared would soon be lost. In the excerpt included here, he describes the Inca understanding of the origins of the world. His "traditional world," however, is heavily influenced by his new Christian faith.

The first white people in the world were brought by God to this country. They were descended from those who survived the flood in Noah's Ark. It is said that they were born in pairs, male and female, and therefore they multiplied rapidly.

These people were incapable of useful work. They could not make proper clothes so they wore garments of leaves and straw. Not knowing how to build houses, they lived in caves and under rocks. They worshipped God with a constant outpouring of sound like the twitter of birds, saying: "Lord how long shall I cry and not be heard?"

In their turn these first people were succeeded by the two castes: the great lords, who were the ancestors of our Inca, and the common people, who were descended from bastards and multiplied rapidly in number.

However barbarous they may have been, our ancestors had some glimmer of understanding of God. Even the mere saying of [God's name] is a sign of faith and an important step forward. Christians have much to learn from our people's good way of life.

Their usual diet consisted of maize, potatoes and other tubers; cress, sorrel, and lupin; pond-weed, laver [a water plant] and a grass with yellow flowers; leaves for chewing; mushrooms, edible grubs, shells, shrimps, crab and various sorts of fish. . . . The burial of the dead was conducted with dignity, but without undue ceremony in vaults constructed for the purpose. There were separate vaults, which were white-washed and painted, for people of high rank. The Indians believed that after death they would have to endure hard labor, torture, hunger, thirst and fire. Thus they had their own conception of Hell, which they called the place under the earth or the abode of demons.

Source: Huamán Poma, *Letter to a King: A Picture History of the Inca Civilization* (New York: E. P. Dutton, 1978), pp. 24–25, 30.

■ The Spanish Conquests

Hernán Cortés (1485–1546) was ambitious to make something of himself in the New World. Of a poor but aristocratic background from the Extremadura region of southwest Spain, he had gone to the West Indies in 1504 to seek his fortune in the service of the governor of Cuba. The governor gave him a commission to lead an expeditionary force to investigate reports of a wealthy and prosperous mainland Indian civilization. From the very beginning, Spanish authorities seem to have distrusted Cortés's aims. He was forced to depart hastily from Cuba to evade formal notification that the governor of Cuba had revoked his commission because of insubordination.

Cortés landed in Mexico at the site of the city he would name Vera Cruz ("True Cross") early in 1519 with a tiny command of five hundred men, sixteen horses, eleven ships, and a few pieces of artillery. Aided by a devastating outbreak of smallpox and Amerindian peoples happy to shake off Aztec control, Cortés and his troops managed to destroy the network of city-states dominated by the Aztecs of Tenochtitlán in two years and lay claim to the Valley of Mexico for the king of Spain. The manner in which Cortés explained and justified his mission can serve as a model against which to measure the adventures of other sixteenth-century Europeans in the Americas.

Cortés, like Machiavelli, believed in the power of truly able leaders (men of virtù) to overcome chance through bold acts. Even so, an attempt to capture a city of 200,000 with an army of 500 appears more foolhardy than bold. Cortés seems to have attempted it simply because he found himself with very little choice. With his commission revoked by the governor of Cuba, Cortés arrived on the mainland as a rebel against both the governor of Cuba and the king of Spain. He burned his ships in Vera Cruz harbor, making clear to all his men that there was no turning back. Much of what he did and said concerning the great Aztec Empire was an attempt to justify his initial act of insubordination and win back royal support. He quickly found allies among native groups who, for their own reasons, wished to see the Aztec Empire destroyed. The allied forces moved toward Tenochtitlán.

Cortés was greatly aided by fortune in the form of Malintzin, a Mexica woman who after her conversion called herself Doña Marina (ca. 1501–1550). Malintzin was Cortés's interpreter and, later, his mistress. Without her, one of Cortés's followers recalled, "We could not have understood the language of New Spain and Mexico." Her story illustrates many of the complex interactions at play in sixteenth-century Mexico. Born a noble Aztec, she was sold by her stepfather and mother, ending up in the hands of Mayas. They gave her, along with twenty other women, to Cortés. Knowing both the Maya and Mexica languages, and quickly learning Spanish, she was the one person who could mediate between Spaniard and native. She changed her name to the Spanish Doña Marina and was baptized as a Christian. After bearing Cortés a son, she finished her life in Spain as the wife of a Spanish gentleman. Like many of the natives who felt no affection for the Aztecs of Tenochtitlán, she did not find it difficult to aid the Spaniard.

Despite the help of Malintzin and Spaniards who had previously lived with the natives, the meeting of Aztecs and Spaniards demonstrated the breadth of the chasm separating the Old World and the New. At first the Aztec king Moctezuma was unconcerned about the coming of the Spaniards. Later he seems to have attempted to buy them off. And finally he and his successors fought desperately to drive them out of Tenochtitlán. The Aztecs' indecision was caused in large part by the fact that in neither words nor gestures did the two groups speak the same language. Hearing that the Spaniards were on the march, Moctezuma sent ambassadors bearing gold, silver, and other costly gifts, which they presented in a most humble fashion to the Spaniards. To a modern ear the gifts sound like (and have often been interpreted to be) desperate attempts to buy off the invaders. To Cortés, or any European or Asian resident of the Old World, such gifts were a sign of submission. But to Moctezuma and most Amerindians, the giving of gifts with great humility by otherwise powerful and proud people could be a show of wealth and status. Seen in that light, Moctezuma's lavish gifts and apparent humility were probably meant to demonstrate the superiority of his civilization, and Cortés's acceptance of the gifts seemed to indicate his recognition of his own inferior status.

Spaniards later claimed that Moctezuma was confounded by the sudden appearance of these peoples from the East. Cortés himself reported to the king of Spain that when he first met Moctezuma, the Aztec leader said, "We have always held that those who descended from [the god Quetzalcoatl°] would come and conquer this land and take us as his vassals." Later Spaniards explained that the Aztecs believed that Quetzalcoatl, the serpent-god symbolically conquered by Huitzilopochtli, had traveled to the East, promising one day to return and reclaim his lands, thus ending Aztec rule. The Spaniards believed that Moctezuma's ambivalence toward them was rooted in his belief in that myth.

Neither story holds up in light of the evidence. There is no surviving preconquest source for Moctezuma's supposed confession, and the myth of the return of Quetzalcoatl was first recorded in Spanish, not Indian, sources long after the conquest. In truth, neither Cortés nor historians can satisfactorily explain in Western terms Moctezuma's initial response to the Spaniards. Cortés took the Aztec leader captive in 1521 and began what would be a two-year battle to take control of the capital and its empire. Although weakened by the arrival of smallpox and other virulent Old World diseases, the Aztecs continued to fight even as more and more of the subject peoples joined the Spanish beseigers. The Spaniards cut off food and water to Tenochtitlán, but still the Aztecs fought.

Different understandings of the rules of war, different traditions of diplomacy, and different cultures prevented the Aztecs and Cortés from reaching any understanding. The peoples of the Valley of Mexico tried to take captives to be sacrificed in temples. The Spaniards, to Aztec eyes, killed indiscriminately and needlessly on the battlefield. Cortés later complained of the Aztecs' refusal to negotiate: "We showed them more signs of peace than have ever been shown to a vanquished people." Thus, to end a war that neither side could resolve in any other way, in

---

Quetzalcoatl (ket-zahl-coh-AH-tal)

August 1523 Cortés and his allies completely destroyed the garden-city of Tenochtitlán.

Cortés's recurring insubordination was an unfortunate model. His own lieutenants later rebelled against his control and attempted to create their own governments as they searched for riches and El Dorado, a mythical city of gold. Later adventurers marched throughout the North American Southwest and Central and South America following rumors of hidden riches. Using private armies and torturing native peoples, veterans of Cortés's army and newly arrived speculators hoped to find wealth that would allow them to live like nobles on their return to Spain. Like Cortés, they claimed to be acting for the monarchy and the church, but in fact they expected that success would justify their most vicious acts.

Francisco Pizarro° (1470–1541) was the most successful of the private adventurers. Poor, illegitimate at birth, he arrived in the Americas ambitious for riches and power. After serving in Balboa's army, participating in several slaving expeditions, and helping to found Panama City, Pizarro was prosperous but still not wealthy. Rumors of Inca wealth filtered through to Central America. Pizarro and a partner resolved in 1530 to lead an expedition down the west coast of South America in search of the Inca capital. Benefiting from disorganization caused by a smallpox epidemic and ensuing civil war, Pizarro was able to find local sympathizers.

Like Cortés, he used numerous Indian allies in his most important battles. Aided by Amerindians eager to throw off Inca domination, he captured and executed the Paca Inca and conquered the capital of Cuzco by 1533. He later built a new capital on the coast at Lima (see Map 13.4) from where he worked to extend his control over all of the old Inca Empire. Pizarro and his Spanish partners seized vast amounts of gold and silver from the Inca. The Spanish eventually found silver mines at Potosí°, which would be a critical source of revenue for the Spanish monarchy. Resistance to Spanish rule continued into the 1570s, when the last of the independent Inca strongholds was finally destroyed.

■ Colonial Organization

The Spanish crown needed to create a colonial government that could control the actions of its headstrong adventurers and create an orderly economy. Although the Spaniards proclaimed that they would "give to those strange lands the form of our own [land]," the resulting political and economic organization of the new Spanish possessions was a curious mixture of old and new.

The head of the administration was the monarchy. As early as the reigns of Ferdinand and Isabella, Spanish monarchs had tried to curb the excesses of the explorers and conquerors who traveled in their name. Isabella initially opposed the enslavement of Amerindians and any slave trade in the new lands. Further, they promoted a broad-based debate about the rights of Amerindians and the nature of religious conversion. It was royal policy that native rights, even the right not to become Christian, were to be protected. Mexicans had to accept missionaries, but they did not have to convert. Royal control, however, was limited by the sheer distance between the court and the new provinces. It could easily take two years for a royal response to a question to arrive at its destination. Things moved so slowly that as one viceroy ruefully noted, "If death came from Madrid, we should all live to a very old age." Given the difficulties of communication, the powers of local administrators had to be very broad.

By 1535 Spanish colonial administration was firmly established in the form it would retain for the next two hundred years. The king created a Council of the Indies located at court, eventually in Madrid, which saw to all legal and administrative issues pertaining to the new possessions. The new territories themselves were eventually divided into the viceroyalty of Mexico (primarily Central America and part of Venezuela) and the viceroyalty of Peru.

In Spain, Castilian conquerors completely dominated newly won lands, but in New Spain, royal administrators created Indian municipalities, or districts, in which Spaniards had no formal right to live or work. Government in these municipalities remained largely in the hands of preconquest native elites. Throughout the sixteenth century, official documents in these communities continued to be written in Nahuatl, the Aztec language. As long as taxes or tribute was paid and missionaries were allowed to circulate, the Spanish government tolerated considerable autonomy in the Indian municipalities.

■ The Colonial Economy

The problem that most plagued the government was the conquerors' desire for laborers to work on the lands and in the mines that they had seized. From Columbus's first visit, the Spanish adopted a system of forced labor developed in Spain. A colonist called an *encomendero*° was offered a grant, or *encomienda*°, of a certain number of

---

Pizarro (pih-ZAR-o)   Potosí (po-to-SEE)

encomendero (en-co-men-DARE-o)
encomienda (en-co-mi-EN-da)

people or tribes who were required to work under his direction. The Spanish government expected that the encomendero was to be a protector of the conquered peoples, someone who would Christianize and civilize them. In theory, Indians who voluntarily agreed to listen to missionaries or to convert to Christianity could not be put under the control of an encomendero. If they refused, however, the Spaniards believed they had the right of conquest. In many areas encomenderos allowed life to continue as it had, simply collecting traditional payments that the preconquest elites had claimed. In other cases, where the subject peoples were forced into mining districts, however, the conditions were brutal. The treatment of native peoples was "more unjust and cruel," one reformer concluded, "than Pharoah's oppression of the Jews."

The pressures exerted by the encomenderos were worsened by the precipitous fall in the indigenous population. Old World diseases such as smallpox and measles swept through populations with no previous exposure to them (see page 454). In central Mexico, where we know most about population changes, the preconquest population was at least 10 or 12 million and may have been twice that. By the mid-sixteenth century, the native pop-

ulation may have declined to just over 6 million, and it probably plunged to less than 1 million early in the seventeenth century before beginning to grow again.

A large population was essential to the Spanish and the Portuguese when they introduced the Old World plantation system to the New World. The Caribbean islands and Brazil were ideal for the production of sugar—a commercial crop in great demand throughout Europe. At first, plantations and mines were worked by Amerindians, but when their numbers shrank, the Spanish and Portuguese imported large numbers of slaves from Africa.

Africans had participated in the initial stages of the conquest. Some had lived in Spain and become Christian; indeed, Amerindians called them "black whitemen." Most Africans, however, were enslaved laborers. African slaves were in Cuba by 1518; they labored in the mines of Honduras by the 1540s. After the 1560s the Portuguese began mass importations of African slaves into Brazil to work on the sugar plantations. It has been estimated that 62,500 slaves were brought into Spanish America and 50,000 into Brazil during the sixteenth century. By 1810, when the movement to abolish the slave trade began to gather momentum, almost 10 million

Caribbean Sugar Plantation
The production of sugar from cane was easily industrialized and centralized. Missing from this depiction of the process are the supervisors who would have overseen the slaves at every step.   *(Courtesy of the John Carter Brown Library at Brown University)*

Africans had been involuntarily transported to the New World to work the fields and the mines on which the colonial economy depended.

The conquerors had hoped to find vast quantities of wealth that they could take back to the Old World. In the viceroyalty of Mexico, the search for El Dorado remained largely unsuccessful. The discovery in 1545 of the silver mines at Potosí in Peru, however, fulfilled the Spaniards' wildest dreams. Between 1550 and 1650, the Spanish probably sent back to Spain 181 tons of gold and 16,000 tons of silver, one-fifth of which was paid directly into the royal treasury.

The tonnage of precious metals was so great that the French scholar Jean Bodin° (see page 532) held this infusion of wealth responsible for the rampant inflation that disrupted the European economy in the late sixteenth century. Although Bodin overestimated the European-wide effect of the precious metals on prices, the flood of silver and gold did have a significant impact on the Continent. The treasure represents one-quarter of the income of King Philip II of Spain in the 1560s and made him the richest monarch in Europe. The New World bonanza funded Spanish opposition to the Protestant Reformation and Spain's attempts to influence the politics of most of its neighbors. And the Spanish coins, the *reales*° and the *reales a ocho*° (the "pieces of eight" prized by English pirates), became the common coin of European traders and even Muslim and Hindu traders in the Indian Ocean. In a world with limited commercial credit, the Spanish treasure allowed for the beginnings of a truly integrated system of world trade.

■ The Debate over Indian Rights

To most conquerors the ruthless pursuit of wealth and power needs little justification, but the more thoughtful among the Spaniards were uneasy. "Tell me," demanded Friar Antonio Montesinos° in 1511, "by what right or justice do you hold these Indians in such cruel and horrible slavery? By what right do you wage such detestable wars on these people who lived idly and peacefully in their own lands?"[5]

Initially the conquerors claimed the right to wage a just war of conquest if Amerindians refused to allow missionaries to live and work among them. Later, on the basis of reports of human sacrifice and cannibalism written by Columbus and other early explorers, Europeans concluded that the inhabitants of the New World

rejected basic natural laws. Juan Gines de Sepulveda°, chaplain of King Charles I of Spain, argued in 1544 that the idolatry and cannibalism of the Indians made them, in Aristotle's terms, natural slaves—"barbarous and inhuman peoples abhorring all civil life, customs and virtue" was how he put it. People lacking "civil life" and "virtue" clearly could not be allowed self-government. Other writers commented that nakedness and cannibalism were both signs of the lack of "civility" among the Amerindians. Sepulveda implied that Indians were merely "humanlike," not necessarily human.

Franciscan and Dominican missionaries were especially vocal opponents of views such as Sepulveda's. To these missionaries, the Indians initially seemed innocent and ideal subjects for conversion to the simple piety of Christ and his first apostles. In their eyes, Indians were like children who could be converted and led by example and, where necessary, by stern discipline. The simple faith of the newly Christian native peoples was to be an example, the missionaries believed, for the lax believers of old Europe. These mendicants saw themselves as advocates for Indians; they desired to protect the natives from the depredations of the Spanish conquerors and the corruptions of European civilization.

The most eloquent defender of Indian rights was Bartolomé de Las Casas (1474–1566), a former encomendero who became a Dominican missionary and eventually bishop of Chiapas in southern Mexico. Las Casas passionately condemned the violence and brutality of the Spanish conquests. In a famous debate with Sepulveda, Las Casas rejected the "humanlike" argument. "All races of the world are men," he declared. All are evolving along a historical continuum. It was wrong, he added, to dismiss any culture or society as outside or beyond natural law. Like all other peoples, Indians had reason. That being the case, even the most brutal could be civilized and Christianized, but by conversion, not coercion. (See the box "Reading Sources: The Rights of Indians.") In the view of Las Casas, the argument for natural slavery was indefensible.

King Charles accepted Las Casas's criticisms of the colonial administration. In 1542 he issued "New Laws" aimed at ending the virtual independence of the most adventurous encomenderos. He further abolished Indian slavery and greatly restricted the transfer of encomiendas.

We should have no illusion, however, that these measures reflected a modern acceptance of cultural pluralism. The very mendicants who protected Indians assumed that Westernization and Christianization would

---

Bodin (bo-DAN)   **reales** (re-AL-es)
reales a ocho (re-AL-es a O-cho)
Montesinos (mon-teh-SEE-nos)

Juan Gines de Sepulveda (HWAN HE-nays de se-PUL-ve-da)

❧ READING SOURCES

The Rights of Indians

Fr. Bartolomé de Las Casas (1474–1566) arrived in the New World as one of the Spanish conquerors. By the time of his death he was Bishop of Chiapas and a passionate defender of Indian rights. In this section of his History of the Indies, *Las Casas criticizes Spanish attempts to Christianize the natives. Christian law made it clear that although no one could be compelled to believe, if a people refused to allow the teaching of Christian doctrine, they abdicated their right to govern themselves.*

Let us examine the substance of this injunction [to require instruction in Christian doctrine]. . . . Supposing the Indians understood our language, what must they have felt when they heard that one God created Heaven, earth and men, believing as they did that the Sun God and the other deities had created them? What reasons, proofs or miracles proved to them that the god of the Spaniards was more God or more Creator than their own? . . . Thus, how could they—especially if they were rulers—love and revere the God of the Spaniards when they heard that St. Peter and his successor the Pope disposed of their territory by giving it to the Castilian King? They believed themselves the true owners of their land by the age-old law of inheritance, and here they were asked to acknowledge a ruler they had never seen or heard of, not knowing whether he was good or bad, whether he intended to govern or steal and destroy, a confusion made the greater by the fierce look of his bearded messengers armed to the teeth with terrible weapons. . . . Therefore, if neither kings nor subjects . . . are under obligation to obey a foreign King, no matter how many injunctions they receive, it is made clear beyond all proof that the threat of an all-out war and captivity of men, women and children intended for slavery is based on neither law nor justice. . . . Hence such wars against such infidels as Indians were, are, and always will be unjust and detestable and condemned by law. . . . [Indians] would, however, serve the King willingly and readily if they had been converted [not by force, but] by the Christian means of peace and love.

Source: Bartolomé de Las Casas, *History of the Indies*, trans. and ed. Andrée Cillard (New York and London: Harper & Row, 1971), pp. 194–196.

 For additional information on this topic, go to http://college.hmco.com.

quickly follow mercy. When it did not, as during revolts in the 1560s, the mendicants themselves sometimes reacted with a puzzled sense of anger, frustration, and betrayal.

THE COLUMBIAN EXCHANGE

HE conquerors, adventurers, and traders who completed the expansion begun by the voyages of Christopher Columbus and Vasco da Gama profoundly altered the Old World and the New. A system of world trade had been in place before 1492, but now, as the Spanish proclaimed, Europe and especially Spain were at the center of economic and political life. As the Spanish and other Europeans moved throughout the world, they carried with them religions, ideas, people, plants, animals, and diseases—forever uniting the Old World and the New. This blending of cultures is known as the "Columbian Exchange."

■ Disease

Columbus and those who followed him brought not only people to the New World but also numerous Old World diseases. "Virgin-soil" epidemics—that is, epidemics of previously unknown diseases—are invariably fierce. Although the New World may have passed syphilis to

Spain, from which it quickly spread throughout the Old World, diseases transferred from the Old World to the New were much more virulent than syphilis. Smallpox spread from Cuba to Mexico as early as 1519. It was soon followed by diphtheria, measles, trachoma, whooping cough, chickenpox, bubonic plague, malaria, typhoid fever, cholera, yellow fever, scarlet fever, amoebic dysentery, influenza, and some varieties of tuberculosis. Disease served as the silent ally of the conquerors. During critical points in the conquest of Tenochtitlán, smallpox was raging in the Aztec population. The disease later moved along traditional trade networks. An epidemic shortly before Pizarro's expedition to Peru carried off the Paca Inca and may have contributed to the unrest and civil war that worked to the advantage of the invaders.

Lacking sources, historians cannot trace accurately the movement of epidemic disease or its effect on the New World populations, yet many archaeologists and historians remain convinced that Old World diseases moved north from Mexico and ravaged and disrupted Amerindian populations in eastern North America long before the arrival of European immigrants. In most of the New World, 90 percent or more of the native population was destroyed by wave after wave of previously unknown afflictions. Explorers and colonists did not so much enter an empty land as an emptied one.

Images of the New World   A mix of fact and fiction characterized many early images of the New World. The text below this illustration claims that these natives share everything, even wives; that they are cannibals; and that they have no government. The woodcut seems to justify Spanish domination.   *(Spencer Collection, New York Public Library)*

It was at least partially because of disease that both the Spanish and the Portuguese needed to import large numbers of African slaves to work their plantations and mines. With the settlement of southeastern North America, plantation agriculture was extended to include the production of tobacco and later cotton. As a result of the needs of plantation economies and the labor shortages caused by epidemics, African slaves were brought in by the thousands, then hundreds of thousands. In the Caribbean and along the coasts of Central and South America, the Africans created an African-Caribbean or African American culture that amalgamated African, European, and American civilizations.

■ Plants and Animals

It became increasingly clear to the Spaniards that the New World had been completely isolated from the Old. The impact of Old World peoples on native populations was immediately evident to all parties. But scholars have recently argued that the importation of plants and animals had an even more profound effect than the arrival of Europeans. The changes that began in 1492 created "Neo-Europes" in what are now Canada, the United States, Mexico, Argentina, Australia, and New Zealand. The flora and fauna of the Old World, accustomed to a relatively harsh, competitive environment, found ideal conditions in the new lands. Like the rabbits that overran the Canary Islands and eventually Australia, Old World plants and animals alike multiplied, driving out many New World species.

The most important meat and dairy animals in the New World—cattle, sheep, goats, and pigs—are imports from Europe. Sailors initially brought pigs or goats aboard ship because they were easily transportable sources of protein. When let loose on the Caribbean islands, they quickly took over. The spread of horses through what is now Mexico, Brazil, Argentina, the United States, and Canada was equally dramatic. To the list of domesticated animals can be added donkeys, dogs, cats, and chickens. The changes these animals brought were profound. Cattle, pigs, and chickens quickly became staples of the New World diet. Horses enabled Amerindians and Europeans to travel across and settle on the vast plains of both North and South America.

The flora of the New World was equally changed. Even contemporaries noted how Old World plants flourished in the New. By 1555, European clover was widely distributed in Mexico—Aztecs called it "Castilian grass."

Old World in the New   The painting of "traditional" Amerindian culture shows animals brought by the Spaniards to the New World. The lives of the Amerindians were changed forever by the introduction of horses, sheep, chickens, and cows, as well as apples, peaches, wheat, and oats.   *(From Martínez Compañon, Trujillo del Peru, vol. II, plate 77. Courtesy, Harvard College Library)*

Other Old World grasses, as well as weeds such as dandelions, quickly followed. Domesticated plants including apples, peaches, and artichokes spread rapidly and naturally in the hospitable new environment. Early in the twentieth century it was estimated that only one-quarter of the grasses found on the broad prairies of the Argentine pampas were native before the arrival of Columbus. Studies of plant life in California, Australia, and New Zealand offer much the same results. The Old World also provided new and widely grown small grains such as oats, barley, and wheat.

The exchange went both ways. Crops from the New World also had an effect on the Old World. By the seventeenth century, maize (or American corn), potatoes, and sweet potatoes had significantly altered the diets of Europe and Asia. It was the addition of maize and potatoes that supported the dramatic population growth that invigorated Italy, Ireland, and Scandinavia. With the addition of the tomato in the nineteenth century, much of the modern European diet became dependent on New World foods. The new plants and new animals, as well as the social and political changes initiated by the Europeans, pulled the Old World and the New more closely together.

■ Culture

One reason for the accommodation between the Old World and the New was that the Europeans and Amerindians tended to interpret conquest and cultural transformation in the same way. The peoples living in the Valley of Mexico believed that their conquest was fated by the gods and that their new masters would bring in new gods. The Spaniards' beliefs were strikingly similar, based on the revelation of divine will and the omnipotence of the Christian God. Cortés, by whitewashing former Aztec temples and converting native priests into white-clad Christian priests, was in a way fulfilling the Aztecs' expectations about their conqueror.

Acculturation was also facilitated by the Spanish tendency to place churches and shrines at the sites of former Aztec temples. The shrine of the Virgin of Guadalupe° (on the northern edge of modern Mexico City), for example, was located on the site of the temple of the goddess Tonantzin°, an Aztec fertility-goddess of childbirth and midwives. The shrine of Guadalupe is a perfect example of the complex mixture of culture. The shrine initially appealed to *creoles*—people of mixed Spanish and Mexican descent. In the seventeenth century and after, it came to symbolize the connection of poor Mexicans to Christianity and was a religious rallying point for resisting state injustices.

The colonists tended to view their domination of the New World as a divine vindication of their own culture and civilization. During the sixteenth century, they set about remaking the world they had found. In the century after the conquest of Mexico, Spaniards founded 190

Guadalupe (gwa-da-LOO-peh)   **Tonantzin** (to-NAN-tzin)

new cities in the Americas. Lima, Bogotá, and many others were proudly modeled on and compared with the cities of Spain. In 1573 King Philip II (r. 1556–1598) established ordinances requiring all new cities to be laid out on a uniform grid with a main plaza, market, and religious center. The new cities became hubs of social and political life in the colonies. In these cities, religious orders founded colleges for basic education much like the universities they had organized in the Old World. And by midcentury, the Crown had authorized the first universities in the New World. The universities of Mexico City and Lima mirrored the great Spanish university of Salamanca. Colonists attempted to re-create in all essentials the society of Spain.

The experience of the Spanish and the Portuguese in the sixteenth century seemed confirmed by the later experiences of the French and English in the seventeenth century. In seventeenth-century New England, the English Puritan John Winthrop concluded, "For the natives, they are nearly all dead of smallpox, so as the Lord hath cleared our title to what we possess."[6] A seventeenth-century French observer came to a similar conclusion: "Touching these savages, there is a thing that I cannot omit to remark to you, it is that it appears visibly that God wishes that they yield their place to new peoples."[7] Political philosophers believed that, in the absence of evidence that the indigenous people were improving the land, the rights to that land passed to those who would make the best use of it. Thus, colonists believed that they had divine and legal sanction to take and to remake these new lands in a European image.

SUMMARY

A S we have seen, there was never a time when Europeans were unaware of or unconcerned about the outside world. Yet the expansion begun by the Portuguese along the coast of Africa and then on to India began a fateful expansion of European economic, political, and cultural influence. For the Portuguese and later for the Spanish, the voyages were almost never adventures of discovery. By rumor and careful reading, they had ideas about what they would find. Nonetheless, they were faced with challenges that led them to adapt their Mediterranean and European ways of organization. The Portuguese developed a trading-post system to control trade in Asia. In the New World, the Spanish developed a system of law and administration that transformed the world they had found. Further, the Euopeans developed a system of plantation slavery that spread throughout the New World.

The expansion of Europe was not the movement of highly developed commercial economies into underdeveloped areas. In Asia, the Portuguese and later the Dutch and English were a military presence long before they were an economic one. In the New World, even as the Spanish conquered people and changed their language, government, and religion, many aspects of Amerindian culture survived in the local Indian municipalities.

Modern historians considering decolonization, economic revolutions in many parts of Asia, and multiculturalism have been changing their thinking about European expansion in the fifteenth century. They have made us very aware of what was lost during the violent and tragic conquests that were part of the European expansions. It is impossible to say whether the economic and technical benefits of the amalgamation of the Old World and the New outweigh the costs.

The economic, political, and cultural changes brought about by the conquest created a hybrid culture. But even those who celebrate the transformation of the New World would probably agree with the conclusions of a Native American in the Pacific Northwest: "I am not sorry the missionaries came. But I wish they had known how to let their news change people's lives from the inside, without imposing their culture over our ways."[8] Tolerance, however, was not yet a hallmark of Western societies. Europeans were incapable of allowing others to change "from the inside." The inability to understand and tolerate others was to be a key to the strife created by the other great event of the sixteenth century, the movement to reform church and society.

■ Notes

1. Quoted in William D. Phillips, Jr., and Carla Rahn Phillips, *The Worlds of Christopher Columbus* (Cambridge: Cambridge University Press, 1992), p. 163.
2. Quoted ibid., p. 166.
3. Quoted in J. H. Parry, ed., *The European Reconnaissance: Selected Documents* (New York: Harper & Row, 1968), p. 242.
4. Quoted in Alfred W. Crosby, *Ecological Imperialism: The Biological Expansion of Europe, 900–1900* (Cambridge: Cambridge University Press, 1986), p. 125.
5. Quoted in Mark A. Burkholder and Lyman L. Johnson, *Colonial Latin America* (Oxford: Oxford University Press, 1990), p. 29.
6. Quoted in Crosby, p. 208.
7. Quoted ibid., p. 215.
8. Quoted in Maria Parker Pascua, "Ozette: A Makah Village in 1491," *National Geographic* (October 1991), p. 53.

■ Suggested Reading

Bethell, Leslie, ed., *The Cambridge History of Latin America.* Vol. 1. 1984. A standard work with excellent discussions of preconquest America and colonial life.

Burkholder, Mark A., and Lyman L. Johnson. *Colonial Latin America.* 1990. A thorough introduction to the conquest and colonization of Central and South America by the Spanish and Portuguese.

Clendinnen, Inga. *Aztecs: An Interpretation.* 1991. A dramatic, beautifully written essay on the Aztecs that shows how daily life, religion, and imperialism were linked.

Crosby, A. W. *Ecological Imperialism: The Biological Expansion of Europe, 900–1900.* 1986. A discussion of how migrating peoples carried plants, animals, and diseases; includes excellent maps and illustrations.

Curtin, P. *The Tropical Atlantic in the Age of the Slave Trade.* 1991. An introductory pamphlet that is an excellent first work for students interested in the history of slavery and the movement of peoples from Africa to the New World.

Elliott, John H. *The Old World and the New, 1492–1650.* 1970. These outstanding essays consider the reciprocal relations between the colonies and the kingdoms of Spain.

Phillips, J. R. S. *The Medieval Expansion of Europe.* 1988. The best survey of European interest in and knowledge of the world beyond Christendom; especially good on European travelers to the East in the thirteenth century.

Phillips, W. D., Jr., and C. R. Phillips. *The Worlds of Christopher Columbus.* 1992. Though written for a popular audience, this is an excellent survey of Columbus and his voyages and an up-to-date summary of recent work on Columbus, maritime technology, and Spanish colonial interests.

Scammell, Geoffrey. *The First Imperial Age: European Overseas Expansion, 1400–1715.* 1989. As the title implies, this is an introductory survey of European colonial interests through the early eighteenth century, with the Spanish and Portuguese explorations discussed in the context of later French and English experiences.

Subrahmanyam, S. *The Portuguese Empire in Asia, 1500–1700: A Political and Economic History.* 1993. A thoughtful introduction to Portuguese expansion by a renowned Indian economic historian.

 For a searchable list of additional readings for this chapter, go to http://college.hmco.com.

The Ships of Exploration

Historians are quite certain that Columbus sailed to the New World in three ships—two caravels and a nao. But what is a caravel? And how does it differ from a nao? We generally assume that caravels are smaller and more maneuverable, but how can we know? The short answer is we cannot know for sure; we are not quite certain what these words mean. And, of course, this leads to a larger problem. How can we visualize objects described in our sources? If we cannot truly understand naval technology, how can we evaluate its impact on the exploration of the New World or on the dominion over the seas by European navies? Unless we can see what they were describing, we are limited to our imaginations.

An important source is surviving examples of early modern ships. Historians can examine ships preserved and displayed in museums throughout Europe to evaluate changes in construction and rigging (the arrangement of sails) and to date the important innovations that led to the creation of the great European sailing ships. The most famous may be the *Mary Rose*, a Tudor warship salvaged in 1982 from the waters off Portsmouth, England, through the financial patronage of Charles, Prince of Wales. The most dramatic is doubtless the *Vasa*, a brilliantly preserved Swedish warship that sank as it left Stockholm on its maiden voyage early in the seventeenth century.

But the least pretentious and yet undoubtedly the most important is the Mataro model—the earliest known example of naval technology by perhaps 150 years. In the second half of the fifteenth century, this model was hung as a votive offering in the church of Saint Simon de Mataro near Barcelona, Spain. It was common for people to leave votive offerings in shrines, churches, and chapels. The sick and injured often left realistic wax images of their afflicted body parts after they had recovered. Sometime after 1450, a shipwright or a sailor made this model, apparently of a specific ship, which was then hung in the church, probably in thanks for the completion of a difficult voyage. It was not the building but the survival and rediscovery of the model that are unusual. In 1929, the model was deposited and eventually given to the Prince Henrik Museum in Rotterdam, where it can still be seen today.

Since the offering was for the safety of a specific ship, it seems likely that the builder made the model as

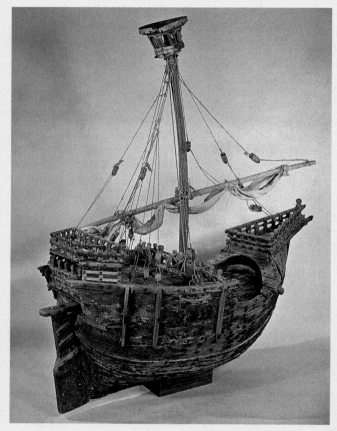

Mataro Model Ship, Fifteenth Century
(Maritiem Museum, Rotterdam)

exact as possible. This is extremely important since we have no blueprints, no complete written descriptions, or any other archaeological remains from this critical period just before Columbus sailed. The few artists who did include ships in their works were not sailors and so did not include the details that would allow us to understand how ships were built. In this respect the model is quite different. It is just over 4 feet long and just under 2 feet wide, which would correspond to a ship about 80 feet by 33 feet. What can we learn about ships and naval technology from this model?

The line drawing shown at right, based on the Mataro model, shows how the boat's hull was attached to its

**The Construction of a Fifteenth-Century
Ship's Hull** *(S. F. Manning)*

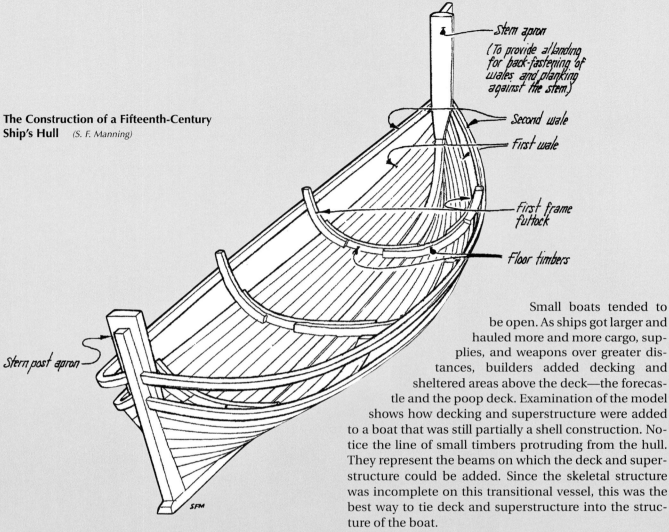

Stem apron
(To provide a landing
for back-fastening of
wales and planking
against the stem.)

Second wale

First wale

First frame
futtock

Floor timbers

Stern post apron

SFM

Small boats tended to be open. As ships got larger and hauled more and more cargo, supplies, and weapons over greater distances, builders added decking and sheltered areas above the deck—the forecastle and the poop deck. Examination of the model shows how decking and superstructure were added to a boat that was still partially a shell construction. Notice the line of small timbers protruding from the hull. They represent the beams on which the deck and superstructure could be added. Since the skeletal structure was incomplete on this transitional vessel, this was the best way to tie deck and superstructure into the structure of the boat.

The Mataro ship model cannot, however, answer all historians' questions. It is critical to know how many masts and what sorts of sails powered the ship. When the model was discovered in the 1920s, it had three crude masts made from twigs with the bark still on them. These had clearly been added at a later date. The model initially had at least two masts, but we cannot tell whether they carried only lateen sails (which made Mediterranean boats highly maneuverable) or the much more efficient combination of square sails with a single small lateen. Large lateen sails could not be handled by a small crew and were virtually unmanageable in heavy weather. It would have been useful to know what our model builder understood about sails and rigging in the mid-fifteenth century. Yet the careful study of the Mataro model and the continued search for other archaeological remains may reveal more fully what contemporaries had in mind when they tell us that Columbus sailed with a nao and two caravels.

frame. This seemingly simple task documents a critically important change in construction. Small boats can be constructed by tying the exterior shell together and then fitting interior supports to the inside. This is still the most efficient way to make small boats. But shell-building does not work for large ships. We know that by sometime in the sixteenth century, builders no longer used shell-building techniques. Construction of large ships began with a skeleton or frame to which the shell was added. Such ships could be larger, could hold more cargo, and, most significantly, could carry heavy deck guns. Size and firepower were critical to European naval power. The Mataro model indicates an early move toward the newer style of construction. As the drawing suggests, in the middle of the fifteenth century, construction began with a partial skeleton, a keel at the bottom with several ribs toward the midsection. The shell was then tied to the frame and finally extra supports were added.

CHAPTER 14

The Age of the Reformation

POPE Clement VII's coronation of Charles V as emperor of the Holy Roman Empire on February 24, 1530, shown here, added a significant dimension to Charles's formidable stature. Charles grips a sword and an orb, symbols of the political and military power he already holds. The crown, to Charles's mind, carried a different authority. It represented a claim to world monarchy, a pre-eminence in the Christian world. The scene was meant to convey something of this global grandeur. Clement's cardinals and other church officials are seated around the carefully constructed dais. Charles's courtiers and flag-bearers are farther in the background. The ceremony took place in San Petronio, a church remodeled during the Renaissance to recall the architecture of the Roman Empire.

The whole ceremony was meant to underline the unity of Christendom under the authority of pope and emperor. Yet by 1556, less than thirty years after the crowning, just the opposite had occurred. Because of religious upheaval throughout Europe and political and military crises in Germany, Charles's empire had disintegrated into a collection of German states. Charles would be the last Holy Roman emperor to be crowned by a pope.

The crisis began with a challenge to the religious authority of the papacy. Debates over the power and authority of the church that raged during this period, however, did not occur in a political vacuum. Support for the old church was an issue of state that profoundly affected the exercise of political authority in the Holy Roman Empire. In England and Scandinavia, in contrast, monarchs viewed the church as a threat to strong royal government, and reformers soon found themselves with royal patrons. Elsewhere, especially in eastern Europe, no strong central governments existed to enforce religious unity, and so a variety of Christian traditions coexisted.

The Reformation Movements, ca. 1517–1545

The Empire of Charles V (r. 1519–1556)

The English Reformation, 1520–1603

France, Scandinavia, and Eastern Europe, 1523–1560

The Late Reformation, ca. 1545–1600

The coronation of Charles V in Bologna.
(Scala/Art Resource, NY)

By the second half of the sixteenth century political and religious authorities concentrated their energies on a process of theological definition and institutionalization that led to the formation of the major Christian religious denominations we know today. They created Roman Catholic, Anglican, and Lutheran Churches as clearly defined confessions, with formally prescribed religious beliefs and practices.

An important aspect of the reform movement was the emphasis on individual belief and religious participation. Far from freeing the individual, however, the Christian churches of the late sixteenth century all emphasized correct doctrine and orderliness in personal behavior. Although early Protestants rejected a system that they accused of oppressing the individual, the institutions that replaced the old church developed their own traditions of control. The increased moral control held by churches accompanied and even fostered the expansion of state power that would characterize the late sixteenth and seventeenth centuries.

QUESTIONS TO CONSIDER

- **Why did the reformers seek to establish entirely new churches outside the Roman Catholic Church?**
- **What political factors limited Charles V's ability to respond to the religious crisis?**
- **What principal Protestant traditions emerged during the sixteenth century, and how did they differ from the Roman Catholic Church?**
- **What were the guiding principles of Catholic reform?**
- **How did social and political interests affect the Reformation?**

TERMS TO KNOW

Charles V	Anabaptists
Martin Luther	Act of Supremacy (1534)
justification by faith	Ignatius Loyola
sola scriptura	*Index of Prohibited Books*
Augsburg Confession	Council of Trent
John Calvin	

THE REFORMATION MOVEMENTS, CA. 1517–1545

 N 1517 Martin Luther, a little-known professor of theology in eastern Germany, launched a protest against practices in the late medieval church. Luther's criticisms struck a responsive chord with many of his contemporaries and led to calls for reform across much of Europe. All the reformers, even the most radical, shared with Luther a sense that the essential sacramental and priestly powers claimed by the late medieval church were illegitimate. These reformers initially had no intention of forming a new church; they simply wanted to return Christianity to what they believed was its earlier, purer form. Although their various protests resulted in the creation of separate and well-defined religious traditions, the differences among the reformers became clear only in the second half of the sixteenth century. Thus, it is appropriate to speak of "Reformation movements" rather than a unified Protestant Reformation.

We call the men and women who joined these new churches "Protestants," but the reformers tended to think of themselves as "evangelical reformed Christians." The word *evangelical* derived from *evangel* (literally, "good news"), the New Testament Gospel. They were evangelical in the sense that they believed that authority derived from the Word of God, the Bible. They were reformed Christians because their aim was to restore Christianity to the form they believed it exhibited in the first centuries of its existence.

■ The Late Medieval Context

Although reformers claimed religious life was in decline before the Reformation, medieval Christianity was, in fact, flourishing. Questions of an individual's salvation and personal relationship to God and to the Christian community remained at the heart of religious practice and theological speculation. Nominalist theologians, the leading thinkers of the late Middle Ages, rejected the key assumption of previous Scholastics—that moral life was circumscribed by universal ideas and generally applicable rules. In the words of William of Ockham (ca. 1285–1347), "No universal reality exists outside the mind." Truth was to be found in daily experience or in revealed Scripture, not in complex logical systems. At the heart is Ockham's method—known as "Ockham's razor"—the observation that what can be explained simply "is vainly explained by assuming more."

Nominalist theologians dismissed ponderous systems of logic, but they held on to the traditional rituals and beliefs that tied together the Christian community. They believed in a holy covenant in which God would save those Christians who, by means of the church's sacraments and through penitential acts, were partners in their own salvation. Foremost among the penitential acts was the feeding of "Christ's Poor," especially on important feast days. The pious constructed and supported hospices for travelers and hospitals for the sick. Christians went on pilgrimages to shrines such as the tomb of Saint Thomas Becket in Canterbury or the church of Saint James of Compostela in Spain. They also built small chapels, called chantry chapels, for the sake of their own souls. To moralists, work itself was in some sense a penitential and ennobling act.

The most common religious practice of the late Middle Ages was participation in religious brotherhoods. Urban brotherhoods were usually organized around a craft guild or neighborhood; rural brotherhoods were more likely to include an entire village or parish. Members vowed to attend monthly meetings, to participate in processions on feast days, and to maintain peaceful and charitable relations with fellow members. Religious brotherhoods often played a political role as well. In the south of France, for example, city governments frequently met in the chapels of the Brotherhoods of the Holy Spirit.

The most typical religious feast was that of *Corpus Christi* (the "Body of Christ"). The feast celebrated and venerated the sacrament of the mass and the ritual by which the bread offered to the laity became the actual body of Christ. Corpus Christi was popular with the church hierarchy because it emphasized the role of the priest in the central ritual of Christianity. The laity, however, equated Corpus Christi with the body of citizens who made up the civic community.

Kingdoms, provinces, and towns all venerated patron saints who, believers thought, offered protection from natural as well as political disasters. At the pinnacle

CHRONOLOGY

1513–1517	Fifth Lateran Council meets to consider reform of the Catholic Church
1517	Luther makes public his "Ninety-five Theses"
1518	Zwingli is appointed people's priest of Zurich
1520	Pope Leo X condemns Luther's teachings
1521	Luther appears at the Diet of Worms
1524–1525	Peasant revolts in Germany
1527	Imperial troops sack Rome
1530	Melanchthon composes the Augsburg Confession summarizing Lutheran belief
1534	Calvin flees from Paris
1534	Loyola founds the Society of Jesus
1535	Anabaptist community of Münster is destroyed
1536	Calvin arrives in Geneva and publishes *Institutes of the Christian Religion*
1545–1563	Council of Trent meets to reform Catholic Church
1555	Emperor Charles V accepts the Peace of Augsburg
1559	Parliament passes Elizabethan Act of Supremacy and Act of Uniformity

were royal saints such as Edward of England, Louis of France, and Olaf of Norway. Festivals in honor of the saints were major events in towns or kingdoms. The most revered saint in the late Middle Ages was the Virgin Mary, the mother of Jesus. The most popular new pilgrimage shrines in the north of Europe were dedicated to the Virgin. It was she, townsmen believed, who protected them from invasion, plague, and natural disasters. It was obviously becoming impossible to distinguish between religion and society, church and state.

Women played a prominent role in late medieval religious life. Holy women who claimed any sort of moral standing often did so because of visions or prophetic gifts such as knowledge of future events or discernment of the status of souls in Purgatory. Reputations for sanctity provided a profound moral authority. The Italian Blessed Angela of Foligno° (ca. 1248–1309) had several visions and became the object of a large circle of devoted followers. She was typical of a number of late medieval religious women who on the death of a spouse turned to religion. They tended to gather "families" around them, people whom they described as their spiritual "fathers" or "children." They offered moral counsel and boldly warned businessmen and politicians of the dangers of lying and sharp dealings. "Oh my sons, fathers, and brothers," counseled Angela, "see that you love one another . . . [and] likewise unto all people."[1]

In the late Middle Ages religious houses for women probably outnumbered those for men. For unmarried or unmarriageable (because of poverty or disabilities) daughters, convents provided an economical, safe, and controlled environment. Moralists denounced the dumping of women in convents: "They give [unmarriageable daughters] to a convent, as if they were the scum and vomit of the world," was the conclusion of Saint Bernardino of Siena (1380–1444). The general public, however, believed that well-run communities of women promoted the spiritual and physical health of the community. In a society in which women were not allowed to control their own property and, except among the nobility, lacked a visible role in political and intellectual life, a religious vocation may have had a compelling appeal. At the least, it permitted women to define their own religious and social relationships; and it offered other advantages, too. Well-to-do or aristocratic parents appreciated the fact that the traditional gift that accompanied a daughter entering a religious house was much smaller than a dowry.

Some women declined to join convents, which required vows of chastity and obedience to a Rule and close male supervision. They could be found among the many pilgrims who visited local shrines, the great churches of Rome, or even the holy city of Jerusalem. Many other women chose to live as anchoresses, or recluses, in closed cells beside churches and hospitals or in rooms in private houses. Men and women traveled from all parts of England seeking the counsel of the Blessed Julian of Norwich (d. after 1413), who lived in a tiny cell built into the wall of a parish church.

The most controversial group of religious women were the Beguines, who lived in communities without taking formal vows and often with minimal connections to the local church hierarchy. By the early fifteenth century, Beguines were suspect because clerics believed that these independent women rejected traditional religious cloistering and the moral leadership of male clergy; consequently, it was thought, they were particularly susceptible to heresy. Critics maintained that unsupervised Beguines held to what was called the "Heresy of the Free Spirit," a belief that one who had achieved spiritual perfection was no longer capable of sin. Fantastic rumors of sexual orgies, spread by fearful clerical opponents, quickly brought suspect women before local church authorities. Although some Beguines may have held such a belief in spiritual perfection, the majority certainly did not. But they were feared by an ecclesiastical hierarchy that distrusted independence.

A more conservative movement for renewal in the church was the Brothers and Sisters of the Common Life founded by the Dutchman Geert Groote° (1340–1384). A popular preacher and reformer, Groote gathered male and female followers into quasi-monastic communities at Deventer in the Low Countries. Eventually a community of Augustinian canons was added at Windesheim. Brothers and Sisters of the Common Life supported themselves as book copyists and teachers in small religious schools in the Low Countries. Members of these communities followed a strict, conservative spirituality that has come to be known as the *devotio moderna,* or "modern devotion." Although they called themselves "modern," their piety was traditional. Their ideas are encapsulated in *The Imitation of Christ,* a popular work of traditional monastic spirituality written by Thomas à Kempis (ca. 1380–1471), a canon of Windesheim. They advocated the contrary ideals of fourteenth-century religious life: broader participation by the laity and strict control by clerical authorities.

Religious life in the late medieval period was broadly based and vigorous. Theologians, lay people, and popular preachers could take heart they were furthering their own salvation and that of their neighbors. Thus the Reformation of the sixteenth century involved more than simple moral change.

■ Martin Luther and the New Theology

Martin Luther (1483–1546) eventually challenged many of the assumptions of late medieval Christians. He seemed to burst onto the scene in 1517, when he objected to the way in which papal indulgences—that is, the

Foligno (fo-LIN-yo)

Geert Groote (HIRT HROW-ta)

Cranach: The True Church and the False   This woodcut was designed to make clear the distinction between the evangelical church and the papacy. On one side Christ and his sacrifice are clearly at the center; on the other the pope and innumerable church officials are caught in the flames of Hell. *(Staatliche Kunstsammlungen Dresden)*

remission of penalties owed for sins—were being bought and sold in the bishopric of Brandenburg. Luther's father, a miner from the small town of Mansfeld, had hoped that his son would take a degree in law and become a wealthy and prestigious lawyer. Luther chose instead to enter a monastery and eventually become a priest.

Throughout his life, Martin Luther seems to have been troubled by a sense of his own sinfulness and unworthiness. According to late medieval theology, the life of a Christian was a continuing cycle of sin, confession, contrition, and penance, and the only way to achieve salvation was to have confessed all one's sins and at least begun a cycle of penance at the time of one's death. Christians lived in fear of dying suddenly, unconfessed. The purchase of indulgences, membership in penitential brotherhoods, ritualized charity, and veneration of popular saints were seen as ways to acquire merit in the eyes of God.

Luther came to believe that the church's requirement that believers achieve salvation by means of con-

fession, contrition, and penance made too great a demand on the faithful. Instead, Luther said, citing the New Testament, salvation (or justification) was God's gift to the faithful. Luther's belief is known as "justification by faith." Acts of charity were important products resulting from God's love, but in Luther's opinion, they were not necessary for salvation. Late in his life, Luther explained how he came by these ideas:

> Though I lived as a monk without reproach, I felt that I was a sinner before God with an extremely disturbed conscience. I could not believe that he was placated by my [acts of penance]. I did not love, yes, I hated the righteous God who punishes sinners. At last, by the mercy of God, I gave context to the words, namely, "In it the righteousness of God is revealed, as it is written, 'He who through faith is righteous shall live.'" There I began to understand that the righteous lives by a gift of God, namely by faith. Here I felt that I was altogether born again and had entered paradise itself through open gates.[2]

Although Luther recalled a sudden, dramatic revelation, it now seems clear that his insight developed slowly over the course of his academic career and during his defense of his teachings. Nonetheless, his recollection conveys a sense of the novelty of his theology and suggests why his attack on the late medieval church proved to be so much more devastating than the complaints of earlier critics.

Others had complained of impious priests, an unresponsive bureaucracy, and a church too much involved in matters of government, but the theology that Luther developed struck at the very doctrinal foundations of the church itself. Luther separated justification from acts of sanctification—from the good works or charity expected of all Christians. In Luther's theology, the acts of piety so typical of the medieval church were quite unnecessary for salvation because Christ's sacrifice had brought justification once and for all. Justification came entirely from God and was independent of human works. Luther argued that the Christian was at the same time sinner and saved, so the penitential cycle and careful preparation for a "good death" were, in his opinion, superfluous.

Luther also attacked the place of the priesthood in the sacramental life of the church and, by extension, the power and authority a church might claim in public life. The church taught that, through the actions of ordained priests, Christ was really present in the bread and wine of the sacrament of Holy Communion. Luther agreed that the sacrament transformed the bread and wine into the body and blood of Christ, but he denied that priests had a role in the transformation. The power of priests was symbolically implied when they distributed only the bread to the laity, reserving the consecrated wine for themselves. Priests, in Luther's view, were not mediators between God and individual Christians. John Wyclif and Jan Hus (see pages 360–361) had argued against the spiritual authority of unworthy priests. Luther, however, directly challenged the role of all clergy, and of the institutional church itself, in the attainment of salvation. Thus he argued for a "priesthood of all believers."

In the years before 1517, Luther's views on salvation and his reservations about the traditional ways of teaching theology attracted little interest outside his own university. Matters changed, however, when he questioned the sale of indulgences. Indulgences were often granted as rewards for pilgrimages, or for noteworthy acts of charity or sacrifice. The papacy frequently authorized the sale of indulgences to pay various expenses. Unscrupulous priests often left the impression that purchase of an indulgence freed a soul from Purgatory. After getting no response to his initial complaints, Luther made his "Ninety-five Theses" public. Luther probably posted his document on the door of the Wittenberg Cas-

tle church, the usual way to announce topics for theological debates. Luther's text created a firestorm when it was quickly translated and printed throughout German-speaking lands. His charges against the sale of indulgences encapsulated German feelings about unworthy priests and economic abuses by the clergy. Luther was acclaimed as the spokesman of the German people.

In a debate with a papal representative in Leipzig in 1519, Luther was forced to admit that in some of his positions he agreed with the Czech reformer Jan Hus, who had been burned at the stake as a heretic in 1415 (see page 361). In the Leipzig debate and in hearings the following year, Luther responded to his critics and tried to explain more fully the nature of the changes he advocated. Three tracts were especially important. In *Address to the Christian Nobility of the German Nation,* Luther urged the princes to reject papal claims of temporal and spiritual authority. (See the box "Reading Sources: Martin Luther's Address to the Christian Nobility of the German Nation.") In *On the Babylonian Captivity of the Church,* he argued for the principle of *sola scriptura—* that is, church authority had to be based on biblical teachings. In *On Christian Freedom,* he explained clearly his understanding of salvation: "A Christian has all he needs in faith and needs no works to justify him." Luther was speaking of spiritual freedom from unnecessary ritual, not social or political freedom. This distinction would later be crucial to Luther's opposition to political and economic protests by peasants and artisans.

In 1520 Pope Leo X (r. 1513–1521) condemned Luther's teachings and gave him sixty days to recant. Luther refused to do so and publicly burned the papal letter. In 1521 Emperor Charles V called an imperial diet, or parliament, at Worms to deal with the religious crisis. Charles demanded that Luther submit to papal authority. Luther, however, explained that religious decisions must be based on personal experience and conscience as both were informed by a study of Scripture:

> Unless I am convicted by the testimony of Scripture or by clear reason, for I do not trust either in the Pope or in councils alone, since it is well known that they have often erred and contradicted themselves, I cannot and will not retract anything, for it is neither safe nor right to go against conscience. I cannot do otherwise, here I stand, may God help me. Amen.[3]

The emperor and his allies, however, stayed firmly in the papal camp (see Map 14.1). The excommunicated Luther was placed under an imperial ban—that is, declared an outlaw. As Luther left the Diet of Worms, friendly princes took him to Wartburg Castle in Saxony, where they could protect him. During a year of isolation

⅔ R E A D I N G   S O U R C E S

Martin Luther's Address to the Christian Nobility of the German Nation

Luther wrote this tract to the rulers of Germany to explain the nature of his conflict with the church over ecclesiastical authority. In this excerpt, he outlines his disagreements with the system of clerical status and immunities that had grown throughout the Middle Ages.

The Romanists have very cleverly built three walls around themselves. In the first place, when pressed by the temporal power, they have made decrees and declared that the temporal power had no jurisdiction over them, but that on the contrary, the spiritual power is above the temporal. In the second place, when the attempt is made to reprove them with the Scriptures, they raise the objection that only the Pope may interpret the Scriptures. In the third place if threatened with a council, their story is that no one may summon a council but the Pope.

Let us begin by attacking the first wall. It is pure invention that the Pope, bishops, priests, and monks are called the spiritual estate while princes, lords, craftsmen, and peasants are the temporal estate. This is indeed a piece of deceit and hypocrisy: all Christians are truly of the spiritual estate. The Pope or bishop anoints, shaves heads, ordains, consecrates, and prescribes garb different from that of the laity, but he can never make a man into a Christian or into a spiritual man by so doing. He might well make a man into a hypocrite or a humbug and a blockhead, but never a Christian or a spiritual man. Therefore a priest in Christendom is nothing else but an office-holder. As long as he holds his office, he takes precedence; where he is deposed, he is a peasant or a townsman like anybody else.

The second wall is still more loosely built and less substantial. The Romanists want to be the only masters of Holy Scripture, although they never learn a thing from the Bible their life long. Besides, if we are all priests, and all have one faith, one gospel, one sacrament, why should we not also have the power to test and judge what is right or wrong in matters of faith?

The third wall falls of itself, when the first two are down. When the Pope acts contrary to the Scriptures, it is our duty to stand by the Scriptures and to reprove him and to constrain him, according to the word of Christ. The Romanists have no basis in Scripture for their claim that the Pope alone was right to call or to confirm a council. This is just their own ruling, and it is only valid so long as it is not harmful to Christendom or contrary to the laws of God.

Source: Martin Luther, *Three Treatises,* in *The American Edition of Luther's Works* (Philadelphia: Fortress Press, 1970), pp. 10–22.

---

at Wartburg, Luther used Erasmus's edition of the Greek New Testament as the basis of a translation into German of the New Testament, which became an influential literary as well as religious work.

■ The Reformation of the Communities

Luther challenged the authority of the clerical hierarchy and called on lay people to take responsibility for their own salvation. His ideas spread rapidly in the towns and countryside of Germany because he and his followers took advantage of the new technology of printing. (See the feature "Weighing the Evidence: A Reformation Woodcut" on pages 494–495) Perhaps 300,000 copies of his early tracts were published in the first years of the protest. Luther's claim that the Scriptures must be the basis of all life and his appeal to the judgment of the laity made sense to the men and women in towns and villages, where councils of local people were accustomed to making decisions based on ideas of the common good. It is also true that townspeople and villagers saw religious and civic life as being inextricably interconnected.

Map 14.1   Reform in Germany, 1517–1555   The pattern of religious reform in Germany was complex. Although some territorial princes, such as the dukes of Bavaria, rejected the reform, most free towns, particularly those in the southwest, adopted it.

For them, the notion of a religiously neutral act was unthinkable.

The impact of Luther's ideas quickly became evident. If the active intercession of the clergy was not necessary for the salvation of individuals, then, according to Luther's followers, there was no reason for the clergy to remain unmarried and celibate, nor for men and women to cloister themselves in monasteries and convents. Also, maintained Luther's partisans, the laity's participation in the sacrament of the Eucharist need not be restricted. Thus, the priest must distribute wine to the congregants along with the bread. With the spread of Luther's ideas came the end of a very visual part of clerical power. Because Luther's followers believed that penitential acts were not prerequisites for salvation, they tended to set aside the veneration of saints and give up pilgrimages to the shrines and holy places all over Europe.

Many historians have referred to the spread of these reform ideas as "the Reformation of the Common Man." In Strasbourg, Nuremberg, Zurich, and other towns, ideas about the primacy of the Bible and attacks on clerical privilege were spread by "people's priests." These individuals were hired by the town government to preach and teach, and to care for the souls in the community. Many of the most famous reformers initially gained a following through preaching. The message then seems to have spread especially quickly among artisan and mercantile groups, which put pressure on town governments to press for reform. Agitation was often riotous. One resident of Augsburg exposed himself during a church service to protest what he believed was an evil and idolatrous service. Women on both sides of the reform stepped out of traditional roles. They wrote tracts advocating reform; and they used shovels and rakes to defend traditional shrines.

To quell disturbances and to arrive at a consensus within their communities, cautious town councils often set up debates between reformers and church representatives. Because the church hierarchy rarely approved of such debates, traditional views were often poorly represented, giving a great advantage to the reformers. The two sides argued over the power of the church hierarchy, the nature of salvation, and whether papal authority and the seven sacraments could be verified in Scripture. At the conclusion of such debates, many town governments ordered that preaching and practice in the town should be according to the "Word of God"—a code for reformed practice. In reformed towns, the city council became a council of elders for the church. Thus, civil government came to play an important role in the local organization of the church.

The case of Zurich is instructive. In 1519 the people's priest of Zurich was Huldrych Zwingli° (1484–1531), son of a rural official from a nearby village. After a university education, he became a typical late medieval country priest, right down to his publically acknowledged mistress. Yet after experiences as a military chaplain and an acquaintance with the humanist writings of Erasmus, Zwingli began to preach strongly biblical sermons. In 1522 he defended a group of laymen who protested by breaking the required Lenten fast. Later in the same year he requested episcopal permission to marry. Early in 1523 he led a group of reformers in a public debate over the nature of the church. The city council declared in favor of the reformers, and Zurich became, in effect, a Protestant city.

Unlike Luther, Zwingli believed that reform should be a communal movement—that town governments should take the lead in bringing reform to the community. Zwingli explained that moral regeneration of individuals was an essential part of God's salvation. In the years following 1523, the reformers restructured church services, abolishing the mass. They also removed religious images from churches and suppressed monastic institutions. Zwingli further disagreed with Luther about the nature of the sacrament of Holy Communion. Whereas Luther, like Catholic theologians, accepted that Christ was truly present in the bread and wine, Zwingli argued that Christ's presence was merely spiritual—the bread and wine merely signified Christ. This disagreement created within the reform movement a division that made a common response to papal or imperial pressure difficult.

The reform message spread from towns into the countryside, but often with effects that the reformers did not expect or desire. Luther thought his message was a spiritual and theological one. Many peasants and modest artisans, however, believed Luther's message of biblical freedom carried material as well as theological meaning.

In many parts of Germany villagers and peasants found themselves under increasing pressure from landlords and territorial princes. Taking advantage of changed economic and political conditions, these lords were intent on regaining claims to ancient manorial rights, on suppressing peasant claims to use common lands, and on imposing new taxes and tithes. Like townspeople, peasants saw religious and material life as closely connected. They argued that new tithes and taxes not only upset tradition but violated the Word of God. Using Luther's argument that authority should be based on the Scriptures, peasants from the district of Zurich, for example, petitioned the town council in 1523–1524, claiming that they should not be required to pay tithes on their produce because there was no biblical justification for doing so. Townsmen rejected the peasants' demand, noting that though the Bible did not stipulate such payments, it also did not forbid them. Accordingly, the peasants should make them "out of love"—that is, because they were traditional.

Demands that landlords and magistrates give up human ordinances and follow "Godly Law" soon turned to violence. Peasants, miners, and villagers in 1524 and 1525 participated in a series of uprisings that began on the borderlands between Switzerland and Germany and spread throughout southwest Germany, upper Austria, and even into northern Italy. Bands of peasants and villagers, perhaps a total of 300,000 in the empire, revolted against their seigneurial lords or even their territorial overlords.

Luther initially counseled landlords and princes to redress the just grievances. As reports of riots and increased violence continued to reach Wittenberg, however, Luther condemned the rebels as "mad dogs" and

---

Zwingli (SVING-lee)

Peasant Freedom The German peasants believed Luther's call for individual freedom of conscience included economic and political freedom. Their revolt of 1524–1525 struck terror in the hearts of German rulers. As this woodcut indicates, the peasant army was lightly armed. Many carried only tools, pitchforks, flails, and scythes. *(Title page of an anonymous pamphlet from the Peasants' War, 1525)*

urged that they be suppressed. Territorial princes and large cities quickly raised armies to meet the threat. The peasants were defeated and destroyed in a series of battles in April 1525. It seems likely that, in response to these rebellions, lords lived in fear of another revolt and were careful not to overburden their tenants. But when it became clear that the reformers were unwilling to follow the implications of their own theology, villagers and peasants lost interest in the progress of the reform. As a townsman of Zurich commented, "Many came to a great hatred of the preachers, where before they would have bitten off their feet for the Gospel."[4]

■ John Calvin and the Reformed Tradition

The revolts of 1524 and 1525 demonstrated the mixed messages traveling under the rubric "true" or "biblical" religion. In the 1530s the theological arguments of the reformers began to take on a greater clarity, mostly because of the Franco-Swiss reformer John Calvin (1509–1564). Calvin had a humanistic education in Paris and became a lawyer before coming under the influence of reform-minded thinkers in France. In 1534 he fled from Paris as royal pressures against reformers increased. He arrived in Geneva in 1536, where he would remain, except for a short exile, until the end of his life.

Because of Geneva's central location and the power of Calvin's theology, it quickly came to rival Wittenberg as a source of Protestant thought. Reformed preachers moved easily from Geneva to France, Scotland, England, and the Low Countries carrying with them Calvin's ideas about salvation and the godly. Until the end of his life, Calvin was a magnet drawing people interested in reform.

The heart of Calvin's appeal lay in his formal theological writings. In 1536 he published the first of many editions of the *Institutes of the Christian Religion*, which was to become the summa of Reformed theology. In it Calvin laid out a doctrine of the absolute power of God and the complete depravity and powerlessness of humanity.

Like Luther, Calvin viewed salvation as a mysterious gift of God. Yet Calvin differed from Luther in a crucial aspect. Salvation was by grace, but it was part of a progressive sanctification. This was a critical difference, for Luther did not believe that human behavior could be transformed. We are, he said, "simultaneously justified and sinners." Calvin, on the other hand, believed that there could be no salvation "if we do not also live a holy life."

Calvin believed it was the church's duty to promote moral progress. Public officials were to be "vicars of God." They had the power to lead and correct both the faithful and the unregenerate sinners who lived in Christian communities. In his years in Geneva, Calvin tried to create a "Christian Commonwealth," but Geneva was far from a theocracy. Calvin's initial attempts to create a Christian community by requiring public confession and allowing church leaders to discipline sinners were rejected by Geneva's city council, which exiled Calvin in 1538.

On his return in 1541 he sought to institute church reforms modeled on those he had observed in the Protestant city of Strasbourg. Calvin's Reformed church hierarchy was made up of four offices: preachers, teachers, deacons, and elders. Preachers and teachers saw to the care and education of the faithful. Deacons, as in the early church, were charged with attending to the material needs of the congregation. The elders—the true leaders of the Genevan church—were selected from the patriciate who dominated the civil government of the city. Thus, it makes as much sense to speak of a church governed by the town as a town dominated by the church. The elders actively intervened in education, charity, and attempts to regulate prostitution. Consistories, or church courts, made up of community elders who enforced community moral and religious values, became one of the most important characteristics of Reformed (Calvinist) communities.

Calvin had suggested the elect would benefit from "signs of divine benevolence," an idea that would have a profound impact on the Calvinist understanding of the relationship of wealth to spiritual life. Calvin believed that good works and a well-ordered society were the result of God's grace. By the seventeenth century, many followers of Calvin in Europe's commercial centers believed that the elect had a duty to work in the secular world and that wealth accumulated in business was a sign of God's favor. It was an idea nicely adapted to the increasingly wealthy world of early modern Europe.

That connection between salvation and material life, however, lay in the future. The aspect of election that most interested Calvin was the creation of a truly Christian community by the elect. To accomplish this, Reformed churches, that is, those who took their lead from Zwingli and Calvin, purged their churches of any manifestation of "superstition." Like Zwinglians, they rejected the idea that Christ was really present in the sacrament of Holy Communion. They rejected the role of saints. They removed from their churches and destroyed paintings and statuary that they believed were indications of idolatry.

Iconoclasm   Calvinists believed that Christians had to live in communities in which "true religion" was practiced. Iconoclasts (image smashers) cleansed churches of all paintings and statuary that might lead people back to the worship of idols—that is, the medieval cult of saints. This illustration shows just how organized iconoclasm really was.   *(The Fotomas Index, U.K.)*

Reformed churchmen reacted promptly and harshly to events that seemed to threaten either church or state. The most famous episode involved the capture, trial, and execution of Michael Servetus (1511–1553), a Spanish physician and radical theologian who rejected traditional doctrines such as the Trinity and specifically criticized many of Calvin's teachings in the *Institutes*. After corresponding with Servetus for a time, Calvin remarked that if Servetus were in Geneva, "I would not suffer him to get out alive." After living in various parts of Europe, Servetus eventually did come anonymously to Geneva. He was recognized and arrested. Calvin was as good as his word. After a public debate and trial, Servetus was burned at the stake for blaspheming the Trinity and the Christian religion. Calvin's condemnation of Servetus was all too typical of Christians in the sixteenth century. Lutherans, Calvinists, and Catholics all believed that protection of true religion required harsh measures against the ignorant, the immoral, and the unorthodox. All too few would have said, as the humanist reformer Sebastion Castellio did, "To burn a heretic is not to defend a doctrine, but to burn a man."[5]

■ The Radical Reform of the Anabaptists

Michael Servetus was but one of a number of extremists who claimed to be carrying out the full reform implied in the teachings of Luther, Zwingli, and Calvin. Called "Anabaptists" (or "rebaptizers" because of their rejection of infant baptism), or simply "radicals," they tended to take biblical commands more literally than the mainline reformers. They believed that baptism should happen only after confession of sin. They believed that Christians should live apart in communities of the truly redeemed. Thus they refused to take civil oaths or hold public office, for to do so would be to compromise with unreformed civil society.

The earliest of the radicals allied themselves with the rebels of 1525. Thomas Müntzer (1490–1525) was an influential preacher who believed in divine revelation through visions and dreams. His visions told him that the poor were the true elect and that the end of the world was at hand. An active participant in the uprisings of 1525, Müntzer called on the elect to drive out the ungodly. After the defeat of the rebels, he was captured and executed by the German princes.

Other radicals, such as the revolutionaries who took control of the north German city of Münster, rejected infant baptism, adopted polygamy, and proclaimed a new "Kingdom of Righteousness." The reformers of Münster instituted the new kingdom in the city by rebaptizing those who joined their cause and expelling those who opposed them. They abolished private property rights in Münster and instituted new laws concerning morality and behavior. Leadership in the city eventually passed to a tailor, Jan of Leiden (d. 1535), who proclaimed himself the new messiah and lord of the world. The Anabaptists were opposed by the prince-bishop of Münster, the political and religious lord of the city. After a sixteen-month siege, the bishop and his allies recaptured the city in 1535. Besieging forces massacred men, women, and children. Jan of Leiden was captured and executed by mutilation with red-hot tongs.

With the destruction of the Münster revolutionaries in 1535, the Anabaptist movement turned inward. Under leaders such as Menno Simons (1495–1561), who founded the Mennonites, and Jakob Hutter (d. 1536), who founded the Hutterian Brethren, they rejected their predecessors' violent attempts to establish truly holy cities. To varying degrees they also rejected connections with civil society, military service, even civil courts. They did, however, believe that their own communities were exclusively of the elect. They tended to close themselves off from outsiders and enforce a strict discipline over their members. The elders of these communities were empowered to excommunicate or "shun" those who violated the group's precepts. Anabaptist communities have proved unusually durable. Hutterian and Mennonite communities continue to exist in western Europe, North America, and parts of the former Soviet Union.

Like Luther, all of the early reformers appealed to the authority of the Bible in their attacks on church tradition. Yet in the villages and towns of Germany and Switzerland, many radicals were prepared to move far beyond the positions Luther had advocated. When they did so, Luther found himself in the odd position of appealing for vigorous action by the very imperial authorities whose previous inaction had allowed his own protest to survive.

THE EMPIRE OF CHARLES V (R. 1519–1556)

 UTHER believed that secular authorities should be neutral in religious matters. In his eyes, the success of the early Reformation was simply God's will:

I simply taught, preached and wrote God's Word; otherwise I did nothing. And while I slept or drank Wittenberg beer with my friends, the Word so greatly

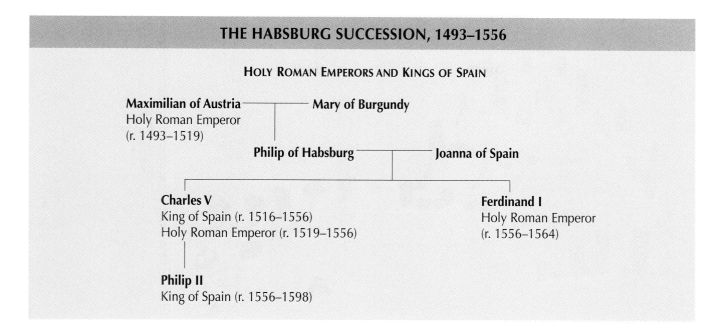

THE HABSBURG SUCCESSION, 1493–1556

HOLY ROMAN EMPERORS AND KINGS OF SPAIN

Maximilian of Austria — Mary of Burgundy
Holy Roman Emperor
(r. 1493–1519)

Philip of Habsburg — Joanna of Spain

Charles V
King of Spain (r. 1516–1556)
Holy Roman Emperor (r. 1519–1556)

Ferdinand I
Holy Roman Emperor
(r. 1556–1564)

Philip II
King of Spain (r. 1556–1598)

weakened the Papacy that no prince or emperor ever inflicted such losses on it.[6]

Luther's belief in the word of God was absolute, yet he must have known even as he drank his beer, that the Holy Roman emperor could have crushed the reform movements if he had been able to enforce imperial decrees. But attempts to resolve religious conflict became entangled with attempts to hold together the family lands of the Habsburg emperor and with political rivalries among the various German princes. The eventual religious settlement required a constitutional compromise that preserved the virtual autonomy of the great princes of Germany. Charles had dreamed of using his imperial office to restore and maintain the political and religious unity of Europe. The political realities of sixteenth-century Europe, however, made nobles afraid of the emperor even when he tried to preserve the unity of the church.

■ Imperial Challenges

Emperor Charles V (r. 1519–1556) was the beneficiary of a series of marriages that, in the words of his courtiers, seemed to re-create the empire of Charlemagne (see Map 15.1, page 506). From his father, Philip of Habsburg, he inherited claims to Austria, the imperial crown, and Burgundian lands that included the Low Countries and the county of Burgundy. Through his mother, Joanna,

the daughter of Ferdinand and Isabella of Spain, Charles became heir to the kingdoms of Castile, Aragon, Sicily, Naples, and Spanish America. During the Italian wars of the early sixteenth century, Charles's holdings in Italy expanded to include the duchy of Milan and most of the rest of Lombardy. By 1506 he was duke in the Burgundian lands; in 1516 he became king of Aragon and Castile; and in 1519 he was elected Holy Roman emperor. Every government in Europe had to deal with one part or another of Charles's empire. His chancellor enthused, "[God] has set you on the way towards a world monarchy, towards the gathering of all Christendom under a single shepherd."

Charles seems to have sincerely desired such a world monarchy, but he faced challenges in each of the areas under his control. In Castile, for example, grandees, townsmen, and peasants felt they had grounds for complaint. They objected that taxes were too heavy and that Charles disregarded the *cortes* and his natural advisers, the old nobility. But most of all they complained that too many of his officials were foreigners whom he had brought with him from his home in Flanders. Protests festered in the towns and villages of Castile and finally broke out into a revolt called the *Comunero* (townsmen's or citizens') movement. Between 1517 and 1522, when religious reform was making dramatic advances in Germany, many of the most important towns of Spain were in open rebellion against the Crown. Charles's forces eventually took control of the situation,

The Capture of Belgrade, 1521 During the sixteenth century Ottoman Turks dominated the Balkans militarily and were a significant force in European diplomacy. They were masters of coordinated attacks combining artillery and infantry. *(Österreichische Nationalbibliothek)*

and by 1522 he had crushed the Comuneros. But in the critical years between 1522 and 1530, he was careful to spend much of his time in his Spanish kingdoms.

Charles's claims in Italy, as well as in the Pyrenees and the Low Countries, brought him into direct conflict with the Valois kings of France. Again in the critical 1520s, the Habsburgs and the Valois fought a series of wars (see page 370). Charles dramatically defeated the French at Pavia in northern Italy in 1525, sacked and occupied Rome in 1527, and became the virtual arbiter of Italian politics. The volatile situation in Italy made for cynical alliances. In the course of the struggle, the Catholic Francis I of France, whose title was "the Most Christian king," found it to his advantage to ally himself with Charles's most serious opponents, the Protestants and the Turks. Francis demonstrated the truth of Machiavelli's dictum that private virtues play a small role in political and diplomatic life. The Habsburg-Valois Wars dragged on until, in exhaustion, the French king Henry II (r. 1547–1559) and the Spanish king Philip II (r. 1556–

1598) signed the Treaty of Cateau-Cambrésis in 1559 (see page 370).

Charles was not the only ruler to claim the title "emperor" and a succession reaching back to the Roman Empire. After the conquest of Constantinople in 1453, the sultan of the Ottoman Turks began to refer to himself as "the Emperor." After consolidating control of Constantinople and the Balkans, Turkish armies under the command of Emperor Suleiman (r. 1520–1566), known as "the Magnificent," resumed their expansion to the north and west. After capturing Belgrade, Turkish forces soundly defeated a Hungarian army at the Battle of Mohács in 1526. Charles appealed for unity within Christendom against the threat. Even Martin Luther agreed that Christians should unite during invasion.

Suleiman's army besieged Vienna in 1529 before being forced to retreat. Turks also deployed a navy in the Mediterranean and, with French encouragement, began a series of raids along the coasts of Italy and Spain. The Turkish fleet remained a threat throughout the sixteenth

⊕ GLOBAL ENCOUNTERS

Duels Among Europeans and Turks

A Flemish diplomat in the service of Ferdinand I of Austria (who became Emperor Ferdinand I after the abdication of Charles V), Augier Ghislain De Busbecq (1522–1592) was twice sent to Constantinople as ambassador. Understanding the Turks and their interests was critical for the Germans as attacks by the Turks in eastern Europe prevented the empire from either suppressing the German Protestants or pressing German claims against the French. The following selection is part of a letter written from Constantinople in 1560. In it, Busbecq discusses violence among the Turks and contrasts it with Europeans' behavior.

The mention I made a while ago of matters in the confines of Hungary, gives me occasion to tell you, what the Turks think of duels, which among Christians are accounted a singular badge of personal valor. There was one Arstambey, a sanjack [district official], who lived on the frontier of Hungary, who was very much famed as a robust person [Arsta signifies a lion in Turkey]. He was an expert with the bow; no man brandished his sword with more strength; none was more terrible to his enemy. Not far from his district there also dwelt one Ulybey, also a sanjack, who was jealous of the same praise. And this jealousy (initiated perhaps by other occasions) at length occasioned hatred and many bloody combats between them. It happened thus, Ulybey was sent for to Constantinople, upon what occasion I know not. When he arrived there, the Pashas [governors] had asked many questions of him in the Divan [court] concerning other matters. At last they demanded how it was that he and Arstambey came to fall out? To put his own cause in the best light, he said that once Arstambey had laid an ambush and wounded him treacherously. Which he said, Arstambey need not have done, if he would have shown himself wor-

thy of the name he bears because Ulybey often challenged him to fight hand to hand and never refused to meet him on the field. The Pashas, taking great offense, replied, "How dare you challenge a fellow soldier to a duel? What? Was there no Christian to fight with? Do both of you eat your emperor's bread? And yet, you attempt to take one another's life? What precedent did you have for this? Don't you know that whichever of you had died, the emperor would have lost a subject?" Whereupon, by their command, he was carried off to prison where he lay pining for many months. And at last, with difficulty, he was released, but with the loss of his reputation.

It is quite different among us Christians. Our people will draw their swords many times against each other before they ever come in sight of a public enemy, and unfortunately, they count it a brave and honorable thing to do. What should one do in such a case? Vice has usurped the seat of virtue and that which is worthy of punishment is counted noble and glorious.

Source: The Four Epistles of A. G. Busbequius Concerning His Embassy to Turkey (London: J. Taylor & J. Wyat, 1694), pp. 196–198.

---

century. The reign of Suleiman marked the permanent entry of Turkey into the European military and diplomatic system. Turkish pressure was yet another reason why Charles was unable to deal with German Protestants in a direct and uncompromising way. (See the box "Global Encounters: Duels Among Europeans and Turks.")

■ German Politics

The political configuration of Germany had an ongoing influence on the course of the religious reform. In 1500 Germany was much less centralized than France or England. Since 1495 seven electoral princes (three archbishops and four lay princes) and a larger circle of

476

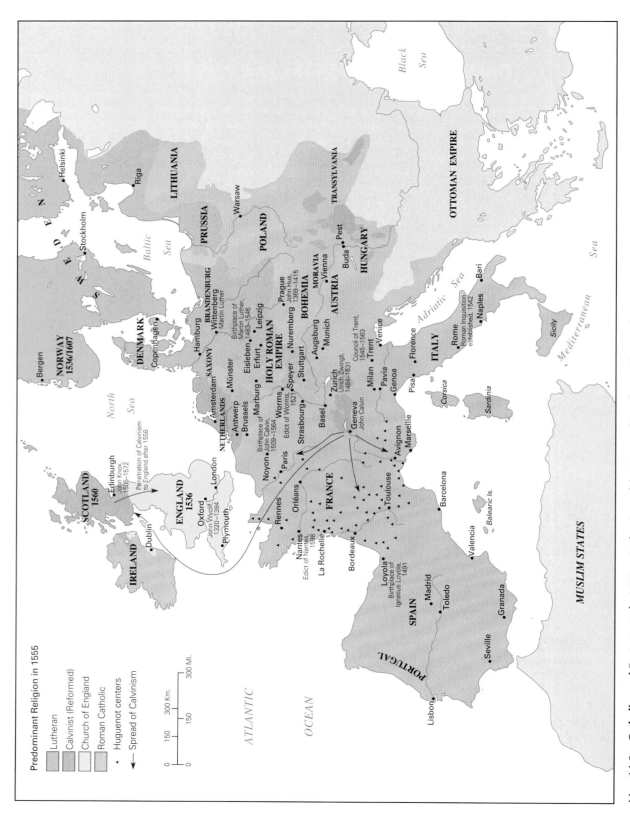

Map 14.2 Catholics and Protestants in 1555 At the time of the Peace of Augsburg, Christendom in western Europe was divided into three major groups. Lutheran influence was largely confined to parts of Germany and Scandinavia, while Calvinist influence was strong in Switzerland, Scotland, the Low Countries, and parts of France. Most of the West, however, remained within the Roman Catholic Church.

Predominant Religion in 1555

- Lutheran
- Calvinist (Reformed)
- Church of England
- Roman Catholic
- ▴ Huguenot centers
- → Spread of Calvinism

0   150   300 Km.
0   150   300 Mi.

NORWAY
1536/1607

DENMARK

SCOTLAND
1560
Edinburgh
John Knox,
1505–1572
Penetration of Calvinism
to England after 1558

ENGLAND
1536
Oxford
John Wyclif,
1320–1384
Plymouth
London

IRELAND
Dublin

Bergen
Bergen

Stockholm

Helsinki

Riga

LITHUANIA

Warsaw

PRUSSIA

POLAND

BRANDENBURG
Wittenberg
Martin Luther
Birthplace of
Martin Luther,
Eisleben, 1483–1546

Hamburg

Copenhagen

SAXONY
Münster

NETHERLANDS
Amsterdam
Antwerp
Brussels

Erfurt
Leipzig

HOLY ROMAN
EMPIRE

Birthplace of Marburg
John Calvin,
1509–1564
Worms
Noyon
Paris
Edict of Worms,
1521

Prague
John Hus,
1369–1415

BOHEMIA

MORAVIA

Nuremberg
Speyer
Stuttgart
Augsburg
Munich

Vienna

AUSTRIA

Council of Trent,
1545–1563

Buda
Pest

HUNGARY

TRANSYLVANIA

OTTOMAN EMPIRE

Strasbourg
Basel

Zurich
Ulrich Zwingli,
1484–1531
Geneva
John Calvin

Milan
Pavia
Genoa

Trent
Venice

Florence
Pisa

ITALY
Rome
Roman Inquisition
established, 1542

Naples
Bari

Sicily

Avignon
Marseille

FRANCE

Rennes
Orléans

Nantes
Edict of Nantes,
1598
La Rochelle

Toulouse

Bordeaux

Loyola
Birthplace of
Ignatius Loyola,
1491

Barcelona

Valencia

Balearic Is.

Corsica

Sardinia

SPAIN
Madrid
Toledo

Seville

Granada

PORTUGAL

Lisbon

MUSLIM STATES

ATLANTIC

OCEAN

North
Sea

Baltic
Sea

Black
Sea

Adriatic
Sea

Mediterranean
Sea

imperial princes had claimed the right to representation in the imperial council, and nearly three hundred other towns or principalities demanded various exemptions from imperial control. The emperor's claims in most areas amounted to the right to collect modest taxes on households and individuals, a court of high justice, and the authority to proclaim imperial truces. Yet the empire lacked a unified legal system, and the emperor himself had only one vote on the imperial council. In many respects political centralization and innovation were characteristics of individual territories, not of the empire as a whole. The power of the emperor depended on his relations with the towns and princes of Germany.

In the first years after Luther issued his Ninety-five Theses, he was defended by the elector Frederick of Saxony, who held a key vote in Charles's quest for election as Holy Roman emperor. As long as Frederick protected Luther, imperial officials had to proceed against the reformer with caution. When Luther was outlawed by the imperial Diet of Worms in 1521, Frederick and many other princes and towns refused to enforce the edict against him and his followers unless their own grievances with the emperor and their complaints about the church were taken up at the same time. At the Diet of Speyer in 1526, delegates passed a resolution empowering princes and towns to settle religious matters in their territories as they saw fit. In effect, this resolution legitimated the reform in territories where authorities chose to follow the new teachings and presaged the final religious settlement in Germany.

German princes took advantage of the emperor's relative powerlessness and made choices reflecting a complex of religious, political, and diplomatic issues. Electoral Saxony and ducal Saxony, the two parts of the province of Saxony, split over the issue of reform. Electoral Saxony, Luther's homeland, was Lutheran. Ducal Saxony was strongly Catholic. Especially in the autonomous towns, many decisions about religion were often made with one eye on the choices made by neighbors and competitors.

Some rulers acted in ways that were even more consciously cynical and self-serving. The Grand Master of the religious order of the Teutonic Knights, Albrecht von Hohenzollern (1490–1568), who controlled the duchy of Prussia, renounced his monastic vows. Then, at the urging of Luther and other reformers, he secularized the order's estates (that is, he transferred them from church to private ownership), which then became East Prussia, hereditary lands of the Hohenzollern family. In other territories, rulers managed to claim the properties of suppressed religious orders. Even when, as in the case of

Count Philip of Hesse (1504–1567), much of the revenue from secularization was used to create hospitals and an organized system of charity, the reforming prince was still enriched.

Some rulers found their personal reservations about Luther reinforced by their fears of popular unrest. Luther's call for decisions based on personal conscience seemed to the dukes of Bavaria, for example, to repudiate princely authority and even to provoke anarchy. In the confused and fluid situation of the 1520s and 1530s, imperial interests were never the primary issue.

■ The Religious Settlement

With the fading of the Turkish threat on Vienna in 1529, Charles V renewed his pressure on the German principalities at a meeting of the imperial diet at Augsburg in 1530. It was for this diet that Philip Melanchthon (1497–1560), Luther's closest adviser, prepared the Augsburg Confession, which would become the basic statement of the Lutheran faith. Melanchthon hoped that the document would form the basis of compromise with Catholic powers, but that possibility was rejected out of hand by the imperial party. Charles aimed to affirm his strength in Germany by forcing the princes to end the reform movement and enforce bans on Luther's teachings.

The Protestant princes responded by forming the League of Schmalkalden. At first, the founders of the league claimed that they were interested in protecting Lutheran preaching, but the league quickly developed as a center of opposition to imperial influence in general. Eventually Charles and a group of allied princes managed to defeat the league at the Battle of Mühlberg in 1547. The emperor was unable to continue pressure on the Protestants, however, because he had depended on the support of some Protestant princes in his battles with the league. As a result, even after military defeat, the Protestant princes were able to maintain religious autonomy. In the Religious Peace of Augsburg of 1555, the emperor formally acknowledged the principle that sovereign princes could choose the religion to be practiced in their territories, *cuius regio, eius religio* ("whose territory, his religion"). There were limits, however: leaders had only two choices—remain under papal authority or adopt the Augsburg Confession outlined by Melanchthon. Reformed churches associated with Zwingli or Calvin were not legally recognized (see Map 14.2).

Shortly after the settlement, Charles abdicated his Spanish and imperial titles. Exhausted by years of political and religious struggle, he ceded the imperial crown to

The Augsburg Confession In this woodcut of the Augsburg Confession being read to Charles V, the artist has included in the background text and images of the Lutheran teachings on the sacraments and the nature of salvation. In contrast are the images on the left of a papal ceremony and court hierarchy in which, the artist implies, Christ is not present. *(Kunstsammlung Veste Coburg)*

his brother, Ferdinand (r. 1556–1564). His possessions in the Low Countries, Spain, Italy, and the New World he transferred to his son, Philip II (r. 1556–1598). Charles had believed his courtiers when they compared his empire to that of the ancient Romans. He had accepted that his duty as emperor was to unite Christendom under one law and one church. But in no part of his empire did he ever command the authority that would have allowed him to unite his lands politically, let alone to re-establish religious unity. Following his abdication, Charles retired to a monastery in Spain, where he died in 1558.

THE ENGLISH REFORMATION, 1520–1603

HE Reformation in England is often called a monarchical Reformation. In contrast with Germany, where reform occurred in spite of imperial opposition, in England the Crown instituted the reform. On the other hand, as in Germany, institutional change in the church followed from both secular issues and reform ideas. In England, an initially hostile monarch began to tolerate reform ideas when he perceived the papacy as an unbiblical, tyrannical force blocking essential state policy. Although reformers were active in England, their success depended entirely on royal support. And by the middle of the sixteenth century, it was royal interest in compromise that brought a settlement that left England a curious hybrid of reformed and traditional religious practices.

■ Henry VIII and the Monarchical Reformation

England was closely tied to Germany. Since the twelfth century, large numbers of German merchants had lived and traded in England, and Cologne was home to a considerable English community. Anglo-German connections became especially significant during the Reformation. Reformers from Wittenberg and other Protestant towns had contact with English merchants from London who traded and traveled on the Continent. One reformer, William Tyndale (ca. 1494–1536), served as a bridge between the Continent and England. He had a humanistic education in classical languages and began working on a translation of the Bible in the 1520s. Forced to flee London by the church hierarchy, he visited Luther in Wittenberg before settling in Antwerp, where he completed his English New Testament. By 1526 copies of his translation and his religious tracts flooded into England. By the 1520s Lutheran influence was noticeable in London and Cambridge. To some extent the ground may have been prepared for the reformers by the few surviving Lollards, followers of Wyclif, who had argued for church reform in the late fourteenth and fifteenth centuries (see page 360). Lollards, who tended to be literate, were an ideal market for Tyndale's English Bible and his numerous reformist tracts.

Henry VIII (r. 1509–1547) began his reign as a popular and powerful king. Handsome, athletic, and artistic, he seemed to be the ideal ruler. Henry took an interest in theology and humanistic culture. At first, he was quite hostile to Luther's reform ideas and wrote *Defense of the Seven Sacraments,* which earned him the title "Defender of the Faith" from a grateful Pope Leo X. Throughout his life Henry remained suspicious of many Protestant ideas, but he led the initial phase of the break with the papacy because of his political problems with the highly orthodox Holy Roman emperor Charles V. The first phase of the English Reformation was thus monarchical.

Henry VII had initiated closer relations with Spain when he married his eldest son, Arthur, prince of Wales, to Ferdinand of Aragon's daughter, Catherine. After Arthur's death, the future Henry VIII was married to his brother's widow in 1509. Henry VIII later tried to further the Anglo-imperial alliance when he arranged a treaty by which the emperor Charles V, who was Catherine of Aragon's nephew, agreed to marry Henry's daughter, Mary Tudor. But by the late 1520s the Anglo-imperial alliance fell apart when Charles, responding to Spanish pressures, renounced the proposed marriage and instead married a Portuguese princess.

Henry's relations with Charles were further hampered by what the English called "the King's Great Matter," that is, his determination to divorce Catherine. Recalling the unrest of the Wars of the Roses, Henry believed that he needed a son to ensure that the Tudors could maintain control of the English crown. By 1527 Henry and Catherine had a daughter, Mary, but no living sons. Henry became convinced that he remained without a male heir because, by biblical standards, he had committed incest by marrying his brother's widow. As Leviticus 20:21 says, "If a man takes his brother's wife, it is impurity; they shall remain childless." Henry desired an annulment. Unfortunately for him, Leo X's successor, Pope Clement VII (r. 1523–1534), was a virtual prisoner of imperial troops who had recently sacked Rome and taken control of most of Italy. As long as Charles supported Catherine of Aragon and his forces occupied Rome, a papal annulment was out of the question.

The king's advisers quickly divided into two camps. Sir Thomas More, the royal chancellor and a staunch Catholic, urged the king to continue his policy of negotiation with the papacy and his efforts to destroy the growing Protestant party. Until his resignation in 1532, More led royal authorities in a vigorous campaign against the dissemination of the newly translated Tyndale Bible and against the spread of Protestant ideas. More was opposed and eventually ousted by a radical party of Protestants led by Thomas Cranmer (1489–1556) and Thomas Cromwell (1485?–1540), who saw in the king's desire for a divorce an effective wedge to pry Henry out of the papal camp. Cromwell, who eventually replaced More as chancellor, advised the king that the marriage problem could be solved by the English clergy without papal interference.

Between 1532 and 1535, Henry and Parliament took a number of steps that effectively left the king in control of the church in England. Early in 1533 Cranmer was named archbishop of Canterbury. Later that year Parliament ruled that appeals of cases concerning wills, marriages, and ecclesiastical grants had to be heard in England. In May an English court annulled the king's marriage to Catherine. Four months later, Henry's new queen, Anne Boleyn, gave birth to a daughter, Elizabeth.

Even before Cromwell became chancellor, Henry had attacked absentee clergy, restricted church courts, and revoked certain papal taxes. After the split began, the king began to seize church properties. Parliamentary action culminated in the passage of the Act of Supremacy in 1534, which declared the king to be "the Protector and only Supreme Head of the Church and the Clergy of England." Henry meant to enforce his control by requiring a public oath supporting the act. Sir Thomas More refused to take the oath and was arrested, tried, and executed for treason. In some respects, Parliament had acted as an instrument of reform, in the manner of the German and Swiss town councils that moderated debates over church reform. In England, however, Parliament and perhaps a majority of the laity perceived this reformation primarily as a political issue.

Cromwell and Cranmer had hoped to use "the King's Great Matter" as a way to begin a Lutheran-style reform of the church. But, though separated from the papal party, Henry remained suspicious of religious changes. Although he continued to object to the aspects of the older tradition that he called "idolatry and other evil and naughty ceremonies," he rejected the Protestant understanding of justification and what anti-Protestant critics called "bibliolatry"—excessive reverence for scriptural ideas. He complained of radicals who "do wrest and interpret and so untruly allege [novel understandings of Scripture] to subvert and overturn as well the sacraments of Holy Church as the power and authority of princes and magistrates." Between 1534 and Henry's death in 1547, neither the Protestant nor the Catholic party was able to gain the upper hand at court or at Canterbury. Substantive changes in the English church would be made by Henry's children.

■ Reform and Counter-Reform Under Edward and Mary

Prince Edward, Henry's only surviving son in 1547, was born to Henry's third wife, Jane Seymour. He was only 10 years old when his father died. By chance, Edward Seymour, who was Prince Edward's uncle, and the Protestant faction were in favor at the time of Henry's death. Seymour was named duke of Somerset and Lord Protector of the young king Edward VI (r. 1547–1553). Under Somerset, the Protestants were able to make significant changes in religious life in England. The Protestant party quickly changed the nature of the Eucharist, allowing the laity to take both bread and wine in the Protestant manner. Edward completed the "dissolution of the monasteries," that is, the process of confiscating properties belonging to chapels and shrines that his father had begun. In an act of great symbolic meaning, priests were legally allowed to marry; many had already done so. Finally, Archbishop Cranmer introduced the first edition of the English *Book of Common Prayer* in 1549. The publication updated some late medieval English prayers and combined them with liturgical and theological ideas taken from Luther, Zwingli, and Calvin. In its beautifully expressive English, it provided the laity with a primer on how to combine English religious traditions with reform theology. Later, continental Protestants were named to teach theology at Oxford and Cambridge. If Edward had not died of tuberculosis in 1553, England's reform would have looked very much like the movement in Switzerland and southern Germany.

Protestant reformers attempted to prevent Mary Tudor (r. 1553–1558), Henry's Catholic daughter, from claiming the throne, but Mary and the Catholic party quickly took control of the court and the church. Mary immediately declared previous reform decrees to be void. Cardinal Reginald Pole (1500–1558), who had advocated reform within the Catholic Church, became the center of the Catholic restoration party in Mary's England. Pole rooted out Protestants within the church. More than eight hundred gentlemen, clerics, and students fled England for the Protestant havens on the Continent. Some officials, including Cranmer, chose to remain, and paid with their lives. In all, three hundred Protestants, mostly artisans and laborers, were tried and executed by church courts, earning the queen her nickname, "Bloody Mary." (See the box "Reading Sources: The Martyrdom of Thomas Cranmer.")

The policies of the queen brought about an abrupt return of the English church to papal authority. Most of the English quickly and easily returned to traditional Roman religious practices. Statues were removed from hiding and restored to places of honor in churches and chapels. Although conclusive evidence is lacking, the queen's initial successes may indicate that the Reformation was not broadly supported by the people. In fact, the restoration of Catholicism by Mary might have worked had the queen not died after little more than six years on the throne. At her death, the final settlement of the reform in England was far from certain.

■ The Elizabethan Settlement

Queen Elizabeth (r. 1558–1603), daughter of Anne Boleyn, succeeded to the throne at the death of her half-sister. The reign of Elizabeth was one of the most enigmatic and successful of English history. At home, she managed to gain control of the various political and religious factions in the country, and abroad, she exploited the rivalries of a variety of international powers to her own advantage. She seems to have clearly recognized the necessity of striking a balance between opposing forces.

Her first pressing task was to effect a religious settlement. Early in her reign she twice left church services at the elevation of the bread by the priest. Since in Catholic thought it was this action of the priest that made Christ present in the bread, she was indicating symbolically her opposition to a purely Catholic understanding of the sacraments. In the next few years she continued to work for the restoration of many features of her father's and her half-brother's reforms. In 1559 the new Act of Supremacy and an Act of Uniformity reinstituted royal control of the English church and re-established uniform liturgical and doctrinal standards. The *Book of Common Prayer* composed by Cranmer was brought back, and final changes were made in the liturgy.

❧ READING SOURCES

The Martyrdom of Thomas Cranmer

Richard Fox (1516–1587) composed his Book of Martyrs *to propound his belief that Protestant reformers were struggling against an evil just as insidious as the early Christian martyrs faced. His book was instrumental in forming English Protestant antipathy toward the Catholic Church. In this section he describes the execution of Thomas Cranmer, the former archbishop of Canterbury.*

Cranmer's open, generous nature was more easily to be seduced by a liberal conduct than by threats and fetters. When Satan finds the Christian proof against one mode of attack, he tries another; and what form is so seductive as smiles, rewards, and power, after a long, painful imprisonment? Thus it was with Cranmer: his enemies promised him his former greatness if he would but recant, as well as the queen's favor, and this at the very time they knew that his death was determined in council. To soften the path to apostasy, the first paper brought for his signature was conceived in general terms; this once signed, five others were obtained as explanatory of the first, until finally he put his hand to the following detestable instrument:

> I, Thomas Cranmer, late archbishop of Canterbury, do renounce, abhor, and detest all manner of heresies and errors of Luther and Zwingli, and all other teachings which are contrary to sound and true doctrine. . . .

The queen's revenge was only to be satiated by Cranmer's blood, and therefore she wrote an order to Dr. Pole [archbishop of Canterbury], to prepare a sermon to be preached March 21, directly before his martyrdom, at St. Mary's, Oxford. At the end of his sermon, Pole asked Cranmer to give a sign of his conversion. After begging God's forgiveness, Cranmer surprised Pole and announced: "And as for the pope, I refuse him as Christ's enemy, and Antichrist, with all his false doctrine."

Upon the conclusion of this unexpected declaration, amazement and indignation were conspicuous in every part of the church. The Catholics were completely foiled, their object being frustrated, Cranmer, like Samson, having completed a greater ruin upon his enemies in the hour of death, than he did in his life.

Cranmer would have proceeded in the exposure of the popish doctrines, but the murmurs of the idolaters drowned his voice, and the preacher gave an order to "lead the heretic away!" . . . A chain was provided to bind him to the stake, and after it had tightly encircled him, fire was put to the fuel, and the flames began soon to ascend.

Then were the glorious sentiments of the martyr made manifest; then it was, that stretching out his right hand, he held it unshrinkingly in the fire until it was burnt to a cinder, even before his body was injured, frequently exclaiming, "This unworthy right hand."

His body did abide the burning with such steadfastness that he seemed to have no more than the stake to which he was bound; his eyes were lifted up to heaven, and he repeated "this unworthy right hand," as long as his voice would suffer him; and using often the words of Stephen [traditionally held to be the first Christian martyr], "Lord Jesus, receive my spirit," in the greatness of the flame, he gave up the ghost.

Source: Richard Fox, *Fox's Book of Martyrs,* ed. William Byron Forbush (Philadelphia & Chicago: John C. Winston, 1926). Spelling modernized by Duane Osheim.

 For additional information on this topic, go to http://college.hmco.com.

Protestants had hoped for a complete victory, but the "Elizabethan Settlement" was considerably less than that. Although figures are lacking, it is likely that a large portion of the English population did not support a return to Henry's and Edward's reforms. After making clear her significant differences with Rome, Elizabeth confounded her most fervent Protestant supporters by offering a number of concessions to Anglo-Catholics. She herself remained celibate, and she ordered the Anglican clergy to do the same—although she could do little to prevent clerical marriage. More important, she and her closest advisers allowed a great variety of customs and practices favored by Anglo-Catholics. These matters, the queen's supporters argued, were not essential to salvation, and thus individuals could be allowed to choose. Many of the prayers in the *Book of Common Prayer,* for example, seemed "papist" to the most radical Protestants. Similarly, many of the traditional clerical vestments and altar furnishings remained unchanged. Elizabeth probably knew that the Protestants had no alternative but to support her and thus felt free to win back the support of the Anglo-Catholics.

The Queen in Parliament
This image was meant to show the willingness of Parliament to support the queen, a key element of the Elizabethan Settlement.
(*Bibliothèque Nationale de France*)

In fact, from the 1570s Elizabeth seems to have been especially concerned to regain control of insubordinate clerics. In these years the main outlines of her religious settlement became clear. She created a reformed liturgy that seemed acceptable to both Protestants and Catholics. At the same time she retained the parish and diocesan structure of the medieval church. She seems to have been most careful to restrict theological debate to the universities.

Toward the end of Elizabeth's reign, Richard Hooker (1554–1600) published his *Laws of Ecclesiastical Polity*, which provides an excellent description of the Anglican (English) Church born of the Elizabethan Settlement. England, Hooker maintains, has its own way of handling religious affairs. Theologically it represents a middle ground between the traditions cultivated by the Roman church and the more radically biblical religion favored by the Lutherans of Germany and the Calvinists of Switzerland. The Church of England moderated Luther's and Calvin's absolute reliance on Scriptures with history and tradition. In areas where tradition was strong, processions and other pre-Reformation traditions continued to animate village life. In other areas, more austere reformed practices were likely to predominate.

FRANCE, SCANDINAVIA, AND EASTERN EUROPE, 1523–1560

 N England and in the empire of Charles V, the success of the new religious reforms depended greatly on the political situation. It would be naive to conclude, as Luther claimed, that "the Word did everything." Yet this complex religious reform movement cannot be reduced to the politics of kings and princes. The issues will be clearer if we survey politics and reform in the rest of Europe, noting whether and to what extent the new ideas took root. In France, for example, the widespread, popular support of the old religion limited the options of the country's political leaders. Similarly, in northern Europe religious reform was an issue of both popular feeling and royal politics.

■ France

Luther's work, and later the ideas of the urban reformers of southwestern Germany and Switzerland, passed quickly into France. Geneva is in a French-speaking area close to the French border. It, like Strasbourg, was easy for French Protestants to reach. Perhaps because of France's proximity to the Calvinists in French-speaking Switzerland or because of the clarity and power of Calvin's *Institutes*, French Protestants, known as Huguenots, were tied more closely to the Calvinists of Geneva than to the Lutherans of Germany.

It is difficult, however, to know how many French Christians were Protestants. At the height of the Reformation's popularity, Protestants probably represented no more than 10 percent of the total population of France. It has been estimated that Protestant congregations numbered about 2,100 in the 1560s—in a country that had perhaps 32,000 traditional parishes. Protestants seem to have comprised a diverse mix that included two of the three most important noble families at court: the Bourbon and the Montmorency families. Clerics interested in moral reform and artisans who worked at new trades, such as the printing industry, also made up a significant portion of the converts. Perhaps reflecting the numerous printers and merchants in their numbers, Protestants tended to be of higher-than-average literacy. The Protestant population was spread throughout the country. Protestants were particularly well represented in towns and probably constituted a majority in the southern and western towns of La Rochelle, Montpellier, and Nîmes. Paris was the one part of the realm in which they had little influence, and their absence in the capital may have been their undoing.

The conservative theologians of the Sorbonne in Paris were some of Luther's earliest opponents. They complained that many masters at the University of Paris were "Lutheran." As early as 1523, Parisian authorities seized and burned books said to be by Luther. But as in Germany, there was no clear understanding of who or what a Lutheran was. The Sorbonne theologians were also suspicious of a number of "pre-reformers," including the humanist editor Jacques Lefèvre d'Étaples (1455–1536; see page 413), who late in life had come to an understanding of justification quite like Luther's. Others were clerics intent on religious reform within the traditional structures. Unlike Luther and the French Protestants, these pre-reformers did not challenge the priests' relationship to the sacraments. They were interested in the piety and behavior of churchmen. They never challenged the role of the clergy in salvation. King Francis's own sister, Margaret of Angoulême° (1492–1549), gathered a group of religious persons at her court, even including several reformers. (See the box "Reading

---

Angoulême (ohn-goo-LEM)

❧ READING SOURCES

The Conversion of Jeanne d'Albret

Jeanne d'Albret was the niece of King Francis I and mother of Henry of Navarre, the future Henry IV. In this letter, written in 1555 to Viscount Gourdon, a Huguenot supporter, she explains the pressures on her to remain Catholic and why she chose to become Protestant. After her conversion, her court became a center of the Huguenot movement.

I am writing to tell you that up to now I have followed in the footsteps of the deceased Queen, my most honored mother—whom God forgive—in the matter of hesitation between the two religions. The said Queen [was] warned by her late brother the King, Francois I of good and glorious memory, my much honored uncle, not to get new doctrines in her head so that from then on she confined herself to amusing stories. Besides, I well remember how long ago, the late King, my most honored father, surprised the said Queen when she was praying in her rooms with the ministers Roussel and Farel, and how with great annoyance he slapped her right cheek and forbade her sharply to meddle in matters of doctrine. He shook a stick at me which cost me many bitter tears and has kept me fearful and compliant until after

they had both died. Now that I am freed by the death of my said father two months ago, a reform seems so right and so necessary that, for my part, I consider that it would be disloyalty and cowardice to God, to my conscience and to my people to remain any longer in a state of suspense and indecision. It is necessary for sincere persons to take counsel together to decide how to proceed, both now and in the future. Knowing that you are noble and courageous and that you have learned persons about you, I beg you to meet me.

Source: Nancy L. Roelker, trans., *Queen of Navarre: Jeanne d'Albret, 1528–1572* (Cambridge, Mass.: Harvard University Press, 1968), p. 127 (slightly adapted).

Sources: The Conversion of Jeanne d'Albret.") But Margaret herself urged that theology be left to scholars; she believed that the laity should stick to simple pieties. Like Margaret, most French Christians had no clear sense that Protestant teachings required a complete break with medieval Christian traditions.

Like previous French kings, Francis I (r. 1515–1547) hoped to extend royal jurisdictions in France and make France an international power. Engaged in the seemingly intractable wars with the Habsburgs, Francis generally ignored religious questions. In 1525 he was taken captive in the wake of a military disaster at Pavia in Lombardy. He was held prisoner for nearly a year, during which time conservatives at the Sorbonne and in Paris moved actively against suspected Protestants. Francis was not initially opposed to what seemed to be moral reform within the church. His own view was that the king's duty was to preserve order and prevent scan-

dal, and at first carrying out that duty meant protecting reformers whom the conservative militants persecuted. The king feared disorder more than he feared religious reform.

On October 18, 1534, however, Francis's attitude changed when he and all Paris awoke to find the city littered with anti-Catholic placards containing, in the words of the writers, "true articles on the horrible, great and insufferable abuses of the Papal Mass." The response of the Parisians was outrage. They attacked foreigners, especially those who by dress or speech seemed "Lutheran"—that is, German or Flemish. Several months later Francis himself led a religious procession through Paris in honor of the Blessed Sacrament. The "Affair of the Placards" changed Francis's ideas about the sources of disorder. Opposition to traditional religious practices became more difficult and more dangerous. John Calvin himself was forced to leave Paris and eventually France because he feared persecution. Between 1534 and 1560, some ten thousand Protestants fled France, many joining Calvin in Geneva.

By the middle of the sixteenth century, it was clear that neither Protestant nor Catholic factions would be able to control religious and political life in France. Francis I died in 1547, and the stage was set for a series of destructive factional struggles over religion and political power that would continue for the rest of the century (discussed in Chapter 15).

■ Scandinavia

All of Scandinavia became Lutheran. Initial influences drifted north from Germany, carried by Hanseatic merchants and students who had studied at the universities of northern Germany. Yet the reform in Sweden and Denmark even more than in England was a monarchical reformation. In both Scandinavian kingdoms the kings began with an attack on the temporal rights and properties of the church. Changes in liturgy and practice came later as reformers gained royal protection.

Since 1397 all Scandinavia had been united in theory in the Union of Kalmar (see page 379). But early in the sixteenth century, the last pretenses of unity were shattered. Christian I of Denmark (r. 1513–1523) invaded Sweden and captured Stockholm, the capital. So great was his brutality that within a few years Gustav Vasa, a leading noble, was able to secure the loyalty of most of the Swedes and in 1523 was elected king of Sweden. Gustav's motto was "All power is of God." Like Henry VIII of England, Gustav (r. 1523–1560) moved carefully in an attempt to retain the loyalty of as many groups as possible. Although he never formally adopted a national confession of faith, the church and Swedish state gradually took on a more Lutheran character. In an effort to secure royal finances, the Riksdag, or parliament, passed the Vasteras Ordinances, which secularized ecclesiastical lands and authorized the preaching of the "Pure Word of God." Olaus Petri (1493–1552), Sweden's principal reform preacher, was installed by royal order in the cathedral of Stockholm.

In Denmark the reformers also moved cautiously. Frederick I (r. 1523–1533) and his son, Christian III (r. 1534–1559), continued the policy of secularization and control that Christian I had initiated. Danish kings seemed interested in reform as a diplomatic means of attack on the Roman church. It seems that in Denmark the old religion simply suffered from a sort of royal indifference. The kings tended to support reformers as a way to attack the political power of the bishops. The Danes finally accepted the Augsburg Confession, which was becoming the most widely accepted exposition of Lutheran belief, in 1538. The transformation of practice proceeded slowly over the next decades.

In the frontier regions of Scandinavia—Finland, Iceland, and Norway—the reform was undertaken as a matter of royal policy. Initially only a handful of local reformers introduced and proselytized the new theology and practice. In many regions resistance to the Reformation continued for several generations. One valley hidden in the mountains of western Norway continued to follow the old religion for three centuries after its contacts with Rome had been severed.

■ Eastern Europe

In some respects, a political vacuum in eastern Europe allowed for the expansion of Protestantism and the creation of a unique religious culture. The church hierarchy was not in a position to enforce orthodoxy. Some rulers were indifferent to religious debates, as were the Muslim Ottoman Turks, who controlled much of eastern Hungary and what is now Romania. Other rulers offered toleration because they could ill afford to alienate any portion of their subject populations.

Protestant ideas initially passed through the German communities of Poland and the trading towns along the Baltic coast. But in the 1540s, Calvinist ideas spread quickly among the Polish nobles, especially those at the royal court. Given the power and influence of some of the noble families, Catholics were unable to suppress the various secret Calvinist congregations. During the first half of the sixteenth century, Protestantism became so well established in Poland that it could not be rooted out. Throughout the sixteenth century, Protestantism remained one of the rallying points for those opposed to the expansion of royal power.

The situation was much the same in Hungary and Transylvania. Among German colonists, Magyars, and ethnic Romanians there were numerous individuals who were interested first in Luther's message and later in Calvin's revisions of the reformed theology. Because no one could hope to enforce uniformity, some cities adopted a moderate Lutheran theology, and others followed a Calvinist confession. By the 1560s the Estates (representative assemblies) of Transylvania had decreed that four religions were to be tolerated—Catholic, Lutheran, Reformed, and Unitarian. Further, when various radical groups migrated from the west in search of toleration, they too were able to create their own communities in Slavic and Magyar areas.

The Reformation was to have virtually no influence farther to the east, in Russia. The Orthodox Church in Russia was much more firmly under government control than was the church in the West. The Russian church followed the traditions of the Greek church, and Western arguments over justification made little sense in Orthodox Churches. Given the historic suspicion of the Orthodox for Rome, the Russians were more tolerant of contacts with the Protestants of northern Europe. But there would be no theological innovation or reform in sixteenth-century Russia.

THE LATE REFORMATION, CA. 1545–1600

N the first half of the sixteenth century, Catholics applied the term *Lutheran* to anyone who was anticlerical. As Francesco Guicciardini (1483–1540), a papal governor in central Italy, remarked:

> I know of no one who loathes the ambition, the avarice, and the sensuality of the clergy more than I. . . . In spite of all this, the positions I have held under several popes have forced me, for my own good, to further their interests. Were it not for that, I should have loved Martin Luther as much as myself—not so that I might be free of the laws based on Christian religion as it is generally interpreted and understood; but to see this bunch of rascals get their just deserts, that is, to be without vices or without authority.[7]

Guicciardini's remarks catch both the frustration many Christians felt with the traditional church and also the very real confusion over just what it was that Luther had said. In parts of Germany by the late 1520s and across Europe by the 1550s, political and religious leaders attempted to explain to the peoples of Europe just what *Lutheran, Reformed,* and *Catholic* had come to mean. It was only in the second half of the sixteenth century that these terms came to have any clarity. After the middle of the sixteenth century, it was true that along with theological and political changes, the Reformation represented a broad cultural movement.

The profound changes that began in the sixteenth century continued into the seventeenth. People began to sort out what it meant to belong to one church instead of to another. Central governments supported religious authorities who desired religious uniformity and control over individual Christians. In all parts of Europe, religious behavior changed. Both Protestants and Catholics became more concerned with the personal rather than the communal aspects of Christianity. After the sixteenth century, the nature of Christianity and its place in public life, whether in Protestant or in Catholic countries, differed profoundly from what it had been in the Middle Ages.

■ Catholic Reform, 1512–1600

Historians commonly speak of both a movement for traditional reform and renewal within the Catholic Church and a "Counter-Reformation," which was a direct response to and rejection of the theological positions championed by the Protestants. It is certainly true that one can categorize certain acts as clearly challenging the Protestants. However, to do so is to miss the point that the energetic actions of the Roman Catholic Church during the sixteenth century both affirmed traditional teachings and created new institutions better fitted to the early modern world.

The idea of purer, earlier church practices to which the "modern" church should return had been a commonplace for centuries. The great ecumenical Council of Constance early in the fifteenth century had called for "reform in head and members" (see page 361). In 1512, five years before Luther made his public protests, Pope Julius II (r. 1503–1513) convened another ecumenical council, the Fifth Lateran Council (1513–1517), which was expected to look into the problems of nonresident clergy, multiple benefices, and a host of other issues. This tradition of moral reform was especially strong in Spain, Portugal, and Italy, lands whose political rulers were either indifferent or opposed to Protestant reforms.

The desire for reform along traditional lines was deeply felt within the Catholic Church. In the wake of the sack of Rome by imperial troops in 1527, one Roman cardinal, Bishop Gian Matteo Giberti° of Verona (1495–1543), returned to his diocese and began a thoroughgoing reform. He conducted visitations of the churches and other religious institutions in Verona, preached tirelessly, worked hard to raise the educational level of his clergy, and required that priests live within their parishes. Giberti believed that morally rigorous traditional reform and renewal could counter the malaise he perceived. Other reforming bishops could be found throughout Catholic Europe.

Giberti (ji-BARE-ti)

A Marian Shrine   Shrines, such as this one in Regensburg dedicated to the Virgin, remained important centers of Catholic piety. As we see here, shrines drew large crowds made up of individuals and religious groups who came in search of spiritual and physical healing. *(Foto Marburg/Art Resource, NY)*

New religious foundations sprang up to renew the church. The Spanish mystic Teresa of Avila (1515–1582) reflected the thinking of many when she lamented, "No wonder the Church is as it is, when the religious live as they do." Members of the new orders set out to change the church through example. The Florentine Filippo Neri (1515–1595) founded the Oratorian order, so named because of the monks' habit of leading the laity in prayer services. Filippo was joined in his work by Giovanni Palestrina (ca. 1525–1594), who composed music for the modest but moving prayer gatherings in Rome. Pales-

trina's music combined medieval plainchants with newer styles of polyphony, creating complex harmonies without obscuring the words and meaning of the text. The popularity of the Oratorians and their services can be measured in part by the fact that oratories, small chapels modeled on those favored by Filippo, remain to this day important centers of the musical life in the city of Rome.

The Catholic reform of the sixteenth century, however, was better known for its mystical theology than for its music. In Italy and France, but especially in Spain, a profusion of reformers chose to reform the church

❧ READING SOURCES

Saint Teresa of Avila on Rapture and Mortification

Teresa de Jesus (1515–1582) was a mystic, reformer, and tireless defender of women's spirituality. Religious authorities were initially suspicious of the daughter of an important converso family, fearing both Judaizing and spiritual teaching by a woman. She was, however, immensely influential. She led a reform movement within the Carmelite order, wrote hundreds of letters of spiritual advice, and analyzed carefully the nature of prayer and meditation. This letter, written in 1577 to her brother, is typical of the counsel she offered to those who sought her guidance.

You must understand that for these last eight days I have been in such a state. . . . Just before I wrote to you, my raptures came on again; and this gives me great trouble, because they sometimes happen in public, and while I am at matins [the first church service of the morning]. To resist is not sufficient, nor can they be concealed. I am so ashamed that I could hide myself I know not where. I earnestly beg of God to deliver me from having them in public; and do you also pray for me, for they are attended with many inconveniences, and it seems to me that prayer does not consist in having them at all. On those days I am almost like one drunk: . . . it is painful to attend to anything more than to what the soul wishes.

I believe I have already given you an answer as to what you said about remaining [after a rapture], as if nothing had happened. . . . I remember now that I sent you an answer, for I have received a great number of letters since I read yours: and even now I have to write so many answers, that I can hardly find time to send this off. At other times, the soul continues in such a state, that she cannot return to herself for many days, and she seems to resemble the sun, whose rays give heat, and yet the sun is not seen:

thus it appears as if the soul dwelt somewhere else, and animated the body without being in it, because some faculty is suspended.

When you cannot recollect yourself properly in the time of prayer, or when you are desirous of doing something for our Lord, I send you this hair-shirt, which will powerfully revive your love. . . . But I recommend this mortification with some fear. As you are of a sanguine temperament, anything might heat your blood; but yet the pleasure is so great which is produced by doing something for God (even should it be a mere nothing, like this is), that I earnestly wish you to try this penance. When the winter is over, you shall do a little more, for I intend taking care of you. Write, and tell me how you like this "trifling!" mortification [remembering what our Lord suffered for us]. . . . I cannot help smiling, to see how you send me sweetmeats, delicacies, and money, and I send you a hair-shirt!

Source: The Letters of Saint Teresa, trans. John Dalton (London: Thomas Baker, 1893), pp. 154–155, 158, 159 (slightly modernized).

---

through austere prayer and contemplative devotions. Teresa of Avila, who belonged to a wealthy converso family, led a movement to reform the lax practices within the religious houses of Spain. Famed for her rigorous religious life, her trances, and her raptures, Teresa animated a movement to reform the order of Carmelite nuns in Spain. Because of her writings about her mystical experiences she was named a "Doctor of the Church," a title re-

served for the greatest of the church's theologians. (See the box "Reading Sources: Saint Teresa of Avila on Rapture and Mortification.")

The most important of the new religious orders was the Society of Jesus, or Jesuits, founded in 1534 by Ignatius Loyola (1491–1556). A conservative Spanish nobleman, Loyola was wounded and nearly killed in battle. During a long and painful rehabilitation, he continuously read accounts of lives of the saints. After recovering, he went on a pilgrimage and experienced a profound conversion.

Loyola initially meant to organize a missionary order directed at converting the Muslims. The structure of his order reflected his military experience. It had a well-defined chain of command leading to the general of the order and then to the pope. To educate and discipline the members, Loyola composed *Spiritual Exercises,* emphasizing the importance of obedience. He encouraged his followers to understand their own attitudes, beliefs, and even lives as less important than the papacy and Roman church. If the church commands it, he concluded, "I will believe that the white object I see is black." He prohibited Jesuits from holding any ecclesiastical office that might compromise their autonomy. After papal approval of the order in 1540, the Jesuits directed their activities primarily to education in Catholic areas and reconversion of Protestants.

Throughout Europe, Jesuits gained fame for their work as educators of the laity and as spiritual advisers to the political leaders of Catholic Europe. In the late sixteenth and early seventeenth centuries, they were responsible for a number of famous conversions, including that of Christina (1626–1689), the Lutheran queen of Sweden, who abdicated her throne in 1654 and spent the rest of her life in Rome. Jesuits were especially successful in bringing many parts of the Holy Roman Empire back into communion with the papacy. They have rightly been called the vanguard of the Catholic reform movement.

Catholic reformers were convinced that one of the reasons for the success of the Protestants was that faithful Christians had no clear guide to orthodox teachings. The first Catholic response to the reformers was to try to separate ideas they held to be correct from those they held to be incorrect. Successive popes made public lists of books and ideas that they considered to be in error. The lists were combined into the *Index of Prohibited Books* in 1559. The climate of suspicion was such that the works of humanists such as Erasmus were prohibited alongside the works of Protestants such as Martin Luther. In times of religious tensions, the *Index* could be vigorously enforced. In general, however, it did little to inhibit the circulation of books and ideas. It was finally suppressed in 1966.

During the first half of the sixteenth century, Catholics joined Protestants in calls for an ecumenical council that all believed would solve the problems dogging the Christian church. But in the unsettled political and diplomatic atmosphere that lasted into the 1540s, it

A Mystical Reformer   Saint Teresa of Avila came from a converso family. She believed that renewal within the Christian church would come through mysticism, prayer, and a return to traditional religious practices. She founded a reformed Carmelite order of nuns to further religious renewal in Spain.   *(Institut Amatller d'Art Hispanic)*

was impossible to find any agreement about where or when a universal council should meet. Finally, in 1545, at a time when the hostilities between the Valois and Habsburgs had cooled, Pope Paul III (r. 1534–1549) was able to convene an ecumenical council in the city of Trent, a German imperial city located on the Italian side of the Alps.

It is difficult to overemphasize the importance of the Council of Trent. It marked and defined Roman Catholicism for the next four hundred years. Reformers within the Catholic Church hoped that it would be possible to create a broadly based reform party within the church and that the council would define theological positions acceptable to the Protestants, making reunion possible. Unfortunately for the reformers, conservatives quickly took over the papal-controlled council.

The Council of Trent sat in three sessions between 1545 and 1563. The initial debates were clearly meant to mark the boundaries between Protestant heresy and the orthodox positions of the Catholic Church. In response to the Protestant emphasis on the Scriptures, the council said that the church always recognized the validity of traditional teaching and understanding. Delegates rejected the humanists' work on the text of the Bible, declaring that the Latin Vulgate edition compiled by Jerome in the late fourth century was the authorized text. In response to the widely held Protestant belief that salvation came through faith alone, the council declared that good works were not merely the outcome of faith but prerequisites to salvation. The council rejected Protestant positions on the sacraments, the giving of wine to the laity during Holy Communion, the marriage of clergy, and the granting of indulgences.

Protestant critics often point to these positions as evidence that the work of the council was merely negative. To do so, however, is to ignore the many ways in which the decrees of the council were an essential part of the creation of the Roman Catholic Church that would function for the next four centuries. The delegates at Trent generally felt that the real cause behind the Protestant movement was the lack of leadership and supervision within the church. Many of the acts of the council dealt with that issue.

First, the council affirmed apostolic succession—the idea that the authority of a bishop is transmitted through a succession of bishops, ultimately leading back through the popes to Saint Peter. Thus, the council underlined the ultimate authority of the pope in administrative as well as theological matters. The council ordered that local bishops should reside in their dioceses; that they should establish seminaries to see to the education of parish clergy; and that, through regular visitation and supervision, they should make certain that the laity participated in the sacramental life of the church. At the final sessions of the council, the nature of the Roman Catholic Church was summed up in the Creed of Pius IV, which like the Lutheran Augsburg Confession expressed the basic position of the church.

■ Confessionalization

The labors of the Jesuits and the deliberations of the Council of Trent at midcentury proved that reconciliation between the Protestant reformers and the Catholic Church was not possible. Signs of the separation include the flight of several important Protestant religious leaders from Italy in the late 1540s and the wholesale migration of Protestant communities from Modena, Lucca, and other Italian towns to France, England, and Switzerland. These actions signify the beginnings of the theological, political, and social separation of "Protestant" and "Catholic" in European

society. Further, the states of Europe saw themselves as the enforcers of religious uniformity within their territories. It is from this time that denominational differences become clearer.

The theological separation was marked in a number of concrete and symbolic ways. Churches in which both bread and wine were distributed to the laity during the sacrament of Holy Communion passed from Catholic to Protestant. Churches in which the altar was moved forward to face the congregation but the statuary was retained were likely to be Lutheran. Churches in which statues were destroyed and all other forms of art were removed were likely to be Reformed (Calvinist), for Calvin had advised that "only those things are to be sculpted or painted which the eye is capable of seeing; let not God's majesty, which is far above the perception of the eyes, be debased through unseemly representations."[8] Even matters such as singing differentiated the churches. Although the Calvinist tradition tended to believe that music, like art, drew the Christian away from consideration of the word, Luther believed that "next to the Word of God, music deserves the highest praise." Lutherans emphasized congregational singing and the use of music within the worship service. Countless pastors in the sixteenth and seventeenth centuries followed Luther in composing hymns and even theoretical tracts on music. This tradition would reach its zenith in the church music of Johann Sebastian Bach (1685–1750), most of whose choral works were composed to be part of the normal worship service.

Music had played an important role in Catholic services since well before the Reformation. It was really architecture that distinguished Catholic churches from Protestant churches in the late sixteenth and seventeenth centuries. In Rome, the great religious orders built new churches in the baroque style (see page 533). Baroque artists and architects absorbed all the classical lessons of the Renaissance and then went beyond them, sometimes deliberately violating them. Baroque art celebrates the supernatural, the ways in which God is not bound by the laws of nature. Where Renaissance art was meant to depict nature, baroque paintings and sculpture seemed to defy gravity. The work celebrated the supernatural power and splendor of the papacy. This drama and power are clear in the construction of the Jesuit Church of the Gesù° in Rome and even more so in Gianlorenzo Bernini's (1598–1680) throne of Saint Peter made for the basilica of Saint Peter in the Vatican. The

Gesu (jeh-SUE)

The Gesu in Rome   This church is the center of the Jesuit order and the burial place of Saint Ignatius Loyola. Its baroque architecture set the tone for many later buildings in Rome and for many new Catholic churches elsewhere.   *(Scala/Art Resource, NY)*

construction of baroque churches, first in Spain and Italy but especially in the Catholic parts of Germany, created yet another boundary between an austere Protestantism and a visual and mystical Catholicism.

■ The Regulation of Religious Life

Because of the continuing religious confusion and political disorder brought on by the reforms, churchmen, like state officials, were intent on maintaining religious order within their territories by requiring what they understood to be the practice of true Christianity. In an ironic twist, both Protestant and Catholic authorities followed much the same program. In both camps, regulation of religion became a governmental concern. Religious regulation and state power grew at the same time. This true religion was much less a public and communal religion than medieval Christianity had been. Medieval Christians had worried greatly about public sins that complicated life in a community. In the age of confessionalization, theologians—both Protestant and Catholic—became preoccupied with the moral status and interior life of individuals. Sexual sins and gluttony now seemed more dangerous than economic sins such as avarice or usury. Even penance was understood less as a "restitution" that would reintegrate the individual into the Christian community than as a process of coming to true contrition for sins.

The Holy Household   One of the most popular ideas among Protestants was that true religion should be taught and preserved in the Christian family, presided over by the father. The detail in this painting shows not only the interior of a Flemish home but also the role of the father and the symbolic importance of meals eaten together.   *(The Shakespeare Birthplace Trust)*

The changed attitude toward penance made the sense of Christian community less important and left individuals isolated and more subject to the influence of the church and secular authorities. In all parts of Europe officials were consumed with the control and supervision of the laity.

All of the major religious groups in the late sixteenth century emphasized education, right doctrine, and social control. In Catholic areas, it was hoped that a renewed emphasis on private confession by the laity would lead to a proper understanding of doctrine. During this period Charles Borromeo, archbishop of Milan (1538–1584), introduced the private confessional box, which isolated priest and penitent from the prying ears

of the community. This allowed confessors time and opportunity to instruct individual consciences with care. As early as the 1520s some Lutheran princes had begun visitations to ensure that the laity understood basic doctrine.

Churchmen in both Protestant and Catholic areas used catechisms—that is, handbooks containing instruction for the laity. The first and most famous was by Luther himself. Luther's *Small Catechism* includes the Lord's Prayer, Ten Commandments, and Apostles' Creed along with simple, clear explanations of what they mean. More than Catholic rulers, Protestant rulers used church courts to enforce discipline within the community. Churchmen began to criticize semireligious popular celebrations such as May Day, harvest feasts, and the Feast of Fools, whose origins lay in popular myths and practices that preceded Christianity. Such observations were now scorned for encouraging superstition and mocking the social and political order with, for example, parodies of ignorant clergy and foolish magistrates.

Religious authorities were also concerned by what seemed to be out-of-control mysticism and dangerous religious practices, especially among women. The impact of the Reformation on the status of women has often been debated. The Protestant position is that the Reformation freed women from the cloistered control of traditional convents. Further, the Protestant attack on state-controlled prostitution reduced one of the basest forms of exploitation. To the realists who argued that young, unmarried men would always need sexual outlets, Luther replied that one cannot merely substitute one evil practice for another. Critics of the Reformation counter that a convent was one of very few organizations that a woman could administer and direct. Women who took religious vows, Catholics point out, could engage in intellectual and religious pursuits similar to those enjoyed by men. The destruction of religious houses for women, Catholics argued, destroyed one of the few alternatives that women had to life in an authoritarian, patriarchal society.

In fact, in the late sixteenth and early seventeenth centuries, both Protestant and Catholic authorities viewed with suspicion any signs of religious independence by women. In the first years of the Reformation, some women did leave convents, eager to participate in the reform of the church. Early in the 1520s some women wrote tracts concerning the morality of the clergy. And for a time, women served as deacons in some Calvinist churches. Yet like the female witches discussed in Chapter 15, these religious women seemed somehow dangerous. Lutheran and Calvinist theologians argued that a woman's religious vocation should be in the Christian care and education of her family. And even the most famous of the sixteenth- and seventeenth-century female Catholic mystics were greeted with distrust and some hostility. Religious women in Catholic convents were required to subordinate their mysticism to the guidance they received from male spiritual advisers. Calvinist theologians exhibited similar suspicions toward the theological and spiritual insights of Protestant women. For the laity in general and for women in particular, the late Reformation brought increased control by religious authorities.

SUMMARY

DURING the age of the Reformation, Europe experienced a number of profound shocks. The medieval assumption of a unified Christendom in the West was shattered. No longer could Europeans assume that at heart they held similar views of the world and the place of individuals in it. Charles V had begun his reign with hopes for one law, one faith, and one empire. He ended it by dividing his empire and retiring to a monastery.

The Protestant challenge did not simply attack the institutional structure or the moral lapses as previous heretical movements had done. The early Protestant reformers rejected the penitential system that was at the heart of the medieval church. Peasants and artisans argued that Luther's message of Christian freedom liberated them from both economic and spiritual oppression. Both Protestant and peasant rejected the traditions of the late Middle Ages.

Monarchies and republics throughout Europe came to view religious institutions and religious choices as matters of state. Many of the small states of Germany, Scandinavia, and the territories that now form Latvia and Estonia became Lutheran. Many of the Swiss cantons, parts of the Low Countries, and Scotland became Reformed, or Calvinist. England followed its own course forming the Anglican Church. Spain, Portugal, Italy, France, and the rest of the Low Country and Germany remained part of the reformed and rejuvenated Roman Catholic Church. Poland and Hungary were predominantly Roman Catholic, while much of the rest of eastern Europe followed no clear pattern. When faced by theological challenges and cries for moral reform, governments reacted in ways that offered religious change and bolstered the claims of secular government. In England and Sweden, calls for reform resulted in the secularization of church property, which put vast new sources of wealth in the hands of the kings. In the towns of Germany and Switzerland, governments redoubled their efforts to regulate religion and moral life. In Catholic countries, the church hierarchy extended its control over the religious life of the laity. Thus, both Reformation and Counter-Reformation brought about a significant strengthening of religious and secular authorities.

Ironically, the reforms that Luther and other Protestants advocated on the basis of individual study and

(continued on page 496)

A Reformation Woodcut

Erhard Schön's 1533 woodcut "There Is No Greater Treasure Here on Earth Than an Obedient Wife Who Desires Honor" and other broadsheets like it informed and amused Europeans of all walks of life in the late fifteenth and sixteenth centuries. Schön's image of a henpecked husband and his wife followed by others would have been instantly recognizable to most people. Accompanying texts clarified the message implied in the woodcut itself. But how may we, centuries later, "read" this message? How does the modern historian analyze Schön's broadsheet to investigate popular ideas about social roles, religion, and politics? What do this and similar broadsheets tell us about popular responses to the social and religious tumults of the sixteenth century?

Look at the simple and clear lines of the woodcut. They give a clue about the popularity of broadsheets. They were cheap and easy to produce and were printed on inexpensive paper. Artists would sketch an image that an artisan would later carve onto a block. A printer could produce a thousand or more copies from a single block. Even famous artists such as Albrecht Dürer (see page 418) sold highly profitable prints on religious, political, and cultural themes.

Almost anyone could afford broadsheets. Laborers and modest merchants decorated their houses with pictures on popular themes. In the middle of the fifteenth century, before the Reformation, most images were of saints. It was widely believed, for example, that anyone who looked at an image of Saint Christopher would not die on that day.

During the political and religious unrest of the sixteenth century, artists increasingly produced images that referred to the debates over religion. Schön himself made his living in Nuremberg producing and selling woodcuts. He and other artists in the city were closely tuned to the attitudes of the local population. One popular image was entitled "The Roman Clergy's Procession into Hell."

Schön's "Obedient Wife" picture reflected a fear shared by both Protestants and Catholics: the rebellious nature of women. Evidence suggests that women in the late fifteenth and sixteenth centuries may have been marrying at a later age and thus were likely to be more independent-minded than their younger sisters. The ranks of single women were swollen by widows and by former nuns who had left convents and liberated themselves from male supervision. Thus, it was not difficult for men in the sixteenth century to spot women who seemed dangerously free from male control.

Let us turn again to the woodcut, to see what worried villagers and townsmen and how Schön depicted their fears. Notice the henpecked husband. He is harnessed to a cart carrying laundry. Both the harness and the laundry were popular images associated with women's duties. During popular festivals, German villagers often harnessed unmarried women to a plow to signify that they were shirking their duty by not marrying and raising children. Doing the laundry was popularly thought to be the first household chore that a powerful wife would force on her weak-kneed husband. Countless other images show women, whip in hand, supervising foolish husbands as they pound diapers with a laundry flail. "Woe is me," says the poor man, all this because "I took a wife." As if the message were not clear enough, look at what the woman carries in her left hand: his purse, his sword, and his pants. (The question "Who wears the pants in the family?" was as familiar then as now.) But the woman responds that he is in this position not because of marriage but because he has been carousing: "If you will not work to support me, then you must wash, spin, and draw the cart."*

The figures following the cart are commenting on the situation. The young journeyman is asking the maiden at his side, "What do you say about this?" She responds coyly, "I have no desire for such power." The woman dressed as a fool counsels the young man never to marry and thus to avoid anxiety and suffering. But an old man, identified as "the wise man," closes the procession and ends the debate. "Do not listen to this foolish woman," he counsels. "God determines how your life to-

---

*Keith Moxey, *Peasants, Warriors and Wives: Popular Imagery in the Reformation* (Chicago: University of Chicago Press, 1989), pp. 108–109; includes a translation of portions of the texts in the broadsheet.

Icein edler schatz ist auff der ert. Dann ein frums weib die eh begert.

Der arm göße.

Ach weh ach weh mir armen narren
Wie hart zeuch ich in disem karren
Darzů hat mich weyb nemen bracht
Ich wolt ich het mirs nie gedacht
So man ist komen in mein hauß
Zeucht mir schwert / brüch vn tasche auß
Nacht vnd tag hab ich kein rhů
Vnd kein gůttes wort darzů
Mein trew ist jr nicht angenehm
Meine wort sind jr gar widerzehm
Also geschicht noch manchem man
Der nichtes hatt / wascht oder kan
Wil doch bey zeyt ein frawen han.

"There Is No Greater Treasure Here on Earth Than an Obedient Wife Who Desires Honor,"
Erhard Schön   *(Gotha, Schlossmuseum)*

gether will be, so stay with her in love and suffering and always be patient."

If we think about this woodcut's images and text, we can understand the contrary hopes and fears in sixteenth-century Germany. Like the young woman, the Christian wife was expected to eschew power either inside or outside the home. Martin Luther concluded that "the husband is the head of the wife even as Christ is head of the Church. Therefore as the Church is subject to Christ, so let wives be subject to their husbands in everything"(Ephesians 5:23–24). Authority was to be in the hands of husbands and fathers. But if the good wife was required to avoid power, the good husband was also expected to follow Luther's precepts for the Christian family. As the wise old man observes, the husband must be a loving and forgiving master.

Schön's woodcut and others similar to it should remind you of the "argument over women" discussed in Chapter 12 (see page 411). The words of the wise man and the young maid bring to mind Christine de Pizan's *Book of the City of the Ladies* when they urge love and understanding, but their hopefulness is undercut by the power and immediacy of the image. As the broadsheet clearly demonstrates, suspicion of women characterized even the most simple literature of Reformation Europe.

 For additional information on this topic, go to http://college.hmco.com.

conscience led to new confessional beliefs and a conviction that right religion was a matter of state interest. Religious power, which to some extent had been a matter of personal conscience and local community, became an issue to be decided by the aggressive states of Europe.

■ Notes

1. Angela of Foligno, *The Book of Divine Consolation of the Blessed Angel of Foligno,* trans. Mary G. Steegmann (New York: Cooper Square Publishers, 1966), p. 260.
2. Martin Luther, *Works,* vol. 34 (Philadelphia: Fortress Press, 1955; reprint, St. Louis: Concordia Publishing House, 1986), pp. 336–337.
3. Quoted in Steven Ozment, *The Age of Reform, 1250–1550* (New Haven: Yale University Press, 1980), p. 245.
4. Quoted in Robert W. Scribner, *The German Reformation* (London: Macmillan, 1986), p. 32.
5. Quoted in Carter Lindberg, *The European Reformations* (New York: Blackwell Publishers, 1996), p. 269.
6. Quoted in Euan Cameron, *The European Reformation* (Oxford: Clarendon Press, 1991), pp. 106–107.
7. Francesco Guicciardini, *Maxims and Reflections (Ricordi),* trans. Mario Domandi (Philadelphia: University of Pennsylvania Press, 1965), p. 48.
8. Quoted in Lindberg, p. 375.

■ Suggested Reading

Bireley, Robert. *The Refashioning of Catholicism: A Reassessment of the Counter Reformation.* 1999. A well-written survey that places the Roman Catholic Church in the context of political, social, and religious developments between 1450 and 1600.

Bossy, John. *Christianity in the West, 1400–1700.* 1985. A subtle, important essay arguing that the Reformation ended communal Christianity and created in its place a more personal religion emphasizing individual self-control.

Cameron, Euan. *The European Reformation.* 1991. The best recent history of the Reformation, emphasizing the common principles of the major reformers.

Dickens, Arthur G. *The English Reformation.* 1991. A classic, clear discussion of English religion, emphasizing the popular enthusiasm for reform, which Dickens believes was connected to the earlier Lollard movements.

Englander, David, Diana Norman, Rosemary O'Day, and W. R. Owens, eds. *Culture and Belief in Europe, 1450–1600: An Anthology of Sources.* 1990. A collection of documents illustrating religious and social values and giving an excellent overview of popular reform.

Haigh, Christopher, ed. *The English Reformation Revised.* 1987. A collection of essays criticizing Dickens's thesis on the popular basis of reform in England; the introduction is especially useful for following what is still an important debate over reform.

McGrath, Alister E. *A Life of John Calvin: A Study in the Shaping of Western Culture.* 1990. An excellent biography emphasizing the definitive role of Calvin's religious thought.

Oberman, Heiko. *Luther: Man Between God and the Devil.* 1989. A brilliant, beautifully written essay connecting Luther to prevailing late medieval ideas about sin, death, and the devil.

Oberman, Heiko, Thomas Brady, and James Tracy, eds. *Handbook of European History, 1400–1600: Late Middle Ages, Renaissance, and Reformation.* 1994–1995. A collection of excellent introductory studies of political, religious, and social life.

Pettegree, Andrew, ed., *The Reformation World.* 2000. A demanding but very comprehensive survey of the most recent work on the Reformation.

 For a searchable list of additional readings for this chapter, go to http://college.hmco.com.

CHAPTER 15

T HREE well-dressed gentlemen stand over a mutilated body; one of them holds up the severed head. Elsewhere sword-wielding men engage in indiscriminate slaughter, even of babies. Corpses are piled up in the background. This painting memorializes the grisly events of August 24, 1572. A band of Catholic noblemen accompanied by the personal guard of the king of France had hunted down a hundred Protestant nobles, asleep in their lodgings in and around the royal palace, and murdered them in cold blood. The king and his counselors had planned the murders as a preemptive political strike because they feared that other Protestant nobles were gathering an army outside Paris. But the calculated attack became a general massacre when ordinary Parisians, overwhelmingly Catholic and believing they were acting in the king's name, turned on their neighbors. About three thousand Protestants were slain in Paris over the next three days.

This massacre came to be called the Saint Bartholomew's Day Massacre for the Catholic saint on whose feast day it fell. Though particularly horrible in its scope, the slaughter was not unusual in the deadly combination of religious and political antagonisms it reflected. Religious conflicts were by definition intractable political conflicts since virtually every religious group felt that all others were heretics who could not be tolerated and must be eliminated. Rulers of all faiths looked to divine authority and religious institutions to uphold their power.

In the decades after 1560, existing political tensions contributed to instability and violence, especially when newly reinforced by religious differences. Royal governments continued to consolidate authority, but resistance to royal power by provinces, nobles, or towns accustomed to independence now might have a religious sanction.

The Saint Bartholomew's Day Massacre.
(Musée Cantonal des Beaux-Arts, Lausanne)

Europe in the Age of Religious Wars 1560–1648

Economic Change and Social Tensions

Imperial Spain and the Limits of Royal Power

Religious and Political Conflict in France and England

The Holy Roman Empire and the Thirty Years' War, 1555–1648

Writing, Drama, and Art in an Age of Upheaval

Warfare over these issues had consumed the Holy Roman Empire in the first half of the sixteenth century. The conflict had now spilled over into France and the Netherlands, and threatened to erupt in England. In the early seventeenth century, the Holy Roman Empire once again was wracked by a war simultaneously religious and political in origin. Regardless of its roots, warfare itself had become more destructive than ever before thanks to innovations in military technology and campaign tactics. Tensions everywhere were also worsened by economic changes, especially soaring prices and grinding unemployment.

A period of tension, even extraordinary violence, in political and social life, the era of the late sixteenth and early seventeenth centuries was also distinguished by great creativity in some areas of cultural and intellectual life. The plays of Shakespeare, for example, mirrored the passions but also reflected on the dilemmas of the day and helped to analyze Europeans' circumstances with a new degree of sophistication.

Economic Change and Social Tensions

 RELIGIOUS strife, warfare, and economic change disrupted the everyday lives of whole communities as well as individuals in the late sixteenth and early seventeenth centuries. Wars were devastating to many areas of western Europe and contributed to especially severe economic decline in parts of the Low Countries (the Netherlands), France, and the Holy Roman Empire. But other factors, most notably a steady rise in prices, also played a role in the dramatic economic and social changes of the century after 1550. A series of economic changes altered power relations in cities, in the countryside, and in the relationship of both to central governments. Ordinary people managed their economic difficulties in a variety of ways: they sought new sources of work; they protested against burdensome taxes; sometimes, they found scapegoats for their distress among their neighbors.

■ Economic Transformation and the New Elites

The most obvious economic change was an unrelenting rise in prices, which resulted in the concentration of wealth in fewer and fewer hands. Sixteenth-century observers attributed rising prices to the inflationary effects of the influx of precious metals from Spanish territories in the New World. Historians now believe that European causes may also have helped trigger this "price revolution." Steady population growth caused a relative shortage of goods, particularly food, and the result was higher prices. Both the amount and the effect of price changes were highly localized, depending on factors such as the structure of local economies and the success of harvests. Between 1550 and 1600, however, the price of grain may have risen between 50 and 100 percent, and sometimes more, in cities throughout Europe—including eastern Europe, the breadbasket for growing urban areas to the west. Wages did not keep pace with prices; historians estimate that wages lost between one-tenth and one-fourth of their value by the end of the century. The political and religious struggles of the era thus took place against a background of increasing want, and economic distress was often expressed in both political and religious terms.

These economic changes affected the wealthy as well as the poor. During this period, monarchs were making new accommodations with the hereditary aristocracy—with the Crown usually emerging stronger, if only through concessions to aristocrats' economic interests. Underlying this new symbiosis of monarchy and traditional warrior-nobles were the effects of the widespread economic changes. These changes would eventually blur lines between the old noble families and the new elites and would simplify power relationships within the state. Conditions in the countryside, where there were fewer resources to feed more mouths, grew less favorable. But at the same time more capital became available to wealthy urban or landholding families to invest in the countryside, by buying land outright on which to live like gentry or by making loans to desperate peasants. This capital came from profits from expanded production and trade and was also an effect of the scarcity of land as population and prices rose. Enterprising landholders raised ground rents wherever they could, or they converted land to the production of wool, grain, and other cash crops destined for distant markets.

As a result, a stratum of wealthy, educated, and socially ambitious "new gentry," as these families were called in England, began growing and solidifying. Many of the men of these families were royal officeholders. Where the practice existed, many bought titles outright or were granted nobility as a benefit of their offices. They often lent money to royal governments. The monumental expense of wars made becoming a lender to government, as well as to individuals, an attractive way to live off personal capital.

No one would have confused this up-and-coming gentry with warrior-aristocrats from old families, but the social distinctions between them are less important (to us) than what they had in common: legal privilege, the security of landownership, a cooperative relationship with the monarchy. Monarchs deliberately favored the new gentry as counterweights to independent aristocrats.

City governments also changed character as wealth accumulated in the hands of formerly commercial families. Town councils became dominated by successive generations of privileged families, now more likely to live from landed than from commercial wealth. By the beginning of the seventeenth century, traditional guild control of government had been subverted in many

CHRONOLOGY

1558–1603	Reign of Elizabeth I
1559	Act of Supremacy (England)
1562–1598	Religious wars in France
1565	Netherlands city councils and nobility ignore Philip's law against heresy
1566	Calvinist "iconoclastic fury" begins
1567	Duke of Alba arrives in the Netherlands
1571	Defeat of Turkish navy at Lepanto
1576	Sack of Antwerp
1579	Union of Utrecht
1588	Defeat of Spanish Armada
1589–1610	Reign of Henry IV
1598	Edict of Nantes
1609	Truce is declared between Spain and the Netherlands
1618–1648	Thirty Years' War
1620	Catholic victory at Battle of White Mountain
1621	Truce between Spain and the Netherlands expires; war between Spain and the Netherlands begins
1629	Peace of Alais
1631	Swedes under Gustav Adolf defeat imperial forces
1632	Death of Gustav Adolf
1635	Peace of Prague
1640–1653	"Long Parliament" in session in England
1648	Peace of Westphalia

places. Towns became more closely tied to royal interests by means of the mutual interests of Crown and town elites. The long medieval tradition of towns serving as independent corporate bodies had come to an end.

■ Economic Change and the Common People

The growth of markets around Europe and in Spanish possessions overseas, as well as population growth within Europe, had a marked effect on patterns of production and the lives of artisans and laborers. Production of cloth on a large scale for export, for example, now required huge amounts of capital—much more than a typical guild craftsman could amass. Cloth production was increasingly controlled by new investor-producers with enormous resources and access to distant markets. These entrepreneurs bought up large amounts of wool and hired it out to be cleaned, spun into thread, and woven into cloth by wage laborers in urban workshops or by pieceworkers in their homes. Thousands of women and men in the countryside around urban centers helped to support themselves and their families in this way.

The new entrepreneurs had sufficient capital entirely to bypass guild production. In towns, guilds still regulated most trades but could not accommodate the numbers of artisans who sought to join them. Fewer and fewer apprentices and journeymen could expect to become master artisans. The masters began to treat apprentices virtually as wage laborers, at times letting them go during slow periods. The household mode of production, in which apprentices and journeymen had worked and lived side by side with the master's family, also began to break down, with profound economic, social, and political consequences.

One of the first reflections of the dire circumstances faced by artisans was an attempt to reduce competition at the expense of the artisans' own mothers, sisters, daughters, and sons. Increasingly, widows were forbidden to continue practicing their husbands' enterprises, though they headed from 10 to 15 percent of households in many trades. Women had traditionally learned and practiced many trades but rarely followed the formal progress from apprenticeship to master status. A woman usually combined work of this kind with household production, with selling her products and those of her husband, and with bearing and nursing children. Outright exclusion of women from guild organization appears as early as the thirteenth century but now began regularly to appear in guild statutes. In addition, town governments tried to restrict women's participation in work such as selling in markets, which they had long dominated. Even midwives had to defend their practices, even though as part of housewifery women were expected to know about herbal remedies and practical medicine. (See the box "Reading Sources: A Woman Defends Her Right to Practice Healing.") Working women

thus began to have difficulty supporting themselves if single or widowed and difficulty supporting their children. In the changing position of such women, we can see the distress of the entire stratum of society that they represent.

Wealth in the countryside was also becoming more stratified. Population growth caused many peasant farms to be subdivided for numerous children, creating tiny plots that could not support the families who lived on them. Countless peasants lost what lands they had to wealthy investors—many of them newly wealthy gentry—who lent them money for renting more land or for purchasing seed and tools, and then reclaimed the land when the peasants failed to repay. Other peasants were simply unable to rent land as rents rose. To survive, some sought work as day laborers on the land of rich landlords or more prosperous farmers. But with the shrinking opportunities for farming, this option became less feasible. Many found their way to cities, where they swelled the ranks of the poor. Others, like some of their urban counterparts, coped by becoming part of the newly expanding network of cloth production, combining spinning and weaving with subsistence farming. However, one bad harvest might send them out on the roads begging or odd-jobbing; many did not long survive such a life.

In eastern Europe, peasants faced other dilemmas, for their lands had a different relationship to the wider European economy. The more densely urbanized western Europe, whose wealth controlled the patterns of trade, sought bulk goods, particularly grain, from eastern Germany, Poland, and Lithuania. Thus, there was an economic incentive for landowners in eastern Europe to bind peasants to the land just as the desire of their rulers for greater cooperation had granted the landlords more power. Serfdom now spread in eastern Europe when precisely the opposite condition—a more mobile labor force—grew in the West.

■ Coping with Poverty and Violence

The common people of Europe did not submit passively to either the economic difficulties or the religious and political crises of their day. Whatever their religion, common people took the initiative in attacking members of other faiths to rid their communities of them. Heretics were considered to be spiritual pollution that might provoke God's wrath, and ordinary citizens believed that they had to eliminate heretics if the state failed to do so. Common people, as well as elites and governments, were thus responsible for the violence that sometimes occurred in the name of religion.

A Woman Defends Her Right to Practice Healing

In this document, Katharine Carberiner testifies to the city council of Munich in defense of her right to her livelihood. Notice that she insists she does not deliberately compete with male doctors. Rather, she has skills that might lead women to choose her over male practitioners. How else does she justify her right to practice healing? Do you think the members of the city government were persuaded by her appeal?

I use my feminine skills, given by the grace of God, only when someone entreats me earnestly, and never advertise myself, but only when someone has been left for lost. . . . I do whatever I can possibly do . . . using only simple and allowable means that should not be forbidden or proscribed in the least. Not one person who has come under my care has a complaint or grievance against me. If the doctors, apothecaries or barber-surgeons have claimed this, it is solely out of spite.

At all times, as is natural, women have more trust in other women to discover their secrets, problems and illnesses, than they have in men—but perhaps this jealousy came from that. Undoubtedly as well, husbands who love and cherish their wives will seek any help and assistance they can, even that from women, if the wives have been given up (by the doctors) or otherwise come into great danger.

Because I know that I can help in my own small way, I will do all I can, even, as according to the Gospel, we should help pull an ox out of a well it has fallen into on Sunday.

Source: Quoted in Merry Wiesner, "Women's Defense of Their Public Role," in Mary Beth Rose, ed., *Women in the Middle Ages and the Renaissance* (Syracuse: Syracuse University Press, 1986), p. 9.

Ordinary people fought in wars not only from conviction but also from the need for self-defense and from economic choice. It was ordinary people who defended the walls of towns, dug siege works, and manned artillery batteries. Although nobles remained military leaders, armies consisted mostly of infantry made up of common people, not mounted knights. Women were part of armies, too. Much of the day-to-day work of finding food and firewood, cleaning guns, and endlessly repairing inadequate clothing was done by women looking after their husbands and lovers among the troops.

Many men joined the armies and navies of their rulers because, given the alternatives, the military seemed a reasonable way of life. Landless farm hands, day laborers, and out-of-work artisans found the prospect of employment in the army attractive enough to outweigh the dangers of military life. Desertion was common; nothing more than the rumor that a soldier's home village was threatened might prompt a man to abandon his post. Battle-hardened troops could threaten their commanders not only with desertion but with mutiny. A mutiny of Spanish soldiers in 1574 was a well-organized affair, for example, somewhat like a strike. Occasionally, mutinies were brutally suppressed; more often, they were successful and troops received some of their back wages.

Townspeople and country people participated in riots and rebellions to protest their circumstances when the situation was particularly dire or when other means of action had failed. The devastation of religious war led to both peasant rebellions and urban uprisings. Former soldiers, prosperous farmers, or even noble landlords whose economic fortunes were tied to peasant profits might lead rural revolts. Urban protests could begin spontaneously when new grievances worsened existing problems. In Naples, in 1585, food riots were provoked not simply by a shortage of grain but by a government decision to raise the price of bread during the shortage. Rebels sometimes seized property—for example, they might distribute looted bread among themselves—and occasionally killed officials. Their protests rarely generated lasting political change and were usually brutally quashed.

Governments at all levels tried to cope with the increasing problem of poverty by changing the administration and scale of poor relief. In both Catholic and Protestant Europe, caring for the poor became more institutionalized and systematic, and more removed from religious impulses. In the second half of the sixteenth century, governments established public almshouses and poorhouses to dispense food or to care for orphans or the destitute in towns throughout Catholic and Protestant Europe. Initially, these institutions reflected

Publicizing Witch Trials   Printed pamphlets, such as this one describing the execution of three women in Essex, England, spread the news of local "outbreaks" of witchcraft. One of the women, Joan Prentis, is also depicted surrounded by her animal familiars. The ferret in Joan's lap, the pamphlet relates, was the Devil himself in animal form.   *(Lambeth Palace Library)*

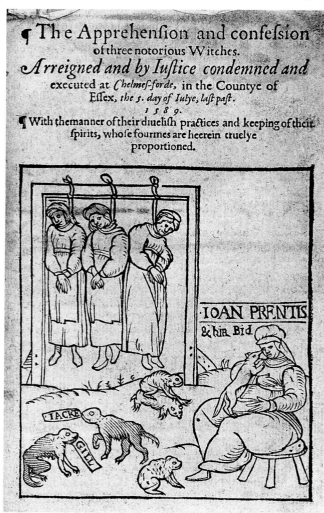

an optimistic vision of an ideal Christian community attentive to material want. But by 1600, the charitable distribution of food was accompanied by attempts to distinguish "deserving" from "undeserving" poor, by an insistence that the poor work for their ration of food, and even by an effort to compel the poor to live in almshouses and poorhouses.

These efforts were not uniformly successful. Begging was outlawed by Catholic and Protestant city governments alike, but never thoroughly suppressed. Catholic religious orders and parishes often resisted efforts at regulating their charitable work—even when they were imposed by Catholic governments. Nonetheless, the trend was clear. From viewing poverty as a fact of life and as an occasional lesson in Christian humility, European elites were beginning to see it as a social problem. And they saw the poor as people in need of control and institutional discipline.

■ The Hunt for Witches

Between approximately 1550 and 1650, Europe saw a dramatic increase in the persecution of women and men for witchcraft. Approximately one hundred thousand people were tried and about sixty thousand executed. The surge in witch-hunting was closely linked to communities' religious concerns and also to the social tensions that resulted from economic difficulties.

Certain types of witchcraft had long existed in Europe. So-called black magic of various kinds—one peasant casting a spell on another peasant's cow—had been common since the Middle Ages. What now made the practice seem particularly menacing, especially to elites, were theories linking black magic to Devil worship. Catholic leaders and legal scholars began to advance such theories in the fifteenth century, and by the late sixteenth century both Catholic and Protestant elites viewed a witch not only as someone who might cast harmful spells but also as a heretic.

The impetus for most individual accusations of witchcraft came from within the communities where the "witch" lived—that is, from common people. Usually targeted were solitary or unpopular people whose difficult relationships with fellow villagers made them seem likely sources of evil. Often, such a person had practiced black magic (or had been suspected of doing so) for years, and the villagers took action only when faced with a community crisis, such as an epidemic.

A majority of accused witches were women. Lacking legal, social, and political resources, women may have been more likely than men to use black magic for self-protection or advancement. Women's work often made them vulnerable to charges of witchcraft since families' food supplies and routine medicines passed through women's hands. The deaths of young children or of domestic animals, such as a milk cow, were among the most common triggers for witchcraft accusation. The increase in poverty during the late sixteenth and early seventeenth centuries made poor women frequent targets of witch-hunts. It was easier to find such a woman menacing—and to accuse her of wrongdoing—than to feel guilty because of her evident need.

Both Christian dogma and humanistic writing portrayed women as morally weaker than men and thus more susceptible to the Devil's enticements. Writings on witchcraft described Devil worship in sexual terms, and the prosecution of witches had a voyeuristic, sexual dimension. The bodies of accused witches were searched for the "Devil's mark"—a blemish thought to be Satan's imprint. In some regions, women accounted for 80 percent of those prosecuted and executed. A dynamic of gender stereotyping was not always at work, however; in other regions, prosecutions were more evenly divided between men and women, and occasionally men made up the majority of those accused.

Because they were often prompted by village disasters or tragedies, individual accusations of witchcraft increased in these decades in response to the crises that beset many communities. In addition, isolated accusations often started localized frenzies of active hunting for other witches. Dozens of "witches" might be identified and executed before the whirlwind subsided. These more widespread hunts were driven, in part, by the anxieties of local elites about disorder and heresy and were facilitated by contemporary legal procedures that they applied. These procedures permitted lax rules of evidence and the use of torture to extract confessions. Torture or the threat of torture led most of those accused of witchcraft to "confess," and to name accomplices or other "witches." In this way, a single initial accusation could lead to dozens of prosecutions. In regions where procedures for appealing convictions and sentences were fragile or nonexistent, witch-hunts could expand with alarming speed. Aggressive hunts were common, for example, in the small principalities and imperial cities of the Holy Roman Empire, which were largely independent of higher political authority.

The widespread witch-hunts virtually ended by the late seventeenth century, in part because the intellectual energies of elites shifted from religious to scientific thought. The practice of witchcraft continued among common folk, although accusations of one neighbor by another never again reached the level of these crisis-ridden decades.

IMPERIAL SPAIN AND THE LIMITS OF ROYAL POWER

T O contemporary observers, no political fact of the late sixteenth century was more obvious than the ascendancy of Spain. Philip II (r. 1556–1598) ruled Spanish conquests in the New World as well as wealthy territories in Europe, including the Netherlands and parts of Italy. Yet imperial Spain did not escape the political, social, and religious turmoil of the era. Explosive combinations of religious dissent and political disaffection led to revolt against Spain in the Netherlands. This conflict revealed the endemic tensions of sixteenth-century political life: nobles, towns, and provinces trying to safeguard remnants of medieval autonomy against efforts at greater centralization—with the added complications of economic strain and religious division. The revolt also demonstrated the material limits of royal power, since even with treasure from the American conquests pouring in, Philip could at times barely afford to keep armies in the field. As American silver dwindled in the seventeenth century, Philip's successors faced severe financial and political strains even in their Spanish domains.

■ The Revolt of the Netherlands

Philip's power stemmed in part from the far-flung territories he inherited from his father, the Habsburg king of Spain and Holy Roman emperor Charles V: Spain, the Low Countries (the Netherlands), the duchy of Milan, the kingdom of Naples, the conquered lands in the Americas, and the Philippine Islands in Asia. (Control of Charles's Austrian lands had passed to his brother, Ferdinand, Philip's uncle; see Map 15.1.) Treasure fleets bearing precious metals from the New World began to reach Spain regularly during Philip's reign. Spain was now the engine powering a trading economy unlike any that had existed in Europe before. To supply its colonies, Spain needed timber and other shipbuilding materials from the hinterlands of the Baltic Sea. Grain from the Baltic fed the urban populations of Spain (where wool was the principal cash crop) and the Netherlands, while the Netherlands, in turn, was a source of finished goods, such as cloth. The major exchange point for all of these goods was the city of Antwerp in the Netherlands, the leading trading center of all of Europe by 1550.

The Netherlands were the jewel among Philip's European possessions. These seventeen provinces (constituting mostly the modern nations of Belgium and the

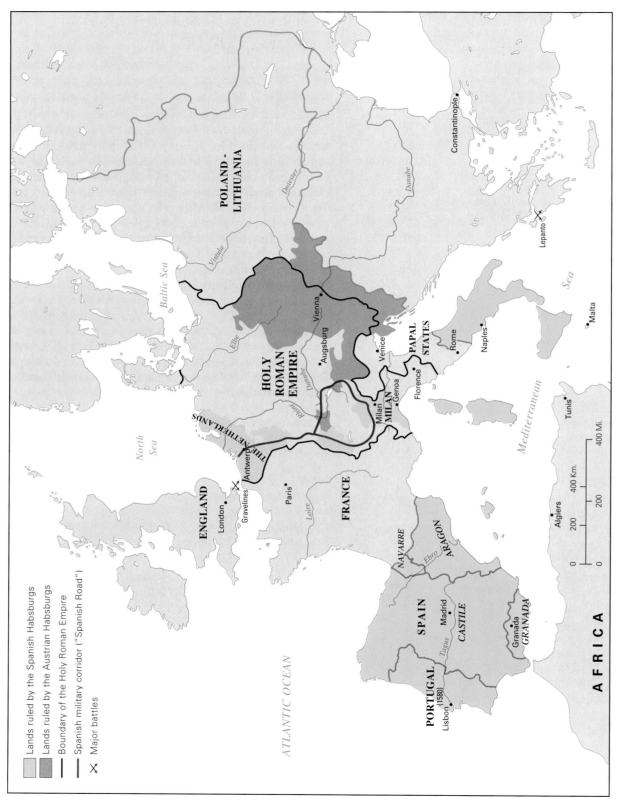

Map 15.1   The Spanish Habsburgs and Europe, ca. 1556   Philip II's control of territories in northern Italy permitted the overland access of Spanish troops to the Netherlands and heightened the Spanish threat to France. Lands bordering the western Mediterranean made the sea a natural sphere of Spanish influence as well. Habsburg lands in central Europe were controlled after 1556 by Charles V's brother Ferdinand and his descendants.

The City of Antwerp   Antwerp, in the southern Netherlands, was the point of sale for Portuguese spices brought around Africa from India, the selling and transshipping center for Baltic goods, including timber, fur, and grain, and the source for manufactured goods such as cloth.   *(Musées royaux des Beaux-Arts de Belgique)*

Netherlands) had been centers of trade and manufacture since the twelfth century and, in the fourteenth and fifteenth centuries, had enjoyed political importance and a period of cultural innovation under the control of the dukes of Burgundy. By the time Philip inherited the provinces from his father, a sort of federal system of government had evolved to accommodate the various centers of power. Each province had an assembly (Estates) in which representatives of leading nobility and towns authorized taxation, but each also acknowledged a central administration in Brussels that represented Philip. Heading the council of state in Brussels was a governor-general, Philip's half-sister, Margaret of Parma.

Philip's clumsy efforts to adjust this distribution of power in his favor pushed his subjects in the Netherlands into revolt. Though conscientious to a fault, Philip was a rigid, unimaginative man. Born and raised in Spain, he had little real familiarity with the densely populated, linguistically diverse Netherlands, and he never visited there after 1559. Early in Philip's reign, tensions in the Netherlands arose over taxation and over Spanish insistence on maintaining tight control. Bad harvests and commercial disruptions occasioned by wars in the Baltic region in the 1560s depressed the Netherlands' economy and made it difficult for the provinces to pay taxes demanded by Spain. When the Peace of Cateau-Cambrésis° of 1559 brought an end to the long struggle between the Habsburgs and the Valois° kings of France, the people of the Netherlands had reason to hope for lower taxes and reduced levels of Spanish control, yet neither was forthcoming. Indeed, Philip had named to the council of state officials who were Spaniards themselves or had close ties to the Spanish court, bypassing local nobles who had fought for Philip and his father before 1559 and who expected positions of influence in his government.

Cateau-Cambrésis (kah-toe kam-bray-SEE)   **Valois** (val-WAH)

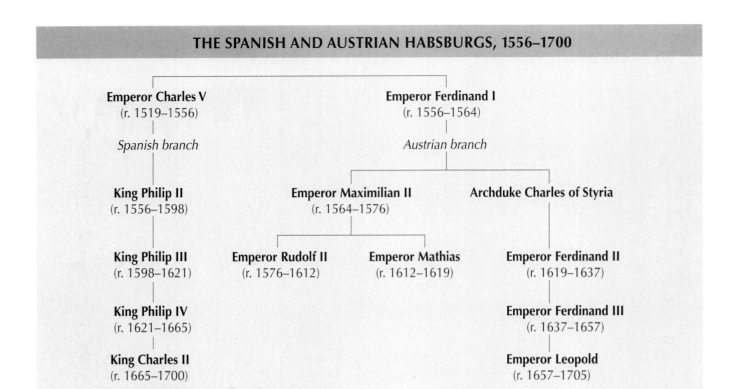

THE SPANISH AND AUSTRIAN HABSBURGS, 1556–1700

Emperor Charles V
(r. 1519–1556)

Spanish branch

Emperor Ferdinand I
(r. 1556–1564)

Austrian branch

King Philip II
(r. 1556–1598)

Emperor Maximilian II
(r. 1564–1576)

Archduke Charles of Styria

King Philip III
(r. 1598–1621)

Emperor Rudolf II
(r. 1576–1612)

Emperor Mathias
(r. 1612–1619)

Emperor Ferdinand II
(r. 1619–1637)

King Philip IV
(r. 1621–1665)

Emperor Ferdinand III
(r. 1637–1657)

King Charles II
(r. 1665–1700)

Emperor Leopold
(r. 1657–1705)

Philip only added to the economic and political discontent by unleashing an invigorated repression of heresy. Unlike his father, Philip directed the hunt for heretics not just at lower-class dissenters but also at well-to-do Calvinists—followers of the French Protestant religious reformer John Calvin—whose numbers were considerable. Punishment for heresy now included confiscation of family property not just execution of the individual. By 1565 municipal councils in the Netherlands were routinely refusing to enforce Philip's religious policies, believing that urban prosperity—as well as their personal security—depended on restraint in the prosecution of heresy. Leading nobles also stopped enforcing the policies on their estates.

Encouraged by greater tolerance, by 1566 Protestants had begun to hold open-air meetings and attracted new converts in many towns. In a series of actions called the "iconoclastic fury," townsfolk around the provinces stripped Catholic churches of the relics and statues deemed idolatrous by Calvinist doctrine. At the same time, reflecting the economic strain of these years, some townsfolk rioted to protest the price of bread. One prominent nobleman warned Philip, "All trade has come to a standstill, so that there are 100,000 men begging for their bread who used to earn it . . . which is [important] since poverty can force people to do things which otherwise they would never think of doing."[1]

In early 1567 armed bands of Calvinist insurgents seized two towns in the southern Netherlands by force of arms in hopes of stirring a general revolt that would secure freedom of worship. Margaret of Parma quelled the uprisings by rallying city governments and loyal nobles, now fearful for their own property and power. But by then, far away in Spain, a decision had been made to send in the Spanish duke of Alba with an army of ten thousand men.

Alba arrived in August 1567 and, to bolster his own shaky standing at the Spanish court, acted more like a conqueror than a peacemaker. He billeted troops in friendly cities, established new courts to try rebels, arrested thousands of people, executed about a thousand rebels (including Catholics as well as prominent Protestants), and imposed heavy new taxes to support his army. Thus, Alba repeated every mistake of Spanish policy that had triggered rebellion in the first place.

Margaret of Parma resigned in disgust and left the Netherlands. Protestants from rebellious towns escaped into exile, where they were joined by nobles who had been declared traitors for resisting Alba's extreme policies. The most important of these was William of Nassau°, prince of Orange (1533–1584), whose lands outside the Netherlands, in France and the empire, lay beyond

Nassau (NAS-saw)

Philip II in 1583   Dressed in the austere black in fashion at the Spanish court, Philip holds a rosary and wears the Order of the Golden Fleece, an order of knighthood, around his neck. At age 56 Philip has outlived four wives and most of his children.   *(Museo del Prado, Madrid)*

Spanish reach and so could be used to finance continued warfare against Spain. A significant community with military capability began to grow in exile.

In 1572 ships of exiled Calvinist privateers known as the "Sea Beggars" began preying on Spanish shipping and coastal fortresses from bases in the northern provinces. The northern provinces, increasingly Calvinist, became the center of opposition to the Spanish, who concentrated their efforts against rebellion in the wealthier southern provinces. Occasionally the French and English lent aid to the rebels.

The war in the Netherlands was a showcase for the new and costly technology of warfare in this period. Many towns in the Netherlands were (or came to be, as a consequence of the revolt) equipped with "bastions,"

newly designed walled defenses that could resist artillery fire; such cities could not be taken by storm. Where bastions had been built, military campaigns consisted of grueling sieges, skirmishes in surrounding areas for control of supplies, and occasional pitched battles between besiegers and forces attempting to break the siege. Vast numbers of men were required both for effective besieging forces and for garrisoning the many fortresses that controlled the countryside and defended access to major towns.

In an attempt to supply the Netherlands with seasoned veterans and materiel from Spain and Spanish territories in Italy, the Spanish developed the "Spanish Road," an innovative string of supply depots where provisions could be gathered in advance of troops marching

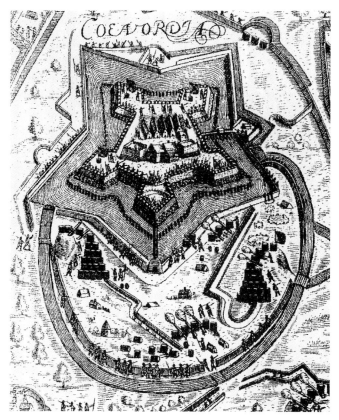

Bastioned Fortress This fortress in the Netherlands was protected by five bastions—the five pentagonal projections around the buildings in the center. The bastions enabled defenders to fire from all angles on besiegers and created a smaller expanse of wall on which besiegers could direct artillery fire. The walls were also lower than those of a medieval fortress and were reinforced with earth. The Dutch took this fortress from the Spanish in 1592—a rare successful attack on a bastioned fortress—by tunneling to the outer wall (*lower right*) and mining it with huge explosive charges. (*From Christopher Duffy,* Siege Warfare: The Fortress in the Early Modern World, 1494–1660 *[London: Routledge]. Reproduced with permission.*)

Map 15.2 The Netherlands, 1559–1609 The seventeen provinces of the Netherlands were strikingly diverse politically, economically, and culturally. Like his father, Philip was, technically, the ruler of each province separately—that is, he was count of Flanders, duke of Brabant, and so forth.

to the Netherlands (see Map 15.1). Maintaining its large armies, however, taxed Spain's resources to the breaking point. Even with American silver at hand, Philip could at times barely afford to keep armies in the field. Inevitably, large numbers of troops also exhausted the countryside, and both soldiers and civilians suffered great privations. On occasion, Spanish troops reacted violently to difficult conditions and to delayed pay (American treasure dwindled badly between 1572 and 1578). In 1576 Spanish troops sacked the hitherto loyal city of Antwerp and massacred about eight thousand people. This event was bitterly remembered afterward as the "Spanish Fury."

The massacre prompted leaders in the southern provinces to raise their own armies to protect themselves against the Spanish. Late in 1576, they concluded an alliance with William of Orange and the northern rebels. But the northern and southern provinces were increasingly divided by religion, and their differences were skillfully exploited by Philip's new commander, Margaret's son Alexander Farnese°, duke of Parma. With galleons from America filling the king's coffers again, Parma wooed the Catholic elites of the southern provinces back into loyalty to Philip, in return for promises to respect their provincial liberties and safeguard their property from troops.

In 1579 the northern provinces united in a defensive alliance, the Union of Utrecht°, against the increasingly unified south. Parma's forces could not surmount the natural barrier of the Rhine River that bisects the Low Countries (see Map 15.2) or meet the increasing costs of

Farnese (far-NAY-zee) **Utrecht** (OO-trekt)

siege warfare in waterlogged terrain, particularly as Spain diverted money to conflicts with England, in 1588, and France, after 1589. In 1609 a truce was finally concluded between Spain and the northern provinces. This truce did not formally recognize the "United Provinces" as an independent entity, though in fact they were. The modern nations of Belgium (the Spanish provinces) and the Netherlands are the distant result of this truce.

The independent United Provinces (usually called, simply, the Netherlands) was a fragile state, an accident of warfare at first. But commercial prosperity began to emerge as its greatest strength. Much of the economic activity of Antwerp had shifted north to Amsterdam in the province of Holland because of fighting in the south and a naval blockade of Antwerp by rebel ships. Philip's policies had created a new enemy nation and had enriched it at his expense.

■ The Failure of the Invincible Armada

The revolt of the Netherlands had lured Spain into wider strategic involvement, particularly against England. England and Spain had a common foe in France and common economic interests, and Philip had married Mary Tudor, the Catholic queen of England (r. 1553–1558). Even after Mary's death and the accession of her Protestant half-sister, Queen Elizabeth (r. 1558–1603), Spanish-English relations remained cordial. Relations started to sour, however, when Elizabeth began tolerating the use of English ports by the rebel Sea Beggars and authorizing attacks by English privateers on Spanish treasure fleets. In response, Spain supported Catholic resistance to Elizabeth within England, including plots to replace Elizabeth on the throne with her Catholic cousin Mary, Queen of Scots. Greater Spanish success in the Netherlands, raids by the Spanish and English on each other's shipping, and Elizabeth's execution of Mary in 1587 prompted Philip to order an invasion of England. A fleet (*armada*) of Spanish warships sailed in 1588.

"The enterprise of England," as the plan was called in Spain, represented an astounding logistical effort. The Armada was supposed to clear the English Channel of English ships in order to permit an invading force—troops under Parma in the Netherlands—to cross on barges. The sheer number of ships required for the undertaking—about 130—meant that some, inevitably, were slower supply ships, or vessels designed for the more protected waters of the Mediterranean. The English also had the advantage in arms, since they had better long-range artillery and better-trained gunners.

When the Armada entered the Channel on July 29, the English harassed the Spanish with artillery from a distance without sustaining much damage themselves. Parma could not get his men readied on their barges quickly enough once the fleet's presence in the Channel had been confirmed by messenger, nor could the fleet protect itself while waiting offshore. On the night of August 7, the English launched eight fire ships—burning vessels set adrift to deliver arson—into the anchored Spanish fleet. At dawn on the next day, they attacked the weakened fleet off Gravelines°, sank many ships, and dispersed what remained. (See the box "Reading Sources: Secret Dispatches from the Venetian Ambassador in Spain.")

The Battle at Gravelines was the first major artillery battle by sailing ships and helped set the future course of naval warfare. It was a disaster for Philip's hopes, and for thousands of sailors and soldiers in Spanish pay. Many of the surviving ships sank in bad weather, or were forced into hostile harbors, as the Armada sailed for home around the northern tip of the British Isles (see Map 15.1). Less than half of Philip's great fleet made it back to Spain.

■ Successes at Home and Around the Mediterranean

Despite his bountiful overseas empire and his preoccupation with the Netherlands, many of Philip's interests still centered on the Mediterranean. Spain and the kingdom of Naples had exchanged trade for centuries. Newer ties had been forged with the duchy of Milan and the city-state of Genoa, whose bankers were financiers to the Spanish monarchy. It was in his kingdoms of Spain and their Mediterranean sphere of interest that Philip made his power felt more effectively, though not without effort.

Philip's father, Charles V, had tried to secure the western Mediterranean against the Turks and their client states along the African coast, but it was under Philip that the Turkish challenge in the western Mediterranean receded. The Spanish allied temporarily with the papacy and Venice—both were concerned with the Turkish naval power in the Mediterranean—and their combined navies inflicted a massive defeat on the Turkish navy at Lepanto, off the coast of Greece, in October 1571 (see Map 15.1). The Turks remained the leading power in the eastern Mediterranean, but their ability to threaten Spain and Spanish possessions in the west was over.

To Philip and his advisers, the Turks represented a potential internal threat as well, since it was feared they might incite rebellion among his Muslim subjects. These

Gravelines (grahv-LEEN)

❧ READING SOURCES

Secret Dispatches from the Venetian Ambassador in Spain

Because it so heavily depended on its trading empire, Venice closely monitored developments at foreign courts. The Venetian ambassador at the Spanish court sent these reports back about the Spanish Armada. Note that the most sensitive material (here, in italics) was sent in code. What differences do you notice between the encoded and other dispatches? What seems to be the ambassador's attitude toward Philip and his invincible fleet? What can you learn from these dispatches about how fast and how accurately news traveled in sixteenth-century Europe?

April 30, 1588

Day by day we are expecting news that the Armada has sailed. It has drawn down the river to Belem at the mouth of the port, three miles from Lisbon. The blessing of the standard [flag] was performed with great pomp and many salvos of artillery.... Here in all the churches they make constant prayers; and the king himself is on his knees two or three hours every day before the sacrament. Everyone hopes that the greater the difficulties, humanly speaking, the greater will be the favor of God.

June 4, 1588

The Armada set sail from Lisbon at length on the twenty-ninth of last month, a Sunday.... They are now waiting the news of its arrival at Corunna to embark more troops, and then to sail. I have from time to time reported the great preparations which have been made; but we here must expect news of its progress from other quarters now, unless the peace is effected in Flanders.

July 12, 1588

The wiser wonder what can induce the king to insist, quite against his natural temper, that the Armada shall give battle to the English, who are known to be awaiting the attack with eager courage, and so they surmise that, over and above the belief that God will be on his side, two motives urge the king to this course; first, that he has some secret understandings which will fail if there is any delay; secondly, that these expenses of a million of gold a month cannot be supported for long, and so he has resolved to try his fortune....

August 20, 1588

Don Bernardino de Mendoza [the Spanish ambassador in France] announces from France, in letters of the second of August, that the Armada has given battle to the English, sunk some of their ships, won a great victory and passed on to join the duke of Parma; but the report is so confused, and that ambassador is so accustomed to deceive himself, that they are waiting confirmation of the news....

September 6, 1588

The bad news received in dispatches from the duke of Parma, and dated the tenth of August . . . pain the king and the court all the more that they were unexpected, and moreover quite contrary to the news sent by [Mendoza], who by three different couriers had confirmed . . . that [the Armada] had sunk many of the enemy and was on the point of effecting a junction with the Duke of Parma.... It is a blessing that the bad news did not reach Spain while the king was suffering from fever, for though His Majesty professes to allow no occurrence to disturb his equanimity, yet this war moves him in such a way as to prove clearly that on other occasions he was only acting and that now he is unable to do so, perhaps because this war is entirely conducted by himself alone and that it should not succeed brings to light all his anxiety.

Source: James C. Davis, ed., *Pursuit of Power: Venetian Ambassadors' Reports on Turkey, France and Spain in the Age of Philip II, 1560–1600* (New York: Harper and Row, 1970), pp. 110–113.

 For additional information on this topic, go to http://college.hmco.com.

were the nominally Christian descendants of the Muslims of Granada who had been conquered by the Spanish in 1492. Called *moriscos,* they had been forced to convert to Christianity in 1504 or be expelled from Spain, but no serious effort had been made to teach them Christian beliefs in their own language (Arabic) and they had not been assimilated into Spanish society. Philip inaugurated a new wave of persecution and provoked a massive rebellion by the moriscos that began on Christmas Day in 1568. The revolt took two years to suppress. After it was crushed, the moriscos of Granada were forcibly exiled and dispersed farther north in Spain.

Philip's power in each of his Spanish kingdoms was limited by the traditional privileges of towns, nobility, and clergy. In Aragon, for example, he could raise revenues only by appealing to local assemblies, the cortes°. Philip made significant inroads into Aragonese independence by the end of his reign, however. Noble feuds and peasant rebellions in Aragon during the 1580s provided a pretext for sending in veteran troops from the Netherlands campaigns to establish firmer royal control. Philip was successful in the long run in Aragon, as he had not been in the Netherlands, because he used adequate force but tempered it afterward with constitutional changes that were cleverly moderate. He cemented the peace by appearing in Aragon in person, in the words of a contemporary, "like a rainbow at the end of a storm."[2]

In Castile, the arid kingdom in the center of the Iberian Peninsula, the king was able to levy taxes with greater ease but only because of concessions that gave nobles undisputed authority over their peasants. Philip established his permanent capital, Madrid, and his principal residence, the Escorial, there. The Spanish Empire became more and more Castilian as the reign progressed, with royal advisers and counselors increasingly drawn only from the Castilian elite. Yet the rural economy of Castile was stunted by the dual oppression of landholders and royal tax collectors.

Philip also invaded and annexed Portugal in 1580, temporarily unifying the Iberian Peninsula. The annexation was ensured by armed force but had been preceded by careful negotiation to guarantee that Philip's claim to the throne—through his mother—would find some support within the country. When Philip died in 1598, he was old and ill, a man for whom daily life had become a painful burden. His Armada had been crushed; the Netherlands had slipped through his fingers. Yet he had learned from his mistakes and had been more successful, by his own standards, in other regions that he ruled.

■ Spain in Decline, 1600–1648

Spain steadily lost ground economically and strategically after the turn of the century. Imports of silver declined. The American mines were exhausted, and the natives forced to work in them were decimated by European diseases and brutal treatment. Spain's economic health was further threatened by the very success of its colonies: local industries in the Americas began to produce goods formerly obtained from Spain. The increasing presence of English, French, and Dutch shipping in the Americas provided colonists with rival sources for the goods they needed. Often, these competitors could offer their goods more cheaply than Spaniards could for Spanish productivity was low and prices were high because of the inflationary effects of the influx of precious metals.

Spain renewed hostilities with the United Provinces in 1621, after the truce of 1609 had expired. Philip IV (r. 1621–1645) also aided his Habsburg cousins in the Thirty Years' War in the Holy Roman Empire (see page 523). Squeezed for troops and revenue for these commitments, other Spanish territories revolted. The uprisings reflected both economic distress and unresolved issues of regional autonomy. Castile bore the brunt of the financial support of the state. The chief minister to Philip IV, Gaspar de Guzmán, Count Olivares° (1587–1645), was an energetic Castilian aristocrat determined to distribute the burdens of government more equitably among the various regions of Spain. His policies provoked rebellions in Catalonia and Portugal.

In Catalonia, a province of the kingdom of Aragon, the revolt began as a popular uprising against the billeting of troops. At one point Catalan leaders invited French troops to defend them and solemnly transferred their loyalty to the French king in the hope that he would respect their autonomy. Spain resumed control only in 1652, after years of military struggle and promises to respect Catalan liberties.

In Portugal, a war of independence began in 1640, also launched by popular revolt. The Spanish government tried to restore order with troops under the command of a leading Portuguese prince, John, duke of Braganza. The duke, however, was the nearest living relative to the last king of Portugal, and he seized this opportunity to claim the crown of Portugal for himself. Although war dragged on until 1668, the Portuguese under John IV (r. 1640–1656) succeeded in winning independence from Spain.

---

cortes (core-TEZ)

Olivares (oh-lih-VAR-ez)

As a result of these uprisings, Count Olivares resigned in disgrace in 1643. In 1647 upheaval would shake Spain's Italian possessions of Sicily and Naples. By mid-century, Spain had lost its position as the pre-eminent state in Europe.

RELIGIOUS AND POLITICAL CONFLICT IN FRANCE AND ENGLAND

 N the second half of the sixteenth century, France was convulsed by civil war that had both religious and political causes. Though a temporary resolution was achieved by 1598, the kingdom was still divided by religion and by military and political challenges to royal authority. England, in contrast, was spared political and religious upheaval in the second half of the century, in part because of the talents and long life of its ruler, Elizabeth I. But in the seventeenth century, constitutional and religious dissent began to reinforce each other in new ways and dramatically threatened royal power.

■ The French Religious Wars, 1562–1598

Civil war wracked France from 1562 until 1598. As in the Netherlands, the conflicts in France had religious and political origins, and international ramifications. The French monarch, like Philip, was unable to monopolize military power. In 1559 the king of France, Henry II (r. 1547–1559), had concluded the Peace of Cateau-Cambrésis with Philip II, ending the Habsburg-Valois Wars, but had died in July of that year from wounds suffered at a tournament held to celebrate the new treaty. His death was a political disaster. Great noble families vied for influence over his 15-year-old son, Francis II (r. 1559–1560). The queen mother, Catherine de' Medici° (1519–1589), worked carefully and intelligently to balance the nobles' interests. She gained greater authority when, in late 1560, the sickly Francis died and was succeeded by his brother, Charles IX—a 10-year-old for whom Catherine was officially the regent. But keeping the conflicts among the great courtiers from boiling over into civil war proved impossible.

In France, as elsewhere, noble conflict invariably had a violent component. Noblemen carried swords and daggers and were accompanied by armed entourages.

Although they relied on patronage and army commands from the Crown, the Crown depended on their services. Provincial landholdings, together with the royal offices they enjoyed, afforded enough resources to support private warfare, and the nobles assumed a right to wage it.

In addition, religious tension was rising throughout France. (Henry II had welcomed the 1559 treaty in part because he wanted to turn his attention to "heresy.") Public preaching by, and secret meetings of, Protestants (known as "Huguenots°" in France) were causing unrest in towns. At court, members of leading noble families—including the Bourbons, who were princes of royal blood—had converted to Protestantism and worshiped openly in their rooms in the palace. In 1561 Catherine convened a national religious council, known as the Colloquy of Poissy°, to reconcile the two faiths. When it failed, she chose provisional religious toleration as the only practical course and issued a limited edict of toleration in the name of the king in January 1562.

The edict led only to further unrest. Ignoring its restrictions, Protestants armed themselves, while townspeople of both faiths insulted and attacked one another at worship sites and religious festivals. In March 1562 the armed retainers of a Catholic duke killed a few dozen Protestants gathered in worship at Vassy° near one of the duke's estates. The killing, in bringing the military power of the nobility to bear on the broader problem of religious division, sparked the first of six civil wars. In some ways, the initial conflict was decisive. The Protestant army lost the principal pitched battle of the war in December 1562. This defeat checked the growth of the Protestant movement by reducing the appeal of the movement to nobles. The peace edict granted in 1563 curtailed the reach of the Huguenot movement; the limited rights granted to Protestants in the Crown's edict made it difficult for Protestants in towns—where the vast majority of them lived—to worship. But if the Protestants were not powerful enough to win, neither were they weak enough to be decisively beaten.

The turning point most obvious to contemporaries came a decade later. The Protestant faction was still represented at court by the Bourbon princes and by the very able and influential nobleman Gaspard de Coligny°, related to the Bourbons by marriage. Coligny was pressing the king for a war against Spain in order to aid Protestant rebels in the Netherlands. Opposed to entanglement in another war against Spain and alarmed by rumors of Huguenot armies massing outside Paris,

---

de' Medici (day MAY-di-chi)

Huguenots (HEW-guh-nots)   **Poissy** (pwa-SEE)   **Vassy** (vah-SEE)   **Gaspard de Coligny** (gas-PAR duh koh-leen-YEE)

≥ READING SOURCES

A Justification for Rebellion Against the King

This is an excerpt from A Defense of Liberty Against Tyrants, *the most important work of Protestant political theory in France, published in 1579. It was probably written by Philippe Duplessis-Mornay, a Huguenot nobleman and confidant of Henry of Navarre who narrowly escaped death in the Saint Bartholomew's Day Massacre. In his tract, the author argues that a contract exists between the sovereign and his people. If the king violates that contract, he thereby becomes a tyrant, and his subjects are no longer obligated to obey him.*

[Must we] always obey God's commandments without any exception, and men's ever with limitation? As there are many princes in these days, calling themselves Christians, which arrogantly assume an unlimited power, over which God himself hath no command, and that they have no want of flatterers, which adore them as gods upon earth, many others also, which for fear or by constraint, either seem or else do believe, that princes ought to be obeyed in all things by all men. And withal, seeing the unhappiness of these times is such that there is nothing so firm, certain or pure which is not shaken, disgraced or polluted; I fear that whosoever shall . . . consider these things will confess this question to be not only most profitable, but also, the times considered, most necessary. . . . Princes exceed their bounds, not contenting themselves with that authority which the almighty and all good God hath given them, but seek to usurp that sovereignty, which he hath reserved to himself over all men, being not content to command the bodies and goods of their subjects . . . but assume license to themselves to enforce the consciences, which appertains chiefly to Jesus Christ. . . .

Now for that we see that God invests kings into their kingdoms, almost in the same manner that vassals are invested into their [fiefs] by their sovereign, we must needs conclude that kings are the vassals of God, and deserve to be deprived of the benefit they receive from their lord if they commit a felony, in the same fashion as rebellious vassals are of their estates. These premises being allowed, this question may easily be resolved; for if God hold the place of the sovereign lord, and the king as vassal, who dare deny but that we must rather obey the sovereign than the vassal? If God commands one thing, and the king commands the contrary, what is that proud man that would term him a rebel who refuses to obey the king, when else he must disobey God?

Source: Harold J. Laski, ed., *A Defense of Liberty Against Tyrants* (Gloucester, Mass.: Peter Smith, 1963), pp. 65–66, 79.

Charles IX (r. 1560–1574) and his mother authorized royal guards to murder Coligny and other Protestant leaders on August 24, 1572—Saint Bartholomew's Day. Coligny's murder touched off a massacre of Protestants throughout Paris and, once news from Paris had spread, throughout the kingdom.

The Saint Bartholomew's Day Massacre revealed the degree to which religious differences had strained the fabric of community life. Neighbor murdered neighbor in an effort to rid the community of heretical pollution; bodies of the dead, including Coligny's, were torn apart,

mutilated. Gathered in the south of France, the remaining Huguenot forces vowed "never [to] trust those who have so often and so treacherously broken faith and the public peace."[3] Huguenot writers published tracts arguing that royal power was by nature limited and that rebellion was justified against tyrants who overstepped their legitimate authority. (See the box "Reading Sources: A Justification for Rebellion Against the King.")

Further war produced the inevitable truces and limited toleration, but many Catholics also renounced reconciliation. Some noblemen formed a Catholic league to fight in place of the weakened monarchy. Charles's brother, Henry III (r. 1574–1589), was another king of limited abilities. Middle-aged, Henry had no children. The heir to his throne was the Protestant Henry of Navarre, and the assumption of the throne by a Protestant was unimaginable to the zealous Catholic faction at court and to many ordinary Catholics. By the end of Henry III's reign, the king had almost no royal authority left to wield. He was forced to cooperate with first one of the warring parties and then with another. In December 1588 he resorted to murdering two courtiers who led the ultra-Catholic faction; in turn, he was murdered by a priest in early 1589.

Henry of Navarre, the Bourbon prince who became Henry IV (r. 1589–1610), had to fight for his throne. He faced Catholic armies now subsidized by Philip II of Spain, an extremist Catholic city government in Paris, and subjects who were tired of war but mainly Catholic, and could count on only meager support from Protestants abroad. Given these obstacles, the politically astute Henry agreed to convert to Catholicism.

After his conversion in 1593, the wars continued for a time, but after thirty years of civil strife, many of Henry's subjects believed that only rallying to the monarchy could save France from chaos. Nobles grew increasingly disposed, for both psychological and practical reasons, to cooperate with the Crown. Service to a successful king could be a source of glory, and Henry was personally esteemed because he was a talented general and brave, gregarious, and charming. The nobility forced the citizens of Paris and other cities to accept Henry's authority. The civil war period thus proved to be an impor-

The Entry of Henry IV into Paris After the Religious Wars   The king is depicted here as the magnanimous victor and the residents of the city as both submissive and grateful.   *(Louvre © R.M.N.)*

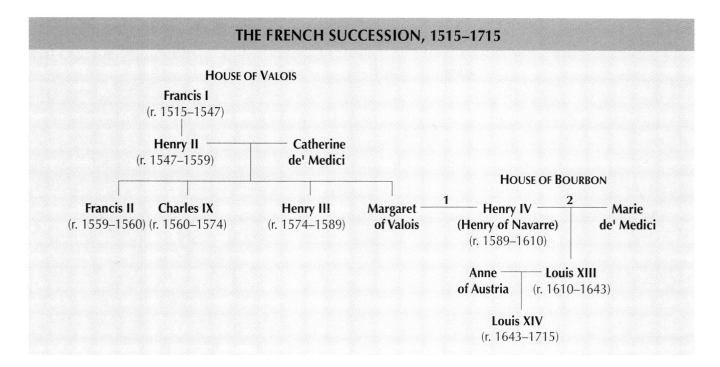

THE FRENCH SUCCESSION, 1515–1715

HOUSE OF VALOIS

Francis I
(r. 1515–1547)

Henry II ——— Catherine
(r. 1547–1559)   de' Medici

HOUSE OF BOURBON

Francis II   Charles IX   Henry III   Margaret —1— Henry IV —2— Marie
(r. 1559–1560) (r. 1560–1574) (r. 1574–1589) of Valois   (Henry of Navarre)   de' Medici
                                                            (r. 1589–1610)

Anne ——— Louis XIII
of Austria   (r. 1610–1643)

Louis XIV
(r. 1643–1715)

tant phase in the incremental accommodation of the nobility to the power of the state.

In April 1598 Henry granted toleration for the Huguenot minority in a royal edict proclaimed in the city of Nantes°. The Edict of Nantes was primarily a repetition of provisions from the most generous edicts that had ended the various civil wars. Nobles were allowed to practice the Protestant faith on their estates; townspeople were granted more limited rights to worship in selected towns in each region. Protestants were guaranteed access to schools, hospitals, royal appointments, and separate judicial institutions to ensure fair treatment. They were also guaranteed rights of self-defense—specifically, the right to maintain garrisons in about two hundred towns. About half of these garrisons would be paid for by the Crown.

The problem was that the Edict of Nantes, like any royal edict, could be revoked by the king at any time. Moreover, the provision allowing Protestants to keep garrisoned towns reflected concessions to Protestant aristocrats who could support their followers by paid garrison duty. These concessions also meant that living peacefully amid religious diversity was not yet thought to be possible. Thus, although Henry IV ended the French religious wars, he had not solved the problem of religious and political division within France.

■ The Consolidation of Royal Authority in France, 1598–1643

During Henry IV's reign, France recovered from the long years of civil war. Population and productivity began to grow; the Crown encouraged internal improvements to facilitate commerce. Henry's chief minister, Maximilien de Béthune°, duke of Sully° (1560–1641), increased royal revenue by nibbling away at traditional local self-government and control of taxation. He succeeded in creating a budget surplus and in extending mechanisms of centralized government.

Yet Henry's regime was stable only in comparison with the preceding years of civil war. The power of the great nobility had not been definitively broken. Moreover, the king had agreed to a provision, known as the *paulette* (named for the functionary who first administered it), that allowed royal officeholders not merely to own their offices but also to pass on those offices to their heirs in return for the payment of an annual fee. Primarily a device to raise revenue after decades of civil war, the paulette also helped cement the loyalty of royal bureaucrats at a critical time, particularly that of the royal judges of the supreme law court, the Parlement of Paris, who had recently agreed to register the Edict of Nantes

Nantes (NAHNT)

Béthune (bay-TOON)   **Sully** (soo-LEE)

only under duress. However, the paulette made royal officeholders largely immune from royal control since their posts were now, in effect, property, like the landed property of the traditional nobility.

In 1610 a fanatical Catholic assassinated Henry IV. Henry's death brought his 9-year-old son, Louis XIII (r. 1610–1643), to the throne with Louis's mother, Marie de' Medici, serving as regent. Marie was disgraced when her unpopular leading minister—resented for monopolizing patronage—was assassinated with Louis's approval in 1617.

Four years later, Louis faced a major rebellion by his Huguenot subjects in southwestern France. Huguenots felt that Louis's recent marriage to a Spanish princess, and other ominous royal policies, meant that royal support for toleration was wavering. Certain Huguenot nobles initiated fighting as a show of force against the king. The wars persisted, on and off, for eight years, as the French troops, like the Spanish in the Netherlands, had difficulty breeching the defenses of even small fortress towns. The main Huguenot stronghold was the well-fortified port city of La Rochelle—which had grown wealthy from European and overseas trade. Not until the king took the city, after a siege lasting more than a year and costing thousands of lives, did the Protestants accept a peace on royal terms.

The Peace of Alais° (1629) reaffirmed the policy of religious toleration but rescinded the Protestants' military and political privileges. It was a political triumph for the Crown because it deprived French Protestants of the means for further rebellion while reinforcing their dependence on the Crown for religious toleration. Most of the remaining great noble leaders began to convert to Catholicism.

The Peace of Alais was also a personal triumph for the king's leading minister, who crafted the treaty and who had directed the bloody siege that made it possible: Armand-Jean du Plessis° (1585–1642), Cardinal Richelieu°. From a provincial noble family, Richelieu had risen in the service of the queen mother. He was admired and feared for his skill in the political game of seeking and bestowing patronage—a crucial skill in an age when elites received offices and honors through carefully cultivated relationships at court. His control of many lucrative church posts gave him the resources to build up a large network of clients. He and the king—whose sensitive temperament Richelieu handled adeptly—formed a lasting partnership that had a decisive impact not only on French policy but also on the entire shape of the French state.

Richelieu favored an aggressive foreign policy to counter what he believed still to be the greatest threat to the French crown: the Spanish Habsburgs. When war resumed between the Netherlands and Spain after their truce expired in 1621 (see page 525), Richelieu sent troops to attack Spanish possessions in Italy. In the 1630s, with the king's full confidence, he superintended large-scale fighting against Spain in the Netherlands itself, as well as in Italy, and he began subsidizing Swedish and German Protestant armies fighting the Habsburgs in Germany.

Richelieu's policies were opposed by many people, who saw taxes double, then triple, in just a few years. Many courtiers and provincial elites favored keeping a tenuous peace with Spain, a fellow Catholic state, and objected to alliances with German Protestants. They were alarmed by the increasing taxes and by the famine, disease, and, above all, the revolts that accompanied the peasants' distress. Their own status was also directly threatened by Richelieu's monopoly of royal patronage and by his creation of new offices, which diluted and undermined their power. In 1632, for example, Richelieu created the office of *intendant*. Intendants had wide powers for defense and administration in the provinces that overrode the established bureaucracy.

By 1640 Richelieu's ambitious foreign policy seemed to be bearing fruit. The French had won territory along their northern and eastern borders by their successes against Habsburg forces. But when Richelieu and Louis XIII died within five months of each other, in December 1642 and May 1643, Richelieu's legacy was tested. Louis XIII was succeeded by his 5-year-old son, and the warrior nobility as well as royal bureaucrats would waste little time before challenging the Crown's new authority.

■ Precarious Stability in England: The Reign of Elizabeth I, 1558–1603

England experienced no civil wars during the second half of the sixteenth century, but religious dissent challenged the stability of the monarchy. In Elizabeth I (r. 1558–1603), England—in stark contrast to France—possessed an able and long-lived ruler. Elizabeth was well educated in the humanistic tradition and was already an adroit politician at the age of 25, when she acceded to the throne at the death of her Catholic half-sister, Mary Tudor (r. 1553–1558).

Elizabeth faced the urgent problem of reaching a policy of consensus in religious matters. Her father, Henry VIII (r. 1509–1547), had broken away from the Catholic Church for political reasons but had retained many Catholic doctrines and practices. A Calvinist-

---

Alais (ah-LAY)   **du Plessis** (doo pleh-SEE)
Richelieu (RISH-el-yeuh)

Elizabeth I: The Armada Portrait
Both serene and resolute, Elizabeth is flanked by "before" and "after" glimpses of the Spanish fleet; her hand rests on the globe in a gesture of dominion that also memorializes the circumnavigation of the globe by her famous captain, Sir Francis Drake, some years before.
(By kind permission of Marquess of Tavistock and Trustees of Bedford Estate)

inspired Protestantism had been prescribed for the Church of England by the advisers of Henry's successor, Elizabeth's young half-brother, Edward VI (r. 1547–1553). True Catholicism, such as Mary had tried to reimpose, was out of the question. The Roman Church had never recognized Henry VIII's self-made divorce and thus regarded Elizabeth as a bastard with no right to the throne.

Elizabeth adopted a cleverly moderate solution and used force, where necessary, to maintain it. In 1559 Parliament passed a new Act of Supremacy, which restored the monarch as head of the Church of England. Elizabeth dealt with opposition to the act by arresting bishops and lords whose votes would have blocked its passage by Parliament. Elizabeth and most of her ministers, moderate realists as was she, were willing to accept some flexibility for personal belief. For example, the official prayer book in use in Edward's day was revised to include elements of both traditional and radical interpretations of communion. But church liturgy, clerical vestments, and, above all, the hierarchical structure of the clergy closely resembled Catholic practices. The Act of Uniformity required all worship to be conducted according to the new prayer book. Yet although uniformity was required in worship, Elizabeth was careful, in her words, not to "shine beacons into her subjects' souls."

Catholicism continued to be practiced, especially by otherwise loyal nobility and gentry in the north of England who worshiped privately on their estates. But priests returning from exile beginning in the 1570s, most newly imbued with the proselytizing zeal of the Counter-Reformation (the Catholic response to the Protestant Reformation), practiced it more visibly, and were zealously prosecuted for their boldness. In the last twenty years of Elizabeth's reign, approximately 180 Catholics were executed for treason, two-thirds of them priests. (By 1585, being a Catholic priest in itself was a crime.)

In the long run, the greater threat to the English crown came from the most radical Protestants in the realm, known (by their enemies initially) as Puritans. Puritanism was a broad movement for reform of church practice along familiar Protestant lines: emphasis on Bible reading, preaching, private scrutiny of conscience, and a de-emphasis on institutional ritual and clerical authority. Most Puritans had accepted Elizabeth's religious compromise for practical reasons but grew increasingly alienated by her insistence on clerical authority and her refusal to change any elements of the original religious settlement. A significant Presbyterian underground movement began to form among them.

Presbyterians wanted to dismantle the episcopacy, the hierarchy of priests and bishops, and govern the church instead with councils, called "presbyteries," that included lay members of the congregation. Laws were passed late in the queen's reign to enable the Crown more easily to prosecute, and even to force into exile, anyone who attended "nonconformist" (non-Anglican) services.

The greatest challenge Elizabeth faced from Puritans came in Parliament, where they were well represented by many literate gentry. Parliament met only when called by the monarch, and in theory members could merely voice opinions and complaints. Initiating legislation and prescribing policy were beyond its purview. However, only Parliament could vote taxes. Further, since it had in effect helped constitute royal authority by means of the two Acts of Supremacy, Parliament's supposedly consultative role had been expanded by the monarchy itself. During Elizabeth's reign, Puritans capitalized on Parliament's enlarged scope, using meetings to press for further religious reform. In 1586 they went so far as to introduce bills calling for an end to the episcopacy and the Anglican prayer book. Elizabeth had to resort to imprisoning one Puritan leader to end debate on the issue and on Parliament's right to address it.

In Elizabeth's reign, efforts at English expansion in the New World began, in the form of unsuccessful attempts at colonization and successful raids on Spanish possessions. However, the main focus of her foreign policy remained Europe itself. Elizabeth, like all her forebears, felt her interests tightly linked to the independence of the Netherlands, whose towns were a major outlet for English wool. Philip II's aggressive policy in the Netherlands increasingly alarmed her, especially in view of France's weakness. She began to send small sums of money to the rebels and allowed their ships access to southern English ports, from which they could raid Spanish-held towns on the Netherlands' coast. In 1585, in the wake of the duke of Parma's successes against the rebellions, she committed troops to help the rebels.

Her decision was a reaction not only to the threat of a single continental power dominating the Netherlands but also to the threat of Catholicism. From 1579 to 1583, the Spanish had helped the Irish fight English domination and were involved in several plots to replace Elizabeth with her Catholic cousin, Mary, Queen of Scots. These threats occurred as the return of Catholic exiles to England peaked. The victory over the Spanish Armada in 1588 was quite rightly celebrated for it ended any Catholic threat to Elizabeth's rule.

The success against the Armada has tended to overshadow other aspects of Elizabeth's foreign policy, particularly with regard to Ireland. Since the twelfth century, an Anglo-Irish state dominated by great princely families had been loosely supervised from England, but most of Ireland remained under the control of Gaelic chieftains. Just as Charles V and Philip II attempted to tighten their governing mechanisms in the Netherlands, so in England did Henry VIII's minister, Thomas Cromwell, streamline control of outlying areas such as Wales and Anglo-Ireland. Cromwell proposed that the whole of Ireland be brought under English control partly by the established mechanism of feudal ties: the Irish chieftains were to pay homage as vassals to the king of England.

Under Elizabeth, this legalistic approach gave way to virtual conquest. Elizabeth's governor, Sir Henry Sidney, appointed in 1565, inaugurated a policy whereby Gaelic lords, by means of various technicalities, could be entirely dispossessed of their lands. Any Englishman capable of raising a private force could help enforce these dispossessions and settle his conquered lands as he saw fit. This policy provoked stiff Irish resistance, which was viewed as rebellion and provided the rationale for further military action, more confiscations of land, and more new English settlers. Eventually, the Irish, with Spanish assistance, mounted a major rebellion, consciously Catholic and aimed against the "heretic" queen. The rebellion gave the English an excuse for brutal suppression and massive transfers of land to English control. The political domination of the Irish was complete with the defeat, in 1601, of the Gaelic chieftain Hugh O'Neill, lord of Tyrone, who had controlled most of the northern quarter of the island. Although the English were unable to impose Protestantism on the conquered Irish, to Elizabeth and her English subjects the conquests in Ireland seemed as significant as the victory over the Spanish Armada.

The English enjoyed relative peace at home during Elizabeth's reign. However, her reign ended on a note of strain. The foreign involvements, particularly in Ireland, had been very expensive. Taxation granted by Parliament more than doubled during her reign, and local taxes further burdened the people. Price inflation related to government spending, social problems caused by returned unemployed soldiers, and a series of bad harvests heightened popular resentment against taxation. Despite her achievements, therefore, Elizabeth passed two problems on to her successors: unresolved religious tensions and financial instability. Elizabeth's successors would also find in Parliament an increasing focus of opposition to their policies.

■ Rising Tensions in England, 1603–1642

In 1603 Queen Elizabeth died and James VI of Scotland, the Protestant son of Mary, Queen of Scots, ascended to the English throne as James I (r. 1603–1625). Religious tensions between Anglicans and Puritans were temporarily quieted under James because of a plot, in 1605, by Catholic dissenters. The Gunpowder Plot, as it was called, was a conspiracy to blow up the palace housing both king and Parliament at Westminster. Protestants of all stripes once again focused not on their differences but on their common enemy, Catholicism.

Financial problems were James's most pressing concern. Court life became more elaborate and an increasing drain on the monarchy's resources. James's extravagance was partly to blame for his financial problems, but so were pressures for patronage from courtiers. Added to the debts left from the Irish conflicts and wars with Spain were new military expenses as James helped defend the claims of his daughter and her husband, a German prince, to rule Bohemia (see page 525).

To raise revenue without Parliament's consent, James relied on sources of income that the Crown had enjoyed since medieval times: customs duties, wardship (the right to manage and liberally borrow from the estates of minor nobles), and the sale of monopolies, which conveyed the right to be sole agent for a particular kind of goods. To rebuild his treasury, James increased the number of monopolies for sale and even created a new noble title—baronet—which he sold to socially ambitious commoners.

The monopolies were widely resented. Merchants objected to the arbitrary restriction of production and trade; common people found that they could no longer afford certain ordinary commodities, such as soap. Resentments among the nobility were sharpened, and general criticism of the court escalated, as James indulged in extreme favoritism of certain courtiers, including the corrupt George Villiers° (1592–1628), duke of Buckingham, who served as the king's first minister.

When James summoned Parliament to ask for funds in 1621, Parliament used the occasion to protest court corruption and the king's financial measures. The members revived the medieval procedure of impeachment and removed two royal ministers from office. In 1624, still faced with expensive commitments to Protestants abroad and in failing health, James again called Parliament, which voted new taxes but also openly debated the wisdom of the king's foreign policy.

Villiers (VIL-yerz)

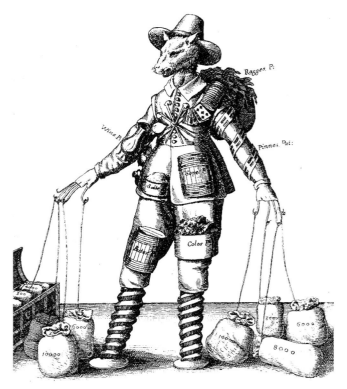

Criticism of Monopolies   Holders of royally granted monopolies were bitterly resented by English consumers and tradespeople alike, as this contemporary print reveals. The greedy beast pictured here controls even ordinary commodities such as pins, soap, and butter.   *(Courtesy of the Trustees of the British Museum)*

Tensions between Crown and Parliament increased under James's son, Charles I (r. 1625–1649). One reason was the growing financial strain of foreign policy as well as the policies themselves. Charles declared war on Spain and supported the Huguenot rebels in France. Many wealthy merchants opposed this aggressive foreign policy because it disrupted trade. In 1626 Parliament was dissolved without granting any monies in order to stifle its objections to royal policies. Instead, Charles levied a forced loan and did not hesitate to imprison gentry who refused to lend their money to the government.

Above all, Charles's religious policies were a source of controversy. Charles was personally inclined toward "high church" practices: an emphasis on ceremony and sacrament reminiscent of Catholic ritual. He also was a believer in Arminianism, a school of thought that rejected the Calvinist notion that God's grace cannot be earned, and hence emphasized the importance of the sacraments and the authority of the clergy. Charles's attempt to fashion the Church of England into an instrument that would reflect and justify royal claims to power put him on a collision course with gentry and aristocrats who leaned toward Puritanism.

Charles's views were supported by William Laud° (1573–1645), archbishop of Canterbury from 1633 and thus leader of the Church of England. He tried to impose changes in worship, spread Arminian ideas, and censor opposing views. He also challenged the redistribution of church property, which had occurred in the Reformation of the sixteenth century, and thereby alienated the gentry on economic as well as religious grounds.

Charles's style of rule worsened religious, political, and economic tensions. Cold and intensely private, he did not inspire confidence or have the charm or the political skills to disarm his opponents. His court was ruled by formal protocol, and access to the king himself was highly restricted—a serious problem in an age when proximity to the monarch was a guarantee of political power.

Revenue and religion dominated debate in the Parliament of 1628–1629, which Charles had called, once again, to get funds for his foreign wars. In 1628 the members of Parliament presented the king with a document called the Petition of Right, which protested his financial policies as well as arbitrary imprisonment. (Seventeen members of Parliament had been imprisoned for refusing loans to the Crown.) Though couched conservatively as a restatement of customary practice, the petition in fact claimed a tradition of expanded parliamentary participation in government. Charles dissolved the Parliament in March 1629, having decided that the money he might extract was not worth the risk.

For eleven years, Charles ruled without Parliament. When he was forced by necessity to summon it again, in 1640, the kingdom was in crisis. Royal finances were in desperate straits even though Charles had pressed collection of revenues far beyond traditional bounds. In 1634, for example, he had revived annual collection of "ship money"—a medieval tax levied on coastal districts to help support the navy during war. England, however, was not at war at that time, and the tax was levied not only on seaports but on inland areas, too.

The immediate crisis in 1640—and the reason for Charles's desperate need for money—was a rebellion in Scotland. Like Philip II in the Netherlands, Charles tried to rule in Scotland through a small council of men who did not represent the local elite. Worse, he also tried to

force his "high church" practices on the Scots. The Scottish Church had been more dramatically reshaped during the Reformation and now was largely Presbyterian in structure. The result of Charles's politics was riots—and rebellion. Unable to suppress the revolt in a first campaign in 1639, Charles was forced to summon Parliament to obtain funds to raise a more effective army.

But the Parliament that assembled in the spring of 1640 provided no help. Instead, members questioned the war with the Scots and other royal policies. Charles's political skills were far too limited for him to re-establish a workable relationship with Parliament under the circumstances. Charles dissolved this body, which is now known as the "Short Parliament," after just three weeks. Even more stinging than Charles's dissolution of the Parliament was the lack of respect he had shown the members: a number of them were harassed or arrested. Mistrust fomented by the eleven years in which Charles had ruled without Parliament thus increased.

Another humiliating and decisive defeat at the hands of the Scots later in 1640 made summoning another Parliament imperative. Members of the "Long Parliament" (it sat from 1640 to 1653) took full advantage of the king's predicament. Charles was forced to agree not to dissolve or adjourn Parliament without the members' consent and to summon Parliament at least every three years. Parliament abolished many of his unorthodox and traditional sources of revenue and impeached and removed from office his leading ministers, including Archbishop Laud. The royal commander deemed responsible for the Scottish fiasco, Thomas Wentworth, earl of Strafford, was executed without trial in May 1641.

The execution of Strafford shocked many aristocrats in the House of Lords (the upper house of Parliament) as well as some moderate members of the House of Commons. Meanwhile, Parliament began debating the perennially thorny religious question. A bare majority of members favored abolition of Anglican bishops as a first step in thoroughgoing religious reform. Working people in London, kept apprised of the issues by the regular publication of parliamentary debates, demonstrated in support of that majority. Moderate members of Parliament, in contrast, favored checking the king's power but not upsetting the Elizabethan religious compromise.

An event that unified public and parliamentary opinion at a crucial time—a revolt against English rule in Ireland in October 1641—temporarily eclipsed these divisions and once again focused suspicion on the king. The broad consensus of anti-Catholicism once again became the temporary driving force in politics. Fearing that Charles would use Irish soldiers against his English

Laud (LAWD)

subjects, Parliament demanded that it have control of the army to put down the rebellion. In November, the Puritan majority introduced a document known as the "Grand Remonstrance," an appeal to the people and a long catalog of parliamentary grievances against the king. It was passed by a narrow margin, further setting public opinion in London against Charles. The king's remaining support in Parliament eroded in January 1642 when he attempted to arrest five leading members on charges of treason. The five escaped and the stage was set for wider violence. The king withdrew from London, unsure he could defend himself there, and began to raise an army. In mid-1642 the kingdom stood at the brink of civil war.

THE HOLY ROMAN EMPIRE AND THE THIRTY YEARS' WAR, 1555–1648

HE Holy Roman Empire enjoyed a period of comparative quiet after the Peace of Augsburg halted religious and political wars in 1555. The 1555 agreement, which permitted rulers of the various states within the empire to impose either Catholicism or Lutheranism in their lands, proved to be a workable solution, for a time, to the problem of religious division. By the early seventeenth century, however, fresh causes of instability brought about renewed fighting. One factor was the rise of Calvinism, for which no provision had been necessary in 1555. Especially destabilizing was the drive by the Austrian Habsburgs to reverse the successes of Protestantism both in their own lands and in the empire at large and to solidify their control of their diverse personal territories.

In the Thirty Years' War (1618–1648), as it is now called, we can see the continuation of conflicts from the sixteenth century—religious tensions, regionalism versus centralizing forces, dynastic and strategic rivalries between rulers. The war was particularly destructive because of the size of the armies and the degree to which army commanders evaded control by the states for which they fought. As a result of the war, the empire was eclipsed as a political unit by the regional powers that composed it.

■ Peace Through Diversity, 1556–ca. 1618

The Austrian Habsburgs ruled over a diverse group of territories in the Holy Roman Empire, as well as northwestern Hungary (see Map 15.3). On his abdication in 1556, Emperor Charles V had granted Habsburg lands in

central Europe to his brother Ferdinand (see the chart on page 508), who had long been the actual ruler there in Charles's stead. On Charles's death in 1558, Ferdinand was duly crowned emperor.

Though largely contiguous, Ferdinand's territories comprised independent duchies and kingdoms, each with its own institutional structure, and included speakers of Italian, German, and Czech, plus a few other languages. The non-German lands of Bohemia (the core of the modern Czech Republic) and Hungary had been distinct kingdoms since the High Middle Ages. Both states bestowed their crowns by election and had chosen Ferdinand, the first Habsburg to rule them, in separate elections in the 1520s and 1530s. Most of Hungary was now under Ottoman domination, but Bohemia, with its rich capital, Prague, was a wealthy center of population and culture.

Unlike the Netherlands, these linguistically and culturally diverse lands were still governed by highly decentralized institutions. Moreover, unlike their Spanish cousins, the Austrian Habsburgs made no attempt to impose religious uniformity in this period. Ferdinand was firmly Catholic but tolerant of reform efforts within the church, including clerical marriage and allowing the laity to receive both wine and bread at communion. Both he and his son, Maximilian II (r. 1564–1576), believed an eventual reunion of the Catholic and Protestant faiths might be possible. During his reign, Maximilian worked to keep religious peace in the empire as a whole and granted limited rights of worship to Protestant subjects within his ancestral lands (separate territories more or less equivalent to modern Austria in extent). Catholicism and many strands of Protestantism flourished side by side in Maximilian's domain, above all in Hungary and Bohemia.

Maximilian's son, Rudolf II (r. 1576–1612), shared the religious style of his father and grandfather. He was an energetic patron of the arts and sponsored the work of scientists. During his reign, as under Maximilian, education, printing, and humanistic intellectual life flourished. Yet Rudolf, a weak leader politically, was challenged for control of the Habsburg lands and the empire itself by his brother and ambitious cousins. Political rivalries as well as renewed religious conflict would soon end the period of relative peace in Habsburg lands and in the empire.

The resurgence of Catholicism in the wake of the Council of Trent (1545–1563) had begun to shift the religious balance. Members of the Jesuit order arrived in Habsburg lands in the reign of Maximilian. Toughminded and well trained, they established Catholic

Map 15.3 Territories of the Austrian Habsburgs, ca. 1556 In addition to the lands constituting modern Austria, Austrian Habsburg lands comprised the Tyrol (modern west Austria and northeast Italy), Carniola (modern Slovenia), part of Croatia, Bohemia (the core of the modern Czech Republic and southern Poland), and Hungary. Most of Hungary had been in Ottoman hands since the Battle of Mohács in 1526.

schools and became confessors and preachers to the upper classes. Self-confident Catholicism emerged as one form of cultural identity among the German-speaking ruling classes and thus as a religious impetus to further political consolidation of all the Habsburg territories.

Resurgent Catholicism was evident, too, in the empire as a whole, where certain princes were confident they might now eliminate Protestantism, as their ancestors had failed to do. In the face of this challenge, certain Protestant princes formed a defensive pact known as the Evangelical Union in 1608; in response, Catholic princes formed an alliance, the Holy League, the next year. A major war between the two alliances over a disputed territory was narrowly averted the following year. Like the

English under Elizabeth, Habsburg subjects and peoples in the empire had enjoyed a period of calm in political and religious matters. Now, as in England, the stage was set for conflict of both kinds.

■ The Thirty Years' War, 1618–1648

The Thirty Years' War was touched off in 1618 by a revolt against Habsburg rule in the kingdom of Bohemia. Bohemia was populous and prosperous; Rudolf II had made its bustling capital, Prague, his imperial capital. The powerful and diverse Protestant community had wrested formal recognition of its rights to worship from Rudolf and from his younger brother, Matthias (r. 1612–1618).

Matthias was quickly succeeded by his cousin Ferdinand II (r. 1619–1637), who was the ideal Counter-Reformation prince, and unlikely to honor these agreements. Educated by the Jesuits, he sincerely believed that reimposing Catholicism was his Christian duty. He once stated that he would "sooner beg than rule over heretics";[4] he had virtually eliminated Protestantism, by persuasion as well as by compulsion, in the small duchy in southern Austria he had governed before assuming the throne.

Ferdinand would not tolerate the political independence of nobles and towns in Bohemia or the religious pluralism that independence defended. As Philip II had done in the Netherlands, Ferdinand appointed a regency council to govern in his name that enforced unpopular policies: the right to build new Protestant churches was denied; Bohemian crown lands were given to the Catholic Church; non-Catholics were barred from serving in government.

On May 23, 1618, delegates to a Protestant assembly that had unsuccessfully petitioned Ferdinand to end his violations of earlier guarantees marched to the palace in Prague where the hated royal officials met. After a confrontation over their demands, the delegates "tried" the officials on the spot for treason and, literally, threw them out the palace window. The incident became known as the Defenestration of Prague (from the Latin *fenestra*, "window"). (The officials' lives were saved only because they fell into a pile of refuse in the moat.) The rebels proceeded to set up their own government.

This upstart Bohemian government officially deposed Ferdinand and elected a new king in 1619: a Protestant, Frederick, elector of the Palatinate, and a Calvinist prince. His selection had implications for the empire as a whole because his territories in west central Germany (called the Lower Palatinate and the Upper Palatinate) conveyed the right to be one of the seven electors who chose the emperor.

Emboldened by these events, Protestant subjects in other Habsburg lands asked for guarantees of freedom of worship similar to those enjoyed by Protestants in Bohemia. Other princes saw their chance to make political gains. For example, rival claimants to Habsburg rule in Hungary took up arms against Ferdinand.

The revolt in Bohemia set off a wider war because foreign rulers also felt their interests to be involved. The English king, James I, supported Frederick because Frederick was married to his daughter. Spain's supply routes north from Italy to the Netherlands passed next to Frederick's lands in western Germany. France's first interest was its rivalry with Spain; thus, France kept its eye on the border principalities that were strategically important to Spain. In addition, France desired to keep Protestant as well as Catholic princes within the empire strong enough to thwart Austrian Habsburg ambitions. Thus, from the outset, the war was a conflict not only over the Habsburgs' power in their own lands but also over the balance of religious and political power in the empire and in Europe (see Map 15.4).

Ferdinand secured aid from the Catholic duke of Bavaria and from his cousin, King Philip III of Spain, by promising them Frederick's lands in the Palatinate. By the fall of 1620 a Catholic army was closing in on Bohemia. On November 8, on a hillside near Prague, the Catholic force faced a Bohemian army that had received little aid from Protestant allies. The Battle of White Mountain was a complete Catholic victory.

Despite the rout, fighting did not cease but became more widespread. The truce between Spain and the Netherlands, established in 1609, expired in 1621, and the nearby Lower Palatinate, now in Spanish hands, offered a staging point for Spanish forces and thus threatened the peace in that corner of the empire. Claiming to be a Protestant champion, the Protestant king of Denmark, Christian IV (r. 1588–1648), who was also duke of Holstein in northern Germany, sought to conquer additional German territory. His goals were to gain greater control over profitable German Baltic seaports and to defend himself against any Catholic attempt to seize northern German territory. Christian received little help from fellow Protestants, however. The Dutch were busy with Spain, the English were wary of fighting after Frederick's defeat, and Denmark's regional rivals, the Swedish, were uninterested in furthering Danish ambitions in the Baltic.

The confusing blend of politics and religion that motivated the Protestant rulers was also evident on the Catholic side. When imperial forces defeated Christian's armies in 1626, Catholic princes became alarmed at the possibility of greater imperial power in northern Germany. Led by the duke of Bavaria, they arranged a truce that led to Denmark's withdrawal from the fighting on relatively generous terms. At the same time, Protestants outside Bohemia learned some of the consequences of imperial victory, and took up arms. As his armies defeated Christian, Ferdinand issued new edicts that in effect voided the religious settlement in place since 1555. His victorious armies brutally enforced his edicts wherever they passed.

Christian's rival, Gustav Adolf, king of Sweden (r. 1611–1632), now assumed the role of Protestant leader. Gustav Adolf hoped to gain territory along the Baltic

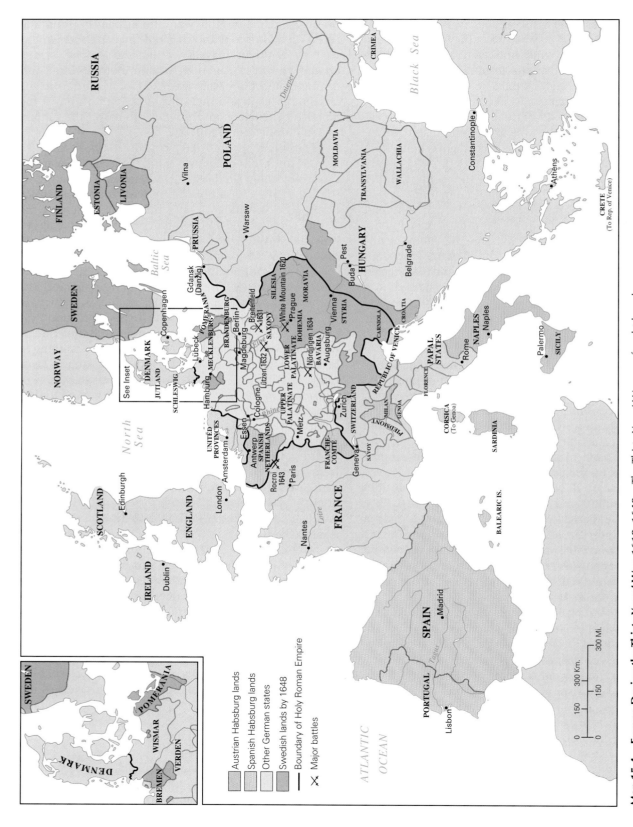

Map 15.4 Europe During the Thirty Years' War, 1618–1648 The Thirty Years' War was fought largely within the borders of the Holy Roman Empire. It was the result of conflicts within the empire as well as the meddling of neighbors for their own strategic advantages.

seacoast, but personal aggrandizement also was one of his goals. An innovative military leader, his campaigns were capped by a victory over an imperial army at Breitenfeld° in Saxony in 1631. After Gustav Adolf was killed in battle in 1632, however, the tide turned in the favor of Ferdinand's forces. A decisive imperial victory over a combined Swedish and German Protestant army, at Nördlingen° in 1634, led to a general peace treaty favorable to the Catholics: the Peace of Prague (1635).

The Peace of Prague brought only a temporary peace, however, because Ferdinand died shortly thereafter, and because French involvement increased now that other anti-Habsburg forces had been eclipsed. France tried to seize imperial territory along its own eastern border and generously subsidized continued fighting within the empire by channeling monies to Protestant princes and mercenaries there. Fighting dragged on. By the end of the Thirty Years' War, order had disintegrated so completely in the wake of the marauding armies that both staunchly Catholic rulers and firmly Protestant ones allied with religious enemies to safeguard their states.

A comprehensive peace treaty became possible when France withdrew its sponsorship of the fighting in order to concentrate on its conflict with Spain. The French wanted only a workable balance of power in the empire, which was achieved once they and their allies convincingly defeated imperial forces in 1645. More urgent to the French was the continued rivalry with the Spanish Habsburgs for control of territory along France's eastern and northern borders and in Italy. A defeat by France in the Spanish Netherlands in 1643 had convinced Spain to concentrate on that rivalry too, and fighting between them continued separately until 1659. Negotiations for peace had begun in 1643 among warweary states of the empire and resulted in a group of agreements known as the Peace of Westphalia° in 1648.

■ The Effects of the War

The Thirty Years' War ruined the economy and decimated the population in many parts of the empire and had long-term political consequences for the empire as a whole. One reason for the war's devastation was a novel application of firepower to warfare that increased both the size of armies and their deadly force in battle. This was the use of volley fire, the arrangement of foot soldiers in parallel lines so that one line of men could fire while another reloaded. This tactic, pioneered in the Netherlands around the turn of the century, was further refined by Gustav Adolf of Sweden. Gustav Adolf amassed large numbers of troops and increased the rate of fire so that a virtually continuous barrage was maintained; he also used maneuverable field artillery to protect the massed infantry from cavalry charges.

Following Gustav Adolf's lead, armies of all the major states adopted these tactics. Despite these new offensive tactics, defensive expertise—as in holding fortresses—remained important, and pitched battles, such as at Nördlingen in 1634, still tended to be part of sieges. The costs in resources and human life of this kind of warfare reached unheard-of dimensions. Popular printed literature and court drama both condemned the horrors of the war.

Where fighting had been concentrated, as in parts of Saxony, between a third and half of the inhabitants of rural villages and major towns may have disappeared. Many starved, were caught in the fighting, or were killed by marauding soldiers. The most notorious atrocity occurred in the aftermath of the siege of Magdeburg° in 1631. After the city surrendered to besieging Catholic forces, long-deprived soldiers ate and drank themselves into a frenzy, raped and killed indiscriminately, and set fires that destroyed the town. Some victims of war migrated to other regions in search of peaceful conditions and work. Some joined the armies in order to survive. Others formed armed bands to fight off the soldiers or to steal back enough goods to live on.

Compounding these effects of war were the actions of armies hired by enterprising mercenary generals for whom loyalty to the princes who paid them took a back seat to personal advancement. They contracted to provide, supply, and lead troops and thus were more willing than the princes would have been to allow troops to live "economically" on plunder. States thus managed to field large armies but had not yet evolved the mechanisms fully to fund, and thus control, them.

The Peace of Westphalia, which ended fighting in the empire, was one of the most important outcomes of the war. The various treaties composing the peace effectively put an end to religious war in the empire. Calvinism was recognized as a tolerated religion. The requirement that all subjects must follow their rulers' faith was retained, but some leeway was allowed for those who now found themselves under new rulers.

In political matters, the treaties reflected some of the recent successes of the Swedish by granting them Baltic

---

Breitenfeld (BRIGHT-un-feld)   **Nördlingen** (NERD-ling-un)
Westphalia (west-FAIL-yuh)

Magdeburg (MAHG-duh-boorg)

coast territory. France gained the important towns of Metz, Toul, and Verdun on its eastern border. Spain formally recognized the independence of the Netherlands.

The most important political outcome of the peace was a new balance of power in the empire. Most of the major Catholic and Protestant rulers extended their territories at the expense of smaller principalities and cities. The son of Frederick, king of Bohemia, received back the smaller of the two Palatine territories that his father had held. The Upper Palatinate—as well as the right to be a new elector of the emperor—was given to the powerful duke of Bavaria. The principalities within the empire were acknowledged, in the peace, to be virtually autonomous, both from the emperor and from one another. In addition, the constitution of the empire was changed to make it very difficult for one prince or a group of princes to disrupt the peace in their own interests. As a result, the agreements at Westphalia were the beginning of one hundred years of peace within the Holy Roman Empire.

Another outcome was that the Habsburgs, though weakened as emperors, were strengthened as rulers of their own hereditary lands on the eastern fringes of the empire. Except in Hungary, Protestantism—and its contrary political baggage—had been eliminated early in the wars, and the peace did not alter these circumstances. The Habsburgs moved their capital back to Vienna from Prague, and the government of their hereditary lands gained in importance as administration of the empire waned.

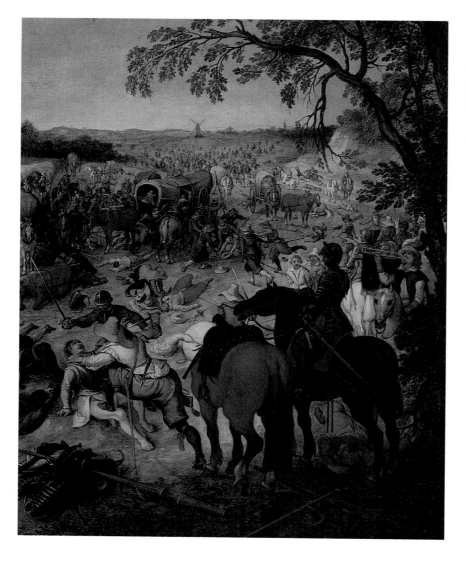

The Horrors of War This painting by a seventeenth-century artist depicts an attack on a supply convoy by opposing troops. Control of supplies to feed and equip the increasing numbers of troops was one of the most important aspects of warfare. *(Staatsgalerie Aschaffenburg [Schloss], Bayerische Staatsgemäldesammlungen/Godwin Alfen-ARTOTHEK)*

WRITING, DRAMA, AND ART IN AN AGE OF UPHEAVAL

BOTH imaginative literature and speculative writing, such as political theory, bear the stamp of their times. In the late sixteenth and early seventeenth centuries, political speculation often concerned questions of the legitimacy of rulers and of the relationship of political power to divine authority—urgent problems in an age when religious division threatened the very foundations of states. Authors and rulers alike often relied on still-prevalent oral modes of communication to convey their ideas. Indeed, some of the greatest literature and some of the most effective political statements of the period were presented as drama and not conveyed in print. Nevertheless, literacy continued to spread and led to greater opportunities for knowledge and reflection. The medium of print became increasingly important to political life. In the visual arts, the dramatic impulse was wedded to religious purposes to create works that conveyed both power and emotion.

■ Literacy and Literature

Traditional oral culture changed slowly under the impact of the spread of printing, education, and literacy. Works of literature from the late sixteenth and early seventeenth century incorporate material from traditional folktales, consciously reflecting the coexistence of oral and literature culture. In *Don Quixote*°, by Spain's Miguel de Cervantes° (1547–1616), the title character and his companion, Sancho Panza, have a long discussion about oral and literate traditions. The squire Panza speaks in the style that was customary in oral culture—a rather roundabout and repetitive style, by our standards, that enabled the speaker and listener to remember what was said. Much of the richness of Don Quixote is due to the interweaving of prose styles and topical concerns from throughout Cervantes' culture—from the oral world of peasants to the refined world of court life. Yet the perspective that enabled Cervantes to accomplish this rich portrayal came about from his own highly developed literacy and the awareness of language that literacy made possible.

The spread of education and literacy in the late sixteenth century had a dramatic impact on attitudes toward literature and on literature itself. The value of education—particularly of the continuing humanist recovery of ancient wisdom—was reflected in much of the literature of the period. Writers found in humanistic education a vision of what it meant to be cultivated and disciplined men of the world. This vision provided the beginnings of a new self-image for members of the warrior class.

It is customary to regard the French author Michel de Montaigne° (1533–1592) as the epitome of the reflective and—more important—the *self*-reflective gentleman. Montaigne was a judge in the parlement (law court) of Bordeaux; he resigned from the court in 1570, however, and retired to his small château, where he wrote his *Essais* (from which we derive the word *essays*), a collection of short reflections that were revolutionary in both form and content. Montaigne invented writing in the form of a sketch, a "try" (the literal meaning of *essai*), which enabled him to combine self-reflection with formal analysis.

Montaigne's reflections ranged from the destructiveness of the French civil wars to the consequences of European exploration of the New World. Toward all of these events and circumstances, Montaigne was able to achieve an analytic detachment remarkable for his day. For example, he noted an irony in Europeans labeling New World peoples "savage," given Europeans' seemingly endless and wanton violence against those "savages" and against one another. (See the box "Global Encounters: Montaigne Discusses Barbarity in the New World and the Old.") Owing to the spread of printing and literacy, Montaigne had—in addition to his own effort and the resources of leisure—a virtually unparalleled opportunity to reflect on the world through reading the wide variety of printed texts available to him. For the first time, it was possible for a leisured lay reader to consider and compare different events, values, and cultures.

His essays also reveal a distancing from himself, and this distancing is another result of literacy—not simply the ability to read and write but the capacity to enjoy long periods of solitude and reflection in the company of other solitary, book-bound, voices. Montaigne's works mark the beginning of what we know as the "invention" of private life, in which an individual is known more by internal character and personality traits than by social role and past behavior.

The works of the great English poet and playwright William Shakespeare (1564–1616) are still compelling to us because of the profundity of the questions he asked about love, honor, and political legitimacy, but he asked

---

Quixote (key-HO-tay)   **Cervantes** (sair-VAHN-tayz)

Montaigne (mon-TEN-yuh)

⊕ G L O B A L   E N C O U N T E R S

Montaigne Discusses Barbarity in the New World and the Old

In one of his most famous essays, Michel de Montaigne ironically compares the customs of Native Americans, about whom he has heard, with the customs of his own society.

They have their wars with [other] nations, to which they go quite naked, with no other arms than bows or wooden spears. . . . It is astonishing that firmness they show in their combats, which never end but in slaughter and bloodshed; for, as to routs and terror, they know nothing of either.

Each man brings back as his trophy the head of the enemy he has killed. . . . After they have treated their prisoner well for a long time with all the hospitality they can think of . . . they kill him with their swords. This done, they roast him and eat him in common and send some pieces to their absent friends.

I am not sorry that we notice the barbarous horror of such acts, but am heartily sorry that . . . we should be so blind to our own. I think there is more barbarity . . . in tearing by tortures and the rack a body still full of feeling, in roasting a man bit by bit, having him bitten and mangled by dogs (as we have not only read but seen within fresh memory . . .

among neighbors and fellow citizens, and what is worse, on the pretext of piety and religion).

Three of these men (were brought to France) . . . and [someone] wanted to know what they had found most amazing. . . . They said that in the first place they thought it very strange that so many grown men, bearded, strong and armed who were around the king . . . should submit to obey a child [the young French king]. . . . Second (they have a way in their language of speaking of men as halves of one another), they had noticed that there were among us men full and gorged with all sorts of good things, and that their other halves were beggars at their doors, emaciated with hunger and poverty; and they thought it strange that these needy halves could endure such injustice.

Source: Donald M. Frame, trans., *The Complete Essays of Montaigne* (Stanford, Calif.: Stanford University Press, 1948), pp. 153, 155–159.

these questions in terms appropriate to his own day. One of his favorite themes—evident in *Hamlet* and *Macbeth*—is the legitimacy of rulers. He was at his most skilled, perhaps, when exploring the contradictions in values between the growing commercial world he saw around him and the older, seemingly more stable world of feudal society. Subtle political commentary distinguishes Shakespeare's later plays, written near and shortly after the death of Queen Elizabeth in 1603, when political and economic problems were becoming increasingly visible and troublesome. Shakespeare explored not only the duties of rulers but also the rights of their subjects. In *Coriolanus* he portrays commoners as poor but neither ignorant nor wretched; they are in fact fully rational and capable of analyzing their situation—

perhaps more capable, Shakespeare hints, than their ruler is. The play is safely set in ancient Rome, but the social and political tensions it depicts clearly applied to the Elizabethan present.

Shakespeare, Cervantes, and other writers of their day were also representatives of what were starting to be self-consciously distinct national literatures. The spread of humanism added a historical dimension to their awareness of their own languages and to their distinct subject matter: their own society and its past. This kind of self-consciousness is evident in Shakespeare's historical plays, such as *Henry V* and *Richard II*. In *Richard II* he depicts the kingdom in terms that reflect the Elizabethan sense of England as a separate and self-contained nation:

This royal throne of kings, this scept'red isle,
This earth of majesty, this seat of Mars,
This other Eden, demi-paradise,
This fortress built by Nature for herself
Against infection and the hand of war,
This happy breed of men, this little world,
This precious stone set in the silver sea . . .
This blessed plot, this earth, this realm, this
    England . . .
(*Richard II*, act 2, sc. 1, lines 40–50)[5]

■ The Great Age of Theater

Shakespeare's extraordinary career was possible because his life coincided with the rise of professional theater. In the capitals of both England and Spain, professional theaters first opened in the 1570s. Some drama was produced at court or in aristocratic households, but most public theaters drew large and very mixed audiences, including the poorest city dwellers. Playwrights, including Shakespeare, often wrote in teams under great pressure to keep acting companies supplied with material. The best-known dramatist in Spain in this period, Lope de Vega° (1562–1635), wrote more than fifteen hundred works on a wide range of topics. Although religious themes remained popular in Spanish theater, as an echo of medieval drama, most plays in England and Spain treated secular subjects and, as in *Coriolanus*, safely disguised political commentary.

Over time, theater became increasingly restricted to aristocratic circles. In England, Puritan criticism of the "immorality" of public performance drove actors and playwrights to seek royal patronage. The first professional theater to open in Paris, in 1629, as political and religious turmoil quieted, quickly became dependent on Cardinal Richelieu's patronage. Inevitably, as court patronage grew in importance, the wide range of subject matter treated in plays began to narrow to those of aristocratic concern, such as family honor and martial glory. These themes were depicted in the works of the Spaniard Pedro Calderón° (1600–1681), who wrote for his enthusiastic patron, Philip IV, and of the Frenchman Pierre Corneille° (1606–1684), whose great tragedy of aristocratic life, *Le Cid*, was one of the early successes of the seventeenth-century French theater.

Drama's significance as an art form is reflected in its impact on the development of music: the opera, which weds drama to music, was invented in Italy in the early seventeenth century. The first great work in this genre is generally acknowledged to be *Orfeo* (*Orpheus*, 1607) by Claudio Monteverdi° (1567–1643). Opera, like drama, reflected the influence of humanism in its secular themes and in its emulation of Greek drama, which had used both words and music. The practice of music itself changed under the dramatic impulse. Monteverdi was the first master of a new musical style known as monody, which emphasized the progression of chords. Monodic music was inherently dramatic, creating a sense of forward movement, expectation, and resolution.

■ Sovereignty in Ceremony, Image, and Word

Whether produced on a public stage or at court or in a less formal setting, drama was a favored method of communication in this era because people responded to and made extensive use of oral communication. Dramatic gesture and storytelling to get a message across were commonplace and were important components of politics.

What we might call "street drama" was an ordinary occurrence: when great noble governors entered major towns, such as when Margaret of Parma entered Brussels, a solemn yet ostentatious formal "entry" was often staged. The dignitary would ride through the main gate, usually beneath a canopy made of luxurious cloth. The event might include staged tableaux in the town's streets, with costumed townspeople acting out brief symbolic vignettes such as David and Goliath, and it might end in an elaborate banquet. A remnant of these proceedings survives today in the ceremony by which distinguished visitors are given "the keys to the city," which, in the sixteenth century, really were functional.

Royalty made deliberate and careful use of dramatic ceremony. Royal entries into towns took on an added weight, as did royal funerals and other such occasions. These dramas reinforced political and constitutional assumptions in the minds of witnesses and participants. Thus, over time, we can see changes in the representations of royal power. In France, for example, the ritual entry of the king into Paris had originally stressed the participation of the leading guilds, judges, and administrators, symbolizing their active role in governing the city and the kingdom. But in the last half of the sixteenth century, the procession began to glorify the king alone.

The very fact that rulers experimented self-consciously with self-representation suggests that issues pertaining to the nature and extent of royal power were

---

Lope de Vega (LOW-pah day VAY-guh)   **Pedro Calderón** (PAY-dro kall-day-ROHN)   **Corneille** (kore-NAY)

Monteverdi (mon-tay-VAIR-dee)

≥▲ R E A D I N G   S O U R C E S

Elizabeth I Addresses Her Troops

The day after English ships dispersed the Spanish Armada in 1588, Elizabeth addressed a contingent of her troops. She used the opportunity to fashion an image of herself as a warrior above all but also as the beloved familiar of her people, unafraid of potential plots against her. Note her willingness to portray herself as androgynous—that is, embodying both female and male qualities.

My loving people, we have been persuaded by some that are careful of our safety, to take heed how we commit ourselves to armed multitudes, for fear of treachery. But I assure you, I do not desire to live to distrust my faithful and loving people. Let tyrants fear. I have always so behaved myself that, under God, I have placed my chiefest strength in the loyal hearts and good will of my subjects; and therefore I am come amongst you, as you see, at this time, not for my reaction or disport, but being resolved, in the midst and heat of the battle, to live or die amongst you all, to lay down for my God, and for my kingdom, and for my people, my honor and my blood, even in the dust. I know I have the body of a weak and feeble woman, but I have the heart and the stomach of a king, and of a king of England too, and think foul scorn that Parma or Spain, or any prince of Europe should dare to invade the borders of my realm; to which, rather than any dishonor shall grow by me, I myself will take up arms, I myself will be your general, judge, and rewarder of every one of your virtues in the field.

Source: J. E. Neale, *Queen Elizabeth I* (New York: Anchor, 1957), pp. 308–309.

---

profoundly important and far from settled. Queen Elizabeth had the particular burden of assuming the throne in a period of great instability. Hence, she paid a great deal of attention to the image of herself that she conveyed in words and authorized to be fashioned in painting. Elizabeth styled herself variously as mother to her people and as a warrior-queen (drawing on ancient myths of Amazon women). She made artful use of the image of her virginity to buttress each of these images—as the wholly devoted, self-sacrificing mother (which, of course, had religious tradition behind it) or as an androgynous ruler, woman but doing the bodily work of man. (See the box "Reading Sources: Elizabeth I Addresses Her Troops.")

More formal speculation about constitutional matters also resulted from the tumult of the sixteenth and seventeenth centuries. As we have seen, the Protestant faction in France advanced an elaborate argument for the limitation of royal power. Alternative theories enhancing royal authority were offered, principally in support of the Catholic position though also simply to buttress the beleaguered monarchy itself. The most fa-

mous of these appeared in *The Six Books of the Republic* (1576), by the legal scholar Jean Bodin° (1530–1596). Bodin was a Catholic but offered a fundamentally secular perspective on the purposes and source of power within a state. His special contribution was a vision of a truly sovereign monarch. Bodin offered a theoretical understanding that is essential to states today and is the ground on which people can claim rights and protection from the state—namely, that there is a final sovereign authority. For Bodin, that authority was the king. He recognized that in practice royal power was constrained by limitations; but he was more intrigued with the theoretical grounding for royal authority, not its practical application.

Contract theory devised by French Protestants to legitimize resistance to the monarchy had to be abandoned when Henry IV granted toleration to the Huguenots in 1598. In England, theoretical justification of resistance to Charles I was initially limited to invoking tradition and precedent. Contract theory as well as other

---

Bodin (bo-DAHN)

Rubens: The Raising of the Cross
This dramatic rendering of the crucifixion of Jesus, part of a three-panel altarpiece in Antwerp Cathedral, is a masterpiece of baroque art. Rubens portrays not a static scene but a moment of action. He creates a sense of movement with the strong diagonal lines of the main figures and focuses our attention with light on the figure of Jesus. *(Onze Lieve Vrouwkwerk, Antwerp Cathedral, Belgium/Peter Willi/Bridgeman Art Library)*

sweeping claims regarding subjects' rights would be more fully developed later in the century.

Bodin's theory of sovereignty, however, was immediately echoed in other theoretical works, most notably that of Hugo Grotius° (1583–1645). A Dutch jurist and diplomat, Grotius developed the first principles of modern international law. He accepted the existence of sovereign states that owed no loyalty to higher authority (such as the papacy) and thus needed new principles to govern their interactions. His major work, *De Jure Belli ac Pacis (On the Law of War and Peace)* (1625), was written in response to the turmoil of the Thirty Years' War.

Grotius argued that relations between states could be based on respect for treaties voluntarily reached between them. In perhaps his boldest move, he argued that war must be justified and developed criteria to distinguish just from unjust wars.

■ Baroque Art and Architecture

Speculation about and celebration of power, as well as of dramatic emotion, also occurred in the visual arts— most notably in painting and architecture, in the style now known as "baroque°." (See the feature "Weighing

Grotius (GROW-shus)

baroque (ba-ROKE)

the Evidence: Art at Court" on pages 536–537.) The word *baroque* comes from the Portuguese *barroco*, used to describe irregularly shaped pearls; the term as applied to the arts was initially derogatory, describing illogic and irregularity. Baroque architecture modified the precision, symmetry, and orderliness of Renaissance architecture to produce a sense of greater dynamism in space. Façades and interiors were both massive and, through clever use of architectural and decorative components, suggestive of movement. Hence baroque churches, for example, were impressively grand and emotionally engaging at the same time. Baroque techniques were pioneered in Italy, first in church design, in the late sixteenth century and spread slowly, with many regional variations, especially throughout Catholic Europe, during the seventeenth century.

One of the primary purposes of baroque architecture and painting was to encourage piety that was not only emotionally involved but also awe-inspired. Italian baroque painting made use of the realism developed in Renaissance art but added dynamism and emotional energy—such as by painting throngs of people or by using light to create direction and energy in the scene portrayed. Dramatic illusion was also a common device, such as painting a chapel ceiling with figures receding as if ascending to heaven. The faithful were emotionally engaged through their senses, yet always aware of divine majesty.

In Italy baroque sculpture and architecture were dominated by the work of Gianlorenzo Bernini° (1598–1680), who designed the sweeping portico outside Saint Peter's Basilica in Rome. He is perhaps best known for his moving sculpture of the sixteenth-century mystic Saint Theresa, known as "St. Theresa in Ecstasy." The most influential baroque painter was Peter Paul Rubens (1577–1640), a native of the southern Netherlands. Rubens's early training in Italy shaped him as an artist and established his secondary career as a diplomat, trusted by princely patrons. Throughout his life, he undertook diplomatic missions for the Habsburg viceroys in the Spanish Netherlands, gaining artistic commissions wherever he traveled. Rubens's subject matter varied widely, including church design and decoration, portraiture, and landscape painting. Baroque technique, of which he was a master, is distinguished by the dramatic use of color and shading and by the dynamic energy of his figures.

Bernini (bare-NEE-nee)

SUMMARY

THE late sixteenth and early seventeenth centuries were an era of intense struggle over political and religious authority. Rulers everywhere, through a variety of expedients, tried to buttress and expand royal power. They were resisted by traditional centers of power, such as independent-minded nobles. But they were also resisted by the novel challenge of religious dissent, which empowered subjects both to claim a greater right to question authority and to risk more in their attempts to oppose it. In some areas of Europe, such as the Holy Roman Empire, the struggles reached some resolution. In other areas, such as England, decades of bloody conflict still lay ahead.

On the whole, these conflicts did little to improve the lives of ordinary people since for the most part victorious elites decided matters of religion and governance in their own interests. In addition, the difficult economic circumstances of these decades meant that working people, desperate for a secure livelihood, rioted or took up arms out of economic as well as religious concerns.

Yet however grim the circumstances people faced, the technology of print and the spread of literacy helped spur speculative and creative works by providing the means for reflection and the audiences to receive and appreciate it. Ironically, the increased importance and grandeur of court life, although a cause of political strain, resulted in a new wave of patronage for art, literature, and drama. Some of the works we still value, such as Rubens's paintings, portray the splendid ambience of royal courts. Other works, such as Shakespeare's plays, both reflect and reflect on the tensions and contradictions in the society of the day: for example, the importance of the stability provided by royal authority as opposed to the dignity and wisdom of ordinary people, who had no claim to power at all.

■ Notes

1. Geoffrey Parker, *The Dutch Revolt* (London: Penguin Books, 1985), p. 288, n. 5.
2. Quoted in A. W. Lovett, *Early Habsburg Spain, 1517–1598* (Oxford: Oxford University Press, 1986), p. 212.
3. Quoted in R. J. Knecht, *The French Wars of Religion, 1559–1598* (London: Longman, 1989), p. 109.
4. Quoted in Jean Berenger, *A History of the Habsburg Empire, 1273–1700*, trans. C. A. Simpson (London and New York: Longman, 1990), p. 239.

5. *The Riverside Shakespeare,* 2d ed. (Boston: Houghton Mifflin, 1997), p. 855.

■ Suggested Reading

Bonney, Richard. *The European Dynastic States, 1494–1660.* 1991. A recent, rich survey of the period that is solid on eastern as well as western Europe; however, written from an English point of view, it does not consider England as part of Europe.

Eagleton, Terry. *William Shakespeare.* 1986. A brief and highly readable interpretation of Shakespeare that emphasizes the tensions in the plays caused by language and by ideas from the new world of bourgeois commercial life.

Hale, J. R. *War and Society in Renaissance Europe.* 1985. An analysis of war as a function of government and as a part of the social, economic, and intellectual life of the sixteenth century.

Holt, Mack P. *The French Wars of Religion, 1562–1629.* 1995. An up-to-date synthesis that evaluates social and political context while not slighting the importance of religion.

Lynch, John. *Spain, 1516–1598: From Nation-State to World Empire.* 1991. A survey covering the reign of Philip II by a leading scholar of Spanish history.

Parker, Geoffrey. *The Military Revolution.* 1988; and Black, Jeremy. *A Military Revolution?* 1991. Two works that disagree about the nature and extent of the changes in military practices and their significance for military, political, and social history. Black tries to refute claims for a dramatic military "revolution."

———. *The Dutch Revolt.* 2d ed. 1985. The best survey of the revolt available in English.

Smith, A. G. R. *The Emergence of a Nation-State: The Commonwealth of England, 1529–1660.* 1984. A good place to start in the immense bibliography on the Elizabethan period.

Wiesner, Merry. *Women and Gender in Early Modern Europe.* 1993. Discusses all aspects of women's experience, including their working lives.

 For a searchable list of additional readings for this chapter, go to http://college.hmco.com.

Art at Court

The painting you see reproduced here (at less than $\frac{1}{25}$ of its original size) is a portrait of the English king Charles I painted by the Flemish painter Anthony Van Dyck about the year 1638. Van Dyck was a pupil of the great baroque painter Peter Paul Rubens. Like Rubens, he enjoyed international fame. Among his greatest works are portraits completed during a long sojourn at the English court in the 1630s. This large portrait was designed to be hung at the end of a long corridor or a similar place so that, from a distance, the observer would have the illusion of actually seeing the king outdoors on horseback. This effect was similar to that achieved by baroque artists who painted church ceilings with receding angels and cherubs, giving the faithful the illusion of gazing up toward heaven.*

How are we meant to interpret and respond to Charles's portrait? What visual cues did Van Dyck include for his contemporaries that we might miss, or misinterpret? Charles's suit of armor was, by itself, a complex image. Aristocrats no longer wore full body armor onto the battlefield since it had been designed for fighting against lances, not guns. Indeed, although his body is fully armored, Charles wears riding boots rather than armor on his shins and feet. The fact that he is about to be handed a magnificently decorated helmet by his attendant further complicates the image. This kind of headgear was worn for a festive mock battle, a typical entertainment at courts throughout Europe. Thus, the king is not portrayed in the unbelievable role of a medieval knight; instead, he is dressed in a costume that any courtier could have identified as "pretend." Both Charles and the artist, Van Dyck, could count on the fact that his courtiers would have *expected* Charles to manipulate images of himself; indeed, they would have expected him to be skillful at it. The mock battles, staged entries, and courtly theatricals that they regularly witnessed or participated in were all vehicles for dramatically displaying royal power.

Although courtiers were familiar with the image of a heroic knight on horseback, it was not commonplace or banal. Van Dyck here drew on a tradition, dating back to

the Roman Empire and recently revived by Renaissance sculptors and painters, of depicting a ruler, particularly the emperor, as a heroic mounted warrior. Equestrian statues of Renaissance generals and princes, aping ancient ones of Roman emperors, were among the great achievements of fifteenth- and sixteenth-century art. The most immediate influence on Van Dyck was a painting of the Holy Roman emperor Charles V by the Renaissance master Titian: to celebrate Charles's victory over Protestant forces, the emperor is portrayed as an armored warrior on horseback. In later decades (see pages 538 and 554), the theme would be overused and this kind of image would be constantly reused, but in the early seventeenth century it was still novel and fresh and must have retained particular force on the imagination.

What use to Charles was a heroic image borrowed from antiquity? Note that behind Charles, fastened to the tree, is a plaque with a Latin inscription. This writing would have been easily legible to anyone viewing the actual, 12-foot-high painting. It reads: *Carolus I Rex Magnae Britaniae*, or Charles I, King of Great Britain. Any courtier viewing the painting would have known of the recent political wrangling about the king's claim to that title. "Great Britain" was a newly coined term referring to the combined kingdoms of England and Scotland. James I, Charles's father, had been king of Scotland when he acceded to the English throne and had referred to himself as "King of Great Britain." But Parliament insisted that his titles be listed separately until the institutions of the two kingdoms had been united to create a truly integrated state—a process Parliament intended to oversee. James used the title "King of Great Britain" anyway, one of the many ways he asserted his prerogative against the power of Parliament. Charles, however, had actually begun to force the integration of the two kingdoms by forcing Anglican Church structure on the Scots. Thus, Van Dyck cleverly reinforces Charles's claim to this quasi-imperial title of King of Great Britain by depicting him as emperor, complete with label.

Van Dyck added yet another symbolic prop to Charles's majesty and authority: the medallion around his neck. This medallion (which carried the image of Saint George and the dragon) identifies him as the leader of the Order of the Knights of the Garter, an

---

*This discussion draws on the work of Roy Strong, *Van Dyck: Charles I on Horseback* (New York: Viking Press, Inc., 1972).

Van Dyck: Charles I on Horseback
(© The National Gallery, London)

English order of knights founded in the Middle Ages. This symbol of the loyalty and valor of ideal knights, and the ceremonies such as celebration of the feast day of Saint George, had a variety of symbolic possibilities. Elizabeth I had used the Garter Festival (on Saint George's day) as an occasion to celebrate the chivalrous loyalty of her subjects for their lady fair—that is, Elizabeth herself. During his reign so far, Charles had emphasized a different aspect of the order's symbolic potential: its religious symbolism. In the Middle Ages, knighthood had always been imbued with religious values. Under Charles, the Garter Festival included a formal procession of magnificently attired knights, clergy, and courtiers, followed by a religious service that was almost unchanged from the days of Catholicism. In other words, Charles used the trappings of the Order of the Garter to sponsor religious services reminiscent of Rome at the court and to help craft an identity as a warrior fighting on God's behalf.

Van Dyck's portrayal of Charles I was thus a highly charged, contentious one. It laid claim symbolically to the powers Charles was trying to exercise in practice, including wider authority over his two kingdoms and the stature of divine agent on earth. Unlike us, the courtiers of his day would have known how to "read" the symbolic references in the painting because the painting borrowed images from court life and ceremony, and from other art forms with which they were familiar. By trying to re-enter the world in which this painting once made symbolic sense, we can appreciate how uncertain were the boundaries of royal power in this epoch and how high were the stakes in representing the king. Van Dyck's extraordinary skill made this particular representation both daring in its claims for royal power and compelling to the viewer.

 For additional information on this topic, go to http://college.hmco.com.

CHAPTER 16

Europe in the Age of Louis XIV ca. 1640–1715

THE portrait of King Louis XIV of France as a triumphant warrior, to the left, was one of hundreds of such images of the king that decorated his palace at Versailles and other sites around his kingdom—where they made his subjects aware of his presence, regardless of whether he was in residence. Louis is dressed as a Roman warrior, and his power is represented by a mixture of other symbols—Christian and pagan, ancient and contemporary. An angel crowns him with a victor's laurel wreath and carries a banner bearing the image of the sun. In his hand, Louis holds a marshal's baton—a symbol of military command—covered with the royal emblem of the fleur-de-lys°. In the background, behind the "Roman" troops following Louis, is an idealized city.

These trappings symbolized the significant expansion of royal power during Louis's reign. He faced down the challenges of warrior-nobles, suppressed religious dissent, and tapped the nation's wealth to wage a series of wars of conquest. A period of cultural brilliance early in his reign and the spectacle of an elaborate court life crowned his achievements. In his prime, his regime was supported by a consensus of elites; such harmony was made possible by the lack of institutional brakes on royal authority. However, as his attention to symbolism suggests, Louis's power was not unchallenged. By the end of the Sun King's reign, the glow was fading: France was struggling under economic distress brought on by the many wars fought for his glory and had missed opportunities for commercial success abroad. Elites throughout France who had once accepted, even welcomed, his rule became trenchant critics, and common people outright rebels.

fleur-de-lys (flur–duh–LEE)

France in the Age of Absolutism

English Civil War and Its Aftermath

New Powers in Central and Eastern Europe

The Expansion of Overseas Trade and Settlement

Louis XIV in Roman armor, by the contemporary artist Charles Le Brun. (Scala/Art Resource, NY)

After the Thirty Years' War, vigorous rulers in central and eastern Europe undertook a program of territorial expansion and state building that led to the dominance in the region of Austria, Brandenburg-Prussia, and Russia. The power of these states derived, in part, from the economic relationship of their lands to the wider European economy. In all the major states of continental Europe, princely governments were able to monopolize military power for the first time, in return for economic and political concessions to noble landholders. In England, by contrast, the Crown faced rebellion by subjects claiming religious authority and political legitimacy for their causes. Resistance to the expansion of royal authority, led by Parliament, resulted in the execution of the king and the establishment of a short-lived republic, the Commonwealth. Although the monarchy was restored, the civil war had long-term consequences for royal power in England.

The seventeenth century also witnessed a dynamic phase of European expansion overseas, following on the successes of the Portuguese and the Spanish in the fifteenth and sixteenth centuries. Eager migrants settled in the Americas in ever increasing numbers, while forced migrants—enslaved Africans—were transported by the thousands to work on the profitable plantations of European colonizers. Aristocrats, merchants, and peasants back in Europe jockeyed to take advantage of—or to mitigate the effects of—the local political and economic impact of Europe's expansion.

QUESTIONS TO CONSIDER

- How did Louis XIV successfully expand royal power in France?

- What were the long-term consequences of the English civil war?

- What economic and political interests led to war in eastern Europe?

- How did the expansion of international trade and colonization affect European states and communities?

TERMS TO KNOW

Louis XIV	Brandenburg-Prussia
absolutism	Treaty of Carlowitz
mercantilism	Great Northern War
Oliver Cromwell	Peter the Great
Interregnum	Dutch East India Company
Glorious Revolution	plantation system

FRANCE IN THE AGE OF ABSOLUTISM

 BSOLUTISM is a term often used to describe the extraordinary concentration of power in royal hands achieved by the kings of France, most notably Louis XIV (r. 1643–1715), in the seventeenth century. Louis continued the expansion of state power begun by his father's minister, Cardinal Richelieu (see page 518). The extension of royal power, under Louis as well as his predecessor, was accelerated by the desire to sustain an expensive and aggressive foreign policy. The policy itself was partly traditional—fighting the perpetual enemy, the Habsburgs, and seeking military glory—and partly new—expanding the borders of France. Louis XIV's successes in these undertakings made him both envied and emulated by other rulers; the French court became a model of culture and refinement. But increased royal authority was not accepted without protest: common French people as well as elites dug in their heels.

■ The Last Challenge to Absolutism: The Fronde, 1648–1653

Louis came to the throne as a 5-year-old child in 1643. Acting as his regent, his mother, Anne of Austria (1601–1666), had to defuse a serious challenge to royal authority during her son's minority. Together with her chief minister and personal friend, Cardinal Jules Mazarin° (1602–1661), she faced opposition from royal bureau-

---

Mazarin (mah-zah-RAHN)

crats and the traditional nobility as well as the common people.

Revolts against the concentration of power in royal hands and against the exorbitant taxation that had prevailed under Louis's father began immediately. In one province, a group of armed peasants cornered the intendant and forced him to agree to lower taxes; elsewhere, provincial parlements tried to abolish special ranks of officials, especially the intendants, created by Richelieu. In 1648, after several more years of foreign war and of financial expedients to sustain it, the most serious revolt began, led by the Parlement° of Paris and the other sovereign law courts in the capital.

The source of the Parlement's leverage over the monarchy was its traditional right to register laws and edicts, which amounted to judicial review. Now, the Parlement, as a guardian of royal authority, attempted to extend this power by debating and even initiating government policy: the sovereign courts sitting together drew up a reform program abolishing most of the machinery of government established under Richelieu and calling for consent to future taxation. The citizens of Paris rose to defend the courts when royal troops were sent against them in October.

Mazarin was forced to accept the proposed reform of government, at least in theory. He also had to avert challenges by great nobles for control of the young king's council. Civil war waxed and waned around France from 1648 until 1653. The main combatants were conventionally ambitious great nobles, but reform-minded urban dwellers often made common cause with them, to benefit from their military power. Meanwhile, middling nobles in the region around Paris began to devise a thoroughgoing reform program and to prepare for a meeting of the Estates General—a representative assembly—to enact it.

These revolts begun in 1648 were derided with the name "Fronde°," which was a popular children's game. However, the Fronde was not child's play: it constituted a serious challenge to the legacy of royal government as it had developed under Richelieu. It ended without a noteworthy impact on the growth of royal power for several reasons. First, Mazarin methodically regained control of the kingdom through armed force and artful concessions to individual aristocrats, who were always eager to trade their loyalty for the fruits of royal service. Meanwhile, the Parlement of Paris, as well as many citizens of the capital, welcomed a return to royal authority when civil war caused starvation as well as political unrest.

Moreover, the Parlement of Paris was a law court, not a representative assembly. Its legitimacy derived

---

Parlement (par-luh-MAWNH)   **Fronde** (FRAWND)

CHRONOLOGY

1602	Dutch East India Company formed
1607	Jamestown colony founded in Virginia
1608	Champlain founds Quebec City
1613	Michael becomes first Romanov tsar in Russia
1620	Pilgrims settle at Plymouth (Massachusetts)
1643	Louis XIV becomes king of France
1642–1648	Civil war in England
1648–1653	Fronde revolts in France
1649	Execution of Charles I
1649–1660	English Commonwealth
1659	Peace of the Pyrenees
1660	Monarchy restored in England
1661	Louis XIV assumes full control of government
1672–1678	Dutch War
1682	Peter the Great becomes tsar of Russia
1685	Edict of Nantes revoked
1688	Glorious Revolution
1699	Treaty of Carlowitz
1700–1721	Great Northern War
1701–1714	War of the Spanish Succession
1713	Peace of Utrecht
1715	Death of Louis XIV

from its role as upholder of royal law, and it could not, over time, challenge the king on the pretext of upholding royal tradition in his name. Parlementaires tended to see the Estates General as a rival institution and helped quash the proposed meeting of representatives. Above all, they wanted to avert such reforms as the abolition of the paulette, a fee guaranteeing the hereditary right to royal office (see page 517).

Unlike in England, there was in France no single institutional focus for resistance to royal power. A strong-willed and able ruler, such as Louis XIV proved to be, could obstruct or override challenges to royal power, particularly when he satisfied the ambitions of aristocrats and those bureaucrats who profited from the expansion of royal power. Moreover, the young Louis had been traumatized by the uprisings of the Fronde and grew up determined never to allow another such challenge to his absolute sovereignty.

■ France Under Louis XIV, 1661–1715

Louis XIV fully assumed control of government at Mazarin's death in 1661. It was a propitious moment. The Peace of the Pyrenees in 1659 had ended in France's favor the wars with Spain that had dragged on since the end of the Thirty Years' War. As part of the peace agreement, Louis married a Spanish princess, Maria Theresa. In the first ten years of his active reign, Louis achieved a degree of control over the mechanisms of government unparalleled in the history of monarchy in France or anywhere else in Europe. Louis was extremely vigorous and proved a diligent king. He put in hours a day at a desk while sustaining the ceremonial life of the court with its elaborate hunts, balls, and other public events.

Louis did not invent any new bureaucratic devices but rather used existing ranks of officials in new ways that increased government efficiency and further centralized control. He radically reduced the number of men in his High Council, the advisory body closest to the king, to include only three or four great ministers of state affairs. This intimate group, with Louis's active participation, handled all policymaking. The ministers of state, war, and finance were chosen exclusively from non-noble men of bourgeois backgrounds whose training and experience fitted them for such positions. Jean-Baptiste Colbert° (1619–1683), perhaps the greatest of them, served as minister of finance and supervised most domestic policy from 1665 until his death; he was from a merchant family and had served for years under Mazarin.

Several dozen other officials, picked from the ranks of up-and-coming lawyers and administrators, drew up laws and regulations and passed them to the intendants for execution at the provincial level. Sometimes, these officials at the center were sent to the provinces on short-term supervisory missions. The effect of this system was to bypass many entrenched provincial bureaucrats, particularly those known as tax farmers. Tax farmers were freelance businessmen who bid for the right to collect taxes in a region in return for a negotiated fee they paid to the Crown. The Crown, in short, did not control its own tax revenues. The money Louis's regime saved by the more efficient collection of taxes (revenues almost doubled in some areas) enabled the government to streamline the bureaucracy: dozens of the offices created over the years to bring cash in were bought back by the Crown from their owners.

The system still relied on the bonds of patronage and personal service, political bonds borrowed from aristocratic life. Officials rose through the ranks by means of service to the great, and family connection and personal loyalty still were essential. Of the seventeen different men who were part of Louis XIV's High Council during his reign, five were members of the Colbert family, for example. In the provinces, important local families vied for minor posts, which at least provided prestige and some income.

Further benefits of centralized administration can be seen in certain achievements of the early years of Louis's regime. Colbert actively encouraged France's economic development. He reduced the internal tolls and customs barriers, which were relics of medieval decentralization—for example, the right of a landholder to charge a toll on all boats along a river under his control. He encouraged industry with state subsidies and protective tariffs. He set up state-sponsored trading companies—the two most important being the East India Company and the West India Company, established in 1664.

Mercantilism is the term historians use to describe the theory behind Colbert's efforts. This economic theory stressed self-sufficiency in manufactured goods, tight control of trade to foster the domestic economy, and the absolute value of bullion. Both capital for development—in the form of hard currency, known as bullion—and the amount of world trade were presumed to be limited in quantity. Therefore, state intervention in the form of protectionist policies was believed necessary to guarantee a favorable balance of payments.

This static model of national wealth did not wholly fit the facts of growing international trade in the seventeenth century. Nevertheless, mercantilist philosophy was helpful to France. France became self-sufficient in the all-important production of woolen cloth, and French industry expanded notably in other sectors. Colbert's greatest success was the systematic expansion of the navy and merchant marine. By 1677 the navy had increased almost sixfold, to 144 ships. By the end of Louis XIV's reign, the French navy was virtually the equal of the English navy.

Colbert and the other ministers began to develop the kind of planned government policymaking that we now take for granted. Partly by means of their itinerant supervisory officials, they tried to formulate and execute

---

Colbert (coal-BEAR)

policy based on carefully collected information. How many men of military age were available? How abundant was this year's harvest? Answers to such questions enabled not only the formulation of economic policy but the deliberate management of production and services to achieve certain goals—above all, the recruitment and supply of the king's vast armies.

Beginning in 1673, Louis tried to bring the religious life of the realm more fully under royal control, claiming for himself—with mixed success—some of the church revenues and powers of ecclesiastical appointment that still remained to the pope. Partly to bolster his position with the pope, he also began to attack the Huguenot community in France. First, he offered financial inducements for conversions to Catholicism. Then he took more drastic steps such as destroying Protestant churches and quartering troops in Huguenots' households to force them to convert. In 1685 he declared that France would no longer abide any Protestant community, and he revoked the Edict of Nantes. A hundred thousand Protestant subjects—including some six hundred army and navy officers—refused even nominal conversion to Catholicism and chose to emigrate.

Meanwhile, Louis faced resistance to his claims against the pope from within the ranks of French clergy. These churchmen represented a movement within French Catholicism known as Jansenism, after the professor of theology named Cornelius Jansen, whose writings were its inspiration. Jansenists practiced an austere style of Catholic religiosity that, in its notions about human will and sinfulness, was akin to some Protestant doctrine. Louis was suspicious of Jansenism, because its adherents included many of his political enemies, particularly among families of parlementary officials. Louis was wary of any threat to the institutional—or symbolic—unity of his regime, such as Protestants and, now, Jansenists represented. At the end of Louis's long reign, another pope obligingly declared many Jansenist doctrines to be heretical as part of a compromise agreement with Louis on matters of church governance and finance. Louis's efforts to exert greater control over the church had brought him modest practical gains, but at the price of weakening the religious basis of his authority in the eyes of many sincere Catholics.

By modern standards, the power of the Crown was still greatly limited. The "divine right" of kingship, a notion formulated by Louis's chief apologist, Bishop Jacques Bossuet° (1627–1704), did not mean unlimited power to rule; rather it meant that hereditary monarchy was the divinely ordained form of government, best suited to human needs. *Absolutism* was not iron-fisted control of the realm but rather the successful focusing of energy, loyalties, and symbolic authority in the Crown. The government functioned well in the opening decades of Louis's reign because his role as the focal point of power and loyalty was both logical, after the preceding years of unrest, and skillfully exploited. Much of the glue holding together the absolutist state lay in informal mechanisms such as patronage and court life, as well as in the traditional hunt for military glory—all of which Louis amply supplied.

■ The Life of the Court

An observer comparing the lives of prominent noble families in the mid-sixteenth and mid-seventeenth centuries would have noticed striking differences. By the second half of the seventeenth century, most sovereigns or territorial princes had the power to crush revolts, and the heirs of the feudal nobility had to accommodate themselves to the increased power of the Crown. The nobility relinquished its former independence but retained economic and social supremacy and, as a consequence, considerable political clout. Nobles also developed new ways to symbolize their privilege by means of cultural refinement. This process was particularly dramatic in France as a strong Crown won out over a proud nobility.

One sign of Louis's success in marshaling the loyalty of the aristocracy was the brilliant court life that his regime sustained. No longer able to wield independent political power, aristocrats lived at court whenever they could. There, they endlessly jostled for patronage and prestige—for commands in the royal army and for honorific positions at court itself. (See the box "Reading Sources: A Courtier Criticizes the King.") A favored courtier might, for example, participate in the elaborate daily *lever* (arising) of the king; he might be allowed to hand the king his shirt—a demeaning task, yet a coveted one for the attention by the king that it implied and guaranteed. Courtiers now defended their honor with private duels, not warfare, and more routinely relied on elegant ceremonial, precise etiquette, and clever conversation to demarcate their political and social distinctiveness. (See the feature "Weighing the Evidence: Table Manners" on pages 571–572.)

As literacy became more widespread, and the power of educated bureaucrats of even humble origin became more obvious, nobles from the traditional aristocracy began increasingly to use reading and writing as a means to think critically about their behavior—in the case of men, to re-imagine themselves as gentlemen rather than warriors. Noblewomen and noblemen alike began to

Bossuet (BOS-soo-way)

❧ READING SOURCES

A Courtier Criticizes the King

Louis de Rouvroy, duke of Saint-Simon (1675–1755), was a favored courtier but one critical of Louis XIV on a number of counts. In this excerpt from his memoirs, Saint-Simon evaluates the character of the king and criticizes his reliance on men of bourgeois backgrounds for his leading ministers. As a member of the traditional aristocracy, Saint-Simon certainly had a reason for disliking this policy. However, this testimony does have the ring of unbiased authenticity in some important respects.

[The king's] ministers, general, mistresses and courtiers learned soon after he became their master that glory, to him, was a foible rather than an ambition. They therefore flattered him to the top of his bent, and in so doing, spoiled him. Praise, or better, adulation . . . were the only road to his favour and those whom he liked owed his friendship to choosing their moments well and never ceasing in their attentions. That is what gave his ministers their power, for they had endless opportunities of flattering his vanity, especially by suggesting that he was the source of all their ideas. . . .

He was well aware that though he might crush a nobleman with the weight of his displeasure, he could not destroy him or his line, whereas a secretary of state or other such minister could be reduced together with his whole family to those depths of nothingness from which he had been elevated. . . . Therein lay the reason for the watchful, jealous attitude of his ministers, who made it difficult for the King to hear any but themselves, although he pleased to think that he was an easy man to approach.

Nevertheless, in spite of the fact that the King had been so spoiled with false notions of majesty and power, that every other thought was stifled in him, there was much to be gained from a private audience, if it might be obtained, and if one knew how to conduct oneself with all the respect due to his dignity and habits. Once in his study, however prejudiced he might be . . . he would listen patiently, good-naturedly, and with a real desire to be informed. You could see that he had a sense of justice and a will to get at the truth. . . . It is therefore enough to make one weep to think of the wickedness of an education designed solely to suppress the . . . intelligence of that prince, and the insidious poison of barefaced flattery which make him a kind of god in the very heart of Christendom.

Source: Louis, duc de Saint-Simon, *Versailles, the Court and Louis XIV,* Lucy Norton, ed. (New York: Harper and Row, 1966), pp. 248–251.

---

reflect on their new roles in letters, memoirs, and the first novels. A prominent theme of these works is the increasing necessity for a truly private life of affection and trust, with which to counterbalance the public façade necessary to an aspiring courtier. The most influential early French novel was *The Princess of Cleves* by Marie-Madeleine Pioche de la Vergne (1634–1693), best known by her title, Madame de Lafayette. Mme. de Lafayette's novel treats the particular difficulties faced by aristocratic women who, without military careers to bring glory and provide distraction, were more vulnera-

ble than men to gossip and slander at court and more trapped by their arranged marriages.

Louis XIV's court is usually associated with the palace he built at Versailles°, southwest of Paris. Some of the greatest talent of the day worked on the design and construction of Versailles from 1670 through the 1680s. It became a masterpiece of luxurious but restrained baroque styling—a model for royal and aristocratic palaces throughout Europe for the next one hundred years.

Versailles (vare-SIGH)

The Château of Versailles   This view of the central section of the palace is taken from the gardens. The reflecting pools you see here are on the first level of an immense terraced garden that, to someone exiting the château, seems to stretch to the horizon. The apparent openness of the king's residence (notice the rows of floor-length windows on the ground floor) is in stark contrast to a fortified castle, and was a dramatic statement of a new kind of royal power.   *(Château de Versailles, France/Peter Willi/The Bridgeman Art Library)*

Before Louis's court in his later years withdrew to Versailles, it traveled among the king's several châteaux around the kingdom, and in this itinerant period of the reign, court life was actually at its most creative and productive. These early years of Louis's personal reign were the heyday of French drama. The comedian Jean-Baptiste Poquelin, known as Molière° (1622–1673), impressed the young Louis with his productions in the late 1650s and was rewarded with the use of a theater in the main royal palace in Paris. Like Shakespeare earlier in the century, Molière explored the social and political tensions of his day. He satirized the pretensions of the aristocracy, the social climbing of the bourgeoisie, the self-righteous piety of clerics. Some of his plays were banned from performance, but most were not only tolerated but extremely popular with the elite audiences they mocked—their popularity

is testimony to the confidence of Louis's regime in its early days.

Also popular at court were the tragedies of Jean Racine° (1639–1699), who was to the French theater what Shakespeare was to the English: the master of poetic language. His plays, which treated familiar classical stories, focused on the emotional and psychological lives of the characters and often stressed the unpredictable, usually unhappy, role of fate, even among royalty. The pessimism in Racine foreshadowed the less successful second half of Louis's reign.

■ **The Burdens of War and the Limits of Power**

Wars initiated by Louis XIV dominated the attention of most European states in the second half of the seventeenth century. Louis's wars sprang from traditional

Molière (mole-YARE)

Racine (rah-SEEN)

causes: the importance of the glory and dynastic aggrandizement of the king and the preoccupation of the aristocracy with military life. But if Louis's wars were spurred by familiar concerns about territorial and economic advantage, they were far more demanding on state resources than any previous wars.

In France and elsewhere, the size of armies grew markedly. And with the countryside still smarting from the rampaging armies of the Thirty Years' War, so did the need for greater management of troops. Louis XIV's victories in the second half of the century are partly traceable to his regime's attention to the bureaucratic tasks of recruitment, training, and supply, which together constituted another phase of the "military revolution." The new offensive tactics developed during the Thirty Years' War (see page 527) changed the character of armies in ways that demanded more resources for training. A higher proportion of soldiers became gunners, and their effectiveness lay in how well they operated as a unit. Armies began to train seriously off the field of battle because drill and discipline were vital to success. France was the first to provide its soldiers with uniforms, which boosted morale and improved discipline. The numbers of men on the battlefield increased somewhat as training increased the effectiveness of large numbers of infantry, but the total numbers of men in arms supported by the state at any time increased dramatically once the organization to support them was in place. Late in the century, France kept more than 300,000 men in arms when at war (which was most of the time).

Louis's first war, in 1667, reflected the continuing French preoccupation with Spanish power on French frontiers. Louis invoked rather dubious dynastic claims to demand, from Spain, lands in the Spanish Netherlands and the large independent county on France's eastern border called the Franche-Comté° (see Map 16.1). After a brief conflict, the French obtained only some towns in the Spanish Netherlands by the terms of the Treaty of Aix-la-Chapelle. Louis had already begun to negotiate with the Austrian Habsburgs over the eventual division of Spanish Habsburg lands, for it seemed likely that the Spanish king, Charles II (r. 1665–1700), would die without an heir. So, for the moment, Louis was content with modest gains at Spain's expense, confident that he would get much more in the future.

Louis's focus then shifted to a new enemy: the Dutch. The Dutch had been allied with France since the beginning of their existence as provinces in rebellion against Spain. The French now turned against the Dutch

for reasons that reflect the growth of the international trading economy: the Dutch dominance of seaborne trade. The French at first tried to offset the Dutch advantage in trade with tariff barriers against Dutch goods. But confidence in the French army led Louis's generals to urge action against the vulnerable Dutch lands. "It is impossible that his Majesty should tolerate any longer the insolence and arrogance of that nation," rationalized the usually pragmatic Colbert in 1670.[1]

The Dutch War began in 1672, with Louis personally leading one of the largest armies ever fielded in Europe—perhaps 120,000 men. At the same time, the Dutch were challenged at sea by England. The English had fought the Dutch over trade in the 1650s; now Louis secretly sent the English king, Charles II, a pension to secure an alliance against the Dutch.

At first, the French were spectacularly successful against the tiny Dutch army. However, the Dutch opened dikes and flooded the countryside, and what had begun as a rout became a soggy stalemate. Moreover, the Dutch were beating combined English and French forces at sea and were gathering allies who felt threatened by Louis's aggression. The French soon faced German and Austrian forces along their frontier, and, by 1674, the English had joined the alliance against France as well.

Nonetheless, the French managed to hold their own, and the Peace of Nijmegen°, in 1678, gave the illusion of a French victory. Not only had the French met the challenge of an enemy coalition, but Spain ceded them further border areas in the Spanish Netherlands as well as control of the Franche-Comté.

Ensconced at Versailles since 1682, Louis seemed to be at the height of his powers. Yet the Dutch War had in fact cost him more than he had gained. Meeting the alliance against him had meant fielding ever increasing numbers of men. Internal reforms in government and finance ended under the pressure of paying for war, and old financial expedients of borrowing money and selling privileges were revived. Other government obligations, such as encouraging overseas trade, were neglected. Colbert's death in 1683 dramatically symbolized the end of an era of innovation in the French regime.

Louis's unforgiving Dutch opponent, William of Orange, king of England from 1689 to 1702, renewed and stirred up anti-French alliances. The war, now known as the Nine Years' War, or King William's War, was touched off late in 1688 by French aggression—an invasion of Germany to claim an inheritance there. In his ongoing dispute with the pope, Louis seized the papal territory of

---

Franche-Comté (FRAWNSH–con-TAY)

Nijmegen (NIME-ay-gehn)

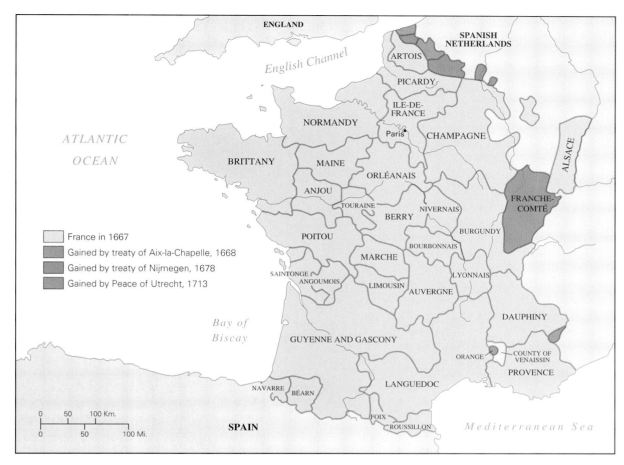

Map 16.1 Territorial Gains of Louis XIV, 1667–1715 Louis's wars, though enormously expensive for France, produced only modest gains of territory along France's eastern and northern frontiers.

Avignon° in southern France. Boldest of all, he helped the exiled Catholic claimant to the English crown mount an invasion to reclaim his throne.

A widespread war began with all the major powers—Spain, the Netherlands, England, Austria, the major German states—ranged against France. The French also carried the fighting abroad by seizing English territory in Canada. As with the Dutch War, the Nine Years' War was costly and, on most fronts, inconclusive. This time, though, there was no illusion of victory for Louis. In the Treaty of Ryswick (1697), Louis had to give up most of the territories in Germany, the Spanish Netherlands, and northern Spain that he managed to occupy at war's end. Avignon went back to the pope, and Louis gave up his contentious claim to papal revenues. The terrible burden of war taxes combined with crop failures in 1693 and

1694 caused widespread starvation in the countryside. French courtiers began to criticize Louis openly.

The final major war of Louis's reign, called the War of the Spanish Succession, broke out in 1701. In some ways it was a straightforward dynastic clash between France and its perennial nemesis, the Habsburgs. Both Louis and Habsburg Holy Roman emperor Leopold I (r. 1657–1705) hoped to claim for their heirs the throne of Spain, left open at the death in 1700 of the last Spanish Habsburg, Charles II. Leopold represented the Austrian branch of the Habsburg family (see the genealogy, page 508), but Charles II bequeathed the throne to Louis's grandson, Philip of Anjou°, by reason of Louis's marriage to the Spanish princess, Maria Theresa. Philip quickly proceeded to enter Spain and claim his new kingdom. War was made inevitable when Louis renounced one of

Avignon (ah-veen-YOHN)

Anjou (ahn-ZHOO)

the conditions of Charles's will: Philip's accession to the throne of Spain, Louis insisted, did not preclude his becoming king of France as well. This declaration was an act of sheer belligerence, for Philip was only third in line for the French throne. The Dutch and the English responded to the prospect of so great a disruption of the balance of power in Europe by joining the emperor in a formal Great Alliance in 1701. The Dutch and English also wanted to defend their colonial interests since the French had already begun to profit from new trading opportunities with the Spanish colonies.

Again the French fought a major war on several fronts on land and at sea. Again the people of France felt the cost in crushing taxes worsened by harvest failures. Major revolts inside France forced Louis to divert troops from the war. For a time it seemed that the French would be soundly defeated, but they were saved by the superior organization of their forces and by dynastic accident: unexpected deaths in the Habsburg family meant that the Austrian claimant to the Spanish throne suddenly was poised to inherit rule of Austria and the empire as well. The English, more afraid of a revival of unified Habsburg control of Spain and Austria than of French domination of Spain, quickly called for peace negotiations.

The Peace of Utrecht in 1713 resolved long-standing political conflicts and helped to set the agenda of European politics for the eighteenth century. Philip of Anjou was recognized as Philip V, the first Bourbon king of Spain, but on the condition that the Spanish and French crowns would never be worn by the same monarch. To maintain the balance of power against French interests, the Spanish Netherlands and Spanish territories in Italy were ceded by a second treaty in 1714 to Austria, which for many decades would be France's major continental rival. The Peace of Utrecht also marked the beginning of England's dominance of overseas trade and colonization. The French gave to England lands in Canada and the Caribbean and renounced any privileged relationship with Spanish colonies. England was allowed to control the highly profitable slave trade with Spanish colonies.

Louis XIV had added small amounts of strategically valuable territory along France's eastern border (see Map 16.1), and a Bourbon ruled in Spain. But the costs in human life and resources were great for the slim results achieved. Moreover, the army and navy had swallowed up capital that might have fueled investment and trade; strategic opportunities overseas were lost, never to be regained. Louis's government had been innovative in its early years but remained constrained by traditional ways of imagining the interest of the state.

ENGLISH CIVIL WAR AND ITS AFTERMATH

 N England, unlike in France, a representative institution—Parliament—became an effective, permanent brake on royal authority. The process by which Parliament gained a secure role in governing the kingdom was neither easy nor peaceful, however. As we saw in Chapter 15, conflicts between the English crown and its subjects, culminating in the Crown-Parliament conflict, concerned control over taxation and the direction of religious reform. Beginning in 1642, England was beset by civil war between royal and parliamentary forces. The king was eventually defeated and executed, and a period followed during which the monarchy was abolished altogether. It was restored in 1660, but Parliament retained a crucial role in governing the kingdom, a role that was confirmed when, in 1688, it again deposed a monarch whose fiscal and religious policies became unacceptable to its members.

■ Civil War and Regicide, 1642–1649

Fighting broke out between the armies of Charles I and parliamentary armies in the late summer of 1642. The Long Parliament (see page 522) continued to represent a broad coalition of critics and opponents of the monarchy, ranging from aristocrats concerned primarily with the abuses of royal prerogative to radical Puritans eager for thorough religious reform and determined to defeat the king. Fighting was halfhearted initially, and the tide of war at first favored Charles.

In 1643, however, the scope of the war broadened. Charles made peace with Irish rebels and brought Irish troops to England to bolster his armies. Parliament, in turn, sought military aid from the Scots in exchange for promises that Presbyterianism would become the religion of England. Meanwhile, Oliver Cromwell (1599–1658), a Puritan member of the Long Parliament and a cavalry officer, helped reorganize parliamentary forces. The eleven-hundred-man cavalry trained by Cromwell and known as the "Ironsides," supported by parliamentary and Scottish infantry, defeated the king's troops at Marston Moor in July 1644. The victory made Cromwell famous.

Shortly afterward, Parliament further improved its forces and created the New Model Army, rigorously trained like Cromwell's Ironsides. Sitting Members of Parliament were barred from commanding troops;

hence upper-class control of the army was reduced. This army played a decisive role not only in the war but also in the political settlement that followed the fighting.

The New Model Army won a convincing victory over royal forces at Naseby in 1645. In the spring of 1646, Charles surrendered to a Scottish army in the north. In January 1647 Parliament paid the Scots for their services in the war and took the king into custody. In the negotiations that followed, Charles tried to play his opponents off against each other, and, as he had hoped, divisions among them widened.

Most members of Parliament were Presbyterians, Puritans who favored a strongly unified and controlled state church along Calvinist lines. They wanted peace with the king in return for acceptance of the new church structure and parliamentary control of standing militias for a specified period. They did not favor expanding the right to vote or other dramatic constitutional or legal change. These men were increasingly alarmed by the rise of sectarian differences and the actual religious freedom that many ordinary people were claiming for themselves. With the weakening of royal authority and the disruption of civil war, censorship was relaxed, and public preaching by ordinary men and even women who felt divinely inspired was becoming commonplace.

Above all, Presbyterian gentry in Parliament feared more radical groups in the army and in London who had supported them up to this point but who favored more thoroughgoing reform. Most officers of the New Model Army, such as Cromwell, were Independents, Puritans who favored a decentralized church, a degree of religious toleration, and a wider sharing of political power among men of property, not just among the very wealthy gentry. In London, a well-organized artisans' movement known as the Levellers favored universal manhood suffrage, law reform, better access to education, and decentralized churches—in short, the separation of political power from wealth and virtual freedom of religion. Many of the rank and file of the army were deeply influenced by Leveller ideas.

In May 1647 the majority in Parliament voted to offer terms to the king and to disband the New Model Army—without first paying most of the soldiers' back wages. This move provoked the first direct intervention by the army in politics. Representatives of the soldiers were chosen to present grievances to Parliament; when this failed, the army seized the king and, in August, occupied Westminster, Parliament's meeting place. Independent and Leveller elements in the army debated the direction of possible reform to be imposed on Parliament. (See the box "Reading Sources: The Putney Debates.")

Oliver Cromwell   Cromwell had seen his own family's income decline under the weight of Charles I's exactions. Elected to Parliament in 1628 and again in 1640, he also brought a long-standing religious zeal to his public life. His opposition to the "tyranny and usurpation" of the Anglican Church hierarchy first prompted him to criticize royal government.   *(In the collection of the Duke of Buccleuch and Queensberry KT)*

However, in November, Charles escaped from his captors and raised a new army among his erstwhile enemies, the Scots, who were also alarmed by the growing radicalism in England. Civil war began again early in 1648. Although it ended quickly with a victory by Cromwell and the New Model Army in August, the renewed war further hardened political divisions and enhanced the power of the army. The king was widely blamed for the renewed bloodshed, and the army did not trust him to keep any agreement he might now sign. When Parliament, still dominated by Presbyterians, once again voted to negotiate with the king, army troops under a Colonel Thomas Pride prevented members who favored Presbyterianism or the king from attending sessions. The "Rump" Parliament that remained after "Pride's Purge" voted to try the king. A hasty trial ensued, and Charles I was executed for "treason, tyranny and bloodshed" against his people on January 30, 1649.

The Putney Debates

In October 1647, representatives of the Leveller movement in the army ranks confronted Independents—largely comprising the officer corps—in formally staged debates in a church at Putney, outside London. The debates reflected the importance of the army in deciding the shape of change. In this exchange the Leveller representative, Thomas Rainsborough, advocates universal manhood suffrage, whereas Cromwell's fellow officer, Henry Ireton, argues for a franchise more restricted to men of some means.

Rainsborough: . . . Really I think that the poorest he that is in England hath a life to live as the greatest he; and therefore truly, sir, I think it's clear, that every man that is to live under a government ought first by his own consent to put himself under that government; and I do think that the poorest man in England is not at all bound in a strict sense to that government that he hath not had a voice to put himself under; and I am confident that, when I have heard the reasons against it, that something will be said to answer those reasons, insomuch that I should doubt whether I was an Englishman or no, that should doubt of these things.

Ireton: . . . I think that no person hath a right to an interest or share in the disposing of the affairs of the kingdom, and in determining or choosing those that shall determine what laws we shall be ruled by here, no person hath a right to this that hath not a permanent fixed interest in this kingdom, and those persons together are properly the represented of this kingdom, who taken together, and consequently are to make up the representers of this kingdom, are the representers, who taken together do comprehend whatsoever is of real or permanent interest in the kingdom, and I am sure there is otherwise (I cannot tell what), otherwise any man can say why a foreigner coming in amongst us, or as many as will be coming in amongst us, or by force or otherwise settling themselves here, or at least by our permission having a being here, why they should not as well lay claim to it as any other. We talk of birthright. Truly birthright there is thus much claim: men may justly have by birthright, by their very being born in En-

gland, that we should not seclude them out of England. That we should not refuse to give them air and place and ground, and the freedom of the highways and other things, to live amongst us, not any man that is born here, though he in birth, or by his birth there come nothing at all that is part of the permanent interest of this kingdom to him. That I think is due to a man by birth. But that by a man's being born here he shall have a share in that power that shall dispose of the lands here, and of all things here, I do not think it a sufficient ground, but I am sure if we look upon that which is the utmost, within man's view, of what was originally the constitution of this kingdom, upon that which is most radical and fundamental, and which if you take away, there is no man hath any land, any goods, you take away any civil interest, and that is this: that those that choose the representers for the making of laws by which this state and kingdom are to be governed, are the persons who taken together, do comprehend the local interest of this kingdom; that is, the persons in whom all land lies, and those in corporations in whom all trading lies. This is the most fundamental constitution of this kingdom, and which if you do not allow, you allow none at all.

Source: G. E. Aylmer, ed., *The Levellers in the English Revolution* (Ithaca: Cornell University Press, 1975), pp. 100–101.

■ The Interregnum, 1649–1660

A Commonwealth—a republic—was declared. Executive power resided in a council of state. The House of Lords having been abolished, legislative power resided in a one-chamber Parliament, the Rump Parliament. Declaring a republic proved far easier than running one, however. The execution of the king shocked most English and Scots people and alienated many elites from the new regime. The legitimacy of the Commonwealth government would always be in question.

The tasks of making and implementing policy were hindered by the narrow political base on which the government now rested. Excluded were the majority of the reformist gentry who had been purged from Parliament. Also excluded were the more radical Levellers; Leveller leaders in London were arrested when they published tracts critical of the new government. Within a few years, many disillusioned Levellers would join a new religious movement called the Society of Friends, or Quakers, which espoused complete religious autonomy. Quakers declined all oaths or service to the state, and they refused to acknowledge social rank.

Above all, the new government was vulnerable to the power of the army, which had created it. In 1649 and 1650 Cromwell led expeditions to Ireland and Scotland, partly for sheer revenge and partly to put down resistance to Commonwealth authority. In Ireland, Cromwell's forces acted with shameful ruthlessness. English control there was strengthened by more dispossession of Irish landholders, which also served to pay off the army's wages. Meanwhile, Parliament could not agree on systematic reforms, particularly the one reform Independents in the army insisted on: more broadly based elections for a new Parliament. Fresh from his victories, Cromwell led his armies to London and dissolved Parliament in the spring of 1652.

In 1653 a cadre of army officers drew up the "Instrument of Government," England's first and only written constitution. It provided for an executive, the Lord Protector, and a Parliament to be based on somewhat wider male suffrage. Cromwell was the natural choice for Lord Protector, and whatever success the government of the Protectorate had was due largely to him.

Cromwell was an extremely able leader who was not averse to compromise. Although he had used force against Parliament in 1648, he had worked hard to reconcile the Rump Parliament and the army before marching on London in 1652. He believed in a state church, but one that allowed for control, including choice of minister, by local congregations. He also believed in toleration

Popular Preaching in England   Many women took advantage of the collapse of royal authority to preach in public—a radical activity for women at the time. This print satirizes the Quakers, a religious movement that attracted many women.   *(Mary Evans Picture Library)*

for other Protestant sects, as well as for Catholics and Jews, as long as no one disturbed the peace.

As Lord Protector, Cromwell oversaw impressive reforms in law that testify to his belief in the limits of governing authority. For example, contrary to the practice of his day, he opposed capital punishment for petty crimes. The government of the Protectorate, however, accomplished little given Parliament's internal divisions and opposition to Cromwell's initiatives. The population at large still harbored royalist sympathizers; after a royalist uprising in 1655, Cromwell divided England into military districts and vested governing authority in army generals.

In the end, the Protectorate could not survive the strains over policy and the challenges to its legitimacy. When Cromwell died of a sudden illness in September

1658, the Protectorate did not long survive him. In February 1660 the decisive action of one army general enabled all the surviving members of the Long Parliament to rejoin the Rump. The Parliament summarily dissolved itself and called for new elections. The newly elected Parliament recalled Charles II, son of Charles I, from exile abroad and restored the monarchy. The chaos and radicalism of the late civil war and *interregnum*—the period between reigns, as the years from 1649 to 1660 came to be called—now spawned a conservative reaction.

■ The Restoration, 1660–1685

Charles II (r. 1660–1685) claimed his throne at the age of 30. He had learned from his years of uncertain exile and from the fate of his father. He did not seek retribution but rather offered a general pardon to all but a few rebels (mostly those who had signed his father's death warrant), and he suggested to Parliament a relatively tolerant religious settlement that would include Anglicans as well as Presbyterians. He was far more politically adept than his father and far more willing to compromise.

That the re-established royal government was not more tolerant than it turned out to be was not Charles's doing but Parliament's. During the 1660s, the "Cavalier" Parliament, named for royalists in the civil war, passed harsh laws aimed at religious dissenters. Anglican orthodoxy was reimposed, including the re-establishment of bishops and the Anglican *Book of Common Prayer*. All officeholders and clergy were required to swear oaths of obedience to the king and to the established church. As a result, hundreds were forced out of office and pulpits. Holding nonconformist religious services became illegal, and Parliament passed a "five-mile" act to prevent dissenting ministers from traveling near their former congregations. Property laws were tightened and the criminal codes made more severe.

The king's behavior, in turn, began to mimic prerevolutionary royalist positions. Charles II began to flirt with Catholicism, and his brother and heir, James, openly converted. Charles promulgated a declaration of tolerance that would have included Catholics as well as nonconformist Protestants, but Parliament would not accept it. Anti-Catholic feeling still united all Protestants. In 1678 Charles's secret treaties with the French became known (see page 546), and rumors of a Catholic plot to murder Charles and reimpose Catholicism became widespread. No evidence of any plot was ever unearthed, though thirty-five people were executed for alleged participation. Parliament focused its attention on anti-Catholicism, passing the Test Act, which barred all but

Anglicans from public office. As a result, the Catholic James was forced to resign as Lord High Admiral.

When Parliament moved to exclude James from succession to the throne, Charles dissolved it. A subsequent Parliament, worried by the specter of a new civil war, backed down. But the legacy of the civil war was a potent one. First, despite the harsh laws, to silence all dissent was not possible. After two decades of religious pluralism and broadly based political activity, it was impossible to reimpose conformity; well-established communities of various sects and a self-confidence bred vigorous resistance. The clearest reflection of the legacy of events was the power of Parliament. Though reluctant to press too far, Parliament had tried to assert its policies against the desires of the king.

Nevertheless, by the end of his reign, Charles was financially independent of Parliament thanks to increased revenue from overseas trade and to secret subsidies from France, his recent ally against Dutch trading rivals. This financial independence and firm political tactics enabled Charles to regain, and retain, a great deal of power. If he had been followed by an able successor, Parliament might have lost a good measure of its confidence and independence. But his brother James's reign and its aftermath further enhanced Parliament's power.

■ The Glorious Revolution, 1688

When James II (r. 1685–1689) succeeded Charles, Parliament's royalist leanings were at first evident. James was granted customs duties for life and was also given funds to suppress a rebellion by one of Charles's illegitimate sons. James did not try to impose Catholicism on England as some had feared, but he did try to achieve toleration for Catholics in two declarations of indulgence in 1687 and 1688. However admirable his goal—toleration—he had essentially changed the law of the realm without Parliament's consent and further undermined his position with heavy-handed tactics. When several leading Anglican bishops refused to read the declarations from their pulpits, he had them imprisoned and tried for seditious libel. However, a sympathetic jury acquitted them.

James also failed because of the coincidence of other events. In 1685, at the outset of James's reign, Louis XIV in France had revoked the Edict of Nantes. The possibility that subjects and monarchs in France and, by extension, elsewhere could be of different faiths seemed increasingly unlikely. Popular fears of James's Catholicism were thus heightened early in his reign, and his later declarations of tolerance, though benefiting Protestant dissenters, were viewed with suspicion. In 1688 not only were the Anglican bishops acquitted but the king's second wife, who was Catholic, gave birth to a son. The birth raised the specter of a Catholic succession.

In June 1688, to put pressure on James, leading Members of Parliament invited William of Orange, husband of James's Protestant daughter, Mary, to come to England. William mounted an invasion that became a rout when James refused to defend his throne. James simply abandoned England and went to France. William called Parliament, which declared James to have abdicated and offered the throne jointly to William and Mary. With French support James eventually invaded Ireland in 1690—bound for Westminster—but was defeated by William at the Battle of Boyne that year.

The substitution of William (r. 1689–1702) and Mary (r. 1689–1694) for James, known as the "Glorious Revolution," was engineered by Parliament and confirmed its power. Parliament presented the new sovereigns with a Declaration of Rights upon their accession and, later that year, with a Bill of Rights that defended freedom of speech, called for frequent Parliaments, and required subsequent monarchs to be Protestant. The effectiveness of these documents was reinforced by Parliament's power of the purse. Parliament's role in the political process was ensured by William's interests in funding his ambitious military efforts, particularly the Netherlands' ongoing wars with France.

The issues that had faced the English since the beginning of the century were common to all European states: religious division and elite power, fiscal strains and resistance to taxation. Yet the cataclysmic events in England—the interregnum, the Commonwealth, the Restoration, the Glorious Revolution—had set it apart from the experience of other states. Consequently, the incremental assumption of authority by a well-established institution, Parliament, made challenge of the English monarchy more legitimate and more effective.

New Powers in Central and Eastern Europe

BY the end of the seventeenth century, three states dominated central and eastern Europe: Austria, Brandenburg-Prussia, and Russia. After the Thirty Years' War, the Habsburgs' dominance in the splintering empire waned, and they focused on expanding and consolidating their power in their hereditary possessions. Brandenburg-Prussia, in northeastern Germany, emerged from obscurity to rival the Habsburg

state. The rulers of Brandenburg-Prussia had gained lands in the Peace of Westphalia, and astute management transformed their relatively small and scattered holdings into one of the most powerful states in Europe. Russia's new stature in eastern Europe resulted in part from the weakness of its greatest rival, Poland, and the determination of one leader, Peter the Great, to assume a major role in European affairs. Sweden controlled valuable Baltic territory through much of the century but eventually was also eclipsed by Russia as a force in the region.

The internal political development of these states was dramatically shaped by their relationship to the wider European economy: they were sources of grain and raw materials for the more densely urbanized west. The development of and the competition among states in central and eastern Europe were closely linked to developments in western Europe.

■ The Consolidation of Austria

The Thirty Years' War (see pages 523–528) weakened the Habsburgs as emperors but strengthened them in their own lands. The main Habsburg lands in 1648 were a collection of principalities comprising modern Austria, the kingdom of Hungary (largely in Turkish hands), and the kingdom of Bohemia (see Map 16.2). In 1714 Austria acquired the Spanish Netherlands, which were renamed the "Austrian Netherlands." Although language and ethnic differences prevented an absolutist state along French lines, Leopold I (r. 1657–1705) instituted political and institutional changes that enabled the Habsburg state to become one of the most powerful in Europe through the eighteenth century.

Much of the coherence that already existed in Leopold's lands had been achieved by his predecessors in the wake of the Thirty Years' War. The lands of rebels in Bohemia had been confiscated and redistributed among loyal, mostly Austrian, families. In return for political and military support for the emperor, these families were given the right to exploit their newly acquired land and the peasants who worked it. The desire to recover population and productivity after the destruction of the Thirty Years' War gave landlords further incentive to curtail peasants' autonomy sharply, particularly in devastated Bohemia. Austrian landlords throughout the Habsburg domains provided grain and timber for the export market and foodstuffs for the Austrian armies, while elite families provided the army with officers. This political-economic arrangement provoked numerous serious peasant revolts, but the peasants were not able to force changes in a system that suited both the elites and the central authority.

Celebrating Habsburg Power   Leopold I is depicted here trampling a Turkish soldier, wearing armor and a medieval order of knighthood around his neck—appropriate garb with which to represent a victory over "the Infidel." Compare this sculpture with the painting of Louis XIV in Roman armor on page 538.   *(Kunsthistorisches Museum, Vienna)*

Although Leopold had lost much influence within the empire itself, an imperial government made up of various councils, a war ministry, financial officials, and the like still functioned in his capital, Vienna. Leopold worked to extricate the government of his own lands from the apparatus of imperial institutions, which were staffed largely by Germans more loyal to imperial than to Habsburg interests. In addition, Leopold used the Catholic Church as an institutional and ideological support for the Habsburg state.

Leopold's personal ambition was to re-establish devout Catholicism throughout his territories. Acceptance of Catholicism became the litmus test of loyalty to the Habsburg regime, and Protestantism vanished among elites. Leopold encouraged the work of Jesuit teachers and members of other Catholic orders. These men and women helped staff his government and administered religious life down to the most local levels.

Leopold's most dramatic success, as a Habsburg and as a religious leader, was his reconquest of the kingdom of Hungary from the Ottoman Empire. Since the mid-sixteenth century, the Habsburgs had controlled only a narrow strip of the kingdom. Preoccupied with countering Louis XIV's aggression, Leopold did not himself choose to begin a reconquest. His centralizing policies, however, alienated nobles and townspeople in the portion of Hungary he did control, as did his repression of Protestantism, which had flourished in Hungary. Hungarian nobles began a revolt, aided by the Turks, aiming for a reunited Hungary under Ottoman protection.

The Habsburgs emerged victorious in part because they received help from the Venetians, the Russians, and especially the Poles, whose lands in Ukraine were threatened by the Turks. The Turks overreached their supply lines to besiege Vienna in 1683. When the siege failed, Habsburg armies slowly pressed east and south, recovering Buda, the capital of Hungary, in 1686 and Belgrade in 1688. The Danube basin lay once again in Christian hands. The Treaty of Carlowitz ended the fighting in 1699, after the first conference where European allies jointly dictated terms to a weakening Ottoman Empire. Austria's allies had also gained at the Ottomans' expense: the Poles recovered the threatened Ukraine, and the Russians gained a vital foothold on the Black Sea.

Leopold gave land in the reclaimed lands to Austrian officers who he believed were loyal to him. The traditions of Hungarian separatism, however, were strong, and the great magnates—whether they had defended the Habsburgs against Turkish encroachment or guarded the frontier for Turkish overlords—retained their independence. The peasantry, as elsewhere, suffered a decline in status as a result of the Crown's efforts to ensure the loyalty of elites. In the long run, Hungarian independence weakened the Habsburg state, but in the short run Leopold's victory over the Turks and the recovery of Hungary itself were momentous events, confirming the Habsburgs as the pre-eminent power in central Europe.

■ The Rise of Brandenburg-Prussia

Three German states, in addition to Austria, gained territory and stature after the Thirty Years' War: Bavaria, Saxony, and Brandenburg-Prussia. By the end of the seventeenth century, the strongest was Brandenburg-Prussia, a conglomeration of small territories held, by dynastic accident, by the Hohenzollern family. The two principal territories were electoral Brandenburg, in northeastern Germany, with its capital, Berlin, and the duchy of Prussia, a fief of the Polish crown along the Baltic coast east of Poland proper (see Map 16.2). In addition the Hohenzollerns ruled a handful of small principalities near the Netherlands. The manipulation of resources and power that enabled these unpromising lands to become a powerful state was primarily the work of Frederick William, known as "the Great Elector" (r. 1640–1688).

Frederick William used the occasion of a war to effect a permanent change in the structure of government. He took advantage of a war between Poland and its rivals, Sweden and Russia (described in the next section), to win independence for the duchy of Prussia from Polish overlordship. When his involvement in the war ended in 1657, he kept intact the general war commissariat, a combined civilian and military body that had efficiently directed the war effort, bypassing traditional councils and representative bodies. He also used the standing army to force the payment of high taxes. Most significantly, he established a positive relationship with the *Junker°*, hereditary landholders, which ensured him both revenue and loyalty. He agreed to allow the Junkers virtually total control of their own lands in return for their agreement to support his government—in short, they surrendered their accustomed political independence in exchange for greater economic and social power over the peasants who worked their lands.

Peasants and townspeople were taxed, but nobles were not. The freedom to control their estates led many nobles to invest in profitable agriculture for the export market. The peasants were serfs who received no benefits from the increased productivity of the land. Frederick William further enhanced his state's power by sponsoring state industries. These industries did not have to fear competition from urban producers because the towns had been frozen out of the political process and saddled with heavy taxes. Although an oppressive place for many Germans, Brandenburg-Prussia attracted many skilled refugees, such as Huguenot artisans fleeing Louis XIV's France.

Bavaria and Saxony, in contrast to Brandenburg-Prussia, had vibrant towns, largely free peasantries, and weaker aristocracies but were relative nonentities in international affairs. Power on the European stage depended on military force. Such power, whether in a large state like France or in a small one like Brandenburg-Prussia, usually came at the expense of the people.

■ Competition Around the Baltic: The Demise of Poland and the Zenith of Swedish Power

The rivers and port cities of the Baltic coast were conduits for the growing trade between the Baltic hinterland and the rest of Europe. Tolls assessed on the passage of timber, grain, naval stores, and furs were an important source of local income, and the commodities themselves brought profits to their producers. This trading system had profound social and political consequences for all of the states bordering the Baltic Sea in the seventeenth century.

First, it was a spur to war: Sweden and Denmark fought over control of the sea-lanes connecting the Baltic and North Seas. Sweden, Poland, and Russia fought for control of the eastern Baltic coastline in the sixteenth and seventeenth centuries. In the seventeenth century, Poland and Russia fought over grain- and timber-producing lands comprising modern Belarus, parts of modern Russia, and Ukraine. Second, profits from the production of grain for export in such volume reinforced the power of large landholders, particularly within Poland, where most of the grain was produced.

In 1600 a large portion of the Baltic hinterland lay under the control of Poland-Lithuania, a dual kingdom at the height of its power, but one that would prove an exception to the pattern of expanding royal power in the seventeenth century (see Map 16.2). A marriage in 1386 had brought the duchy of Lithuania under a joint ruler with Poland; earlier in the fourteenth century, Lithuania had conquered Belarus and Ukraine. Poland-Lithuania commanded considerable resources, including the Vistula and Nieman Rivers and the ports of Gdansk and Riga on the Baltic coast. Like the neighboring Habsburg lands, it was a multi-ethnic state, particularly in the huge duchy of Lithuania, where Russian-speakers predominated. Poland was Catholic but had large minorities of Protestants and Jews. Owing to ties with Poland, Lithuanians themselves were mostly Catholic (and some were Protestant), but Russian-speakers were Orthodox. German-speaking families dominated trade in most coastal cities.

Internal strains and external challenges began to mount in Poland-Lithuania in the late sixteenth century. The commercial power of Polish landlords gave them considerable political clout; the king was forced to grant concessions that weakened urban freedoms and bound impoverished peasants to the nobles' estates. In 1572 the sudden death of the very able but childless king, Sigismund II (r. 1548–1572), only enhanced the nobles' position. Sigismund's successors would be elected, which dramatically limited their power: they would have no control over succession to the throne and would be closely supervised by noble counselors.

The spread of the Counter-Reformation, encouraged by the Crown, created tensions with both Protestant and Orthodox subjects in the diverse kingdom. In Ukraine, communities of Cossacks, nomadic farmer-warriors,

Junker (YUNG-kur)

Map 16.2   New Powers in Central and Eastern Europe, to 1725   The balance of power in central and eastern Europe shifted with the strengthening of Austria, the rise of Brandenburg-Prussia, and the expansion of Russia at the expense of Poland and Sweden.

grew as Polish and Lithuanian peasants fled harsh conditions to join them. The Cossacks had long been tolerated because they served as a military buffer against the Ottoman Turks to the south, but now Polish landlords wanted to reincorporate the Cossacks into the profitable political-economic system that they controlled. Meanwhile, the Crown was involved in several wars. From 1609 to 1612 Polish armies tried but failed to impose a Polish king on the Russians during a dispute over the succession. While aiding Austria in the Thirty Years' War against the Turks, their common enemy, the Poles lost Livonia (modern Latvia) and other bits of northern territory to the aggressive Gustav Adolf of Sweden.

In 1648 the Polish crown faced revolt and invasion that it could not counter. The Cossacks, with the Crimean Tatars and their Ottoman overlords as allies, staged a major uprising, defeated Polish armies, and established an independent state. In 1654 the Cossacks transferred their allegiance to Moscow and became part of a Russian invasion of Poland that, by the next year, had engulfed much of the eastern half of the dual kingdom. At the same time, the Swedes seized central Poland and competed with the Russians for control elsewhere; the Swedes were helped by Polish and Lithuanian aristocrats acting like independent warlords.

Polish royal armies managed to recover much territory—most important, the western half of Ukraine. But the invasions and subsequent fighting were disastrous. The population of Poland may have declined by as much as 40 percent, and vital urban economies were in ruins. The Catholic identity of the Polish heartland had been a rallying point for resistance to the Protestant Swedes and the Orthodox Russians, but the religious tolerance that had distinguished the Polish kingdom and had been mandated in its constitution was now abandoned. In addition, much of its recovery of territory was only nominal. In parts of Lithuania inhabited by Russian-speaking peoples, the Russian presence during the wars had achieved local transfers of power from Lithuanian to Russian landlords loyal to Moscow.

The elective Polish crown passed in 1674 to the brilliant military commander Jan Sobieski° (r. 1674–1696), known as "Vanquisher of the Turks" for his role in raising the siege of Vienna in 1683. Given Poland's internal weakness, however, Sobieski's victories in the long run helped the Ottomans' other foes—Austria and Russia—more than they helped the Poles. His successor, Augustus II of Saxony (r. 1697–1704, 1709–1733), dragged Poland back into war, from which Russia would emerge the clear winner in the power struggle in eastern Europe.

On the Baltic coast, however, Sweden remained the dominant player through most of the seventeenth century. Swedish efforts to control Baltic territory began in the sixteenth century, first to counter the power of its perennial rival, Denmark, in the western Baltic. It then competed with Poland to control Livonia, whose principal city, Riga°, was an important trading center for goods from both Lithuania and Russia. By 1617, under Gustav Adolf, the Swedes gained the lands to the north surrounding the Gulf of Finland (the most direct outlet for Russian goods) and in 1621 displaced the Poles in Livonia itself. Swedish intervention in the Thirty Years' War came when imperial successes against Denmark both threatened the Baltic coast and created an opportunity to strike at Sweden's old enemy. The Treaty of Westphalia (1648) confirmed Sweden's earlier gains and added control of further coastal territory, mostly at Denmark's expense.

The port cities held by Sweden were profitable but simply served to pay for the costly wars necessary to seize and defend them. Indeed, Sweden's efforts to hold Baltic territory were driven by dynastic and strategic needs as much as economic objectives. The ruling dynasty struggled against Denmark's control of western Baltic territory in order to safeguard its independence from the Danes, who had ruled the combined kingdoms until 1523. Similarly, competition with Poland for the eastern Baltic was part of a dynastic struggle after 1592. Sigismund Vasa, son of the king of Sweden, had been elected king of Poland in 1587 but also inherited the Swedish throne in 1592. Other members of the ruling Swedish Vasa family fought him successfully to regain rule over Sweden and extricate Swedish interests from Poland's continental preoccupations. Sigismund ruled Poland until his death in 1632, but a Vasa uncle replaced him on the Swedish throne in 1604.

The one permanent gain that Sweden realized from its aggression against Poland at mid-century was the renunciation of the Polish Vasa line to any claim to the Swedish crown. Owing to its earlier gains, Sweden reigned supreme on the Baltic coast until the end of the century, when it was supplanted by the powerful Russian state.

■ The Expansion of Russia

The Russian state expanded dramatically through the sixteenth century. Ivan IV (r. 1533–1584) was proclaimed "Tsar of All the Russias" in 1547. This act was the culmination of the accumulation of land and authority by the princes of Moscow through the late Middle Ages, when

---

Sobieski (so-BYESS-key)

Riga (REE-guh)

Peter the Great   This portrait by a Dutch artist captures the tsar's "Westernizing" mission by showing Peter in military dress according to European fashions of the day. (*Rijksmuseum-Stichting, Amsterdam*)

Moscow had vied for pre-eminence with other Russian principalities. Ivan IV's grandfather, Ivan III (r. 1462–1505), the first to use the title *tsar,* had absorbed neighboring Russian principalities and ended Moscow's subservience to Mongol overlords.

Ivan IV, also known as Ivan "the Terrible"(in Russian, *groznyi,* more accurately translated as "awe-inspiring"), was the first actually to be crowned tsar and routinely to use the title. His use of the title aptly reflected his imperial intentions, as he continued Moscow's push westward and, especially, eastward against the Mongol states of central Asia. Two of the three Mongol states to the east and south fell, and Russian hegemony edged eastward over the Ural Mountains to Siberia for the first time.

Within this expanding empire, Ivan IV ruled as an autocrat. Part of his authority stemmed from his own personality. He was willing—some suggest because of mental imbalance—to use ruthless methods, including the torture and murder of thousands of subjects, to enforce his will. The practice of gathering tribute for Mon-

gol overlords had put many resources in the hands of Muscovite princes. Ivan IV was able to bypass noble participation and intensify the centralization of government by creating ranks of officials, known as the service gentry, loyal only to him.

A period of disputed succession known as the Time of Troubles followed Ivan's death in 1584, not unlike similar crises in other European states, where jealous aristocrats vied for power during periods of royal weakness. In this case, aristocratic factions fought among themselves as well as against armies of Cossacks and other common people who disputed nobles' ambitions and desired less oppressive government. Nonetheless, the foundations of the large and cohesive state laid by Ivan enabled Michael Romanov° to rebuild autocratic government with ease after being chosen tsar in 1613.

The Romanovs were an eminent aristocratic family related to Ivan's. Michael (r. 1613–1645) was selected to rule by an assembly of aristocrats, gentry, and commoners who were more alarmed at the civil wars and recent Polish incursions than at the prospect of a return to strong tsarist rule. Michael was succeeded by his son, Alexis (r. 1645–1676), who presided over the extension of Russian control to eastern Ukraine in 1654 and developed interest in cultivating relationships with the West.

Shifting the balance of power in eastern Europe and the Baltic in Russia's favor was also the work of Alexis's son, Peter I, "the Great" (r. 1682–1725). Peter accomplished this by military successes against his enemies and by forcibly reorienting Russian government and society toward involvement with the rest of Europe.

Peter was almost literally larger than life. Nearly 7 feet tall, he towered over most of his contemporaries and had physical and mental energy to match his size. He set himself to learning trades and studied soldiering by rising through the ranks of the military like a common soldier. He traveled abroad to learn as much as he could about western European economies and governments. He wanted the revenue, manufacturing output, technology and trade, and, above all, the up-to-date army and navy that other rulers enjoyed. In short, Peter sought for Russia a more evolved state system because of the strength it would give him.

Immediately on his accession to power, Peter initiated a bold series of changes in Russian society. His travels had taught him that European monarchs coexisted with a privileged but educated aristocracy and that a brilliant court life symbolized and reinforced the rulers' authority. So he set out to refashion Russian society in what amounted to an enforced cultural revolution. He

Romanov (ROH-man-off)

Resistance to Peter the Great

Many of his subjects resisted Peter's policies, including nobles who despised the enforced cultural changes and peasants who chafed under Peter's more traditional demand of heavy taxes. This letter, from July 1705, reflects the efforts of one group of resisters, city dwellers from Astrakhan, a port on the Caspian Sea, to join forces with another, the Cossacks of the Don River region, to their west. Many citizens of Astrakhan had been at odds with the tsars since the seventeenth century over church reforms. Note that their objections to Peter's cultural reforms, which included European dress and other matters of style (such as being clean-shaven and using tobacco), are thus couched in religious terms. What other concerns does this document reveal? Why might the citizens of Astrakhan have forged an alliance with the Cossacks?

To [the Chief] and to all the Don Cossack Host, we . . . all the city folk of Astrakhan . . . send our greetings. We wish to inform you of what has happened in Astrakhan on account of our Christian faith, because of beard-shaving, German dress, and tobacco; how we, our wives and our children were not admitted into churches in our old Russian dress; how men and women who entered the holy church had their clothes shorn and were expelled and thrown out. . . . Moreover, in the last year, they imposed on us and collected a [new] tax: one ruble "bath money" apiece; and they also ordered us to pay [a certain tax] per seven feet of cellar space. . . . The [local governor] together with other men in authority, colonels and captains, took away all of our firearms and wanted to kill us. . . . They also took away from us, without orders, our bread allowance and forbade that it be issued to us. We endured all this for a long time. [At last,] after taking counsel among ourselves . . . moved by our great distress, for we could endure it no more to be in danger of losing our Christian faith, we resisted: we killed some of them and have put some others in prison. You, the Cossack [Chief] and all the Host of the Don, please deliberate among yourselves and stand up together with us to defend the Christian faith, and send a message about your decision to us at Astrakhan. We are awaiting you . . . and we rely upon you.

Source: Alfred J. Andrea and James H. Overfield, *The Human Record: Sources of Global History,* vol. 2: *Since 1500,* 2d ed. (Boston: Houghton Mifflin, 1994), pp. 168–169.

provoked a direct confrontation with Russia's traditional aristocracy over everything from education to matters of dress. He elevated numerous new families to the ranks of gentry and created an official ranking system for the nobility to encourage and reward service to his government.

Peter's effort to reorient his nation culturally, economically, and politically toward Europe was most apparent in the construction of the city of St. Petersburg on the Gulf of Finland, which provided access to the Baltic Sea (see Map 16.2). In stark contrast to Moscow, dominated by the medieval fortress of the Kremlin and churches in the traditional Russian style, St. Petersburg was a modern European city with wide avenues and palaces designed for a sophisticated court life.

But although Peter was highly intelligent, practical, and determined to create a more productive and better-governed society, he was also cruel and authoritarian. Peasants already were bearing the brunt of taxation, but their tax burden worsened when they were assessed arbitrarily by head and not by output of the land. The building of St. Petersburg cost staggering sums in money and in workers' lives. Peter's entire reform system was carried out tyrannically; resistance was brutally suppressed. Victims of Peter's oppression included his son, Alexis, who died after torture while awaiting execution for questioning his father's policies.

Peter faced elite as well as populist rebellions against the exactions and the cultural changes of his regime. The most serious challenge, in 1707, was a revolt of Cossacks of the Don River region against the regime's tightened controls. (See the box "Reading Sources: Resistance to Peter the Great.") A major reason for the high cost of Peter's government to the Russian people was his ambition for territorial gain—hence his emphasis on an improved, and costly, army and navy. Working side by side with workers and technicians, many of whom he had recruited while abroad, Peter created the Russian navy from scratch. At first, ships were built in the south to contest Turkish control of the Black Sea; later, they were built in the north to secure and defend the Baltic. Peter also modernized the Russian army by employing tactics, training, and discipline he had observed in the West. He introduced military conscription and munitions plants. By 1709 Russia was able to manufacture most of the up-to-date firearms its army needed.

Russia waged war virtually throughout Peter's reign. Initially with some success, he struck at the Ottomans and their client state in the Crimea. Later phases of these conflicts brought reverses, however. Peter was spectacularly successful against his northern competitor, Sweden, for control of the weakened Polish state and the Baltic Sea. The conflicts between Sweden and Russia, known as the Great Northern War, raged from 1700 to 1709 and, in a less intense phase, lasted until 1721. By the Treaty of Nystadt in 1721, Russia gained its present-day territory in the Gulf of Finland near St. Petersburg, plus Livonia and Estonia. These acquisitions gave Russia a secure window on the Baltic and, in combination with its gains of Lithuanian territory earlier in the century, made Russia the pre-eminent Baltic power, at Sweden's and Poland's expense.

THE EXPANSION OF OVERSEAS TRADE AND SETTLEMENT

B Y the beginning of the seventeenth century, competition from the Dutch, French, and English was disrupting the Spanish and Portuguese trading empires in Asia and the New World. During the seventeenth century, European trade and colonization expanded and changed dramatically. The Dutch not only became masters of the spice trade but broadened the market to include many other commodities. In the Americas, a new trading system linking Europe, Africa, and the New World came into being with the expansion of tobacco and, later, sugar production. French and English colonists began settling in North America in increasing numbers. By the end of the century, trading and colonial outposts around the world figured regularly as bargaining chips in disagreements between European states. More important, overseas trade had a crucial impact on life within Europe: on patterns of production and consumption, on social stratification, and on the distribution of wealth.

■ The Growth of Trading Empires: The Success of the Dutch

By the end of the sixteenth century, the Dutch and the English were making incursions into the Portuguese-controlled spice trade with areas of India, Ceylon, and the East Indies. Spain had annexed Portugal in 1580, but the drain on Spain's resources from its wars with the Dutch and French prevented Spain from adequately defending its enlarged trading empire in Asia. The Dutch and, to a lesser degree, the English rapidly supplanted Portuguese control of this lucrative trade (see Map 16.3).

The Dutch were particularly well placed to be successful competitors in overseas trade. They already dominated seaborne trade within Europe, including the most important long-distance trade, which linked Spain and Portugal—with their wine and salt, as well as spices, hides, and gold from abroad—with the Baltic seacoast, where these products were sold for grain and timber produced in Germany, Poland-Lithuania, and Scandinavia. The geographic position of the Netherlands and the fact that the Dutch consumed more Baltic grain than any other area, because of their large urban population, help to explain their dominance of this trade. In addition, the Dutch had improved the design of their merchant ships to maximize their profits. By 1600 they were building the *fluitschip* (flyship) to transport cargo economically; it was a vessel with a long, flat hull, simple rigging, and cheap construction.

The Dutch were successful in Asia because of institutional as well as technological innovations. In 1602 the Dutch East India Company was formed. The company combined government management of trade, typical of the period, with both public and private investment. In the past, groups of investors had funded single voyages or small numbers of ships on a one-time basis. The formation of the Dutch East India Company created a permanent pool of capital to sustain trade. After 1612 investments in the company were negotiable as stock. These greater assets allowed proprietors to spread the risks and delays of longer voyages among larger numbers of investors. In addition, more money was available for warehouses, docks, and ships. The English East India Company, founded in 1607, also supported trade, but more modestly. It had one-tenth the capital of the Dutch company and did not use the same system of permanent

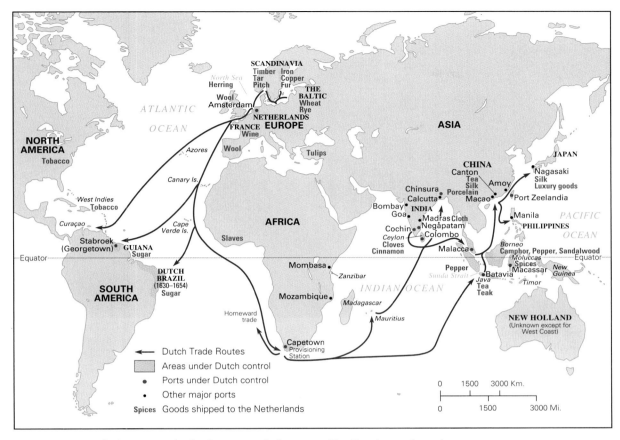

Map 16.3   Dutch Commerce in the Seventeenth Century   The Dutch supplanted Portuguese control of trade with Asia and dominated seaborne trade within Europe.

capital held as stock by investors until 1657. The Bank of Amsterdam, founded in 1609, became the depository for the bullion that flowed into the Netherlands with the flood of trade. The bank established currency exchange rates and issued paper money and instruments of credit to facilitate commerce.

A dramatic expansion of trade with Asia resulted from the Dutch innovations, so much so that by 1650 the European market for spices was glutted, and traders' profits had begun to fall. To control the supply of spices, the Dutch seized some of the areas where they were produced. The Dutch and English further responded to the oversupply of spices by diversifying their trade. The proportion of spices in cargoes from the East fell from about 70 percent at midcentury to just over 20 percent by the century's end. New consumer goods such as tea, coffee, silks, and cotton fabrics took their place. The demand of ordinary people for inexpensive yet serviceable Indian cottons grew steadily. Eventually, the Dutch and

the English, alert for fresh opportunities in the East, entered the local carrying trade among Asian states. Doing so enabled them to make profits even without purchasing goods, and it slowed the drain of hard currency from Europe—currency in increasingly short supply as silver mines in the Americas were depleted.

■ The "Golden Age" of the Netherlands

The prosperity occasioned by the Netherlands' "mother trade" within Europe and its burgeoning overseas commerce helped to foster social and political conditions unique among European states. The concentration of trade and shipping sustained a healthy merchant oligarchy and also an extensive and prosperous artisanal sector. Disparities of wealth were smaller here than anywhere else in Europe. The shipbuilding and fishing trades, among others, supported large numbers of workers with a high standard of living for the age.

Dutch Strength at Sea   This painting by Dutch artist Van der Velde the Younger celebrates a Dutch victory over a combined French and English fleet in 1673. The Dutch had fought their primary commercial rivals, the English, during the 1650s and had built up their fleet of warships in response. Like most major sea battles of the era, this one was fought close to home, off the Dutch coast near the sea-lanes to Amsterdam. *(HarperCollins Publishers/The Art Archive)*

The Netherlands appeared to contemporaries to be an astonishing exception to the normal structures of politics. Political decentralization in the Netherlands persisted. The Estates General (representative assembly) for the Netherlands as a whole had no independent powers of taxation. Each of the seven provinces retained considerable autonomy. Wealthy merchants in the Estates of the province of Holland in fact constituted the government for the entire nation for long periods because of Holland's economic dominance. The head of government was the executive secretary, known as the pensionary, of Holland's Estates.

Holland's only competition in the running of affairs came from the House of Orange, aristocratic leaders of the revolt against Spain (see pages 505–511). They exercised what control they had by means of the office of *stadholder*°—a kind of military governorship—to which they were elected in individual provinces. Their principal interest was the traditional one of military glory and self-promotion. Therein lay a portion of their influence, for they continued to lead the defense of the Netherlands against Spanish attempts at reconquest until the Peace of Westphalia in 1648, and against French aggres-

sion after 1672. Their power also came from their status as the only counterweight within the Netherlands to the dominance of Amsterdam's (in Holland) mercantile interests. Small towns dependent on land-based trade or rural areas dominated by farmers and gentry looked to the stadholders of the Orange family to defend their interests.

As elsewhere, religion was a source of political conflict. The stadholders and the leading families of Holland, known as regents, vied for control of the state church. Pensionaries and regents of Holland generally favored a less rigid and austere form of Calvinism than did the stadholders. Their view reflected the needs of the diverse urban communities of Holland, where thousands of Jews as well as Catholics and various kinds of Protestants lived. Foreign policy was also disputed: Hollanders desired peace in order to foster commerce, whereas stadholders willingly engaged in warfare for territory and dynastic advantage.

These differences notwithstanding, Dutch commercial dominance involved the Netherlands in costly wars throughout the second half of the century. Between 1657 and 1660 the Dutch defended Denmark against Swedish ambitions in order to safeguard the sea-lanes and port cities of the Baltic. More costly conflicts arose because of

---

stadholder (STAHT-hole-der)

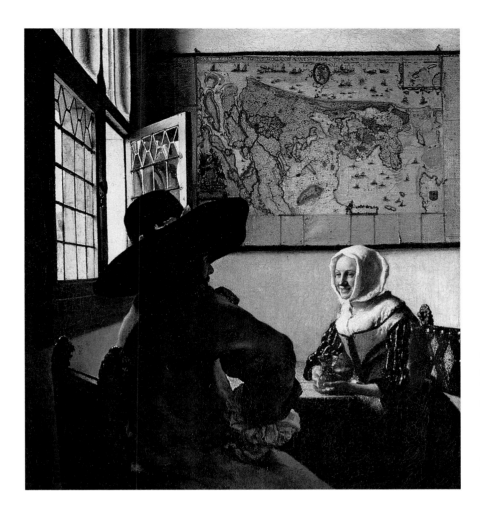

Vermeer: The Soldier and the Laughing Girl This is an early work by one of the great artists of the Dutch "Golden Age." Dutch art was distinguished by its treatment of common, rather than heroic, subjects. The masterful use of light and perspective in paintings such as this one would not be equaled until the invention of photography.
(Copyright The Frick Collection, New York)

rivalry with the more powerful England and France. Under Cromwell, the English attempted to close their ports to the Dutch carrying trade. In 1672 the English under Charles II allied with the French, assuming that together they could destroy Dutch power and perhaps even divide the Netherlands' territory between them. The Dutch navy, rebuilt since Cromwell's challenge, soon forced England out of the alliance.

Owing largely to the land war with France, the Estates in Holland lost control of policy to William of Nassau (d. 1702), prince of Orange after 1672. William drew the Netherlands into his family's long-standing close relationship with England. Like other members of his family before him, William had married into the English royal family: his wife was Mary, daughter of James II.

Ironically, after William and Mary assumed the English throne, Dutch commerce suffered more in alliance with England than in its previous rivalry. William used Dutch resources for the land war against Louis XIV and reserved for the English navy the fight at sea. By the end of the century, Dutch maritime strength was being eclipsed by English sea power.

The Growth of Atlantic Colonies and Commerce

In the seventeenth century, the Dutch, the English, and the French joined the Spanish as colonial and commercial powers in the Americas. The Spanish colonial empire, in theory a trading system closed to outsiders, was in fact vulnerable to incursion by other European traders. Spanish treasure fleets were themselves a glittering attraction. In 1628, for example, a Dutch captain seized the entire fleet. But by then Spain's goals and those of its competitors had begun to shift. The limits of an economy based on the extraction, rather than the production, of wealth became clear with the declining output of the Spanish silver mines during the 1620s. In response, the Spanish and their Dutch, French, and English competitors expanded the production of the cash crops of tobacco, dyestuffs, and, above all, sugar.

The European demand for tobacco and sugar, both addictive substances, grew steadily in the seventeenth century. The plantation system—the use of forced labor to produce cash crops on vast tracts of land—had been

Sugar Manufacture in Caribbean Colonies   Production of sugar required large capital outlays, in part because the raw cane had to be processed quickly, on site, to avoid spoilage. This scene depicts enslaved workers operating a small sugar mill on the island of Barbados in the seventeenth century. In the background a press crushes the cane; in the foreground, the juice from the cane is boiled down until sugar begins to crystallize.   *(Mary Evans Picture Library)*

developed on Mediterranean islands in the Middle Ages by European entrepreneurs, using slaves procured in Black Sea ports by Venetian and Genoese traders. Sugar production by this system had been established on Atlantic islands, such as the Cape Verde Islands, using African labor, and then in the Americas by the Spanish and Portuguese. Sugar production in the New World grew from about 20,000 tons in 1600 to about 200,000 tons by 1770.

In the 1620s, while the Dutch were exploiting Portuguese weakness in the eastern spice trade, they were also seizing sugar regions in Brazil and replacing the Portuguese in slaving ports in Africa. The Portuguese were able to retake most of their Brazilian territory in the 1650s. But the Dutch, because they monopolized the carrying trade, were able to become the official supplier of slaves to Spanish plantations in the New World and the chief supplier of slaves as well as other goods to most other regions. (See the box "Global Encounters: Journal of a Dutch Slave Ship.") The Dutch were able to make handsome profits dealing in human cargo until the end of the seventeenth century, when they were supplanted by the British.

The Dutch introduced the techniques of sugar cultivation to the French and English after learning it themselves in Brazil. Sugar plantations began to supplant tobacco cultivation as well as subsistence farming on the Caribbean islands the English and the French controlled. Beginning late in the sixteenth century, English and French seamen had seized island territories to serve as provisioning stations and staging points for raids against or commerce with Spanish colonies. Some island outposts had expanded into colonies and attracted European settlers—some, as in North America, coming as indentured servants—to work the land. Sugar cultivation, though potentially more profitable than tobacco, demanded huge outlays of capital and continual supplies of unskilled labor, and it drastically transformed the settlements' characters. Large plantations owned by wealthy, often absentee landlords and dependent on slave labor replaced smaller-scale independent farming. The most profitable sugar colonies were, for the French, the islands of Martinique° and Guadeloupe°, and for the English, Barbados° and Jamaica.

Martinique (mar-tih-NEEK)   **Guadeloupe** (gwah-dah-LOO-puh)   **Barbados** (bar-BAY-dose)

Journal of a Dutch Slave Ship

These excerpts from a journal kept by the captain of the Dutch ship St. Jan *record a 1659 slave-trading voyage that began in Africa and ended on Curaçao, a Dutch island colony in the Caribbean. A companion document reveals that 110 of the 219 captive men, women, and children died during the voyage across the Atlantic. Note the fate of those who were still alive by journey's end: why was a pirate able to escape with so many of the slaves?*

The 8th [of March]. We arrived with our ship on Saturday before Arda [in modern Benin] to take on board the surgeon's mate, and tamarinds as refreshment for the slaves. We set sail the next day to continue our voyage to Rio Reael.

The 22nd [of May]. We weighed anchor again and sailed out of the Rio Reael. . . . We acquired there in trade two hundred and nineteen slaves, men and women, boys as well as girls; and we set our course for [islands in the Gulf of Biafra] in order to seek food for the slaves, because nothing was to be had in Rio Reael.

The 26th ditto. On Monday we arrived [on the islands]. We spent seven days there looking but barely obtained enough for the slaves' daily consumption; therefore we decided to sail [up a nearby river] to see whether any food could be found there.

The 29th [of June]. On Sunday we decided to continue our voyage because there was also little food [up the river mouth] for the slaves because of the heavy rain which we had daily and because many slaves were suffering from dysentery caused by the bad food supplied to us at [St. George del Mina, a Dutch fort established to serve the slave trade]. . . .

The 11th [of August]. We lay sixteen days at Cape Lopez [modern Gabon] in order to take on water and firewood. Among the water barrels some forty were taken apart to be repaired because our cooper died . . . [and] we had no one who could repair them.

The 24th [of September]. On Friday we arrived at the island of Tobago [in the Caribbean] where we took on water and also bought some bread for our crew because for three weeks they have had no rations.

The 1st of November. We lost our ship on the reef [east of Curaçao] and our crew fled in the boat immediately. There was no chance to save the slaves because we had to abandon the ship on account of heavy surf.

The 4th ditto. We arrived with the boat at . . . Curaçao. The [governor] dispatched two sloops to retrieve the slaves from the shipwreck. One of the sloops was taken by a pirate together with eighty-four slaves.

Source: Charles T. Gehring and J. A. Schiltkamp, eds., *New Netherlands Documents*, vol. 17 (Interlaken, N.Y.: Heart of the Lakes Publishing, 1987), pp. 128–131.

 For additional information on this topic, go to http://college.hmco.com.

Aware of the overwhelming Spanish territorial advantage in the New World, and yet still hoping for treasures such as the Spanish had found, the English, French, and Dutch were also eager to explore and settle North America. From the early sixteenth century, French, Dutch, English, and Portuguese seamen had fished and traded off Newfoundland. By 1630 small French and Scottish settlements in Acadia (near modern Nova Scotia) and on the St. Lawrence River and English settlements in Newfoundland were established to systematically exploit the timber, fish, and fur of the north Atlantic coasts.

In England rising unemployment as well as religious discontent created a large pool of potential colonists,

⚜ READING SOURCES

The Disappointments of the Virginia Colony

In this letter sent to the Virginia Company back in London in 1608, Captain John Smith (1580–1631) explains somewhat angrily that the colony cannot produce the profits that the investors had hoped for. He notes the folly of carrying boats west over the fall line of the Virginia rivers—where, it had been assumed, they might sight the Pacific Ocean as the Spaniards had done in Panama. He reports no sign of the colony of Sir Walter Raleigh, which vanished after being planted in North Carolina in 1585. He also notes the difficulties of mere survival, let alone extracting wealth.

I have received your letter, wherein you write that . . . we feed you but with ifs and ands and hopes, and some few proofs . . . and that we must expressly follow your instructions sent by Captain Newport [the commander of the supply ship], the charge of whose voyage . . . we cannot defray.

For the quartered boat to be borne by the soldiers over the falls, Newport had 120 of the best men. . . . If he had burned her to ashes, one might have carried her in a bag, but as she is, five hundred cannot, to a navigable place above the falls. And for him, at that time to find in the South Sea a mine of gold, or any of them sent by Sir Walter Raleigh, at our consultation I told them was as likely as the rest. . . . In their absence I followed the new begun works of pitch and tar, glass, [potash, and lumber],

whereof some small quantities we have sent you. But if you rightly consider, what an infinite toil it is in Russia and [Sweden], where the woods are proper for naught else [and where] there be the help of both man and beast . . . yet thousands of those poor people can scarce get necessaries to live. . . .

From your ship we had not provision in victuals worth twenty pound, and we are more than two hundred to live upon this. . . . Though there be fish in the sea, fowls in the air, and beasts in the woods . . . they are so wild and we so weak and ignorant, we cannot much trouble them.

Source: Philip L. Barbour, ed., *The Complete Works of Captain John Smith* (1580–1631), vol. 2 (Chapel Hill: University of North Carolina Press, 1986), pp. 187–189.

---

some of whom were initially attracted to the Caribbean. The first of the English settlements to endure in what was to become the United States was established at Jamestown, named for James I, in Virginia in 1607. ("Virginia," named for Elizabeth I, the "Virgin Queen," was an extremely vague designation for the Atlantic coast of North America and its hinterland.)

The Crown encouraged colonization, but a private company similar to those that financed long-distance trade was established to organize the enterprise. The directors of the Virginia Company were London businessmen. Investors and would-be colonists purchased shares. Shareholders among the colonists could participate in a colonial assembly, though the governor appointed by the company was the final authority.

The colonists arrived in Virginia with ambitious and optimistic instructions. They were to open mines, establish profitable cultivation, and search for sea routes to Asia. But at first the colonists struggled merely to survive. (See the box "Reading Sources: The Disappointments of the Virginia Colony.") The indigenous peoples in Virginia, unlike those in Spanish-held territory, were not organized in urbanized, rigidly hierarchical societies that, after conquest, could provide the invaders with a labor force. Indeed, much of the local native population was quickly wiped out by European diseases. The introduction of tobacco as a cash crop a few years later saved the colonists economically—though the Virginia Company had already gone bankrupt and the Crown had assumed control of the colony. With the cultivation of tobacco, the

Virginia colony, like the Caribbean islands, became dependent on forced, eventually slave, labor.

Among the Virginia colonists were impoverished men and women who came as servants indentured to those who had paid their passage—that is, they were bound by contract to pay off their debt by several years of labor. Colonies established to the north, in what was called "New England," also drew people from the margins of English society. Early settlers there were religious dissidents. The first to arrive were the Pilgrims, who arrived at Plymouth (modern Massachusetts) in 1620. They were a community of religious Separatists who had originally immigrated to the Netherlands from England for freedom of conscience.

Following the Pilgrims came Puritans escaping escalating persecution under Charles I. The first, in 1629, settled under the auspices of another royally chartered company, the Massachusetts Bay Company. Among their number were many prosperous Puritan merchants and landholders. Independence from investors in London allowed them an unprecedented degree of self-government once the Massachusetts Bay colony was established.

Nevertheless, the colonies in North America were disappointments to England because they generated much less wealth than expected. Shipping timber back to Europe proved too expensive, though New England forests did supply some of the Caribbean colonists' needs. The fur trade became less lucrative as English settlement pushed westward the Native Americans who did most of the trapping and as French trappers to the north encroached on the trade. Certain colonists profited enormously from the tobacco economy, but the mother country did so only moderately because the demand in Europe for tobacco never grew as quickly as the demand for sugar. The English settlements did continue to attract more migrants than other colonizers' outposts. By 1640 Massachusetts had some fourteen thousand European inhabitants. Through most of the next century, the growth of colonial populations in North America would result in an English advantage over the French in control of New World territory.

The French began their settlement of North America at the same time as the English, in the same push to compensate for their mutual weakness vis-à-vis the Spanish (see Map 16.4). The French efforts, however, had very different results, owing partly to the sites of their settlements but mostly to the relationship between the mother country and the colonies. The French hold on territory was always tenuous because of the scant number of colonists who could be lured from home. There

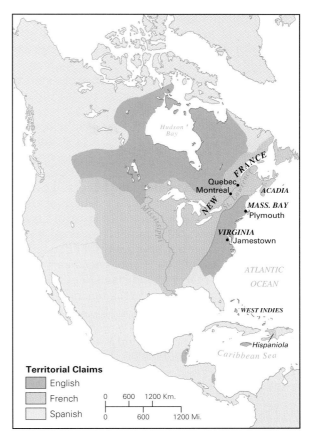

Map 16.4   English and French in North America, ca. 1700 By 1700 a veritable ring of French-claimed territory encircled the coastal colonies of England. English-claimed areas, however, were more densely settled and more economically viable.

seems to have been less economic impetus for colonization from France than from England. And, after the French crown took over the colonies, any religious impetus evaporated, for only Catholics were allowed to settle in New France. Moreover, control by the Crown forced a traditional hierarchical political organization on the French colonies. A royal governor directed the colony, and large tracts of land were set aside for privileged investors. Thus, North America offered little to tempt French people of modest means who were seeking a better life.

The first successful French colony was established in Acadia in 1605. This settlement was an exception among the French efforts because it was founded by Huguenots, not by Catholics. A few years later, the explorer Samuel de Champlain (1567?–1635) navigated the

St. Lawrence River and founded Quebec City (1608). He convinced the royal government, emerging from its pre-occupations with religious wars at home, to promote the development of the colony. French explorers went on to establish Montreal, farther inland on the St. Lawrence (1642), and to explore the Great Lakes and the Mississippi River basin (see Map 16.4).

Such investment as the French crown was able to attract went into profitable trade, mainly in furs, and not into the difficult business of colonization. French trappers and traders who ventured into wilderness areas were renowned for their hardiness and adaptability, but they did not bring their families and establish settled, European-style towns. Quebec remained more of a trading station, dependent on shipments of food from France, than a growing urban community. Added to the commercial dimension of New France was the church's interest: much of the energy of French colonization was expended by men and women of religious orders—the "Black Robes"—bringing their zeal to new frontiers. By the middle of the seventeenth century, all of New France had only about three thousand European inhabitants.

The seeming weakness of the French colonial effort in North America was not much noticed at the time. French and English fishermen, trappers, and traders competed intensely, and the French often reaped the greater share of profits, owing to their closer ties with native American trading systems. Outright battles occasionally erupted between English and French settlements. But for both England and France, the major profits and strategic interests in the New World lay to the south, in the Caribbean. The Dutch experience reveals the degree to which North America was of secondary importance, for all colonial powers, to the plantation profits farther south. In 1624 the Dutch founded a trading center, New Amsterdam, at the site of modern-day New York City. Fifty years later they relinquished New Amsterdam—the cornerstone of their northern enterprise—to the English in return for recognition of the Dutch claims to sugar-producing Guiana (modern Suriname°) in South America.

Consequently, by far the largest group of migrants to European-held territories in the Americas were forced migrants: African men and women sold into slavery and transported across the Atlantic to work the plantations established by Europeans. A conservative estimate is that approximately 1,350,000 Africans were forcibly transported as slave labor to the New World during the seventeenth century.

Suriname (SIR-ih-nam)

■ The Beginning of the End of Traditional Society

Within Europe, the economic impact of overseas trade was profound. Merchants and investors in a few of Europe's largest cities reaped great profits. Mediterranean ports such as Venice, once the heart of European trade, did not share in the bonanza from the new trade with Asia or the Americas. Atlantic ports such as Seville, through which most Spanish commerce with the New World flowed, and, above all, Amsterdam began to flourish. The population of Amsterdam increased from about 30,000 to 200,000 in the course of the seventeenth century.

All capital cities, however, not just seaports, grew substantially during the 1600s. Increasing numbers of government functionaries, courtiers and their hangers-on, and people involved in trade lived and worked in capital cities. These cities also grew indirectly from the demand such people generated for services and products, ranging from fashionable clothing to exotic foodstuffs. For the first time, cities employed vast numbers of country people. Perhaps as much as one-fifth of the population of England passed through London at one time or another, creating the mobile, volatile community so active in the English civil war and its aftermath.

The economy became more productive and flexible as it expanded, but social stratification intensified. Patterns of consumption in cities reflected the economic gulfs between residents. Most people could not afford to buy imported pepper or sugar. Poverty increased in cities, even in vibrant Amsterdam, because cities attracted people fleeing rural unemployment with few skills and fewer resources. As growing central governments heaped up tax burdens on peasants, many rural people were caught in a cycle of debt; the only escape was to abandon farming and flock to cities.

Peasant rebellions occurred throughout the century as a result of depressed economic conditions and heavy taxation, reflecting expansion of royal power and expensive royal military ambitions. Some small-scale revolts involved direct action, such as seizing the tax collector's grain or stopping the movement of grain to the great cities. Urban demand often caused severe food shortages in rural areas in western Europe, despite the booming trade in grain with eastern Europe via the Baltic.

The typical peasant revolt in western Europe during the seventeenth century, however, was directed against escalating taxation. Tax rebellions often formed spontaneously, perhaps as tax officials passed through a village, but they were not mere chaotic gatherings of rabble. Countryfolk were accustomed to defending themselves as communities—against brigands and marauding soldiers, for example. Local gentry or prosperous farmers who ordinarily fulfilled the function of local constable led such revolts from time to time, convinced that they represented the legitimate interests of the community against rapacious officials higher up. The scale of peasant violence meant that thousands of troops sometimes had to be diverted from a state's foreign wars. As a matter of routine, soldiers accompanied tax officials and enforced collection all over Europe. Thus, as the ambitions of rulers grew, so too did resistance of ordinary people to the exactions of the state.

SUMMARY

 THE beginning of the seventeenth century was marked by religious turmoil and by social and political upheaval. By the end of the century, the former had faded as a source of collective anxiety, and the latter was largely resolved. States troubled by religious and political turmoil or on the political margins early in the century had evolved into secure and dynamic centers of power: the Netherlands, the Habsburg domains, Brandenburg-Prussia, and Russia. Following the most powerful monarchy in Europe, France, most states had moved from internal division—with independent provinces and aristocrats going their own way—to greater coherence. This stability was both cause and consequence of rulers' desires to make war on an ever larger scale. By the end of the century, only those states able to field massive armies were competitive on the European stage. The Netherlands, a stark exception to the pattern of centralized royal control, began more closely to resemble other states under the pressure of warfare by century's end.

At the beginning of the century, overseas trade and colonization had been the near monopoly of Spain and Portugal; at the century's end, the English, French, and Dutch had supplanted the Iberian states in controlling trade with Asia and were reaping many profits in the Americas, especially from the extension of plantation agriculture. Beneath all these developments lay subtle but significant economic, social, and cultural shifts. One effect of the increased wealth generated by overseas trade and the increased power of governments to tax their subjects was a widening gulf between rich and poor. New styles of behavior and patterns of consumption highlighted differences between social classes. Long-term effects of overseas voyages on Old World attitudes, as well as fundamental changes in world-views that were paving the way for modern science, would have a revolutionary impact on Europeans and their cultures.

■ Notes

1. Quoted in D. H. Pennington, *Europe in the Seventeenth Century,* 2d ed. (London: Longman, 1989), p. 508.

■ Suggested Reading

Collins, James B. *The State in Early Modern France.* 1995. An up-to-date synthesis by one of the leading scholars of French absolutism.

De Vries, Jan. *The Economy of Europe in an Age of Crisis, 1600–1750.* 1976. The single most important work on the development of the European economy in this period, integrating European developments with the growth of overseas empires.

Howard, Michael. *War in European History.* 1976. A general study of warfare emphasizing the relationship between war making and state development.

Kishlansky, Mark. *A Monarchy Transformed.* 1996. The most recent, full scholarly treatment of political events in England.

Oakley, Stewart P. *War and Peace in the Baltic, 1560–1790.* 1992. An excellent survey of the Baltic region in the early modern period.

Pennington, D. H. *Europe in the Seventeenth Century.* 2d ed. 1989. A general history of the century.

Riasanovsky, Nicolas V. *A History of Russia.* 6th ed. 2000. A reliable and readable survey of Russian history from medieval times; includes an extensive bibliography of major works available in English.

Schama, Simon. *The Embarrassment of Riches: An Interpretation of Dutch Culture in the Golden Age.* 1997. An innovative study of Dutch culture that explores the social and psychological tensions created by its growing wealth in the seventeenth century.

Wolf, Eric R. *Europe and the People Without History.* 1982. A survey of European contact with and conquest of peoples after 1400; includes extensive treatments of non-European societies and detailed explanations of the economic and political interests of the Europeans.

 For a searchable list of additional readings for this chapter, go to http://college.hmco.com.

Table Manners

If you were to sit down in a fancy restaurant, order a juicy steak, and then eat it with your bare hands, other diners would undoubtedly stare, shocked by your bad manners. It has not always been the case that table manners meant very much—were able to signal social status, for example. It was not always the case that table manners existed at all in the sense that we know them. How did they evolve? How did they come to have the importance that they do? And why should historians pay any attention to them?

Imagine that you have been invited to dinner at a noble estate in the year 1500. As you sit down, you notice that there are no knives, forks, and spoons at your place at the table, and no napkins either. A servant (a young girl from a neighboring village) sets a roast of meat in front of you and your fellow diners. The lords and ladies on either side of you hack off pieces of meat with the knives that they always carry with them, and then they eat the meat with their fingers. Hunks of bread on the table in front of them catch the dripping juices.

One hundred fifty years later, in 1650, dinner is a much more "civilized" meal. Notice the well-to-do women dining in this engraving by the French artist Abraham Bosse (1602–1676). The table setting, with tablecloths, napkins, plates, and silverware, is recognizable to us. The lady at the extreme right holds up her fork and napkin in a somewhat forced and obvious gesture. These diners have the utensils that we take for granted, but the artist does not take them for granted: they are intended to be noticed by Bosse's elite audience.

In the seventeenth century, aristocrats and gentry signaled their political and social privilege with behavior that distinguished them from the lower classes in ways their more powerful ancestors had found unnecessary. Historians have called this the invention of civility. As we have seen, proper courtesy to one's superiors at court was considered essential. It marked the fact that rituals of honor and deference were increasingly taking the place of armed conflict as the routine behavior of the upper classes. Also essential, however, were certain standards of physical privacy and delicacy. Something as seemingly trivial as the use of a fork became charged with symbolic significance. As the actual power of the aristocrats was circumscribed by the state, they found new expressions of status. Since the sixteenth century, new kinds of manners had been touted in handbooks, reflecting changes that already had occurred at Italian courts. During the seventeenth century, these practices became more widespread and opened up a gulf between upper- and lower-class behavior.

Some of the new behaviors concerned bodily privacy and discretion. A nobleman now used a handkerchief instead of his fingers or coat sleeve, and he did not urinate in public. The new "rules" about eating are particularly interesting. Why did eating with a fork seem refined and desirable to aristocrats trying to buttress their own self-images? As any 3-year-old knows, eating with a fork is remarkably inefficient.

Using a fork kept you at a distance—literal and symbolic—from the animal you were eating. Napkins wiped away all trace of bloody juices from your lips. Interestingly, as diners began to use utensils, other eating arrangements changed in parallel ways. Sideboards had been in use for a long time, but pieces of meat were now discreetly carved on the sideboard and presented to diners in individual portions. The carcass was brought to the sideboard cut into roasts instead of unmistakably whole, and it was often decorated—as it is today—to further disguise it.

The new aristocrat was increasingly separated from the world of brute physical force, both in daily life and on the battlefield. In warfare, brute force was no longer adequate. Training, discipline, and tactical knowledge were more important and heightened the significance of rank, which separated officers from the vast numbers of common soldiers (see page 546). Aristocrats now lived in a privileged world where violence—except for an occasional duel—was no longer a fact of life. Their new behavior codes signaled their new invulnerability to others. Above all, they worked to transform a loss—of the independence that had gone hand in hand with a more violent life—into a gain: a privileged immunity to violence.

Specific manners became important, then, because they were symbols of power. The symbolic distance be-

Table Manners of the Upper Class in the Seventeenth Century   *(Courtesy of the Trustees of the British Museum)*

tween the powerful and the humble was reinforced by other changes in habits and behavior. A sixteenth-century warrior customarily traveled on horseback and often went from place to place within a city on foot, attended by his retinue. A seventeenth-century aristocrat was more likely to travel in a horse-drawn carriage. The presence of special commodities from abroad—such as sugar—in the seventeenth century created further possibilities for signaling status.

It is interesting to note that other personal habits still diverged dramatically from what we would consider acceptable today. Notice the large, stately bed in the same room as the dining table in Bosse's engraving. Interior space was still undifferentiated by our standards, and it was common for eating, talking, sleeping, and estate management all to go on in a single room. The grand bed is in the picture because, like the fork, it is a mark of status. Like virtually everything else, what is "proper" varies with historical circumstance.

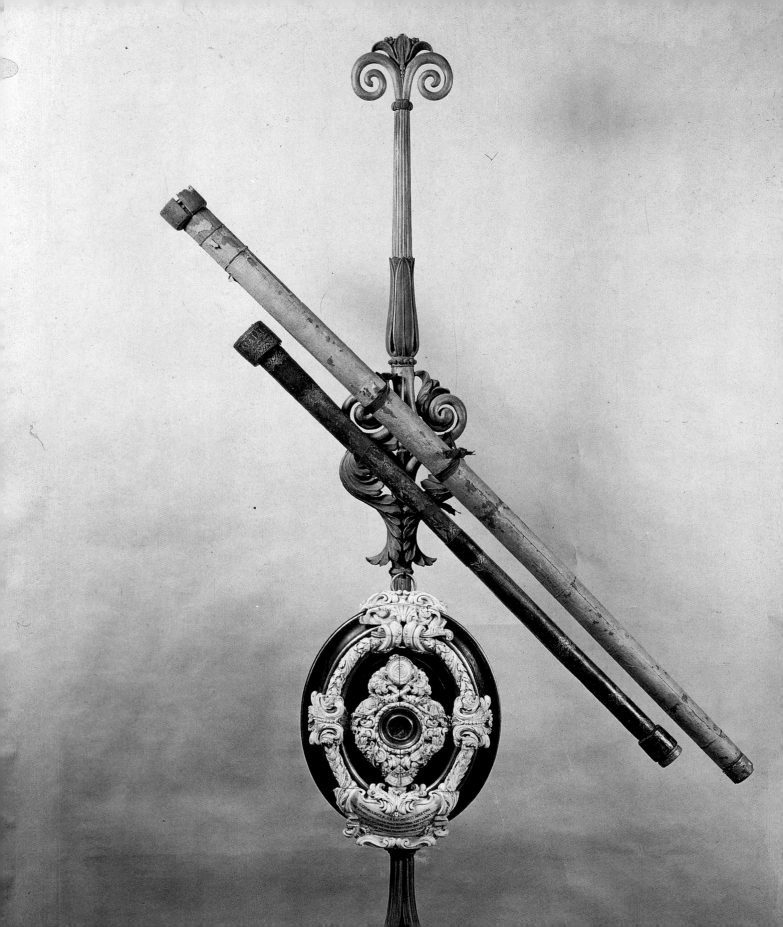

CHAPTER 17

A Revolution in World-View

PRESERVED in the Museum of Science in Florence, Italy, are two narrow cylinders mounted on an ornate stand. They are two of the telescopes built in the seventeenth century by the astronomer Galileo. Galileo's telescopes permitted the first enhanced views of heavenly bodies in human history. They seem very simple instruments to our eyes, but the twenty-fold magnification provided by the smaller instrument enabled Galileo to make celestial observations that would help revolutionize humans' understanding of their physical world. These telescopes were also enormously popular devices. Galileo made dozens of them in his lifetime and gave many away to interested colleagues and would-be patrons. The Scientific Revolution, as we now label the dramatic shifts in scientific explanation that occurred in this era, was a complex cultural movement that included both the specialized work of individuals such as Galileo and the involvement and support of patrons, other scholars, and learned amateurs.

By the end of the seventeenth century, a vision of an infinite but orderly cosmos appealing to human reason had, among educated Europeans, largely replaced the medieval vision of a closed universe centered on earth and suffused with Christian purpose. Religion became an increasingly subordinate ally of science as confidence in an open-ended, experimental approach to knowledge came to be as strongly held as religious conviction. It is because of this larger shift in world-view, not simply because of particular scientific discoveries, that the seventeenth century may be labeled the era of the scientific *revolution.*

The revolution was initiated within the sciences in the sixteenth century by the astronomical calculations and hypotheses of Nicholas Copernicus, who posited that the earth moves around the sun.

The Revolution in Astronomy, 1543–1632

The Scientific Revolution Generalized, ca. 1600–1700

The New Science: Society, Politics, and Religion

Lens and telescopes of Galileo.
(Scala/Art Resource, NY)

573

Galileo and others eventually proved this hypothesis true, overturning principles of physics and philosophy that had held sway since ancient times. Later generations of scientists and philosophers labored to construct new principles to explain the way the physical universe behaves. The readiness of scientists, their patrons, and educated lay people to push Copernicus's hypothesis to these conclusions came from several sources: their exposure to the intellectual innovations of Renaissance thought; the intellectual challenges and material opportunities represented by the discovery of the New World; and the challenge to authority embodied in the Reformation. Also, the new science offered prestige and technological advances to the rulers who sponsored it.

Because religious significance had been attached to previous explanations, and religious authority defended them, the new astronomy automatically led to an enduring debate about the compatibility of science and religion. But the revolution in world-view was not confined to astronomy or even to science generally. As philosophers gained confidence in human reason and the intelligibility of the world, they turned to new speculation about human af-

fairs. They began to challenge traditional justifications for the hierarchical nature of society and the sanctity of authority just as energetically as Copernicus and his followers had overthrown old views about the cosmos.

QUESTIONS TO CONSIDER

- ■ Why did new theories about astronomy lead to a broader Scientific Revolution?

- ■ What were some of the features of the new "mechanistic" world-view?

- ■ How did religious, political, and social conditions shape the work of scientists?

- ■ What were the implications for political thought of the new scientific approach to the world?

TERMS TO KNOW

Nicholas Copernicus	Francis Bacon
heliocentrism	empirical reasoning
Johannes Kepler	Isaac Newton
Galileo Galilei	laws of motion
René Descartes	Thomas Hobbes
mechanistic world-view	John Locke

THE REVOLUTION IN ASTRONOMY, 1543–1632

THE origins of the seventeenth-century revolution in world-view lie, for the most part, in developments in astronomy. Because of astronomy's role in the explanations of the world and of human life that had been devised by ancient and medieval scientists and philosophers, any advances in astronomy were bound to have widespread intellectual repercussions. By the early part of the seventeenth century, fundamental astronomical beliefs had been successfully challenged. The consequence was the undermining of both the material (physics) and the philosophical (metaphysics) explanations of the world that had been standing for centuries.

■ The Inherited World-View and the Sixteenth-Century Context

Ancient and medieval astronomy accepted the perspective on the universe that unaided human senses support—namely, that the earth is fixed at the center of the universe and the celestial bodies rotate around it. The regular movements of heavenly bodies and the obvious importance of the sun for life on earth made astronomy a vital undertaking for both scientific and religious purposes in many ancient societies. Astronomers in ancient Greece carefully observed the heavens and learned to calculate and to predict the seemingly circular motion of the stars and the sun about the earth. The orbits of the planets were more difficult to explain, for the planets seemed to travel both east and west across the sky at various times and with no regularity that could be mathematically understood. Indeed, the very word *planet* comes from a Greek word meaning "wanderer."

We now know that all the planets simultaneously orbit the sun at different speeds in paths that are at different distances from the sun. The relative positions of the planets thus constantly change; sometimes other planets are "ahead" of the earth and sometimes "behind." In the second century A.D. the Greek astronomer Ptolemy° attempted to explain the planets' occasional "backward" motion by attributing it to "epicycles"—small circular orbits within the larger orbit. Ptolemy's mathematical explanations of the imagined epicycles were extremely complex, but neither Ptolemy nor medieval mathematicians and astronomers were ever able fully to account for planetary motion.

Ancient physics, most notably the work of the Greek philosopher Aristotle° (384–322 B.C.), explained the fact that some objects (such as cannonballs) fall to earth but others (stars and planets) seem weightless relative to the earth because of their composition: different kinds of matter had different inherent tendencies and properties. In this view, all earthbound matter (like cannonballs) falls because it is naturally attracted to earth—heaviness being a property of earthbound things.

In the Christian era, the Aristotelian explanation of the universe was infused with Christian meaning and purpose. The heavens were said to be made of different, pure, matter because they were the abode of the angels. Both earth and the humans who inhabited it were changeable and corruptible. Yet God had given human beings a unique and special place in the universe. The universe was thought to be literally a closed world with the stationary earth at the center. Revolving around the earth in circular orbits were the sun, the moon, the stars, and the planets. The motion of all lesser bodies was caused by the rotation of all the stars together in the vast crystal-like sphere in which they were embedded.

A few ancient astronomers theorized that the earth moved about the sun. Some medieval philosophers also adopted this heliocentric thesis (*helios* is the Greek word for "sun"), but it remained a minority view because it seemed to contradict both common sense and observed data. The sun and stars *appeared* to move around the earth with great regularity. Moreover, how could objects fall to earth if the earth was moving beneath them? Also, astronomers detected no difference in angles from which observers on earth viewed the stars at different times. Such differences would exist, they thought, if the earth changed positions by moving around the sun. It

---

Ptolemy (TOL-eh-mee)   Aristotle (AIR-is-tot-il)

CHRONOLOGY	
1543	Copernicus, *De Revolutionibus Orbium Caelestium;* Vesalius, *On the Fabric of the Human Body*
1576	Construction of Brahe's observatory begins
1603	Accadèmia dei Lincei founded in Rome
1609	Kepler's third law of motion
1610	Galileo, *The Starry Messenger*
1620	Bacon, *Novum Organum*
1628	Harvey, *On the Motion of the Heart*
1632	Galileo, *Dialogue on the Two Chief Systems of the World*
1633	Galileo condemned and sentenced to house arrest
1637	Descartes, *Discourse on Method*
1651	Hobbes, *Leviathan*
1660	Boyle, *New Experiments Physico-Mechanical*
1660	Royal Society of London founded
1666	Académie Royale des Sciences founded in France
1686	Fontenelle, *Conversations on the Plurality of Worlds*
1687	Newton, *Principia (Mathematical Principles of Natural Philosophy)*
1690	Locke, *Two Treatises on Government* and *Essay on Human Understanding*
1702	Bayle, *Historical and Critical Dictionary*

was inconceivable that the universe could be so large and the stars so distant that the earth's movement would produce no measurable change in the earth's position with respect to the stars.

Several conditions of intellectual life in the sixteenth century encouraged new work in astronomy and led to revision of the earth-centered world-view. The most important was the work of Renaissance humanists in recovering and interpreting ancient texts. Now able to work with new Greek versions of Ptolemy, mathematicians and astronomers noted that his explanations for

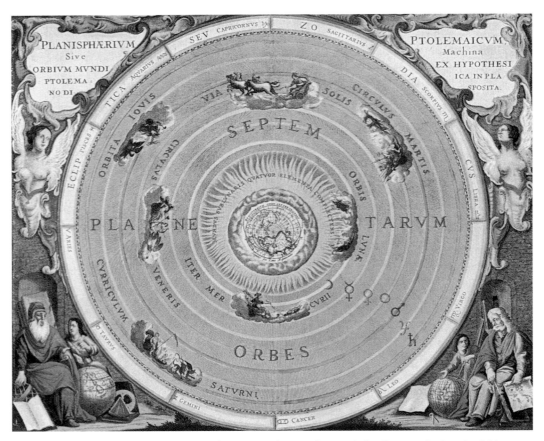

The Traditional Universe   In this print from around 1600, heavenly bodies are depicted orbiting the earth in perfectly circular paths. In fact, the ancient astronomer Ptolemy believed that the planets followed complex orbits-within-orbits, known as *epicycles,* moving around the stationary earth. *(Hulton-Getty/Liaison)*

the motions of the planets were imperfect and not simply inadequately transmitted, as they had long believed. Also, the discovery of the New World dramatically undercut the assumption that ancient knowledge was superior. The existence of the Americas specifically undermined Ptolemy's authority once again, for it disproved many of the assertions in his *Geography,* which had just been recovered in Europe the previous century.

The desire to explain heavenly motions better was still loaded with religious significance in the sixteenth century and was heightened by the immediate need for reform of the Julian calendar (named for Julius Caesar). Ancient observations of the movement of the sun, though remarkably accurate, could not measure the precise length of the solar year. By the sixteenth century, the cumulative error of this calendar had resulted in a change of ten days: the spring equinox fell on March 11 instead of March 21. An accurate and uniform system of dating was necessary for all rulers and their tax collec-

tors and recordkeepers. And because the calculation of the date of Easter was at stake, a reliable calendar was the particular project of the church.

Impetus for new and better astronomical observations and calculations arose from other features of the intellectual and political landscape as well. Increasingly as the century went on, princely courts became important sources of patronage for and sites of scientific activity. Rulers eager to buttress their own power by symbolically linking it to dominion over nature sponsored investigations of the world, as Ferdinand and Isabella had so successfully done, and displayed the marvels of nature at their courts. Sponsoring scientific inquiry also yielded practical benefits: better mapping of the ruler's domains and better technology for mining, gunnery, and navigation.

Finally, schools of thought fashionable at the time, encouraged by the humanists' critique of received tradition, hinted at the possibilities of alternative physical

the work of one another, were the Dane Tycho Brahe (1546–1601), the German Johannes Kepler (1571–1630), and the Italian Galileo Galilei (1564–1642).

Like generations of observers before him, Tycho Brahe° had been stirred by the majesty of the regular movements of heavenly bodies. After witnessing a partial eclipse of the sun, he abandoned a career in government befitting his noble status and became an astronomer. Brahe was the first truly post-Ptolemaic astronomer because he was the first to improve on the data that the ancients and all subsequent astronomers had used. Ironically, *no* theory of planetary motion could have reconciled the data that Copernicus had used: they were simply too inaccurate, based as they were on naked-eye observations, even when errors of translation and copying, accumulated over centuries, had been corrected.

In 1576 the king of Denmark showered Brahe with properties and pensions enabling him to build an observatory, Uraniborg, on an island near Copenhagen. At Uraniborg, Brahe improved on ancient observations with large and very finely calibrated instruments that permitted precise measurements of celestial movements by the naked eye. His attention to precision and frequency of observation produced results that were twice as accurate as any previous data had been.

As a result of his observations, Brahe agreed with Copernicus that the various planets did rotate around the sun, not around the earth. He still could not be persuaded that the earth itself moved, for none of his data supported such a notion. Brahe's lasting and crucial contribution was his astronomical data. They would become obsolete as soon as data from telescopic observations were accumulated about a century later. But in the meantime, they were used by Johannes Kepler to further develop Copernicus's model and arrive at a more accurate heliocentric theory.

Kepler was young enough to be exposed to Copernican ideas from the outset of his training, and he quickly recognized in Brahe's data the means of resolving the problems in Copernican analysis. Though trained in his native Germany, Kepler went to Prague, where Brahe spent the last years of his life, at the court of the Holy Roman emperor after a quarrel with the Danish king. There, Kepler became something of an apprentice to Brahe. After Brahe's death in 1601, Kepler kept his mentor's records of astronomical observation and continued to work at the imperial court as Rudolf II's court mathematician.

Kepler's contribution to the new astronomy, like that of Copernicus, was fundamentally mathematical. In it,

we can see the stamp of the Neo-Platonic conviction about the purity of mathematical explanation. Kepler spent ten years working to apply Brahe's data to the most intricate of all the celestial motions—the movement of the planet Mars—as a key to explaining all planetary motion. Mars is close to the earth but its orbital path is farther from the sun. This combination produces very puzzling and dramatic variations in the apparent movement of Mars to an earthly observer.

The result of Kepler's work was laws of planetary motion that, in the main, are still in use. First, Kepler eliminated the need for epicycles by correctly asserting that planets follow elliptical and not circular orbits. Elliptical orbits could account, both mathematically and visually, for the motions of the planets when combined with Kepler's second law, which described the *rate* of a planet's motion around its orbital path. Kepler noted that the speed of a planet in its orbit slows proportionally as the planet's distance from the sun increases. A third law demonstrated that the distance of each planet from the sun and the time it takes each planet to orbit the sun are in a constant ratio.

Kepler's work was a breakthrough because it mathematically confirmed the Copernican heliocentric hypothesis. In so doing, the work directly challenged the ancient world-view, in which heavenly bodies constantly moved in circular orbits around a stationary earth. Hence, Kepler's laws invited speculation about the properties and motion of heavenly and terrestrial bodies alike. A new physics would be required to explain the novel motions that Kepler had posited. Kepler himself, in Neo-Platonic fashion, attributed planetary motion to the sun: "[The sun] is a fountain of light, rich in fruitful heat, most fair, limpid and pure . . . called king of the planets for his motion, heart of the world for his power. . . . Who would hesitate to confer the votes of the celestial motions on him who has been administering all other movements and changes by the benefit of the light which is entirely his possession?"[2]

■ Galileo and the Triumph of Copernicanism

Galileo Galilei° holds a pre-eminent position in the development of astronomy because, first, he provided compelling new evidence to support Copernican theory and, second, he contributed to the development of a new physics—or, more precisely, mechanics—that could account for the movement of bodies in new terms. In short, he began to close the gap between the new astronomy and new explanations for the behavior of matter.

Brahe (BRAH)

Galileo Galilei (gal-ih-LAY-oh gal-ih-LAY-ee)

Galileo   This portrait of Galileo appeared as the frontispiece in two of his publications. He is identified as "philosopher and mathematician of the Grand Duke of Tuscany." The cherubs above the portrait hold a military compass and a telescope—both Galileo's inventions that he gave to his patrons.   *(Ann Ronan Picture Library)*

Just as important, his efforts to publicize his findings and his condemnation by the church spurred popular debate about Copernican ideas in literate society and helped to determine the course science would take.

Galileo's career also illustrates, in dramatic fashion, the dependence of scientists on and their vulnerability to patronage relationships. Born to a minor Florentine noble family, Galileo began studying medicine at the University of Pisa at the age of 17 but became intrigued by problems of mechanics and mathematics. He began studying those disciplines at Pisa under the tutelage of a Tuscan court mathematician and himself became a lecturer in mathematics there in 1589, at 25, after publishing promising work in mechanics. Three years later, well-connected fellow mathematicians helped him secure a more lucrative and prestigious professorship at the University of Padua, where Copernicus had once

studied. Galileo skillfully cultivated the learned Venetian aristocrats (Venice ruled Padua at this time) who controlled academic appointments and secured renewals and salary raises over the next eighteen years.

During his years at Pisa and Padua, Galileo pursued his revolutionary work in mechanics, although he did not publish the results of his experiments until much later. Galileo's principal contribution to mechanics lay in his working out of an early theory of inertia. As a result of a number of experiments with falling bodies (balls rolling on carefully constructed inclines—not free-falling objects that, according to myth, he dropped from the Leaning Tower of Pisa), Galileo ventured a new view of what is "natural" to objects. Galileo's view was that uniform motion is as natural as a state of rest. In the ancient and medieval universe, all motion needed a cause, and all motion could be explained in terms of purpose. "I hold," Galileo countered, "that there exists nothing in external bodies . . . but size, shape, quantity and motion."[3] Galileo retained the old assumption that motion was somehow naturally circular. Nevertheless, his theory was a crucial step in explaining motion according to new principles and in fashioning a world-view that accepted a mechanical universe devoid of metaphysical purpose.

The results of this work were, for the most part, not published until the end of his life. In the meantime, Galileo became famous for his astronomical observations, which he began in 1609 and which he parlayed into a position at the Florentine court. Early that year, Galileo learned of the invention of a primitive telescope (which could magnify distant objects only three times) and quickly improved on it to make the first astronomically useful instrument. In *Sidereus Nuncius* (*The Starry Messenger,* 1610) he described his scrutiny of the heavens with his telescope in lay language. He documented sighting previously undetectable stars as well as moons orbiting the planet Jupiter. In another blow to ancient descriptions of the universe, he also noted craters and other "imperfections" on the surface of the moon. Three years later he published his solar observations in *Letters on Sunspots.* Sunspots are regions of relatively cool gaseous material that appear as dark spots on the sun's surface. For Galileo sunspots and craters on the moon proved that the heavens were not perfect and changeless but rather were like the supposedly "corrupt" and changeable earth. His telescopic observations also provided further support for Copernican heliocentrism. Indeed, Galileo's own acceptance of Copernicanism can be dated to this point because magnification revealed that each heavenly body rotated on its axis: sunspots, for example, could be tracked across the visible surface of the sun as the sun rotated.

🐌 R E A D I N G   S O U R C E S

Galileo Reassures a Patron

After Galileo's work on sunspots was released, many learned followers grew anxious about the implications of the new science. In the letter excerpted here, published in 1615 and widely circulated, Galileo reassures the mother of Cosimo, the dowager grand duchess, that the new science does not contradict Christianity. The confident, almost arrogant tone is typical of Galileo's writing. The fact that he presumed to judge the work of theologians as well as to interpret Scripture would be used against him by the Inquisition.

But I do not feel obliged to believe that the same God who has endowed us with senses, reason and intellect has intended to forgo their use and by some other means to give us knowledge which we can attain by them. He would not require us to deny sense and reason in physical matters which are set before our eyes and minds by direct experience or demonstrations. This must be especially true in those sciences of which but the faintest trace . . . is to be found in the Bible. Of astronomy, for instance, so little is found that none of the planets except Venus are so much as mentioned. . . .

Now, if the Holy Spirit has purposely neglected to teach us propositions of this sort as irrelevant to the highest goal (that is, to our salvation), how can anyone affirm that it is obligatory to take sides on them, and that one belief is required by faith, while another side is erroneous? . . . I would assert here something that was heard from [a respected cleric]: . . . "the intention of the Holy Ghost is to teach us how to go to heaven, not how heaven goes."

But let us again consider the degree to which necessary demonstrations and sense experience ought to be respected in physical conclusions, and the authority they have enjoyed at the hands of . . .

learned theologians. [For example] in St. Augustine we read: "If anyone shall set the authority of Holy Writ against clear and manifest reason, . . . he opposes to the truth not the meaning of the Bible, which is beyond his comprehension, but rather his own interpretation. . . ."

Moreover, we are unable to affirm that all interpreters of the Bible speak with divine inspiration, for if that were so there would exist no differences between them about the sense of a given passage. Hence [it would be wise] not to permit anyone to usurp scriptural texts and force them in some way to maintain any physical conclusion to be true, when at some future time the senses . . . may show the contrary. Who indeed will set bounds to human ingenuity? Who will assert that everything in the universe capable of being perceived is already discovered and known?

Source: Stillman Drake, *The Discoveries and Opinions of Galileo* (New York: Doubleday, 1957), pp. 183–187.

 For additional information on this topic, go to http://college.hmco.com.

Galileo had already been approached by various Italian princes and in turn sought to woo their support with gifts of some of his earlier inventions, such as a military compass. He aimed his *Starry Messenger* at the Medici dukes of Florence, naming Jupiter's moons the "Medicean Stars" and publishing the work to coincide with the accession of the young Cosimo II, whom he had tutored as a youth. In 1610 he returned in triumph to his native Tuscany as court philosopher to the grand

duke. Soon, however, his own fame and the increasing acceptance of Copernicanism, especially vindicated by his work on sunspots, aroused opposition. In 1615 Galileo was denounced to the Inquisition by a Florentine friar. (See the box "Reading Sources: Galileo Reassures a Patron.") After an investigation, the geokinetic theory (that the earth moves) was declared heretical, but Galileo himself was not condemned. He could continue to use Copernican theory, but only as a theory.

Indeed, a number of the most fervent practitioners of the new science continued to be clergymen who followed Galileo's work with interest. A new pope, elected in 1623, was a Tuscan aristocrat and an old friend of Galileo's; Galileo dedicated his work on comets, *The Assayer* (1624), to Urban VIII in honor of his election.

Now in his sixties, Galileo began to work on a book that summarized his life's work: *Dialogue on the Two Chief Systems of the World* (1632), structured as a conversation among three characters debating the merits of Copernican theory. Given the work's sensitive subject matter, Galileo obtained explicit permission from the pope to write it and cleared some portions with censors before publication. The work was the most important single source in its day for the popularization of Copernican theory, but it led to renewed concerns in Rome. Galileo had clearly overstepped the bounds of discussing Copernicanism in theory only and indeed appeared to advocate it: Simplicio, the character representing the old world-view, was, as his name suggests, an example of ignorance not wisdom.

Moreover, the larger political context affecting Galileo's patrons and friends had changed. The pope was being threatened by the Spanish and Austrian Habsburgs for his tepid support in the Thirty Years' War, in which Catholic forces were now losing to Protestant armies and he could no longer be indulgent with his friend Galileo. (The pope tended to favor French foreign policy as a counterweight to the enormous power of the Habsburgs.) Galileo was forced to stand trial for heresy in Rome in 1633. When, in a kind of plea-bargain arrangement, he pled guilty to a lesser charge of inadvertently advocating Copernicanism, Pope Urban intervened to insist on a weightier penalty. Galileo's book was banned, he was forced to formally renounce his "error," and he was sentenced to house arrest. Galileo lived confined and guarded, continuing his investigations of mechanics, until his death seven years later.

THE SCIENTIFIC REVOLUTION GENERALIZED, CA. 1600–1700

 ALILEO'S work found such a willing audience in part because Galileo, like Kepler and Brahe, was not working alone. Dozens of other scientists were examining old problems from the fresh perspective offered by the breakthroughs in astronomy. Some analyzed the nature of matter, now that it appeared that all matter in the universe was somehow the same despite its varying appearances. Many of these thinkers addressed the metaphysical issues that their investigations inevitably raised. They began the complex intellectual and psychological journey toward a new world-view, one that accepted the existence of an infinitely large universe of undifferentiated matter with no obvious place in it for humans.

■ The Promise of the New Science

No less a man than Francis Bacon (1561–1626), lord chancellor of England during the reign of James I, wrote a utopian essay extolling the benefits of science for a peaceful society and for human happiness. In *New Atlantis,* published one year after his death, Bacon argued that science would produce "things of use and practice for man's life."[4] In *New Atlantis* and in *Novum Organum* (1620), Bacon revealed his faith in science by advocating patient, systematic observation and experimentation to accumulate knowledge about the world. He argued that the proper method of investigation "derives axioms from . . . particulars, rising by gradual and unbroken ascent, so that it arrives at the most general axioms of all. This is the true way but untried."[5]

Bacon himself did not undertake experiments, though his widely read works were influential in encouraging both the empirical method (relying on observation and experimentation) and inductive reasoning (deriving general principles from particular facts). Indeed, Bacon was a visionary. Given the early date of his writings, it might even seem difficult to account for his enthusiasm and confidence. In fact, Bacon's writings reflect the widespread interest and confidence in science within his elite milieu, an interest actively encouraged by the state. In another of his writings he argued that a successful state should concentrate on effective "rule in religion *and nature,* as well as civil administration."[6]

Bacon's pronouncements reflected the fact that an interest in exploring nature's secrets and exercising "dominion over nature" had become an indispensable part of princely rule. Princely courts were the main source of financial support for science and a primary site of scientific work during Bacon's lifetime. Part of the impetus for this development had come from the civic humanism of the Italian Renaissance, which had celebrated the state and service to it and had provided models both for educated rulers and for cultivated courtiers. Attention to science and to its benefits for the state also reflected the scope, and pragmatism, of princely resources and ambitions: the desire of rulers for technical expertise in armaments, fortification, construction, navigation, and mapmaking. (See the feature "Weighing the Evidence: Modern Maps" on pages 600–601.)

The promise of the New World and the drive for overseas trade and exploration especially encouraged princely support of scientific investigation. A renowned patron of geographic investigation, from mapmaking to navigation, was Henry, prince of Wales (d. 1612), eldest son of James I. Prince Henry patronized technical experts such as experienced gunners and seamen as well as those with broader and more theoretical expertise. One geographer at his court worked on the vital problem of calculating longitude, sketched the moon after reading and emulating Galileo's work with the telescope, and—in a spirit of empiricism often associated with Bacon—compiled information about the new territory Virginia, including the first dictionary of any Native American language.

Science was an ideological as well as a practical tool for power. Most courts housed collections of marvels, specimens of exotic plants and animals, and mechanical contrivances. These demonstrated the ruler's interest in investigation of the world—in other words, his or her status as an educated individual. These collections and the work of court experts also enhanced the ruler's reputation as a patron and person of power. Galileo was playing off such expectations when he named his newly discovered moons of Jupiter "Medicean Stars." Like all patronage relationships, the status was shared by both partners; indeed, the attention of a patron was a guarantor of the researcher's scientific credibility.

By the beginning of the seventeenth century, private salons and academies where investigators might meet on their own were another significant milieu of scientific investigation. These, too, had their roots in the humanist culture of Italy, where circles of scholars without university affiliations had formed. Though also dependent on private resources, these associations were an important alternative to princely patronage, since a ruler's funds

A Collection of Naturalia   Displays of exotica, such as these specimens in Naples, symbolized the ruler's authority by suggesting his or her power over nature.   *(From Ferrante Imperato, Dell' Historia Naturale [Naples, 1599]. By permission of the Houghton Library, Harvard University)*

might wax and wane according to his or her other commitments. Private organizations could avoid the stark distinctions of rank that were inevitable at courts, yet mimicked courts in the blend of scholars and educated courtiers they embraced. This more collegial but still privileged environment also fostered a sense of legitimacy for the science pursued there: legitimacy came from the recognition of fellow members and, in many cases, from publication of work by the society itself.

The earliest academy dedicated to scientific study was the *Accadèmia Segreta* (Secret Academy) founded in Naples in the 1540s. The members pursued experiments together, in order, in the words of one member, "to make a true anatomy of the things and operations of nature itself."[7] During the remainder of the sixteenth century and on into the seventeenth, such academies sprang up in many cities. The most celebrated was the *Accadèmia dei Lincei°*, founded in Rome by an aristocrat in 1603. Its most famous member, Galileo, joined in 1611. The name "Lincei," from *lynx,* was chosen because of the legendary keen sight of that animal, an appropriate mascot for "searchers of secrets."

Galileo's notoriety and the importance of his discoveries forced all such learned societies to take a stand for or against Copernicanism. Throughout the seventeenth century, specific investigation of natural phenomena would continue in increasingly sophisticated institutional settings. The flowering of scientific thought in the seventeenth century occurred because of the specific innovations in astronomy and the general spread of scientific investigation that had been achieved by the end of Bacon's life.

■ Scientific Thought in France: Descartes and a New Cosmology

Philosophers, mathematicians, and educated elites engaged in lively debate and practical investigation throughout Europe in the first half of the seventeenth century. In France the great questions about cosmic order were being posed, ironically, at a time of political disorder. The years following the religious wars saw the murder of Henry IV, another regency, and further civil war in the 1620s (see pages 517–518). In this environment, questions about order in the universe and the possibilities of human knowledge took on particular urgency. It is not surprising that a Frenchman, René Descartes° (1596–1650), created the first fully articulated alternative world-view.

Descartes's thinking was developed and refined in dialogue with a circle of other French thinkers. His work became more influential among philosophers and lay people than the work of some of his equally talented contemporaries because of its thoroughness and rigor, grounded in Descartes's mathematical expertise, and because of his graceful, readable French. His system was fully presented in his *Discours de la méthode* (*Discourse on Method,* 1637). Descartes described some of his intellectual crises in his later work, *Meditations* (1641).

Descartes accepted Galileo's conclusion that the heavens and the earth are made of the same elements. In his theorizing about the composition of matter, he drew on ancient atomic models that previously had not been generally accepted. His theory that all matter is made up of identical bits, which he named "corpuscles," is a forerunner of modern atomic and quantum theories. Descartes believed that all the different appearances and behaviors of matter (for example, why stone is always hard and water is always wet) could be explained solely by the size, shape, and motion of these "corpuscles." Descartes's was an extremely mechanistic explanation of the universe. It nevertheless permitted new, more specific observations and hypotheses and greater understanding of inertia. For example, because he re-imagined the universe as being filled with "corpuscles" free to move in any direction, "natural" motion no longer seemed either circular (Galileo's idea) or toward the center of the earth (Aristotle's idea). The new understanding of motion would be crucial to Isaac Newton's formulations later in the century.

In his various works, Descartes depicts and then firmly resolves the crisis of confidence that the new discoveries about the universe had produced. The collapse of the old explanations about the world made Descartes and other investigators doubt not only what they knew but also their capacity to know anything at all. Their physical senses—which denied that the earth moved, for example—had been proved untrustworthy. Descartes's solution was to re-envision the human rational capacity, the mind, as completely distinct from the world—that is, as distinct from the human body—and the unreliable perceptions it offers the senses. In a leap of faith, Descartes presumed that he could count on the fact that God would not have given humans a mind if that mind consistently misled them. For Descartes, God became the guarantor of human reasoning capacity, and humans, in Descartes's view, were distinguished by that capacity. This is the significance of his famous claim, "I think, therefore I am." (See the box "Reading Sources: Descartes: 'I think, therefore I am.'")

Accadèmia dei Lincei (ack-uh-DAY-mee-uh day-ee lin-CHAY-ee) **Descartes** (day-KART)

Descartes at the Swedish Court   In 1649 René Descartes (shown here pointing to the drawing on the table) accepted an invitation from Queen Christina to reside at the Swedish Court. He discovered that the queen was an eager but demanding patron, requiring him to lecture on scientific topics at 5 A.M. each day. Descartes died in Stockholm of pneumonia after a few short months of residence. *(Versailles/Bulloz)*

Descartes thus achieved a resolution of the terrifying doubt about the world, a resolution that exalted the role of the human knower. The Cartesian universe was one of mechanical motion, not purpose or mystical meaning, and the Cartesian human being was pre-eminently a mind that could apprehend that universe. In what came to be known as "Cartesian dualism," Descartes was proposing the human mind is detached from the world yet at the same time can objectively analyze the world.

Descartes's ambitious view of human reason emphasized deductive reasoning (a process of reasoning in which the conclusion follows necessarily from the stated premises), a natural consequence of his philosophical rejection of sense data. The limits of deductive reasoning

for scientific investigation would be realized and much of Cartesian physics itself supplanted by the end of the century. Nevertheless, Descartes's assumption about the objectivity of the observer would become an enduring part of scientific practice. In Descartes's day, the most radical aspect of his thought was the reduction of God to the role of guarantor of knowledge. Many fellow scientists and interested lay people were fearful of Descartes's system because it seemed to encourage "atheism." In fact, a profound faith in God was necessary for Descartes's creativity in imagining his new world system—but the system did work without God.

Although Descartes would have been surprised and offended by charges of atheism, he knew that his work

❧ READING SOURCES

Descartes: "I think, therefore I am"

In the passages leading up to this one in his Discourse on Method, *Descartes has made it clear that he does not advocate, or anticipate, any social or political upheaval as a consequence of his search for truth. On the contrary, he acknowledges his duty to abide by the tenets of religion and the laws of his country. The only status quo he wants to challenge is the habits of his own mind, in order to build a sure foundation for reasoning. Notice that he assumes his senses may deceive him and therefore sure knowledge cannot be based on sensory data.*

For a long time I had remarked that it is sometimes requisite in common life to follow opinions which one knows to be most uncertain, as [I have stated] above. But because in this case I wished to give myself entirely to the search for Truth, I thought that it was necessary for me to take an apparently opposite course, and to reject as absolutely false everything as to which I could imagine the least ground of doubt, in order to see afterwards if there remained anything in my belief that was entirely certain. Thus, because our senses sometimes deceive us, I wished to suppose that nothing is just as they cause us to imagine . . . and judging that I was as subject to error as was any other [man], I rejected as false all the reason formerly accepted by me as demonstrations. . . . I resolved to assume that everything that ever entered into my mind was no more true than the illusions of my dreams. But immediately afterwards I noticed that whilst I thus wished to think all things false, it was absolutely essential that the "I" who thought this should be somewhat, and remarking that this truth, "I think, therefore I am" was so certain and so assured that all the most extravagant suppositions brought forward by the skeptics were incapable of shaking it, I came to the conclusion that I could receive it without scruple as the first principle of the Philosophy for which I was seeking.

Source: Discourse on the Method of Rightly Conducting the Reason, trans. Elizabeth S. Haldane and G. R. T. Ross, in Mortimer Adler, ed., *Great Books of the Western World,* vol. 28 (Chicago: Encyclopaedia Britannica, 1990), p. 275.

would antagonize the church. He moved to the Netherlands to study in 1628, and his *Discourse* was first published there. He had lived in the Netherlands and in Germany earlier in his life; fearful of the tense atmosphere during the renewed war against French Protestants, he now left France virtually for good. Unlike Galileo, Descartes enjoyed personal wealth that enabled him to travel widely, work in solitude, and sample the intellectual environment of courts and universities without depending on powerful patrons. Long residence in the Netherlands led him to advocate religious toleration late in his life.

A contemporary of Descartes, fellow Frenchman Blaise Pascal° (1623–1662), drew attention in his writings

and in his life to the limits of scientific knowledge. Son of a royal official, Pascal was perhaps the most brilliant mind of his generation. A mathematician like Descartes, he stressed the importance of mathematical representations of phenomena, built one of the first calculating machines, and invented probability theory. He also carried out experiments to investigate air pressure, the behavior of liquids, and the existence of vacuums.

Pascal's career alternated between periods of intense scientific work and religious retreat. Today he is well known for his writings that justified the austere Catholicism known as Jansenism and explored the human soul and psyche. His *Pensées* (*Thoughts,* 1657) consists of the published fragments of his defense of Christian faith, which remained unfinished at the time

---

Pascal (pahss-KAHL)

of his early death. Pascal's appeal for generations after him may lie in his attention to matters of faith and of feeling. His most famous statement, "The heart has its reasons which reason knows not," can be read as a declaration of the limits of the Cartesian world-view.

■ Science and Revolution in England

The new science had adherents and practitioners throughout Europe by 1650. Dutch scientists in the commercial milieu of the Netherlands, for example, had the freedom to pursue practical and experimental interests. The Dutch investigator Christiaan Huygens° (1629–1695) worked on a great variety of problems, including air pressure and optics. He invented and patented the pendulum clock in 1657, the first device accurately to measure small units of time, essential for a variety of measurements.

England proved a unique environment for the development of science in the middle of the century. In a society torn by civil war, differing positions on science became part and parcel of disputes over Puritanism, church hierarchy, and royal power. Scientific investigation and speculation were spurred by the urgency of religious and political agendas. Scientific, along with political and religious, debate was generally encouraged by the collapse of censorship beginning in the 1640s.

In the 1640s natural philosophers with Puritan leanings were encouraged in their investigations by dreams that science, of the practical Baconian sort, could be the means by which the perfection of life on earth could be brought about and the end of history, the reign of the saints preceding the return of Christ, accelerated. Their concerns ranged from improved production of gunpowder (for the armies fighting against Charles I) to surveying and mapmaking. Perhaps the best-known member of this group was Robert Boyle (1627–1691). In his career we can trace the evolution of English science through the second half of the seventeenth century.

Boyle and his colleagues were theoretically eclectic, drawing on Cartesian mechanics and even Paracelsian chemical theories. They attacked the English university system, still under the sway of Aristotelianism, and proposed widespread reform of education. They were forced to moderate many of their positions, however, as the English civil wars proceeded. Radical groups such as the Levellers used Hermeticism and the related Paracelsianism as part of their political and religious tenets. The

Levellers and other radical groups drew on the hermetic notion that matter is imbued with divine spirit; they believed that each person was capable of divine knowledge and a godly life without the coercive hierarchy of church and state officials.

Boyle and his colleagues responded to these challenges. They gained institutional power, accepting positions at Oxford and Cambridge. They formed the core of the Royal Society of London, which they persuaded Charles II to recognize and charter on his accession to the throne in the Restoration of 1660. They worked to articulate a theoretical position that combined the orderliness of mechanism, a continued divine presence in the world, and a Baconian emphasis on scientific progress. This unwieldy set of notions was attractive to the educated elite of their day, who embraced the certainties of science but also clung to certain authoritarian aspects of the old Christian world-view.

Their most creative contribution, both to their own cause and to the advancement of science, was their emphasis on and refinement of experimental philosophy and practice. In 1660 Boyle published *New Experiments Physico-Mechanical*. The work described the results of his experiments with an air pump he had designed, and it laid out general rules for experimental procedure. Descartes had accounted for motion by postulating that "corpuscles" of matter interact, thereby eliminating the possibility of a vacuum in nature. Recent experiments on air pressure suggested otherwise, however, and Boyle tried to confirm their findings with his air pump.

Boyle's efforts to demonstrate that a vacuum could exist—by evacuating a sealed chamber with his pump—were not successes by modern standards because they could not readily be replicated. Boyle tied the validity of experimental results to the agreement of witnesses to the experiment—a problematic solution, for only investigators sympathetic to his hypothesis and convinced of his credibility usually witnessed the results. In response to a Cambridge scholar who criticized his interpretation of one of his experiments, Boyle replied that he could not understand his critic's objections, ". . . the experiment having been tried both before our whole society [the Royal Society of London], and very critically, by its royal founder, his majesty himself."[8] Rather than debate differing interpretations, Boyle appealed to the authority and prestige of the participants themselves. In English science of the mid-seventeenth century, therefore, we have a further example of the fact that new truths, new procedures for determining truth, and new criteria for practitioners were all being established simultaneously.

Huygens (HI-ghenz)

Isaac Newton   Pictured here about fifteen years after the publication of the *Principia,* Newton was also one of the developers of calculus. The cumbersome mathematics he still relied on, however, has led one scholar to ponder: "What manner of man he was who could use as a weapon what we can scarcely lift as a burden."[9]   *(By courtesy of the National Portrait Gallery, London)*

■ The Newtonian Synthesis: The Copernican Revolution Completed

The Copernican revolution reached its high point with the work of the Englishman Isaac Newton (1643–1727), born one year almost to the day after Galileo died. Newton completed the new explanation for motion in the heavens and on earth that Copernicus's work had initiated and that Kepler, Galileo, and others had sought.

After a difficult childhood and an indifferent education, Newton entered Cambridge University as a student in 1661. Copernicanism and Cartesianism were being hotly debated, though not yet officially studied. Newton made use of Descartes's work in mathematics to develop his skill on his own and, by 1669, he had invented calculus. (He did not publish his work at the time and another mathematician, Gottfried von Leibniz°, later independ-

Leibniz (LIBE-nits)

ently developed calculus and vied with Newton for credit.)

Newton was elected to a fellowship at Cambridge in 1667 and, in 1669, was made professor of mathematics at the recommendation of a retiring professor with whom Newton had shared his work on calculus. With less demanding teaching assignments, he was able to devote much of the next decade to work on optics—an important area of study for testing Descartes's corpuscular theory of matter.

In the 1680s, Newton experienced a period of self-imposed isolation from other scientists after a particularly heated exchange with one colleague, provoked by Newton's difficult temperament. During this decade, he returned to the study of alternative theories about matter. As a student at Cambridge he had been strongly influenced by the work of a group of Neo-Platonists who were critical of Cartesian dualism. This controversial theory posited God as a cause of all matter and motion but removed God, or any other unknown or unknowable force, as an explanation for the behavior of matter. Their concerns were both religious and scientific. As Newton says in some of his early writing while a student, "However we cast about we find almost no other reason for atheism than this [Cartesian] notion of bodies having . . . a complete, absolute and independent reality."[10]

Newton now read treatises in alchemy and hermetic tracts and began to imagine explanations for the behavior of matter (such as for bits of cloth fluttered from a distance by static electricity) that Cartesian corpuscular theory could not readily explain. Precisely what the forces were that caused such behavior he was not sure, but his eclectic mind and his religious convictions enabled him to accept their existence.

It was this leap that allowed him to propose the existence of gravity—a mysterious force that accounts for the movement of heavenly bodies in the vacuum of space. Others had speculated about the existence of gravity; indeed, the concept of inertia as so far elaborated by Galileo, Descartes, and others suggested the need for the concept of gravity. Otherwise, if a planet were "pushed" (say, in Kepler's view, by the "motive force" of the sun), it would continue along that course forever unless "pulled back" by something else.

Newton's extraordinary contribution to a new mechanistic understanding of the universe was the mathematical computation of the laws of gravity and planetary motion, which he combined with a fully developed concept of inertia. In 1687 Newton published *Philosophia Naturalis Principia Mathematica* (*Mathematical Principles of Natural Philosophy*; usually called *Principia*). In this mathematical treatise—so intricate that it was baffling to lay people, even those able to read Latin—Newton laid out his laws of motion and expressed them as mathematical theorems that can be used to test future observations of moving bodies. Then he demonstrated that these laws also apply to the solar system, confirming the data already gathered about the planets and even predicting the existence of an as-yet-unseen planet. His supreme achievement was his law of gravitation, with which he could predict the discovery of the invisible planet. This law states that every body, indeed every bit of matter, in the universe exerts over every other body an attractive force proportional to the product of their masses and inversely proportional to the square of the distance between them. Newton not only accounted for motion but definitively united heaven and earth in a single scheme and created a convincing picture of an orderly nature.

Neither Newton nor anyone else claimed that his theorems resolved all questions about motion and matter. Exactly what gravity is and how it operates were not clear, as they still are not. Newton's laws of motion are taught today because they still adequately account for most problems of motion. The fact that so fundamental a principle as gravity remains unexplained in no way diminishes Newton's achievement but is clear evidence about the nature of scientific understanding: science provides explanatory schemas that account for many—but not all—observed phenomena. No schema explains everything, and each schema contains open doorways that lead both to further discoveries and to blind alleys. Newton, for example, assumed that the forces that accounted for gravity would mysteriously work on metals so that, as alchemists predicted, they might "quickly pass into gold."[11]

After the publication of the *Principia,* Newton was more of a celebrated public figure than a practicing scientist. He helped lead resistance to James II's Catholicizing policies in the university, and he became the familiar of many other leading minds of his day, such as John Locke (see page 596). In 1703 Newton became the president of the Royal Academy of Sciences and was knighted in 1705, the first scientist to be so distinguished. By the end of Newton's life, universities in England were dominated by men who acclaimed and built on his work: the transformation of the institutional structure of science in England was complete.

■ Other Branches of Science

The innovations in astronomy that led to the new mechanistic view of the behavior of matter did not automatically spill over to other branches of science. In astronomy, innovation came after the ancient and medieval inheritance had been fully assimilated and its errors disclosed. Other branches of science followed their own paths, though all were strongly influenced by the mechanistic world-view.

In chemistry, the mechanistic assumption that all matter was composed of small, equivalent parts was crucial to understanding the properties and behavior of compounds (combinations of elements). But knowledge of these small units of matter was not yet detailed enough to be of much use in advancing chemistry conceptually. Nevertheless, the flawed conceptual schema did not hold back all chemical discovery and development. Lack of understanding of gases, and of the specific elements in their makeup, for example, did not prevent the development and improvement of gunpowder. Indeed, unlike the innovations in astronomy, eventual conceptual innovation in chemistry and biology owed a great deal to the results of plodding experiment and the slow accumulation of data.

A conceptual leap forward was made in biology in the sixteenth and seventeenth centuries. Because biological knowledge was mostly a byproduct of the practice of medicine, biological studies remained very practical and experimental. The recent discovery of *On Anatomical Procedures,* a treatise by the ancient physician Galen, encouraged dissection and other practical research. Andreas Vesalius° (1514–1564), in particular, made important advances by following Galen's exhortation to anatomical research. Born in Brussels, Vesalius studied at the nearby University of Louvain, and then at Padua, where he was appointed professor of surgery. He ended his career as physician to Emperor Charles V and his son, Philip II of Spain. In his teaching at Padua Vesalius acted on the newly recovered Galenic teachings by doing dissections himself rather than giving the work to technicians. In 1543 he published versions of his lectures as an illustrated compendium of anatomy, *De Humani Corporis Fabrica* (*On the Fabric of the Human Body*).

The results of his dissections of human corpses, revealed in this work, demonstrated a number of errors in Galen's knowledge of human anatomy, much of which had been derived from dissection of animals. Neither Vesalius nor his immediate successors, however, questioned overall Galenic theory about the functioning of the human body, any more than Copernicus had utterly rejected Aristotelian physics.

The slow movement from new observation to changed explanation is clearly illustrated in the career of

---

Vesalius (vuh-SAY-lee-us)

the Englishman William Harvey (1578–1657). Much like Vesalius, Harvey was educated first in his own land and then at Padua, where he benefited from the tradition of anatomical research. He also had a career as a practicing physician in London and at the courts of James I and Charles I.

Harvey postulated the circulation of the blood—postulated rather than discovered because, owing to the technology of the day, he could not observe the tiny capillaries where the movement of arterial blood into the veins occurs. After conducting vivisectional experiments on animals that revealed the actual functioning of the heart and lungs, he reasoned that circulation must occur. He carefully described his experiments and his conclusions in *Exercitatio Anatomica de Motu Cordis et Sanguinis in Animalibus* (1628), usually shortened to *De Motu Cordis* (*On the Motion of the Heart*).

Harvey's work challenged Galenic anatomy and, like Copernicus's discoveries, created new burdens of explanation. According to Galenic theory, the heart and the lungs helped each other to function. The heart sent nourishment to the lungs through the pulmonary artery, and the lungs provided raw material for the "vital spirit," which the heart gave to the blood to sustain life. The lungs also helped the heart sustain its "heat." This heat was understood to be an innate property of organs, just as "heaviness," in traditional physics, had been considered an innate property of earthbound objects.

From his observations, Harvey came to think of the heart in terms consonant with the new mechanistic notions about nature: as a pump to circulate the blood. But he adjusted, rather than abandoned, Galenic theories concerning "heat" and "vital spirit." The lungs had been thought to "ventilate" the heart by providing air to maintain "heat," just as a bellows aerates a fire. In light of his discovery of the pulmonary transit (that all of the blood is pumped through the lungs and back through the heart), Harvey suggested instead that the lungs carried out some of these functions for the blood, helping it to concoct the "vital spirit." Only in this sense did he think of the heart as a machine, circulating this life-giving material throughout the body.

Harvey's explanation of bodily functions in light of his new knowledge thus did not constitute a rupture with Galenic tradition. But by the end of his life, Harvey's own adjustments of Galenic theory were suggesting new conceptual possibilities. His work inspired additional research in physiology, chemistry, and physics. Robert Boyle's efforts to understand vacuums can be traced in part to questions Harvey raised about the function of the lungs and the properties of air.

THE NEW SCIENCE: SOCIETY, POLITICS, AND RELIGION

 CIENTISTS wrestled with questions about God and human capacity every bit as intently as they attempted to find new explanations for the behavior of matter and the motion of the heavens. Eventually, the profound implications of the new scientific world-view would affect thought and behavior throughout society. Once people no longer thought of the universe in hierarchical terms, they could question the hierarchical organization of society. Once people questioned the authority of traditional knowledge about the universe, the way was clear for them to begin to question traditional views of the state, the social order, and even the divine order. Such profound changes of perspective took hold very gradually, however. The advances in science did lead to revolutionary cultural change, but until the end of the seventeenth century, traditional institutions and ideologies limited its extent.

■ The Beginnings of Scientific Professionalism

Institutions both old and new supported the new science developing in the sixteenth and seventeenth centuries. Some universities were the setting for scientific breakthroughs, but court patronage, a well-established institution, also sponsored scientific activity. The development of the Accadèmia dei Lincei, to which Galileo belonged, and other academies was a step toward modern professional societies of scholars, although these new organizations depended on patronage.

In both England and France, royally sponsored scientific societies were founded in the third quarter of the century. The Royal Society of London, inaugurated in 1660, received royal recognition but no money and remained an informal institution sponsoring amateur scientific interests as well as specialized independent research. The Académie Royale des Sciences in France, established in 1666 by Jean-Baptiste Colbert, Louis XIV's minister of finance (see page 542), sponsored research and supported chosen scientists with pensions. These associations were extensions to science of traditional kinds of royal recognition and patronage. Thus, the French Académie was well funded but tightly controlled by the government of Louis XIV, and the Royal Society of London received little of Charles II's scarce resources or precious political capital. Like the earlier academies, these royally sponsored societies published their fellows' work; in England, the *Philosophical Transactions of the Royal Society* began in 1665.

The practice of seventeenth-century science took place in so many diverse institutions—academies, universities, royal courts—that neither *science* nor *scientist* was rigorously defined. Science as a discipline was not yet detached from broad metaphysical questions. Boyle, Newton, Pascal, and Descartes all concerned themselves with questions of religion, and all thought of themselves not as scientists but, like their medieval forebears, as natural philosophers. These natural philosophers were still members of an elite who met in aristocratic salons to discuss literature, politics, or science with equal ease and interest. Nevertheless, the beginnings of a narrowing of the practice of science to a tightly defined, truly professional community are evident in these institutions.

The importance of court life and patronage to the new science had at first enabled women to be actively involved. Women ran important salons in France; aristocratic women everywhere were indispensable sources of patronage for scientists; and women themselves were scientists, combining, as did men, science with other pursuits. Noblewomen and daughters of gentry families had access to education in their homes, and a number of such women were active scientists—astronomers, mathematicians, and botanists. The astronomer Maria Cunitz° (1610–1664), from Silesia (a Habsburg-controlled province, now in modern Poland), learned six languages with the encouragement of her father, who was a medical doctor. Later, she published a useful simplification of some of Kepler's mathematical calculations. Women from artisanal families might also receive useful training at home. Such was the case of the German entomologist Maria Sibylla Merian (1647–1717). Merian learned the techniques of illustration in the workshop of her father, an artist in Frankfurt. She later used her artistic training and her refined powers of observation to study and record the features and behavior of insects and plants in the New World.

Margaret Cavendish, duchess of Newcastle (1623–1673), wrote several major philosophical works, including *Grounds of Natural Philosophy* (1668). She was a Cartesian but was influenced by Neo-Platonism. She believed matter to have "intelligence" and thus disagreed with Cartesian dualism, but she criticized fellow English philosophers on the grounds that, like Descartes, she distrusted sensory knowledge as a guide to philosophy.

Women were routinely accepted as members of Italian academies, but they were excluded from formal

Cunitz (KOO-nits)

Astronomers Elisabetha and Johannes Hevelius   The Heveliuses were one of many collaborating couples among the scientists of the seventeenth century. Women were usually denied pensions and support for their research when they worked alone, however.   *(From Hevelius,* Machinae coelestis. *By permission of the Houghton Library, Harvard University)*

membership in the academies in London and Paris, though they could use the academies' facilities and received prizes from the societies for their work. One reason that women were barred was the purse: the amount of available patronage was limited, and coveted positions automatically went to men. Moreover, the hierarchical distinction signified by gender made the exclusion of women a useful way to define the academies as special and privileged.

Margaret Cavendish was aware of the degree to which her participation in scientific life depended on informal networks and on the resources available to her

❧ R E A D I N G   S O U R C E S

Margaret Cavendish Challenges Male Scientists

In her preface to her earliest scientific work, The Philosophical and Physical Opinions *(1655), Cavendish addresses scholars at Oxford and Cambridge Universities with deceptive humility. She implies that the seeming limitations of women's abilities are in fact the consequence of their exclusion from education and from participation in worldly affairs.*

Most Famously Learned,

I here present to you this philosophical work, not that I can hope wise school-men and industrious laborious students should value it for any worth, but to receive it without scorn, for the good encouragement of our sex, lest in time we should grow irrational as idiots, by the dejectedness of our spirits, through the careless neglects and despisements of the masculine sex to the female, thinking it impossible we should have either learning or understanding, wit or judgment, as if we had not rational souls as well as men, and we out of a custom of dejectedness think so too, which makes us quit all industry towards profitable knowledge, being imployed only in low and petty imployments which take away not only our abilities towards arts but higher capacities in speculations, so that we are become like worms, that only live in the dull earth of ignorance, winding ourselves sometimes out by the help of some refreshing rain of good education, which seldome is given us, for we are kept like birds in cages, to hop up and down in our houses . . . ; thus by an opinion, which I hope is but an erroneous one in men, we are shut out of all power and authority by reason we are never imployed either in civil or martial affairs, our counsels are despised and laughed at and the best of our actions are trodden down with scorn, by the over-weening conceit men have of themselves and through a despisement of us.

Source: Moira Ferguson, ed., *First Feminists: British Women Writers, 1578–1799* (Bloomington and New York: Indiana University Press and The Feminist Press, 1985), pp. 85–86.

because of her aristocratic status. (See the box "Reading Sources: Margaret Cavendish Challenges Male Scientists.") Women scientists from more modest backgrounds, without Cavendish's resources, had to fight for the right to employment as public institutions gained importance as settings for the pursuit of science. The German astronomer Maria Winkelman° (1670–1720), for example, tried to succeed her late husband in an official position in the Berlin Academy of Sciences in 1710, after working as his unofficial partner during his tenure as astronomer to the academy. The academy withheld an official position from Winkelman after her husband's death, however, despite her experience and accomplishments (she had discovered a new comet, for example, in 1702). The secretary of the academy stated: "That she be kept on in an official capacity to work on the calendar or to continue with observations simply will not do. Already during her husband's lifetime the society was burdened with ridicule because its calendar was prepared by a woman. If she were now to be kept on in such a capacity, mouths would gape even wider."[12]

Winkelman worked in private observatories, but was able to return to the Berlin Academy only as the unofficial assistant to her own son, whose training she herself had supervised. As the new science gained in prestige, women scientists often found themselves marginalized.

■ The New Science, the State, and the Church

The new natural philosophy had implications for traditional notions about the state. The new world-view that all matter was identical and answerable to discernible natural laws gradually undermined political systems resting on a belief in the inherent inequality of persons

Winkelman (VINK-el-mahn)

and on royal prerogative. By the middle of the eighteenth century, a fully formed alternative political philosophy would argue for more "rational" government in keeping with the rational, natural order of things. But the change came slowly, and while it was coming, traditional rulers found much to admire and utilize in the new science.

Technological possibilities of the new science were very attractive to governments. Experiments with vacuum pumps had important applications in the mining industry, for example. Governments also sponsored pure, and not only applied, scientific research. A French naval expedition to Cayenne, in French Guiana, led to refinements of the pendulum clock but had as its main purpose progressive observations of the sun to permit the calculation of the earth's distance from the sun.

Members of the elite saw the opportunity not only for practical advances but also for prestige and, most important, confirmation of the orderliness of nature. It is hard to overestimate the psychological impact and intellectual power of this fundamental tenet of the new science—namely, that nature is an inanimate machine that reflects God's design not through its purposes but simply by its orderliness. Thus, in the short run, the new science supported a vision of order that was very pleasing even to a monarch of absolutist pretensions such as Louis XIV.

As we have seen, scientists themselves flourished in close relationships with princes and actively sought their patronage for its many benefits. Christiaan Huygens left the Netherlands to accept the patronage of Louis XIV, producing in France some of his most important work in

Science and Royal Power   This painting memorializes the founding of the French Académie des Sciences and the building of the royal observatory in Paris. Louis himself is at the center of the painting, reflecting the symbolic importance of royal power in the sponsorship of science. *(Château de Versailles/Laurie Platt Winfrey, Inc.)*

optics and mechanics. Huygens had learned from his father, secretary to the princes of Orange in the Netherlands, that a princely court not only offered steady
support, but also opened doors to other royal academies
and salons. Huygens published some of his early research through the Royal Society in London, thanks to
contacts his father had established. When Galileo left his
position at Padua for the Medici court in Florence, he
wrote to a friend, "It is not possible to receive a salary
from a Republic [Venice] . . . without serving the public,
because to get something from the public one must satisfy it and not just one particular person; . . . no one can
exempt me from the burden while leaving me the income; and in sum I cannot hope for such a benefit from
anyone but an absolute prince."[13]

Scientists and scientific thought also remained
closely tied to religion in both practical and institutional
ways during the seventeenth century. Both religion and
the Catholic Church as an institution were involved with
scientific advancement from the time of Copernicus.
Copernicus himself was a cleric, as were many philosophers and scientists active after him. This is not surprising, for most research in the sciences to this point had
occurred within universities sponsored and staffed by
members of religious orders, who had the education,
time, and resources necessary for scientific investigation. Some of Descartes's closest collaborators were clerics, as were certain of Galileo's aristocratic patrons and
his own protégés. Moreover, religious and metaphysical
concerns were central to the work of virtually every scientist. The entire Cartesian edifice of reasoning about
the world, for example, was grounded in Descartes's
certainty about God. Copernicus, Kepler, Newton, and
others perceived God's purpose in the mathematical regularity of nature.

The notion that religion was the opponent of science in this era is a result of Galileo's trial, and represents
a distortion even of that event. It is true that the new astronomy and mechanics challenged traditional interpretations of Scripture as well as the fundamentals of
physics and metaphysics that were taught in universities. Thus, in its sponsorship of universities, the church
was literally invested in the old view, even though
individual clerics investigated and taught Copernican
ideas.

The rigid response of the church hierarchy to Galileo
is partially explained by the aftermath of the Protestant
Reformation, which, in the minds of many churchmen—
including Galileo's accusers and some of his judges—
had demonstrated the need for a firm response to any

challenge to the church's authority. Galileo seemed particularly threatening because he was well known, wrote
for a wide audience, and, like the Protestants, presumed
on the church's right to interpret the Scriptures. Galileo
may well have escaped punishment entirely had it not
been for the political predicament faced by the pope co-
incident with his trial, however.

The condemnation of Galileo shocked many clerics,
including the three who had voted for leniency at his
trial. Clerics who were also scientists continued to study
and teach the new science where and when they could.
Copernicanism was taught by Catholic missionaries
abroad. (See the box "Global Encounters: Jesuits and
Astronomy in China.") To be sure, Galileo's trial did have
a chilling effect on scientific investigation in most
Catholic regions of Europe. Investigators could and did
continue their research, but many could publish results
only by smuggling manuscripts to Protestant lands.
Many of the most important empirical and theoretical
innovations in science occurred in Protestant regions after the middle of the seventeenth century.

Protestant leaders, however, were also not initially
receptive to Copernican ideas because they defied scriptural authority as well as common sense. In 1549 one of
Martin Luther's associates wrote: "The eyes are witnesses that the heavens revolve in the space of twenty-
four hours. But certain men, either from love of novelty
or to make a display of ingenuity, have concluded that
the earth moves. . . . Now it is want of honesty and de-
cency to assert such notions publicly and the example is
pernicious. It is part of a good mind to accept the truth as
revealed by God and to acquiesce in it."[14]

Protestant thinkers were also as troubled as
Catholics by the metaphysical dilemmas that the new
theories seemed to raise. In 1611, one year after Galileo's
Starry Messenger appeared, the English poet John
Donne (1573–1631) reflected on the confusion that now
reigned in human affairs, with the heavenly hierarchy
dismantled:

> [The] new Philosophy calls all in doubt,
> The Element of fire is quite put out;
> The Sun is lost, and th'earth, and no man's wit
> Can well direct him where to look for it.
> . . . .
> Tis all in pieces, all coherence gone;
> All just supply, and all Relation:
> Prince, Subject, Father, Son, are things forgot,
> For every man alone thinks he hath got
> To be a Phoenix, and that then can be
> None of that kinde, of which he is, but he.[15]

⊕ GLOBAL ENCOUNTERS

Jesuits and Astronomy in China

The Italian Matteo Ricci (1552–1610) was one of the first Jesuit missionaries to establish himself at the imperial court in China. He was appreciative as well as critical of Chinese science, but his remarks are more interesting to us because they reveal that Ricci himself regarded expertise in mathematics and astronomy as worthy of esteem. Ricci's own scientific knowledge was crucial to his acceptance at court; Jesuit missionaries who followed Ricci in the seventeenth century found their scientific expertise equally valued, and several openly taught Copernican theory in the East. Chinese interest in European knowledge was itself new; in previous centuries, Europeans had eagerly borrowed from China—including knowledge of papermaking and printing.

The Chinese have not only made considerable progress in moral philosophy but in astronomy and in many branches of mathematics as well. At one time they were quite proficient in arithmetic and geometry, but in the study and teaching of these branches of learning they labored with more or less confusion. They divide the heavens into constellations in a manner somewhat different from that which we employ. Their count of the stars outnumbers the calculations of our astronomers by fully four hundred, because they include in it many of the fainter stars which are not always visible. And yet with all this, the Chinese astronomers take no pains whatever to reduce the phenomena of celestial bodies to the discipline of mathematics. Much of their time is spent in determining the moment of eclipses and the mass of the planets and the stars, but here, too, their deductions are spoiled by innumerable errors. Finally they center their whole attention on that phase of astronomy which our scientists term astrology, which may be accounted for the fact that they believe that everything happening on this terrestrial globe of ours depends upon the stars.

Some knowledge of the science of mathematics was given to the Chinese by the Saracens [Mongols], who penetrated into their country from the West, but very little of this knowledge was based upon definite mathematical proofs. What the Saracens left them, for the most part, consisted of certain tables of rules by which the Chinese regulated their calendar and to which they reduced their calculations of planets and the movements of the heavenly bodies in general. The founder of the family which at present regulates the study of astrology prohibited anyone from indulging in the study of this science unless he were chosen for it by hereditary right. The prohibition was founded upon fear, lest he who should acquire a knowledge of the stars might become capable of disrupting the order of the empire and seek an opportunity to do so.

Source: Louis J. Gallagher, trans., *China in the Sixteenth Century: The Journals of Matthew Ricci: 1583–1610* (New York: Random House, 1953), pp. 30–31.

The challenge of accounting in religious terms for the ideas of Copernicus and Descartes became more urgent for Protestants as the ideas acquired an anti-Catholic status after the trial of Galileo in 1633, and as they became common scientific currency by about 1640. A religious certainty about divine force that could account for the motion of bodies in a vacuum enabled Newton to develop his theories on motion and gravity. In short, religion did not merely remain in the scientists' panoply of explanations; it remained a fundamental building block of scientific thought and central to most scientists' lives, whether they were Catholic or Protestant.

■ The New Science and Human Affairs at the End of the Seventeenth Century

Traditional institutions and ideologies checked the potential effects of the new science for a time, but by the middle of the seventeenth century, political theory was beginning to reflect the impact of the mechanistic world-view. Political philosophers began to doubt that either the world or human society was an organic whole in which each part was distinguished in nature and function from the rest. Thomas Hobbes, John Locke, and others recast the bonds that link citizens to each other and to their rulers.

Because of the political turmoil in England, Thomas Hobbes (1588–1679) spent much of his productive life on the Continent. After the beginnings of the parliamentary rebellion, he joined a group of royalist émigrés in France. He met Galileo and lived for extended periods in Paris, in contact with the circle of French thinkers that included Descartes. Like Descartes, he theorized about the nature and behavior of matter and published a treatise on his views in 1655.

Hobbes is best known today for *Leviathan*° (1651), his treatise on political philosophy. *Leviathan* applies to the world of human beings his mostly Cartesian view of nature as composed of "self-motivated," atomlike structures. Hobbes viewed people as mechanistically as he viewed the rest of nature. In his view, people were made up of appetites of various sorts—the same kind of innate forces that drove all matter. The ideal state, concluded Hobbes, is one in which a strong sovereign controls the disorder that inevitably arises from the clash of desires. Unlike medieval philosophers, Hobbes did not draw analogies between the state and the human body (the king as head, judges and magistrates as arms, and so forth). Instead, Hobbes compared the state to a machine that "ran" by means of laws and was kept in good working order by a skilled technician—the ruler.

Hobbes's pessimism about human behavior and his insistence on the need for restraint imposed from above reflect, as does the work of Descartes, a concern for order in the wake of political turmoil. This concern was one reason he was welcomed into the community of French philosophers, who were naturally comfortable with royalty as a powerful guarantor of order. But Hobbes's work, like theirs, was a radical departure because it envisioned citizens as potentially equal and constrained neither by morality nor by natural obedience to authority.

Leviathan (luh-VIE-uh-thun)

Another Englishman, John Locke (1632–1704), offered an entirely different vision of natural equality among people and, consequently, of social order. Locke's major works, *Essay on Human Understanding* (1690) and *Two Treatises on Government* (1690), reflect the experimentalism of Robert Boyle, the systematizing rationality of Descartes, and other strands of the new scientific thought. In the *Essay*, Locke offered a view of human knowledge more pragmatic and utilitarian than the rigorous mathematical model of certainty used by many other philosophers. He argued that human knowledge is largely the product of experience. He agreed with Descartes that reason orders and explains human experience but, unlike Descartes, doubted that human reason had unlimited potential to comprehend the universe. Locke, however, offered a more optimistic vision of the possible uses of reason. Whereas Descartes was interested in mentally ordering and understanding the world, Locke was interested in actually functioning *in* the world.

Locke's treatises on government reflect his notion of knowledge based on experience as well as his particular experiences as a member of elite circles following the Restoration of monarchy in England. Trained in medicine, he served as personal physician and general political assistant to one of the Members of Parliament most opposed to Charles II's pretensions to absolutist government. When James II acceded to the throne in 1685, Locke remained in the Netherlands, where he had fled to avoid prosecution for treason. He became an adviser to William of Orange and returned to England with William and Mary in 1688. Locke's view of the principles of good government, then, came to reflect the pro-parliamentary stance of his political milieu.

Unlike Hobbes, Locke argued that people are capable of self-restraint and mutual respect in their pursuit of self-interest. The state arises, he believed, from a contract that individuals freely enter into to protect themselves, their property, and their happiness from possible aggression by others. They can invest the executive and legislative authority to carry out this protection in monarchy or any other governing institution, though Locke believed the English Parliament was the best available model. Because sovereignty resides with the people who enter into the contract, rebellion against abuse of power is justified. At the core of Locke's schema was thus a revolutionary vision of political society based on human rights.

Locke's experience as an English gentleman is apparent in his emphasis on private property, which he considered a fundamental human right. Nature, he believed, could not benefit humankind unless it was worked by human hands, as in a farm, for example; private ownership of property guaranteed its productivity and entitled the owner to participate in his imagined contract. Indeed, his political vision is unequivocal, and unbending, on the nature of property. Locke even found a justification for slavery. He also did not consider women to be political beings in the same way as men. The family, he felt, was a separate domain from the state, not bound by the same contractual obligations.

Locke and many other seventeenth-century thinkers were unable to imagine a new physical or political reality without invoking a notion of gender as a "natural" principle of order and hierarchy. Although Margaret Cavendish (see page 591) and other women disputed the validity of such gender distinctions, men frequently used them. Locke's use of gender as an arbitrary organizing principle gave his bold new vision of rights for certain men a claim to being "natural." The use of gender-specific vocabulary to describe nature itself had the effect of making the new objective attitude toward the world seem "natural." Works by seventeenth-century scientists are filled with references to nature as a woman who must be "conquered," "subdued," or "penetrated."

Traditional gender distinctions limited and reinforced most facets of political thought, but in other areas the fact of uncertainty and the need for tolerance were embraced. Another of Locke's influential works was the impassioned *Letter on Toleration* (1689). In it he argued that religious belief is fundamentally private and that only the most basic Christian principles need be accepted by everyone. Others went further than Locke by entirely removing traditional religion as necessary to morality and public order. Fostering this climate of religious skepticism were religious pluralism in England and the self-defeating religious intolerance of Louis XIV's persecution of Protestants.

Pierre Bayle (1647–1706), a Frenchman of Protestant origins, argued that morality can be wholly detached from traditional religion. Bayle cited as an example of morality the philosopher Baruch Spinoza° (1632–1677). Spinoza believed the state to have a moral purpose and human happiness to have spiritual roots. Yet he was not a Christian at all but a Dutch Jew who had been ejected from his local synagogue for supposed atheism! One need hardly be a Christian of any sort in order to be a moral being, Bayle concluded.

Bayle's skepticism toward traditional knowledge was more wide ranging than his views on religion. His

Spinoza (spin-OH-za)

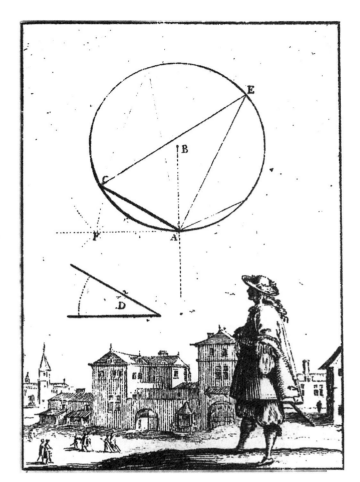

Gentleman Surveying a Town   This illustration appeared in a seventeenth-century book on surveying by a mathematician who helped design the gardens at Versailles. The book aimed to teach elites the math necessary for precise measurements of landscapes—for example, for the purpose of siege warfare. The presence of the gentleman in the foreground, estimating the proportions of the town by sight, reveals that the author expected his audience to be interested in the mathematical computations he sought to teach them.   *(Bibliothèque Nationale de France)*

best-known work, *Dictionnaire historique et critique* (*Historical and Critical Dictionary*, 1702), was a compendium of observations about and criticisms of virtually every thinker whose works were known at the time, including such recent and lionized figures as Descartes and Newton. Bayle was the first systematic skeptic, and he relentlessly exposed errors and shortcomings in all received knowledge. His works were very popular with elite lay readers.

Science Gains an Audience   This illustration from Bernard de Fontenelle's major work popularized the new science. It reveals the audience for which the work was intended. A gentleman, sitting with a lady in a formal garden, gestures to a depiction of the solar system as it was now understood; the lady is presumed to understand and to be interested in the information.   *(By permission of Houghton Library, Harvard University)*

Bayle's fellow countryman Bernard de Fontenelle° (1657–1757), secretary to the Académie des Sciences from 1699 to 1741, was the greatest popularizer of the new science of his time. His *Entretiens sur la Pluralités des Mondes* (*Conversations on the Plurality of Worlds*, 1686) was, as the title implies, an informally presented description of the infinite universe of matter. A great success, it went through numerous editions and transla-

---

Fontenelle (fon-tuh-NEL)

tions. As secretary to the Académie, Fontenelle continued his work as popularizer by publishing descriptions of the work of the Académie's scientists. At his death (at age 99) in 1757 it was said that "the Philosophic spirit, today so much in evidence, owes its beginnings to Monsieur de Fontenelle."[16]

SUMMARY

FONTENELLE is a fitting figure with whom to end a discussion of the Scientific Revolution because he represents, and worked to accomplish, the transference of the new natural philosophy into political and social philosophy—a movement we know as the "Enlightenment." The Scientific Revolution began, as innovation in scientific thinking often does, with a specific research problem whose answer led in unexpected directions. Copernicus's response to traditional astronomical problems led to scientific and philosophical innovation because of his solution and because of the context into which it was received. Recent recoveries of new ancient texts in the Renaissance and the discovery of previously unknown lands in the New World made it possible to imagine challenging ancient scientific authority. The interest of princes in both the prestige and the practical use of science helped support the work of scientists.

Other scientists, following Copernicus, built on his theories, culminating in the work of Galileo, who supported Copernican theory with additional data and widely published his findings. The Frenchman Descartes was the first to fashion a systematic explanation for the operations of nature to replace the medieval view. The political and intellectual climate in England, meanwhile, encouraged the development of experimental science and inductive reasoning. Isaac Newton provided new theories to explain the behavior of matter and expressed them in mathematical terms that could apply to either the earth or the cosmos; with his work, traditional astronomy and physics were overturned. In their place was a vision of the universe of matter that behaved, not according to higher purposes, but rather as a machine. New institutions in the form of private as well as officially sponsored scientific societies rose up to support scientists' work. These were particularly important before the new science became accepted in universities; they excluded some practitioners of the new science, however, particularly women.

Rulers made use of the new science for the practical results it offered despite the ideological challenge it presented to their power. The relationship of religion to the new science was equally complex and contrary. Some religious leaders scorned the new science; most scientists, whether Catholic or Protestant, worked to accommodate both the new science and their religious beliefs. Indeed, religious faith, in the case of Newton, for example, was a spur to innovation. By the end of the seventeenth century, the hierarchical Christian world-view grounded in the old science was being challenged on many fronts, most notably in the work of political philosophers Hobbes and Locke. A fully articulated secular world-view would be the product of the Enlightenment in the next century.

■ Notes

1. Quoted in *The New Encyclopaedia Britannica*, 15th ed., vol. 9 (Chicago, 1992), p. 135.
2. Quoted in Thomas S. Kuhn, *The Copernican Revolution* (Cambridge, Mass.: Harvard University Press, 1985), p. 131.
3. Quoted in Margaret C. Jacob, *The Cultural Meaning of the Scientific Revolution* (Philadelphia: Temple University Press, 1988), p. 18.
4. Quoted ibid., p. 33.
5. Quoted in Alan G. R. Smith, *Science and Society in the Sixteenth and Seventeenth Centuries* (New York: Science History Publications, 1972), p. 72.
6. Quoted in Jacob, p. 32 (emphasis added).
7. Quoted in Bruce T. Moran, ed., *Patronage and Institutions: Science, Technology and Medicine at the European Court* (Rochester, N.Y.: Boyden Press, 1991), p. 43.
8. Quoted in Steven Shapin, *A Social History of Truth* (Chicago: University of Chicago Press, 1994), p. 298.
9. Quoted in Smith, p. 130.
10. Quoted in Jacob, p. 89.
11. Quoted ibid., p. 25.
12. Quoted in Londa Schiebinger, *The Mind Has No Sex?* (Cambridge, Mass.: Harvard University Press, 1989), p. 92.
13. Quoted in Richard S. Westfall, "Science and Patronage," *ISIS* 76(1985): 16.
14. Quoted in Kuhn, p. 191.
15. *Complete Poetry and Selected Prose of John Donne*, ed. John Hayward (Bloomsbury, England: Nonesuch Press, 1929), p. 365, quoted in Kuhn, p. 194.
16. Quoted in Paul Edwards, ed., *The Encyclopedia of Philosophy*, vol. 3 (New York: Macmillan, 1967), p. 209.

■ Suggested Reading

Biagioli, Mario. *Galileo, Courtier.* 1993. A new study that stresses the power of patronage relations to shape scientific process.

Kuhn, Thomas. *The Copernican Revolution.* 1985. A classic treatment of the revolution in astronomy that lucidly explains the Aristotelian world-view; to understand the Copernican revolution, start here.

Schiebinger, Londa. *The Mind Has No Sex?* 1989. An examination of the participation of women in the practice of science and an explanation of how science began to reflect the exclusion of women in its values and objects of study—above all, in its claims about scientific "facts" about women themselves.

Shapin, Steven. *The Scientific Revolution.* 1996. An elegant short introduction with a lengthy bibliography; emphasizes the intellectual, social, and political contexts that shaped the development of the new science.

———, and Simon Schaffer. *Leviathan and the Air-Pump.* 1985. One of the most important studies of seventeenth-century science: traces the conflict between Cartesian science, as represented by Hobbes, and experimental science, in the work of Boyle; and shows the relationship of Hobbes and Boyle to their respective contexts and the widespread philosophical implications of each school of thought.

Westfall, R. *Never at Rest: A Biography of Isaac Newton.* 1993. A biography by one of the best-known historians of science.

 For a searchable list of additional readings for this chapter, go to http://college.hmco.com.

Modern Maps

We take for granted that contemporary maps will provide accurate representations of geography and present information in standardized ways we can easily read. But how did these standards of clarity and accuracy come about?

Modern mapping was developed during the Scientific Revolution. Like most of the changes we have labeled the "Scientific Revolution," changes in mapping were the result of several influences: innovations in Renaissance art, knowledge gleaned from voyages of exploration, the impact of new astronomical discoveries, and the interest and support of princely patrons. All of these factors enabled Europeans of this era to have a literally new view of their world.

Let us look at Christopher Saxton's map of Somerset, a county in England. This map was printed in 1579 in one of the first atlases ever published. We might be struck by how different this map appears from contemporary maps; many of its features seem decorative or even quaint. Ships, not drawn to scale, ride at anchor or sail off the coast. Towns are represented not by dots of various sizes but by miniature town buildings. Relief in the landscape is depicted with hills drawn, like the town buildings, from a side view inconsistent with the aerial perspective of the map as a whole. The large royal coat of arms that occupies the upper left quadrant of the map seems the most antiquated and irrelevant feature.

But is it irrelevant? Let us try to appreciate what a striking and powerful image this map must have been for its original viewers. Because the features are represented in ways that we consider decorative, it is easy for us to overlook the fact that this map illustrates a revolutionary method of depicting space. Saxton provides an aerial view of an entire county, with all locales arrayed in accurate spatial relationship to one another. This accurate rendering of space was, first, the result of the discovery of linear perspective by Renaissance artists. This discovery, which enabled space to be imagined from the perspec-

Map of the County of Somerset, England, 1579 *(British Library)*

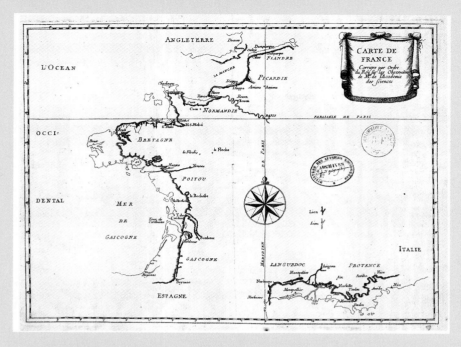

Map of the French Coastline, 1693
(Bibliothèque Nationale de France)

tive of a distanced observer, created the illusion of three-dimensional space in Renaissance paintings. Saxton's maps—and the few others published at about the same time—represented the first time Europeans could take "visual possession" of the land they lived in, in the way we now take for granted whenever we buy a road map.*

Precise measurement of land forms—the location of hills in this map, for example—still relied on the established craft of systematic surveying. And here is where the royal coat of arms enters the picture, literally. Saxton's surveying and the production of his atlas were sponsored by the government of Queen Elizabeth. Thus, just as this map enabled contemporary observers to envision for the first time, in its entirety, the land they lived in, it simultaneously marked royal power over that land.

Now let us look at a 1693 map of the coastline of France. We immediately note that most decorative elements are gone: no ships sail the abundant seas, for example. The figure of a compass marks the Paris meridian—the site of the city, we are shown, has been precisely determined by means of its longitude and latitude. More accurate calculation of longitude had been made possible by the work of Kepler and Galileo, whose mapping of heavenly bodies provided known points in

the night sky from which to calculate the longitude of the observer's position on earth. (Calculation of latitude had always been easier, since it involved only determining the angle of the sun above the horizon, but it was also improved by better instrumentation in the seventeenth century.) After 1650, French cartographers, among others, systematically collected astronomical observations from around the world so they could map all known lands more precisely.

This map superimposes a corrected view (the darker line) of the coastline of France over an older rendering. The power of this coastline map, then, lies in the way it dramatically advertises the progress of mapmaking itself. Royal power remains connected to scientific effort: the title reads, "Map of France, corrected by order of the King by the observations of Messieurs of the Academy of Sciences."

Thus, both of these maps glorify royal power: one by linking it with a new visualization of the land it ruled, the other by presenting royalty as a patron and guarantor of knowledge. But in the second map, royal identity is no longer pictured along with the land it claims. Instead, the king is mentioned discreetly, in what came to be a standardized label.

Like all innovations of the Scientific Revolution, those in mapmaking had unintended consequences. Claims to royal power articulated on maps lost their force as the information the maps conveyed was increasingly valued for itself. Royal power had many practical and ideological uses for the new science but, in the end, would be undermined by the world-view the new science made possible.

---

*Richard Helgerson, "The Land Speaks: Cartography, Chorography, and Subversion in Renaissance England," *Representations* 16 (Fall 1986): 51. This discussion of Saxton's map and the evolution of mapmaking is drawn from Helgerson and from Norman J. W. Thrower, *Maps and Civilization* (Chicago: University of Chicago Press, 1996), chaps. 5 and 6.

CHAPTER 18

Europe on the Threshold of Modernity ca. 1715–1789

DRINKS are set before these gentlemen on their table, but something tells us this is more than just a social gathering. The men are absorbed in intense conversation. One man raises his hand, perhaps to emphasize his point, while another listens with a skeptical smirk. Several others eagerly follow their conversation. Other animated discussions go on at nearby tables. The setting depicted here was altogether new in the eighteenth century, when this picture was made, and a caption that originally accompanied the illustration speaks to its importance: "Establishment of the new philosophy: our cradle was the café."

Cafés were one of the new settings in which literate elites could discuss the "new philosophy"—what we now call Enlightenment philosophy—and could explore its implications for social and political life. Men gathered in clubs and cafés; women directed private gatherings known as salons. Both men and women read more widely than ever before. The Enlightenment was the extension into political and social thought of the intellectual revolution that had already occurred in the physical sciences. Hence, it constituted a revolution in political philosophy, but it was also much more. The era witnessed the emergence of an informed body of public opinion, critical of the prevailing political system. The relationship between governments and the governed had begun to change: subjects of monarchs were becoming citizens of nations.

The notion that human beings, using their rational faculties, could not only understand nature but might also transform their societies

The Enlightenment

European States in the Age of Enlightenment

The Widening Scope of Warfare

Economic Expansion and Social Change

Café society in the eighteenth century.
(The Art Archive/Musée Carnavalet, Paris/Dagli Orti)

was appealing to rulers as well, in part for the traditional reason—strengthening state power. Frederick the Great of Prussia, Catherine the Great of Russia, and other monarchs self-consciously tried to use Enlightenment precepts to guide their efforts at governing. They had mixed success because powerful interests opposed their efforts at reform and because, ultimately, their own hereditary and autocratic power was incompatible with Enlightenment perspectives.

Profound changes in economic and social life accompanied this revolution in intellectual and political spheres. Economic growth spurred population growth, which in turn stimulated industry and trade. The increasing economic and strategic importance of overseas colonies made them important focal points of international conflict. As the century closed, Europe was on the threshold of truly revolutionary changes in politics and production that had their roots in the intellectual, economic, and social ferment of eighteenth-century life.

QUESTIONS TO CONSIDER

■ What were the most important notions in Enlightenment thought, and what were some of the intellectual, social, and political conditions that favored its development?

■ To what extent did the activities of "enlightened despots" reflect Enlightenment precepts, and to what extent did they reflect traditional concerns of state power?

■ How did warfare itself, and the causes of war, change in the eighteenth century?

■ How was European agriculture transformed in this era, and what further transformations did it bring in its wake?

TERMS TO KNOW

philosophes	Frederick the Great
Voltaire	Maria Theresa
Adam Smith	Catherine the Great
Jean-Jacques Rousseau	agricultural revolution
salon, salonnière	putting-out system
enlightened despotism	

THE ENLIGHTENMENT

T HE Enlightenment was an intellectual movement that applied to political and social thought the confidence in the intelligibility of natural law that Newton and other scientists had recently achieved. Following Descartes and Locke, Enlightenment thinkers believed that human beings could discern and work in concert with the laws of nature for the betterment of human life. Perhaps the most significant effect of this confidence was the questioning of traditional social and political bonds. A belief grew that society must be grounded on rational foundations to be determined by humans, not arbitrary foundations determined by tradition and justified by religious authority.

The Enlightenment was a social and cultural movement: Enlightenment thought was received and debated in the context of increasingly widespread publications and new opportunities for exchanging views in literary societies, salons, and cafés. This context shaped the potential radicalism of the Enlightenment by helping to ensure that informed public opinion would become a new force in political and cultural life. Given this broad base, Enlightenment thinking was certain to challenge the very foundations of social and political order.

■ Voltaire: The Quintessential *Philosophe*

A wide range of thinkers participated in the Enlightenment. In France they were known as *philosophes*°, a term meaning not a formal philosopher but rather a thinker and critic. The most famous of the philosophes was Voltaire (1694–1778). A prolific writer, critic, and reformer, Voltaire was lionized by admirers throughout Europe, including several rulers. Born François-Marie Arouet to a middle-class family, he took the pen name Voltaire in 1718, after one of his early plays was a critical success. Like many philosophes, Voltaire moved in courtly circles but

---

philosophes (fee-low-ZOHFS)

was often on its margins. His mockery of the regent for the young French king earned him a year's imprisonment in 1717, and an exchange of insults with a leading courtier some years later led to enforced exile in Great Britain for two years.

After returning from Britain, Voltaire published his first major philosophical work. *Lettres philosophiques* (*Philosophical Letters*, 1734) revealed the influence of his British sojourn and helped to popularize Newton's achievement. To confidence in the laws governing nature Voltaire added cautious confidence in humans' attempts to discern truth. From Locke's work (see page 596) he was persuaded to trust human educability tempered by awareness of the finite nature of the human mind. These elements gave Voltaire's philosophy both its passionate conviction and its sensible practicality.

Voltaire portrayed Great Britain as a more rational society than France. He was particularly impressed with the relative religious and intellectual toleration evident across the Channel. The British government had a more workable set of institutions; the economy was less crippled by the remnants of feudal privilege; and education was not in the hands of the church. (See the box "Reading Sources: Voltaire on Britain's Commercial Success.") Voltaire was one of many French thinkers who singled out the Catholic Church as the archenemy of progressive thought. Philosophes constantly collided with the church's negative views of human nature and resented its control over most education and its still strong sway in political life. Typical of Voltaire's castigation of the church is his stinging satire of the clerics who condemned Galileo: "I desire that there be engraved on the door of your holy office: Here seven cardinals assisted by minor brethren had the master of thought of Italy thrown into prison at the age of seventy, made him fast on bread and water, because he instructed the human race."

After the publication of his audacious *Lettres*, Voltaire was again forced into exile from Paris, and he resided for some years in the country home of a woman with whom he shared a remarkable intellectual and emotional relationship: Emilie, marquise du Châtelet° (1706–1749). Châtelet was a mathematician and a scientist. She prepared a French translation of Newton's *Principia* while Voltaire worked at his accustomed variety of writing, which included a commentary on Newton's work. Because of Châtelet's tutelage, Voltaire became more knowledgeable about the sciences and more serious in his efforts to apply scientific rationality to human affairs. He was devastated by her sudden death in 1749.

Châtelet (shot-uh-LAY)

CHRONOLOGY

1715–1774	Reign of Louis XV in France
1722–1741	Walpole first British "prime minister"
1734	Voltaire, *Philosophical Letters*
1740–1748	War of the Austrian Succession
1740–1780	Reign of Maria Theresa of Austria
1740–1786	Reign of Frederick the Great of Prussia
1746	Battle of Culloden
1748	Montesquieu, *The Spirit of the Laws*
1748	Hume, *Essay on Human Understanding*
1751–1765	Diderot, editor, *The Encyclopedia*
1756–1763	Seven Years' War
1758	Voltaire, *Candide*
1762	Rousseau, *The Social Contract*
1762–1796	Reign of Catherine the Great of Russia
1772	First partition of Poland
1776	Smith, *The Wealth of Nations*
1780–1790	Reign of Joseph II of Austria
1792	Wollstonecraft, *A Vindication of the Rights of Woman*

Shortly afterward, he accepted the invitation of the king of Prussia, Frederick II, to visit Berlin. His stay was stormy and brief because of disagreements with other court philosophers. He resided for a time in Geneva, until his criticisms of the city's moral codes forced yet another exile on him. He spent most of the last twenty years of his life at his estates on the Franco-Swiss border, where he could be relatively free from interference by any government. These were productive years. He produced his best-known satirical novelette, *Candide*, in 1758. It criticized aristocratic privilege and the power of clerics as well as the naiveté of philosophers who took "natural law" to mean that the world was already operating as it should.

Voltaire Visits Frederick the Great of Prussia   Voltaire leans forward, at left, to discuss a point
of philosophy with Frederick. Skill at witty conversation enabled philosophes such as Voltaire to
advance fundamental criticisms of society even to elite audiences.   *(Bildarchiv Preussischer Kulturbesitz)*

Voltaire's belief that only by struggle are the accumulated habits of centuries overturned is also reflected in
his political activity. Voltaire became involved in several
celebrated legal cases in which individuals were pitted
against the authority of the church, which was still
backed by the authority of the state. In pursuit of justice
in these cases and in relentless criticism of the church,
Voltaire added a stream of straightforward political pamphlets to his literary output. He also worked closer to
home, initiating agricultural reform on his estates and
working to improve the status of peasants in the vicinity.

Voltaire died in Paris in May 1778, after a triumphal
welcome for the staging of one of his plays. By then, he
was no longer leader of the Enlightenment in strictly intellectual terms. Thinkers and writers more radical than
he had earned prominence during his long life and had
dismissed some of his beliefs, such as the notion that
a monarch could introduce reform. But Voltaire had
provided a crucial stimulus to French thought with his
Lettres philosophiques. His importance lies also in his
embodiment of the critical spirit of eighteenth-century
rationalism: its confidence, its increasingly practical
bent, its wit and sophistication. Until the end of his life,
Voltaire remained a bridge between the increasingly diverse body of Enlightenment thought and the literate
elite audience.

❧ READING SOURCES

Voltaire on Britain's Commercial Success

In this excerpt from Philosophical Letters, *Voltaire compares British trade and sea power with the commercial activities of the German and French elites, who scorned trade in order to engage in aristocratic pretentiousness and court politics. Voltaire's admiration for England and his penchant for criticizing irrationalities of all sorts are evident, as is his famed wit. Wit and irony were important tools, enabling Voltaire to advance trenchant criticism when seeming only to poke fun.*

Commerce, which has brought wealth to the citizenry of England, has helped to make them free, and freedom has developed commerce in its turn. By means of it the nation has grown great; it is commerce that little by little has strengthened the naval forces that make the English the masters of the seas. . . . Posterity may learn with some surprise that a little island with nothing of its own but a bit of lead, tin . . . and coarse wool became, by means of its commerce, powerful enough to send three fleets at one time to three different ends of the earth.

All this makes the English merchant justly proud; moreover, the younger brother of a peer of the realm does not scorn to enter into trade. . . . [In Germany], they are unable to imagine how [an aristocrat could enter trade since they have] as many as thirty Highnesses of the same name, with nothing to show for it but pride and a coat of arms.

In France anybody who wants to can [act the part of marquis] and whoever arrives in Paris with money to spend and a [plausible name] may indulge in such phrases as "a man of my rank and quality" and with sovereign eye look down upon a wholesaler. . . . Yet I don't know which is the more useful to a state, a well-powdered lord who knows precisely what time the king gets up in the morning . . . and who gives himself airs of grandeur while playing the role of slave in a minister's antechamber, or a great merchant who enriches his country.

Source: Ernest Dilworth, trans. and ed., *Voltaire: Philosophical Letters* (New York: Bobbs-Merrill, 1961), pp. 39–40.

■ The Variety of Enlightenment Thought

Differences among philosophes grew as the century progressed. In the matter of religion, for example, there was virtual unanimity of opposition to the Catholic Church among French thinkers, but no unanimity about God. Voltaire was a theist—believing firmly in God, creator of the universe, but not a specifically Christian God. To some later thinkers, God was irrelevant—the creator of the world, but a world that ran continuously according to established laws. Some philosophes were atheists, arguing that a universe operating according to discoverable laws needs no higher purpose and no divine presence to explain, run, or justify its existence. In Protestant areas of Europe, in contrast to France, Enlightenment thought was often less hostile to Christianity.

Questions about social and political order, as well as about human rationality itself, were also pondered. Charles de Secondat (1689–1755), baron of Montesquieu°, a French judge and legal philosopher, combined the belief that human institutions must be rational with Locke's assumption of human educability. Montesquieu's treatise *De L'Esprit des lois* (*The Spirit of the Laws,* 1748) was published in twenty-two printings within two years. In it Montesquieu maintained that laws were not meant to be arbitrary rules but derived naturally from human society: the more evolved a society was, the more liberal were its laws. This notion that progress is possible within society and government deflated Europeans' pretensions with regard to other

Montesquieu (mawn-tess-KYUH)

societies, for a variety of laws could be equally "rational" given differing conditions. Montesquieu is perhaps best known to Americans as the advocate of the separation of legislative, executive, and judicial powers that later became enshrined in the U.S. Constitution. To Montesquieu, this scheme seemed to parallel in human government the balance of forces observable in nature; moreover, the arrangement seemed best to guarantee liberty.

Enlightenment philosophers also investigated the "laws" of economic life. In France economic thinkers known as *physiocrats* proposed ending "artificial" control over land use in order to free productive capacity and permit the flow of produce to market. Their target was traditional forms of land tenure, including collective control of village lands by peasants and seigneurial rights over land and labor by landlords. The freeing of restrictions on agriculture, manufacture, and trade was proposed by the Scotsman Adam Smith in his treatise *An Inquiry into the Nature and Causes of the Wealth of Nations* (1776).

Smith (1723–1790), a professor at the University of Glasgow, is best known in modern times as the originator of "laissez-faire" economics. *Laissez faire,* or "let it run on its own," assumes that an economy will regulate itself, without interference by government and, of more concern to Smith, without the monopolies and other economic privileges common in his day. Smith's schema for economic growth was not merely a rigid application of natural law to economics. His ideas grew out of an optimistic view of human nature and rationality that was heavily indebted to Locke. Humans, Smith believed, have drives and passions that they can direct and govern by means of reason and inherent mutual sympathy. Thus, Smith suggested, in seeking their own achievement and well-being, people are often "led by an invisible hand" simultaneously to benefit society as a whole.

Throughout the century, philosophers of various stripes disagreed about the nature and the limits of human reason. Smith's countryman and friend David Hume (1711–1776) was perhaps the most radical in his critique of the human capacity for knowing. He was the archskeptic, taking Locke's view of the limitations on pure reason to the point of doubting the efficacy of any sensory data. His major exposition of these views, *Essay Concerning Human Understanding* (1748), led to important innovations later in the century in the work of the German philosopher Immanuel Kant. At the time, though, Hume's arguments were almost contrary to the prevailing spirit that embraced empirical knowledge. Hume himself separated this work from his other efforts in moral,

political, and economic philosophy, which were more in tune with contemporary views.

Mainstream confidence in empirical knowledge and in the intelligibility of the world is evident in the production of the *Encyclopédie* (*Encyclopedia*). This seventeen-volume compendium of knowledge, criticism, and philosophy was assembled by leading philosophes in France and published there between 1751 and 1765. The volumes were designed to contain state-of-the-art knowledge about arts, sciences, technology, and philosophy. The guiding philosophy of the project, set forth by its chief editor, Denis Diderot° (1713–1784), was a belief in the advancement of human happiness through the advancement of knowledge. The *Encyclopédie* was a history of the march of knowledge as well as a compendium of known achievements. It was revolutionary in that it not only intrigued and inspired intellectuals but assisted thousands of government officials and professionals.

The encyclopedia project illustrates the political context of Enlightenment thought as well as its philosophical premises. The Catholic Church placed the work on the *Index of Prohibited Books,* and the French government might have barred its publication but for the fact that the official who would have made the decision was himself drawn to Enlightenment thinking. Many other officials, however, worked to suppress it. By the late 1750s, losses in wars overseas had made French officials highly sensitive to political challenges of any kind. Thus, like Voltaire, the major contributors to the *Encyclopédie* were admired by certain segments of the elite and persecuted by others in their official functions.

The *Encyclopédie* reflects the complexities and limitations of Enlightenment thought on another score—the position of women. One might expect that the Enlightenment penchant for challenging received knowledge and traditional hierarchies would lead to revised views of women's abilities and rights. Indeed, some contributors blamed women's inequality with men not on inherent gender differences but rather on the customs and laws that had kept women from education and the development of their abilities. However, other contributors blamed women, and not society, for their plight, or they argued that women had talents that fit them only for the domestic sphere.

Both positions were represented in Enlightenment thought as a whole. The assumption of the natural equality of all people provided a powerful ground for arguing the equality of women with men. Some thinkers, such as Mary Astell (1666–1731), challenged Locke's sep-

---

Diderot (DEED-uh-row)

🐌 READING SOURCES

An Enlightenment Thinker Argues for the Equality of Women

In these passages from A Vindication of the Rights of Woman, *Mary Woll-stonecraft argues that just as living as aristocratic courtiers corrupts men, so too does dependence on men corrupt women. Wollstonecraft argued, in a move very radical for her day, that even to be good wives and mothers women must be economically independent. She was extending to women the connection between independence and virtue that Locke and Rousseau, among others, applied to men.*

It is vain to expect virtue from women till they are in some degree independent from men; nay, it is vain to expect that strength of natural affection which would make them good wives and mothers. Whilst they are absolutely dependent on their husbands, they will be cunning, mean and selfish. . . . Yet whilst wealth enervates men, and women live, as it were, by their personal charms, how can we expect them to discharge those ennobling duties which equally require exertion and self-denial? . . . the society is not properly organized which does not compel men and women to discharge their respective duties, by making it the only way to acquire that countenance [respect] from their fellow creatures which every human being wishes some way to attain. . . .

But to render [woman] really virtuous and useful, she must not . . . want, individually, the protection of civil laws; she must not be dependent on her husband's bounty for her subsistence during his life

or support after his death—for how can a being be generous who has nothing of its own? Or virtuous, who is not free? . . .

Business of various kinds they might likewise pursue, if they were educated in a more orderly manner. . . . Women would not then marry for a support, as men accept of places under government, and neglect the implied duties; nor would an attempt to earn their own subsistence . . . sink them almost to the level of those poor abandoned creatures who live by prostitution.

Source: Moira Ferguson, ed., *First Feminists: British Women Writers, 1578–1799* (Bloomington: Indiana University Press, 1985), pp. 423–429.

 For additional information on this topic, go to http://college.hmco.com.

---

aration of family life from the public world of free, contractual relationships. "If absolute authority be not necessary in a state," she reasoned, "how comes it to be so in a family?" Most such thinkers advocated increased education for women, if only to make them more fit to raise enlightened children. By 1800 the most radical thinkers were advocating full citizenship rights for women and equal rights to property, along with enhanced education.

The best-known proponent of those views was an Englishwoman, Mary Wollstonecraft (1759–1797), who authored *A Vindication of the Rights of Woman* (1792). She assumed that most elite women would devote themselves to domestic duties, but she argued that without the responsibilities of citizenship, the leavening of education, and economic independence, women could be nei-

ther fully formed individuals nor worthy of their duties. Working women, she concluded, needed these rights simply to survive. (See the box "Reading Sources: An Enlightenment Thinker Argues for the Equality of Women.")

A more limited view of women's capacities was one element in the influential work of Jean-Jacques Rousseau° (1712–1778). Like Locke, Rousseau could conceive of the free individual only as male, and he grounded his scorn of the old order and his novel political ideas in an arbitrary division of gender roles. Rousseau's view of women was linked to a critique of the artificiality of elite, cosmopolitan society in which Enlightenment thought was then flourishing, and in which aristocratic women

Rousseau (roo-SO)

❧ READING SOURCES

Rousseau Discusses the Benefits of Submitting to the General Will

In this excerpt from his Social Contract, *Rousseau describes the relationship of individuals to the general will. Notice the wider-ranging benefits Rousseau believes men will enjoy in society as he envisions it; Rousseau is clearly interested in intellectual, moral, and emotional well-being.*

I assume that men reach a point where the obstacles to their preservation in a state of nature prove greater than the strength that each man has to preserve himself in that state. Beyond this point, the primitive condition cannot endure, for then the human race will perish if it does not change its mode of existence. . . .

"How to find a form of association which will defend the person and goods of each member with the collective force of all, and under which each individual, while uniting himself with the others, obeys no one but himself, and remains as free as before." This is the fundamental problem to which the social contract holds the solution. . . .

The passing from the state of nature to the civil society produces a remarkable change in man; it puts justice as a rule of conduct in the place of instinct, and gives his actions the moral quality they previously lacked. . . . And although in civil society man surrenders some of the advantages that belong to the state of nature, he gains in return far greater ones; his faculties are so exercised and developed, his mind is so enlarged, his sentiments so ennobled, and his whole spirit so elevated that . . . he should constantly bless the happy hour that lifted him for ever from the state of nature and from a stupid, limited animal made a creature of intelligence and a man. . . .

For every individual as a man may have a private will contrary to, or different from, the general will that he has as a citizen. His private interest may speak with a very different voice from that of the public interest; his absolute and naturally independent existence may make him regard what he owes to the common cause as a gratuitous contribution, the loss of which would be less painful for others than the payment is onerous for him; and fancying that the artificial person which constitutes the state is a mere fictitious entity (since it is not a man), he might seek to enjoy the rights of a citizen without doing the duties of a subject. The growth of this kind of injustice would bring about the ruin of the body politic.

Hence, in order that the social pact shall not be an empty formula, it is tacitly implied in that commitment—which alone can give force to all others—that whoever refuses to obey the general will shall be constrained to do so by the whole body, which means nothing other than that he shall be forced to be free; for this is the necessary condition which, by giving each citizen to the nation, secures him against all personal dependence, it is the condition which shapes both the design and the working of the political machine, and which alone bestows justice on civil contracts—without it, such contracts would be absurd, tyrannical and liable to the grossest abuse.

Source: Jean-Jacques Rousseau, *The Social Contract*, trans. Maurice Cranston (London: Penguin Books, 1968), pp. 59–60, 63–65.

were fully involved. Rousseau believed in the educability of men but was as concerned with issues of character and emotional life as with cognitive knowledge. Society—particularly the artificial courtly society—was corrupting, he believed. The true citizen had to cultivate virtue and sensibility, not manners, taste, or refinement.

Rousseau designated women as guarantors of the "natural" virtues of children and as nurturers of the emotional life and character of men—but not as fully formed beings in their own right.

Rousseau's emphasis on the education and virtue of citizens was the underpinning of his larger political vision, set forth in *Du Contrat social* (*The Social Contract,* 1762). He imagined an egalitarian republic—possible particularly in small states such as his native Geneva—in which men would consent to be governed because the government would determine and act in accordance with the "general will" of the citizens. The "general will" was not majority opinion but rather what each citizen *would* want if he were fully informed and were acting in accordance with his highest nature. The "general will" became apparent whenever the citizens met as a body and made collective decisions, and it could be imposed on all inhabitants. (See the box "Reading Sources: Rousseau Discusses the Benefits of Submitting to the General Will.") This was a breathtaking vision of direct democracy—but one with ominous possibilities, for Rousseau rejected the institutional checks on state authority proposed by Locke and Montesquieu.

Rousseau's emphasis on private emotional life anticipated the romanticism of the early nineteenth century. It also reflected Rousseau's own experience as the son of a humble family, always sensing himself an outcast in the brilliant world of Parisian salons. He had a love-hate relationship with this life, remaining attached to several aristocratic women patrons even as he decried their influence. His own personal life did not match his prescriptions for others. He completely neglected to give his four children the nurture and education that he argued were vital; indeed, he abandoned them all to a foundling home. He was nevertheless influential as a critic of an elite society still dominated by status, patronage, and privilege. Rousseau's work reflects to an extreme degree the tensions in Enlightenment thought generally: it was part of elite culture as well as its principal critic.

■ The Growth of Public Opinion

It is impossible to appreciate the significance of the Enlightenment without understanding the degree to which it was a part of public life. Most of the philosophes were of modest origin. They influenced the privileged elite of their day because of the social and political environment in which their ideas were elaborated. Indeed, the clearest distinguishing feature of the Enlightenment may be the creation of an informed body of public opinion that stood apart from court society.

Increased literacy and access to books and other printed materials are an important part of the story. Perhaps more important, the kinds of reading that people favored began to change. We know from inventories made of people's belongings at the time of their deaths (required for inheritance laws) that books in the homes of ordinary people were no longer just traditional works such as devotional literature. Ordinary people now read secular and contemporary philosophical works. As the availability of such works increased, reading itself evolved from a reverential encounter with old ideas to a critical encounter with new ideas. Solitary reading for reflection and pleasure became more widespread.

Habits of reading and responding to written material changed not only because of these increased opportunities to read but also because of changes in the social environment. In the eighteenth century, forerunners of the modern lending libraries made their debut. In Paris, for a fee, one could join a *salle de lecture* (literally, a "reading room") where the latest works were available to any member. Booksellers, whose numbers increased dramatically, found ways to meet readers' demands for inexpensive access to reading matter. One might pay for the right to read a book in the bookshop itself. In short, new venues encouraged people to see themselves not just as readers but as members of a reading public.

Among the most famous and most important of these venues were the Parisian salons, regular gatherings in private homes, where Voltaire and others read their works in progress aloud and discussed them. Several Parisian women—mostly wealthy, but of modest social status—invited courtiers, bureaucrats, and intellectuals to meet in their homes at regular times each week. The *salonnières*° (salon leaders) themselves read widely in order to facilitate the exchange of ideas among their guests. This mediating function was crucial to the success of the salons. Manners and polite conversation had been a defining feature of aristocratic life since the seventeenth century, but they had largely been means of displaying status and safeguarding honor. The leadership of the salonnières and the protected environment they provided away from court life enabled a further evolution of "polite society" to occur: anyone with appropriate manners could participate in conversation as an equal. The assumption of equality, in turn, enabled conversation to turn away from maintaining the status quo to questioning it.

The influence of salons was extended by the wide correspondence networks the salonnières maintained. Perhaps the most famous salonnière in her day, Marie-Thérèse Geoffrin° (1699–1777) corresponded with Catherine the Great, the reform-minded empress of Russia, as well as with philosophes outside Paris and with interested would-be members of her circle. The ambassador of Naples regularly attended her salon while in Paris and exchanged weekly letters with her when home in Italy. He

salonnières (sal-on-YAIR) **Geoffrin** (zhoh-FRAN)

The Growth of the Book Trade Book ownership dramatically increased in the eighteenth century, and a wide range of secular works—from racy novelettes to philosophical tracts—was available in print. In this rendering of a bookshop, shipments of books have arrived from around Europe. Notice the artist's optimism in the great variety of persons, from the peasant with a scythe to a white-robed cleric, who are drawn to the shop by "Minerva" (the Roman goddess of wisdom). *(Musée des Beaux-Arts de Dijon)*

reflected on the importance of salon leaders such as Geoffrin when he wrote from Naples lamenting, "[our gatherings here] are getting farther away from the character and tone of those of France, despite all [our] efforts. . . . There is no way to make Naples resemble Paris unless we find a woman to guide us, organize us, *Geoffrinise* us."[1]

Various clubs, local academies, and learned and secret societies, such as Masonic lodges, copied some features of the salons of Paris. Hardly any municipality was without a private society that functioned both as a forum for political and philosophical discussion and as an elite social club. Here mingled doctors, lawyers, local officials—some of whom enjoyed the fruits of the political system in offices and patronage. In Scotland universities were flourishing centers of Enlightenment thought, but political clubs in Glasgow and Edinburgh enriched debate and the development of ideas.

Ideas circulated beyond the membership of the multitude of clubs by means of print. Newsletters reporting the goings-on at salons in Paris were produced by some participants. Regularly published periodicals in Great Britain, France, and Italy also served as important means for the dissemination of enlightened opinion in the form of reviews, essays, and published correspondence. Some of these journals had been in existence since the second half of the seventeenth century, when they had begun as a means to circulate the new scientific work. Now, subscribers included Americans anxious to keep up with intellectual life in Europe. Europeans who could not afford the annual subscriptions could peruse the journals in the newly opened reading rooms and libraries. In addition to newsletters and journals, newspapers, which were regularly published even in small cities throughout western and central Europe, circulated ideas. (See the feature "Information Technology: Newspapers.")

In all these arenas Enlightenment ideas encouraged, and lended legitimacy to, a type of far-reaching political debate that had never before existed, except possibly in England during the seventeenth century. The greatest impact of the Enlightenment, particularly in France, was not

The Cult of Sensibility in Art   This painting, *The Swing,* by the Frenchman Fragonard, depicts a moment of playful and sensuous intimacy. This style of painting was an elaboration of baroque style known as *rococo*. It began to be considered too excessive and lighthearted and was replaced by the more serious neoclassical style as the century wore on.   *(Wallace Collection, London/Art Resource, NY)*

the creation of any specific program for political or social change. Rather its supreme legacy was an informed body of public opinion that could generate change.

■ Art in the Age of Reason

The Enlightenment reverberated throughout all aspects of cultural life. Just as the market for books and the reading public expanded, so did the audience for works of art in the growing leisured urban circles of Paris and other great cities. The modern cultured public—a public of concert goers and art gallery enthusiasts—began to make its first appearance and constituted another arena in which public opinion was shaped. The brilliant and sophisticated courts around Europe continued to sponsor composers, musicians, and painters by providing both patronage and audiences. Yet some performances of concerts and operas began to take place in theaters and halls outside the courts in venues more accessible to the public.

Beginning in 1737 one section of the Louvre° palace in Paris was devoted annually to public exhibitions of painting and sculpture (though by royally sponsored and

approved artists). In both France and Britain, public discussion of art began to take place in published reviews and criticisms: the role of art critic was born. Works of art were also sold by public means, such as auctions. As works became more available, demand grew and production increased.

In subject matter and style these various art forms exhibited greater variety than works in preceding centuries had shown. We can nevertheless discern certain patterns and tendencies in both the content and the form of eighteenth-century European art. Late baroque painters contributed to an exploration of private life and emotion sometimes called the "cult of sensibility." Frequently, they depicted private scenes of upper-class life, especially moments of intimate conversation or flirtation.

The cult of sensibility was fostered by literature as well. The private life of emotion was nurtured by increased literacy, greater access to books, and the need to retreat from the elaborate artifice of court life. The novel became an increasingly important genre as a means of exploring social problems and human relationships. In English literature the novels of Samuel Richardson (1689–1761)—*Pamela* (1740) and *Clarissa* (1747–1748)— explored personal psychology and passion. Other novelists,

---

Louvre (LOO-vruh)

Newspapers

The invention of printing in the fifteenth century greatly expanded the kinds of information available to Europeans. In addition to books, thousands of pamphlets and single-page "reports" of startling news appeared, such as the 1513 "Trew Encountre" describing a battle between the English and Scots, and detailing the heroic deeds of the combatants. Along with these other short, occasional publications, the newspaper was born in the seventeenth century. By the eighteenth century newspapers had become firmly established as a means of spreading news of European and world affairs, as well as of local concerns, within European society. Newspapers represented an application of printing technology that, under new conditions and for new purposes, constituted a real innovation in communication—and one with long-term consequences.

News had commercial as well as entertainment value. Even before printing technology had taken hold, the agents of great merchant families dispatched detailed news of products and harvests, as well as of timely political issues. In the sixteenth century, the Venetian government charged citizens a small fee to hear official news of battles against its great rival, the Turks. (A common name for newspaper—gazette—comes from *gazetta,* the coin Venetians used to pay for their news.) One of the first true newspapers was the Dutch paper *Nieuwe Tidjingen.* It began publication early in the seventeenth century about the same time the Dutch East India Company was formed; the same ships that brought goods back from abroad brought news of the world, too.

Dutch publishers had an advantage over many other publishers around Europe since the Netherlands' highly decentralized political system made its censorship laws very difficult to enforce. Throughout Europe in the seventeenth century governments began recognizing the revolutionary potential of the free press and began requiring licenses of newspapers—to control who was able to publish news. Another tactic, in France and elsewhere on the Continent from the 1630s onward, was for governments to sponsor official newspapers. These state publications met the increasing demand for news but always supported the governments' views of the events of the day.

By the eighteenth century new conditions allowed newspapers to flourish as never before. First, demand for news increased as Europe's commercial and political interests spread around the globe. Merchants in London, Liverpool, or Glasgow, for example, depended on early news of Caribbean harvests and gains and losses in colonial wars. Europe's growing commercial strength also increased distribution networks for newspapers; there were more and better roads, and more carters who could deliver newspapers in cities and convey them to outlying towns. Newspaper publishers made use of the many new sites where the public expected to read; newspapers were delivered to cafés and sold or delivered by booksellers.

Second, many European states had established effective postal systems by the eighteenth century. It was through the mails that readers outside major cities and their environs—and virtually all readers in areas where press censorship was firmly in control—received their newspapers. One of the most successful newspapers in Europe was a French-language paper (one of the many known as "la Gazette") published in Leiden in the Netherlands, which boasted a wide readership in France and among elites throughout Europe. Censorship thus had a dwindling effect on well-educated readers anywhere in Europe.

Finally, press censorship faltered in one of the most important markets for news—England—at the turn of the eighteenth century. After the Glorious Revolution, debates raged about whether Parliament or the Crown had the right to control the press, and in the confusion the press flourished. The emergence of political parties further hampered control of the press because political decisions in Parliament now always involved compromise and many members believed an active press was useful to that process. British control of the press was reduced to a tax (one of the Stamp Acts so hated by American colonists) that drove some papers out of business.

such as Daniel Defoe in *Robinson Crusoe* (1717), used realism for purposes of social commentary.

Rousseau followed Richardson's lead in structuring his own novels, *La Nouvelle Héloïse* (1761) and *Emile* (1762). The cult of sensibility was not mere entertainment; it also carried the political and philosophical message that honest emotion was a "natural" virtue and that courtly manners, by contrast, were irrational and degrading. The enormous popularity of Rousseau's novels, for example, came from the fact that their intense emotional appeal was simultaneously felt to be uplifting.

A revival of classical subjects and styles after the middle of the century evoked what were thought to be the pure and timeless values of classical heroes. This re-

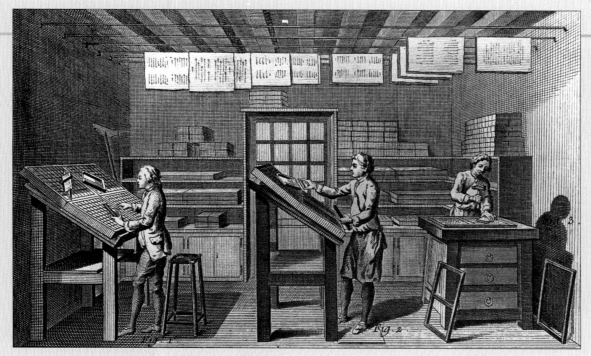

Producing a Newspaper This illustration of the process of typesetting by hand in a newspaper printshop appears in Diderot's *Encyclopedia*. Notice the finished printed sheets drying above the workers' heads. *(Division of Rare & Manuscript Collections/Cornell University Library)*

Eighteenth-century newspapers were modest products, by our standards. Many were published only once or twice a week instead of every day, in editions of only a few thousand copies. Each newspaper was generally only four pages long. Illustrations were rare, and headlines had not yet been invented. Hand-operated wooden presses were used to print the papers, just as they had been used to print pamphlets and books since the invention of printing in the fifteenth century.

Yet these newspapers had a dramatic impact on their reading public. Regular production of newspapers (especially of many competing newspapers) meant that news was presented to the public at regular intervals and in manageable amounts. Even strange and threatening news from around the world became increasingly easy for readers to absorb and interpret. The more sophisticated reader of the eighteenth century would respond to news more skeptically than had readers of the harrowing "Trew Encountre."

Newspaper readers also felt themselves part of the public life about which they were reading. This was true partly because newspapers, available in public reading rooms and in cafés, were one kind of reading that occupied an increasingly self-aware and literate audience. Newspapers were also uniquely responsive to their readers, however. They began to carry advertisements, which both produced revenue for papers and widened the readers' exposure to their own communities. Even more important was the inauguration of letters to the editor. Newspapers themselves thus became venues for the often rapid exchange of news and opinions. They were a vital tool of Europe's "enlightened" citizenries.

vival revealed the influence of Enlightenment thought because the artists assumed the educability of their audience by means of example. Classical revival architecture illustrated a belief in order, symmetry, and proportion. Americans are familiar with its evocations because it has been the architecture of their republic, but even churches were built in this style in eighteenth-century Europe. The classical movement in music reflected both the cult of sensibility and the classicizing styles in the visual arts. Embodied in the works of Austrians Franz Josef Haydn (1732–1809) and Wolfgang Amadeus Mozart (1756–1791), this movement saw the clarification of musical structures, such as the modern sonata and symphony, and enabled melody to take center stage.

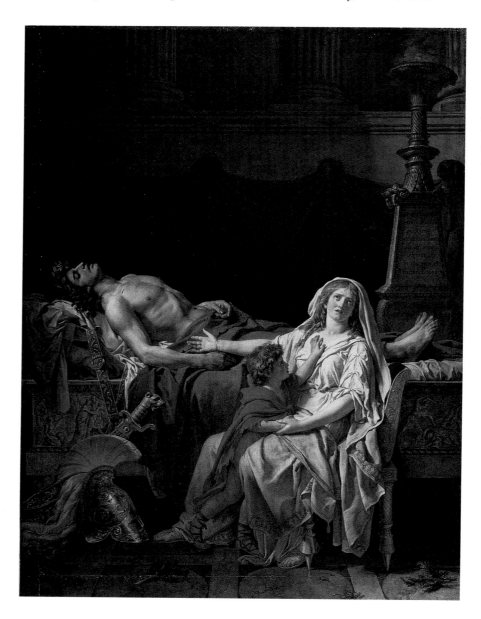

The Moralizing Message of Neoclassical Art The French painter Jacques-Louis David portrays the mourning of Trojan hero Hector by his wife, Andromache. David was well known for depicting his subjects with simple gestures—such as the extended arm of Andromache here—that were intended to portray honest and sincere emotion. *(Private Collection/The Stapleton Collection/Bridgeman Art Library)*

Another trend in art and literature was a fascination with nature and with the seemingly "natural" in human culture—less "developed" or more historically distant societies. One of the most popular printed works in the middle of the century was the alleged translation of the poems of Ossian°, a third-century Scots Highland poet. Early English, German, Norse, and other folktales were also "discovered" (in some cases invented) and published, some in several editions during the century. Folk life, other cultures, and untamed nature itself thus be-

gan to be celebrated at the very time they were being more definitively conquered. (See the feature "Weighing the Evidence: Gardens" on pages 638–639.) Ossian, for example, was celebrated just as the Scottish Highlands were being punished and pacified by the English after the clans' support for a rival claimant to the English throne. Once purged of any threat, the exotic image of another culture (even the folk culture of one's own society) could be a spur to the imagination. Thus the remote became romantic, offering a sense of distance from which to measure one's own sophistication and superiority.

Ossian (AHSH-un)

EUROPEAN STATES IN THE AGE OF ENLIGHTENMENT

MINDFUL of the lessons to be learned from the civil war in England and the achievements of Louis XIV, European rulers in the eighteenth century continued their efforts to govern with greater effectiveness. Some, like the rulers of Prussia and Russia, were encouraged in their efforts by Enlightenment ideas that stressed the need for reforms in law, economy, and government. In the main they, like Voltaire, believed that monarchs could be agents for change. In Austria significant reforms, including the abolition of serfdom, were enacted. The changes were uneven, however, and at times owed as much to traditional efforts at better government as to enlightened persuasion.

In all cases, rulers' efforts to govern more effectively meant continual readjustments in relationships with traditional elites. Whether elites had formal roles in the governing process by means of established institutions such as the English Parliament, royal governments everywhere still depended on their participation. However limited their "enlightened" policies, monarchs were changing their views of themselves and their public images from diligent but self-aggrandizing absolutist to servant of the state. In this way, monarchs actually undermined their dynastic claims to rule by re-founding their regimes on a utilitarian basis. The state was increasingly seen as separate from the ruler, with dramatic consequences for the future.

■ France During the Enlightenment

It is one of the seeming paradoxes of the era of the Enlightenment that critical thought about society and politics flourished in France, an autocratic state. Yet France was blessed with a well-educated elite, a tradition of scientific inquiry, and a legacy of cultured court life that, since the early days of Louis XIV, had become the model for all Europe (see pages 543–545). French was the international intellectual language, and France was the most fertile center of cultural life. Both Adam Smith and David Hume, for example, spent portions of their careers in Paris and were welcomed into Parisian salons. In fact, the French capital was an environment that encouraged debate and dissent precisely because of the juxtaposition of the new intellectual climate with the difficulties the French state was facing and the institutional rigidities of its political system. In France, access to power was wholly through patronage and privilege, a system that excluded many talented and productive members of the elite.

The French state continued to embody fundamental contradictions. As under Louis XIV, the Crown sponsored scientific research, subsidized commerce and exploration, and tried to rationalize the royal administration. Royal administrators tried to chip away at the privileges, accrued since the Middle Ages, that hampered effective government—such as the exemption most nobles enjoyed from taxation. However, the Crown also continued to claim the right to govern autocratically, and the king was supported both ideologically and institutionally by the Catholic Church. A merchant in the bustling port of Bordeaux might be glad of the royal navy's protection of the colonies, and of the Crown's efforts to build better roads for the movement of goods within France. However, with his fellow Masons, he would fume when church officials publicly burned the works of Rousseau and be continually frustrated over his exclusion from any formal role in the political process.

The problems facing the French government were made worse by two circumstances: first, the strength of the privileged elites' defense of the old order, and second, mounting state debt from foreign wars that made fiscal reform increasingly urgent. Louis XIV was followed on the throne by his 5-year-old great-grandson, Louis XV (r. 1715–1774). During the regency early in his reign, the supreme law courts, the parlements, reclaimed the right of remonstrance—that is, the right to object to royal edicts and thus to exercise some control over the enactment of law. Throughout Louis XV's reign, his administration often locked horns with the parlements, particularly as royal ministers tried various expedients to cope with financial crises.

The power of the parlements came not only from their routine role in government but also from the fact that parlementaires were all legally noble and owned their offices just as a great nobleman owned his country estate. In addition, the parlements were the only institutions that could legitimately check royal power. As such, the parlements were often supported in their opposition to royal policies by the weight of public opinion. On the one hand, enlightened opinion believed in the rationality of doing away with privileges such as the ownership of offices. On the other hand, the role of consultative bodies and the separation of powers touted by Montesquieu, himself a parlementaire, were much prized. And even our Bordeaux merchant, who had little in common with privileged officeholders, might nevertheless see the parlementaires' resistance as his best protection from royal tyranny. The parlementaires, however, usually used their power for protecting the status quo.

Further hampering reform efforts was the character of the king himself. Louis XV displayed none of the kingly qualities of his great-grandfather. He was neither pleasant nor affable, and he was lazy. By the end of his reign, he was roundly despised. He did not give the "rationality" of royal government a good name. By the late 1760s, the weight of government debt from foreign wars finally forced the king into action. He threw his support behind the reforming schemes of his chancellor, Nicolas de Maupeou°, who dissolved the parlements early in 1771 and created new law courts whose judges would not enjoy independent power.

The Crown lost control of reform when Louis died soon after, in 1774. His 20-year-old grandson, Louis XVI, well-meaning but insecure, allowed the complete restoration of the parlements. Further reform efforts, sponsored by the king and several talented ministers, came to naught because of parlementary opposition. Not surprisingly, from about the middle of the century, there had been calls to revive the moribund Estates General, the representative assembly last convened in 1614, as well as for the establishment of new councils—local, decentralized representative assemblies. By the time an Estates General was finally called in the wake of further financial problems in 1788, the enlightened elites' habit of carrying on political analysis and criticism outside the actual corridors of power, and their accumulated mistrust of the Crown, had given rise to a volatile situation.

■ Monarchy and Constitutional Government in Great Britain

After the deaths of William (d. 1702) and Mary (d. 1694), the British crown passed to Mary's sister, Anne (r. 1702–1714), and then to a collateral line descended from Elizabeth Stuart (d. 1662), sister of the beheaded Charles I. Elizabeth had married Frederick, elector of the Palatinate (and had reigned with him briefly in Bohemia at the outset of the Thirty Years' War; see page 525), and her descendants were Germans, now electors of Hanover. The new British sovereign in 1714, George I (r. 1714–1727), was both a foreigner and a man of mediocre abilities. Moreover, his claim to the throne was immediately contested by Catholic descendants of James II, who attempted to depose him in 1715 and later his son, George II (r. 1727–1760), in 1745.

The 1745 attempt to depose the Hanoverian kings was more nearly successful. The son of the Stuart claimant to the throne, Charles (known in legend as Bonnie Prince Charlie), landed on the west coast of Scotland, with French assistance, and marched south into England. Most of the British army, and George II himself, was on the Continent, fighting in the War of the Austrian Succession (see page 626). Scotland had been formally united with England in 1707 (hence the term *Great Britain* after that time), and Charles found some support among Scots dissatisfied with the economic and political results of that union.

But the vast majority of Britons did not want the civil war that Charles's challenge inevitably meant, especially on behalf of a Catholic pretender who relied on support from Britain's great rival, France. Charles's army, made up mostly of poor Highland clansmen, was destroyed at the Battle of Culloden° in April 1746 by regular army units returned from abroad. Charles fled back to France, and the British government used the failed uprising as justification for the brutal and forceful integration of the still-remote Highlands into the British state.

Traditional practices, from wearing tartans to playing bagpipes, were forbidden. Control of land was redistributed to break the social and economic bonds of clan society. Thousands of Highlanders died at the battle itself, in prisons or deportation ships, or by deliberate extermination at the hands of British troops after the battle.

Despite this serious challenge to the new dynasty and the harsh response it occasioned, the British state, overall, enjoyed a period of relative stability as well as innovation in the eighteenth century. The events of the seventeenth century had reaffirmed both the need for a strong monarchy and the role of Parliament in defending elite interests. The power of Parliament had recently been reinforced by the Act of Settlement, by which the Protestant heir to Queen Anne had been chosen in 1701. By excluding the Catholic Stuarts from the throne and establishing the line of succession, this document reasserted that Parliament determined the legitimacy of the monarchy. In addition, the act claimed greater parliamentary authority over foreign and domestic policy in the wake of the bellicose William's rule (see page 563).

Noteworthy in the eighteenth century were the ways in which cooperation evolved between monarchy and Parliament as Parliament became a more sophisticated and secure institution. Political parties—that is, distinct groups within the elite favoring certain foreign and domestic policies—came into existence. Two groups, the Whigs and the Tories, had begun to form during the

---

Maupeou (mo-POO)

Culloden (cull-AH-dun)

reign of Charles II (d. 1685). The Whigs (named derisively by their opponents with a Scottish term for horse thieves) had resisted Charles's pro-French policies and his efforts to tolerate Catholicism and had wholly opposed his brother and successor, James II. Initially, the Whigs favored an aggressive foreign policy against continental opponents, particularly France. The Tories (whose name was also a taunt, referring to Irish cattle rustlers) tended to be staunch Anglicans uninterested in Protestant anti-Catholic agitation. They leaned toward a conservative view of their own role, favoring isolationism in foreign affairs and deference toward monarchical authority. Whigs generally represented the interests of the great aristocrats or wealthy merchants or gentry. Tories more often represented the interests of provincial gentry and the traditional concerns of landholding and local administration.

The Whigs were the dominant influence in government through most of the century to 1770. William and Mary as well as Queen Anne favored Whig religious and foreign policy interests. The loyalty of many Tories was called into question by their support for a Stuart, not Hanoverian, succession at Anne's death in 1714. The long Whig dominance of government was also ensured by the talents of Robert Walpole, a Member of Parliament who functioned virtually as a prime minister from 1722 to 1742.

Walpole (1676–1745) was from a minor gentry family and was brought into government in 1714 with other Whig ministers in George I's new regime. An extremely talented politician, he took advantage of the mistakes of other ministers over the years and, in 1722, became both the first lord of the treasury and chancellor of the exchequer. No post or title of "prime minister" yet existed, but the great contribution of Walpole's tenure was to create that office in fact, if not officially. He chose to maintain peace abroad when and where he could and thus presided over a period of recovery and relative prosperity that enhanced the stability of government.

Initially, Walpole was helped in his role as go-between for king and Parliament by George I's own limitations. The king rarely attended meetings of his own council of ministers and, in any case, was hampered by his limited command of English. Gradually, the Privy Council of the king became something resembling a modern cabinet dominated by a prime minister. By the end of the century the notions of "loyal opposition" to the Crown within Parliament and parliamentary responsibility for policy had taken root.

In some respects, the maturation of political life in Parliament resembled the lively political debates in the

Political Satire in England   This gruesome image, showing England being disemboweled by members of the government, criticizes the government's acceptance of a treaty with France. Satirical images such as this one were increasingly part of the lively and more open political life in eighteenth-century England.   *(Courtesy of the Trustees of the British Museum)*

salons of Paris. In both cases, political life was being legitimized on a new basis. In England, however, that legitimation was enshrined in a legislative institution, which made it especially effective and resilient.

Parliament was not yet in any sense representative of the British population, however. Because of strict property qualifications, only about 200,000 adult men could vote. In addition, representation was very uneven, heavily favoring traditional landed wealth. Some constituencies with only a few dozen voters sent members to Parliament. Many of these "pocket boroughs" were under the control of (in the pockets of) powerful local families who could intimidate the local electorate, particularly in the absence of secret ballots.

Movements for reform of representation in Parliament began in the late 1760s as professionals, such as doctors and lawyers, with movable (as opposed to landed) property and merchants in booming but underrepresented cities began to demand the vote. As the burden of taxation grew—the result of the recently concluded Seven Years' War (discussed below)—these groups felt increasingly deprived of representation. Indeed, many felt kinship and sympathy with the American colonists who opposed increased taxation by the British government on these same grounds and revolted in 1775.

However, the reform movement faltered over the issue of religion. In 1780 a tentative effort by Parliament to extend some civil rights to British Catholics provoked rioting in London (known as the Gordon Riots, after one of the leaders). The riots lasted for eight days and claimed three hundred lives. Pressure for parliamentary reform had been building as Britain met with reversals in its war against the American rebels, but this specter of a popular movement out of control temporarily ended the drive for reform by disenfranchised elites.

■ "Enlightened" Monarchy

Arbitrary monarchical power might seem antithetical to Enlightenment thought. After all, the Enlightenment stressed the reasonableness of human beings and their capacity to discern and act in accord with natural law. Yet monarchy seemed an ideal instrument of reform to Voltaire and to many of his contemporaries. The work of curtailing the influence of the church, reforming legal codes, and eliminating barriers to economic activity might be done more efficiently by a powerful monarch than by other available means. Historians have labeled a number of rulers of this era "enlightened despots" because of the arbitrary nature of their power and the enlightened or reformist uses to which they put it.

"Enlightened despotism" aptly describes certain developments in the Scandinavian kingdoms in the late eighteenth century. In Denmark the Crown had governed without significant challenge from the landholding nobility since the mid-seventeenth century. The nobility, however, like its counterparts in eastern Europe, had guaranteed its supremacy by means of ironclad domination of the peasantry. In 1784 a reform-minded group of nobles, led by the young crown prince Frederick (governing on behalf of his mentally ill father), began to apply Enlightenment remedies to the kingdom's economic problems. The reformers encouraged freer trade and sought, above all, to improve agriculture by elevating the status of the peasantry. With improved legal status and

with land reform, which enabled some peasants to own the land they worked for the first time, agricultural productivity in Denmark rose dramatically. These reforms constitute some of the clearest achievements of any of the "enlightened" rulers.

In Sweden, in 1772, Gustav III (r. 1771–1796) staged a coup with army support that overturned the dominance of the Swedish parliament, the Diet. In contrast to Denmark, Sweden had a relatively unbroken tradition of noble involvement in government, stemming in part from its marginal economy and the consequent interest of the nobility in participation in the Crown's aggressive foreign policy. Since Sweden's eclipse as a major power after the Great Northern War (see page 560), factions of the Diet, not unlike the rudimentary political parties in Great Britain, had fought over the reins of government. After reasserting his control, Gustav III began an ambitious program of reform of the government. Bureaucrats more loyal to parliamentary patrons than to the Crown were replaced; restrictions on trade in grain and other economic controls were liberalized; the legal system was rationalized; the death penalty was strictly limited; and legal torture was abolished.

Despite his abilities, Gustav III suffered the consequences of the contradictory position of advancing reform by autocratic means in a kingdom with a strong tradition of representative government. Gustav eventually tried to deflect the criticisms of the nobility by reviving grandiose—but completely untenable—schemes for the reconquest of Baltic territory. However, in 1796 he was mortally wounded by an assassin hired by disgruntled nobles.

Another claimant to the title "enlightened despot" was Frederick II of Prussia (r. 1740–1786), "the Great." Much of the time, Frederick resided in his imperial electorate of Brandenburg, near its capital, Berlin. His scattered states, which he extended by seizing new lands, are referred to as Prussia rather than as Brandenburg-Prussia because members of his family were now kings of Prussia thanks to their ambitions and the weakness of the Polish state, of which Prussia had once been a dependent duchy. In many ways, the Prussian state *was* its military victories, for Frederick's bold moves and the policies of his father, grandfather, and great-grandfather committed the state's resources to a military presence of dramatic proportions. Prussia was on the European stage at all only because of that driving commitment.

The institutions that constituted the state and linked the various provinces under one administration were dominated by the needs of the military. Frederick II's father, Frederick William (r. 1713–1740), had added an efficient provincial recruiting system to the state's central institutions, which he also further consolidated. But in many other respects, the Prussian state was in its infancy. There was no tradition of political participation—even by elites—and little chance of cultivating any. Nor was there any political or social room for maneuver at the lower part of the social scale. The rulers of Prussia had long ago acceded to the aristocracy's demand for tighter control over peasant labor on their own lands in return for their support of the monarchy. The rulers relied on nobles for local administration and army commands. Thus, the kinds of social, judicial, or political reforms that Frederick could hope to carry out without undermining his own power were starkly limited.

Frederick tried to modernize agricultural methods and simultaneously to improve the condition of peasants, but he met stiff resistance from noble landholders. He did succeed in abolishing serfdom in some regions. He tried to stimulate the economy by sponsoring state industries and trading monopolies, but too few resources and too little initiative from the tightly controlled merchant communities stymied his plans. Simplifying and codifying the inherited jumble of local laws was a goal of every ruler. A law code published in 1794, after Frederick's death, was partly the product of his efforts.

Frederick's views of the role of Enlightenment thought reflect the limitations of his situation. One doesn't have to lead a frontal assault on prejudices consecrated by time, he thought; instead, one must be tolerant of superstition because it will always have a hold on the masses. Perhaps his most distinctive "enlightened" characteristic was the seriousness with which he took his task as ruler. He was energetic and disciplined to a fault. In his book *Anti-Machiavel* (1741) he argued that a ruler has a moral obligation to work for the betterment of the state. He styled himself as the "first servant" or steward of the state. However superficial this claim may appear, Frederick compares favorably with Louis XV of France who, having a far more wealthy and flexible society to work with, did much less.

■ Enlightenment and Tradition: The Case of Austria

One of the most effective rulers of the eighteenth century was the Habsburg ruler Maria Theresa of Austria (r. 1740–1780). A devout Catholic, she was guided more by traditional concerns for effective rule and compassion for her subjects than by Enlightenment ideas. After surviving the near dismemberment of Austrian territories in the War of the Austrian Succession (see page 626), she embarked on an energetic program of reform to remedy the weaknesses in the state that the war had revealed. "Austria," it must be remembered, is a term of convenience; the state was a very medieval-looking hodgepodge that included present-day Austria, the kingdoms of Bohemia and Hungary, the Austrian Netherlands, and lands in northern Italy. In addition, since the sixteenth century, a male member of the Habsburg family had almost always been elected emperor of the Holy Roman Empire.

Maria Theresa streamlined and centralized administration, finances, and defense, particularly in Bohemia and Austria, where she was able to exercise her authority relatively unchecked, compared with her other domains. Above all, she reformed the assessment and collection of taxes to tap the wealth of her subjects more effectively and thus better defend all her domains. She improved her subjects' access to justice and limited the exploitation of serfs by landlords. She made primary schooling universal and compulsory, in order better to train peasants for the army. Although the policy was far from fully implemented at the time of her death (only about half of Austrian children were in school, and far fewer in Hungary and elsewhere), hers was the first European state with so ambitious an education policy. Maria Theresa accomplished all of this without being particularly "enlightened" personally. For example, she had a traditional fear of freedom of the press and cherished orthodoxy in religious matters.

Maria Theresa's policies were implemented by a group of ministers, bureaucrats, and officers who shared her concern for effective government and defense, and who were well-versed in "enlightened" ideas for reform. The diverse character of the Habsburg lands meant that some members of the governing elite came from the Netherlands and from Italy, where sympathy for the Enlightenment was well rooted by comparison with the relatively poorer and more rural society of the Austrian hinterland. Moreover, the language of the Habsburg court was French (Maria Theresa spoke it fluently), thus no amount of local censorship—which, in any case, Maria Theresa relaxed—could prevent the governing class from reading and absorbing Enlightenment philosophy in its original language.

Maria Theresa was followed on the throne by her two sons Joseph II (r. 1780–1790) and Leopold II (r. 1790–1792). Each son counted himself a follower of the Enlightenment and each, as was the family custom, served a period of "apprenticeship" governing Habsburg territories where he could attempt to implement reform. After his mother's death, Joseph II carried out a variety of bold initiatives that she had not attempted, including freedom of the press, significant freedom of religion, and the abolition of serfdom in Habsburg lands. During his ten-year reign, the political climate in Vienna began to resemble that in Paris, London, and other capitals where political life was no longer confined to the royal court.

Like Frederick the Great, Joseph regarded himself as a servant of the state. Like Frederick, his reform program was limited by the economic and social rigidities of the society he ruled: Austria had but a small middle class to insist on reform, and Joseph could not directly assault the privileges of great landholders, on whose wealth the state depended. In addition, Joseph was by temperament an inflexible autocrat, whose methods antagonized many of these powerful subjects. Joseph's policies provoked simmering opposition, even open revolt, and some of his reforms were repealed even before his death. His more able brother, Leopold, had implemented many reforms while ruling as grand duke in Tuscany (Italy) before assuming the throne in 1790. Much of his brief two-year reign was spent dexterously saving reforms enacted by his mother and brother in the face of mounting opposition.

■ Catherine the Great and the Empire of Russia

Another ruler with a claim to the title "enlightened despot" was Catherine, empress of Russia (r. 1762–1796). Catherine the Great, as she came to be called, was the true heir of Peter the Great in her abilities, policies, and

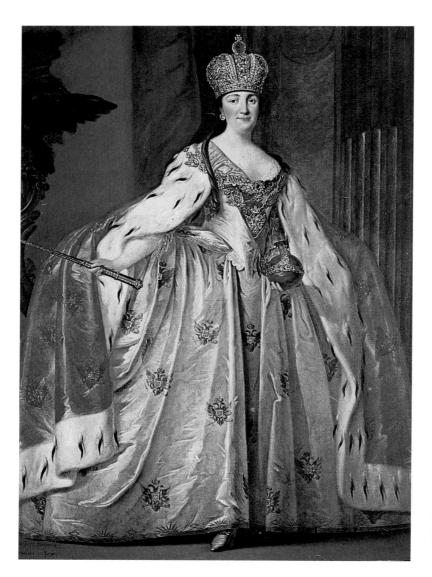

Catherine the Great   Catherine was a German princess who had been brought to Russia to marry another German, Peter of Holstein-Gottorp, who was being groomed as heir to the Russian throne. Russia had crowned several monarchs of mixed Russian and German parentage since the time of Peter the Great's deliberate interest in and ties with other European states. *(The Luton Hoo Foundation)*

Map 18.1 **The Partition of Poland and the Expansion of Russia** Catherine the Great acquired present-day Lithuania, Belarus, and Ukraine, which had once constituted the duchy of Lithuania, part of the multi-ethnic Polish kingdom.

ambitions. Her determination and political acumen were obvious early in her life at the Russian court, where she had been brought from her native Germany in 1745. Brutally treated by her husband, Tsar Peter III, Catherine engineered a coup in which he was killed, then ruled alone for more than thirty years.

Like any successful ruler of her age, Catherine counted territorial aggrandizement among her chief achievements. With regard to the major European powers, Russia tended to ally with Britain (with which it had important trading connections, including the provision of timber for British shipbuilding) and with Austria

(against their common nemesis, Turkey), and against France, Poland, and Prussia. In 1768 Catherine initiated a war against the Turks from which Russia gained much of the Crimean coast. She also continued Peter's efforts to dominate the weakened Poland. She was aided in this goal by Frederick the Great, who proposed the deliberate partitioning of Poland to satisfy his own territorial ambitions as well as those of his competitors Russia and Austria. In 1772 portions of Poland were gobbled up in the first of three successive "grabs" of territory (see Map 18.1). Warsaw itself eventually landed in Prussian hands, but Catherine gained all of Belarus, Ukraine, and modern Lithuania—which had constituted the duchy of Lithuania.

Nevertheless, Catherine also counted herself a sincere follower of the Enlightenment. While young, she had received an education that bore the strong stamp of the Enlightenment. Like Frederick, she attempted to take an active role in the European intellectual community, corresponding with Voltaire over the course of many years and acting as patron to encyclopedist Diderot. One of Catherine's boldest political moves was the secularization of church lands. Although Peter the Great had extended government control of the Russian Orthodox Church, he had not touched church lands. Catherine also licensed private publishing houses and permitted a burgeoning periodical press. The number of books published in Russia tripled during her reign. This enriched cultural life was one of the principal causes of the flowering of Russian literature that began in the early nineteenth century.

The stamp of the Enlightenment on Catherine's policies is also clearly visible in her attempts at legal reform. In 1767 she convened a legislative commission and provided it with a guiding document, the *Instruction,* which she had penned. The commission was remarkable because it included representatives of all classes, including peasants, and provided a place for the airing of general grievances. Catherine hoped for a general codification of law as well as reforms such as the abolition of torture and capital punishment—reforms that made the *Instruction* radical enough to be banned from publication in other countries. She did not propose changing the legal status of serfs, however, and class differences made the commission unworkable in the end. Most legal reforms were accomplished piecemeal and favored the interests of landed gentry.

Like the Austrian rulers, Catherine undertook far-reaching administrative reform to create more effective local units of government. Here again, political imperatives were fundamental, and reforms in local government strengthened the hand of the gentry. The legal subjection of peasants in serfdom was also extended as a matter of state policy to help win the allegiance of landholders in newly acquired areas—such as Ukrainian territory gained in the partition of Poland. Gentry in general and court favorites in particular, on whom the stability of her government depended, were rewarded with estates and serfs to work them.

In Russia, as in Prussia and Austria, oppression of the peasantry was perpetuated because the monarch wanted to ensure the allegiance of the elites who lived from their labor. Catherine particularly valued the coop-

eration of elites because the Russian state was in a formative stage in another sense as well. It was trying to incorporate new peoples, such as the Tatars in the Crimea, and to manage its relationships with border peoples such as the Cossacks. Catherine's reign was marked by one of the most massive and best-organized peasant rebellions of the century. Occurring in 1773, the rebellion expressed the grievances of the thousands of peasants who joined its ranks and called for the abolition of serfdom. The revolt took its name, however, from its Cossack leader, Emelian Pugachev° (d. 1775), and reflected the dissatisfaction with the Russian government of this semi-autonomous people.

The dramatic dilemmas faced by Catherine illustrate both the promise and the costs of state formation throughout Europe. State consolidation permitted the imposition of internal peace, of coordinated economic policy, of reform of justice, but it came at the price of greater—in some cases much greater—control and coercion of the population. Thus, we can see from the alternative perspective of Russia the importance of the political sphere that was opening up in France and was being consolidated in England. It was in that environment, rather than in Russia, that the Enlightenment philosophy could find most fertile ground.

THE WIDENING SCOPE OF WARFARE

IN the eighteenth century a new constellation of states emerged to dominate politics in Europe. Alongside the traditional powers of England, France, and Austria were Prussia in central Europe and Russia to the east (see Map 18.1); these five states would dominate European politics until the twentieth century. Certain characteristics common to all these states account for their dominance. None is more crucial than their various abilities to field effective armies. In the eighteenth century most wars were launched to satisfy traditional territorial ambitions. Now, however, the increasing significance of overseas trade and colonization also made international expansion an important source of conflict, particularly between England and France. As warfare widened in scope, governments increasingly focused on recruiting and maintaining large navies and armies, with increasingly devastating effects on ordinary people.

Pugachev (poo-guh-CHOFF)

■ A Century of Warfare: Circumstances and Rationales

The large and small states of Europe continued to make war on one another for both strategic and dynastic reasons. States fought over territory that had obvious economic and strategic value. War over the Baltic coastline, for example, absorbed Sweden and Russia early in the century. Dynastic claims, however, were still major causes of war. Indeed, the fundamental instability caused by hereditary rule accounts for many of the major wars of the eighteenth century. The century opened with the War of the Spanish Succession, and later the succession of the Austrian Habsburgs provoked a continent-wide war. Often, these conflicts were carried out in arbitrary ways that reflected a dynastic, rather than wholly strategic, view of territory. Although rational and defensible "national" borders were important, collecting isolated bits of territory was also still the norm. The wars between European powers thus became extremely complex strategically. France, for example, might choose to strike a blow against Austria by invading an Italian state in order to use the conquered Italian territory as a bargaining chip in eventual negotiations. Wars were preceded and carried out with complex systems of alliances and were followed by the adjustments of many borders and the changing control of small scattered territories. Rulers of lesser states in Germany and Italy, particularly, remained important as allies and as potential rivals of the great powers. The rise of Prussia, after all, had demonstrated the benefits of zealous ambition.

The state of military technology, tactics, and organization shaped the outcomes of conflicts as well as the character of the leading states themselves. In the eighteenth century weapons and tactics became increasingly refined. More reliable muskets were introduced. A bayonet that could slip over a musket barrel without blocking the muzzle was invented. Coordinated use of bayonets required even more assured drill of troops than volley fire alone to ensure disciplined action in the face of enemy fire and charges. Artillery and cavalry forces were also subjected to greater standardization of training and discipline in action. Increased discipline of forces meant that commanders could exercise meaningful control over a battle for the first time, but such battles were not necessarily decisive, especially when waged against a comparable force. Indeed, training now was so costly that commanders were, at times, ironically reluctant to hazard their fine troops in battle at all.

Thus, one sure result of the new equipment and tactics was that war became a more expensive proposition than ever before and an ever greater burden on a state's resources and administration. It became increasingly difficult for small states such as Sweden to compete with the forces that others could mount. Small and relatively poor states, such as Prussia, that were able to support large forces did so by means of an extraordinary bending of civil society to the economic and social needs of the army. In Prussia twice as many people were in the armed forces, proportionally, as in other states, and a staggering 80 percent of meager state revenue went to sustain the army.

Most states introduced some form of conscription in the eighteenth century. In all regions, the very poor often volunteered for army service to improve their lives. However, conscription of peasants, throughout Europe but particularly in Prussia and Russia, imposed a significant burden on peasant communities and a sacrifice of productive members to the state. Governments everywhere supplemented volunteers and conscripts with mercenaries and even criminals, as necessary, to fill the ranks without tapping the wealthier elements of the community. Thus, common soldiers were increasingly seen not as members of society but as its rejects. Said Frederick II, "Useful hardworking people should [not be conscripted but rather] be guarded as the apple of one's eye," and a French war minister agreed that armies had to consist of the "scum of people and of all those for whom society has no use."[2] Brutality became an accepted tool for governments to use to manage such groups of men. From the eighteenth century, the army increasingly became an instrument of social control used to contain and make use of individuals who otherwise might disrupt their own communities.

But the costs of maintaining these forces had other outcomes as well. Wars could still be won or lost not on the battlefield but on the supply line. Incentive still existed to bleed civilian populations and to exploit the countryside. Moreover, when supply lines were disrupted and soldiers not equipped or fed, the armies of a major power could be vulnerable to smaller, less disciplined armies of minor states. Finally, even supplies, training, and sophisticated tactics could not guarantee success. Not until 1746, at Culloden, could the British army decisively defeat the fierce charge and hand-to-hand fighting of Highland clansmen by holding its position and using disciplined volley fire. Warfare became increasingly professional but was still an uncertain business with unpredictable results, despite its staggering cost.

■ The Power of Austria and Prussia

Major wars during the mid-eighteenth century decided the balance of power in German-speaking Europe for the next hundred years: Prussia emerged as the equal of Austria in the region. The first of these wars, now known as the War of the Austrian Succession, began shortly after the death of the Emperor Charles VI in 1740. Charles died without a male heir, and his daughter, Maria Theresa, succeeded him. Charles VI had worked to shore up his daughter's position as his heir (versus other female relatives who also had claims) by means of an act called the Pragmatic Sanction, which he had painstakingly persuaded allies and potential opponents to accept. When Charles VI died, rival heiresses and their husbands challenged Maria Theresa for control of her various lands. They were supported by France, the Habsburgs' perennial rival.

The Austrian lands were threatened with dismemberment. Indeed, Charles himself had negotiated away the wealthy Bohemian province of Silesia°, promising it to Prussia in return for acceptance of his heir (see Map 18.1), and had not left his armies or his treasury well equipped to fight such a war. When Frederick the Great's troops marched into Silesia in 1740, Maria Theresa's rivals saw their chance and invaded other Habsburg territories.

Maria Theresa proved a more tenacious opponent than anyone had anticipated, and she was helped by Great Britain, which saw the possibility of gains against its colonial rival, France. Fighting eventually spread throughout Habsburg territories, including the Netherlands and in Italy, as well as abroad to British and French colonies. In a preliminary peace signed in 1745, Frederick the Great was confirmed in possession of Silesia, but the throne of the Holy Roman Empire was returned to the Habsburgs—given to Maria Theresa's husband, Francis (Franz) I (r. 1745–1765). A final treaty in 1748 ended all the fighting that had continued since 1745, mostly by France and Britain overseas. The Austrian state had survived dismemberment, but Maria Theresa now embarked on the administrative and military reforms necessary to make her state less vulnerable in the future. Prussia, because of the annexation of Silesia and the psychological imprint of victory, emerged as a power of virtually equal rank to the Habsburgs.

The unprecedented threat that Austria now felt from Prussia led to a revolution in alliances across Europe. In order to isolate Prussia, Maria Theresa agreed to an alliance with France, the Habsburgs' long-standing enemy.

Silesia (sigh-LEE-zhee-uh)

Sweden and Russia, with territory to gain at Prussia's expense, joined as well.

Frederick the Great himself initiated what came to be known as the Seven Years' War in 1756, hoping to prevent consolidation of the new alliances. Instead, he found that he had started a war against overwhelming odds. What saved him, in part, was limited English aid. The English, engaged with France in the overseas conflict that Americans call the French and Indian War, wanted France to be heavily committed on the Continent. Prussia managed to emerge intact—though strained economically and demographically. Prussia and Austria were confirmed as the two states of European rank in German-speaking Europe. Their rivalry would dominate German history until the late nineteenth century. Austria's and Prussia's narrow escapes from being reduced to second-class status reveal how fragile even successful states could be; Prussia's emergence as a major power was by no means ensured.

■ The Atlantic World: Trade, Colonization, Competition

The importance of international trade and colonial possessions to the states of western Europe grew enormously in the eighteenth century. Between 1715 and 1785, Britain's trade with North America rose from 19 to 34 percent of its total trade, and its trade with Asia and Africa rose from 7 to 19 percent of the total. By the end of the century, more than half of all British trade was carried on outside Europe; for France, the figure was more than a third.

European commercial and colonial energies were concentrated in the Atlantic world in the eighteenth century because there the profits were greatest. The population of British North America grew from about 250,000 in 1700 to about 1.7 million by 1760. The densely settled New England colonies provided a market for manufactured goods from the mother country, though they produced little by way of raw materials or bulk goods on which traders could make a profit. The colonies of Maryland and Virginia produced tobacco, the Carolinas rice and indigo (a dyestuff). England re-exported all three throughout Europe at considerable profit.

The French in New France, only 56,000 in 1740, were vastly outnumbered by the British colonists. Nevertheless, the French had successfully expanded their control of territory in Canada. Settlements sprang up between the outposts of Montreal and Quebec on the St. Lawrence River. Despite resistance, the French extended their fur trapping—the source of most of the profits New France generated—west and north along the Great

⊕ G L O B A L   E N C O U N T E R S

An African Recalls the Horrors of the Slave Ship

Olaudah Equiano (ca. 1750–1797) was one of several Africans sold into slavery in the Americas to leave a written record of his experiences. An Ibo from the Niger region, he first experienced slavery as a boy when kidnapped from his village by other Africans. But nothing prepared him for the brutality of the Europeans who bought and shipped him to Barbados, in the British West Indies. He eventually regained his freedom and received an education.

The first object which saluted my eyes when I arrived on the [African] coast was the sea and a slave-ship . . . waiting for its cargo. . . . When I was carried on board I was immediately handled, and tossed up, to see if I were sound, by some of the crew. . . . I was soon put down under the decks, and there I received such a salutation in the nostrils as I had never experienced in my life; so that with the loathsomeness of the stench . . . I became so sick and low that I was not able to eat. . . . I now wished for the last friend, death, to relieve me; but soon, to my grief, two of the white men offered me eatables; and, on my refusing to eat, one of them held me fast by the hands and laid me across, I think, the windlass, and tied my feet while the other flogged me severely.

One day, when we had a smooth sea and a moderate wind, two of my wearied countrymen, who were chained together, preferring death to such a life of misery, somehow made through the nettings and jumped into the sea; immediately another dejected fellow who [was ill and so not in irons] followed their example. . . . Two of the wretches were drowned, but they got the other and afterwards flogged him unmercifully for thus attempting to prefer death to slavery. In this manner we continued to undergo more hardships than I can now relate. Many a time we were near suffocation for want of fresh air. . . . This, and the stench of the necessary tubs, carried off many.

Source: Philip D. Curtin, *Africa Remembered* (Madison University of Wisconsin Press, 1967), pp. 92–96.

Lakes, consolidating their hold by building forts at strategic points. They penetrated as far as the modern Canadian province of Manitoba, where they cut into the British trade run out of Hudson Bay to the north. The French also contested the mouth of the St. Lawrence River and the Gulf of St. Lawrence with the British. The British held Nova Scotia and Newfoundland; the French controlled parts of Cape Breton Island; and both states fished the surrounding waters.

The commercial importance of all of these holdings, as well as those in Asia, was dwarfed by the European states' Caribbean possessions, however. The British held Jamaica and Barbados; the French, Guadeloupe and Martinique; the Spanish, Cuba and San Domingo; and the Dutch, a few small islands. Sugar produced by slave labor was the major source of profits, along with other cash crops such as coffee, indigo, and cochineal (another dyestuff). The concentration of shipping to this region in-dicates the region's importance. By the 1760s the British China trade occupied seven or eight ships. In the 1730s British trade with Jamaica alone drew three hundred ships. The tiny Dutch possession of Guiana on the South American coast required twice as many visits by Dutch ships as the Dutch East India Company sent into Asia.

The economic dependence of the colonies on slave labor meant that the colonies were tied to their home countries not with a two-way commercial exchange but with a three-way, or "triangle," trade (see Map 18.2). Certain European manufactures were shipped to ports in western Africa, where they were traded for slaves. Captive Africans were transported to South America, the Caribbean, or North America, where planters bought and paid for them with profits from their sugar and tobacco plantations. (See the box "Global Encounters: An African Recalls the Horrors of the Slave Ship.") Sugar and tobacco were then shipped back to the mother country

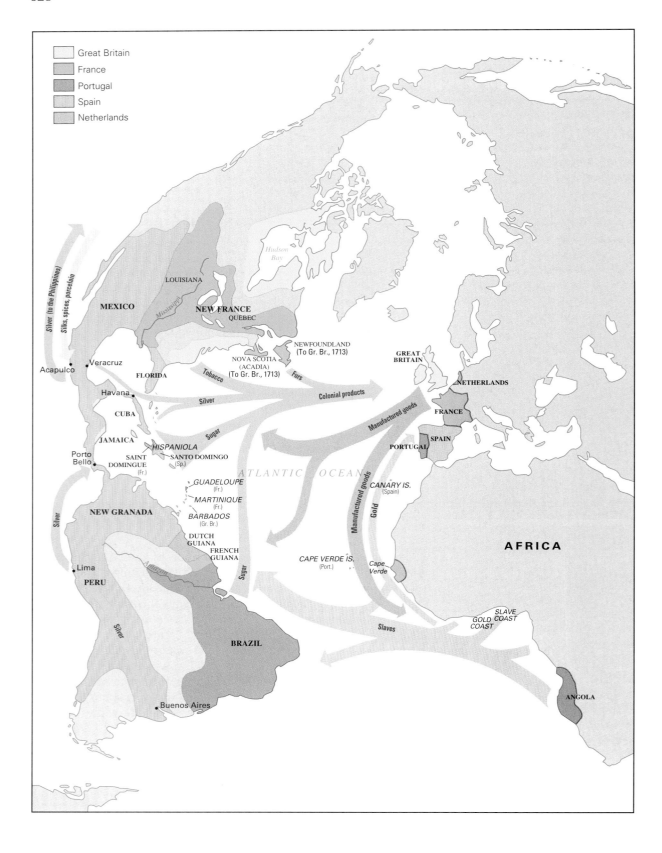

Great Britain
France
Portugal
Spain
Netherlands

Silver (to the Philippines)
Silks, spices, porcelain

LOUISIANA

Hudson Bay

MEXICO

NEW FRANCE
QUEBEC

Mississippi

Acapulco

Veracruz

FLORIDA

NEWFOUNDLAND
(To Gr. Br., 1713)

NOVA SCOTIA
(ACADIA)
(To Gr. Br., 1713)

GREAT
BRITAIN

Tobacco

Havana

Silver

Furs

Colonial products

NETHERLANDS

CUBA

Sugar

Manufactured goods

FRANCE

JAMAICA

HISPANIOLA

SAINT
DOMINGUE
(Fr.)

SANTO DOMINGO
(Sp.)

PORTUGAL

SPAIN

Porto
Bello

ATLANTIC OCEAN

GUADELOUPE
(Fr.)

MARTINIQUE
(Fr.)

Manufactured goods

Gold

CANARY IS.
(Spain)

NEW GRANADA

BARBADOS
(Gr. Br.)

DUTCH
GUIANA

AFRICA

FRENCH
GUIANA

CAPE VERDE IS.
(Port.)

Cape
Verde

Silver

Amazon

Sugar

Lima

PERU

Silver

*SLAVE
COAST*

GOLD
COAST

BRAZIL

Slaves

Buenos Aires

ANGOLA

to be re-exported at great profit throughout Europe. A variety of smaller exchanges also took place. For example, timber from British North America was traded in the Caribbean for sugar or its byproducts, molasses and rum. Individual planters in the colonies were not the only ones whose fortunes and status depended on these networks. Merchants in cities such as Bordeaux in France and Liverpool in England were also heavily invested in the slave trade and the re-export business.

◼ Great Britain and France: Wars Overseas

The proximity and growth of French and British settlements in North America ensured conflict (see Map 18.3). The Caribbean and the coasts of Central and South America were strategic flashpoints as well. At the beginning of the eighteenth century, several substantial islands remained unclaimed by any power. The British were making incursions along the coastline claimed by Spain and were trying to break into the monopoly of trade between Spain and Spain's vast possessions in the region. Public opinion in both Britain and France became increasingly sensitive to colonial issues. For the first time, tensions abroad would fuel major conflicts between two European states.

During this century England became the dominant naval power in Europe. Its navy protected its far-flung trading networks, its merchant fleet, and the coast of England itself. England's strategic interests on the Continent lay in promoting a variety of powers there, none of which (or no combination of which) posed too great a threat to England or to its widespread trading system. A second, dynastic consideration in continental affairs was the electorate of Hanover, the large principality in western Germany that was the native territory of the Hanoverian kings of England. Early in the century especially, the interests of this German territory were a significant factor in British foreign policy. Unable to field a large army, given their maritime interests, the British sought protection for Hanover in alliances and subsidies for allies' armies on the Continent and paid for these ventures with the profits on trade.

Map 18.2 The Atlantic Economy, ca. 1750 The triangle trade linked Europe, Africa, and European colonies in the Americas. The most important component of this trade for Europe was the plantation agriculture of the Caribbean islands, which depended on enslaved Africans for labor.

After the death of Louis XIV in 1715, England's energies centered on colonial rivalries with France, its greatest competitor overseas. Conflict between England and France in colonial regions played out in three major phases. The first two were concurrent with the major land wars in Europe: the War of the Austrian Succession (1740–1748) and the Seven Years' War (1756–1763). The third phase coincided with the rebellion of British colonies in North America—the American Revolution—beginning in the 1770s. France was inevitably more committed to affairs on the Continent than were the British. The French were able to hold their own successfully in both arenas during the 1740s, but by 1763, though pre-eminent on the Continent, they had lost many of their colonial possessions to the English.

In the 1740s France was heavily involved in the War of the Austrian Succession while Britain vied with Spain for certain Caribbean territories. Both France and England also tested each other's strength in scattered colonial fighting, which produced a few well-balanced gains and losses. Their conquests were traded back when peace was made in 1748.

Tension was renewed almost immediately at many of the strategic points in North America. French and British naval forces harassed each other's shipping in the Gulf of St. Lawrence. The French reinforced their encirclement of British colonies with more forts along the Great Lakes and the Ohio River. When British troops (at one point led by the colonial commander George Washington) attempted to strike at these forts, beginning in 1754, open fighting between the French and the English began.

In India, meanwhile, both the French and the British attempted to strengthen their commercial footholds by making military and political alliances with local Indian rulers. The disintegration of the Mogul Empire heightened competition among regional Indian rulers and sparked a new level of ambition on the part of the European powers with interests in Asia. A British attack on a French convoy provoked a declaration of war by France in May 1756, three months before fighting in the Seven Years' War broke out in Europe. For the first time, a major war between European nations had started and would be fought in their empires, signifying a profound change in the relation of these nations to the world.

The French had already committed themselves to an alliance with Austria and were increasingly involved on the Continent after Frederick II initiated war there in August 1756. Slowly, the drain of sustaining war both on the Continent and abroad began to tell, and Britain scored

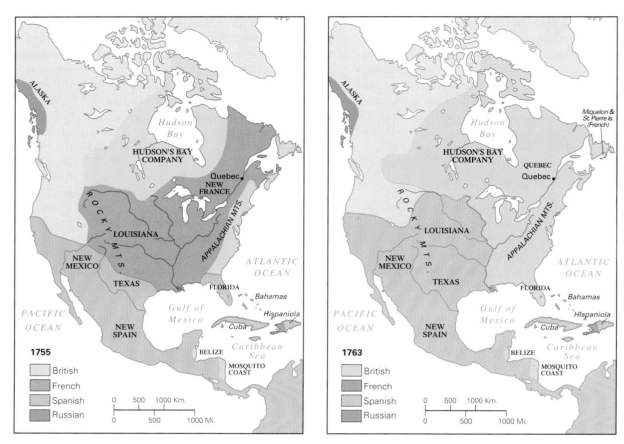

Map 18.3   British Gains in North America   The British colonies on the Atlantic coast were effective staging posts for the armies that ousted the French from North America by 1763. However, taxes imposed on the colonies to pay the costs of the Seven Years' War helped spark revolt—the American Revolution—a decade later.

major victories against French forces after an initial period of balanced successes and failures. The French lost a number of fortresses on the Mississippi and Ohio Rivers and on the Great Lakes and, finally, also lost the interior of Canada with the fall of Quebec and of Montreal in 1759 and 1760, respectively (see Map 18.3).

In the Caribbean, the British seized Guadeloupe, a vital sugar-producing island. Superior resources in India enabled the British to take several French outposts there, including Pondicherry°, the most important. The cost of involvement on so many fronts meant that French troops were short of money and supplies. They were particularly vulnerable to both supply and personnel shortages—especially in North America—because they were

weaker than the British at sea and because New France remained sparsely settled and dependent on the mother country for food.

By the terms of the Peace of Paris in 1763, France regained Guadeloupe; the most profitable of its American colonies—the sugar islands—thus remained in French control. In India, France retained many of its trading stations but lost its political and military clout. British power in India was dramatically enhanced not only by French losses but also by victories over Indian rulers who had allied with the French. In the interior Britain now controlled lands that had never before been under the control of any European power. British political rule in India, as opposed to merely a mercantile presence, began at this time. The British now also held Canada. They emerged from the Seven Years' War as the pre-eminent world power among European states.

Pondicherry (pon-dih-CHAIR-ee)

The Death of General Wolfe at Quebec   General Wolfe commanded British troops that in 1759 defeated the French at Quebec in Canada. Wolfe's death at the battle was memorialized ten years later by American-born artist Benjamin West. This image became widely popular after West sold cheap engraved versions. Notice West's sympathetic treatment of the Native American earnestly focused, like his British allies, on the death of the commander.   *(National Gallery of Canada, Ottawa. Transfer from the Canadian War Memorials)*

ECONOMIC EXPANSION AND SOCIAL CHANGE

HE eighteenth century was an era of dramatic change, though that change was not always apparent to those who lived through it. The intellectual and cultural ferment of the Enlightenment laid the groundwork for domestic political changes to come, just as British victories in the Seven Years' War shifted the balance of power abroad. More subtle and potentially more profound changes were occurring in the European countryside, however. Population, production,

and consumption were beginning to grow beyond the bounds that all preceding generations had lived within and taken for granted.

■ More Food and More People

Throughout European history, a delicate balance had existed between available food and numbers of people to feed. Population growth had accompanied increases in the amount of land under cultivation. From time to time, however, population growth surpassed the ability of the land to produce food, and people became malnourished and prey to disease. In 1348 the epidemic outbreak of bubonic plague known as the Black Death struck just such a vulnerable population in decline.

Europeans had few options for increasing the productivity of land. Peasants safeguarded its fertility by alternately cultivating some portions while letting others lie fallow or using them as pasture. Manure provided fertilizer, but during the winter months livestock could not be kept alive in large numbers. Limited food for livestock meant limited fertilizer, which in turn meant limited production of food for both humans and animals.

After devastating decline in the fourteenth century, the European population experienced a prolonged recovery, and in the eighteenth century the balance that had previously been reached began to be exceeded for the first time. Infant mortality remained as high as ever. No less privileged a person than Queen Anne of England outlived every one of the seventeen children she bore, and all but one of them died in infancy. Population growth occurred because of a decline in the death rate for adults and a simultaneous increase in the birthrate in some areas owing to earlier marriages.

Adults began to live longer partly because of a decline in the incidence of plague. However, the primary reason adults were living longer, despite the presence of various epidemic diseases, was that they were better nourished and thus better able to resist disease. More and different kinds of food began to be produced. The increase in the food supply also meant that more new families could be started.

Food production increased because of the introduction of new crops and other changes in agricultural practices. The cumulative effect of these changes was so

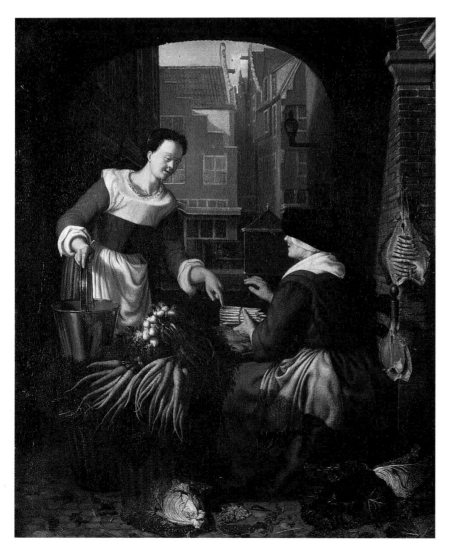

Gérard Dou: The Vegetable Seller
The specialization of agriculture meant that a more varied diet was available to increasing numbers of Europeans. *(Musée des Beaux-Arts, Nimes/Giraudon/Art Resource, NY)*

dramatic that historians have called them an "agricultural revolution." The new crops included fodder, such as clover, legumes, and turnips, which did not deplete the soil and could be fed to livestock over the winter. The greater availability of animal manure, in turn, boosted grain production. The potato, introduced from the Americas in the sixteenth century, is nutrient-dense and can feed more people per acre than can grain. In certain areas, farming families produced potatoes to feed themselves while they grew grain to be sold and shipped elsewhere.

More food being produced meant more food available for purchase. The opportunity to buy food freed up land and labor. A family that could purchase food might decide to convert its farm to specialized use, such as raising dairy cattle. In such a case, many families might be supported from a piece of land that had previously supported only one. Over a generation or two, a number of children might share the inheritance of what had previously been a single farm, yet each could make a living from his or her share, and population could grow as it had not done before.

Farmers had known about and experimented with many of the crops used for fodder for centuries. However, the widespread planting of these crops, as well as other changes, was long in coming and happened in scattered areas. A farmer had to have control over land in order to implement change. In the traditional open-field system, peasants had split up all the land in each community so that each family might have a piece of each field. Making effective changes was hard when an entire community had to act together. Most important, changing agriculture required capital for seed and fertilizer and for the greater number of people and animals needed to cultivate the new crops. Only prosperous farmers had spare capital. Few were inclined to take risks with the production of food and to trust the workings of the market. The bad condition of roads alone was reason enough not to rely on distant markets.

Yet where both decent roads and growing urban markets existed, some farmers—even entire villages working together—were willing to produce for urban populations. Capital cities, like London and Amsterdam, and trading centers such as Glasgow and Bordeaux were booming. These growing cities demanded not only grain but also specialized produce such as dairy products and fruits and vegetables. Thus, farmers had an incentive to make changes such as to dairy farming. Urbanization and improved transportation networks also encouraged agriculture because human waste produced by city dwellers—known as "night soil"—could be collected and distributed in the surrounding agricultural regions as fertilizer. By the late eighteenth century, pockets of intensive, diversified agriculture existed in England, northern France, the Rhineland in Germany, the Po Valley in Italy, and Catalonia in Spain.

In other areas, changes in agriculture were often accompanied by a shift in power in the countryside. Wealthy landlords began to invest in change in order to reap the profits of producing for the new markets. Where the traditional authority of the village to regulate agriculture was weak, peasants were vulnerable. In England a combination of weak village structure and the attraction of urban markets created a climate that encouraged landlords to treat land speculatively. To make their holdings more profitable, they raised the rents that farmers paid. They changed cultivation patterns on the land that they controlled directly. They appropriated the village common lands, a process known as "enclosure," and used them for cash crops such as sheep (raised for their wool) or beef cattle. Among other ramifications, the clans of Scotland completely disintegrated as meaningful social units as markets for beef, wool, and other Highland commodities drew chieftains' resources and turned what remained of their traditional clan relationships into exploitative commercial ones.

Thus, although the agricultural revolution increased the food supply to sustain more people in Europe generally, it did not create general prosperity. The growth of population did not mean that most people were better off. Indeed, many rural people were driven off the land or made destitute by the loss of the resources of common lands. Peasants in eastern Europe produced grain for export to the growing urban centers in western Europe, but usually by traditional methods. In both eastern and western Europe, the power and profits of landlords were a major force in structuring the rural economy.

■ The Growth of Industry

Agricultural changes fostered change in other areas of economic and social life. As more food was grown with less labor, that labor was freed to take on other productive work. If enough people could be kept employed making useful commodities, then the nonagricultural population could continue to grow. If population grew, more and more consumers would be born, and the demand for more goods would help continue the cycle of population growth, changes in production, and economic expansion. This is precisely what happened in the eighteenth century. A combination of forces increased the numbers of people who worked at producing a few essential materials and products (see Map 18.4).

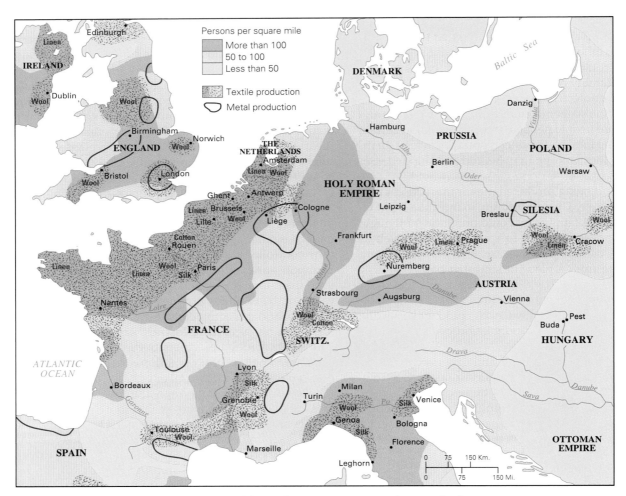

Map 18.4   Population and Production in Eighteenth-Century Europe   The growth of cottage industry helped to support a growing population. With changes in agriculture, more land-poor workers were available in the countryside to accept work as spinners, knitters, and weavers.

Especially significant was the expansion in the putting-out system. Also known as cottage industry, putting out involved the production in the countryside of thread and cloth by spinners and weavers working in their own homes for an entrepreneur who bought raw materials and "put them out" to be finished by individual workers. The putting-out system expanded in the eighteenth century as the agricultural economy was transformed. All agricultural work was seasonal, demanding intensive effort and many hands at certain times but not at others. The labor demands of the new crops meant that an even larger number of people might periodically need nonfarm work in order to make ends meet. Rural poverty, whether as a result of tradi-

tional or new agricultural methods, made manufacturing work in the home attractive to more and more people.

Overseas trade also stimulated the expansion of production by spurring the demand in Europe's colonies for cloth and other finished products and increasing the demand at home for manufactured items, such as nails to build the ships that carried the trade. The production of cloth expanded also because heightened demand led to changes in the way cloth was made. Wool was increasingly combined with other fibers to make less expensive fabrics. By the end of the century, wholly cotton fabrics were being made cheaply in Europe from cotton grown in America by slave labor.

&♠ R E A D I N G   S O U R C E S

A Peasant Protests Forced Labor

Generally, the condition of agricultural workers was worst in eastern Europe, where political and economic forces kept them bound in serfdom. In A Journey from St. Petersburg to Moscow *(1790), the reform-minded nobleman Alexander Radishchev (1749–1802) describes an encounter with a Russian serf who, like most serfs, was forced to work the lord's lands at the expense of his own.*

A few steps from the road I saw a peasant plowing a field. It was now Sunday, [about midday]. The ploughing peasant, of course, belonged to a landed proprietor, who would not let him pay a commutation tax. The peasant was plowing very carefully. The field . . . was not part of the master's land. He turned the plow with astonishing ease.

"God help you," I said, walking up to the ploughman, who, without stopping, was finishing the furrow he had started. . . . "Have you no time to work during the week, then, and can you not have any rest on Sundays, in the hottest part of the day, at that?"

"In a week, sir, there are six days, and we go six times a week to work on the master's field; in the evening, if the weather is good, we haul to the master's house the hay that is left in the woods. . . . God

grant that it rains this evening. If you have peasants of your own, sir, they are praying for the same thing."

"But how do you manage to get food enough [for your family] if you have only the holidays free?"

"Not only the holidays, the nights are ours too."

"Do you work the same way for your master?"

"No, sir, it would be a sin to work the same way. On his fields there are a hundred hands for one mouth, while I have two for seven mouths: you can figure it out for yourself."

Source: Alexander Radishchev, *A Journey from St. Petersburg to Moscow,* trans. Leo Wiener, ed. Roderick Page Thaler (Cambridge, Mass.: Harvard University Press, 1958; quoted in Robert and Elborg Forster, eds., *European Society in the Eighteenth Century* (New York: Harper and Row, 1969), pp. 136–139.

Steady innovation in textile production allowed woven goods to be aimed at broader markets. In the Middle Ages, weavers produced luxury-quality cloth, and their profits came not from demand, which was relatively low, but from the high price that affluent consumers paid. In the eighteenth century, cloth production became a spur to a transformed industrial economy because cheaper kinds of cloth were made for mass consumption. Producing in great quantities became important, and innovations that promoted productivity were welcomed.

A crucial innovation was increased mechanization. The invention of machines to spin thread in the late eighteenth century brought a marked increase in the rate of production. Machines likewise brought profound changes to the lives of rural workers who had been juggling agricultural and textile work according to season and need. The selected areas of England, France, and the

Low Countries where the new technologies were introduced stood, by the end of the century, on the verge of a massive industrial transformation that would have unprecedented social consequences.

■ Control and Resistance

The economic changes of the century produced both resistance and adaptation by ordinary people and, at times, direct action by state authorities. (See the box "Reading Sources: A Peasant Protests Forced Labor.") Sometimes ordinary people coped in ways that revealed their desperation. In many cities numbers of abandoned children rose greatly because urban families, particularly recent immigrants from the countryside, could not support all their offspring. The major cities of Europe put increasing resources into police forces and

An Idle Apprentice Is Sent to Sea, 1747   In one of a series of moralizing engravings by William Hogarth, the lazy apprentice, Tom, is sent away to a life at sea. The experienced seamen in the boat introduce him to some of its terrors: on the left one dangles a cat-o'-nine-tails—the instrument used for flogging—and on the distant promontory is a gallows, where pirates and mutineers meet their fate.   *(From the Collections of Lauinger Library, Georgetown University)*

city lighting schemes. Charitable institutions run by cities, churches, and central governments expanded. By 1789, for example, there were more than two thousand *hôpitaux*°—poorhouses for the destitute and ill—in France. The poor received food and shelter but were forced to work for the city or to live in poorhouses against their will. Men were sometimes taken out of poorhouses and forced to become soldiers.

Resistance and adaptation were particularly visible wherever the needs of common people conflicted with the states' desire for order and revenue. This scenario was evident on the high seas, for example, in the cru-

sade to suppress piracy. Piracy had been a way of life for hundreds of Europeans and colonial settlers since the sixteenth century. From the earliest days of exploration, European rulers had authorized men known as privateers to commit acts of war against specific targets. The Crown took little risk and was spared the cost of arming the ships but shared in the plunder. True piracy—outright robbery on the high seas—was illegal, but in practice the difference between piracy and privateering was negligible. As governments and merchants grew to prefer regular trade over the irregular profits of plunder, and as national navies developed in the late seventeenth century, a concerted effort to eliminate piracy began.

---

hôpitaux (op-ee-TOE)

Life on the seas became an increasingly vital part of western European economic life in the eighteenth century; English-speaking seamen alone numbered about thirty thousand around the middle of the century. Sea life began to resemble life on land in the amount of compulsion it entailed. Sailors in port were always vulnerable to forcible enlistment in the navy by impressment gangs, particularly during wartime. A drowsy sailor sleeping off a rowdy night in port could wake up to find himself aboard a navy ship. Press gangs operated throughout England and not just in major ports, for authorities were as interested in controlling "vagrancy" as in staffing the navy. Merchant captains occasionally filled their crews by such means, particularly when sailing unpopular routes.

Like soldiers in the growing eighteenth-century armies, sailors in the merchant marine as well as the navy could be subjected to brutal discipline and appalling conditions. Merchant seamen attempted to improve their lot by trying to regulate their relationship with ships' captains. Contracts for pay on merchant ships became more regularized, and seamen often negotiated their terms very carefully, including, for example, details about how rations were to be allotted. Sailors might even take bold collective action aboard ship. The modern term for a work stoppage, *strike,* comes from the sailing expression "to strike sail," meaning to lower the sails so that they cannot fill with wind. Its use dates from the eighteenth century, from "strikes" of sailors protesting unfair shipboard conditions.

Seafaring men were an unusually large and somewhat self-conscious community of wage workers. Not until industrialization came into full swing a century later would a similar group of workers exist within Europe itself (see Chapter 21). But economic and political protest by ordinary people on the Continent also showed interesting parallel changes. Peasant revolts in the past had ranged from small-scale actions against local tax collectors to massive uprisings that only an army could suppress. The immediate goals of the rebels were usually practical. For example, they aimed not to eliminate taxation altogether but might protest the collection of a particularly burdensome tax. The political rationale behind such actions was not a hope that the system would disappear but rather a hope that it would operate more fairly, as it presumably had in the past. Where there was a revolutionary vision, it was usually a utopian one—a political system with no kings, landlords, taxes, or state of any kind.

Peasant revolts continued to follow those patterns in the eighteenth century. They were also driven by the localized unemployment caused by agricultural reforms or by objections to press gangs. In certain cases, however, peasants, like sailors, began to confront the state in new ways. Peasants often attacked not state power but the remnants of landlords' power, wielded over them in the shape of forced labor and compulsory use of landlords' mills. As weapons, they increasingly marshaled legal devices to maintain control over their land and to thwart landlords' efforts to enclose fields and cultivate cash crops. This change, though subtle, was important because it signaled an effort to bring permanent structural change to the system and was not simply a temporary redress of grievances. In part, the trend toward "enlightened" revolt reflects increased access to information and the circulation of ideas about reform. A major peasant rebellion in 1775 in Austrian lands, for example, followed several years of bad harvests but specifically protested the delay in implementing changes—the subject of earnest debate among elites—in compulsory labor by peasants.

SUMMARY

 T is important not to exaggerate the degree to which circumstances of life changed in the eighteenth century. The economy was expanding and the population growing beyond previous limits, and the system of production was being restructured. But these developments occurred incrementally over many decades and were not recognized for the fundamental changes they were.

Most of the long-familiar material constraints were still in place. Roads, on which much commerce depended, were generally impassable in bad weather. Shipping was relatively dependable and economical— but only relatively. Military life likewise reflected traditional constraints. Despite technological changes and developments of the administrative and economic resources of the state to equip, train, and enforce discipline, the conduct of war was still hampered by problems of transport and supply that would have been familiar to warriors two centuries before.

Similarly, though some rulers were inspired by precepts of the Enlightenment, all were guided by traditional concerns of dynastic aggrandizement and strategic advantage. One new dimension of relations between states was the importance of conflict over colonies abroad, but the full economic and strategic impact of British colonial gains would not be felt until the next century.

(continued on page 640)

Gardens

What is a garden? We first think of intensely culti-vated flower gardens, such as the famous Rose Garden at the White House. We usually don't think of the yards around houses as gardens, yet that is what they are. The landscaping around most ordinary American homes derives from English landscape gardening of the eighteenth century and after—a fact that is reflected in the British custom of calling the "yards" around their homes "gardens." Like most of the art forms that we see habitually, the garden, reproduced in the American backyard, is difficult to analyze or even to think of as an art form. Like the buildings they surround, however, gar-dens have much to tell us about human habits and val-ues. Let us examine their eighteenth-century ancestors for evidence of contemporaries' attitudes toward nature and their relationship with it.

Look at the two English-style gardens illustrated here. The first is next to the Governor's Mansion in Williamsburg, the capital of the English colony of Vir-ginia. Construction of this garden began at the end of the seventeenth century; the photograph shows the restored gardens that tourists may visit today. The second garden, from the private estate of West Wycombe in England, looks very different—much more like a natural land-scape. The engraving reproduced here dates from the 1770s. The two gardens represent distinct epochs in the development of the garden, hence the differences be-tween them. However, each of these gardens in its own way celebrates human domination of nature.

This symbolic domination of nature is more obvious to us in the Williamsburg garden. The lawns and hedges are trimmed in precise geometrical shapes and are laid out, with the walkways, in straight lines. This "palace gar-den" was a small English variant of the classical garden developed in France—most spectacularly at Versailles Palace—and then imitated throughout Europe during the seventeenth century. At Versailles, the garden is so vast that at many points all of nature visible to the eye is nature disciplined by humans.

We can think of such gardens as pieces of architec-ture, because that is how they were originally conceived: The design originated in the enclosed courtyard gardens of the homes of classical antiquity. The straight lines and squared shapes of these gardens mimic the buildings

they are attached to. In fact, these seventeenth- and eigh-teenth-century gardens were usually laid out as an exten-sion of the building itself. Notice the wide staircase that descends from the central axis of the Governor's Mansion into the central walkway of the garden. Other architec-tural details, such as the benches positioned at the ends of various walkways, add to the sense of the garden as an exterior room. Elsewhere, this sense was enhanced by the construction of devices such as grottoes, such as that at Versailles. The garden symbolizes the taming of nature into a pleasing vision of order and regularity.

The later, eighteenth-century garden represents even greater confidence in the human relationship with nature, although it does not appear to do so at first glance. The extensive gardens at first seem to be nature itself plus a few added details, such as the statuary, and a few improvements, such as the grass kept trim by the workers in the foreground. Our familiarity with such landscapes—in our own suburban yards—keeps us from immediately perceiving how contrived such a landscape is. Nature, however, does not intersperse dense stands of trees or clumps of shrubbery with green expanses of lawns. Nor does nature conveniently leave portions of a hillside bare of trees to provide a view of the water from the palatial house, to the left on the hill. Note also that the waterfall cascading over rocks and statuary flows from an artificial lake, neatly bordered by a path.

This kind of garden reflects Enlightenment optimism about humans' ability to understand and work with na-ture. Such gardens were asymmetrical: paths were usu-ally curved, and lakes and ponds were irregularly shaped, as they would be in nature. Trees and shrubs were al-lowed to maintain their natural form. Nevertheless, this landscaping conveys a powerful message of order. Hu-mans cannot bend or distort nature to their own ends, but they can live in harmony with it as they manage it and enjoy its beneficence. People were freed from regarding nature as hostile and needing to be fought. In this garden, one lives with nature but improves on it. The workers cut-ting the grass do not detract from the engraving but rather make the scene more compelling.

This brand of landscape gardening appeared in English colonies across the Atlantic by the end of the eighteenth century. One of the best examples is at Mon-

ticello, Thomas Jefferson's Virginia estate, first designed
in the 1770s and constructed and improved over the remainder of Jefferson's life (1743–1826). If you tour Mon-
ticello, you will notice a curving garden path bordered by
flowers in season, with mature trees scattered here and
there. Jefferson, we know, planned every inch of this
largely random-looking outdoor space, just as he
planned the regimented fruit and vegetable garden that
borders it. The older, classical style of the Williamsburg
garden is partly explained by its earlier date and also because this more aggressively controlling style lasted
longer in the American colonies than in Europe, perhaps
because "nature" seemed more wild and still more formidable in the New World. You might wish to consider
the curious blend of "nature" and order that is evident in
the landscapes we create and live with today.

The most visible change would happen first in politics, where goals and expectations nurtured by Enlightenment philosophy clashed with the rigid structure of the French state and triggered the French Revolution. The Enlightenment was not simply an intellectual movement that found fault with society. It also encompassed the public and private settings in which "enlightened" opinion flourished. The revolutionary potential of Enlightenment thought came from belief in its rationality and from the fact that it was both critical of its society and fashionable to practice.

■ Notes

1. Quoted in Dena Goodman, *The Republic of Letters: A Cultural History of the French Enlightenment* (Ithaca, N.Y.: Cornell University Press, 1994), p. 89.
2. Quoted in M. S. Anderson, *Europe in the Eighteenth Century, 1713–1783*, 3d ed. (London: Longman, 1987), pp. 218–219.

■ Suggested Reading

Anderson, M. S. *Europe in the Eighteenth Century, 1713–1783.* 4th ed. 2000. A general history covering political, economic, social, and cultural developments.

Black, Jeremy. *European Warfare, 1660–1815.* 1994. One of several recent books by this military historian known particularly for his studies of the seventeenth and eighteenth centuries.

Cipolla, Carlo. *Before the Industrial Revolution.* 1976. A comprehensive treatment of the development of the European economy and technology through this period.

Colley, Linda. *Britons: Forging the Nation, 1707–1837.* 1992. A history of the British that emphasizes the interrelationships of political, social, and cultural history.

Goodman, Dena. *The Republic of Letters: A Cultural History of the French Enlightenment.* 1994. Useful for understanding the social context of the Enlightenment, especially the role of women as salon leaders.

Kennedy, Paul. *The Rise and Fall of British Naval Mastery.* 1976. A comprehensive work on the rise of British sea power from the sixteenth century to modern times.

Porter, Roy. *The Enlightenment.* 1990. A brief introduction.

Roche, Daniel. *France in the Enlightenment.* 1998. An indispensable study of state and society in France by an eminent French scholar.

 For a searchable list of additional readings for this chapter, go to http://college.hmco.com.

CHAPTER 19

An Age of Revolution 1789–1815

T HESE militiamen marching off to defend France against the invader in September 1792 appear to be heroes already. Adoring women in the crowd hand them laurel wreaths as they pass; the men march by, resolute and triumphant. Symbols of the ongoing revolution stand out as well: the prominent tricolor flag, the tricolor cockade in each man's hat. In fact, that September, France's citizen armies for the first time defeated the army of a foreign monarch poised to breach its borders and snuff out its revolution. The painting celebrates this triumph about to happen and thereby inspires confidence in the Revolution and pride in its citizen-soldiers.

Today the French Revolution is considered the initiation of modern European as well as modern French history. The most powerful monarch in Europe was forced to accept constitutional limits to his power by subjects convinced of their right to demand them. Eventually, the king was overthrown and executed, and the monarchy abolished. Events in France reverberated throughout Europe because the overthrow of one absolute monarchy threatened fellow royals elsewhere. Revolutionary fervor on the part of ordinary soldiers enabled France's armies unexpectedly to best many of their opponents. By the late 1790s the armies of France would be led in outright conquest of other European states by one of the most talented generals in European history: Napoleon Bonaparte. He brought to the continental European nations that his armies eventually conquered a mixture of imperial aggression and revolutionary change. Europe was transformed both by the shifting balance of power and by the spread of revolutionary ideas.

The Beginnings of Revolution, 1775–1789

The Phases of the Revolution, 1789–1799

The Napoleonic Era and the Legacy of Revolution, 1799–1815

The National Guard of Paris leaves to join the army, September 1792 (detail). (Château de Versailles/Hubert Josse)

Understanding the French Revolution means understanding not only its origins but also its complicated course of events, and their significance. Challenges to the power of the king were not new, but the Revolution overthrew his right to rule at all. The notion that the people constituted the nation, were responsible as citizens, and had some right to representation in government became irresistible. The republican system it conjured up replaced a government by inherited privilege. Louis XVI was transformed from the divinely appointed father of his people to an enemy of the people, worthy only of execution. Central to the Revolution was the complex process by which public opinion was shaped and, in turn, shaped events. Change was driven, in part, by the power of symbols—flags, rallying cries, inspiring art—to challenge an old political order and to legitimize a new one.

QUESTIONS TO CONSIDER

- What factors led to the beginning of revolution in France in 1789?

- Why did the Revolution take a more radical direction from 1792 until 1794?

- What was the impact of Napoleon's rule on France?

- What were the major effects of the French Revolution and Napoleonic rule on the rest of Europe and overseas?

TERMS TO KNOW

Third Estate	Maximilien Robespierre
National Assembly	the Terror
Tennis Court Oath	Society of Revolutionary
Declaration of the	Republican Women
Rights of Man	Directory
and the Citizen	Napoleon Bonaparte
Jacobins	the Civil Code
sans-culottes	François Toussaint-Louverture

THE BEGINNINGS OF REVOLUTION, 1775–1789

 AM a citizen of the world," wrote John Paul Jones, captain in the fledgling United States Navy, in 1778. He was writing to a Scottish aristocrat, apologizing for raiding the lord's estate while marauding along the British coast during the American Revolution. Jones (1747–1792), himself born a Scotsman, was one of the thousands of cosmopolitan Europeans who were familiar with European cultures on both sides of the Atlantic. As a sailor, Jones literally knew his way around the Atlantic world, but he was a "citizen of the world" in another sense as well. When the Scotsman wrote back to Jones, he expressed surprise that his home had been raided because he was sympathetic to the American colonists. Like Jones, he said, he was a man of "liberal sentiments."[1] Both Jones and the Scottish lord felt they belonged to an international society of gentlemen who recognized certain Enlightenment principles regarding just and rational government.

In the Atlantic world of the late eighteenth century, both practical links of commerce and shared ideals about "liberty" were important shaping forces. The strategic interests of the great European powers were also always involved. Thus, when the American colonists actively resisted British rule and then in 1776 declared their independence from Britain, the consequences were widespread and varied: British trading interests were challenged, French appetites for gains at British expense were whetted, and illusive notions about "liberty" seemed more plausible. The victory of the American colonies in 1783, followed by the creation of the U.S. Constitution in 1787, further heightened the appeal of liberal ideas elsewhere. Attempts at liberal reform were mounted in several states, including Ireland, the Netherlands, and Poland. However, the American Revolution had the most direct impact on later events in France because the French had been directly involved in the American effort.

■ Revolutionary Movements in Europe

While the British government was facing the revolt of the American colonies, it also confronted trouble closer to home. The war against the American colonies was not firmly supported by Britons. Like many Americans, many Britons had divided loyalties, and many who did favor armed force to subdue the rebellion were convinced that the war was being mismanaged. The prosecution of the war against the American colonies proceeded amid calls for reform of the ministerial government. In this setting, a reform movement sprang up in Ireland in 1779. The reformers demanded greater autonomy from Britain. Like the Americans, Irish elites felt like disadvantaged junior partners in the British Empire. They chafed over British policies that favored British imperial interests over those of the Irish ruling class: for example, the exclusion of Irish ports in favor of English and Scottish trading stops and the granting of political rights to Irish Catholics so that they might fight in Britain's overseas armies.

Protestant Irish landlords, threatened by such policies, expressed their opposition not only in parliamentary debates but also in military defiance. Following the example of the American rebels, middle- and upper-class Anglo-Irish set up a system of locally sponsored voluntary militia to resist British troops if necessary. The Volunteer Movement was neutralized when greater parliamentary autonomy for Ireland was granted in 1782, following the repeal of many restrictions on Irish commerce. Unlike the Americans, the Irish elites faced an internal challenge to their own authority—the Catholic population whom they had for centuries dominated. That challenge forced them to reach an accommodation with the British government.

Meanwhile, a political crisis with constitutional overtones was also brewing in the Netherlands. Tensions between the aristocratic stadholders of the House of Orange and the merchant oligarchies of the major cities deepened during the American Revolution. The Dutch were then engaged in a commercial war against the British, to whom the stadholder was supposed to be sympathetic. The conflict ceased to be wholly traditional for two reasons. First, the representatives of the various cities, calling themselves the Dutch "Patriot" Party, defended their position on the grounds of traditional balance of power within the Netherlands and invoked wider claims to American-style "liberty." Second, the challenge to traditional political arrangements widened when middling urban dwellers, long disenfranchised by these oligarchies, demanded "liberty," too—that is, political enfranchisement within the cities—and briefly took over the Patriot movement. Just as many Irish rebels accepted the concessions of 1782, many Patriot oligarchs in the Netherlands did nothing to resist an invasion in 1787 that restored the power of the stadholder, the prince of Orange, and thereby ended the challenge to their own control of urban government.

Both the Irish volunteers and the Dutch Patriots, though members of very limited movements, echoed

CHRONOLOGY

1775–1783	American Revolutionary War
1779–1782	Irish Volunteer Movement
1788	United States Constitution ratified
	Reform movement begins in Poland
	"Patriot" movement ends in the Netherlands
1789	French Estates General meets in Versailles (May)
	Third Estate declares itself the National Assembly (June)
	Storming of the Bastille (July)
1790	Polish constitution
1791	French king Louis XVI captured attempting to flee
	Slave revolt begins in Saint Domingue
1792	France declares war on Austria; revolutionary wars begin (April)
	Louis XVI arrested; France declared a republic (August–September)
1793	Louis XVI guillotined
1793–1794	Reign of Terror in France
1799	Napoleon seizes power in France
1802	Napoleon declared consul for life
1804	Napoleon crowned emperor
	Napoleonic Civil Code
	Independence of Haiti (Saint Domingue) declared
1805	Battle of Trafalgar
	Battle of Austerlitz
1806	Dissolution of Holy Roman Empire
1812	French invasion of Russia
1814	Napoleon abdicates and is exiled
	French monarchy restored
1815	Hundred Days (February–June)
	Battle of Waterloo

the American rebels in practical and ideological ways. Both were influenced by the economic and political consequences of Britain's relationship with its colonies. Both were inspired by the success of the American rebels and their thoroughgoing claims for political self-determination.

Desire for political reform flared in Poland as well during this period. Reform along lines suggested by Enlightenment precepts was accepted as a necessity by Polish leaders after the first partition of Poland in 1772 had left the remnant state without some of its wealthiest territories (see Map 18.1 on page 623). Beginning in 1788, however, reforming gentry in the *sejm*° (representative assembly) went further; they established a commission to write a constitution, following the American example. The resulting document, known as the May 3 (1791) Constitution, was the first codified constitution in Europe; it was read and admired by George Washington.

Poles thus established a constitutional monarchy in which representatives of major towns as well as gentry and nobility could sit as deputies. The *liberum veto*, which had allowed great magnates to obstruct royal authority at will, was abolished. However, Catherine the Great, empress of Russia, would not tolerate a constitutional government operating so close to her own autocratic regime; she ordered an invasion of Poland in 1792. The unsuccessful defense of Poland was led by a veteran of the American Revolution, Tadeusz Kosciuszko° (1746–1817). The second, more extensive partition of Poland followed, to be answered in turn in 1794 by a widespread insurrection against Russian rule, again spearheaded by Kosciuszko. The uprising was mercilessly suppressed by an alliance of Russian and Prussian troops. Unlike the U.S. Constitution from which they drew inspiration, the Poles' constitutional experiment was doomed by the power of its neighbor.

■ The American Revolution and the Kingdom of France

As Britain's greatest commercial and political rival, France naturally was drawn into Britain's struggle with its North American colonies. In the Seven Years' War (1756–1763), the French had lost many of their colonial settlements and trading outposts to the English (see page 630). Stung by this outcome, certain French courtiers and ministers pressed for an aggressive colonial policy that would regain for France some of the riches in trade that Britain now threatened to monopolize. The American Revolution seemed to offer the perfect opportunity. The French extended covert aid to the Americans from the very beginning of the conflict in 1775. After the first major defeat of British troops by the Americans—at the Battle of Saratoga in 1777—France formally recognized the independent United States and established an alliance with them. The French then committed troops as well as funds for the American cause. John Paul Jones's most famous ship, the *Bonhomme Richard*°, was purchased and outfitted in France at French government expense, as were many other American naval vessels during the war. French support was decisive. In 1781 the French fleet kept reinforcements from reaching the British force besieged by George Washington at Yorktown. The American victory at Yorktown effectively ended the war; the colonies' independence was formally recognized by the Treaty of Paris in 1783.

The consequences for France of its American alliance were momentous. Aid for the Americans saddled France with a debt of about 1 billion *livres* (pounds), which represented as much as one-quarter of the total debt that the French government was trying to service. A less tangible impact of the American Revolution derived from the direct participation of about nine thousand French soldiers, sailors, and aristocrats. The best known is the Marquis de Lafayette°, who became an aide to George Washington and helped command American troops. For many humble men, the war was simply employment. For others, it was a quest of sorts. For them, the promise of the Enlightenment—belief in human rationality, natural rights, and universal laws by which society should be organized—was brought to life in America.

Exposure to the American conflict occurred at the French court, too. Beginning in 1775, a permanent American mission to Versailles lobbied hard for aid and later managed the flow of that assistance. The chief emissary of the Americans was Benjamin Franklin (1706–1790), a philosophe by French standards whose writings and scientific experiments were already known to European elites. His talents—among them, a skillful exploitation of a simple, Quaker-like demeanor—succeeded in promoting the idealization of America at the French court.

The U.S. Constitution, the various state constitutions, and the debates surrounding their ratifications were all published in Paris and much discussed in salons and at court, where lively debate about reform of French institutions had been going on for decades. America became the prototype of the rational republic—the embodiment of Enlightenment philosophy. It was hailed as the place where the irrationalities of inherited privilege did not prevail. A British observer, Arthur Young (1741–1820), believed that "the American revolution has laid

---

sejm (SAME)
Tadeusz Kosciuszko (tah-DAY-oosh kos-USE-ko)

Bonhomme Richard (bon-OHM ree-SHARD)
Marquis de Lafayette (mar-KEE duh la-fye-ET)

Marie-Joseph, Marquis de Lafayette   The marquis is depicted commanding troops during the American Revolution. Called the "hero of two worlds," Lafayette returned to France to become one of the most imortant aristocratic reformers during the French Revolution. He favored a constitutional monarchy and opposed republican rule.   *(Jean-Loup Charmet)*

the foundation of another in France, if [the French] government does not take care of itself."[2]

By the mid-1780s there was no longer a question of whether the French regime would experience reform but rather what form the reform would take. The royal government was almost bankrupt. A significant minority of the politically active elite was convinced of the fundamental irrationality of France's system of government. Nevertheless, a dissatisfied elite and a financial crisis—even fanned by a successful revolt elsewhere—do not necessarily lead to revolution. Why did the French government—the *Ancien Régime°*, or "Old Regime," as it became known after the Revolution—not "take care of itself"?

■ The Crisis of the Old Regime

The Old Regime was brought to the point of crisis in the late 1780s by three factors: (1) heavy debts that dwarfed an antiquated system for collecting revenue; (2) institutional constraints on the monarchy that defended privileged interests; and (3) public opinion that envisioned thoroughgoing reform and pushed the monarchy in that direction. Another factor was the ineptitude of the king, Louis XVI (r. 1774–1793).

Louis came to the throne in 1774, a year before the American Revolution began. He was a kind, well-meaning man better suited to carry out the finite responsibilities of a petty bureaucrat than to be king. The queen, the Austrian Marie Antoinette (1755–1793), was unpopular. She was regarded with suspicion by the many who despised the "unnatural" alliance with Austria the marriage had sealed. She, too, was politically inept, unable to negotiate the complexities of court life and widely rumored to be selfishly wasteful of royal resources despite the realm's financial crises.

The fiscal crisis of the monarchy had been a long time in the making and was an outgrowth of the system in which the greatest wealth was protected by traditional privileges. At the top of the social and political pyramid were the nobles, a legal grouping that included warriors and royal officials. In France, nobility conferred exemption from much taxation. Thus, the royal government could not directly tax its wealthiest subjects.

This situation existed throughout much of Europe, a legacy of the individual contractual relationships that had formed the political and economic framework of medieval Europe. Unique to France, however, was the strength of the institutions that defended this system. Of particular importance were the royal law courts, the parlements°, which claimed a right of judicial review over royal edicts. All the parlementaires—well-educated lawyers and judges—were noble and loudly defended the traditional privileges of all nobles. Louis XV (d. 1774), near the end of his life, had successfully undermined the power of the parlements by a bold series of moves. Louis XVI, immediately after coming to the throne, buckled under pressure and restored the parlements to full strength.

Deficit financing had been a way of life for the monarchy for centuries. After early efforts at reform, Louis XIV (d. 1715) had reverted to common fund-raising expedients such as selling offices, which only added to the weight of privileged investment in the old order. England had established a national bank to free its government from the problem, but the comparable French

---

Ancien Régime (ahn-SYEN ray-ZHEEM)

parlements (par-luh-MAWHN)

The Common People Crushed by Privilege In this contemporary cartoon, a nobleman in military dress and a clergyman crush a commoner under the rock of burdensome taxes and forced labor (*corvées*). The victim's situation reflects that of the peasantry, but his stylish clothes would allow affluent towns-people to identify with him. *(Musée Carnavalet, Paris/Giraudon/Art Resource, NY)*

effort early in the century had been undercapitalized and had failed. Late in the 1780s, under Louis XVI, one-fourth of the annual operating expenses of the government was borrowed, and half of all government expenditure went to paying interest on its debt. Short-term economic crises, such as disastrous harvests, added to the cumulative problem of government finance.

The king employed able finance ministers who tried to institute fundamental reforms, such as replacing the tangle of taxes with a simpler system in which all would pay and eliminating local tariffs, which were stifling commerce. The parlements and many courtiers and aristocrats, as well as ordinary people, resisted these policies. Peasants and townsfolk did not trust the "free market" (free from traditional trade controls) for grain; most feared that speculators would buy up the grain supply and people would starve. Trying to implement such reforms in times of grain shortage almost guaranteed their failure. Moreover, many supported the parlements simply because they were the only institution capable of standing up to the monarchy. Yet not all members of the elite joined the parlements in opposing reform. The imprint of "enlightened" public opinion was apparent in the thinking of some courtiers and thousands of educated commoners who believed that the government and the economy had to change and openly debated the nature and extent of reform needed.

In 1787 the king called an "Assembly of Notables"—an ad hoc group of elites—to support him in facing down the parlements and proceeding with some changes. He found little support even among men known to be sympathetic to reform. Some did not support particular proposals, and many were reluctant to allow the monarchy free rein. Others, reflecting the influence of the American Revolution, maintained that a "constitutional" body such as the Estates General, which had not been called since 1614, needed to make these decisions.

Ironically, nobles and clergy who were opposed to reform supported the call for the Estates General, confident they could control its deliberations. The three Estates met and voted separately by "order"—clergy (First Estate), nobles (Second Estate), and commoners (Third Estate). The combined votes of the clergy and nobles would presumably nullify whatever the Third Estate might propose.

In 1788 popular resistance to reform in the streets of Paris and mounting pressure from his courtiers and bureaucrats induced Louis to summon the Estates General. On Louis's orders, deputies were to be elected by local assemblies, which were chosen, in turn, by wide male suffrage. Louis mistakenly assumed he had widespread support in the provinces, and he wished to tap into it by means of this grass-roots voting. Louis also agreed that

⌘ READING SOURCES

Lists of Grievances for the Estates General

In preparation for the meeting of an Estates General, communities throughout France prepared lists of grievances that they hoped the deputies would address. Among the following petitions compiled by a town in Normandy in 1789, we can note deference to the king but also radical proposals reflecting the impact of Enlightenment thought. The document denounces certain special privileges associated with nobility, in particular the burdensome remnants of medieval property control, and clearly recognizes the Estates as the legitimate voice of the nation. Note also the initial demand: that, contrary to the king's plans, voting in the Estates should occur by head.

. . . [T]he inhabitants decreed that their wishes were:

1. That in the assembly of the Estates-General, opinions be counted by head and not by order. . . .

2. That only the assembled nation may consent to taxes, loans and new offices, and no corporation, organization, not even provincial estates will be allowed to represent the nation.

3. That, in keeping with his majesty's promise, the Estates-General will assemble at fixed and determined periods, that taxes may only be consented to by the Estates until the period of their next meeting, and that each new assembly of estates will be preceded by a new choosing of deputies, so that no citizen can perpetually represent the nation. . . .

7. That all privileges and pecuniary exemptions be abolished, and taxes be collected without discrimination in the same proportion from all orders within the province.

8. That, to facilitate commerce, tollgates be removed to the frontiers of the realm, that his majesty be entreated to remedy the obstacles to commerce occasioned by differences in weights and measures. . . .

10. That the right of *franc fief* [fee payable by commoners to the king for the right of holding a noble fief] be suppressed, as humiliating to the Third Estate.

11. That, at the same time, his majesty be humbly entreated to recall that decision . . . which excludes from his majesty's service all citizens who cannot prove four degrees of nobility; that his majesty equally be entreated to bring about a reform of the [Parlement's] decisions whereby a gentleman is sought for an office which confers nobility before a candidate's merits are considered, in consequence of which merit will become sufficient grounds to enter the different estates.

Source: Annales du Centre Régional de Documentation Pédagogique de Caen, *Les Cahiers de Doléances de 1789 dans le Calvados.* Nouvelle série #6. Service Éducatif des Archives départementales du Calvados. Translated by Laura Mason. Reprinted in Laura Mason and Tracey Rizzo, eds., *The French Revolution: A Document Collection* (Boston: Houghton Mifflin, 1999), pp. 56–57.

---

the Third Estate should have twice as many deputies as the other two Estates, but he did not authorize voting by head rather than by order, which would have brought about the dominance of the Third Estate. Nevertheless, the king hoped that the specter of drastic proposals put forth by the Third Estate would frighten the aristocrats and clergy into accepting some of his reforms. (See the box "Reading Sources: List of Grievances for the Estates General.")

Louis's situation was precarious when the Estates General convened in May 1789. As ever, he faced immediate financial crisis. He also faced a constitutional crisis. Already a groundswell of sentiment confirmed the legitimacy of the Estates General, the role of the Third Estate, and the authority of the Third Estate to enact change. Political pamphlets abounded arguing that the Third Estate deserved enhanced power because it carried the mandate of the people. The most important of these was

What Is the Third Estate? (1789) by Joseph Emmanuel Sieyès° (1748–1836), a church official from the diocese of Chartres. The sympathies of Abbé Sieyès, as he was known, were with the Third Estate: his career had suffered and stalled because he was not noble. Sieyès argued that the Third Estate represented the nation because it did not reflect special privilege.

Among the deputies of the first two Estates—clergy and nobility—were men, such as the Marquis de Lafayette (1757–1834), who were sympathetic to reform. More important, however, the elections had returned to the Third Estate a large majority of deputies who reflected the most radical political thought possible for men of their standing. Most were lawyers and other professionals who were functionaries in the government but, like Sieyès, of low social rank. They frequented provincial academies, salons, and political societies. They were convinced of the validity of their viewpoints and determined on reform, and they had little stake in the system as it was. When this group convened and met with resistance from the First and Second Estates and from Louis himself, they seized the reins of government and a revolution began.

■ 1789: A Revolution Begins

As soon as the three Estates convened at the royal palace at Versailles, conflicts surfaced. The ineptness of the Crown was immediately clear. On the first day of the meetings in May, Louis and his ministers failed to introduce a program of reforms for the deputies to consider. This failure raised doubt about the monarchy's commitment to reform. More important, it allowed the political initiative to pass to the Third Estate. The deputies challenged the Crown's insistence that the three Estates meet and vote separately. Deputies to the Third Estate refused to be certified (that is, to have their credentials officially recognized) as members of only the Third Estate rather than as members of the Estates General as a whole.

For six weeks the Estates General was unable to meet officially, and the king did nothing to break the impasse. During this interlude, the determination of the deputies of the Third Estate strengthened. More and more deputies were won over to the notion that the three Estates must begin in the most systematic way: France must have a written constitution.

By the middle of June, more than thirty reformist members of the clergy were sitting jointly with the Third Estate, which had invited all deputies from all three Estates to meet and be certified together. On June 17 the

Third Estate simply declared itself the National Assembly of France. At first, the king did nothing, but when the deputies arrived to meet on the morning of June 20, they discovered they had been locked out of the hall. Undaunted, they assembled instead in a nearby indoor tennis court and produced the document that has come to be known as the "Tennis Court Oath." It was a collective pledge to meet until a written constitution had been achieved. Only one deputy refused to support it. Sure of their mandate, the deputies had assumed the reins of government.

The king continued to handle the situation with both ill-timed self-assertion and feeble attempts at compromise. As more and more deputies from the First and Second Estates joined the National Assembly, Louis "ordered" the remaining loyal deputies to join it, too. Simultaneously, however, he ordered troops to come to Paris. He feared disorder in the wake of the recent disturbances throughout France and believed that any challenge to the legitimacy of arbitrary monarchical authority would be disastrous.

This appeal for armed assistance stirred unrest in the capital. Paris, with a population of about 600,000 in 1789, was one of the largest cities in Europe. It was the political nerve center of the nation—the site of the publishing industry, salons, the homes of parlementaires and royal ministers. It was also a working city, with thousands of laborers of all trades plus thousands more—perhaps one-tenth of the inhabitants—jobless recent immigrants from the countryside. The city was both extremely volatile and extremely important to the stability of royal power. The king's call for troops aroused Parisians' suspicions. Some assumed a plot was afoot to starve Paris and destroy the National Assembly. Already they considered the Assembly to be a guarantor of acceptable government.

It took little—the announcement of the dismissal of a reformist finance minister—for Paris to erupt in demonstrations and looting. Crowds besieged City Hall and the royal armory, where they seized thousands of weapons. A popular militia formed as citizens armed themselves. Armed crowds assailed other sites of royal authority, including the huge fortified prison, the Bastille, on the morning of July 14. The Bastille now held only a handful of petty criminals, but it still remained a potent symbol of royal power and, it was assumed, held large supplies of arms. Like the troops at the armory, the garrison at the Bastille had received no firm orders to fire on the crowds if necessary. The garrison commander at first mounted a hesitant defense, then decided to surrender after citizens managed to secure cannon and drag them to face the prison. Most of the garrison were

Sieyès (say-EZ)

The Tennis Court Oath   It was raining on June 20 when the deputies found themselves barred from their meeting hall and sought shelter in the royal tennis court. Their defiance created one of the turning points of the Revolution; the significance was recognized several years later by this painting's artist. *(Photographie Bulloz)*

allowed to go free, although the commander and several officers were murdered by the crowd.

The citizens' victory was a great embarrassment to royal authority. The king immediately had to embrace the popular movement. He came to Paris and in front of crowds at City Hall donned the red and blue cockade worn by the militia and ordinary folk as a badge of resolve and defiance. This symbolic action signaled the reversal of the Old Regime—politics would now be based on new principles.

Encouraged by events in Paris, inhabitants of cities and towns around France staged similar uprisings. In many areas, the machinery of royal government completely broke down. City councils, officials, and even parlementaires were thrown out of office. Popular militias took control of the streets. A simultaneous wave of uprisings shook the countryside. Most of them were the result of food shortages, but their timing added momentum to the more strictly political protests in cities. These events forced the members of the National Assembly to

work energetically on the constitution and to pass legislation to satisfy popular protests against economic and political privileges.

On August 4 the Assembly issued a set of decrees abolishing the remnants of powers that landlords had enjoyed since the Middle Ages, including the right to co-opt peasant labor and the bondage of serfdom itself. Although largely symbolic, because serfdom and forced labor had been eliminated in much of France, these changes represented a dramatic inroad into the property rights of the elite as they had been traditionally construed. The repeals were hailed as the "end of feudalism." A blow was also struck at established religion by eliminating the tithe. At the end of August, the Assembly issued a Declaration of the Rights of Man and the Citizen. It was a bold assertion of the foundations of a newly conceived government, closely modeled on portions of the U.S. Constitution. Its preamble declared "that [since] the ignorance, neglect or contempt of the rights of man are the sole cause of public calamities and the corruption of governments," the deputies were "determined to set forth in a solemn declaration the natural, inalienable and sacred rights of man. . . ."[3]

In September the deputies debated the king's role in a new constitutional government. Monarchists favored a government rather like England's, with a two-house legislature, including an upper house representing the hereditary aristocracy and a royal right to veto legislation. More radical deputies favored a single legislative chamber and no veto power for the king. After deliberation, the Assembly reached a compromise. The king was given a three-year suspensive veto—the power to suspend legislation for the sitting of two legislatures. This was still a formidable amount of power but a drastic curtailment of his formerly absolute sovereignty.

Again, Louis resorted to troops. This time, he called them directly to Versailles, where the Assembly sat. News of the troops' arrival provoked outrage, which heightened with the threat of another grain shortage. Early on the morning of October 5, women in the Paris street markets saw the empty grocers' stalls and took immediate collective action. "We want bread!" they shouted at the steps of City Hall. Because they were responsible for procuring their families' food, women often led protests over bread shortages. This protest, however, went far beyond the ordinary. A crowd of thousands gathered and decided to walk all the way to Versailles, accompanied by the popular militia (now called the "National Guard"), to petition the king directly for sustenance.

At Versailles, they presented a delegation to the National Assembly, and a joint delegation of the women and deputies was dispatched to see the king. Some of the women fell at the feet of the king with their tales of hardship, certain that the "father of the people" would alleviate their suffering. He did order stored grain supplies distributed in Paris, and he also agreed to accept the constitutional role that the Assembly had voted for him.

Storming the Bastille   The crowd was convinced that the Bastille held political prisoners as well as a large supply of arms. In fact, it held neither. Thousands of Parisians—including artisans and shopkeepers and not merely desperate rabble—surrounded the fortress and forced the garrison to surrender.   *(Photographie Bulloz)*

That very night members of the National Guard, which had replaced the royal guard around the person of the king, saved Louis's life. A mob broke into the palace and managed to kill two members of the royal guard still in attendance outside the queen's chamber. The king agreed to return to Paris so that he could reassure the people. But the procession back to the city was a curious one. The royal family was escorted by militia and bread protesters, and the severed heads of the dead royal guardsmen were carried on pikes.

The king was now in the hands of his people. Already, dramatic change had occurred as a result of a complex dynamic among the three Estates, the Crown, and the people of Paris. The king was still assumed to be the fatherly guardian of his people's well-being; but his powers were now limited, and his authority was badly shaken. The Assembly had begun to govern in the name of the "nation" and, so far, had the support of the people.

THE PHASES OF THE REVOLUTION, 1789–1799

HE French Revolution was a complicated affair. It was a series of changes, in a sense a series of revolutions, driven not by one group of people but by several groups. Even among elites convinced of the need for reform the range of opinion was wide. The people of Paris continued to be an important force for change. Country people also became active, primarily in resisting changes forced on them by the central government.

All of the wrangling within France was complicated by foreign reaction. Managing foreign war soon became a routine burden for the fragile revolutionary governments. In addition, they had to cope with the continuing problems that had precipitated the Revolution in the first place: the government's chronic indebtedness, economic difficulties, and recurrent grain shortages. Finally, the Revolution itself was an issue in that, once the traditional arrangements of royal government had been altered, momentum for further change was unleashed.

■ The First Phase Completed, 1789–1791

At the end of 1789, Paris was in ferment, but for a time forward progress blunted the threat of disastrous divisions between king and Assembly and between either of those and the people of Paris. The capital continued to be the center of lively political debate. Salons continued

to meet; academies and private societies proliferated. Deputies to the Assembly swelled the ranks of these societies or helped to found new ones. Several would be important throughout the Revolution—particularly the Jacobin° Club, named for the monastic order whose buildings the members used as a meeting hall.

These clubs represented the gamut of revolutionary opinion. Some, in which ordinary Parisians were well represented, focused on economic policies that would directly benefit common people. Women were active in a few of the more radical groups. Monarchists dominated other clubs. At first similar to the salons and debating societies of the Enlightenment era, the clubs quickly became both sites of political action and sources of political pressure on the government. A bevy of popular newspapers also contributed to the vigorous political life in the capital.

The broad front of revolutionary consensus began to break apart as the Assembly forged ahead with decisions about the constitution and with policies necessary to remedy France's still-desperate financial situation. The largest portion of the untapped wealth of the nation lay with the Catholic Church, an obvious target for anticlerical reformers. The deputies did not propose to dismantle the church, but they did make sweeping changes: They kept church buildings intact and retained the clergy as salaried officials of the state. They abolished all monasteries and pensioned the monks and nuns to permit them to continue as nurses and teachers where possible. With the depleted treasury in mind, the Assembly seized most of the vast lands of the church and declared them national property (*biens nationaux*) to be sold for revenue.

Economic and political problems ensued. Revenue was needed faster than the property could be inventoried and sold, so government bonds (*assignats*°) were issued against the eventual sale of church properties. Unfortunately, in the cash-strapped economy, the bonds were treated like money, their value became inflated, and the government never realized the hoped-for profits. A greater problem was the political divisiveness generated by the restructuring of the church. Many members of the lower clergy, living as they did near ordinary citizens, were among the most reform-minded of the deputies. These clergy were willing to go along with many changes, but the required oath of loyalty to the state made a mockery of clerical independence.

The Civil Constitution of the Clergy, as these measures were called, was passed by the Assembly in July 1790 because the clerical deputies opposing it were outvoted.

Jacobin (JACK-oh-bin)   **assignats** (ah-see-NYAH)

CHRONOLOGY

The French Revolution

1789	**May 5**	Estates General meets in Versailles
	June 17	Third Estate declares itself the National Assembly
	June 20	Tennis Court Oath
	July 14	Storming of the Bastille
	August 27	Declaration of the Rights of Man and the Citizen
	October 5–6	Women's march on Versailles Louis XVI returns to Paris
1790	**July**	Civil Constitution of the Clergy
1791	**June**	Louis XVI captured attempting to flee
	August	Declaration of Pillnitz
	September	New constitution implemented
1792	**April**	France declares war on Austria
	August 10	Storming of the Tuileries Louis XVI arrested
	September 21	National Convention declares France a republic
1793	**January 21**	Louis XVI guillotined
	May	First Law of the Maximum
	July	Terror inaugurated
1794	**July**	Robespierre guillotined Terror ends
1795	**October**	Directory established
1799	**November**	Napoleon seizes power

More than half of the churchmen did take the oath of loyalty. Those who refused, concentrated among the higher clergy, were in theory thrown out of their offices. A year later (April 1791) the pope declared that clergy who had taken the oath were suspended from their offices. Antirevolutionary sentiment grew among thousands of French people, particularly in outlying regions, to whom the church was still vital as a source of charity and a center of community life. This religious opposition worked to undermine the legitimacy of the new government.

Meanwhile, the Assembly proceeded with administrative and judicial reform. The deputies abolished the medieval provinces as administrative districts and replaced them with uniform *départements* (departments). They declared that local officials would be elected—a revolutionary dispersal of power that had previously belonged to the king.

As work on the constitution drew to a close in the spring of 1791, the king decided that he had had enough. Royal authority, as he knew it, had been virtually dismantled. Louis himself was now a virtual prisoner in the Tuileries° Palace in the very heart of Paris. Afraid for himself and his family, he and a few loyal aides worked out a plan to flee France. The king and the members of his immediate family set out in disguise on June 20, 1791. However, the party missed a rendezvous with a troop escort and was stopped—and recognized—in the town of Varennes°, near the eastern border of the kingdom.

Louis and his family were returned to Paris and held under lightly disguised house arrest. The circumstances of his flight were quickly discovered. He and the queen had sent money abroad ahead of themselves. He had left behind a document condemning the constitution. His intention was to invade France with Austrian troops if necessary. Thus, in July 1791, just as the Assembly was completing its proposal for a constitutional monarchy, the constitution it had created began to seem unworkable because the monarch was not to be trusted.

Editorials and protests against the monarchy increased. In one incident known as the Massacre of the Champ (Field) de Mars°, government troops led by Lafayette fired on citizens at an antimonarchy demonstration that certain Parisian clubs had organized; about fifty men and women died. This inflammatory incident both reflected and heightened tensions between moderate reformers satisfied with the constitutional monarchy, such as Lafayette, and outspoken republicans who wanted to eliminate the monarchy altogether.

On September 14 the king swore to uphold the constitution. He had no choice. The event became an occasion for celebration, but the tension between the interests of the Parisians and the provisions of the new constitution could not be glossed over. Though a liberal document for its day, the constitution reflected the views of the elite deputies who had created it. The right to vote, based on a minimal property qualification, was given to about half of all adult men. However, these men only chose electors, for whom the property qualifications were higher. The electors in turn chose deputies to

Tuileries (TWEE-lair-ee)   **Varennes** (vah-REN)
Champ de Mars (SHOM duh MARSS)

Declaration of the Rights of Woman

This retort to the new constitution, in which rights for women were conspicuously absent, was written in 1791 by Olympe de Gouges (1748?–1793), a self-educated butcher's daughter from southwestern France. The document reflects the complexity of political life during the Revolution. Gouges's declaration urges the extension to women of the Revolution's broad-based challenge to tradition. Yet Gouges dedicates the declaration to the queen, Marie-Antoinette, drawing on the tradition of aristocratic patronage. Ironically, given Article 10, Gouges died on the scaffold for her revolutionary sympathies.

Man, Are you capable of being just? It is a woman who poses the question; at least you will not take away this right. Tell me, what gives you the sovereign empire to oppress my sex? Your strength? Your talents? Observe the Creator in his wisdom; look at nature in all her grandeur, with whom you seem to want to be in harmony, and give me, if you dare, an example of this tyrannical empire. . . . Bizarre, blind, bloated with science and degenerated—in a century of light and wisdom—in the crassest ignorance, he wants to command as a despot a sex which has received all intellectual faculties; he pretends to enjoy the Revolution and reclaim his rights to equality only to say nothing more about it.

1. Woman is born free and lives equal to man in her rights. Social distinctions may be founded only upon common utility.

2. The purpose of any political association is the conservation of the natural and imprescriptible rights of woman and man; these rights are liberty, property, security, and above all resistance to oppression.

3. The principle of all sovereignty resides essentially in the Nation, which is nothing other than the union of woman and man: no body, no individual can exercise authority which does not emanate from it.

4. Liberty and justice consist of rendering all that belongs to others; thus, the exercise of the natural rights of woman has only been limited by the perpetual tyranny that man opposes to them; these limits should be reformed by the laws of nature and reason. . . .

10. No one should be troubled for holding basic opinions; woman has the right to mount the scaffold; she must equally have the right to mount the podium. . . .

Source: Olympe de Gouges, *Écrits politiques, 1788–1791* (Paris: Côte-femmes, 1993), pp. 204–210. Translated by Tracey Rizzo. Reprinted in Laura Mason and Tracey Rizzo, eds., *The French Revolution: A Document Collection* (Boston: Houghton Mifflin, 1999), pp. 110–112.

---

national bodies as well as local officials. Although in theory any eligible voter could be an elected deputy or official, the fact that elite electors determined every officeholder meant that few ordinary citizens would become deputies or local administrators. The Declaration of Rights that accompanied the constitution reflected a fear of the masses that had not existed when the Declaration of the Rights of Man and the Citizen was first promulgated in 1789. Freedom of the press and freedom of assembly, for example, were not fully guaranteed.

Further, no political rights were accorded to women. Educated women had joined Parisian clubs such as the *Cercle sociale* (Social Circle), where opinion favored extending rights to women. Through such clubs, these women had tried to influence the National Assembly. But the Assembly granted neither political rights nor legal equality to women, nor did it pass other laws beneficial to women such as legalizing divorce or mandating female education. The prevailing view of women among deputies seemed to reflect those of the Enlightenment philosophe Rousseau, who imagined women's competence to be entirely circumscribed within the family. A Declaration of the Rights of Woman was drafted by a woman named Olympe de Gouges° to draw attention to the treatment of women in the constitution. (See the box "Reading Sources: Declaration of the Rights of Woman.")

Olympe de Gouges (oh-LAMP duh GOOZH)

Very soon after the constitution was implemented, the fragility of the new system became clear. The National Assembly declared that its members could not serve in the first assembly to be elected under the constitution. Thus, the members of the newly elected Legislative Assembly, which began to meet in October 1791, lacked any of the cohesiveness that would have come from collective experience. Also, unlike the previous National Assemblymen, they did not represent a broad range of opinion but were mostly republicans.

In fact, the Legislative Assembly was dominated by republican members of the Jacobin Club. They were known as Girondins°, after the region in southwestern France from which many of the club's leaders came. The policies of these new deputies and continued pressure from the ordinary citizens of Paris would cause the constitutional monarchy to collapse in less than a year.

■ The Second Phase and Foreign War, 1791–1793

An additional pressure on the new regime soon arose: a threat of foreign invasion and a war to counter the threat. Antirevolutionary aristocratic émigrés, including the king's brothers, had taken refuge in nearby German states and were planning to invade France. The emperor and other German rulers did little actively to aid the plotters. Austria and Prussia, however, in the Declaration of Pillnitz of August 1791, declared, as a concession to the émigrés, that they would intervene if necessary to support the monarchy in France.

The threat of invasion, when coupled with distrust of the royal family, seemed more real to the revolutionaries in Paris than it may actually have been. Indeed, many deputies hoped for war. They assumed that the outcome would be a French defeat, which would lead to a popular uprising that would rid them, at last, of the monarchy. In April 1792, under pressure from the Assembly, Louis XVI declared war against Austria. From this point, foreign war would be an ongoing factor in the Revolution.

At first, the war was a disaster for France. The army had not been reorganized into an effective fighting force after the loss of many aristocratic officers and the addition of newly self-aware citizens. On one occasion, troops insisted on putting an officer's command to a vote. The French lost early battles in the Austrian Netherlands, but the Austrians did not press their advantage and invade France because they were preoccupied with problems in eastern Europe.

Girondins (zhih-ron-DEHN)

Louis XVI in 1792   The king, though a kindly man, had neither the character nor the convictions necessary to refashion royal authority symbolically as the Revolution proceeded. When Parisian crowds forced him to wear the "liberty cap," the monarchy was close to collapse.   *(Metropolitan Museum of Art, The Elisha Whittelsey Collection, The Elisha Whittelsey Fund, 1962)*

The defeats emboldened critics of the monarchy, who demanded action. Under the direction of the Girondins, the Legislative Assembly began to press for the deportation of priests who had been leading demonstrations against the government. The Assembly abolished the personal guard of the king and summoned provincial national guardsmen to Paris. The king's resistance to these measures, as well as fears of acute grain shortages owing to a poor harvest and the needs of the armies, created further unrest. Crowds staged boisterous marches near the royal palace, physically confronted the king, and forced him to don the "liberty cap," a symbol of republicanism. The king's authority and prestige were now thoroughly undermined.

By July 1792, tensions had become acute. The grain shortage was severe, Austrian and Prussian troops committed to saving the royal family were threatening to invade, and, most important, the populace was better organized and more determined than ever before. In each of the forty-eight "sections"—administrative wards—of Paris a miniature popular assembly thrashed out all the events and issues of the day just as deputies in the nationwide Legislative Assembly did. Derisively called *sans-culottes*° ("without knee pants") because they could not afford elite fashions, the ordinary Parisians in the section assemblies included shopkeepers, artisans, and laborers. Their political organization enhanced their influence with the Assembly, the clubs, and the newspapers in the capital. By late July most sections of the city had approved a petition calling for the exile of the king, the election of new city officials, the exemption of the poor from taxation, and other radical measures.

In August the sans-culottes took matters into their own hands. On the night of August 9, after careful preparations, representatives of the section assemblies constituted themselves as a new city government with the aim of "saving the state." They then assaulted the Tuileries Palace, where the royal family was living. In the bloody confrontation, hundreds of royal guards and citizens died. After briefly taking refuge in the Legislative Assembly itself, the king and his family were imprisoned in one of the fortified towers in the city, under guard of the popularly controlled city government.

The storming of the Tuileries inaugurated the second major phase of the Revolution: the establishment of republican government in place of the monarchy. By their intimidating numbers, the people of Paris now controlled the Legislative Assembly. Some deputies had fled. Those who remained agreed under pressure to dissolve the Assembly and make way for another body to be elected by universal manhood suffrage. On September 20, that assembly—known as the National Convention—began to meet. The next day, the Convention declared the end of the monarchy and set to work crafting a constitution for the new republic.

Coincidentally, that same September day, French forces won their first genuine victory over the allied Austrian and Prussian invasion forces. Though not a decisive battle, it was a profound psychological triumph. A citizen army had defeated the professional force of a ruling prince. The victory bolstered the republican government and encouraged it to put more energy into the wars. Indeed, maintaining armies in the field became a weighty factor in the delicate equilibrium of revolutionary government. The new republican regime let it be known that

---

sans-culottes (sahn–koo-LOT)

its armies were not merely for self-defense but for the liberation of all peoples in the "name of the French Nation."

The Convention faced the divisive issue of what to do with the king. Louis had not done anything truly treasonous, but some of the king's correspondence, discovered after the storming of the Tuileries, provided the pretext for charges of treason. The Convention held a trial for him, lasting from December 11, 1792, through January 15, 1793. He was found guilty of treason by an overwhelming vote (683 to 39); the republican government would not compromise with monarchy. Less lopsided was the sentence: Louis was condemned to death by a narrow majority, 387 to 334.

The consequences for the king were immediate. On January 21, 1793, Louis mounted the scaffold in a public square near the Tuileries and was beheaded. The execution split the ranks of the Convention and soon resulted in the breakdown of the institution itself.

■ The Faltering Republic and the Terror, 1793–1794

In February 1793 the republic was at war with virtually every state in Europe; the only exceptions were the Scandinavian kingdoms and Russia. Moreover, the regime faced massive and widespread counterrevolutionary uprisings within France. Vigilance against internal and external enemies became a top priority. The Convention established an executive body, the Committee of Public Safety. In theory, this executive council was answerable to the Convention as a whole. As the months passed, however, it acted with greater and greater autonomy not only to institute policies but also to eradicate enemies. The broadly based republican government represented by the Convention began to disintegrate.

The first major narrowing of control came in June 1793. Pushed by the Parisian sections, a group of extreme Jacobins purged the Girondin deputies from the Convention, arresting many of them. The Girondins were republicans who favored an activist government in the people's behalf, but they were less radical than the Jacobins, less insistent on central control of the Revolution, and less willing to share power with the citizens of Paris. After the purge, the Convention still met, but most authority lay with the Committee of Public Safety.

New uprisings against the regime began. Added to counterrevolutionary revolts by peasants and aristocrats were new revolts by Girondin sympathizers. As resistance to the government mounted and the foreign threat continued, a dramatic event in Paris led the Committee

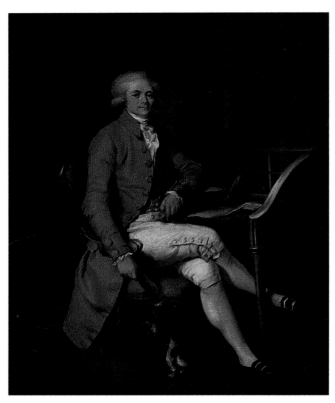

Robespierre the Incorruptible   A lawyer who had often championed the poor, Robespierre was elected to the Estates General in 1789 and was a consistent advocate of republican government from the beginning of the Revolution. His unswerving loyalty to his political principles earned him the nickname "the Incorruptible." *(Musée des Beaux-Arts, Lille)*

of Public Safety officially to adopt a policy of political repression. A well-known figure of the Revolution, Jean Paul Marat (1743–1793), publisher of a radical republican newspaper very popular with ordinary Parisians, was murdered on July 13 by Charlotte Corday (1768–1793), a young aristocratic woman who had asked to meet with him. Shortly afterward, a long-time member of the Jacobin Club, Maximilien Robespierre° (1758–1794), joined the Committee and called for "Terror"—the systematic repression of internal enemies. He was not alone in his views. Members of the section assemblies of Paris led demonstrations to pressure the government into making Terror the order of the day.

Terror meant the use of intimidation to silence dissent. Since the previous autumn, the guillotine had been at work against identified enemies of the regime, but now a more energetic apparatus of terror was instituted. A Law of Suspects was passed that allowed citizens to be arrested simply on vague suspicion of counterrevolutionary sympathies. Revolutionary tribunals and an oversight committee made arbitrary arrests and rendered summary judgments. In October a steady stream of executions began, beginning with the queen, imprisoned since the storming of the Tuileries the year before. The imprisoned Girondin deputies followed, and then the beheadings continued relentlessly. Paris witnessed about 2,600 executions from 1793 to 1794.

Around France the verdicts of revolutionary tribunals led to approximately 14,000 executions. Another 10,000 to 12,000 people died in prison. Ten thousand or more were killed, usually by summary execution, after the defeat of counterrevolutionary uprisings. For example, 2,000 people were summarily executed in Lyon when a Girondin revolt collapsed there in October. The aim of the Terror was not merely to stifle active resistance; it was also to silence simple dissent. The victims in Paris included not only aristocrats or former deputies but also sans-culottes. The radical Jacobins wanted to seize control of the Revolution from the Parisian citizens who had lifted them to power.

Robespierre himself embodied all the contradictions of the policy of Terror. He was an austere, almost prim, man who lived very modestly—a model, of sorts, of the virtuous, disinterested citizen. The policies followed by the government during the year of his greatest influence, from July 1793 to July 1794, included generous, rational, and humane actions to benefit ordinary citizens as well as the atrocities of official Terror. (See the box "Reading Sources: Robespierre Justifies the Terror.") Indeed, the Terror notwithstanding, the government of the Committee of Public Safety was effective in providing direction for the nation at a critical time. In August 1793 it instituted the first mass conscription of citizens into the army (*levée en masse°*), and a consistently effective popular army came into existence. In the autumn of 1793 this army won impressive victories. In May the Convention had instituted a Law of the Maximum, which controlled the price of grain so that city people could afford their staple food—bread. In September the Committee extended the law to apply to other necessary commodities. Extensive plans were made for a system of free and universal primary education. Slavery in the French colonies was abolished in February 1794. Divorce, first legalized in 1792, was made easier for women to obtain.

Robespierre (ROBES-pee-air)

levée en masse (leh-VAY ohn MAHSS)

❧ READING SOURCES

Robespierre Justifies the Terror

In this excerpt from a speech before the Convention in December 1793, Robespierre justifies the revolutionary government's need to act in an extraconstitutional manner. He echoes Rousseau's notion of a highly abstract sense of the public good. He also warns against challenges to the Revolution within France posed by foreign powers.

The defenders of the Republic must adopt Caesar's maxim, for they believe that "nothing has been done so long as anything remains to be done." Enough dangers still face us to engage all our efforts. It has not fully extended the valor of our Republican soldiers to conquer a few Englishmen and a few traitors. A task no less important, and one more difficult, now awaits us: to sustain an energy sufficient to defeat the constant intrigues of all the enemies of our freedom and to bring to a triumphant realization the principles that must be the cornerstone of public welfare.... Revolution is the war waged by liberty against its enemies; a constitution ... crowns the edifice of freedom once victory has been won and the nation is at peace.... The principal concern of a constitutional government is civil liberty; that of a revolutionary government, public liberty. [A] revolutionary government is obliged to defend the state itself against the factions that assail it from every quarter. To good citizens revolutionary government

owes the full protection of the state; to the enemies of the people it owes only death.

Is a revolutionary government the less just and the less legitimate because it must be more vigorous in its actions and freer in its movement than ordinary government? ... It also has its rules, all based on justice and public order.... It has nothing in common with arbitrary rule; it is public interest which governs it and not the whims of private individuals.

Thanks to five years of treason and tyranny, thanks to our credulity and lack of foresight ... Austria and England, Russia, Prussia, and Italy had time to set up in our country a secret government to challenge the authority of our own.... We shall strike terror, not in the hearts of patriots, but in the haunts of foreign brigands.

Source: George Rudé, ed., *Robespierre* (Englewood Cliffs, N.J.: Prentice-Hall, 1967), pp. 58–63.

In the name of "reason," traditional rituals and rhythms of life were changed. One reform of long-term significance was the introduction of the metric system of weights and measures. Although people continued to use the old, familiar measures for a very long time, the change was eventually accomplished, leading the way for standardization throughout Europe. Equally "rational" but not as successful was the elimination of the traditional calendar; weeks and months were replaced by forty-day months and *decadi* (ten-day weeks with one day of rest), and all saints' days and Christian holidays were eliminated. The years had already been changed— Year I had been declared with the founding of the republic in the autumn of 1792.

Churches were rededicated as "temples of reason." Believing that outright atheism left people with no basis for personal or national morality, Robespierre sought instead to promote a cult of the Supreme Being. The new public festivals were solemn civic ceremonies intended to ritualize and legitimize the new political order. These and other innovations of the regime were not necessarily welcomed. The French people generally resented the elimination of the traditional calendar. In the countryside massive peasant uprisings protested the loss of poor relief, community life, and familiar ritual.

Divorce law and economic regulation were a boon, especially to urban women, but women's participation in sectional assemblies and in all organized political activity—which had been energetic and widespread—was banned in October 1793. The particular target of the regime was the Society of Revolutionary Republican Women, a powerful club representing the interests of female sans-culottes. By banning women from political life, the regime helped to ground its legitimacy, since the seemingly "natural" exclusion of women might make the new system of government appear part of the "natural" order. (See the feature "Weighing the Evidence: Political Symbols" on pages 674–675.) Outlawing women's clubs and barring women from section assemblies also eliminated a source of popular power, from which the regime was now trying to distance itself.

The Committee and the Convention were divided over religious and other policies, but the main policy differences concerned economic matters: how far to go to assist the poor, the unemployed, and the landless. Several of the temperate critics of Robespierre and his allies were guillotined for disagreeing with these policies and for doubting the continuing need for the Terror itself. Their deaths helped precipitate the end of the Terror by causing Robespierre's power base to shrink so much that it had no further legitimacy.

Deputies to the Convention finally dared to move against Robespierre in July 1794. French armies had scored a major victory over Austrian troops on June 26, so there was no longer any need for the emergency status that the Terror had thrived on. In late July the Convention voted to arrest Robespierre, the head of the revolutionary tribunal in Paris, and their closest associates and allies in the city government. On July 28 and 29, Robespierre and the others—about a hundred in all—were guillotined, and the Terror ended.

■ Thermidorian Reaction and the Directory, 1794–1799

After the death of Robespierre, the Convention reclaimed many of the executive powers that the Committee of Public Safety had seized. The Convention dismantled the apparatus of the Terror, repealed the Law of Suspects, and forced the revolutionary tribunals to adopt ordinary legal procedures. The Convention also passed into law some initiatives, such as expanded public education, that had been proposed in the preceding year but not enacted. This post-Terror phase of the Revolution is called the "Thermidorian Reaction" because it began in the revolutionary month of Thermidor (July 19–August 17).

Lacking the weapons of the Terror, the Convention was unable to enforce controls on the supply and price of bread. Thus, economic difficulties and a hard winter produced famine by the spring of 1795. The people of Paris tried to retain influence with the new government. In May crowds marched on the Convention chanting "Bread and the Constitution of '93," referring to the republican constitution drafted by the Convention but never implemented because of the Terror. The demonstrations were met with force and were dispersed.

Members of the Convention remained fearful of a renewed, popularly supported Terror, on the one hand, or a royalist uprising, on the other. Counterrevolutionary uprisings had erupted in the fall of 1794, and landings on French territory by émigré forces occurred the following spring. The Convention drafted a new constitution that limited popular participation in government, as had the first constitution of 1791. The new plan allowed fairly widespread (but not universal) male suffrage, but only for electors, who would choose deputies for the two houses of the legislature. The property qualifications for being an elector were very high, so all but elite citizens were effectively disenfranchised. The Convention also decreed, at the last minute, that two-thirds of its members must serve in the new legislature, regardless of the outcome of elections. Though this maneuver enhanced the stability of the new regime, it undermined the credibility of the new ballot.

Governance under the provisions of the new constitution, beginning in the fall of 1795, was called the Directory, for the executive council of five men chosen by the upper house of the new legislature. To avoid the concentration of authority that had produced the Terror, the members of the Convention had tried to enshrine separation of powers in the new system. However, the governments under the Directory were never free from attempted coups or from their own extraconstitutional maneuvering.

The most spectacular external challenge, the Conspiracy of Equals, was led by extreme Jacobins who wanted to restore popular government and aggressive economic and social policy on behalf of the common people. The conspiracy ended with arrests and executions in 1797. When elections in 1797 and 1798 returned many royalist as well as Jacobin deputies, the Directory itself abrogated the constitution to forestall challenges to its authority: many undesirable deputies were arrested, sent into exile, or denied seats.

The armies of the republic did enjoy some spectacular successes during these years, for the first time carrying the fighting—and the effects of the Revolution—onto foreign soil. French armies conquered the Dutch in 1795. In 1796–1797 French armies led by the young general

Napoleon Bonaparte° wrested control of northern Italy from the Austrians. Both regions were transformed into "sister" republics, governed by local revolutionaries but under French protection. By 1799, however, conditions had once again reached a critical juncture. The demands of the war effort, together with rising prices and the continued decline in the value of the assignats, brought the government again to the brink of bankruptcy. The government also seemed to be losing control of the French countryside; there were continued royalist uprisings, local political vendettas between moderates and Jacobins, as well as outright banditry.

Members of the Directory had often turned to sympathetic army commanders to suppress dissent and to carry out arrests and purges of the legislature. They now invited General Bonaparte to help them form a government that they could more strictly control. Two members of the Directory plotted with Napoleon and his brother, Louis Bonaparte, to seize power on November 9, 1799.

THE NAPOLEONIC ERA AND THE LEGACY OF REVOLUTION, 1799–1815

 TALENTED, charming, and ruthless, Napoleon Bonaparte (1769–1821) was the kind of person who gives rise to myths. His audacity, determination, and personal magnetism enabled him to profit from the political instability and confusion in France and to ensconce himself in power. Once in power, he temporarily stabilized the political scene by fixing in law the more conservative gains of the Revolution. He also used his power and his remarkable abilities as a general to continue wars of conquest against France's neighbors, which helped deflect political tensions at home.

Napoleon's troops, in effect, exported the Revolution as they conquered most of Europe. In most states that came under French control, law codes were reformed, governing elites opened to talent, and public works upgraded. Yet French conquest also meant domination, pure and simple, and involvement in France's rivalry with Britain. The Napoleonic era left Europe an ambiguous legacy—war and its complex aftermath yet also revolution and its goad to further change.

***

Napoleon Bonaparte (nuh-POLE-ee-un BONE-uh-part)

■ Napoleon: From Soldier to Emperor, 1799–1804

Napoleon was from Corsica, a Mediterranean island that had passed from Genoese to French control in the eighteenth century. The second son of a large gentry family, he was educated at military academies in France, and he married the politically well-connected widow Joséphine de Beauharnais (1763–1814), whose aristocratic husband had been a victim of the Terror.

Napoleon steered a careful course through the political turmoil of the Revolution. By 1799 his military victories had won him much praise and fame. He had demonstrated his reliability and ruthlessness in 1795 when he ordered troops guarding the Convention to fire on a Parisian crowd. He had capped his successful Italian campaign of 1796–1797 with an invasion of Egypt in an attempt to strike at British influence and trade connections in the eastern Mediterranean. The Egyptian campaign failed in its goals, but individual spectacular victories during the campaign ensured Napoleon's military reputation. In addition, Napoleon had demonstrated his widening ambitions. He had taken leading scientists and skilled administrators with him to Egypt in order to export the seeming benefits of French civilization—and to install a more lasting bureaucratic authority.

Napoleon's partners in the new government after the November 1799 coup soon learned of his great political ambition and skill. In theory, the new system was to be a streamlined version of the Directory: Napoleon was to be first among equals in a three-man executive—First Consul, according to borrowed Roman terminology. But Napoleon quickly asserted his primacy among them and began not only to dominate executive functions but also to bypass the authority of the regime's various legislative bodies.

Perhaps most important to the success of his increasingly authoritarian rule was his effort to include, among his ministers, advisers, and bureaucrats, men of many political stripes—Jacobins, reforming liberals, even former Old Regime bureaucrats. He welcomed many exiles back to France, including all but the most ardent royalists. He thus stabilized his regime by healing some of the rifts among ruling elites. Napoleon combined toleration with ruthlessness, however. Between 1800 and 1804 he imprisoned, executed, or exiled dozens of individuals for alleged Jacobin agitation or royalist sympathies. His final gesture to intimidate royalist opposition came in 1804 when he kidnapped and coldly murdered a Bourbon prince who had been living in exile in Germany.

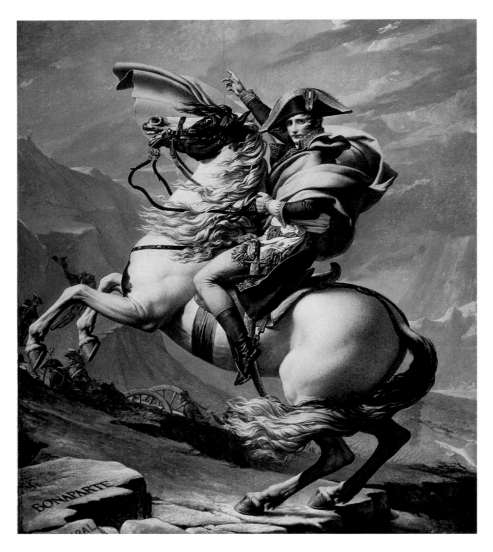

Napoleon Crossing the Great St. Bernard   This stirring portrait by the great neoclassical painter Jacques-Louis David memorializes Napoleon's 1796 crossing of the Alps before his victorious Italian campaign, as a general under the Directory. In part because it was executed in 1801–1802, the painting depicts the moment heroically rather than realistically. (In truth, Napoleon wisely crossed the Alps on a sure-footed mule, not a stallion.) Napoleon, as First Consul, wanted images of himself that would justify his increasingly ambitious claims to power.   *(Réunion des Musées Nationaux/Art Resource, NY)*

Under Napoleon's regime, any semblance of free political life ended. Legislative bodies lost all initiative in the governing process, becoming rubber stamps for the consuls' policies. In any case, there were no meaningful elections. Voters chose only candidates for a kind of pool of potential legislators, from which occasional replacements were chosen by sitting legislators! Political clubs were banned; the vibrant press of the revolutionary years wilted under heavy censorship. Napoleon also further centralized the administrative system, set up by the first wave of revolutionaries in 1789, by establishing the office of prefect to govern the départements. All prefects and their subordinates were appointed by Napoleon, thus extending the range of his power and undermining autonomous local government.

Certain administrative changes that enhanced central control, such as for tax collection, were more uniformly positive in their effects. Napoleon oversaw the establishment of the Bank of France, modeled on the Bank of England. The bank provided capital for investment and helped the state stabilize the French currency. Perhaps the most important achievement early in his regime was the Concordat of 1801. The aim of this treaty with the pope was to solve the problem of church-state relations that for years had provoked counterrevolutionary rebellions. The agreement allowed for the resumption of Catholic worship and the continued support of the clergy by the state, but also accepted the more dramatic changes accomplished by the Revolution. Church lands that had been sold were guaranteed to their new owners. Protestant churches were also allowed and their clergy were paid, although Catholicism was recognized as the "religion of the majority of Frenchmen." Later, Napoleon granted new rights to Jews also. Nonetheless, the Concordat removed one of the most important grounds for counterrevolutionary upheaval in the countryside and defused royalist resistance from abroad.

The law code that Napoleon established in 1804 was much like his accommodation with the church in its limited acceptance of revolutionary gains. His Civil Code (also known as the *code napoléon*, or Napoleonic Code) honored the revolutionary legacy in its guarantee of equality before the law and its requirement for the taxation of all social classes; it also enshrined modern forms of property ownership and civil contracts. Neither the code nor Napoleon's political regime fostered individual rights, especially for women. Fathers' control over their families was enhanced. Divorce was no longer permitted except in rare instances. Women lost all property rights when they married, and they generally faced legal domination by fathers and husbands.

Napoleon was careful, though, to avoid heavy-handed displays of power. He cleverly sought ratification of each stage of his assumption of power through national plebiscites (referendums in which all eligible voters could vote for or against proposals)—one plebiscite for a new constitution in 1800 and another when he claimed consulship for life in 1802. He approached his final political coup—declaring himself emperor—with similar dexterity. Long before he claimed the imperial title, Napoleon had begun to sponsor an active court life appropriate to imperial pretensions. The empire was proclaimed in May 1804 with the approval of the Senate; it was also endorsed by another plebiscite. Members of Napoleon's family were given princely status, and a number of his favorites received various titles and honors. The titles brought no legal privilege but signaled social and political distinctions of great importance. Old nobles were allowed to use their titles on this basis.

Many members of the elite, whatever their persuasions, tolerated Napoleon's claims to power because he safeguarded fundamental revolutionary gains yet reconfirmed their own status. War soon resumed against political and economic enemies—principally Britain, Austria, and Russia—and, for a time, Napoleon's success on the battlefield continued. Because military glory was central to the political purpose and self-esteem of elites, Napoleon's early successes as emperor further enhanced his power.

■ Conquering Europe, 1805–1810

Napoleon maintained relatively peaceful relations with other nations while he consolidated power at home, but the truces did not last. Tensions with the British quickly re-escalated when Britain resumed aggression against French shipping in 1803, and Napoleon countered by seizing Hanover, the ancestral German home of the English king. England was at war on the high seas with Spain and the Netherlands, which Napoleon had forced to enter the fray. Napoleon began to gather a large French force on the northern coast of France; his objective was to invade England.

The British fleet, commanded by Horatio Nelson (1758–1805), intercepted the combined French and Spanish fleets that were to have been the invasion flotilla and inflicted a devastating defeat off Cape Trafalgar in southern Spain (see Map 19.1) on October 21, 1805. The victory ensured British mastery of the seas and, in the long run, contributed to Napoleon's demise. In the short run, the defeat at Trafalgar paled for the French beside Napoleon's impressive victories on land. Even as the French admirals were preparing for battle, Napoleon had abandoned the plans to invade England and in August had begun to march his army east through Germany to confront the great continental powers, Austria and Russia.

In December 1805, after some preliminary, small-scale victories, Napoleon's army routed a combined Austrian and Russian force near Austerlitz°, north of Vienna (see Map 19.1). The Battle of Austerlitz was Napoleon's most spectacular victory. Austria sued for peace. In further battles in 1806, French forces defeated Prussian as well as Russian armies once again. Prussia was virtually dismembered by the subsequent Treaty of Tilsit (1807), but Napoleon tried to remake Russia into a contented ally. His hold on central Europe would not be secure with a hostile Russia, nor would the anti-British economic system that he envisioned—the Continental System (see page 666)—be workable without Russian participation.

French forces were still trying to prevail in Spain, which had been a client state since its defeat by revolutionary armies in 1795 but was resisting outright rule by a French-imposed king. In 1808, however, Napoleon turned his attention to more fully subduing Austria. Napoleon won the Battle of Wagram° in July 1809, and Austria, like Russia, accepted French political and economic hegemony in a sort of alliance. By 1810 Napoleon had transformed most of Europe into allied or dependent

Austerlitz (AW-stir-lits)   **Wagram** (VAHG-rahm)

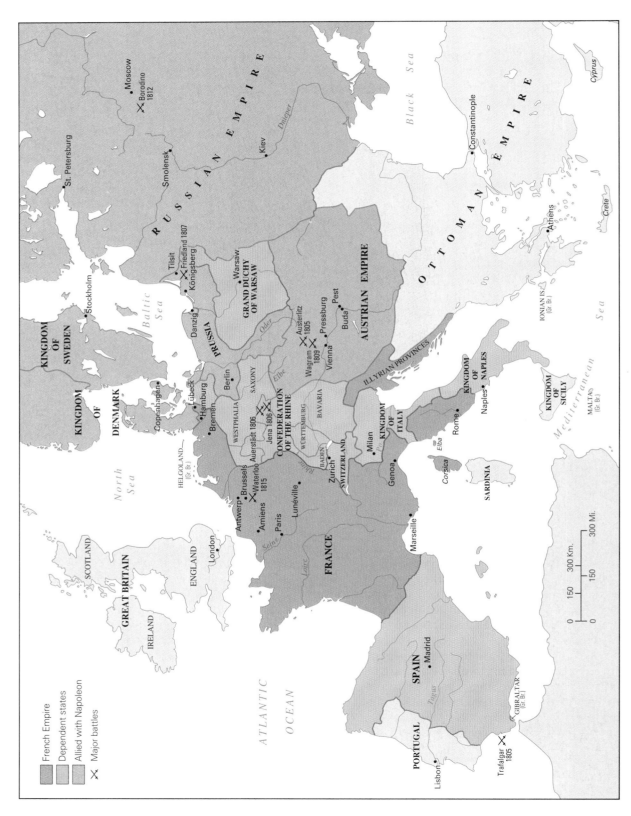

Map 19.1 Napoleonic Europe, ca. 1810 France dominated continental Europe after Napoleon's victories.

states (see Map 19.1). The only exceptions were Britain and the parts of Spain and Portugal that continued, with British help, to resist France.

The states least affected by French hegemony were its reluctant allies: Austria, Russia, and the Scandinavian countries. Denmark had allied with France in 1807 only for help in fending off British naval supremacy in the Baltic. Sweden had reluctantly made peace in 1810 after losing control of Finland to Napoleon's ally, Russia, and only minimally participated in the Continental System. At the other extreme were territories that had been incorporated into France. These included the Austrian Netherlands, territory along the Rhineland, and sections of Italy that bordered France. These regions were occupied by French troops and were treated as though they were départements of France itself.

In most other areas, some form of French-controlled government was in place, usually headed by a member of Napoleon's family. In both northern Italy and the Netherlands, where "sister" republics had been established after French conquests under the Directory, Napoleon imposed monarchies. Rulers were also installed in the kingdom of Naples and in Spain. Western German states

of the Holy Roman Empire that had allied with Napoleon against Austria were organized into the Confederation of the Rhine, with Napoleon as its "Protector." After a thousand years, the Holy Roman Empire ceased to exist. Two further states were created, largely out of the defeated Prussia's territory: the kingdom of Westphalia in western Germany and the grand duchy of Warsaw in the east (see Map 19.1).

Napoleon's domination of these various regions had complex, and at times contradictory, consequences. On the one hand, Napoleonic armies essentially exported the French Revolution, in that French domination brought with it the Napoleonic Civil Code, and with it political and economic reform akin to that of the early phases of the Revolution. Equality before the law was decreed following the French example; this meant the end of noble exemption from taxation in the many areas where it existed. In general, the complex snarl of medieval taxes and tolls was replaced with straightforward property taxes that were universally applied. As a consequence, tax revenues rose dramatically—by 50 percent in the kingdom of Italy, for example. Serfdom and forced labor were also abolished, as they had been in France in August 1789.

In most Catholic regions, the church was subjected to the terms of the Concordat of 1801. The tithe was abolished, church property seized and sold, and religious orders dissolved. Though Catholicism remained the state-supported religion in these areas, Protestantism was tolerated and Jews were granted rights of citizenship. Secular education, at least for males, was encouraged.

On the other hand, Napoleon would countenance in the empire only those aspects of France's revolutionary legacy that he tolerated in France itself. Just as he had suppressed any meaningful participatory government in France, so too did he suppress it in conquered regions. This came as a blow in states such as the Netherlands, which had experienced its own democratizing "Patriot" movement and which had enjoyed republican self-government after invasion by French armies during the Revolution itself. Throughout the Napoleonic Empire, many of the benefits of streamlined administration and taxation were offset by the drain of continual warfare; deficits rose three- and fourfold, despite increased revenues. In addition, one of the inevitable costs of empire was political compromise to secure allies. In the duchy of Warsaw, reconstituted from lands Prussia had seized in the eighteenth century, Napoleon tampered little with either noble privileges or the power of the church. And, throughout Europe, Napoleon randomly allotted lands to reward his greatest generals and ministers, thereby exempting those lands from taxation and control by his own bureaucracy.

If true self-government was not allowed, a broad segment of the elite in all regions was nevertheless won over to cooperation with Napoleon by being welcomed into his bureaucracy or into the large multinational army, called the *Grande Armée*. Their loyalty was cemented when they bought confiscated church lands.

The impact of Napoleon's Continental System was equally mixed. Under this system, the Continent was in theory closed to all British shipping and British goods. The effects were widespread but uneven, and smuggling to evade controls on British goods became a major enterprise. Regions heavily involved in trade with Britain or its colonies or dependent on British shipping suffered in the new system, as did overseas trade in general when Britain gained dominance of the seas after Trafalgar. However, the closing of the Continent to British trade, combined with increases in demand to supply Napoleon's armies, spurred the development of continental industries, at least in the short run. This industrial growth, enhanced by the improvement of roads, canals, and the like, formed the basis for further industrial development.

■ Defeat and Abdication, 1812–1815

Whatever its achievements, Napoleon's empire was ultimately precarious because of the hostility of Austria and Russia, as well as the belligerence of Britain. Russia was a particularly weak link in the chain of alliances and subject states because Russian landowners and merchants were angered when their vital trade in timber for the British navy was interrupted and when supplies of luxury goods, brought in British ships, began to dwindle. A century of close alliances with German ruling houses made alliance with a French ruler an extremely difficult political option for Tsar Alexander I.

It was Napoleon, however, who ended the alliance by provoking a breach with Russia. He suddenly backed away from an arrangement to marry one of Alexander's sisters and accepted the Austrian princess Marie Louise instead. (He had reluctantly divorced Joséphine in 1809 because their marriage had not produced an heir.) Also, he seized lands along the German Baltic seacoast belonging to a member of Alexander's family. When Alexander threatened rupture of the alliance if the lands were not returned, Napoleon mounted an invasion. Advisers warned him about the magnitude of the task he seemed so eager to undertake—particularly about the preparations needed for winter fighting in Russia—but their alarms went unheard.

Napoleon's previous military successes had stemmed from a combination of strategic innovations and pure audacity. Napoleon divided his forces into independent corps. Each corps included infantry, cavalry, and artillery. Organized in these workable units, his armies could travel quickly by several separate routes and converge in massive force to face the enemy. Leadership on the battlefield came from a loyal and extremely talented officer corps that had grown up since army commands had been thrown open to nonaristocrats during the Revolution. The final ingredient in the success formula was the high morale of French troops. Since the first victory of the revolutionary armies in September 1792, citizen-soldiers had proved their worth. Complicated troop movements and bravery on the battlefield were possible when troops felt they were fighting for their *nation*, not merely their ruling dynasty. Napoleon's reputation as a winning general added a further measure of self-confidence.

The campaign against Russia began in June 1812. It was a spectacular failure. Napoleon had gathered a force of about 700,000 men—about half from France and half from allied states—a force twice as large as Russia's. The strategy of quickly moving independent corps and assembling massive forces could not be implemented: simply mustering so many men along the border was already the equivalent of gathering them for battle. Bold victories had often enabled Napoleon's troops to live off the countryside while they waited for supplies to catch up to the front line. But when the enemy attacked supply lines, when the distances traveled were very great, when the countryside was impoverished, or when battles were not decisive, Napoleon's ambitious strategies proved futile. In varying degrees, these conditions prevailed in Russia.

By the time the French faced the Russians in the principal battle of the Russian campaign—at Borodino°, west of Moscow (see Map 19.1)—the Grande Armée had been on the march for two and a half months and stood at less than half its original strength. After the indecisive but bloody battle, the French occupied and pillaged Moscow but found scarcely enough food and supplies to sustain them. When Napoleon finally led his troops out of Moscow late in October, the fate of the French forces was all but sealed. As they retreated, French and allied soldiers who had not died in battle died of exposure or starvation or were killed by Russian peasants when they wandered away from their units. The talents of generals and the determination of troops were focused on sheer survival. Of the original 700,000 troops of the Grand Armée, fewer than 100,000 made it out of Russia. (See the box "Reading Sources: A Napoleonic Soldier Recounts the Horrors of the Russian Campaign.")

Napoleon left his army before it was fully out of Russia. A coup attempt in Paris prompted him to return to his governing duties before the French people realized the extent of the disaster in the east. The collapse of his reign had begun, spurred by a coincidental defeat in Spain. Since 1808 Spain had been largely under French domination, with Napoleon's brother, Joseph, as king. A rebel cortes (national representative assembly), however, continued to meet in territory that the French did not control, and British troops were never expelled from the Iberian Peninsula. In 1812, as Napoleon was advancing against Russia, the collapse of French control accelerated. By the time Napoleon reached Paris at the turn of the new year, Joseph had been expelled from Spain, and an Anglo-Spanish force led by the duke of Wellington was poised to invade France.

Napoleon lost his last chance to stave off a coalition of all major powers against him when he refused an Aus-

trian offer of peace for the return of conquered Austrian territories. With Britain willing to subsidize the allied armies, Tsar Alexander determined to destroy Napoleon, and the Austrians now anxious to share the spoils, Napoleon's empire began to crumble. Imperial forces—many now raw recruits—were crushed in a massive "Battle of Nations" near Leipzig in October, during which some troops from German satellite states deserted him on the battlefield. The allies invaded France and forced Napoleon to abdicate on April 6, 1814.

Napoleon was exiled to the island of Elba, off France's Mediterranean coast, but was still treated somewhat royally. He was installed as the island's ruler and was given an income drawn on the French treasury. Meanwhile, however, the restored French king was having his own troubles. Louis XVIII (r. 1814–1824) was the brother of the executed Louis XVI; he took the number eighteen out of respect for Louis XVI's son, who had died in prison in 1795. The new monarch had been out of the country and out of touch with its circumstances since the beginning of the Revolution. In addition to the delicate task of establishing his own legitimacy, he faced enormous practical problems, including pensioning off thousands of soldiers now unemployed and still loyal to Napoleon.

Napoleon, bored and almost penniless on his island kingdom (the promised French pension never materialized), took advantage of the circumstances and returned surreptitiously to France on February 26, 1815. His small band of attendants was joined by the soldiers sent by the king to halt his progress. Louis XVIII abandoned Paris to the returned emperor.

Napoleon's triumphant return lasted only one hundred days, however. Though many soldiers welcomed his return, many members of the elite were reluctant to throw in their lot with Napoleon again. Many ordinary French citizens had also become disenchanted with him since the defeat in Russia, and with the high costs, in conscription and taxation, of raising new armies. In any case, Napoleon's reappearance galvanized the divided allies, who had been haggling over a peace settlement, into unity. Napoleon tried to strike first, but he lost against English and Prussian troops in his first major battle, at Waterloo (in modern Belgium; see Map 19.1) on June 18, 1815. When Napoleon arrived in Paris after the defeat, he discovered the government in the hands of an ad hoc committee that included the Marquis de Lafayette. Under pressure, he abdicated once again. This time, he was exiled to the tiny, remote island of St. Helena in the South Atlantic, from which escape would be impossible. He died there in 1821.

Borodino (bore-uh-DEE-no)

🐌 R E A D I N G   S O U R C E S

A Napoleonic Soldier Recounts the Horrors
of the Russian Campaign

Jakob Walter, a stonemason from western Germany, was conscripted in 1806 into the army of a German prince, an ally of Napoleon against Prussia and Austria. In 1812, aged 24, he marched into Russia with the massive Grande Armée and was one of the lucky few to survive the campaign. Some years afterward, Walter recorded his memoirs of military life in the citizen army—including its appalling dehumanization. In this passage, he describes the fleeing army's crossing of the Berezina River (in modern Belarus). Thousands managed to ford the Berezina thanks to the heroic work of French engineers, many of whom died constructing the bridges. But the horror of the crossing, in Walter's experience, almost overshadows the fact that part of the army was saved. This excerpt also provides a glimpse of the extreme privation that the soldiers endured.

When I had gone somewhat further . . . I met a man who had a sack of raw bran in which there was hardly a dust of flour. I begged him ceaselessly to sell me a little of the bran, pressing a silver ruble into his hand; so he put a few handfuls in my little cloth. . . . When I and my master came closer to the Beresina, we camped on a near-by hill and by contributing wood I obtained a place at the fire. I immediately mixed some snow with my bran . . . [and] allowed it to heat red on the outside in order to obtain something like bread from the inside. . . .

After a time . . . the Russians pressed nearer and nearer from every side, and the murdering and torturing seemed to annihilate everyone. . . . When it became day again, we stood near the stream approximately a thousand paces from the two bridges. . . . However, one could not see the bridges because of the crowd of people, horses and wagons. Everyone crowded together into a solid mass, and nowhere could one see a way out or a means of rescue. From

morning til night we stood unprotected from the cannonballs and grenades which the Russians hurled at us from two sides. . . . I had to kneel on [my horse] in order not to have my feet crushed off, for everything was so closely packed that in a quarter of an hour one could move only four or five steps forward. To be on foot was to lose all hope of rescue. . . . Everyone was screaming under the feet of the horses, and everywhere was the cry, "Shoot me. . . ." Finally, toward four o'clock in the evening, when it was almost dark, I came to the bridge. . . . Now it is with horror, but at that time it was with a dull, indifferent feeling, that I looked at the masses of horses and people that lay dead, piled upon the bridge.

Source: Jakob Walter, *The Diary of a Napoleonic Footsoldier,* ed. by Marc Raeff (New York: Penguin Books, 1993), pp. 83–86.

 For additional information on this topic, go to http://college.hmco.com.

■ The Legacy of Revolution for France and the World

The process of change in France between 1789 and 1815 was so complex that it is easy to overlook the overall impact of the Revolution. Superficially, the changes seemed to come full circle—with first Louis XVI on the

throne, then Napoleon as emperor, and then Louis XVIII on the throne. Even though the monarchy was restored, however, the Revolution had discredited absolute monarchy in theory and practice. Louis XVIII had to recognize the right of "the people," however narrowly defined, to participate in government and to enjoy due process of law. Another critical legacy of the Revolution and the Napoleonic era was a centralized political system of départements rather than a patchwork of provinces. For the first time, a single code of law applied to all French people. Most officials—from département administrators to city mayors—were appointed by the central government until the late twentieth century. The conscientious attention of the government, at various stages of the Revolution, to advances for France generally reflects the positive side of this centralization. The government sponsored national scientific societies, a national library and archives, and a system of teachers' colleges and universities. Particularly under Napoleon, a spate of canal- and road-building projects drastically improved transport systems.

Napoleon's legacy, like that of the Revolution itself, was mixed. His self-serving reconciliation of aristocratic pretensions with the opening of careers to men of talent ensured the long-term success of revolutionary principles from which the elite as a whole profited. His reconciliation of the state with the Catholic Church helped to stabilize his regime and cemented some revolutionary gains. The restored monarchy could not renege on these gains. Yet whatever his achievements, Napoleon's overthrow of constitutional principles worsened the problem of political instability. His brief return to power in 1815 reflects the degree to which his power had always been rooted in military adventurism and in the loyalty of soldiers and officers. Similarly, the swiftness of his collapse suggests that although the empire under Napoleon may have seemed an enduring solution to the political instability of the late 1790s, it was no more secure than any of the other revolutionary governments.

Although Louis XVIII acknowledged the principle of constitutionalism at the end of the Revolution, the particular configuration of his regime rested on fragile footing. Indeed, the fragility of new political systems was one of the most profound lessons of the Revolution. There was division over policies, but even greater division over legitimacy—that is, the acceptance by a significant portion of the politically active citizenry of a particular government's right to rule. Before the Revolution started, notions about political legitimacy had undergone a significant shift. The deputies who declared themselves to be the National Assembly in June 1789 already believed that they had a right to do so. In their view, they represented "the nation," and their voice had legitimacy for that reason. The shift reflects not the innate power of ideas but the power of ideas in context. These deputies brought to Versailles not only their individual convictions that "reason" should be applied to the political system but also their experience in social settings where those ideas were well received. In their salons, clubs, and literary societies, they had experienced the familiarity, trust, and sense of community that are essential to effective political action.

The deputies' attempt to transplant their sense of community into national politics was not wholly successful. Factions, competing interests, and clashes of personality can be fatal to an insecure system. The National Assembly had scarcely been inaugurated when its deputies guaranteed its failure by disqualifying themselves from standing for office under the new constitution. The king also actively undermined the system because he disagreed with it in principle. The British parliamentary system, by comparison, though every bit as elitist as the narrowest of the representative systems during the French Revolution, had a long history as a workable institution for lords, commoners, and rulers. This shared experience was an important counterweight to differences over fundamental issues, so that Parliament as an institution both survived political crises and helped resolve them. The Revolution thus left a powerful yet ambiguous legacy for France. Politics was established on new principles, yet still lacking were the practical means to achieve the promise inherent in those principles.

Throughout Europe and overseas, the Revolution left a powerful and equally complex legacy. France's continental conquests were the least enduring of the changes of the revolutionary era. Nevertheless, French domination had certain lasting effects: elites were exposed to modern bureaucratic management, and equality under the law transformed social and political relationships. Although national self-determination had an enemy in Napoleon, the breaking down of ancient political divisions provided important practical grounding for later cooperation among elites in nationalist movements. In Napoleon's kingdom of Italy, for example, a tax collector from Florence for the first time worked side by side with one from Milan. The most important legacy of the revolutionary wars, however, was the change in warfare itself made possible by the citizen armies of the French. Citizen soldiers who identified closely with their nation, even when conscripts, proved able to maneuver and attack on the battlefield in ways that the brutishly disciplined poor conscripts in other armies would not. In response, other states tried to build competing armies; the mass national armies that fought the world wars of the twentieth century were the result.

Naturally, the most important legacy of the French Revolution, as of the American, was the success of the revolution itself. The most powerful absolute monarchy in Europe had succumbed to the demands of its people for dramatic social and political reforms. Throughout

Haitian Leader Toussaint-Louverture   Son of an educated slave, Toussaint-Louverture had himself been freed in 1777 but took on a leadership role when the slave revolt began on Saint Domingue in 1791. His military skill and political acumen were vital to the success of the revolt and to ruling the island's diverse population afterward.   *(Stock Montage, Inc.)*

of the French-controlled Caribbean islands, Saint Domingue°, the Revolution inspired a successful rebellion by the enslaved plantation workers.

The National Assembly in Paris had delayed abolishing slavery in French colonies, despite the moral appeal of such a move, because of pressure from the white planters and out of fear that the financially strapped French government would lose some of its profitable sugar trade. But the example of revolutionary daring in Paris and confusion about ruling authority as the Assembly and the king wrangled did not go unnoticed in the colonies—in either plantation mansions or slave quarters. White planters on Saint Domingue simply hoped for political and economic "liberty" from the French government and its mercantilist trade policies. White planter rule was challenged, in turn, by wealthy people of mixed European and African descent who wanted equal citizenship, hitherto denied them. A civil war broke out between these upper classes and was followed by a full-fledged slave rebellion, beginning in 1791. (See the box "Global Encounters: A Planter's Wife on the Haitian Slave Revolt.") Britain sent aid to the rebels when it went to war against the French revolutionary government in 1793. Only when the republic was declared in Paris and the Convention abolished slavery did the rebels abandon alliances with France's enemies and attempt to govern in concert with the mother country.

Though it recovered other colonies from the British, France never regained control of Saint Domingue. Led by a former slave, François Dominique Toussaint-Louverture° (1743–1803), the new government of the island tried to run its own affairs, though without formally declaring independence from France. Napoleon, early in his rule, decided to tighten control of the profitable colonies by reinstituting slavery and ousting the independent government of Saint Domingue. In 1802 French forces fought their way onto the island. They captured Toussaint-Louverture, who died shortly thereafter in prison. But in 1803 another rebellion provoked by the threat of renewed slavery expelled French forces for good. A former aide of Toussaint's declared the independence of the colony under the name Haiti—the island's Native American name—on January 1, 1804.

The French Revolution and Napoleonic rule, and the example of the Haitian revolution, had a notable impact on Spanish colonies in the Americas also. Like other American colonies, the Spanish colonies wanted to loosen the closed economic ties the mother country tried to impose. In addition, the liberal ideas that had helped

Europe, in the nineteenth century, ruling dynasties faced revolutionary movements that demanded constitutional government, among other changes, and resorted to force to achieve it. European colonies overseas felt the impact of the Revolution and subsequent European wars in several ways. The British tried to take advantage of Napoleon's preoccupation with continental affairs by seizing French colonies and the colonies of the French-dominated Dutch. In 1806 they seized the Dutch colony of Capetown—crucial for support of trade around Africa—as well as French bases along the African coast. In 1811 they grabbed the island of Java. In the Caribbean, the French sugar-producing islands of Martinique and Guadeloupe were particularly vulnerable to English sea power while Napoleon was executing his brilliant victories on the Continent after 1805. On the most productive

Saint Domingue (SAHN dome-ANGUE)
Toussaint-Louverture (too-SAHN–loo-ver-TOUR)

A Planter's Wife on the Haitian Slave Revolt

The following are excerpts from two letters of Madame de Rouvray, a wealthy planter's wife living in the French colony of Saint Domingue (the western half of the island of Hispaniola), to her married daughter in France. The decree of May 15, 1791, that Madame de Rouvray mentions in her first letter granted civil rights to free persons of mixed race. The decree affected only a few hundred persons on Saint Domingue (many of whom themselves owned slaves), but white planters feared any breach in the barriers between the races. Tensions between white planters, on the one hand, and mulattos and modest white settlers who favored revolutionary changes, on the other, enabled the well-organized slave rebellion to be dramatically successful. It began in late August 1791 and is the backdrop to Madame de Rouvray's second letter. Madame de Rouvray and her husband fled the island for the United States in 1793.

July 30, 1791

I am writing to you from Cap [a city on the island] where I came to find out what the general mood is here. . . . All the deputies who make up the general assembly [of the colony] left here the day before yesterday to gather at Léogane [another city]. If they conduct themselves wisely their first action should be to send emissaries to all the powers who have colonies with slaves in order to tell them of the decree [of May 15] and of the consequences that will follow from it, and ask for help from them in case it happens that the National Assembly actually abolishes slavery too, which they will surely do. After their decree of May 15, one cannot doubt that that is their plan. And you understand that all the powers who have slave colonies have a common interest in opposing such a crazy plan because the contagion of liberty will soon infect their colonies too, especially in nearby Jamaica. It is said that [the English] will send a ship and troops [which] would be wonderful for us. Your father thinks it won't be long before the English take control here.

September 4, 1791

If news of the horrors that have happened here since the 23rd of last month have reached you, you must have been very worried. Luckily, we are all safe. We can't say whether our fortunes are also safe because we are still at war with the slaves who revolted [and] who have slaughtered and torched much of the countryside hereabouts. . . . All of this will gravely damage our revenues for this year and for the future, because how can we stay in a country where slaves have raised their hands against their masters? . . . You have no idea, my dear, of the state of this colony; it would make you tremble. Don't breathe a word of this to anyone but your father is determined, once the rebels have been defeated, to take refuge in Havanna.

Source: M. E. McIntosh and B. C. Weber, *Une Correspondance familiale au temps des troubles de Saint-Domingue* (Paris: Société de l'Histoire des Colonies Françaises et Librairie Larose, 1959), pp. 22–23, 26–28. Trans. by Kristen B. Neuschel.

spawn the French Revolution spurred moves toward independence in Spanish America. Taking advantage of the confusion of authority in Spain, some of these colonies were already governing themselves independently in all but name. Echoes of radical republican ideology and of the Haitian experience resounded in some corners. For

example, participants in two major rebellions in Mexico espoused the end of slavery and championed the interests of the poor against local and Spanish elites. The leaders of these self-declared revolutions were executed (in 1811 and 1815), and their movements were crushed by local elites in alliance with Spanish troops. The efforts of local elites to become self-governing—the attempted liberal revolutions—were little more successful. Only Argentina and Paraguay broke away from Spain at this time.

But as in Europe, a legacy remained of both limited and more radical revolutionary activity, and of its risks. Slave rebellions rocked British Caribbean islands in subsequent decades. Other colonies had learned a lesson from the Haitian revolution and were determined to avoid the horrors that had surrounded that struggle for freedom. In some regions dominated by plantations, such as some British possessions and the Spanish island of Cuba, planters were reluctant to disturb the prevailing order with any liberal political demands.

■ The View from Britain

Today the city of Paris is dotted with public monuments that celebrate Napoleon's victories. In London another hero and other victories are celebrated. In Trafalgar Square stands a statue of Lord Nelson, the British naval commander whose fleet destroyed a combined French and Spanish navy in 1805. Horatio Nelson was a brilliant tactician, whose innovations in maneuvering ships in the battle line resulted in stunning victories at Trafalgar and, in 1798, at the Nile Delta, which limited French ambitions in Egypt and the eastern Mediterranean. Trafalgar looms large in British history because it ensured British mastery of the seas, which then forced Napoleon into economic policies that strained French ties to France's allies and satellites. Virtually unchallenged sea power enabled the British to seize colonies formerly ruled by France and its allies.

Britain's maritime supremacy and seizure of French possessions expanded British trading networks overseas—though in some cases only temporarily—and closer to home, particularly in the Mediterranean. As long as the British had been involved in trade with India, the Mediterranean had been important for economic and strategic reasons: it marked the end of the land route for trade from the Indian Ocean. Especially after Napoleon's aggression in Egypt, the British redoubled their efforts to control strategic outposts in the Mediterranean, such as ports in southern Italy and on the island of Malta.

The British economy would expand dramatically in the nineteenth century as industrial production soared. The roots for growth were laid in this period in the coun-

The Funeral of Lord Nelson, January 8, 1806 Nelson had been mortally wounded on the deck of his flagship at the Battle of Trafalgar in October. Rather than being buried at sea, as was the custom, his body was returned to London for an impressive state funeral, commemorated here in a contemporary engraving. *(National Maritime Museum, London)*

tryside of Britain, where changes in agriculture and in production were occurring. These roots were also laid in Britain's overseas possessions as tighter control of foreign sources of raw materials, notably raw Indian cotton, meant rising fortunes back in Britain. In regions of India, the East India Company was increasing its political domination, and hence its economic stranglehold on Indian commodities. The export of Indian cotton rose significantly during the revolutionary period as part of an expanding trading system that included China, the source of tea.

However, economic expansion was not the sole motive for British aggression. In fact, economic expansion was often a by-product of increased British control of particular regions or sea-lanes, and the reasons for it were as much strategic as economic. Not every conquest had direct economic payoffs, but British elites were sure that strategic domination was a desirable step, wherever it could be managed. One Scottish landholder, writing in the opening years of the nineteenth century, spoke for many when he said that Britain needed an empire to ensure its greatness and that an empire of the sea was an effective counterweight to Napoleon's empire on land. Much as the French were at that moment exporting features of their own political system, the British, he said, could export their constitution wherever they conquered territory.

Thus, England and France were engaged in similar phases of expansion in this period. In both, the desire for power and profit drove policy. In each, myths about heroes and about the supposed benefits of domination masked the state's self-interest. For both, the effects of conquest would become a fundamental shaping force in the nineteenth century.

SUMMARY

HE French Revolution was a watershed in European history because it successfully challenged the principles of hereditary rule and political privilege by which all European states had hitherto been governed. The Revolution began when a financial crisis forced the monarchy to confront the desire for political reform by a segment of the French elite. Political philosophy emerging from the Enlightenment and the example of the American Revolution moved the French reformers to action. In its initial phase, the French Revolution established the principle of constitutional government and ended many of the traditional political privileges of the Old Regime.

Then, because of the intransigence of the king, the threat of foreign invasion, and the actions of republican legislators and Parisian citizens, the Revolution moved in more radical directions. Its most extremist phase, the Terror, produced the most effective legislation for ordinary citizens but also the worst violence of the Revolution. A period of unstable conservative rule that followed the Terror ended when Napoleon seized power.

Though Napoleonic rule solidified some of the gains of the Revolution, it also subjected France and most of Europe to the great costs of wars of conquest. After Napoleon, the French monarchy was restored but henceforth its power would not be absolute—and the people would not be refused a voice in government—as a result of the Revolution. Indeed, hereditary rule and traditional social hierarchies remained in place in much of Europe, but they would not be secure in the future. The legacy of revolutionary change would prove impossible to contain in France or anywhere else.

■ Notes

1. Quoted in Samuel Eliot Morrison, *John Paul Jones: A Sailor's Biography* (Boston: Little, Brown, 1959), pp. 149–154.
2. Quoted in Owen Connelly, *The French Revolution and the Napoleonic Era* (New York: Holt, Rinehart and Winston, 1979), p. 32.
3. James Harvey Robinson, *Readings in European History* (Boston: Ginn, 1906), p. 409.

■ Suggested Reading

Baker, Keith Michael. *Inventing the French Revolution.* 1990. A series of essays situating the Revolution amid the dramatic changes in eighteenth-century political culture.

Hunt, Lynn. *The French Revolution and Human Rights: A Brief Documentary History.* 1996. A well-presented short collection of documents, useful for a greater understanding of the impact of the Revolution on the development of human rights.

Jordan, D. P. *The King's Trial.* 1979. An engaging study of Louis XVI's trial and its importance for the Revolution.

Landes, Joan. *Women and the Public Sphere in the Age of the French Revolution.* 1988. An analysis of the uses of gender ideology to fashion the new political world of the revolutionaries.

Langley, Lester D. *The Americas in the Age of Revolution, 1750–1850.* 1996. A survey of all the American states and colonies and the impact of the Atlantic revolutions.

Popkin, Jeremy. *A Short History of the French Revolution.* 1995. A compact and readable recent synthesis of research.

 For a searchable list of additional readings for this chapter, go to http://college.hmco.com.

Political Symbols

An Armed Citizen, ca. 1792 *(Bibliothèque Nationale de France)*

During the French Revolution, thousands of illustrations in support of various revolutionary (or counterrevolutionary) ideas were reproduced on posters, on handbills, and in pamphlets. Some satirized their subjects, such as Marie Antoinette, or celebrated revolutionary milestones, such as the fall of the Bastille. The etching here of the woman armed with a pike, dating from 1792, falls into this category. Other pictures, such as the representation from 1795 of Liberty as a young woman wearing the liberty cap, symbolized or reinforced various revolutionary ideals.*

Political images like these are an invaluable though problematic source for historians. Let us examine these two images of women and consider how French people during the Revolution might have responded to them. To understand what they meant to contemporaries, we must know something about the other images that these would have been compared to. We must also view the images in the context of the events of the Revolution itself. Immediately, then, we are presented with an interpretive agenda. How ordinary and acceptable was this image of an armed woman? If women were not citizens coequal with men, how could a woman be a symbol of liberty? What, in short, do these political images reveal about the spectrum of political life in their society?

The woman holding the pike stares determinedly at the viewer. Many details confirm what the original caption announced: This is a French woman who has become free. In her hat she wears one of the symbols of revolutionary nationhood: the tricolor cockade. The badge around her waist celebrates a defining moment for the revolutionary nation: the fall of the Bastille. Her pike itself is inscribed with the words "Liberty or death!"

---

*This discussion draws on the work of Joan Landes, "Representing the Body Politic: The Paradox of Gender in the Graphic Politics of the French Revolution," and Darlene Gay Levy and Harriet B. Applewhite, "Women and Militant Citizenship in Revolutionary Paris," in Sara E. Melzer and Leslie W. Rabine, eds., *Rebel Daughters: Women and the French Revolution* (New York: Oxford University Press, 1992), pp. 15–37, 79–101.

The woman appears to be serving not merely as a symbol of free women. She comes close to being the generic image of a free citizen, willing and able to fight for liberty—an astonishing symbolic possibility in a time when women were not yet treated equally under the law or granted the same political rights as the men of their class. Other images prevalent at the time echo this possibility. Many contemporary representations of the women's march on Versailles in 1789 show women carrying arms, active in advancing the Revolution. By the time this image was created (most likely in 1792), many other demonstrations and violent confrontations by ordinary people had resulted in the creation of dozens of popular prints and engravings that showed women acting in the same ways as men.

Repeatedly during 1792, women proposed to the revolutionary government that they be granted the right to bear arms. Their request was denied, but it was not dismissed out of hand. There was debate, and the issue was in effect tabled. Nevertheless, women's actions in the Revolution had created at least the possibility of envisaging citizenship with a female face.

The image of liberty from 1795 does not reflect the actions of women but rather represents their exclusion from political participation. It is one of a number of images of Liberty that portray this ideal as a passive, innocent woman, here garbed in ancient dress, surrounded by a glow that in the past had been reserved for saints. Liberty here is envisaged as a pure and lofty goal, symbolized as a pure young woman.

Late in 1793, during the Terror, women were excluded from formal participation in politics with the disbanding of women's organizations. Nor did they gain political rights under the Directory, which re-established some of the limited gains of the first phase of the Revolution. The justification offered for their exclusion in 1793 was borrowed from Rousseau: it is contrary to nature for women to be in public life (see page 611). Women "belong" in the private world of the family, where they will nurture male citizens. Women embody ideal qualities such as patience and self-sacrifice; they are not fully formed beings capable of action in their own right.

Such notions made it easy to use images of women to embody ideals for public purposes. A woman could represent Liberty precisely because actual women were not able to be political players.

The two images shown here thus demonstrate that political symbols can have varying relationships to "re-

"Liberty" as a Young Woman, ca. 1795 *(S. P. Avery Collection, Miriam and Ira D. Wallach Division of Art, Prints, and Photographs, The New York Public Library, Astor, Lenox, and Tilden Foundations)*

ality." The pike-bearing citizen is the more "real." Her image reflects the way of thinking about politics that became possible for the first time because of their actions. The other woman reflects not the attributes of actual women but an ideal type spawned by the use of arbitrary gender distinctions to legitimize political power. In these images we can see modern political life taking shape: the sophistication of its symbolic language, the importance of abstract ideas such as liberty and nationhood—as well as the grounding of much political life in rigid distinctions between public and private, male and female.

 For any additional information on this topic, go to http://college.hmco.com.

CHAPTER 20

The Industrial Transformation of Europe 1750–1850

WITH fires spewing from factory chimneys, it was hard to distinguish day from night. At night the sky was so lit up it might be daytime. During the day smoke and smog so obscured the sunlight that it might be night. Shropshire, England, a region previously renowned for its natural beauty, was transformed by industrial activity by 1788, when this painting was made. Containing in proximity both coal and iron deposits, Shropshire was the ideal site for establishing ironworks. Here Abraham Darby (1676–1717) and his descendants built one of the largest and most important concentrations of ironworks in Britain. The dramatic rise in the use of new machinery, which led to previously unheard of levels in production of iron and textiles, struck contemporaries. In the 1830s the French socialist Louis Blanqui° (see page 720) would propose a descriptive term, suggesting that just as France had recently experienced a political revolution, so Britain was undergoing an "industrial revolution." Eventually, that expression entered the general vocabulary to describe the advances in production that occurred first in England and then dominated most of western Europe by the end of the nineteenth century. Many economic historians now emphasize how gradual and cumulative the changes were and question the appropriateness of the term. Indeed, it seems best to discuss the changes not as an industrial revolution but as a continuous process of economic transformation.

Industrial development left its mark on just about every sphere of human activity. Scientific and rational methods altered production. Economic activity became increasingly specialized. The unit of production changed from the family to a larger and less personal group. Significant numbers of workers left farming to enter mining and

Blanqui (blahn-KEE)

George Robertson, *Nat-Y-Glo Iron Works.*
(National Museums & Galleries of Wales)

manufacturing, and major portions of the population moved from rural to urban environments. Machines replaced or supplemented manual labor.[1]

The economic changes brought about by industrial development physically transformed Europe. Greater levels of production were achieved, and more wealth was created, than ever before. Factory chimneys belched soot into the air. Miners in search of coal, iron ore, and other minerals cut deep gashes into the earth. Cities, spurred by industrialization, grew quickly, and Europe became increasingly urban.

Industrialization simultaneously created unprecedented advancement and opportunity as well as unprecedented hardships and social problems. Workers, with a growing sense of solidarity, struggled to protect and advance their interests.

QUESTIONS TO CONSIDER

- Why did Europe industrialize before the rest of the world?
- Which inventions appear to have been the most important in launching industrialization?
- What impact did industrialization have on the environment?
- What did workers gain and what did they lose as a result of industrialization?

TERMS TO KNOW

industrialization	urbanization
steam engine	friendly societies
entrepreneurship	proletariat
factories	Luddite
mass production	

SETTING THE STAGE FOR INDUSTRIALIZATION

NO one can say with certainty what conditions were necessary for the industrialization of Europe. Nevertheless, we do know why industrialization did not spread widely to the rest of the world in the nineteenth century. A certain combination of conditions—geographic, cultural, economic, demographic—helped make industrialization possible in Europe.

■ Why Europe?

A unique set of circumstances seems to explain why Europe was the stage for industrial development. With the development of legal due process, rich merchants did not run the risk of having their wealth confiscated—as they did, for instance, in the Ottoman Empire, where sultans and corrupt officials on a whim grabbed wealth. Hence in the West accumulating wealth was a worthwhile endeavor. The unfolding of state power in Europe reduced the frequency of highway robbery—still common in many parts of the world—and thus encouraged trade.

In Europe, disparities of wealth, though serious, were less extreme than in other parts of the world; thus, there was a better market for goods. At the time western Europe industrialized, the average yearly income per person was equivalent to $500—more than the amount in many non-Western societies even today. And nearly half of the population was literate, again a very high proportion compared with non-Western societies.

Although Europe's population grew during the eighteenth century, late marriages and limited family sizes kept its rise in check. European society was therefore rarely overwhelmed by population pressure; because all of its energies were not absorbed feeding its people, Europe could mobilize for other production.

Compared with Asia, Europe enjoyed greater cultural, political, and social diversity. Challenges to dominant religious and political powers had brought some diversity—a rarity in Asia, where large territories tended to be dominated by a single ruler and faith. Diversity encouraged a culture that tolerated and eventually promoted innovation. Competitiveness drove states to try to outdo one another. Governments actively encouraged industries and commerce to enrich their countries and make them more powerful than their neighbors. None of these factors alone explains why industrialization occurred, but their combination seems to have facilitated the process when it did occur.[2]

The industrialization of Europe radically transformed power relationships between the industrial West and nonindustrial Africa, Asia, and South America. By 1900 the West had overwhelmed the other regions with its economic and military power. Within Europe, power shifted to the most industrial nation. Britain, the first to industrialize, was the dominant political power throughout the nineteenth century. The rest of Europe admired Britain and regarded it not only as an economic model but also as a political and cultural one. As France had been the dominant power in the eighteenth century, so Britain dominated the nineteenth, a stellar accomplishment for a small island nation.

■ Transformations Accompanying Industrialization

A number of transformations preceded or accompanied and helped define the industrializing era. Changes in commerce, agriculture, transportation, and behavior of the population, if not always creating the preconditions of industrial development directly, were at least the major stimuli making them possible.

Changes in agriculture increased the productivity of the land. Farmers more frequently used fertilizer and improved the rotation of their crops, easing the exhaustion of the soil. New, more efficient plows enabled them to cultivate more land than ever before. In the eighteenth century, new crops that provided high yields even in poor soil were introduced into Europe: maize (corn) and potatoes from the Americas. The wealth created by agriculture allowed for investment in industry and for expenditures on infrastructure, such as roads and canal systems, useful to industry. More prosperous farmers could purchase manufactured goods such as iron plows and even machine-woven textiles, thus providing an impetus for industry. Most important, the new crops and the more efficient cultivation of traditional ones increased the capacity to feed a growing population and freed many people to go to the city and work in the industries.

In the seventeenth and eighteenth centuries, European trade had grown significantly, enriching entrepreneurs and making them aware of the fortunes to be made by marketing high-demand goods not just locally but even far away. A new dynamic ethos inspired entrepreneurs to venture into untried fields of economic endeavor.

During the years of the industrial transformation, population grew, enough to promote industrialization, yet not so much as to put a brake on economic expansion. The first spurt in population growth occurred in the mid-eighteenth century, before the effects of industrialization could be widely felt. Thereafter the population of

Europe increased dramatically throughout the industrial era: from 1750 to 1850 it doubled.

This growth was largely due to a lowering of the death rate. Infant mortality had been very high from diseases such as smallpox, diphtheria, and tuberculosis. Although none of these diseases had been medically conquered, improved standards of living after 1750, such as greater food intake, enabled children to better resist killer diseases. Better employment opportunities led to earlier marriages and thus higher fertility. Most of the population increase occurred in the countryside. This growing group of people supplied the labor force for the new industries and provided the large surge in consumers of various industrial goods.

CHRONOLOGY

1712	Newcomen invents steam-operated water pump
1733	Kay invents flying shuttle
1750–1800	3 million Africans are brought to the Americas as slaves
1753	First steam engine in the Americas
1760s	Hargreaves invents spinning jenny
1765	Watt improves steam engine with separate condenser
1769	Arkwright invents water frame
1777	Watt and Arkwright build power loom
1793	Whitney invents cotton gin
1811–1812	Luddites
1825	Börsig builds first steam engine in Germany
1832	Cholera epidemic
1831, 1834	Workers' uprising in Lyon
1834	Creation of German Customs Union, the Zollverein
1844	Workers' uprising in Silesia
1851	Majority of Britain's population becomes urban

In the countryside industrialization was foreshadowed by a form of production that had developed beginning in the seventeenth century—the putting-out system, or cottage industry. During the winter and at other slack times, peasants took in handwork such as spinning, weaving, or dyeing. Often they were marginal agriculturists, who on a part-time basis were able to augment their incomes. Entrepreneurs discovered that some individuals were better than others at specific tasks. Rather than have one household process the wool through all the steps of production until it was a finished piece, the entrepreneur would buy wool from one family, then take it to another to spin, a third to dye, a fourth to weave, and so on. Some historians believe that this form of production, also called protoindustrialization, laid the basis for industrial manufacture. Both protoindustrialization and industrial manufacture depended on specialization; both of them supplied goods to a market beyond the producers' needs. Although cottage industry was an important contributor to industrialization in some regions, that was not the case everywhere.

A less ambiguous prerequisite for industry was a good transportation network. Transportation improved significantly in the eighteenth century. Better roads were built; new coaches and carriages could travel faster and carry heavier loads. Government and private companies built canals linking rivers to each other or to lakes. Road- and canal-building were important preconditions for industrialization, hastening and cheapening transportation and making possible the movement of raw materials to manufacture and products to market without too great an increase in the price of the finished good. In Great Britain these transformations occurred simultaneously with industrialization; on the Continent they were actual precursors to economic change.

In Britain industrialization preceded the development of railroads; yet once railroad expansion occurred, beginning in the 1830s, the order for iron rails, steam engines, and wagons sustained and advanced industrial growth. (See the box "Global Encounters: A Persian Discovers the British Rail System.") On the Continent rail-building stimulated industrialization, notably in Germany and later in Italy.

First Railroad, from Manchester to Liverpool   The engineer George Stephenson (1781–1848) first built engines that could pull coal at mines; then in 1821 he constructed the first "locomotive" for public transportation. Four years later the first regular railroad line, connecting Manchester with Liverpool, was erected.   *(Private Collection/The Bridgeman Art Library, London and New York)*

⊕ G L O B A L E N C O U N T E R S

A Persian Discovers the British Rail System

In 1836 a delegation of three Persian princes visited England. Traveling widely, they had the opportunity to meet important Englishmen and to inspect and experience some of the country's latest technological advances, including the railroad. One of the princes, Najaf-Kuli Mirza, wrote down his observations. In this entry on the new British rail system, he attempts to describe its workings to fellow Persians.

All the wonderful arts which require strong power are carried on by means of steam, which has rendered immense profits and advantages. The English then began to think of steam coaches, which are especially applicable to their country, because it is small, but contains an enormous population. Therefore, in order to do away with the necessity for horses, and that the land which is sown with horse-corn [rye] should be cultivated with wheat, so as to cause it to become much more plentiful (as it is the most important article of food), and that England might thereby support a much greater population, they have with their ingenious skill invented this miraculous wonder, so as to have railroads from the capital to all parts of the kingdom.

Thus, by geometrical wisdom, they have made roads of iron, and where it was necessary these roads are elevated on arches. The roads on which the coaches are placed and fixed are made of iron bars. The coach is so fixed that no air or wind can do it any harm and twenty or thirty coaches may be fixed to the first in the train, and these one after the other.

All that seems to draw these coaches is a box of iron, in which they put water to boil, as in a fire-place; underneath this iron box is like an urn, and from it rises the steam which gives the wonderful force: when the steam rises up, the wheels take their motion, the coach spreads its wings, and the travellers become like birds. In this way these coaches go the incredible distance of forty miles an hour.

We actually travelled in this coach, and we found it very agreeable, and it does not give more but even less motion than horses; whenever we came to the sight of a distant place, in a second we passed it. The little steam engine possesses the power of eighteen horses.

Source: Najaf-Kuli Mirza, *Journal of a Residence in England and of a Journey to and from Syria* II (London: 1839; reprint, Farnborough, England: Gregg International Publishers, 1971), pp. 11–12.

INDUSTRIALIZATION AND EUROPEAN PRODUCTION

SEVERAL important technological advances powered European industry, and breakthroughs in one field often led to breakthroughs in others. The first two industries to be affected by major technological breakthroughs were textiles and iron. New forms of energy drove the machinery; novel methods of directing labor and organizing management further enhanced production. At first limited to the British Isles, industry spread to the Continent, a development that occurred unevenly in various regions and at different times.

■ Advances in the Cotton Industry

A series of inventions in the eighteenth century led the way to the mass manufacture of textiles. One of the earliest was the flying shuttle, introduced in Britain in 1733 by John Kay (1704–1764). (A shuttle carries the thread back and forth on a loom.) Kay's flying shuttle accelerated the weaving process to such an extent that it increased the demand for thread. This need was met in the 1760s by James Hargreaves (d. 1778), who invented the

British Cotton Manufacture Machines simultaneously performed various functions. The carding machine (*front left*) separated cotton fibers, readying them for spinning. The roving machine (*front right*) wound the cotton onto spools. The drawing machine (*rear left*) wove patterns into the cloth. Rich in machines, this factory needed relatively few employees; most were women and children. *(The Granger Collection, New York)*

spinning jenny, a device that spun thread from wool or cotton. Improvements, such as the "mule" of Samuel Crompton (1753–1827), made the spinning jenny increasingly efficient, and by 1812 one jenny could produce as much yarn as two hundred hand spinners. In 1769 Richard Arkwright (1732–1792), a barber and wigmaker, invented the water frame. It was installed in a single establishment with three hundred employees, forming the first modern factory. The frame was originally powered by horses or by a waterfall, but in 1777 Arkwright had James Watt construct a steam engine to operate it, the first power loom. With these innovations, cotton manufacturing was fully mechanized; its output increased 130-fold between 1770 and 1841.

The cotton manufacturing industry in Great Britain was an important departure from traditional production. For the first time in history a staple industry was based on a natural resource that was not domestically produced. Grown mainly in the U.S. South, cotton was transformed into cloth in Britain. Manufactured cotton was comfortable to wear and easy to wash; it became so cheap that it competed effectively with all handmade textiles. The popularity of cotton may have improved public health as well, for it enabled people to own several changes of clothing and keep them clean. Everyone was eager to buy British cottons. The higher demand for raw material put pressure on cotton growers in the U.S. South, who opened up new land.

In 1793 the American Eli Whitney (1765–1825) invented the cotton gin, a device that mechanically removed the seeds from cotton, formerly a laborious hand process. The cotton gin meant that more cotton could be processed and thus more could be grown. Almost overnight the machine heightened the profitability of the United States's southern plantation economy, and that situation increased the attractiveness of slave labor.

Between 1750 and 1800 approximately 3 million Africans were forcibly transported to the New World. The demographic loss to Africa was great; at least 10 percent of the captives died in the "middle passage," while being transported to the Americas, and an unknown number died in the wars triggered by slavers. Since predominantly young men were enslaved, villages were often left without their most productive workers and became vulnerable to famine, which also may have decimated the population.

The slave economy in the Americas influenced Britain's economy in several ways. Sugar produced by slave labor in the West Indies and cotton in the American South shifted Britain's trade patterns from Asia to the Atlantic. The sophisticated administrative skills that went into organizing and operating the slave trade provided invaluable management experience to the more conventional sectors of the British economy. Although some historians have argued that Britain's industrialization was founded on the wealth generated by the traffic in humans, the evidence is far from conclusive. Yet, once industrialized, Britain's economy benefited enormously from processing sugar and cotton, staples produced by slaves.

In ways beneficial and not, people were interconnected by the cotton trade; later other products would also link the economies of various nations and peoples. No longer, as in preindustrial trade, were all goods locally made, nor did the consumer meet producers and buy from them. Increasingly, specialization became the norm. Those most skilled performed a particular function efficiently and productively. The results were high production and low prices for the finished products.

■ Iron, Steam, and Factories

Industrial production was facilitated by the use of a new energy source, coal. Traditionally, charcoal had fueled the smelting of iron. Britain, however, ran low on wood—the source for charcoal—before other European countries did and needed an alternative fuel. There was plenty of coal, but it contained impurities, particularly sulfur, which contaminated the materials with which it came into contact. In 1708 the English ironmaster Abraham Darby discovered that coal in a blast furnace could smelt iron without these attending complications. His discovery triggered the iron industry's use of coal. In 1777 the introduction of a steam engine to operate the blast furnace considerably increased efficiency. In 1783 a

steam engine was first used to drive a forge hammer to shape the iron; three years later, steam-driven rollers flattened the iron into sheets. With these innovations, the output of the English iron industry doubled between 1788 and 1796 and again in the following eight years.

The greater supply of iron stimulated other changes. Relatively cheap and durable iron machines replaced wooden machines, which wore out rapidly. The new machines opened the door to further advances. Improvements in manufacturing methods and techniques led to the production of ever larger amounts of goods, usually at lower prices. Industrial change started with cotton, but breakthroughs in the use of iron and coal continued and sustained these changes.

Before the age of industry, the basic sources of power were humans, animals, wind, and water. Humans and animals were limited in their capacities to drive the large mills needed to grind grain or cut wood. Wind was unreliable because it was not constant. Water-driven mills depended on the seasons—streams dried up in the summer and froze in the winter. And water mills could be placed only where a downward flow of water was strong enough to drive a watermill. Clearly the infant industries needed a power source that was constant and not confined to riverbanks. The steam engine, invented and improved on in Britain, met that need and stoked the island's industrial growth. As late as the 1860s people, animals, and wind- and water-operated machines still supplied more than half of the energy needs of manufacturing in Great Britain and the United States. But the steam engine was clearly the wave of the future.

The steam engine was first used to pump water out of coal mines. As mining shafts were dug ever deeper through groundwater, drainage became a critical factor. In 1712 Thomas Newcomen (1663–1729) invented a steam-operated water pump. Its use spread rapidly. The first steam engine in the Americas was a Newcomen engine installed in New Jersey in 1753. James Watt (1736–1819) improved on the Newcomen engine considerably, making it twice as efficient in energy output. Eventually, by developing a separate condenser, Watt devised an engine that could convert the reciprocating motion of the piston to the more functional rotary motion. This breakthrough enabled the steam engine to power a variety of machines. (See the box "Reading Sources: James Watt Receives a Patent for the Steam Engine.") Thus, steam engines could operate mills that had previously been powered by water or wind. The high-pressure steam engine was even more powerful and energy-efficient. The use of steam engines spread in Britain, to the Continent, and to the United States.

Newcomen Engine Thomas Newcomen, a hardware merchant, produced the first successful operating steam engine in 1712. Steam was introduced into a cylinder that was then cooled, creating a partial vacuum. The pressure of the atmosphere forced the piston down, pulling down one end of the beam and creating a pumping stroke. The engine could make as many as fourteen pumping strokes a minute. *(The Fotomas Index, U.K.)*

The steam engine centralized the workplace. With the machine as a central power source, it became practical and commonplace to organize work in a factory. Locating a manufacturing plant where it was most convenient eliminated the expense of transporting raw materials to be worked on at a natural but fixed power source such as a waterfall. The central factory also reinforced work discipline. These factories were large, austere edifices, sometimes inspired by military architecture and therefore resembling barracks. With the introduction of blast furnaces and other heat-producing manufacturing methods, the tall factory chimney became a common sight on the industrial landscape.

The steam engine powered a dramatic growth in production. It increased the force of blast furnaces and the mechanical power of machinery used to forge iron and to produce equipment for spinning and weaving. Assisted by machines, workers were enormously more productive than when they depended solely on hand-operated tools. In 1700 spinning 100 pounds of cotton took 50,000 worker-hours; by 1825, it took only 135—a 370-fold increase in productivity capacity per worker.

■ Inventions and Entrepreneurs

Inventions triggered the industrial age, and the continued flow of new ones sustained it. In the decade 1700–1709, 22 patents had been issued in Britain; between 1840 and 1849, 4,581 were issued. Something revolutionary was occurring. People were seeing in their lifetimes sizable growth in productivity, both in the factory and on the farm. Rather than cling to traditional methods, many entrepreneurs consciously and persistently challenged tradition and attempted to find new ways of improving production. In this age of invention, innovation was prized as never before.

The early industrialists came from a variety of backgrounds. In Britain very few were landed nobles, industrial workers, or artisans. A large number of the early manufacturers were university educated, a fact suggesting that even in the early stages of industry, scientific knowledge was valuable. Most came from the merchant class, since also in these early years the possession of capital was a distinct advantage in launching an industrial enterprise.

Entrepreneurs such as Arkwright and Watt pioneered innovations and became famous, but most who advanced the cause of industrial production were not particularly inventive. They just replicated methods of production that had proved profitable to others. Truly successful entrepreneurs, however, seemed to share one attribute: they were driven by a nearly insatiable appetite for innovation, work, and profit.

Entrepreneurs took the financial risk of investing in new types of enterprises. Most industrialists ran a single plant by themselves or with a partner, but even in the early stages, some ran several plants. In 1788 Richard Arkwright and his partners ran eight mills. Some enterprises were vertically integrated, controlling production at many stages. The Peels in Britain owned operations ranging from spinning to printing and even banking. The entrepreneurs' dynamism and boldness fostered the growth of the British industrial system, making that small nation the "workshop of the world."

⁊⬥ READING SOURCES

James Watt Receives a Patent for the Steam Engine

British laws encouraged innovation by promoting and protecting patents, which guaranteed inventors sole rights to profit from their inventions for a set time. Watt had first received a patent for a fourteen-year period in 1769, but by 1775 after lots of experiments, he was uncertain that his efforts to develop an even more efficient engine would succeed. So he sought and received a twenty-five-year extension. This document, granting the extension, expresses the state's vested interest in industrialization and explains its willing support of men such as Watt.

And whereas, the said James Watt hath employed many years, and . . . whereas, in order to manufacture these engines with the necessary accuracy, and so that they may be sold at moderate prices, a considerable sum of money must be previously expended in erecting mills, and other apparatus; and as several years, and repeated proofs, will be required before any considerable part of the publick can be fully convinced of the utility of the invention, and of their interest to adopt the same, the whole term granted by the said Letters Patent may probably elapse before the said James Watt can receive an advantage adequate to his labour and invention:

And whereas, by furnishing mechanical powers at much less expense, and in more convenient forms, than has hitherto been done, his engines may be of great utility in facilitating the operations in many great works and manufacturers of this kingdom; yet it will not be in the power of the said James Watt to carry his invention into that complete execution which he wishes, and so as to render the same of the highest utility to the publick of which it is capable, unless the term granted by the said Letters patent be prolonged . . . be it enacted, by the King's Most Excellent Majesty . . . that the said *James Watt*, his executors, administrators, and assigns, shall and lawfully may have and enjoy the whole profit, benefit, commodity and advantage, from time to time coming, growing, accruing, and arising, by reason of these his said inventions, for the said term of twenty-five years, to have, hold, receive and enjoy the same, for and during and to the full end and term of twenty-five years as aforesaid. . . .

Source: B. W. Clapp, H. E. S. Fisher, and A. R. J. Jurica, eds. *Documents in English History* (London: G. Bell & Sons, 1976), pp. 147–149.

■ Britain's Lead in Industrial Innovation

Britain led the way industrially for many reasons. It was the first European country to have a standard currency, tax, and tariff system. Although Britain was by no means an egalitarian society, it accommodated some movement between the classes. Ideas and experiments were readily communicated among entrepreneurs, workers, and scientists.

In addition, England had gained an increasing share of international trade since the seventeenth century. This trade provided capital for investment in industrial plants. The world trade network also ensured that Britain had a market beyond its borders, and because total demand was relatively high, mass manufacture was feasible. The international trade network also enabled Britain to import raw materials for its industry, the most important of which was cotton.

Earlier than its competitors, Britain had a national banking system that could finance industries in areas where private funding fell short. In addition to numerous London banks lending mainly in the capital, six hundred provincial banks serviced the economy by 1810. The banking system reflected the growth of the economy as much as it contributed to it. Banking could flourish because Britons had wide experience in trade,

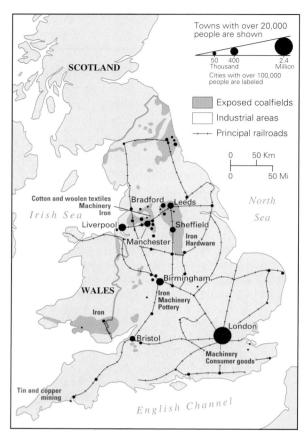

Map 20.1 The Industrial Transformation in England, ca. 1850 Industry developed in the areas rich in coal and iron fields. Important cities sprang up nearby and were soon linked by a growing rail network.

had accumulated considerable amounts of wealth, and had found a constant demand for credit.

Geographically, Britain was also fortunate. Coal and iron were located close to each other (see Map 20.1). A relatively narrow island, virtually all of Britain has easy access to the sea—no part of the country is more than 70 miles from a seacoast. This was a strategic advantage, for water was by far the cheapest means of transportation. Compared with the Continent, Britain had few tolls, and moving goods was relatively easy and inexpensive.

On the whole, British workers were better off than their continental counterparts. They were more skilled, earned higher wages, and had discretionary income to spend on the manufactured goods now for sale. But because labor was more costly than on the Continent, British business owners had an incentive to find labor-saving devices and reduce the number of workers needed for production.

Population growth in Great Britain—in part the result of industrial growth—increased by 8 percent in each decade from 1750 to 1800. This swelling population expanded the market for goods. The most rapid growth occurred in the countryside, causing a steady movement of people from rural to urban areas. The presence of this work force was another contributing factor in Britain's readiness for change.

Britain was far more open to dissent than were other European countries at the time. The lack of conformity was reflected in religion, and also in a willingness to try new methods of production. In fact, the two often went together. A large proportion of British entrepreneurs were Quakers or belonged to one of the dissenting (non-Anglican) religious groups—for instance, the iron-making Darby family; the engineer of the steam engine, James Watt; and the inventor of the "mule," Samuel Crompton. Perhaps dissenters were accustomed to questioning authority and treading new paths. They were also well educated and, as a result of common religious bonds, inclined to provide mutual aid, including financial support.

The timing of the industrial transformation in Britain was also influenced by plentiful harvests in the years 1715–1750, creating low food prices and thus making possible low industrial wages. The demand for industrial goods was reasonably high. Farmers with good earnings could afford to order the new manufactured iron plows. It is likely that income from farming helped bring about changes associated with industrialization, such as population growth, improvements to the transportation system, and the growing availability of capital for investment. Thus, each change triggered more change; the cumulative effect was staggering.

■ The Spread of Industry to the Continent

The ideas and methods that were changing industry in Britain spread to the Continent by direct contact and by emulation. Visitors came to Britain, studied local methods of production, and returned home to set up blast furnaces and spinning works inspired by British design. The German engineer August Börsig° (1804–1854), after studying steam engines in Britain, built the first German steam engine in 1825 and the first German locomotive in 1842. Some visitors even resorted to industrial espionage, smuggling blueprints of machines out of Britain. Although a British law forbade local artisans to emigrate, some did leave, including entrepreneurs who helped set up industrial plants in France and Belgium. By the 1820s

Börsig (BEUR-sick)

British technicians were all over Europe—in Belgium, France, Germany, and Austria.

In the eighteenth century France had seemed a more likely candidate for economic growth than Britain. France's overseas trade was growing faster than Britain's. In 1780 France's industrial output was greater than Britain's, though production per person was less. In the nineteenth century, however, while Britain's industry boomed and it became the workshop of the world, France lagged behind. Why?

Historians have suggested several reasons. The wars and revolutions of the late eighteenth century were certainly contributing factors. They slowed economic growth and cut France off from the flow of information and new techniques from Britain. Moreover, in the 1790s, when the French peasants pressured for legislation to ease their situation, the revolutionaries responded positively. Thus, the misery of the peasantry was somewhat relieved, and peasants were comfortable enough to feel no urgency to leave the land and provide the kind of cheap and ready labor that Britain had. Further, the Napoleonic Code of 1804 abolished primogeniture, so that when a peasant died, his younger sons were not forced off the land.

Population figures suggest another reason for France's relatively low economic growth. Between 1800 and 1914, the population of France grew at half the average rate experienced by the rest of the Continent. In Britain during this period, much of the labor that left the land and worked the factories and mills came from the rural population explosion. But no such phenomenon occurred in the French countryside, and thus the labor force in France was not poised for industrial growth.

Traditionally France had produced high-quality luxury goods, and French entrepreneurs who sought to emulate British accomplishments faced serious difficulties.

The Börsig Ironworks in the 1840s   August Börsig, an artisan, founded these ironworks in Berlin. The factory expanded to meet the needs of the burgeoning German rail system. By the time of Börsig's death in 1854, his factory had built five hundred locomotives.   *(Bildarchiv Preussischer Kulturbesitz)*

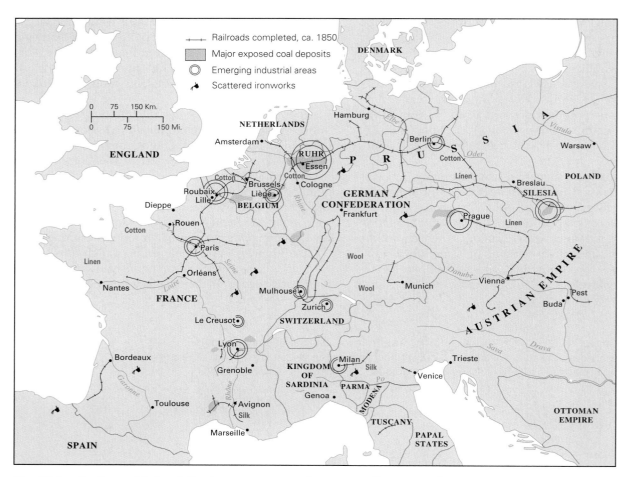

Map 20.2 Continental Industrialization, ca. 1850 Industry was still sparse on the Continent, but important regions had developed near major coal deposits in Liège, the Ruhr, and Silesia.

Iron and coal deposits in France were not close together (see Map 20.2). Because labor was still quite cheap, many goods could be manufactured inexpensively by hand; thus the incentive to invest in labor-saving devices was absent. Soon, however, French manufacturers found themselves facing British competition. By being the first to industrialize, the British had the advantage of being able to manufacture goods and to corner markets efficiently and relatively cheaply. The French were the first to feel the negative effects of being industrial latecomers.

The invasions of Germany by Napoleon caused considerable destruction, but they also brought some positive economic benefits. The example of the French Revolution led to important socioeconomic changes. Restrictive guilds declined. The French occupiers suppressed the small German states with their many tariffs

and taxes, established a single unified legal system—which survived even after 1815—and introduced a single standard of measurement based on the metric system.

Government in Germany played an important role in the adoption of improved methods of manufacturing. The Prussian state, eager for industrial development, sent an official to Britain to observe the puddling process (the method by which iron is freed of carbon) and bring that know-how back home. The Prussian government promoted industrial growth by investing in a transportation network to carry raw materials for processing and finished goods to their markets. To spur both trade and industrial growth, Prussia took the lead in creating a customs union, the *Zollverein*°, which abolished

Zollverein (TZOLL-fair-eyn)

tariffs among its members. By 1834 a German market embracing eighteen German states with a population of 23 million had been created.

German industrial growth accelerated dramatically in the 1850s. Massive expenditures on railways created a large demand for metal, which pressured German manufacturers to enlarge their plant capacities and increase efficiency. The German states were not yet politically unified, but the German middle classes saw economic growth as the means by which their country could win a prominent place among Europe's nation-states.

Germany's growth was phenomenal. It successfully emulated Britain, overtook France, and toward the end of the nineteenth century pioneered in the electrical engineering and chemical industries. If France experienced the disadvantages of being a latecomer, Germany reaped the benefits of that status. The Germans were able to avoid costly and inefficient early experimentation and to adopt the latest, proven, methods; moreover, Germany entered fields that Britain had neglected.

Even by the end of the century, however, progress remained slow in many areas of Europe. As long as Russia retained serfdom (until 1861), it would lack the mobile labor force needed for industrial growth. And until late in the century, the ruling Russian aristocracy hesitated to adopt an economic system in which wealth was not based on land. In Austria, Bohemia was the only important industrial center; otherwise, Austria remained heavily agrarian (see Map 20.2).

The impoverished southern Mediterranean countries experienced little economic growth. With mostly poor soil, their agriculture yielded only a meager surplus. Spain, lacking coal and access to other energy sources, could not easily diversify its economic base. Some industry emerged in Catalonia, especially around Barcelona, but it was limited in scope and did not have much impact on the rest of the country. The Italian peninsula was still industrially underdeveloped in the middle of the nineteenth century. There were modest advances, but growth was too slow to have a measurable positive impact on the Italian economy. In 1871, 61 percent of the population of Italy was still agrarian.

Although by midcentury only a few European nations had experienced industrialization to any great extent, many more would do so by the end of the century, pressured by vigorous competition from their more advanced neighbors (see Figure 20.1). The potential threat was political and military as well as economic, for the industrialized nations had the backing of military might

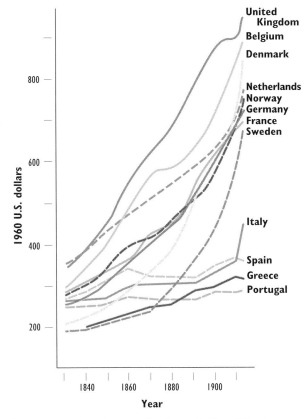

Figure 20.1   The Increase in Gross National Product per Capita in Principal European Countries, 1830–1913
The countries that industrialized rapidly—such as the United Kingdom in particular, and also Belgium, France, and Germany—experienced dramatic increase in per capita income during the nineteenth century. Other countries such as Greece and Portugal economically trailed the industrial leaders, and per capita income there remained essentially flat.   *(Source: Norman J. G. Pounds,* An Historical Geography of Europe, *1800–1914 [New York: Cambridge University Press, 1985], p. 32. Used by permission of Cambridge University Press.)*

and superiority. Compared with the rest of the world, the European continent in the nineteenth century had acquired a distinct material culture that was increasingly based on machine manufacture or was in the process of becoming so. The possession of "skillful industry," one Victorian writer exulted, was "ever a proof of superior civilization." Although only some regions of Europe were industrialized, many Europeans came to view themselves as obviously "superior," while deeming all other races "inferior."

THE TRANSFORMATION OF EUROPE AND ITS ENVIRONMENT

NDUSTRY changed the traditional methods of agriculture, commerce, trade, and manufacture. It also transformed people's lives, individually and collectively. It altered how they made a livelihood, where and how they lived, even how they thought of themselves. Industry's need of people with specialized skills created new occupations. Because industry required specialization, the range of occupations that people adopted expanded dramatically.

The advent of industry transformed the way society functioned. Until the eighteenth century, the basis of influence and power was hereditary privilege, which meant aristocratic birth and land. The aristocracy did not disappear overnight. From the late eighteenth century on, however, it was challenged by a rising class of people whose wealth was self-made and whose influence was based on economic contributions to society rather than on bloodlines. Increased social mobility opened opportunities even for some workers. Industrialization transformed both the social and the natural environment. Cities experienced extraordinary growth as a result of industrialization. Europeans faced not only urban problems but also the dangerous pollution of their air and water.

■ Urbanization and Its Discontents

A sociologist at the end of the nineteenth century observed, "The most remarkable social phenomenon of the present century is the concentration of population in cities."[3] The number and size of cities grew as never before. The major impetus for urban growth was the concentration of industry in cities and the resulting need of large numbers of urban workers and their families for goods and services (see Map 20.3).

Industrialization was not the only catalyst. France provides many examples of urban growth with little industry. Increased commercial, trading, and administrative functions led to the growth of cities such as Toulouse, Bordeaux, and Nancy. Neither Holland, Italy, nor Switzerland witnessed much industrial development in the first half of the nineteenth century, yet their cities grew. In general, however, industry transformed people from rural to urban inhabitants. People wanted to live near their work, and as industries concentrated in cities, so did populations.

Urban growth in some places was explosive. In the entire eighteenth century, London grew by only 200,000;

but in the first half of the nineteenth century, it grew by 1.4 million, more than doubling its size. Liverpool and Manchester experienced similar growth in the same period. Census figures show that by 1851 Britain was a predominantly urban society, the first country to have as many people living in cities as in the countryside. For Germany that date was 1891, and for France it was not until 1931. Although the proportion of people who were urban varied from place to place, the trend was clear and has continued.

As the pace of industry governed in part urban growth, it was fueled in turn by urbanization. Large cities provided convenient markets for goods and a labor pool for manufacturing. The concentration of people encouraged the exchange of ideas. A large city was likely to have scientific societies and laboratories where engineers and scientists could share new ideas and new inventions that would encourage industrial production. After midcentury, industrialization was driven more and more by scientific and technological breakthroughs made in urban environments.

Cities pulled in people from near and far. Usually, the larger the city, the stronger its ability to attract migrants from great distances. The medium-sized French town of Saint-Etienne° drew resettlers from the nearby mountains, whereas Paris drew from the entire country. Industrial centers even attracted people from beyond the nation's borders. The Irish arrived in large numbers to work in the factories of Lancashire, in northwestern England; Belgians came for mine work in northern France; and Poles sought employment in the Ruhr Valley region of western Germany. Industrial activity stimulated the growth of world trade and shipping across the seas, taking merchant sailors far from home. Many large cities were marked by heterogeneous populations, which included people with different native languages, religions, and national origins, as well as, in some cases, people of different races. Africans and Asians inhabited port cities such as Amsterdam, Marseille, and Liverpool.

With the growth of cities came a multitude of urban ills. In the first half of the nineteenth century, mortality rates were higher in the cities than in the countryside. In the 1840s Britain as a whole had a death rate of 22 per thousand, but Liverpool averaged 39.2 and Manchester 33.1. In France national mortality rates were around 22 per thousand, but in some French cities the rate was as high as 35 per thousand. Social inequality in the face of death was startling. Including the high child mortality rate, the average age at death for members of gentry

Saint-Etienne (sen–et-YEN)

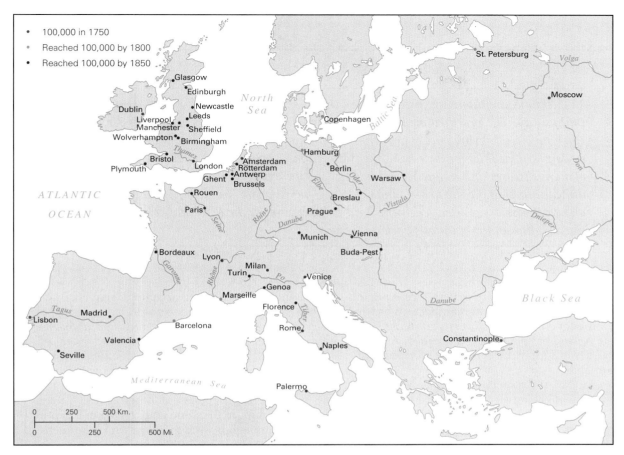

- 100,000 in 1750
- Reached 100,000 by 1800
- Reached 100,000 by 1850

Map 20.3   Cities Reaching Population Level of 100,000 by 1750, 1800, and 1850   In 1750 the largest cities owed their existence to factors other than industry, but thereafter the development of industry often determined the growth of cities. England, the leading industrial nation, contained many of the largest cities.   *(Source: Data from Tertius Chandler,* Four Thousand Years of Urban Growth: An Historical Census *[Lewistown, N.Y.: St. David's University Press, 1987], pp. 22–24.)*

families in Liverpool in 1842 was 35; for members of laborers' families it was 15. In 1800 boys living in urban slums were 8 inches shorter than the sons of rich urban dwellers.

The rapid growth of the cities caught local authorities unprepared, and in the early stages of industrialization, city life was particularly severe for the poor. Urban slums developed. The most notorious London slum was St. Giles, which became a tourist attraction because of its squalor. In many cities, large numbers of people were crammed into small areas. The houses were built back to back on small lots and had insufficient lighting and ventilation. Overcrowding was the norm. (See the box "Reading Sources: A Slum in Manchester.")

Sanitation was rudimentary or nonexistent. A single privy in a courtyard was likely to serve dozens of tenants—in some notorious cases in Britain and France, a few hundred. Waste from the privy might drain through open sewers to a nearby river, which was likely to be the local source of drinking water. Or the privy might be connected to a cesspool from which wastewater would seep and contaminate nearby wells. Some tenants lacked toilets and relieved themselves in the streets. In the 1830s people living in the poorest sections of Glasgow stored human waste in heaps alongside their houses and sold it as manure. Water in the cities was scarce and filthy. Piped water was reserved for the rich. The poor had to supply themselves from public fountains or wells and were often obliged to carry water a considerable distance.

In manufacturing towns factory chimneys spewed soot, and everything was covered with dirt and grime.

❧ READING SOURCES

A Slum in Manchester

The terrible conditions in urban slums were captured by the physician James Philips Kay, who practiced medicine in the newly industrialized city of Manchester, England. The dizzying pace of growth made it impossible for the city to provide basic sanitary facilities for its inhabitants. At the time Kay wrote, in 1832, the causes of many diseases such as typhus and tuberculosis were not known. He attributed the unhealthiness of the city to dirt, and, in a way, he was right. In the dirt, dampness, and darkness of crowded tenements and polluted streets, the fleas that communicated typhus and tuberculosis bacteria thrived.

Manchester, properly so called, is chiefly inhabited by shopkeepers and the labouring classes. Those districts where the poor dwell are of very recent origin. The rapid growth of the cotton manufacture has attracted hither operatives from every part of the kingdom, and Ireland has poured forth the most destitute of her hordes to supply the constantly increasing demand for labour. . . .

The state of the streets powerfully affects the health of their inhabitants. Sporadic cases of typhus chiefly appear in those which are narrow, ill ventilated, unpaved, or which contain heaps of refuse, or stagnant pools. The confined air and noxious exhalations, which abound in such places, depress the health of the people. And on this account contagious diseases are also most rapidly propagated there. The operation of these causes is exceedingly promoted by their reflex influence on the manners. The houses, in such situations, are unclean, ill provided with furniture; an air of discomfort if not of squalid and loathsome wretchedness pervades them, they are often dilapidated, badly drained, damp; and the habits of their tenants are gross—they are ill-fed, ill-clothed. . . .

A whole family is often accommodated on a single bed, and sometimes a heap of filthy straw and a covering of old sacking hide them in one undistinguished heap, debased alike by penury, want of economy and dissolute habits. Frequently, the inspectors found two or more families crowded into one small house, containing only two apartments, one in which they slept, and another in which they eat; and often more than one family lived in a damp cellar, containing only one room, in whose pestilential atmosphere from twelve to sixteen persons were crowded. To these fertile sources of disease were sometimes added the keeping of pigs and other animals in the house, with other nuisances of the most revolting character.

Source: J. P. Kay, *The Moral and Physical Condition of the Working Classes Employed in the Cotton Manufacture in Manchester* (London: James Ridgway, 1832), pp. 6, 14–15, 19.

Smoke was a major ingredient of the famous London fog, which not only reduced visibility but posed serious health risks. City streets were littered with refuse; rotting corpses of dogs and horses were common sights. In 1858 the stench from sewage and other rot was so putrid that the British House of Commons was forced to suspend its sessions.

It is not surprising that cholera, a highly infectious disease transmitted through contaminated water, swept London and other European urban centers. In the 1830s one of the first epidemics of modern times struck Europe, killing 100,000 in France, 50,000 in Britain, and 238,000 in Russia. A generation later, the cholera epidemic of 1854 killed 150,000 in France. Typhoid fever, also an acute infectious disease, struck mostly the poor but did not spare the privileged. Queen Victoria of Great Britain nearly died of it; her husband, Prince Albert, did.

St. Giles   The most notorious London slum was St. Giles, whose human squalor made it a tourist attraction.   *(From Thomas Beames,* The Rookeries of London. *Courtesy Harvard University Library)*

For most of its denizens, the city provided a crowded and squalid environment. Only in the second half of the nineteenth century would any attempts be made to bring order to the chaos of urban life.

■ The Working Classes and Their Lot

In 1842 a middle-class observer traveling in industrial Lancashire noted that around the mills and factories there had developed a "population [that] like the system to which it belongs is NEW . . . hourly increasing in breadth and strength."[4] A French countess, using the pen name Daniel Stern, wrote in her memoirs of France in the 1830s and 1840s of the emergence of "a class apart, as if it were a nation within the nation," working in factories and mines, called "by a new name: the industrial proletariat."[5] Originally used to designate the poorest propertyless wretches in Roman society, the term *proletariat* became synonymous with the class of workers developing in the burgeoning factories. What distinguished this growing class throughout the nineteenth century was that it was relatively unskilled and totally dependent on the factory owners for its livelihood. In earlier eras

apprentices appear to have occupied a similar situation. But guild rules and traditions gave apprentices some protection from arbitrariness, and they could escape their lowly position by eventually becoming master artisans themselves, owning their own tools and being masters of their own time—a possibility denied the members of the working class.

As industry advanced and spread, more and more people depended on it for a livelihood. In the putting-out system, during an agricultural downturn, a cottager could spend more time on hand labor; and when demand for piecework slacked off, the cottager could devote more time to the land. But people living in industrial cities had no such backup. And neither skilled nor unskilled workers were assured of regular employment: any downturn in the economy translated into layoffs or job losses.

In addition, the introduction of new industries often devastated laborers in older forms of production. The mechanization of cotton production reduced the earning power of weavers in England and in Flanders, for instance. The production of linen was mechanized in Belgium by the 1840s, but cotton production was so much cheaper that in order to price their wares competitively, linen producers drastically reduced their workers' wages.

Most factory work was dirty and laborious in grim plants with heavy, noisy machinery. Sixteen-hour workdays were common. Child labor was widespread. With no safety provisions, the workers were prone to accidents. Few factory owners protected their workers against dangerous substances or circumstances. Mercury used in hat manufacturing gradually poisoned the hatmakers and often led to dementia, hence the term "mad hatters." Lead used in paints and pottery also had a devastating impact on workers' health.

Usually physically lighter than boys and often underfed, young girls were faced with heavy labor that undermined their health. In 1842, 18-year-old Ann Eggley, a mineworker since the age of 7, hauled carriages loaded with ore weighing 800 pounds, for twelve hours a day. She testified to a parliamentary commission that she was so tired from her work that when she came home, she often fell asleep before even going to bed. Isabel Wilson, another mineworker, testified that she had given birth to ten children and had suffered five miscarriages. These women were overworked, exhausted, and vulnerable to disease, and faced premature death.

Did industrialization improve the workers' lot? Perhaps this question is best answered by another question:

What would the workers have done without industrial employment? A population explosion meant that many did not have enough land to make a living, and more efficient farming methods lessened the need for farm hands. It is not clear that these workers could have made a better living, or any at all, if they had remained in the country.

Until the mid-nineteenth century, information on workers' income and expenses is incomplete. The best evidence comes from Britain, where an average family of five needed at least 21 shillings a week to fend off poverty. Skilled workers, who were in demand, might earn as much as 30 shillings a week, but most workers were unskilled. And even skilled workers enjoyed little security: if they became less productive because of illness or old age, their wages fell. If women and children did not always need to work to help the family meet its minimum needs, at some point they usually did have to pitch in. Women, even when they were the main breadwinners, almost never received wages sufficient to meet a family's total needs.

Incomes were so low that workers normally spent between two-thirds and three-fourths of their budget on food. Those who lived in rural areas might raise chickens or pigs or have a plot of potatoes. Bread was the largest single item consumed, varying between one and two pounds a day per person. In Britain and Germany people also ate a lot of potatoes. A little bacon or other meat

Children Toiling in Mines
Able to crawl in narrow mine shafts, many children were employed underground. In this woodcut, a woman joins a child in his labor. Often, whole families worked together and were paid a fixed price for the amount of coal extracted.
(Hulton Getty/Liaison)

gave flavor to the soup in which people dipped their bread or potatoes, but meat was rarely consumed as a main course. Because men were the chief breadwinners and tended to have the most strenuous occupations, they received the choice piece of meat and the largest amount of food. Women and children ate what was left.

From the beginning, industrialization increased society's wealth. But did it benefit workers? "Optimist" historians argue that some of the new wealth trickled down to the lower levels of society. "Pessimist" historians say that a downward flow did not necessarily occur. Statistics suggest that by the 1840s workers' lives in Britain did improve. Their real income rose by 40 percent between 1800 and 1850.

Factory workers benefited not only from increased earnings but from the relatively low prices of many basic goods. In London the price of 4 pounds of household bread fell from 15 pennies at the beginning of the nineteenth century to 8½ pennies in the 1830s. As the cost of cloth declined, the dress of working-class people noticeably improved. On the Continent, the lot of workers improved a little later than in Britain, but the process followed the same pattern. (See the feature "Weighing the Evidence: Workers' Wages" on pages 704–705.)

■ Industrialization and the Family

Industrialization dramatically changed the character of the working-class family and household. Job segregation reserved the best-paying jobs for men; men were supervisors and ran machinery such as the jenny. Especially in the textile industries, factory owners employed children and women in the lowliest positions. They were thought to be more pliable than men, and their wages were considerably lower. Women generally received from 30 to 50 percent of men's wages, children from 5 to 25 percent. In 1839 Thomas Heath, a weaver in Spitalfields, a London neighborhood, earned 15 shillings a week, his wife but 3 shillings.

Factory work often undermined the ability of women to take care of their children. As farmers or cottagers, women had been able simultaneously to work and to supervise their children; the factory, however, often separated mothers from their children. Many children were given heavy responsibilities at an early age, and it was not uncommon for an older child, sometimes only 5 or 6 years old, to be entrusted with the care of a younger sibling.

Other workers resorted to more dangerous methods of child-care. They might send newborns to "baby-farms," run by individuals in the countryside who were paid to take care of infants. Very often these babies were neglected, and their mortality rate was extremely high. In many cases, babyfarming was no more than a camouflaged form of infanticide. Mothers who kept their children but were obliged to leave them unwatched at home during factory hours sometimes pacified the children by drugging them with mixtures of opium, readily available from the local apothecary.

Working-class women carried an exhausting burden in the family. In addition to sometimes working outside the home, they were responsible for running the household, managing the family income, and taking care of the children, providing most of the nurture and supervision they required.

Because of the many demands on married women, their employment pattern often was affected by the life cycle. Young women might work before marriage, or before giving birth, then stay home until the children were older, and then return to work. Factory work had a harsh impact on women's lives, but it should be remembered that relatively few women were in the wage market—by 1850 only about a quarter in both Britain and France. And of that quarter few worked in factories; far more were in agriculture, crafts industries (which still flourished despite poor working conditions), and domestic service, with many of these women working part-time while their children were small. Some sectors of industry employed a large proportion of women—for instance, textiles. Other sectors, such as the metal and mining industries, were heavily male-dominated.

The textile industry found employment for children once they were over the age of 5 or 6. Their size and agility made them useful for certain jobs, such as reaching under machines to pick up loose cotton. Because of their small hands they were also hired as "doffers," taking bobbins off frames and replacing them. Elizabeth Bentley began work as a doffer in 1815 at the age of 6. At the age of 23, when she testified before a parliamentary commission, she was "considerably deformed . . . in consequence of this labor." (See the box "Reading Sources: The Young Girl in the Factory.") Child labor certainly did not start with the industrial transformation; it had always existed. What was new was the stern industrial discipline imposed on the very young. Children were subject to the clock, closely supervised and prevented from taking long breaks, or mixing work and play—as had been possible in an earlier era.

Although children were common in British textile industries, overall less than 10 percent of working children were in industry. Most were in agriculture or the service sector. In the early stages of industrialization, children were primarily employed in textile mills to pick up waste and repair broken threads. As technological

The Young Girl in the Factory

Reformers in Parliament, among them Michael Sadler, denounced the appalling conditions in the factories. Sadler was appointed to head the commission that investigated the matter. Workers who appeared before the panel gave vivid descriptions of their lot. Public and parliamentary outrage at the conditions revealed by these hearings led to the Factory Act of 1833. Among the witnesses was Elizabeth Bentley, a 23-year-old weaving machine operative, who gave the following testimony. Note the extent to which the questions and answers deal with time. Both employers and employees had developed a strong sense of time. As Bentley's testimony shows, employees who ignored the clock risked retribution.

What age are you?—23. . . .

What time did you begin to work in a factory?—When I was 6 years old. . . .

What were your hours of labor? . . . —From 5 in the morning till 9 at night, when they were thronged [busy].

For how long have you worked that excessive length of time?—For about half a year.

What were your usual hours of labor when they were not so thronged?—From 6 in the morning till 7 at night.

What time was allowed for your meals?—40 minutes at noon. . . .

Your labor is very excessive?—Yes, you have not time for anything.

Suppose you flagged a little, or were too late, what would they do?—Strap us. . . .

Girls as well as boys?—Yes.

Severely?—Yes.

Could you eat your food well in that factory? —No, indeed, I had not much to eat, and the little I had I could not eat it, my appetite was so poor, and being covered with dust; and it was no use taking it home, I could not eat it. . . .

Did you live far from the mill?—Yes, two miles.

Had you a clock?—No, we had not. . . .

Were you generally there in time?—Yes; my mother has been up at four o'clock in the morning and at two o'clock; the colliers used to go to their work at about three or four o'clock, and when she heard them stirring she has got up out of her warm bed, and gone out and asked them the time; and I have sometimes been at Hunslet Car at 2 o'clock when it was steaming down with rain, and we have had to stay till the mill was opened [at 5 A.M.].

Source: Great Britain, Sessional Papers, House of Commons, Hearing of June 4, 1832, vol. XV (1831–1832), pp. 195–197.

 For additional information on this topic, go to http://college.hmco.com.

advances relieved both problems, the need for children lessened.

Improved technology and the growth of industries other than textiles increased the employment of adult men. In iron and later steel plants, physical strength was essential. Despite the higher labor costs that resulted when men were employed, managers had no choice but to hire them. However, in France, where textiles were still the predominant product after the turn of the nine-

teenth century, women made up two-thirds of the textile industry work force as late as 1906.

In some cases, industrialization meant a transformation in the authority structure of workers' households, undermining the influence of the male as head of the household. A woman could make a living independent of her spouse, and children at a reasonably early age could emancipate themselves from their parents and make a go of it working in a factory or a mine. These

Table 20.1
Coal Production in Industrializing Nations

	Millions of Tons	Kilograms per Inhabitant
1700	4	26
1750	7	16
1800	16	76
1830	30	120
1860	129	390

Source: Based on B. R. Mitchell, "Statistical Appendix, 1700–1914," in Carlo Cippola, ed., *The Fontana Economic History of Europe,* vol. 4 (London: Collins, 1973), pp. 747, 770; and Norman J. G. Pounds, *An Historical Geography of Europe, 1500–1840* (New York: Cambridge University Press, 1979), pp. 268–269.

options were not possible in agriculture or in the putting-out system. As in the putting-out system, however, often whole families were hired as a group to perform a specific function. Contemporaries sometimes denounced industry for dissolving family bonds, but the family remained an effective work unit.

If not participating in the wage market, wives and children contributed in other ways to the household budget—by making clothes, raising a pig, tending a potato patch, and performing daily household chores. Grandparents often moved from the country to live with the family and take care of children. When industrial workers married, they frequently settled with their spouses on the same street or in the same neighborhood where their parents lived. Although industry had the potential to break up traditional family structures, the historical evidence is that the family adjusted and survived the challenges posed by the new economic system.

■ The Land, the Water, and the Air

Industrialization seriously disturbed the environment, transforming the surface of the earth, the water, and the air. To run the new machinery, coal was mined in increasing amounts (see Table 20.1). Iron and other minerals were also in great demand. The exploitation of coal ushered in the modern age of energy use, in which massive amounts of nonrenewable resources are consumed.

To extract coal and other minerals, miners dug deep tunnels, removing millions of tons of earth, rock, and other debris. This material, plus slag and other waste from the factories, was heaped up in mounds that at times covered acres of land, creating new geological formations.

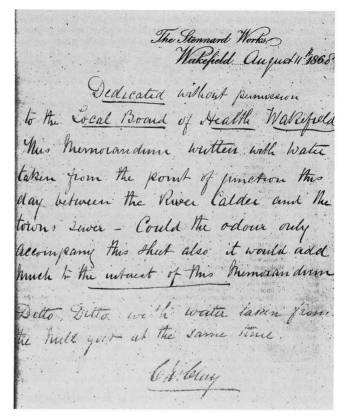

A Letter Written with Polluted Water In 1868 an irate Englishman wrote the health board, using water drawn from the Calder River in northern England to make his point about the condition of the river. As the letter writer points out, readers of the missive will miss one dimension of the situation— the river's stench. *(The British Library)*

With axes and saws people cut down trees, depleting forests to supply the wood needed to build shafts for coal, iron, and tin mines, or to make the charcoal necessary for glassmaking. Between 1750 and 1900, industrial and agricultural needs led to the clearing of 50 percent of all the forests ever cleared. Many of Europe's major forests disappeared or were seriously diminished. Deforestation in turn sped up soil erosion.

Industry changed the physical environment in which people lived. Forests, lakes, rivers, and air—as well as people themselves—showed the harmful effects of industry. Centrifugal pumps drained large marshes in the Fenland in eastern England. A contemporary lamented, "The wind which, in the autumn of 1851 was curling the blue water of the lake, in the autumn of 1853 was blowing in the same place over fields of yellow

Manchester, England, 1851   A small, unimportant town of 20,000 in the 1750s, Manchester—as a result of industrialization—had 400,000 inhabitants in 1850. In this 1851 painting, the polluted industrial city is contrasted with its idealized pastoral suburb.   *(The Royal Collection © 2001 Her Majesty Queen Elizabeth II)*

corn." Factories dumped waste ash into rivers, changing their channels and making them considerably shallower. Because of pollution from industrial and human waste, by 1850 no fish could survive in the lower Thames River. Some rivers were so polluted that their water could be used as ink. Alkali, used for making glass, when released into the atmosphere killed trees for several miles around. Smoke and soot darkened the skies, intensifying the fog over London and other cities. Foul odors from factories could be detected at several miles' distance. Not merely unpleasant, various air pollutants caused cancer and lung diseases, though the connection between pollutants and disease was not yet understood.

■ Changing Sense of Time

In agrarian societies time was measured in terms of natural occurrences, such as sunrise and sunset, or the time it might take to milk a cow. With industrialization, punctuality became essential. Shifts of labor had to be rotated to keep the smelters going; they could not stop, or the

molten iron would harden at the bottom of the hearths. The interactive nature of industrial production, in which workers with differing specialties each performed a particular task in finishing a product, made it necessary for employees to be at the factory at an appointed time. They could not be late.

Clocks were installed in church towers and municipal buildings as early as the fourteenth century, but they were not very reliable until the eighteenth century. Watches were commonly owned by men of property and even by some artisans. By the mid-nineteenth century— at least in Britain—as the price of watches came down, many workers could afford them. And even when workers did not own timepieces, they were intensely aware of time. Those who ignored time were fined or fired from their jobs. People listened for the church bell or factory whistle, or asked a neighbor or passer-by for the time. (See the box "Reading Sources: The New Discipline of the Factory System." See also "The Young Girl in the Factory" on page 696.) Western societies increasingly regularized and internalized the sense of time.

✍ READING SOURCES

The New Discipline of the Factory System

The new factories regimented the work force and were likely to impose stiff penalties for infractions of the rules. This document lists some of the regulations of the Berlin Foundry and Engineering Works of the Royal Overseas Trading Company of 1844. Note how obsessed with efficient use of time the factory rules are. The worker is left little room for personal initiative.

The normal working day begins at all seasons at 6 A.M. precisely and ends, after the usual break of half an hour for breakfast, an hour for dinner, and half an hour for tea, at 7 P.M., and it shall be strictly observed.

Five minutes before the beginning of the stated hours of work until their actual commencement, a bell shall ring and indicate that every worker employed in the concern has to proceed to his place of work, in order to start as soon as the bell stops.

The doorkeeper shall lock the door punctually at 6 A.M., 8:30 A.M., 1 P.M., and 4:30 P.M.

Workers arriving 2 minutes late shall lose half an hour's wages; whoever is more than 2 minutes late may not start work until after the next break, or at least shall lose his wages until then. . . .

Repeated irregular arrival at work shall lead to dismissal. This shall also apply to those who are found idling by an official or overseer, and refuse to obey their order to resume work. . . .

All conversation with fellow-workers is prohibited. . . .

Smoking in the workshops or in the yard is prohibited during working-hours; anyone caught smoking shall be fined five silver groschen for the sick fund.

Natural functions must be performed at the appropriate places. . . .

It goes without saying that all overseers and officials of the firm shall be obeyed without question, and shall be treated with due deference. Disobedience will be punished by dismissal.

Immediate dismissal shall also be the fate of anyone found drunk in any of the workshops. . . .

The gatekeeper and the watchman, as well as every official, are entitled to search the baskets, parcels, aprons, etc. of the women and children who are taking the dinners into the works, on their departure, as well as search any worker suspected of stealing any article whatever. . . .

A free copy of these rules is handed to every workman, but whoever loses it and requires a new one, or cannot produce it on leaving, shall be fined 2½ silver groschen.

Source: S. Pollard and C. Holmes, eds., *Documents of European Economic History*, vol. 1 (New York: St. Martin's Press, 1968), pp. 534–536.

RESPONSES TO INDUSTRIALIZATION

PEOPLE in the new industrial classes living at subsistence levels were disquieting evidence of the impact of industrialization. What should be done about the working classes—or for them? These new classes developed their own sense of a common interest and fate. The result was a resounding cry for political and social democracy that began in the first half of the nineteenth century and became increasingly insistent. Many solutions were proffered.

■ The Growth of Working-Class Solidarity

Hardest hit by economic changes, workers sought to improve their conditions by organizing and articulating their needs. In the preindustrial economy, artisans and craftsmen lived in an accepted hierarchy with prescribed rules. They began by serving for a certain number of years as apprentices to a master, next became journeymen, and finally with hard work and good fortune became masters of their trades. As tradesmen with common interests, they tended to band together into brotherhoods, promising one another help and trying to improve their working conditions.

With industrialization, guilds declined. Unlike the skilled handicrafts that required years of apprenticeship, few aspects of industrial production demanded extensive training. The system of dependence between apprentice and master became irrelevant. Guilds trying to protect their members often resisted new technologies and came to be seen as a hindrance to economic development. Liberals viewed guilds as constraints on trade and the free flow of labor. In France the revolutionaries abolished the guilds and all workers' coalitions. Throughout the eighteenth century the British Parliament passed various acts against "combinations" by workmen.

While guilds faded in importance, the solidarity and language born of the guild continued to shape workers' attitudes throughout much of the nineteenth century. New experiences also reinforced the sense of belonging to a group and sharing common aspirations.

Cultural forces fostered workers' sense of solidarity. The common language of religion and shared religious practice united workers. Religious sects flourished in an environment of despair punctuated by hopes of deliverance. Some historians believe that the growth of Methodism in England in the 1790s (see page 713) was a response to grim economic conditions. Emphasis on equality before God fueled the sense of injustice in a world where a privileged few lived in luxury while others were condemned to work along with their children for a pittance. Joanna, a self-proclaimed prophet active in the 1810s in England, announced both salvation and the coming of a new world of material well-being. In France workers believed the new society would come about by their martyrdom; like Jesus, the workers would suffer, and from their suffering would emerge a new, better society. Ideas of social justice were linked in the countryside with religious broadsides speaking of "Jesus the worker." Religious themes and language continued to be important in labor organization for many years.

Other cultural and social factors created bonds among workers. Housing was increasingly segregated. Workers lived in low-rent areas—in slums in the center

Leisure Activity for the Working Poor   Some harsh forms of entertainment turned up in the industrial period. Scores of working-class spectators came to see the celebrated dog "Billy" kill a hundred rats at one time at the Westminster Pit in London in 1822.   *(The British Library)*

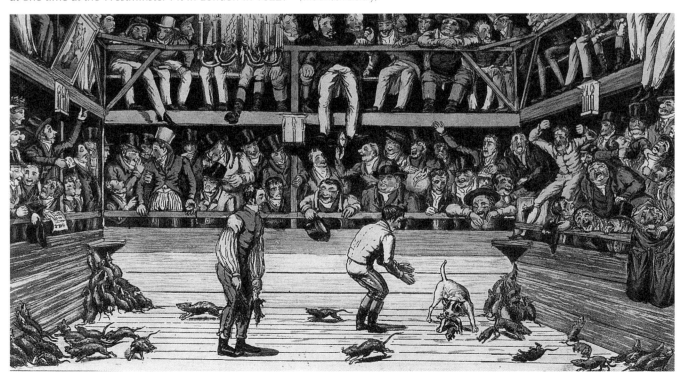

of cities or in outlying areas near the factories. Thus, urban workers lived close together, in similar conditions of squalor and hardship. Workers grew close by spending their leisure time together, drinking in pubs, attending theaters and new forms of popular entertainment such as the circus, or watching traditional blood sports such as boxing or cockfights. Sports became popular as both spectator and participatory events in the 1880s. Soccer, which developed in England at this time, drew players and fans overwhelmingly from the working class.

Social institutions also encouraged class unity. In the eighteenth century both husband and wife were usually in the same craft. By 1900 it became more common for workers to marry across their crafts, thereby strengthening the sense of solidarity that encompassed the working classes as a whole.

Faced with the uncertainties of unemployment and job-related accidents, in addition to disease and other natural catastrophes, workers formed so-called friendly societies in which they pooled their resources to provide mutual aid. These societies, descendants of benefit organizations of the Middle Ages and Renaissance, combined business activity with feasts, drinking bouts, and other social functions.

Friendly societies had existed as early as the seventeenth century, but they became increasingly popular and important after industrialization. Their strength in a region often reflected the degree to which the area was industrialized. First started to provide aid for workers in a particular trade, they soon included members in several crafts. In time, they federated into national organizations, so that a worker who moved to a new town could continue membership in the new locale. Connected by common membership in friendly societies, workers expressed a feeling of group solidarity beyond their individual occupations. Though far from solidified, a working class was in the making.

■ Collective Action

Militant and in some cases violent action strengthened workers' solidarity. In politics, workers expressed common grievances, and some of their disappointments in the political arena underscored their common situation.

In the face of hardships, artisans organized for collective action. In 1811–1812 British hand weavers, faced with competition from mechanized looms, organized in groups claiming to be led by a mythical General Ned Ludd. In the name of economic justice and to protect their livelihood, the "Luddites," as the general's followers were called, smashed machines or threatened to do so. In Saxony in eastern Germany in the 1830s and 1840s,

weavers went on machine-crushing campaigns. These movements revealed the militance of labor and its willingness to resort to violence.

In Lyon, France, in 1831 and 1834, workers led uprisings demanding fair wages for piecework. Angered when the silk merchants lowered the amount they would pay, the workers marched in the streets bearing banners proclaiming "Live Working or Die Fighting." Troops were brought in to restore order to the riot-torn city. Although conditions of the silk trade had been the immediate impetus for the uprising, the workers appealed for help to their fellow workers in other trades, who joined in the protests.

Labor agitation in much of Europe increased in the 1840s: A major strike wave involving twenty thousand workers broke out in Paris in 1840. In the summer of 1842, an industrial downturn in England led to massive unemployment and rioting. During the summer of 1844 in Silesia, in eastern Prussia, linen handloom weavers, desperate because of worsening conditions brought on by competition from machine-made cotton fabrics, attacked the homes of the wealthy. In 1855 in Barcelona, the government tried to dissolve unions, and fifty thousand workers went on strike carrying placards that warned "Association or Death."

Workers had to conform to severe discipline and rigid rules not only in the workplace but also away from it. Workers in some factories were forbidden to read certain newspapers, had to attend religious services, and could marry only with the owners' permission. Workers resisted these attempts at control and resented employers' intrusiveness.

Workers' actions in the early nineteenth century clearly showed that they wanted both freedom from intrusive regulation by their employers and the security of employment at a decent wage. Unions provided a means to these goals.

Many of the friendly societies struggled to improve their members' working conditions, acting very much as labor unions would. They organized strikes and provided support to members during work stoppages. The advantages offered by unions were well understood—by both sides. Unions were illegal in Britain until 1825, in Prussia until 1859, and in France until the 1860s. As a French workers' paper declared in 1847, "If workers came together and organized . . . nothing would be able to stop them." An organized force could threaten to withhold labor if the employer did not grant decent wages and acceptable conditions. Unions made workers a countervailing force to the factory owners.

The process of unionization was difficult. By 1850 many countries had passed laws supporting employers

Unionization   This certificate signifies membership in the first professional union in Britain, the Amalgamated Society of Engineers. With references to classical antiquity, British inventors, and various trades, the document highlights the nobility of the trade.   *(The Art Archive)*

against the workers. Censorship and the use of force against organized strikes were not uncommon. Population growth made it difficult for workers to withhold labor lest they be replaced by others only too willing to take their places. Foreign workers—for example, the Irish who streamed into England and the Belgians and Italians who migrated to France—were often desperate for work and not well informed about local conditions.

In many countries, workers formed unions before unions were legalized. Although there were early attempts in Britain to organize unions on a national basis, most were centered around a single craft or a single industry. Because labor unions originated in the crafts tradition, the earliest members were skilled craftsmen who organized to protect their livelihoods from the challenge that industrialization posed. These craftsmen were usually literate and long-time residents of their communities. They provided the labor movement with much of its leadership and organization. Skilled craft workers also played a strong role in developing a sense of class-consciousness. The language and institutions that they had developed over decades and sometimes over centuries became the common heritage of workers in general.

Workers looked to political action as the means to improve their situations. In the 1830s and 1840s British and French workers agitated for the right to vote; they saw voting as a way to put themselves on equal footing with the privileged and to win better conditions. Their disappointment at their failure to win political representation strengthened their class solidarity against the wealthy, privileged upper classes. Politically, organized workers played a major role in the revolutions that would rock Europe in 1848 (see pages 732–735), sometimes helping to instigating the uprisings, often influencing their course. However vague their ideas, European workers showed that their organizations were legitimate representatives of the people and that the lot of the worker should be the concern of government. In general, workers upheld the ideal of a moral economy—one in which all who labored got a just wage and every person was assured a minimum level of well-being.

The working classes were never a monolithic group. They consisted of people with varying skills, responsibilities, and incomes. Artisans with valuable skills were the segment that employers most respected and favored in pay and in working conditions. In contrast, unskilled workers were poorly paid, harshly treated, and often given only temporary work. Many skilled workers looked with contempt on the unskilled.

If both sexes worked side by side, it created little solidarity between them. Men worried that women were undermining their earning power by accepting lower wages. They often excluded women from their unions. Men even went on strike to force employers to discharge women.

Nor was there solidarity across nationalities. Foreign workers were heartily despised. British workers were hostile to their Irish colleagues, the French to the Belgians and Italians in their midst. The hostility often led to fisticuffs. In London anti-Irish riots were common. Many forces fostered dissension among the working classes in the nineteenth century, and unity among workers was far from achieved. Nevertheless, various experiences, including the spread of industry, broadened and deepened workers' sense of a shared fate and common goal.

The middle classes came to believe that all workers formed a single class. By the mid-nineteenth century, they had developed a clear fear of workers, not only as individuals but as a group, as a class. It was not unusual for members of the elite to refer to workers as "the swinish multitude" or, as the title of a popular English book put it, *The Great Unwashed* (1868). In France reference was alternately made to "the dangerous classes" and "the laboring classes." Not just workers but even the privileged seemed to see relations between the groups as a form of class war.

SUMMARY

 TS industrial transformation altered the face of Europe. This process, which started around 1750 in parts of England, spread by 1850 to other states of Europe. Material and cultural factors combined with a number of fortuitous circumstances explain why industrial production originated in England. The proximity of coal and iron, the relative ease of domestic transportation, a culture open to innovation and entrepreneurship, and the existence of an already relatively dynamic economy help explain why Britain was the first nation to industrialize.

Economies based on industry changed power relations within Europe and altered the relationship of Europe to the rest of the world. As a result of the transformation in its economy, Britain became in the nineteenth century the most powerful nation in Europe and achieved worldwide influence. Although Europe was industrialized only in certain areas, many Europeans came to think of their continent as economically and technologically superior to the rest of the world. Being industrial became synonymous for many with Europe's identity.

Industry changed the nature of work for large numbers of Europeans. Machines replaced human energy in the workplace. By the application of science and technology, manufacturing productivity increased significantly. A decreasing number of people worked in agriculture, and more entered manufacturing. Population patterns changed; cities grew dramatically, and for the first time European cities had over a million inhabitants.

The massing of workers in factories and urban areas aggravated their misery but called attention to their potential power. Eager to improve their lives and working conditions, workers began to express their solidarity. They organized into associations that were more broadly based and therefore more powerful than workers' groups of the past. As workers began to think of themselves as a class, the dominant elites within society began to perceive them as such. The new proletarian class, shaped by industrialization, was a growing force that would challenge the existing order throughout the nineteenth century and much of the next.

■ Notes

1. Phyllis Deane, *The First Industrial Revolution* (Cambridge: Cambridge University Press, 1965), p. 1.
2. These ideas are provocatively developed in E. L. Jones, *The European Miracle: Environments, Economies and Geopolitics of Europe and Asia* (Cambridge: Cambridge University Press, 1981).
3. Adna Ferrin Weber, *The Growth of Cities in the Nineteenth Century: A Study in Statistics* (New York: Macmillan, 1899; reprint, Ithaca, N.Y.: Cornell University Press, 1963), p. 1.
4. Cooke Taylor, *Notes of a Tour in the Manufacturing Districts of Lancashire, in a Series of Letters to His Grace the Archbishop of Dublin* (London, 1842), pp. 4–6, quoted in E. P. Thompson, *The Making of the English Working Class* (New York: Vintage, 1963), p. 191.
5. Marie de Flavigny d'Agoult [Daniel Stern], *Histoire de la Révolution de 1848*, 2d ed., vol. 1 (Paris, 1862), p. 7, quoted in Theodore S. Hamerow, *The Birth of a New Europe: State and Society in the Nineteenth Century* (Chapel Hill: University of North Carolina Press, 1983), pp. 206–207.

■ Suggested Reading

Chinn, Carl. *Poverty Amidst Prosperity: The Urban Poor in England, 1834–1914.* 1995. Concentrates on the harsher aspects of industrialization.

Hopkins, Eric. *Industrialisation and Society.* 2000. A survey that considers the social and political impact of industry on British society.

Jones, E. L. *The European Miracle.* 1981. A broad comparative work that considers the forces leading to the industrialization of the West.

Landes, David S. *The Wealth and Poverty of Nations.* 1999. Explores why Europe industrialized as compared with the rest of the world.

Mokyr, Joel. *The Lever of Riches: Technological Creativity and Economic Progress.* 1990. A comparative study of Western and Chinese technology, emphasizing cultural elements as explanations for the industrialization of the West.

Sylla, Richard, and Gianni Toniolo, eds. *Patterns of European Industrialization.* 1991. A comparative perspective on the patterns of industrialization.

Thompson, E. P. *The Making of the English Working Class.* 1963. Emphasizes the cultural factors that encouraged the development of working-class consciousness in England.

 For a searchable list of additional readings for this chapter, go to http://college.hmco.com.

Workers' Wages

In 1869 the Chamber of Commerce of Verviers°, a town in eastern Belgium, published a report on workers' wages. In the seventeenth century, Verviers, located on the Vesdre° River, had become a major producer of woolens. The river provided water for power, for washing the cloth, and for carrying away industrial waste. Thus, the site was ideal for finishing textiles, and the merchants of Verviers drew on the labor of spinners and weavers in the surrounding farm areas. With a population of 4,500 in the mid-seventeenth century, Verviers had 10,000 inhabitants by the end of the eighteenth.

Two local entrepreneurs brought the Englishman John Cockerill to town. In 1802 he set up the first spinning machine on the Continent and in 1816 the first steam engine in Belgium. Thirty years later, Verviers boasted forty factories and the population had increased to 23,000.

Industrialization transformed the people's lives in many ways. The table of wages reveals the existence of a variegated, hierarchical work force with clear, separate functions and specified salaries. It indicates the uneven ways in which people benefited from industry, depending on their skills, age, and gender.

For example, this list allows us to compare the wages of industrial workers and artisans. Industry made it difficult for the artisans to survive; unable to compete with machine manufacture, many had to give up their trade or tighten their belts to make ends meet. The new machine age, however, created an increased demand for the services of some artisans. Early in the nineteenth century the new machines eliminated hand spinning, for example, but inexpensive yarn at first increased the demand for handloom weavers. Notice that handloom weavers ("hand weavers" in the table) were relatively well paid in 1836. This is due to the uneven introduction of mechanical production. Weaving of high-quality woolens proved to be more difficult to mechanize than cotton goods. Power looms did not become common in Verviers until the 1860s, and we see the relative wages of handloom weavers decline in 1869. Joiners and ironsmiths not only did the work they had traditionally done but found new opportunities building and repairing machines. The ironsmiths, joiners, and carpenters of Verviers were all paid better than other workers.

Even among the factory workers we find some significant wage discrepancies. Compare, for example, the wages of the nonspecialized laborer to the wages of the other, specialized industrial workers.

Changes in technology, productivity, labor supply, and market demand for certain goods increased the relative wages of workers over time. Thus the relative wages of jobs changed between 1836 and 1869. Notice that a wool washer in 1869 was making 174 percent more than a wool washer made in 1836, but in the same period the wages paid to a warper had increased by 300 percent.

Let us next consider women in the labor force. Notice that the list is divided into "male occupations," "female occupations," and finally "children's occupation." Work is divided according to gender and age. Look at the list of women's industrial occupations. The absence of spinning female occupations in this list is significant. Spinning had been a female occupation since antiquity, but the spinning machines in Verviers were tended by men. Notice how little differentiation is evident among women's work; far fewer industrial occupations are listed for women than for men. Also look at the wages. Women's wages were all equally depressed, with the one exception of menders' wages, hovering in 1836 around .7 francs but climbing by 1869 to 2.25 francs, an increase of over 300 percent. Among men's occupations the spread of salaries was far greater. In 1869 the highest-paid women (menders) received 40 percent more than the lowest-paid women in 1836 (scourers), but the highest-paid men (ironsmiths) received 138 percent more than the lowest-paid men (wool washers) in 1836. By 1869 the wage gap had somewhat diminished for both men and women, but it was still far larger for men (72 percent) than for women (28 percent).

Some male artisans—carpenters, for example—consistently received wages higher than the wages of many machine operators. But notice the one female artisan occupation: seamstress. Although a seamstress was probably quite skilled, she was paid no more than the women in the factories. Special crafts, still prized for some men, were not given much monetary value when practiced by women. Note the wage differences overall

---

Verviers (ver-VYAY)   Vesdre (VEH-druh)

Wage Differentials in Verviers, Belgium, 1836–1869

		Wages (francs per day)				
		1836	1846	1856	1863	1869
Male Occupations	Ironsmith*	1.73	2.25	2.50	3.00	3.87
	Carpenter*	1.90	2.25	2.65	2.87	3.50
	Dyer	1.40	1.46	1.60	2.60	3.37
	Spinner	1.80	1.90	2.90	3.12	3.40
	Carder	1.47	1.75	2.30	3.25	3.30
	Tanner*	1.83	2.00	2.25	3.00	3.25
	Warper	0.80	0.95	1.57	1.65	3.25
	Hand weaver*	1.97	1.70	2.85	3.00	3.00
	Joiner*	1.98	2.00	2.25	2.75	3.00
	Tenterer	—	1.25	1.40	2.34	3.00
	Presser	1.47	1.78	1.78	2.15	3.00
	Machine weaver	—	—	—	—	2.75
	Comber	0.84	1.27	1.50	1.75	2.65
	Fuller	1.40	1.50	1.75	2.30	2.67
	Laborer	—	1.25	1.50	1.87	2.50
	Wool washer	1.15	1.25	1.40	1.75	2.25
Female Occupations	Mender	0.73	0.80	1.10	1.40	2.25
	Wool sorter	0.98	1.08	1.70	1.85	2.00
	Gigger	0.75	0.80	0.80	1.25	2.00
	Burler	0.77	1.00	1.20	1.70	1.80
	Seamstress*	0.73	0.80	1.10	1.40	—
	Scourer	0.70	0.75	0.85	1.35	1.62
Children's Occupation	Piecener	—	0.70	0.90	1.10	1.60

*Artisans. (Those not starred were industrial workers.)

Source: Chamber of Commerce of Verviers, *Rapport général sur la situation du commerce et de l'industrie en 1868* (Verviers, 1869), p. 69; repr. in George Alter, *Family and the Female Life Course—The Women of Verviers, Belgium, 1849–1880* (Madison: University of Wisconsin Press, 1988), p. 103. © 1988. Reprinted by permission of The University of Wisconsin Press.

between male and female workers. In 1836 the average female worker received wages equivalent to 53.2 percent of the average male worker's wages. By 1869 there was some improvement: the difference had declined by 11 percentage points; still, women earned only 64 percent of men's pay.

The table lists only one occupation for children: piecener. Small and nimble, children were paid to splice broken threads. They worked in many other capacities as well. Some were paid wages by their employers; others helped their parents in a factory or workshop. The wages of some adults probably included compensation for their children's labor.

We can learn much from a statistical table such as this about the impact of industrialization on the labor force. Some workers benefited, and others were harmed by the adoption of industry; over time workers experienced changes in their circumstances. If statistical tables are informative on such issues, they also have their limits. They do not tell us how workers interpreted and understood their experience. As workers suffered daily hardships, they had to try to make sense of their changing world, an effort no table can count.

 For additional information on this topic, go to http://college.hmco.com.

CHAPTER 21

Restoration, Reform, and Revolution 1814–1848

REVOLUTION struck Berlin in March 1848. King Friedrich Wilhelm IV (r. 1840–1861), who initially opposed the revolutionaries' demands for political liberties and a unified nation, surprised his subjects on March 21 by announcing support for a united, free, constitutional Germany. This print, distributed by the thousands, shows the king, on horseback, being acclaimed by a grateful people. The black, red, and gold flags, the symbol of German unity since the Napoleonic Wars, are prominently displayed. The king is preceded by a businessman he had appointed as chief minister. People from most walks of life appear united in purpose. Notice the depiction of well-dressed middle-class citizens as well as humble artisans. The print captures a moment of hope and great possibilities. Soon, however, the forces that made the revolution possible fell into disunion, and the Prussian king was able to turn back the tide of change. As in Prussia, the first moments of exhilarating possibilities in the rest of Europe nearly always were followed by failure and disappointment as the forces of reaction won the upper hand.

In 1848 Europe experienced a revolutionary wave, unprecedented in over a half century since the heady days of the French Revolution. These revolutions erupted in protest against the reactionary regimes established after the fall of Napoleon. The political order in western Europe started changing by the 1830s; the pace of change was slower, however, in eastern Europe.

Despite European statesmen's dogged attempts to set the clock back, the forces unleashed by the French Revolution proved irrepressible. Conservatism attempted to bolster the old order, but new

The Search for Stability: The Congress of Vienna, 1814–1815

Ideological Confrontations

Restoration, Reform, and Reaction

The Revolutions of 1848

King Friedrich Wilhelm IV (*center*) announcing his devotion to German unity (detail). (Germanisches National Museum Nuremberg)

ideologies such as romanticism, nationalism, liberalism, and socialism challenged it. (An ideology is a structured, organized set of ideas that reflects a group's thinking about life or society.) The forces revealing themselves in 1848 suggested the outline of Europe's development in the second half of the century.

At the end of the Napoleonic Wars, in 1815, the victorious Great Powers—Austria, Great Britain, Prussia, and Russia—tried to re-establish as much of the old European state system as possible. The international arrangements they carved out at the Congress of Vienna were soon shaken by outbreaks of nationalist fervor. Nationalists aimed either to create larger political units, as in Italy and Germany, or to win independence from foreign rule, as in Greece.

The attempt to set the clock back had only limited success. The conservatism of European rulers and their opposition to change were at odds with the new dynamism of European society. Between 1800 and 1850, Europe's population increased by nearly 50 percent, from around 190 million to 280 million. Population growth and surging industrialization had turned small towns into large cities. Factory manufacturing was on the rise, promising to reshape class structures and the lives of workers. Romanticism, liberalism, and other systems of thought were redefining the relationship of the individual to society. Sporadic outbreaks of collective violence reached a crescendo when the revolutions of 1848 swept most of Europe, undermining the established order in state after state. Revolutionaries did not win all their goals, and in many cases the forces of order crushed them. Yet by midcentury, major intellectual, social, and political changes had occurred.

QUESTIONS TO CONSIDER

- **What were the goals of the restorations that followed the Napoleonic era?**

- **What major ideologies developed in the first half of the nineteenth century?**

- **What were the main causes of the revolutions of 1848, and what roles did nationalism and liberalism play in inciting and sustaining revolution?**

- **What new and permanent features were created by the revolutions of 1848?**

TERMS TO KNOW

Congress of Vienna	socialism
conservatism	Marxism
romanticism	July Revolution
nationalism	Decembrists
liberalism	Great Reform Bill
laissez faire	Chartism
utilitarian	Frankfurt Assembly

THE SEARCH FOR STABILITY: THE CONGRESS OF VIENNA, 1814–1815

HE defeat of Napoleon put an end to French dominance in Europe. In September 1814 the victorious Great Powers—Austria, Great Britain, Prussia, and Russia—convened an international conference in Vienna to negotiate the terms of peace. The victors sought to draw territorial boundaries advantageous to themselves and to provide long-term stability on the European continent. Although many small powers attended the Congress of Vienna, their role was reduced to ratifying the large states' decisions. Having faced a powerful France, which had mobilized popular forces with revolutionary principles, the victors decided to erect an international system that would remove such threats. One method was to restore the European order that had existed before the French Revolution. Thus, following principles of "legitimacy and compensation," they redrew the map of Europe (see Map 21.1). Rulers who had been overthrown were restored to their thrones. The eldest surviving brother of Louis XVI of France became King Louis XVIII. In Spain, Ferdinand VII

Metternich   The consummate statesman and aristocrat, the Austrian prince Metternich tried to quell revolution at home and abroad. Some called his era the Metternichean age.
(The Royal Collection © 2001 Her Majesty Queen Elizabeth II)

CHRONOLOGY

1808	Beethoven, *Pastoral* Symphony
1814–1815	Congress of Vienna
1819	Peterloo massacre
1819	Carlsbad Decrees
1821	Spanish revolt
1821	Greek revolution
1821–1825	Spanish colonies in the Americas win independence
1823	Monroe Doctrine
1824	Owen establishes New Harmony
1825	Decembrists in Russia
1830	July Revolution in France
1830	Ottoman Empire recognizes Serbian autonomy
1832	Great Reform Bill in Britain
1833	Abolition of slavery in British colonies
1834	Turner, *Fire at Sea*
1838	"People's charter" in Great Britain
1839	Anti–Corn Law League
1845–1848	Hungry '40s
1848	Marx and Engels, *Communist Manifesto*
1848	Revolutions of 1848

was restored to the throne from which Napoleon had toppled him and his father. The restoration, however, was not so complete as its proponents claimed. After the French Revolution, certain new realities had to be recognized. For example, Napoleon had consolidated the German and Italian states; the process was acknowledged in the former with the creation of a loose German Confederation. In Italy the number of independent states had shrunk to nine. Also, unlike earlier French kings, Louis XVIII could not be an absolute monarch.

Negotiations at the Congress of Vienna strengthened the territories bordering France, enlarged Prussia and created the kingdom of Piedmont-Sardinia, joined Belgium to Holland, and provided the victors with spoils and compensation for territories bartered away. Austria received Venetia and Lombardy in northern Italy to compensate for the loss of Belgium (to the Netherlands) and parts of Poland (to Russia) and to strengthen its position in general. Prussia was also allowed annexations in compensation for giving up parts of Poland. England

acquired a number of colonies and naval outposts. Thus, with one hand these conservative statesmen swore their loyalty to the prerevolutionary past, and with the other they nevertheless changed the map of Europe.

The leading personality at the Congress of Vienna was the Austrian foreign minister, Prince Clemens von Metternich° (1773–1859), who presided over the meetings. An aristocrat in exile from the Rhineland, which had been annexed by revolutionary France, he had gone into the service of the Habsburg Empire and risen to become its highest official. Personal charm, tact, and representation of a state that for the time being was satisfied

---

Metternich (MEH-ter-nick)

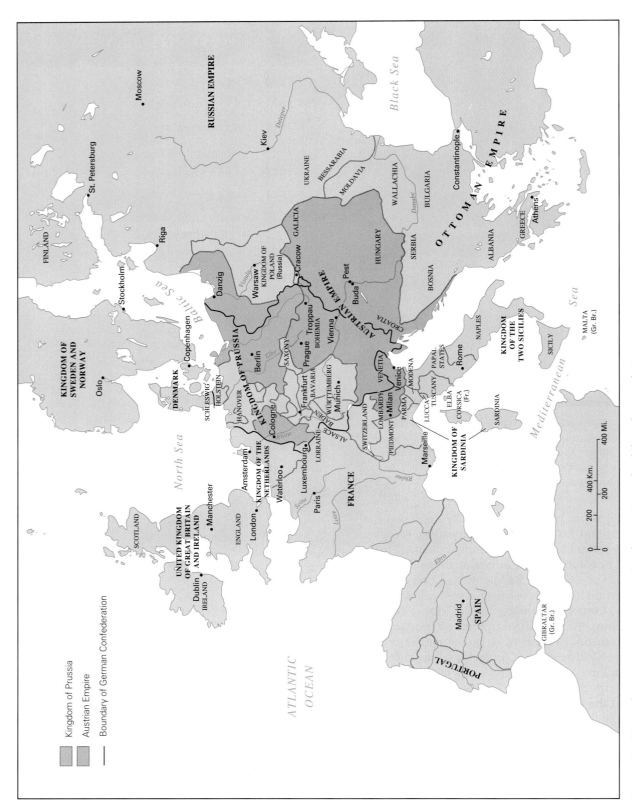

Map 21.1 Europe in 1815 Intent on regaining the security and stability of prerevolutionary years, the Great Powers redrew the map of Europe at the Congress of Vienna.

with its territories made Metternich seem a disinterested statesman. His influence at the congress was great.

Because it was Napoleon's belligerent imperialism that had brought the powers together in Vienna, France was at first treated as an enemy at the conference. By the end, however, France managed to join the other states and be included with them as one of the five Great Powers jointly known as the "Concert of Europe." The Concert continued to function for nearly forty years, meeting and resolving international crises, and preventing any major European war from breaking out. Underlying the states' cooperation was the principle of a common European destiny.

IDEOLOGICAL CONFRONTATIONS

 HE international and domestic political system established in 1815 was modified by a series of challenges, even revolts, culminating in revolutions throughout Europe in 1848. The order established in 1815 was inspired by conservatism. Its challengers advocated competing ideologies: romanticism, nationalism, liberalism, and socialism.

■ Conservatism

The architects of the restoration justified their policies with doctrines based on the ideology of conservatism, emphasizing the need to preserve the existing order of monarchies, aristocracy, and an established church. As a coherent movement, conservatism sprang up during and after the French Revolution to resist the forces of change. Before the American and French Revolutions, the existing political institutions appeared to be permanent. When the old order faced serious challenges in the late eighteenth and early nineteenth centuries, an ideology justifying traditional authority emerged.

Edmund Burke (1729–1797), a British statesman and political theorist, launched one of the first intellectual assaults on the French Revolution. The revolutionary National Assembly had asserted that ancient prerogatives were superseded by the rights of man and principles of human equality based on appeals to natural law. In *Reflections on the Revolution in France* (1790), Burke countered that such claims were abstract and dangerous and that the belief in human equality undermined the social order. Government should be anchored in tradition, he argued. No matter how poorly the French monarchy and its institutions had served the nation,

they should be preserved; their very longevity proved their usefulness. Burke's writings were widely read and influential on the Continent.

In the English-speaking world, one of the most popular writers was Hannah More (1745–1833), who with her four sisters ran a prosperous school. More saw piety as a rampart against rebellion. In a series of pamphlets entitled *Cheap Repository Tracts,* she advocated the acceptance of the existing order and the solace of religious faith. Costing but a penny, the moral tracts were often handed out by the rich together with alms or food to the poor. More was the first writer in history to sell over a million copies; within three years her sales doubled. Conservative values thus spread to a very large audience in both Britain and the United States, where one of her works appeared in thirty editions.

A more extreme version of conservatism was the counterrevolutionary or ultraroyalist ideology. Unlike Burke, who was willing to tolerate some change, counterrevolutionaries wanted to restore society to its prerevolutionary condition. The most extreme counterrevolutionaries were those with personal experience of the upheavals of the Revolution. Count Joseph de Maistre° (1753–1821), a Savoyard (from the Franco-Italian border region) nobleman whose estates were occupied by the invading French, described monarchy as a God-given form of government in his *Considerations on France* in 1796. Any attempt to abolish or even limit it was a violation of divine law. According to de Maistre and his fellow reactionaries, the authority of church and state was necessary to prevent human beings from falling into evil ways. De Maistre advocated stern government control, including the generous use of the death penalty, to keep people loyal to throne and altar.

Conservatism was also influenced by romanticism, with its glorification of the past, taste for pageantry, and belief in the organic unity of society. Nor were conservative ideas limited to intellectual circles; at times they had mass appeal. (See the box "Reading Sources: A Spanish Carlist Appeals to the Peasantry.")

■ Romanticism

The long-lived romantic movement had emerged in the 1760s as a rebellion against rationalism and persisted until the 1840s. It was primarily a movement in the arts. Writers, painters, composers, and others consciously rebelled against the Enlightenment and its rationalist values. In contrast to the philosophes and their emphasis on reason,

Maistre (MESS-treh)

A Spanish Carlist Appeals to the Peasantry

The conservatism of political thinkers became current enough that its language was used in a popular appeal to rally support in Spain for Don Carlos, the brother of Ferdinand VII. A conservative, Don Carlos challenged the right of his niece Isabella to the throne and precipitated the Carlist war (1834–1839). Carlism was defeated but its ideas were an influential part of Spanish conservatism. Notice the appeals made to tradition, religion, and history, the underpinnings of conservatism.

. . . Policies which alter the laws of the state without need or utility are found most often when they are influenced by other nations; there is general agreement to reject these changes, as they shock public opinion; Holy Religion is the ultimate, sublime principle of the people, who desire a pious prince, who will restore the old ways and revive the blessed days of our fathers. . . . Don Carlos, protected by God, will defeat the revolution, and under his paternal rule, we will see the hoped for restoration; the restoration of principles and doctrines, of laws and institutions, of habits, of customs. . . . The Holy Faith in all its dignity and purity; the sovereignty of the king, without the checks that destroy it or hinder his good deeds; . . . the vigour of the old laws and *fueros* [local and provincial privileges]; the extinction of administrative abuses and vices; the noble and honourable independence of the nation and the prosperity of all classes: these are his aims. . . . We turn to religion as the basic foundation of society and we see the legitimate authority of the prince as its powerful and healthy influence on society, the best and most secure guarantee against the fury of popular passion and the degradation of true liberty . . . by tyranny. . . . What is irrational or extremist in this? . . . that the monarchy might be made strong through a united sovereign will of the people rather than by armed force and a mass of civil servants; that the abuses of public administration which enrage the people and the excesses that warp and corrupt the government be destroyed. There is no surer road to these ends than the preservation of old, essentially conservative institutions. . . . [We demand] nothing more than to be left in active possession of our immemorial legitimate rights; and that, in accord with the wise counsel of public law, no innovations be introduced without grave need. . . .

Source: A. Bullon de Mendoza, *La primera Guerra Carlista* (Madrid, 1992), pp. 560–562, in Michael Broers, trans. and ed., *Europe After Napoleon: Revolution, Reaction and Romanticism, 1814–1848* (1996), pp. 129–130.

---

romantics praised emotion and feeling. Jean-Jacques Rousseau's strong appeal to sentiment was taken up by the German writer Johann Wolfgang von Goethe° (1749–1832), who declared, "Feeling is everything." Goethe's *Sorrows of Young Werther* (1774), the most widely read book of the era—Napoleon had a copy by his bedside—depicted the passions of the hero, who, depressed over unrequited love, kills himself. Many young men dressed in "Werther clothes"—tight black pants, blue vest, and an open yellow shirt—and in some cases emulated the tragic hero by committing suicide.

Whereas the Enlightenment had studied nature for the principles it could impart, romantics worshiped nature for its inherent beauty. The German composer Ludwig van Beethoven° (1770–1827) wrote his *Pastoral Symphony* in praise of idyllic nature, depicting the passions one might feel in contemplating its loveliness and serenity. The English poets William Wordsworth (1770–1850) and Samuel Taylor Coleridge (1772–1834) treated untamed wilderness as a particular subject of wonder. Fellow Englishman Joseph Mallord William Turner (1775–1851) displayed the raw passions of the sea in such paintings as *Fire at Sea* (1834) and *Snowstorm: Steamboat off a Harbour's Mouth* (1842). Before painting the latter, Turner is said to have tied himself to a ship's mast and braved a snowstorm for four hours.

In pursuit of the authentic and the ancient, of feeling rather than rationality, many romantics rediscovered

---

Goethe (GOE-teh)

Beethoven (BATE-ho-ven)

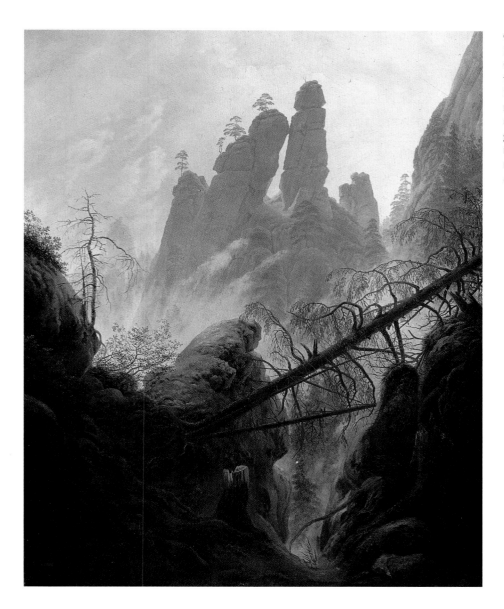

Caspar David Friedrich: Rocky Landscape (1822–1823) The German romantic painter evokes the mystery, majesty, and awe-inspiring natural beauty of the mountains. The dead tree reminds us of our mortality, while the young growths on the left remind us of the miracle of life—two themes that the romantics also often evoked.
(Osterreichische Galerie Belvedere Vienna)

religion. In some areas of Europe, popular religion had anticipated the artists' and intellectuals' romantic sensibilities. France experienced a revival of Catholicism. In the German states, pietism, which had emerged in the seventeenth and eighteenth centuries, stressed the personal relationship between the individual and God, unimpeded by theological formalities or religious authorities. The influence of pietism, with its emphasis on spirituality and emotion, spread throughout central Europe in schools and churches.

In England, emotionalism in religion expressed itself in the popularity of Methodism. Founded in the 1730s by the English preacher John Wesley (1703–1791), this movement emphasized salvation by a faith made active in one's life, a method of living. Appealing especially to the poor and desperate, Methodism by the 1790s had

gained seventy thousand members; within a generation it quadrupled its flock.

The classicism of the Enlightenment had required an audience well versed in the traditional texts. Since the mid-eighteenth century, however, the reading public had grown to include people without access to elite culture. Appeals to emotion and sentiment were congenial to these new audiences, and a new interest developed in folklore and rustic life. In his short but productive life, Franz Schubert (1797–1828) composed, among other forms of music, over 600 *lieder*°, or songs, that echo the simplicity of folk tunes. Although living in Paris, Frédéric Chopin° (1810–1849) composed works influenced by the peasant music of his native Poland.

---

lieder (LEE-der)   **Chopin** (sho-PEHN)

🕮 READING SOURCES

Franz Liszt, Passionate Piano Virtuoso

Franz Liszt (1811–1886) was both a composer and virtuoso pianist. With the demise of aristocratic patronage, artists who wanted to make a living had to beguile their audiences and make piano playing a dramatic enough event to woo sponsors and commissions. A Viennese news account vividly describes Liszt's performance, which fulfilled many of the expectations of romanticism, with its emphasis on youth, spontaneity, feeling, and genius.

Vienna, end of April [1838].—Unusual events require an extraordinary report. The present one is prompted by the wholly unexpected arrival of the famous pianist Franz Liszt, whom Vienna had not seen since his 12th year and who, like a *Deus ex machina* [an unhoped-for savior], came to us quite suddenly from the slopes of the Apennines [he had spent the winter in Italy].

We have now heard him, the strange wonder, whom the superstition of past ages, possessed by the delusion that such things could never be done without the help of the Evil One, would undoubtedly have condemned without mercy to the stake—we have heard him, and seen him too, which, of course, makes a part of the affair. Just look at the pale, slender youth in his clothes that signal the nonconformist; the long, sleek, drooping hair, the thin arms, the small, delicately formed hands; the almost gloomy and yet childlike pleasant face—those features so strongly stamped and full of meaning, in this respect. . . .

Liszt knows no rule, no form, no law; he creates them all himself. He remains an inexplicable phenomenon, a compound of such heterogeneous, strangely mixed materials, that an analysis would inevitably destroy what lends the highest charm, the individual enchantment, namely, the inscrutable secret of the chemical mixture of genial coquetry and childlike simplicity, of whimsy and divine nobleness.

After the concert he stands there like a conqueror on the field of battle . . . vanquished pianos lie about him, broken strings flutter . . . the hearers look at each other in mute astonishment as after a storm . . . and he, the Prometheus [the titan in Greek mythology who stole the fire of the gods] who creates a form from every note . . . who now treats his beloved, the piano, tenderly, then tyrannically; caresses, pouts, scolds, strikes, drags by the hair, and then, all the more fervently, with all the fire and glow of love, throws all his arms around her with a shout, and away with her through all the spaces; he stands there bowing his head, leaning languidly on a chair, with a strange smile, like an exclamation mark after the burst of universal admiration: this is Franz Liszt!

Source: Allgemeine musikalische Zeitung (May 1838), in Pierro Weiss and Richard Taruskin, eds., *Music in the Western World— A History in Documents* (New York: Schirmer Books, 1984), pp. 363, 365.

Whereas the philosophes had decried the Middle Ages, the romantics celebrated the medieval period. Painters frequently took Gothic buildings or ruins as their theme. Architects imitated the Gothic style in both private and public buildings. Sir Walter Scott (1771–1832) in Scotland and Victor Hugo° (1802–1885) in France recaptured chivalry and the age of faith in such popular works as *Ivanhoe* (1819) and *The Hunchback of Notre Dame* (1831). The opera *William Tell* by Gioacchini Rossini (1792–1868) is based on the legendary tale of a freedom-loving peasant who supposedly lived in thirteenth-century Switzerland. Thus it also had a liberal and nationalistic appeal.

The romantics sought displacement not only in time but also in place. The exotic had great appeal to them. Recently conquered Algeria in North Africa provided exotic scenes for French painters, among them Eugène Delacroix° (1798–1863) and Jean Ingres° (1780–1867).

Hugo (U-go)

Delacroix (de-la-KRWAH)   **Ingres** (AENG-reh)

Senegal in West Africa, which the French recovered from the British in 1815, offered the setting for Théodore Géricault's° powerful *Raft of the "Medusa."* (See the feature "Weighing the Evidence: Raft of the 'Medusa'" on pages 738–739.) In music Franz Liszt (1811–1886) composed Hungarian rhapsodies that were considered exotic since they were based on gypsy music. (See the box "Reading Sources: Franz Liszt, Passionate Piano Virtuoso.")

Romanticism exalted mythical figures as embodiments of human energy and passion. In the dramatic poem *Faust,* Goethe retold the legend of a man who sells his soul to the devil in exchange for worldly success. Several composers set that story to powerful music. In the poetic drama *Prometheus Unbound,* the English romantic poet Percy Bysshe Shelley (1792–1822) celebrated Prometheus°, who, according to Greek mythology stole fire from the gods and gave it to human beings. In much the same spirit, many romantics lionized Napoleon, who had overthrown kings and states. Delacroix, who witnessed the July Revolution of 1830 in Paris (see pages 723–724), celebrated the heroism and passion of the revolutionaries in his huge canvas *Liberty Leading the People* (1830).

Romantics often challenged existing power relations, including relations between the sexes. The French writer Amandine-Aurore Dupin° (1804–1876), better known by her pen name, George Sand°, spoke for the emancipation of women from the oppressive supervision of their husbands, fathers, and brothers. In her personal life, Sand practiced the freedom she preached, dressing like a man, smoking cigars, and openly pursuing affairs with a number of well-known artists. The English writer Mary Ann Evans (1819–1892), like George Sand, adopted a male pseudonym, George Eliot. She conducted her life in a nonconformist manner, living with a married man. The use of male pen names by both writers attests to the hostility that intellectual women still faced.

After the French Revolution, nobles and monarchs ceased sponsoring art on a grand scale and were expected to conduct their lives soberly. Cut off from royal patronage, artists had to depend on members of the new middle classes to buy paintings and books and attend plays and musical performances. If earning a livelihood had often been difficult for artists in the past, it now became even more so. Forced to live marginally, they cultivated the image of the artist as unconventional. In their lifestyles and their work, they deliberately rejected the norms of society. The romantic period gave rise to the

---

Géricault (jair-ih-KO)   Prometheus (pro-MEETH-ee-us)
Amandine-Aurore Dupin (ah-man-DEEN–oh-ROR du-PAEN)
Sand (SAN)

Lord Byron in Albanian Costume   The British romantic poet had himself painted in exotic garb. Romantics were attracted to what were believed to be the mysteries of the East, representing a truer, more authentic existence.   *(Courtesy of the National Portrait Gallery, London)*

notion of the starving genius, alienated from society, loyal only to his all-consuming art.

Romantics of many stripes declared their determination to overthrow the smug present and create a new world. Victor Hugo called for "no more rules, no more models" to constrain the human imagination. Romantic painters and musicians consciously turned their backs on the classical tradition in both subject matter and style. Old methods were discarded for new ones. The English poet George Gordon, Lord Byron (1788–1824), declared war on kings, on established religion, and on the international order; a nationalist as well as a romantic, he died while fighting for the independence of Greece.

■ Nationalism

The ideology of nationalism emerged in, and partly shaped, this era. Nationalism is the belief that people derive their identity from their nation and owe it their primary loyalty. A list of criteria for nationhood is likely to include a common language, religion, and political authority, as well as common traditions and shared historical experiences. Some nineteenth-century nationalists found any one of those criteria sufficient. Others insisted that all of them had to be present before a group could consider itself a nation.

In an era that saw the undermining of traditional religious values, nationalism offered a new locus of faith. To people who experienced the social turmoil brought about by the erosion of the old order, nationalism held out the promise of a new community. Nationalism became an ideal espoused as strongly as religion. The Italian nationalist Giuseppe Mazzini° (1805–1872) declared that nationalism was "a faith and mission" ordained by God. The Polish romantic poet and nationalist Adam Mickiewicz° (1798–1855) compared perpetually carved-up Poland to the crucified Christ. The religious intensity of nationalism helps explain its widespread appeal.

Many forces shaped nationalism. Its earliest manifestation, cultural nationalism, had its origins in Rousseau's ideas of the organic nature of a people. Johann Gottfried Herder (1744–1833), Rousseau's German disciple, elaborated on his mentor's ideas, declaring that every people has a "national spirit." To explore the unique nature of this spirit, intellectuals all over Europe began collecting local folk poems, songs, and tales. In an effort to document the spirit of the German people, the Grimm brothers, Jacob (1785–1863) and Wilhelm (1786–1859), compiled fairy tales and published them between 1812 and 1818; among the better known are "Little Red Riding Hood" and "Snow White."

Political nationalism, born in the era of the French Revolution, injected urgency and passion into the new ideology. In the 1770s, French aristocrats resisted attempts by the French monarchy to impose taxes, claiming that they embodied the rights of "the nation" and could not be taxed without its consent. Thus, the concept of nation was given general currency. When revolutionary France was attacked by neighboring countries, which were ruled by kings and dukes, the Legislative Assembly called on the French people to rise and save the nation. The realm of the king of France had become the French nation.

In reaction to the French threat, intellectuals in Germany and Italy embraced the spirit of nationalism. In Germany the philosopher Johann Gottlieb Fichte° (1762–1814) delivered his series of *Addresses to the German Nation* after the Prussian defeat at Jena, calling on all Germans to stand firm against Napoleon. He argued

that Germans were endowed with a special genius that had to be safeguarded for the well-being of all humankind. In Italy the writer Vittorio Alfieri (1749–1803) challenged France's claim to the right to lead the peoples of Europe. That right, Alfieri insisted, properly belonged to Italians, the descendants and heirs of ancient Rome.

For the most part, however, after the French Revolution and the Napoleonic era, early-nineteenth-century nationalism was generous and cosmopolitan in its outlook. Herder and Mazzini believed that each of Europe's peoples was destined to achieve nationhood by forming its own political identity and that the nations of Europe would then live peacefully side by side. The members of dedicated nationalist groups such as Young Germany and Young Italy were also members of Young Europe. Many nationalists in the 1830s and 1840s were likewise committed to the ideal of a "Europe of free peoples." Victor Hugo even envisioned a "European republic" with its own parliament.

It is important to remember, however, that although many intellectuals found nationalism attractive, in the first half of the nineteenth century most people were likely to feel local and regional affinities more than national identities. Only as the result of several decades of propaganda by nationalists and governments was this ideology to win wide support, and only then did it become natural for Europeans to think of dying for their nations.

■ Liberalism

Liberalism was a direct descendant of the Enlightenment's critique of eighteenth-century absolutism. Nineteenth-century liberals believed that individual freedom was best safeguarded by reducing government powers to a minimum. They wanted to impose constitutional limits on government, to establish the rule of law, to sweep away all restrictions on individual enterprise—specifically, state regulation of the economy—and to ensure a voice in government for men of property and education. Liberalism was influenced by romanticism, with its emphasis on individual freedom and the imperative of the human personality to develop to its full potential. Liberalism was also affected by nationalism, especially in multinational autocratic states such as Austria, Russia, and the Ottoman Empire, in which free institutions could be established only if political independence were wrested from, respectively, Vienna, St. Petersburg, and Istanbul. (Nationalism challenged the established order in the first half of the century, but in the second half, conservatives were to use nationalism as a means to stabilize their rule.)

Mazzini (mat-SEE-nee)   **Mickiewicz** (MISS-kyev-ich)
Fichte (FISH-te)

❧ READING SOURCES

Adam Smith Describes the Workings of the Market Economy

In An Inquiry into the Nature and Causes of the Wealth of Nations, *Adam Smith explained how individuals working to maximize their own interests cause the economy as a whole to expand and society to benefit. Among the various economic activities, trade and specialization particularly contribute to the well-being of both society and the individual. Notice the reciprocal nature of self-interest. Smith is building a model that he believed was true in all societies and at all times. Characterized by a mixture of theory and down-to-earth examples, his writings remain a pleasure to read.*

In almost every other race of animals each individual, when it is grown up to maturity, is entirely independent, and in its state has occasion for the assistance of no other living creature. But man has almost constant occasion for the help of his brethren, and it is in vain for him to expect it from their benevolence only. He will be more likely to prevail, if he can interest their self-love in his favour, and shew them that it is for their advantage to do for him what he requires of them. Whoever offers to another a bargain of any kind, proposes to do this. Give me that which I want, and you shall have this which you want, is the meaning of every such offer; and it is in this manner that we obtain from one another the far greater part of those good offices which we stand in need of. It is not from the benevolence of the butcher, the brewer, or the baker, that we expect our dinner, but from their regard to their own interest. We address ourselves, not to their humanity, but to their self-love, and never talk to them of our own necessities, but of their advantages. Nobody but a beggar chooses to depend chiefly upon the benevolence of his fellow-citizens. . . .

So it is this same trucking [trading] disposition which originally gives occasion to the division of labour. In a tribe of hunters or shepherds a particular person makes bows and arrows, for example, with more readiness and dexterity than any other. He frequently exchanges them for cattle or venison with his companions; and he finds at last that he can in this manner get more cattle and venison, than if he himself went to the field to catch them. From a regard to his own interest, therefore, the making of bows and arrows grows to be his chief business, and he becomes a sort of armourer. Another excels in making the frames and covers of their little huts or moveable houses. He is accustomed to be of use in this way to his neighbours, who reward him in the same manner with cattle and with venison, till at last he finds it in his interest to dedicate himself entirely to this employment, and to become a sort of house-carpenter. In the same manner a third becomes a smith or a brazier, a fourth a tanner or dresser of hides of skin, the principal part of the clothing of savages. And thus the certainty of being able to exchange all that surplus part of the produce of his own labour, which is over and above his own consumption, for such parts of the produce of other men's labour as he may have occasion for, encourages every man to apply himself to a particular occupation. . . .

Source: Adam Smith, *An Inquiry into the Nature and Causes of the Wealth of Nations* (London: W. Strahan, 1776), pp. 17–18.

Liberalism was both an economic and a political theory. In 1776 Adam Smith (1723–1790), the influential Scottish economist, published *An Inquiry into the Nature and Causes of the Wealth of Nations*, a systematic study of the economic knowledge of his era. Smith advocated freeing national economies from the fetters of the state. (See the box "Reading Sources: Adam Smith Describes the Workings of the Market Economy.") Under the mercantilist system, prevalent throughout Europe until about 1800, the state regulated the prices and conditions of manufacture. Smith argued for letting the free forces of the marketplace shape economic decisions. He believed that economics was subject to basic unalterable laws that could be discerned and applied in the same fashion as natural laws. Chief among them, in Smith's view, was the compatibility of economic self-interest and the general good. He argued that entrepreneurs who lower prices sell more products, thus increasing their own profits *and* providing the community with affordable wares. In this way, an individual's drive for profit benefits society as a whole. The economy is driven as if "by an invisible hand." This competitive drive for profits, Smith predicted, would expand the "wealth of nations." In France, advocates of nonintervention by government in the economy were called supporters of *laissez faire* (meaning "to leave alone, to let run on its own").

Smith and his disciples formed what came to be known as the school of classical economy, emphasizing the importance of laissez faire. Smith had been relatively optimistic about the capacities of the free market. Those who followed him, and who witnessed more of the negative results of industrialization, were more gloomy. Thomas Malthus (1766–1834), a parson, published in 1798 *An Essay on the Principle of Population*, which suggested that population was outstripping resources. Unless people voluntarily limited their family sizes, they would suffer starvation. By their failure to exercise sexual restraint, the poor, Malthus declared, "are themselves the cause of their own poverty." The laws of economics suggested to Malthus that factory owners could not improve their workers' lot by increasing wages or providing charity because higher living standards would lead to more births, which in turn would depress wages and bring greater misery.

David Ricardo (1772–1823) made his fortune in the stock market, retired young, and wrote on economics, his best-known work being *Principles of Political Economy* (1817). Ricardo argued that capitalists' profits depended on wages paid to workers; to be profitable, industrialists had to compete in limiting the wages they offered. The capitalist offering the lowest wages was likely to be most successful. The "iron law of wages" seemed to provide, as had Malthus, scientific justification for the exploitation of workers.

Even supporters of laissez faire had some reservations about the market economy. In France in the first half of the nineteenth century, commentators on the factory system, including industrialists, expressed fear that factory work would undermine the stability of family life and hence of society itself. Philanthropic intervention, they hoped, would resolve the problems they had identified.

Even some of the British classical economists doubted the wisdom of allowing the market economy to operate entirely without regulation and of trusting it to provide for human happiness. Smith warned that the market tended to form monopolies, and he suggested that government intervene to prevent this occurrence. According to Smith, the marketplace could not provide for all human needs; the government needed to supply education, road systems, and an equitable system of justice.

John Stuart Mill (1806–1873), the leading British economic and political thinker at midcentury, voiced strong support for laissez-faire economics in the first edition of his *Principles of Political Economy* (1848). If left alone, the individual could carry on economic functions better than the government, Mill insisted. In subsequent editions, however, he remarked that the state had an obligation to relieve human misery. Nor could the free market satisfactorily address every human need. Once wealth was produced, he noted, its distribution was subject to traditions and to decisions made by those in power. Thus, presumably, wealth could be shared by society as a whole. Toward the end of his life, Mill seemed to be leaning toward socialism.

Mill's about-face reflected and presaged changing attitudes among the proponents of laissez faire. In the face of unsanitary urban conditions, child labor, stark inequities in wealth, and other alarming results of industrialization, at least some liberals around midcentury called on the state to intervene in areas of concern that would have been unthinkable a half-century earlier.

In their political positions, liberals were firm throughout the century, constant in their support for limiting government power to prevent despotism. Enlightened eighteenth-century monarchs had declared that the purpose of their rule was to promote the public good. In even more ringing terms, the French Revolution had proclaimed that the purpose of government is to ensure the happiness of humankind. As Thomas Jefferson (1743–1826), another child of the Enlightenment, asserted in the Declaration of Independence (1776), among the "unalienable rights" of individuals are "life, liberty, and the pursuit of happiness." The purpose of government is to safeguard and promote those rights.

The Enlightenment had posited natural law as the basis of government. French liberals in the nineteenth century continued to see human liberty as founded on natural law, but their English counterparts were less theoretical in outlook. Jeremy Bentham (1748–1832) argued that the purpose of government is to provide "the greatest happiness of the greatest number" and that governments should be judged on that basis. Bentham and his disciples believed that the test of government is its usefulness; thus they were known as "Utilitarians."

Democracy was implicit in Bentham's philosophy: the greatest number could ensure its own happiness only by voting for its rulers. John Stuart Mill, a disciple of Bentham, was the foremost proponent of liberalism, seeing it as guaranteeing the development of a free society. Individuals could best develop their talents if they were unhampered by state interference. In his essay *On Liberty,* one of the fundamental documents of nineteenth-century liberalism, Mill argued for the free circulation of ideas—even false ideas. For in the free marketplace of ideas, false ideas will be defeated, and truth vindicated, in open debate. Mill also asserted that a free society should be free for all its members. Influenced by Harriet Taylor (1807–1856), who was to become his wife, he wrote in *On the Subjection of Women* (1861) that women should be permitted to vote and should have access to equal educational opportunities and the professions. Such equality not only would be just but also would have the advantage of "doubling the mass of mental faculties available for the higher service of humanity." Mill, the foremost male proponent of women's rights in his generation, helped win a broader audience for the principle of equality between the sexes.

Despite Mill's influence, many liberals, especially in the early nineteenth century, feared the masses and therefore vigorously opposed democracy. They feared that the common people, uneducated and supposedly gullible, would easily be swayed by demagogues who might become despotic or who, in a desire to curry favor with the poor, might attack the privileges of the wealthy. The French liberal Benjamin Constant denounced democracy as "the vulgarization of despotism"; the vote, he declared, should be reserved for the affluent and educated. When less fortunate Frenchmen denounced the property requirements that prevented them from voting, the liberal statesman François Guizot (1787–1874) smugly replied, "Get rich."

In the twelfth and thirteenth centuries, a new wealthy class based on urban occupations emerged; its members were called "burgers" or "bourgeois." This class fully developed in the nineteenth century. If unsympathetic to extending suffrage to the lower classes, the *bourgeoisie*° championed liberalism, which justified its own right to participate in governance. Economic liberalism was also attractive to merchants and manufacturers, who wished to gather wealth without state interference.

If originating in and justifying middle-class interests, the basic tenets of liberalism—the belief in the sanctity of human rights, freedom of speech and freedom to organize, the rule of law and equality before the law—eventually became so widely accepted that even conservative and socialist opponents of liberalism accepted them as fundamental rights.

■ Socialism

The notion that human happiness can best be ensured by the common ownership of property had been suggested in earlier times by individuals as different as the Greek philosopher Plato (427?–347 B.C.) and Sir Thomas More (1478–1535), the English author of *Utopia.* Troubled by the harsh condition of the working classes, thinkers in Britain and France came to espouse theories that, beginning in the 1820s, were called "socialist." Socialists believed that the "social" ownership of property, unlike private ownership, would benefit society as a whole. During the first half of the nineteenth century, most workers, even in industrializing England, where manufacturing was increasingly large scale, were artisans. It was in a later era that socialism would address the issues raised by industry.

In 1796, during the French Revolution, Gracchus Babeuf° (1760–1797), a minor civil servant, participated in the Conspiracy of Equals (see page 660). The Revolution, however haltingly, had proclaimed political equality for its citizens, but it had failed to bring economic equality. Babeuf decided to resort to revolution to bring about a "communist" society—a society in which all property would be owned in common and private property would be abolished. Work would be provided for everyone; medical services and education would be free to all. Babeuf's plot was discovered, and he was guillotined, but his theories and example of conspiratorial revolutionary action would influence later socialists.

Several other important French thinkers made contributions to European socialism. Curiously, it was a French aristocrat, Henri de Saint-Simon° (1760–1825), who emphasized the need "to ameliorate as promptly and as quickly as possible the moral and physical existence of the most numerous class." The proper role for the state, Saint-Simon declared, was to ensure the welfare of the masses. The course of history, he suggested, was in the direction of expertise. No longer could people rule solely on the basis of their birth. Rather, Europe

---

bourgeoisie (boor-zhwa-ZEE)

Gracchus Babeuf (GRAH-kus bah-BOEF)
Saint-Simon (saen–see-MON)

should come to be governed by a council of qualified artists and scientists who would oversee the economy and ensure that everyone enjoyed a minimum level of well-being.

Another vital contribution to socialist thought came from thinkers who tried to imagine an ideal world. They were later derisively dismissed as dreamers, as builders of utopias, fantasy worlds (the Greek word *utopia* means "nowhere"). Their schemes varied, but they shared the view that property should be owned in common and used for the common good. They also believed that society should rest on principles of cooperation rather than competitive individualism.

One of the earliest and most notable utopians was the Welsh mill-owner Robert Owen (1771–1859). Beginning in 1800 he ran a prosperous cotton mill in New Lanark, Scotland. He also provided generously for his workers, guaranteeing them jobs and their children decent educations. In his writings Owen suggested the establishment of self-governing communities owning the means of production. Essentials would be distributed to all members according to their needs. Owen's ideas for the new society included equal rights for women.

Owen received little support from fellow manufacturers and political leaders, and his own attempt in 1824 to establish an ideal society in the United States at New Harmony, Indiana, ended in failure after four years.

Another influential contributor to early socialist theory was the Frenchman Charles Fourier° (1772–1837). A clerk and salesman, Fourier wrote out in great detail his vision of the ideal future society. It would consist of cooperative organizations called "phalansteries," each with 1,600 inhabitants who would live in harmony with nature and with one another. Everyone would be assured gainful employment, which would be made enjoyable by rotating jobs. Because cooperative communes often faced the issue of who would carry out the distasteful tasks, everyone would share the pleasant *and* unpleasant work. Fourier thought that because children enjoy playing with dirt, they should be put in charge of picking up garbage.

Fourier had an important female following because of his belief in the equality of the sexes, and some of these women tried to put his ideas into action. In Belgium the activist Zoé Gatti de Gamond° (1806–1854) cofounded a phalanstery for women. She believed that if women could be assured of economic well-being, other rights would follow. Also inspired by Fourier, Flora Tristan (1801–1844) was an effective advocate for workers'

rights. In her book *Union Ouvrière (Workers' Union),* she suggested that all workers should contribute to establish a "Worker's Palace" in every town. In the palace, the sick and disabled would have shelter, and the workers' children could receive a free education. Crossing France on foot, she spread the word of workers' solidarity and self-help.

There were other approaches. The French socialist journalist Louis Blanc° (1811–1882) saw in democracy the means of bringing into existence a socialist state. By securing the vote, the common people could win control over the state and require it to serve their needs. The state could be induced to buy up banks, insurance companies, and railway systems and set up a commercial and retail chain that would provide jobs for workers and offer goods and services at prices unaffected by the profit motive. Once the workers controlled the state by the ballot, the state in turn would establish social workshops in which the workers would be responsible for production and supervision of business matters. Society should be established according to (from the socialist viewpoint) fundamental fairness: "Let each produce according to his aptitudes and strength; let each consume according to his need."

Blanc's contemporary Louis Blanqui° (1805–1882) suggested a more violent mode of action. He advocated seizure of the state by a small, dedicated band of men who were devoted to the welfare of the working class and who would install communism, for the equality of all. Blanqui was a perpetual conspirator, confined to state prisons for much of his long life. His ideas strengthened the notion of class warfare, and his own life served as a symbol of this struggle. The thought and example of Blanqui and the other socialists would play a major role in shaping the thinking of the most important socialist of the nineteenth century, Karl Marx.

Karl Marx (1818–1883), the son of a lawyer, grew up in the Rhineland, in western Germany, an industrializing area that was particularly open to political ideas and agitation. The Rhineland had been influenced by the ideas of the French Revolution and was primed for political radicalism. As a young man Marx studied philosophy at the University of Berlin and joined a group known as the "Young Hegelians," self-declared disciples of the idealist philosopher G. W. F. Hegel (1770–1831). Hegel taught that reality is mainly based on the ability of the mind to conceive of it. Marx, by contrast, was a materialist, believing that material realities impose themselves on the mind.

Fourier (foor-YAY)   **Gamond** (gay-MON)

Blanc (BLAHN)   **Blanqui** (blahn-KEE)

Marx showed an early interest in political liberty and socialism. In 1842–1843 he edited a newspaper that spoke out for freedom and democracy in Germany. The following year, in Paris, he met several of the French socialist writers. Even when he was a young man, his contemporaries perceived him as bright but unyielding in his determination.

Because of his radical journalism, he was exiled from the Rhineland and lived briefly in Paris, then Brussels. In 1849 he settled in London, where he lived for the rest of his life, dedicated to establishing his ideas on what he viewed as scientific bases. Deriving a modest income from writing for the *New York Daily Tribune* and from funds provided by his friend and collaborator Friedrich Engels (1820–1895), Marx was never able to provide well for his family, which constantly lived on the edge of poverty. Of the six children born to the Marx household, three died in infancy.

In 1848 Marx and Engels published the *Communist Manifesto*. A pamphlet written for the Communist League, a group of Germans living in exile, the manifesto was an appeal to the working classes of the world. The league deliberately called itself "Communist" rather than "Socialist." Communism was a radical program, bent on changing property relations by violence; socialism was associated with more peaceful means of transformation. The pamphlet laid out Marx's basic ideas, calling on the proletariat to rise—"You have nothing to lose but your chains"—and create a society that would end the exploitation of man by man. (See the box "Reading Sources: Karl Marx's *Communist Manifesto*.")

A number of political and polemical works flowed from Marx's pen, but most of them remained unpublished during his lifetime. The first volume of his major work, *Capital*, was published in 1867; subsequent volumes appeared posthumously. Marxism, the body of Marx's thought, is complex and sometimes contradictory. *Capital* is written in an obscure style, difficult to penetrate. But certain basic concepts resound throughout and were embraced by Marx's followers.

Marx agreed with Hegel and many of his contemporaries that human history has a direction and a goal. Hegel believed that the goal was the realization of the world spirit. Marx believed that it was the abolition of capitalism, the victory of the proletariat, the disappearance of the state, and the ultimate liberation of all humankind.

Whereas Hegel thought that ideas govern the world, Marx insisted that material conditions determine it. Hegel said that history evolves by the "dialectic": a principle, say despotism, has within it ideas that oppose it; in

Karl Marx   Through his writings and agitation, Marx transformed the socialism of his day and created an ideology that helped shape the nineteenth and twentieth centuries. *(Corbis)*

the struggle between despotism and its opposite, a higher ideal emerges—freedom, the ultimate goal of history. Following Hegel, Marx posited a world of change but insisted that it was embedded in material conditions, not in a clash of ideas. Hence, the process of history was grounded on the notion of "dialectical materialism." Ideas, to Marx, were but a reflection of the material world.

Marx grouped human beings into classes based on their relationship to the means of production. Capitalists were one class because they owned the means of production. Workers were a separate class—the proletariat—because they did not own any of the means of production and their income came only from their own

✎ READING SOURCES

Karl Marx's *Communist Manifesto*

The Communist Manifesto *provides a preview of the major themes that would inform Marx and Engels's later writings: the concept of class formation and class antagonism, the privileged role of the proletariat, and the inevitability of the proletariat's success.*

The history of all hitherto existing society is the history of class struggles.

Freeman and slave, patrician and plebeian, lord and serf, guild-master and journeyman, in a word, oppressor and oppressed, stood in constant opposition to one another, carried on an uninterrupted, now hidden, now open fight, that each time ended, either in a revolutionary reconstitution of society at large, or in the common ruin of the contending classes. . . .

In ancient Rome we have patricians, knights, plebeians, slaves; in the Middle Ages, feudal lords, vassals, guild-masters, journeymen, apprentices, serfs; in almost all of these classes, again, subordinate gradations.

The modern bourgeois society that has sprouted from the ruins of feudal society, has not done away with class antagonisms. It has but established new classes, new conditions of oppression, new forms of struggle in place of the old ones. . . .

Society as a whole is more and more splitting up into two great hostile camps, into two great classes directly facing each other: Bourgeoisie and Proletariat. . . .

With the development of industry the proletariat not only increases in number; it becomes concentrated in greater masses, its strength grows and it feels that strength more. . . . [T]he collisions between individual workmen and individual bourgeois take more and more the character of collisions between two classes. . . .

Of all the classes that stand face to face with the bourgeoisie today, the proletariat alone is a really revolutionary class. The other classes decay and finally disappear in the face of modern industry; the proletariat is its special and essential product.

All previous historical movements were movements of minorities. The proletarian movement is the self-conscious, independent movement of the immense majority. The proletariat, the stratum of our present society, cannot stir, cannot raise itself up, without the whole superincumbent strata of official society being sprung into the air. . . .

. . . The development of modern industry, therefore, cuts from under its feet the very foundation on which the bourgeoisie produces and appropriates products. What the bourgeoisie therefore produces, above all, are its own grave-diggers. Its fall and the victory of the proletariat are equally inevitable.

Source: Karl Marx and Friedrich Engels, *Communist Manifesto* (1848; reprint, New York: International Publishers, 1948), pp. 9, 17, 20–21.

---

hands. Because these two classes had different relationships to the means of production, they had different—in fact, antagonistic—interests and were destined (Marx believed) to engage in a class struggle.

Some of Marx's contemporaries lamented the increasing hostility between workers and capitalists. Marx, however, saw the conflict as necessary to advance human history, and he sought to validate his thesis by the study of the past. In the Middle Ages, he pointed out, the feudal class dominated society but eventually lost the struggle to the commercial classes. Now, in turn, the capitalists were destined to be overwhelmed by the rising proletariat.

In his study of history and economics, Marx found not only justification for but irrefutable proof of the "scientific" basis of his ideas. Capitalism was itself creating the forces that would supplant it. The large industrial plants necessitated an ever greater work force with a growing sense of class interest. The inherently competitive nature of capitalism would inevitably drive an increasing number of enterprises out of business, and a form of monopoly capitalism would emerge, abusive of both consumers and workers. As a result of ever more savage competition, more businesses would fail, and consequently more workers would become unemployed. Angered and frustrated by their lot, workers would overthrow the system that had abused them for so long: "The knell of private property has sounded. The expropriators will be expropriated." The proletariat would take power and, to solidify its rule, would temporarily exercise the "dictatorship of the proletariat." Once that had taken place, the state would wither away. With the coming to power of the proletariat, the history of class war would end and the ideal society would prevail. Ironically, Marx, who spent his life writing about the nature and history of social change, envisaged a time when change would cease, when history, as it were, would stop.

Many protested the evils of industrialism, but Marx described economic change in dramatic terms as a necessary stage for humankind to traverse on its way to liberation. The suffering of the workers was not in vain. Rather, it was a necessary process, part of the drama that would finally lead to human emancipation. Unlike some of the utopians who deplored industrialism, Marx accepted it and saw it as part of the path that history was fated to follow.

Marx's study of economics and history proved to him that the coming of socialism was not only desirable—as the utopians had thought—but inevitable. The laws of history dictated that capitalism, having created the rising proletariat, would collapse. By labeling his brand of socialism as scientific, Marx gave it the aura it needed to become the faith of millions of people. To declare ideas scientific in the nineteenth century, when science was held in such high esteem, was to ensure their popularity.

RESTORATION, REFORM, AND REACTION

DESPITE the new ideologies that emerged to challenge the existing order, efforts at restoration appeared successful until at least 1830. Indeed in central and eastern Europe, from the German states to Russia and the Ottoman Empire, the political systems established in 1815 would persist virtually unchanged until midcentury. In western Europe, however, important transformations would occur by the 1830s as reaction gave way to reform. Then in 1848, widespread

revolutions would break out on much of the Continent. The language of liberalism and nationalism and even the newer idiom of socialism would be heard on the barricades, in popular assemblies, and in parliamentary halls.

■ Western Europe: From Reaction to Liberalism, 1815–1830

Most of Europe until the 1830s experienced the heavy hand of reaction. Then western Europe saw more liberal regimes come into their own. Revolution and the threat of revolution helped dismantle the worst features of the restored regimes. The more liberal western European states faced continuing discontents of various sorts—mainly social and political—which they managed to negotiate with varying degrees of success.

The most dramatic restoration of the older order occurred in France. The restored Bourbons turned the clock back, not to 1789 but closer to 1791, when the country had briefly enjoyed a constitutional monarchy, and it went beyond that in maintaining the Napoleonic Code with its provisions of legal equality. The Bourbon constitution provided for a parliament with an elected lower house, the Chamber of Deputies, and an appointed upper house, the Chamber of Peers. Although suffrage to the Chamber of Deputies was limited to a small elite of men with landed property—100,000 voters, about 0.2 percent of the population—this constitution was a concession to representative government that had not existed in the Old Regime (see page 647). Louis XVIII (r. 1814–1824) stands out among European rulers because he realized that it would be necessary to compromise on the principles of popular sovereignty proclaimed by the French Revolution. His intention was to "popularize the monarchy" and "royalize the nation." A moderate, Louis was succeeded by his ultrareactionary brother, Charles X (r. 1824–1830), who alienated the middle classes. More general disenchantment came with an economic downturn in 1827, marked by poor harvests and increased unemployment in the cities. Discontent brought to Parliament a liberal majority that refused to accept the reactionary ministers the king appointed. On July 26, 1830, after the humiliating defeat of his party at the polls, the king issued a set of decrees suspending freedom of the press, dissolving the Chamber of Deputies, and stiffening property qualifications for voters in subsequent elections. The king appeared to be engineering a coup against the existing political system.

The first to protest were the Parisian journalists and typesetters, directly threatened by the censorship laws. On July 28, others joined the protest and began erecting barricades across many streets. After killing several

Louis XVIII as Military Leader   The French king, returned to his throne by France's foreign enemies, had no military glory attached to his reign. But in 1823 France successfully invaded Spain, helping its reactionary king suppress a liberal revolt. This painting celebrates the return of the victorious French troops.   *(Château de Versailles/Laurie Platt Winfrey, Inc.)*

hundred protesters, the king's forces lost control of the city. The uprising, known as "the three glorious days," drove the king into exile.

Alarmed by the crowds' clamor for a republic, the liberal opposition—consisting of some of the leading newspaper editors and sympathetic deputies—quickly drafted the duke of Orléans, Louis Philippe (r. 1830–1848), known for his liberal opinions, to occupy the throne.

Compared with the rest of Europe, Great Britain enjoyed considerable constitutional guarantees and a parliamentary regime. Yet liberals and radicals found their government retrograde and repressive. Traumatized by the French Revolution, the ruling class clung to the past, certain that advocates for change were Jacobins in disguise. Change seemed to invite revolution.

Social unrest beset Britain as it faced serious economic dislocation. The arrival of peace in 1815 led to a sudden drop in government expenditures, the return into the economy of several hundred thousand men who had been away at war, financial disarray, and plummeting prices. The poor and the middle classes were especially incensed over the clear economic advantages that the landed classes, dominating Parliament, had secured for themselves in 1815 in passing the Corn Law. This legislation imposed high tariffs on imported "corn"—that is, various forms of grain. It thus shielded the domestic market from international competition and allowed landowners to reap huge profits at the expense of consumers. All these issues were cause for demonstrations, petitions, protest marches, and other challenges to the authorities.

In August 1819, sixty thousand people gathered in St. Peter's Fields in Manchester to demand universal suffrage for men and women alike, an annual Parliament, and other democratic reforms. The crowd was peaceful and unarmed, yet mounted soldiers charged, killing eleven and wounding four hundred. Using military force against the people as if against the French at Waterloo was seen as wrong, and the confrontation was branded "the battle of Peterloo." The British public was shocked by this use of violence against peaceful demonstrators; Parliament responded by passing the so-called Six Acts, which outlawed freedom of assembly and effectively imposed censorship. Through much of the 1820s Britain appeared resistant to reform until news of revolution across the channel in 1830 brought about change.

The term *liberal* was first coined in Spain, where the fate of liberals prefigured what would happen elsewhere in continental Europe. In 1812 a national parliament, the Cortes, elected during the Napoleonic occupation, issued a democratic constitution that provided for universal manhood suffrage and a unicameral legislature with control over government policy. Supporters and admirers of the constitution in Spain and elsewhere were known as "liberals," or friends of liberty.

Napoleon had ousted the Bourbon king of Spain, Ferdinand VII (r. 1808, 1814–1833). Ferdinand returned to power in 1814, promising to respect the liberal 1812 constitution. But Ferdinand was by temperament hostile to the new order, and he was a believer in the divine right of kings. He drew his support from the aristocracy and from segments of the general population still loyal to the call of throne and altar. Liberals were arrested or driven into exile.

Ferdinand's plan to restore Spain to its earlier prominence included a reassertion of control over its American colonies. The Spanish dominions had grown restless in the eighteenth century, for they had witnessed the advent of an independent United States and the French occupation of Spain itself. Spain's emboldened colonies had refused to recognize the Napoleonic regime in Madrid and became increasingly self-reliant. Their attitude did not change when French control of Spain ended. Ferdinand refused to compromise with the overseas territories. Instead, he gathered an army to subdue them. Some liberal junior officers, declaring the army's loyalty to the constitution of 1812, won support from the rank and file, who balked at going overseas. This military mutiny coincided with a sympathetic provincial uprising to produce the "revolution of 1820," the first major assault on the European order established in 1815 at the Congress of Vienna. Ferdinand appealed to the European powers for help. France intervened on his behalf and crushed the uprising.

Ferdinand restored his reactionary regime but could not regain Spain's American colonies. The British,

"Peterloo" Massacre   In August 1819 at St. Peter's Fields in Manchester, a crowd demanding parliamentary reform was charged by government troops, leading to bloodshed. Many English people derided the event and called it "Peterloo." *(Public Record Office)*

sympathetic to the cause of Latin American independence and eager for commercial access to the region, opposed reconquest, and their naval dominance of the seas kept Spain in its place. The United States, meanwhile, had recognized the independence of the Latin American republics and wished to see their independence maintained. In 1823 President James Monroe issued the statement known as the Monroe Doctrine, prohibiting European colonization or intervention in the affairs of independent republics in the Americas. Of course, the United States had no military muscle to back this proclamation, but the British navy effectively enforced it. By 1825 all of Spain's colonies on the mainland in Central and South America had won their freedom.

The newly independent states patterned their regimes on models of Spanish liberalism; all had constitutions stipulating separation of powers and guaranteeing human rights. Brazil, the Portuguese empire in the Americas, was a monarchy for most of the rest of the nineteenth century, as was Mexico for a short time, but all the other states became republics, opting for what was then an unusual form of government. Although most of the Latin regimes eventually became dictatorships, they continued to pay lip service to liberal values.

■ Western Europe, 1830–1848

For the political systems of western Europe, the 1830s marked a time of modification. The threat, and occasionally the sting, of revolt produced more liberal regimes, but except for Britain and Spain, most governments were unable to stem the tide of discontent, which became revolution in 1848.

As a result of the 1830 revolution in Paris, a more liberal regime was installed in France. Louis Philippe proclaimed himself "King of the French," thus acknowledging that he reigned at the behest of the people. Freedom of the press was reinstated. Suffrage was extended to twice as many voters as before, 200,000 men. The July Monarchy, named after the month in which it was established by revolution, justified itself by celebrating the great Revolution of 1789. Louis Philippe commissioned huge canvases glorifying great moments of the Revolution. On the site where the Bastille had been razed in 1789, the government erected a large column with the names of the victims of the July 1830 revolution, thus suggesting a continuity between those who had fought tyranny in 1789 and 1830.

Identification with the Revolution appeared to legitimize the regime but also had the potential to subvert it. Fearful that the cult of revolution would encourage violence against the new monarchy, the regime censored

artistic production, promoting only works that extolled the period from 1789 to 1791, when the revolutionaries had attempted to found a constitutional monarchy. Now that the revolution of 1830 had established a constitutional monarchy, the regime was suggesting, any further uprisings were illegitimate. If the July Monarchy turned out not to be as liberal as its founders had hoped, foreign visitors coming from more authoritarian societies were nonetheless impressed by France's apparently liberal institutions. (See the box "Global Encounters: A Moroccan Describes the French Freedom of the Press.") Many French liberals, however, saw the regime as a travesty of the hopes and promises it had represented on coming to power in 1830.

The major political problem facing Britain in the early nineteenth century was the composition of Parliament, which did not reflect the dramatic population shifts that had occurred since the seventeenth century. Industrialization had transformed mere villages into major cities—Manchester, Birmingham, Leeds, Sheffield—but those cities had no representation in Parliament. Localities that had lost population, however, were still represented. In districts known as "pocket boroughs," single individuals owned the right to a seat in Parliament. In districts known as "rotten boroughs," a handful of voters elected a representative.

News of the July 1830 revolution in Paris encouraged British liberals to push for reform. Fearing the same fate as the hapless Charles X, some conservatives silently yielded. The government introduced a reform bill abolishing or reducing representation for sparsely populated areas while granting seats for the populous and unrepresented cities. The bill also widened the franchise by lowering property qualifications to include many middle-class men. Following a prolonged, bitter political battle between the government and middle classes on one side and the aristocracy on the other, the House of Lords finally passed what came to be known as the Great Reform Bill of 1832.

The reform was not particularly radical. Only the upper layers of the middle class were enfranchised, or one in seven adult males. By establishing national criteria for the vote and eliminating local variations, some people, including some women, actually lost the vote. Yet despite its shortcomings, the reform demonstrated the willingness of the political leaders to acknowledge the increasing economic importance of manufacturing. Parliament became a more representative forum whose makeup better reflected the shift of economic power from agricultural landowners to the industrial and commercial classes. The bill passed as a result of nationwide agitation, evidence that the political

⊕ GLOBAL ENCOUNTERS

A Moroccan Describes French Freedom of the Press

In 1845–1846 a Moroccan diplomatic mission visited Paris; the ambassador's secretary, Muhammad as-Saffar (d. 1881), wrote an account of the visit. Impressed by many aspects of French society, in the following passage he praises France's press. The "Sultan" as-Saffar refers to is King Louis Philippe. To this Moroccan observer, the extent to which the French enjoyed constitutional government was striking.

The people of Paris, like all the French indeed, like all of [Europe] are eager to know the latest news and events that are taking place in other parts [of the world]. For this purpose they have the gazette. [In] these papers . . . they write all the news that has reached them that day about events in their own country and in other lands both near and far.

This is the way it is done. The owner of a newspaper dispatches his people to collect everything they see or hear in the way of important events or unusual happenings. Among the places where they collect the news are the two Chambers, the Great and the Small, where they come together to make their laws. When the members of the Chamber meet to deliberate, the men of the gazette sit nearby and write down everything that is said, for all debating and ratifying of laws is matter for the gazette and is known to everyone. No one can prevent them from doing this. . . .

. . . [I]f someone has an idea about a subject but he is not a member of the press, he may write about it in the gazette and make it known to others, so that the leaders of opinion learn about it. If the idea is worthy they may follow it, and if its author was out of favor it may bring him recognition.

No person in France is prohibited from expressing his opinion or from writing it and printing it, on condition that he does not violate the law. . . .

In the newspapers they write rejoinders to the men of the two Chambers about the laws they are making. If their Sultan demands gifts from the notables or goes against the law in any way, they write about that too, saying that he is a tyrant and in the wrong. He cannot confront them or cause them harm. Also, if someone behaves out of the ordinary, they write about that too, making it common knowledge among people of every rank. If his deeds were admirable, they praise and delight in him, lauding his example; but if he behaved badly, they revile him to discourage the like.

Moreover, if someone is being oppressed by another, they write about that too, so that everyone will know the story from both sides just as it happened, until it is decided in court. One can also read in it what their courts have decided.

Source: Susan Gilson Miller, ed. and trans., *Disorienting Encounters: Travels of a Moroccan Scholar in France in 1845–1846. The Voyage of Muhammad as-Saffar* (Berkeley: University of California Press, 1992), pp. 150–153.

---

system could respond to grievances and bring about reform peacefully.

Parliament justified the population's newfound faith in its efficacy by undertaking several more reforms. In 1835 Parliament passed the Municipal Corporation Act, which provided for more representative municipal councils with increased decision-making powers in local affairs.

A series of colonial reforms also showed Parliament's willingness to adapt to changing circumstances. Opposition to slavery had been voiced since the 1780s. (See the box "Reading Sources: A Plea to Abolish Slavery in the British Colonies.") Slavery, the very opposite of human freedom, was an affront to liberal principles. Moreover, its persistence threatened the empire—in 1831, 60,000 slaves rebelled in Jamaica. Parliament heeded the call for change and in 1833 abolished slavery throughout the British Empire.

In addition, the British began to review their imperial administration. Their control over Canada had been challenged in an uprising in 1837; London sent out a fact-finding mission headed by Lord Durham (1806–1848). As a result of the *Durham Report*, the

ஃ READING SOURCES

A Plea to Abolish Slavery in the British Colonies

Among the causes that British reformers embraced was the abolition of slavery. The slave trade had been abolished in 1807; one more step was left—ending in the colonies the institution of slavery itself. In this petition to Parliament in 1823, the Society for the Mitigation and Gradual Abolition of Slavery Throughout the British Dominions explains the harsh and degrading nature of the institution. Trading in slaves had already been abolished as immoral and unnatural; here the petitioners remind Parliament that holding slaves is no less abhorrent. Under the pressure of this type of agitation, Parliament in 1833 abolished slavery in the British Empire.

In the colonies of Great Britain there are at this moment upwards of 800,000 human beings in a state of degrading personal slavery.

These unhappy persons, whether young or old, male or female, are the absolute property of their master, who may sell or transfer them at his pleasure, and who may also regulate according to his discretion (within certain limits) the measure of their labour, their food, and their punishment.

Many of the slaves are (and all may be) branded like cattle, by means of a hot iron, on the shoulder or other conspicuous part of the body, with the initials of their master's name; and thus bear about them in indelible characters the proof of their debased and servile state. . . .

It can hardly be alleged that any man can have a right to obtain his fellow creatures in a state so miserable and degrading as has been described. And the absence of such right will be still more apparent, if we consider how these slaves were originally obtained. They, or their parents, were the victims of the Slave Trade. They were obtained, not by lawful means, or under any colourable pretext, but by the most undisguised rapine, and the most atrocious fraud. Torn from their homes and from every dear relation in life, barbarously manacled, driven like herds of cattle to the sea-shore, crowded into the potential holds of slave-ships, they were transported to our colonies and there sold in bondage. . . .

The Government and Legislature of this country have on various occasions, and in the most solemn and unequivocal terms denounced the Slave Trade as immoral, inhuman, and unjust; but the legal perpetuation of that state of slavery, which has been produced by it, is surely, in its principle, no less immoral, inhuman and unjust, than the trade itself. . . .

Source: Reprinted in *Circular Letters of the Society for the Mitigation and Gradual Abolition of Slavery Throughout the British Dominions* (April 1823).

 For additional information on this topic, go to http://college.hmco.com.

British government promulgated self-government for Canada in 1839 and 1841; eventually all the British colonies with a majority of white settlers were given similar rights of self-rule. The idea of self-government for nonwhites in the colonies was as yet an unimaginable proposition.

Reforms solidified Britain's influence overseas. In Canada they reduced opposition to British rule. The antislavery campaign led to the extension of British power into Africa. Having abolished the slave trade in 1807, the British worked to compel other nations to end the trade. With the largest navy in the world, Britain was well equipped to patrol the coast of West Africa, trying to suppress the traffic in humans and hinder its colonial rivals from benefiting from the trade. Needing bases for these patrols, the British established a number of minor settlements in West Africa, becoming the predominant European power along the coast. Although unimportant when acquired, these possessions foreshadowed the increasing European intrusion into African affairs.

Parliament's reforming zeal stimulated support for Chartism, a movement intended to transform Britain from essentially an oligarchy—rule by a few—into a democracy. In 1838 political radicals with working-class support drew up a "people's charter" calling for universal male suffrage; electoral districts with equal population; salaries and the abolition of property qualifications for members of Parliament; the secret ballot; and annual general elections. The Chartists hoped that giving workers the vote would end the dominance of the much smaller upper classes in Parliament and ensure an improvement in the workers' lot.

Chartism won wide support among men and women in the working class, sparking demonstrations and petition drives of unprecedented size. Women participated to a larger extent than in any other political movement of the day, founding over a hundred female Chartist chapters. Some Chartists, especially female members, asked for women's suffrage, but this demand failed to gain overall adherence from the membership. Winning mass support during particularly hard economic years, Chartism lost followers during a temporary economic upswing. The movement also fell under the sway of advocates of violence, who scared off many artisans and potential middle-class supporters. It lost credibility too by criticizing British institutions for being unresponsive to the needs of the working class, whereas in fact Parliament had introduced a number of significant reforms, including the Factory Act of 1833, which provided some protection to laborers. Lacking popular support, Chartism failed as a political movement; yet it drew public attention to an integrated democratic program whose main provisions (except for yearly elections) would be adopted piecemeal over the next half-century.

In 1839 urban businessmen founded the Anti–Corn Law League for the purpose of abolishing the Corn Law of 1815, which was increasing the price of grain. The Corn Law was unpopular with manufacturers, who knew that low food prices would allow them to pay low wages. It was also unpopular with workers, who wanted bread at a price they could afford. The anti–Corn Law movement proved more effective than Chartism because it had the support of the middle classes. Alarmed by the threat of famine after the poor harvest of 1845, Parliament repealed the Corn Law in 1846.

In the end, this action did not affect the price of grain. Nevertheless, repeal of the Corn Law was a milestone in British history, demonstrating the extent to which organized groups could bring about economic improvements. A popular, mass organization had been able to shape public policy—a far cry from the days of Peterloo, when the government had not only ignored the public but attacked it with bayonets fixed.

■ The Absolutist States of Central and Eastern Europe, 1815–1848

Having seen the turmoil unleashed by the French Revolution and suffered at the hands of the Grande Armée, the states of central and eastern Europe were particularly committed to maintaining absolute government. In contrast to many parts of western Europe, which saw important political changes in the 1830s, the absolutist states were able to preserve themselves essentially unchanged until 1848—and in some cases even beyond.

The Austrian Empire's far-flung territories seemed to its Habsburg rulers to require a firm hand (see Map 21.1). Liberalism, which challenged imperial power, could not be countenanced. Nor, in this multinational empire, could nationalism be tolerated. The emperor, Francis I (r. 1792–1835), was opposed to any change; his motto was "Rule and change nothing." Prince Metternich, Francis's chief minister, viewed the French Revolution of 1789 and its aftermath as a disaster and believed his task was to hold the line against the threat of revolution. Quick to interpret protests or the desire for change as a threat to the fundamental order, Metternich established a network of secret police and informers to spy on the imperial subjects and keep them in check.

In most of the German states, the political order was authoritarian and inflexible. The states of Baden and Württemberg in the southwest and Bavaria in the south had granted their subjects constitutions, although effective power remained in the hands of the ruling houses. The king of Prussia had repeatedly promised a constitution, but none had materialized. A central, representative Diet would not meet there until 1847. Prussia was ruled by an alliance of the king and the *Junkers°*, the landowning aristocrats who staffed the officer corps and the bureaucracy. Both the officer corps and the bureaucracy were efficient enough to serve as models for the rest of Europe. Where Prussia lagged by liberal standards was in its political institutions.

Throughout the German states, the urban middle classes, intellectuals, journalists, university professors, and students were frustrated with the existing system. They were disappointed by the lack of free institutions and the failure of the patriotic wars against Napoleon to create a united Germany. University students formed *Burschenschaften°*, or brotherhoods, whose slogan was "Honor, Liberty, Fatherland." Metternich imposed a policy of reaction on the German Confederation and pushed through the Carlsbad Decrees in July 1819, establishing

---

Junkers (YUNG-kurz)
Burschenschaften (BOOR-shen-shaft-en)

close supervision over the universities, censorship of the press, and dissolution of the youth groups. Wholesale persecution of liberals and nationalists followed. The Prussian king dismissed his more enlightened officials.

The outbreak of revolution in Paris in 1830 inspired further political agitation and repression in several German states. Mounting opposition to local despots and agitation for national unity led to the prosecution of outspoken liberals. Many associated with the nationalist "Young Germany" movement fled abroad, particularly to Paris.

Renewed nationalist agitation swept the German states in the 1840s. A mass outpouring of patriotic sentiment erupted in response to possible French ambitions on the Rhine during a diplomatic crisis in 1840. Two patriotic songs were penned: "The Watch on the Rhine" and *"Deutschland, Deutschland über alles"* ("Germany, Germany above all"), the latter becoming Germany's national anthem half a century later. German rulers, who in the past had been reluctant to support the national idea, now attempted to co-opt it. In Bavaria the crown prince, who later became King Ludwig I (r. 1825–1848), built Walhalla, named after the hall in which fallen heroes gather in Germanic lore. Ludwig's Walhalla was to be a "sacred monument" to German unity adorned with statues of famous Germans. Cologne's unfinished cathedral became a symbol of German enthusiasm; from all over Germany donations poured in to finish it. These events suggested a broadening base for nationhood, which potentially could replace the existing system of a fragmented Germany. But with minor exceptions, the system established in 1815 prevailed until 1848.

Austria exercised considerable power over Italy through its possession of Italian territory, by dynastic ties to several ruling houses in the central part of the peninsula, and by political alliances with others, including the papacy. The only ruling house free of Austrian ties—and hence eventually looked to by nationalists as a possible rallying point for the independence of the peninsula—was the Savoy dynasty of Piedmont-Sardinia.

Italy consisted of eight political states, and it was in Austria's interest to maintain disunity. Many Italian governments—notably the papacy, the kingdom of Naples, and the central Italian duchies—imposed repressive policies, knowing that they could count on Austrian assistance to squelch any uprising. Indeed, Metternich did crush rebellions that were intended to bring about freer institutions and a unified Italy. His interventions generated hatred of Austria among Italian liberals and nationalists.

By far the most autocratic of the European states was tsarist Russia. Since 1801 Alexander I (r. 1801–1825) had been tsar. An enigmatic character whose domestic

policy vacillated between liberalism and reaction and whose foreign policy wavered between brutal power politics and apparently selfless idealism, Alexander puzzled his contemporaries. When the Congress of Vienna gave additional Polish lands to the tsar, establishing the Kingdom of Poland, he demonstrated his liberalism to the world (and curried favor with his new subjects) by granting Poland a liberal constitution. But he offered no such constitution to his own people and within a few years violated the Polish constitution, refusing to call the diet into session. Alexander and his council discussed terms for the abolition of serfdom in Russia in 1803 and again in 1812, but like so many of his plans, this one was not implemented. Although he earnestly desired freedom for the serfs, the tsar was unwilling to impose any policy detrimental to the interests and privileges of the landed gentry.

Toward the end of his rule, Alexander became increasingly authoritarian and repressive, probably in response to growing opposition. Western liberal ideas, including constitutionalism, were adopted by Russian military officers who had served in western Europe, by Russian Freemasons who had corresponded with Masonic lodges in western Europe, and by Russian intellectuals who read Western liberal political tracts. These groups formed secret societies with varying agendas. Some envisioned Russia as a republic, others as a constitutional monarchy, but all shared a commitment to the abolition of serfdom and the establishment of a freer society.

Alexander died in December 1825, without designating which of his brothers would succeed him. Taking advantage of the confusion, the military conspirators declared in favor of the older brother, Constantine, in the belief that he favored a constitutional government. The younger brother, Nicholas, claimed to be the legal heir. The St. Petersburg garrison rallied to the conspirators' cause. Taking their cue from the Spanish uprising of 1820, the officers little doubted that the military could bring about change on its own in a country in which popular participation in governance was unknown.

The "Decembrist uprising," as it is known, quickly failed. The military revolt in the Russian capital was badly coordinated with uprisings planned in the countryside, and Nicholas moved quickly to crush the rebellion. He had the leaders executed, sent to Siberia, or exiled. In spite of its tragic end, throughout the nineteenth century the Decembrist uprising served as an inspiration to Russians resisting tsarist oppression.

Coming to the throne under such circumstances, Nicholas I (r. 1825–1855) was obsessed with the danger of revolution and determined to suppress all challenges to his authority. The declared goal of his rule was to uphold "orthodoxy, autocracy, and nationality." Nicholas created a stern, centralized bureaucracy to control all facets of Russian life. He originated the modern Russian secret police, called the "Third Section"; a state within the state, it was above the law. Believing in the divine right of monarchs, Nicholas refused to accept limits to his imperial powers. The tsar supported the primacy of the Russian Orthodox Church within Russian society; the church in turn upheld the powers of the state. Nicholas also used nationalism to strengthen the state, exalting the country's past and trying to Russify non-Russian peoples. After a nationalist rebellion in 1831 in Poland attempted to shake loose Russian control, Nicholas abrogated the kingdom's constitution and tried to impose the Russian language on its Polish subjects.

Russia's single most overwhelming problem was serfdom. Economically, serfdom had little to recommend it; free labor was far more efficient. Moreover, public safety was threatened by the serfs' dissatisfaction with their lot. Nicholas's thirty-year reign was checkered with over six hundred peasant uprisings, half of them put down by the military. Nicholas understood that serfdom had to be abolished for Russia's own good, but he could envision no clear alternative to it. Emancipation, he believed, would only sow further disorder. Except for a few minor reforms, he did nothing. Nicholas's death, followed by Russia's defeat in the Crimean War (see page 742), eventually brought to an end the institution that had held nearly half of the Russian people in bondage.

In its sheer mass, the Ottoman Empire continued to be a world empire. It extended over three continents. In Africa it ran across the whole North African coast. In Europe it stretched from Dalmatia (on the Adriatic coast) to Istanbul. In Asia it extended from Mesopotamia (present-day Iraq) to Anatolia (present-day Turkey). But it was an empire in decline, seriously challenged from inside by nationalist movements and from outside by foreign threats.

The Ottoman bureaucracy, once the mainstay of the government, had fallen into decay. In the past, officials had been recruited and advanced by merit; now lacking funds, Constantinople sold government offices. Tax collectors ruthlessly squeezed the peasantry. By the eighteenth century, the Janissaries, formerly an elite military force, had become an undisciplined band that menaced the peoples of the Ottoman Empire—especially those located at great distances from the close control of the capital. The reform-minded Sultan Selim III (r. 1789–1807) sought to curb the army, but he was killed by rebellious Janissaries, who forced the new ruler, Mahmud

Mehemet Ali   Painted by the famed British artist Sir David Wilkie, this portrait depicts the Egyptian leader at the height of his powers. Mehemet challenged the Ottoman Empire, winning for Egypt virtual independence and bringing Syria under his control.   *(Tate Gallery, London/Art Resource, NY)*

II (r. 1808–1839), to retract most of the previous improvements. The worst features of the declining empire were restored.

Most of the Ottoman Empire was inhabited by Muslims, but in the Balkans Christians were in the majority. Ottoman officials usually treated religious minorities such as Jews and Orthodox with tolerance. But the Christian subject people found in their religion a means of collectively resisting a harsh and at times capricious rule. Some Christian peoples in the Balkans looked back nostalgically to earlier eras—the Greeks to their great Classical civilization or the Serbs to their era of self-rule. The ideas of nationalism and liberty that triggered changes in western Europe also stirred the peoples of the Balkans.

The Serbs were the first people to revolt successfully against Ottoman rule. A poor, mountainous region, Serbia suffered greatly from the rapaciousness of the Janissaries. In protest, a revolt broke out in 1804. At first the Ottomans were able to contain the insurrection, but in 1815 they had to recognize one of its leaders, Milosh Obrenovich (r. 1815–1839), as governor and allow the formation of a national assembly. In 1830, under pressure from Russia, which took an interest in fellow Slavs and members of the Orthodox faith, Constantinople recognized Milosh as hereditary ruler over an autonomous Serbia.

The Greeks' struggle led to complete independence from Ottoman rule. Greeks served as administrators throughout the Ottoman lands and, as merchants and seafarers, traveled widely throughout the Mediterranean world and beyond. They had encountered the ideas of the French Revolution and, in the 1790s, were affected by the nationalism spreading in Europe. Adamantios Koraïs° (1748–1833), an educator living in revolutionary Paris, reformed written Greek to make it more consonant with ancient Greek by removing foreign accretions. Koraïs created a new, more elegant Greek and edited Greek classics to connect his fellow countrymen with their ancient and illustrious past. Greek cultural nationalism found an echo among some intellectuals. The *Philike Hetairia* (Society of Friends), a conspiratorial group, founded in 1814, dedicated itself to restoring Greek independence by political means.

Greek peasants were not particularly interested in politics, but they were hostile to the Ottoman Turks, who had accumulated vast landholdings at their expense. This in part motivated Greek peasants to join the anti-Turkish revolt that began in 1821. Greeks killed large numbers of defenseless Turks in the Morea, a region in central Greece. The Turkish authorities hanged the patriarch, the leader of the Orthodox Church, in Constantinople and massacred or sold into slavery the population of the Aegean island of Chios. The war continued fitfully. By 1827 the Ottomans, aided by their vassal Mehemet Ali (1769–1849) of Egypt, controlled most of the Balkan peninsula. The rest of Europe, excited by the idea of an independent Greece restored to its past greatness, widely supported the Greek movement for freedom. The Great Powers intervened in 1827, sending their navies to intercept supplies intended for the Ottoman forces. At Navarino Bay, in the southwest of the Peloponnesus, the Ottoman navy fired on the allies, who returned fire and sank the Turkish ships. The destruction of Ottoman power ensured the independence of Greece. In 1830 an international agreement spelled out Greek independence.

Losing influence in the Balkans, the Ottoman Empire was also challenged elsewhere. In Egypt, Mehemet Ali, nominally subordinate to Constantinople, actually ruled Egypt as if it were independent. He wrested Syria away in 1831 and threatened to march against his over-

Koraïs (KOOR-ay-iss)

lord, the sultan. Britain and Russia, concerned that an Ottoman collapse would upset the region's balance of power, intervened on the empire's behalf. Constantinople won back Syria but in 1841 had to acknowledge Mehemet Ali as the hereditary ruler of Egypt. The survival of the Ottoman Empire was beginning to depend on the goodwill—or self-interest—of the Great Powers.

THE REVOLUTIONS OF 1848

 ROM France in the west to Poland in the east, at least fifty separate revolts and uprisings shook the Continent in 1848, the most extensive outbreak of popular violence in nineteenth-century Europe (see Map 21.2). The revolt had an impact far beyond Europe's borders. Inspired by the example of the European revolutions, Brazilians rose up against their government. In Bogota, Colombia, church bells rang, and in New York public demonstrations enthusiastically greeted the announcement of a republic in France. And as a result of the Parisian revolution, slaves in French colonies were emancipated.

■ Roots of Rebellion

At no time since 1800 had so many Europeans been involved in collective action. Many reasons account for this widespread outbreak of discontent. In the countryside, restrictions in access to land such as enclosure frustrated peasants. Although in the past many had enjoyed free access to village commons, these were coming increasingly under private control, or the peasants faced competition for their use. Formerly a peasant might have grazed sheep in the commons, but now a peasant's two or three animals competed with herds of sometimes hundreds of sheep owned by a rich farmer. Also, the poor once had relatively free access to forests to forage for firewood, but the limitation of this right also now led to frequent conflicts.

Points of friction were made worse by growing populations that put pressure on available resources. In the urban environment a crisis erupted in the handicrafts industry, which dominated city economies. Urban artisans were being undercut by the putting-out system or cottage industry, in which capitalists had goods produced in the countryside by cottagers—part-time artisans who supported themselves partly through agriculture and were thus willing to work for lower wages. Crises in the crafts hurt the journeymen who wanted to be masters; they had to serve far longer apprenticeships and in many cases could never expect promotion. Where the

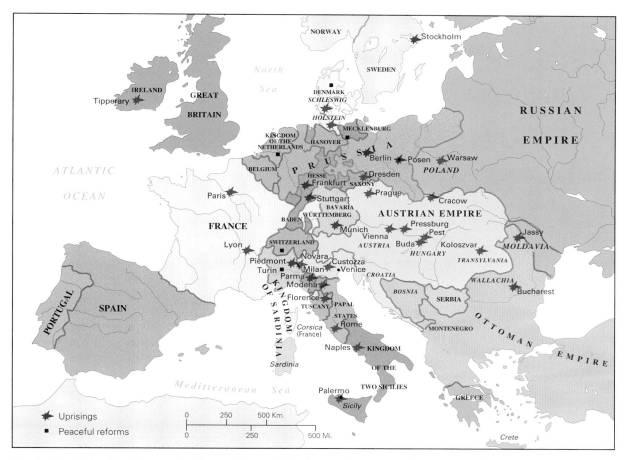

Map 21.2   Major Uprisings and Reforms, 1848–1849   In no other year had as many revolts broken out simultaneously; in many cases the revolutions led to reforms and new constitutions.

guild system still existed, it was in decline, unable to protect the economic interests of artisans anxious about their futures.

These developing concerns came to a crisis point as a result of the economic depression of 1845–1846. In 1845 a crop disaster, including the spread of potato blight, destroyed the basic food of the poor in northern Europe. The most notorious catastrophe was in Ireland. In the last famine in western Europe, 1 million Irish starved to death between 1844 and 1851 as a result of the blight. The poor harvests doubled the price of food from the 1840 level. An industrial downturn accompanied these agricultural disasters, creating massive unemployment. Municipal and national governments seemed unable to deal with the crowding, disease, and unsanitary conditions that were worsening already high tensions in the cities, the sites of national governments. People were ready to heed those who called for the overthrow of the existing regimes. The established political and adminis-

trative elites were disoriented and found they could not count on their traditional sources of support. Revolts were triggered not only by discontent, but also by the hope for change.

The revolutions of 1848 were sparked by the revolution in Paris in February. News of the fall of Louis Philippe triggered a ripple effect, spreading turbulence to over fifty localities in Europe. In France the revolution was for political and social rights. In several other countries, another issue was added to the combustible situation—nationalism. Once the revolution in the Germanies had started, the demands arose for national unification. Throughout the Italian peninsula, national unity was the goal; northern Italians added their desire for independence from the Habsburg Empire. In other Habsburg lands the cry went out for national independence: the Hungarians, Poles, and Czechs all wanted to be masters of their own destinies, and free from Vienna's control.

■ Liberals: From Success to Defeat

The revolutions of 1848 went through a number of stages. In the first stage liberal demands for more political liberties joined with popular demands for social justice. In France the victors declared a republic, which provided basic constitutional freedoms and granted universal male suffrage (the first European regime to do so). The provisional government included a working man in the cabinet and instituted national workshops to give work to the urban unemployed. Inspired by the example of Paris, crowds in Vienna demonstrated and petitioned the emperor. Having lost control over the capital, Metternich resigned and fled to England. On March 15, 1848, the Austrian imperial court, faced with continued agitation by students and workers, announced its willingness to issue a constitution. Even more important was Aus-

Ballots, Not Bullets   This print of 1848 informs the revolutionary of the barricade to put away his rifle and trust the democratic process. Pointing to the rifle, our French revolutionary announces, "this is for the external enemy." "As for the internal ones," he says, indicating the election urn, "this is how one fairly competes with them."   *(Harlingue-Viollet)*

Ça, c'est pour l'ennemi du dehors ; pour le dedans, voici comme l'on combat loyalement les adversaires....

tria's decision to abolish serfdom. Some had feared a serf uprising, but the relatively generous terms of the emancipation mollified the peasantry.

In Germany news of the February uprising in Paris also acted as a catalyst for change in the German states. The forces of change seemed irresistible. As the king of Württemberg observed, "I cannot mount on horseback against ideas." The wisest course appeared to be compromise. He and many of his fellow dukes and princes changed their governments, dismissing their cabinets and instituting constitutions.

Up to this point Prussia was conspicuous for being untouched by the revolutionary wave. But when news of Metternich's fall reached Berlin on March 16, middle-class liberals and artisans demonstrated for reforms. To appease his subjects, King Friedrich Wilhelm IV appointed the liberal Rhenish businessman who in the ceremonial march through Berlin (see the illustration on page 706) walked ahead of the king. Representative government was introduced, and suffrage was extended, though it was still restricted to men of property. No longer the exclusive preserve of the aristocracy, government was opened to men from the liberal professions and the business classes. As in Austria, the German countryside was appeased by reducing some of the feudal arrangements that still existed in many areas.

The second stage of the revolution marked a breakdown in the unity that had initially formed against the old regimes. With the enemy defeated or compliant, the middle classes, peasants, and workers discovered they no longer shared a common goal. In France the peasants, who at least had not opposed the revolution, by April 1848 were hostile to the new republic. They decried the additional taxes that had to be levied to pay for the national workshops supporting unemployed urban workers. Armed with the vote, the peasants elected conservative landowners, lawyers, and notaries—a group nearly identical to the pre-1848 deputies. In June the new parliament decided to terminate the costly national workshops. The workers, in despair, revolted. The government carried out a bloody repression, killing 1,500 and arresting 12,000. The re-election of conservative forces revealed that universal suffrage could serve as a means to mobilize moderate public opinion against radicalism in Paris. The advent of railroads allowed the government to muster military support from outside the city. Thereafter, it would be far more difficult for radical Parisian crowds to dictate policies to the rest of the country.

The propertied classes, feeling menaced by the poor, looked to authority for security. Of the several candidates for president in 1848, Louis Napoleon (1808–1873), a nephew of Napoleon Bonaparte, appealed to the largest cross section of the population. The middle class was attracted by the promise of authority and order. Peasants, disillusioned by the tax policies of the republic, remained loyal to the memory of Napoleonic glory. Workers embittered by the government's repression of the June uprisings were impressed by Louis Napoleon's vaguely socialistic program. Louis Napoleon was elected president; three years later, he dissolved the National Assembly by force and established a personal dictatorship. In 1852 he declared himself Emperor Napoleon III.

In Austria and Germany the middle classes became wary of the lower classes; the class conflict in Paris intensified their concern. Once the peasants had won their freedom from feudal dues in Germany and from serfdom in the Austrian Empire, they were no longer interested in what was occurring in the capital. Thus the alliance in favor of change disappeared, and it could not even serve as a bulwark against the return of conservative forces. In Austria the reactionary forces around the court, led by General Windischgrätz, reconquered Vienna in October 1848 for the emperor and suspended the liberals' constitution. In December the king of Prussia, who had appeared to bow to liberal opinion, regained his courage and dismissed the elected assembly. Most of the liberal forces were spent and overcome by the end of the year.

■ The Nationalist Impulse

The revolutions did not break out because of nationalism, but once they erupted, the nationalist cause helped shape the outcome in several regions. Faced with internal turmoil, Prussia and Austria—which both opposed German unification lest it undermine their power—could not prevent the question of a united Germany from coming to the fore. In March 1848 a self-appointed national committee invited five hundred prominent German liberals to convene in Frankfurt to begin the process of national unification. In addition to fulfilling a long-standing liberal dream, a united German nation would consolidate the liberal victory over absolutism. The gathering called for suffrage based on property qualifications, thus excluding most Germans from the political process and alienating them from the evolving new order. The first all-German elected legislature met in May 1848 in Frankfurt to pursue unification. It faced the thorny issue of the shape of this new Germany: which regions should be included and which excluded? The most ambitious plan envisioned a *Grossdeutschland°*, or large Germany, consisting of all the members of the German Confederation, including the German-speaking parts of Austria and the German parts of Bohemia. Such a solution would include many non-Germans, including Poles, Czechs, and Danes. The proponents of *Kleindeutschland°*, or small Germany, which would exclude Austria and its possessions, saw their solution as a more likely scenario, although it would exclude many Germans. They succeeded in the end, largely because the reassertion of Austrian imperial power in the fall of 1848 put the non-German areas under Vienna's control out of reach.

The Prussian reassertion of royal power, though partial, was a signal for other German rulers in late 1848 to dismiss their liberal ministers. The moment for liberalism and national unification to triumph had passed by the time the Frankfurt Assembly drew up a constitution in the spring of 1849. Having opted for the *Kleindeutsch* solution, the parliament offered the throne to Friedrich Wilhelm IV, king of Prussia. Although the king was not a liberal, he ruled the largest state within the designated empire. If power could promote and protect German unity, he possessed it in the form of the Prussian army. But Friedrich Wilhelm feared that accepting the throne would lead to war with Austria. Believing in the principle of monarchy, he also did not want an office offered by representatives of the people, and so he refused the offer. Lacking an alternative plan, most members of the Frankfurt Assembly went home. A rump parliament and a series of uprisings in favor of German unity were crushed by the Prussian army. So German unification failed. Liberalism alone was unable to bring about German unity; other means would be required to do so.

In Italy, too, nationalist aspirations emerged once a revolt triggered by social and economic grievances had broken out. In the years before 1848, nationalists and liberals hoped somehow to see their program of a united and free Italy implemented. News of the Paris uprising in February galvanized revolutions in Italy. Italians under Austrian rule forced the Austrians to evacuate their Italian possessions. Revolts and mass protests in several Italian states led rulers to grant, or at least promise, a constitution. The king of Piedmont, Charles Albert (r. 1831–1849), granted his people a constitution, the Statuto. Charles Albert hoped to play a major part in unifying Italy. In Austrian Italy, the middle classes, although eager to be free of foreign rule, feared radical elements among the laborers. They believed that annexation to nearby Piedmont would provide security from both Austria and the troublesome lower classes. The king of Piedmont decided to unite Italy under his

---

Grossdeutschland (Grose-DOYT-shlant)

Kleindeutschland (Kline-DOYT-shlant)

Constitutional Government in Denmark   On March 21, 1848, fifteen thousand Danes, inspired by
the example of Paris, marched on the palace to demand constitutional rights. Unlike in the French
capital, however, this event was peaceful and led to the establishment of constitutional government.
This painting honors the new parliament that came into being after the liberal constitution was
adopted in 1849.   *(Statens Museum for Kunst, Copenhagen)*

throne if doing so would prevent the spread of radicalism to his kingdom. On March 24, 1848, he declared war
on Austria but was defeated in July and had to sue for an
armistice. The continued spread of nationalist and revolutionary sentiment tempted Charles Albert to declare
war on Austria once again, in March 1849. The outcome
for Piedmont was even worse than it had been a year
earlier. Within six days its army was defeated. Humiliated, Charles Albert resigned his throne to his son, Victor Emmanuel II (r. 1849–1878). The Austrians quickly
reconquered their lost provinces and reinstated their
puppet governments. The dream of a united Italy was
dashed.

In the multinational empire of the Habsburgs, nationalism manifested itself in the form of demands for
national independence from foreign rule. With Austria's
power temporarily weakened as a result of revolution in
Vienna, nationalist revolts broke out not only in Italy, but
simultaneously in Hungary, the Czech lands, and Croa-

tia. The Austrian emperor yielded in Hungary, giving it
virtual independence; it was joined to the empire solely
by personal union to the ruler. Constitutional government was established in Hungary, but participation in
the political process was limited to Magyars, who were
the single largest ethnic group, constituting 40 percent of
the population. The other nationalities in Hungary—Romanians, Slovaks, Croats, and Slovenes—preferred the
more distant rule of Austrian Vienna to Magyar authority. The Czech lands also witnessed agitation, but there
and elsewhere the tide favoring the nationalists turned.
The revolt against the empire was not coordinated, and
the nationalisms were often in conflict with one another.
Once the emperor re-established his power in Vienna,
he could move against his rebellious subjects. The Austrian Empire practiced a policy of divide and rule; it re-
established its authority in Italy, bombarded Prague into
submission, and with Russian help brought Hungary to
heel. If the nationalist fires had been quenched, the dan-

gers nationalism posed to the survival of the Habsburg Empire were also revealed.

In the large sweep of revolutions that washed across Europe, three major countries were spared. In Great Britain the government had proven sufficiently capable of adjusting to some of the major popular demands; revolution seemed unnecessary. In Russia the repressive tsarist system prevented any defiance from escalating into an opposition mass movement. Successive military officers governed in Spain, including General Ramón Narváez° (1799–1868), who brutally ran the country from 1844 to 1851. When he was on his deathbed, the priest asked him whether he forgave his enemies. He answered, "I have no enemies. I have shot them all!" So in 1848, no revolution disturbed Spain.

SUMMARY

 HE revolutions of 1848 released many of the forces for change that had been gathering strength since 1815. In spite of the Congress of Vienna's effort to restore the old order after Napoleon's fall, the generation after 1815 established a new order. The ideas of change that had powered the French Revolution of 1789 continued to shape an era that claimed to be rolling history back to prerevolutionary times. Liberalism contested authoritarianism.

Reform-minded regimes in Europe improved the lives of people in colonies overseas, abolishing slavery in British and then French colonies and providing self-rule for Canada. Some states even turned away from monarchy and experimented with republicanism, a form of government that until then many had thought fit only for small states. All of the Latin American colonies except Mexico and Brazil became republics on gaining independence. In Europe during 1848–1849, the French, German, Hungarian, and Roman republics were proclaimed. Although they did not last, these experiments suggested new modes of political organization that were to become common in the following century.

The generation after 1815 experienced revolutions frequently and broadly. These uprisings usually failed, and the forces of order in most cases were able to recapture power. Yet the status quo was altered. In many cases absolutist rulers had to grant constitutions and accept ministers who were not their choices. Even though most of these arrangements were temporary, they established an impor-

tant precedent. If unusual in the first half, constitutions became the norm in the second half of the century.

Nationalism arose in these years. The desire for national independence and unity found expression in Italy, Germany, Hungary, Poland, and the land of the Czechs. To free themselves from Madrid's rule, the Spanish colonies in the Americas employed a nationalist discourse borrowed from Europe. In the second half of the century, Europe would have to contend more rigorously with the forces of nationalism that first appeared after 1814.

Socialist ideas challenged private property. In 1848 some might have pointed to the institution of the temporary workshops in Paris as an effort to realize a part of the socialist program. But that was a modest effort; socialist ideas would come into full expression—and their power become formidable—toward the end of the century.

The middle classes found their position strengthened after 1848. They did not dominate the political system, but their influence increased with the growth of entrepreneurship. Middle-class professionals were recruited into the civil services of states determined to streamline their operations in order to withstand revolution more effectively. Revolutionary fervor waned after 1848, but the current of economic and social change continued to transform Europe.

■ Suggested Reading

Broers, Michael. *Europe After Napoleon: Revolution, Reaction, and Romanticism, 1815–1848.* 1996. Evaluates the era from the point of view of the participants.

Hobsbawm, E. J. *The Age of Revolution, 1789–1848.* 1962. Presents compelling arguments that the era was dominated by two simultaneous revolutions, the French Revolution and the industrial transformation.

Johnson, Paul. *The Birth of the Modern World Society, 1815–1830.* 1991. A weighty but readable book providing a panoramic view of the era; includes biographical sketches of some of the major figures of the time.

Laven, David, and Lucy Riall, eds. *Napoleon's Legacy: Problems of Government in Restoration Europe.* 2000. Essays on the Restoration experience in different European countries.

Sperber, Jonathan. *The European Revolutions, 1848–1851.* 1994. The best up-to-date synthesis, which includes some new emphases, such as the role of rural and religious discontent in shaping the revolts.

Wheen, Francis. *Karl Marx: A Life.* 2000. A lively biography that, in addition to discussing Marxian thought, emphasizes the man's personal life.

Narváez (NAR-va-yes)

 For a searchable list of additional readings for this chapter, go to http://college.hmco.com.

Raft of the "Medusa"

In September 1816 the French were shocked at the news of the disaster that had befallen the government ship *Méduse* (Medusa) as it headed for Senegal in West Africa the previous July. Including the ship's crew, 400 passengers had boarded the vessel.

The captain of the ship was a nobleman, Duroys de Chaumareys°, whom the restoration government had appointed solely on the basis of his family and political connections. Inexperienced as a seaman, the captain clumsily ran his ship aground on the Mauritanian coast, off West Africa, on July 2. The *Medusa* had only six lifeboats capable of carrying a total of 250 people; for the rest of the passengers a raft was rigged with planks, beams, and ropes. The captain and his officers forcibly took over the lifeboats, abandoning 150 passengers, including one woman, to the less secure raft. With no navigational tools and insufficient food and water, the passengers of the raft were at the mercy of stormy seas and a brutal sun. Anger at officers for having abandoned them led seamen on the raft to murder some of their superiors. By the third day, driven by thirst and hunger, some passengers ate their dead companions—killed by exposure or drowned by huge waves. On the sixth day, the strongest among the survivors, fearing that their rations were dwindling, banded together and murdered the weaker ones. On the thirteenth day, the French frigate *Argus* spotted the raft and rescued fifteen survivors. Five died soon after, leaving only ten survivors out of the raft's original 150 passengers.

Although the government tried to suppress information about the event, the French press exposed the incompetence and cowardice of Captain de Chaumareys. The event was understood to reflect the weakness of the regime that had appointed him. The selfish act of the captain and his fellow officers suggested the narrow class interest of the restoration government, favoring aristocracy at the cost of the common people.

The French painter Théodore Géricault (1791–1824) befriended the ship's surgeon Henri Savigny, one of the lucky ten who survived the harrowing experience on the raft of the *Medusa*. In addition to press reports, Géricault

Duroys de Chaumareys (du-RWAH duh sho-mah-RAY)

thus had a direct eyewitness account of the event. The painter shared Savigny's sense of outrage against the government for having appointed the incompetent captain and for having treated the survivors callously—at one point the government arrested Savigny for publicizing the tragedy. The light prison sentence imposed on the captain was another source of grievance.

Since 1815 the French government had sought to bring distinction to itself by displaying art in salon expositions. That of 1819 was intended to be larger, more glorious than any previous one. Among its paintings was Géricault's huge canvas—the largest in that year's exposition—measuring 16 feet high by 24 feet wide, innocently titled "Scene of Shipwreck." Carelessly, the regime had wanted to gain glory for itself by exhibiting this impressive artwork, while at the same time keeping hidden its real subject. But the stratagem failed; everyone recognized the painting to be the *Raft of the "Medusa"* and an attack on the Bourbon regime.

The painting, reproduced here, depicts the moment the survivors have spotted the frigate, the *Argus,* barely visible in the horizon. Notice the figure of an African standing at the fore of the raft, waving a red-and-white cloth to attract the ship's attention. In this painting the nobility and symbol of hope the African symbolizes is an attack on the slave trade, which Britain had abolished but which France was still engaged in. And so by including the African, the painting is implicitly criticizing the restoration regime for sanctioning commerce in humans. Just as the *Argus* is coming to the rescue of the shipwrecked, the painting appears to suggest, so Africans will see the day when their enslavement will be ended.

Historians often regard the *Raft of the "Medusa"* as the most important painting of French romanticism, and it includes nearly all the major themes of the movement. By locating the scene off the coast of Africa, Géricault incorporates an element of exoticism. Nature—cruel and unforgiving—is central to the scene, reflected in the turbulent sea, dark clouds, and imperiled raft. The canvas includes an extraordinary range of passions: Observe, for example, the inconsolable grief of the figure at the bottom left, a father cradling the dead body

Géricault: Raft of the "Medusa" *(Erich Lessing/Art Resource, NY)*

of his son. Other figures express despair and terror, and still others limitless hope. The painting evokes the dark passions lurking in the human heart. Although it does not show the scenes of insanity, murder, and cannibalism that the survivors had witnessed, they undoubtedly came to the mind of the viewers, who were familiar with the tragic events. The painting was a powerful indictment of Enlightenment faith in humans as creatures of reason and balance.

Romantic artists wanted to engage the passions of those viewing, reading, or hearing their works. *Raft of the "Medusa"* purposely stages the events in the foreground in order to pull viewers into the picture and make them participants in the drama; they thus share in the alternating feelings of terror and hope that swept the raft.

The fate of the painting and the artist followed a romantic script. When Géricault started the painting, he intended it as an indictment of the restoration government. He poured energy into it in an effort to take his mind off a disastrous love affair, and as his work proceeded he came to see the painting as an allegory of larger human passions and concerns. Yet when it was displayed, much to his disappointment, the painting was understood mainly in political terms. Disillusioned by this reaction, Géricault thereafter painted no major works. He grew sickly, rarely bestirred himself, and died of bone tuberculosis in 1824, aged 33. He illustrated the romantics' view of a heroic life—the genius who performs a major feat and then dies young, before realizing his potential. To the romantics, human intent and effort often appeared thwarted by larger forces. This painting, originally meant to criticize the regime, was after Géricault's death purchased by the restoration government and hung in France's national museum, the Louvre.

CHAPTER 22

Nationalism and Political Reform 1850–1880

I N 1885, on the occasion of the seventieth birthday of the German Chancellor Otto von Bismarck, Kaiser Wilhelm I gave the chancellor this painting, depicting the proclamation of German unification in the Hall of Mirrors in Versailles in 1871. On the podium, standing just behind the newly declared kaiser, is Crown Prince Friedrich Wilhelm (later Kaiser Friedrich III). To the kaiser's left, with his arm upraised, is the grand duke of Baden. In the middle of the scene, resplendent in his white uniform, is Bismarck, the political architect of German unification, and on the right nearby, Field Marshal Helmuth von Moltke°, the military genius who provided the series of military victories allowing Prussia to unify Germany under its aegis. The new state was proclaimed by the crowned heads of Germany; no popular vote or parliament sanctioned the founding event. By war, Germany had become a united nation. Wars and the threat of wars brought about the emergence of several new states on the European scene: Italy, Romania, and Bulgaria. In the generation after 1850 the contours of European politics were being changed—new states appeared on the map, and within their national borders a good number of states reformed their political institutions. As Europe changed, a much enlarged and more powerful United States and a united Canada also emerged.

To meet the demand for popular participation in government so forcefully expressed in 1848, every European state except the Ottoman and Russian Empires found it necessary to have a parliament. Rare before midcentury, such institutions became common thereafter. No longer was the demand for popular participation seen as a threat to the existing political and social order. In fact, popular participation, or the appearance of it, gave the existing order a legitimacy

---

von Moltke (fon molt-KEH)

Wilhelm I is proclaimed ruler of the German Empire at Versailles, 1871.
(Friedrichsruh, Bismarck-Museum/AKG London)

it had not enjoyed since before the French Revolution. Nationalism flourished during this period, emerging as a decisive force in European affairs and in the United States, where it promoted territorial expansion and fired a determination to preserve the Union.

These political transformations occurred in an era of unprecedented economic growth and prosperity. Industrial production expanded the economy; the discovery of gold in California in 1848 led to the expansion of credit (since currencies were backed by gold), which led to the founding of new banks and mass investments in growing industries. The standard of living rose significantly in industrializing nations. Industrial production in Great Britain increased by 90 percent, and in France by 50 percent, between 1850 and 1880. The middle classes expanded dramatically.

In the first half of the century, international relations had been dominated by the congress system, in which representatives of the major European states met periodically to refine and preserve the balance of power. This system disappeared in the second half of the century, as political leaders pursued the narrow interests of their respective states. Instead of negotiating with one another, a new generation of leaders employed brute military force—or the threat of its use—to resolve international conflicts. The new age was dominated not by ideals but by force, announced Prussian chancellor Otto von Bismarck, the main practitioner of what became known as *Realpolitik,* a policy in which war became a regular instrument of statecraft.

QUESTIONS TO CONSIDER

- How did the Crimean War affect international relations?

- How did political leaders in Prussia and Piedmont harness the forces of nationalism to achieve German and Italian national unity?

- Why did Russia abolish serfdom, and what was the impact of this action?

- Why was comprehensive political reform, especially the expansion of democracy, possible in some countries, but only limited reforms in others?

TERMS TO KNOW

Realpolitik	Tanzimat
congress system	Young Turks
risorgimento	glasnost
trasformismo	mir
Otto von Bismarck	manifest destiny
February Patent	Paris Commune
Compromise of 1867	Second Reform Bill

THE CHANGING NATURE OF INTERNATIONAL RELATIONS

 HE Crimean War and its aftermath shaped European international relations for several decades. Following the 1815 Congress of Vienna (see Chapter 21), European states attempted to work out their differences by negotiation, avoiding situations in which one state triumphed at the cost of another. The Crimean War and subsequent realignments raised mutual suspicions, leading nations to act in their own self-interests and to ignore the concerns of the other major players in the international system. This reorientation facilitated the emergence of nation-states.

■ The Crimean War, 1854–1856

The Crimean War had many causes. Principally, however, it was ignited by the decision of French and British statesmen to contain Russian power in the Balkans and keep it from encroaching on the weakening Ottoman Empire. Russian claims to have the right to intervene on behalf of Ottoman Christians had led to war between the two states in October 1853. The defeat of the Ottoman navy at Sinope° in November left the Ottoman Empire defenseless.

British and French statesmen had considerable interest in the conflict. Britain had long feared that the collapse of the Ottoman Empire would lead Russia to seek territorial gains in the Mediterranean. Such a move would challenge Britain's supremacy. An explosion of public sentiment against Russia also obliged the British government to take an aggressive stance. Meanwhile, the French emperor, Napoleon III, viewed defeat of Russia as a way to eclipse one of the states most dedicated to preserving the current European borders. He wanted to undermine existing power relations, hoping that a new order would lead to increased French power and influence. Napoleon also imagined that fighting side by side with Britain could lay the foundation for Anglo-French friendship. And so England and France rushed to defend the Ottoman Empire and declared war on Russia in March 1854.

The war was poorly fought on all sides. Leadership was woefully inadequate, and five times more casualties resulted from disease than from enemy fire. Although the Russians had a standing army of a million men, their poor communications and supply systems prevented them from ever fielding more than a quarter of their forces. In Britain the press and Members of Parliament denounced their side's inadequate materiel and incompetent leadership. For the first time the press played an active role in reporting war, and photography brought to readers at home the gruesome realities of battle. One of the few heroic figures to emerge from this conflict was the English nurse Florence Nightingale (1820–1910), who organized a nursing service to care for the British sick and wounded. Later, her wartime experience allowed her to pioneer nursing as a professional calling. (See the box "Reading Sources: Florence Nightingale in the Crimean War.")

After almost two years of fighting in the Balkans and the Crimean peninsula, Russia abandoned the key fortress of Sevastopol in September 1855. Militarily defeated, the Russians also were alarmed at Austria's posture. Tsar Nicholas I had expected Austrian assistance in the war in return for his help in crushing the Hungarian rebellion in 1849. Instead, Austria's leaders not only withheld aid but even threatened to join the Western alliance.

The Crimean conflict killed three-quarters of a million people—more than any European war between the

---

Sinope (see-NO-pay)

CHRONOLOGY

1840s	Tanzimat in the Ottoman Empire
1851	Louis Napoleon's coup d'état
1854–1856	Crimean War
1860	Italy united under Piedmontese rule
1861–1865	U.S. Civil War
1861	Great Reforms in Russia
1862	Bismarck appointed minister president of Prussia
1864	Austria and Prussia attack Denmark and occupy Schleswig-Holstein
1866	Austro-Prussian War
1866	Abolition of estate system in Sweden
1867	Second Reform Bill in England
1867	North America Act creates Canadian federation
1867	Austro-Hungarian compromise
1870	Franco-Prussian War
1870	Rome, joined to Italy, becomes its capital
1870	Declaration of French Third Republic
1871	Unification of German Empire
1871	Paris Commune
1876	Bulgarian horrors
1878	Congress of Berlin

end of the Napoleonic Wars and World War I. It was a particularly futile, senseless war whose most important consequence was political: it unleashed dramatic new changes in the international order that allowed for the emergence of the new nation-states.

■ The Congress of Paris, 1856

The former combatants met in Paris in February 1856 to work out a peace treaty. Their decisions—which pleased no one—shaped relations among European states for the next half-century. Russian statesmen were especially discontented, as their country was forbidden from

Crimean War   This photograph shows the interior of the Sevastapol fortress after it had been battered into surrender. The Crimean War was the first conflict to be documented by photographers.
(Courtesy of the Board of Trustees of the Victoria & Albert Museum)

having a fleet in the Black Sea. Nor did French leaders feel their nation had benefited. Although holding the congress in Paris flattered the emperor's pride, no other clear advantages emerged for France. The north Italian state of Piedmont°, which had joined the allies, gained from the congress only a vague statement on the unsatisfactory nature of the existing situation in Italy. Prussia was invited to attend the congress only as an afterthought and hence also felt slighted.

Although the war seemed to have sustained the integrity of the Ottoman Empire, the peace settlement weakened it indirectly by dictating reforms in the treatment of its Christian populations. These reforms impaired the empire's ability to repress the growing nationalist movements in the Balkans. British political leaders, galled by the heavy sacrifices of the war, moved toward isolationism in foreign policy. Austrian policymakers, who had hoped to gain the aid of Britain and France in preserving the Habsburg Empire, found them

Piedmont (PEED-mont)

Florence Nightingale   This photograph was taken in 1856, shortly after Nightingale returned to England from the Crimean War. Her privileged background provided the official connections that helped the success of her nursing services.   *(Courtesy, Florence Nightingale Museum, St. Thomas' Hospital, London. Photo: London Metropolitan Archives)*

🕮 R E A D I N G   S O U R C E S

Florence Nightingale in the Crimean War

Nightingale used her influential family connections to win an appointment to the Crimean battlefield. Once there, she organized nursing for the wounded and was able to secure additional personnel and medical supplies for her hospital. Women were supposed to be sheltered from the harsh realities of the outside world, but as this letter indicates, Nightingale was not spared war in its cruelest aspects.

We have no room for corpses in the wards. The Surgeons pass on to the next, an excision of the shoulder-joint—beautifully performed and going on well—[cannon] ball lodged just in the head of the joint, and fracture starred all round. The next poor fellow has two stumps for arms—and the next has lost an arm and leg. As for the balls, they go in where they like, and do as much harm as they can in passing. That is the only rule they have. The next case has one eye put out, and paralysis of the iris of the other. He can neither see nor understand. But all who can walk come into us for Tobacco, but I tell them that we have not a bit to put into our own mouths. Not a sponge, nor a rag of linen, not anything have I left. Everything is gone to make slings and stump pillows and shirts. These poor fellows have not had a clean shirt nor been washed for two months before they came here, and the state in which they arrive from the transport is literally crawling. I hope in a few days we shall establish a little cleanliness. But we have not a basin nor a towel nor a bit of soap nor a broom—I have ordered 300 scrubbing brushes. But one half the Barrack is so sadly out of repair that it is impossible to use a drop of water on the stone floors, which are all laid upon rotten wood, and would give our men fever in no time. . . .

I am getting a screen now for the Amputations, for when one poor fellow, who is to be amputated to-morrow, sees his comrade today die under the knife it makes impression—and diminishes his chance. But, anyway, among these exhausted frames the mortality of the operations is frightful.

Source: Letter to Dr. William Bowman, November 14, 1854, in Sue M. Goldie, ed., *"I Have Done My Duty": Florence Nightingale in the Crimean War, 1854–56* (Iowa City: University of Iowa Press, 1987), pp. 37–38.

---

hostile instead, a stance that encouraged the forces undermining Habsburg hegemony. At the time the peace treaty was signed, few people foresaw the enormous results that would flow from it.

In the first half of the century, the congress system had tried to ensure that no major state was dissatisfied enough to subvert the existing distribution of power. The international order had been upheld in part by the cooperation of the rulers of the conservative Eastern powers: Russia, Austria, and Prussia. Now these powers were rivals, and their competition contributed to growing instability in the international system. By and large, the decisions reached in Paris would be disregarded or unilaterally revised. This new international climate also allowed new states to take shape without international sanction.

ITALIAN UNIFICATION, 1859–1870

N Metternich's memorable phrase, Italy at midcentury was nothing but a "geographic expression." The revolution of 1848 (see pages 735–736) had revealed an interest in national unification, but the attempt had failed. Yet within a dozen years what many believed to be impossible would come to pass. Idealists such as Giuseppe Mazzini (see page 716) had preached that Italy would be unified not by its rulers but by its people, who would rise and establish a free republic. Instead, the deed was done by royalty, by war, and with the help of a foreign state. Although ideals were not absent from the process of unification, cynical manipulation and scheming also came into play.

Since the late eighteenth century, some Italians had been calling for a *risorgimento°*, a political and cultural renewal of Italy. By the mid-nineteenth century the idea was actively supported by a small, elite group consisting of the educated middle class, urban property owners, and members of the professions. For merchants, industrialists, and professionals, a unified state would provide a larger stage on which to pursue their ambitions.

■ Cavour Plots Unification

After the failed 1848 revolution, most Italian rulers resorted to repression. Only the north Italian kingdom of Piedmont kept the liberal constitution adopted during the 1848 revolution, and it welcomed political refugees from other Italian states. Not only politically but economically, it was a beacon to the rest of Italy, establishing modern banks and laying half the rail lines on the peninsula.

The statesman who was to catapult Piedmont into a position of leadership in the dramatic events leading to Italian unification was Count Camillo di Cavour° (1810–1861). The son of a Piedmontese nobleman and high government official, he grew up speaking French, the language of the royal court and formal education in Piedmont, and mastered Italian only as an adult. Cosmopolitan in his interests, Cavour knew more about Britain and France than about Italy. He was sympathetic to the aspirations of the middle class and saw in Britain and France models of what Italy ought to become, a liberal and economically advanced society.

Short, fat, and near-sighted, Cavour hardly cut a heroic figure. Yet he was ambitious, hard-working, and driven to succeed. A well-known journalist, the editor of the newspaper *Risorgimento,* he joined the government in 1850. Two years later King Victor Emmanuel appointed him prime minister. He shared the enthusiasm of the middle classes for an Italian nation, but his vision did not include the entire Italian peninsula, only its north and center, which then could dominate the rest of the peninsula in a loose federation. One lesson he had learned from the failures of 1848 was that foreign help, especially French assistance, would be necessary to expel the Austrians from the peninsula.

When the Crimean War broke out in 1854, Cavour steered Piedmont to the allied side, hoping to advance his cause. He sent twenty thousand troops to the Crimea, one-tenth of whom died. This act gained him a seat at the Congress of Paris, where his presence boosted the kingdom's prestige—and where he and Napoleon III had an opportunity to meet and size up each other.

Napoleon III favored the cause of Italian liberation from Austrian rule and some form of unification of the peninsula. Austria had been France's traditional opponent; destroying Austria's power in Italy might strengthen France. Thus in July 1858 the French emperor and the Piedmontese prime minister met secretly at Plombières°, a French spa, to discuss how Italian unity could be achieved. They agreed that Piedmont would stir up trouble in one of Austria's Italian territories in an effort to goad the Austrians into war. France would help the Piedmontese expel Austria from the peninsula, and the new Piedmont, doubled in size, would become part of a confederation under the papacy. In exchange, the French emperor demanded the Piedmontese provinces of Nice° and Savoy, which bordered France.

This demand presented difficulties: Savoy was the heartland of the Piedmont kingdom, the ancestral home of the royal family; and Nice had a mostly Italian, not French, population. Napoleon's other condition was that the king of Piedmont, who headed the oldest reigning house in Europe, the Savoy, allow his 15-year-old daughter to marry the emperor's 38-year-old dissipated cousin. To accept these terms seemed a betrayal of national honor and conventional morality. But scruples gave way to political ambition, and Cavour assented. (See the box "Reading Sources: Cavour Outlines a Deal with Napoleon III.")

War between Austria and Piedmont broke out in April 1859. By June the combined Piedmontese and French forces had routed the Austrians at Magenta and Solferino (see Map 22.1). The bloodiness of these battles impressed contemporaries: the color magenta was named after the deep red of the soaked battlefield, and when a Swiss humanitarian, Henri Dunant° (1828–1901), organized emergency services for both French and Austrians wounded at Solferino, he proposed the founding of voluntary relief societies in every nation, called the Red Cross.

Instead of pressing on after these two victories, Napoleon III decided to end the fighting. He was shocked by the bloodshed he had witnessed and alarmed by the Prussian mobilization on the Rhine on behalf of Austria. In addition, his plan for Italy was threatening to develop in unforeseen directions. Several states in central Italy had appealed for annexation to Piedmont, which would have resulted in a larger inde-

---

risorgimento (ree-sor-djee-MEN-toe)   **Cavour** (kah-VOOR)

Plombières (plom-bee-YAIR)   **Nice** (NEECE)
Dunant (dew-NAN)

Map 22.1 The Unification of Italy, 1859–1870 Piedmontese leadership and nationalist fervor united Italy.

pendent state than Napoleon III had anticipated. These factors led Napoleon to sign an armistice with the Austrians, allowing Austria to remain in northern Italy and participate in an Italian confederation. Cavour was outraged by Napoleon's betrayal and resigned as prime minister; he returned to office, however, in January 1860.

■ Unification Achieved, 1860

Cavour had envisioned no more than a united northern Italy. Unexpected events in the south, however, dramatically expanded that vision. The centuries-old misgovernment of the kingdom of Naples led to an uprising in

☙ READING SOURCES

Cavour Outlines a Deal with Napoleon III

In July 1858 Cavour and Napoleon III met at Plombières in France to plot war against Austria. In this note written to the military aide of the king of Savoy, Cavour reports on the negotiations. The king's young daughter was to be given in marriage to cement the Piedmontese-French alliance. Notice the lack of concern for the 15-year-old princess; she is to be sacrificed on the altar of Realpolitik.

The Emperor entered into many particulars on the problems of the war, which it is my duty to tell you about, and which I shall report to you orally. He seemed to me to have studied the matter rather better than his generals, and to have sensible ideas in that regard. He talked of direct command questions—of how to manage the Pope—of the administrative system for stabilizing the occupied countries—of methods of finance. In a word of all the essential things for our grand project. We were in accord on everything.

The only undefined point is that of the marriage of the Princess Clotilde. The King had authorized me to agree to that, but only in the case that the Emperor had made it a condition *sine qua non* of the alliance. The Emperor not having pushed his insistence to that extreme, I did not, as a gentleman, undertake pledges. But I remain convinced that he lays very great importance on the matrimonial question, and that on it depends, if not the alliance, then its final outcome. It would be an error and a very grave error

to commit oneself to the Emperor and at the same time to give him an affront which would never fade. . . . I have written strongly to the King not to risk the finest undertaking of modern times out of sour aristocratic scruples. I beg you, if he consults you, to join your voice to mine. Perhaps this enterprise should not be attempted, in which the crown of our King and the fate of our people are jeopardized; but if it is attempted, then for the love of heaven let nothing be neglected which could decide the final outcome.

I left Plombières in very serene spirits. If the King consents to the marriage I am confident, let me say almost certain, that within two years you will enter Vienna at the head of our victorious columns.

Source: Letter from Cavour to La Marmora, 24 July 1858, repr. in Mack Walker, ed., *Plombières: Secret Diplomacy and the Rebirth of Italy* (New York: Oxford University Press, 1968), p. 227.

Sicily in April 1860. The revolutionary firebrand Giuseppe Garibaldi° (1807–1882), a rival of Cavour, set sail for Sicily in May 1860, with but a thousand poorly armed, red-shirted followers, to help the island overthrow its Bourbon ruler. Winning that struggle, Garibaldi's forces crossed to the mainland in August. Victory followed victory, and enthusiasm for Garibaldi grew. His army swelled to 57,000 men, and he won the entire kingdom of Naples.

Threatened by the advance of Garibaldi's power and fearing its reach into the Papal States, Cavour sent his army into the area in September 1860. This brutal attack on a weak state that had not harmed Piedmont was viewed by many Catholics as aggression against the

pope and the church. However, as Cavour explained to his parliament, political necessity required it. Morality was less important than the interests of Piedmont and the about-to-be-born Italy. Although Garibaldi was a republican, he was convinced that Italy could best achieve unity under the king of Piedmont, and he willingly submitted the southern part of Italy, which he controlled, to the king, Victor Emmanuel II (r. 1849–1878). Thus by November 1860, Italy had been united under Piedmontese rule (see Map 22.1). The territories that had come under Piedmont's control affirmed their desire to be part of the new Italy in plebiscites based on universal male suffrage. The 1848 constitution of Piedmont became the constitution of the newly united Italy. The statesman who had engineered the nation's unification lived to relish his handiwork only a few months, dying of an undiagnosed

---

Garibaldi (gar-ih-BALL-dee)

Garibaldi Leading His "Red Shirts" to Victory over the Neapolitan Army, May 1860   Garibaldi's successful conquests in the south and Cavour's in the north opened the way for Italian unification. *(Museo di Risorgimento, Milan/Scala/Art Resource, NY)*

illness in May 1861; Cavour's last words were "Italy is made—all is safe."

Still to be joined to the new state were Austrian-held Venetia in the northeast and Rome and its environs, held by the pope with the support of a French garrison. But within a decade, a favorable international situation enabled the fledgling country to acquire both key areas. After Austria was defeated in the Austro-Prussian War in 1866, it ceded Venetia to Italy. Then the Franco-Prussian War forced the French to evacuate Rome, which they had occupied since 1849. Rome was joined to Italy and became its capital in 1870. With that event, unification was complete.

■ The Problems of Unified Italy

National unity had been achieved, but it was frail. The uprisings in the south that had led to its inclusion in a united Italy were motivated more by hatred of the Bour-

bons than by fervor for national union. And once the union was achieved, the north behaved like a conquering state—sending its officials to the south, raising taxes, and imposing its laws. In 1861 an uprising of disbanded Neapolitan soldiers and brigands broke out. To crush the revolt, half the Italian army was sent south; the civil war lasted five years and produced more casualties than the entire effort of unification.

Other major divisions remained. In 1861 only 2.5 percent of the population spoke the national language, Florentine Italian. The economy also remained divided. The north was far more industrialized than the rural south. In the south, child mortality was higher, life expectancy was lower, and illiteracy was close to 90 percent. The two regions seemed to belong to two different nations. Piedmont imposed strong central control, resolutely refusing a federal system of government, which many Italians in an earlier era had hoped for. This choice reflected the determination of Piedmont to project its power onto the rest of the peninsula, as well as fear that any other form of government might lead to disintegration of the new state. The United States, with its federal system of government, was wracked by secessionism so strident that in early 1861 it led to the Civil War (see page 763). Piedmont wanted to save the new Italian state from such a fate.

Piedmont imposed its constitution on unified Italy, which limited suffrage to men of property and education, less than 2 percent of the population. Further, although parliamentarism was enshrined in the constitution, Cavour's maneuvering as prime minister had kept governments from being answerable to the parliament. Instead of parliamentary majorities designating the government, Cavour created majorities in parliament to support the cabinet. He cajoled and bribed parliamentarians, transforming previous foes into supporters. This system of manipulation, known as *trasformismo°*, would characterize Italian government for the next several decades. Nevertheless, the new unified Italy was a liberal state that guaranteed legal equality and freedom of association, and provided more freedom for its citizens than the Italian people had seen for centuries.

The Catholic Church remained hostile to the new Italian state. The popes, left to rule a tiny domain—a few square blocks around the papal palace known as the Vatican—considered themselves prisoners; they denounced their "captor" and all its supporters, including anyone who participated in elections. Thus many Italian Catholics refused to recognize the new state for decades, thwarting its legitimacy. With its 27 million people in 1870, Italy was the sixth-most-populous European nation. It was too small to be a great power and too large to accept being a small state. Italian statesmen found it difficult to define their country's role in international politics, and they lacked a firm consensus on Italy's future.

GERMAN UNIFICATION, 1850–1871

 IKE Italy, Germany had long been a collection of states. Since 1815 the thirty-eight German states had been loosely organized in the German Confederation. Like Piedmont in Italy, one German state, powerful Prussia, led the unification movement. And just as Italy had in Cavour a strong leader who imposed his will, so did German unification have a ruthless and cunning champion: Otto von Bismarck, minister

trasformismo (trass-for-MEES-mo)

president of Prussia. Cavour, however, for all his wiliness was committed to establishing a liberal state; Bismarck, on the other hand, was wedded to autocratic rule.

The revolutionaries of 1848 had failed in their attempt to achieve German unification when the king of Prussia refused to accept a throne offered by the elected Frankfurt Assembly. As the painting at the beginning of this chapter illustrates, German unification was ratified not by the ballot as it was in Italy, but rather by the acclamation of the crowned heads of Germany. The nation was united by the use of military force and the imposition of Prussian absolutism over the whole country.

■ The Rise of Bismarck

Austria under Metternich had always treated Prussia as a privileged junior partner. After Metternich's fall in 1848, however, rivalry erupted between the two German states. Each tried to manipulate for its own benefit the desire for national unity that had become manifest during the revolution of 1848.

In March 1850 a number of German states met in Erfurt to consider unification under Prussian sponsorship. Austria, which had been excluded, insisted that the "Erfurt Union" be dissolved and that Prussia remain in the German Confederation. Austrian leaders, supported by Russia, threatened war. Since the Prussian military was not strong enough to challenge Austria, Prussia agreed to scuttle the Erfurt Union and accept Austrian leadership in Germany. The new Prussian king, Wilhelm I (r. 1861–1888), was determined to strengthen Prussia by expanding the size and effectiveness of the army. He wanted to reduce the reserve army, increase the professional army, and expand the training period from two to three years. These measures needed parliamentary approval, but the parliament, which was dominated by liberals, opposed the increased costs.

When the parliament refused to accept the king's proposals, he dissolved it. But new elections produced an even stronger liberal majority. The issue was not purely military, but rather one of who should govern the country—the king or the elected representatives. To get his way, the king appointed Count Otto von Bismarck as minister president.

Bismarck was a Junker, a Prussian aristocrat known for his reactionary views, who had opposed the liberal movement in 1848. As Prussian emissary to the German Confederation, he had challenged Austrian primacy. Devoted to his monarch, Bismarck sought to heighten Prussian power in Germany and throughout Europe. He faced down the parliament, telling the Budget Commission in 1862, "The position of Prussia in Germany will be

❧ READING SOURCES

Bismarck Lectures Parliament on Royal Prerogatives

In 1862–1863, a showdown pitted the Prussian king against his country's parliament. The latter claimed it had the right to control the budget and, if it wished, to veto the military reforms proposed by the king. The newly appointed minister president, Otto von Bismarck, insisted that the king had the final word. Prussia was not going to submit to parliamentarism, as Britain had.

If you, gentlemen, had the exclusive right finally to determine the total amount and the particulars of the budget, if you had the right to demand of His Majesty the King the dismissal of those ministers who do not retain your confidence, if you had the right through your resolutions concerning the budget to determine the strength and organization of the army, if you had the right—as constitutionally you do not have, although you claim it in the Address—to control the relationship of the executive power of the government to its officials, then you would in fact possess the complete governmental power in this country (Prussia). Your Address is based upon these claims, if it has any basis at all. I believe, therefore, that its practical significance can be characterized in a few words: "Through this Address the Royal House of Hohenzollern is requested to transfer its constitutional governing rights to the majority of this House.". . .

You know as well as anyone in Prussia that the ministry acts in Prussia in the name of and on behalf of His Majesty the King, and that in this sense it has executed those acts in which you see a violation of the constitution. You know that in this connection a

Prussian ministry has a different position from that of the English. An English ministry, call it what you will, is a parliamentary one, a ministry of the parliamentary majority; but we are ministers of His Majesty the King. . . . Theories about what is lawful when no budget is passed have been advanced, and I do not intend to evaluate them here. . . .

It is sufficient for me to recognize the necessity of state and not pessimistically allow to come to pass a situation in which the treasury is closed. Necessity alone is decisive, and we have taken this necessity into account . . . we shall reject, and we shall steadfastly protect the rights of the Crown against your claims.

The Prussian monarchy has not yet fulfilled its mission; it is not yet ripe for becoming a purely ornamental decoration of your constitutional edifice, not yet ready to be integrated like a lifeless, mechanical part into the mechanism of a parliamentary regime.

Source: Bismarck Speech to the Prussian Parliament, January 27, 1863, repr. in Eugene N. Anderson, Stanley Pincetl, Jr., and Donald Ziegler, eds. *Europe in the Nineteenth Century—A Documentary Analysis of Change and Conflict,* Vol. I (Indianapolis: Bobbs Merrill, 1961), pp. 261–262, 265–267.

---

decided not by its liberalism but by its power . . . not through speeches and majority decisions are the great questions of the day decided—that was the mistake of 1848 and 1849—but by iron and blood."[1]

Bismarck tried to win over the liberals by suggesting that with military force at its disposal, Prussia could lead German unification. But the liberals resisted, and the parliament voted against the military reforms. Unphased, Bismarck carried out the military measures anyway and ordered the collection of the necessary taxes. (See the box "Reading Sources: Bismarck Lectures Parlia-

ment on Royal Prerogatives.") The citizens acquiesced, and paid to upgrade their army.

German liberals faced a dilemma: Which did they value more: the goal of nationhood or the principles of liberty? Fellow liberals elsewhere lived in existing nation-states in which statehood had preceded the development of liberalism. And in Italy, unification had been led by the liberal state of Piedmont. That was not the case in Germany, where the natural leader, Prussia, had a long tradition of militarism and authoritarianism. To oppose Bismarck effectively, German liberals knew they would have to join with the working classes, but they feared them and forestalled such an alliance. Germany appeared embarked on an illiberal course.

Bismarck's genius was to exploit the growing desire for German unification. During the Franco-Austrian War of 1859 that launched Italian unification, Germans had feared that the French would attack across the Rhine River. Many came to believe that only a strong, united Germany could give its inhabitants security. Economically a united Germany was developing under Prussian leadership with the *Zollverein*, a customs union of most German states, excluding Austria. Founded in 1834, the customs union had become more extensive with the passage of time; even states that were politically hostile to Prussia joined to protect their economic interests. Germans began to think in all-German terms. Professional and cultural organizations now often extended beyond a single state to the wider, "national" context: the German Commercial Association, the Congress of German Jurists, and the German Sharpshooters League, for example. Although it had yet to find much resonance among the lower classes, the idea of a united Germany had gained a substantial audience by the 1860s.

■ Prussian Wars and German Unity

Having established the supremacy of royal power in Prussia, Bismarck was ready to enlarge Prussia's role in Germany at the expense of Austria. A crisis over Schleswig-Holstein° (see Map 22.2) gave him an opening. These two provinces, ethnically and linguistically German (except for northern Schleswig), were ruled by the king of Denmark. Historically and by previous treaty agreements, Schleswig and Holstein were legally inseparable. When in 1863 the Danish king, contrary to earlier treaty obligations, attempted to annex Schleswig to Denmark, Holstein felt threatened. Holstein was a member of the German Confederation, so it called on the confederation for protection. Acting on behalf of the confederation, Prussia and Austria intervened, sending troops that won a quick, cheap victory. Prussia occupied Schleswig, and Austria took Holstein.

Prussia and Austria continued to be bitter rivals for domination of Germany. Bismarck believed war was the only means to win this contest, and conflicts over the administration of Schleswig and Holstein served as a pretext. With no declaration of war, Prussia attacked Austrian-administered Holstein in June 1866. The Austro-Prussian War lasted a scant seven weeks. The de-

cisive victory of the new, reformed Prussian army was the Battle of Sadowa° on July 3. With a much more advanced industry than Austria, Prussia had equipped its soldiers with the new breech-loading rifles, known as needle guns; their advantage was that troops could fire from a prone position, while the Austrians, with their muzzle loaders, had to stand up to shoot. Prussia's superiority in arms and Moltke's superb military leadership defeated Austria, forcing it to accept peace on Prussian terms.

Prussia annexed its smaller neighbors who had supported Austria, creating a contiguous state linking Prussia with the Rhineland. In Bismarck's scheme this enlarged Prussia would dominate the newly formed North German Confederation, comprising all the states north of the Main° River. From now on, Austria was excluded from German affairs.

The triumph of Sadowa made Bismarck a popular hero. Elections held on the day of the battle returned a conservative pro-Bismarck majority to the Prussian parliament. The legislature, including a large number of liberals mesmerized by the military victory, voted to legalize retroactively the illegal taxes that had been levied since 1862 to upgrade the military. Enthusiastic at the prospect of achieving German unity at last, most liberals compromised their principles. They rationalized that national unity ought to be gained first, with liberal constitutional institutions secured later. Their optimism proved to be a miscalculation.

The unification of Germany, like that of Italy, was facilitated by a favorable international situation. The Crimean War had estranged Russia from Austria. In 1850 Austrian resistance to Prussian attempts to lead Germany had been backed by Russia, but by the time the Austro-Prussian War broke out in 1866, Austria stood alone. Although it would have been opportune for France to intervene on the Austrian side, the French emperor was indecisive and in the end did nothing. He also had been lulled into inaction by vague Prussian promises of support for French plans to annex Luxembourg. Once the war was won, Bismarck reneged on these promises. France was left with the problem of a strong, enlarged Prussia on its eastern border, which threatened France's position as a Great Power. British leaders likewise did not intervene in the unification process. Disillusioned by the results of the Crimean War, they were in an isolationist mood. Moreover, Britain's government was sympathetic to the rise of a fellow Protestant power.

Bismarck's design was almost complete. Only the southern German states remained outside the North

---

Schleswig (SHLES-vik)   **Holstein** (HOLL-shteyn)   **Sadowa** (SAH-doe-wah)   **Main** (MINE)

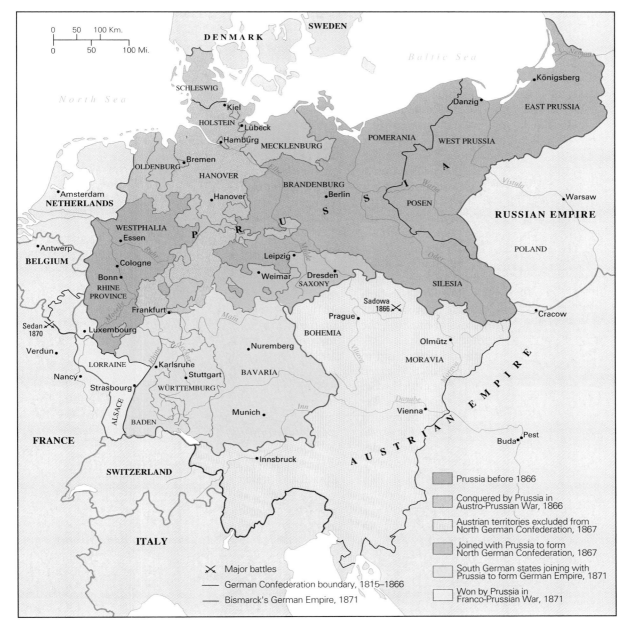

Map 22.2   The Unification of Germany, 1866–1871   A series of military victories made it possible for Prussia to unite Germany under its domain.

German Confederation. He obliged them to sign a military treaty with Prussia and established a customs parliament for all the members of the Zollverein (the customs union), including the southern German states. The southern states, which were Catholic and sympathetic to Austria, were reluctant to see German unity advance any further. Only some dramatic event could remove their resistance.

■ The Franco-Prussian War and Unification, 1870–1871

French leaders were also determined to prevent German unity. They feared the loss of influence in the southern German states that had traditionally been France's allies. Moreover, since the mid-seventeenth century, French security had relied on a weak and divided Germany.

Both Berlin and Paris anticipated war. And war came soon enough, precipitated by a crisis over the Spanish succession. In 1868 a military coup had overthrown the Spanish queen Isabella, and the provisional government offered the throne to a Catholic member of the Hohenzollerns°, the reigning Prussian monarch's family. The French viewed this candidacy as an unacceptable expansion of Prussian power and influence. Fearing a two-front war with Prussia in the east and Spain in the south, they insisted the Hohenzollerns refuse the proffered throne. As passions heated, Bismarck was elated at the prospect of war. But King Wilhelm was not. On July 12, 1870, he engineered the withdrawal of the young prince's candidacy, removing the cause for war. Bismarck was bitterly disappointed.

Not content with this diplomatic victory, the French pushed their luck further. On July 13 the French ambassador met the king of Prussia at Ems and demanded guarantees that no Hohenzollern would ever again be a candidate for the Spanish throne. Unable to provide any more concessions without a serious loss of prestige, the Prussian king refused the French petition.

Wilhelm telegraphed an account of his meeting to Chancellor Bismarck. The chancellor immediately seized the opportunity this message provided. He edited what became known as the Ems dispatch, making the exchange between king and ambassador seem more curt than it actually had been; then he released it to the press. As he hoped, the French interpreted the report as a deliberate snub to their ambassador and overreacted. Napoleon III was deluged with emotional demands that he avenge the imagined slight to French national honor; on July 15 he declared war.

The Prussians led a well-planned campaign. An army of 384,000 Prussians was rushed by rail to confront a force of 270,000 Frenchmen. The French had the advantage of better rifles, but the Prussians were equipped with heavier cannon, which could pulverize French positions from a distance. Within a few weeks, Prussia won a decisive victory at Sedan°, taking the French emperor prisoner on September 2. The French continued the struggle, despite difficult odds. Infuriated by the continuation of the war, the Prussians resorted to extreme measures. They took hostages and burned down whole villages, and they laid siege to Paris, starving and bombarding its beleaguered population.

Throughout Germany the outbreak of the war aroused general enthusiasm for the Prussian cause. Exploiting this popular feeling, Bismarck called on leaders of the southern German states to accept the unification of Germany under the Prussian king. Reluctant princes, such as the king of Bavaria, were bought off with bribes. On January 18, 1871, the German princes met in the Hall of Mirrors at the Versailles palace, symbol of past French greatness, and acclaimed the Prussian king as German emperor, Kaiser Wilhelm I.

In May 1871 the Treaty of Frankfurt established the peace terms (see Map 22.1). France was forced to give up the provinces of Alsace and Lorraine and to pay Germany a heavy indemnity of 5 billion francs. These harsh terms embittered the French, leading many to desire revenge and establishing a formidable barrier to future Franco-German relations.

■ The Character of the New Germany

German unity had been won through a series of wars—against Denmark in 1864, Austria in 1866, and France in 1870. The military had played a key role in forging German unity, and it remained a dominant force in the new nation. Italian unity had been sanctioned by plebiscites and a vote by an elected assembly accepting the popular verdict. The founding act of the new German state, as the opening illustration to this chapter shows, was the acclamation of the German emperor by German rulers on the soil of a defeated neighbor. Thus the rulers placed themselves above elected assemblies and popular sanction.

On the surface the constitution of the new Germany was remarkably democratic. It provided for an upper, appointed house, the *Bundesrat*°, representing the individual German states, and a lower house, the *Reichstag*°, which was elected by universal manhood suffrage. The latter might seem a surprising concession from Bismarck, the authoritarian aristocrat. But he knew the liberals lacked mass support and gambled that, with appropriate appeals, he would be able to create majorities that could be manipulated for his purposes.

The dominant state in the new Germany was, of course, Prussia, which was home to two-thirds of its population. The king of Prussia occupied the post of emperor, and the chancellor and other cabinet members were responsible not to parliament but to him. Only the emperor could make foreign policy and war, command the army, and interpret the constitution. The authoritarianism of Prussia had been projected onto all of Germany.

The emergence of a strong, united Germany shattered the European balance of power. In February 1871

Hohenzollerns (HO-en-tsoll-ernz)   **Sedan** (seh-DAEN)

Bundesrat (BOON-tes-raht)   **Reichstag** (RYSH-stak)

the British political leader Benjamin Disraeli observed that the unification of Germany was a "greater political event than the French revolution of last century. . . . There is not a diplomatic tradition which has not been swept away. You have a new world. . . . The balance of power has been entirely destroyed."[2] Germany had become the dominant power on the Continent.

PRECARIOUS EMPIRES

T HE three large empires of central and eastern Europe, battered by aggressive behavior from other European states and challenged by internal tensions, attempted to weather the endless crises they confronted. The Austrian, Ottoman, and Russian Empires labored to fortify their regimes with political reforms, restructuring their institutions, but only Austria tried to accommodate democratic impulses by establishing a parliament. The Ottoman sultans and the Russian tsars clung tenaciously to their autocratic traditions.

■ The Dual Monarchy in Austria-Hungary

Emperor Franz Joseph (r. 1848–1916) had come to the throne as an 18-year-old in that year of crisis, 1848. He was a well-meaning monarch who took his duties seriously. His upbringing was German, he lived in German-speaking Vienna, and he headed an army and a bureaucracy that was mostly German, but Franz Joseph was markedly cosmopolitan. He spoke several of his subjects' languages and thought of himself as the emperor of all his peoples. A much-loved, regal figure, Franz Joseph provided a visible symbol of the state. He lacked imagination, however, and did little more than try to conserve a disintegrating empire coping with the modern forces of liberalism and nationalism.

After the war with Piedmont and France (see page 746), Austrian statesmen sensed the vulnerability of their empire. To give the government credibility, in February 1861, Franz Joseph issued what became known as the February Patent, which guaranteed civil liberties and provided for local self-government and an elected parliament.

The need to safeguard the remaining territories was clear. By 1866 the Austrian Habsburgs were no longer a German or Italian power (Venetia had been handed over to a united Italy). The strongest challenge to Habsburg rule came from Hungary, where the Magyars insisted on self-rule, a claim based on age-old rights and Vienna's

initial acceptance of autonomy in 1848. Since Magyar cooperation was crucial for the well-being of the Habsburg Empire, the government entered into lengthy negotiations with Magyar leaders in 1867. Empress Elizabeth, sympathetic to the Magyars, helped convince the emperor to take a conciliatory stance. The outcome was "the Compromise of 1867," creating new structures for the empire that lasted until 1918. The agreement divided the Habsburg holdings into Austria in the west and Hungary in the east (see Map 22.3). Each was independent, but they were linked by the person of the emperor of Austria, Franz Joseph, who was also king of Hungary. Hungary had full internal autonomy and participated jointly in imperial affairs—state finance, defense, and foreign relations. The new state created in 1867 was known as the dual monarchy of Austria-Hungary.

The compromise confirmed Magyar dominance in Hungary. Although numerically a minority, Magyars controlled the Hungarian parliament, the army, the bureaucracy, and other state institutions. They opposed self-rule by the Croats, Serbs, Slovaks, Romanians, and others in the kingdom and attempted a policy of Magyarization—teaching only Magyar in the schools, conducting all government business in Magyar, and giving access to government positions only to those fully assimilated in Magyar culture. This arrangement created frustrations and resistance among the various nationalities under their rule.

The terms of the compromise also gave the Hungarians a voice in imperial foreign policy. Magyars feared that Slavic groups outside the empire, who planned to form independent states or had already done so, would inspire fellow Slavs in Austria-Hungary to revolt. To prevent that, the Hungarians favored an expansionist foreign policy in the Balkans, which the monarchy embraced (see Map 22.3). Having lost its influence in Germany, Austria-Hungary saw the Balkans as an area in which to assert itself. The policy was fraught with risks and, by bringing more discontented Slavs into the empire, led to hostility with other states.

■ The Ailing Ottoman Empire

At midcentury the Ottoman Empire was still one of the largest European powers, but it faced unrest within its borders and threats from the expansionist designs of its neighbors. The ailing empire was commonly referred to as "the sick man of Europe." Over the next twenty-five years, the empire shed some of its territory and modernized its government, but nothing could save it from decline in the face of nationalist uprisings in its Balkan possessions.

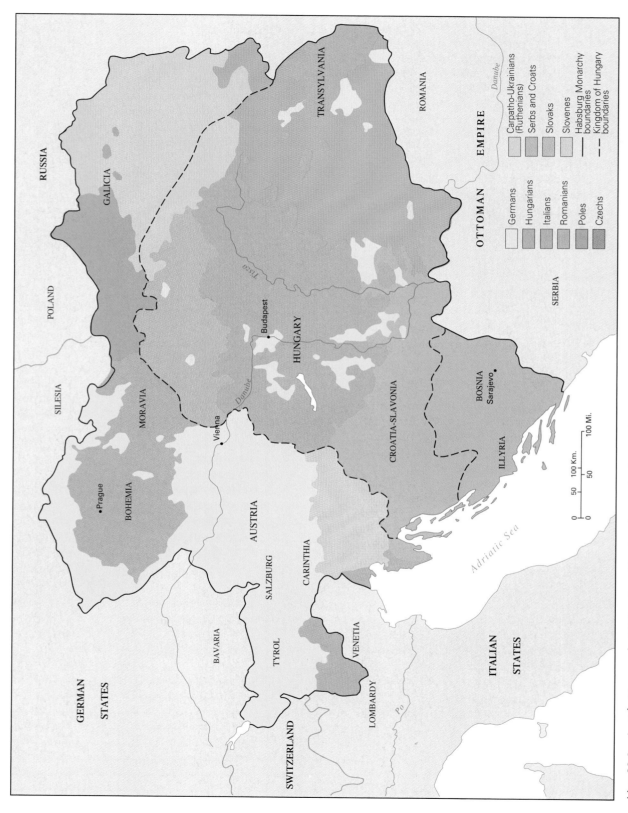

Map 22.3 Austria-Hungary in 1878 A multinational state, the Austro-Hungarian Empire occupied Bosnia in 1878, bringing more dissatisfied peoples under its rule. Tensions in the Balkans would lead to the outbreak of world war in 1914.

Legend:

Germans
Hungarians
Italians
Romanians
Poles
Czechs
Carpatho-Ukrainians (Ruthenians)
Serbs and Croats
Slovaks
Slovenes
Habsburg Monarchy boundaries
Kingdom of Hungary boundaries

Map labels:

RUSSIA
OTTOMAN EMPIRE
GERMAN STATES
ITALIAN STATES
SWITZERLAND
GALICIA
POLAND
SILESIA
MORAVIA
BOHEMIA
Prague
Vienna
AUSTRIA
SALZBURG
BAVARIA
TYROL
CARINTHIA
VENETIA
LOMBARDY
Po
Adriatic Sea
ILLYRIA
CROATIA-SLAVONIA
BOSNIA
Sarajevo
SERBIA
ROMANIA
TRANSYLVANIA
HUNGARY
Budapest
Danube
Tisza
100 Mi.
100 Km.
50
50
0
0

As early as the 1840s, the Ottoman Empire had begun various reform movements to bring more security to its subjects. Known as the *Tanzimat°*, these changes were initiated by Sultan Abdul Mejid° (r. 1839–1861), with the help of his able prime minister, Reshid Mustafa Pasha° (1800–1858). Reshid had served as the Ottoman ambassador in London and Paris and was familiar with Western institutions, which he admired and wished to emulate. The reforms introduced security of property, equity in taxation, and equality before the law regardless of religion. Government officials—who previously had been free to collect taxes arbitrarily, sending the required amount to the central government and keeping the rest—were given fixed salaries and subjected to regular inspections.

These reforms were strengthened after the Crimean War by further imperial edicts. Contacts with the West encouraged Turks to think of transforming their empire into a more modern, Westernized state. Many young intellectuals were impatient with the pace of change, however, and critical of the sultan. Unable freely to express their opinions at home, some went into exile in the late 1860s to Paris and London. Their hosts called them the "Young Turks," an expression that became synonymous with activists for change and improvement.

Alarmed by challenges to its authority, the central government began to turn away from reform, and in 1871 the sultan decided to assert his personal rule. His inability successfully to wage war and hold onto the empire led to dissatisfaction, and in the spring of 1876 rioters demanded and won the establishment of constitutional government. Within a year, however, the new sultan, Abdul Hamid II (r. 1876–1909), dismissed the constitutional government and reverted to personal rule.

Part of the administration's problem was financial. The Crimean War had forced the empire to borrow money abroad. The easy terms of foreign credit lured the sultan into taking out huge loans to finance extravagant projects. By 1875 more than half the annual income of the empire went to pay the interest on the debt. In spite of a drought and famine, the authorities raised taxes, fostering widespread discontent.

Opposition to the government increased, fueled by nationalist fervor. The empire tolerated religious diversity and did not persecute people because of their religion. But the central administration had lost control over its provincial officials, who were often corrupt and tyran-

nical. Christians, the majority population in the Balkans, blamed their suffering on Islamic rule, and many were inspired by the 1821 Greek war of independence and the revolutions of 1848 to seek their own independence.

The Romanians, who lived mainly in the adjoining provinces of Moldavia in the north and Wallachia° in the south, began to express nationalist sentiments in the late eighteenth century. These sentiments were nurtured by Western-educated students, who claimed for their countrymen illustrious descent from Roman settlers of antiquity. News of revolution in Paris in 1848 helped trigger a revolt in both provinces demanding unification and independence. This uprising was quickly crushed by the Turks.

In 1856 the Congress of Paris removed Russia's right of protection over Moldavia and Wallachia and provided for a referendum to determine their future. In 1859 the two provinces chose a local military officer, Alexander Cuza° (r. 1859–1866), as ruler of each territory. In 1862, the Ottoman Empire recognized the union of the two principalities in the single, autonomous state of Romania. At the Congress of Berlin in 1878, Romania's full independence was recognized. Thus, in less than a quarter-century, two provinces of the Ottoman Empire had gained full sovereignty.

The path to independence was much more violent for the Bulgarians. Influenced by neighboring Serbia and encouraged by the Russians, revolutionary committees spread propaganda and agitated against Ottoman rule. An uprising in Bulgaria broke out in May 1876. The Christian rebels attacked not only symbols of Ottoman authority but also peaceable Turks living in their midst. The imperial army, aided by local Turk volunteers, quickly re-established Ottoman authority. Incensed by the massacre of fellow Muslims, the volunteers resorted to mass killing, looting, and burning of Christian villages. The "Bulgarian horrors" shocked Europe and made the continuation of Turkish rule unacceptable.

The Bulgarian crisis was resolved by the Balkan wars of 1876–1878, which were provoked by the uprising of the westernmost Ottoman provinces of Bosnia and Herzegovina. Since many of the inhabitants of these two provinces were Serbs, they had the sympathy of Serbia, which hoped to unify the southern Slavs. Together with the neighboring mountain state of Montenegro, Serbia declared war on the Ottoman Empire. They were savagely defeated by the Turks.

Russia, which saw itself as the protector of the Slavic peoples, reacted to the Bulgarian horrors by declaring

---

Tanzimat (tan-zee-MAT)   **Abdul Mejid** (Ab-DOOL med-JEED)
Reshid Mustafa Pasha (ray-SHEED moo-STAH-fah PAH-shah)

Wallachia (vall-AK-yah)   **Cuza** (KOO-sah)

Nationalistic Uprising in Bulgaria   In this 1879 lithograph, Bulgaria is depicted in the form of a maiden—protected by the Russian eagle, breaking her chains, and winning liberty from the Ottoman Empire.   *(St. Cyril and Methodius National Library, Sofia)*

war on the empire in April 1877. At first progress was slow; then the Russians broke through the Turkish lines and forced the sultan to sue for peace. The resulting Treaty of San Stefano, signed in March 1878, created a huge, independent Bulgaria as essentially a Russian protectorate.

The British, Austrians, and French were shocked at the extent to which the San Stefano treaty favored Russia. Under their pressure, the European powers met in Berlin in 1878 to reconsider the treaty. The Congress of Berlin reduced the size of the Bulgarian territory, returning the rest to the Ottomans. Bosnia and Herzegovina were removed from Ottoman rule, henceforth to be administered by Austria-Hungary (see Map 24.4 on page 837). The sultan was forced to acknowledge the legal independence of Serbia, Montenegro, and Romania and

the autonomy of Bulgaria. The British insisted on being allowed to administer the island of Cyprus in the eastern Mediterranean as an outpost for checking further Russian challenges to the existing balance of power.

Thus Turkey was plundered, not only by its enemies but also by powers that had intervened on its behalf. When France complained that it received no compensation, it was given the chance to grab Tunisia, another land under Ottoman rule. Russia, which had signed an alliance with Romania and promised to respect its territorial integrity, ignored its obligations and took southern Bessarabia from its ally. The devious work of the congress reflected the power politics that now characterized international affairs. Statesmen shamelessly used force against both foe and friend for the aggrandizement of their own states. Neither morality nor international law restrained ambition.

■ Russia and the Great Reforms

Russia's defeat in the Crimean War and its distrust of the Western powers forced the tsar to consider ways of strengthening Russia by restructuring its institutions. Beginning in 1861, a series of measures known collectively as the Great Reforms began to change the face of Russia.

Already by the 1840s, concern about the archaic nature and structure of Russian government was mounting. Many officials lamented the tendency of a timid bureaucracy to lie to and mislead the public. Defeat in the Crimean War widened the critique of Russian institutions. Calls for *glasnost*—greater openness—became the leading motif in the Great Reforms. The chief problem that needed resolution was serfdom. Educated opinion had long denounced serfdom as immoral, but conscience was not the principal reason for its abolition. Serfdom was abolished because it presented clear disadvantages in both the domestic and international domains. The new tsar, Alexander II (r. 1855–1881), feared that if serfdom was not abolished from above, it would be overthrown from below—by a serf rebellion that would sweep away everything in its path, including the autocracy itself.

Serfdom also held Russia back in its competition with the rest of the world. Defeat in the Crimean War by Britain and France suggested that soldiers with a stake in their society fought harder than men bound to lifetime servitude. In addition, the victorious Western states had won in part because their industrial might translated into more and better guns, ammunition, and transportation. Industrial progress required a mobile labor force,

ॐ R E A D I N G   S O U R C E S

The Tsar Demands the Freeing of the Serfs

In January 1861, Tsar Alexander II addressed the Council of State, an advisory body that he had asked four years earlier to prepare a draft law emancipating the serfs. After this forceful speech, a workable proposal emerged that was implemented six weeks later. Notice that the council's opinion is only advisory; the tsar is indicating his "absolute will." While he gives lip service to the serfs' interests, the power of Russia and the future of the tsarist regime are Alexander's prime concerns.

The matter of the liberation of the serfs, which has been submitted for the consideration of the State Council, I consider to be a vital question for Russia, upon which will depend the development of her strength and power. . . . [T]his matter cannot be postponed . . . I repeat—and this is my absolute will—that this matter should be finished right away. . . .

[Y]ou will assure yourselves that all that can be done for the protection of the interests of the nobility has been done . . . but I ask you only not to forget that the basis of the whole work must be the improvement of the life of the peasants—an improvement not in words alone or on paper but in actual fact. . . .

My predecessors felt all the evils of serfdom and continually endeavored, if not to destroy it completely, to work toward the gradual limitation of the arbitrary power of the estate owners.

Already in 1856, before the coronation, while in Moscow I called the attention of the leaders of the nobility of the Moscow *guberniia* [region] to the necessity for them to occupy themselves with improving the life of the serfs, adding that serfdom could not continue forever and that it would therefore be better if the transformation took place from above rather than from below. . . .

I have the right to demand one thing from you: that you, putting aside all personal interests, act not like estate owners but like imperial statesmen invested with my trust. Approaching this important matter I have not concealed from myself all those difficulties that awaited us and I do not conceal them now.

Source: Speech of January 28, 1861, in George Vernadsky et al., eds., *A Sourcebook for Russian History from Early Times to 1917*, vol. 3. Copyright © 1972. Reprinted by permission of the publisher, Yale University Press.

---

not one tied to the soil by serfdom. With a free labor force, rural populations, as in the West, could become the abundant labor supply that drove industrial production. Many educated Russians felt that the defeat in the Crimea had revealed Russia's general backwardness. To catch up with the West, they argued, Russia needed to shed its timeworn institutions, particularly serfdom.

In April 1861 Alexander II issued a decree freeing the serfs. (See the box "Reading Sources: The Tsar Demands the Freeing of the Serfs.") At one stroke, he emancipated 22 million people from a system that allowed them to be bought and sold, separated from their families, and treated in the cruelest ways imaginable. Emancipation represented a compromise with the gentry, which had re-

luctantly agreed to liberate its serfs but insisted on compensation. As a result, the newly liberated peasants had to reimburse the government with mortgage payments lasting fifty years. The peasants received some land, but its value was vastly overrated and its quantity insufficient for peasant families. To make ends meet, most freed peasants continued working for their former masters.

The mortgage payments and taxes imposed on the peasants by the central government were handled by the local commune, the *mir*°. The mir determined how the land was to be used, and it paid collectively for the mortgage and taxes on the land. As a consequence,

---

mir (MEER)

A Critique of Russian Serfdom   The French artist Gustave Doré reveals how landowners viewed their serfs as mere property that could be won and lost with a draw of the cards.
(Miriam and Ira D. Wallach Division of Art, Prints and Photographs, The New York Public Library, Astor, Lenox and Tilden Foundations)

the commune was reluctant for the peasants to leave the land, and they could do so only with its permission. Freed from serfdom, the peasants still suffered many constraints. In fact, the emancipation declaration was accompanied by massive peasant uprisings that had to be put down by force.

The tsar and his advisers feared the large mass of uneducated peasants as a potential source of anarchy and rebellion. They depended on the mir to preserve control even though the commune system had some inherent economic disadvantages. Since increased productivity benefited the commune as much as the individual peasant, there was little incentive for peasants to improve their land, and agricultural yields remained low.

Alexander, lauded as the "tsar emancipator" by his contemporaries, remained wedded to the principles of autocracy. His aim in abolishing serfdom and introducing other reforms was to modernize and strengthen Russia and stabilize his divinely mandated rule. Like most Russians, Alexander believed that only the firm hand of autocracy could hold together a large, ethnically diverse

country. The peasant uprisings that accompanied emancipation only confirmed his beliefs. Clearly, however, the sudden freedom of 22 million illiterate peasants threatened to overwhelm existing institutions, and some changes had to be made. Although he surrendered no powers, Alexander did institute a number of reforms, altering the government and the judicial and military systems so they could deal more effectively with the totally remodeled Russian society.

Government reform had paramount importance. Between 1800 and 1850, the Russian population had increased from 36 to 59 million, and it had become more and more difficult to administer this vast country. Overcentralized, with a poorly trained civil service, the government was unable to cope effectively with the problems of its people. Emancipation of the serfs greatly exacerbated this situation. Thus in 1864 a law was passed providing for local governments, or *zemstvos°*, at

---

zemstvos (SEMST-vose)

the village and regional levels, giving Russians the authority and the opportunity to use initiative in local matters.

The zemstvos were largely controlled by the gentry and not particularly democratic. They were forbidden to debate political issues, and their decisions could be overridden or ignored by local officials appointed by the tsar. Some hoped that zemstvos could become the basis for self-government at the national level and looked for the creation of an all-Russian zemstvo, but such hopes were firmly squelched by the tsar, who jealously insisted on undivided and undiminished autocracy. Nonetheless, the zemstvos were a viable attempt to modernize an overburdened central government.

The tsar also created an independent judiciary that ensured equality before the law, public jury trials, and uniform sentences. Russian political leaders recognized that public confidence in the judiciary and the rule of law was a prerequisite for the development of commerce and industry. Businessmen would no longer fear arbitrary intervention by capricious officials and could develop enterprises in greater security.

In addition, censorship of the press was abolished. Under the previous tsar, Nicholas I, all ideas that did not conform to government policy were censored. Such censorship prevented the central government from being well informed about public opinion or about the effects of its policies on the country. Under Alexander, openness in the press was viewed as a remedy for corruption and misuse of power. People could be punished only for specific violations after publication, and they would face trial in an independent court.

Reform also extended to the Russian army. Its structure and methods became more Western. Military service, previously limited to peasants, became the obligation of all Russian men. All men submitted to a lottery, and those with an "unlucky" number entered the service. In an effort to make military service more attractive, the length of service was drastically cut and corporal punishment was abolished. Access to the officer corps was to be by merit rather than by social connection. The Ministry of War also improved the system of reserves, enabling Russia to mobilize a larger army with more modern weapons in case of war.

The Great Reforms represented considerable change for Russia. Serfdom had been abolished, self-government was established on the local level, the rule of law was adopted, and army service was made more humane. But above the change, the tsarist regime remained autocratic and repressive, flexible only to the degree that its rulers had the will and wisdom to be.

THE EMERGENCE OF NEW POLITICAL FORMS IN THE UNITED STATES AND CANADA, 1840–1880

 CROSS the seas a new power emerged in these years, the United States. It enlarged its territories, strengthened its national government, and broadened its democracy by including a large category of people previously excluded from the political process—African Americans. But these achievements were the result of the bloodiest conflict in all of American history, the Civil War.

■ Territorial Expansion and Slavery

In the early years of its existence, the United States was confined to the land east of the Mississippi River, but in the nineteenth century it gained much territory through westward expansion (see Map 22.4). In 1803 President Thomas Jefferson secured the Louisiana Purchase from the French, which nearly doubled the size of the United States. In 1819 Florida was acquired from Spain. Some Americans looked even farther westward. Some began to insist that the United States had a "manifest destiny" to occupy the whole North American continent from coast to coast.

The U.S. government used the settlements of American citizens in Mexican- and British-held territories as pretexts for expansion. In 1845 Congress voted to annex Texas, which had gained independence from Mexico in 1836. As a result of negotiation with Britain, the United States in 1846 acquired Oregon country south of the forty-ninth parallel. Declaring war on Mexico in the same year, and quickly winning, the United States added California and the Southwest in 1848. Manifest destiny or not, the United States now spanned the continent from the Atlantic to the Pacific.

Beginning in the 1820s the United States saw serious sectional clashes between east and west as well as north and south. The latter were more important. Many issues divided the two regions, notably a conflict between the industrial interests of the North and the agrarian interests of the South. What sharpened this divide, however, was the issue of slavery. As the United States annexed new territories, the question of whether they would be slave or free divided the nation. The North opposed the extension of the "peculiar institution," while much of the South favored it. Southerners believed that if the new areas were closed to slavery, the institution would weaken in the South; slaveholding would eventually disappear, and with it southern prosperity. They would then be unable to withstand the political and economic pressure of an economically richer and more populous North, unsympathetic to slavery.

The issue of slavery was passionately debated for decades. Some Americans wanted slavery abolished throughout the United States; if that could not be done, some of the most committed abolitionists, especially in New England, advocated the secession of free states from the Union. On the other side, southerners threatened that if their way of life—meaning a society based on slavery—were not assured, then the South would secede. The threat of secession was lightly and frequently made by partisans of various causes for many decades.

In November 1860 Illinois Republican Abraham Lincoln (1809–1865) was elected president in a highly contested four-way race. Lincoln opposed the spread of slavery beyond its existing borders and hence appeared to threaten its future in the South itself. For many southerners his election to the highest office was the final blow.

Beginning in December 1860 most southern state legislatures voted to secede from the Union, forming in February 1861 the Confederate States of America. The South defined its cause as defending states' rights, claiming that the people of each state had the right to determine their destiny, free from what they viewed as the tyranny of the national government. Southern states seized federal funds and property, and in April 1861 the Confederates bombarded federally held Fort Sumter. Lincoln, inaugurated in March 1861, was determined to preserve the Union and to put down the insurrection. The long-dreaded civil war had begun.

Map 22.4   U.S. Expansion Through 1853   In eight short years, from 1845 to 1853, the United States increased its territorial size by a third. The principle of manifest destiny appeared to be fulfilled, as the United States now stretched from the Atlantic to the Pacific.

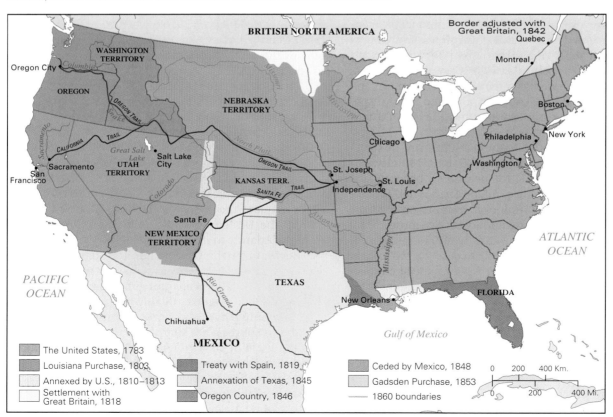

■ Civil War and National Unity, 1861–1865

The North had many advantages. It had nearly three times as many people as the South, a strong industrial base that could supply an endless stream of weapons, and a far more extensive rail system for transporting men and materiel to the front. Although blue and gray armies clashed in a number of important military engagements, the North effectively blockaded the South, leading it toward the end of the war to be desperately short of men, money, and supplies.

During the war, Lincoln's government took measures that centralized power in Washington, changing the nation from a loose federation of states to a more centrally governed entity. As one historian has noted, the United States changed from "they" to "it." The federal government intruded into areas of life from which it had before been absent. With the National Banking Act of 1863, state banks were driven out of business and replaced by a uniform national banking system. The federal government provided massive subsidies for a national railroad system. Lincoln established the National Academy of Sciences to advise him on scientific matters. The word *national* came into increasing use. Senator John Sherman of Ohio declared during the war that "the policy of this country ought to be to make everything national as far as possible."

When the main Confederate army surrendered in 1865, the principle of state sovereignty, proclaimed by the South, was roundly defeated. With the passage of the Thirteenth Amendment to the U.S. Constitution the same year, slaves, previously considered property, were declared to be free. The North occupied the South in an attempt to "reconstruct" it. Reconstruction included efforts to root out the Confederate leadership and ensure full civil and political rights for the newly emancipated African Americans. The government also embarked on a short-lived campaign to provide freed slaves with enough land to ensure them a livelihood— another example of federal authority at work. At the end of Reconstruction, federal power retreated and many states with impunity denied African Americans their rights. But certainly the nation was more centralized, and its citizens were more enfranchised, after the Civil War than before.

■ The Frontiers of Democracy

One of the major transformations in the United States from the 1820s through the 1860s was the inclusion of an ever greater number of people in the political process. By the late 1820s, under the impact of popular pressure, states abandoned restrictions on voting, and most adult white men received the vote. Symbolic of this new "age of the common man" was the election of Andrew Jackson as U.S. president in 1828. All his predecessors had been men of education and property—some were even described as "Virginia aristocrats"—but Jackson represented himself as a self-made man, a rugged frontiersman. State legislatures had in the past elected members to the presidential Electoral College, but in response to public calls for change, state legislatures altered the system so that Electoral College members were selected by direct popular vote.

National presidential campaigns became rough-and-tumble affairs, with emotional appeals to the public. Scurrilous attacks, many untrue, were mounted against opponents. In 1828, for instance, during President John Quincy Adams's re-election campaign, his opponents charged him with corruption, although once he was defeated, they admitted he had been one of the nation's most honest officeholders. Campaigns began to revolve around easily grasped symbols, and when William Henry Harrison ran for president in 1840 he was depicted as a simple frontiersman. His supporters wore log-cabin badges, sang log-cabin songs, and dragged log-cabin replicas on floats in parades. Such paraphernalia became a common sight in American elections. If some contemporary observers, such as the Frenchman Alexis de Tocqueville (1805–1859), were disappointed at the lack of a thoughtful and deliberate process in choosing political leaders, they recognized that democracy was nowhere in the world as fully developed as in the United States, where it foreshadowed the future of other societies.

When Abraham Lincoln was elected U.S. president in 1860, nobody of his social standing occupied an equivalent position in Europe. At the news of his assassination in 1865, workmen and artisans, seeing in the dead president a kindred spirit, stood for hours in line outside the U.S. legation in London and the consul general's office in Lyon (France) to sign a book of condolence to express their sorrow. It was also a form of tribute to the nation that had elected a backwoodsman, born in a log cabin, to its highest office.

The frontiers of democracy appeared to have widened after the Civil War when amendments to the U.S. Constitution granted African Americans full equality with whites. Slavery was forbidden throughout the United States, and regardless of "race, color, or previous

Bingham: The Verdict of the People   In George Caleb Bingham's 1855 painting set in the American West, voters await election results. Unlike in Europe, where religious and property barriers to suffrage continued throughout the nineteenth century, many U.S. states had universal white male suffrage by the 1820s.   *(From the Art Collection of NationsBank)*

condition of servitude," all Americans were declared to be citizens. During the first few years of Reconstruction, whites who had supported the Confederacy were deprived of the right to vote, and African Americans represented a voting bloc in the South. As a result, for the first time the United States saw the election of blacks to positions as varied as lieutenant governor, U.S. senator, congressman, postmaster, and innumerable county and town offices. After the end of military occupation of the South, however, local white power reasserted itself and the rights of African Americans were sharply curtailed. Yet, compared with their status before the Civil War, African Americans had advanced significantly. They were no longer slaves but citizens, they were free to move

where they wanted, and in some places they were able to participate in the political process.

By 1880 the United States not only had seen four decades of territorial expansion but had been transformed by the ordeal of the Civil War, which brought about the extension of federal authority and—however hesitatingly—of the rights of citizenship to new groups. A large, powerful democracy had arisen in the North American continent.

■ The Northern Neighbor: Canada

Just north of the United States, in Canada, some similar processes unfolded during the 1800s that also resulted

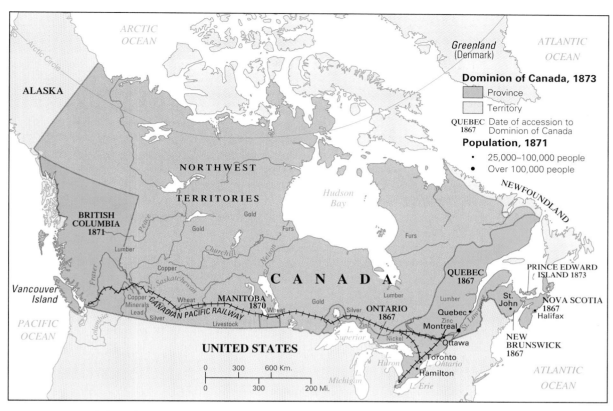

Map 22.5   Dominion of Canada, 1873   By 1873 Canada had become a vast territory with the addition of the western territories. Like the United States, Canada reached from the Atlantic to the Pacific.

in a larger, freer, and more centralized society. Though Canada was spared a civil war, a popular uprising did occur as citizens chafed under the oligarchical grip of British colonial rule, in which authority was in the hands of a few families. Lord Durham, the new governor, suggested in 1839 a series of reforms (see pages 727–728) that in the end were implemented, uniting Upper and Lower Canada, and providing for an elected assembly and a government responsible to it. The British North America Act in 1867 created a federal system of government, with each province exercising considerable autonomy. With the purchase of the Northwest Territories from the private Hudson Bay Company in 1869 and the gradual attachment of other provinces, Canada gained in size; by 1871, the country stretched from the maritime provinces in the east to the Pacific (see Map 22.5). The building of a transcontinental railroad in the 1880s helped unite the huge nation. By the end of the nineteenth century, Canada was virtually self-governing, having full control over all its affairs, except for defense and foreign affairs.

THE DEVELOPMENT OF WESTERN DEMOCRACIES

 N the generation after 1850, Britain, France, and several smaller states in northern Europe made major strides forward in creating democratic political systems and cultures. Although universal manhood suffrage had been instituted only in France, all these countries' governments were responsible to elected representatives of the voters. Lincoln had spoken of the United States enjoying "government of the people, by the people, for the people." As a result of a series of political reforms, this goal was in the process of being attained in many European countries.

■ Victorian Britain

The mid-nineteenth century was a period of exceptional wealth and security for Britain, as the population as a whole began to share in the economic benefits of

⊕ G L O B A L   E N C O U N T E R S

A Japanese View of the British Parliament

In 1862 the Japanese government sent its first diplomatic mission to Europe. Accompanying the delegation was its young translator, Fukuzawa Yukichi (1835–1901). Intrigued by what he saw and eager to interest his fellow Japanese in the West, Fukuzawa published several books. In fact, all books about the West in Japan came to be known as "Fukuzawa-bon." Toward the end of his life in his Autobiography, *he described how, while in London, he had tried to understand the workings of the British Parliament.*

Of political situations at that time, I tried to learn as much as I could from various persons that I met in London . . . though it was often difficult to understand things clearly as I was as yet unfamiliar with the history of Europe. . . . A perplexing institution was representative government. When I asked a gentleman what the "election law" was and what kind of an institution the Parliament really was, he simply replied with a smile, meaning I suppose that no intelligent person was expected to ask such questions. But these were the things most difficult of all for me to understand. In this connection, I learned that there were different political parties—the Liberal and the Conservative—who were always "fighting" against each other in the government.

For some time it was beyond my comprehension to understand what they were "fighting" for, and what was meant, anyway, by "fighting" in peace

time. "This man and that man are 'enemies' in the House," they would tell me. But these "enemies" were to be seen at the same table, eating and drinking with each other. I felt as if I could not make much out of this. It took me a long time, with some tedious thinking, before I could gather a general notion of these separate mysterious facts. In some of the more complicated matters, I might achieve an understanding five or ten days after they were explained to me. But all in all, I learned much from this initial tour of Europe.

Source: The Autobiography of Fukuzawa Yukichi, trans. Eiichi Kiyooka (Tokyo: Hokuseida Press, 1948), pp. 138, 143–144.

For additional information on this topic, go to http://college.hmco.com.

industrialization. Britain enjoyed both social and political peace. The political system was not challenged as it had been in the generation after the Napoleonic Wars. A self-assured, even smug, elite—merchants, industrialists, and landowners—developed a political system reflecting liberal values.

Although suffrage was still very restricted, the parliamentary system was firmly established, with a government clearly responsible to the electorate. The importance of Parliament was symbolized by the new building in which it met, finished in 1850 on the site of previous parliamentary buildings but of unprecedented splendor and size. The form of government developed in its halls after midcentury aroused the curiosity and envy

of much of the world. (See the box "Global Encounters: A Japanese View of the British Parliament.")

In the twenty years after 1846, five different political parties vied for power. Depending on the issue, parties and factions coalesced to support particular policies. After 1867, however, a clear two-party system emerged: Liberal and Conservative (Tory), both with strong leadership. This development gave the electorate a distinct choice. The Conservatives were committed to preserving traditional institutions and practices, whereas the Liberals were more open to change.

Heading these parties were the two strong-minded individuals who dominated British political life for over a generation: William E. Gladstone (1809–1898), a Liberal, and Benjamin Disraeli° (1804–1881), a Conservative. Gladstone came from a family of industrialists and married into the aristocracy; Disraeli was the son of a Jewish man of letters who had converted to Christianity. His father's conversion made his career possible—before the 1850s Jews were barred from Parliament. Prior to heading their parties, Gladstone and Disraeli both served in important cabinet positions. They were master debaters; Parliament and the press hung on their every word. Each was capable of making speeches lasting five hours or more and of conducting debates that kept the house in session until 4 A.M. The rivalry between the two men thrilled the nation and made politics a popular pastime.

The Conservatives' electoral base came from the landed classes, Anglicans, and from England, rather than the rest of the United Kingdom. The Liberals' base came from the middle classes, from Christian groups other than the Church of England, and from Scotland and Wales. In the House of Commons both parties had a large number of members from the landed aristocracy, but cabinet members were increasingly chosen for political competence rather than family background. Aristocratic birth was no longer a requirement for reaching the pinnacle of power, as Gladstone and Disraeli so clearly illustrated.

The competition for power between the Liberals and Conservatives led to an extension of suffrage in 1867. The Second Reform Bill lowered property qualifications, extending the vote from 1.4 to 2.5 million people out of a population of 22 million, and gave new urban areas better representation by equalizing the electoral districts— henceforth the same size population was required for each district sending a member to Parliament. Although some in Parliament feared that these changes would lead to the masses capturing political power—"a leap into the dark," one member called it—in fact no radical change ensued. Extending the vote to clerks, artisans, and other skilled workers made them feel more a part of society, and thus bolstered the existing system. John Stuart Mill, then a Member of Parliament, championed the cause of women's suffrage, but he had few allies and that effort failed.

As the extension of voting rights increased the size of the electorate, parties became larger and stronger. Strong party systems meant alternation of power between the Liberals and the Conservatives. With an obvious majority and minority party, the monarch could no longer play favorites in choosing a prime minister. The leader of the majority party had to be asked to form a government. Thus, even though Queen Victoria (r.

Disraeli (diz-RAY-lee)

Disraeli and Gladstone: Victorian Political Rivals   This 1868 cartoon from *Punch* magazine captures the politicians' personalities. Disraeli was known as vain and theatrical, while Gladstone was dour and moralistic.   *(Mary Evans Picture Library)*

1837–1901) detested Gladstone, she had to ask him to form governments when the Liberals won parliamentary elections. (See the feature "Weighing the Evidence: An Engraving of the British Royal Family" on pages 772–773.)

The creation of a broad-based electorate also meant that politicians had to make clear appeals to the public and its interests. In the past, oratory had been limited to the halls of Parliament, but after the electoral reforms, it occurred in the public arena as well. Public election campaigns became part of the political scene in Britain. The democratic, "American" style of campaigning appealed to the common man. Also borrowed from across the seas was the "Australian ballot"—the secret ballot— adopted in 1872. This protected lower-class voters from intimidation by their employers, landowners, or other social superiors. In 1874 the first two working-class members of Parliament were elected, sitting as Liberals.

Although their victory represented a very modest gain for workers' representation, it presaged the increasingly democratic turn England was to take.

■ France: From Empire to Republic

Unlike Britain, which was transformed gradually into a parliamentary democracy, France took a more tumultuous path. Revolutions and wars overthrew existing political systems and inaugurated new ones. Each time the French seemed to have democracy within reach, the opportunity slipped away.

The constitution of the Second French Republic provided for a single four-year presidential term. Frustrated by this limitation of power, Louis Napoleon by a coup d'état extended his presidency to a ten-year term in 1851. The following year, he called for a plebiscite to confirm him as Napoleon III (r. 1852–1870), emperor of the French. Both of these moves were resisted in the countryside, particularly in the south, but the resistance was put down by massive repression.

In the rest of the country, huge majorities of voters endorsed first the prolonged presidency and then the imperial title. The new emperor seemed different from his predecessors. He believed in the principle of popular sovereignty (he maintained universal male suffrage, introduced in 1848), he did not pretend to reign by divine right, and he repeatedly tested his right to rule by an appeal to the popular vote. He seemed to combine order and authority with the promises of the Revolution—equality before the law, careers open to talent, and the abolition of hereditary rights.

The mid-nineteenth century was a period of prosperity for most Frenchmen, including urban workers and peasants. Louis Napoleon, in his youth the author of a book on pauperism, introduced measures congenial to labor. On the one hand, workers were required to keep a booklet in which employers recorded their conduct; on the other hand, workers were granted limited rights to strike, and labor unions were virtually legalized. The emperor expressed his desire to improve the workers' lot, and the government initiated a few concrete measures, such as providing some public housing. Although slum clearance during the rebuilding of Paris drove many from their homes to the outskirts of the city, it did provide healthier towns for those who stayed behind, and the ambitious urban projects provided work for many (see page 791). Other public works projects, such as ports, roads, railroads, and monumental public buildings, also created jobs. Railroad mileage in France increased tenfold, enabling peasants to market their harvests more widely. If some peasants had initially opposed Louis Napoleon, most supported him once he was in power. Not only were they a cautious group, preferring stable authority, but they saw in the emperor—the heir to the great Napoleon—an incarnation of national glory.

Not all the French supported the emperor; many republicans could not forget that he had usurped the constitution of 1848. In protest, some had gone into exile, including the poet Victor Hugo. Trying to win over the opposition, Napoleon made some concessions in 1860, easing censorship and making his government more accountable to the parliament. Instead of winning him new support, however, liberalization allowed the expression of mounting opposition. A coordinated republican opposition strongly criticized the economic policies of the empire, notably the decision to sign a free-trade treaty with England. Free trade helped wine and silk exporters, but it left iron and textile manufacturers unprotected. Businessmen in these fields rallied their workers against the imperial regime.

A number of other issues—including widespread hostility to the influence of the Catholic Church and the desire for more extensive freedoms of expression and assembly—also helped forge a republican alliance of the middle classes and workers. This alliance was strongest in the large cities and in some southern regions notorious for their opposition to central government control. Republicanism was better organized than in earlier years and had a more explicit program. Moreover, its proponents were now better prepared to take over the government, if the opportunity arose.

By 1869 the regime of Napoleon III, which declared itself a "liberal empire," had evolved into a constitutional monarchy, responsible to the Legislative Corps, the lower house of the parliament. In a plebiscite in May 1870, Frenchmen supported the liberal empire by a vote of five to one. It might have endured had Napoleon III not rashly declared war against Prussia two months later in a huff over the supposedly insulting Ems dispatch (see page 754). Defeat at the hands of Bismarck brought down the empire. In September, at news of the emperor's capture, the republican opposition in the Legislative Corps declared a republic. It continued the war but had to sign an armistice in January 1871.

The leader of the new government was an old prime minister of Louis Philippe, Adolphe Thiers° (1797–1877). Before signing a definitive peace, the provisional government held elections. The liberals, known as republicans since they favored a republic, were identified with con-

---

Thiers (tee-YAIR)

tinuing the war; the conservatives, mostly royalists, favored peace. Mainly because of their position on this issue, the royalists won a majority from a country discouraged by defeat.

The new regime had no time to establish itself before a workers' uprising in the spring of 1871 shook France, while reminding the rest of Europe of revolutionary dangers. The uprising was called the Paris Commune, a name that harked back to 1792–1794, when the Paris crowds had dictated to the government. The Commune insisted on its right to home rule. Radicals and conservatives greeted the Commune as a workers' revolt intended to establish a workers' government. Marx described it as the "bold champion of the emancipation of labor." To an even larger degree than during the revolution of 1848, women took an active part, fighting on the barricades, pouring scalding water on soldiers, posting revolutionary broadsides. The main woman's leader was Louise Michel (1830–1905), a schoolteacher, who while agitating for both socialism and women's rights, took an active part in the fighting.

Although labor discontent played a role in the Paris Commune, other forces also contributed, notably the Prussian siege of Paris during the Franco-Prussian War. Paris had become radicalized during the siege: the rich had evacuated the city, leaving a power vacuum quickly filled by the lower classes. Parisians suffered much because of the siege, and angered that their economic needs went unmet and their courage against the Prussians unnoticed, they rose up against the new French government. Food was the paramount issue sparking the massive women's participation in the uprising. The Commune, composed largely of artisans, now governed the city.

In March 1871 the Commune declared itself free to carry out policies independent of the central government in Versailles. Its goals were quite moderate: it sought free universal education, a fairer taxation system, a minimum wage, and disestablishment of the official Catholic Church. But this was too radical for the conservative French government, which sent in the army. It suppressed the Commune, massacring 25,000 people, arresting 40,000, and deporting several thousand more.

The crushing of the Paris Commune and some of its sister communes in southern France, which had also asserted local autonomy, signified the increasing power of the centralized governments. One mark of the emerging modern state was its capacity to squelch popular revolts that, in the past, had constituted serious threats. Western Europe would not again witness a popular uprising of this magnitude.

Napoleon III   This is an example of official art glorifying the emperor. The emperor is framed by a Roman statue on his right and the imperial eagle on his left, both symbols of strength and glory.   *(Giraudon/Art Resource, NY)*

Despite its brutality, the suppression of the Commune reassured many Frenchmen. "The Republic will be conservative, or it will not be," declared Thiers. The question now at hand was what form the new government would take. The monarchist majority offered the throne to the Bourbon pretender. However, he insisted he would become king only if the *tricouleur*—the flag of the Revolution, which long since had become a cherished national symbol—were discarded and replaced by the white flag of the house of Bourbon. This was unacceptable, so France remained a republic. The republic, as Thiers put it, "is the regime which divides us the least."

By 1875 the parliament had approved a set of basic laws that became the constitution of the Third Republic. Ironically, a monarchist parliament had created a liberal, democratic parliamentary regime. A century after the French Revolution, the republican system of government in France was firmly launched.

■ Scandinavia and the Low Countries

France and especially Britain served as models of parliamentary democracy for the smaller states in northern Europe. Norway, Sweden, Denmark, Belgium, and Holland recast their political institutions at midcentury. Several of the states were affected by the 1848 revolutions: Stockholm saw minor riots, Denmark a peaceful protest demanding enlarged political participation (see page 736) , and in Holland, the king feared that his country would be affected by revolution as in the neighboring German states. In Copenhagen King Frederick VII (r. 1848–1863), who had no stomach for a confrontation, yielded and accepted a constitution providing for parliamentary government. "Now I can sleep as long as I like," he is reputed to have said.

Sweden's parliamentary system, established in the Middle Ages, had representation by estates—noble, clergy, burgher, and peasant. The 11,000 nobles were weighted in the same manner as the 2.5–3 million peasants. After the riots of 1848, liberal aristocrats recognized that abolition of the estates system would best preserve their privileges, removing the major issue that had provoked popular resentments. With some delays, this conviction, born in 1848, was finally carried out in 1866. The estates were replaced by a parliament with two houses; the upper was restricted to the wealthiest landowners and the lower to men of property, providing the vote to 20 percent of adult men. While the king was not constitutionally obligated to choose a government reflecting parliamentary currents, desiring to avoid conflict, he usually did.

Norway had been joined to Sweden in 1814 under the Swedish king , but it had a separate parliament and made its own laws. Swedish rule rankled the Norwegians, however, and their Liberal Party in the 1850s began to insist that the king should not have the final word in governance, but rather parliament, representative of the Norwegian people, should be supreme. In 1883 the principle that government officials are responsible to parliament won out. In 1905 Norway peacefully separated from Sweden and became an independent state.

In the Netherlands as a result of the revolutions of 1848, the king recognized the need to strengthen support for his crown by acceding to liberals' demands for parliamentary government. By midcentury, government in the Netherlands was responsible to parliament, rather than the king. A new constitution guaranteed the principles of freedom of speech, assembly, and religion.

Belgium had enjoyed a liberal constitution from the time it became an independent state in 1830, but because no strong party system materialized, the king was able to appoint to government whom he pleased. In the 1840s the liberals organized, and the king, reluctantly, had to invite them to govern in 1848. The new government reduced property qualifications for voting, thus increasing the electorate.

Unlike the reforms that had followed the revolutions of 1848, only to be rolled back in conservative backlashes, these sweeping reforms in northern European states became the basis for their evolution into full democracies.

For full democracy, the electorate had to be broadened. These years witnessed much agitation for universal male suffrage. Property qualifications, wherever they were instituted, were questioned and resisted. For instance, in Sweden the stipulation that a man had to earn 800 crowns a year to be a voter unleashed a pamphlet war: What if a man earned only 799 crowns? Did that make him less qualified? What if a man qualified one year, but through no fault of his own, for instance a natural disaster, did not earn that much the following year? Should he then be barred from voting? Belgium in the 1880s saw a mass movement in favor of universal suffrage; the letters "SU," standing for universal suffrage in French, became emblematic of the hopes for the masses for a better life. While suffrage remained as yet limited in these countries, it was only a matter of time before democracy would be achieved.

SUMMARY

 OVEL configurations of power appeared on the West's chessboard in the period from about 1850 to 1880 as new or enlarged states were created through warfare or the threat of force. Liberal nationalists in the early nineteenth century had believed that Europe would be freer and more peaceful if each people had a separate nation, but they were now proved wrong. The Crimean War and its aftermath replaced the congress system, which had sought a balance of power among partners, with a system of rival states in pursuit of their own self-interest. The international order was severely shaken as Italy and Germany emerged from the center of Europe and as Romania and Bulgaria were carved out of the Ottoman Empire in the east.

Both new and existing states faced a choice between federalism and centralized rule. In the process of unification, Italy and Germany could have opted for a loose federal union, but both Piedmont and Prussia chose central control. And the crushing of the Paris Commune spelled the doom of those who wanted a France of decentralized self-governing units. Strong, centralized governments increasingly became the norm. That was also the case across the ocean in the United States, where North and South fought a bloody Civil War over the issues of slavery and state sovereignty, and the victorious federal government imposed its will on the rebellious states. Canada became a large state, stretching across the continent, and acquired self-government.

To achieve legitimacy, however, governments had to appear to be enjoying the consent of their peoples. Hence all European rulers except those of the Ottoman and Russian Empires found it necessary to have a parliament. France, Britain, and several northern European states became increasingly democratic in these years, answerable to a growing electorate. In other states parliaments had only limited powers, but once they were in place, it could be argued—and was—that more power should be shifted toward them and that they should be chosen by an expanded electorate. In the United States whites already enjoyed freer and more open institutions than existed anywhere else, and the post–Civil War era marked a further enlargement of political participation when African American men were granted the right to vote.

Two major changes that liberals in 1848 had agitated for had become reality: freer political institutions and the organization of nation-states. Although neither of these was fully implemented everywhere, both appeared to have been successfully established. Many Europeans could easily believe they were living in an age of optimism.

■ Notes

1. Quoted in Otto Pflanze, *Bismarck and the Development of Germany*, vol. 1 (Princeton: Princeton University Press, 1990), p. 184.
2. Quoted in William Flavelle Monypenny and George Earle Buckle, *The Life of Benjamin Disraeli: Earl of Beaconsfield*, vol. 2 (London: John Murray, 1929), pp. 473–474.

■ Suggested Reading

Alter, Peter. *The German Question and Europe. A History*. 2000. Explains the international context within which German unity was possible and its impact on European diplomacy.

Blackbourn, David. *The Long Nineteenth Century—A History of Germany, 1780–1918*. 1998. Particularly strong on the social aspects and consequences of German unification.

Jelavich, Charles and Barbara. *The Establishment of the Balkan National States, 1804–1920*. 1977. Traces the emergence of independent states from the Ottoman Empire.

Lincoln, W. Bruce. *Great Reforms*. 1990. Shows the reforms to be part of a general program of modernization.

Matthew, Colin, ed. *The Nineteenth Century: The British Isles, 1815–1901*. 2000. An up-to-date collection of articles on major themes in British history.

 For a searchable list of additional readings for this chapter, go to http://college.hmco.com.

An Engraving of the British Royal Family

Why were Queen Victoria and her family depicted in the manner shown in this popular engraving? The illustration might well have been of an upper-middle-class family. Note the family's attire. The queen is plainly dressed; her husband, Prince Albert, wears a dark business suit; the children are clothed in simple outfits. The image extends from the royal family to the rest of England, depicted as a quaint farm, some cottages, and a grouping of common people. Notice the crown hovering over this idyllic scene. Victoria's reign was the longest of any British monarch; the manner in which she conducted herself, and her subjects' image of her, shaped the monarchy and people's expectations of it.

Illustrations of this type familiarized the British with their monarch. Surrounded by her husband and children, the queen seemed to have an endearing common touch. In the past representations of the monarchy had suggested power and intimidation. The aura of the close-knit, nuclear royal family, not unlike the families of the queen's middle-class subjects, suggested a serenity that was reassuring to those subjects.

Victoria cultivated the image of herself as contented mother, but in reality she resented much about motherhood. She complained of the extent to which her pregnancies interfered with her daily routines, preventing her from traveling and from being with her beloved Albert as much as she would have liked. She described childbearing as an "annoyance" that made her feel "so pinned down—one's wings clipped." She also refused to romanticize birthing, seeing it as an animal-like act, reducing a woman to "a cow or a dog." Biology put women in an inauspicious position; "I think our sex a most unenviable one," she lamented. And Victoria continued viewing the children, once they were no longer babies, as a burden, describing them as "an awful plague and anxiety for which they show one so little gratitude very often!" But such views were expressed strictly privately, and the public never suspected Victoria's ambivalence toward her role as mother.

Whatever her complaints about children, Victoria's family life was in strong contrast to that of her predecessors, projecting a new image of the monarchy. Her grandfather George III (r. 1760–1820) had been plagued with bouts of insanity. Her uncle George IV (r. 1820–1830) was a notorious philanderer. George IV and his brothers, the duke of Clarence (later to be William IV [r. 1830–1837]) and the duke of Kent (Victoria's father), were bigamists. They fathered a large brood of illegitimate children and were implicated in numerous public scandals.

The character of Victoria's three predecessors and of the various other men in line to the throne had strengthened opposition to the monarchy. Public outrage at their excesses had led to a call for the abolition of the institution. When the 18-year-old Victoria came to the throne, it would have been difficult to imagine that she would on her death leave the monarchy considerably strengthened.

The image of Victoria shown here intentionally contrasts her reign with those of her predecessors. Victoria is surrounded by four of her children (eventually she would have nine). Her predecessors had died leaving no legitimate direct heirs and thus endangering the regular succession to the throne. The engraving announces that the royal line is assured. English people wary of a female ruler can find solace in knowing that Victoria would be succeeded by one of her sons. Later, Victoria's children and their progeny would intermarry with the rest of Europe's royalty, and by the end of her reign most of Europe's crowned heads would be related to one another.

Although Victoria's uncles and father were wastrels and bankrupts, the queen and her husband lived frugally by royal standards and conducted an exemplary family life. Under the wise administration of Prince Albert, royal wealth increased; he carefully administered various royal estates and investments. Instead of being subject to various debtors, the British royal house became one of the wealthiest landowners in Great Britain, achieving financial independence and winning social prestige. Among the large landowning magnates of Britain, the royal house became the most prominent.

The model royal family appealed to the growing middle class of Victorian society. Consider how the simple terms in which the monarch is depicted here and in many other illustrations reflect the increasingly democratic

Illustration from *A Book of English Song*

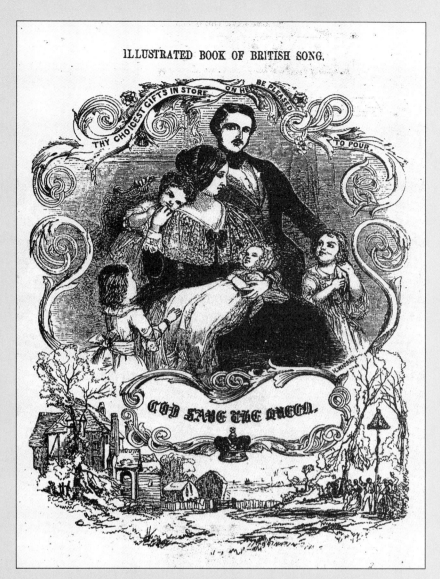

spirit of the era. The ruler and her family appear in a common scene. Victoria is queen, but she also is a mother and wife. There is no sign here of pomp and ceremony.

Given the disrepute into which the monarchy had fallen and the rise of republican sentiment, the coming to the throne of a woman in 1837 may have substantially lessened antimonarchical sentiment. The last woman to rule England, Elizabeth I (r. 1558–1603), had been one of its greatest monarchs, one who had provided stability and brought glory to her kingdom. A young, seemingly frail woman coming to the throne lent a certain gallantry to the royal household. Also, because of her gender Victoria was seen as less of a threat to constitutional liberties.

Under Victoria's rule, Britain completed the process of becoming a constitutional monarchy. Although Victoria's predecessors had been openly partisan, the queen cultivated the image of being above party, a symbol of national unity and the state. Fellow monarchs in central and eastern Europe exercised greater power, but after World War I they were all toppled. In Britain, monarchy in its constitutional form endured. Victoria established a pattern of public and private behavior by which members of subsequent generations of the British royal family were to be judged.

 For additional information on this topic, go to http://college.hmco.com.

CHAPTER 23

The Age of Optimism 1850–1880

THE first department store in Paris, which served as a model for others in France and abroad, *Le Bon Marché* (the "good buy") opened its doors in the 1850s. The store bought goods in mass quantities and thus could sell them at low prices. Constructed of glass and iron, Le Bon Marché represented the new, modern age. It combined under one roof a large range of products that previously had been available only in separate specialty shops—a time-saving convenience in an increasingly harried age. The store also had a large catalog sales department for customers too busy or distant to shop in person. Filled with toys, bed linens, furniture, crystal, and other items, the department store was a symbol of the new opulence of the middle classes.

This new type of store would not have been possible in an earlier age. It serves as a summary of the various technological and social changes that the more prosperous regions of the West experienced as industrialization advanced in the second half of the nineteenth century. Industrial innovation had lowered the price of glass and steel, so that these new, huge commercial emporiums could be built at reasonable cost. Railroads brought into the city large quantities of increasingly mass-produced goods, as well as out-of-town customers. In town, trams and omnibuses transported shoppers to the store. The penny press provided advertising for the department store, which in turn supported the emergence of this new medium. The expansion of the postal system facilitated catalog sales and the mailing of parcels to customers. And the higher incomes available to many people allowed them to purchase more than just the necessities. A phenomenon

Felix Valloton, *Le bon marché.*
(Private Collection/Edimedia)

775

began that would become predominant in the West a century later—the consumer society.

As industrialization spread throughout western Europe, rising productivity brought greater wealth to more social groups and nations. This wealth not only led to more consumer spending but also contributed to a change in attitudes. The second half of the nineteenth century was an era shaped to a large extent by the growing middle classes, who were filled with optimism and convinced they were living in an age of progress. John Stuart Mill proclaimed that in his era "the general tendency is and will continue to be . . . one of improvement—a tendency towards a better and happier state." Across the Channel in France, the social thinker Auguste Comte° (1798–1857) concurred, confidently stating, "human development brings . . . an ever growing amelioration." The successful application of science and technology to social problems gave many men and women confidence in the human ability to improve the world. People controlled their environments to a degree never before possible. On farms they increased the fertility of the soil; to the burgeoning cities they brought greater order. Scientists used new methods to study and combat disease. Public authorities founded schools, trained teachers, and reduced illiteracy. Transportation and communication rapidly improved.

In reality, not all of society benefited from the fruits of progress. The new wealth was far from equally shared. Eastern and southern Europe changed little, and even in the western regions a large part of the population still lived in great misery. If some cities carried out ambitious programs of urban renewal, others continued to neglect slums. Public sanitation programs did not affect the majority of Europeans who lived in rural areas. Despite spectacular advances in science, much of the population maintained a traditional belief in divine intervention. Many intellectuals strongly denounced the materialism and smugness of the age, stressing the meanness and ignorance that lay just beneath the surface.

Still, the tone of the age was set by the ascendant middle classes in western Europe, which embraced change and believed that the era was heading toward even more remarkable improvements. Their optimism was all the greater because the ultimate effects of the social and technological changes taking place in Europe were not yet known. Of the major processes that unfolded between 1850 and 1880, many were still in their infancy in 1880. What lay beyond the horizon would certainly be even more wonderful.

QUESTIONS TO CONSIDER

- **What technological changes led to the expansion of the European economy after the mid-nineteenth century?**

- **How did the economic expansion affect the various social classes, and city versus rural areas, differently?**

- **In what ways did the state increasingly intervene in people's daily lives?**

- **How did Charles Darwin both reflect and shape the intellectual trends of his era?**

TERMS TO KNOW

second industrial revolution
bourgeois century
professionalization
Victorian morality
separate spheres
solidarism
social Catholics
positivism

impressionism
Darwinism
Social Darwinism

Auguste Comte (oh-GOOST KONT)

INDUSTRIAL GROWTH AND ACCELERATION

EGINNING in the 1850s, western Europe experienced an unprecedented level of economic expansion. Manufacturers created new products and harnessed new sources of energy. An enlarged banking system provided more abundant credit to fund this expansion. Scientific research was systematically employed to improve methods of manufacture. A revolution in transportation speedily delivered goods and services to distant places. For many Europeans, daily life was profoundly changed by technological innovations.

■ The "Second Industrial Revolution"

The interrelated cluster of economic changes that began in the generation after 1850 is often called the "second industrial revolution." It was characterized by a significant speedup in production and by the introduction of new materials such as mass-produced steel, synthetic dyes, and aluminum. Manufacturers replaced the traditional steam engine with stronger steam-powered turbines or with machines powered by new forms of energy—petroleum and electricity.

The invention of new products and methods of manufacture spurred this industrial expansion. The second half of the nineteenth century has often been called the "age of steel." Up to then, steel production had been limited by the expense involved in its manufacture, but in 1856, Sir Henry Bessemer (1813–1898) discovered a much cheaper method, which produced in twenty minutes the same amount of steel previously produced in twenty-four hours. Ten years later, William Siemens° (1823–1883) in England and Pierre Martin (1824–1915) in France developed an even more efficient technique of steel production, the open-hearth process. The Thomas-Gilchrist method, invented in 1878, made possible the use of phosphor-laden iron ore, which previously had been economically unfeasible.

The results were dramatic. In Great Britain steel production increased fourfold, and the price of steel fell by more than 50 percent between the early 1870s and the following decade. Greater steel production made possible the expansion of the rail system, the creation of a steamship fleet, and an explosive growth in the building industry. No longer was steel a rare alloy used only for the

Siemens (SEE-menz)

CHRONOLOGY

1818	Gas street lamps in London
1820s	Omnibuses introduced in France
1829	Stephenson runs the *Rocket*
1830	Lyell founds the principles of modern geology
1831	Faraday discovers electromagnetic induction
1833	Telegraph invented
1840	Penny stamp introduced
1848	England adopts first national health legislation
1850s	Age of clipper ships
	Trams added to public transportation systems
1851	Crystal Palace
1852–1870	Rebuilding of Paris
1859	Darwin, *On the Origin of Species*
1863	Europe's first underground railroad, in London
1864	Pope Pius IX issues *Syllabus of Errors*
1865	Transoceanic telegraph cable installed
	Lister initiates antiseptic surgery
	University of Zurich admits women
1869	Opening of Suez Canal
	Mendeleev produces periodic table of elements
1874	Impressionist exhibition
1875	Bell invents telephone
	Electric lights in Paris
1881	Pasteur proposes germ theory of disease
1891	Pope Leo XIII issues *Rerum novarum*

The Suez Canal   Opened in 1869, the canal significantly shortened the voyage by ship from Europe to East Asia. The Suez Canal exemplified the speeding up of transportation and communication in the second half of the nineteenth century.   *(AKG London)*

finest swords and knives; it became the material that defined the age.

Significant changes in the supply of credit further stimulated economic expansion. Discovery of gold in California and Australia led to the inflow of huge amounts of the precious metal to Europe, expanding the supply of money and credit. This led to the establishment of the modern banking system.

Each advance made possible additional changes. Increased wealth and credit accelerated further expansion of industrial plants and the financing of an ambitious infrastructure of roads, railroads, and steamships, which in turn boosted trade. Between 1800 and 1840, the value of world trade had doubled. In the twenty years following 1850, it increased by 260 percent.

By the 1880s important scientific discoveries fueled industrial improvements. Electricity began to be more widely used, replacing coal as a source of energy. Synthetic dyes revolutionized the textile industry, as did alkali in the manufacture of soap and glass. Dynamite, invented by the Swedish chemist Alfred Nobel° (1833–1896) in the 1860s, made it possible to level hills and blast tunnels through mountains, facilitating construc-

Nobel (no-BELL)

tion. Five years after Nobel's death, his will established a prestigious prize named after its donor, to honor significant contributions to science and peace.

■ Transportation and Communications

The rail system grew dramatically in the middle decades of the nineteenth century. When the English engineer Robert Stephenson (1803–1859) demonstrated the feasibility of his steam locomotive, the *Rocket,* in 1829, it ran at 5 miles per hour on a track that was 1½ miles long. By 1880 total European railroad mileage was 102,000 (see Map 23.1). In 1888 the Orient Express line opened, linking Constantinople to Vienna and thus to the rest of Europe. Distance was conquered by speed as well: by midcentury, trains ran 50 miles per hour, ten times as fast as when they were invented. The cost of rail transport steadily decreased, allowing for its greater use. Between 1850 and 1880 in Germany, the number of rail passengers increased tenfold and the volume of goods eightyfold. In France and Great Britain, the increases were nearly as impressive.

Ocean transportation was also revolutionized. In 1869 the French built the Suez Canal across Egyptian territory, linking the Mediterranean to the Red Sea and the Indian Ocean. The canal reduced by 40 percent the

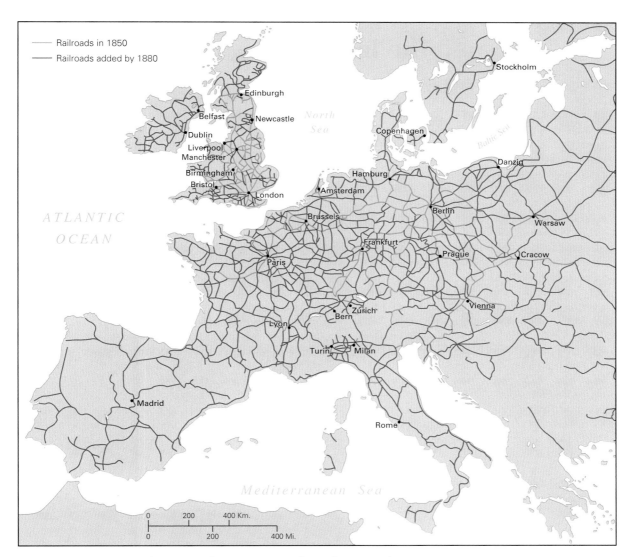

Map 23.1   European Rails, 1850 and 1880   During the mid-nineteenth century, European states built railroads at an increasing rate, creating a dense network by the 1880s.   *(Adapted from Norman J. G. Pounds,* An Historical Geography of Europe, 1800–1914 *[New York: Cambridge University Press, 1985].)*

thirty-five-day journey between London and Bombay. More efficient ships were developed; by midcentury, the so-called clipper ship could cross the Atlantic in fourteen days, half the previous length of time. Steamships were also built, although they did not dominate ocean traffic until the 1890s. By 1880 European shipping carried nearly three times the cargo it had thirty years earlier.

The optimism born of conquering vast distances was reflected in a popular novel by the French writer Jules Verne° (1828–1905), *Around the World in Eighty Days*

Jules Verne (DJOOL VAIRN)

(1873). The hero, Phineas Fogg, travels by balloon, llama, and ostrich, as well as by the modern steam locomotive and steamship to accomplish in eighty days a feat that, only thirty years earlier, would have taken at least eleven months. In 1889 the New York newspaper *The World* in a publicity gambit to increase readership sent its reporter Nellie Bly (1867–1922) on an around-the-world trip to see if she could beat Phineas Fogg's record. Readers breathlessly kept up with reports of her progress. She circled the globe in 72 days, 6 hours, 11 minutes, and 14 seconds. Such was the impact of the steamship, the locomotive, the Suez Canal—and the newspaper.

The Telegraph

The telegraph radically altered the speed with which information could be collected and spread around the world. In 1793 two young Frenchmen, Claude Chappe (1763–1805) and his brother, Ignace (1760–1829), built a device with large wooden arms that, by their location, designated letters of the alphabet in a pre-arranged code. A lookout, equipped with a telescope and stationed on a tower mounted on a tall building or a hill, would take down the message and relay it to the next lookout, as far as 6 miles away. The system was called the *telegraph,* meaning "far, or long-distance writing" in Greek. This system was cumbersome, depending as it did on the messengers' ability to read and retransmit the signals. It could obviously not be used at night or in bad weather.

The Chappes' invention was to be replaced by something more powerful and functional, but that retained the name telegraph. In the 1830s the American Samuel F. B. Morse (1791–1872) surmised that electricity could be used to send messages over long distances. With funding from Congress, in 1844 he built a line 40 miles long from Washington, D.C., to Baltimore. Morse sent electrical impulses in combinations representing letters of the alphabet—sequences of "dots" and "dashes" that became known as the Morse code. A clerk would transcribe the signals into the alphabetical letters they represented, spelling out a message, and have it delivered to the recipient.

In England two events popularized the telegraph, showing its benefits. In 1844, forty minutes after the palace announced that Queen Victoria had given birth to her second son, the *Times* was able to share the happy news with the nation. The following year, a John Tawell murdered his mistress in Slough. Fleeing the police, he took the train for London. Alerted by telegraph, the police arrested the murderer as he got off the train in Paddington Station. The utility of the telegraph had been convincingly demonstrated.

Telegraph wires were rapidly expanded. In the 1850s the telegraph in Britain crossed the English Channel. The following decade the telegraph spread across the North American continent and connected it in turn with Europe via the transatlantic cable. From a few dozen miles in the 1840s, telegraph lines thirty years later were 650,000 miles long, connecting twenty thousand towns and villages across the world to one another.

Newspapers prided themselves on being "wired" and so able to give their readers the latest news fast; many a newspaper adopted a name such as the *Daily Telegraph.* In the 1840s newspapers had printed news from overseas that was often obsolete, or at best outrageously outdated. News from Cape Town, South Africa, in the *London Times* was eight weeks old, from Brazil six weeks old. A couple of decades later, thanks to the telegraph, international news had happened only yesterday.

Governments found the telegraph useful in collecting information and issuing orders to subordinates. Imperial authority over distant territories was now better assured. In the 1840s it had taken ten weeks for a message and a reply to go from London to Bombay and back; thirty years later, the exchange took four minutes.

The telegraph was also a tool of warfare. The first war in which the telegraph played a crucial role was the Crimean; the British and French high commands in London and Paris were able to communicate with their officers in the Crimea, directing operations from afar. In the Austro-Prussian War the Prussians directed their pincer attack leading to the victory at Sadowa by telegraph. Battle plans could be modified quickly as the telegram informed commanders of how the fighting was developing. The telegraph was widely used in the American Civil War, helping shape many a battle; during that conflict 6 million telegrams were sent.

The most common early use for the telegraph was to coordinate the railroads. Still in their infancy, most rail lines had single tracks, and collisions were frequent. One station could inform another by telegram of a train's departure, so that managers could decide which train had the right of way

Along with the new speed, advances in refrigeration changed food transport. Formerly, refrigeration could be achieved only with natural ice, cut from frozen ponds and lakes, but this changed in the 1870s with the introduction of mechanical ice-making machines. By the 1880s dairy products and meat were being transported vast distances by rail and even across the seas by ship. Thanks to these advances, the surplus food of the Americas and Australia, rich in grasslands, could offer Europe a cheaper and far more varied diet.

Regular postal service was also a child of the new era of improved transportation. In 1840 Britain instituted a postage system based on standard rates. Replacing the earlier practice in which the recipient paid for the delivery of a letter, the British system enabled the sender to buy a stamp—priced at just one penny—and drop

The Telegraph and War
Although serving mainly civilian purposes, the telegraph was repeatedly used in warfare after its invention in the 1840s, notably in the U.S. Civil War. Here, linemen string wire for the Union Army near Brandy Station, Va., in 1864. The belligerents used 16,000 miles of telegraph wire during the Civil War. *(National Archives, NWDNS-165-SP-62)*

and take appropriate precautions. The telegraph spread with the rail lines, usually built alongside them. Train travel became safer and more speedy, for with good communications between stations, trains could be more readily dispatched.

Even so, railroads found it impossible to schedule trains traveling across large nations properly because each area had its own local time. The setting of a standard time was facilitated by the telegraph: at a given moment a telegraphic message indicated the exact time to the second, and every town along the line was able to set its time accordingly.

Until the advent of the telegraph it was difficult for merchants to know trade conditions in distant lands. With the new device, business people could collect market information, such as the cheapest price of commodities, and offer their wares competitively to potential buyers around the world. The telegraph brought instant information to merchants, allowing them to expand their markets and lower their costs, thus fostering the development of the consumer society.

Used by governments and businesses, the telegram also became a means for frequent and immediate communica-

tion between individuals. Lovers sent each other messages, parents proudly announced children's births, people shared the sad news of a death in the family. Telegraph operators in the dead of night when there was no traffic on the wires would share jokes or play chess. With greater use, the cost of sending telegrams went down; by 1885 in Britain, a short message was priced at 6 pence, an amount within reach of most people. Lower cost allowed for greater use. Within half a century after 1851, the number of telegrams sent each year in Britain rose from 100,000 to over 90 million.

The telegraph was one of the technological advances of the nineteenth century that, along with the train and steamship, conquered distances. Charles Dickens described the telegraph as "of all our modern wonders the most wonderful." Even more than improved transportation, it transformed the world into an instant, global village. As the governor of New York said at a commemorative event a generation after Samuel Morse's invention, "Men speak to one another now, though separated by the width of the earth, with lightning's speed and as if standing face to face."

the letter into a mailbox. It was collected, transported speedily by the new railroads, and delivered. The efficiency and low cost of mail led to a huge increase in use.

The post combined with transoceanic telegraphs and the invention of the telephone to transform the world of information. In the late 1830s the telegraph was invented, and by 1864, 80,000 miles of telegraph wire had been laid on the European continent. (See the feature "Information

Technology: The Telegraph.") In 1875 the American inventor Alexander Graham Bell (1847–1922) invented a machine capable of transmitting the human voice by electrical impulses; in 1879 the first telephones were installed in Germany; two years later they appeared in France. At first a curiosity, used to listen to a musical or theatrical production at a distance, the phone began to be installed in homes for people to communicate with each other.

CHANGING CONDITIONS AMONG SOCIAL GROUPS

NDUSTRIAL advances transformed the traditional structure of European society. Fewer people worked the land; more worked in industry. The social and political influence of the landed aristocracy waned as wealth became far less dependent on property ownership. To varying degrees, this influence now had to be shared with the growing middle classes. Generally, life for both industrial and farm workers improved in this period. However, great disparities persisted, and many people continued to suffer from profound deprivation.

■ The Declining Aristocracy

Always a small, exclusive group, the European aristocracy in the nineteenth century represented less than 1 percent of the population. Many of those of noble birth were quite poor and economically indistinguishable from their non-noble neighbors. Others owned vast estates and were fabulously wealthy.

Some ennoblements were of recent origin. In England, most titles were less than a hundred years old, having originally been conferred on individuals in recognition of service to the state, the arts, or the economy. In France both Napoleons had bestowed titles on persons they wished to honor. In Germany Chancellor Otto von Bismarck ennobled the Jewish banker Gerson Bleichröder° (1822–1893) for helping finance the wars of the Prussian state and for relieving the German chancellor of personal financial worries by making profitable investments for him. Distinctions between aristocrats and members of the upper middle class became increasingly blurred. Noble families in financial straits often married their children to the offspring of wealthy merchants. And many nobles who previously had shunned manufacture participated in the new economy by becoming industrialists and bankers. Idle members of the nobility were now somewhat rare. Although many aristocrats still enjoyed a lavish lifestyle, others had adopted the habits of successful business people.

Despite the theories of egalitarianism sweeping Europe in the aftermath of the French Revolution and the rapidly changing social structure engendered by industrialization, the power of the aristocracy did not disap-

pear altogether. In Prussia some of the wealthiest industrialists came from the highest aristocracy. The heavily aristocratic officer corps played an important role in running the Prussian state and unified Germany. In France about 20 to 25 percent of officers and many diplomats were aristocrats. In Britain officers, diplomats, and high-ranking civil servants were usually of noble birth. In Austria and Russia, aristocratic origin was the norm for government service.

Nonetheless, nobles no longer asserted privileges based exclusively on birth. In most European states, such claims had become anachronisms.

■ The Expanding Middle Classes

Up to the eighteenth century, society had been divided into legally separate orders on the basis of birth. In the nineteenth century, it became more customary to classify people by their economic functions. The "middle class" belonged neither to the nobility nor to the peasantry nor to the industrial working class. It included such people as wealthy manufacturers, country physicians, and bank tellers. Given this diversity, it has become common to use the plural and think of all these people as forming the "middle classes." Another term frequently used to describe these people is *bourgeois*.

The nineteenth century has often been described as "the bourgeois century." Although such a label may be too broad, after the midcentury mark it is appropriate enough to use as a shorthand term to describe the dominance of the bourgeois elites. This situation was especially prevalent in western Europe, where the middle classes helped fashion much of society.

The middle classes expanded dramatically in the wake of industrialization. More trade and manufacture meant more entrepreneurs and managers, while the increasingly complex society called for more engineers, lawyers, accountants, and bankers. New standards of comfort and health demanded more merchants and doctors. Urban improvements in the generation after 1850 created a need for architects and contractors, among other professionals.

The middle and lower levels of middle-class society grew most rapidly as business, the professions, and government administration created more jobs. In the 1870s about 10 percent of urban working-class people reached lower-middle-class status by becoming storekeepers, lower civil servants, clerks, or salespeople. Faster growth occurred for white-collar workers than for their blue-collar counterparts. As industries matured, the increasing use of machinery and better industrial organization

---

Bleichröder (BLY-shro-der)

meant a need for fewer additional laborers and more clerks and bureaucrats. Large import-export businesses, insurance companies, and department stores provided opportunities of this kind. So did the expansion of government services.

The social impact of job growth was great. The men and women staffing these new positions often came from modest backgrounds. For the son or daughter of peasants to become village postmaster, schoolteacher, or clerk in a major firm signified social ascension, however modest. And for the family, such a position, even more than income, meant joining the lower stratum of the middle classes. Accessibility to its ranks was certainly one of the strengths of the bourgeoisie, an ever growing group whose promise of social respectability and material comfort exercised a compelling force of attraction over the lower classes.

A widening subgroup of the middle classes consisted of members of the professions, those whose prestige rested on the claim of exclusive expertise in a particular field. In the early nineteenth century, requirements for exercising a profession varied, depending on the country. In France and Prussia, for example, government regulation stipulated the necessary qualifications to practice medicine; while in England only the Royal Colleges did. Medicine in the United States was unregulated by either governmental or medical schools. As the professions attempted to create a monopoly for themselves and eliminate rivals, they established stricter standards. Medical doctors, for instance, began requiring specialized education to distinguish themselves from herbalists, midwives, bone-setters, healers, and other competitors, and they insisted on their exclusive right to exercise their profession. The medical profession controlled access to its ranks by establishing powerful professional associations—for example, the British Medical Association (1832) and the German Medical Association (1872).

Although the professionalization of medicine did not create better doctors immediately, as the science of medicine taught at universities improved, so did the preparation and expertise of doctors. Similarly, in other professions, such as law, architecture, and engineering, common standards and requirements encouraged professional practice and expertise. By midcentury either professional associations or the state itself accredited members of the professions. Women had limited access to these professions; typically their opportunities were confined to lower teaching positions. After the Crimean War, as a result of Florence Nightingale's efforts (see page 743), nursing became an increasingly popular profes-

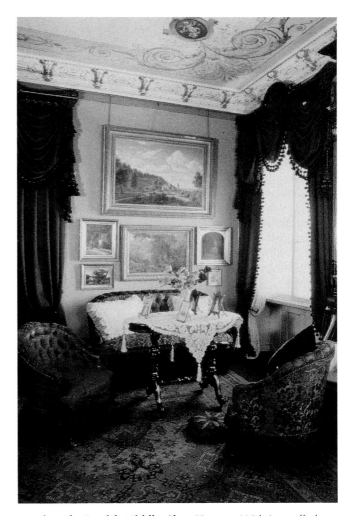

Interior of a Danish Middle-Class Home   With its stuffed furniture, lace curtains and tablecloths, and gilt-edged framed paintings, this living room provided a comfortable and pleasing escape from the grimy exterior of the industrial city. *(National Museum of Denmark)*

sion for women. But the dominant view in the middle classes was to discourage women from all employment.

The growing role of the state in society led to bureaucratic expansion. More and more, civil servants were selected by merit rather than through patronage. By the eighteenth century, Prussia had instituted a civil service examination system. After the Revolution, France instituted educational requirements for certain government corps, and by the 1880s it established civil service exams for all government positions. Beginning in 1870, Britain introduced the civil service examination and eliminated patronage.

◼ Middle-Class Lifestyles

The standard of living of the growing middle classes varied considerably, from the wealthy entrepreneur who bought a château, or built one, to the bourgeois who dwelled in a modest apartment. But they all lived in new standards of comfort. Their homes had running water, upholstered furniture, and enough space to provide separate sleeping and living quarters. They owned several changes of clothing and consumed a varied diet that included meat and dairy products, sugar, coffee, and tea. They read books and subscribed to newspapers and journals. Having at least one servant was a requisite for anyone who wished to be counted among the middle classes in the mid-nineteenth century.

By 1900 servants were still common among bourgeois households, but they were fewer in proportion to the population as a whole. As service industries developed, the need for servants decreased. With the growth of cab services, for instance, a family could dispense with a coachman and groom. And many families went without servants. Toward the end of the century, domestics' wages rose as competing forms of employment vied for their service, and only the upper layers of the bourgeoisie still employed domestic help.

In some areas suburban living became fashionable. The wealthy lived in large, imposing houses; the less well-off lived in smaller houses with a garden for privacy and quiet. Some owned two homes—one in the city and one in the countryside, providing a respite from the hectic urban environment.

For further relief from the crowded cities, visits to resorts became popular. Throughout Europe, resort towns sprang up, devoted principally to the amusement of the well-off. It became fashionable to "take the waters"—to bathe in hot springs and drink the mineral waters thought to have special attributes—and gamble in resorts such as Baden-Baden in Germany and Vichy in France. For the first time, tourism became big business. Thomas Cook (1808–1892), an Englishman, organized tours to the Crystal Palace exhibition of 1851 in London, the largest world exposition, which highlighted industrial accomplishments. Discovering the large market for guided travel, Cook began running tours in England and

The Crystal Palace   Built in 1851, this building was the largest glass and steel structure of its time. Site of the first great international exposition, the Crystal Palace displayed the inventiveness and opulence of the age.   *(Courtesy of the Trustees of the British Museum)*

on the Continent. In the eighteenth century the European tour had been a custom of the aristocracy, but now many members of the middle classes demanded this experience as well.

New wealth and leisure time led as well to more hotels, restaurants, and cafés. In 1869 Paris had 20,000 cafés and 4,000 hotels and lodging houses; the largest hotel offered 700 well-appointed rooms to discriminating guests. Vienna's National Hotel, with 300 rooms, had steam heat, spring water on every floor, and an icehouse providing cool drinks. For the traveler's convenience, many hotels, such as the monumental Charing Cross Hotel in London, were located next to train stations. At home or away, the bourgeois valued comfort.

The middle classes shared certain attitudes about the conduct of their lives. They believed their successes were due not to birth but to talent and effort. They wanted to be judged by their merits, and they expected their members to abide by strict moral principles. Their lives were supposed to be disciplined, especially with regard to sex and drink. The age was called "Victorian" because the middle classes in Britain saw in the queen who reigned for two-thirds of the century a reflection of their own values. (See the feature "Weighing the Evidence: An Engraving of the British Royal Family" in Chapter 22, on pages 772–773.) "Victorian morality," widely preached but not always practiced, was often viewed as hypocritical by social critics. Yet as the middle classes came to dominate society, their values became the social norms. Public drunkenness was discouraged, and anti-alcohol movements vigorously campaigned against drinking. Public festivals were regulated, making them more respectable and less rowdy.

In spite of their differences in education, wealth, and social standing, most of the bourgeoisie resembled one another in dress, habits of speech, and deportment. Bourgeois men dressed somberly, in dark colors, avoiding any outward signs of luxury. Their clothing fit closely and eschewed decoration—an adjustment to the machine age, in which elaborate dress hampered activity. It also reflected a conscious attempt to emphasize the frugal and achievement-oriented attitudes of the bourgeoisie in contrast to what was seen as the frivolous nobility.

Bourgeois conventions regarding women's dress were less reserved. Extravagant amounts of colorful fabrics used to fashion huge, beribboned hoop dresses reflected the newfound wealth of the middle classes and confirmed their view of women as ornaments whose lives were to be limited to the home and made easier by servants. This era was dominated by domesticity, by the ideal of the home. While the man was out in the secular

Josephine Grey Butler   An important Victorian reformer, Butler agitated for several causes, most notably abolition of the Contagious Diseases Act. This act empowered the police to arrest any woman it suspected of prostitution and to force her to be examined for venereal disease. Largely as a result of Butler's efforts, this act was repealed in 1886.
(Fawcett Library/Mary Evans Picture Library)

world earning a living and advancing his career, the bourgeois woman was to run her household, providing her family with an orderly, comfortable shelter from the storms of daily life. (See the box "Reading Sources: Advice on Running the Middle-Class Household.") She decorated the rooms, changed curtains with the seasons and the styles, supervised the servants, kept the accounts, oversaw the children's homework and religious education, and involved herself in charitable works. In the decades around midcentury, the notion of two separate spheres—one male and public, the other female and private—reached its height.

In spite of the relatively passive role assigned to women, many bourgeois women were very active. Some took up philanthropic causes, helping the sick and the poor. In England, Josephine Grey Butler (1828–1906), a member of a family of reformers, fought for the spread of education to impoverished women. She also waged a fierce battle against prostitution. Many bourgeois women helped their husbands or fathers in the office, the business, or the writing of scientific treatises. Others

Advice on Running the Middle-Class Household

In 1861 Isabella Mary Mayson Beeton, a London housewife, published Mrs. Beeton's Book of Household Management, *which in Britain was outsold only by the Bible. Her popular book provided British middle-class women with advice on running their households and reflected their values concerning discipline, frugality, and cleanliness.*

As with the commander of an army, or the leader of an enterprise, so is it with the mistress of a house. Her spirit will be seen through the whole establishment; and just in proportion as she performs her duties intelligently and thoroughly, so will her domestics follow in her path. Of all those acquirements, which more particularly belong to the feminine character, there are none which take a higher rank, in our estimation, than such as enter into a knowledge of household duties; for on these are perpetually dependent the happiness, comfort, and well-being of a family. . . .

Early rising is one of the most essential qualities which enter into good Household Management, as it is not only the parent of health, but of innumerable other advantages. Indeed, when a mistress is an early riser, it is almost certain that her house will be orderly and well-managed. . . .

Cleanliness is indispensable to health, and must be studied both in regard to the person and the house, and all that it contains. . . .

Frugality and economy are home virtues, without which no household can prosper. . . .

Charity and benevolence are duties which a mistress owes to herself as well as to her fellow-creatures; and there is scarcely any income so small, but something may be spared from it. . . . Great ad-

vantages may result from visits paid the poor, for there being, unfortunately, much ignorance, generally amongst them with respect to all household knowledge, there will be opportunities for advising and instructing them in a pleasant and unobtrusive manner, in cleanliness, industry, cookery, and good management. . . .

A housekeeping account-book should invariably be kept, and kept punctually and precisely. . . .

. . . The treatment of servants is of the highest possible moment as well to the mistress as to the domestics themselves. On the head of the house the latter will naturally fix their attention; and if they perceive that the mistress's conduct is regulated by high and correct principles, they will not fail to respect her. If, also a benevolent desire is shown to promote their comfort, at the same time that a steady performance of their duty is exacted, then their respect will not be unmingled with affection, and they will be more solicitous to continue to deserve her favour.

Source: Isabella Mary Mayson Beeton, *Mrs. Beeton's Book of Household Management* (London: S. O. Beeton, 1861), pp. 1–6.

 For additional information on this topic, go to http://college.hmco.com.

achieved success on their own terms, running their own businesses, writing, painting, teaching.

The expectation that middle-class women would be married and taken care of by their husbands led to the provision of inferior education for girls and young women. Even bright and intellectually curious young girls could not receive as good an education as their brothers, nor as

a consequence pursue as interesting a career—a situation that had prevailed for centuries.

Various liberal movements in the nineteenth century insisted on legal equality among men, removing disabilities aimed against members of a particular social class or religion. Such discrimination, many had insisted, should also not be based on gender. Proponents

Ladies' Bicycling Fashion   This new mode of transportation suggested possibilities for female emancipation. Free, on her bicycle, the young woman is contrasted with a man, who rides only a tricycle.   *(From Karin Helm [ed.],* Rosinen aus der Gartenlaube *[Gütersloh: Signum Verlag, n.d.]. Reproduced with permission.)*

Telephone Operators in London   New technologies opened up new employment opportunities for women. Telephone operators formed a completely feminized profession.   *(Boyer-Viollet)*

of women's rights demanded equal access to education and the professions. Slowly, secondary and university education was made available to young women. In Europe the University of Zurich in Switzerland was the first university to admit women in 1865. Although British universities admitted women, the University of London did not grant them degrees until after 1878; and the most prestigious British institutions, Oxford and Cambridge, did not grant degrees to women until after World War I. In spite of discriminatory laws, harassment by male students, and initial obstruction by professional and accrediting groups, a few female doctors and lawyers practiced in England by the 1870s and on the Continent in the following decades.

Women more easily penetrated lower levels of middle-class occupations. Expanding school systems, civil services, and businesses provided new employment opportunities for women. By the 1890s, two-thirds of primary school teachers in England and half the post office staff in France were women; by 1914 nearly half a million women worked as shop assistants in England. Some new technologies created jobs that became heavily feminized, such as the positions of typist and telephone operator.

■ The Workers' Lot

The increased prosperity and greater productivity of the period gradually improved the conditions of both female and male workers in the generation after 1850. Their wages and standards of living rose, and they enjoyed more job security. In Britain the earning power of the average worker rose by one-third between 1850 and 1875. For the first time, workers were able to put money aside to tide them over in hard times.

The workers' increased income permitted a better diet. In France the average number of calories consumed per adult male increased by one-third between 1840 and

1890. In Britain, between 1844 and 1876, per capita consumption of tea tripled, and that of sugar quadrupled. The quality of food as well as the amount also improved: people consumed more meat, fish, eggs, and dairy products.

Legislation gradually reduced the length of the workweek. The British workweek, typically 73 hours in the 1840s, was reduced to 56 hours in 1874. In France it was reduced to 10 hours a day, in Germany to 11. But these improvements were accompanied by an increased emphasis on efficiency at the workplace. Fewer informal breaks were allowed as industrialists insisted on greater worker productivity. New machines increased the tempo of work, frequently leading to exhaustion and accidents.

As workers had more time and more money, their leisure patterns changed. Some leisure activities that previously had been limited to the upper classes became available to workers. The introduction of rail connections to resort towns such as Brighton in England or Trouville and Dieppe in France enabled workers to visit such places. New music and dance halls, popular theaters, and other forms of public entertainment sprang up to claim workers' increased spending money.

Although most workers believed their lot had improved, they were also aware that a vast gulf remained between them and the middle and upper classes. In the 1880s in the northern French industrial city of Lille, the combined estate of twenty thousand workers equaled that of one average industrialist. Life expectancies still varied dramatically according to income; in Bordeaux in 1853, the life expectancy of a male bourgeois was twenty years greater than that of a male laborer.

The disparity between rich and poor was especially striking in the case of domestics. Most servants were female, and they led tiring and restricted lives under the close supervision of their employers. Their hours were overly long: a six-and-one-half-day week was not uncommon. Housed in either the basement or the attic, servants experienced extremes of cold, heat, and humidity. Sometimes they were subjected to physical or sexual abuse by the master of the house, his sons, or the head of the domestic staff. And yet, for impoverished rural women with little chance of finding better work, domestic service was a risky but often necessary option. It provided free housing, food, and clothing and allowed the servant to save an annual sum equivalent to an amount between one-third and one-half of a worker's yearly wages. These savings often served as a dowry and allowed the young woman to make an advantageous match. Two out of five female wage earners in England were in domestic employ in 1851.

Although a few members of the working class managed to enter the lower levels of the middle classes, most remained mired in the same occupations as their grandparents. Poverty was still pervasive. In the 1880s about one-third of Londoners were living at or below the subsistence level. Industrial and urban diseases, such as tuberculosis, were common among workers. Compared with the healthier, better-fed, and better-housed middle classes, the workers continued living in shabby and limited circumstances.

■ The Transformation of the Countryside

Before the nineteenth century, the countryside had hardly changed at all, but beginning at midcentury it was radically transformed. Especially in western Europe, an increasing number of people left the land. In 1850, 20 percent of the population of Britain were agricultural workers; by 1881 only 11 percent were. The decrease of the agricultural population led in many places to labor shortages and therefore higher wages for farm hands.

Agriculture became increasingly efficient, and the food supply grew significantly. More land was put under the plow. Not only was more land cultivated but the yield per acre increased. In 1760 an agricultural worker in England could feed himself and one other person; by 1841 he could feed himself and 2.7 others. The population of Europe nearly doubled between 1800 and 1880, and yet it was nourished better than ever before.

Higher yields were the result of an increased use of manure, augmented in the 1870s by saltpeter imported from Chile and, beginning in the 1880s, by chemical fertilizers manufactured in Europe. Innovations in tools also improved productivity. The sickle, which required the laborer to crouch to cut grass or wheat, was replaced by the long-handled scythe, which allowed the field hand to stand and use the full weight of the body to swing the instrument through the grain. This new method increased efficiency fourfold. In the 1850s steam-driven threshing machinery was introduced in some parts of western Europe. Organizational techniques borrowed from industrial labor, including specialization and regular schedules, also contributed to greater productivity on the land.

Improved roads and dramatically expanded rail lines enabled farmers to extend their markets. No longer did they need to produce only for the local area; they could depend on a national market and beyond for customers.

While the prices of farm products rose, those of industrial products fell, allowing farmers to purchase machinery to work the land as well as items providing personal convenience such as cast-iron stoves. Owners of medium and large farms did particularly well. For the first time, many qualified for credit, and the availability of fire and weather insurance buffered some from the unpredictability of farming.

Life in the countryside became less insular. Not only did rail lines connect farms to cities, but national school systems brought teachers into the villages. Local dialects and in some cases even distinct languages that peasants had spoken for generations were replaced by a standardized national language. Local provincial costumes became less common as styles fashionable in the cities spread to the countryside via mail order catalogs. The farm girls who went to the cities as maids to work in middle-class homes returned to their villages with urban and middle-class ideals. The military draft brought the young men of the village into contact with urban folk and further spread urban values to the countryside.

Even so, the rural world remained very distinct from urban society. Many of the forces seen as contributing to modernity actually aggravated rural conditions. The expansion of manufacturing in cities contributed to the decline of cottage industry in rural areas, where agricultural workers had relied on the putting-out system to provide supplementary income. Thus farm workers were idle during slack seasons, and rural unemployment grew. In many cases railroads bringing goods made elsewhere wiped out some of the local markets on which these cottage industries had depended. The steamship lowered the cost of transporting freight, including grain from distant Canada and Argentina, which often undersold wheat grown in Europe. The resultant crisis, worsened by a rural population explosion, led to the emigration of millions, who left the land for towns and cities or even migrated across the seas to the Americas and Australia (see page 820). Although this process was painful for large segments of the rural population, for those who were able to remain on the land, the situation eventually improved.

These trends had a striking effect in the rural areas of western Europe. Eastern Europe, in contrast, was hardly touched by them. In Russia agriculture remained backward; the average yield per acre in 1880 was one-quarter that of Great Britain. The land sheltered a large surplus population that was underemployed and contributed little to the rural economy. In the Balkans, most peasants were landless and heavily indebted.

Steam-Powered Thresher   This image shows the thresher being operated in the French countryside in 1860. It would be decades before this kind of technology became a common sight in Europe, but it was a harbinger of the change coming to the rural world.   *(Bibliothèque Nationale de France)*

Pissarro: L'avenue de l' Opéra, Sunlight, Winter Morning   Camille Pissarro, one of the leading impressionists, portrayed the broad new avenue designed by Baron Haussmann. The avenue leads to the new opera, in background, also planned during the Second Empire.   *(Musée Saint-Denis, Reims/Giraudon/Art Resource, NY)*

URBAN PROBLEMS AND SOLUTIONS

BY 1851 the majority of English people lived in cities; by 1891 the majority of Germans did as well. To cope with urban growth and its attendant problems—epidemics, crowding, traffic jams—cities developed public health measures and introduced planning and rebuilding programs. They adapted the new technologies to provide such urban amenities as streetlights, public transportation, water and sewer systems, and helped make the city safer by establishing large, more efficient police forces. Cities gradually became safer and more pleasant places to live, although for a long time city dwellers continued to suffer high mortality rates.

■ City Planning and Urban Renovation

Most of Europe's cities had begun as medieval walled cities and had grown haphazardly into major industrial centers. Their narrow, crooked streets could not accommodate the increased trade and daily movement of goods and people, and traffic snarls were common. City

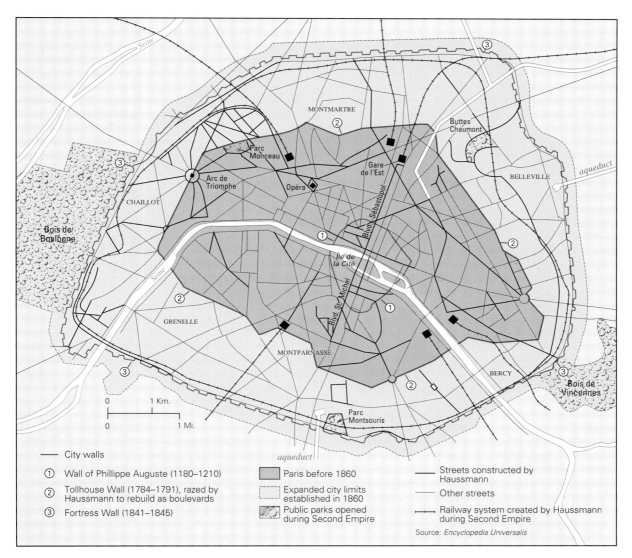

Map 23.2   Haussmann's Paris, 1850–1870   During the reign of Napoleon III, Baron Georges Haussmann reshaped the city of Paris, replacing its narrow medieval streets with a system of broad avenues and public parks and encircling the city with a railway.

officials began to recognize that broad, straight avenues would help relieve the congestion and also bring sunlight and fresh air into the narrow and perpetually dank lanes and alleys. In the 1820s, London saw the first ambitious street-widening initiative. On Regency Street, old hovels were torn down and replaced with fancy new houses; the poor were displaced. Later projects followed this pattern. (See the feature "Weighing the Evidence: The Modern City and Photography" on pages 806–807.)

The most extensive program of urban rebuilding took place in midcentury Paris. Over a period of eighteen years, Napoleon III and his aide, Baron Georges Haussmann (1809–1891), transformed Paris from a dirty medieval city to a beautiful modern one (see Map 23.2). Haussmann and his engineers carved broad, straight avenues through what had been dingy slums. They built elegant houses on the new tree-lined avenues. Public monuments and buildings, such as the new opera house, enhanced the city. The tremendous costs of this ambitious scheme kept the city of Paris in debt for decades. In addition, the slum-removal program drove tens of thousands of the poorest Parisians to the outskirts of the city, leading to greater social segregation than had previously existed.

Haussmann's extensive work in Paris served as a model for other cities, and although none was rebuilt as extensively, many underwent significant improvements. The cities of Europe began to display an expansive grace and sense of order, supporting the belief of the middle classes that theirs was an age of progress.

◼ The Introduction of Public Services

Beginning at midcentury, government at the central and local levels helped make cities more livable by legislating sanitary reforms and providing public transportation and lighting. Medical practitioners in the 1820s had observed that disease and higher mortality were related to dirt and lack of clean air, water, and sunshine. Since diseases spreading from the poorer quarters of town threatened the rich and powerful, there was a general interest in improving public health by clearing slums, broadening streets, and supplying clean air and water to the cities.

Reform began in England, where the lawyer and civil servant Edwin Chadwick (1800–1895) drafted important plans for reform that became the basis for legislation. The Public Health Bill of 1848 established national standards for urban sanitation and required cities to regulate the installation of sewers and the disposal of refuse. The 1875 Health Act mandated certain basic health standards for water and drainage. Armed with these laws, cities and towns took the initiative: Birmingham cleared 50 acres of slums in the 1870s, for example.

London was also a leader in supplying public water, a service later adopted by Paris and many other cities. Berlin had a municipal water system in 1850, but it took several decades before clean water was available in every household. As late as the 1870s, Berlin's sewage was carried in open pipes. In Paris, which typically led France in innovations, 60 percent of the houses had running water in 1882. The French capital did not have a unitary sewer system until the 1890s, however.

As running water in the home became a standard rather than a luxury, bathing became more common. The English upper classes had learned the habit of daily baths from their colonial experience in India; on the Continent it did not become the custom until about the third quarter of the nineteenth century. The French artist

Edgar Degas° (1834–1917) frequently painted bath scenes, portraying the new European habit.

All these changes had a direct impact on the lives of city dwellers. Life became healthier, more comfortable, and more orderly. Between the 1840s and 1880, London's death rate fell from 26 per thousand to 20 per thousand. In Paris for the same period the decline was from 29.3 to 23.7 per thousand. The decline in the incidence of diseases associated with filthy living conditions was even more immediate. Improved water supplies provided a cleaner environment and reduced the prevalence of waterborne diseases such as cholera and typhoid.

Other improvements also contributed to a better quality of life. With the introduction of urban transportation, city dwellers no longer had to live within walking distance of their workplaces. An early example of public transportation was the French omnibus service of the 1820s—a system of horse-drawn carriages available to the public on fixed routes. In the 1850s the tram was introduced. A carriage drawn on a rail line by horses, a tram could pull larger loads of passengers faster than the omnibus. Because of the many rail stations in London and the difficulty of getting from one station to another in time to make a connection, London built an underground railway in 1863, the predecessor of the subway system. Technological improvements made the bicycle a serious means of transportation for some city dwellers. By the mid-1880s, nearly 100,000 bicycles were being pedaled around Great Britain, and a decade later, 375,000 in France—rising to a million by 1900.

Improvements in public transportation enabled workers to move out of the inner city into the less dense and less expensive suburbs. This trend in turn led to a decrease in urban population density and eventually helped make the city a healthier place to live.

Gaslights also improved city life, making it easier and safer to be outside at night. (Prior to gaslights, city dwellers depended mainly on moonlight or, rarely, expensive and time-consuming oil lamps—which had to be lit one at a time.) In 1813 London was the first city to be illuminated by gas; Berlin followed in 1816. Electrical lights were introduced in Paris in 1875, although they were not common until the end of the century.

Cities also significantly expanded police forces to impose order, to control criminal activity, and to discourage behavior deemed undesirable, such as dumping garbage on the street, relieving oneself in public, or carousing late at night. In 1850 London was the best-policed city in Europe with a 5,000-man force. Paris had around 3,000 police officers.

Degas (DAY-gah)

SOCIAL AND POLITICAL INITIATIVES

EW institutions and groups emerged to tackle the unequal distribution of wealth and critical urban problems that followed in the wake of economic growth. The state intervened in the economy in new ways. Private charitable groups sprang up. Socialist political parties, exclusively dedicated to improving the workers' lot, gained in numbers and strength.

■ State Intervention in Welfare

The difficult conditions industry imposed on workers led to debates in several countries about the need for the state to protect the workers. The growing militancy of organized labor also forced the established authority to consider ways to meet the workers' needs. While some rejected government intervention in the free operation of market forces, others argued that the laws of supply and demand had caused the exploitation of many who ought to have been protected—especially very young children and pregnant women. Britain led the way with Factory Acts regulating child and female labor; similar acts were passed later in Prussia and France. In much of Europe, however, the state did little to improve the welfare of the working class. In eastern Europe, where industry was still in its infancy, workers had no protection.

Fear of social upheaval and the rising strength of socialist political parties prompted some governments to act. In France moderate bourgeois liberals attempted to defuse class war by advocating "solidarism." With the motto "Every man, his neighbor's debtor," solidarism insisted on the mutual responsibility of classes and individuals for one another's well-being. Guided by such sentiments, French Republicans passed a number of laws toward the end of the century that improved the lot of the working class. In newly unified Germany, the government wanted to impress workers with state benefits so they would abandon the growing Socialist Party and back the kaiser's authoritarian government. Chancellor Otto von Bismarck embarked on a deliberate program to tame the workers and win their support for the existing political and economic institutions. Thus, in the 1880s the new German government provided a comprehensive welfare plan that included health insurance and old-age pensions. In addition to the welfare initiatives by state and city governments, middle and upper classes also worked to better the workers' lot. Concern among these groups and individuals arose from a mixture of pity for

workers' conditions, religious teachings about their responsibilities for the less fortunate, and fear of the consequences of unrelieved misery.

Women participated heavily in volunteer charity work. By the end of the nineteenth century, as many as half a million English women contributed their time to provide charity to the less fortunate. In Sweden by the 1880s, women had founded refuges for the destitute, old-age homes, a children's hospital, an asylum for the mentally handicapped, and various societies to promote female industry.

In Catholic and Protestant countries, the Christian churches traditionally had identified with the rights of employers and seemed to ignore the lot of the workers. However, a number of Christians, lay and clerical, began to emphasize the church's need to address social issues. Pope Leo XIII (r. 1878–1903) reflected this trend and reinforced it among Catholics when in 1891 he issued his encyclical *Rerum novarum* ("Of New Things"), which defined society's responsibility for the well-being of the poor. His message was taken up in France, Italy, and Spain among what became known as "social Catholics." (See the box "Reading Sources: Leo XIII Calls for Concern for the Working Classes.") In England, Protestants' concern for the poor was evidenced by the founding of the Salvation Army in 1878. Religious groups also hoped they could win converts among the less privileged by alleviating their plight.

Increasingly, municipalities, volunteer groups, and churches accepted responsibility for the well-being of others. Among their many activities, private charitable groups furnished cheap housing for the poor, church groups visited them, providing advice and some monetary assistance, municipalities opened free medical dispensaries. In many cases these pioneering efforts in aiding the poor were later taken over by the state, which, in amplified form, led to the development—in much of twentieth-century Europe—of the welfare state.

■ Educational and Cultural Opportunities

At the beginning of the nineteenth century, governments took little responsibility for providing education. Some upper-class children were educated with private tutors, and others attended elite schools. All schools were segregated by social class and all but a few charity schools for the poor charged tuition. In England the education of the masses became a national responsibility after the Second Reform Bill of 1867. This legislation extended the vote to the artisan classes and prompted a movement to ensure that the new voters were educated. In 1870 the

❧ READING SOURCES

Leo XIII Calls for Concern for the Working Classes

In his 1891 encyclical Rerum Novarum (Of New Things), *Pope Leo XIII called on the propertied classes and the state to show concern for the poor. Leo reminded his readers of the central Christian message: charity. Note also how he appears to present the church as a solution to the growing class conflicts of the late nineteenth century.*

The momentous seriousness of the present state of things just now fills every mind with painful apprehension . . . and there is nothing which has a deeper hold on public attention. . . .

. . . There is nothing more powerful than religion (of which the Church is the interpreter and guardian) in drawing rich and poor together, by reminding each class of its duties to the other, and especially of the duties of justice. Thus religion teaches the labouring man and the workman to carry out honestly and well all equitable agreements freely made; never to injure capital, or to outrage the person of an employer. . . . Religion teaches the rich man and the employer that their work people are not their slaves; that they must respect in every man his dignity as a man and as a Christian. . . . [T]he employer must never tax his work people beyond their strength, nor employ them in work unsuited to their sex or age. . . . [R]ich men and masters should remember this—that to exercise pressure for the sake of gain upon the indigent and the destitute and to make one's profit out of the need of another is condemned by all laws, human and divine. To defraud anyone of wages that are his due is a crime which cries to the avenging anger of Heaven.

Rights must be religiously protected wherever they are found; and it is the duty of the public authority to prevent and punish injury, and to protect each one in the possession of his own. Still, when there is question of protecting the rights of individuals, the poor and helpless have a claim to special consideration. The richer population have many ways of protecting themselves, and stand less in need of help from the State; those who are badly off have no resources to fall back upon, and must chiefly rely upon the assistance of the State. And it is for this reason that wage-earners, who are undoubtedly among the weak and necessitous, should be specially cared for and protected by the commonwealth.

Source: Francesco Nitti, *Catholic Socialism*, trans. Mary Mackintosh (New York: Macmillan & Co., 1895), pp. 404, 409, 415.

English government began to provide significant subsidies for education, to set educational standards, and to establish a national inspection system to enforce them. England and France initiated mandatory primary school education in the 1880s.

Public education included not only reading, writing, and arithmetic but other skills as well. By insisting on punctuality and obliging students to carry out repetitive tasks such as copying letters, words, or sentences, schools encouraged people to fit into the emerging industrial society. The obedience and respect for authority learned at school shaped the soldiers and factory workers of the future. And regardless of political inclination, each regime took advantage of its control of the educational system to inculcate in the young the love of country and of its form of government.

Secondary education was, on the whole, available only to the privileged few in the upper middle classes. It confirmed their social status and won them access to the universities and the professions. For a very small number from the lower middle classes, secondary school attendance provided the means to ascend socially. The lower middle class was sparsely represented in universities, and the children of workers and peasants were totally absent.

Public education spread from the schools to other institutions, which made culture available to the masses in new ways. Between 1840 and 1880, the number of large libraries in Europe increased from 40 to 500. The French national public library, the *Bibliothèque Nationale*, was established in Paris in the 1860s. This iron and glass building, radical for its time, was an impressive monument to the desire to make reading available to an expanded public. Many provincial cities, as well as the glittering capitals of Europe, were endowed with new libraries. Less grandiose, but probably more important for mostly rural populations, were the traveling libraries.

Museums and art galleries, which in the previous century had been open to only a select few, gradually became accessible to the general public. The first museum to open to the public was the Louvre in Paris after the French Revolution. Other European countries lagged behind in making their cultural heritages available to the masses, but in the later part of the century even the poorer classes gained access to these temples of culture.

CULTURE IN AN AGE OF OPTIMISM

T HE improving economic and material conditions of the second half of the nineteenth century buoyed European thinkers. Many believed that men and women were becoming more enlightened, and they expressed faith in humankind's ability to transform the world with a parade of scientific and technological breakthroughs. The world seemed knowable and perfectible. This faith advanced secularism while it undermined the certainties of traditional religion. The arts reflected these new values, emphasizing realism and science—as well as an underlying foreboding about the dark side of this "age of optimism."

■ Darwin and Evolution

By midcentury most thinkers accepted the notion of change and transformation of society—and, by analogy, of the natural environment. The French thinker Comte championed the notion that human development—human history—proceeded through distinct and irreversible stages. Human progress, inscribed in the laws of nature, leads inexorably upward to the final and highest stage of development, the positive—or scientific—stage. Widely read throughout Europe and Latin America, Comte's writings helped bolster the era's faith in science, and the very progress science made seemed to confirm its precepts. Comte's philosophy, known as positivism, dominated the era. While the romantics had emphasized feeling, positivists upheld the significance of the measurable, the palpable, the verifiable. Scientific methods, the positivists were confident, would ensure the continued progress of humanity. Hadn't science already proved that the world was evolving to ever higher forms?

Charles Darwin, Proponent of Evolution   This portrait was made in 1840, when the young scientist was wrestling with the meaning of the evidence he had collected in the Galápagos Islands. His observations there became the basis for *On the Origin of Species by Means of Natural Selection* (1859), the most important scientific work of the nineteenth century. *(Down House/The Bridgeman Art Library, London and New York)*

In the field of geology, the Englishman Charles Lyell (1797–1875) maintained that the earth was far older than the biblical story of Genesis suggested. He argued that its geological formations—the mountains, valleys, and seas—were subject to natural forces that, over hundreds of thousands, even millions, of years, had shaped them. Most educated people accepted his theory, which led many to wonder if it might also be true that the animal kingdom had evolved gradually over long periods of time.

Although evolution in the biological realm had been suggested as early as the end of the eighteenth century, Charles Darwin (1809–1882) was the first to offer a plausible explanation of the process. As the naturalist on an official British scientific expedition in the

🔖 READING SOURCES

Darwin's Basic Laws of Evolution

Writing in an age of vast transformations, Darwin could imagine the mutability of all nature, including species, over time. And like his contemporaries, he could imagine that evolution would lead to improvement, to increasing "perfection" of various species. A religious man who lost much of his faith as a result of his scientific investigations, Darwin was anxious to reassure Christians, hence his attempt to portray evolution as part of God's divine plan.

Nothing at first can appear more difficult to believe than that the more complex organs and instincts have been perfected, not by means superior to, though analogous with, human reason, but by the accumulation of innumerable slight variations, each good for the individual possessor. Nevertheless, this difficulty, though appearing to our imagination insuperably great, cannot be considered real if we admit the following propositions, namely, that all parts of the organisation and instincts offer, at least, individual differences—that there is a struggle for existence leading to the preservation of profitable deviations of structure or instinct—and, lastly, that gradations in the state of perfection of each organ may have existed, each good of its kind. The truth of these propositions cannot, I think, be disputed. . . .

As geology plainly proclaims that each land has undergone great physical changes, we might have expected to find that organic beings have varied under nature, in the same way as they have varied under domestication. And if there has been any variability under nature, it would be an unaccountable fact if natural selection had not come into play. . . .

There is grandeur in this view of life, with its several powers, having been originally breathed by the Creator into a few forms or into one; and that, whilst this planet has gone cycling on according to the fixed law of gravity, from so simple a beginning endless forms most beautiful and most wonderful have been, and are being evolved.

Source: Charles Darwin, *On the Origin of Species by Means of Natural Selection*, 6th ed., vol. 2 (1872; reprint, New York: Appleton, 1923), pp. 267–268, 279, 305–306.

1830s, he had visited the Galápagos Islands off the western coast of South America. On these islands he found species similar to but different from those on the mainland and even different from one another. Could they be the results of separate creations? Or was it more likely that in varying environments they had adapted differently? Darwin proposed that closely related species compete for food and living space. In this struggle, those in each species that are better adapted to the environment have the advantage over the others and hence are more likely to survive. In the "struggle for existence," only the fittest endure. Those surviving, Darwin surmised, pass on the positive traits to their offspring. He called the mechanism that explained the evolution and development of new species "natural selection," a process that he proposed was imperceptible but continuous. (See the box "Reading Sources: Darwin's Basic Laws of Evolution.")

Darwin's theory of the inevitability of evolution in nature echoes the era's confidence in change and its conviction that the present represented a more developed stage of the past. His work was seen as confirming the notion that societies—like species—were preordained to evolve toward progressively higher stages. Darwin at first avoided the question of whether human beings, too, were affected by the laws of evolution. To do so would be to question humanity's uniqueness, its separation from the rest of creation by its possession (in the

Christian view) of a soul. But in *The Descent of Man* (1871), Darwin did confront this issue, clearly stating his belief that humanity, too, was subject to these natural laws. The recognition that human beings were members of the animal kingdom like other species disturbed him, and the admission, he wrote, "is like confessing a murder." Nonetheless, for Darwin scientific evidence took precedence over all other considerations.

Many Christians were shocked by these assertions, and some denounced the new scientific findings. Some argued that science and faith belonged to two different worlds. Others claimed that there was no reason why God could not have created the world through natural forces. In the long run, however, Darwinism seemed to undermine the certainties of religious orthodoxies by showing their incompatibility with scientific discovery.

Some contemporaries applied Darwin's theories to human society. Social Darwinists argued that human societies evolved in the same way as plants and animals. Just as species, so some human societies—races, classes, nations—were destined to survive, while others were condemned to fade away. And from these harsh laws a better humanity would evolve. The British social theorist Herbert Spencer (1820–1903), who coined the expression "survival of the fittest," believed that society should be established in such a way that the strongest and most resourceful would survive. The weak, poor, and improvident were not worthy of survival, and if the state helped them survive—for instance by providing welfare—it would only perpetuate the unfit. Poverty was a sign of biological inferiority, wealth a sign of success in the struggle for survival. In Europe and the United States (where Spencer was extremely popular, selling hundreds of thousands of books), Social Darwinism was thus used to justify callousness toward the poor at home and imperial conquest abroad. Since in the colonizing game the white races were the subjugators of Africans and Asians and not vice versa, whites were clearly superior, argued Social Darwinists. People of color were seen as inferior, poorly endowed to compete in the race for survival (see Chapter 24).

■ Physics, Chemistry, and Medicine

Dramatic scientific breakthroughs occurred in the nineteenth century, confirming the prevalent belief that human beings could understand and control nature. Since the seventeenth century, scientists had attempted to study nature by careful observation, by seeking regularities in nature, and by developing theories to explain what they had observed. Scientific truths had their own rules, independent of the investigator, who had to remain impartial and objective. The scientific method yielded major breakthroughs in the nineteenth century. In physics, laws regarding electricity and magnetism were articulated by Michael Faraday (1791–1867) and James Clerk Maxwell (1831–1879) in the 1830s and 1850s, respectively. Their work established the field of electrical science. In the 1840s, Hermann von Helmholtz (1821–1894) in Germany and James Joule (1818–1889) in Great Britain defined the nature of energy in the laws of thermodynamics. In chemistry, new elements were discovered almost every year, and individual findings contributed to the understanding of larger patterns. In 1869 Russian chemist Dmitri Mendeleev° (1834–1907) developed the periodic table, in which the elements are arranged by their atomic weight. He left blank spaces for elements still unknown but that he was confident existed. Within ten years, three of these elements were discovered, affirming the belief that scientific knowledge not only can be experimentally tested but also has predictive value. Such triumphs further enhanced science's prestige.

Prolific research yielded discoveries in one field of knowledge that could be transferred to another. For example, chemists produced new color dyes, enabling biologists to stain slides of microorganisms and better study their evolution. Scientific breakthroughs also led to technical achievements; for instance, inventions in chemistry led to the development of the first artificial fertilizers in 1842, while in physics the discovery of electromagnetism formed the basis of the telegraph and later the commercial uses of electricity.

Science also became increasingly specialized. In the eighteenth century, the scientist had been a learned amateur practicing a hobby. In the nineteenth century, as the state and industry became more involved in promoting scientific research, the scientist became a professional employed by a university, a hospital, or some other institution. New theories and discoveries were disseminated by scientific journals and at meetings of scientific associations and congresses. Around the mid-century mark, a number of important breakthroughs occurred in medicine. Before the development of anesthesia, surgical intervention was limited. With only alcohol to dull the patient's pain, even the swiftest surgeons could perform only modest surgical procedures. In the

---

Mendeleev (men-del-LAY-ef)

1840s, however, the introduction of ether and then chloroform allowed people to undergo more extensive surgery. It also was used to relieve pain in more routine procedures and in childbirth; Queen Victoria asked for chloroform when in labor.

Increasingly, the experimental method in science was applied to medicine, and as a result physicians became concerned not simply with treating diseases but with discovering their origins. Louis Pasteur (1822–1895) achieved notable breakthroughs when he discovered that microbes, small organisms invisible to the naked eye, cause various diseases. Pasteur found that heating milk to a certain temperature kills disease-carrying organisms. This process, called pasteurization, reduced the incidence of certain diseases that were particularly harmful to children. Pasteur initiated other advances as well in the prevention of disease. Vaccination against smallpox had started in England in the eighteenth century, but Pasteur invented vaccines for other diseases and was able to explain the process by which the body, inoculated with a weak form of bacilli, developed antibodies that successfully overcame more serious infections. In England the surgeon Joseph Lister (1827–1912) developed an effective disinfectant, carbolic acid, to kill the germs that cause gangrene and other infections in surgical patients. Lister's development of germ-free procedures transformed the science of surgery. By reducing the patient's risk, more ambitious surgery could be attempted. Eventually, midwives and doctors, by washing their hands and sterilizing their instruments, began to reduce the incidence of the puerperal, or "childbed," fever that killed so many women after childbirth. The increasingly scientific base of medicine and its visible success in combating disease improved its reputation.

Science was now fashionable. In 1869 Empress Eugénie in France had Louis Pasteur come to tea, draw blood from her finger, and examine it under a microscope, all to the astonishment of her guests. Some frogs, brought in for experimentation, escaped down palace corridors. The spectacle of science as the chic entertainment of an empress was a reminder of the increasing authority it commanded in the later nineteenth century.

■ Birth of the Social Sciences

The scientific method, so dramatically effective in uncovering the mysteries of nature, was also applied to the human enterprise. Just as the secrets of nature were unlocked, the workings of society, it was thought, could be understood in a scientific manner.

No field in the human sciences flourished as much in the nineteenth century as history. In an era undergoing vast transformations, many people became interested in change over time. They were eager to employ the methods of the scientist to explore their past. The father of modern historical writing is the German Leopold von Ranke° (1795–1886). Departing from the tradition of earlier historians, who explained the past as the ongoing fulfillment of an overarching purpose—divine will, the liberation of humanity, or some other goal—Ranke insisted that the role of the historian was to "show how things actually were." Like a scientist, the historian must be objective and dispassionate. By viewing humankind of all eras and environments on their own terms, and not those of others, historians could arrive at a better understanding of humanity.

This perspective transformed the study of history into a discipline with recognizable common standards of evidence. Historians studied and interpreted original (or "primary") sources; they collected and published their findings; they founded professional organizations and published major journals.

Other social sciences also developed in this period. Anthropology, the comparative study of people in different societies, had been the subject of speculative literature for hundreds of years. Increased contacts with non-European societies in the nineteenth century—the effect of burgeoning trade, exploration, and missionary activities—stimulated anthropological curiosity. In 1844 the Society of Ethnology was founded in Paris, followed by the Anthropological Society (1859). London, Berlin, and Vienna quickly followed suit, establishing similar societies in the 1860s. Consisting of medical doctors, biologists, and travelers, these societies speculated on the causes of the perceived differences among human races, mainly attributing the variations to their physical structures. Anthropologists gave apparent "scientific" backing to the era's racism, explaining that non-Europeans were condemned to an existence inferior to the white races.

In Britain, the main anthropological theorist was Edward Tylor (1832–1917), the son of a brass manufacturer. Through his travels, Tylor came into contact with non-European peoples, who aroused his curiosity. Strongly influenced by the evolutionary doctrines of his day, Tylor believed that the various societies of humankind were subject to discoverable scientific laws. Tylor posited that if one could travel back in time, one would find humankind increasingly unsophisticated; so,

---

von Ranke (fon RANG-key)

too, the farther one traveled from Europe, the more primitive humankind became. The contemporary African was at a level of development similar to that of Europeans in an earlier era.

Tylor was not technically a racist, since he argued that the conditions of non-Europeans were not due to biology but rather were a function of their institutions. Eventually, they would "evolve" and become akin to Europeans. Like racists, however, evolutionists believed in the superiority of the European over other races. Anthropology gave "scientific" sanction to the idea of a single European people, sharing either a similar biological structure or a common stage of social development, which distinguished them from non-Europeans.

Anthropology gradually gained recognition and legitimacy as a profession. In 1872 in France, Paul Broca founded a journal devoted to physical anthropology. In 1876 he founded a school of anthropology with six chaired professors. In 1884 Tylor—who was so closely identified with anthropology it was called "Mr. Tylor's science"—was appointed to the first university chair in anthropology in Britain.

The term *sociology* was coined by Auguste Comte. A number of ambitious thinkers, among them the English "social philosopher" Herbert Spencer (see page 797), had considered how individuals are affected by the society in which they live. In the 1840s various social reformers published detailed statistical investigations revealing relationships between, for instance, income and disease and death rates. A few decades later, the theoretical principles underlying sociology were spelled out. Among the first researchers to do so was Emile Durkheim° (1858–1917), who insisted that sociology was a verifiable science. He occupied the first chair of sociology at a French university in 1887. A few years later he founded a journal of sociology and mentored a corps of disciples who ensured the success of sociology as a professionalized discipline.

Whereas in the past, history, anthropology, and sociology were the purview of amateurs, now professional historians, anthropologists, and sociologists were engaged full-time in research and teaching at universities or research institutes. The professionalization that had occurred in medicine and physics also transformed the social sciences. Professionalization and specialization led to significant advances in several disciplines, but it also led to the fragmentation and compartmentalization of knowledge. People of broad learning and expertise became far less common.

■ The Challenge to Religion

The scientific claims of the era seemed to clash with the traditions of religion. A number of scientists, including Darwin himself, found their Christian faith undermined by theories on evolution. Although most Europeans continued to be strongly influenced by traditional religious beliefs, they appeared less confident than in earlier eras.

After the revolutions of 1848, religion was seen as a bulwark of order. In France Napoleon III gave the Catholic Church new powers over education, and the bourgeoisie flocked to worship. In Spain moderates who had been anticlerical (opposed to the clergy) began to support the church, and in 1851 they signed a concordat (an agreement with the papacy) declaring Roman Catholicism "the only religion of the Spanish nation." In Austria in 1855, the state surrendered powers it had acquired in the 1780s, returning to bishops full control over the clergy, the seminaries, and the administration of marriage laws.

In 1848 the papacy had been nearly overthrown by revolution, and in 1860 it lost most of its domains to Italy. Thus Pope Pius IX became a sworn enemy of liberalism, and in 1864, in the *Syllabus of Errors*, he condemned a long list of perceived errors, among them "progress," "liberalism," and "modern civilization." To establish full control over the clergy and believers, the Lateran Council in 1870 issued the controversial doctrine of papal infallibility, declaring that the pope, when speaking officially on matters of faith and morals, was incapable of error. This doctrine became a target of anticlerical opinion.

The political alliance the Catholic Church struck with reactionary forces meant that when new political groups came to power, they moved against the church. In Italy, since the church had discouraged national unification, conflict raged between the church and the new state. In Germany, Catholics had either held on to their regional loyalties or favored unification under Austrian auspices. When Protestant Prussia unified Germany, Chancellor Bismarck viewed the Catholics with suspicion as unpatriotic and launched a campaign against them, the *Kulturkampf*° ("cultural struggle"). Bismarck expelled the Jesuits and attempted to establish state control over the Catholic schools and appointment of bishops. Not satisfied, he seized church property and imprisoned or exiled 1,800 priests.

In France the republicans, who finally won the upper hand over monarchists in 1879, bitterly resented the church's support of the monarchist party. They were also

---

Durkheim (DIRK-hime)

Kulturkampf (KOOL-toor-kampf)

strongly influenced by Comte's ideas of positivism, believing that France would not be a free country until the power of the church was diminished and its nonscientific or antiscientific disposition was overcome. The republican regime reduced the role of the church in education as well as some other clerical privileges.

Greater religious tolerance, or perhaps indifference to religion in general, led to more acceptance of religious diversity. In 1854 and 1871 England opened university admission and teaching posts at all universities to non-Anglicans. Anti-Catholicism, at times a popular and virulent movement, declined in the 1870s. In France, too, the position of religious minorities improved. Some of the highest officials of the Second Empire were Protestants, as were some early leaders of the Third Republic and some important business leaders and scientists.

Legal emancipation of Jews, started in France in 1791, subsequently spread to the rest of the Continent. England removed restrictions on Jews when the House of Commons, in 1858, and the House of Lords the following decade allowed Jews to hold parliamentary seats. In the 1860s Germany and Austria-Hungary granted Jews the rights of citizenship. Social discrimination continued, however, and Jews were not accepted as social equals in most of European society. Although some Jews occupied high office in France and Italy, in Germany and Austria-Hungary they had to convert before they could aspire to such positions. In other fields, access was easier. Some of the major European banking houses were founded by Jews—the Rothschilds in France, Britain, and Germany, and the Warburgs in Germany, for instance.

In the expanding economy of western Europe, where the condition of most people was improving, the enhanced opportunity of a previously despised minority aroused relatively little attention. In other parts of Europe, Jews were not so fortunate. When they seized economic opportunities in eastern Europe and moved into commerce, industry, and the professions, they were resented. Outbreaks of violence against them, called *pogroms*, occurred in Bucharest, capital of Romania, in 1866 and in the Russian seaport of Odessa in 1871. Although economic rivalries may have fueled anti-Jewish feelings, they do not completely explain it. In most cases anti-Jewish sentiment occurred in the areas of Europe least exposed to liberal ideas of human equality and human rights.

The emphasis on science and reason transformed religion in the nineteenth century, but, as the continued anti-Semitism demonstrates, it by no means always led to increased tolerance or weakened religious fervor. On the contrary, in certain cases religiosity grew. French

people reported frequent sightings of the Virgin Mary. In 1858 a shepherd girl claimed to have seen and spoken with her at Lourdes°, which became an especially important shrine whose waters were reputed to heal the lame and the sick. In 1872 construction of a rail line allowed 100,000 people a year to visit the town.

Church attendance continued to be high, especially in rural areas. In England villagers usually attended church, many twice or more each Sunday. Children dutifully attended Sunday schools. Advances in printing made it possible to distribute large quantities of inexpensive religious tracts to a sizable and avid readership. The faithful eagerly funded proselytizing, sending large numbers of missionaries into all corners of the globe.

■ Culture in the Age of Material Change

The era's admiration of technology and science, and its idolization of progress, were reflected in the arts. Some artists optimistically believed they could more accurately portray reality by adopting the methods of the scientist, coolly depicting their subjects. A minority, however, were disillusioned by the materialism of the age and warned against its loss of values.

Photography had a direct impact on painting. Various experiments in the late eighteenth century, plus the inventions of the Frenchman Louis Daguerre° (1789–1851), made the camera relatively usable by the 1830s. It was still a large, cumbersome object, however, until the dry plate and the miniature camera were introduced in the 1870s. Twenty years later, with the invention of celluloid film, the camera came into wide use, the best-known mass-produced version being the Kodak camera invented by the American George Eastman (1854–1932). Unlike painting and sculpture, photography was affordable for the public. Photographic services were in high demand; by the 1860s, thirty thousand people in Paris made a living from photography and allied fields. Many Europeans became amateur photographers—Queen Victoria and Prince Albert had a darkroom at Windsor Castle (see the feature "Weighing the Evidence: The Modern City and Photography").

The ability of photography to depict a scene with exactitude had a significant impact on art. On the one hand, it encouraged many artists to be true to reality, to reproduce on the canvas a visual image akin to that of a photograph. On the other hand, other artists felt that such realism was no longer necessary in their sphere. However, the great majority of the public, which now

---

Lourdes (LOORD)   **Daguerre** (dah-GAIR)

Courbet: The Stone Breakers   This realistic 1849 painting depicts the rough existence of manual laborers. The bleakness of the subject matter and the style in which it was carried out characterized much of the realist school of art.   *(Staatliche Kunstsammlungen, Dresden/The Bridgeman Art Library, London and New York)*

had wide access to museum exhibitions, was accustomed to photographic accuracy and desired art that was representative and intelligible. Realistic works of art met this need, at least superficially.

Discarding myths and symbols, many artists portrayed the world as it actually was, or at least as it appeared to them—a world without illusions, everyday life in all its grimness. The realist painter Gustave Courbet° (1819–1877) proclaimed himself "without ideals and without religion." His fellow Frenchman, Jean-François Millet° (1814–1875), held a similar opinion. Instead of romanticizing peasants in the manner of earlier artists, he painted the harsh physical conditions under which they labored. In England the so-called pre-Raphaelites took as their model the painters of Renaissance Italy prior to Raphael, who presumably had depicted the realistic simplicity of nature. In painting historical scenes,

these artists emphasized meticulous research of the landscape, architecture, fauna, and costumes of their subjects. To paint the Dead Sea in *The Scapegoat,* English artist Holman Hunt (1827–1910) traveled all the way to Palestine to guarantee accurate portrayal of the site.

In the past, artists had been concerned about composition and perspective. But under the influence of photography, they began to paint incomplete, off-center pictures. *Orchestra of the Paris Opera* by French artist Edgar Degas looks as if it has been cropped, with only half a musician showing on each edge and the top half of the ballet dancers missing.

On April 15, 1874, six French artists—Edgar Degas (1834–1917), Claude Monet° (1840–1926), Camille Pissarro (1830–1903), Auguste Renoir° (1840–1919), Alfred Sisley (1839–1899), and Berthe Morisot° (1841–1895)—

Courbet (koor-BAY)   **Millet** (mil-LAY)

Monet (moh-NAY)   **Renoir** (ren-WOIR)
Morisot (mor-ee-SO)

opened an exhibition in Paris that a critic disparagingly called "impressionist," after the title of one of Monet's paintings, *Impression: Sunrise.* The impressionists were influenced by new theories of physics that claimed images were transmitted to the brain as small light particles that the brain then reconstituted. The impressionists wanted their paintings to capture what things looked like before they had been "distorted" by the brain. In their search for realism, impressionist painters ceased painting in their studios and increasingly went outdoors to paint objects exactly as they looked when light hit them at a certain angle. Monet, for example, emphasized outdoor painting and the need for spontaneity—for reproducing subjects without preconceptions about how earlier artists had depicted them—and seeking to show exactly how the colors and shapes struck the eye. Monet was particularly interested in creating multiple paintings of the same scene—from different viewpoints, under different weather conditions, at different times of day—to underscore that no single "correct" depiction could possibly capture a subject.

The school of realism also influenced literature, especially the novel. In realist novels, life was not glorified or infused with mythical elements; the stark existence of daily life was seen as a suitable subject. Charles Dickens (1812–1870), who came from a poor background and had personally experienced the inhumanity of the London underworld, wrote novels depicting the lot of the poor with humor and sympathy. The appalling social conditions he described helped educate his large middle-class audience on the state of the poor. He also provided numerous examples of individuals who by hard work were able to rise above their circumstances. In fact, the income from Dickens' many novels provided him with a comfortable income; by the pen he was able to join the middle class himself.

Another realist, the French novelist Gustave Flaubert° (1821–1880), consciously debunked the romanticism of his elders. His famous novel, *Madame Bovary*°, describes middle-class life as bleak, boring, and meaningless. The heroine seeks to escape the narrow confines of provincial life by adulterous and disastrous affairs.

Emile Zola (1840–1902), another Frenchman, belonged to the naturalist school of literature. The writer, he declared, should be like a surgeon or chemist, providing a scientific cause and record of human behavior; his work, in Zola's words, is similar to "the analysis that surgeons make on cadavers." (See the box "Reading Sources: Emile Zola on the Novelist as Scientist.") In his Rougon-Macquart° series, which describes in detail the experience of several generations of a family, Zola's major theme is the impact of environment and heredity on his characters' lives of degradation and vice. His characters seem locked in a Darwinian struggle for survival: some are doomed by the laws of biology to succeed, others to succumb.

The Russian novelist Leo Tolstoy (1828–1910) brought a new perspective to the historical novel in *War and Peace*. Instead of a heroic approach to battle, he showed individuals trapped by forces beyond their control. Small and insignificant events as well as major ones seemed to govern human destiny. Another Russian novelist often associated with the realist school, Feodor Dostoyevsky (1821–1881), aimed to portray realistically the psychological dimensions of his characters in novels such as *Crime and Punishment* (1866), *The Idiot* (1868), and *The Brothers Karamazov* (1879–1880).

In music realism was less evident. Johannes Brahms (1833–1897), while not sympathetic to some of the romantic composers, himself wrote music that evoked folk themes, such as his *Hungarian Dances* or his *Love Songs,* just as the romantics had done. The major musician whose work might be labeled as paralleling the realist movement in the other arts is the Russian Modest Mussorgsky (1839–1881), whose music was consciously realistic. Mussorgsky attempted to capture the accents of natural speech, gestures, and the sound of crowds in piano pieces such as *Pictures at an Exhibition* and the opera *Boris Godunov.*

Although this era generally celebrated material progress, a number of intellectuals reacted against it. They were alarmed by the prospect of the popular masses achieving political power through winning the vote and by mass production and consumption. They denounced the smug and the self-satisfied, who saw happiness in acquisition and consumption. Some condemned the age in severe terms. Dostoyevsky railed against the materialism and egotism of the West, branding its civilization as driven by "trade, shipping, markets, factories." In Britain—the nation that seemed to embody progress—the historian Thomas Carlyle (1795–1881) berated his age as one not of progress but of selfishness. Parliamentarism he saw as a sham, and he called for a strong leader to save the nation from endless debates and compromises. Unlike most of his contemporaries, who saw in material plenty a sign of progress, Carlyle saw the era as one of decline, bereft of spiritual values.

Flaubert (flo-BEAR)   **Bovary** (bo-vah-REE)

Rougon-Macquart (roo-ZHON–mah-KAR)

❧ READING SOURCES

Emile Zola on the Novelist as Scientist

Emile Zola believed that the novelist should act like a scientist, experimenting with characters' reactions to differing circumstances in order to determine the laws that govern thought and emotion. Zola wanted to be the literary equivalent of the great French scientist, Claude Bernard (1813–1878), one of the founders of experimental science. The title of this essay, "The Experimental Novel," published in 1880, echoes the title of Bernard's Introduction to Experimental Medicine *(1865).*

Here you have scientific progress. In the last century, a more exact application of the experimental method creates chemistry and physics which free themselves from the irrational and the supernatural. Profound studies lead to the discovery that there are established laws; phenomena are mastered. Then a fresh step is taken. Living bodies, in which the vitalists still admitted a mysterious influence, are in their turn reduced to the general mechanism of matter.

Science proves that the conditions of life of all phenomena are the same in matter and in living bodies; hence, physiology gradually acquires the same certitude as chemistry and physics. But will we stop at that? Evidently not.

When we have proved that the body of man is a machine, which we shall one day be able to take to pieces and put together again at the experimenter's will, then it will be time to pass on to the sentimental and intellectual activities of man. This means that we should enter a realm which, until now, belonged wholly to philosophy and literature; it will be the decisive victory of science over the hypotheses of philosophers and writers. We already have experimental chemistry and physics; we are going to have experimental physiology; and then, later, we shall have the experimental novel. This is a necessary progression, and one whose end can easily be foreseen today. Everything is related, one had to start from the determinism of matter to arrive at the determinism of living bodies. . . . The same determinism must rule the stones in the roadway and the brains of man. . . .

It follows that science already enters our domain—the domain of writers like us, who are at the moment the students of man in his private and social activities. By our observations, by our experiments, we carry forward the work of the physiologist who had continued that of physicists and chemists.

Source: Eugen Weber, ed. and trans., *Paths to the Present* (New York: Dodd, Mead & Co., 1960), p. 170.

Another Englishman, John Ruskin (1819–1900), looked back to the Middle Ages as an ideal era in human history. People then did not produce with machines but exercised a fine sense of craftsmanship. People then supposedly had a better sense of community and labored for the common good. Ruskin was one of the founders of the arts and crafts movement, which aimed to produce goods for daily use with an eye for beauty and originality. "Industry without art is brutality," Ruskin warned.

In France republicans saw in the ostentation of the Second Empire a sign of depravity and decline. Defeat in war in 1870 and the outbreak of the Commune furthered a mood of pessimism among many intellectuals. Flaubert detested his own age, seeing it as petty and mean. The characters in Zola's Rougon-Macquart novels slide steadily downward as each generation's mental faculties, social positions, and morals degenerate. And some abroad were also unimpressed with developments in Europe. (See the box "Global Encounters: A Chinese Official's Views of European Material Progress.")

Not all were optimistic in this age of optimism. If many people celebrated what they viewed as an age of progress, others claimed that under the outer trappings of material comfort lay a frightening ignorance of aesthetic, moral, and spiritual values.

⊕ GLOBAL ENCOUNTERS

A Chinese Official's Views of European Material Progress

Educated in European universities, Ku Hung-Ming rose to become a high official in the Chinese court. His essays were penned under the impact of the European military intervention in China during the Boxer Rebellion in 1900. Ku denounced European notions of superiority over Asia, arguing that material progress was an inappropriate measure of a civilization's value.

In order to estimate the value of a civilization, it seems to me, the question we must finally ask is not what great cities, what magnificent houses, what fine roads it has built and is able to build; what beautiful and comfortable furniture, what clever and useful implements, tools and instruments it has made and is able to make; no, not even what institutions, what arts and sciences it has invested: the question we must ask, in order to estimate the value of a civilization,—is, what type of humanity, what kind of men and women it has been able to produce. In fact, the man and woman,— the type of human beings—which a civilization produces, it is this which shows the essence, the personality, so to speak, the soul of that civilization. Now if the men and women of a civilization show the essence, the personality and soul of that civilization, the language which the men and women in that civilization speak, shows the essence, the personality, the soul of the men and women of that civilization. . . .

To Europeans, and especially to unthinking practical Englishmen, who are accustomed to take what modern political economists call "the standard of living" as the test of the moral culture of or civilization of a people, the actual life of the Chinese and of the people of the East at the present day, will no doubt appear very sordid and undesirable. But the standard of living by itself is not a proper test of the civilization of a people. The standard of living in America at the present day, is, I believe, much higher than it is in Germany. But although the son of an American millionaire, who regards the simple and comparatively low standard of living among the professors of a German University, may doubt the value of the education in such a University, yet no educated man, I believe, who has travelled in both countries, will admit that the Germans are a less civilized people than the Americans.

Source: Ku Hung-Ming, *The Spirit of the Chinese People,* 2d ed. (Beijing: Commercial Press, 1922), pp. 1, 144–145.

SUMMARY

 DURING the second half of the nineteenth century, advances in industry created for many westerners an era of material plenty, providing more riches and comforts to a larger population than ever before. This self-confident age believed in progress and anticipated further improvements in its material and intellectual environment. It appeared to be an age of unbounded optimism.

Economic changes transformed the class structure of many European countries, and middle-class values and tastes defined the second half of the century. The new wealth and technologies led to improvements in both the countryside and the cities; in both, life became more comfortable and safer. Governments provided new services such as public education, cultural facilities, and expanded welfare services.

The material changes in society were reflected in intellectual currents. Change and evolution were embraced as an explanation for the origin of species. A new confidence in scientific research led to many scientific and technological breakthroughs. Novelists and painters aimed to dissect like scientists the world around them, adopting realism in the arts. Some intellectuals, however, were repulsed by the crass self-satisfaction of the bourgeoisie, and they despised their age's worship of industry and materialism.

Progress, as Europeans were to learn in a later era, was two-edged: the very forces that improved life for many also threatened it. The same breakthroughs in chemistry that led to the development of artificial fertilizers also provided more powerful military explosives. The expansion of education and reduction of illiteracy meant an end to ignorance but also the creation of a public that could more easily absorb messages of hate against a rival nation or against religious or ethnic minorities at home. Material progress and well-being continued, but there were new forces in the shadows that would ultimately undermine the comforts, self-assurance, and peace of this age.

■ Suggested Reading

Auerbach, Jeffrey A. *The Great Exhibition of 1851.* 1999. Brings alive the great exhibition.

Cannadine, David. *The Rise and Fall of Class in Britain.* 1999. Reveals the importance of class in nineteenth-century British society.

Clark, Linda L. *The Rise of Professional Women in France.* 2000. A fine study delineating the increasing role of women in the professions, especially public administration.

Goodman, David, and Colin Chant, eds. *European Cities and Technology Reader.* 1999. Emphasizes the importance of technological breakthroughs in the modernization of cities.

Hobsbawm, Eric J. *The Age of Capital, 1848–1875.* 1979. Particularly strong on social and economic developments.

Nord, Philip. *Impressionists and Politics.* 2000. Sets the French impressionists in their political and social contexts.

Standage, Tom. *The Victorian Internet.* 1998. A brief, popular history of the telegraph.

 For a searchable list of additional readings for this chapter, go to http://college.hmco.com.

The Modern City and Photography

This photo of Piccadilly Center in Manchester was taken in 1886. It documents the modernization of the nineteenth century city and at the same time conveys the sense of immediacy that a new means of representation, the photograph, provided.

Manchester in the nineteenth century became a wealthy textile city, manufacturing and marketing textiles to the rest of Britain and the world. The first rail lines in Britain were built in Manchester; by 1840 six rail lines connected it to the rest of the kingdom. The city grew dramatically, from 43,000 in 1774 to 271,000 in 1831. By 1900 it had reached the 600,000 mark.

Piccadilly, the commercial center of Manchester, had warehouses and offices where buyers purchased textiles that they would in turn sell to retail consumers. Fancy stores were also located here, and in some cases elegant dwellings were situated in the upper floors. Piccadilly was a large open square allowing for the easy movement of pedestrians and wagons. City planners in the nineteenth century created squares and broad, straight avenues, such as those gracing Piccadilly, by tearing down old slums and narrow alleys. These broad avenues eased the flow of traffic and admitted fresh air and sunlight, which diminished exposure to killer diseases such as cholera and tuberculosis.

As it grew, Manchester needed public transportation to move people quickly on the broad new avenues. Notice the rails for the horse-drawn tramways. Horse-drawn carriages called omnibuses, which had been introduced in the 1820s, were the first means of mass transportation within the city. Trams ran on rails that reduced friction and allowed a horse to pull a far greater load; in this case the tram, located in the center of the photo, is a double-decker.

An industrial town, Manchester was not a particularly pleasant city to live in. Visitors complained of its grime, pollution, and foul smells. Many members of the commercial classes lived in wealthy suburbs and commuted by tram to work in the center with little waste of time. Sometime after this picture was taken, the horse-drawn tram was replaced by the electrical tram, which could transport more people faster than its predecessor. Its lower cost also meant that it was accessible even to most workers. With the advent of the electrical tram, workers too began to move to the suburbs, making the center less crowded.

The large modern city required ease of communication at night as well as in the daytime. Street lighting provided that convenience, as well as making the streets more secure by discouraging crime. Street lamps became the norm in large cities, especially in the better neighborhoods. The elegant gas lights that adorn the square were replaced a few years later by electrical ones that were cheaper to operate and allowed for the spread of city lighting. In lighting, public transport, police, sanitation, and other municipal services, it was quite common to discriminate in favor of the richer neighborhoods, while neglecting the poorer ones. The latter were usually the last to be served. By the 1880s, when the franchise was enlarged, municipalities became more sensitive to the needs of new voters of every class. In Manchester, as in many British cities, public services such as lighting, water supplies, and the tram system were municipalized, thus reducing the cost of these amenities and making them available to a larger proportion of the citizenry.

This photo,* taken in the 1880s, is also evidence of the great progress that had taken place in photography since its invention half a century earlier. In 1839 Louis Daguerre publicized the method of fixing an image on silvered copperplate. At first, the cameras and equipment were so cumbersome that photography was confined to studios; photographers could not take pictures anywhere else. Thus the only images were portraits of people, or the occasional still life. As the camera became simpler, photographers could leave the studio and take pictures outdoors. Improvements in film, most significantly the introduction of the dry plate method in the 1870s, made it far more sensitive to light, reducing exposure time to a fraction of a second. Now a photograph could capture movement without reducing it to a blur, as in this bustling city scene.

---

*The advice of Thomas Prasch in the choice of this photo is gratefully acknowledged.

Originally, photography had been regarded as a more exact, and less expensive, form of illustration and so was influenced by the conventions of painting. Most early photographs, even outdoor shots, were staged. Given the slowness of taking pictures and the obvious presence of the photographer with all the equipment, it could hardly have been different. But soon thereafter, thanks to technical innovations, photographers could capture a scene even without the cooperation of the subject. None of the subjects in this photo has eye contact with the camera. In fact, they seem unaware of the presence of the photographer as they go about their daily business.

If the modern photograph was different from a painting, photography still adhered to some of the traditions of painting—notably composition. The photographer has composed this image, has made choices as to what to put in the foreground. We get a sense of the harried merchant crossing the well-ordered street with its backdrop of amenities.

The new chemical and optical breakthroughs that made the camera such an effective new tool were implemented by inventors in cities such as London, Paris, Berlin. Photographers, in turn, took pictures of some of the great technical feats of their era. The modern aspects of the city, such as this scene, were frequent subjects for the photographer's lens. With a modern device, the camera, the photographer captured the new modern metropolis that was so much more efficient—and exciting—than its predecessor.

Piccadilly Square, Manchester, ca. 1886   *(Topham Picturepoint/The Image Works)*

CHAPTER 24

Escalating Tensions 1880–1914

I N April 1912, the *Titanic*, the largest and most technologically advanced passenger ship ever built, sailed from Southampton, England, for New York. Its owners, the White Star Line, boasted that the building of this majestic vessel testified to "the progress of mankind" and would "rank high in the achievements of the twentieth century." Hailed as "virtually unsinkable," the *Titanic* struck an iceberg on the night of April 12, south of Newfoundland, and rapidly sink. More than 1,500 of the 2,100 people aboard perished in the icy North Atlantic waters. The overconfident captain had not taken warnings of icebergs in the ship's path seriously enough.

Two years later European society was hit by a major disaster, the outbreak of a world war. That such a disaster would end the era called by contemporaries the *belle époque°*, "the beautiful epoch," was as unimaginable as *Titanic*'s fate. The booming economy had been expanding opportunities for many. The arts flourished and were celebrated. Parliamentary government continued to spread, and more nations seemed to be adapting to democracy as suffrage was extended. Yet hand in hand with these trends of apparent progress appeared troubling tendencies. Under the surface were forces threatening the stability of European society. There was peace, but in 1914 a lone assassin's bullet set off a series of reactions that ultimately led to war and the crash of the pre-1914 world.

In many societies, governing became more complex as populations increased. The population of Europe jumped from 330 million in 1880 to 460 million by 1914. A larger population coupled with extended

---

belle époque (BELL eh-POK)

The *Titanic* proudly announces its maiden voyage.
(Corbis)

suffrage meant that more people participated in the political system, but it became harder to reach consensus. The example of democracy in some countries led to discontent in the autocratic ones at their failure to move toward freer institutions. In the same way that prosperity and economic growth aroused resentment in those who did not share in the benefits, some groups became frustrated at their exclusion from the political system.

Intellectuals revolted against what they viewed as the smug self-assuredness of earlier years. They no longer felt certain that the world was knowable, stable, or subject to comprehension and, ultimately, to mastery by rational human beings. Some jettisoned rationality, imagining that they had made strides in sophistication by glorifying emotion, irrationality, and in some cases violence. The works of painters and writers seemed to anticipate the impending destruction of world order.

The anxieties and tensions that beset many Europeans took a variety of forms. Ethnic minorities became targets of hatred. European states embarked on a race for empire throughout the world, forcibly putting non-Europeans under white domination. On the Continent, states felt increasingly insecure, worried that they would be subject to attack. They established standing armies, shifted alliances, drafted war plans, and, in the end, went to war.

QUESTIONS TO CONSIDER

- What were the main motivations for European imperialism?

- In what ways did the world-view of intellectuals living in the *belle époque* differ from that of a generation earlier?

- In what ways did British and Russian political institutions reveal an inability to resolve the issues facing society?

- To what extent did social problems undermine the Russian regime?

- What responsibility did each of the Great Powers have for the outbreak of war in 1914?

TERMS TO KNOW

"new imperialism"	suffragists
Second International	*Weltpolitik*
anti-Semitism	Bolshevik
Zionism	Triple Alliance
Sigmund Freud	Triple Entente
avant-garde	

THE NEW IMPERIALISM AND THE SPREAD OF EUROPE'S POPULATION

 ART of Europe's self-confidence during the period from the 1880s to 1914 was based on the unchallenged sway it held over the rest of the globe. Europeans brought under political control large swathes of land across the seas and also marked the globe by massive migrations.

The age of empire building that started in Europe in the sixteenth century seemed to have ended by 1750. Then, in the 1880s, the European states launched a new era of expansionism, conquering an unprecedented amount of territory. In only twenty-five years, Europeans subjugated 500 million people—one half of the world's non-European population. European expansion was also manifest in a massive movement of people: between 1870 and 1914, 55 million Europeans moved overseas, mainly to Australia, the United States, Canada, and Argentina.

This era of ambitious conquest is often called the "new imperialism" to differentiate it from the earlier stage of empire building. Whereas the earlier imperialism focused on the Americas, nineteenth-century imperialism centered on Africa and Asia. And unlike the colonizing of the earlier period, the new imperialism occurred in an age of mass participation in politics and was accompanied by expressions of popular enthusiasm.

■ Economic and Social Motives

The hope of profit overseas was crucial in the dynamic of the new imperialism. Most of these hopes were illusory, but the desire for huge markets was instrumental in stirring an interest in empire. Colonies, it was believed, would provide eager buyers for European goods that would stimulate production at home. "Colonial policy is the daughter of industrial policy," declared French prime minister Jules Ferry° in 1884. Yet colonies did not represent large markets for the mother countries. In 1914 France's colonies represented only 12 percent of its foreign trade. Great Britain's trade with its colonies represented a considerable one-third of its foreign trade, but most of that was with the settlement colonies, such as Canada and Australia, not those acquired in the era of the new imperialism. As for Germany, colonial trade represented less than 1 percent of its exports. Even protective tariffs imposed on colonies by no means secured monopoly of trade. Far more than their colonies, France, Germany, and Great Britain continued to be one another's best customers.

Some proponents of empire, known as social imperialists, argued that possession of an empire could resolve social as well as economic issues. An empire could be an outlet for a variety of domestic frustrations, especially for those nations concerned about overpopulation. German and Italian imperialists often argued that their nations needed colonies in which to resettle their multiplying poor. Once the overseas territories were acquired, however, few found them attractive for settlement.

■ Nationalistic Motives

To a large extent, empire building was triggered by the desire to assert national power. At the end of the nineteenth century, two major powers emerged, Russia and the United States. Compared with these giants, western European nations seemed small and insignificant, and many of their leaders believed that to compete effectively on the world stage they needed to become large territorial entities. Empires would enable them to achieve that goal.

The British Empire, with India as its crown jewel, constituted the largest, most powerful, and apparently the wealthiest of all the European domains. It was the envy of Europe. Although the real source of Britain's wealth and power was the country's industrial economy,

---

Ferry (feh-REE)

CHRONOLOGY	
1873	Three Emperors' League
1882	Britain seizes Egypt
	Triple Alliance of Germany, Italy, and Austria-Hungary
1884	Three Emperors' League renewed
1890	Kaiser Wilhelm II dismisses Bismarck as chancellor
1894	Franco-Russian Alliance
	Beginning of the Dreyfus affair
1900	King of Italy assassinated
1903	Emmeline Pankhurst founds the Women's Social and Political Union
1904	Anglo-French Entente
1905	Einstein proposes theory of relativity
	Revolution in Russia
1907	Anglo-Russian Entente
1908	Young Turk rebellion in Ottoman Empire
1911	Italy grabs Libya
	Second Moroccan crisis
June 28, 1914	Archduke Franz Ferdinand is assassinated
August 4, 1914	With the entry of Britain, Europe is at war

many people believed possession of a vast empire explained Britain's success. And so the British example stimulated other nations to carve out empires. Their activities, in turn, triggered British anxieties. Britain and France unleashed a scramble for Africa and Asia; in Asia Britain also competed with Russia.

France, defeated by Prussia in 1870, found in its colonies proof that it was still a Great Power. Germany and Italy, which formed their national identities relatively late, cast a jealous eye on the British and French empires and decided that if they were to be counted as

Great Powers, they too would need overseas colonies. Belgium's King Leopold II (r. 1876–1909) spun out various plans to acquire colonies to compensate for his nation's small size. And Britain, anxious at the emergence of rival economic and political powers in the late nineteenth century, found in its colonies a guarantee for the future.

In the race for colonies, worldwide strategic concerns stimulated expansion. Because the Suez Canal ensured the route to India, the British established a protectorate over Egypt in 1882. Beginning in the next decade, fearing that a rival power might threaten their position by encroaching on the Nile, they established control over the Nile Valley all the way south to Uganda (see Map 24.1). Russian expansion southward into central Asia toward Afghanistan was intended to avert a British takeover of this area, while the British movement northwestward to Afghanistan had the opposite intention—to prevent Russia from encroaching on India. The "great game" played by Russia and Britain in central Asia lasted the entire nineteenth century, ending only in 1907, with the signing of the Anglo-Russian Entente.

Much of this expansion was driven by the desire to control the often turbulent frontiers of newly acquired areas. Once those frontiers had been brought under control, there were, of course, again new frontiers that had to be subdued. As a Russian foreign minister said of such an incentive for expansion, "The chief difficulty is to know where to stop." The imperial powers rarely did.

The bitter rivalry among the Great Powers helps explain the division of the globe, but it also protected some regions from falling under European domination. In an effort to contain their rivalry in southeast Asia, Britain and France established Siam (now Thailand) as a buffer state. Russia seriously violated China's sovereignty by usurping large chunks of territory as it moved southward and eastward. The Western powers seized Chinese "treaty ports" and insisted on the right of their merchants and missionaries to move freely through the country. Yet most of China survived because the European powers held one another's ambitions in check. No state alone could conquer all of China; none would allow the others to do so either.

◼ Other Ideological Motives

In addition to the search for profit and nationalistic pride, Europeans used a strong sense of mission to rationalize imperialism. Because Europeans had gained technological and scientific know-how, many imperialists believed it was Europe's duty to develop Africa and

Asia for the benefit of colonizer and colonized. Railroads, telegraphs, hospitals, and schools would transform colonial peoples by opening them to what were seen as the beneficent influences of Europe. If necessary, these changes would be realized by force.

At the same time that Europeans were making substantial material progress as a result of industrialization, their wide-scale expansion overseas brought them into contact with Africans and Asians who had not created an industrial economy. They assumed that the dramatic disparity between their own material culture and that of colonial peoples was proof of their own innate superiority. Africans and Asians were seen as primitive, inferior peoples, still in their evolutionary "infancy." (See the feature "Weighing the Evidence: The Layout of the British Museum" on pages 840–841.)

Influenced by Darwin and his theory of the struggle for survival (see pages 795–797), many argued that just as competition among species existed in nature, so did groups of humans struggle for survival. Dubbed "Social Darwinists," these thinkers envisioned a world of fierce competition. They believed that the most serious struggle was among the races and, further, that the outcome was predetermined: the white race was destined to succeed, the nonwhites to succumb.

Many Europeans paternalistically believed they had a duty to "develop" these "infant" peoples. The British bard of imperialism, Rudyard Kipling (1865–1936), celebrated this view in his poem "White Man's Burden" (1899):

> Take up the White Man's burden—
> Send forth the best ye breed—
> Go bind your sons to exile
> To serve your captives' need.

Each nation was certain that providence had chosen it for a colonial mission. France, its leaders announced, had a civilizing mission to fulfill in the world; Prime Minister Ferry declared it the duty of his country "to civilize the inferior races." Although European states were colonial rivals, they also believed they were engaged in a joint mission overseas. Empire building underscored the belief in a common European destiny, as opposed to the ascribed savagery and backwardness of non-Europeans.

Map 24.1   Africa in 1914   European powers in the late nineteenth century conquered most of Africa. Only Liberia and Ethiopia were left unoccupied at the start of the war.

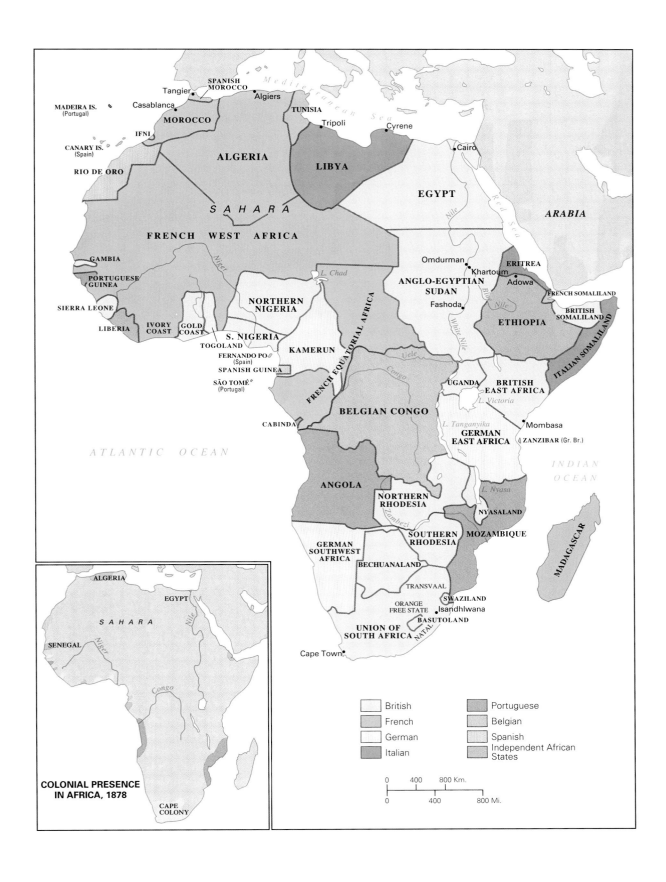

MADEIRA IS.
(Portugal)

CANARY IS.
(Spain)

SPANISH
MOROCCO
Tangier
Casablanca
MOROCCO
IFNI

RIO DE ORO

GAMBIA
PORTUGUESE
GUINEA
SIERRA LEONE
LIBERIA
IVORY
COAST
GOLD
COAST
TOGOLAND
FERNANDO PO
(Spain)
SPANISH GUINEA
SÃO TOMÉ
(Portugal)

Mediterranean Sea
Algiers
TUNISIA
Tripoli
Cyrene

ALGERIA

S A H A R A

FRENCH   WEST   AFRICA

Niger
L. Chad

**NORTHERN
NIGERIA**

S. NIGERIA

KAMERUN

LIBYA

EGYPT

Cairo

Nile

Omdurman
Khartoum
**ANGLO-EGYPTIAN
SUDAN**
Fashoda

White Nile
Blue Nile

ERITREA
Adowa
FRENCH SOMALILAND
BRITISH
SOMALILAND

ETHIOPIA

ARABIA

Red Sea

FRENCH EQUATORIAL AFRICA

Uele

Congo

CABINDA

BELGIAN CONGO

UGANDA
**BRITISH
EAST AFRICA**

L. Victoria

L. Tanganyika
Mombasa

**GERMAN
EAST AFRICA**
ZANZIBAR (Gr. Br.)

ITALIAN SOMALILAND

A T L A N T I C   O C E A N

*I N D I A N
OCEAN*

ANGOLA

**NORTHERN
RHODESIA**

L. Nyasa

NYASALAND

Zambezi

**SOUTHERN
RHODESIA**

MOZAMBIQUE

MADAGASCAR

**GERMAN
SOUTHWEST
AFRICA**

BECHUANALAND

TRANSVAAL

ORANGE
FREE STATE
Isandhlwana
SWAZILAND
BASUTOLAND
NATAL

**UNION OF
SOUTH AFRICA**

Cape Town

Legend

British	Portuguese
French	Belgian
German	Spanish
Italian	Independent African States

0   400   800 Km.
0   400   800 Mi.

Inset map

ALGERIA
EGYPT
S A H A R A
Nile
SENEGAL
Niger
Congo

**COLONIAL PRESENCE
IN AFRICA, 1878**

CAPE
COLONY

Dutch Colonial Officials in the Dutch East Indies In this club in an outpost of empire (in present-day Indonesia), the comforts of European bourgeois life were lovingly re-created. Absent from this photo are the countless Indonesian servants who were part of the colonial officials' lives. *(Royal Tropical Institute, Amsterdam)*

Pointing to historical antecedents, imperialists colored their activities with a hue of heroism. Many Europeans took satisfaction in the idea that their country performed feats akin to those of ancient Rome or the Crusaders, spreading "civilization" to far-flung empires. Colonial literature celebrated white men of action who, by their heroism, conquered and administered what had been large kingdoms or empires in Africa and Asia. Even novelists such as Kipling who tried to be sympathetic to "natives" nonetheless portrayed them as simple, almost childlike people, thus reinforcing European superiority.

Colonial acquisitions triggered public support for further expansion of the empire—support that was expressed by the founding of various colonial societies. Britain's Primrose League, which lobbied for empire as well as other patriotic goals, had 1 million members. The German Colonial Society, founded in 1888, had 43,000 members by 1914. The French and Italian groups were limited in size but had influential contacts with policymakers. Colonial societies generally drew their member-

ship from the professional middle classes—civil servants, professors, and journalists—who were quite open to nationalist arguments. These societies produced a steady stream of propaganda favoring empire building.

Much of the literature celebrating empire building described it in masculine terms. European men were seen as proving their virility by going overseas, conquering, and running empires. They contrasted their manliness with the supposed effeminacy of the colonial peoples. And in building empires, Europeans asserted their manliness in comparison with their wives, sisters, or mothers. Women were to stay home; if later they came overseas, it was as helpmates to male colonial officials. A few women heroically explored distant lands; the Englishwoman Mary Kingsley (1862–1900) went on two exploration trips into Africa. (See the box "Reading Sources: Mary Kingsley Decries Racism but Defends Imperialism.") Her books were popular and focused British interest on overseas territories, but they in no way shook the established view that empire was a man's enterprise.

Mary Kingsley Decries Racism but Defends Imperialism

Mary Kingsley belonged to a small but hardy group of women who, despite the Victorian ideal of the woman as homebody, went exploring overseas. In two separate expeditions she visited the western part of Africa. Her observations of Africans represent a mixture of views: if she believes that Africans are different from Europeans, and even inferior in some respects, she also sees them as excelling in other fields. Kingsley bases her views on differences of culture, rather than of biology. She suggests that because Africans are less developed than Europeans, Britain has a special duty and obligation to them.

I openly and honestly own I sincerely detest touching on this race question. For one thing, Science has not finished with it; for another, it belongs to a group of enormous magnitude, upon which I have no opinion, but merely feelings, and those of a nature which I am informed by superior people would barely be a credit to a cave man of the paleolithic period. . . . I am often cornered for the detail view, whether I can reconcile my admiration for Africans with my statement that they are a different kind of human being to white men. Naturally I can, to my own satisfaction, just as I can admire an oak tree or a palm; but it is an uncommonly difficult thing to explain. All that I can say is, that when I come back from a spell in Africa, the thing that makes me proud of being one of the English is not the manners of customs up here, certainly not the houses or the climate; but it is the thing embodied in a great railway engine. I once came home on a ship with an Englishman who had been in South West Africa, for seven unbroken years; he was sane and in his right mind. But no sooner did we get ashore at Liverpool, than he rushed at and threw his arms round a postman, to that official's embarrassment and surprise. Well, that is how I feel about the first magnificent bit of machinery I come across: it is the manifestation of the superiority of my race.

In philosophic moments I call superiority difference, from a feeling that it is not mine to judge the grade in these things. Careful scientific study has enforced on me, as it has on other students, the recognition that the African mind naturally approaches all things from a spiritual point of view. . . . [H]is mind works along the line that things happen because of the action of spirit upon spirit. . . . We think along the line that things happen from action of matter upon matter. . . . This steady sticking to the material side of things, I think, has given our race its dominion over matter; the want of it has caused the African to be notably behind us in this. . . .

This seems to me simply to lay upon us English for the sake of our honour that we keep clean hands and a cool head, and be careful of Justice; to do this we must know what there is we wish to wipe out of the African, and what there is we wish to put in, and so we must not content ourselves by relying materially on our superior wealth and power, and morally on catch phrases. All we need to look to is justice.

Source: Mary H. Kingsley, *West African Studies* (London: Macmillan, 1899), pp. 329–331.

■ Conquest, Administration, and Westernization

Industrialization gave Europeans the means to conquer overseas territories. They manufactured rapid-fire weapons. Their steam-driven gunboats and ocean-going vessels effectively projected power overseas. Telegraphic communications tied the whole world into a single network, allowing Europeans to gather information and coordinate military and political decision making. (See the feature "Information Technology: The Telegraph" in Chapter 23, pages 780–781.) Such advantages made Europeans virtually invincible in a colonial conflict. One remarkable exception was the defeat of the Italians in Adowa in 1896 at the hands of an Ethiopian force that was not only superior in numbers but better armed.

Conquest was often brutal. In September 1898, British-led forces at the Battle of Omdurman slaughtered 20,000 Sudanese. From 1904 to 1908, an uprising in southwest Africa against German rule led to the killing of an estimated 60,000 of the Herero people. The German general, who had expressly given an order to exterminate the whole population, was awarded a medal by Kaiser Wilhelm II.

Colonial governments could be brutally insensitive to the needs of the indigenous peoples. (See the box "Global Encounters: Chief Montshiwa Petitions Queen Victoria.") To save administrative costs in the 1890s, France put large tracts of land in the French Congo under the control of private rubber companies, which systematically and savagely coerced the local people to collect the sap of the rubber trees. When the scandal broke in Paris, the concessionary companies were abolished and the French state re-established its control. The most notorious example of exploitation, terror, and mass killings was connected with the Belgian Congo. Leopold II of Belgium had acquired it as a personal empire: it was his private domain, and he was not accountable to anyone for his actions there. To his shame, Leopold mercilessly exploited the Congo and its people. An international chorus of condemnation finally forced the king to surrender his empire and put it under the administration of the Belgian government, which abolished some of the worst features of Leopold's rule.

Brutal and abusive, imperialism spread Western technologies, institutions, and values. By 1914 Great Britain had built 40,000 miles of rail in India—nearly twice as much as in Britain. In India and Egypt, the British erected hydraulic systems that irrigated previously arid lands. Colonials built cities often modeled on the European grid system. In some cases they were graced with large, tree-lined avenues, and some neighborhoods were equipped with running water and modern sanitation. Schools, patterned after those in Europe, taught the imperial language and spread Western ideas and scientific knowledge—though only to a small percentage of the local population.

The European empire builders created political units that had never existed before. Although there had been many efforts in the past to join the whole Indian subcontinent under a single authority, the British were the first to accomplish this feat (see Map 24.2). Through a common administration, rail network, and trade, Britain gave Indians the sense of a common condition, leading in 1885 to the founding of the India Congress Party. The Congress Party platform included the demand for constitutional government, representative assemblies, and the rule of law—concepts all based on Western theory and practice. While initially demanding reforms within the British colonial system, eventually the Congress Party became India's major nationalist group.

In contact with the colonizers, intellectuals in colonial societies adopted a European ideology, nationalism. Nationalism was one of the major values Europeans successfully exported to its overseas possessions. In India, it

Empire and Advertising   Empire had become so much a part of European life that advertisements for biscuits included colonial scenes. Media such as advertisement made colonial domination seem normal, part of the natural order of things. *(The Robert Opie Collection)*

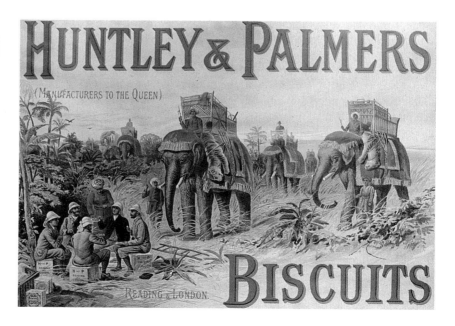

Chief Montshiwa Petitions Queen Victoria

In 1885 Bechuanaland in southern Africa became a British protectorate. The Bechuana leaders saw British protection as a means to prevent takeover by the Boers, Dutch-speaking white settlers who were aggressively expanding in South Africa. The British were cavalier about their responsibilities, however, and a few years later allowed the British South Africa Company, a particularly exploitive enterprise, to take control of Bechuanaland. In protest, Chief Montshiwa (1815–1896), a major chief of the Baralong people, petitioned Queen Victoria for redress. His petition was supported by missionary lobbying, and most of Bechuanaland was saved from the clutches of the company.

Mafeking, 16 August, 1895

To the Queen of England and Her Ministers:

We send greetings and pray that you are all living nicely. You will know us; we are not strangers. We have been your children since 1885.

Your Government has been good, and under it we have received much blessing, prosperity, and peace. . . .

We Baralong are very astonished because we hear that the Queen's Government wants to give away our country in the Protectorate to the Chartered Company; we mean the B[ritish] S[outh] A[frica] Company.

Our land there is a good land, our fathers lived in it and buried in it, and we keep all our cattle in it. What will we do if you give our land away? My people are increasing very fast and are filling the land.

We keep all the laws of the great Queen; we have fought for her; we have always been the friends of her people; we are not idle; we build houses; we plough many gardens; we sow. . . .

Why are you tired of ruling us? Why do you want to throw us away? We do not fight against your laws. We keep them and are living nicely.

Our words are No: No. The Queen's Government must not give my people's land in the Protectorate to the Chartered Company. . . .

Peace to you all, we greet you;
Please send a good word back.

I am etc,

Montshiwa

Source: S. M. Molema, *Montshiwa, 1815–1896* (Cape Town: G. Struik, 1966), pp. 181–182.

---

was those Indians who had been most exposed to British influence, by having studied in British schools or visited Britain, who were most likely to be nationalists. They founded a movement, known as Young India, harking back to Young Italy and other European nationalist movements founded in Mazzini's lifetime (see Chapter 21). Similarly, in French Algeria before World War I a movement named Young Algerians sprang up.

It was to be several decades before nationalism successfully challenged the European empires. In the meantime, Europeans took great satisfaction in their achievements overseas, confirming their sense of themselves as agents of progress, building a new and better world. Europeans arrogantly believed they knew what was best for other people; and they accepted force as a means of implementing their ideas. Such attitudes may also have colored the increasingly caustic relations between European states.

The ties of empire affected metropolitan cultures. The Hindi word for *bandit* became the English word *thug;* the Hindi number five, denoting the five ingredients necessary for a particular drink, became *punch.* Scenes from the colonial world often were the themes of European art, such as Paul Gauguin's° paintings of Tahiti and advertising

---

Gauguin (go-GEYN)

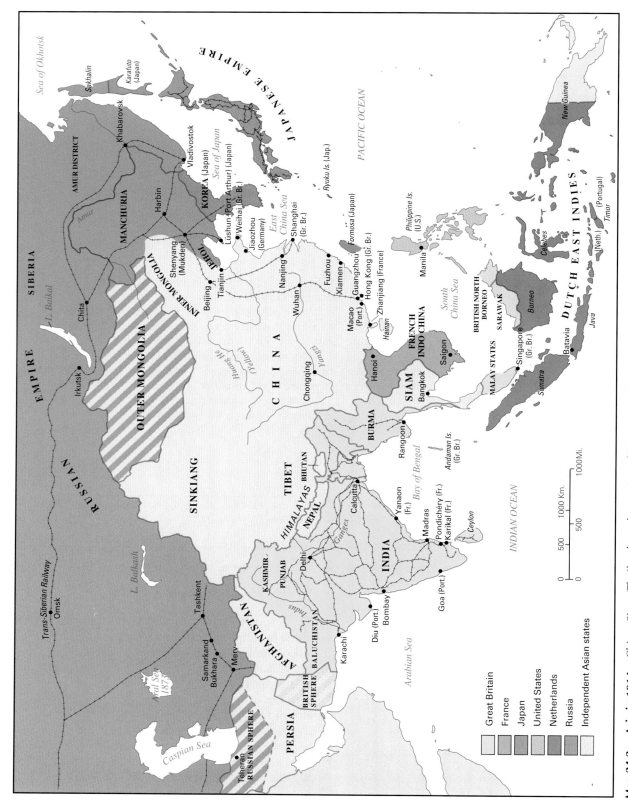

Map 24.2   Asia in 1914   China, Siam (Thailand), and a portion of Persia were the only parts of Asia still independent after the Great Powers, including the United States and Japan, subjugated the continent to alien rule.

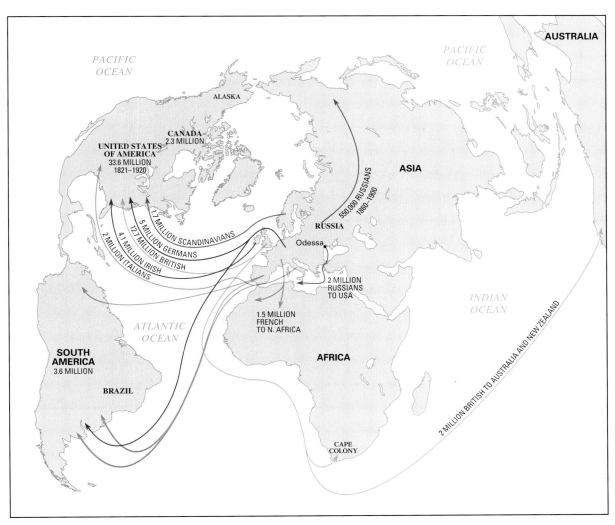

Map 24.3   European Migrations, 1820–1910   Throughout the nineteenth century, millions of Europeans left home for overseas; most headed for the United States.   *(Source:* The Times Atlas of World History, *3d ed. Copyright © HarperCollins Publishers, Ltd. Reprinted by permission of the publisher. Some data from Eric Hobsbawm,* The Age of Empire, 1875–1914 *[New York: Pantheon, 1987].)*

posters for products as different as soap and whiskey. After the turn of the century, Pablo Picasso's° cubism reflected his growing familiarity with African art. In running the largest empire in the world, the British emphasized the need to develop masculine virtues. They cultivated competitive sports and stern schooling, which, they believed, would develop "character" and leadership. To administer their overseas colonies, Europeans developed sophisticated means of gathering and managing information that benefited metropolitan societies. A growing number of people from the colonies also came to live in European

cities. By 1900 some former colonial subjects, despite various forms of discrimination, had become full participants in the lives of their host countries; two East Indians won election to the British Parliament in the 1890s.

■ Overseas Migrations and the Spread of European Values

The nineteenth century saw a phenomenal expansion in European overseas migrations, adding to Europe's impact on other societies (see Map 24.3). Europeans had always migrated. They left villages for towns or, in the case of migrant farm laborers, traveled from village to village

Picasso (pih-KAH-so)

Petersen: Emigrants Preparing to Depart   Edward Petersen's 1890 painting depicts Danish emigrants readying to leave their homeland. Between 1860 and 1914, 300,000 people emigrated from the small country of Denmark, most of them to the United States.   *(Courtesy of the Aarhus Kunstmuseum. Reproduced with permission of Thomas, Poul, and Ole Hein Pedersen, Aarhus.)*

as the seasons changed and different crops needed to be harvested. With the expansion of European power abroad beginning in the sixteenth century, Europeans migrated overseas; between the sixteenth and eighteenth centuries around 6 million people left Europe. These numbers pale, however, when compared with the nineteenth-century figures: between 1870 and 1914, 55 million Europeans left the Continent for the Americas, Australia, and New Zealand.

Certain European groups migrated to specific areas. Scandinavians settled in the upper midwestern United States, Italians in Argentina, Germans in Paraguay, Britons in South Africa, Portuguese in Brazil, each group leaving its imprint on its adopted land. The upper Midwest was known as "the great desert," but Scandinavians used farm techniques from their homelands to cultivate these dry lands. German Mennonites settled in Kansas and brought with them a strain of wheat that became the basis of the state's prosperity. Immigrants made similar impacts on urban sites. Durban in South Africa

looks like an English city, and some towns in Paraguay resemble Alpine villages of southern Germany. The Germans who came to Milwaukee, Wisconsin, made it a city of beer and strong socialist convictions, reminiscent of home.

Emigration scattered peoples and extended cultures overseas. By 1914 nearly half of all Irish and Portuguese lived outside Europe. The settlers consumed many European goods and in turn produced for the European market, increasing the centrality of Europe in the world economy. The migrations across the globe reinforced imperial conquest, further imprinting Europe's stamp on peoples and societies abroad.

If Europe appeared triumphant, its supremacy rested on frail foundations—mainly force. From the start, local resistance and even expressions of protonationalist sentiments challenged Europe's supremacy. Imperial powers, worried that their European rivals or their colonial subjects might cause trouble, looked to force to assure the future of their empires.

From Optimism to Anxiety: Politics and Culture

 MANY of the beliefs and institutions that had seemed so solid in the "age of optimism" found themselves under attack in the next generation. Forces hostile to liberalism became increasingly vocal. In the arts and philosophy, the earlier confidence was replaced by doubt, relativism, and a desire to flee the routines of everyday life.

■ The Erosion of the Liberal Consensus

In 1850 liberalism appeared to be the ascendant ideology, and liberals assumed that with the passage of time more and more people would be won over to their world-view. By 1900, however, liberalism faced serious challenges. Principles eroded within the liberal camp, and in addition, various ideas and movements—some new, some rooted in the past—chipped away at the liberal consensus. Prominent among these were socialism, anarchism, a new political right, racism, and anti-Semitism.

The undermining of the liberal consensus began among liberals themselves, who, in the face of changing circumstances, retreated from some of their basic tenets. For example, one of the principal emphases of liberalism had always been free trade. But under the pressure of economic competition, liberals supported tariffs at home and created closed markets for the mother country overseas in the empire.

Historically, liberals had typically stood for an expansion of civil liberties, yet several groups were denied their rights. Power remained an exclusively male domain, and liberal males saw nothing wrong or inconsistent in continuing to deny women both the vote and free access to education and professional advancement. In the face of labor agitation, many liberals no longer unconditionally supported civil liberties for workers and favored instead the violent crushing of strikes.

Similarly, liberals had always upheld the sanctity of private property, but under the pressure of events, they abandoned this principle as an absolute goal. To ensure workers' safety, they placed limits on employers by passing legislation on working conditions. In some countries, some supported progressive income taxes, which other liberals perceived as a serious invasion of private property. When it became clear that a free market was unable to meet many human needs, welfare programs were instituted in several countries. These reforms were intended to strengthen the state by winning support from the masses. But because they reflected the liberals' willingness to breach fundamental principles, these measures also revealed the apparent inability of liberal ideology to deal with the real-life problems of the day.

■ The Growth of Socialism and Anarchism

Among the groups challenging the power and liberal ideology of the middle classes were the socialist parties, both Marxist and non-Marxist, whose goal was to win the support of workers by espousing their causes. Socialists varied in their notions of how their goals should be achieved: some favored pursuing objectives gradually and peacefully; others were dedicated to a violent overthrow of capitalist society.

In Britain, where the Liberal Party was more open to the needs of workers than in other European states, a separate socialist party, the Independent Labour Party, was established relatively late, in 1893. Not until the 1920s did this party gain any particular electoral success. More influential in the late nineteenth century was the Fabian Society, founded in 1884 and named after the Roman general Fabian, who was noted for winning by avoiding open, pitched battles. The Fabians criticized the capitalist system as inefficient, wasteful, and unjust. They believed that by gradual, democratic means, Parliament could transfer factories and land from the private sector to the state, which would manage them for the benefit of society as a whole. Socialism was a desirable system that would replace capitalism because it was more efficient and more just. It would come into being not through class war but through enlightened ideas. This gradualist approach became the hallmark of British socialism, shaping the ideology of the Labour Party.

In Germany various strands of socialism came together when a single united party was formed in 1875. But within a few years a debate that was to break out in most socialist parties rent the German party: Could socialism come about by gradual democratic means, or, as Marx had contended, would it require a violent revolution? The German socialist leader, Eduard Bernstein° (1850–1932), who had visited England and had soaked up the influence of the Fabians, argued for gradualism in a book with the telling English title *Evolutionary Socialism* (1898). Marx had been wrong, said Bernstein, to suggest that capitalism necessarily led to the increasing wretchedness of the working class. The capitalist economy had in fact expanded and been able to provide for steadily improved conditions. Workers would not need to seize power by some cataclysmic act. Rather, by piecemeal democratic action they could win more

Bernstein (BURN-stine)

Jean Jaurès   An ideological moderate, the French socialist leader Jean Jaurès (1859–1914) was a firebrand as a speaker, one of France's greatest orators. Much of his socialism was based on ethical notions about social justice, rather than on Marxist doctrine. Here Jaurès addresses a socialist gathering in 1913.   *(Roger-Viollet)*

power and legislate on behalf of their interests. Since he argued for a revision of Marxist theory, Bernstein was labeled a "revisionist." Opposing him in this great debate was the party theoretician Karl Kautsky° (1854–1938). Kautsky insisted that nothing short of a revolution would institute socialism.

Like most other socialists in Europe, the German socialists rejected revisionism and claimed to embrace the doctrine of a violent proletarian revolution, but in fact pursued revisionist policies. Socialists in practice had become another parliamentary party that hoped to reach its goals through legislation.

Another movement that sought to liberate the downtrodden was anarchism, which proclaimed that humans could be free only when the state had been abolished. According to anarchist theory, in a stateless society people would naturally join together in com-

munes and share the fruits of their labor. Some anarchists believed they could achieve their goal by educating people. Others were more impatient and hoped to speed up the process by making direct attacks on existing authority. The Russian nobleman Michael Bakunin° (1814–1876), frustrated at the authoritarianism of his homeland, became a lifelong anarchist. He challenged tsarism at home and participated in the 1848 revolutions throughout Europe. He viewed all governments as repressive and declared unilateral war on them: "The passion for destruction is also a creative passion." His ideas were particularly influential in Italy, Spain, and parts of France, especially among the artisan classes.

Many anarchists of this period wanted to bring about the new society by "propaganda of the deed." An attack on the bastions of power, these anarchists believed, could bring about the dissolution of the state. They formed secret terrorist organizations that assassinated heads of state or those close to them. Between 1894 and 1901, anarchists killed a president of France, a prime minister of Spain, an empress of Austria, a king of Italy, and a president of the United States. These murders fixed the popular image of anarchism as a violence-prone ideology. More important, such manifestations of the "propaganda of the deed" produced no particular improvement in the lives of the working-class people on whose behalf these deadly campaigns had supposedly been launched.

Without accepting the anarchists' methods, some in the labor movement shared their hostility toward parliamentary institutions. A working-class program, labor activists argued, could be implemented only by a pure workers' movement, such as unionization. Workers should shun the political arena and concentrate on direct action. According to this line of thought, known as "syndicalism°" (after the French word for unions), workers should amass their power in unions, and at the right moment carry out a general strike, crippling capitalist society and bringing it down. Syndicalism was particularly popular in Mediterranean countries, where its more militant form, anarcho-syndicalism, radicalized labor and made a sizable number of workers hostile to parliamentarism.

European socialism also attempted an international presence. In 1864 Marx had participated in the founding of the International Workers' Association, which fell prey to internal dissension and dissolved after a few years. Known as the First International, it was followed by a more robust organization, the Second International, in 1889. The International met yearly and debated issues of concern to socialists in general, including the worsening relations among European states. As early as 1893 the International urged European states to resolve their conflicts by mandatory arbitration. In 1907, sensing impending war, the International called on the workers to strike and refuse military service in case of international conflict. The International saw itself as a bulwark of peace; it did not realize that once war broke out, Europeans, including socialists, would be swept up in nationalist fervor and would willingly go to war. Although most socialists advocated peace at home and abroad, many had contributed to a militant discourse with their class war rhetoric.

■ The New Right, Racism, and Anti-Semitism

The traditional opponents of liberalism on the political right were the conservatives, wedded to preserving the existing order. Beginning in the 1880s, however, a "new right" emerged that was populist and demagogic. Although conservatives had been wary of nationalism, the new right embraced it. Alienated by industry, democracy, and social egalitarianism, many in this new right rejected doctrines of human equality and embraced racist ideologies.

Racist thinking was common in the nineteenth century. Many Europeans believed human races were not only different physiologically but also—as a result of these biological variations—differently endowed in intelligence and other qualities (see pages 798–799). Europeans were often ethnocentric, convinced they were the epitome of humankind, whereas members of other races belonged to lesser groups. In midcentury the Frenchman Arthur de Gobineau° (1816–1882) published his *Essay on the Inequality of Human Races,* declaring that race "dominates all other problems and is the key to it." Biologists and early anthropologists made similar statements, thus giving racism a "scientific" aura. Throughout the second half of the nineteenth century, race was thought to be the principal explanation for the differences that were discovered among human groupings.

These racist ideas helped fuel anti-Semitism. For centuries Jews had been the object of suspicion and bigotry. Originally, the basis of the prejudice was religious. As early as the Middle Ages, however, the argument emerged that "Jewish blood" was different. And with the popularization of pseudoscientific racist thinking in the nineteenth century, Jews were commonly viewed as a separate, inferior race, unworthy of the same rights as the majority of the population.

Historically, Christians had relegated the Jews in their midst to marginal positions. In the Middle Ages, when land was the basis of wealth and prestige, Jews had been confined to such urban trades as cattle trading and moneylending. They incurred high risks by lending money: they often were not paid back and faced unsympathetic courts when they tried to collect their debts. To counteract these risks, Jewish moneylenders charged high interest rates that earned them their unpopular reputation as usurers.

The emancipation of the Jews, which began in France with the Revolution and spread to Germany and Austria by the 1860s, provided them opportunities they had not had before. Some members of society found it hard to adjust to the prominence a few Jews gained. Because their increased social standing and success were concurrent with the wrenching social transformations brought by industrialization and urbanization, anti-Semites pointed to the Jews as the perpetrators of these unsettling changes.

Many people perceived Jews as prototypical of the new capitalist class. Although most Jews were of modest means, resentment of the rich often was aimed at Jews. Earlier in the century, many anti-Semites were socialists, speaking on behalf of the working class. Later they came from among the petty bourgeois—small shopkeepers and artisans—who felt threatened by economic change.

Political movements based on anti-Semitism were founded in the 1880s. They depicted Jews as dangerous and wicked and called for their exclusion from the political arena and from certain professions. In some cases proponents suggested that Jews be expelled from the state. Karl Lueger (1844–1928) was elected mayor of Vienna, on an anti-Semitic platform. In Berlin the emperor's chaplain, Adolf Stöcker° (1835–1909), founded an anti-Semitic party, hoping to make political inroads among the working-class supporters of socialism. In France Edouard Drumont (1844–1917) published one of the best-sellers of the second half of the nineteenth century, *Jewish France,* in which he blamed all the nation's misfortunes on the Jews.

In Russia organized *pogroms,* or mass attacks, on Jews killed two thousand in the 1880s and one thousand in 1905, frightening 2 million Jews into exile, mostly to the United States. Russian Jews lived under social as well as legal disabilities; condemned to second-class citizenship, they won full emancipation only with the Bolshevik Revolution of 1917.

In the face of growing hostility, some Jews speculated that they would be safe only in their own nation. The

---

Gobineau (go-bee-NO)

Stöcker (SHTOE-kur)

❧ READING SOURCES

Nietzsche Declares God to Be Dead

By pronouncing God dead, Nietzsche believed he had liberated people from tradition and conventions. Fully free, they can explore all the potentialities of human existence, test the boundaries of what is possible—if, indeed, there are any boundaries. Consider the deliberate shock value of Nietzsche's formulation.

The greatest recent event—that "God is dead," that the belief in the Christian God has ceased to be believable—is even now beginning to cast its first shadows over Europe. For the few, at least, whose eyes, whose *suspicion* in their eyes, is strong and sensitive enough for this spectacle, some sun seems to have set just now. . . . In the main, however, this may be said: the event itself is much too great, too distant, too far from the comprehension of the many even for the tidings of it to be thought of as having *arrived* yet, not to speak of the notion that many people might know what has really happened here, and what must collapse now that this belief has been undermined—all that was built upon it, leaned on it, grew into it; for example our European morality.

Indeed, we philosophers and "free spirits" feel as if a new dawn were shining on us when we receive the tidings that "the old god is dead"; our heart overflows with gratitude, amazement, anticipation, expectation. At last the horizon appears free again to us, even granted that it is not bright; at last our ships may venture out again, venture out to face any danger; all the daring of the lover of knowledge is permitted again; the sea, *our* sea, lies open again; perhaps there has never yet been such an "open sea."

Source: Walter Kaufmann, ed., *The Portable Nietzsche* (New York: Viking Press, 1954), pp. 447–448.

Austrian Jewish journalist Theodore Herzl° (1860–1904), outraged by the Dreyfus affair in France, in which a Jewish officer was imprisoned on trumped-up charges of treason (see page 828), founded the Zionist movement. He advocated establishing a Jewish state in the Jews' ancient homeland of Israel. In the beginning, the Zionist movement won a following only in eastern Europe, where the Jews were particularly ill-treated, but by 1948, Zionism culminated in the creation of the state of Israel.

Various manifestations of anti-Semitism revealed the vulnerability of tolerance, one of the basic ideas of liberalism. It became eminently clear that racism, with its penchant for irrationality and violence, could easily be aroused.

■ Irrationality and Uncertainty

In contrast to the confidence in reason and science that had prevailed at midcentury, the era starting in the 1880s wrestled with the issues of irrationality and uncer-

tainty—in philosophy, in science, in the arts, even in religion. The positivism of the earlier era had emphasized surface reality of "progress" but neglected inner meaning and ignored the emotional and intuitive aspects of life. By the 1890s a neoromantic mood, emphasizing emotion and feeling, stirred major intellectual movements. The spotlight was no longer on reason, but on instinct.

In philosophy the tension between reason and emotion was vividly expressed in the work of the German philosopher Friedrich Nietzsche° (1844–1900), who proclaimed that rationality had led humankind into a meaningless abyss. Reason would not resolve human problems, nor would any preconceived ideas. "God is dead," Nietzsche announced. With no God, humankind was free of all outside constraints, free to overthrow all conventions. (See the box "Reading Sources: Nietzsche Declares God to Be Dead.") Nietzsche admonished his readers to challenge existing institutions and accepted truths and to create new ones.

Herzl (HER-tsl)

Friedrich Nietzsche (FREED-reesh NEET-sheh)

The French philosopher Henri Bergson° (1859–1940) argued that science—and indeed life—must be interpreted not rationally but intuitively. "Science," Bergson declared, "can teach us nothing of the truth; it can only serve as a rule of action." Humans could best understand meaningful truths—such as the truth of religion, literature, and art—by relying on their feelings.

Various disciplines of knowledge subscribed to the notion that humans were often irrational, motivated by deep-seated instinctive forces. The Austro-Hungarian Sigmund Freud° (1856–1939) founded psychoanalysis, a method of treating psychic disorders by exploring the unconscious. Freud believed that people were motivated not only by observed reality but also by their unconscious feelings and emotions. Whereas earlier physicians had described the mental condition of "hysteria" as a physical ailment, Freud saw its roots as psychological, the result of unresolved inner conflicts. Although Freud's work was influenced by rational methods, he stressed that irrational forces played a significant role in human behavior.

The social theorist Gaetano Mosca (1858–1941) in his book *Elements of Political Science* (1891) posited that in all societies—even democratic ones—an elite minority rules over the majority. The desire to dominate is a basic part of human nature; even in democratic or socialist societies, this thirst for power is never slaked. Beneath slogans touting the public good lies selfish ambition. Thus, as did Freud, Mosca suggested that surface appearances are deceptive and at heart humans are guided by irrational forces.

The scientists of this period seemed to underscore the conclusions of contemporaries who questioned the knowableness of the world through reason. In 1905 Albert Einstein (1879–1955) proposed the theory of relativity, which undermined the certainties of Newtonian physics. Einstein's theory demonstrated that time and space are not absolute but exist relative to the observer. Much of the research in atomic theory also revealed variations and unexplained phenomena. For example, the work of German physicist Max Planck (1858–1947) upset fundamental theories about the nature of the atom with his quantum theory. Planck showed that energy in the form of electrons is absorbed or emitted not continuously, as previously assumed, but rather discontinuously. A subatomic particle such as an electron could be in two places at the same time, until measured. The stability of nature was questioned; waves could be particles, but particles could also be waves; causes were not necessarily linked to effects. Some scientists no longer shared

Freud in 1909   Although much of Sigmund Freud's career still lay ahead of him, he already had established a reputation as the founder of modern psychology.   *(Sigmund Freud Copyrights/ Mary Evans Picture Library)*

the self-confidence that their colleagues had maintained half a century earlier, finding it increasingly difficult to believe in absolute certainties.

In the arts, the idea of being *avant-garde*—French for "forefront"—took hold among creative people. Breaking the taboos of society and the conventions of one's craft seemed to be signs of artistic creativity. Artistic movements proclaimed idiosyncratic manifestos and constantly called for the rejection of existing forms of expression and the creation of new ones. The symbolists in France and Italy, the expressionists in Germany, the futurists in Italy, and the secessionists in Austria all reflected the sense that they were living through a fractured period.

In protest against the mass culture of their day, artists focused on images that were different and unique. Unlike earlier art, which had a clear message, the art of this era did not. Many artists no longer believed their role was to portray or spread ideals. Rather, they tended to be introspective and even self-absorbed. The public at

---

Bergson (BERK-sohn)   **Freud** (FROYD)

Munch: The Scream   Painted in 1893, this work reflects the fear and horror that some intellectuals experienced at the end of the nineteenth century.   *(Edvard Munch,* The Scream, *1893. Tempera and oil pastel on cardboard. 91 × 73.5 cm. Photo: J. Lathion, Nasjonalgalleriet, Oslo. Copyright Munch Museum, Oslo, 1993)*

large found it difficult to decipher the meaning of the new art, but bewildered or not, a number of patrons supported the avant-garde artists' talent and insight.

Unlike the realists who preceded them, artists in the 1890s surrendered to neoromanticism, trying to investigate and express inner forces. As the French painter Paul Gauguin (1848–1903) noted, the purpose of painting was to communicate not how things looked but the emotions they conveyed. The Russian Wassily Kandinsky° (1866–1944) asked viewers of his art to "look at the picture as a graphic representation of a mood and not as a representation of objects." Artists appeared to be examining the hidden anxieties of society. The Frenchman Gustave Moreau° (1826–1898) displayed monsters, creations of nightmare, byproducts of the unconscious. The

Austrian artist Egon Schiele° (1890–1918) and the Norwegian painter Edvard Munch° (1863–1944) emphasized scenes of violence, fear, and sheer horror.

Musicians too stretched the traditional forms of their art. Claude Debussy° (1862–1918) defied established rules of tone and harmony of Western music and its usage of orchestral instruments in works such as *Prelude* and *Afternoon of a Faun* (1894) and his opera *Pelléas and Mélisande* (1902). Rather than being cerebral, he insisted, his work was instinctive.

Religion, too, felt the effects of intellectual challenge. Although large numbers of people still held traditional religious beliefs and followed traditional practices, indifference to organized religion spread. In urban areas of western Europe, church attendance declined; as these regions urbanized, they became increasingly secular. But with the decline of traditional Christian practices, various forms of mysticism became more widespread. Some people were attracted to Eastern religions such as Buddhism and Hinduism and to other mystical beliefs. These attitudes may have reflected a loss of faith in Western culture itself. As the century came to an end, a number of intellectuals argued that their culture, like the century, was destined for decline.

VULNERABLE DEMOCRACIES

BY the end of the nineteenth century, most of Europe's political systems floundered in crisis. The major powers with democratic institutions—Great Britain, France, and Italy—confronted volatile public opinion and had difficulty winning a broad consensus for their policies. They struggled with new challenges emerging from an expanded electorate that was at times frustrated by the failure of the system to respond to its demands. Turning away from the democratic precept of resolving differences through the ballot and legislation, many people—both in government and out—were willing to resort to extraparliamentary means, including violence, to see their interests prevail.

■ Great Britain

In Great Britain the Reform Bill of 1884 transformed the political landscape by giving the vote to two of every three adult men, doubling suffrage to 5 million. The appeal of this enlarged electorate tempted politicians to

---

Wassily Kandinsky (vass-IH-lee kan-DIN-skee)
Moreau (mo-RO)

Egon Schiele (EYE-gohn SHE-lee)   **Munch** (MOONGK)
Debussy (day-bew-SEE)

make demagogic promises, which were often broken later, to the exasperation of their constituents. It was also more difficult to reach compromises in a Parliament that no longer consisted of a fairly limited class of people with common interests and values. The British political system was faced with issues it was unable to resolve peacefully, and it was obliged—uncharacteristically—to resort to force or the threat of force.

As in earlier periods, Ireland proved to be a persistent problem. The political consciousness of the Irish had risen considerably, and they seethed under alien rule. In an attempt to quell Irish opposition in 1886, Prime Minister William Gladstone° proposed autonomy, or "home rule," for Ireland. There were many objections to such a plan, the most serious being that if Ireland, a predominantly Catholic country, ruled itself, the local Protestant majority in Ulster, the northeast part of the island, would be overwhelmed and likely to fall under Catholic control. "Home rule is Rome rule," chanted the supporters of Ulster Protestantism. Among Gladstone's own Liberals, many opposed changing the existing relationship between England and its neighboring possession. They seceded from the Liberals and formed the Unionist Party, which, in coalition with the Conservatives, ruled the country from 1886 to 1905. When the Liberals returned to power in 1906, they again proposed home rule. In 1911 the House of Commons finally passed a home rule bill, but it was obstructed in the House of Lords and was not slated to go into effect until September 1914.

In the process of wrangling over the Irish issue, many segments of British society showed they were willing to resort to extralegal and even violent means. Fearing Catholic domination, Protestants in northern Ireland armed themselves, determined to resist home rule. In the rest of Ireland, Catholic groups took up arms, too, insisting on the unity of the island; they were ready to fight for home rule for the whole of Ireland. The Conservative Party in Britain, which opposed home rule, called on Ulster to revolt. British officers threatened to resign their commissions rather than fight Ulster. The behavior of the Conservatives and the army indicated a breakdown of order and authority, a disregard for tradition by two of its bulwarks. Only the outbreak of world war in 1914 delayed a showdown over Ireland, and then by only a few years.

Once back in power in 1906, the Liberals committed themselves to an impressive array of social reforms but were frustrated by the difficulty of getting their program through the House of Lords. The feisty Liberal chancellor of the exchequer, David Lloyd George (1863–1945), ex-

pressed his outrage that the will of the people was being thwarted by a handful of magnates in the House of Lords, sitting there not by election but by hereditary right.

The Liberals' social reform program included old-age pensions. To finance them, Lloyd George proposed raising income taxes and death duties and levying a tax on landed wealth. A bill with these measures easily passed the House of Commons in 1909 but was stymied in the upper chamber, where many members were prominent landowners. The House of Lords technically had the power to amend or reject a bill passed by Commons, but for nearly 250 years it had been tacitly understood that the Lords did not have the right to reject a money bill. Nonetheless, motivated by economic self-interest and personal spite against the Liberals, a majority in the House of Lords disregarded convention and voted against the bill. This decision provoked a major constitutional crisis.

The Liberal government wanted not only to pass its bill but also to reduce the power of the Lords. In 1911 it sponsored a bill, quickly passed by the House of Commons, to limit the House of Lords to a suspensive veto. This would mean that a bill defeated in the House of Lords could be prevented from going into effect for only a predetermined period—in this case, two years. The House of Lords refused at first to pass such a law. But at the request of the government, the king threatened to appoint four hundred new lords. Reluctantly, the House of Lords passed the bill.

During the debate over the bill, Conservatives—the representatives of British traditionalism and the upholders of decorum—resorted to brawling and refused to let the prime minister speak. It was the first time in British parliamentary history that such breach of conduct had occurred. The British Parliament, considered the model for supporters of free institutions, had shown itself unable to resolve issues in a civil manner.

Violence also appeared in another unlikely place: the women's suffrage movement. Most liberal males, when speaking of the need to extend human liberty, had excluded women. Toward the end of the nineteenth century, that bastion, too, was under siege. Women began to organize into groups devoted to winning the vote but had little initial success. In 1903 Emmeline Pankhurst (1858–1928) and her two daughters founded the Women's Social and Political Union, whose goal was immediate suffrage.

Angered and frustrated by their lack of progress, in 1906 the suffragists (often referred to by contemporaries as "suffragettes"), led by the Pankhursts, began a more militant program of protest—disturbing proceedings in

---

Gladstone (GLAD-sten)

A Suffragist Attempts to Chain Herself to the Gates of Buckingham Palace, London, 1914   In their effort to win the vote, women resorted to public protests and the police often violently intervened. *(Popperfoto/Archive Photos)*

Parliament, breaking windows at the prime minister's residence, slashing canvases at the National Gallery, burning down empty houses, dropping acid into mailboxes, and throwing bombs. They even threatened the lives of the prime minister and the king. Suffragists who were arrested often engaged in hunger strikes. Fearing they would die, the authorities force-fed the women—a painful and humiliating procedure. Female protesters were also physically attacked by male thugs. (See the box "Reading Sources: Pankhurst Testifies on Women's Rights.") That women would resort to violence, and that men in and outside of the government would retaliate in kind, demonstrated how widespread the cult of force had become.

■ France

The Third French Republic, founded in 1870 after France's humiliating military defeat at the hands of the Prussians, also struggled with an ongoing series of crises. Challenged by enemies on the political left and right

who continually called for the abolition of democracy, the regime found itself buffeted from all sides.

The French government itself contributed to the unstable political situation by its lack of strong leadership. The need to build coalitions among the several parties in the parliament rewarded those politicians who had moderate programs and were flexible. Thus there was little premium on firm ideas and commitments, and the prime minister was often more a conciliator than a leader. Further, lackluster leadership appealed to republicans, who continued to fear that a popular leader might—as Louis Napoleon had in 1851—exploit his support to make himself dictator.

The regime seemed to lurch from scandal to scandal. The most notorious was the Dreyfus affair. In October 1894, Captain Alfred Dreyfus° (1859–1935) of the French army was arrested and charged with passing military secrets to the German embassy. Dreyfus seems to have attracted suspicion because he was the only Jewish

Dreyfus (DRY-fooss)

Pankhurst Testifies on Women's Rights

In 1908 the suffragists, led by Emmeline Pankhurst, issued a handbill calling on the people of London to "rush" Parliament and win the vote for women. The legal authorities interpreted their action as a violation of the peace, and several suffragists, including Pankhurst, were put on trial. They put up a spirited defense, in which Pankhurst movingly explained her motives for leading the suffragist cause.

I want you to realise how we women feel; because we are women, because we are not men, we need some legitimate influence to bear upon our lawmakers. Now, we have tried every way. We have presented larger petitions than were ever presented for any other reform, we have succeeded in holding greater public meetings than men have ever had for any reform, in spite of the difficulty which women have in throwing off their natural diffidence, that desire to escape publicity which we have inherited from generations of our foremothers; we have broken through that. We have faced hostile mobs at street corners, because we were told that we could not have that representation for our taxes which men have won unless we converted the whole of the country to our side. Because we have done this, we have been misrepresented, we have been ridiculed, we have had contempt poured upon us. The ignorant mob at the street corner has been incited to offer us violence, which we have faced unarmed and unprotected by the safeguards which Cabinet Ministers have. We know that we need the protection of the vote even more than men have needed it. . . .

We believe that if we get the vote it will mean better conditions for our unfortunate sisters. We know what the condition of the woman worker is . . . and we have been driven to the conclusion that only through legislation can any improvement be effected, and that that legislation can never be effected until we have the same power as men have to bring pressure to bear upon our representatives and upon Governments to give us the necessary legislation. . . .

I should never be here if I had the same kind of power that the very meanest and commonest of men have—the same power that the wife-beater has, the same power that the drunkard has. I should never be here if I had that power, and I speak for all the women who have come before you and other magistrates. . . .

If you had power to send us to prison, not for six months, but for six years, for sixteen years, or for the whole of our lives, the Government must not think that they can stop this agitation. It will go on. . . .

We are here not because we are law-breakers; we are here in our efforts to become lawmakers.

Source: F. W. Pethick Lawrence, ed. *The Trial of the Suffragette Leaders* (London: The Women's Press, 1909), pp. 21–24.

officer on the general staff. The evidence was flimsy—a handwritten letter that some thought Dreyfus had penned, although other experts testified that the handwriting was not that of the young officer.

This letter, and materials that later turned out to be forged, led the French army to court-martial Dreyfus and sentence him to life imprisonment on Devil's Island off the coast of South America. By March 1896, the general staff had evidence that another officer, Major Esterhazy, was actually the spy. But to reopen the case would be to admit the army had made an error, and that the general staff refused to do.

By late 1897, when the apparent miscarriage of justice became widely known, French society split over "the affair." The political left, including many intellectuals, argued for reopening the case. For them it was crucial that justice be carried out. The army and its supporters, right-wing politicians, royalists, and zealous Catholics, argued that the decision should stand. As the bulwark against internal and foreign threats, the army should be above challenge, and the fate of a single man—guilty or innocent—was immaterial.

The affair unleashed a swirl of controversy and rioting, which led the government to order a retrial in 1899.

Riots in Italian Parliament   Party strife and conflicts between individuals in the Italian parliament were so severe that often they degenerated into fisticuffs. This illustration catches a particularly violent moment of a parliamentary debate. *(Madeline Grimoldi)*

But the court again found Dreyfus guilty—this time with "extenuating circumstances" and the recommendation that he be pardoned. Finally, in 1906, Dreyfus was fully exonerated. He ended his days as a general in the army that had subjected him to so much suffering.

The strong encouragement many Catholics gave to those who supported the original verdict confirmed the republicans' belief that the church was a menace to the regime. The Radical Party, the staunchest backers of Dreyfus, won the elections in 1898. Despite its title, the Radical Party backed moderate social reforms. It was uncompromising, however, in its anticlericalism, determined to wreak vengeance on Catholics and end the influence of the church once and for all. In 1905 the parliament passed a law separating church and state, thus ending the privileged position the Catholic Church had enjoyed. Violent language and physical confrontations

on both sides accompanied this division. Catholics trying to prevent state officials from entering churches to take required inventories sometimes resorted to force, using weapons or, in one case, a bear chained to the church. Armed soldiers broke down church doors and dragged priests away.

Labor problems also triggered repeated confrontations with the government. Increased labor militancy produced long, drawn-out strikes, which in 1904 alone led to the loss of 4 million workdays. There was agitation in the countryside, too, particularly in 1907 in the Midi, the south of France. This region suffered from a crisis in the wine industry caused by a disease that attacked the vines, competition from cheap foreign wines, and fraud. More important, the region witnessed increased rural proletarianization as population grew and larger land-holdings were concentrated in fewer hands. Rural militancy led to revolt in 1907. Troops were sent in, killing dozens and winning for the Radical regime the title "government of assassins."

■ Italy

The third major power in Europe to adopt parliamentary government also had grave problems. Although unification took place in 1860, Italy found genuine unity elusive. The country was plagued by regionalism, social strife, and an unrepresentative political system. As in the past, the south especially challenged the central government. Assertive regionalism, crime, and poverty made this area resistant to most government programs.

The parliamentary system established in 1860 was far from democratic. Property qualifications limited suffrage to less than 3 percent of the population. And as a result of the persistence of *trasformismo* (see Chapter 22)—the practice by which government corrupted and co-opted the opposition—electoral choice was short-circuited.

Between 1870 and 1890 the Italian government introduced some important reforms, but it was difficult to improve the general standard of living for a people undergoing rapid population growth. In the fifty years after unification, the population increased from 25 to 35 million, and the country had limited resources to deal with such growth. In the south, a few wealthy landowners held large *latifundia*°, or private estates, while the majority of the peasants were landless and forced to work the land for minimum wages. In the north, industrialization had started, but the region was not rich in coal or iron. To be competitive, industry paid very low wages, and the workers lived in abject misery.

---

latifundia (lah-tee-FOON-dya)

Conditions on the land and in the factory led to widespread protests, followed by stern government repression. In 1893 a Sicilian labor movement won the adherence of 300,000 members, who seized land and attacked government offices. The government responded with massive force and declared martial law. In 1896, with unrest spreading throughout the peninsula, the government placed half of the provinces under military rule. A cycle of violence and counterviolence gripped the nation. In this turbulent atmosphere, an anarchist killed King Umberto I on July 29, 1900.

After the turn of the century, a new prime minister, Giovanni Giolitti° (1842–1928), tried to bring an end to the upheaval. He used government force more sparingly and showed a spirit of cooperation toward the workers. Seeking to broaden his popularity by an appeal to nationalist fervor, Giolitti launched an attack on Libya in 1911, wresting it from the ailing Ottoman Empire. The territory was arid and bereft of economic promise, but its conquest was championed as a test of national virility and the foundation of national greatness. The imperialists proudly proclaimed force the arbiter of the nation's future.

Domestically, the nation also returned to force. A wave of workers' discontent seized the nation again, and in June 1914 a national strike led to rioting and workers' seizing power in several municipalities. In the Romagna, in northern Italy, an independent workers' republic was proclaimed. It took 100,000 government troops ten days to restore order. The workers' restlessness and brazen defiance led some nationalist right-wing extremists to form groups of "volunteers for the defense of order," anticipating the vigilante thugs who were to make up the early bands of Italian fascism.

Autocracies in Crisis

 OUR major autocracies dominated central and eastern Europe: Germany, Austria-Hungary, the Ottoman Empire, and Russia. If the democracies encountered difficulties in these years, the autocracies faced even more vehement opposition. Although many groups in the parliamentary regimes grew impatient at the slowness of change, theoretically at least they could believe that someday their goals would be realized. Not so in the autocracies. In authoritarian states, the demands for more democracy were growing louder; opponents sought by all means, including violence, to challenge the existing order. Governments in turn were willing to use violence to maintain themselves.

The severity of autocratic rule varied from state to state, ranging from the absolutism of the Ottoman Empire to the semiparliamentary regime of Germany, but the ruler had the final political say in all of them. Resistance to the autocracies included broad popular challenges to the German imperial system, the reduction of Austria-Hungary into a nearly ungovernable empire, and revolution in the Russian and Ottoman Empires.

■ Germany

Although Germany had a parliament, the government was answerable to the kaiser, not the people's electoral representatives. And in the late nineteenth century, Prussia, the most reactionary part of the country, continued to dominate.

To rule effectively, Chancellor Otto von Bismarck maneuvered and intrigued to quell opposition. In the face of socialist growth, he used an attempt to assassinate the emperor as the excuse to ban the Socialist Party in 1879. He succeeded in simultaneously winning over conservative agrarian and liberal industrial interests by supporting tariffs on both imported foodstuffs and industrial goods. He also turned against the Catholics, who were lukewarm toward Protestant Prussia, persecuting them and their institutions. These measures, however, did not prevent the growth of the Socialist and Catholic Center Parties.

Unfortunately for Bismarck, whose tenure in office depended on the goodwill of the emperor, Wilhelm I died in 1888, to be succeeded first by his son Friedrich, who ruled only a few months, and then by his grandson, Wilhelm II (r. 1888–1918). The young Kaiser Wilhelm intended to rule as well as reign, but he was ill fit to govern. Convinced of his own infallibility, he bothered to learn very little. Born with a crippled hand, Wilhelm seemed to want to compensate for this infirmity by appearing forceful, even brutal. He hated any hints of limitation to his powers, announcing, "There is only one ruler in the Reich and I am he. I tolerate no other." A restless individual, Wilhelm changed uniforms eight times daily and traveled ceaselessly among his seventy-five castles and palaces. Dismayed by Bismarck's proposals of reprisals against the socialists and the chancellor's unwillingness to take on a clearly pro-Austrian and anti-Russian foreign policy, the kaiser dismissed him. But he also did so to rid himself of a formidable, intimidating individual.

Wilhelm II was determined to make Germany a world power whose foreign policy would have a global

Giovanni Giolitti (jo-VAH-nee jo-LEE-tee)

Wilhelm II   The German emperor liked to be viewed in a heroic and military posture. His crippled left hand is turned away from the viewer.   *(Landesbildstelle, Berlin)*

impact. He wanted Germany to have colonies, a navy, and major influence among the Great Powers. This policy, *Weltpolitik,* or "world politics," greatly troubled Germany's neighbors, partly because they already worried about a new, assertive power in central Europe and partly because German moves were accompanied by the kaiser's bombastic threats. Within Germany, however, *Weltpolitik* won support. Steel manufacturers and shipbuilders received lucrative contracts; workers, in some industries at least, seemed assured of employment.

Although the nationalist appeals impressed many Germans, the nation could not be easily managed. The emperor's autocratic style was challenged, and his behavior was increasingly viewed as irresponsible. In the elections of 1912, one-third of all Germans voted for Socialist Party candidates. Thus the largest single party in the Reichstag was at least rhetorically committed to the downfall of the capitalist system and autocracy. Labor militancy also reached new heights. In 1912, 1 million workers—a record number—went on strike. More and

more Germans pressed for a parliamentary system with a government accountable to the people's elected representatives.

The emperor could not tolerate criticism of his behavior. He had come to Bismarck's conclusions and frequently talked about using the military to crush socialists and the parliament. These violent thoughts were echoed in the officer corps and in government circles. To some observers it seemed likely that the days of German autocracy were numbered—or that the army and the people would come to blows.

■ Austria-Hungary

The neighboring Austro-Hungarian Empire was also wracked by a series of crises. In an age of intense nationalism, a multinational empire was an anomaly, as the emperor Franz Joseph (r. 1848–1916) himself acknowledged. Although the relationship between the two halves of the empire was regulated by the Compromise of 1867 (see page 755), the agreement did not prevent conflict between Austria and Hungary, particularly over control of their joint army. The insistence on separate Hungarian interests had developed to such a degree that, had it not been for the outbreak of the world war, Hungary probably would have broken loose from the dual monarchy.

In the Hungarian half of the empire, the Magyars found it increasingly difficult to maintain control. Other nationalities opposed Magyarization—the imposition of the Magyar language and institutions—and insisted on the right to use their own languages in their schools and administrations. The Hungarian government resorted to censorship and jailings to silence nationalist leaders. In the Austrian half of the empire, the treatment of nationalities was less harsh, but the government was equally strife-ridden.

There were no easy solutions to the many conflicts the empire faced. Since much of the national agitation was led by middle-class intellectuals, the Habsburg government introduced universal male suffrage in 1907 in an effort to undercut their influence. However, the result was an empire even more difficult to govern. It became nearly impossible to find a workable majority within a parliament that included thirty ethnically based political parties.

The virulence of debate based on nationality and class divisions grew to unprecedented extremes. Within the parliament, deputies threw inkwells at each other, rang sleigh bells, and sounded bugles. Parliament ceased to be relevant. By 1914 the emperor had dissolved it and several regional assemblies. Austria was being ruled by decree. Emperor Franz Joseph feared the empire would not survive him.

■ Ottoman Empire

In the generation before 1914, no political system in Europe suffered from so advanced a case of dissolution as the Ottoman Empire, undermined by both secessionist movements within its own borders and aggression from other European powers. Sultan Abdul Hamid° II (r. 1876–1909) ruled the country as a despot and authorized mass carnage against those who contested his rule, earning him the title "the Great Assassin."

Young, Western-educated Turks—the so-called Young Turks—disgusted at one-man rule and the continuing loss of territory and influence, overthrew Abdul Hamid in a coup in July 1908. They set up a government responsible to an elected parliament. The Young Turks hoped to stem the loss of territory by establishing firmer central control, but their efforts had the opposite effect. The various nationalities of the empire resented the attempts at "Turkification," the imposition of Turkish education and administration. Renewed agitation broke out in Macedonia, in Albania, and among the Armenians. The government carried out severely repressive measures to end the unrest, killing thousands of Armenians.

For foreign powers, the moment seemed propitious to plunder the weakened empire. In 1911 Italy occupied Libya, an Ottoman province. Greece, Bulgaria, and Serbia—impatient to enlarge their territories—formed an alliance, the Balkan League, which in 1912 prosecuted a successful war against the empire. Albania became independent, and Macedonia was partitioned among members of the league. Thus, except for the capital, Constantinople, and a narrow strip of surrounding land, the empire was stripped of most of its European possessions.

■ Russia

Through the Great Reforms of the 1860s, the Russian autocracy had attempted to resolve many of the problems troubling its empire and people. But the reforms and the major social changes of the period unleashed new forces, making it even more difficult for the tsars to rule.

The needs of a modernizing country led to an increase in the number of universities and students. The newly educated Russian youths almost instantly began an ardent, sustained critique of autocracy. In the absence of a large group upholding liberal, advanced ideas, university students and graduates, who came to be known as the *intelligentsia*, saw it as their mission to transform Russia.

In the 1870s, university youths by the thousands organized a populist movement, hoping to bring change to the countryside. These young idealists intended to educate the peasants and make them more politically aware. But they met with suspicion from the peasantry and repression by the government. Large numbers of populists were arrested and put on trial. Frustrated at the difficulty of bringing about change from below by transforming the people, disaffected radicals formed the People's Will, which turned to murdering public officials to hasten the day of revolution.

Although the regime intensified repression, it also sought to broaden its public support. In 1881 Tsar Alexander II decided to create an advisory committee that some thought would eventually lead to a parliamentary form of government. In March 1881, as he was about to sign the decree establishing this committee, the tsar was assassinated by members of the People's Will.

The new ruler, Tsar Alexander III (r. 1881–1894), who had witnessed the assassination, blamed his father's leniency for his death. By contrast, he was determined to uphold autocracy firmly. He sought to weaken his father's reforms, reducing local self-rule in the process.

When Alexander's son, Nicholas II (r. 1894–1917), succeeded his father on the throne in 1894, he declared he would be as autocratic as his father. However, he lacked the methodical, consistent temperament such a pledge required. A pleasant man, he wanted to be liked, and he lacked the forcefulness to establish a coherent policy for his troubled country.

Since the Great Reforms, serious problems had accumulated that threatened the stability of the regime. In the countryside the situation worsened steadily as the population exploded and pressure on the land increased. The provisions that had accompanied the freeing of the serfs left considerable discontent. The peasants were not free to come and go as they pleased; they had to have the permission of the village council. Agriculture remained inefficient, far inferior to that of western Europe. Hence the allotted land was insufficient to feed the peasants, creating a constant demand for more land.

Although Russia remained largely agrarian, pockets of industrial growth sprang up. Some factories and mining concerns were unusually large, with as many as six thousand employees. When workers grew incensed at their condition and insistent on winning the same rights and protection as their counterparts in western Europe, they engaged in massive strikes that crippled industry.

Political dissatisfaction with the autocracy grew. Members of the expanding middle classes began to clamor that, like their contemporaries in western Europe, they should be given the opportunity to participate in governance. Increasingly, aristocrats also demanded a right to political participation.

Abdul Hamid (ab-DOOL ah-MEED)

ॐ READING SOURCES

Lenin Urges a Conspiratorial Revolutionary Party

The Russian Socialist Party was wracked by internal debates over the direction and means by which a socialist revolution could be created. The majority favored a broad-based party, but in his 1902 essay, "What Is to Be Done?" Lenin explained why revolution in Russia could succeed only if it were led by a cadre of professional revolutionaries, organized into a tightly knit conspiratorial group. As Lenin presses for a tightly organized party, notice the practical reasons he enumerates as well as the self-serving nature of his argument.

We must have a committee of professional revolutionaries . . . irrespective of whether they are students or working men. I assert: 1) That no movement can be durable without a stable organization of leaders to maintain continuity; 2) that the more widely the masses are drawn into the struggle and form the basis of the movement, the more necessary it is to have such an organization and the more stable it must be—otherwise it is much easier for demagogues to sidetrack the more backward sections of the masses; 3) that the organization must consist chiefly of persons engaged in revolution as a profession; 4) that in a country with a despotic government, the more we restrict the membership of this organization to persons who are engaged in revolution as a profession and who have been professionally trained in the art of combating the political police, the more difficult will it be to catch the organization; and 5) the wider will be the circle of men and women of the working class or of other classes of society able to join the movement and perform active work in it. . . .

It is . . . argued against us that the views on organization here expounded contradict the "principles of democracy."

Ponder a little over the real meaning of the high-sounding phrase . . . and you will realize that "broad democracy" in party organization, amidst the gloom of autocracy and the domination of the gendarmes, is nothing more than a useless and harmful toy. It is a useless toy, because as a matter of fact, no revolutionary organization has ever practiced broad democracy, nor could it, however much it desired to do so.

The only serious organizational principle the active workers of our movement can accept is: Strict secrecy, strict selection of members and the training of professional revolutionists.

Source: Vladimir Ilich Lenin, "What Is to Be Done?" *Collected Works,* vol. 4 (New York: International Publishers, 1929), pp. 198–199, 210–213.

 For additional information on this topic, go to http://college.hmco.com.

Various revolutionary groups committed to socialism continued to flourish. The heirs to the People's Will were the Social Revolutionaries, who emerged as a political force in the 1890s. They believed that the peasants would bring socialism to Russia. In 1898 the Russian Social Democratic Party was founded; a Marxist party, it promoted the industrial working class as the harbinger of socialism. In 1903 that party split into the Menshevik and the Bolshevik factions. The Mensheviks insisted that Russia had to go through the stages of history Marx had outlined—to witness the full development of capitalism

and its subsequent collapse before socialism could come to power. The Bolsheviks, a minority group, were led by Vladimir Ilich Lenin (1870–1924), a zealous revolutionary and Marxist. Rather than wait for historical forces to undermine capitalism, he insisted that a revolutionary cadre could seize power on behalf of the working class. Lenin favored a small, disciplined, conspiratorial party, like the People's Will, while the Mensheviks favored a more open, democratic party. (See the box "Reading Sources: Lenin Urges a Conspiratorial Revolutionary Party.")

Workers' Demonstration in Moscow, 1905   In 1905 workers as well as peasants protested against the Russian autocracy. To bring the revolution under control, Nicholas II was obliged to grant several concessions.   *(Novosti)*

At the turn of the century these groups were still quite small and played a limited role in the mounting opposition to tsarism. But popular opposition soon grew in the face of Russian military ineptitude in the war against Japan, which had broken out in February 1904 in a dispute over control of northern Korea. Antagonism to the tsarist regime escalated as a result of social tensions, heightened by an economic slowdown.

Beginning in January 1905, a series of demonstrations, strikes, and other acts of collective violence erupted. Together, they were dubbed "the revolution of 1905." One Sunday in January 1905, 400,000 workers seeking redress of their grievances gathered in front of the tsar's St. Petersburg palace. Rather than hear their protests, officials ordered soldiers to fire on them, resulting in 150 deaths and hundreds more wounded. "Bloody Sunday" inflamed the populace. The tsar, instead of being viewed as an understanding, paternal authority, had become the murderer of his people. Unrest spread to most of the country. As reports reached Russia of more defeats in the war with Japan, the regime's prestige deteriorated

further. By September 1905, Russia had to sue for peace and admit defeat. Challenged in the capital, where independent workers' councils called *soviets* had sprung up, the government also lost control over the countryside, the site of widespread peasant uprisings.

Fearing for his regime, Nicholas hoped to disarm the forces challenging tsarism by meeting the demands for parliamentary government and granting major constitutional and civil liberties, including freedom of religion, speech, assembly, and association. At the end of October, the tsar established an elective assembly, the Duma, with restricted male suffrage and limited political power. It was far from the Western-style parliament that Russian liberals had desired, but it quickly became the arena for criticism of autocracy. Wanting to create a more pliant instrument, the tsar suspended the assembly, changing its electoral base and its rules of operations. Even many conservatives were disillusioned with the tsar's backtracking and his breach of the promise he had made in 1905 to establish constitutionalism and parliamentarism.

The government reduced the peasants' financial obligations; the power of the commune, or *mir* (see pages 759–760), was weakened; and local self-rule was extended to the peasants. But these changes did little to alleviate a worsening relationship between population and land. Between emancipation and 1914, the peasant population grew by 50 percent, but it acquired only 10 percent more land. Rural poverty was widespread; in 1891 famine broke out in twenty provinces, killing a quarter of a million people. Rural discontent was deep and widespread.

Labor unrest also mounted among industrial workers. In 1912, walkouts had involved 725,000 strikers, but by the first half of 1914, that number had doubled. When the French president visited St. Petersburg on the eve of the outbreak of the First World War, barricades were rising in the workers' neighborhoods.

Internally, the authoritarian states of Europe were fighting strong challenges. It was unclear how long they could maintain their respective grips.

THE COMING WAR

 NSTABILITY and upheaval characterized international relations in the years between 1880 and 1914. But the outbreak of war was by no means inevitable. Good common sense dictated against it, and some intelligent people predicted that in the new modern era, war would become so destructive that it would be unthinkable. Finally, no European state wanted a war, although the Great Powers carried on policies that brought them to its brink.

■ Power Alignments

Germany enjoyed an unchallenged position in the international order of the 1870s and 1880s. It was united in an alliance with the two other eastern conservative states—Russia and Austria-Hungary—in the Three Emperors' League, formed in 1873 and renewed by treaty in 1884. And it was part of the Triple Alliance with Austria and Italy. France stood alone, without allies. Britain, with little interest in continental affairs, appeared to be enjoying a "splendid isolation."

However, Germany's alliance system was not free from problems. Two of its allies, Austria-Hungary and Russia, were at loggerheads over control of the Balkans. How could Germany be the friend of both? Wary of apparent German preference for Austria, Bismarck signed the Reinsurance Treaty in 1887, assuring Russia that Ger-

many would not honor its alliance with Austria if the latter attacked Russia. After Bismarck's resignation in 1890, Kaiser Wilhelm allowed the Reinsurance Treaty to lapse. Alarmed, the Russians turned to France and, in January 1894, signed the Franco-Russian Alliance, by which each side pledged to help the other should either be attacked by Germany.

The Great Powers on the Continent were now divided into two alliances, the Triple Alliance and the Franco-Russian Alliance. Britain formally belonged to neither, but if it favored any side, it would be the German-led alliance. Britain's strongest competitors in the 1880s and 1890s were France and Russia. Both rivaled Britain for influence in Asia, while France vied with Britain for control of Africa.

By its actions in the 1890s Germany lost British goodwill. Launching his *Weltpolitik*, Wilhelm II built up the German navy. Over the years, Britain had developed a navy second to none. An island nation, dependent on international trade for its economic survival, Britain saw a strong navy as a necessity, the German naval buildup as a threat to its security.

In the face of what they viewed as a mounting German menace, Britain and France decided to resolve their difficulties overseas: in 1904 they signed an understanding, or *entente,* resolving their rivalries in Egypt. In 1907 Great Britain and Russia regulated their competition for influence in Persia (present-day Iran) with the Anglo-Russian Entente. Europe was still loosely divided into two groups, but now according to a different configuration: the Triple Alliance of Germany, Austria-Hungary, and Italy, and the Triple Entente of Great Britain, France, and Russia.

■ The Momentum Toward War

Only through a series of crises did these alignments solidify to the point where their members were willing to go to war to save them. France's attempts to take over Morocco twice led to conflict with Germany. In 1905 Germany insisted that an international conference discuss the issue and deny France this kingdom adjacent to its colony of Algeria. When France grabbed Morocco anyway, in 1911, Germany accepted the situation only after extorting compensation from the French, who deeply resented what they viewed as German bullying.

The heightened international rivalry forced the European states to increase their arms expenditures, which added in turn to their sense of insecurity. In 1906 Britain introduced a new class of ships with the launching of the *Dreadnought*. Powered by steam turbines, it was the fastest ship afloat; heavily armored, it could not be sunk easily; and its ten 12-inch guns made it a menace on the seas. The British had thought the Germans could not build equivalent ships, but they did, wiping out British supremacy—older British ships could easily be sunk by German dreadnoughts. No longer able to depend on its past supremacy, Britain was feeling less secure than at any time since the Napoleonic Wars, and it continued an expensive and feverish naval race with Germany.

In Germany the growing war-making capacity of Russia created great anxieties. The Japanese defeat of the tsarist empire in 1905 revealed the Russian military to be inferior—a lumbering giant, slow to mobilize and maneuver. As a result Germany had not been particularly afraid of its eastern neighbor. But stung by its humiliation in 1905, Russia quickly rebuilt its army and planned an extensive rail network in the west. To many in Germany, their country now appeared encircled by a hostile Russia to the east and an equally unfriendly France to the west. Germany became genuinely worried, and beginning in 1912 many in the military and within the government started thinking about a preventive war. If war was inevitable, many Germans argued, it should occur before Russia became even stronger. Fear of the future military balance made some of the highest policymakers see the crisis that broke out in the summer of 1914 as an opportunity to go to war and throttle Russia.

Many political leaders viewed the escalating arms race as a form of madness. Between 1904 and 1913, French and Russian arms expenditures increased by 80 percent; those of Germany by 120 percent; those of Austria-Hungary by 50 percent; and those of Italy by 100 percent. British foreign secretary Sir Edward Grey (1862–1933) warned that if the arms race continued, "It will submerge civilization." But no way was found to stop it.

On the whole warfare was not feared. Except for short victorious colonial wars, the Western powers had not experienced a major conflict since the Crimean War. Russia had successfully warred against the Ottoman Empire in 1876. Its war against Japan in 1905 had been a calamity, but Russia refused to believe that such a disaster would happen again. Most policymakers believed that the next war would be short. The wars that had so dramatically changed the borders of European states in the second half of the nineteenth century, notably the Austro-Prussian War of 1866 and the Franco-Prussian War of 1870, had been decided within a few short weeks. Few imagined that the next war, if it came, would be very brutal or very lengthy. And therefore many of Europe's leaders did not dread war enough to make a major effort to prevent or avoid it.

It was the territorial rivalry between Austria and Russia that triggered international disaster. For decades

Map 24.4   The Balkans in 1914   By 1914 the Ottoman Empire was much diminished, containing virtually no European territory. Political boundaries did not follow nationality lines. Serbia was committed to unite all Serbs at the expense of the Austro-Hungarian Empire.

enmity had been growing between the two empires over control of the Balkans (see Map 24.4). In 1903, following a bloody military coup that killed the king and queen of Serbia, a pro-Russian party took control of the Serbian government. In 1908 Russia, still not recovered from its defeat in 1905, was surprised when Austria unilaterally declared the annexation of the province of Bosnia (which it had administered since the Congress of Berlin in 1878; see page 758). The annexation appeared to spell an end to Serbia's dream of annexing Bosnia, which had many Serb inhabitants. Fearing war, Russia had to accept diplomatic defeat and abandoned its ally, Serbia. But Russia determined it would not cave in again.

Undeterred, Serbia spread anti-Austrian propaganda and sought to unify under its banner Slavs living

The Shot Heard 'Round the World
The young Serb nationalist Gavril Princip shoots Franz Ferdinand, the heir to the Austro-Hungarian throne, and his consort. The assassination unleashed the outbreak of World War I. *(Österreichische Nationalbibliothek, Vienna)*

in the Balkans, including those under Austrian rule. As a result, many Austrian officials were convinced that the survival of the Austro-Hungarian Empire required the destruction of Serbia. Talk of an attack on Serbia filled the Austrian court in 1914.

On June 28, 1914, the heir to the Habsburg throne, Archduke Franz Ferdinand, visited Sarajevo in Austrian-ruled Bosnia. A young Bosnian-Serb nationalist hostile to Austrian rule, who had been trained and armed by a Serb terrorist group called the Black Hand, assassinated the archduke and his wife.

The assassination of the heir to the throne provided Austria with an ideal pretext for military action. The German kaiser, fearing that failure to support Vienna would lead to Austrian collapse and a Germany bereft of any al-

lies, urged Austria to attack Serbia. On July 23, Austria issued an ultimatum to Serbia, deliberately worded in such a way as to be unacceptable. When Serbia refused the ultimatum, Austria declared war on July 28.

Perceived self-interest motivated each state's behavior in the ensuing crisis. Although in the past Russia had failed to protect Serbia, now it was resolved to help. Russia's status as a Great Power demanded that it not allow its client state to be humiliated, much less obliterated. In the past the French government had acted as a brake on Russian ambitions in the Balkans. On the very eve of the war in 1914, France counseled restraint, but it did not withhold its aid. Since 1911, France had increasingly feared isolation in the face of what it perceived as growing German aggression. Its only ally on the Continent was Russia. To remain a Great Power, France needed to preserve its friendship with Russia and help that country maintain its own Great Power status.

Germany could not allow Austria, its only ally, to be destroyed. Its leaders may also have seen the crisis as a propitious moment to begin a war that was going to occur sooner or later anyway. The Germans no doubt also thought it expedient to strike before the entente powers, especially Russia, became stronger. As the German prime minister put it, his country was about to take "a leap in the dark," and he declared war on Russia. Assuming that France would come to the aid of Russia, Germany invaded France through Belgium. The British, concerned by the threat to their ally France, and outraged by the violation of Belgian neutrality to which all the Great Powers had been signatories since 1839, declared war on Germany. Events had hurtled forward between the Austrian declaration of war on Serbia on July 28 and the British decision on August 4. Europe was at war. Eventually so would be much of the world.

SUMMARY

 N the surface, the years from 1880 to 1914 seemed comfortable. More people than ever before enjoyed material advantages and improved standards of living. Literacy spread. Death rates went down. Life expectancy rose.

Europe appeared to dominate the globe. In their relations with Africa and Asia, Europeans resorted to force to an unprecedented degree, conquering most of the African and much of the Asian continents. Europe intended to exploit the new empires as new sources of wealth, trade, and the trappings of power. But colonial rivals and subjects challenged the future of these empires, leading to various anxieties.

With improved conditions in Europe, a revolution of rising expectations had been created. People grew more demanding, insisting in sometimes violent ways on their political and economic rights. Although mass movements such as socialism and the women's suffrage movement generally used peaceful means in their campaigns to change society, some of their members advocated and employed force. Anarchism appeared to stalk Europe. In turn, states did not hesitate to use force in efforts to quell various protest movements, even resorting to martial law.

Reflecting these trends, intellectuals such as Freud and Bergson and artists such as Munch and Moreau suggested that a hidden, irrational dimension of life lurked beneath the tranquil surface appearances. Behind the façade of security and conformity lay many disturbing impulses such as racism, anti-Semitism, and tyranny.

Although most Europeans were confident and optimistic about their futures, such self-assuredness was not universally shared. Intellectuals spoke of decadence and decline. Policymakers worried about the future of their countries and, anxious to avoid the threat of decline, resorted to extreme measures such as empire building overseas and armed competition in Europe. Among European thinkers and leaders, force had become widely accepted as the means to an end; some leaders—notably those of Austria-Hungary and Germany—favored war over negotiation in July 1914.

The major powers—except Britain, confident in its naval dominance—built up large standing armies with millions of men and lethal modern equipment. Europe's network of alliances led inexorably to the larger conflict. If some leaders still feared war, more dreaded the consequences of not fighting, believing that war would save their regimes from the internal and external challenges they faced. Few could foresee the dire consequences of such a choice.

■ Suggested Reading

Burrow, J. W. *The Crisis of Reason: European Thought, 1848–1914*. 2000. Strong emphasis on individual intellectuals and their contributions.

Carrère d'Encaussé, Hélène. *Nicholas II*. 2000. A biography of the tsar, set within the context of an increasingly difficult country to govern.

Hobsbawm, Eric. *The Age of Empire, 1875–1914*. 1987. A fine survey, emphasizing social change, by a leading British historian.

Hochschild, Adam. *King Leopold's Ghost*. 1998. A dramatic account of Leopold II's brutal rule over the Congo.

Jay, Mike, and Michael Neve, eds. *1900. A fin de siècle Reader*. 1999. A rich collection of documents on how people imagined the new century.

Johnson, Martin P. *The Dreyfus Affair*. 1999. A brisk review of the major events shaping the affair.

Joll, James. *The Origins of the First World War*. 1984. A clear, concise, readable history tracing how strategic interests and nationalist passions led to the outbreak of the war.

Schorske, Carl E. *Fin de Siècle Vienna—Politics and Culture*. 1980. A critically acclaimed work on the arts and social and political thought in the Habsburg capital at the turn of the century.

 For a searchable list of additional readings for this chapter, go to http://college.hmco.com.

The Layout of the British Museum

The British Museum was founded in the mid-eighteenth century when the government acquired some private collections. The museum increased the size of its collections, largely through donations, bringing in objects from around the world. In its early years the museum was located in a converted private mansion; then in 1847, to house its growing collection, the museum moved into a monumental building with a neoclassical façade. Until the 1830s public access was limited to the upper classes, mainly the learned. By the mid-nineteenth century, however, a million people a year were visiting the museum. Displays of materials gathered from non-European cultures drew particularly large audiences.

Consider how the exhibits reflected British imperialism. In the first half of the nineteenth century, objects from Oceania, reflecting British activities in the Pacific, were acquired. African materials became more plentiful with the British conquest of much of Africa after the 1880s; the British military expedition to Nigeria in 1897 led to the acquisition of the fabulous Benin bronzes.

While imperial adventures were shaping the museum collection, the museum in turn was supporting imperialism. Museum officials declared that increased knowledge about regions overseas would fuel enthusiasm for the imperial venture and make the British people better fit to rule their new subjects.

Plan of the Upper Floor of the British Museum, ca. 1880 *(Based on map in Henry C. Shelley,* The British Museum: Its History and Treasures *[Boston: L. C. Page, 1911], pp. 274–275.)*

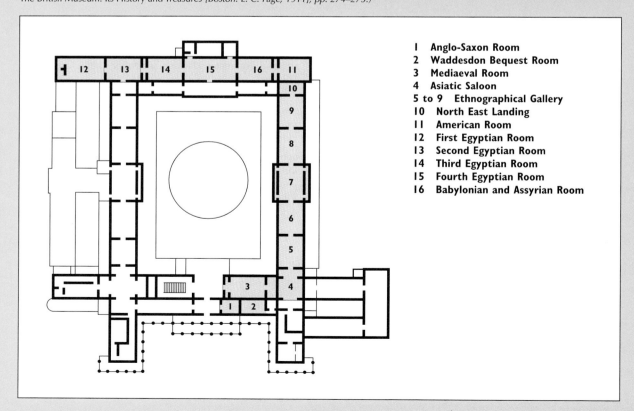

1 Anglo-Saxon Room
2 Waddesdon Bequest Room
3 Mediaeval Room
4 Asiatic Saloon
5 to 9 Ethnographical Gallery
10 North East Landing
11 American Room
12 First Egyptian Room
13 Second Egyptian Room
14 Third Egyptian Room
15 Fourth Egyptian Room
16 Babylonian and Assyrian Room

The manner in which the British Museum displayed some of its possessions reflected the intellectual currents of the times. In the late eighteenth and early nineteenth centuries the museum grouped its non-European objects with "natural history"; non-Europeans were associated with nature, with the beasts of the earth. Running out of space, the museum moved the natural history collection to a separate Natural Museum in South Kensington, and in the 1880s ethnography, the branch of anthropology devoted to human cultures, constituted a separate collection.

The late-nineteenth-century plan of the upper floor of the museum shown here reflects the racial views of imperial Britain. After climbing the stairs from the ground floor, we start at the room labeled 1, the Anglo-Saxon Room, which celebrates England's early history. Then comes the Waddesdon Bequest Room, which houses various artifacts of ancient and medieval English and European history (the room is named after the Rothschild mansion, where the collection was previously housed). Next we arrive at the Mediaeval Room itself. Using the route most visitors would then take, we come to the Asiatic Saloon, filled with pottery, porcelain, and other works of art from Japan, China, Persia, and India.

What is the significance of this juxtaposition of rooms? The British and other Europeans had developed an ethnocentric view of the human races, believing that the white race was by far superior to all others. This belief seemed confirmed by the material accomplishments of Europeans, especially impressive in the nineteenth century. Of the non-Europeans, Asians had won the grudging respect of the British and other Europeans. China, with its thousands of years of recorded history and sophisticated government structures, was one of several Asian societies that impressed them. Because many African societies lacked a written culture and had government and religious systems dramatically different from the Europeans', the British and other Europeans often considered Africans ignorant and primitive.

Biologists, anthropologists, and others speculating about the human races offered two different explanations for racial variations. These hypotheses competed with each other for public acceptance. According to the first, biology determined the level of civilization of each people. According to the second, different peoples were at different levels of development. In this view, Europeans were most developed, Africans least; but eventually Asians and Africans would progress and reach a level similar to that of Europeans. In the meantime non-Europeans illustrated European life at earlier stages of development.

It is interesting that the Asiatic Saloon, with its swords, shields, and other elaborate Asian objects, was next to the Mediaeval Room. The positioning invites consideration that some nineteenth-century Asian societies were at a level of development akin to medieval England.

An empty corridor separated this part of the museum from the Ethnographical Gallery, giving visitors the sense that what they would view was separate from medieval England and selected Asian societies. The Ethnographical Gallery displayed objects from Asia, Oceania, Africa, and the Americas. They tended to be objects of daily life such as household wares, weapons, and clothing. The stress was on their simplicity and primitiveness—presumably reflections of the primitive culture of their makers. The objects were not differentiated chronologically; pre-Columbian artifacts from the Americas were displayed beside modern African crafts. Ethnographic items were seldom dated, implying that the peoples who created them did not develop and had no history. The museum guidebook invited nineteenth-century viewers to consider how close the development of these peoples was to that of the earliest Europeans.

After passing through the Ethnographical Gallery, a visitor would arrive at the North East Landing and then enter the American Room. It contained items from Eskimos, Native Americans, and other peoples whom Victorians considered "primitives," but it also included artifacts from the Aztecs and Incas, whom the British considered to have been highly developed.

The Aztec and Inca collections abutted the room devoted to two ancient civilizations with monumental architecture, the Babylonian and Assyrian Room. Next came four Egyptian rooms. In the nineteenth century the greatness of ancient Egyptian culture was recognized. The British Museum allotted ancient Egypt ample space far removed from what were seen as the "primitive" peoples represented in the Ethnographical Gallery.

In 1972 the ethnographic collection was moved out of the Brtitish Museum and now constitutes the Museum of Mankind. With the loss of empire and the decline of confidence in the superiority of the white race, the old uses for the objects collected overseas had become obsolete.*

* The author is grateful to Thomas Prasch, Washburn University, for his help and advice and for making available two of his unpublished papers on this subject.

CHAPTER 25

War and Revolution 1914–1919

MUD. It was not what soldiers had in mind when they headed off to war in August 1914 amid visions of glory, gallantry—and quick victory. But after heavy rain and constant shelling, mud was a fact of life for those fighting on the western front—Belgium and northern France—during the fall of 1917. The mud was so pervasive, in fact, that soldiers literally drowned in it. These Canadian troops are holding the line on November 14, 1917, at the end of the Battle of Passchendaele°, a British-led assault that began late in July. That assault pushed the Germans back a mere 5 miles—at the cost of 300,000 lives. There was no end to the war in sight.

Some had thought a major war impossible in rational, civilized Europe. Others had devoutly wished for war—precisely to break out of the stifling bourgeois conventions of rational, civilized Europe. When war actually began early in August 1914, the European mood was generally enthusiastic, even festive. No one was prepared for what this war would bring, including the hellish scenes of mud, smoke, artillery craters, blasted trees, decaying bodies, and ruined buildings that came to frame the daily experience of those on the western front. A far wider and more destructive war would follow within a generation, but it was World War I, known to contemporaries as "the Great War," that shattered the old European order, with its comfortable assumptions of superiority, rationality, and progress. After this war, neither Westerners nor non-Westerners could still believe in the privileged place of Western civilization in quite the same way.

Passchendaele (PAH-shun-dale)

The Unforeseen Stalemate, 1914–1917

The Experience of Total War

Two Revolutions in Russia: March and November 1917

The New War and the Allied Victory, 1917–1918

The Outcome and the Impact

Passchendaele, Belgium, 1917
(By courtesy of the Trustees of the
Imperial War Museum)

843

The war that began in August was supposed to be over by Christmas. The British government promised "business as usual." But the fighting bogged down in a stalemate during the fall of 1914, then continued for four more years. By the time it ended, in November 1918, the war had strained the whole fabric of life, affecting everything from economic organization to literary vocabulary, from journalistic techniques to the role of women.

Partly because the war grew to become the first "world war," it proved the beginning of the end of European hegemony. The intervention of the United States in 1917 affected the military balance and seemed to give the war more idealistic and democratic purposes. The geographic reach of the war was itself unprecedented, especially after the intervention of the Ottoman Empire spread the fighting to the Middle East. Because of European colonial networks, the war also involved many other non-Europeans in combat or support roles. Although the old colonialism continued into the postwar era, the war nourished the forces that would later overthrow it.

Because of all the strains it entailed, the war had many unintended consequences. Revolutions dramatically changed the political landscape first in Russia, then in Germany. The Habsburg and Ottoman Empires collapsed. So when the victors met early in 1919 to shape the peace, they confronted a situation that could not have been foreseen in 1914. And their effort to determine the contours of the postwar world, and thus the immediate meaning of the war, left much unresolved.

QUESTIONS TO CONSIDER

- How did geography affect the shape and outcome of World War I?

- Why did this prove a total war, making necessary new forms of socioeconomic coordination and even systematic propaganda?

- What was the relationship between the war and the two revolutions in Russia in 1917?

- What factors shaped the peace settlement that the victors imposed on Germany in 1919?

TERMS TO KNOW

Sacred Union	Vladimir Lenin
British blockade	Wilson's "Fourteen
total war	Points"
Kriegsrohstoffabteilung	Treaty of Brest-Litovsk
(KRA), war raw	"stab in the back" myth
materials office	Treaty of Versailles
Petrograd Soviet	League of Nations
provisional government	

THE UNFORESEEN STALEMATE, 1914–1917

WHEN the war began in August 1914, enthusiasm and high morale, based on expectations of quick victory, marked both sides. But fighting on the crucial western front led to a stalemate by the end of 1914, and the brutal encounters of 1916 made it clear that this was not the sort of war most had expected. By early 1917 the difficulties of the war experience brought to the surface underlying questions about what all the fighting was for—and whether it was worth the price.

■ August 1914: The Domestic and Military Setting

Although some, including Helmuth von Moltke° (1848–1916), chief of the German general staff, worried that this would prove a long, destructive war testing the very fabric of Western civilization, the outbreak of fighting early in August produced a wave of euphoria and a remarkable degree of domestic unity. To many, war came almost as a relief; at last, the issues that had produced tension and intermittent crisis for the past decade would find a definitive solution. Especially among educated young

---

Moltke (MOLT-kuh)

people, this settling of accounts seemed to offer the prospect of renewal, even a kind of redemption, for themselves and their societies. The war promised an escape from the stifling bourgeois world and, in response to the common danger, an end to the bickering and divisiveness of everyday politics. (See the box "Reading Sources: The Joys of August 1914.")

An unexpected display of patriotism from the socialist left reinforced the sense of domestic unity and high morale. Forgetting their customary rhetoric about international proletarian solidarity, members of the socialist parties of the Second International rallied to their respective national war efforts almost everywhere in Europe. To socialists and workers, national defense against a more backward aggressor seemed essential to the eventual creation of socialism. French socialists had to defend France's democratic republic against autocratic and militaristic Germany; German socialists had to defend German institutions, and the strong socialist organizations that had proven possible within them, against repressive tsarist Russia. When, on August 4, the German Socialist delegation in the Reichstag voted with the other parties to give the government the budgetary authority to wage war, it was clear that the Second International had failed in its long-standing commitment to keep the workers of Europe from slaughtering each other.

In France, the government had planned, as a precaution, to arrest roughly one thousand trade union and Socialist leaders in the event of war, but no such arrests were necessary. The order of the day was "Sacred Union," which meant that French leaders from across the political spectrum agreed to cooperate for the duration of the war. Rather than seek to sabotage the war, Socialist leaders joined the new government of national defense. Germany enjoyed a comparable "Fortress Truce," including an agreement to suspend labor conflict during the war, although no Socialist was invited to join the war cabinet.

In 1914 the forces of the Triple Entente outnumbered those of Germany and Austria-Hungary. Russia had an army of over 1 million men, the largest in Europe, and France had 700,000. Britain, which did not introduce conscription until 1916, had about 250,000. Germany led the Central Powers with 850,000; Austria-Hungary contributed 450,000. Though outnumbered, the Central Powers had potential advantages in equipment, coordination, and speed over their more dispersed adversaries. The outcome was hardly a foregone conclusion in August 1914.

After the fighting began, a second group of nations intervened one by one, expanding the war's scope and complicating the strategic alternatives. In November 1914 the Ottoman Empire, fearful of Russia, joined the Central

CHRONOLOGY

August 1914	Fighting begins
September 1914	French forces hold off the German assault at the Marne
August–September 1914	German victories repel Russian invasion on eastern front
May 1915	Italy declares war on Austria-Hungary
February–December 1916	Battle of Verdun
July–November 1916	Battle of the Somme
January 1917	Germans resume unrestricted submarine warfare
March 1917	First Russian revolution: fall of the tsar
April 1917	U.S. declaration of war
July 1917	German Reichstag war-aims resolution
November 1917	Second Russian revolution: the Bolsheviks take power
March 1918	Treaty of Brest-Litovsk between Germany and Russia
March–July 1918	Germany's last western offensive
June 1918	Initial outbreak of "Spanish flu"
July 1918	Second Battle of the Marne
November 1918	Armistice: fighting ends
January 1919	Paris Peace Conference convenes
June 1919	Victors impose Treaty of Versailles on Germany

Powers, thereby extending the war along the Russo-Turkish border and on to Mesopotamia and the approaches to the Suez Canal in the Middle East. For Arabs disaffected with Ottoman Turkish rule, the war presented an opportunity to take up arms—with the active

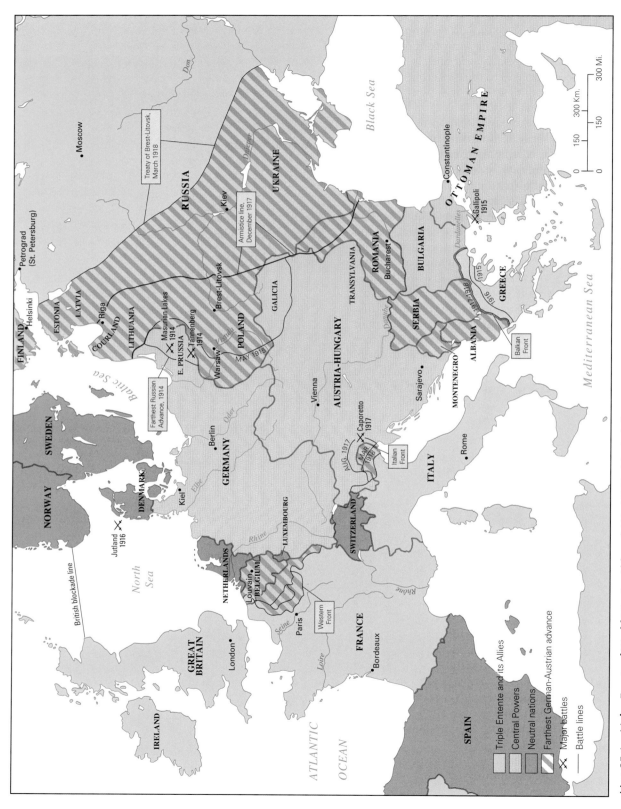

Map 25.1 Major Fronts of World War I Although World War I included engagements in East Asia and the Middle East, it was essentially a European conflict, encompassing fighting on a number of fronts. A vast territory was contested in the east, but on the western front, which proved decisive, fighting was concentrated in a relatively small area.

≈& R E A D I N G   S O U R C E S

The Joys of August 1914

In an autobiography published in 1943, writer Stefan Zweig (1881–1942) recalled the remarkable enthusiasm that accompanied the outbreak of war in his native Vienna in 1914. The popular mood reflected a naive faith, yet Zweig sensed that something more troubling was at work as well.

[I]n Vienna I found the entire city in a tumult. The first shock at the news of war—the war that no one, people or government, had wanted—the war which had slipped, much against their will, out of the clumsy hands of the diplomats who had been bluffing and toying with it, had suddenly been transformed into enthusiasm. There were parades in the streets, flags, ribbons, and music burst forth everywhere, young recruits were marching triumphantly, their faces lighting up at the cheering. . . .

And to be truthful, I must acknowledge that there was a majestic, rapturous, and even seductive something in this first outbreak of the people from which one could escape only with difficulty. And in spite of all my hatred and aversion for war, I should not like to have missed the memory of those first days. As never before, thousands and hundreds of thousands felt what they should have felt in peace time, that they belonged together. A city of two million, a country of nearly fifty million, in that hour felt that they were participating in world history, in a moment which would never recur, and that each one was called upon to cast his infinitesimal self into the glowing mass, there to be purified of all selfishness. All differences of class, rank, and language were flooded over at that moment by the rushing feeling of fraternity. Strangers spoke to one another in the streets, people who had avoided each other for

years shook hands. . . . [T]he clerk, the cobbler, had suddenly achieved a romantic possibility in life; he could become a hero, and everyone who wore a uniform was already being cheered by the women. . . . But it is quite possible that a deeper, more secret power was at work in this frenzy. So deeply, so quickly did the tide break over humanity that, foaming over the surface, it churned up the depths, the subconscious primitive instincts of the human animal—that which Freud so meaningfully calls "the revulsion from culture," the desire to break out of the conventional bourgeois world of codes and statutes, and to permit the primitive instincts of the blood to rage at will.

. . . [T]he people had unqualified confidence in their leaders; no one in Austria would have ventured the thought that the all-high ruler Emperor Franz Josef, in his eighty-third year, would have called his people to war unless from direct necessity, would have demanded such a sacrifice of blood unless evil, sinister, and criminal foes were threatening the peace of the Empire.

Source: Stefan Zweig, *The World of Yesterday: An Autobiography* (New York: Viking, 1943), pp. 223–225.

 For additional information on this topic, go to http://college.hmco.com.

---

support of Britain and France. Italy, after dickering with both sides, committed itself to the Entente in the Treaty of London of April 1915. This secret agreement specified the territories Italy would receive—primarily the Italian-speaking areas still within Austria-Hungary—in the event of Entente victory. In September 1915 Bulgaria entered the war on the side of the Central Powers, seeking territorial advantages at the expense of Serbia, which

had defeated Bulgaria in the Second Balkan War in 1913. Finally, in August 1916, Romania intervened on the side of the Entente, hoping to gain Transylvania, then part of Hungary.

Thus the war was fought on a variety of fronts (see Map 25.1). This fact, combined with uncertainties about the role of sea power, led to ongoing debate among military decision makers about strategic priorities. Because

No Trenches in Sight   Spirits were high early in August 1914, as soldiers like these in Paris marched off to war. None foresaw what fighting this war would be like. None grasped the long-term impact the war would have.   *(Archives Larousse-Giraudon)*

of the antagonism that the prewar German naval buildup had caused, some expected that Britain and Germany would quickly be drawn into a decisive naval battle. Britain promptly instituted an effective naval blockade on imports to Germany, but the great showdown on the seas never materialized. Even the most significant naval encounter between them, the Battle of Jutland in 1916, was inconclusive. Despite the naval rivalry of the prewar years, World War I proved fundamentally a land war.

Germany faced not only the long-anticipated two-front war against Russia in the east and France and Britain in the west; it also had to look to the southeast, given the precarious situation of its ally Austria-Hungary, which was fighting Serbia and Russia, then also Italy and Romania as well. On the eastern front, Germany was largely successful, forcing first Russia, then Romania, to seek a separate peace by mid-1918. But it was the western front that proved decisive.

■ Into the Nightmare, 1914

With the lessons of the wars of German unification in mind, both sides had planned for a short war based on rapid offensives, a war of movement. According to the Schlieffen° Plan, drafted in 1905, Germany would concentrate first on France, devoting but one-eighth of its forces to containing the Russians, who would need longer to mobilize. After taking just six weeks to knock France out of the war, Germany would then concentrate on Russia. French strategy, crafted by General Joseph Joffre° (1852–1931), the commander-in-chief of the French forces, similarly relied on rapid offensives. The boys would be home by Christmas—or so it was thought.

Although German troops encountered more opposition than expected from the formerly neutral Belgians, they moved swiftly through Belgium into northern France during August. By the first week of September they had reached the Marne River, threatening Paris and forcing the French government to retreat south to Bordeaux°. But French and British troops under Joffre counterattacked September 6–10, forcing the Germans to fall back and begin digging in along the Aisne° River. By holding off the German offensive at this first Battle of the Marne, the Entente had undercut the Schlieffen Plan—and with it, it turned out, any chance of a speedy victory by either side.

Schlieffen (SHLEE-fyn)   **Joffre** (JOFF-ruh)
Bordeaux (bor-DOH)   **Aisne** (ENN)

Trench Warfare Grim though they were, the trenches proved effective for defensive purposes. Here a British soldier guards a trench at Ovillers, on the Somme, in July 1916. *(Trustees of the Imperial War Museum)*

During the rest of the fall of 1914, each side tried—unsuccessfully—to outflank the other. When, by the end of November, active fighting ceased for the winter, a military front of about 300 miles had been established, all the way from Switzerland to the coast of the North Sea in Belgium (see Map 25.2 on page 864). This line failed to shift more than 10 miles in either direction over the next three years. So the result of the first six weeks of fighting on the western front was not a gallant victory but a grim and unforeseen stalemate.

Virtually from the start, the war took a fiercely destructive turn. In northern France in September 1914, the Germans fired on the cathedral at Reims°, severely damaging its roof and nave, because they believed—apparently correctly—that the French were using one of its towers as an observation post. If such a catastrophe could happen to one of the great monuments in Europe, what else might this war bring?

The two sides were forced to settle into a war of attrition relying on an elaborate network of defensive trenches. Although separated by as much as 5 miles in some places, enemy trenches were sometimes within shouting distance, so there was occasionally banter back

and forth, even attempts to entertain the other side. But the trenches quickly became almost unimaginably gruesome—filthy, ridden with rats and lice, noisy and smoky from artillery fire, and foul-smelling, partly from the odor of decaying bodies.

As defensive instruments, however, the trenches proved quite effective. Each side quickly learned to take advantage of barbed wire, mines, and especially machine guns to defend its positions. A mass of barbed wire, 3 to 5 feet high and 30 yards wide, guarded a typical trench. The machine gun had been developed before the war as an offensive weapon; few foresaw the decided advantage it would give the defense. But with machine guns, soldiers could defend trenches even against massive assaults—and inflict heavy casualties on the attackers.

In 1916 the British sent the first shipment of tanks to France as an antidote to the machine gun, but, as skeptics had warned, tanks proved too ungainly and unreliable to be widely effective. Although the French used them to advantage in the decisive Allied offensive in 1918, tanks were not crucial to the outcome of the war.

Though the defensive trenches had formidable advantages, neither side could give up the vision of a decisive offensive to break through on the western front.

Reims (RAANZ)

❧ READING SOURCES

Into the Trenches

As the initial offensives on the western front turned into stalemate, ordinary soldiers on both sides began to experience unprecedented forms of warfare in an eerie new landscape. Writing home to his family from France in November 1914, a young German soldier, Fritz Franke (1892–1915), sought to convey what this new war was like. He was killed six months later.

Yesterday we didn't feel sure that a single one of us would come through alive. You can't possibly picture to yourselves what such a battle-field looks like. It is impossible to describe it, and even now, when it is a day behind us, I myself can hardly believe that such bestial barbarity and unspeakable suffering are possible. Every foot of ground contested; every hundred yards another trench; and everywhere bodies—rows of them! All the trees shot to pieces; the whole ground churned up a yard deep by the heaviest shells; dead animals; houses and churches so utterly destroyed by shellfire that they can never be of the least use again. And every troop that advances in support must pass through a mile of this chaos, through this gigantic burial ground and the reek of corpses.

In this way we advanced on Tuesday, marching for three hours, a silent column, in the moonlight, toward the Front and into a trench as Reserve, two to three hundred yards from the English, close behind our own infantry.

There we lay the whole day, a yard and a half to two yards below the level of the ground, crouching in the narrow trench on a thin layer of straw, in an overpowering din which never ceased all day or the greater part of the night—the whole ground trem-

bling and shaking! There is every variety of sound—whistling, whining, ringing, crashing, rolling . . . [ellipses in the original] the beastly things pitch right above one and burst and the fragments buzz in all directions, and the only question one asks is: "Why doesn't one get me?" Often the things land within a hand's breath and one just looks on. One gets so hardened to it that at the most one ducks one's head a little if a great, big naval-gun shell comes a bit too near and its grey-green stink is a bit too thick. Otherwise one soon just lies there and thinks of other things. . . .

One just lives from one hour to the next. For instance, if one starts to prepare some food, one never knows if one may'nt have to leave it behind within an hour. . . .

. . . Above all one acquires a knowledge of human nature! We all live so naturally and unconventionally here, every one according to his own instincts. That brings much that is good and much that is ugly to the surface.

Source: A. F. Wedd, ed., *German Students' War Letters*, translated and arranged from the original edition of Dr. Philipp Witkop (London: Methuen, 1929), pp. 123–125.

Thus the troops were periodically called on to go "over the top" and then across "no man's land" to assault the dug-in enemy. Again and again, however, such offensives proved futile, producing incredibly heavy casualties: "Whole regiments gambled away eternity for ten yards of wasteland."[1]

For the soldiers on the western front the war became a nightmarish experience in a hellish landscape. Bombardment by new, heavier forms of artillery scarred the terrain with craters, which became muddy, turning the landscape into a near swamp. (See the box "Reading

Sources: Into the Trenches.") Beginning early in 1915, tear gas, chlorine gas, and finally mustard gas found use on both sides. Although the development of gas masks significantly reduced the impact of this menacing new chemical warfare, the threat of poison gas added another nightmarish element to the experience of those who fought the war.

The notions of patriotism, comradeship, duty, and glory that had been prevalent in 1914 gradually dissolved as soldiers experienced the horrors of warfare. A French soldier, questioning his own reactions after battle in

1916, responded with sarcasm and irony: "What sublime emotion inspires you at the moment of assault? I thought of nothing other than dragging my feet out of the mud encasing them. What did you feel after surviving the attack? I grumbled because I would have to remain several days more without *pinard* [wine]. Is not one's first act to kneel down and thank God? No. One relieves oneself."[2]

Although the Germans had been denied their quick victory in the west, by the end of 1914 they occupied much of Belgium and almost one-tenth of France, including major industrial areas and mines producing most of France's coal and iron. On the eastern front, as well, the Germans won some substantial advantages in 1914—but not a decisive victory.

The first season of fighting in the east suggested that the pattern there would not be trench warfare but rapid movement across a vast but thinly held front. When the fighting began in August, the Russians mustered more quickly than anticipated, confronting an outnumbered German force in a menacing, if reckless, invasion of East Prussia. But by mid-September German forces under General Paul von Hindenburg (1847–1934) and his chief

of staff General Erich Ludendorff (1865–1937) repelled the Russian advance, taking a huge number of prisoners and seriously demoralizing the Russians.

As a result of their victory in East Prussia, Hindenburg and Ludendorff emerged as heroes, and they would play major roles in German public life thereafter. Hindenburg, the senior partner, became chief of staff of the entire German army in August 1916, and the able and energetic Ludendorff remained at his side. Ludendorff proved to be the key figure as this powerful duo gradually assumed undisputed control of the whole German war effort, both military and domestic.

■ Seeking a Breakthrough, 1915–1917

After the campaigns of 1915 proved inconclusive, German leaders decided to concentrate in 1916 on a massive offensive against the great French fortress at Verdun, intending to inflict a definitive defeat on France. To assault the fortress, the Germans gathered 1,220 pieces of artillery for attack along an 8-mile front. Included were thirteen "Big Bertha" siege guns, weapons so large that nine tractors were required to position each of them; a

Paul von Hindenburg and Erich Ludendorff
The talents of Hindenburg (*left*) and Ludendorff meshed effectively to carry them from success on the eastern front in 1914 to a predominant role in the German war effort. They are shown here at a reception in honor of Hindenburg's seventieth birthday in October 1917.   *(AKG London)*

crane was necessary to insert the shell, which weighed over a ton. The level of heavy artillery firepower that the Germans applied at Verdun was unprecedented in the history of warfare.

German forces attacked on February 21, taking the outer defenses of the fortress, and appeared poised for victory. The tide turned, however, when General Philippe Pétain° (1856–1951) assumed control of the French defense at Verdun. Pétain had the patience and skill necessary to organize supply networks for a long and difficult siege. Furthermore, he proved able, through considerate treatment, to inspire affection and confidence among his men. By mid-July the French army had repelled the German offensive, although only in December did the French retake the outer defenses of the fortress. The French had held firm in what would prove the war's longest, most trying battle—one that killed over 700,000 men on both sides. For the French the Battle of Verdun would remain the epitome of the horrors of World War I.

To relieve pressure on Verdun, the British led a major attack at the Somme River on July 1, 1916. On that day alone the British suffered almost 60,000 casualties, including 21,000 killed. Fighting continued into the fall, but the offensive proved futile in the end. One-third of those involved, or over 1 million soldiers, ended up dead, missing, or wounded.

Dominated by the devastating battles at Verdun and the Somme, the campaigns of 1916 finally extinguished the high spirits of the summer of 1914. Both sides suffered huge losses—apparently for nothing. By the end of 1916, the front had shifted only a few miles from its location at the beginning of the year.

In light of the frustrating outcome so far, the French turned to new military leadership, replacing Joffre as commander-in-chief with Robert Nivelle (1856–1924), who promptly sought to prove himself with a new offensive during the spring of 1917. Persisting even as it became clear that this effort had no chance of success, Nivelle provoked increasing resistance among French soldiers, some of whom were refusing to follow orders by the end of April.

With the French war effort in danger of collapse, the French government replaced Nivelle with General Pétain, the hero of the defense of Verdun. Pétain reestablished discipline by adopting a conciliatory approach—improving food and rest, visiting the troops in the field, listening, offering encouragement, urging patience, even dealing relatively mercifully with most of the resisters themselves. To be sure, many of the soldiers who had participated in this near-mutiny were court-

martialed, and over 3,400 were convicted. But of the 554 sentenced to death, only 49 were executed.

After the failure of the Nivelle offensive, the initiative fell to the British under General Douglas Haig (1861–1928), who was convinced, despite skepticism in the British cabinet, that Nivelle's offensive had failed simply because of tactical mistakes. Beginning near Ypres° in Belgium on July 31, 1917, and continuing until November, the British attacked. As before, the effort yielded only minimal territorial gains—about 50 square miles—at a horrifying cost, including 300,000 British and Canadian casualties. Known as the Battle of Passchendaele, the British offensive of 1917 ranks with the Battles of Verdun and the Somme as the bloodiest of the war.

■ 1917 as a Turning Point

Meanwhile, the Germans decided to concentrate on the eastern front in 1917 in an effort to knock Russia out of the war. This intensified German military pressure helped spark revolution in Russia, and in December 1917 Russia's new revolutionary regime asked for a separate peace (see page 862). The defeat of Russia freed the Germans at last to concentrate on the west, but by this time France and Britain had a new ally.

On April 6, 1917, the United States entered the war on the side of the Entente, in response to Germany's controversial use of submarines. Germany did not have enough surface ships to respond to Britain's naval blockade, whether by attacking the British fleet directly or by mounting a comparable blockade of the British Isles. So the Germans decided to use submarines to interfere with shipping to Britain. Submarines, however, were too vulnerable to be able to surface and confiscate goods, so the Germans had to settle for sinking suspect ships with torpedoes. In February 1915 they declared the waters around the British Isles a war zone and served notice that they would torpedo not only enemy ships but also neutral ships carrying goods to Britain.

The German response was harsh, but so was the British blockade, which violated a number of earlier international agreements about the rights of neutral shipping and the scope of wartime blockades. The British had agreed that only military goods such as munitions and certain raw materials, not such everyday goods as food and clothing, were to be subject to confiscation. Yet in blockading Germany, the British refused to make this distinction, prompting the sarcastic German quip that Britannia not only rules the waves but waives the rules.[3]

Pétain (puh-TANH)

Ypres (EE-pray)

In May 1915 a German sub torpedoed the *Lusitania*, a British passenger liner, killing almost 1,200 people and producing widespread indignation. Partly because 128 of those killed were Americans, U.S. president Woodrow Wilson issued a severe warning, which contributed to the German decision in September 1915 to pull back from unrestricted submarine warfare. But as German suffering under the British blockade increased, pressure mounted on Berlin to put the subs back into action.

The issue provoked bitter debate. Chancellor Theobald von Bethmann-Hollweg° and the civilian authorities opposed resumption out of fear it would provoke the United States to enter the war. But Ludendorff and the military finally prevailed, partly with the argument that even if the United States did intervene, U.S. troops could not get to Europe in sufficient numbers, and in sufficient haste, to have a major impact. Germany announced it would resume unrestricted submarine warfare on January 31, 1917, and the United States responded with a declaration of war on April 6.

Many on both sides doubted that U.S. intervention would make a pivotal difference; most assumed—correctly—that it would take at least a year for the American presence to materialize in force. Still, the entry of the United States gave the Entente at least the promise of more fighting power. And the United States seemed capable of renewing the sense of purpose on the Entente side, showing that the war had a meaning that could justify the unexpected costs and sacrifice.

THE EXPERIENCE OF TOTAL WAR

A S the war dragged on, the distinction between the military and civilian spheres blurred. Suffering increased on the home front, and unprecedented governmental mobilization of society proved necessary to wage war on the scale that had come to be required. Because it became "total" in this way, the war decisively altered not only the old political and diplomatic order, but also culture, society, and the patterns of everyday life.

■ Hardship on the Home Front

The war meant food shortages, and thus malnutrition, for ordinary people in the belligerent countries, although Britain and France, with their more favorable geographic positions, suffered considerably less than others. Germany was especially vulnerable, and the British naval blockade exacerbated an already dire situation. With military needs taking priority, the Germans encountered shortages of the chemical fertilizers, farm machinery, and draft animals necessary for agricultural production. The government began rationing bread, meat, and fats during 1915. The increasing scarcity of food produced sharp increases in diseases such as rickets and tuberculosis and in infant and childhood mortality rates.

The need to pay for the war produced economic dislocations as well. Government borrowing covered some of the cost for the short term, but to underwrite the rest, governments all over Europe found it more palatable to inflate the currency, by printing more money, than to raise taxes. The notion that the enemy would be made to pay once victory had been won seemed to justify this decision. But this way of financing the war meant rising prices and severe erosion of purchasing power for ordinary people all over Europe. In France and Germany, the labor truces of 1914 gave way to increasing strike activity during 1916.

With an especially severe winter in 1916–1917 adding to the misery, there were serious instances of domestic disorder, including strikes and food riots, in many parts of Europe during 1917. In Italy, major strikes developed in Turin and other cities over wages and access to foodstuffs. The revolution that overthrew the tsarist autocracy in Russia that same year began with comparable protests over wartime food shortages.

The strains of war even fanned the flames in Ireland, where an uneasy truce over the home-rule controversy accompanied the British decision for war in 1914. Partly because of German efforts to stir up domestic trouble for Britain, unrest built up again in Ireland, culminating in the Easter Rebellion in Dublin in 1916. The brutality with which British forces crushed the uprising intensified demands for full independence—precisely what Britain would be forced to yield to the Irish Republic shortly after the war.

Moreover, new technologies made civilians ever less immune to wartime violence. Although bombing from aircraft began with an immediate military aim—to destroy industrial targets or to provide tactical support for other military units—it quickly became clear that night bombing, especially, might demoralize civilian populations. In 1915 German airplanes began bombing English cities, provoking British retaliation against cities in the German Ruhr and Rhineland areas. These raids had little effect on the course of the war, but they showed that new technologies could make warfare more destructive even for civilians.

Bethmann-Hollweg (BETT-mahn–HOHL-veg)

■ Domestic Mobilization

Once it became clear that the war would not be over quickly, leaders on both sides also realized that the outcome would not be determined on the battlefield alone. Victory required mobilizing all of the nation's resources and energies. So World War I became a total war, involving the entire society.

The British naval blockade on Germany, which made no distinction between military and nonmilitary goods, was a stratagem characteristic of total war. The blockade would not affect Germany's immediate strength on the battlefield, but it could damage Germany's long-term war-making capacity. The blockade was effective partly because Germany had not made adequate preparations—including stockpiling—for a protracted war of attrition.

In peacetime, Germany had depended on imports of food, fats, oils, and chemicals, including the nitrates needed for ammunition. With the onset of war, these goods were immediately in short supply, as was labor. Thus Germany seemed to need stringent economic coordination and control. By the end of 1916, the country had developed a militarized economy, with all aspects of economic life coordinated for the war effort. Under the supervision of the military, state agencies, big business, and the trade unions were brought into close collaboration. The new system included rationing, price controls, and compulsory labor arbitration, as well as a national service law enabling the military to channel workers into jobs deemed vital to the war effort.

The Germans did not hesitate to exploit the economy of occupied Belgium, requisitioning foodstuffs even to the point of causing starvation among the Belgians themselves. They forced 62,000 Belgians to work in German factories under conditions of virtual slave labor. By the time this practice was stopped in February 1917, nearly a thousand Belgian workers had died in German labor camps.

The body coordinating Germany's war economy was the Kriegsrohstoffabteilung° (KRA), or war raw materials office. Led initially by the able Jewish industrialist Walther Rathenau° (1867–1922), this agency came to symbolize the unprecedented coordination of the German economy for war. Recognizing that Germany lacked the raw materials for a long war, Rathenau devised an imaginative program that included the development of synthetic substitute products and the creation of new

mixed (private and government) companies to allocate raw materials. The KRA's effort was remarkably successful—a model for later economic planning and coordination in Germany and elsewhere.

Although Germany presented the most dramatic example of domestic coordination, the same pattern was evident everywhere. In Britain, the central figure was David Lloyd George (1863–1945), appointed to the newly created post of minister of munitions in 1915. During his year in that office, ninety-five new factories opened, soon overcoming the shortage of guns and ammunition that had impeded the British war effort until then. His performance made Lloyd George seem the one person who could organize Britain for victory. Succeeding Herbert Asquith as prime minister in December 1916, he would direct the British war effort to its victorious conclusion.

■ Accelerating Socioeconomic Change

Everywhere the war effort quickened the long-term socioeconomic change associated with industrialization. Government orders for war materiel fueled industrial expansion. In France, the Paris region became a center of heavy industry for the first time. The needs of war spawned new technologies—advances in food processing and medical treatment, for example—that would carry over into peacetime.

With so many men needed for military service, women were called on to assume new economic roles—such as running farms in France, or working in the new munitions factories in Britain. (See the box "Reading Sources: Domestic Mobilization and the Role of Women.") During the course of the war, the number of women employed in Britain rose from 3.25 million to 5 million. In Italy, 200,000 women had war-related jobs by 1917. Women also played indispensable roles at the front, especially in nursing units.

The expanded opportunities of wartime intensified the debate over the sociopolitical role of women that the movement for women's suffrage had stimulated. The outbreak of war led some antiwar feminists to argue that women would be better able than men to prevent wars, which were essentially masculine undertakings. Women should have full access to public life, not because they could be expected to respond as men did but because they had a distinctive—and valuable—role to play. At the same time, by giving women jobs and the opportunity to do many of the same things men did, the war undermined the stereotypes that had long justified restrictions on women's political roles and life choices.

Kriegsrohstoffabteilung (kreegs-ROH-stoff-AHB-ty-loong)
Rathenau (RAT-un-ow)

﴾ R E A D I N G   S O U R C E S

Domestic Mobilization and the Role of Women

Early in 1917, British writer Gilbert Stone published a remarkable collection of statements intended to illuminate the new experiences that British women were encountering in the workplace. The following passage by Naomi Loughnan, a well-to-do woman who worked in a munitions factory, makes it clear that the new work experience during the war provoked new questions about both gender and class.

Engineering mankind is possessed of the unshakable opinion that no woman can have the mechanical sense. If one of us asks humbly why such and such an alteration is not made to prevent this or that drawback to a machine, she is told, with a superior smile, that a man has worked her machine before her for years, and that therefore if there were any improvement possible it would have been made. As long as we do exactly as we are told and do not attempt to use our brains, we give entire satisfaction, and are treated as nice, good children. Any swerving from the easy path prepared for us by our males arouses the most scathing contempt in their manly bosoms. . . . Women have, however, proved that their entry into the munitions world has increased the output. Employers who forget things personal in their patriotic desire for large results are enthusiastic over the success of women in the shops. But their workmen have to be handled with the utmost tenderness and caution lest they should actually imagine it was being suggested that women could do their work equally well, given equal conditions of training—at least where muscle is not the driving force. This undercurrent of jealousy rises to the surface rather often, but as a general rule the men behave with much kindness, and are ready to help with muscle and advice whenever called upon. If eyes are very bright and hair inclined to curl, the muscle and advice do not even wait for a call.

The coming of the mixed classes of women into the factory is slowly but surely having an educative effect upon the men. "Language" is almost unconsciously becoming subdued. There are fiery exceptions who make our hair stand up on end under our close-fitting caps, but a sharp rebuke or a look of horror will often bring to book the most truculent. . . . It is grievous to hear the girls also swearing and using disgusting language. Shoulder to shoulder with the children of the slums, the upper classes are having their eyes pried open at last to the awful conditions among which their sisters have dwelt. Foul language, immorality, and many other evils are but the natural outcome of overcrowding and bitter poverty. If some of us, still blind and ignorant of our responsibilities, shrink horrified and repelled from the rougher set, the compliment is returned with open derision and ribald laughter. . . . On the other hand, attempts at friendliness from the more understanding are treated with the utmost suspicion, though once that suspicion is overcome and friendship is established, it is unshakable.

Source: Naomi Loughnan, "Munition Work," in Gilbert Stone, ed., *Women War Workers: Accounts Contributed by Representative Workers of the Work Done by Women in the More Important Branches of War Employment* (New York: Thomas Y. Crowell, 1917), pp. 35–38.

For many women, doing a difficult job well, serving their country in this emergency situation, afforded a new sense of accomplishment, as well as a new taste of independence. Women were now much more likely to have their own residences and to go out on their own, eating in restaurants, even smoking and drinking. Yet while many seized new opportunities and learned new skills, women frequently had to combine paid employment with housework and child rearing, and those who left home—to serve in nursing units, for example—often felt guilty about neglecting their traditional family roles.

Working Women and the War All over Europe, governments recruited women to work in munitions factories. This Russian government poster uses an image of working women to rally support for the war. The text reads, "Everything for the war effort! Subscribe to the war loans at 5½ percent." *(Eileen Tweedy, The Art Archive)*

■ Propaganda and the "Mobilization of Enthusiasm"

Because the domestic front was crucial to sustaining a long war of attrition, it became ever more important to shore up civilian morale as the war dragged on. The result was what the historian Elie Halévy called the "mobilization of enthusiasm"—the deliberate manipulation of collective passions by national governments on an unprecedented scale. Every country instituted extensive censorship, even of soldiers' letters from the front. Because of concerns about civilian morale, the French press carried no news of the Battle of Verdun, with its horrifying numbers of casualties. In addition, systematic propaganda included not only patriotic themes but also attempts to discredit the enemy, even through outright falsification of the news. British anti-German propaganda helped draw the United States into the war in 1917.

At the outset of the war, the brutal behavior of the German armies in Belgium made it easy for the French and the British to demonize the Germans. Having expected to pass through neutral Belgium unopposed, the Germans were infuriated by the Belgian resistance they encountered. At Louvain late in August 1914 they responded to alleged Belgian sniping by shooting a number of hostages and setting the town on fire, destroying the famous old library at the university. This notorious episode led the *London Times* to characterize the Germans as "Huns," a reference to the central Asian tribe that began invading Europe in the fourth century. Stories about German soldiers eating Belgian babies began to circulate.

Devastation at Louvain   Unexpected destruction at the outset of the war fanned the flames of hatred and changed the stakes of the conflict. Located in the path of the first German advance, the Belgian city of Louvain was particularly hard hit.   *(Trustees of the Imperial War Museum)*

In October 1914 ninety-three German intellectuals, artists, and scientists signed a manifesto, addressed to "the World of Culture," justifying Germany's conduct in Belgium and its larger purposes in the war. As passions heated up, major intellectuals on both sides—from the German theologian Adolf von Harnack (1851–1930) to the French philosopher Henri Bergson (1859–1941)—began denigrating the culture of the enemy and claiming a monopoly of virtue for their own sides.

As the war dragged on, some came to believe that real peace with an adversary so evil, so abnormally different, was simply not possible. There must be no compromise but rather total victory, no matter what the cost. At the same time, however, war-weariness produced a countervailing tendency to seek a "white peace," a peace without victory for either side. But in 1917, as Europeans began earnestly debating war aims, the Russian Revolution and the intervention of the United States changed the war's meaning for all the belligerents.

Two Revolutions in Russia: March and November 1917

STRAINED by war, the old European order cracked first in Russia in 1917. Initially the overthrow of the tsarist autocracy seemed to lay the foundations for parliamentary democracy. But by the end of the year, the Bolsheviks, the smallest and most extreme of Russia's major socialist parties, had taken power, an outcome that was hardly conceivable when the revolution began.

■ The Wartime Crisis of the Russian Autocracy

The Russian army performed better than many had expected during the first year of the war. As late as June 1916, it mounted a successful offensive against Austria-Hungary. Russia had industrialized sufficiently by 1914 to sustain a modern war, at least for a while, and the country's war production increased significantly by 1916. But Russia suffered from problems of leadership and organization—in transportation, for example—that made it less prepared for a long war than the other belligerents. Even early in 1915, perhaps a fourth of Russia's newly conscripted troops were sent to the front without weapons; they were told to pick up rifles and supplies from the dead.

In August 1915, Tsar Nicholas II (1868–1918) assumed personal command of the army, but his absence from the capital only accelerated the deterioration in government and deepened the divisions within the ruling clique. With the tsar away, the illiterate but charismatic Siberian "holy man" Grigori Rasputin (ca. 1872–1916) emerged as the key political power within the circle of the German-born Empress Alexandra (1872–1918). He won her confidence because of his alleged ability to control the bleeding of her hemophiliac son, Alexis, the heir to the throne. Led by Rasputin, those around the empress made a shambles of the state administration. Many educated Russians, appalled at what was happening, assumed—incorrectly—that pro-German elements at court were responsible for the eclipse of the tsar and the increasing chaos in the government. Asked one Duma deputy of the government's performance, "Is this stupidity, or is it treason?"

Finally, late in December 1916, Rasputin was assassinated by aristocrats seeking to save the autocracy from these apparently pro-German influences. This act indicated how desperate the situation was becoming, but eliminating Rasputin made little difference.

By the end of 1916, the difficulties of war had combined with the strains of rapid wartime industrialization to produce a revolutionary situation in Russia. The country's urban population had mushroomed, and now, partly because of transport problems, the cities faced severe food shortages. Strikes and demonstrations spread from Petrograd (the former St. Petersburg, whose name was abandoned as too German at the start of the war) to other cities during the first two months of 1917. In March renewed demonstrations in Petrograd, spearheaded by women protesting the lack of bread and coal, led to revolution.

■ The March Revolution and the Fate of the Provisional Government

At first, the agitation that began in Petrograd on March 8, 1917, appeared to be just another bread riot. Even when it turned into a wave of strikes, the revolutionary parties (see page 834) expected it to be crushed by the government troops stationed at the Petrograd garrison. But

when they were called out to help the police break up the demonstrations, the soldiers generally avoided firing at the strikers. Within days, they were sharing weapons and ammunition with the workers; the garrison was going over to what was now becoming a revolution.

Late in the afternoon of March 12, leaders of the strike committees, delegates elected by factory workers, and representatives of the socialist parties formed a *soviet,* or council, following the example of the revolution of 1905, when such soviets had first appeared. Regiments of the Petrograd garrison also began electing representatives, soon to be admitted to the Petrograd Soviet, which officially became the Council of Workers' and Soldiers' Deputies. This soviet was now the ruling power in the Russian capital. It had been elected and was genuinely representative—though of a limited constituency of workers and soldiers. Following the lead of Petrograd, Russians elsewhere promptly began forming soviets, so that over 350 local units were represented when the first All-Russian Council of Soviets met in Petrograd in April. The overwhelming majority of their representatives were Mensheviks and Socialist Revolutionaries; about one-sixth were Bolsheviks.

On March 14 a committee of the Duma, recognizing that the tsar's authority had been lost for good, persuaded Nicholas to abdicate, then formed a new provisional government. This government was to be strictly temporary, paving the way for an elected constituent assembly, which would write a constitution and establish fully legitimate governmental institutions.

Considering the strains in the autocratic system that had produced the revolution of 1905 after the Russo-Japanese War, it was hardly surprising that the system would shatter now, in light of this far more trying war and the resulting disarray within the tsarist government. Russia had apparently experienced, at last, the bourgeois political revolution necessary to develop a Western-style parliamentary democracy. Even from an orthodox Marxist perspective, the immediate priority was to help consolidate the new democratic order, which would then provide the framework for the longer-term pursuit of socialism.

Although the fall of the tsarist order produced widespread relief, Russia's new leaders faced difficult questions about priorities. Should they focus their efforts on revitalizing the Russian war effort? Or, given the widespread war-weariness in the country, should they focus on domestic political reform? For now, the Petrograd Soviet was prepared to give the provisional government a chance to govern. But the soviet was a potential rival for power if the new government failed to address Russia's immediate problems.

Lenin as Leader Although he was in exile during much of 1917, Lenin's leadership was crucial to the Bolshevik success in Russia. He is shown here addressing a May Day rally in Red Square, Moscow, on May 1, 1919. *(ITAR-TASS/Sovfoto)*

The provisional government took important steps toward Western-style liberal democracy, establishing universal suffrage, civil liberties, autonomy for ethnic minorities, and labor legislation, including provision for an eight-hour workday. But the government failed in two key areas, fostering discontents that the Bolsheviks soon exploited. First, it persisted in fighting the war. Second, it dragged its feet on agrarian reform.

The provisional government's determination to renew the war effort stemmed from genuine concern about Russia's obligations to its allies, about the country's national honor and position among the great powers. The long-standing goal of Russian diplomacy—an outlet to the Mediterranean Sea through the Dardanelles Strait—seemed within reach if Russia could continue the war and contribute to an Entente victory. The educated, well-to-do Russians who led the new government expected that ordinary citizens, now free, would fight with renewed enthusiasm, like the armies that had grown from the French Revolution over a century before. These leaders failed to grasp how desperate the situation of ordinary people had become.

Although the March revolution began in the cities, the peasantry soon moved into action as well, seizing land, sometimes burning the houses of their landlords. By midsummer, a full-scale peasant war seemed to be in the offing in the countryside, and calls for radical agrarian reform became increasingly urgent. Partly from expediency, partly from genuine concern for social justice, the provisional government promised a major redistribution of land. But it insisted that the reform be carried out legally—not by the present provisional government, but by a duly elected constituent assembly.

Calling for elections would thus seem to have been the first priority. The new political leaders kept putting it off, however, waiting for the situation to cool before giving up power to a newly elected assembly. But playing for time was a luxury they could ill afford. As unrest grew in the countryside, the authority of the provisional government diminished and the soviets gained in stature. But what role were the soviets to play?

■ The Bolsheviks Come to Power

In the immediate aftermath of the March revolution, the Bolsheviks had not seemed to differ substantially from their rivals within the socialist movement, at least on matters of immediate concern—the war, land reform, and the character of the revolution itself. But the situation began to change in April when Lenin, assisted by the German military, returned from exile in Switzerland. The Germans assumed—correctly, it turned out—that the Bolsheviks would help undermine the Russian war effort. Largely through the force of Lenin's leadership, the Bolsheviks soon took the initiative within the still-developing revolution in Russia.

Lenin (1870–1924), born Vladimir Ilich Ulianov, came from a comfortable upper-middle-class family. He was university-educated and trained as a lawyer. But after an older brother was executed in 1887 for participating in a plot against the tsar's life, Lenin followed him into revolutionary activity. Arrested for the first time in 1895, he was confined to Siberia until 1900. He then lived in exile abroad for almost the entire period before his return to Russia in 1917.

The Bolshevik Party was identified with Lenin from its beginning in 1903, when it emerged from the schism in Russian Marxist socialism. Because of his emphases, Bolshevism came to mean discipline, organization, and a special leadership role for a revolutionary vanguard. Lenin proved effective because he was a stern and somewhat forbidding figure, disciplined, fiercely intelligent, sometimes ruthless. As a Bolshevik colleague put it, Lenin was "the one indisputable leader . . . a man of iron will, inexhaustible energy, combining a fanatical faith in the movement, in the cause, with an equal faith in himself."[4]

Still, Lenin's reading of the situation when he returned to Petrograd in April astonished even many Bolsheviks. He argued that the revolution was about to pass from the present bourgeois-democratic stage to a socialist phase, involving dictatorship of the proletariat in the form of government by the soviets. So the Bolsheviks should begin actively opposing the provisional government, especially by denouncing the war as fundamentally imperialist and by demanding the distribution of land from the large estates to the peasants. This latter measure had long been identified with the Socialist revolutionaries; most Bolsheviks had envisioned collectivization and nationalization instead.

As Lenin saw it, under the strains of war, all of Europe was becoming ripe for revolution. A revolution in Russia would provide the spark to ignite wider proletarian revolution, especially in Germany. He did not envision backward Russia seeking to create socialism on its own. Although some remained skeptical of Lenin's strategy, he promptly won over most of his fellow Bolsheviks. And thus the Bolsheviks began actively seeking wider support by promising peace, land, and bread.

In April 1917 moderate socialists still had majority support in the soviets, so the Bolsheviks sought to build support gradually, postponing any decisive test of strength. But events escaped the control of the Bolshevik leadership in mid-July when impatient workers, largely Bolshevik in sympathy, took to the streets of Petrograd on their own. The Petrograd Soviet refused to support the uprising, and the provisional government had no difficulty getting military units to put it down, killing two hundred in the process. Though the uprising had developed spontaneously, Bolshevik leaders felt compelled to offer public support, and this gave the government an excuse to crack down on the Bolshevik leadership. Lenin

managed to escape to Finland, but a number of his colleagues were arrested and jailed.

With the Bolsheviks on the defensive, counterrevolutionary elements in the Russian military decided to seize the initiative with a march on Petrograd in September. To resist this attempted coup, the provisional government, now led by the young Socialist revolutionary Alexander Kerensky (1881–1970), had to rely on whoever could offer help, including the Bolsheviks. And thanks to Bolshevik propaganda, the soldiers under the command of the counterrevolutionaries refused to fight against the upholders of the revolution in Petrograd. Thus the coup was thwarted. Within days, the Bolsheviks won their first clear-cut majority in the Petrograd Soviet, then shortly gained majorities in most of the other soviets as well.

During the fall of 1917, the situation became increasingly volatile, eluding control by anyone. People looted food from shops; peasants seized land, sometimes murdering their landlords. Desertions and the murder of officers increased within the Russian military.

With the Bolsheviks now the dominant power in the soviets, and with the government's control diminishing, Lenin, from his hideout in Finland, urged the Bolshevik central committee to prepare for armed insurrection. Although some found this step too risky, the majority accepted Lenin's argument that the provisional government would continue dragging its feet, inadvertently giving right-wing officer cadres time for another coup.

Because Lenin remained in hiding, the task of organizing the seizure of power fell to Leon Trotsky (1870–1940), who skillfully modified Lenin's aggressive strategy. Lenin wanted the Bolsheviks to rise in their own name, in opposition to the provisional government, but Trotsky linked the insurrection to the cause of the soviets and played up its defensive character against the ongoing danger of a counterrevolutionary coup. With the political center at an impasse, the only alternative to such a coup seemed to be a Bolshevik initiative to preserve the Petrograd Soviet, by now the sole viable institutional embodiment of the revolution and its promise. Trotsky's interpretation led people who wanted simply to defend the Soviet to support the Bolsheviks' initiative.

During the night of November 9, armed Bolsheviks and regular army regiments occupied key points in Petrograd, including railroad stations, post offices, telephone exchanges, power stations, and the national bank. Able to muster only token resistance, the provisional government collapsed. Kerensky escaped and mounted what quickly proved a futile effort to rally troops at the front for a counterattack against the Bolsheviks. In contrast to the March revolution, which had taken about a week, the Bolsheviks took over the

❧ READING SOURCES

The Bolsheviks in Power, November 1917

John Reed (1887–1920), an American journalist and communist leader from Port-land, Oregon, was in Russia during the fall of 1917, when the second revolution be-gan. His enthusiastic firsthand account, which drew the praise of Lenin himself, conveys the drama and excitement of the revolution. In the following passage, Reed provides a sense of the emergency, improvisation, and revolutionary enthusiasm that marked the Bolsheviks' first days in power.

Having settled the question of power, the Bolshe-viki turned their attention to problems of practical administration. First of all, the city, the country, the Army must be fed. Bands of sailors and Red Guards scoured the warehouses, the railway terminals, even the barges in the canals, unearthing and con-fiscating thousands of *poods* [a *pood* equals 36 pounds] of food held by private speculators. Emis-saries were sent to the provinces, where with the assistance of the Land Committees they seized the storehouses of the great grain dealers. Expeditions of sailors, heavily armed, were sent out in groups of five thousand to the South, to Siberia, with roving commissions to capture cities still held by the White Guards, establish order and *get food* [italics in the original]. . . .

Towards the end of November occurred the "wine-pogrom"—looting of the wine cellars—begin-ning with the plundering of the Winter Palace vaults. For days there were drunken soldiers on the streets. In all this was evident the hand of the counterrevo-lutionists, who distributed among the regiments plans showing the location of the stores of liquor. The Commissars of Smolny began by pleading and arguing, which did not stop the growing disorder, followed by pitched battles between soldiers and Red Guards. Finally the Military Revolutionary Commit-tee sent out companies of sailors with machine-guns, who fired mercilessly upon the rioters, killing many; and by executive order the wine cellars were invaded by Committees with hatchets, who smashed the bot-tles—or blew them up with dynamite.

. . . In all quarters of the city small elective Rev-olutionary Tribunals were set up by the workers and soldiers to deal with petty crime. . . .

Alert and suspicious, the working class of the city constituted itself a vast spy system, through the servants prying into bourgeois households, and reporting all in-formation to the Military Revolutionary Committee, which struck with an iron hand, unceasing. In this way was discovered the Monarchist plot led by a former Duma-member Purishkevich and a group of nobles and officers, who had planned an officers' uprising. . . .

Still the strike of the Ministries went on, still the sabotage of the old officials, the stoppage of normal economic life. Behind Smolny was only the will of the vast, unorganized popular masses; and with them the Council of People's Commissars dealt, di-recting revolutionary mass action against its ene-mies. In eloquent proclamations, couched in simple words and spread over Russia, Lenin explained the Revolution, urged the people to take the power into their own hands, by force to break down the resist-ance of the propertied classes, by force to take over the institutions of Government. Revolutionary order! Revolutionary discipline! Strict accounting and con-trol! No strikes! No loafing!

Source: John Reed, *Ten Days That Shook the World* (London: Pen-guin, 1977), pp. 244–246.

capital, overthrowing the Kerensky government, literally overnight, and almost without bloodshed.

But though the Bolsheviks enjoyed considerable support in the network of soviets, it was not clear that they could extend their control across the whole Russian Empire. (See the box "Reading Sources: The Bolsheviks in Power, November 1917.") Moreover, from their own perspective, the revolution's immediate prospects, and its potential wider impact, were bound up with the course of the war. Would the Bolshevik Revolution in Russia prove the spark for revolution elsewhere in war-weary Europe, as Lenin anticipated?

■ The Russian Revolution and the War

Having stood for peace throughout the revolution, the Bolsheviks promptly moved to get Russia out of the war, agreeing to an armistice with Germany in December 1917. They hoped that Russia's withdrawal would speed the collapse of the war effort on all sides and that this, in turn, would intensify the movement toward revolution elsewhere in Europe. The Russian Revolution was but a chapter in this larger story. As Lenin noted to Trotsky, "If it were necessary for us to go under to assure the success of the German revolution, we should have to do it. The German revolution is vastly more important than ours." Indeed, said Lenin to the Bolsheviks' party congress of March 1918, "It is an absolute truth that we will go under without the German revolution."[5]

After assuming control in November, the Bolsheviks published the tsarist government's secret agreements specifying how the spoils were to be divided in the event of a Russian victory. They hoped to inflame revolutionary sentiment elsewhere by demonstrating that the war had been, all along, an imperialist offensive on behalf of capitalist interests. This Bolshevik initiative added fuel to the controversy already developing in all the belligerent countries over the war's purpose and significance.

THE NEW WAR AND THE ALLIED VICTORY, 1917–1918

ECAUSE the stakes of the war changed during 1917, the outcome, once peace finally came in November 1918, included consequences that Europeans could not have foreseen in 1914. German defeat brought revolution against the monarchy and the beginning of a new democracy. Austro-Hungarian defeat brought the collapse of the Habsburg monarchy and thus the opportunity for its national minorities to form nations of their own. As the old European order fell, grandiose new visions competed to shape the postwar world.

■ The Debate over War Aims

The French and British governments publicly welcomed the March revolution in Russia, partly because they expected Russia's military performance to improve under new leadership, but also because the change of regime seemed to have highly favorable psychological implications. With Russia no longer an autocracy, the war could be portrayed—and experienced—as a crusade for democracy. At the same time, the March revolution could only sow confusion among the many Germans who had understood their own war effort as a matter of self-defense against reactionary Russia. But the November revolution required a deeper reconsideration for all the belligerents.

Allied war aims agreements, such as the Treaty of London that brought Italy into the war in 1915, had remained secret until the Bolsheviks published the tsarist documents. Products of old-style diplomacy, those agreements had been made by a restricted foreign policy elite within the governing circles of each country; even members of the elected parliaments generally did not know their contents. The debate over war aims that developed in 1917 thus became a debate over decision making as well. Many assumed that a more democratic approach to foreign policy would minimize the chances of war since the people would not agree to wars for dynastic or business interests. In addition, there were exhortations for all the parties in the present war to renounce annexations and settle for a white peace. It was time to call the whole thing off and bring the soldiers home.

Seeking to counter such sentiments, especially the Russian contention that the war was not worth continuing, the idealistic U.S. president, Woodrow Wilson (1856–1924), insisted on the great potential significance of an Allied victory. First in his State of the Union speech of January 1918, and in several declarations thereafter, Wilson developed the "Fourteen Points" that he proposed should guide the new international order. Notable among them were open diplomacy, free trade, reduced armaments, self-determination for nationalities, a league of nations, and a recasting of the colonial system to ensure for the indigenous populations rights equal to those of the colonizers.

Lenin and Wilson, then, offered radically different interpretations of the war, with radically different implications for present priorities. Yet, compared with the old diplomacy, they had something in common. Together, they seemed to represent a whole new approach to international relations—and the possibility of a more peaceful world. Thus, they found an eager audience among the war-weary peoples of Europe.

Despite the strains of the war, Sacred Union in France did not weaken substantially until April 1917, with General Nivelle's disastrous offensive. But then, as near-mutiny began to develop within the army, rank-and-file pressures forced Socialist leaders to demand clarification, and perhaps revision, of French war aims. Suddenly the French government was under pressure to suggest that the war had idealistic and democratic purposes. Doubts about the government's goals were threatening to turn into active opposition to the war.

The same pressures were at work in Germany. Antiwar sentiment grew steadily within the Social Democratic Party (SPD) until the antiwar faction split off and formed the Independent Socialist party (USPD) in April 1917. A large-scale debate on war aims, linked to considerations of domestic political reform, developed in the Reichstag by the summer of 1917. On July 19, a solid 60 percent majority passed a new war aims resolution, which affirmed that Germany's purposes were solely defensive, that Germany had no territorial ambitions. Germany too seemed open to a white peace.

But just as the dramatic events of 1917 interjected new pressures for moderation and peace, pressures in the opposite direction also mounted as the war dragged on. It seemed to some that this war was only the beginning of a new era of cutthroat international competition; the old rules would no longer apply. War aims grew more grandiose as nations tried to gain the leverage for success in the postwar world. The present war offered a precious opportunity to secure advantages for that more contentious world, which would surely entail further war before long.

The shape of the current war convinced top German officials that Germany's geography and dependence on imports made it especially vulnerable in a long war. So Germany had to seize the present opportunity to conquer the means to fight the next war on a more favorable footing. Responding in February 1918 to calls for a white peace, General Ludendorff stressed that "if Germany makes peace without profit, it has lost the war." Germany, insisted Ludendorff, must win the military and economic basis for future security—to "enable us to contemplate confidently some future defensive war."[6] Many German officials believed that Germany could achieve parity with Britain, and thus the basis for security and peace, only if it maintained control of the Belgian coast. German expansion into Russian Poland and up the Baltic coast of Lithuania and Latvia seemed essential as well.

When, in response to the Russian request for an armistice, Germany was able to dictate the peace terms, as specified in the Treaty of Brest-Litovsk of March 1918, it became clear how radically annexationist Germany's war aims had become. European Russia was to be largely dismembered, leaving Germany in direct or indirect control of 27 percent of Russia's European territory, 40 percent of its population, and 75 percent of its iron and coal. All the Reichstag parties except the Socialists accepted the terms of the treaty, which, in fact, produced a renewed determination to push on to victory after the disillusionment that had led to the Reichstag war aims resolution of July 1917.

France, less vulnerable geographically than Germany, tended to be more modest. But news of the terms the Germans had imposed at Brest-Litovsk inflamed the French, reinforcing their determination to fight on to an unqualified victory. Only thus could France secure the advantages necessary to ward off an ongoing German menace.

■ The Renewal of the French War Effort

The domestic division in France that followed the failure of Nivelle's offensive reached its peak during the fall of 1917. In November, with pressures for a white peace intensifying and France's ability to continue fighting in doubt, President Raymond Poincaré° called on Georges Clemenceau° (1841–1929) to lead a new government. The 76-year-old Clemenceau was known as a "hawk"; his appointment portended a stepped-up prosecution of the war. His message was simple as he appeared before the Chamber of Deputies on November 20, 1917: "If you ask me about my war aims, I reply: my aim is to be victorious." For the remainder of the war, France was under the virtual dictatorship of Clemenceau and his cabinet.

Clemenceau moved decisively on both the domestic and military fronts. By cracking down on the antiwar movement—imprisoning antiwar leaders, suppressing defeatist newspapers—he stiffened morale on the home front. Understanding that lack of coordination between French and the British military leaders had hampered the Allied effort on the battlefield, Clemenceau persuaded the British to accept the French general Ferdinand Foch° (1851–1929) as the first supreme commander of all Allied forces in the west. In choosing Foch, known for his commitment to aggressive offensives, Clemenceau was pointedly bypassing Pétain, whom he found too passive, even defeatist. After some initial friction, Clemenceau let Foch have his way on the military level, and the two proved an effective leadership combination.

■ The German Gamble, 1918

As the military campaigns of 1918 began, Germany seemed in a relatively favorable position: Russia had been knocked out of the war, and American troops were yet to arrive. Moderates in Germany wanted to seize the opportunity to work out a compromise peace while there was still a chance. But the military leadership persuaded Kaiser Wilhelm II that Germany could win a definitive victory on the western front if it struck quickly,

---

Poincaré (PWAN-cah-RAY)   **Clemenceau** (KLEM-ahn-SOH)
Foch (FOHSH)

before U.S. help became significant. Since Germany would be out of reserves by summer, the alternative to decisive victory in the west would be total German defeat.

The German gamble almost succeeded. From March to June 1918, German forces seized the initiative with four months of sustained and effective attacks. By May 30 they had again reached the Marne, where they had been held in 1914. Paris, only 37 miles away, had to be evacuated again (see Map 25.2). As late as mid-July, Ludendorff remained confident of victory, but by mid-August it was becoming clear that Germany lacked the manpower to exploit the successes of the first several months of 1918.

Those successes had caused mutual suspicion between the French and the British at first, but under Foch's leadership the Western allies eventually managed fuller and more effective coordination. By mid-1918 American involvement was also becoming a factor. On June 4, over a year after the U.S. declaration of war, American troops went into action for the first time, bolstering French forces along the Marne. This was a small operation, in which the Americans' performance was amateurish when compared with that of their battle-seasoned allies. But as the Allied counterattack proceeded, 250,000 U.S. troops were arriving per month, considerably boosting Allied morale and battlefield strength.

By June 1918 Europe was experiencing the first outbreak of a virulent new influenza virus, promptly dubbed the "Spanish flu" though it had originated in South Africa. Because of their inferior diets, German soldiers proved far more susceptible to the disease than their adversaries, a fact that significantly affected Germany's combat performance during the crucial summer of 1918.

Germany lost the initiative for good during the second Battle of the Marne, which began on July 15 with yet another German attack. Foch launched a sustained counterattack on July 18, using tanks to good advantage, and maintained the momentum thereafter. By early August the whole western front began to roll back. With astonishing suddenness, the outcome was no longer in doubt, although most expected the war to drag on into 1919. Few realized how desperate Germany's situation had become.

Meanwhile, Germany's allies began falling one by one. In the Balkans an Allied offensive broke through the German-Bulgarian line in September, prompting the Bulgarians to ask for an armistice. The Turkish military

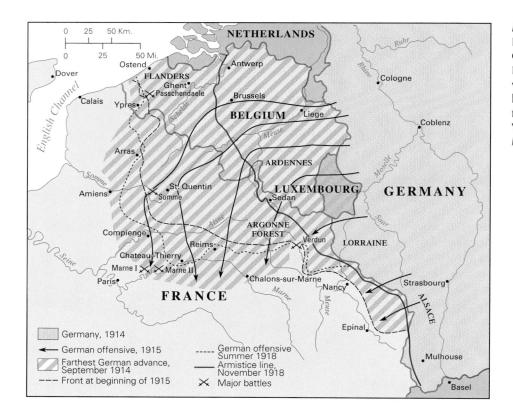

Map 25.2   Stalemate and Decision on the Western Front On the western front, in northern France and Belgium, trench warfare developed and the best known battles of the war were fought. Notable sites include Verdun, Passchendaele, and the Marne and Somme Rivers.

effort collapsed in October. With the defeat of Russia in 1917, the Habsburg Empire of Austria-Hungary redoubled its effort on the Italian front, inflicting a devastating defeat on the Italians at Caporetto late in 1917. But the Italians held, resisted, and then began driving the Austrians back. The Italian victory at Vittorio Veneto forced Austria's unconditional surrender on November 3, 1918. But by this point the armies of the Habsburg Empire, a central pillar of the old European order, were disintegrating along nationality lines. And the impending collapse of this centuries-old empire gave its various national minorities the chance to form states of their own.

■ Military Defeat and Political Change in Germany

By late September it was clear to Ludendorff that his armies could not stop the Allied advance. On September 29 he informed the government that to avoid invasion, Germany would have to seek an immediate armistice. Hoping to secure favorable peace terms and to foist responsibility for the defeat onto the parliamentary politicians, Hindenburg and Ludendorff asked that a government based on greater popular support be formed. A leading moderate, Prince Max von Baden° (1867–1929), became chancellor, and he promptly replaced Ludendorff with General Wilhelm Groener° (1867–1939), who seemed more democratic in orientation. By now it was clear that ending the war could not be separated from the push for political change in Germany, especially because it was widely assumed that a more democratic Germany could expect more favorable peace terms.

After securing a written request for an armistice from Hindenburg, Prince Max sent a peace note to President Wilson early in October, asking for an armistice based on Wilson's Fourteen Points. During the month that followed, Prince Max engineered a series of measures, passed by the Reichstag and approved by the emperor, that reformed the constitution, abolishing the three-class voting system in Prussia and making the chancellor responsible to the Reichstag. At last Germany had a constitutional monarchy. Not completely satisfied, President Wilson encouraged speculation that Germany could expect better peace terms if Wilhelm II were to abdicate and Germany became a republic.

But a far more radical outcome seemed possible during late 1918 and early 1919. As negotiations for an armistice proceeded in October, the continuing war effort produced instances of mutiny in the navy and breaches of discipline in the army. By early November

workers' and soldiers' councils were being formed all over Germany, just as in Russia the year before. On November 7, antiwar socialists in Munich led an uprising of workers and soldiers that expelled the king of Bavaria and proclaimed a new Bavarian republic. Its provisional government promptly sought its own peace negotiations with the Allies. On November 9, thousands of workers took to the streets of Berlin to demand immediate peace, and the authorities could not muster enough military resources to move against them.

The senior army leadership grew concerned that the collapse of government authority would undermine the ability of officers even to march their troops home. So Hindenburg and Groener persuaded the emperor to abdicate. Having lost the support of the army, Wilhelm II accepted the inevitable and left for exile in the Netherlands.

With the German right, including the military, in disarray, and with the centrist parties discredited by their support for what had become an annexationist war, the initiative passed to the socialists. They, at least, had been in the forefront of the movement for peace. But the socialists had divided in 1917, mostly over the question of response to the war. The mainstream of the SPD, by supporting the war for so long, had irrevocably alienated the party's leftist socialist wing. The most militant of these leftist socialists, led by Karl Liebknecht (1871–1919) and Rosa Luxemburg (1870–1919), envisioned using the workers' and soldiers' councils as the basis for a full-scale revolution, more or less on the Bolshevik model.

The SPD, on the other hand, clung to its reformist heritage and insisted on working within parliamentary institutions. Party leaders argued that a Bolshevik-style revolution was neither appropriate nor necessary under the circumstances. So SPD moderates proclaimed a parliamentary republic on November 9, just hours before the revolutionaries proclaimed a soviet-style republic. The next day the soldiers' and workers' councils in Berlin elected a provisional executive committee, to be led by the moderate socialist Friedrich Ebert° (1871–1925). As the new republic sought to consolidate itself, the radical leftists continued to promote further revolution. For Germany the end of the war meant a leap into an unfamiliar democratic republic, which had to establish itself in conditions not only of military defeat and economic hardship but also of incipient revolution on the extreme left.

Birth from military defeat was especially disabling for the new republic because the German people were so little prepared for defeat when it came. Vigorous censorship had kept the public in the dark about Germany's real situation, so the request for an armistice early in October came as a shock. At no time during the war had Germany been invaded from the west, and by mid-1918 the German army had seemed on the brink of victory. It appeared inconceivable that Germany had lost a military decision, plain and simple. Thus the "stab in the back" myth, the notion that political intrigue and revolution at home had sabotaged the German military effort, developed to explain what otherwise seemed an inexplicable defeat. This notion would prove a heavy burden for Germany's new democracy to bear.

THE OUTCOME AND THE IMPACT

FTER the armistice officially ended the fighting on November 11, 1918, it was up to the war's four victors—France, Britain, Italy, and the United States—to establish the terms of peace and, it was to be hoped, a new basis for order at the same time. But the peacemakers had to deal with a radically new political and territorial situation. Revolution had undermined, or threatened to undermine, the old political order in much of Europe. And the war had come to involve non-European powers and peoples in unprecedented ways. After all that had happened since August 1914, it was not clear what a restoration of peace and order would require. But it was evident that Europe would no longer dominate world affairs in quite the way it had.

■ The Costs of War

Raw casualty figures do not begin to convey the war's human toll, but they afford some sense of the magnitude of the catastrophe that had befallen Europe and much of the world. Estimates differ, but it is generally agreed that from 10 to 13 million military men lost their lives, with another 20 million wounded. In addition, between 7 and 10 million civilians died as a result of the war and its hardships. In the defeated countries especially, food shortages and malnutrition continued well after the end of the fighting. Thus the Spanish flu that had affected the balance on the battlefield early in the summer of 1918 returned with particularly devastating results during the fall. The influenza pandemic killed perhaps 30 million people worldwide.

Germany suffered the highest number of military casualties, but France suffered the most in proportional terms. Two million Germans were killed, with another 4 million wounded. Military deaths per capita for France

were roughly 15 percent higher than for Germany—and twice as severe as for Britain. Of 8 million Frenchmen mobilized, over 5 million were killed or wounded. Roughly 1.5 million French soldiers, or 10 percent of the active male population, were killed—and this in a country already concerned about demographic decline. The other belligerents suffered less, but still in great numbers. Among the military personnel killed were 2 million Russians, 500,000 Italians, and 114,000 Americans.

Economic costs were heavy as well. In addition to the privations suffered during the years of war, Europeans found themselves reeling from inflation and saddled with debt, especially to the United States, once the war was over. Although the immediate transition to a peacetime economy did not prove as difficult as many had feared, the war and its aftermath produced an economic disequilibrium that lingered, helping to produce a worldwide depression by the 1930s.

■ The Search for Peace in a Revolutionary Era

The war had begun because of an unmanageable nationality problem in Austria-Hungary, and it led not simply to military defeat for Austria-Hungary but to the breakup of the Habsburg system (see Map 25.3). In east-central Europe, the end of the war brought bright hopes for self-determination to peoples like the Czechs, Slovaks, Poles, Serbs, and Croats. Even before the peacemakers opened deliberations in January 1919, some of these ethnic groups had begun creating a new order on their own. For example, a popular movement of Czechs and Slovaks established a Czechoslovak republic on October 29, 1918, and a new Yugoslavia and an independent Hungary similarly emerged from indigenous movements. Czechoslovakia and Yugoslavia were made up of different ethnic groups that found cooperation advantageous now but that might well disagree in the future. Moreover, many of these countries lacked traditions of self-government, and they had reason to feud among themselves. With the Habsburg system no longer imposing one form of stability, a power vacuum seemed likely in this potentially volatile part of Europe.

Map 25.3   The Impact of the War: The Territorial Settlement in Europe and the Middle East   The defeat of Russia, Austria-Hungary, Germany, and Ottoman Turkey opened the way to major changes in the map of east-central Europe and the Middle East. A number of new nations emerged in east-central Europe, while in the Arab world the end of Ottoman rule meant not independence but new roles for European powers.

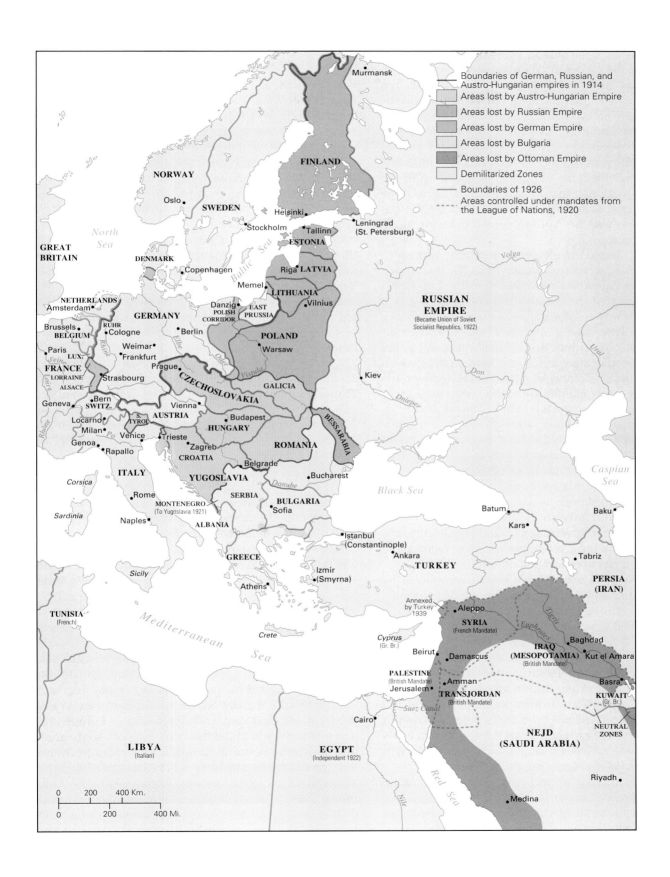

Boundaries of German, Russian, and Austro-Hungarian empires in 1914
Areas lost by Austro-Hungarian Empire
Areas lost by Russian Empire
Areas lost by German Empire
Areas lost by Bulgaria
Areas lost by Ottoman Empire
Demilitarized Zones
Boundaries of 1926
Areas controlled under mandates from the League of Nations, 1920

Murmansk

NORWAY

Oslo

SWEDEN

Helsinki

FINLAND

Stockholm

Leningrad (St. Petersburg)

North Sea

GREAT BRITAIN

Tallinn

ESTONIA

DENMARK

Copenhagen

Baltic Sea

Riga LATVIA

Memel

LITHUANIA

Vilnius

Volga

RUSSIAN EMPIRE
(Became Union of Soviet Socialist Republics, 1922)

NETHERLANDS
Amsterdam

GERMANY

Danzig

POLISH CORRIDOR

EAST PRUSSIA

Brussels

RUHR
Cologne

BELGIUM

Berlin

Oder

Vistula

POLAND

Warsaw

Kiev

Ural

Paris

LUX.

Weimar
Frankfurt

Elbe

Prague

Ural

FRANCE

LORRAINE

Strasbourg

CZECHOSLOVAKIA

GALICIA

Dnieper

ALSACE

Rhine

Seine

Bern
SWITZ.

Vienna

Don

Geneva

Rhône

Locarno

S. TYROL

AUSTRIA

Budapest

BESSARABIA

Milan

Po

Venice

Trieste

HUNGARY

Genoa

Rapallo

Zagreb

ROMANIA

CROATIA

Caspian Sea

ITALY

Belgrade

Corsica

Rome

YUGOSLAVIA

Bucharest

Danube

Black Sea

Sardinia

Naples

SERBIA

MONTENEGRO
(To Yugoslavia 1921)

ALBANIA

BULGARIA

Sofia

Batum

Baku

Kars

GREECE

Istanbul (Constantinople)

Ankara

TURKEY

Tabriz

Izmir (Smyrna)

Sicily

Athens

PERSIA (IRAN)

Crete

Cyprus (Gr. Br.)

Annexed by Turkey 1939

Aleppo

SYRIA
(French Mandate)

Tigris

Baghdad

TUNISIA
(French)

Mediterranean Sea

Beirut

Damascus

Euphrates

IRAQ (MESOPOTAMIA)
(British Mandate)

Kut el Amara

PALESTINE
(British Mandate)

Jerusalem

Amman

Basra

TRANSJORDAN
(British Mandate)

KUWAIT
(Gr. Br.)

Suez Canal

NEUTRAL ZONES

Cairo

LIBYA
(Italian)

EGYPT
(Independent 1922)

NEJD (SAUDI ARABIA)

Red Sea

Nile

Riyadh

Medina

0   200   400 Km.

0   200   400 Mi.

The Bolshevik Revolution in Russia immeasurably complicated the situation. The unsettled conditions in Germany and the former Habsburg territories in the wake of defeat seemed to invite the spread of revolution—precisely according to Lenin's script. Shortly after taking power, Lenin and his party had begun calling themselves "communists," partly to jettison the provincial Russian term *bolshevik,* but especially to underline their departure from the old reformist socialism of the Second International. In adopting "communism," they wanted to make it clear that they stood for a revolutionary alternative, and they actively sought to inspire revolution elsewhere.

Outside Russia, the greatest communist success in the wake of the war was in Hungary, where a communist regime under Béla Kun (1885–1937) governed Budapest and other parts of the country from March to August 1919, when it was put down by Allied-sponsored forces. At about the same time, communist republics lasted for months in the Slovak part of Czechoslovakia and in the important German state of Bavaria. Even in Italy, which had shared in the victory, Socialists infatuated with the Bolshevik example claimed that the substantial labor unrest that developed during 1919–1920 was the beginning of full-scale revolution.

Meanwhile, fears that the Russian Revolution might spread had fueled foreign intervention in Russia itself beginning in June 1918, when 24,000 French and British troops landed at Murmansk, in northern Russia. As long as the war with Germany lasted, military concerns helped justify this course, but after the armistice of November 1918, the intervention became overtly anticommunist, intended to help topple the new regime and undercut its effort to export revolution.

Further complicating the postwar situation were the defeat and dissolution of the Turkish Ottoman Empire, which had controlled much of the Middle East in 1914. The Arab revolt against the Turks that developed in the Arabian peninsula in 1916 did not achieve its major military aims, though it endured, causing some disruption to the Turkish war effort. Its success was due partly to the collaboration of a young British officer, T. E. Lawrence (1888–1935), who proved an effective military leader and an impassioned advocate of the Arab cause. The support that Britain had offered the Arabs suggested that independence, perhaps even a single Arab kingdom, might follow from a defeat of the Ottoman Empire.

But British policy toward the Arabs was uncertain and contradictory. Concerned about the Suez Canal, the British government sought to tighten its control in Egypt by declaring it a protectorate in 1914, triggering increased anti-British sentiment in the region. The secret Sykes-Picot Agreement of May 1916, named for the British and French diplomats who negotiated it, projected a division of the Ottoman territories of the Middle East into colonial spheres of influence. France would control Syria and Lebanon, while Britain would rule Palestine and Mesopotamia, or present-day Iraq.

Potentially complicating the situation in the region was Zionism, the movement to establish a Jewish state in Palestine. Led by Chaim Weizmann (1874–1952), a remarkable Russian-born British chemist, the Zionists reached an important milestone when British foreign secretary Arthur Balfour (1848–1930) cautiously announced, in the Balfour Declaration of November 1917, that the British government "looked with favor" on the prospect of a "Jewish home" in Palestine. At this point, British leaders sympathetic to Zionism saw no conflict in simultaneously embracing the cause of the Arabs against the Ottoman Turks; indeed, Arabs and Jews, each seeking self-determination, could be expected to collaborate.

In the heat of war, the British established their policy for the former Ottoman territories without careful study. Thus, they made promises and agreements that were not entirely compatible. After the war, the victors' effort to install a new order in the Middle East would create fresh conflicts.

■ The Peace Settlement

The peace conference took place in Paris, beginning in January 1919. Its labors led to five separate treaties, with each of the five defeated states, known collectively as the Paris peace settlement. The first and most significant was the Treaty of Versailles with Germany, signed in the Hall of Mirrors of the Versailles Palace on June 28, 1919. Treaties were also worked out, in turn, with Austria, Bulgaria, Hungary, and finally Turkey, in August 1920.

This was to be a dictated, not a negotiated, peace. Germany and its allies were excluded, as was renegade Russia. The passions unleashed by the long war had dissolved the possibility of a more conciliatory outcome, a genuinely negotiated peace. Having won the war, France, Britain, the United States, and Italy were to call the shots on their own, with the future of Europe and much of the world in the balance. However, spokesmen for many groups—from Slovaks and Croats to Arabs, Jews, and pan-Africanists—were in Paris as well, seeking a hearing for their respective causes. Both the Arab Prince Faisal (1885–1933), who would later become king of Iraq, and Colonel T. E. Lawrence were on hand to plead for an independent Arab kingdom. (See the box "Global Encounters: Prince Faisal at the Peace Confer-

An Arab in Paris   Prince Faisal (*foreground*) attended the Paris Peace Conference, where he lobbied for the creation of an independent Arab kingdom from part of the former Ottoman Turkish holdings in the Middle East. Among his supporters was the British officer T. E. Lawrence (*middle row, second from the right*), on his way to legend as "Lawrence of Arabia."   *(Trustees of the Imperial War Museum)*

ence.") The African American leader W. E. B. Du Bois° (1868–1963), who took his Ph.D. at Harvard in 1895, led a major pan-African congress in Paris concurrently with the peace conference.

The fundamental challenge for the peacemakers was to reconcile the conflicting visions of the postwar world that had emerged by the end of the war. U.S. President Wilson represented the promise of a new order that could give this terrible war a lasting meaning. As he toured parts of Europe on his way to the peace conference, Wilson was greeted as a hero. Clemenceau, in contrast, was a hard-liner concerned with French security and dismissive of Wilsonian ideals. Since becoming prime minister in 1917, he had stressed that only permanent French military superiority over Germany, and not some utopian league of nations, could guarantee a lasting peace. The negotiations at Paris centered on this fundamental difference between Wilson and Clemenceau. Although Britain's Lloyd George took a hard line on certain issues, he also sought to mediate, helping engineer the somewhat awkward compromise that resulted. When, after the peace conference, he encountered criticism for the outcome, Lloyd George replied, "I think I did as well as might be expected, seated as I was between Jesus Christ and Napoleon Bonaparte."[7]

Du Bois (doo BOYS)

The Victors and the Peace   In June 1919 the leaders of the major victorious powers exude confidence after signing with Germany the Treaty of Versailles, the most important of the five treaties that resulted from the Paris Peace Conference. From the left are David Lloyd George of Britain, Georges Clemenceau of France, and Woodrow Wilson of the United States.   *(Corbis-Bettmann)*

⊕ G L O B A L   E N C O U N T E R S

Prince Faisal at the Peace Conference

With the war nearing its end in October 1918, British authorities, in line with provisions of the Sykes-Picot agreement, permitted Faisal ibn-Husayn (1885–1933) to set up a provisional Arab state, with its capital at Damascus. As head of a delegation from this area to the Paris Peace Conference, Faisal claimed to speak for all Arab Asia, but some in the Arabian peninsula challenged his claim. In the memorandum of January 1919 that follows, he outlined the Arab position, mixing pride and assertiveness with a recognition that the Arabs would continue to need the support and help of Western powers. After the peace was concluded, Faisal found himself caught up in British and French rivalries as he was installed as king first of Syria, then of Iraq. But his efforts were central to the eventual achievement of Arab independence in the Middle East.

We believe that our ideal of Arab unity in Asia is justified beyond need of argument. If argument is required, we would point to the general principles accepted by the Allies when the United States joined them, to our splendid past, to the tenacity with which our race has for 600 years resisted Turkish attempts to absorb us, and, in a lesser degree, to what we tried our best to do in this war as one of the Allies. . . .

The various provinces of Arab Asia—Syria, Irak, Jezireh, Hedjaz, Nejd, Yemen—are very different economically and socially, and it is impossible to constrain them into one frame of government.

We believe that Syria, an agricultural and industrial area thickly peopled with sedentary classes, is sufficiently advanced politically to manage her own internal affairs. We feel also that foreign technical advice and help will be a most valuable factor in our national growth. We are willing to pay for this help in cash; we cannot sacrifice for it any part of the freedom we have just won for ourselves by force of arms.

. . . The world wishes to exploit Mesopotamia rapidly, and we therefore believe that the system of government there will have to be buttressed by the men and material resources of a great foreign Power. We ask, however, that the Government be Arab, in principle and spirit, the selective rather than the elective principle being necessarily followed in the neglected districts, until time makes the broader basis possible. . . .

In Palestine the enormous majority of the people are Arabs. The Jews are very close to the Arabs in blood, and there is no conflict of character between the two races. In principles we are absolutely at one. Nevertheless, the Arabs cannot risk assuming the responsibility of holding level the scales in the clash of races and religions that have, in this one province, so often involved the world in difficulties. They would wish for the effective super-position of a great trustee, so long as a representative local administration commended itself by actively promoting the material prosperity of the country. . . .

In our opinion, if our independence be conceded and our local competence established, the natural influences of race, language, and interest will soon draw us together into one people; but for this the Great Powers will have to ensure us open internal frontiers, common railways and telegraphs, and uniform systems of education. To achieve this they must lay aside the thought of individual profits, and of their old jealousies. In a word, we ask you not to force your whole civilisation upon us, but to help us to pick out what serves us from your experience. In return we can offer you little but gratitude.

Source: J. C. Hurewitz, *Diplomacy in the Near and Middle East: A Documentary Record: 1914–1956* (Princeton, N.J.: D. Van Nostrand, 1956), vol. 2, pp. 38–39.

In Article 231 of the final treaty, the peacemakers sought to establish a moral basis for their treatment of Germany by assigning responsibility for the war to Germany and its allies. On this basis, the Germans were required to pay reparations to reimburse the victors for the costs of the war, although the actual amount was not established until 1921. The determination to make the loser pay for what had ended up a fabulously expensive war was one of the factors militating against a compromise peace on both sides by 1917.

Germany was also forced to dismantle much of its military apparatus. The army was to be limited to a hundred thousand men, all volunteers. The treaty severely restricted the size of the German navy as well, and Germany was forbidden to manufacture or possess military aircraft, submarines, tanks, heavy artillery, or poison gas.

France took back Alsace and Lorraine, the provinces it had lost to Germany in 1871 (see Map 25.3). But for France, the crucial security provision of the 1919 peace settlement was the treatment of the adjacent Rhineland section of Germany itself. For fifteen years Allied troops were to occupy the west bank of the Rhine River in Germany—the usual military occupation of a defeated adversary. But this would only be temporary. The long-term advantage for France was to be the permanent demilitarization of all German territory west of the Rhine and a strip of 50 kilometers along its east bank. Germany was to maintain no troops on this part of its own soil; in the event of hostilities French forces would be able to march unopposed into this economically vital area of Germany.

French interests also helped shape the settlement in east-central Europe. Wilsonian principles called for self-determination, but in this area of great ethnic complexity, ethnic differences were not readily sorted out geographically. This made it easier for the French to bring their own strategic concerns to bear on the situation. To ensure that Germany would again face potential enemies from both the east and the west, French leaders envisioned building a network of allies in east-central Europe. The first was the new Poland, created from Polish territories formerly in the German, Russian, and Austro-Hungarian Empires. That network might come to include Czechoslovakia, Yugoslavia, and Romania as well. These states would be weak enough to remain under French influence but, taken together, strong enough to replace Russia as a significant force against Germany.

Partly as a result of French priorities, Poland, Czechoslovakia, Yugoslavia, and Romania ended up as large as possible, either by combining ethnic groups or by incorporating minorities that, on ethnic grounds, be-

Map 25.4   Ethnicity in East-Central Europe, 1919
Ethnic diversity made it hard to create homogeneous nation-states in east-central Europe. The new states that emerged after World War I mixed ethnic groups, and ethnic tensions would contribute to future problems.

longed with neighboring states. The new Czechoslovakia included not only Czechs and Slovaks but also numerous Germans and Magyars. Indeed, Germans, mostly from the old Bohemia, made up 22 percent of the population of Czechoslovakia. On the other hand, Austria, Hungary, and Bulgaria, as defeated powers, found themselves diminished (see Map 25.4). What remained of Austria, the German part of the old Habsburg Empire, was prohibited from choosing to join Germany, an obvious violation of the Wilsonian principle of self-determination.

Desires to contain and weaken communist Russia were also at work in the settlement in east-central Europe. A band of states in east-central Europe, led by

France, could serve not only as a check to Germany but also as a shield against the Russian threat. Romania's aggrandizement came partly at the expense of the Russian Empire, as did the creation of the new Poland. Finland, Latvia, Estonia, and Lithuania, all part of the Russian Empire for over a century, became independent states (see Map 25.3).

The territorial settlement cost Germany almost 15 percent of its prewar territory, but German bitterness over the peace terms stemmed above all from a sense of betrayal. In requesting an armistice, German authorities had appealed to Wilson, who had not emphasized war guilt and reparations. He seemed to be saying that the whole prewar international system, not one side or the other, had been responsible for the current conflict. Yet the peacemakers placed the primary blame on Germany, so for Germans the terms of the peace greatly intensified the sting of defeat.

Wilson had been forced to compromise with French interests in dealing with east-central Europe, but he achieved a potentially significant success in exchange—the establishment of a League of Nations, embodying the widespread hope for a new international order. According to the League covenant worked out by April, disputes among member states were no longer to be settled by war but by mechanisms established by the new assembly. Other members were to participate in sanctions, from economic blockade to military action, against a member that went to war in violation of League provisions.

How could Wilsonian hopes for a new international order be squared with the imperialist system, which seemed utterly at odds with the ideal of self-determination? Elites among the colonial peoples had tended to support the war efforts of their imperial rulers, but often in the hope of winning greater autonomy or even independence. The Indian leader Mohandas Gandhi (1869–1948), who had been educated in the West and admitted to the English bar in 1889, even helped recruit Indians to fight on the British side. But his aim was to speed Indian independence, and he led demonstrations that embarrassed the British during the war. (See the box "Global Encounters: Gandhi Advocates Nonviolence" in Chapter 27 on page 919.)

Colonial peoples participated directly in the war on both sides. In sub-Saharan Africa, for example, German-led Africans fought against Africans under British or French command. France brought colonial subjects from West and North Africa into front-line service during the war. But the resulting expansion of political consciousness led more of those subject to European imperialism to question the whole system.

The hope that support for the Western powers in wartime would eventually be rewarded led China and Siam (now Thailand) to associate with the Allied side in 1917, in an effort to enhance their international stature. Each was seeking to restore full sovereignty in the face of increasing Western influence. China sent 200,000 people to work in France to help ease France's wartime labor shortage.

At the peace conference, spokesmen for the non-Western world tended to be moderate in their demands. And prodded by Wilson, the peacemakers made some concessions. German colonies and Ottoman territories were not simply taken over by the victors, in the old-fashioned way, but were placed under the authority of the League. The League then assigned them as mandates to one of the victorious powers, which was to report to the League annually on conditions in the area in question. Classes of mandates varied, based on how prepared for sovereignty the area was judged to be. In devising this system, the Western powers formally recognized for the first time that non-Western peoples under Western control had rights and interests of their own and that, in principle, they were progressing toward independence.

Still, the mandate approach to the colonial question was a halting departure at best. Although Britain granted considerable sovereignty to Iraq in 1932, the victorious powers generally operated as before, assimilating the new territories into their existing systems of colonial possessions. After the hopes for independence raised in the Arab world during the war, this outcome produced a sense of betrayal among Arab leaders.

The Chinese similarly felt betrayed. Despite China's contribution to the Allied war effort, the victors acquiesced in special rights for Japan in China, causing a renewed sense of humiliation among Chinese elites and provoking popular demonstrations and a boycott of Japanese goods. Although Western leaders were allowing a non-Western power, Japan, access to the imperial club, they were hardly departing from imperialism. For Chinese, Arabs, and others, the West appeared hypocritical. Those whose political consciousness had been raised by the war came to believe not only that colonialism should end, but that the colonial peoples would themselves have to take the lead in ending it.

The incongruities of the postwar settlement prompted Marshal Foch to proclaim, "This is not peace. It is an armistice for twenty years."[8] Would the principal victors have the resolve, and the capacity, to preserve the new order they had solidified at Paris? Debate over the American role promptly developed in the United States as President Wilson sought Senate ratification of the Versailles treaty, which entailed U.S. membership in the League of Nations as well as commitments to France and Britain. Wilson's opponents worried that League membership would compromise U.S. sovereignty, but other nations managed to overcome such concerns and join the new organization. American reluctance stemmed especially from the isolationist backlash that was developing against the U.S. intervention in the European war. Late in 1919, at the height of the debate, Wilson suffered a disabling stroke. The Senate then refused to ratify the peace treaty, thereby keeping the United States out of the League of Nations.

American disengagement stemmed partly from the doubts about the wisdom of the peace settlement that quickly developed in both Britain and the United States. During the peace conference, a member of the British delegation, the economist John Maynard Keynes° (1883–1946), resigned to write *The Economic Consequences of the Peace* (1920), which helped undermine confidence in the whole settlement. Keynes charged that the shortsighted, vindictive policy of the French, by crippling Germany with a punishing reparations burden, threatened the European economy and thus the long-term peace of Europe. For some, then, the challenge was not to enforce the Versailles treaty but to revise it. This lack of consensus about the legitimacy of the peace made it especially hard to anticipate the longer-term consequences of the war.

■ The Cultural Impact of the Great War

The war touched virtually everyone, but it marked for life those who had experienced the nightmare of the trenches. At first, traditional notions of glory, heroism, and patriotic duty combined with images of fellowship and regeneration to enable the soldiers to make a certain sense of their wartime experience. But as the war dragged on, such sentiments gradually eroded, giving way, in many cases, to resignation and cynicism. (See the feature "Weighing the Evidence: The Poetry of World War I" on pages 876–877.) But others, such as the young German soldier and writer Ernst Jünger (1895–1998), lauded the war as the catalyst for a welcome new era of steel, hardness, discipline, organization, and machine precision.

After the war, many of those who had fought it felt a sense of ironic betrayal; their prewar upbringing, the values and assumptions they had inherited, had not equipped them to make sense of what they had lived through. But the effort to find meaning involved not only the survivors but also the families and friends of those killed or maimed. There was much effort to recast traditional, often-religious categories and images for the near-universal experience of bereavement, which transcended national and class divisions.

Beginning in the late 1920s a wave of writings about the war appeared. Many were memoirs, such as *Goodbye to All That* by the English writer Robert Graves (1895–1985) and *Testament of Youth* by Vera Brittain (1893–1970), who had served as a British army nurse at the front. But easily the most famous retrospective was the novel *All Quiet on the Western Front* (1929) by the German Erich Maria Remarque (1898–1970), which sold 2.5 million copies in twenty-five languages in its first eighteen months in print. Remarque provided a gripping portrait of the experience of ordinary soldiers on the western front, but his book also reflected the disillusionment that had come to surround the memory of the war by the late 1920s. Not only were many friends dead or maimed for life, but all the sacrifices seemed to have been largely in vain, a sentiment that fueled determination to avoid another war in the future.

The novel forms of warfare introduced during World War I intensified fears of renewed war. Thanks to modern technology, which had been central to the West's confident belief in progress, Europeans had now experienced machine-gun fire, poison gas attacks, and the terror-bombing of civilians from airplanes. A generation later, to be sure, the advent of the nuclear age occasioned a measure of terror hardly imaginable earlier, but the experience of World War I was the turning point, the end of an earlier innocence.

What followed from the war, most fundamentally, was a new sense that Western civilization was neither as secure nor as superior as it had seemed. The celebrated French poet Paul Valéry (1871–1945), speaking at Oxford shortly after the war, observed that "we modern civilizations have learned to recognize that we are mortal like the others. We had heard . . . of whole worlds vanished, of empires foundered. . . . Elam, Nineveh, Babylon were vague and splendid names; the total ruin of these worlds, for us, meant as little as did their existence. But France, England, Russia . . . these names, too, are splendid. . . . And now we see that the abyss of history is deep enough to bury all the world. We feel that a civilization is as fragile as a life."[9] Valéry went on to warn that the coming transition to peace would be even more difficult and disorienting than the war itself. So traumatic might be the convulsion that Europe might lose its leadership and

---

Keynes (KAINZ)

Severini: Armoured Train In this painting from 1915, the Italian futurist Gino Severini (1883–1996) conveys the hard, steel-like imagery and the sense of disciplined modern efficiency that became associated with war, making it attractive to some young Europeans. *(Richard S. Zeisler Collection, New York/The Bridgeman Art Library, London and New York)*

be shown up for what it was in fact—a pathetically small corner of the world, a mere cape on the Asiatic landmass. Astounding words for a European, yet even Valéry, for all his foresight, could not anticipate what Europe would experience in the decades to follow.

Summary

 HE war that began in August 1914 was supposed to be over in a few months, but it quickly bogged down in stalemate in the west, which proved the decisive military front. Germany had to fight a two-front war, and it almost immediately began suffering under Britain's naval blockade. But the Germans defeated Russia in 1917 and then, in 1918, mounted a last-ditch offensive in the west that came close to succeeding as well. By 1918, however, lack of food, provisions, and manpower was fatally weakening the German effort, and U.S. intervention gave the anti-German coalition the long-term advantage in any case. Though it entailed a far greater effort than anyone had expected at the outset, the war reached a definitive outcome with the defeat of Germany and its allies by November 1918.

So great were the strains of the war that radical political changes accompanied military defeat, first in Russia, then in Turkey, Austria-Hungary, and Germany. In destroying the Habsburg Empire and the imperial regime in Germany, that outcome addressed the problems that seemed to have caused the war in the first place. But with so many pillars of the old order falling in the wake of the war, the future remained uncertain indeed even after the major provisions of the peace settlement were established in 1919.

Because it proved so much longer and more difficult than expected, this first "world war" proved a total war, calling forth new forms of socioeconomic coordination and even systematic propaganda. Partly as a result, the war accelerated processes, from technological development to women's suffrage, that many deemed progressive. But coming after a century of relative peace and apparent progress, this unexpectedly long and brutal war ended up shaking Europe's social and cultural foundations. The number of casualties, the advent of terrifying new weapons, the destruction of famous old monuments—all gave the war an apocalyptic aura that heightened its psychological impact. So despite a widespread desire to return to normal once the war was over, many were plagued by a deeper sense that the world could never be the same again. Troubling new uncertainties mixed with exciting new possibilities as Europe and the West looked to the future.

■ Notes

1. Thus wrote the German poet Ivan Goll in 1917; quoted in Modris Eksteins, *Rites of Spring: The Great War and the Birth of the Modern Age* (Boston: Houghton Mifflin, 1989), p. 144.
2. The remarks of Raymond Joubert, as quoted in John Ellis, *Eye-Deep in Hell: Trench Warfare in World War I* (Baltimore: Johns Hopkins University Press, 1989), p. 104.
3. Brian Bond, *War and Society in Europe, 1870–1970* (New York: Oxford University Press, 1986), p. 114.
4. By A. N. Potresov, as quoted in Richard Pipes, *The Russian Revolution* (New York: Random House, Vintage, 1991), p. 348.
5. Both statements are quoted in Koppel S. Pinson, *Modern Germany: Its History and Civilization,* 2d ed. (New York: Macmillan, 1966), p. 337.
6. Quoted in Arno J. Mayer, *Political Origins of the New Diplomacy, 1917–18* (New York: Random House, Vintage, 1970), p. 135.
7. Quoted in Walter Arnstein, *Britain Yesterday and Today: 1830 to the Present,* 6th ed. (Lexington, Mass.: D. C. Heath, 1992), p. 266.
8. Quoted in P. M. H. Bell, *The Origins of the Second World War* (London and New York: Longman, 1986), p. 14.
9. Paul Valéry, *Variety,* 1st series (New York: Harcourt, Brace, 1938), pp. 3–4.

■ Suggested Reading

Chickering, Roger. *Imperial Germany and the Great War, 1914–1918.* 1998. A balanced, comprehensive introduction to the German war effort and experience, especially good on the interpenetration of military and sociopolitical concerns.

Ellis, John. *Eye-Deep in Hell: Trench Warfare in World War I.* 1989. A compelling account of life and death in the trenches, covering topics from trench construction to eating, drinking, and sex; includes striking photographs.

Figes, Orlando. *A People's Tragedy: The Russian Revolution, 1891–1924.* 1997. A lengthy, comprehensive but gripping account of the revolutionary trajectory, from the famine of 1891 to the death of Lenin in 1924. Seeks to reveal the complexity of the whole process, its many episodes and forms of agency.

Fitzpatrick, Sheila. *The Russian Revolution, 1917–1932.* 2d ed. 1994. An ideal introductory work that places the events of 1917 in the sweep of Russian history.

Keegan, John. *The First World War.* 1999. A comprehensive and accessible study by a widely read military historian.

Robbins, Keith. *The First World War.* 1985. An accessible, balanced, and comprehensive treatment, covering everything from military operations to the domestic impact of the war.

Sharp, Alan. *The Versailles Settlement: Peacemaking in Paris, 1919.* 1991. A brief, clear, and balanced overview that seeks to do justice to the magnitude of the task the peacemakers faced.

Wall, Richard, and Jay Winter, eds. *The Upheaval of War: Family, Work and Welfare in Europe, 1914–1918.* 1988. A series of essays that sheds much new light on the war's domestic impact, from nutrition and standards of living to social and labor policy.

Winter, J. M. *The Experience of World War I.* 1989. A beautifully illustrated work that proceeds via concentric circles from politicians to generals to soldiers to civilians, then to the war's longer-term effects.

Winter, Jay. *Sites of Memory, Sites of Mourning.* 1995. Using an effective comparative approach, a leading authority argues that Europeans relied on relatively traditional means of making sense of the bloodletting of World War I.

 For a searchable list of additional readings for this chapter, go to http://college.hmco.com.

The Poetry of World War I

We don't normally think of poetry and war together, and World War I, with its unexpected brutality and severe hardship, may seem the least poetic of wars. Yet even during the war, soldiers like Englishmen Rupert Brooke (1887–1915) and Wilfred Owen (1893–1918) sought to shape their experiences into poetic imagery. What does such poetry tell us about what the war meant to those who fought it? How has poetic testimony affected our understanding of the place of World War I in the Western experience?

In Brooke's wartime poetry what strikes us first is his gratitude that his generation had come of age at this dramatic historical moment:

> Now, God be thanked Who has matched us with
> His hour,
> And caught our youth, and wakened us from
> sleeping

But why would a young man like Brooke welcome war? He seemed to envision release, deliverance—but from what?

When the war broke out, Brooke promptly volunteered, even pulling strings to get into a combat unit.

Seeing action for the first time, in Belgium in October 1914, he was excited by the intensity of battle and pleased by his own calm self-control. Back in England for further training shortly thereafter, he wrote several sonnets, including "Peace," the one reproduced here, expressing his feelings about the war. But he died of blood poisoning on the way to battle in April 1915—without ever fully experiencing trench warfare.

Although most of the young Englishmen who took up arms with such enthusiasm in 1914 assumed that their country was in the right, that Germany was at fault, they gave little thought to the purposes of the war or the larger historical impact it might have. Brooke understood that the war would not accomplish all that was claimed for it, but he was grateful for the personal experience it made possible. Somehow it meant "peace," as the title of his sonnet suggests, and even cleanliness:

> To turn, as swimmers into cleanness leaping,
> Glad from a world grown old and cold and weary

Brooke's sense of deliverance responded to personal frustrations, yet he spoke for others of his generation who also were finding it difficult to assume a place in

Rupert Brooke (1887–1915)   *(Mansell/Time Inc.)*

PEACE

Now, God be thanked Who has matched us with His hour,
  And caught our youth, and wakened us from sleeping,
With hand made sure, clear eye, and sharpened power,
  To turn, as swimmers into cleanness leaping,
Glad from a world grown old and cold and weary,
  Leave the sick hearts that honour could not move,
And half-men, and their dirty songs and dreary,
  And all the little emptiness of love!

Oh! we, who have known shame, we have found release there,
  Where there's no ill, no grief, but sleep has mending.
    Naught broken save this body, lost but breath;
Nothing to shake the laughing heart's long peace there
  But only agony, and that has ending;
    And the worst friend and enemy is but Death.

Rupert Brooke

Wilfred Owen (1893–1918) *(© Hulton Getty/Corbis)*

ANTHEM FOR DOOMED YOUTH

What passing-bells for these who die as cattle?
  —Only the monstrous anger of the guns.
  Only the stuttering rifles' rapid rattle
Can patter out their hasty orisons.
No mockeries now for them; no prayers nor bells;
  Nor any voice of mourning save the choirs,—
The shrill, demented choirs of wailing shells;
  And bugles calling for them from sad shires.

What candles may be held to speed them all?
  Not in the hands of boys but in their eyes
Shall shine the holy glimmers of goodbyes.
  The pallor of girls' brows shall be their pall;
Their flowers the tenderness of patient minds,
And each slow dusk a drawing-down of blinds.

Wilfred Owen

adult society at that particular time. Though they came from educated, upper-middle-class families, they were contemptuous of the routines and compromises of the respectable, everyday world to which they were expected to adjust. Thus Brooke welcomed the chance to

> Leave the sick hearts that honour could not move,
> And half-men, and their dirty songs and dreary

Yet those of Brooke's generation were equally troubled by their own uncertainty about values and commitments—to marriage, career, a place in society. Thanks to the overwhelming, inescapable reality of the war, values that had seemed empty—honor, country, duty, fellowship—now seemed meaningful after all. To his surprise and relief, Brooke found that he himself was capable of courage, commitment, and sacrifice. With its promise of cleanliness and renewal, the war was worth even its highest price, which was merely death.

Unlike Brooke, Wilfred Owen hated the war from the start. He was quickly struck by its sheer ugliness, as manifested in the landscape, the noise, the coarse language of the soldiers themselves. Yet he served with distinction, was decorated for bravery, and was killed by machine-gun fire just one week before the armistice in November 1918.

Owen, then, experienced the reality of World War I in a way that Brooke did not. The sonnet here, "Anthem for Doomed Youth," was written during September and October 1917, after the war had come to entail a terrible bloodletting. Thus Owen sought to shape sentiments very different from Brooke's—a sense of waste, of loss, of incongruity between suffering endured and results achieved. Whereas Brooke had brushed aside the possibility of death, Owen saw death as relentless, carrying off a generation of innocent youth, dying like cattle.

In a sense, even the dignity of death had become a casualty of the war. Thus Owen mixed funeral images with the new horror that this war had brought forth: the only mourning was "The shrill, demented choirs of wailing shells." Mocking the ongoing effort to sweeten the reality of death at the front through reference to nobility and sacrifice, Owen drowned out his initial suggestion of bells with the new and awful sounds of machine-gun fire:

> —Only the monstrous anger of the guns.
> Only the stuttering rifles' rapid rattle

Quite apart from its military and political outcome, World War I has assumed a particular place in our collective memory, thanks partly to those like Brooke and Owen who managed to frame their wartime experiences in the memorable language of poetry. At first, Brooke's poetry helped to justify the alarming slaughter to those who began questioning the war's purpose as it claimed the lives of their sons. Yet by now we find it hard to grasp the ideals that inspired his poetic testimony, for they were in one sense consumed by the war and the era of violence that it began. We still live in the world that emerged from that war, so Owen, with his tragic cynicism, is far more our contemporary. Brooke may still reveal for us something of the innocence that was lost, but it is especially through Owen's way of conveying the tragedy, the sense of betrayal and lost innocence, that World War I has continued to haunt the memory of Western civilization.

CHAPTER 26

The Illusion of Stability 1919–1930

I N 1925 Josephine Baker (1906–1975), a black entertainer from St. Louis, moved from the chorus lines of New York to the bistros of Paris, where she quickly became a singing and dancing sensation. Also a favorite in Germany, she was the most famous of the African American entertainers who took the cultural capitals of Europe by storm during the 1920s. After the disillusioning experience of war, many Europeans found a valuable infusion of vitality in Baker's jazz music, exotic costumes, and "savage," uninhibited dancing (see the photo on page 897).

The European attraction to African Americans as primitive, vital, and sensual reflected a good deal of racial stereotyping, but there really *was* something fresh and uninhibited about American culture, especially its African American variant. And even as they played to those stereotypes, black performers like Baker had great fun ironically subverting them. Many realized they could enjoy opportunities in parts of Europe that were still denied them in the United States. Baker herself was a woman of great sophistication who became a French citizen in 1937, participated in progressive causes, and was decorated for her secret intelligence work in the anti-Nazi resistance during World War II.

The prominence of African Americans in European popular culture was part of a wider infatuation with things American as Europeans embraced the new during the 1920s. Lacking the cultural baggage of Europe, America seemed to offer revitalization and modernity at the same time. With so many old conventions shattered by the war, the ideal of being "modern" became widespread among Europeans, affecting everything from sex education to furniture design. "Modern" meant no-nonsense efficiency, mass production, and a vital popular culture, expressed in jazz, movies, sport, and even advertising. (See the feature "Weighing the Evidence: Advertising" on pages 910–911.)

The West and the World After the Great War

Communism, Fascism, and the New Political Spectrum

Toward Mass Society

Weimar Germany and the Trials of the New Democracies

The Search for Meaning in a Disordered World

Kees van Dongen, *Au cabaret nègre* (detail).
(Collection Christie's/Edimedia)

But Europeans themselves had pioneered modernism in many areas of the arts and sciences, and innovation continued after the war. Paris held its own as an international cultural center, hosting a decorative arts exhibition in 1925 that produced art deco, the sleek, "modernistic" style that helped give the decade its distinctive flavor. And in the unsettled conditions of postwar Germany, Berlin emerged to rival Paris for cultural leadership during what Germans called "the Golden Twenties." Innovations ranged from avant-garde drama to a sophisticated cabaret scene with a prominent homosexual dimension.

Still, something dizzying, even unnerving, marked the eager embrace of the new during the 1920s. Some European cultural observers saw the vogue of black American entertainers as a symptom of decadence that would only undermine further the best of European civilization. Even in embracing the new, many were seeking a new basis for order and security, but where their efforts would lead remained unclear.

Although the immediate disruptions of wartime carried over to 1923, a more hopeful era of relative prosperity and international conciliation followed, continuing until 1929. But there was much that called into question the ideal of a "world safe for democracy" that had surrounded the end of the war. Revolutionary Russia remained an uncertain force, even as it began seeking to build socialism on its own. In Italy, the democracy that had emerged in the nineteenth century gave way to the

first regime to call itself fascist, and some of the new democracies in east-central Europe did not survive the decade. The postwar efforts at economic restabilization, apparently successful for a while, masked growing strains in the international economy. In one sphere after another, postwar restabilization was fragile—and could quickly unravel.

QUESTIONS TO CONSIDER

- How did the differing priorities of Britain and France affect international relations during the 1920s?
- How and why did the priorities of the Russian communist regime change from 1919 to 1930?
- Why did Italy turn from parliamentary democracy to fascism even after sharing in the victory in World War I?
- What were the sources of the political instability that made the future of the new German democracy so uncertain during the 1920s?

TERMS TO KNOW

Maginot Line
fascism
Benito Mussolini
Comintern (Third,
   or Communist,
   International)
New Economic Policy
   (NEP)

Joseph Stalin
Matteotti murder
corporative state,
   corporativism
Gustav Stresemann
Treaty of Locarno
surrealism
Bauhaus

THE WEST AND THE WORLD AFTER THE GREAT WAR

LTHOUGH the United States and Japan were becoming important, the major international players before 1914 had been the European powers, who had apportioned much of the non-Western world in imperial networks. But the war and the peace

had weakened—and to some extent discredited—the belligerent countries of Europe, who now found themselves saddled with foreign debts and unbalanced economies. Though the United States pulled back from a direct political role in Europe in 1919, it became far more active in world affairs, helping to engineer major conferences on arms limitation and international economic relations during the 1920s. But in crucial respects, the shape of the postwar international order still depended on Europeans. And colonial concerns continued to affect the balance of power in Europe, where it fell to the two major victors in the war, France and Britain, to enforce the controversial peace settlement.

■ The Erosion of European Power

Emerging from the war as the principal power in East Asia was a non-Western country, Japan, whose claims to the German bases in the region and to special rights in China were formally recognized at the Paris Peace Conference. With the Washington treaty of 1922, Japan won naval parity with Britain and the United States in East Asia. The Western nations were recognizing Japan as a peer, a great power—even a threat. Aspects of the Washington agreements were intended to block Japanese expansion in East Asia. If a new international system was to emerge, it would not be centered in Europe to the extent the old one had been.

After the slaughter of the war and the hypocrisy of the peace, Europeans could no longer claim to embody civilization with the same arrogance. And as the old Europe lost prestige, President Wilson's ideals of self-determination and democracy were greeted enthusiastically outside the West—in China, for example. At the same time, the Russian revolutionary model appealed to those in the colonial world seeking to understand the mainsprings of Western imperialism—and the means of overcoming it. To some Chinese intellectuals by the early 1920s, Leninism was attractive because it showed the scope for mass mobilization by a revolutionary vanguard.

Non-Western elites were learning to pick and choose from among the elements of the Western tradition. In the 1920s, ever greater numbers of colonial subjects were traveling to western Europe, often for education. Paris was a favored destination, partly because France made an effort to assimilate its colonial peoples. Although those educated in Europe were subject to Westernization, that did not necessarily make them more supportive of Western rule. Many began not only to question colonialism but also to take a fresh look at their own traditions, asking how they might serve the quest for a postcolonial order.

By the 1920s, a generation of anticolonialist, nationalist intellectuals was emerging to lead the non-Western world. Some were more radical than others, but most agreed that the challenge was to learn from the West and to modernize, but without simply copying the West and losing distinctive cultural identities. It was imperative to sift through tradition, determining what needed to be changed and what was worth preserving. The pioneering

CHRONOLOGY	
March 1919	Founding of the Italian fascist movement
November 1920	Russian civil war ends
March 1921	New Economic Policy announced at Russian Communist Party congress
October 1922	Mussolini becomes Italian prime minister
January 1923	French-led occupation of the Ruhr
November 1923	Peak of inflation in Germany
January 1924	First Labour government in Britain
	Death of Lenin
August 1924	Acceptance of the Dawes Plan on German reparations
October 1925	Treaty of Locarno
May 1926	Pilsudski's coup d'état in Poland
	Beginning of general strike in Britain
May 1927	Lindbergh completes first transatlantic solo flight
January 1929	Stalin forces banishment of Trotsky from Soviet Union
April 1929	Soviets adopt first economic Five-Year Plan
August 1929	Acceptance of the Young Plan on German reparations
October 1929	Death of Stresemann

Chinese nationalist Sun Yixien (Sun Yat-sen, 1866–1925) was typical in recognizing the need to adopt the science and technology of the West. But China, he insisted, could do so in its own way, without sacrificing its unique cultural and political traditions. (See the box "Global Encounters: Sun Yixien on Chinese Nationalism.")

As the greatest imperial power, Britain was especially vulnerable to the growing anticolonial sentiment. The struggle to hang on to its empire drew British energies away from the problems of Europe after the peace settlement.

⊕ G L O B A L   E N C O U N T E R S

Sun Yixien on Chinese Nationalism

Sun Yixien (Sun Yat-sen), widely regarded as the father of modern China, founded the Guomindang (Kuomintang), the Chinese nationalist movement, in 1912. Educated by Western missionaries in China, he lived in the United States for extended periods and came to admire the West in important respects. But he insisted that China, to make the best use of what the West offered, had to reconnect with its own unique traditions. Variations on this argument would be heard for decades as the rest of the world sought to come to terms with the seemingly more advanced West. The following passages are from an influential series of lectures that Sun Yixien presented in China in the early 1920s.

What is the standing of our nation in the world? In comparison with other nations we have the greatest population and the oldest culture, of four thousand years' duration. We ought to be advancing in line with the nations of Europe and America. But the Chinese people have only family and clan groups; there is no national spirit. Consequently, in spite of four hundred million people gathered together in one China, we are in fact but a sheet of loose sand. We are the poorest and weakest state in the world, occupying the lowest position in international affairs; the rest of mankind is the carving knife and the serving dish, while we are the fish and the meat. Our position now is extremely perilous; if we do not earnestly promote nationalism and weld together our four hundred millions into a strong nation, we face a tragedy—the loss of our country and the destruction of our race. To ward off this danger, we must espouse Nationalism and employ the national spirit to save the country. . . .

But even if we succeed in reviving our ancient morality, learning, and powers, we will still not be able, in this modern world, to advance China to a first place among the nations. . . . [W]e will still need to learn the strong points of Europe and America before we can progress at an equal rate with them. Unless we do study the best from foreign countries, we will go backward. With our own fine foundation of knowledge and our age-long culture, with our own native intelligence besides, we should be able to acquire all the best things from abroad. The strongest point of the West is its science. . . .

As soon as we learn Western machinery we can use it anytime, anywhere; electric lights, for example, can be installed and used in any kind of Chinese house. But Western social customs and sentiments are different from ours in innumerable points; if, without regard to customs and popular feelings in China, we try to apply Western methods of social control as we would Western machinery—in a hard and fast way—we shall be making a serious mistake. . . .

. . . For the governmental machinery of the United States and France still has many defects, and does not satisfy the desires of the people nor give them a complete measure of happiness. So we in our proposed reconstruction must not think that if we imitate the West of today we shall reach the last stage of progress and be perfectly contented. . . .

Only in recent times has Western culture advanced beyond ours, and the passion for this new civilization has stimulated our revolution. Now that the revolution is a reality, we naturally desire to see China excel the West and build up the newest and most progressive state in the world. We certainly possess the qualifications necessary to reach this ideal, but we must not merely imitate the democratic systems of the West.

Source: Sun Yat-sen, *San Min Chu I: The Three Principles of the People* (Taipei, Taiwan: China Cultural Service, 1953), pp. 5, 46, 109–113, 136, 138–139.

In light of the strong Indian support for the British war effort, the British government promised in 1917 to extend the scope for Indian involvement in the colonial administration in India. Growing expectations as the war was ending provoked episodes of violence against the British, whose troops retaliated brutally in April 1919, firing indiscriminately into an unarmed crowd. This Amritsar Massacre helped galvanize India's independence movement, even though the British, seeking conciliation in the aftermath, extended self-rule by entrusting certain less essential government services to Indians. Another milestone was reached in 1921, when Mohandas Gandhi, the British-educated leader of the Indian independence movement, shed his European clothes in favor of simple Indian attire. But it was on the basis of Western egalitarianism, not some indigenous value, that Gandhi demanded political rights for the "untouchables," the lowest group in India's long-standing caste system.

In Egypt a full-scale anti-British insurrection broke out in 1919. After British troops suppressed the rebellion, British authorities offered to grant moderate concessions, as in India. But Egyptian nationalists demanded independence, which was finally granted in 1922. Egypt gradually evolved into a constitutional monarchy, with representative government and universal suffrage. But Britain retained a predominant influence in Egypt until the nationalist revolution of 1952 (see Chapter 29).

At the same time, nationalism was growing among West Africans who had studied in England. In March 1919 Western-educated Africans in the Gold Coast asked the British governor to establish representative institutions so that Africans could at least be consulted about governmental affairs. The West African National Congress, formed in 1920, made similar demands. The British agreed to new constitutions for Nigeria in 1923 and the Gold Coast in 1925 that took significant steps in that direction. They also agreed to build more schools, though they tended to promote practical education, including African languages and agriculture, whereas the African leaders wanted students to learn the Western classics that "made gentlemen." Such conflicting priorities indicate the complexities of the relationships between colonial rulers and the emerging elites among the colonized peoples.

Anticolonialism in the Middle East   Syria became a League of Nations mandate under French control after World War I. Friction began immediately between the French and Arab nationalists, who had wanted independence. A major nationalist uprising during the fall of 1925 produced the destruction shown here and forced the French to grant concessions. After long negotiations, the French agreed to a treaty granting autonomy for Syria in 1936.   *(Topham Picturepoint/The Image Works)*

■ Enforcing the Versailles Settlement

It was up to France and Britain to make sure the new international order worked, but it was not clear that either had the will and resources to do so. Cooperation between them was essential, yet sometimes their differences—in geography, in values, and in perceptions—seemed to doom them to work at cross-purposes.

France was the dominant power on the European continent after World War I, and until well into the 1930s it boasted the strongest army in the world. Yet even in the early 1920s a sense of hollowness, artificiality, tarnished France's image of strength—and thus the shrillness and the defensiveness that came to mark French thinking and French policy.

In light of Germany's larger population and stronger industrial base, France's long-term security seemed to require certain measures to tip the scales in its favor. By imposing German disarmament and the demilitarization of the Rhineland, the Versailles treaty gave France immediate military advantages. Yet how long could these measures be maintained, once the passions of war had died down and Germany no longer seemed such a threat? France had hoped for British help in enforcing the treaty, but Britain was pulling back from the Continent to concentrate on its empire, just as it had after other major European wars.

In particular, the British wanted to avoid getting dragged into the uncertain situation in east-central Europe, where vital national interests did not seem to be at stake. Yet the French, to replace their earlier link with Russia, promptly developed an alliance system with several of the new or expanded states of the region, including Poland, Czechoslovakia, Romania, and Yugoslavia. France's ties to east-central Europe made the British especially wary of binding agreements with the French.

At first, France felt confident enough to take strong steps even without British support. In response to German foot-dragging in paying reparations, Prime Minister Raymond Poincaré decided to get tough in January 1923. Declaring the Germans in default, he sent French troops at the head of an international force to occupy the Ruhr industrial area and force German compliance. But the move backfired. The Germans adopted a policy of passive resistance in response, and the costs of the occupation more than offset the increase in reparations that France received. The French government ended up having to raise taxes to pay for the venture. Moreover, the move alienated the British, whose lack of support bordered on active hostility.

British leaders now viewed French policy as unnecessarily vindictive and bellicose, and they increasingly saw the Versailles treaty as counterproductive. Instead, they placed great store in the League of Nations and in the international arms reduction effort gaining momentum by the later 1920s. So France found itself with ever less support from its wartime allies as it sought to enforce the peace settlement. The Ruhr occupation of 1923 proved the last time the French dared to go it alone.

From that point on, France gradually lost the advantages it had gained by defeating Germany, and self-confidence gave way to defensiveness and resignation. The defensive mentality found physical embodiment in the Maginot° Line, a system of fortifications on the country's eastern border. Remembering the defensive warfare of World War I and determined to preclude the sort of invasion France had suffered in 1914, the military convinced France's political leaders to adopt a defensive strategy based on a fortified line. Construction began in 1929, and the Maginot system reached preliminary completion in 1935, when it extended along France's border with Germany from Switzerland to the border with Belgium.

This defensive system was not consistent with the other major strands of French policy, especially its alliances with states in east-central Europe. If France emphasized defense behind an impregnable system of forts, what good were French security guarantees to such new allies as Poland and Czechoslovakia?

Still, the situation remained fluid during the 1920s. In France, as in Britain, national elections in 1924 produced a victory for the moderate left, ending a period of conservative nationalist dominance since the war. In each country, international relations became a major issue in the elections, and the outcome forecast a more conciliatory tack, especially in relations with Germany. If democracy was taking root in Germany, then perhaps France's fears about the European power balance were misguided.

COMMUNISM, FASCISM, AND THE NEW POLITICAL SPECTRUM

 N making their revolution in 1917, the Russian Bolsheviks had expected to spark wider revolution, and hopes—and fears—that the revolution would spread were palpable in the immediate postwar period. The Russian communists initially enjoyed extraordinary prestige on the European left; but as

---

Maginot (MAH-zhih-noh)

the nature of Leninist communism became clearer, some Marxists grew skeptical or hostile, and the Russian model eventually produced a damaging split in international socialism. By the end of the 1920s revolution elsewhere was nowhere in sight, and it seemed that, for the foreseeable future, the communist regime in Russia would have to go it alone.

By then, a new and unexpected political movement had developed in Italy, expanding the political spectrum in a different direction. The groundswell was fascism, which brought Benito Mussolini to power in 1922. Emerging directly from the war, the fascist movement was violent and antidemocratic—and thus disturbing to many. Stressing national solidarity and discipline, the fascists were hostile not only to liberal individualism and the parliamentary system, but also to Marxist socialism, with its emphasis on class struggle and the special role of the working class. Claiming to offer a modern alternative to both, Italian fascism quickly attracted the attention of those in other countries who were disillusioned with parliamentary politics and hostile to the Marxist left. The interplay of communism and fascism, as new political experiments, added to the uncertainties of novel postwar world.

◼ Changing Priorities in Communist Russia, 1918–1921

Even after leading the revolution that toppled the provisional government in November 1917, the Bolsheviks could not claim majority support in Russia. When the long-delayed elections to select a constituent assembly were held a few weeks after the revolution, the Socialist Revolutionaries won a clear majority while the Bolsheviks ended up with fewer than one-quarter of the seats. But the Bolsheviks' new Red Army simply dispersed the assembly when it met in January 1918. And over the next three years the Communists, as the Bolsheviks renamed themselves, gradually consolidated their power, establishing a centralized and nondemocratic regime. Power lay not with the soviets, nor with some coalition of socialist parties, but solely with the Communist Party.

During its first years, the new communist regime encountered a genuine emergency that seemed to require a monopoly of power. During 1918–1920, in what became a brutal civil war, the communist "Reds" battled counterrevolutionary "Whites," people who had been dispossessed by the revolution or who had grown disillusioned with the Communists. Appointed People's Commissar for War in April 1918, Leon Trotsky forged a loyal and disciplined Red Army. The Whites drew support from foreign intervention and from separatist senti-

ment, as several of the non-Russian nationalities of the old Russian Empire sought to free themselves from Russian and communist control.

A series of thrusts, involving troops from fourteen countries at one time or another, struck at Russia from a variety of points along its huge border. The Whites and the foreign troops never forged a coordinated strategy, but the dogged counterrevolutionary assault seriously threatened the young Communist regime and the territorial basis of the state it had inherited from the tsarist autocracy. In the final analysis, however, the Whites proved unable to rally much popular support. Peasants feared, plausibly enough, that a White victory would mean a restoration of the old order, including the return of their newly won lands to the former landlords. By the end of active fighting in November 1920, the Communist regime had not only survived but regained most of the territory it had lost early in the civil war (see Map 26.1).

The need to launch the new communist regime in this way, fighting counterrevolutionaries supported by foreign troops, inevitably affected Communist perceptions and priorities. Separatist sentiment might continue to feed counterrevolutionary efforts, so the new regime exerted careful control over the non-Russian nationalities. Thus, when the Union of Soviet Socialist Republics (USSR) was organized in December 1922, it was only nominally a federation of autonomous republics; strong centralization from the Communists' new capital in Moscow was the rule from the start.

In the midst of the civil war the Russian communists founded the Third, or Communist, International—commonly known as the Comintern—in March 1919, to make clear their break with the seemingly discredited strategies of the Second International. Through the Comintern, the Russian communists expected to translate their success in Russia into leadership of the international socialist movement. However, many old-line Marxists elsewhere were not prepared to admit that the leadership of European socialism had passed to the Bolshevik rulers of backward Russia. (See the box "Reading Sources: A Marxist Critique of Communism.")

From its founding in March 1919 until the spring of 1920, as a wave of leftist political agitation and labor unrest swept Europe, the Comintern actively promoted the wider revolution that Lenin had envisioned. Seeking to win mass support, the organization accented leftist solidarity and reached out to the rank and file in the labor unions. By the spring of 1920, however, it seemed clear that further revolution was not imminent. Thus, Comintern leaders began concentrating on improving organization and discipline for a more protracted revolutionary struggle.

Boundary of the Russian Empire 1914
Boundary of area controlled by the Bolsheviks August 1918
Boundary of area controlled by the Bolsheviks October 1919
Boundary of Soviet territory March 1921
Boundary of area controlled by the anti-Bolshevik forces May 1920
White Russian armies
Non-Russian anti-Bolshevik forces

Entente fleet

Murmansk
BRITISH
FRENCH
CANADIANS
ITALIANS
SERBS

CANADIANS
AMERICANS

Archangel
BRITISH
FRENCH

NORWAY

SWEDEN

FINLAND
(Independent)
1917

FINNS

Perm

Helsinki
Kronstadt
Petrograd (Leningrad)

Yudenich
1918–20

British fleet

ESTONIA

Pskov

LETTS

LATVIA   Riga   BALTIC
                     GERMANS

LITHUANIA

BOLSHEVIK   RUSSIA

Volga

Kazan

Kolchak 1918–19

CZECHS

Nizhniy-Novgorod

Moscow

Baltic Sea

GERMANY
(E. PRUSSIA)

Minsk

Smolensk

Mogilev

Kaluga

Penza

Samara

Orenburg

Vistula

Warsaw

Brest-
Litovsk

POLAND

POLES

Gomel

Orel

Tambov

Saratov

Ural

Zhitomir

Kiev

Denikin
1919

Kharkov

Poltava

Voronezh

Don

Tsaritsyn
(Stalingrad)

Volga

COSSACKS
1918–20

CZECHOSLOVAKIA

HUNGARY

ROMANIANS

UKRAINE

BESSARABIA

Dnieper

Dniester

Yekaterinoslav

Rostov-on-Don

Novocherkassak

Astrakhan

ROMANIA

Odessa

FRENCH

Cossacks

YUGOSLAVIA

Simferopol
FRENCH

Novorossiysk
BRITISH

BULGARIA

Danube

BRITISH
Batum

Tiflis

Baku

Krasnovodsk
BRITISH

GREECE

Entente fleet

Kars

BRITISH

BRITISH

TURKEY

Tabriz

1918–19

PERSIA

0   200   400 Km.

0   200   400 Mi.

A Marxist Critique of Communism

Karl Kautsky (1854–1938) was the leading spokesman for orthodox Marxism within the German Social Democratic Party, the most influential Marxist party in the world during the era of the Second International. Thus it is striking that he harshly criticized Leninist Bolshevism, or communism, as a heretical departure that could lead only to disaster. Kautsky's Terrorism and Communism, *written in 1919, was central to a volley of charges and countercharges that pitted him first against Lenin, then against Trotsky.*

The hereditary sin of Bolshevism has been its suppression of democracy through a form of government, namely, the dictatorship, which has no meaning unless it represents the unlimited and despotic power, either of one single person, or of a small organization intimately bound together. . . . It is as easy to begin a dictatorship as it is to begin war, if one has the State power under control. But when once such steps have been taken, it is as difficult at will to stop the one as the other. . . .

. . . [W]herever Socialism does not appear to be possible on a democratic basis, and where the majority of the population rejects it, its time has not yet fully come. Bolshevism, on the other hand, argues that Socialism can only be introduced by being forced on a majority by a minority. . . . The Bolsheviks are prepared, in order to maintain their position, to make all sorts of possible concessions to bureaucracy, to militarism, and to capitalism, whereas any concession to democracy seems to them to be sheer suicide. And yet that alone offers any possibility . . . of leading Russia along paths of economic progress and prosperous development towards some higher form of existence. . . .

. . . [S]ince the rise of the Soviet Republic, a new wedge has been driven through the Socialist ranks of Germany by Bolshevik propaganda, which has demanded that our Party should relinquish the essential claims of democracy. . . .

. . . It was only after long and bitter struggle that the proletariat succeeded in acquiring universal and equal suffrage—a perfectly well-known fact, which, however, all communists and their friends seem to have completely forgotten. Democracy, with its universal equal suffrage, is the method to transform the class-struggle out of a hand-to-hand fight into a battle of intelligence, in which one particular class can triumph only if it is intellectually and morally on a level with its opponent. Democracy is the one and only method through which the higher form of life can be realised. . . .

Source: Karl Kautsky, *Terrorism and Communism: A Contribution to the Natural History of Revolution* (Westport, Conn.: Hyperion Press, 1973), pp. 217–218, 220–222, 226, 229, 231.

Map 26.1   Foreign Intervention and Civil War in Revolutionary Russia, 1918–1920   By mid-1918 the new communist regime was under attack from many sides, by both foreign troops and anticommunist Russians. Bolshevik-held territory shrank during 1919, but over the next year the Red Army managed to regain much of what had been lost and to secure the new communist state. Anton Deniken, Alexander Kolchak, and Nicholas Yudenich commanded the most significant counterrevolutionary forces.
(Source: Adapted from The Times Atlas of World History, *3d ed. Copyright © HarperCollins Publishers, Ltd. Reprinted by permission of the publisher.)*

The Russians felt that poor organization and planning had undermined the wider revolutionary possibility in Europe during 1919 and 1920. The Comintern would therefore cut through all the revolutionary romanticism to show what the Leninist strategy, or communism, meant in fact. The Russians themselves would have to call the shots because what communism meant, above all, was tight organization and discipline.

The second Comintern congress, during the summer of 1920, devised twenty-one conditions for Comintern affiliation. Most notably, any socialist party seeking membership had to accept the Comintern's authority, adopt a centralized organization, and purge its reformists. By early 1921, the Comintern's aggressive claim to leadership had split the international socialist movement, for the Comintern attracted some, but not all, of the members of the existing socialist parties. Those who now called themselves "communists" accepted the Leninist model and affiliated with the Comintern. Those who retained the "socialist" label rejected Comintern leadership; they still claimed to be Marxists but declined to embrace the Bolshevik strategy for taking power.

At first, many European socialists had difficulty assessing the Comintern objectively. The Russian communists enjoyed great prestige because they had made a real revolution, while elsewhere socialists had talked and compromised, even getting swept up in wartime patriotism. When the French Socialist Party debated Comintern membership at its national congress in December 1920, about 70 percent of the delegates voted to join and agreed to the twenty-one points, while a minority walked out to form a new socialist party. But as the implications of Comintern membership became clearer over the next few years, the balance shifted in favor of the socialists. Membership in the French Communist Party, which stood at 131,000 in 1921, declined to 28,000 by 1932.

Late in 1923 the Comintern finally concluded that revolution elsewhere could not be expected any time soon. The immediate enemy was not capitalism or the bourgeoisie, but the socialists, the communists' rivals for working-class support. The communists' incessant criticism of the socialists, whom they eventually dubbed "social fascists," demoralized and weakened the European left, especially in the face of the growing threat of fascism by the early 1930s. The schism on the left remained an essential fact of European political life for half a century.

■ From Lenin to Stalin, 1921–1929

To win the civil war, the communist regime had adopted a policy of "war communism," a rough-and-ready controlled economy in which food and supplies were commandeered for the Red Army. At the beginning of 1921, the economy was in crisis. Industrial production equaled only about one-fifth the 1913 total, workers in key factories went on strike, and peasants were resisting further requisitions of grain. In March 1921 sailors at the Kronstadt naval base near Petrograd mutinied, suffering considerable loss of life as governmental control was reestablished.

With the very survival of the revolution in question, Lenin replaced war communism with the New Economic Policy (NEP) in March 1921. Although transport, banking, heavy industry, and wholesale commerce remained under state control, the NEP restored considerable scope for private enterprise, especially in the retail sector and in agriculture. Peasants could again sell some of their harvest. The economy quickly began to revive and by 1927 was producing at prewar levels.

But what about the longer term? If revolution elsewhere was not on the immediate horizon, could the Soviet Union—relatively backward economically and scarred by over a decade of upheaval—build a genuinely socialist order on its own? Certain measures were obvious: The new regime engineered rapid improvements in literacy, for example. But the Marxist understanding of historical progress required industrialization, and so debate focused on how to promote industrial development under Soviet conditions. That Soviet industrialization was somehow bound up with the creation of socialism was taken for granted.

This debate about priorities became intertwined with questions about the leadership of the new regime. Lenin suffered the first of a series of strokes in May 1922 and then died in January 1924, setting off a struggle among his possible successors. Leon Trotsky, an effective organizer and powerful thinker, was by most measures Lenin's heir apparent. Although he favored tighter economic controls to speed industrial development, Trotsky insisted that the Soviet Union's top priority should be spreading the revolution to other countries.

In contrast, Nikolai Bukharin (1888–1938) wanted to concentrate on the gradual development of the Soviet Union, based on a more open and conciliatory strategy than Trotsky envisioned. Rather than tightening controls to squeeze a surplus from agricultural producers, the government should promote purchasing power by allowing producers to profit. By the time of his death Lenin had apparently begun thinking along the same lines. And he had come to have considerable misgivings about the man who would win this struggle to direct the fragile new Soviet regime, Joseph Stalin (1879–1953).

Stalin was born Josef Djugashvili into a lower-class family in Georgia, in the Caucasus region. As an ethnic Georgian, he did not learn to speak Russian until he was 11 years old. From the position of party secretary, which he had assumed in 1922, Stalin established his control within the Soviet system by 1929. Though he lacked Trotsky's charisma and knew little of economics, he was highly intelligent and proved a master of backstage po-

Rivals for the Soviet Leadership   In July 1926 in Moscow, Soviet leaders carry the coffin of Feliks Dzerzhinsky, the first head of the secret police. Among them are Trotsky (*with glasses, center left*), Stalin (*right foreground*), and Bukharin (*with mustache, at far right*), rivals for the Soviet leadership after Lenin's death. The winner, Stalin, would eventually have his two competitors killed. *(David King Collection)*

litical maneuvering. Stalin first outmaneuvered Trotsky and his allies, removing them from positions of power and forcing Trotsky himself into exile in 1929. Bitterly critical of Stalin to the end, Trotsky was finally murdered by Stalin's agents in Mexico in 1940. Stalin's victory over those like Bukharin was more gradual, but ultimately just as decisive. And his victory proved decisive for the fate of Soviet communism.

By the latter 1920s, those who believed in the communist experiment were growing disillusioned with the compromises of the NEP. It was time for the Soviet Union to push ahead to a new order, leaving capitalism behind altogether. Even if revolution was not imminent elsewhere, the Soviet Union could seize the lead and build "socialism in one country." And genuine enthusiasm greeted the regime's turn to centralized economic planning in 1927, and its subsequent adoption of the first Five-Year Plan early in 1929. Central planning led to a program of crash industrialization, favoring heavy industry, by the end of that year. But this new, more radical direction was not fully thought through, and it soon caused incredible suffering.

To buy the necessary plants and equipment, the state seemed to require better control of agricultural output than had been possible under the New Economic

Policy. The key was to squeeze the agricultural surplus from the peasantry on terms more favorable to the government. By forcing peasants into large, state-controlled collective farms, government leaders could more readily extract the surplus, which would then be sold abroad, earning the money to finance factories, dams, and power plants.

Stalin's effort to mobilize society for the great task of rapid industrialization affected the whole shape of the regime—including cultural and artistic policy. During the 1920s, the possibility of building a new socialist society in the Soviet Union had attracted a number of modernist artists, who assumed that artistic innovation went hand in hand with the radical socioeconomic transformation the communists were seeking to engineer. These artists wanted to make art more socially useful and more central to the lives of ordinary people. With Soviet cultural officials welcoming their experiments, such Soviet artists as Vladimir Tatlin (1885–1956) and Kasimir Malevich (1878–1935) developed striking new cultural forms.

But in 1929 Soviet officials began mobilizing the cultural realm to serve the grandiose task of building socialism in one country. No longer welcoming experiment and innovation, they demanded "socialist realism," which portrayed the achievements of the ongoing Soviet

Tatlin: Monument to the Third International Vladimir Tatlin created this model for a monument to the Third International, or Comintern, during 1919 and 1920. He envisioned a revolving structure, made of glass and iron, and twice as tall as the later Empire State Building. Although the monument was never built, Tatlin's bold, dynamic form symbolized the utopian aspirations of the early years of the communist experiment in Russia. *(David King Collection)*

revolution in an inspiring, heroic light. Modernism, in contrast, they denounced as decadent and counterrevolutionary.

In retrospect, it is clear that a Stalinist revolution within the Soviet regime began in 1929, but where it was to lead was by no means certain—not even to Stalin himself. Still, the Soviet Union was pulling back, going its own way by the end of the 1920s. For the foreseeable future, the presence of a revolutionary regime in the old Russia would apparently be less disruptive for the rest of Europe than it had first appeared.

■ The Crisis of Liberal Italy and the Creation of Fascism, 1919–1925

Fascism emerged directly from the Italian experience of World War I, which proved especially controversial because the Italians could have avoided it altogether. No one attacked Italy in 1914, and the country could have received significant territorial benefits just by remaining neutral. Yet it seemed to many, including leading intellectuals and educated young people, that Italy could not stand idly by in a European war, especially one involving Austria-Hungary, which still controlled significant Italian-speaking areas. To participate in this major war would be the test of Italy's maturity as a nation. In May 1915 Italy finally intervened on the side of the Triple Entente. The government's decision stemmed not from vague visions of renewal but from the commitment of tangible territorial gains that France and Britain made to Italy with the secret Treaty of London in April.

Despite the near collapse of the Italian armies in October 1917, Italy lasted out the war and contributed to the victory over Austria-Hungary. Supporters of the war felt that this success could lead to a thoroughgoing renewal of Italian public life. Yet many Italians had been skeptical of claims for the war from the outset, and the fact that it proved so much more difficult than expected hardly won them over. To socialists, Catholics, and many left-leaning liberals, intervention itself had been a tragic mistake. Thus, despite Italy's participation in the victory, division over the war's significance immensely complicated the Italian political situation after the war was over.

Their skepticism was only confirmed when Italy did not secure all the gains it sought at the Paris Peace Conference. Italy got most of what it had been promised in the Treaty of London, but appetites increased with the dissolution of the Austro-Hungarian Empire. To some Italians, the disappointing outcome of the peace conference simply confirmed that the war had been a mistake, its benefits not worth the costs. But others were outraged at what seemed a denigration of the Italian contribution by France, Britain, and the United States. The outcome fanned resentment not only of Italy's allies but also of the country's political leaders, who seemed too weak to deliver on what they had pledged.

The established leaders of Italy's parliamentary democracy also failed at the task of renewing the country's political system in light of the war experience. To be sure, in a spirit of democratic reform, Italy adopted proportional representation to replace the old system of small, single-member constituencies in 1919. The new system meant a greater premium on mass parties and party discipline at the expense of the one-to-one bargaining that had characterized the earlier *trasformismo*. But the new multiparty system quickly reached an impasse—partly because of the stance of the Italian Socialist Party.

In contrast to the French and German parties, the Italian Socialists had never supported the war, and they did not accept the notion that the war experience could yield political renewal in the aftermath. So rather than reaching out to idealistic but discontented war veterans,

Socialist leaders talked of imitating the Bolshevik Revolution. And the Italian situation seemed at least potentially revolutionary during 1919 and 1920, when a wave of national strikes culminated in a series of factory occupations. But despite their revolutionary rhetoric, Italy's Socialist leaders did not understand the practical aspects of Leninism and did not carry out the planning and organization that might have produced an Italian revolution.

The established parliamentary system was at an impasse, and the Socialist Party seemed at once too inflexible and too romantic to lead some sort of radical transformation. It was in this context that fascism emerged, claiming to offer a third way. It was bound to oppose the Socialists and the socialist working class because of conflict over the meaning of the war and the kind of transformation Italy needed. And this antisocialist posture made fascism open to exploitation by reactionary interests. By early 1921 landowners in northern and central Italy were footing the bill as bands of young fascists drove around the countryside in trucks, beating up workers and burning down socialist meeting halls. But fascist spokesmen claimed to offer something other than mere reaction—a new politics that all Italians, including the workers, would eventually find superior.

At the same time, important sectors of Italian industry, which had grown rapidly thanks to government orders during the war, looked with apprehension toward the more competitive international economy that loomed now that the war was over. With its relative lack of capital and raw materials, Italy seemed to face an especially difficult situation. Nationalist thinkers and business spokesmen questioned the capacity of the present parliamentary system to provide the vigorous leadership that Italy needed. Prone to short-term bickering and partisanship, ordinary politicians lacked the vision to pursue Italy's international economic interests and the will to impose the necessary discipline on the domestic level. Thus the government's response to the labor unrest of 1919 and 1920 was hesitant and weak. (See the box "Reading Sources: Toward Fascism: Alfredo Rocco on the Weakness of the Liberal Democratic State.")

Postwar Italy, then, witnessed widespread discontent with established forms of politics, but those discontented were socially disparate, and their aims were not entirely compatible. Some had been socialists before the war, others nationalists hostile to socialism. While some envisioned a more intense kind of mass politics, others thought the masses already had too much power. Still, these discontented groups agreed on the need for an alternative to both conventional parliamentary politics

🐦 READING SOURCES

Toward Fascism: Alfredo Rocco on the Weakness of the Liberal Democratic State

As Italy's minister of justice from 1925 to 1932, the Italian legal scholar Alfredo Rocco (1875–1935) spearheaded the construction of the new fascist state. Speaking in November 1920, he revealed why he would seek to replace parliamentary democracy with a new, stronger form of government. Rocco was troubled, most immediately, by the apparent weakness of the liberal state in the face of strikes by unions, or syndicates, of public service employees. But the deeper problem he saw was liberal individualism, linked to shortsighted pursuit of personal advantage.

There is a crisis within the state; day by day, the state is dissolving into a mass of small particles, parties, associations, groups and syndicates that are binding it in chains and paralysing and stifling its activity: one by one, with increasing speed, the state is losing its attributes of sovereignty. . . . The conflict of interests between groups and classes is now being settled by the use of private force alone. . . . The state stands by impassively watching these conflicts which involve countless violations of public and private rights. This neutrality which, in liberal doctrine, was intended to allow free play for economic law in the clash of interests between the classes is now being interpreted as allowing the state to abandon its essential function of guardian of public order and agent of justice. . . .

. . . The eighteenth-century reaction against the state . . . came to a head politically in the explosion of the French Revolution. . . . From that time onwards, the claims of individualism knew no bounds. The masses of individuals wanted to govern the state and govern it in accordance with their own individual interests. The state, a living organism with a continuous existence over the centuries that extends beyond

successive generations and as such the guardian of the immanent historical interests of the species, was turned into a monopoly to serve the individual interests of each separate generation. . . .

Now there can be no doubt that one of the most serious consequences of liberal agnosticism was the emergence of syndicalism, a syndicalism that was at once violent, subversive, and opposed to the state.

. . . The state must return to its traditions, interrupted by the triumph of liberal ideology, and treat the modern syndicates exactly as it treated the medieval corporations. It must absorb them and make them part of the state. . . . On the one hand, syndicates must be recognized as essential and on the other they must be placed firmly beneath the control of the state. . . . But above all, it is necessary to change them from aggressive bodies defending particular interests into a means of collaboration to achieve common aims.

Source: Adrian Lyttelton, ed., *Italian Fascisms from Pareto to Gentile* (New York: Harper & Row, Harper Torchbooks, 1975), pp. 269, 273–275, 278–280.

and conventional Marxist socialism. And all found the germs of that alternative in the Italian war experience.

The person who seemed able to translate these aspirations into a new political force was Benito Mussolini (1883–1945), who had been a prominent socialist journalist before the war. Indeed, he was so talented that he was made editor of the Socialist Party's national newspaper in 1912, when he was only 29 years old. At that point

many saw him as the fresh face needed to revitalize Italian socialism.

His concern with renewal made Mussolini an unorthodox socialist even before 1914, and he was prominent among those on the Italian left who began calling for Italian intervention once the war began. The fact that socialists in France, Germany, and elsewhere had immediately rallied to their respective national war efforts

Benito Mussolini   The founder of fascism is shown with other fascist leaders in 1922, as he becomes prime minister of Italy. Standing at Mussolini's right (*with beard*) is Italo Balbo, later a pioneering aviator and fascist Italy's air force minister.   *(Corbis)*

raised new questions about conventional socialism, based on international proletarian solidarity. But the Italian Socialist Party refused to follow his call for intervention, remaining neutralist and aloof, so Mussolini found himself cut off from his earlier constituency.

However, through his new newspaper, *Il popolo d'Italia (The People of Italy)*, Mussolini helped rally the disparate groups that advocated Italian participation in the war. He saw military service once Italy intervened, and after the war he seemed a credible spokesman for those who wanted to translate the war experience into a new form of politics. Amid growing political unrest, he founded the fascist movement in March 1919, taking the term *fascism* from the ancient Roman *fasces,* a bundle of rods surrounding an ax that guards carried at state occasions as a symbol of power and unity.

But fascism was not a major force at first. And even as it gathered force in violent reaction against the socialist labor organizations by 1921, the movement's direc-

tion was something of a mystery. Although young fascist militants wanted to replace the established parliamentary system with a new political order, Mussolini seemed ever more prone to use fascism as his personal instrument to achieve power within the existing system. When his maneuvering finally won him the prime minister's post in October 1922, it was not at all clear that a change of regime, or a one-party dictatorship, was at hand.

At that point, Mussolini, like most Italians, emphasized normalization and legality. Fascism had apparently been absorbed within the political system, perhaps to provide an infusion of youthful vitality after the war. With Mussolini as prime minister, there would be changes, but not revolutionary changes. Government would become more vigorous and efficient; the swollen Italian bureaucracy would be streamlined; the trains would run on time. But those who had envisioned more sweeping change were frustrated that nothing more had come of fascism than this.

A crisis in 1924 forced Mussolini's hand. In June the moderate socialist Giacomo Matteotti° rose in parliament to denounce the renewed fascist violence that had accompanied recent national elections. His murder by fascist thugs shortly thereafter produced a great public outcry, though the responsibility of Mussolini and his government was unclear. Many establishment figures who had tolerated Mussolini as the man who could keep order now deserted him. A growing chorus called for his resignation.

Mussolini sought at first to be conciliatory, but more radical fascists saw the crisis as an opportunity to end the compromise with the old liberal order and to begin creating a whole new political system. The crisis came to a head on December 31, 1924, when thirty-three militants called on Mussolini to demand that he make up his mind. In their view, the way out of the crisis was not to delimit the scope of fascism but to expand it. Mussolini was not an ordinary prime minister but the leader of fascism, *Il Duce*°. In that role he would have to accept responsibility even for his movement's violent excesses and finally begin implementing a full-scale fascist revolution.

Mussolini committed himself to this more radical course in a speech to the Chamber of Deputies a few days later, on January 3, 1925. Defiantly claiming the "full political, moral, and historical responsibility for all that has happened," including "all the acts of violence," he promised to accelerate the transformation that he claimed to have initiated with his agitation for intervention in 1914 and 1915.[1] And now began the creation of a new fascist state, although the compromises continued and the direction was never as clear as committed fascists desired.

■ Innovation and Compromise in Fascist Italy, 1925–1930

Early in 1925, the fascist government began to undermine the existing democratic system by imprisoning or exiling opposition leaders and outlawing nonfascist parties and labor unions. But fascism was not seeking simply a conventional monopoly of political power; the new fascist state was to be totalitarian, all-encompassing, limitless in its reach. Under the old liberal regime, the fascists charged, the state had been too weak to promote the national interest, and Italian society had been too fragmented to achieve its full potential. So Mussolini's regime both expanded the state's sovereignty and mobilized the society to create a deeper sense of national identity and shared purpose. To settle labor disputes, a new system of labor judges replaced the right to strike, which, the fascists claimed, had fostered neither productivity nor long-term working-class interests. And the Fascist Party founded new organizations—for youth, for women, for leisure-time activities—that would make possible new forms of public participation.

The centerpiece of the new fascist state was corporativism, which entailed mobilizing people as producers, through organization of the workplace. Groupings based on occupation, or economic function, were gradually to replace parliament as the basis for political participation and decision making. Beginning in 1926, corporativist institutions were established in stages until a Chamber of Fasces and Corporations at last replaced the old Chamber of Deputies in 1939.

Especially through this corporative state, the fascists claimed to be fulfilling their grandiose mission and providing the world with a third way, beyond both outmoded democracy and misguided communism. The practice of corporativism never lived up to such rhetoric, but the effort to devise new forms of political participation and decision making was central to fascism's self-understanding and its quest for legitimacy. And that effort attracted much attention abroad, especially with the Great Depression of the 1930s.

Despite the commitment to a new regime, however, fascism continued to compromise with pre-existing elites and institutions. The accommodation was especially evident in the arrangements with the Catholic Church that Mussolini worked out in 1929, formally ending the dispute between the church and the Italian state that had festered since national unification in 1870. With the Lateran Pact, Mussolini restored a measure of sovereignty of the Vatican; with the Concordat, he conceded to the church autonomy in education and supremacy in marriage law.

This settlement of an old and thorny dispute afforded Mussolini a good deal of prestige among nonfascists at home and abroad. But compromise with the church could only displease committed fascists, who complained that giving this powerful, autonomous institution a role in Italian public life undermined the totalitarian aspirations of fascism. Such complaints led to a partial crackdown on Catholic youth organizations in 1931, as Mussolini continued trying to juggle traditionalist compromise and revolutionary pretension.

Matteotti (mah-tay-OH-tee) **Il Duce** (eel DOO-chay)

By the end of the 1920s, then, it remained unclear whether Italian fascism was a form of restoration or a form of revolution. It had restored order in Italy, overcoming the labor unrest of the immediate postwar years, but it was order on a new, antidemocratic basis. Yet the fascists claimed to be implementing a revolution of their own at the same time. Fascism could be violent and disruptive, dictatorial and repressive, but Mussolini seemed dynamic and creative. Though its ultimate direction remained nebulous, fascism attracted those elsewhere who were discontented with liberal democracy and Marxist socialism. It thus fed the volatility and ideological polarization that marked the European political order after World War I.

TOWARD MASS SOCIETY

FTER a few years of wild economic swings just after the war, Europe was enjoying renewed prosperity by the later 1920s. Common involvement in the war had blurred class lines and accelerated the trend toward what contemporaries began to call "mass society." As the new prosperity spread the fruits of industrialization more widely, ordinary people increasingly set the cultural tone, partly through new mass media such as film and radio. To some, the advent of mass society portended a welcome revitalization of culture and a more authentic kind of democracy, whereas others saw only a debasement of cultural standards and a susceptibility to populist demagoguery. But though the contours of mass society now became evident, social change did not keep up with the promise of—and the requirements for—democratic politics.

■ Economic Readjustment and the New Prosperity

In their effort to return to normal, governments were quick to dismantle wartime planning and control mechanisms. But the needs of war had stimulated innovations that helped fuel the renewed economic growth of the 1920s. The civilian air industry, for example, developed rapidly during the decade by taking advantage of wartime work on aviation for military purposes. More generally, newer industries such as chemicals, electricity, and advanced machinery led the way to a new prosperity in the 1920s, which significantly altered patterns of life in the more industrialized parts of the West. The automobile, a luxury plaything for the wealthy before the war, began to be mass-produced in western Europe. In France, automobile production shot up dramatically, from 40,000 in 1920 to 254,000 in 1929.

But the heady pace masked problems that lay beneath the relative prosperity of the 1920s, even in victorious Britain and France. While new industries prospered, old ones declined in the face of new technologies and stronger foreign competition. In Britain, the industries responsible for Britain's earlier industrial pre-eminence—textiles, coal, shipbuilding, and iron and steel—were now having trouble competing. Rather than investing in new technologies, companies in these industries demanded government protection and imposed lower wages and longer hours on their workers. At the same time, British labor unions resisted the mechanization necessary to make these older industries more competitive.

Rather than realistically assessing Britain's prospects in the more competitive international economy, British leaders sought to return to the prewar situation, based on the gold standard, with London the world's financial center. For many Britons, the government's announcement in 1925 that the British pound was again freely convertible to gold at 1914 exchange rates was the long-awaited indication that normality had returned at last. Yet the return to 1914 exchange rates overvalued the pound relative to the U.S. dollar, making British goods more expensive on export markets and making it still more difficult for aging British industries to compete. Further, Britain no longer had sufficient capital to act as the world's banker. By trying to do so, Britain became all the more vulnerable when the international economy reached a crisis in 1929.

The structural decline of older industries was clearest in Britain, but inflation and its psychological impact was most prominent in Germany and France. By the summer of 1923, Germany's response to the French occupation of the Ruhr had transformed an already serious inflationary problem, stemming from wartime deficit spending, into one of the great hyperinflations in history. At its height in November, when it took 4.2 trillion marks to equal a dollar, Germans were forced to cart wheelbarrows of paper money to stores to buy ordinary grocery items. By the end of 1923, the government managed to stabilize prices through currency reform and drastically reduced government spending—a combination that elicited greater cooperation from the victors. But the rampant inflation, and the readjustment necessary to control it, had wiped out the life savings of ordinary people while profiting speculators and those in debt, including some large industrialists. This inequity left scars that remained even as Germany enjoyed a measure of prosperity in the years that followed.

Inflation was less dramatic in France, but there, too, it affected perceptions and priorities in significant ways. For over a century, from the Napoleonic era to the outbreak of war in 1914, the value of the French franc had remained stable. But the war started France on an inflationary cycle that shattered the security of its many small savers—those, such as teachers and shopkeepers, who had been the backbone of the Third Republic. To repay war debts and rebuild war-damaged industries, the French government continued to run budget deficits,

and thereby cause inflation, even after 1918. Runaway inflation threatened during 1925 and 1926, but the franc was finally restabilized in 1928, though at only about one-fifth its prewar value.

On the international level, war debts and reparations strained the financial system, creating problems with the financing of trade. But in the course of the 1920s, experts made adjustments that seemed to be returning the international exchange system to equilibrium. Only in retrospect, after the international capitalist system fell into crisis late in 1929, did it become clear how potent those strains were—and how inadequate the efforts at readjustment.

The Legacy of Inflation in Germany
Packets of worthless old banknotes serve as children's building blocks in November 1923. The German government had just introduced a new currency in an effort to check a price inflation that had reached 2,500 percent a month. Although the inflation was brought under control by the end of the year, it produced lasting scars. Many ordinary Germans found their savings wiped out entirely.   *(© Hulton-Deutsch Collection/Corbis)*

■ Work, Leisure, and the New Popular Culture

The wartime spur to industrialization produced a large increase in the industrial labor force all over Europe, and a good deal of labor unrest accompanied the transition to peacetime. Some of that agitation challenged factory discipline and authority relationships. Seeking to re-establish authority on a new basis for the competitive postwar world, business leaders and publicists fostered a new cult of efficiency and productivity, partly by adapting Taylorism and Fordism, influential American ideas about mass production. On the basis of his "time-and-motion" studies of factory labor, Frederick W. Taylor (1856–1915) argued that breaking down assembly-line production into small, repetitive tasks was the key to maximizing worker efficiency. In contrast, Henry Ford (1863–1947) linked the gospel of mass production to mass consumption. In exchange for accepting the discipline of the assembly line, the workers should be paid well enough to be able to buy the products they produced—even automobiles. Sharing in the prosperity that mass production made possible, factory workers would be loyal to the companies that employed them. Not all Europeans, however, welcomed the new ideas from America. In the new cult of efficiency and mass production, some saw an unwelcome sameness and a debasement of cultural standards.

In light of the major role women had played in the wartime labor force, the demand for women's suffrage proved irresistible in Britain, Germany, and much of Europe, though not yet in France or Italy. In Britain, where the call for women's suffrage had earlier met with controversy (see page 827), the right to vote was readily conceded in 1918, though at first only to women over 30. By now women no longer seemed a threat to the political system. And in fact British women, once they could vote, simply flowed into the existing parties, countering earlier hopes—and fears—that a specifically feminist political agenda would follow from women's suffrage.

Although female employment remained higher than before the war, many women were willing to return home, yielding their jobs to the returning soldiers. The need to replace the men killed in the war lent renewed force to the traditional notion that women served society, and fulfilled themselves, by marrying and rearing families. Still, the spirit of innovation brought into the public arena subjects with significant implications for gender roles—subjects largely taboo before the war. The desire to be "modern" produced, for example, a more open, unsentimental, even scientific discussion of sexuality and reproduction.

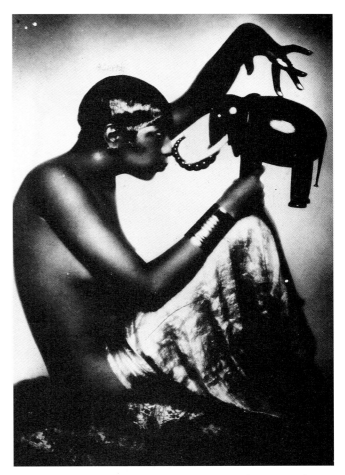

The Sensational Josephine Baker   A native of St. Louis, the African American Josephine Baker moved to Paris in 1925 and quickly created a sensation in both France and Germany as a cabaret dancer and singer. Playing on the European association of Africa with the wild and uninhibited, she featured unusual poses and exotic costumes.   *(Hulton Getty/Liaison)*

The new "rationalization of sexuality" fed demands that governments provide access to sex counseling, birth control, and even abortion as they assumed ever greater responsibilities for promoting social health. This trend was especially prominent in Germany, although German innovators learned from experiments in the new Soviet Union and from the birth control movement that Margaret Sanger (1883–1966) was spearheading in the United States.

The more open and tolerant attitude toward sexuality affected popular entertainment. Thus, for example, Josephine Baker's dancing and costumes—unthinkable before the war. Another result was the emergence of a more visible gay subculture, prominent especially in the vibrant cabaret scene in Berlin during the 1920s.

Weimar Cinema   This poster advertises Fritz Lang's film *Metropolis,* which explored the dehumanization and exploitation of the modern city.   *(Schulz-Neudamm, Metropolis, 1926. Lithograph, 83" × 36½". The Museum of Modern Art, New York. Gift of Universum Film Aktiengesellschaft.)*

Mass consumption followed from the mass production that created the new prosperity of the 1920s. As it became possible to mass-produce the products of the second industrial transformation, more people could afford automobiles, electrical gadgets such as radios and phonographs, and clothing of synthetic fabrics, developed through innovations in chemistry. First came rayon, produced in small quantities since 1891 but mass-produced beginning in the 1920s. In this new artificial form, silk, long one of the trappings of wealth, was now within the means of ordinary people.

With the eight-hour workday increasingly the norm, growing attention was devoted to leisure as a positive source of human fulfillment—for everyone, not just the wealthy. European beach resorts grew crowded as more people had the time, and the means, to take vacations. An explosion of interest in soccer among Europeans paralleled the growth of professional baseball and college football in the United States. Huge stadiums were built across Europe.

The growth of leisure was linked to the development of mass media and mass culture. During the early 1920s radio became a commercial venture, reaching a mass audience in Europe, as in the United States and Canada. Although movies had begun to emerge as vehicles of popular entertainment even before the war, they came into their own during the 1920s, when the names of film stars became household words for the first time.

The rapid development of film showed that new, more accessible media could nurture extraordinary innovation. Germany led the way with such films as *The Cabinet of Dr. Caligari* (1920), *Metropolis* (1927), and *The Blue Angel* (1930), but the Russian Sergei Eisenstein (1898–1948) became perhaps the most admired film maker of the era with *Battleship Potemkin* (1925), his brilliant portrayal of the Russian revolution of 1905. In some spheres, however, America was beginning to outdo both Paris and Berlin. Marlene Dietrich (1901–1992), famous as Lola Lola in *The Blue Angel,* was among a number of German film celebrities who went to Hollywood.

Exploiting the new popular fascination with air travel, the American Charles Lindbergh (1902–1974) captured the European imagination in 1927 with the first solo flight across the Atlantic. Lindbergh's feat epitomized the affirmative side of the decade—the sense that there were new worlds to conquer and that there still were heroes to admire, despite the ironies of the war and the ambiguities of the peace.

■ Society and Politics in the Victorious Democracies

France and Britain seemed the best positioned of the major European countries to take advantage of renewed peace and stability to confront the sociopolitical problems of the postwar era. And during the 1920s, each seemed to return to normal. But was normal good enough, in light of the rupture of the war and the challenges of the emerging mass society?

Victory in the Great War seemed to belie France's prewar concerns about decadence and decline. In the immediate aftermath of the war, Clemenceau and other French leaders were confident in dealing with radical labor unrest and aggressive in translating the battlefield victory into a dominant position on the European continent. But the tremendous loss of French lives had produced a new fear—that France could not withstand another such challenge. The renewed confidence thus proved hollow.

Although some in prewar France had worried about falling behind rapidly industrializing Germany, victory seemed to have vindicated France's more cautious, balanced economy, with its blend of industry and agriculture. Thus the prewar mistrust of rapid industrial development continued. Rather than foster a program of economic modernization that might have promoted genuine security, the French pulled back even from the measure of state responsibility for the economy that had developed during the war.

To be sure, in France, as elsewhere, the 1920s was a decade of relative prosperity. Led by the oil and electricity industries, the economy grew at an annual rate of 4.6 percent between 1923 and 1929, double the prewar rate. Industrial production by 1929 was 40 percent higher than it had been in 1913. But, with the exception of Britain, other Western economies grew more rapidly during the 1920s, and the opportunity that growth afforded to modernize the French economy was not seized. Although government grants helped reconstruct almost eight thousand factories, most were simply rebuilt as they had been before the war. Moreover, the working class benefited little from the relative prosperity of the 1920s. Housing remained poor, wages failed to keep up with inflation, and France continued to lag other countries in social legislation.

Britain, too, made certain adjustments after the war but missed the chance to make others. The government's handling of the Easter Rebellion in Ireland in 1916 (see page 853) intensified anti-British feeling and fed further violence. But the British finally forged at least a provisional resolution. The first step was to partition Ireland, creating a separate Ulster, or Northern Ireland, from those counties with Protestant majorities. Ulster then remained under the British crown when a new independent Republic of Ireland was established in the larger, majority Catholic part of the island in 1922.

The British political system remained stable between the wars, although the Labour Party supplanted the Liberals to become the dominant alternative to the Conservatives by the early 1920s. The Labour Party even got a brief taste of power when Ramsay MacDonald (1866–1937) formed Britain's first Labour government in January 1924. The coming of Labour to power resulted in a significant expansion of the governmental elite to incorporate those, like MacDonald himself, with genuinely working-class backgrounds.

The rise of Labour was striking, but it was the Conservative leader, Stanley Baldwin (1867–1947), who set the tone for British politics between the wars in three stints as prime minister during the years from 1923 to 1937. Although the wealthy son of a steel manufacturer, Baldwin deliberately departed from the old aristocratic style of British Conservative politics. More down-to-earth and pragmatic than his predecessors, he was the first British prime minister to use radio effectively, and he made an effort to foster good relations with workers. Yet Baldwin's era was one of growing social tension.

With exports declining, unemployment remained high in Britain throughout the interwar period, never falling below 10 percent. The coal industry, though still the country's largest employer, had become a particular trouble spot in the British economy. As coal exports declined, British mine owners became ever more aggressive in their dealings with labor, finally, in 1926, insisting on a longer workday and a wage cut of 13 percent to restore competitiveness. The result was a coal miners' strike in May that promptly turned into a general strike, involving almost all of organized labor—about 4 million workers—in the most notable display of trade-union solidarity Britain had ever seen. For nine days the economy stood at a virtual standstill. But threats of arrest and a growing public backlash forced the union leadership to accept a compromise. The miners continued the strike on their own, but they finally returned to work six months later at considerably lower wages.

Although for somewhat different reasons, Britain and France both failed during the 1920s to take advantage of what would soon seem, in retrospect, to have been a precious opportunity to adjust their economies, heal social wounds, and create more genuinely democratic political systems. The lost opportunity would mean growing social tensions once the relative prosperity of the decade had ended.

WEIMAR GERMANY AND THE TRIALS OF THE NEW DEMOCRACIES

THE war was supposed to have paved the way for democracy, and the fall of the monarchies in Russia, Germany, and Austria-Hungary seemed almost made-to-order invitations. But events quickly overwhelmed the new democracy in Russia in 1917. After the war was over, circumstances seemed more favorable in Germany, Poland, and elsewhere in central Europe, but almost everywhere the new democracies led tortured lives and soon gave way to more authoritarian forms of government. So the postwar decade did not see the extension and consolidation of the political democracy that optimistic observers associated with the emerging mass society.

The most significant test took place in Germany, which adopted its first fully democratic constitution in 1919, as the new Weimar Republic emerged from the provisional revolutionary republic proclaimed in November 1918. But the Weimar democracy had great difficulty establishing its legitimacy, and it was suffering serious strains by 1930.

■ Democracy Aborted in East-Central Europe

New democracies were established in much of central and eastern Europe after the war, but except in Czechoslovakia and Finland the practice of parliamentary government did not match the initial promise. Democracy seemed divisive and ineffective, so one country after another adopted a more authoritarian alternative during the 1920s and early 1930s.

Poland offers the most dramatic example. Although its democratic constitution of 1921 established a cabinet responsible to a parliamentary majority, the parliament fragmented into so many parties that instability proved endemic from the start. Poland had fourteen different ministries from November 1918 to May 1926, when Marshal Josef Pilsudski led a coup d'état that replaced parliamentary government with an authoritarian regime stressing national unity. This suppression of democracy came as a relief to many Poles—and was welcomed even by the trade unions. After Pilsudski's death in 1935, a group of colonels ruled Poland until the country was conquered by Nazi Germany in 1939.

Democracy proved hard to manage in east-central Europe partly because of the economic difficulties resulting from the breakup of the Habsburg system. New national borders meant new economic barriers that disrupted long-standing economic relationships. Industrial centers such as Vienna and Budapest found themselves cut off from their traditional markets and sources of raw materials. In what was now Poland, Silesians had long been oriented toward Germany, Galicians toward Vienna, and those in eastern Poland toward Russia. Thus the new Polish nation-state was hardly a cohesive economic unit.

The countries of east-central Europe remained overwhelmingly agrarian, and this, too, proved unconducive to democracy. Land reform that accompanied the transition to democracy made small properties the norm in much of the region. But because these units were often too small to be efficient, agricultural output actually decreased after land was redistributed, most dramatically in Romania and Yugoslavia. When agricultural prices declined in the late 1920s, many peasants had no choice but to sell out to larger landowners. What had seemed a progressive and democratic reform thus failed to provide a stable agrarian smallholder base for democracy.

■ Germany's Cautious Revolution, 1919–1920

Meanwhile, in Germany, the Weimar Republic began under particularly difficult circumstances. Born of military defeat, it was promptly forced to take responsibility for the harsh and dictated Treaty of Versailles in 1919. During its first years, moreover, the regime encountered severe economic dislocation, culminating in the hyperinflation of 1923, as well as ideological polarization that threatened to tear the country apart.

Although Germany had strong military and authoritarian traditions, the initial threat to the new democracy came not from the right, disoriented and discredited, but from the left, stimulated by the Russian example. Those seeking further revolution, and those who feared it, could easily equate the proclamation of a German republic with the first revolution in Russia; as in Russia, the new, more democratic order could prove a mere prelude to communist revolution.

Spearheaded by Karl Liebknecht and Rosa Luxemburg in Berlin, revolutionary unrest reached its peak in Germany during December 1918 and January 1919. But even after Liebknecht and Luxemburg were captured and murdered in January, a serious chance of further revolution persisted through May 1919, and communist revolutionary agitation continued to flare up until the end of 1923.

As it turned out, there was no further revolution, partly because the parallel between Germany and Russia carried only so far. The new German government had made peace, whereas the leaders of the provisional government in Russia had sought to continue the war. Furthermore, those who ended up controlling the councils that sprang up in Germany during the fall of 1918 favored political democracy, not communist revolution, and therefore they supported the provisional government.

Even so, the revolutionary minority constituted a credible threat. And the new government made repression of the extreme left a priority—even if it meant leaving in place some of the institutions and personnel of the old imperial system. In November 1918, at the birth of the new republic, the moderate socialist leader Friedrich Ebert had agreed with General Wilhelm Groener, the new army leader, to preserve the old imperial officer corps to help prevent further revolution. But when the regular army, weakened by war and defeat, proved unable to control radical agitation in Berlin in December, it seemed the republic would have to take extraordinary measures to defend itself from the revolutionary left. With the support of Ebert and Groener, Gustav Noske (1868–1946), the minister of national defense, began to organize "Free Corps," volunteer paramilitary groups to be used against the revolutionaries. Noske, who was a socialist, but one long supportive of the military, noted that "somebody will have to be the bloodhound—I won't shirk the responsibility."[2]

During the first five months of 1919, the government unleashed the Free Corps to crush leftist movements all over Germany, often with wanton brutality. In relying on right-wing paramilitary groups, the republic's leaders were playing with fire, but the immediate threat at this point came from the left. In 1920, however, the government faced a right-wing coup attempt, the Kapp Putsch. The army declined to defend the republic, but the government managed to survive thanks largely to a general strike by leftist workers. The republic's early leaders had to juggle both extremes because, as one of them put it, the Weimar Republic was "a candle burning at both ends."

Though sporadic street fighting by paramilitary groups continued, the republic survived its traumatic birth and achieved an uneasy stability by 1924. But Germany's postwar revolution had remained confined to the political level. There was no program to break up the car-tels, with their concentrations of economic power. Even on the level of government personnel, continuity was more striking than change. There was no effort to build a loyal republican army, and no attempt to purge the bureaucracy and the judiciary of antidemocratic elements from the old imperial order. When right-wing extremists assassinated prominent leaders, such as the Jewish industrialist Walther Rathenau in 1922, the courts often proved unwilling to prosecute those responsible. In general, those who ran the new government day to day were often skeptical of democracy, even hostile to the new regime.

In light of the republic's eventual failure, the willingness of its early leaders to leave intact so much from the old order has made them easy targets for criticism. It can be argued, however, that the course they followed—heading off the extreme left, reassuring the established elites, and playing for time—was the republic's best chance for success. The new regime might establish its legitimacy by inertia, much like the Third Republic in France, which had similarly been born of defeat. Even lacking the sentimental fervor that had earlier surrounded democratic ideals, Germans might gradually become "republicans of reason," recognizing that this regime could be a framework for prosperity and renewed German prominence in international affairs. In the event of an early crisis, however, a republic consolidating itself in this cautious way might well find fewer defenders than opponents.

Elections in January 1919 produced a constituent assembly that convened in Weimar, a town associated with what seemed the most humane German cultural traditions, to draft a democratic constitution. The elections took place before the peace conference had produced the widely detested Treaty of Versailles. When the first regular parliamentary elections finally were held in June 1920, the three moderate parties that had led the new government, and that had been forced to accept the treaty, suffered a major defeat, dropping from 76 to 47 percent of the seats. These were the parties most committed to democratic institutions, but they were never again to achieve a parliamentary majority.

The 1920 elections revealed the problems of polarization and lack of consensus that would bedevil, and eventually ruin, the Weimar Republic. Because the electorate found it difficult to agree, or even to compromise, Germany settled into a multiparty system that led to unstable coalition government. And the strength, or potential strength, of the extremes immeasurably complicated political life for those trying to make the new democracy work. On the left, the Communists constantly criticized

Hopes for Peace Foreign ministers Aristide Briand (*left*) of France and Gustav Stresemann of Germany spearheaded the improved international relations that bred optimism during the later 1920s. *(Corbis)*

the more moderate Socialists for supporting the republic. On the right, the Nationalist Party (DNVP) played on nationalist resentments and fears of the extreme left—but the result was similarly to dilute support for the new republic. To the right even of the Nationalists were Adolf Hitler's National Socialists, or Nazis, who were noisy and often violent, but they attracted little electoral support before 1930.

■ Gustav Stresemann and the Scope for Gradual Consolidation, 1920–1929

All was not necessarily lost for the republic when the three moderate, pro-Weimar parties were defeated in 1920. Germans who were unsupportive or hostile at first might be gradually won over. After the death of President Ebert in 1925, Paul von Hindenburg, the emperor's field marshal, was elected president. Depending on the circumstances, having a conservative military leader from the old order in this role could be advantageous, or

damaging, for the future of democracy. As long as scope for consolidation remained, Hindenburg's presidency suggested to skeptics that the new regime was legitimate and a worthy object of German patriotism. But when crisis came by 1930, Hindenburg was quick to give up on parliamentary government—with devastating results.

The individual who best exemplified the possibility of winning converts to the Weimar Republic was Gustav Stresemann° (1878–1929), the leader of the German People's Party (DVP), a conservative party that did not support the republic at the outset. But it was relatively flexible and offered at least the possibility of broadening the republic's base of support. As chancellor, and especially as foreign minister, Stresemann proved the republic's leading statesman.

Stresemann's background and instincts were not democratic, but by the end of 1920 Germany's postwar

---

Stresemann (STRAY-zuh-mahn)

political volatility had convinced him that if the new republic should go under, the outcome would not be the conservative monarchy he preferred but the triumph of the extreme left. Moreover, it had become clear that the new democratic republic was not likely to be revolutionary on the socioeconomic level. It made sense, then, to work actively to make the new regime succeed. From within this framework Germany could pursue its international aims, negotiating modifications of the Versailles treaty and returning to great power status.

Stresemann became chancellor in August 1923, when inflation was raging out of control. Within months his government managed to get the German economy functioning effectively again, partly because the French agreed that an international commission should review the reparations question, specifying realistic amounts based on Germany's ability to pay. During the summer of 1924, a commission led by the American financier Charles G. Dawes produced the Dawes Plan, which remained in force until 1929. The plan worked well by pinpointing revenue sources, lowering payments, providing loans, and securing the stability of the German currency. With the expiration of the Dawes Plan in 1929, the Young Plan, conceived by American businessman Owen D. Young, removed Allied controls over the German economy and specified that Germany pay reparations until 1988. The annual amount was less than Germany had been paying, so it was expected that this plan constituted a permanent, and reasonable, settlement.

Quite apart from the immediate economic issue, Stresemann understood that better relations with the victors, starting with France, had to be a priority if Germany was to return to the councils of the great powers. French foreign minister Aristide Briand° (1862–1932) shared Stresemann's desire for improved relations, and together they engineered a new, more conciliatory spirit in international affairs. Its most substantial fruit was the Treaty of Locarno of 1925. France and Germany accepted the postwar border between the two countries, which meant that Germany gave up any claim to Alsace-Lorraine. France, for its part, renounced the sort of direct military intervention in Germany that it had attempted with the Ruhr invasion of 1923 and agreed to begin withdrawing troops from the Rhineland ahead of schedule. On the other hand, Germany freely accepted France's key advantage, the demilitarization of the Rhineland, and Britain and Italy now explicitly guaranteed the measure.

By accepting the status quo in the west, Stresemann was freeing Germany to concentrate on eastern Europe,

where he envisioned gradual but substantial revision in the territorial settlement that had resulted from the war. Especially with the creation of Poland, that settlement had come partly at Germany's expense. Stresemann, then, was pursuing German interests, not subordinating them to some larger European vision. But he was willing to compromise and, for the most part, to play by the rules as he did so.

With the Locarno treaty, the victors accepted Germany as a diplomatic equal for the first time since the war. Germany's return to good graces culminated in its entry into the League of Nations in 1926. The new spirit of reconciliation was widely welcomed. Indeed, Stresemann and Briand were joint winners of the Nobel Peace Prize for 1926.

Still, those to the right in Germany continually exploited German resentments by criticizing Stresemann's compromises with Germany's former enemies—in accepting the Dawes and Young plans, for example. Even when successful from Stresemann's own perspective, these negotiations continually cost his party electoral support. The controversy that surrounded Stresemann, a German conservative pursuing conventional national interests, indicates how volatile the German political situation remained, even with the improved economic and diplomatic climate of the later 1920s. Still, Stresemann's diplomatic successes were considerable, and his death in October 1929, at the age of 51, was a severe blow to the republic.

■ An Uncertain Balance Sheet

Although Weimar Germany was considerably better off in 1929 than it had been in 1923, the political consensus remained weak, the political party system remained fragmented, and unstable coalition government remained the rule. Although the immediate threat from the extreme left had been overcome by 1923, many German conservatives continued to fear that the unstable Weimar democracy would eventually open the way to a socialist or communist regime.

The Weimar Republic epitomized the overall European situation during the 1920s. As long as prosperity and international cooperation continued, the new democracy in Germany might endure, even come to thrive. But the new institutions in Germany, like the wider framework of prosperity and stability, were fragile indeed. At the first opportunity, antidemocratic elites, taking advantage of their access to President Hindenburg, would begin plotting to replace the Weimar Republic with a more authoritarian alternative.

Briand (bree-AHN)

THE SEARCH FOR MEANING IN A DISORDERED WORLD

OR all its vitality, the new culture of the 1920s had something brittle about it: the frenetic pace masked a deeper sense that things had started to come apart and might well get worse. The war had accelerated the long-term modernization process toward large industries, cities, and bureaucracies, and toward mass politics, society, and culture. That process was positive, even liberating, in certain respects, but it was also disruptive and disturbing. So the postwar sense of release and excitement combined with an anxious longing for stability, for a return to order. And thus the emphases of intellectuals and artists differed dramatically in the 1920s.

■ Anxiety, Alienation, and Disillusionment

Concern about the dangers of the emerging mass civilization was especially clear in the *Revolt of the Masses* (1930), by the influential Spanish thinker José Ortega y Gasset (1883–1955). In his view, contemporary experience had shown that ordinary people were incapable of creating standards and content with the least common denominator. Communism and fascism indicated the violent, intolerant, and ultimately barbaric quality of the new mass age. But Ortega found the same tendencies in American-style democracy. Much of Europe seemed to be moving toward the mass politics and culture of the United States, but, as far as Ortega was concerned, that was a symptom of the deeper problem, not a solution.

Concern with cultural decline was part of a wider pessimism about the condition of the West, which stood in stark contrast to the belief in progress, and the attendant confidence in Western superiority, that had been essential to Western self-understanding before 1914. The German thinker Oswald Spengler (1880–1936) made concern with decline almost fashionable with his bestseller of the immediate postwar years, *The Decline of the West* (1918), which offered a cyclical theory purporting to explain how spirituality and creativity were giving way to a materialistic mass-based culture in the West.

To Sigmund Freud, the eruption of violence and hatred during the war and afterward indicated a deep, instinctual problem in the human makeup. In his gloomy essay *Civilization and Its Discontents* (1930), Freud suggested that the progress of civilization requires individuals to bottle up their aggressive instincts, which are directed inward as guilt but may erupt in violent outbursts. This notion raised fundamental questions not only about the scope for continued progress but also about the plausibility of the Wilsonian ideals that had surrounded the end of the war. Perhaps, with civilization growing more complex, the Great War had been only the beginning of a new era of hatred and violence. (See the box "Reading Sources: Probing the Limits of Civilization and Progress.")

The sense that something incomprehensible, even nightmarish, haunted modern civilization, with its ever more complex bureaucracies, technologies, and cities, found vivid expression in the work of the Czech Jewish writer Franz Kafka (1883–1924), most notably in the novels *The Trial* and *The Castle*, published posthumously in the mid-1920s. In a world that claimed to be increasingly rational, Kafka's individual is the lonely, fragile plaything of forces utterly beyond reason, comprehension, and control. In such a world, the quest for law, or meaning, or God, is futile, ridiculous.

Especially in the unsettled conditions of Weimar Germany, the anxiety of the 1920s tended to take extreme forms, from irrational activism to a preoccupation with death. Suicides among students increased dramatically. Youthful alienation prompted the novelist Jakob Wassermann (1873–1934) to caution German young people in 1932 that not all action is good simply because it is action, that feeling is not always better than reason and discipline, and that youth is not in itself a badge of superiority.

■ Recasting the Tradition

Expressions of disillusionment revealed something about human experience in the unsettled new world, but they were sometimes morbid and self-indulgent. Other cultural leaders sought to be more positive; the challenge was not to give vent to new anxieties but to find antidotes to them. One direction was to recast traditional categories—in the arts, in religion, in politics—to make them relevant to contemporary experience. Although not all were optimistic about human prospects, many found such a renewal of tradition to be the best hope for responding to the disarray of the postwar world.

Among artists, even those who had been prominent in the modernist avant-garde before the war now pulled back from headlong experimentation and sought to pull things back together, though on a new basis. In music, composers as different as Igor Stravinsky (1882–1971) and Paul Hindemith (1895–1963) adapted earlier styles, although often in a somewhat ironic spirit, as they sought to weave new means of expression into familiar

✺ READING SOURCES

Probing the Limits of Civilization and Progress

Writing at the end of the 1920s, Sigmund Freud, the founder of psychoanalysis, sought to probe the sources, and the wider implications, of the violence and aggressiveness that had been unleashed by the war and that had continued into the 1920s. His account of the wellsprings of violence challenged the long-standing Western belief in continued progress based on human rationality.

[Human beings] are not gentle creatures who want to be loved, and who at the most can defend themselves if they are attacked; they are, on the contrary, creatures among whose instinctual endowments is to be reckoned a powerful share of aggressiveness. As a result, their neighbor is for them not only a potential helper or sexual object, but also someone who tempts them to satisfy their aggressiveness on him, to exploit his capacity to work without compensation, to use him sexually without his consent, to seize his possessions, to humiliate him, to cause him pain, to torture and kill him. . . . Anyone who calls to mind the atrocities committed during the racial migrations or the invasion of the Huns, . . . or at the capture of Jerusalem by the pious Crusaders, or even, indeed, the horrors of the recent World War—anyone who recalls these things to mind will have to bow humbly before the truth of this view.

. . . In consequence of this primary mutual hostility of human beings, civilized society is perpetually threatened with disintegration. The interest of work in common would not hold it together; instinctual passions are stronger than reasonable interests. Civilization has to use its utmost efforts in order to set limits to man's aggressive instincts and to hold the manifestations of them in check. . . .

The communists believe that they have found the path to deliverance from our evils. According to them, man is wholly good and is well-disposed to his neighbor; but the institution of private property has corrupted his nature. . . . I have no concern with any economic criticisms of the communist system. . . . But I am able to recognize that the psychological premises on which the system is based are an untenable illusion. In abolishing private property we deprive the human love of aggression of one of its instruments, . . . but we have in no way altered the differences in power and influence which are misused by aggressiveness, nor have we altered anything in its nature. Aggressiveness was not created by property. It reigned almost without limit in primitive times, when property was still very scanty, and it already shows itself in the nursery. . . .

. . . [I]t is precisely communities with adjoining territories, and related to each other in other ways as well, who are engaged in constant feuds and in ridiculing each other—like the Spaniards and the Portuguese, for instance, the North Germans and South Germans, the English and Scotch, and so on. I gave this phenomenon the name of "the narcissism of minor differences." . . . We can now see that it is a convenient and relatively harmless satisfaction of the inclination to aggression, by means of which cohesion between the members of a community is made easier.

. . . We may expect gradually to carry through such alterations in our civilization as will better satisfy our needs and will escape our criticisms. But perhaps we may also familiarize ourselves with the idea that there are difficulties attaching to the nature of civilization which will not yield to any attempt at reform.

Source: Sigmund Freud, *Civilization and Its Discontents,* trans. James Strachey (New York: W. W. Norton, 1961), pp. 68–72, 74.

forms. The overall tendency toward neoclassicism during the period was an effort to give musical composition a renewed basis of order.

One of the most striking responses to the anxieties of this increasingly secular age was a wave of neo-orthodox religious thinking, most prominent in Protestants like the German-Swiss theologian Karl Barth (1886–1968). In his *Epistle to the Romans* (1919), Barth reacted against the liberal theology, the attempt to marry religious categories to secular progress, that had become prominent by the later nineteenth century. The war, especially, had seemed to shatter the liberal notion that the hand of God was at work in history, and Barth emphasized the radical cleft between God and this, the human world of history, sunken in sin. Recalling the arguments of Augustine and Luther, he portrayed humanity as utterly lost, capable only of a difficult relationship with God, through faith, grace, and revelation.

With democracy faring poorly in parts of Europe, and with fascism and communism claiming to offer superior alternatives, some sought to make new sense of the democratic tradition. In Italy, Benedetto Croce° (1866–1952) agreed with critics that the old justifications for liberal democracy, based on natural law or utilitarianism, were deeply inadequate, but he also became one of Europe's most influential antifascists. He insisted that the most significant innovations in modern thought show us why democratic values, institutions, and practices are still appropriate. We human beings are free, creative agents of a history that we make as best we can, without quite understanding what will result from what we do. Humility, tolerance, and equal access to political participation are essential to the process whereby the world is endlessly remade.

The new political challenges also stimulated fresh thinking within the Marxist tradition. By showing that Marxism could encompass consciousness as well as economic relationships, the Hungarian Georg Lukács (1885–1971) invited a far more sophisticated Marxist analysis of capitalist culture than had been possible before. Lukács accented the progressive role of realistic fiction and attacked the disordered fictional world of Kafka, which seemed to abandon all hope for human understanding of the forces of history. Though more eclectic, the Institute for Social Research, founded in Frankfurt, Germany, in 1923, gave rise to an influential tradition of criticism of capitalist civilization in what came to

be known as the Frankfurt School. These innovations helped give the Marxist tradition a new lease on life in the West, even as it was developing in unforeseen ways in the Soviet Union.

■ The Search for a New Tradition

While some intellectuals sought renewal from within the European tradition, others insisted that a more radical break was needed—but also that the elements for a viable new cultural tradition were available.

Reflecting on the situation of women writers in 1928, the British novelist Virginia Woolf (1882–1941) showed how women in the past had suffered from the absence of a tradition of writing by women. By the 1920s, women had made important strides, but Woolf suggested that further advance required a more self-conscious effort by women to develop their own tradition. Most basically, women needed greater financial independence so that they could have the time for scholarship, the leisure of cultivated conversation, and the privacy of "a room of one's own." Woolf also envisioned a new sort of historical inquiry, focusing on how ordinary women lived their lives, that could show contemporary women where they came from—and thus deepen their sense of identity. (See the box "Reading Sources: Tradition and Women: The Conditions of Independence.")

A very different effort to establish a new tradition developed in Paris, where the poet André Breton (1896–1966) spearheaded the surrealist movement in literature and the visual arts. Surrealism grew directly from Dada, an artistic movement that had emerged in neutral Zurich, Switzerland, and elsewhere during the war. Radically hostile to the war, Dada artists developed shocking, sometimes nihilistic forms to deal with a reality that now seemed senseless and out of control. Some made collages from gutter trash; others indulged in nonsense or relied on chance to guide their art. By the early 1920s, however, the surrealists felt it was time to create a new and deeper basis of order after the willful disordering of Dada. Having learned from Freud about the subconscious, they sought to adapt Dada's novel techniques—especially the use of chance—to gain access to the subconscious mind, which they believed contains a deeper truth, without the overlay of logic, reason, and conscious control.

But other artists, seeking to embrace the modern industrial world in a more positive spirit, found surrealism merely escapist. Among them was Walter Gropius

---

Croce (CROH-chay)

❧ READING SOURCES

Tradition and Women:
The Conditions of Independence

Speaking in 1928 about the situation of women writers, British novelist Virginia Woolf raised questions that were relevant to all women seeking the opportunity to realize their potential. Indeed, her reflections about the value of difference, and the need for particular traditions, inspired those seeking equal opportunity for decades to come. And her question about why we know so little about women's lives in the past helped stimulate later historians to investigate the experiences of ordinary people.

Woman . . . pervades poetry from cover to cover; she is all but absent from history. . . .

Occasionally an individual woman is mentioned, an Elizabeth, or a Mary; a queen or a great lady. But by no possible means could middle-class women with nothing but brains and character at their command have taken part in any one of the great movements which, brought together, constitute the historian's view of the past. . . . What one wants . . . is a mass of information; at what age did she marry; how many children had she as a rule; what was her house like; had she a room to herself; did she do the cooking; would she be likely to have a servant? All these facts lie somewhere, presumably, in parish registers and account books; the life of the average Elizabethan woman must be scattered about somewhere, could one collect it and make a book of it. It would be ambitious beyond my daring, I thought, looking about the shelves for books that were not there, to suggest to the students of those famous colleges that they should re-write history, though I own that it often seems a little queer as it is, unreal, lopsided. . . .

But whatever effect discouragement and criticism had upon their writing—and I believe they had a very great effect—that was unimportant compared with the other difficulty which faced them (I was still considering those early nineteenth-century novelists) when they came to set their thoughts on paper—that is that they had no tradition behind them, or one so short and partial that it was of little help. For we think back through our mothers if we are women. It is useless to go to the great men writers for help, however much one may go to them for pleasure. . . .

. . . [W]omen have sat indoors all these millions of years, so that by this time the very walls are permeated by their creative force, which has, indeed, so overcharged the capacity of bricks and mortar that it must needs harness itself to pens and brushes and business and politics. But this creative power differs greatly from the creative power of men. And one must conclude that it would be a thousand pities if it were hindered or wasted, for it was won by centuries of the most drastic discipline, and there is nothing to take its place. It would be a thousand pities if women wrote like men, or lived like men, or looked like men. . . . Ought not education to bring out and fortify the differences rather than the similarities?

Source: Virginia Woolf, *A Room of One's Own* (San Diego: Harcourt Brace Jovanovich, Harvest/HBJ, 1989), pp. 43–45, 76, 87–88.

 For additional information on this topic, go to http://college.hmco.com.

The Bauhaus Building, Dessau The Bauhaus, an influential but controversial German art school, was established in Weimar in 1919 and then moved to Dessau in 1925. Walter Gropius, its founding director, spearheaded the design of its new headquarters building, constructed in 1925–1926. The building immediately became a symbol of the Weimar modernism that some admired and others detested. *(Vanni/Art Resource, NY)*

(1883–1969), a pioneering modernist architect and leader of an influential German art school, the Bauhaus, during the 1920s. Gropius held that it was possible to establish new forms of culture, even a new tradition, that could be affirmative and reassuring in the face of the postwar cultural disarray. Rather than putting up familiar neoclassical or neo-Gothic buildings, "feigning a culture that has long since disappeared," we must face up to the kind of civilization we have become—industrial, technological, efficient, urban, democratic, mass-based. If we pick and choose carefully from among the elements of our new machine-based civilization, we can again have a culture that works, an "integrated pattern for living."[3]

This "constructive," promodern impulse was particularly prominent in Germany, but it could be found all over—in the modernists of the Russian Revolution, in the French painter Fernand Léger° (1881–1955), in the Swiss architect Le Corbusier° (1887–1965). Whereas many of their contemporaries were at best ambivalent about the masses, these artists sought to bring high art and mass society together in the interests of both. And they welcomed the new patterns of life that seemed to be emerging in the modern world of mass production and fast-paced cities.

Léger (leh-ZHAY) **Le Corbusier** (luh cor-BOO-zee-ay)

SUMMARY

HE 1920s proved a contradictory period of vitality and despair, pacifism and violence, restabilization and instability. The era began with bright hopes for democracy, yet the outcome of the democratic experiment in central and eastern Europe was disappointing. In Germany, the improved economic and diplomatic situation by 1924 enhanced the prospects for democracy, but the new Weimar Republic remained fragile, unstable, and on the defensive. Even Italy, heir to a respectable tradition of democracy, gave rise to the troubling new phenomenon of fascism. A hopeful new spirit of international conciliation drew France and Germany closer together by the end of 1925, but France and Britain seemed to drift apart as the British, preoccupied with colonial concerns, distanced themselves from politics on the Continent.

Still, Europe seemed on its way to restabilization by early 1929. Of the three most volatile and potentially disruptive of the major countries, Italy and Germany seemed to be settling down, and the Soviet Union, though embarking on an unprecedented experiment in socioeconomic engineering, was by now looking inward rather than seeking to export revolution. When the decade is taken on its own terms, it is clear that the vitality, the renewed prosperity, and the diplomatic goodwill were all real. But so also were the unresolved problems that made the 1920s a prelude to the more difficult 1930s, when the notion that Europe had returned to normal came to seem but a fairy tale.

■ Notes

1. Benito Mussolini, speech to the Italian Chamber of Deputies, January 3, 1925, from Charles F. Delzell, ed., *Mediterranean Fascism, 1919–1945* (New York: Harper & Row, 1970), pp. 59–60.
2. Quoted in Robert G. L. Waite, *Vanguard of Nazism: The Free Corps Movement in Postwar Germany, 1918–1923* (New York: W. W. Norton, 1969), pp. 14–15.
3. Walter Gropius, *Scope of Total Architecture* (New York: Collier Books, 1962), pp. 15, 67.

■ Suggested Reading

Gay, Peter. *Weimar Culture: The Outsider as Insider.* 1970. An influential study providing a good sense of the conflicting impulses—the embrace of modernity, the nostalgia for wholeness, the sense of foreboding—that made German culture so intense and vital during the 1920s.

Gentile, Emilio. *The Sacralization of Politics in Fascist Italy.* 1996. Engaging account of the rituals, symbols, and myths that, beginning in Italy during the 1920s, fed the first overtly totalitarian experiment.

Kitchen, Martin. *Europe Between the Wars: A Political History.* 1988. A clear narrative of international and domestic political developments from a leftist perspective.

Kolb, Eberhard. *The Weimar Republic.* 1988. Provides a good overall survey, then pinpoints the recent trends in research and the questions at issue among historians of the period.

Morgan, Philip. *Italian Fascism, 1919–1945.* 1995. A good introductory survey.

Pedersen, Susan. *Family, Dependence, and the Origins of the Welfare State: Britain and France, 1914–1945.* 1993. An effective comparative study showing how concerns about gender roles and family relations helped shape discussion and policy as government assumed greater responsibility for social welfare. Detailed but readable, a landmark in the new gender history.

Peukert, Detlev. *The Weimar Republic: The Crisis of Classical Modernity.* 1992. Accessible interpretive study, accenting the strains stemming from the rapid modernization of the 1920s. Stresses the loss of political legitimacy even before the onset of Depression.

Stites, Richard. *Revolutionary Dreams: Utopian Visions and Experimental Life in the Russian Revolution.* 1989. A vivid account of the utopian aspirations that gave the new communist regime emotional force from 1917 to 1930.

Tucker, Robert C. *Stalin as Revolutionary, 1879–1929: A Study in History and Personality.* 1973. A pioneering account of Stalin's early years and rise to power, probing the sources of the elements of character and personality that helped shape his subsequent rule.

 For a searchable list of additional readings for this chapter, go to http://college.hmco.com.

Advertising

A sleek new automobile. A stylish "new woman" who'd adore a Christmas gift of jewelry. These images from the 1920s catch our eye even today, but why? The designs look "modern" somehow, and they convey particular messages about efficiency and the good life. What do such advertisements tell us about the changes at work in Western cultures after World War I?

Advertising in one form or another is as old as civilization itself. But the advent of printing expanded possibilities, and the second industrial revolution led to a big boost in advertising by the 1890s, as ads for new products like bicycles and sewing machines appeared in newspapers and magazines. But it was during the 1920s that modern advertising came into its own. As mass consumption grew, advertising budgets expanded dramatically, and professional ad agencies emerged to study tastes and determine how to shape the desires of consumers. Moreover, the advent of commercial radio in 1920 opened a whole new set of possibilities, including the scope for musical jingles.

Mass consumption required advertising to show people what to want. And during the 1920s, ad agencies began offering images of the good life, seeking to define the popular sense of what it meant to be "modern." They often drew from the United States, which stood for efficiency and a fast-paced life of fun, pleasure, and consumerist abundance. So eager were the Germans to follow the U.S. lead in advertising that they adopted the term *sex appeal,* leaving it untranslated.

The new products featured in the print and broadcast media ran the gamut from the automobile to cosmetics, from rayon apparel to chewing gum. When the Wrigley Company of Chicago opened a factory in Germany in 1925, chewing gum quickly became associated with Americanization—and its use increased dramatically. But luxury goods were prominent as well, as in elegant ads such as the two shown here. Even for the many who could not afford expensive jewelry or the six-cylinder Opel, images of the good life stimulated the desire to buy less costly versions. Automobile consumption rose sharply during the 1920s, thanks also to the new techniques of mass production that Henry Ford had pioneered in the United States.

Although advertising served the economic interests of business by stimulating consumption, many began to view it as an art form as well. Far more attention was paid to its design, so the advertising "look" of the 1920s differed dramatically from anything seen before. As in the examples here, the new ads were often self-consciously modern, using simplified typefaces and stylized images suggesting the sleek efficiency and precision of the new machine age. The jewelry ad features an elegant contemporary typeface, and the German automobile ad of 1928 relies on crisp, bold forms and a clean, modern design.

The new prominence of advertising raised issues that were debated all over, but especially in Weimar Germany, where conditions remained unsettled even as a measure of prosperity returned by 1924. From cultural standards to gender roles, much was being called into question, and the wider implications of advertising were central to the "culture wars" of the period.

At an international advertising congress in Berlin in 1929, critics charged that advertising was furthering the debasement of standards already associated with mass culture and Americanization. Defenders countered that advertising was rejuvenating the mainstream culture, which had grown either stale and conventional or overblown and elitist. The fact that advertising served a commercial purpose need not have to mean cultural debasement. On the contrary, they argued, this new meshing of the best design with popular culture was healthy. In 1928 G. F. Hartlaub, a leading German art dealer, summed up a widespread view when he observed that advertising was a "truly social, collective, mass art: the only one we now have. It shapes the visual habits of that anonymous collectivity: the public. Little by little an artistic attitude is hammered into the mass soul by billboards."*

A particular advertising target was the "new woman," with her liberated lifestyle, bobbed hair, and short skirts. But the image of women in advertisements was controversial, especially in Weimar Germany. Partly because of the simplification of female attire, images of

---

*Quoted in John Willett, *Art and Politics in the Weimar Period: The New Sobriety, 1917–1933* (New York: Pantheon, 1978), p. 137. Translation modified slightly.

the new woman in popular magazines provoked much concern about the "masculinization" of women by the mid-1920s. Some men found such images aggressive, even threatening.

Yet at the same time advertising often assumed women to be master consumers—or perhaps merely mindless shoppers. In the holiday advertisement here, the woman is chic and liberated in one sense, but she is urged to drape herself with jewelry—to indulge in conventional ornament. This was also an age that claimed to value efficiency purified of ornament, as with the stripped-down typeface in the automobile ad. So though

gender differentiation and women's roles were very much at issue in advertising, the relationship between portrayals of the new woman and genuine liberation remained uncertain.

Despite tensions and contradictions, advertising helped bring new issues to center stage after World War I. Although the ads of the 1920s assumed a prosperity that proved fleeting, the cultural change proved enduring. Eye-catching images of the sleek, the chic, the new—all bathed in "sex appeal"—became the staples of twentieth-century advertising, bound up with the new culture of mass consumption.

Advertising the Six-Cylinder Opel, 1928 *(From Bärbel Schrader and Jürgen Schebera, The "Golden" Twenties: Art and Literature in the Weimar Republic [New Haven: Yale University Press, 1990]. Reproduced with permission.)*

Jewelry for the New Woman
(AKG London)

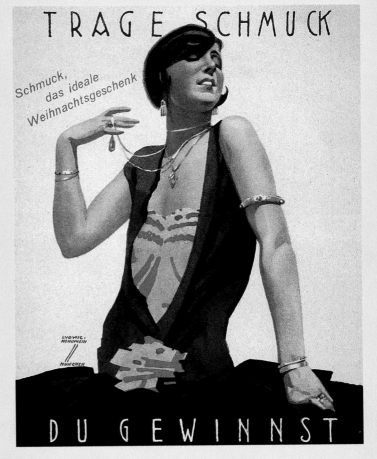

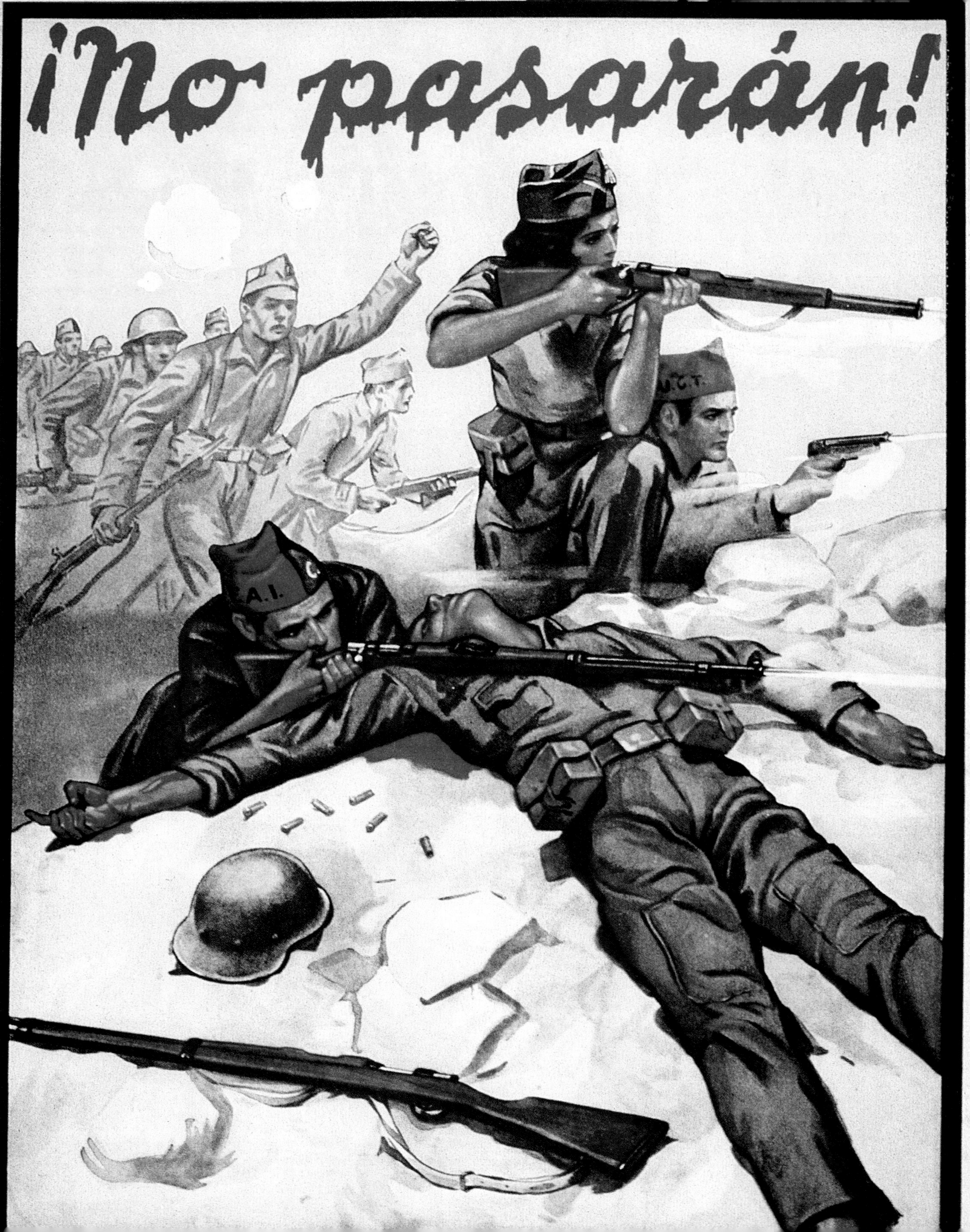
¡No pasarán!

CHAPTER 27

The Tortured Decade 1930–1939

T"HEY shall not pass," proclaimed the charismatic Spanish communist Dolores Ibarruri° (1895–1989), whose impassioned speeches and radio broadcasts helped inspire the heroic defense of Madrid during the civil war that gripped Spain, and captured the attention of the world, during the later 1930s. Known as *La Pasionaria*—the passion flower—Ibarruri became a living legend for her role in defending the Spanish republic against the antidemocratic nationalists seeking to overthrow it. But the Republican side lost, and she spent thirty-eight years in exile before returning to Spain in 1977, after the end of the military dictatorship that had resulted from the Spanish civil war.

In her effort to rally the Republican side, Ibarruri stressed the political power of women, and indeed women were prominent in the citizen militias defending Madrid and other Spanish cities. Women fought for the republic partly because it seemed to open new opportunities for them, especially as it became more radical by 1936. But just as some women welcomed the new direction, others became politically active on the opposing Nationalist side—to support the church, to combat divorce, to defend a separate sphere for women as the guardians of private life and family values.

The ideological polarization that characterized the Spanish civil war reflected the expanding reach of politics in the 1930s, when economic depression and the challenge from new, antidemocratic governments immeasurably complicated the European situation. The mechanisms used to realign the international economy after World War I had seemed effective for most of the 1920s, but by 1929, they

Ibarruri (ee-bah-RUHR-ee)

The Great Depression

The Stalinist Revolution in the Soviet Union

Hitler and Nazism in Germany

Fascist Challenge and Antifascist Response, 1934–1939

The Coming of World War II, 1935–1939

¡**No pasarán!** ("They shall not pass"): Defending the democratic republic during the Spanish civil war. (Biblioteca Nacional, Madrid)

were beginning to backfire, helping to trigger the Great Depression. During the early 1930s the economic crisis intensified sociopolitical strains all over the Western world—and even beyond, heightening anti-Western feeling. In Germany the Depression helped undermine the Weimar Republic and opened the way for the new Nazi regime under Adolf Hitler, whose policies led through a series of diplomatic crises to a new European war.

German Nazism paralleled Italian fascism in its reliance on a single charismatic leader, its willingness to use violence, and its hostility to both parliamentary democracy and Marxist socialism. But Nazism emphasized racism and anti-Semitism in a way that Italian fascism did not, and it more radically transformed its society.

At the same time, Stalin's communist regime in the Soviet Union seemed to converge, in some ways, with these new fascist regimes—especially with German Nazism. So though they expressed widely different aims, Stalinism and Nazism are sometimes lumped together as instances of "totalitarianism." Both apparently sought control over all aspects of society, partly through the use of secret police agencies. But on closer inspection, the forms of coercion and violence in the Soviet and the German regimes by the later 1930s were quite different, and the extent to which each can be understood as an instance of totalitarianism remains controversial.

Fascism, Nazism, and communism seemed able to sidestep—or surmount—the ills of the Depression, yet they stood opposed to the parliamentary democracy that had long seemed the direction of progressive political change. So the democratic movement appeared to lose its momentum in the face of the political and economic challenges of the 1930s. The defeat, by early 1939, of the democratic republic in Spain by the authoritarian Nationalists seemed to exemplify the political direction of the decade.

QUESTIONS TO CONSIDER

- How did the new international economic interdependence after World War I help produce the Great Depression?

- Why did the Stalinist attempt to build "socialism in one country" lead to the "terror-famine" of 1932–1933 and the "great terror" of 1937–1938?

- Through what measures did the Nazi regime claim to be improving the quality of the German population?

- Why did the other major countries not stop Hitler's Germany before it was strong enough to start a new European war in 1939?

TERMS TO KNOW

collectivization	"euthanasia" program
gulag	popular front
show trials	Rome-Berlin Axis
Adolf Hitler	remilitarization of the
National Socialist	Rhineland
(Nazi) Party	appeasement
Schutzstaffel (SS)	Nazi-Soviet Pact

THE GREAT DEPRESSION

 ALTHOUGH the stock market crash of October 1929 in the United States helped usher in the world economic crisis of the early 1930s, it had this effect only because the new international economic order after World War I was extremely fragile. By October 1929, in fact, production was already declining in all the major Western countries except France.

The economies of Germany and the states of east-central Europe remained particularly vulnerable after World War I, and in the increasingly interdependent economic world, their weaknesses magnified problems that started elsewhere. The crash of the U.S. stock market led to a restriction of credit in central Europe, which triggered a more general contraction in production and trade. Facing cruel dilemmas, policymakers proved unable to master the situation for the first few years of the crisis. The consequences—both human and political—were profound.

■ Sources of the Economic Contraction

Certain economic sectors, especially coal mining and agriculture, were already suffering severe problems by the mid-1920s, well before the stock market crash of 1929. British coal exports fell partly because oil and hydroelectricity were rapidly developing as alternatives. Unemployment in Britain was never less than 10 percent even in the best of times between the wars. In agriculture high prices worldwide during the war produced oversupply, which, in turn, led to a sharp drop in prices once the war was over. During the later 1920s, bumper harvests of grain and rice in many parts of the world renewed the downward pressure on prices. The result of low agricultural prices was a diminished demand for industrial goods, which impeded growth in the world economy.

Throughout the 1920s, finance ministers and central bankers had difficulty juggling the economic imbalances created by the war, centering on war debts to the United States and German reparations obligations to France, Britain, and Belgium. The strains in the system finally caught up with policymakers by 1929, when an international restriction of credit forced an end to the international economic cooperation that had been attempted throughout the decade.

The shaky postwar economic system depended on U.S. bank loans to Germany, funneled partly by international agreements but also drawn by high interest rates. By 1928, however, U.S. investors were rapidly withdrawing their capital from Germany in search of the higher returns that could be made in the booming U.S. stock market. This shift tightened credit in Germany. And then the crash of the overpriced U.S. market in October 1929 deepened the problem by forcing suddenly strapped American investors to pull still more of their funds out of Germany. This process continued over the next two years, weakening the major banks in Germany and the other countries of central Europe, which were closely tied to the German economy. In May 1931 the bankruptcy of Vienna's most powerful bank, the Credit-Anstalt, made it clear that a crisis of potentially catastrophic proportions was in progress.

Despite attempts at adjustment on the international level, fears of bank failure or currency devaluation led to runs on the banks and currencies of Germany and east-central Europe. To maintain the value of the domestic currency in world markets, and thereby to resist the withdrawal of capital, government policymakers raised

CHRONOLOGY

October 1929	U.S. stock market crash helps trigger Great Depression
December 1929	Forced collectivization in Soviet agriculture begins
June 1930	Smoot-Hawley Tariff Act (U.S.)
May 1931	Bankruptcy of Vienna's Credit-Anstalt
January 1933	Hitler becomes German chancellor
December 1934	Assassination of Kirov
March 1935	Hitler announces rearmament
October 1935	Italy invades Ethiopia
March 1936	Germany remilitarizes the Rhineland
May 1936	Blum becomes French popular front prime minister
July 1936	Spanish civil war begins
March 1938	Third Moscow show trial; Bukharin and others convicted and executed
March 1938	Anschluss: Germany absorbs Austria
September 1938	"Appeasement": Munich conference ends Sudetenland crisis
November 1938	Crystal Night pogrom
March 1939	Dismemberment of Czechoslovakia
May 1939	Pact of Steel binds fascist Italy and Nazi Germany
August 23, 1939	Nazi-Soviet nonaggression pact
September 1, 1939	German invasion of Poland
September 3, 1939	Britain and France declare war on Germany

Unemployment in Britain
The Depression hit Britain hard—and its effects continued to be felt throughout the 1930s. These unemployed ship-yard workers from Jarrow, in northeastern England, are marching to London in 1936 to present a protest petition. *(Hulton Getty/ Liaison)*

interest rates. This measure was not sufficient to stem the capital hemorrhage, but by restricting credit still more, it further dampened domestic economic activity.

Finally, the Germans seemed to have no choice but to freeze foreign assets—that is, to cease allowing conversion of assets held in German marks to other currencies. In this atmosphere, investors seeking the safest place for their capital tried to cash in currency for gold—or for British pounds, which could then be converted to gold. Europe's flight to gold, however, soon put such pressure on the British currency that Britain was forced to devalue the pound and sever it from the gold standard in September 1931. This proved the definitive end of the worldwide system of economic exchange based on the gold standard that had gradually crystallized during the nineteenth century.

The absence of a single standard of exchange, combined with various currency restrictions, made foreign trade more difficult and uncertain, thereby diminishing it further. So did the scramble for tariff protection that proved a widespread response to the developing crisis. Crucial was the U.S. Smoot-Hawley Tariff Act of June 1930, which raised taxes on imports by 50 to 100 percent, forcing other nations to take comparable steps. Even Britain, long a bastion of free trade, adopted a peacetime tariff for the first time in nearly a century with the Import Duties Act of 1932, which imposed a 10 percent tax on most imports.

The decline of trade spread depression throughout the world economic system. By 1933 most major Euro-

pean countries were able to export no more than two-thirds, and in some cases as little as one-third, of the amount they had sold in 1929. At the same time, losses from international bank failures contracted credit and purchasing power and furthered the downward spiral, until by 1932 the European economies had shrunk to a little over half their 1929 size. This was the astonishing outcome of the short-lived prosperity of the 1920s.

■ Consequences and Responses

The Depression was essentially a radical contraction in economic activity; with less being produced and sold, demand for labor declined sharply. In Germany industrial production by early 1933 was only half what it had been in 1929, and roughly 6 million Germans, or one-third of the labor force, were unemployed.

Although its timing and severity varied, the Depression profoundly affected the lives of ordinary people throughout the Western world and beyond. (See the box "Reading Sources: Working-Class Life During the Great Depression.") Unemployment produced widespread malnutrition, which led, in turn, to sharp increases in such diseases as tuberculosis, scarlet fever, and rickets. The decline in employment opportunities helped produce a backlash against the ideal of "the new woman," working outside the home, which had been a prominent aspect of the new freedom of the 1920s in Germany and elsewhere. Even those men and women who hung on to jobs

❧ READING SOURCES

Working-Class Life During the Great Depression

During the Depression, the Left Book Club, an important movement of left-leaning British intellectuals, commissioned George Orwell (1903–1950) to write a report on the conditions of unemployed miners in the north of England. Published in 1937, Orwell's study of responses to the Depression offered pioneering insights into the dynamics of relative poverty in the modern world. The P.A.C. to which he refers is the British Public Assistance or welfare system.

. . . It is noticeable everywhere that the anomalous position created by unemployment—the man being out of work while the woman's work continues as before—has not altered the relative status of the sexes. . . . Practically never . . . will you see the man doing a stroke of the housework. Unemployment has not changed this convention, which on the face of it seems a little unfair. The man is idle from morning to night but the woman is as busy as ever—more so, indeed, because she has to manage with less money. Yet so far as my experience goes the women do not protest. I believe that they, as well as the men, feel that a man would lose his manhood if, merely because he was out of work, he developed into a "Mary Ann."

But there is no doubt about the deadening, debilitating effect of unemployment on everybody, married or single, and upon men more than women. . . .

I remember the shock of astonishment it gave me, when I first mingled with tramps and beggars, to find that a fair proportion, perhaps a quarter, of these beings whom I had been taught to regard as cynical parasites, were decent young miners and cotton-workers gazing at their destiny with the same sort of dumb amazement as an animal in a trap. They simply could not understand what was happening to them. They had been brought up to work, and behold! it seemed as though they were never going to have the chance of working again. In their circumstances it was inevitable, at first, that they should be haunted by a feeling or personal degradation. That was the attitude toward unemployment in those days: it was a disaster which happened to *you* as an individual and for which *you* were to blame. . . .

. . . When people live on the dole for years at a time they grow used to it, and drawing the dole, though it remains unpleasant, ceases to be shameful. . . . In the back streets of Wigan and Barnley I saw every kind of privation, but I probably saw less *conscious* misery than I should have seen ten years ago. The people have at any rate grasped that unemployment is a thing they cannot help. It is not only Alf Smith who is out of work now; Bert Jones is out of work as well, and both of them have been "out" for years. It makes a great deal of difference when things are the same for everybody.

So you have whole populations settling down, as it were, to a lifetime on the P.A.C. And what I think is admirable, perhaps even hopeful, is that they have managed to do it without going spiritually to pieces. . . . [T]hey realize that losing your job does not mean that you cease to be a human being. So that in one way things in the distressed areas are not so bad as they might be. Life is still fairly normal, more normal than one really has the right to expect. Families are impoverished, but the family-system has not broken up. The people are in effect living a reduced version of their former lives. . . .

But they don't necessarily lower their standards by cutting out luxuries and concentrating on necessities; more often it is the other way about—the more natural way, if you come to think of it. Hence the fact that in a decade of unparalleled depression, the consumption of all cheap luxuries has increased. The two things that have probably made the greatest difference of all are the movies and the mass-production of cheap smart clothes since the war. . . . You may have three halfpence in your pocket and not a prospect in the world, and only the corner of a leaky bedroom to go home to; but in your new clothes you can stand on the street corner, indulging in a private daydream of yourself as Clark Gable or Greta Garbo, which compensates for a great deal.

Source: George Orwell, *The Road to Wigan Pier* (San Diego: Harcourt Brace, 1958), pp. 81–82, 85–88.

suffered from growing insecurity. In his aptly titled *Little Man, What Now?* (1932), the German novelist Hans Fallada (1893–1947) explored the effects of the Depression on members of the lower middle class—store clerks, shop owners, civil servants. Such people were first resentful, then resigned, as their dreams of security, of "order and cleanliness," fell apart.

During the first years of the Depression, central bankers everywhere sought to balance budgets in order to reassure investors and stabilize currencies. With economies contracting and tax revenues declining, the only way to balance the budget was to sharply reduce government spending. In addition, governments responded to the decline in exports by forcing wages down, seeking to enhance competitiveness abroad. But by cutting purchasing power at home, both these measures reinforced the slowdown in economic activity.

Economic policymakers based their responses on the "classical" economic model that had developed from the ideas of Adam Smith in the eighteenth century (see page 717). According to this model, a benign "invisible hand" ensured that a free-market price for labor, for capital, and for goods and services would produce an ongoing tendency toward economic equilibrium. A downward turn in the business cycle was a normal and necessary adjustment; government interference would only upset this self-adjusting mechanism.

By 1932, however, it was clear that the conventional response was not working, and governments began seeking more actively to stimulate the economy. Strategies varied widely. In the United States, Franklin D. Roosevelt (1882–1945) defeated the incumbent president, Herbert Hoover, in 1932 with the promise of a New Deal—a commitment to increase government spending to restore purchasing power. In fascist Italy, a state agency created to infuse capital into failing companies proved a reasonably effective basis for collaboration between government and business. In Germany, economics minister Hjalmar Schacht (1877–1970) mounted an energetic assault on the economic problem after Hitler came to power in 1933. Government measures sealed off the German mark from international fluctuations, stimulated public spending, partly on rearmament, and kept wages low. By 1935 Germany was back to full employment. This success added tremendously to Hitler's popularity.

High unemployment in Norway, Sweden, and Denmark helped social democrats win power in all three of these Scandinavian countries by the mid-1930s. The new left-leaning governments responded to the economic crisis not by a frontal assault on capitalism but by pioneering the "welfare state," providing such benefits as health care, unemployment insurance, and family al-

lowances. To pay for the new welfare safety net, the Scandinavian countries adopted a high level of progressive taxation and pared military expenditures to a minimum. The turn to a welfare state in Scandinavia eased the immediate human costs of the Depression and helped restore production by stimulating demand. At the same time, the Scandinavian model attracted much admiration as a "third way" between free-market capitalism and the various dictatorial extremes.

In the other European democracies the Depression proved more intractable. Although Britain saw some recovery by the mid-1930s, it was especially the rearmament of the later 1930s, financed by borrowing, or deficit spending, that got the British economy growing again. France, less dependent on international trade, experienced the consequences of the world crisis only gradually. But by the early 1930s, France, too, was suffering its effects, which lingered to the end of the decade, helping to poison the political atmosphere.

The Depression also had a major impact on the non-Western world and its relations with the West. The radical restriction of international trade meant a sharp decline in demand for the basic commodities that colonial and other regions exported to the industrialized West. Economic strains fed nationalist, anti-Western sentiments in colonial nations. The increase in misery among rural villagers in India, for example, spread the movement for national independence from urban elites to the rural masses. In this context Mohandas Gandhi°, who had become known by 1920 for advocating noncooperation with the British, became the first leader to win a mass following throughout the Indian subcontinent. Encouraging villagers to boycott British goods, Gandhi accented simplicity, self-reliance, and an overall strategy of nonviolent civil disobedience based on Indian traditions. (See the box "Global Encounters: Gandhi Advocates Nonviolence.")

In Japan, the strains of the Great Depression helped produce precisely the turn to imperialist violence that Gandhi sought to counter. Densely populated yet lacking raw materials, Japan was particularly dependent on international trade and thus reacted strongly as increasing tariffs elsewhere cut sharply into Japanese exports. Led by young army officers who were already eager for their country to embrace a less subservient form of Westernization, Japan turned to aggressive imperialism, seeking to justify its course by claiming to spearhead a wider struggle to free East Asia from Western imperialism. Attacking in 1931, Japanese forces quickly reduced Manchuria to a puppet state, but the Japanese met stubborn resistance

---

Gandhi (GAHN-dee)

Gandhi Advocates Nonviolence

Mohandas Gandhi, a successful English-educated lawyer, emerged as a major force in the movement for Indian independence just after World War I. Calling first for a strategy of noncooperation with the British colonial overlords, Gandhi gradually developed a philosophy of nonviolent civil disobedience, which won widespread sympathy for the cause of Indian independence. The following excerpts from articles published in 1935 and 1939—years notable for outbreaks of violence elsewhere— explain the significance of nonviolence to Gandhi's overall strategy.

Non-violence to be a creed has to be all-pervasive. I cannot be non-violent about one activity of mine and violent about others. That would be a policy, not a life-force. That being so, I cannot be indifferent about the war that Italy is now waging against Abyssinia. . . . India had an unbroken tradition of non-violence from times immemorial. But at no time in her ancient history, as far as I know it, has it had complete non-violence in action pervading the whole land. Nevertheless, it is my unshakeable belief that her destiny is to deliver the message of non-violence to mankind. . . .

. . . India as a nation is not non-violent in the full sense of the term. . . . Her non-violence is that of the weak. . . . She lacks the ability to offer physical resistance. She has no consciousness of strength. She is conscious only of her weakness. If she were otherwise, there would be no communal problems, nor political. If she were non-violent in the consciousness of her strength, Englishmen would lose their role of distrustful conquerors. We may talk politically as we like and often legitimately blame the English rulers. But if we, as Indians, could but for a moment visualize ourselves as a strong people disdaining to strike, we should cease to fear Englishmen whether as soldiers, traders or administrators, and they to distrust us. Therefore if we became truly non-violent we should carry Englishmen with us in all we might do. In other words, we being millions would be the greatest moral force in the world, and Italy would listen to our friendly word. . . .

. . . [W]hen society is deliberately constructed in accordance with the law of non-violence, its structure will be different in material particulars from what it is today. But I cannot say in advance what the government based wholly on non-violence will be like.

What is happening today is disregard of the law of non-violence and enthronement of violence as if it were an eternal law. The democracies, therefore, that we see at work in England, America and France are only so called, because they are no less based on violence than Nazi Germany, Fascist Italy or even Soviet Russia. The only difference is that the violence of the last three is much better organized than that of the three democratic powers. Nevertheless we see today a mad race for outdoing one another in the matter of armaments. And if and when the clash comes, as it is bound to come one day, the democracies win, they will do so only because they will have the backing of their peoples who imagine that they have a voice in their own government whereas in the other three cases the peoples might rebel against their own dictatorships.

Holding the view that without the recognition of non-violence on a national scale there is no such thing as a constitutional or democratic government, I devote my energy to the propagation of non-violence as the law of our life—individual, social, political, national and international. I fancy that I have seen the light, though dimly. I write cautiously, for I do not profess to know the whole of the Law. If I know the successes of my experiments, I know also my failures. But the successes are enough to fill me with undying hope. I have often said that if one takes care of the means, the end will take care of itself. Non-violence is the means, the end for every nation is complete independence.

Source: Raghavan Iyer, ed., *The Essential Writings of Mahatma Gandhi* (Delhi: Oxford University Press, 1991), pp. 245–247, 262–263.

Collectivization in Soviet Agriculture At the "New Life" collective farm, not far from Moscow, women stand for the morning roll call. The Soviet collectivization effort of the 1930s rested in important measure on the forced mobilization of peasant women. *(Endeavor Group UK)*

when they began seeking to extend this conquest to the rest of China in 1937.

Japanese pressure indirectly advanced the rise of the Chinese communist movement, led by Mao Zedong (Mao Tse-tung; 1893–1976). Securing a base in the Yanan district in 1936, Mao began seeking to apply Marxism-Leninism to China through land reform and other measures to link the communist elite to the Chinese peasantry. Mao was notable among those adapting Western ideas to build an indigenous movement that would at once overcome Western imperialism and create an alternative to Western liberal capitalism.

The Depression, and the halting responses of the democracies in dealing with it, enhanced the prestige of the new regimes in the Soviet Union, Italy, and Germany. These three despotic powers appeared either to have avoided the economic crisis or to be dealing with it more creatively. But each of these new regimes was an experiment, and the innovations of each added to the uncertainties of the decade.

THE STALINIST REVOLUTION IN THE SOVIET UNION

HOUGH it won the admiration of some, the Soviet Union, in particular, experienced a decade of unprecedented upheaval during the 1930s. Seeking to build "socialism in one country," Joseph Stalin led the Soviet Union during the 1930s

through an astounding transformation that mixed achievement with brutality and terror in often tragic ways. The resulting governmental system, which gave Stalin unprecedented power, proved crucial to the outcome of the great experiment that had begun with the Russian Revolution of 1917. But whether the fateful turn of the 1930s had been implicit in the Leninist revolutionary model all along, or stemmed mostly from unforeseen circumstances and Stalin's idiosyncratic personality, remains uncertain.

■ Crash Industrialization and Forced Collectivization

Stalin's program of rapid industrialization based on forced collectivization in agriculture began in earnest at the beginning of 1930. It entailed an assault on the better-off peasants, or *kulaks,* who were often sent to labor camps in Siberia while their lands were taken over by the government. The remaining peasants were herded into new government-controlled collective farms. So unpopular was this measure that many peasants simply killed their livestock or smashed their farm implements rather than have them collectivized. During the first two months of 1930, as many as 14 million head of cattle were slaughtered, resulting in an orgy of meat eating and a shortage of draft animals. By 1934 the number of cattle in the Soviet Union was barely half what it had been in 1928.

Collectivization served, as intended, to squeeze from the peasantry the resources needed to finance industrialization, but it was carried out with extreme brutality.

Carrying Out the Stalinist Revolution

Lev Kopelev (b. 1912), who came from a middle-class Jewish family, was an enthusiastic communist as a young man. Believing that the Soviet Communist Party embodied the progressive movement of history, he eagerly assisted in the forced collectivization drive of the early 1930s, which caused such suffering and death in his native Ukraine. But after World War II, he became critical of Soviet communism, and he was finally exiled from the Soviet Union in 1980.

Our great goal was the universal triumph of Communism, and for the sake of that goal everything was permissible. . . . And to hesitate or doubt about all this was to give in to "intellectual squeamishness" and "stupid liberalism," the attributes of people who "could not see the forest for the trees."

. . . I saw what "total collectivization" meant—how . . . mercilessly they stripped the peasants in the winter of 1932–33. I took part in this myself, scouring the countryside, searching for hidden grain, testing the earth with an iron rod for loose spots that might lead to buried grain. With the others, I emptied out the old folks' storage chests, stopping my ears to the children's crying and the women's wails. For I was convinced that I was accomplishing the great and necessary transformation of the countryside; that in the days to come the people who lived there would be better off for it; that their distress and suffering were a result of their own ignorance or the machinations of the class enemy; that those who sent me—and I myself—knew better than the peasants how they should live, what they should sow and when they should plow.

In the terrible spring of 1933 I saw people dying from hunger. I saw women and children with distended bellies, turning blue, still breathing but with vacant, lifeless eyes. . . .

Nor did I lose my faith. As before, I believed because I wanted to believe. Thus from time immemorial men have believed when possessed by a desire to serve powers and values above and beyond humanity. . . .

That was how we thought and acted—we, the fanatical disciples of the all-saving ideals of communism. When we saw the base and cruel acts that were committed in the name of our exalted notions of good, and when we ourselves took part in those actions, what we feared most was to lose our heads, fall into doubt or heresy and forfeit our unbounded faith. . . .

. . . The concepts of conscience, honor, humaneness we dismissed as idealistic prejudices, "intellectual" or "bourgeois," and, hence, perverse.

Source: Lev Kopelev, *No Jail for Thought* (London: Secker & Warburg, 1977), pp. 11–13.

What was being squeezed was not merely a surplus—the state's extractions cut into subsistence. So while Soviet agricultural exports increased after 1930, large numbers of peasants starved to death. The great famine that developed during 1932–1933 resulted in between 5 and 6 million deaths, over half of them in Ukraine. This "terror-famine" went unrecorded in the Soviet press, and the Soviets refused help from international relief agencies. (See the box "Reading Sources: Carrying Out the Stalinist Revolution.")

By 1937 almost all Soviet agriculture took place on collective farms—or on state farms set up in areas not previously under agriculture. However, restrictions on private plots and livestock ownership were eased slightly after 1933, and partly as a result, agriculture rebounded and living standards began to rise. By the late 1930s, moreover, significant increases in industrial output had established solid foundations in heavy industry, including the bases for military production.

In pursuing this program, Stalin played up the great historical drama surrounding the Soviet experiment, with its incredible targets and goals. Suggestions by some that the pace could not be maintained only proved grist for Stalin's mill: "No, comrades," he told a workers' conference early in 1931, "the tempo must not be reduced. On the contrary, we must increase it as much as is within our powers and capabilities. . . . To slow the tempo would mean falling behind. And those who fall behind get beaten. . . . Do you want our socialist fatherland to be beaten and to lose its independence? . . . We are fifty or a hundred years behind the advanced countries. We must make good this distance in ten years. Either we do this or they will crush us."[1]

Soviet propaganda, including art in the official socialist realist style, glorified the achievements of the new Soviet industrial and agricultural workers. "Stakhanovism°," named for a coal miner who had heroically exceeded his production quota in 1935, became the term for the prodigious economic achievements that the regime valued as it proclaimed the superiority of the communist system. Indeed, the fact that in the Soviet Union state management seemed to produce results while much of the world languished in depression helps explain the prestige that communism developed among intellectuals, in both the Western and non-Western worlds, during the 1930s.

But, whatever its successes, this forced development program created many inefficiencies and entailed tremendous human costs. The Soviet Union could probably have done at least as well, with much less suffering, through other strategies of industrial development. Moreover, Stalin's program departed from certain socialist principles—egalitarianism in wages, for example—that the regime had taken very seriously during the late 1920s. By 1931, bureaucratic managers, concerned simply with maximizing output, were openly favoring workers in certain industries. Collective bargaining and the right to strike had vanished from the workers' arsenal.

■ From Opposition to Terror, 1932–1938

Stalin's radical course, with its brutality and uncertain economic justification, quickly provoked opposition. During the summer of 1932, a group centered around M. N. Ryutin° (1890–1937) circulated among party leaders a two-hundred-page tract calling for a retreat from Stalin's economic program and a return to democracy within the party. It advocated readmitting those who had been expelled—including Stalin's archenemy, Leon Trotsky. Moreover, the document strongly condemned Stalin personally, describing him as "the evil genius of the Russian Revolution, who, motivated by a personal desire for power and revenge, brought the Revolution to the verge of ruin."[2]

Stalin promptly had Ryutin and his associates ousted from the party, then arrested and imprisoned. But especially as the international situation grew menacing during the 1930s, Stalin became ever more preoccupied with the scope for further opposition. Both Germany and Japan exhibited expansionist aims that might threaten Soviet territories. Trotsky from exile might work with foreign agents and Soviet dissidents to sabotage the Soviet development effort.

In December 1934 the assassination of Sergei Kirov° (1888–1934), party leader of Leningrad (the former Petrograd), gave Stalin an excuse to intensify the crackdown against actual and potential opponents. The eventual result was a series of bizarre show trials, deadly purges, and, ultimately, a kind of terror, with several categories of Soviet citizens vulnerable to arbitrary arrest by the secret police. By the time it wound down, early in 1939, this "great terror" had significantly changed the communist regime—and Soviet society. But though the bare facts are clear, what to make of them is not.

In the three Moscow show trials, which took place during a twenty-month period from 1936 to 1938, noted Bolsheviks including Nikolai Bukharin and major functionaries such as Genrikh Yagoda, recently removed as chief of the secret police, confessed to a series of sensational trumped-up charges: that they had been behind the assassination of Kirov, that they would like to have killed Stalin, that they constituted an "anti-Soviet, Trotskyite center," spying for Germany and Japan and preparing to sabotage Soviet industry in the event of war. Almost all the accused, including Bukharin and others who had been central to the 1917 revolution, were convicted and executed. Soviet authorities did not dare risk public trial for the few who refused, even in the face of torture, to play their assigned roles and confess. Among them was Ryutin, who was shot in secret early in 1937.

During 1937 a purge wiped out much of the top ranks of the army, with half the entire officer corps shot or imprisoned in response to unfounded charges of spying and treason. The Communist Party underwent several purges, culminating in the great purge of 1937 and 1938. Of the roughly two thousand delegates to the 1934 congress of the Communist Party, over half were shot during the next few years. The most prominent were especially vulnerable. Indeed, 114 of the 139 central committee members elected at the 1934 party congress had been shot or sent to a forced labor camp by 1939.

The first such camps were established under Lenin in 1918, during the civil war, but the camp system expanded exponentially under Stalin during the 1930s,

---

Stakhanovism (stah-KAH-nov-izm)   **Ryutin** (ree-YOU-tin)   **Kirov** (KIH-roff)

coming to play a major economic role. This network of forced labor camps—there were eventually at least 476 of them—became known as the *gulag*, originally an acronym for "main camp administration."

Although considerable controversy remains over the number of victims of the gulag, and of the Stalinist revolution more generally, the totals were clearly staggering. According to one influential high-end estimate, 8.5 million of the approximately 160 million people in the Soviet Union were arrested during 1937 and 1938, and of these perhaps 1 million were executed by shooting. Half the total membership of the Communist Party—1.2 million people—were arrested; of these, 600,000 were executed, and most of the rest died in gulag camps. Altogether, the terror surrounding the several purges resulted in approximately 8 million deaths. Estimates of the death toll from all of Stalin's policies of the 1930s, including the forced collectivizations, range as high as 20 million.

■ Communism and Stalinism

What was going on in this bizarre and lethal combination of episodes? Obviously Stalinism was one possible outcome of Leninist communism, but was it the logical, even the inevitable, outcome? Leninism had accented centralized authority and the scope for human will to force events, so it may have created a framework in which Stalinism was likely to emerge. Yet Stalin's personal idiosyncrasies and growing paranoia seem to have been crucial for the Soviet system to develop as it did. But though he ended up the regime's undisputed leader, Stalin was part of a wider dynamic.

It was long assumed that Stalin was pursuing a coordinated policy of terror to create a system of total control. Yet recent research has shown that he was often merely improvising, responding to a situation that had become chaotic, out of control, as the communists tried to carry through a revolution in a backward country. No one had ever attempted this sort of forced industrialization based on a centrally planned economy. At once idealistic, inexperienced, and suspicious, the regime's leaders really believed that failures must be due to sabotage—that "wreckers" were seeking to undermine the heroic Soviet experiment. Moreover, though Stalin tended to blow them out of proportion, there were genuine threats to the Soviet regime and his own leadership by the mid-1930s.

Whereas the terror was long viewed as almost random, it is now clearer that those in the upper and middle reaches of the Soviet system were the most vulnerable.

Top officials encouraged ordinary workers to provide information about plant managers and local party officials who seemed incompetent or corrupt. And although some workers did so to serve the revolution, others to vent personal resentments, they often took the initiative in denouncing their superiors, thereby playing important roles in the dynamic that developed.

But what explains the "confessions" that invariably resulted from the bizarre show trials? The accused sometimes succumbed to torture, and to threats to their families. But some, at least, offered false confessions because they believed that in doing so they were still serving the communist cause. All along, the revolution had required a willingness to compromise personal scruples, including "bourgeois" concerns about personal honor and dignity. Even though false, these confessions could help the communist regime ward off the genuine dangers it faced. So in confessing, the accused would be serving the long-term cause, which they believed to be bigger than Stalin and the issues of the moment. What some could not see—or admit—was that the triumph of Stalinism was fatally compromising the original revolutionary vision.

Surrounded by great propaganda, the show trials were central to the unending talk of foreign intrigues, assassination plots, and "wrecking" by the later 1930s. And all the talk had its effect, leading many ordinary citizens to believe that a vast conspiracy was indeed at work, responsible for the shortages and economic misfortunes that had accompanied the crash industrialization program.

Although much was unplanned and even out of control, Stalin's ultimate responsibility for the lethal dynamic of the later 1930s is undeniable. At the height of the terror, he personally approved lists for execution, and he took advantage of the chain of events to crush all actual or imagined opposition. By 1939 Stalin loyalists constituted the entire party leadership.

In a sense, the outcome was the triumph of Stalin over the Communist Party, which had held to the original Bolshevik ideal of collective leadership by a revolutionary vanguard. But even this outcome did not snuff out the revolutionary idealism that had helped carry the communist regime through the upheavals of the 1930s. Though some turned away in disillusionment or despair, others found the regime's ruthlessness in rooting out its apparent enemies evidence of its ongoing revolutionary purpose. And whereas Stalin was not a charismatic leader like Hitler or Mussolini, he was coming for many to embody the ongoing promise of the communist experiment.

HITLER AND NAZISM IN GERMANY

ESET with problems from the start, the Weimar Republic lay gravely wounded by 1932. Various antidemocratic groups competed to replace it. The winner was the Nazi movement, led by Adolf Hitler, who became chancellor in January 1933. It was especially Hitler's new regime in Germany that made the 1930s so tortured, for Hitler not only radically transformed German society but fundamentally altered the power balance in Europe.

Nazism took inspiration from Italian fascism, but Hitler's regime proved more dynamic—and more troubling—than Mussolini's. Nazism was not conventionally revolutionary, in the sense of mounting a frontal challenge to the existing socioeconomic order. Some of its themes were traditionalist and even antimodernizing. But in the final analysis Nazism was anything but conservative. Indeed, it constituted a direct assault on what had long been held as the best of Western civilization.

■ The Emergence of Nazism and the Crisis of the Weimar Republic

The National Socialist German Workers' Party (NSDAP), or Nazism, emerged from the turbulent situation in Munich just after the war. A center of leftist agitation, the city also became a hotbed of the radical right, nurturing a number of new nationalist, militantly anticommunist political groups. One of them, a workers' party founded under the aegis of the right-wing Thule Society early in 1919, attracted the attention of Adolf Hitler, who soon gave it his personal stamp.

Adolf Hitler (1889–1945) had been born not German but Austrian, the son of a middling government official. As a young man he had gone to Vienna, hoping to become an artist, but he failed to gain admission to the Viennese Academy of Fine Arts. By 1913 he had become a German nationalist hostile to the multinational Habsburg Empire, and he emigrated to Germany to escape service in the Austrian army. He was not opposed to military service per se, however, and when war broke out in 1914, he immediately volunteered for service in the German army.

Corporal Hitler experienced firsthand the fighting at the front and, as a courier, performed bravely and effectively. Indeed, he was in a field hospital being treated for gas poisoning when the war ended. Although his fellow soldiers considered him quirky and introverted, Hitler found the war experience crucial; it was during the war, he said later, that he "found himself."

Following his release from the hospital, Hitler worked for the army in routine surveillance of extremist groups in Munich. In this role he joined the infant German Workers' Party late in 1919. When his first political speech at a rally in February 1920 proved a resounding success, Hitler began to believe he could play a special political role. From this point, he gradually developed the confidence to lead a new nationalist, anticommunist, and anti-Weimar movement.

But Hitler jumped the gun in November 1923 when, with Erich Ludendorff at his side, he led the Beer Hall Putsch in Munich, an abortive attempt to launch a march on Berlin to overthrow the republic. On trial after this effort failed, Hitler gained greater national visibility as he denounced the Versailles treaty and the Weimar government. Still, *Mein Kampf* (My Battle), the political tract that he wrote while in prison during 1924, sold poorly. To most, Hitler was simply a right-wing rabble-rouser whose views were not worth taking seriously.

His failure in 1923 convinced Hitler that he should exploit the existing political system, but not challenge it directly, in his quest for power on the national level. Yet Hitler did not view the NSDAP as just another political party, playing by the same rules as the others within the Weimar system. Thus, most notably, the Nazi Party maintained a paramilitary arm, the *Sturmabteilung* (SA), which provoked a good deal of antileftist street violence. Still, the Nazis remained confined to the margins of national politics in 1928, when they attracted only 2.6 percent of the vote in elections to the Reichstag.

The onset of the economic depression by the end of 1929 produced problems that the Weimar democracy could not handle—and that radically changed the German political framework. The pivotal issue was unemployment insurance, which became a tremendous financial burden for the government as unemployment grew. The governing coalition fell apart over the issue in March 1930, and this proved to be the end of normal parliamentary government in Weimar Germany.

President Paul von Hindenburg called on Heinrich Brüning (1885–1970), an expert on economics from the Catholic Center Party, to become chancellor. Brüning was to spearhead a hard-nosed, deflationary economic program intended to stimulate exports by lowering prices. Like most of the German middle classes, Brüning feared inflation, disliked unemployment insurance, and believed that Germany could not afford public works projects to pump up demand—the obvious alternative to his deflationary policy. But when he presented his program to the Reichstag, he encountered opposition not only from those on the left but also from conservatives, eager to undermine the republic altogether. As a result, Brüning

The Coming of Nazism The last years of the Weimar Republic saw accelerating street violence between the SA, the Nazi Party's paramilitary arm, and the Communist and trade-unionist left. When the Nazis came to power in January 1933, they immediately cracked down on their leftist enemies. Here SA members line up leftist political prisoners at gunpoint. *(Mary Evans Picture Library)*

could get no parliamentary majority. Rather than resigning or seeking a compromise, he invoked Article 48, the emergency provision of the Weimar constitution, which enabled him to govern under presidential decree.

When this expedient provoked strenuous protests, Brüning dissolved the Reichstag and scheduled new elections for September 1930. At this point there was still some chance that a more conciliatory tack would have enabled the chancellor to build a new parliamentary majority—and save parliamentary government. The Socialists were seeking to be more cooperative in the face of the deepening economic crisis and the prospect of new parliamentary elections, which, under these difficult circumstances, seemed to invite trouble. However, Brüning persisted, believing the electorate would vindicate him.

In fact, the outcome of the elections of September 1930 was disastrous—for Brüning, and ultimately for Germany as well. While two of the democratic, pro-Weimar parties lost heavily, the two extremes, the Communists and the Nazis, improved their totals considerably. Indeed, this was a major breakthrough for the Nazis, whose share of the vote jumped from 2.6 percent to 18.3 percent of the total.

Brüning continued to govern, still relying on President Hindenburg and Article 48 rather than majority support in the Reichstag. But his program of raising taxes and decreasing government spending failed to revive the economy. Meanwhile, the growth of the political extremes helped fuel an intensification of the political violence and street fighting that had bedeviled the Weimar Republic from the beginning. As scuffles between Nazis and Communists sometimes approached

pitched battles, the inability of the government to keep order further damaged the prestige of the republic. And as the crisis deepened in 1932, conservative fears of a Marxist outcome played into Hitler's hands.

By this point, conservatives close to Hindenburg sensed the chance to replace the fragmented parliamentary system with some form of authoritarian government. A new, tougher regime would not only attack the economic crisis but also stiffen governmental resistance against the apparent threat from the extreme left. In May 1932 those advisers finally persuaded Hindenburg to dump Brüning, and two of them, Franz von Papen° (1878–1969) and General Kurt von Schleicher° (1882–1934), each got a chance to govern in the months that followed. But neither succeeded, partly because of the daring strategy Hitler adopted.

When, following the ouster of Brüning, new elections were held in July 1932, the Nazis won 37.3 percent of the vote and the Communists 14.3 percent. Together, the two extremes controlled a majority of the seats in the Reichstag. Hitler, as the leader of what was now the Reichstag's largest party, refused to join any coalition—unless he could lead it as chancellor. Meanwhile, the authoritarian conservatives around President Hindenburg wanted to take advantage of the Nazis' mass support for antidemocratic purposes. Finally, in January 1933, with government at an impasse, Papen lined up a new coalition that he proposed to Hindenburg to replace Schleicher's government. Hitler would be chancellor, Papen himself vice-chancellor, and Alfred Hugenberg (1865–

Papen (PAH-pin)   **Schleicher** (SHLY-shur)

1951), the leader of the Nationalist Party, finance minister. For months, Hindenburg had resisted giving Hitler a chance to govern, but he felt this combination might work to establish a parliamentary majority, to box out the left—and to contain Nazism. So Hindenburg named Hitler Germany's chancellor on January 30, 1933.

It became clear virtually at once that the outcome of the crisis was a dramatic change of regime, the triumph of Hitler and Nazism. But though the Nazis had always wanted to destroy the Weimar Republic, they were not directly responsible for overthrowing it. The rise of Nazism was more a symptom than a cause of the crisis of Weimar democracy.

In one sense, the Weimar Republic collapsed from within, largely because the German people disagreed fundamentally about priorities after the war—and then again with the onset of the Depression. Thus the new democracy produced unstable government based on multiparty coalitions, and it fell into virtual paralysis when faced with the economic crisis by 1930. At the same time, however, those around Hindenburg were particularly quick to begin undercutting democratic government in 1930, as the economic crisis seemed to intensify the threat from the extreme left.

As unemployment grew during the first years of the 1930s, both the Nazis and the Communists gained electoral support, but the Germans voting for the Nazis were not simply those most threatened economically. Nor did the Nazi Party appeal primarily to the uneducated or socially marginal. Rather, the party served as a focus of opposition for those growing alienated from the Weimar Republic itself. Although the Nazis did relatively poorly among Catholics and industrial workers, they put together a broad, fairly diverse base of electoral support, ranging from artisans and small shopkeepers to university students and civil servants. But though Hitler was clearly anti-Weimar, anticommunist, and anti-Versailles, his positive program remained vague, so those who voted for the Nazis were not clear what they might be getting. In light of economic depression and political impasse, however, it seemed time to try something new.

■ The Consolidation of Hitler's Power, 1933–1934

When Hitler became chancellor, it was not obvious that a change of regime was beginning. Like his predecessors, he could govern only with the president's approval, and governmental institutions like the army, the judiciary, and the diplomatic corps, though hardly bastions of democracy, were not in the hands of committed Nazis.

But even though an element of caution and cultivated ambiguity remained, a revolution quickly began, creating a new regime, the Third Reich.

On February 23, just weeks after Hitler became chancellor, a fire engulfed the Reichstag building in Berlin. It was set by a young Dutch communist acting on his own, but it seemed to suggest that a communist uprising was imminent. This sense of emergency gave the new Hitler government an excuse to restrict civil liberties and imprison leftist leaders, including the entire Communist parliamentary delegation. Even in this atmosphere of crisis the Nazis could not win a majority in the Reichstag elections of March 5. But support from the Nationalists and the Catholic Center Party enabled the Nazis to win Reichstag approval for an enabling act granting Hitler the power to make laws on his own for the next four years, bypassing both the Reichstag and the president.

Although the Weimar Republic was never formally abolished, the laws that followed fundamentally altered government, politics, and public life in Germany. The other parties were either outlawed or persuaded to dissolve, so that in July 1933 the Nazi Party was declared the only legal party. When President Hindenburg died in August 1934, the offices of chancellor and president were merged, and Germany had just one leader, Adolf Hitler, holding unprecedented power. Members of the German armed forces now swore loyalty to him personally.

During this period of power consolidation, Hitler acted decisively but carefully, generally accenting normalization. To be sure, his methods occasionally gave conservatives pause, most notably when he had several hundred people murdered in the "blood purge" of June 30, 1934. But this purge was directed especially against the SA, led by Ernst Röhm (1887–1934), who had had pretensions of controlling the army. His removal seemed evidence that Hitler was taming the radical elements in his own movement. In fact, however, this purge led to the ascendancy of the *Schutzstaffel*, or SS, the select Nazi elite, led by Heinrich Himmler (1900–1945). Linked to the Gestapo, the secret political police, the SS became the institutional basis for the most troubling aspects of Nazism.

■ Hitler's World-View and the Dynamics of Nazi Practice

In achieving the chancellorship and in expanding his power thereafter, Hitler showed himself an adept politician, but he was hardly a mere opportunist, seeking to amass power for its own sake. Power was only the instrument for the grandiose transformation he believed necessary. And what most troubles us about Nazism, from personal dictatorship to the eventual effort to exterminate the Jews of Europe, stemmed from an overall vision of the world that radiated from Hitler himself.

Hitler acted on the basis of a world-view that coalesced by about 1924—and that remained extremely important to him. This is not to say that he was an original thinker or that his ideas were true—or even plausible. But he sought to make systematic sense of things, and the most disturbing features of his political activity stemmed directly from the resulting world-view. His most committed followers shared certain of his ideas, although fanatical loyalty to Hitler himself was more important for some of them. The central components of Hitler's thinking—geopolitics, biological racism, anti-Semitism, and Social Darwinism—were by no means specifically German. They could be found all over the Western world by the early twentieth century.

Geopolitics claimed to offer a scientific understanding of world power relationships based on geographical determinism. In his writings of the 1920s, Hitler warned that Germany faced imminent decline unless it confronted its geopolitical limitations. To remain fully sovereign in the emerging new era of global superpowers like the United States, Germany would have to act quickly to expand its territory. Otherwise it would end up like Switzerland or the Netherlands.

For decades German imperialists had argued about whether Germany was better advised to seek overseas colonies or to expand its reach in Europe. As Hitler saw it, Germany's failure to make a clear choice had led to its defeat in World War I. Now choice was imperative, and current geopolitical thinking suggested the direction for expansion. Far-flung empires relying on naval support were said to be in decline. The future lay with land-based states—unified, geographically contiguous, with the space necessary for self-sufficiency. By expanding eastward, into Poland and the Soviet Union, Germany could conquer the living space, or *Lebensraum,* necessary for agricultural-industrial balance—and ultimately for self-sufficiency.

Though limited and mechanistic, this geopolitical way of thinking is at least comprehensible, in light of the German vulnerabilities that had indeed surfaced during World War I. The other three strands of Hitler's worldview were much less plausible, though each had become prominent during the second half of the nineteenth century. Biological racism insisted that built-in racial characteristics determine what is most important about any individual. Anti-Semitism went beyond racism in claim-

ing that Jews have played, and continue to play, a special and negative role in history. The fact that the Jews were dispersed and often landless indicated that they were different—and parasitical. Finally, Social Darwinism, especially in its German incarnation, accented the positive role of struggle—not among individuals, as in a prominent American strand, but among racial groups.

The dominant current of racist thinking labeled the "Aryans" as healthy, creative, superior. Originally the Sanskrit term for "noble," *Aryan* gradually came to indicate the ancient language assumed to have been the common source of the modern Indo-European languages. An Aryan was simply a speaker of one of those languages. By the late nineteenth century, however, the term had become supremely ill defined. In much racist thinking, Germanic peoples were somehow especially Aryan, but race mixing had produced impurity—and thus degeneration. Success in struggle with the other races was the ultimate measure of vitality, the only proof of racial superiority for the future.

Hitler brought these themes together by emphasizing that humanity is not special, but simply part of nature, subject to the same laws of struggle and selection as the other animal species. Humanitarian ideals are thus dangerous illusions. As he put it to a group of officer cadets in 1944:

> Nature is always teaching us . . . that she is governed by the principle of selection: that victory is to the strong and that the weak must go to the wall. She teaches us that what may seem cruel to us, because it affects us personally or because we have been brought up in ignorance of her laws, is nevertheless often essential if a higher way of life is to be attained. Nature . . . knows nothing of the notion of humanitarianism, which signifies that the weak must at all costs be protected and preserved even at the expense of the strong.
>
> Nature does not see in weakness any extenuating reasons . . . on the contrary, weakness calls for condemnation.[3]

To Hitler, the Jews were not simply another of the races involved in this endless struggle. Rather, as landless parasites, they embodied the principles—from humanitarianism to class struggle—that were antithetical to the healthy natural struggle among unified racial groups. "Jewishness" was bound up with the negative, critical intellect that dared suggest things ought to be not natural but just, even that it was up to human beings to change the world, to make it just. The Jews were the virus keeping the community from a healthy natural footing. Marxist communism, embodying divisive class struggle as well as utopian humanitarian ideals, was fundamentally Jewish.

The central features of Nazism in practice, from personal dictatorship to the extermination of the Jews, followed from Hitler's view of the world. First, the racial community must organize itself politically for this ceaseless struggle. Individuals are but instruments for the success of the racial community. Parliamentary democracy, reflecting short-term individual interests, fostered selfish materialism and division, thereby weakening that community. The political order must rest instead on a charismatic leader, united with the whole people through bonds of common blood.

Hitler and Children   Adolf Hitler was often portrayed as the friend of children. This photograph accompanied a story for an elementary school reader that described how Hitler, told it was this young girl's birthday, picked her from a crowd of well-wishers to treat her "to cake and strawberries with thick, sweet cream."   *(From* Jugend um Hitler, *Heinrich Hoffman © "Zeitgeschichte" Verlag und Vertriebs-Gesellschaft Berlin. Reproduced with permission. Photo courtesy Wiener Library, London)*

■ Nazi Aims and German Society

Although Hitler's world-view provided the underlying momentum for the Nazi regime, it did not specify a consistent program that could be implemented all at once. Moreover, the regime sometimes found it necessary to adopt short-term expedients that conflicted with its long-term aims. Thus it was possible for Germans living under Nazi rule in the 1930s to embrace aspects of Nazism in practice without seeing where it was all leading.

Hitler's special leadership function was based on a charismatic relationship with the German people, a nonrational bond resting on common race. But to create a genuine racial community, or *Volksgemeinschaft*, it was necessary to unify society and instill Nazi values, thereby making the individual feel part of the whole—and ultimately an instrument to serve the whole. This entailed more or less forced participation in an array of Nazi organizations, from the Women's Organization to the Hitler Youth, from the Labor Front to the Strength Through Joy leisure-time organization.

Common participation meant shared experiences such as weekend hikes and a weekly one-dish meal. Even the most ordinary, once-private activities took on a public or political dimension. Moreover, the Nazis devised unprecedented ways to stage-manage public life, using rituals like the Hitler salute, symbols like the swastika, new media like radio and film, and carefully orchestrated party rallies—all in an effort to foster this sense of belonging. (See the feature "Weighing the Evidence: Film as Propaganda" on pages 944–945.)

Hitler's regime enjoyed considerable popular support, but even after Hitler was well entrenched in power, most Germans did not grasp the regime's deeper dynamic. Certainly some welcomed the sense of unity, the feeling of belonging and participation, especially after what had seemed the alienation and divisiveness of the Weimar years. Moreover, Hitler himself was immensely popular, partly because of his personal charisma, partly because his apparently decisive leadership was a welcome departure from the near paralysis of the Weimar parliamentary system. But most important, before the coming of war in 1939, he seemed to go from success to success, surmounting the Depression and repudiating the major terms of the hated Versailles treaty.

Hitler's propaganda minister, Joseph Goebbels (1897–1945), played on these successes to create a "Hitler myth," which made Hitler seem at once heroic and a man of the people, even the embodiment of healthy German ideals against the corruptions of the Nazi Party. This myth became central to the Nazi regime, but it merely provided a façade behind which the real Hitler could pursue hidden, longer-term aims. These aims were not publicized directly because the German people did not seem ready for them. In this sense, then, support for Hitler and his regime was broad but shallow during the 1930s.

Moreover, resistance increased as the regime became more intrusive. Youth gangs actively opposed the official Hitler Youth organization as it became more overbearing and militaristic by the late 1930s. But people resisted especially by minimizing their involvement with the regime, retreating into the private realm, in response to the Nazi attempt to make everything public.

Did such people feel constantly under threat of the Gestapo, the secret police? In principle, the Gestapo could interpret the will of the *Führer*, or leader, and decide whether any individual citizen was "guilty" or not. And the Gestapo was not concerned about due process; on occasion it simply bypassed the regular court system. But the Gestapo did not terrorize Germans at random. Its victims were generally members of specific groups, people suspected of active opposition, or people who protected those the Gestapo had targeted.

Moreover, changes and contradictions in Nazi goals allowed considerable space for personal choice. During the struggle for power, the Nazis had emphasized the woman's role as wife and mother and deplored the ongoing emancipation of women. Once Hitler came to power, concerns about unemployment reinforced these views. (See the box "Reading Sources: The Nazi Revolution and the Role of Women.") Almost immediately Hitler's government began offering interest-free loans to help couples set up house if the woman agreed to leave the labor force. Such efforts to increase the German birthrate reinforced the emphasis on child rearing in Nazi women's organizations. Nonetheless, the size of the family continued to decrease in Germany as elsewhere in the industrialized world during the 1930s.

Beginning in 1936, when rapid rearmament began to produce labor shortages, the regime did an about-face and began seeking to attract women back to the workplace, especially into jobs central to military preparation. These efforts were not notably successful, and by 1940 the military was calling for conscription of women into war industries.

Further, the Nazis valued the family only insofar as it was congruent with the "health" of the racial community, and efforts to promote that health also compromised traditional family values. The regime regulated marriage and sought actively to eliminate the "unhealthy," those deemed unfit. Just months after coming to power in 1933, Hitler brushed aside the objections of Vice Chancellor Franz von Papen, a Catholic, and engineered a law mandating the compulsory sterilization of persons suffering from certain allegedly hereditary diseases. Medical personnel sterilized some 400,000, the vast majority of them "Aryan" Germans, during the Nazi years.

Hitler's regime also began immediately to single out the Jews, although Nazi Jewish policy remained an improvised hodgepodge prior to World War II. Within weeks after Hitler became chancellor in 1933, new restrictions limited Jewish participation in the civil service, in the professions, and in German cultural life—and quickly drew censure from the League of Nations. The Nuremberg Laws, announced at a party rally in 1935, included prohibition of sexual relations and marriage between Jews and non-Jewish Germans. Beginning in 1938, the Jews had to carry special identification cards and to add "Sarah" or "Israel" to their given names.

But though Hitler and other Nazi leaders claimed periodically to be seeking a definitive solution to Germany's "Jewish problem," the dominant objective during the 1930s was to force German Jews to emigrate. About 60,000 of Germany's 550,000 Jews left the country during 1933 and 1934, and perhaps 25 percent had gotten out by 1938. The fact that the regime stripped emigrating Jews of their assets made emigration more difficult. Potential host countries, concerned about unemployment during the Depression, were especially unwilling to take in substantial numbers of Jews if they were penniless.

On November 9, 1938, using the assassination of a German diplomat in Paris as a pretext, the Nazis staged the *Kristallnacht* (Crystal Night) pogrom, during which almost all the synagogues in Germany and about seven thousand Jewish-owned stores were destroyed. Between 30,000 and 50,000 relatively prosperous Jews were arrested and forced to emigrate after their property was confiscated. Although the German public had generally acquiesced in the earlier restrictions on Jews, this pogrom, with its wanton violation of private property, shocked many Germans.

Concentration camps—supplementary detention centers—had become a feature of the Nazi regime virtually at once, but prior to 1938 they were used primarily to hold political prisoners. As part of the Crystal Night pogrom, about 35,000 Jews were rounded up and sent to the camps, but most were soon released as long as they could document their intention to emigrate. When World War II began in 1939, the total camp population was about 25,000. The systematic physical extermination of the Jews began only during the war, in newly constructed death camps.

❧ READING SOURCES

The Nazi Revolution and the Role of Women

Hitler and the Nazis trumpeted a highly traditionalist conception of women's roles. In doing so, they were reacting sharply against the emancipation of women that had been a hallmark of the 1920s, especially in Germany. Although a shortage of labor would force some compromise later in the decade, Hitler made the official Nazi view of women unmistakably clear in a speech to the women's section of the Nazi Party on September 8, 1934.

. . . The slogan "Emancipation of women" was invented by Jewish intellectuals and its content was formed by the same spirit. In the really good times of German life the German woman had no need to emancipate herself. She possessed exactly what nature had necessarily given her to administer and preserve; just as the man in his good times had no need to fear that he would be ousted from his position in relation to the woman.

In fact the woman was least likely to challenge his position. Only when he was not absolutely certain in his knowledge of his task did the eternal instinct of self and race-preservation begin to rebel in women. There then grew from this rebellion a state of affairs which was unnatural and which lasted until both sexes returned to the respective spheres which an eternally wise providence had preordained for them.

If the man's world is said to be the State, his struggle, his readiness to devote his powers to the service of the community, then it may perhaps be said that the woman's is a smaller world. For her world is her husband, her family, her children, and her home. But what would become of the greater world if there were no one to tend and care for the smaller one? . . . [O]nly on the basis of this smaller world can the man's world be formed and build up. The two worlds are not antagonistic. They complement each other, they belong together just as man and woman belong together.

We do not consider it correct for the woman to interfere in the world of the man, in his main sphere. We consider it natural if these two worlds remain distinct. To the one belongs the strength of feeling, the strength of the soul. To the other belongs the strength of vision, of toughness, of decision, and of the willingness to act. In the one case this strength demands the willingness of the woman to risk her life to preserve this important cell and to multiply it, and in the other case it demands from the man the readiness to safeguard life.

The sacrifices which the man makes in the struggle of his nation, the woman makes in the preservation of that nation in individual cases. What the man gives in courage on the battlefield, the woman gives in eternal self-sacrifice, in eternal pain and suffering. Every child that a woman brings into the world is a battle, a battle waged for the existence of her people. And both must therefore mutually value and respect each other when they see that each performs the task that Nature and Providence have ordained. And this mutual respect will necessarily result from this separation of the functions of each.

It is not true, as Jewish intellectuals assert, that respect depends on the overlapping of the spheres of activity of the sexes; this respect demands that neither sex should try to do that which belongs to the sphere of the other. It lies in the last resort in the fact that each knows that the other is doing everything necessary to maintain the whole community. . . .

So our women's movement is for us not something which inscribes on its banner as its programme the fight against men, but something which has as its programme the common fight together with men. For the new National Socialist national community acquires a firm basis precisely because we have gained the trust of millions of women as fanatical fellow-combatants, women who have fought for the common life in the service of the common task of preserving life, who in that combat did not set their sights on the rights which a Jewish intellectualism put before their eyes, but rather on the duties imposed by nature on all of us in common.

Source: J. Noakes and G. Pridham, *Nazism: A History in Documents and Eyewitness Accounts, 1919–1945,* vol. 1 (New York: Schocken, 1990), pp. 449–450.

However, the killing of others deemed superfluous or threatening to the racial community began earlier, with the so-called euthanasia program initiated under volunteer medical teams in 1939. Its aim was to eliminate chronic mental patients, the incurably ill, and people with severe physical handicaps. Those subject to such treatment were overwhelmingly ethnic Germans, not Jews or foreigners. Although the regime did all it could to make it appear the victims had died naturally, a public outcry developed, especially among relatives and church leaders. Thus the program was discontinued in 1941, but by then it had claimed 100,000 lives—and seems essentially to have achieved its initial objectives.

This "euthanasia" program was based on the sense, fundamental to radical Nazism, that war was the norm and readiness for war the essential societal imperative. In war, societies send individuals to their deaths and, on the battlefield, make difficult distinctions among the wounded, letting some die in order to save those most likely to survive and return to battle. Struggle necessitates selection, which requires overcoming humanitarian scruples—especially the notion that "weakness" calls for special protection. Thus it was desirable to kill even ethnic Germans who were deemed unfit, as "life unworthy of life."

Preparation for war was the core of Nazism in practice. The conquest of living space in the east would make possible a more advantageous agricultural-industrial balance. The result would be not only the self-sufficiency necessary for sovereignty but also the land-rootedness necessary for racial health. Such a war of conquest would strike not only the Slavic peoples of the region but also communism, centered in the Soviet Union.

The point of domestic reorganization was to marshal the community's energies and resources for war. Because German business interests generally seemed congruent with Nazi purposes, Nazi aims did not appear to require some revolutionary assault on business elites or the capitalist economy. But the Nazis had their own road to travel, and beginning in 1936 they proved quite prepared to bend the economy, and to coordinate big business, to serve their longer-term aims of war-making.

The Nazi drive toward war during the 1930s transformed international relations in Europe. The other European powers sought to understand Hitler's Germany in terms of the increasingly polarized political context of the period. Before considering the fortunes of Hitler's foreign policy, we must consider fascism as a wider phenomenon—and the efforts of the democracies, on the one hand, and the Soviet Union, on the other, to come to terms with it.

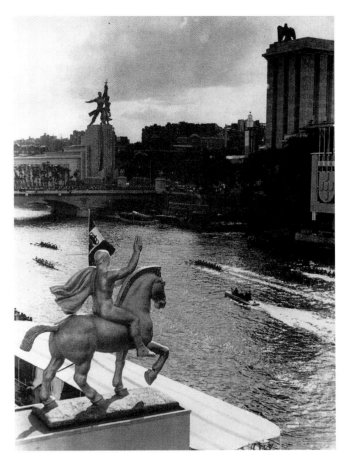

Ideological Confrontation   At a major international exhibition in Paris in 1937, the new antidemocratic political regimes of the interwar period made bold propaganda statements. With a sculpture from fascist Italy's pavilion in the foreground, we look across the Seine River to a classic representation of the ideological warfare of the 1930s: the Soviet Pavilion, on the left, facing the German Pavilion, on the right. *(AP/Wide World Photos)*

FASCIST CHALLENGE AND ANTIFASCIST RESPONSE, 1934–1939

 OMMUNISM, fascism, and Nazism all repudiated the parliamentary democracy that had been the West's political norm. Each seemed subject to violence and excess, yet each had features that some found attractive, especially in light of the difficult socioeconomic circumstances of the 1930s. Yet communists and adherents of the various forms of fascism were bitterly hostile to each other, and the very presence of these new political systems caused polarization all over Europe.

Beginning in 1934 communists sought to join with anyone who would work with them to defend the democratic framework, and thus a role for communist parties, against further fascist assaults. This effort led to new antifascist coalition governments in Spain and France. In each case, however, the Depression restricted maneuvering room, and these governments ended up furthering the polarization they were seeking to avoid. By mid-1940, democracy had fallen in Spain, after a brutal civil war, and even in France, in the wake of military defeat.

■ European Fascism and the Popular Front Response

Although fascism attracted some of those elsewhere who were disaffected with democracy and hostile to communism, the line between fascism and conservative authoritarianism blurred in the volatile political climate of the 1930s. To some, any retreat from democracy appeared a step toward fascism.

In east-central Europe, political distinctions became especially problematic. Movements like the Arrow Cross in Hungary and the Legion of the Archangel Michael in Romania modeled themselves on the Italian and German prototypes, but they never achieved political power. Those who controlled the antidemocratic governments in Hungary and Romania, as in Poland, Bulgaria, and Yugoslavia, were authoritarian traditionalists, not fascists. Still, many government leaders in the region welcomed the closer economic ties with Germany that Hitler's economics minister, Hjalmar Schacht, engineered. The difference between authoritarianism and fascism remained clearest in Austria, where Catholic conservatives undermined democracy during 1933 and 1934. They were actively hostile to the growing pro-Nazi agitation in Austria, partly because they wanted to keep Austria independent.

In France various nationalist, anticommunist, and anti-Semitic leagues gathered momentum during the early 1930s. They covered a spectrum from monarchism to outspoken profascism, but together they constituted at least a potential threat to French democracy. In February 1934, right-wing demonstrations against the Chamber of Deputies provoked a bloody clash with police and forced a change of ministry. As it began to seem that even France might be vulnerable, those from the center and left of the political spectrum began to think about collaborating to resist fascism. The Communists, especially, took the initiative by promoting "popular fronts" of all those seeking to preserve democracy.

This was a dramatic change in strategy for international communism. Even as Hitler was closing in on the German chancellorship in the early 1930s, German Communists, following Comintern policy, continued to attack their socialist rivals rather than seek a unified response to Nazism. From the communist perspective, fascism represented the crisis phase of monopoly capitalism, so a Nazi government would actually be useful to strip away the democratic façade hiding class oppression in Germany. But by 1934 the threat of fascism seemed so pressing that the Communists began actively promoting electoral alliances and governing coalitions with Socialists and even liberal democrats to resist its further spread. From 1934 until 1939, Communists everywhere consistently pursued this "popular front" strategy.

But by the 1930s it was becoming ever harder to be sure what was fascist, what was dangerous, what might lead where. As fears intensified, perceptions became as important as realities. Popular front governments, intended to preserve democracy against what appeared to be fascism, could seem, to conservatives, to be leaning too far to the left. Ideological polarization made democracy extraordinarily difficult. The archetypal example proved to be Spain, where a tragedy of classical proportions was played out.

■ From Democracy to Civil War in Spain, 1931–1939

Spain became a center of attention in the 1930s, when its promising new parliamentary democracy, launched in 1931, led to civil war in 1936 and the triumph of a repressive authoritarian regime in 1939. An earlier effort at constitutional monarchy had fizzled by 1923, when King Alfonso XIII (1886–1941) supported a new military dictatorship. But growing opposition led first to the resignation of the dictator in 1930 and then, in April 1931, to the end of the monarchy and the proclamation of a republic. The elections for a constituent assembly that followed in June produced a solid victory for a coalition of liberal democrats and Socialists, as well as much hope for substantial reform.

A significant agrarian reform law was passed in 1932, but partly because of the difficult depression economic context, the new government was slow to implement it. Feeling betrayed, Socialists and agricultural workers became increasingly radical, producing growing upheaval in the countryside. Radicalism on the left made it harder for the moderates to govern and, at the same time, stimulated conservatives to become more politically active.

A right-wing coalition known as the CEDA, led by José Maria Gil Robles° (1898–1980), grew in strength, becoming the largest party in parliament with the elections of November 1933. In light of its parliamentary strength, the CEDA had a plausible claim to a government role, but it was kept from participation in government until October 1934. It seemed to the left, in the ideologically charged atmosphere of the time, that the growing role of the CEDA was a prelude to fascism. To let the CEDA into the government would be to hand the republic over to its enemies.

A strong Catholic from the traditional Spanish right, Gil Robles refused to endorse the democratic republic as a form of government, but he and the CEDA were willing to work within it. So the Spanish left may have been too quick to see the CEDA as fascist—and to react when the CEDA finally got its government role. However, Mussolini and Hitler had each come to power more or less legally, from within parliamentary institutions. The German left had been criticized for its passive response to the advent of Hitler; the Spanish left wanted to avoid the same mistake.

Thus, when the CEDA finally got a role in the government, the left responded during the fall of 1934 with quasi-revolutionary uprisings in Catalonia and Asturias, where a miners' commune was put down only after two weeks of heavy fighting. In the aftermath, the right-leaning government of 1935 began undoing some of the reforms of the left-leaning government of 1931–1933, though still legally, within the framework of the parliamentary republic.

In February 1936 a popular front coalition to ward off fascism won a narrow electoral victory, sufficient for an absolute majority in parliament. As would be true in France a few months later, electoral victory produced popular expectations that went well beyond the essentially defensive purposes of the popular front. Hoping to win back the leftist rank and file and head off what seemed a dangerous attempt at revolution, the new popular front government began to implement a progressive program, now including the land reform that had been promised but not implemented earlier. But it was too late to undercut the growing radicalization of the masses.

A wave of land seizures began in March 1936, followed by the most extensive strike movement in Spanish history, which by June was becoming clearly revolution-

ary in character. To many, the government's inability to keep order had become the immediate issue. By the early summer of 1936, leaders of the democratic republic had become isolated between the extremes of left and right, each preparing an extralegal solution.

Finally, in mid-July, several army officers initiated a military uprising against the government. Soon led by General Francisco Franco (1892–1975), these Nationalist insurgents took control of substantial parts of Spain. Elsewhere they failed to overcome the resistance of the Republican Loyalists, those determined to defend the republic. So the result was not the intended military takeover but a brutal civil war (see Map 27.1). The substantial Italian fascist and Nazi German intervention on the Nationalist side by the end of 1936 intensified the war's ideological ramifications. At the same time, the remarkable, often heroic resistance of the Loyalists captured the imagination of the world. Indeed, forty thousand volunteers came from abroad to fight to preserve the Spanish republic.

It proved a war of stunning brutality on both sides. Loyalist anticlericalism led to the murder of twelve bishops and perhaps one-eighth of the parish clergy in Spain. On the other side, the German bombing of the Basque town of Guernica° on a crowded market day in April 1937, represented unforgettably in Pablo Picasso's painting, came to symbolize the violence and suffering of the whole era.

Republican Loyalists assumed that Franco and the Nationalists represented another instance of fascism. In fact, however, Franco was no fascist, but rather a traditional military man whose leadership role did not rest on personal charisma. He was an authoritarian emphasizing discipline, order, and Spain's Catholic traditions.

Still, in their effort to rally support during the civil war, Franco's forces found it expedient to take advantage of the appeal of the Falange°, a genuinely fascist movement that had emerged under the leadership of the charismatic young José Antonio Primo de Rivera (1903–1936). Although extremely weak at the time of the elections in February 1936, the Falange grew rapidly in opposition to the leftist radicalism that followed the popular front victory. As street fighting between left and right intensified that spring, the republic arrested José Antonio, as he was called, and he was in prison when the civil war began.

José Antonio decided his best hope was alliance with the military. Although he was contemptuous of their

---

Gil Robles (heel ROH-blayce)

Guernica (gher-NEE-kah, in Spanish; GWAIR-nee-kah, as customarily rendered in English)   **Falange** (fah-LAHN-hay)

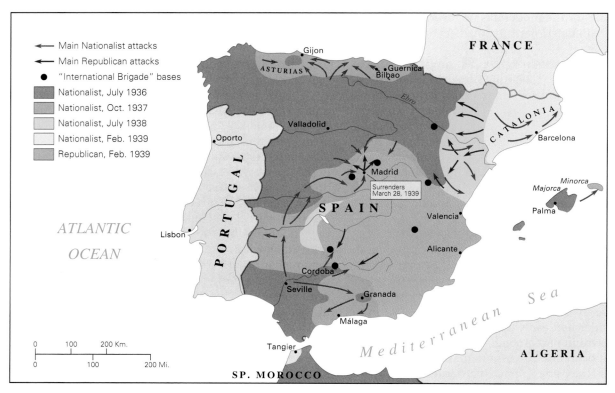

Map 27.1   The Spanish Civil War, 1936–1939   The Nationalist insurgents quickly took over most of northern and eastern Spain in 1936 and then gradually expanded their territory. The fall of Madrid early in 1939 marked the end of fighting. The revolutionary effort of 1936–1937 within the Republican zone was centered in Barcelona.   *(Source: Adapted from* The Times Atlas of World History, *3d ed.* Copyright © HarperCollins Publishers, Ltd. Reprinted by permission of the publisher.)

shortsighted conservatism, he felt their very absence of ideas afforded an opening for the Falange to provide direction, a genuine alternative. But it worked out the other way. In November 1936, José Antonio was tried and executed for conspiring to overthrow the republic, and the Nationalists promptly began using the trappings of the Falange, including the memory of José Antonio, to increase their popular appeal.

Meanwhile, the Republicans had to fight a civil war while dealing with continuing revolution in their own ranks. Developing especially in Catalonia from the uprisings of 1936, that revolution was not communist but anarchist and syndicalist in orientation. The Communists, true to popular front principles, insisted that this was no time for such "infantile leftist" revolutionary experiments. What mattered, throughout the Republican zone, was the factory discipline necessary to produce essential war materiel. So the Communists, under Stalin's

orders, were instrumental in putting down the anarchist revolution in Catalonia in June 1937.

Under these extraordinary circumstances, the Communists, at first a distinct minority on the Spanish left, gradually gained the ascendancy on the Republican side, partly because they were disciplined and effective, partly because Soviet assistance enhanced their prestige. However, this single-minded prosecution of the civil war did not prove enough to defeat the military insurgency, despite the considerable heroism on the Loyalist side. The war ended with the fall of Madrid to the Nationalists in March 1939. General Franco's authoritarian regime governed Spain until his death in 1975.

In Spain, as in Weimar Germany, the initial lack of consensus in a new republic made parliamentary democracy difficult, and the wider ideological framework magnified the difficulties. With the political boiling point so low, the left and the right each saw the other in

Picasso: Guernica   Created for the Spanish Pavilion at the famed 1937 Paris Exhibition, Picasso's painting conveyed horror and outrage—his response to the German bombing of Guernica on a crowded market day in 1937, during the Spanish civil war. Picasso's stark, elemental imagery helped define this era of violence and suffering for the generations that followed.   *(Pablo Picasso, Guernica [1937, May–early June]. Oil on canvas. © Art Resource, NY. © ARS, NY)*

extreme terms and assumed that extraordinary response to the other was necessary. Thus the left tended to view even conservatives operating within a parliamentary framework as "fascist." And each side was relatively quick to give up on a democratic republic that seemed to be tilting too far in the other direction.

■ France in the Era of the Popular Front

In France, as in Spain, concern to arrest the spread of fascism led to a popular front coalition, here including Socialists, Communists, and Radicals, that governed the country from 1936 to 1938. Although it did not lead to civil war, the popular front was central to the French experience of the 1930s, producing polarization and resignation, and undermining confidence in the Third Republic.

Beginning in 1934, the French Communists took the initiative in approaching first the Socialists, then the Radicals, to develop a popular front coalition against fascism. In reaching out to the Radicals, the Communists stressed French patriotism and made no demand for significant economic reforms. Stalin gave this effort a major push in 1935 when, in a stunning change in the commu-

nist line, he stressed the legitimacy of national defense and explicitly endorsed French rearmament.

In the elections of April and May 1936, the popular front won a sizable majority in the Chamber of Deputies, putting the Socialists' leader, Léon Blum (1872–1950), in line to become France's first Socialist prime minister. The Communists pledged full support of the new Blum government but, to avoid fanning fears, they did not participate directly. However, despite the popular front's moderate and essentially defensive aims, the situation quickly began to polarize after the elections.

Fearing that the new Blum government would be forced to devalue the French currency, and thereby diminish the value of assets denominated in francs, French investors immediately began moving their capital abroad. At the same time, the popular front victory produced a wave of enthusiasm among workers that escaped the control of popular front leaders and culminated in a spontaneous strike movement, the largest France had ever seen. By early June it had spread to all major industries nationwide. Although the workers' demands—for collective bargaining, a forty-hour week, and paid vacations—were not extraordinary, the movement involved sit-down strikes as well as the normal

Léon Blum   The French Socialist leader appears in an enthusiastic moment after the popular front victory in 1936. He was about to become France's first Socialist prime minister, but in that role he encountered one dilemma after another. By 1938, the high spirits of 1936 had dissolved.   *(Archives Ringart)*

creases as a direct result of Matignon, then a forty-hour week and paid vacations in a reform package promptly passed by parliament.

In the enthusiasm of the summer of 1936, other reforms were enacted as well, but after that the popular front was forced onto the defensive. Two problems undermined its energy and cohesion: the noncooperation of French business and the Spanish civil war. The cautious response of Blum, the Socialist prime minister, is striking in each case, but he faced a situation with little maneuvering room.

From the outset Blum stressed that he had no mandate for revolution, and as France's first Socialist prime minister, he felt it essential to prove that a Socialist could govern responsibly. Thus, Blum did not respond energetically to the capital flight, even though it produced serious currency and budgetary difficulties. Perhaps, as critics suggest, he should have acted more aggressively to overhaul the French banking and credit system. But Blum shied away from any such drastic measures, both to prove he could be moderate and to avoid antagonizing business.

Blum was also uncertain as he faced the dilemmas surrounding the Spanish civil war. The key question was whether the French government should help the beleaguered Spanish republic, at least by sending supplies. Although he initially favored such help, Blum changed his mind under pressure from three sides. The Conservative government of Stanley Baldwin in Britain was against it. So was the French right; some even suggested that French intervention would provoke civil war in France as well. Moreover, the Radicals in his own coalition were generally opposed to helping the Spanish republic, so intervention would jeopardize the cohesion of the popular front itself.

Thus, rather than help supply the Spanish republic, Blum promoted a nonintervention agreement among the major powers, including Italy and Germany. Many Socialists and Communists within the popular front disliked Blum's cautious policy, however, especially as it became clear that Mussolini and Hitler were violating their hands-off pledges. As Blum stuck to nonintervention, the moral force of the popular front dissolved.

In 1938 a new government under the Radical Edouard Daladier° (1884–1970), still nominally a creature of the popular front, began dismantling some of the key gains of 1936, even attacking the forty-hour week. Citing productivity and national security concerns, Daladier adopted probusiness policies and succeeded in at-

walkouts and thus seemed quasi-revolutionary in character. The major trade union confederation, the Communists, and most Socialists, including Blum himself, saw the strikes as a danger to the popular front, with its more modest aims of defending the republic, and eagerly pursued a settlement.

That settlement, the Matignon° Agreement of June 8, 1936, was a major victory for the French working class. Having been genuinely frightened by the strikes, and now reassured that the popular front government would at least uphold the law, French industrialists were willing to make significant concessions. So the workers got collective bargaining, elected shop stewards, and wage in-

---

Matignon (mah-tin-YAWN)

Daladier (dah-lah-dee-YAY)

tracting capital back to France. But workers, watching the gains they had won in 1936 slip away, felt betrayed. At the same time, businessmen and conservatives began blaming the workers' gains—such as the five-day week—for slowing French rearmament. Although such charges were not entirely fair, they indicated how poisoned the atmosphere in France had become in the wake of the popular front.

As France began to face the possibility of a new war, the popular front was widely blamed for French weakness. When war came at last, resignation and division were prevalent, in contrast with the patriotic unity and high spirits of 1914. It was partly for that reason that France was so easily defeated by Germany in 1940. And when France fell, the democratic Third Republic fell with it.

THE COMING OF WORLD WAR II, 1935–1939

VEN as the Great Depression added to their burdens, Western leaders faced the challenge of maintaining the peace during the 1930s. But despite the promising adjustments of the 1920s, many of the problems that accompanied the World War I peace settlement were still in place when Hitler came to power. And Hitler had consistently trumpeted his intention to overturn that settlement. What scope was there for peaceful revision? Could Hitler be stopped by threat of war? By the last years of the 1930s, these questions tortured the Western world as Hitler went from one success to another, raising the possibility of a new and more destructive war. And the power balance rested on the responses not only of the Western democracies, but of fascist Italy and the communist Soviet Union as well.

■ The Reorientation of Fascist Italy

During its first decade in power, Benito Mussolini's fascist regime in Italy concentrated on domestic reconstruction, especially the effort to mobilize people through their roles as producers within a new corporative state (see page 894). But though corporativist institutions were gradually constructed, with great rhetorical fanfare, they bogged down in bureaucratic meddling. Corporativism proved more the vehicle for regimentation than for a more genuine kind of participation. Mussolini offered assurances that, despite the necessary compromises, fascism's corporativist revolution was

continuing, but many committed fascists were sharply critical of the new system. Fascism seemed to have stalled, partly as the result of compromise with prefascist elites and institutions, and partly as the result of its own internal contradictions.

Mussolini was never merely the instrument of the established elites, but neither was he a consistent ideologue like Hitler. By the early 1930s, he sometimes seemed satisfied with ritual, spectacle, and the cult of his own infallibility as he juggled the contending forces in fascist Italy. But the limitations he had encountered on the domestic level increasingly frustrated him. On the international level, in contrast, the new context after Hitler came to power offered some welcome space for maneuver. So as the fascist revolution in Italy faltered, Mussolini concentrated increasingly on foreign policy.

Though Italy, like Germany, remained dissatisfied with the territorial status quo, it was not obvious that fascist Italy and Nazi Germany had to end up in the same camp. For one thing, Italy was anxious to preserve an independent Austria as a buffer with Germany, whereas many Germans and Austrians favored the unification of the two countries. Such a greater Germany might then threaten the gains Italy had won at the peace conference at Austria's expense. When, in 1934, Germany seemed poised to absorb Austria, Mussolini helped stiffen the resistance of Austria's leaders and played a part in forcing Hitler to back down. Mussolini even warned that Nazism, with its racist orientation, posed a significant threat to the best of European civilization.

As it began to appear that France and Britain might have to work with the Soviet Union to check Hitler's Germany, French and British conservatives pushed for good relations with Mussolini's Italy to provide ideological balance. So Italy was well positioned to play off both sides as Hitler began shaking things up on the international level after 1933. In 1935, just after Hitler announced significant rearmament measures, unilaterally repudiating provisions of the Versailles treaty for the first time, Mussolini hosted a meeting with the French and British prime ministers at Stresa, in northern Italy. In an overt warning to Hitler's Germany, the three powers agreed to resist "any unilateral repudiation of treaties which may endanger the peace of Europe."

However, Mussolini was already preparing to extend Italy's possessions in East Africa to encompass Ethiopia (formerly called Abyssinia). He assumed that the French and British, who needed his support against Hitler, would not offer significant opposition. Ethiopia had become a League of Nations member in 1923—sponsored by Italy, but opposed by Britain and France because it still practiced slavery. After a border incident in December 1934, Italian troops invaded in October 1935, prompting the League to announce sanctions against Italy.

These sanctions were applied haphazardly, largely because France and Britain wanted to avoid irreparable damage to their longer-term relations with Italy. In any case, the sanctions did not deter Mussolini, whose forces prevailed through the use of aircraft and poison gas by May 1936. But they did make Italy receptive to German overtures in the aftermath of its victory. And the victory made Mussolini more restless. Rather than seeking to play again the enviable role of European balancer, he sent Italian troops and materiel to aid the Nationalists in the Spanish civil war, thereby further alienating democratic opinion elsewhere.

Conservatives in Britain and France continued to push for accommodation with Italy, hoping to revive the "Stresa front" against Hitler. Some even defended Italian imperialism in East Africa. But Italy continued its drift toward Germany. Late in 1936 Mussolini spoke of a new Rome-Berlin Axis for the first time. During 1937 and 1938 he and Hitler exchanged visits. Finally, in May 1939, Italy joined Germany in an open-ended military alliance, the Pact of Steel, but Mussolini made it clear that Italy could not be ready for a major European war before 1943.

To cement this developing relationship, fascist Italy adopted anti-Semitic racial laws, even though Italian fascism had not originally been anti-Semitic. Indeed, the party had attracted Jewish Italians to its membership in about the same proportion as non-Jews. Although the imperial venture in Ethiopia had been popular among the Italian people, the increasing subservience to Nazi Germany displeased even many committed fascists. Such opposition helped keep Mussolini from intervention when war broke out in September 1939.

■ Restoring German Sovereignty, 1935–1936

During his first years in power, through 1936, Hitler could be understood as merely restoring German sovereignty, revising a postwar settlement that had been misconceived in the first place. However uncouth and abrasive he might seem, it was hard to find a basis for opposing him. Yet in commencing German rearmament in 1935, and especially in remilitarizing the Rhineland in March 1936, Hitler fundamentally reversed the power balance established in France's favor at the peace conference.

France's special advantage had been the demilitarization of the entire German territory west of the Rhine River and a 50-kilometer strip on the east bank. The measure had been reaffirmed at Locarno in 1925, now with Germany's free agreement, and it was guaranteed by Britain and Italy. Yet on a Saturday morning in March 1936, that advantage disappeared as German troops moved into the forbidden area. The French and British acquiesced, uncertain of what else to do. After all, Hitler was only restoring Germany to full sovereignty.

But Hitler was not likely to stop there. As a result of the war and the peace, three new countries—Austria, Czechoslovakia, and Poland—bordered Germany (see Map 27.2). In each, the peace settlement had left trouble spots involving the status of ethnic Germans; in each, the status quo was open to question.

■ Austria, Czechoslovakia, and Appeasement

As early as 1934, Hitler had moved to encompass his homeland, Austria, but strenuous opposition from Italy led him to back down. The developing understanding with Italy by 1936 enabled Hitler to focus again on Austria—initiating the second, more radical phase of his prewar foreign policy. On a pretext in March 1938, German troops moved into Austria, which was promptly incorporated into Germany. This time Mussolini was willing to acquiesce, and Hitler was genuinely grateful.

The Treaty of Versailles had explicitly prohibited this *Anschluss,* or unity of Austria with Germany, though that prohibition violated the principle of self-determination. It was widely believed in the West, no doubt correctly, that most Austrians favored unity with Germany now that the Habsburg Empire had broken up. The Anschluss could thus be justified as revising a misconceived aspect of the peace settlement.

Czechoslovakia presented quite a different situation. Although it had preserved democratic institutions, the country included restive minorities of Slovaks, Magyars, Ruthenians, Poles, and—concentrated especially in the Sudetenland, along the German and Austrian borders—about 3.25 million Germans. After having been part of the dominant nationality in the old Habsburg Empire, those Germans were frustrated with their minority status in the new Czechoslovakia. Worse, they seemed to suffer disproportionately from the Depression. Hitler's agents actively stirred up their resentments.

Leading the West's response, when Hitler began making an issue of Czechoslovakia, was Neville Chamberlain (1869–1940), who followed Stanley Baldwin as Britain's prime minister in May 1937. An intelligent, vigorous, and public-spirited man from the progressive wing of the Conservative party, Chamberlain has long been derided as the architect of the "appeasement" of Hitler at the Munich conference of 1938, which settled

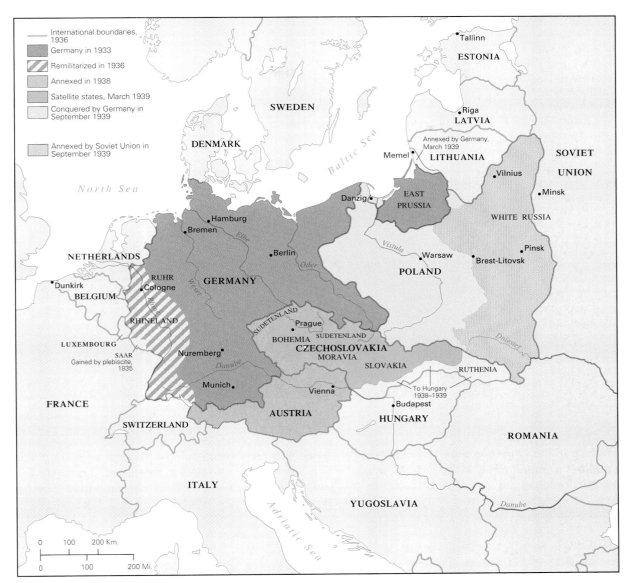

Map 27.2   The Expansion of Nazi Germany, 1936–1939   Especially with the remilitarization of the Rhineland in 1936, Hitler's Germany began moving, step by step, to alter the European power balance. In September 1939 the Soviet Union also began annexing territory, capitalizing on its agreement with Germany the month before.

the crisis over Czechoslovakia. Trumpeted as the key to peace, the Munich agreement proved but a step to the war that broke out less than a year later. Yet though it failed, Chamberlain's policy of appeasement stemmed not from cowardice or mere drift, and certainly not from some unspoken pro-Nazi sentiment.

Rather than let events spin out of control, as seemed to have happened in 1914, Chamberlain sought to master the difficult international situation through creative bargaining. The excesses of Hitler's policy resulted from the mistakes of Versailles; redo the settlement on a more realistic basis, and Germany would behave responsibly. The key, Chamberlain felt, was to pinpoint the sources of Germany's frustrations and, as he put it, "to remove the danger spots one by one."

Moreover, in Britain as elsewhere, there were some who saw Hitler's resurgent Germany as a bulwark against communism, which might spread into east-central

The Illusion of Peace Neville Chamberlain, returning home to Britain from Munich to a hero's welcome, waves the peace declaration that was supposed to have brought "peace in our time." This was late September 1938. Less than a year later, Europe was again at war. *(Hulton Getty/Liaison)*

Europe—especially in the event of another war. Indeed, the victor in another war might well be the revolutionary left. To prevent such an outcome was worth a few concessions to Hitler.

The Czechs, led by Eduard Beneš° (1884–1948), made some attempt to liberalize their nationality policy. But by April 1938 they were becoming ever less sympathetic to Sudeten German demands for autonomy, especially as German bullying came to accompany them. Tensions between Czechoslovakia and Germany mounted, and by late September 1938 war appeared imminent, despite Chamberlain's efforts to mediate. (See the box "Reading Sources: Toward Appeasement: The Longing for Peace.") Both the French and the British began mobilizing, with French troops manning the Maginot Line for the first time.

A 1924 treaty bound France to come to the aid of Czechoslovakia in the event of aggression. Moreover, the Soviet Union, according to a treaty of 1935, was bound to assist Czechoslovakia if the French did so. And throughout the crisis, the Soviets pushed for a strong stand in de-

Beneš (BAY-naish)

fense of Czechoslovakia against German aggression. For both ideological and military reasons, however, the British and French were reluctant to line up for war on the side of the Soviet Union. The value of the Soviet military was uncertain, at best, at a time when the Soviet officer corps had just been purged.

By September, Hitler seemed eager to smash the Czechs by force, but when Mussolini proposed a four-power conference, he was persuaded to talk again. At Munich late in September, Britain, France, Italy, and Germany settled the matter, with Czechoslovakia—and the Soviet Union—excluded. Determined not to risk war over what seemed Czech intransigence, the British ended up agreeing to what Hitler had wanted all along—not merely autonomy for the Sudeten Germans but German annexation of the Sudetenland.

The Munich agreement specified that all Sudeten areas with German majorities be transferred to Germany. Plebiscites were to be held in areas with large German minorities, and Hitler pledged to respect the sovereignty of the now diminished Czechoslovak state. Chamberlain and his French counterpart, Edouard Daladier, each returned home to a hero's welcome, having transformed

ᘓ READING SOURCES

Toward Appeasement: The Longing for Peace

Late in September 1938, the crisis that developed over Germany's demands on Czechoslovakia produced an emotional roller coaster for Europeans. Central to the continuing effort to preserve the peace was the British prime minister, Neville Chamberlain, who flew to Germany twice to meet with Hitler before the crisis reached its climax. At first, Chamberlain thought he had found a formula for peace, but then Hitler upped his demands. Thus, Chamberlain's tone was somber when he addressed the British people by radio shortly after his second trip, on September 27, at what proved the height of the crisis.

First of all I must say something to those who have written to my wife or myself in these last weeks to tell us of their gratitude for my efforts and to assure us of their prayers for my success. Most of these letters have come from women—mothers or sisters of our own countrymen. But there are countless others besides—from France, from Belgium, from Italy, even from Germany, and it has been heartbreaking to read of the growing anxiety they reveal. . . .

If I felt my responsibility heavy before, to read such letters has made it seem almost overwhelming. How horrible, fantastic, incredible it is that we should be digging trenches and trying on gas masks here because of a quarrel in a far-away country between people of whom we know nothing. It seems still more impossible that a quarrel which has already been settled in principle should be the subject of war.

I can well understand the reasons why the Czech Government have felt unable to accept the terms which have been put before them in the German memorandum. Yet I believe after my talks with Herr Hitler that, if only time were allowed, it ought to be possible for the arrangements for transferring the territory that the Czech government has agreed to give to Germany to be settled by agreement under condi-

tions which would assure fair treatment to the population concerned. . . .

However much we may sympathise with a small nation confronted by a big and powerful neighbor, we cannot in all circumstances undertake to involve the whole British Empire in war simply on her account. If we have to fight it must be on larger issues than that. . . . [I]f I were convinced that any nation had made up its mind to dominate the world by fear of its force, I should feel that it must be resisted. . . . But war is a fearful thing, and we must be very clear, before we embark on it, that it is really the great issues that are at stake. . . .

For the present I ask you to await as calmly as you can the events of the next few days. As long as war has not begun, there is always hope that it may be prevented, and you know that I am going to work for peace to the last moment. Good night.

Source: Neville Chamberlain, *In Search of Peace: Speeches (1937–1938)* (London: Hutchinson, 1939), pp. 274–276.

 For additional information on this topic, go to http://college.hmco.com.

what had seemed certain war to, in Chamberlain's soon-to-be-notorious phrase, "peace in our time."

Rather than settle the nationality questions bedeviling Czechoslovakia, the Munich agreement only provoked further unrest. Poland and Hungary, eager to exploit the new weakness of Czechoslovakia, agitated successfully to annex disputed areas with large numbers of their respective nationalities. Then unrest stemming from Slovak separatism afforded a pretext for Germany to send troops into Prague in March 1939. The Slovak areas were spun off as a separate nation, while the Czech areas became the Protectorate of Bohemia and Moravia.

Less than six months after the Munich conference, most of what had been Czechoslovakia had landed firmly within the Nazi orbit (see Map 27.2). It was no longer possible to justify Hitler's actions as an effort to unite all Germans in one state.

■ Poland, the Nazi-Soviet Pact, and the Coming of War

With Poland, the German grievance was still more serious, for the new Polish state had been created partly at German expense. Especially galling to Germans was the Polish corridor, which cut off East Prussia from the bulk of Germany in order to give Poland access to the sea. The city of Danzig (now Gdansk), historically Polish but part of Germany before World War I, was left a "free city," supervised by the League of Nations.

Disillusioned by Hitler's dismemberment of Czechoslovakia, and angered by the Germans' menacing rhetoric regarding Poland, Chamberlain announced to the House of Commons on March 31, 1939, that Britain and France would intervene militarily should Poland's independence be threatened. Chamberlain was not only abandoning the policy of appeasement; he was making a clear commitment to the Continent, of the sort that British governments had resisted since 1919. He could do so partly because Britain was rapidly rearming. By early 1940, in fact, Britain was spending nearly as large a share of its national income on the military as Germany was.

Chamberlain's assertive statement was not enough to deter Hitler, who seems to have been determined to settle the Polish question by force. In an effort to localize the conflict, however, Hitler continued to insist that German aims were limited and reasonable. Germany simply wanted Danzig and German transit across the corridor; it was the Polish stance that was rigid and unreasonable. Hitler apparently believed that Polish stubbornness would alienate the British and French, undercutting their support. And as the crisis developed by mid-1939, doubts were increasingly expressed, on all sides, that the British and French were really prepared to aid Poland militarily—that they had the will "to die for Danzig."

Although they had been lukewarm to Soviet proposals for a military alliance, Britain and France began to negotiate with the Soviet Union more seriously during the spring and summer of 1939. But reservations about the value of a Soviet alliance continued to gnaw at Western leaders. For one thing, Soviet troops could gain access to Germany only by moving through Poland or Romania. But each had territory gained at the expense of Russia in the postwar settlement, so the British and French, suspicious of Soviet designs on both, were reluctant to insist that Soviet troops be allowed to pass through them.

Even as negotiations between the Soviet Union and the democracies continued, the Soviets came to their own agreement with Nazi Germany on August 23, 1939, in a pact that astonished the world. Each side had been denouncing the other, and although Hitler had explored the possibility of Soviet neutrality in May, serious negotiations began only that August, when the Soviets got the clear signal that a German invasion of Poland was inevitable. It now appeared that no Soviet alliance with Britain and France could prevent war. Under these circumstances, a nonaggression pact with Germany seemed better to serve Soviet interests than a problematic war on the side of Britain and France. So the Soviets agreed with the Germans that each would remain neutral in the event that either became involved in a war with some other nation.

The Soviet flip-flop stemmed partly from disillusionment with the British and French response to the accelerating threat of Nazism. The democracies seemed no more trustworthy, and potentially no less hostile, than Nazi Germany. Moreover, a secret protocol to the Nazi-Soviet Pact apportioned major areas of east-central Europe between the Soviet Union and Germany. As a result, the Soviets soon regained much of what they had lost after World War I, when Poland, Finland, and other states had been created or aggrandized with territories that had formerly been part of the Russian Empire.

The Nazi-Soviet Pact seemed to give Hitler the free hand he wanted in Poland. With the dramatic change in alignment, the democracies were surely much less likely to intervene. But Chamberlain, again determined to avoid the hesitations of 1914, publicly reaffirmed the British guarantee to Poland on August 25. Britain would indeed intervene if Germany attacked. And after Hitler ordered the German invasion of Poland on September 1, the British and French responded with declarations of war on September 3.

With each step on the path to war, Hitler had vacillated between apparent reasonableness and wanton aggressiveness. Sometimes he accented the plausibility of his demands in light of problems with the postwar settlement; sometimes he seemed to be actively seeking war. Even in invading Poland, he may still have hoped to localize hostilities. But he was certainly willing to risk a more general European war, and the deepest thrust of his policy was toward an all-out war of conquest—first against Poland, but ultimately against the Soviet Union. War was essential to the Nazi vision, and only when the assault on Poland became a full-scale war did the underlying purposes of Nazism become clear.

SUMMARY

HE 1930s made a cruel mockery of the hopes for restabilization that had followed World War I. The Depression and the challenges from new political regimes called both capitalism and democracy into question. Hitler's Germany, especially, presented an unprecedented challenge to the European order, but the leading democracies, Britain and France, were slow to respond. Eagerness to avoid another war affected their reactions, as did the ideological polarization of the decade. Led by Britain, the democracies began seriously resisting the Nazi challenge only in 1939.

During the 1930s the democracies had to respond to three novel regimes—Italian fascism, German Nazism, and Stalinist communism—that did not play by the expected rules. Although their originating purposes differed, each was totalitarian in seeking the total political mobilization of the population, so that even leisure-time activities took on a public or political dimension. And each claimed to be superior partly because of its capacity to mobilize people for great collective projects as democratic regimes could not. But though they did involve ordinary people in new ways, each of the three regimes concentrated power in the hands of dictators. Thus they were at once dynamic and unpredictable—and thus, in part, the hesitancy and uncertainty of the democracies in dealing with them.

At the same time, the hesitations of the democracies during the 1930s tended to confirm the view of the three dictators that democracy was weak, decadent, passé. Such contempt inclined Mussolini and Hitler to ever greater recklessness, and persuaded Stalin finally to make his own deal with the Nazis in August 1939. When he invaded Poland on September 1, Hitler seriously believed the democracies would let him have his way. It was hardly clear that this would end up another European war, let alone the most destructive, cataclysmic war the world had ever seen.

■ Notes

1. Quoted in Martin McCauley, *The Soviet Union Since 1917* (London and New York: Longman, 1981), pp. 72–73.
2. Quoted in Robert Conquest, *The Great Terror: A Reassessment* (New York: Oxford University Press, 1990), p. 24.
3. Quoted in Helmut Krausnick et al., *Anatomy of the SS State* (New York: Walker, 1968), p. 13.

■ Suggested Reading

Bell, P. M. H. *The Origins of the Second World War in Europe.* 2d ed. 1997. A well-organized and fair-minded survey.

Boffa, Giuseppe. *The Stalin Phenomenon.* 1992. An invaluable historiographical survey—thorough, balanced, and accessible.

Burleigh, Michael, and Wolfgang Wippermann. *The Racial State: Germany 1933–1945.* 1991. Influential, thoroughly researched study of the Nazi quest for "race hygiene."

Fischer, Klaus P. *Nazi Germany: A New History.* 1995. Comprehensive and well researched, this is perhaps the best one-volume treatment of Nazism in English.

Fitzpatrick, Sheila. *Everyday Stalinism, Ordinary Life in Extraordinary Times: Soviet Russia in the 1930s.* 1999. An engaging, balanced account of urban life in the Soviet Union in the context of the upheavals of the 1930s.

Kershaw, Ian. *Hitler,* Vol. 1: *1889–1936, Hubris,* and Vol. 2: *1936–1945, Nemesis.* 1999, 2000. A thorough, very readable biography by a leading authority on Nazism.

Payne, Stanley G. *A History of Fascism, 1914–1945.* 1995. A comprehensive account with historical and interpretive sections, as well as an epilogue on the scope for neofascism.

Watt, Donald Cameron. *How War Came: The Immediate Origins of the Second World War, 1938–1939.* 1989. Detailed but readable narrative account, based on thorough research.

Weber, Eugen. *The Hollow Years: France in the 1930s.* 1994. A lively account of French life and manners during a decade that led to humiliation and defeat.

 For a searchable list of additional readings for this chapter, go to http://college.hmco.com.

Film as Propaganda

One of the extraordinary pieces of evidence from the Nazi period is *Triumph of the Will,* a documentary film on the sixth Nazi Party rally, which took place September 4–10, 1934, in the historic city of Nuremberg, by this time the official site for such party rallies. Directed by a talented young woman, Leni Riefenstahl (b. 1902), *Triumph of the Will* has long been recognized as one of the most compelling propaganda films ever made. What can we learn from this film about how the Nazis understood and used propaganda? What was the Nazi regime trying to convey in sponsoring the film, with the particular images it contained?

A sense of the scope for political propaganda was one of the defining features of the Nazi movement virtually from its inception. In his quest for power Hitler allotted an especially significant role to his future propaganda minister, Joseph Goebbels. Both Hitler and Goebbels saw that new media and carefully orchestrated events might be used to shape the political views of masses of people.

The Nazi Party held the first of what would become annual conventions in Nuremberg in 1927. From the start, these meetings were rallies of the faithful, intended to give the Nazi movement a sense of cohesion and common purpose; but they increasingly became carefully staged propaganda spectacles, with banners and searchlights, parades and speeches. When, by 1934, the regime had completed the task of immediate power consolidation, it seemed time to seize the potential of the film medium to carry the spectacle beyond those present in Nuremberg. The intention to make a film thus influenced the staging of the 1934 rally. Film would transform the six-day event into a single potent work of art.

When Hitler came to power, Goebbels, as propaganda minister, assumed control of the German film industry, and he was particularly jealous of his prerogatives in this sphere. If there was to be a film of one of the Nuremberg rallies, he assumed that he would be in charge. So he objected strenuously when Hitler decided that Riefenstahl, who was not even a party member, should film the 1934 rally.

Already popular as an actress, Riefenstahl had established her own film-making company in 1931, before she turned 30. Her first film won the admiration of Hitler, who sought her out and eventually proposed that she direct the film of the party rally. Although she was an artist with no special interest in politics, Riefenstahl, like many Germans, believed at this point that Hitler might be able to revive Germany's fortunes. So despite considerable reluctance, she bowed to Hitler's persistence and agreed to do the film—though only after she was guaranteed final control over editing. Her relations with Goebbels remained strained, but Hitler continued to support her as she made *Triumph of the Will.*

Riefenstahl developed the 107-minute film by editing sixty-one hours of footage that covered everything from Hitler's arrival and motorcade to the closing parades and speeches. As depicted on film, the party rally does not convey an overt ideological message. We hear Hitler not attacking Jews or glorifying conquest but simply trumpeting German renewal. What strikes us in Riefenstahl's portrayal are the unity and epic monumentality that Nazism had apparently brought to Germany thanks to Hitler's leadership.

The film opens as Hitler emerges from dramatic cloud formations to arrive by airplane, descending from the sky like a god. He appears throughout the film as an almost superhuman figure, even, as in the shot shown here, as inspired, possessed, uncanny. Above all, he is a

As seen in *Triumph of the Will,* the Leader . . .

. . . and the Disciplined, Tightly Knit Community of Followers *(Both photos from the Museum of Modern Art/Film Stills Archive)*

creator who shapes reality by blending will and art, forging masses of anonymous individuals into one people, one racial community, ready for anything. Those individuals seem, from one perspective, to lose their individuality in a monolithic mass, as in the shot of the parade grounds. But their sense of involvement in grandiose purposes charges them emotionally, even gives them a kind of ecstasy. The symbols, the massed banners, the ritualistic show of conformity, all strengthened this sense of participation in the new people's community. But unity and community were not ends in themselves; the film exalted military values and depicted a disciplined society organized for war.

Triumph of the Will extended participation in the spectacle to those who were not actually present in Nuremberg. The film chiseled the sprawling event into a work of art, so seeing the film was in some ways more effective than being there. The Nazis looked for every means possible to involve the whole society in ritualistic spectacles that could promote a sense of belonging and unity. In addition to film, they made effective use of radio, even subsidizing the purchase of radio sets, or "people's receivers." Such new media were to help ordinary Germans feel a more meaningful kind of belonging than possible under the democracy of the Weimar Republic. But this was only an emotional involvement, not the active participation of free citizens invited to make rational choices.

Triumph of the Will had its premiere in March 1935, with Hitler in the audience. It won several prizes in Germany and abroad but enjoyed only mixed success with the German public, especially outside the large cities. For some, it was altogether too artistic, and the Nazi regime did not use it widely for overt propaganda purposes. Still, the Nazis commissioned no other film about Hitler, for *Triumph of the Will* captured the way he wanted to be seen. Indeed, Hitler praised the film as an "incomparable glorification of the power and beauty of our Movement."

 For additional information on this topic, go to http://college.hmco.com.

CHAPTER 28

The Era of the Second World War 1939–1949

T HE effects could well be called unprecedented, magnificent, beautiful, stupendous and terrifying. No manmade phenomenon of such tremendous power had ever occurred before. . . . Thirty seconds after the explosion came first, the air blast pressing hard against the people and things, to be followed almost immediately by the strong, sustained, awesome roar which warned of doomsday and made us feel that we puny things were blasphemous to dare tamper with the forces heretofore reserved to The Almighty."[1]

So wrote Brigadier General Thomas F. Farrell, who had just witnessed the birth of the atomic age. On July 16, 1945, watching from a shelter 10,000 yards away, Farrell had seen the first explosion of an atomic bomb at a remote, top-secret U.S. government testing ground near Alamogordo, New Mexico. Such a weapon had been little more than a theoretical possibility when World War II began, and it required a remarkable concentration of effort, centered first in Britain, then in the United States, to make possible the awesome spectacle that confronted General Farrell. Exceeding most expectations, the test revealed a weapon of unprecedented power and destructiveness.

Within weeks, the United States dropped two other atomic bombs—first on Hiroshima, then on Nagasaki—to force the surrender of Japan in August 1945. Thus ended the Second World War, the conflict that had begun six long years earlier with the German invasion of Poland. At first Germany enjoyed remarkable success, prompting Italy to intervene—and encouraging Japanese aggressiveness as well. But Britain held on even after its ally, France, fell to Germany in 1940. Then

Atomic bombing of Nagasaki, August 9, 1945. When this photo was taken, from an observation plane 6 miles up, thirty-five thousand people on the ground had already died.
(By courtesy of the Trustees of the Imperial War Museum)

the war changed character in 1941 when Germany attacked the Soviet Union and Japan attacked the United States.

Britain, the United States, and the Soviet Union quickly came together in a "Grand Alliance," which spearheaded the victorious struggle against the Axis powers, Germany, Italy, and Japan. In Europe, the Soviet victory in a brutal land war with Germany proved decisive. In East Asia and the Pacific, the Americans gradually prevailed against Japan. The American use of the atomic bomb to end the war was the final stage in an escalation of violence that made World War II the most destructive in history. What the advent of this terrifying new weapon would mean for the future remained unclear in the war's immediate aftermath.

The ironic outcome of the Second World War was a new cold war between the two major victors, the United States and the Soviet Union. Emerging from the war with far greater power and prestige, each assumed a world role that would have been hard to imagine just a few years earlier. By the end of the 1940s, these two new superpowers had divided Europe into competing spheres of influence. Indeed, the competition between the United States and the Soviet Union almost immediately became global in scope, creating a bipolar world. And the cold war between them was especially terrifying because, seeking military advantage, they raced to stockpile ever more destructive nuclear weapons. Thus the threat of nuclear annihilation helped define the cold war era.

World War II led to the defeat of Italy, Germany, and Japan and in this sense resolved the conflicts that had caused it. But the experience of this particular war changed the world forever. Before finally meeting defeat, the Nazis were sufficiently successful to begin implementing their "new order" in Europe, especially in the territories they conquered to the east. As part of this effort, in what has become known as the Holocaust, they began systematically murdering Jews in extermination camps, eventually killing as many as 6 million. The most destructive of the camps was at Auschwitz°, in what had been Poland. Often paired after the war, Auschwitz and Hiroshima came to stand for the incredible new forms of death and destruction that the war had spawned—and that continued to haunt the world long after it had ended, posing new questions about the meaning of Western civilization.

QUESTIONS TO CONSIDER

- How did the Allies manage to defeat Germany in World War II, after Germany's remarkable successes during the war's first two years?

- Does it make sense to link the Holocaust and the atomic bombing of Japan as radically new forms of violence emerging from the Second World War, or are they better seen as fundamentally dissimilar?

- What are the arguments for and against the Allied policy of forcing Nazi leaders to stand trial after Germany's military defeat?

- What was the relationship between the Allied victory in World War II and the coming of the cold war?

TERMS TO KNOW

Vichy France
Winston Churchill
Auschwitz-Birkenau
Stalingrad
"the Great Patriotic War"
Franklin Delano Roosevelt
lend-lease
D-Day
Yalta conference

United Nations
Potsdam conference
Nuremberg trials
cold war
Truman Doctrine

Auschwitz (OWSH-vits)

THE VICTORY OF NAZI GERMANY, 1939–1941

 NSTEAD of the enthusiasm evident in 1914, the German invasion of Poland on September 1, 1939, produced a grim sense of foreboding, even in Germany. Well-publicized incidents such as the German bombing of civilians during the Spanish civil war and the Italian use of poison gas in Ethiopia suggested that the frightening new technologies introduced in World War I would now be used on a far greater scale. The new conflict would be a much uglier war, more directly involving civilians.

Still, as in 1914, there were hopes that this war could be localized and brief—that it would not become a "world war." Hitler and the Germans envisioned a *Blitzkrieg,* or "lightning war," and the initial outcome seemed to confirm these expectations. Poland fell quickly, and Hitler publicly offered peace to Britain and France, seriously thinking that might be the end of it. The British and French refused to call off the war, but from 1939 through 1941 the Nazis won victory after victory, establishing the foundation for their new order in Europe.

■ Initial Conquests and "Phony War"

The Polish army was large enough to have given the Germans a serious battle. But in adapting the technological innovations of World War I, Germany had developed a new military strategy based on rapid mobility. This Blitzkrieg strategy employed swift, highly concentrated offensives based on mobile tanks covered with concentrated air support, including dive-bombers that struck just ahead of the tanks. In Poland this strategy proved decisive. The French could offer only token help, and the last Polish unit surrendered on October 2, barely a month after the fighting had begun. The speed of the German victory stunned the world.

Meanwhile, the Soviets began cashing in on the pact they had made with Nazi Germany a few weeks before. It offered a precious opportunity to undo provisions of the World War I settlement that had significantly diminished the western territories of the former Russian Empire. On September 17, with the German victory in Poland assured, Stalin sent Soviet forces westward to share in the spoils. Soon Poland was again divided between Germany and Russia, just as most of it had been before 1914. The Baltic states of Estonia, Latvia, and Lithuania soon fell as well.

CHRONOLOGY

September 1, 1939	Germany invades Poland
1939–1940	Soviets wage "Winter War" against Finland
1940	Germany attacks Denmark and Norway (April)
	Germany attacks the Netherlands, Belgium, and France (May 10)
1941	Germany attacks the Soviet Union (June 22)
	Churchill and Roosevelt agree to the Atlantic Charter (August)
December 7, 1941	Japan attacks Pearl Harbor
August 1942– February 1943	Battle of Stalingrad
November 1942	Allied landings in North Africa
April–May 1943	Warsaw ghetto revolt
1943	Soviet victory in Battle of Kursk-Orel (July)
	Allied landings in Sicily; fall of Mussolini; Italy asks for an armistice (July)
	Teheran conference (November)
June 6, 1944	D-Day: Allied landings in Normandy
February 1945	Yalta conference
May 7–8, 1945	Germany surrenders
June 1945	Founding of the United Nations
July–August 1945	Potsdam conference
August 6, 1945	U.S. atomic bombing of Hiroshima
August 14, 1945	Japan surrenders
March 1947	Truman Doctrine
June 1948–May 1949	Berlin blockade and airlift
August 1949	First Soviet atomic bomb
September 1949	Founding of the Federal Republic in West Germany

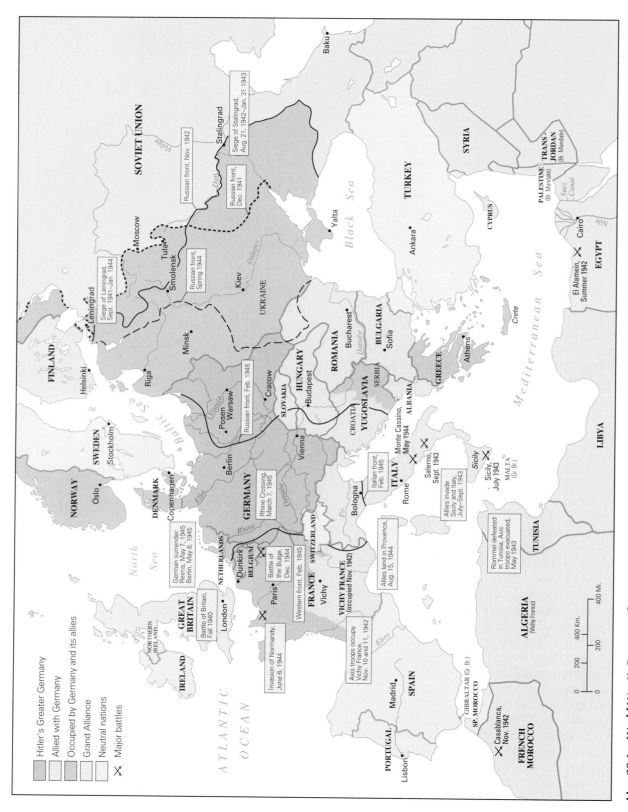

Map 28.1 World War II: European Theaters Much of Europe saw fighting during World War II, although different fronts were important at different times. What proved decisive was the fighting that ensued in the vast expanse of the Soviet Union after the Germans invaded in June 1941.

When Finland proved less pliable, the Soviets invaded in November 1939. In the ensuing "Winter War," the Finns held out bravely, and only by taking heavy casualties did the Soviets manage to prevail by March 1940. These difficulties seemed to confirm suspicions that Stalin's purge during the mid-1930s had substantially weakened the Soviet army. Still, by midsummer 1940 the Soviet Union had regained much of the territory it had lost during the upheavals surrounding the revolution of 1917.

In the west, little happened during the strained winter of 1939–1940, known as the "Phony War." Then, on April 9, 1940, the Germans attacked Norway and Denmark in a surprise move to preempt a British and French scheme to cut off the major route for the shipment of Swedish iron ore to Germany. Denmark fell almost at once, while the staunch resistance in Norway was effectively broken by the end of April. The stage was set for the German assault on France.

■ The Fall of France, 1940

The war in the west began in earnest on May 10, 1940, when the Germans attacked France and the Low Countries. They launched their assault on France through the Ardennes Forest, above the northern end of the Maginot Line—terrain so difficult the French had discounted the possibility of an enemy strike there (see page 884). As in 1914, northern France quickly became the focus of a major war pitting French forces and their British allies against invading Germans. But this time, in startling contrast to World War I, the Battle of France was over in less than six weeks, a humiliating defeat for the French.

The problem for France was not lack of men and materiel, but strategy: how men and materiel were used. For example, Germany had only a slight numerical advantage in tanks. But in France, as in Poland, Germany took advantage of mobile tanks and dive-bombers to mount rapid, highly concentrated offensives. Germany achieved the essential breakthrough partly because the French command underestimated the speed with which the German army could move through Belgium.

Anticipating another long, defensive war, France had dispersed its tanks among infantry units along a broad front. Once the German tank column broke through the French lines, it quickly cut through northern France toward the North Sea. France's poor showing convinced the British that rather than commit troops and planes to a hopeless battle in France, they should get out and regroup for a longer global war. Finally, 200,000

British troops—as well as 130,000 French—escaped German encirclement and capture through a difficult evacuation at Dunkirk early in June (see Map 28.1).

By mid-June, Germany had won a decisive victory. As the French military collapsed, the French cabinet resigned, to be replaced by a new government under Marshal Philippe Pétain, who had led the successful French effort in the Battle of Verdun during World War I. Pétain's government first asked for an armistice and then engineered a change of regime. The French parliament voted by an overwhelming majority to give Pétain exceptional powers, including the power to draw up a new constitution. So ended the parliamentary democracy of the Third Republic, which seemed responsible for France's weakness. The republic gave way to the more authoritarian Vichy° regime, named after the resort city to which the government retreated as the Germans moved into Paris. The end of the fighting in France resulted in a kind of antidemocratic revolution, but one in which the French people, stunned by military defeat, at first acquiesced.

According to the armistice agreement, the French government was not only to cease hostilities but also to collaborate with the victorious Germans. French resistance began immediately, however. In a radio broadcast from London on June 18, Charles de Gaulle° (1890–1970), the youngest general in the French army, called on French forces to rally to him to continue the fight against Nazi Germany. The military forces stationed in the French colonies, as well as the French troops that had been evacuated at Dunkirk, could form the nucleus of a new French army. Under the circumstances of military defeat and political change, de Gaulle's appeal seemed quixotic at best, and most French colonies went along with what seemed the legitimate French government at Vichy. For the new Vichy government, de Gaulle was a traitor. Yet a new Free French force grew from de Gaulle's remarkable appeal, and its subsequent role in the war helped overcome the humiliation of France's quick defeat in 1940.

What next for Hitler and the Germans, who seemed virtually invincible after their conquest of France? Ultimately decisive would be the assault on the Soviet Union in June 1941, but two chains of events after the Battle of France influenced the timing of the assault—perhaps in crucial ways. Britain proved a more implacable foe, and Italy a more burdensome friend, than Hitler had expected.

Vichy (VEE-shee)   **de Gaulle** (duh GOHL)

■ Winston Churchill and the Battle of Britain

With the defeat of France, Hitler seems to have expected that Britain, now apparently vulnerable to German invasion, would come to terms. And certainly some prominent Britons did question the wisdom of remaining at war. But the British war effort found a new and effective champion in Winston Churchill (1874–1965), who replaced Neville Chamberlain as prime minister on May 10, when the German invasion of western Europe began. Although Churchill had been prominent in British public life for years, his career to this point had not been noteworthy for either judgment or success. He was obstinate, difficult, something of a curmudgeon. Yet he rose to the wartime challenge, becoming one of the notable leaders of the modern era. In speeches to the House of Commons during the remainder of 1940, he inspired his nation with some of the most memorable words of the war. Though some found a negotiated settlement with Germany even more sensible in light of the outcome in France, Churchill's dogged promise of "blood, toil, tears, and sweat" helped rally the British people, so that later he could say, without exaggeration, that "this was their finest hour."

After the fall of France, Churchill's Britain promptly moved to full mobilization for a protracted war. Indeed, Britain developed the most thoroughly coordinated war economy of all the belligerents, producing more tanks, aircraft, and machine guns than Germany did between 1940 and 1942. The National Service Act of 1941 subjected men aged 18 to 50 and women aged 20 to 30 to military or civilian war service. The upper age limits were subsequently raised to meet the demand for labor. Almost 70 percent of the 3 million people added to the British work force during the war were women.

Britain, then, intended to continue the fight even after France fell. Hitler weighed his options and decided to attack. In light of British naval superiority, he hoped to rely on aerial bombardment to knock the British out of the war without an actual invasion. The ensuing Battle of

British Resistance   At the height of the German bombing of Britain in 1940, Winston Churchill surveys the damage in London.   *(Hulton Getty/Tony Stone Images)*

Britain culminated in the nightly bombing of London from September 7 through November 2, 1940, killing fifteen thousand and destroying thousands of buildings. But the British held. Ordinary people holed up in cellars and subway stations, while the fighter planes of the Royal Air Force fought back effectively, inflicting heavy losses against German aircraft over Britain.

Although the bombing continued into 1941, the British had withstood the worst the Germans could deliver, and Hitler began looking to the east, his ultimate objective all along. In December 1940 he ordered preparations for Operation Barbarossa, the assault on the Soviet Union. Rather than continuing the attack on Britain directly, Germany would use submarines to cut off shipping—and thus the supplies the British needed for a long war. Once Germany had defeated the Soviet Union, it would enjoy the geopolitical basis for world power, while Britain, as an island nation relying on a dispersed empire, would sooner or later be forced to come to terms.

■ Italian Intervention and the Spread of the War

Lacking sufficient domestic support, and unready for a major war, Mussolini could only look on as the war began in 1939. But as the Battle of France neared its end, it seemed safe for Italy to intervene, sharing in the spoils of what appeared certain victory. Thus in June 1940 Italy entered the war, expecting to secure territorial advantages in the Mediterranean, starting with Corsica, Nice, and Tunisia at the expense of France. Italy also hoped eventually to supplant Britain in the region—and even to take the Suez Canal.

Although Hitler and Mussolini got along reasonably well, their relationship was sensitive. When Hitler seemed to be proceeding without Italy during the first year of the war, Mussolini grew determined to show his independence and finally, in October 1940, ordered Italian forces to attack Greece. But the Greeks mounted a strong resistance, thanks partly to the help of British forces from North Africa.

Meanwhile, Germany had established its hegemony in much of east-central Europe without military force, often by exploiting grievances over the outcome of the peace conference in 1919. In November 1940 Romania and Hungary joined the Axis camp, and Bulgaria followed a few months later. But in March 1941, just after Yugoslavia had similarly committed to the Axis, a coup overthrew the pro-Axis government in Yugoslavia, and the new Yugoslav government prepared to aid the Allies.

By this point Hitler had decided it was expedient to push into the Balkans with German troops, both to reinforce the Italians and to consolidate Axis control of the area. As the war's geographic extent expanded, its stakes increased, yet the Germans continued to meet every challenge. By the end of May 1941 they had taken Yugoslavia and Greece (see Map 28.1).

At the same time, the war was spreading to North Africa and the Middle East because of European colonial ties. The native peoples of the area sought to take advantage of the conflict among the Europeans to pursue their own independence. Iraq and Syria became involved as Germans operating from Syria, administered by Vichy France, aided anti-British Arab nationalists in Iraq. But most important proved to be North Africa, where Libya, an Italian colony since 1912, lay adjacent to Egypt, where the British presence remained strong.

In September 1940 the Italian army drove 65 miles into Egypt, initiating almost three years of fighting across the North African desert. A British counteroffensive from December 1940 to February 1941 drove the Italians back 340 miles into Libya, prompting Germany to send some of its forces from the Balkans into North Africa. Under General Erwin Rommel (1891–1944), the famous "Desert Fox," Axis forces won remarkable successes in North Africa from February to May 1941. But successful though they had been to this point, the German forays into the Balkans and North Africa had delayed the crucial attack on the Soviet Union.

THE ASSAULT ON THE SOVIET UNION AND THE NAZI NEW ORDER

ERMAN troops invaded the Soviet Union on June 22, 1941, initiating what proved the decisive confrontation of World War II. Although the Nazis enjoyed the expected successes for a while, the Soviets eventually prevailed, spearheading the Allied victory in Europe. Supplies from their new Allies—Britain and eventually the United States—aided the Soviet cause, but the surprising strength of the Soviet military effort was the most important factor in the eventual outcome. In the process, though, the Soviets suffered incredible casualties, and after they gained the initiative, they proceeded with particular brutality as they forced the invading Germans back into Germany.

In doing so, the Soviets were responding to the unprecedented form of warfare that the Nazis had unleashed. In preparing for the attack on the Soviet Union, Hitler had made it clear to the Nazi leadership that this was to be no ordinary military engagement but a war of racial-ideological extermination. And the Germans penetrated well into the Soviet Union, reaching the apex of

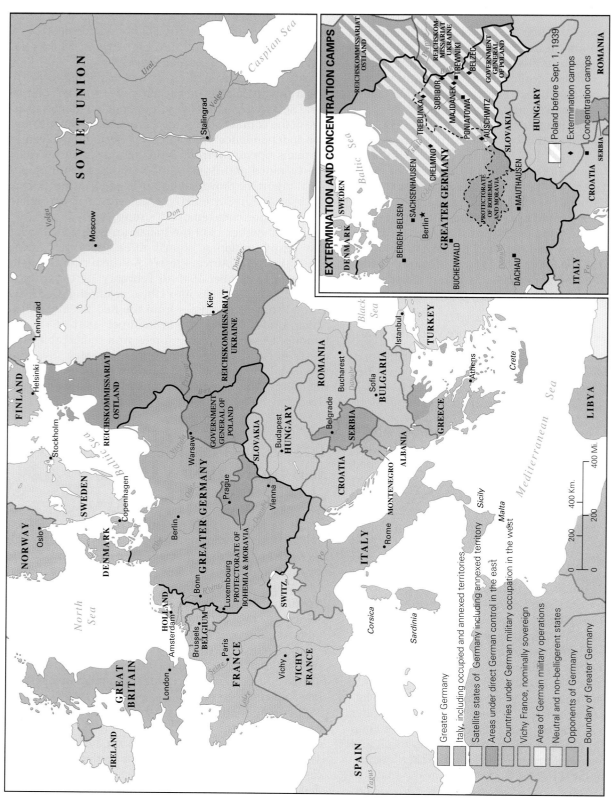

Map 28.2   The Nazi New Order in Europe, 1942   At the zenith of its power in 1942, Nazi Germany controlled much of Europe. Concerned most immediately with winning the war, the Nazis sought to coordinate the economies of their satellite states and conquered territories. But they also began establishing what was supposed to be an enduring new order in eastern Europe. The inset shows the location of the major Nazi concentration camps and of the six extermination camps the Nazis constructed in what had been Poland.

Forgive me, comrade . . .   On June 23, 1941, the day after Nazi Germany attacked the Soviet Union, the London *Daily Mail* published this cartoon depicting Hitler's betrayal of his 1939 pact with Stalin.   *(Daily Mail, London, 23 June 1941. Reprinted with permission of Solo Syndication Limited)*

their power late in 1942. German conquests by that point enabled Hitler to begin constructing the new, race-based European order he had dreamed of. Although in western Europe the Nazis generally sought the collaboration of local leaders, in the Soviet Union, as in Poland, the new order meant brutal subjugation of local populations. As part of this process, the Nazis began systematically killing Jews, first by shooting, then by mass gassing in specially constructed death camps.

■ An Ambiguous Outcome, 1941–1942

In ordering preparations for Operation Barbarossa in December 1940, Hitler decided to risk attacking the Soviet Union before knocking Britain out of the war. Then he invaded the Balkans and North Africa in what may

have been an unnecessary diversion. In retrospect, it is easy to pinpoint that combination as his fatal mistake. But in light of the Soviet purges of the 1930s and what seemed the poor performance of the Soviet army against Finland, Hitler had reason to believe the Soviet Union would crack relatively easily. Western military experts had come to similar conclusions, estimating that German forces would need but six weeks to take Moscow. And if Germany were to defeat the Soviet Union with another Blitzkrieg, it could gain control of the oil and other resources required for a longer war against Britain and, if necessary, the United States.

Attacking the Soviet Union on June 22, 1941, German forces achieved notable successes during the first month of fighting, partly because Stalin was so unprepared for this German betrayal. Ignoring warnings of an impending German assault, he had continued to live up to his end of the 1939 bargain with Hitler, even supplying the Germans with oil and grain. After the attack, Russia's defenses were at first totally disorganized, and by late November, German forces were within 20 miles of Moscow.

But the Germans were ill equipped for Russian weather, and as an early and severe winter descended, the German offensive bogged down. In December the Soviets mounted a formidable surprise counterattack near Moscow. The German Blitzkrieg, which had seemed a sure thing in July, had failed; Germany might still prevail, but a different strategy would be required.

Although their initial assault had stalled, the Germans still had the advantage. German forces failed to take the key city of Leningrad in 1941, but they cut it off by blockade and, until early 1944, kept it under siege with relentless bombing and shelling. And during the summer of 1942, they mounted another offensive, moving more deeply into the Soviet Union than before, reaching Stalingrad in November. But this proved the deepest penetration of German forces—and the zenith of Nazi power in Europe.

■ Hitler's New Order

By the summer of 1942, Nazi Germany dominated the European continent as no power ever had before (see Map 28.2). German military successes allowed the Nazi regime to begin building a new order in the territories under German domination. Satellite states in Slovakia and Croatia, and client governments in Romania and Hungary, owed their existence to Nazi Germany and readily adapted themselves to the Nazi system. Elsewhere in the Nazi orbit, some countries proved eager collaborators; others did their best to resist; still others were given no opportunity to collaborate but were ruthlessly subjugated instead.

The Nazis' immediate aim was simply to exploit the conquered territories to serve the continuing war effort. Precisely as envisioned, access to the resources of so much of Europe made Germany considerably less vulnerable to naval blockade than it had been during World War I. France proved a particularly valuable source of raw materials; by 1943, for example, 75 percent of French iron ore went to German factories.

But the deeper purposes of the war were also clear in the way the Nazis treated the territories under their control, especially in the difference between east and west. Western Europe experienced plenty of atrocities, but Nazi victory there still led to something like conventional military occupation. The Germans tried to enlist the cooperation of local authorities in countries like Denmark, the Netherlands, and France, though with mixed results. And though the Nazis exploited the economy of France, for example, it never became clear what role France might play in Europe after a Nazi victory. However, in Poland and later in the conquered parts of the Soviet Union, there was no pretense of cooperation, and it was immediately clear what the Nazi order would entail.

After the conquest of Poland, the Germans annexed the western part of the country outright and promptly executed, jailed, or expelled members of the Polish elite—professionals, journalists, business leaders, and priests. The Nazis prohibited the Poles from entering the professions and restricted even their right to marry. All the Polish schools and most of the churches were simply closed.

In the rest of Poland, known as the General Government, Nazi policy was slightly less brutal at first. Most churches remained open, and Poles were allowed to practice the professions, but the Nazis closed most schools above the fourth grade, as well as libraries, theaters, and museums as they sought to root out every expression of Polish culture. Some Poles in this area were forced into slave labor, but a final decision as to whether the Polish population was to be exterminated, enslaved, or shipped off to Siberia was postponed—to be made after the victory. (See the box "Reading Sources: Toward the Nazi New Order.")

With the conquest of Poland, Nazi leaders proclaimed that a new era of monumental resettlement in eastern Europe had begun for Germany. Germans selected for their racial characteristics were now resettled in the part of Poland annexed to Germany. Most were ethnic Germans who had been living outside Germany. During the fall of 1942, Heinrich Himmler's *Schutzstaffel*

(SS), the select Nazi elite, began to arrest and expel peasants from the rest of Poland to make way for further German resettlement. By 1943 perhaps 1 million Germans had been moved into what had been Poland.

After the assault on the Soviet Union, Hitler made it clear that eastern Europe as far as the Ural Mountains was to be opened for German settlement. War veterans were to be given priority, partly because the German settlers would have to be tough to resist the Slavs, who would be concentrated east of the Urals. To prepare for German colonization, Himmler told SS leaders that Germany would have to exterminate 30 million Slavs in the Soviet Union. After the German invasion, the SS promptly began executing prisoners of war, as well as any Soviet leaders they could find. However, the Nazis expected that several generations would be required for the resettlement of European Russia.

■ The Holocaust

Conquest of the east also opened the way to a more radical solution to the "Jewish problem" than the Nazis had ever contemplated before. Under the cover of war, they began actually killing the Jews within their orbit. Thus began the process, and the experience, that has come to be known as the Holocaust.

When and why this radical policy was chosen remains controversial. Although prewar Nazi rhetoric occasionally suggested the possibility of actual physical extermination, talk of a "final solution to the Jewish problem" seemed to mean forced emigration. Although the precise chain of events that led to a more radical approach will no doubt remain uncertain, it was surely bound up with the fortunes of the war.

The conquest of Poland, with a Jewish population of 3.3 million, gave the Nazis control over a far greater number of Jews than ever before. In 1940, as part of their effort to create a new order, the Nazis began confining Polish Jews to ghettos set up in Warsaw and five other cities. Although much brutality, and many deaths, accompanied this process, the Nazis had not yet adopted a policy of systematic killing. Indeed, at first no one knew what was to become of these Jews. At this point the Nazis were concentrating on removing, or even killing, non-Jewish Poles to make way for German resettlement into former Polish lands. The fate of the Jews would be decided later.

After the defeat of France, Himmler and the SS made tentative plans to develop a kind of superghetto for perhaps 4 million Jews on the island of Madagascar, at that point still a French colony, once the war had been won. However, as the Polish ghettos grew more crowded and

‍ READING SOURCES

Toward the Nazi New Order

After Nazi Germany conquered much of Poland in 1939, the SS assumed major responsibility for creating a new Nazi order in the conquered territories. In a memorandum dated May 15, 1940, and endorsed by Hitler, the SS leader Heinrich Himmler offered "some thoughts on the treatment of the alien population in the east." The passages that follow make clear the racist basis of Nazi wartime policy.

In our treatment of the foreign ethnic groups in the east we must . . . fish out the racially valuable people from this mishmash, take them to Germany and assimilate them there.

. . . The non-German population of the eastern territories must not receive any education higher than that of elementary school with four forms [grades]. The objective of this elementary school must simply be to teach: simple arithmetic up to 500 at the most, how to write one's name, and to teach that it is God's commandment to be obedient to the Germans and to be honest, hard-working, and well-behaved. I consider it unnecessary to teach reading.

There must be no schools at all in the east apart from this type of school. Parents who wish to provide their children with a better education both in the elementary school and later in a secondary school, must make an application to the higher SS and Police Leader. . . . If we recognize such a child as being of our blood then the parents will be informed that the child will be placed in a school in Germany and will remain in Germany indefinitely. . . .

The parents of these children of good blood will be given the choice of either giving up their child . . . or they would have to agree to go to Germany and become loyal citizens there. . . .

Apart from the examination of the petitions which parents put forward for a better education, all 6–10 year olds will be sifted each year to sort out those with valuable blood and those with worthless blood. Those who are selected as valuable will be treated in the same way as the children who are admitted on the basis of the approval of the parents' petition.

. . . [T]he moment the children and parents arrive in Germany they should not be treated in school and life as outcasts but—after changing their names and despite being treated with vigilance—should be integrated into German life on the basis of trust. The children must not be made to feel rejected; for, after all, we believe in our own blood, which through the mistakes of German history has flowed into a foreign nation, and are convinced that our ideology and ideals will find an echo in the souls of these children which are racially identical to our own. . . . Abusive expressions such as "Polack" or "Ukrainian" and such like must be out of the question. . . .

After these measures have been systematically implemented during the next ten years, the population of the General Government will inevitably consist of an inferior remnant. . . . This population will be available as a leaderless laboring class and provide Germany with migrant and seasonal labor for special work projects (road-building, quarries, construction); even then they will get more to eat and have more from life than under Polish rule.

Source: J. Noakes and G. Pridham, *Nazism, 1919–1945: A Documentary Reader,* vol. 3: *Foreign Policy, War and Racial Extermination* (Exeter: University of Exeter Press, 1988).

difficult to manage, Nazi officials in Poland began pressing for a more immediate solution.

At the same time, Hitler made it clear, in preparing for the invasion of the Soviet Union, that Barbarossa would be an escalation—a racial-ideological war of annihilation. And accompanying the military forces were specially trained SS units, essentially mobile killing squads, assigned to get rid of Communist Party officials and adult male Jews. But some were soon murdering Jewish women and children as well. By late November 1941, the Nazis had killed 136,000 Jews, most by shooting, in the invaded Soviet territories. But this mode of

The End of the Warsaw Ghetto   In April 1943 the sixty thousand Jews remaining in the Warsaw ghetto revolted rather than face shipment to the extermination camps. Many died in the ensuing fighting; others perished as the Germans set fire to the ghetto. Almost all the rest were captured and sent to their deaths at Treblinka. Before it was put down in May, the uprising killed at least three hundred Germans.   *(AP/Wide World Photos)*

killing proved both inefficient and psychologically burdensome—even for these specially trained killers. Their experience in the Soviet Union combined with the problems in the Polish ghettos to lead Nazi leaders to begin seeking a more systematic and impersonal method of mass extermination by late summer 1941.

The most likely scenario is that Hitler settled on physical extermination of the Jews in the thrill of what seemed impending victory over the Soviet Union. At the end of July 1941, Reinhard Heydrich of the SS began developing a detailed plan, and by fall the Nazis were sending German and Austrian Jews to the ghettos in Poland and actively impeding further Jewish emigration from Europe.

Heydrich explained his plan for the extermination of the Jews in January 1942 at a conference of high-ranking officials at Wannsee, a suburb of Berlin. The conference had been postponed from November, and by now the operation had already begun. The Nazis took advantage of the personnel and the methods, and especially the

deadly Zyklon-B gas, that had proven effective during the "euthanasia" campaign of 1939 through 1941 in Germany (see page 931). By March 1942 they had constructed several extermination camps with gas chambers and crematoria, intended to kill large numbers of Jews and dispose of their bodies as efficiently as possible. And now they began full-scale mass killing, targeting first the Polish Jews who had already been confined to ghettos. The Nazis brutally suppressed attempts at resistance, like the Warsaw ghetto uprising of April and May 1943.

During the course of the war the Nazis constructed six full-scale death camps, although not all were operating at peak capacity at the same time. All six were located in what had been Poland (see inset, Map 28.2). Horrifying though they were, the concentration camps in Germany, such as Dachau, Buchenwald, and Bergen-Belsen, were not extermination camps, although many Jews died in them late in the war.

The largest of the six death camps was the Auschwitz-Birkenau complex, which became the principal extermination center in 1943. The Nazis shipped Jews from all over Europe to Auschwitz, which was killing about twelve thousand people a day at the height of its operation in 1944. Auschwitz was one of two extermination camps that included affiliated slave-labor factories, in which Jews most able to work were literally worked to death. Among the companies profiting from the arrangement were two of Germany's best known, Krupp and IG Farben.

The Jews typically arrived at one of the camps crammed into cattle cars on special trains. SS medical doctors subjected new arrivals to "selection," picking some for labor assignments and sending the others, including most women and children, to the gas chambers. Camp personnel made every effort to deceive the Jews who were about to be killed, to lead them to believe they were to be showered and deloused. Even in camps without forced-labor factories, Jews were compelled to do much of the dirty work of the extermination operation. But under the brutal conditions of the camps, those initially assigned to work inevitably weakened; most were then deemed unfit and put to death.

The Nazis took every precaution to hide what was going on in the death camps. The SS personnel involved were sworn to silence. Himmler insisted that if secrecy was to be maintained, the operation would have to be quick—and total, to include women and children, "so that no Jews will remain to take revenge on our sons and grandsons." Indeed, Himmler constantly sought to accelerate the process, even though it required labor and transport facilities desperately needed for the war effort. Indeed, as the fortunes of war turned against Germany, the extermination of the Jews became a kind of end in itself.

Himmler and the other major SS officials, such as Rudolf Höss°, the commandant at Auschwitz, or Adolf Eichmann°, who organized the transport of the Jews to the camps, cannot be understood simply as sadists who enjoyed humiliating their victims. Rather, they took satisfaction in doing what they believed was their duty without flinching, without signs of weakness. Addressing a group of SS members in 1943, Himmler portrayed the extermination of the Jews as a difficult "historical task" that they, the Nazi elite, must do for their racial community: "Most of you know what it means to see a hundred corpses piled up, or five hundred, or a thousand. To have gone through this and—except for cases of human weakness—to have remained decent, that has made us tough. This is an unwritten, never to be written, page of glory in our history."[2]

Höss (HOESS)   **Eichmann** (IKE-mahn)

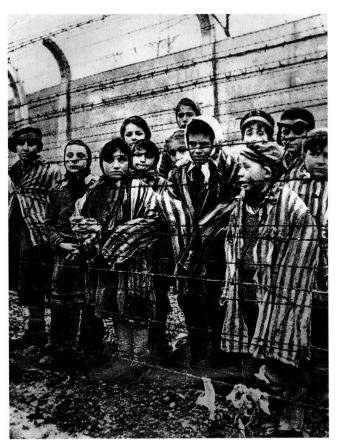

Children at Auschwitz   Images from the Nazi camps haunted the decades that followed the Second World War. The Auschwitz-Birkenau complex proved the largest and most destructive of the camps that the Nazis created specifically for mass killing. The overwhelming majority of those sent to these camps were Jews, most of whom were killed by gassing shortly after their arrival. Those deemed fit for work might be spared, at least for a while, but children were typically killed at once.   *(Hulton Getty/Liaison)*

However, as Himmler's casual reference to "cases of human weakness" suggests, a minority of camp guards and others failed to live up to this image and indulged in wanton cruelty, toward their helpless victims. For some, the extermination process became the occasion to act out sadistic fantasies. But though this dimension is surely horrifying, the bureaucratic, factorylike nature of the extermination process has seemed still more troubling in some respects, for it raises questions about the nature of modern rationality itself. The mass killing of Jews required the expertise of scientists, doctors, and lawyers; it required the bureaucratic organization of the modern state—all to provide the most efficient means to a monstrous end.

Despite the overriding emphasis on secrecy, reports of the genocide reached the West almost immediately in 1942. At first, however, most tended to discount them as wartime propaganda of the sort that had circulated during World War I, when stories about Germans eating Belgian babies whipped up war fever. Skepticism about extermination reports was easier because there were a few concentration camps, like Theresienstadt° in the former Czechoslovakia, that housed Jews who had been selected for special treatment. These camps were not used for extermination and were not secret; the Red Cross was even allowed to inspect Theresienstadt several times. Those outside, and the German people as well, were led to believe that all the Jews were being interned, for the duration of the war, in camps like these, much as Japanese-Americans were being interned in camps in the western United States at the same time. But even as the evidence grew, Allied governments, citing military priorities, refused pleas from Jewish leaders in 1944 to bomb the rail line into Auschwitz.

The Nazis' policy of actually murdering persons deemed undesirable or superfluous did not start with, and was not limited to, the Jews. First came the "euthanasia" program in Germany, and the war afforded the Nazis the chance to do away with an array of other "undesirables," including Poles, Sinti and Roma ("Gypsies"), communists, homosexuals, and vagrants. So the most radical and appalling aspect of Nazism did not stem from anti-Semitism alone. This must not be forgotten, but neither must the fact that the Jews constituted by far the largest group of victims—perhaps 5.7 to 6 million, almost two-thirds of the Jews in Europe. (See the feature "Weighing the Evidence: Holocaust Testimony" on pages 982–983.)

Collaboration in Nazi Europe

In rounding up Jews for extermination, and in establishing their new order in Europe, the Nazis found willing collaborators among some of the countries within their orbit. Several of them found collaboration with the victorious Nazi regime the best way to pursue their own nationalist agendas. Croatia, earlier part of the new state of Yugoslavia, was eager to round up Jews and Gypsies, as well as to attack Serbs, as part of its effort to establish itself as a nation-state. But national circumstances varied across Europe, and so did degrees of collaboration. In Denmark, Norway, and the Netherlands, the Nazis

thought racial kinship would matter, but they never found sufficient support to make possible genuinely independent collaborationist governments. Denmark did especially well at resisting the German effort to round up Jews, as did Italy and Bulgaria.

Vichy France was somewhere in the middle, and thus it has remained particularly controversial. When the Vichy regime was launched during the summer of 1940, Marshal Pétain, its 84-year-old chief of state, enjoyed widespread support. Pétain promised to maximize French sovereignty and shield his people from the worst aspects of Nazi occupation. At the same time, the Vichy government claimed to be implementing its own "national revolution," returning France to authority, discipline, and tradition after the shambles of the Third Republic. Vichy's revolution was anti-Semitic and hostile to the left, so it seemed compatible, up to a point, with Nazism. And at first Germany seemed likely to win the war. Thus, Pétain's second-in-command, Pierre Laval (1883–1945), was willing to collaborate actively with the Nazis. The Vichy regime ended up doing much of the Nazis' dirty work for them—rounding up workers for forced shipment to German factories, hunting down members of the anti-German resistance, and picking up Jews to be sent to the Nazi extermination camps.

After the war, Pétain, Laval, and others were found guilty of treason by the new French government. Because of his advanced age, Pétain was merely imprisoned, while Laval and others were executed. But the shame of Vichy collaboration continued to haunt the French, deepening the humiliation of the defeat in 1940.

Toward the Soviet Triumph

The import of what happened elsewhere in Europe depended on the outcome of the main event, the German invasion of the Soviet Union. Although the German Sixth Army, numbering almost 300,000 men, reached Stalingrad by late 1942, the Germans could not achieve a knockout. The Soviets managed to defend the city in what was arguably the pivotal military engagement of World War II. While some Soviet troops fought street by street, house by house, others counterattacked, encircling the attacking German force. Hitler refused a strategic retreat, but his doggedness backfired. By the end of January 1943, the Soviets had captured what remained of the German force, about 100,000 men, very few of whom survived to return to Germany. Perhaps 240,000 German soldiers died in the Battle of Stalingrad or as prisoners afterward. But the price to the Soviets for their victory was far greater: a million Soviet soldiers and civilians died at Stalingrad.

Theresienstadt (teh-REZ-ay-en-shtat)

Although the Germans resumed the offensive on several fronts during the summer of 1943, the Soviets won the tank battle of Kursk-Orel in July, and from then on Stalin's Red Army moved relentlessly westward, forcing the Germans to retreat. By February 1944 Soviet troops had pushed the Germans back to the Polish border, and the outcome of the war was no longer in doubt (see Map 28.1).

The Soviet victory on what proved the decisive front of World War II was incredible, in light of the upheavals of the 1930s and the low esteem in which most held the Soviet military in 1941. Portraying the struggle as "the Great Patriotic War" for national defense, Stalin managed to rally the Soviet peoples as the Germans attacked. Rather than emphasize communist themes, he recalled the heroic defenses mounted against invaders in tsarist times, including the resistance to Napoleon in 1812. But though the Soviets ultimately prevailed, the cost in death, destruction, and suffering was almost unimaginable. For example, by the time Soviet forces finally broke the siege of Leningrad in January 1944, a million people in the city had died, most from starvation, freezing, or disease. And the Soviets won on the battlefield partly by taking incredible numbers of casualties.

The invading Germans gained access to major areas of Soviet industry and oil supply, and by the end of 1941 the country's industrial output had been cut in half. Yet the Soviet Union was able to weather this blow and go on to triumph. Outside help contributed, but only 5 to 15 percent of Soviet supplies came from the West. Between 1939 and 1941, Soviet leaders had begun building a new industrial base east of the Urals. And when the Germans invaded in 1941, the plant and equipment of 1,500 enterprises were dismantled and shipped by rail for reassembly farther east, out of reach of German attack. Then, beginning in 1942, thousands of brand-new factories were constructed in eastern regions as well.

Moreover, the earlier purges of the armed forces proved to have done less long-term damage than outside observers had expected. If anything, the removal of so many in the top ranks of the military hierarchy made it easier for talented young officers like Georgi Zhukov (1896–1974), who would become the country's top military commander, to rise quickly into major leadership positions.

When the United States entered the war in December 1941, the Soviets were fighting for survival. They immediately began pressuring the United States and Britain to open another front in Europe, preferably by landing in northern France, where an Allied assault could be expected to have the greatest impact. But the Allies did not invade northern France and open a major second front until June 1944. By then the Soviets had turned the tide in Europe on their own.

Stalingrad, November 1942   From September 1942 until the German surrender early in February 1943, this city on the Volga River saw some of the heaviest fighting of World War II. The Soviet victory, in the face of incredible casualties, was arguably the turning point in the war in Europe.   *(Sovfoto/Eastfoto)*

A GLOBAL WAR, 1941–1944

WORLD War II proved unprecedented in its level of violence partly because it eclipsed even World War I in its geographical reach. The European colonial presence quickly drew the war to North Africa and the Middle East. But the war's early results in Europe also altered the power balance in East Asia and the Pacific, where the Russians and the Japanese had long been antagonists. During the 1930s, the United States had also become involved in friction with Japan. By 1941 President Franklin Roosevelt was openly favoring the anti-Axis cause, though it took a surprise attack by the Japanese in December 1941 finally to bring the United States into the war.

■ Japan and the Origins of the Pacific War

As a densely populated island nation lacking the raw materials essential for industry, Japan had been especially concerned about foreign trade and spheres of economic influence as it modernized after 1868. By the interwar period, the Japanese had become unusually reliant on exports of textiles and other products. During the Depression of the 1930s, when countries all over the world adopted protectionist policies, Japan suffered from increasing tariffs against its exports. This situation tilted the balance in Japanese ruling circles from free-trade proponents to those who favored a military-imperialist solution.

To gain economic hegemony by force, Japan could choose either of two directions. The northern strategy, concentrating on China, would risk Soviet opposition as well as strong local resistance. The southern strategy, focusing on southeast Asia and the East Indies, would encounter the imperial presence of Britain, France, the Netherlands, and the United States.

Japan opted for the northern strategy in 1931, when it took control of Manchuria, in northeastern China. But the Japanese attempt to conquer the rest of China, beginning in 1937, led only to an impasse by 1940. Japanese aggression in China drew the increasing hostility of the United States, a strong supporter of the Chinese nationalist leader Jiang Jieshi (Chiang Kai-shek) (1887–1975), as well as the active opposition of the Soviet Union. Clashes with Soviet troops along the border between Mongolia and Manchuria led to significant defeats for the Japanese in 1938 and 1939. The combination of China and the Soviet Union seemed more than Japan could handle.

By 1941, Germany's victories in Europe had seriously weakened Britain, France, and the Netherlands, the major European colonial powers in southeast Asia and the East Indies. The time seemed right for Japan to shift to a southern strategy. To keep the Soviets at bay, Japan agreed to a neutrality pact with the Soviet Union in April 1941. Rather than worry about China and the areas of dispute with the Soviet Union, the Japanese would seek control of southeast Asia, a region rich in such raw materials as oil, rubber, and tin—precisely what Japan lacked.

Japan had already joined with Nazi Germany and fascist Italy in an anticommunist agreement in 1936. In September 1940, the three agreed to a formal military alliance. For the Germans, alliance with Japan was useful to help discourage U.S. intervention in the European war. Japan, for its part, could expect the major share of the spoils of the European empires in Asia. However, diplomatic and military coordination between Germany and Japan remained minimal.

The United States began imposing embargoes on certain exports to Japan in 1938, in response to the Japanese aggression in China. After Japan had assumed control of Indochina, nominally held by Vichy France, by the summer of 1941, the United States imposed total sanctions, and the British and Dutch followed, forcing Japan to begin rapidly drawing down its oil reserves. Conquest of the oil fields of the Dutch East Indies now seemed a matter of life and death to the Japanese.

These economic sanctions heightened the determination of Japanese leaders to press forward aggressively now, when the country's likely enemies were weakened or distracted. But the Japanese did not expect to achieve a definitive victory over the United States in a long, drawn-out war. Rather, they anticipated, first, that their initial successes would enable them to grab the resources to sustain a longer war if necessary, and, second, that Germany would defeat Britain, leading the United States to accept a compromise peace allowing the Japanese what they wanted—a secure sphere of economic hegemony in southeast Asia.

Some Japanese leaders—diplomats, businessmen, naval officers, and even the emperor and some of his circle—were dismayed by the prospect of war with the United States. But as the influence of the military grew during the 1930s, it became ever more difficult for those opposing Japan's new imperialist direction to make themselves heard. By 1941, a conformist confidence in victory was demanded, and dissenters dared not speak out for fear of being labeled traitors.

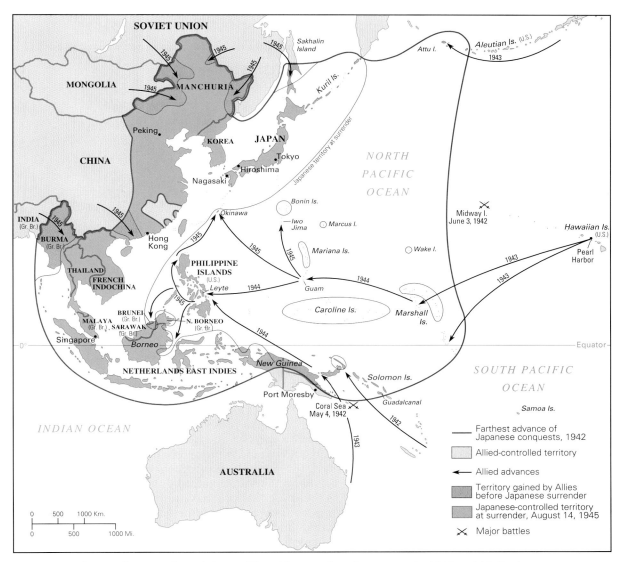

Map 28.3   The War in East Asia and the Pacific   After a series of conquests in 1941 and 1942, the Japanese were forced gradually to fall back before advancing U.S. forces. When the war abruptly ended in August 1945, however, the Japanese still controlled much of the territory they had conquered.

The Japanese finally provoked a showdown on December 7, 1941, with a surprise attack on Pearl Harbor, a U.S. naval base in Hawaii. The next day, Japanese forces seized Hong Kong and Malaya, both British colonies, and Wake Island and the Philippines, both under U.S. control. The United States promptly declared war; in response, Hitler kept an earlier promise to Japan and declared war on the United States. World War II was now unprecedented in its geographic scope (see Map 28.3).

Much like their German counterparts, Japanese forces got off to a remarkably good start. By the summer of 1942, Japan had taken Thailand, the Dutch East Indies, the Philippines, and the Malay Peninsula. Having won much of what they had been seeking, the Japanese began devising the Greater East Asia Co-Prosperity Sphere, their own new order in the conquered territories. (See the box "Global Encounters: Japan's 'Pan-Asian' Mission.")

⊕ G L O B A L E N C O U N T E R S

Japan's "Pan-Asian" Mission

With the coming of war against the Western powers in 1941, the Japanese could claim to be freeing Asians from Western imperialism and establishing a new economic order in East Asia and the Pacific. This selection from an essay entitled "Our Present War and Its Cultural Significance," written just after the bombing of Pearl Harbor by the well-known author Nagayo Yoshio (1888–1961), accents Japan's anti-Western mission in the region. Yoshio understood, especially from his country's recent experience in China, that Asians might find Japanese hegemony just as oppressive as Western domination. Although it served Japan's own economic interests and was often applied brutally, Japanese "Pan-Asianism" helped fuel the reaction against Western imperialism in Asia and the Pacific, with lasting results after the war.

Whenever Japan has faced a powerful enemy it has been the *yamato damashii* [Japanese national spirit] which provided the basis of our courage. Now that we can talk in retrospect of the Sino-Japanese War, I am afraid our national spirit has not been given a proper chance to be aroused, due to the deplorable fact that we had to fight with China, our sister nation, with no foreseeable conclusion to look forward to. . . . While desperately fighting with a country which we made our enemy only reluctantly we were trying to find out a principle, an ethic based upon a new view of the world, which would justify our course of action. . . . The China incident was not only insufficient to fulfill this goal but also met with insurmountable obstacles. Consequently, time and opportunity ripened to declare war against the United States and England. . . .

. . . We would have nothing to say for ourselves if we were merely to follow the examples of the imperialistic and capitalistic exploitation of Greater East-Asia by Europe and the United States. . . .

. . . It is true that the science of war is one manifestation of a nation's culture. But from this time on we have to realize the increasing responsibility on our part if we are to deserve the respect of the people of East-Asian countries as their leaders, in the sphere of culture in general (not only the mere fusion and continuance of Western and Oriental cultures but something surpassing and elevating them while making the most out of them) such as the formation of national character, refinement, intellect, training to become a world citizen, etc. . . .

The sense of awe and respect with which the Orientals have held the white race, especially the Anglo-Saxons, for three hundred years is deep-rooted almost beyond our imagination. It is our task to realize this fact and deal this servility at its root, find out why the white people became the objects of such reverence. It goes without saying that we cannot conclude simplemindedly that their shrewdness is the cause. Also we have to be very careful not to impose the *hakko ichiu* [the gathering of the whole world under one roof] spirit arbitrarily upon the Asians. If we make this kind of mistake we might antagonize those who could have become our compatriots and thus might also blaspheme our Imperial rule. . . .

To sum up, we have finally witnessed the dawn of a new principle which we had been searching for over ten years. . . . [T]he phrase "Greater East-Asian Coprosperity Sphere" is no longer a mere abstract idea.

Source: William H. McNeill and Mitsuko Iriye, eds., *Modern Asia and Africa* (New York: Oxford University Press, 1971), pp. 232–236.

The United States in Europe and the Pacific

During the first years of the war in Europe, the United States did not have armed forces commensurate with its economic strength; in 1940, in fact, its army was smaller than Belgium's. But the United States could be a supplier in the short term, and, if it chose to intervene, a major player over the longer term. With the Lend-Lease Act of March 1941, intended to provide war materiel without the economic dislocations of World War I, the United States lined up on the side of Britain against the Axis powers. In August 1941 a meeting between Churchill and Roosevelt aboard a cruiser off the coast of Newfoundland produced the Atlantic Charter, the first tentative agreement about the aims and ideals that were to guide the anti-Axis war effort. The Americans extended lend-lease to the Soviet Union the next month.

But though President Roosevelt was deeply committed to the anti-Axis cause, isolationist sentiment remained strong in the United States. The Japanese attack on Pearl Harbor in December inflamed American opinion and enabled Roosevelt at last to bring his country into the war as an active belligerent. By May 1942 the United States had joined with Britain and the Soviet Union in a formal military alliance against the Axis powers.

The two democracies had joined with Stalin's Soviet Union in a marriage of expediency, and mutual suspicions marked the relationship from the start. Initially, Britain and the United States feared that the Soviet Union might even seek a separate peace, as Russia had in World War I. The Soviets, for their part, worried that these newfound allies, with their long-standing anti-communism, might hold back from full commitment or even seek to undermine the Soviet Union.

In response to pressure from Stalin, Britain and the United States agreed to open a second front in Europe as soon as possible. But the Nazis dominated the Continent, so opening such a front required landing troops from the outside. It proved far more difficult to mount an effective assault on Europe than either Churchill or Roosevelt anticipated in 1942. The resulting delays furthered Stalin's suspicions that his allies were only too eager to have the Soviets do the bulk of the fighting against Nazi Germany—and weaken themselves in the process.

The United States agreed with its new allies to give priority to the war in Europe. But because it had to respond to the direct Japanese assault in the Pacific, the United States was not prepared to act militarily in Europe right away. What it could do, however, was supply the British with the ships needed to overcome German submarines, which seriously threatened shipping to Britain by 1942.

In the Pacific theater, in contrast, it was immediately clear that the United States would bear the brunt of the fighting against Japan. Although the Japanese went from one success to another during the first months of the war, they lacked the long-term resources to exploit their initial victories. In May 1942 the Battle of Coral Sea—off New Guinea, north of Australia—ended in a stalemate, stopping the string of Japanese successes. Then in June, the United States defeated the Japanese navy for the first time in the Battle of Midway, northwest of Hawaii. After the United States stopped attempted Japanese advances in the Solomon Islands and New Guinea early in 1943, U.S. forces began steadily advancing across the islands of the Pacific toward Japan (see Map 28.3).

The Search for a Second Front in Europe

As the Soviet army fought the Germans in the Soviet Union, the United States and Britain tried to determine how they could help tip the scales in Europe, now an almost impregnable German fortress. Stalin kept urging a direct assault across the English Channel, which, if successful, would have the greatest immediate impact. Churchill, however, advocated attacking the underbelly of the Axis empire by way of the Mediterranean, which would first require winning control of North Africa. And it was that strategy that the Allies tried first, starting in 1942.

By May 1943, step one of Churchill's plan had succeeded, but North Africa was valuable only as a staging ground for an Allied attempt to penetrate Europe from the south (see Map 28.1). Meeting at the Moroccan city of Casablanca in January 1943, Churchill and Roosevelt agreed that British and American forces would proceed from North Africa to Sicily and on up through Italy. The Soviets, still pushing for an invasion across the English Channel into France, objected that the Germans could easily block an Allied advance through the long, mountainous Italian peninsula.

Crossing from North Africa, Allied troops landed in Sicily in July 1943, leading to the arrest of Mussolini and the collapse of the fascist regime. Supported by King Victor Emmanuel III, the Italian military commander, Pietro Badoglio°, formed a new government to seek an armistice. Meanwhile, Allied forces moved on to the Italian mainland, but the Germans quickly occupied much of Italy in response. They even managed a daring rescue of Mussolini and promptly re-established him as puppet

Badoglio (bah-DOHL-yo)

D-Day, 1944 Allied forces land at Normandy, early in the morning of June 6, 1944, at last opening a major second front in Europe. *(National Archives, Washington)*

leader of a new rump republic in northern Italy, now under German control. Just as the Soviets had warned, the Germans sought to block the Italian peninsula, and it was only nine months later, in June 1944, that the Allies reached Rome. So Churchill's strategy of assaulting Europe from the south proved less than decisive.

Only when Churchill, Roosevelt, and Stalin met for the first time, at Teheran, Iran, in November 1943, did they agree that the next step would be to invade western Europe from Britain. Preparations had been underway since early 1942, but the operation was complex and hazardous in the extreme. Finally, Allied troops crossed the English Channel to make an amphibious landing on the beaches of Normandy, in northern France, on June 6, 1944, known to history as D-Day. And partly by deceiving the Germans seeking to defend the area, they were quickly able to consolidate their positions.

The success of the D-Day invasion opened a major second front in Europe at last. Now American-led forces from the west and Soviet forces from the east worked systematically toward Germany. The one substantial German counterattack in the west, the Battle of the Bulge in December 1944, slowed the Allies' advance, but

on March 7, 1945, Allied troops crossed the Rhine River (see Map 28.1).

By June 1944, when Allied forces landed at Normandy, Soviet forces had already crossed the 1939 border with Poland as they moved steadily westward. But in August the Soviets stopped before reaching Warsaw, and the major Soviet thrust began cutting south, through Romania, which surrendered in August, and on into the Danube valley in Hungary and Yugoslavia during the fall. The Soviets resumed their advance westward through Poland and toward Germany only in January 1945.

Now, with the defeat of Germany simply a matter of time, Allied concern shifted to the postwar order. Churchill, especially, worried about the implications of the Soviet advances in east-central Europe and the Balkans. As a supplement to the D-Day landings, he wanted to strike from Italy through Yugoslavia into east-central Europe. But the Americans resisted; Churchill's priorities, they felt, reflected old-fashioned concerns over spheres of influence that were no longer appropriate. So the Allies concentrated instead on a secondary landing in southern France in August 1944. This assault, in which Free French forces were prominent, led quickly to the liberation of Paris.

But because the Allies made both their landings in France, and not in southeastern Europe, the Western democracies were involved only in the liberation of western Europe. It was the Soviets who drove the Germans from east-central Europe and the Balkans. This fact, and the resulting geographic distribution of military strength, fundamentally affected the postwar order in Europe.

THE SHAPE OF THE ALLIED VICTORY, 1944–1945

THE leaders of the Soviet Union, Britain, and the United States sought to mold that postwar order at two notable conferences in 1945. Even as they brought different aspirations for the postwar world, they had to deal together with the legacy of a war of unprecedented violence and destruction. At the same time, they also had to face the hard military realities that had resulted from the fighting so far: each country had armies in certain places but not in others. The result was an informal division of Europe into spheres of influence among the victors.

The most serious question the Allies faced concerned Germany, which was widely held responsible for the two world wars, as well as for Nazism with all its atrocities—including the concentration and extermina-

tion camps, discovered with shock and horror by the advancing Allied armies in 1945. Germany was to be forced to surrender unconditionally; there would be no negotiation or armistice. But what should be done with the country over the longer term?

In the Pacific theater, as in Europe, the way the war ended had major implications for the postwar world. The United States decided to use the atomic bomb, a weapon so destructive that it forced a quick Japanese surrender. The suddenness of the ending helped determine the fate of the European empires in Asia.

■ The Yalta Conference: Shaping the Postwar World

When Stalin, Roosevelt, and Churchill met at Yalta, a Soviet Black Sea resort, in February 1945, Allied victory was assured, and the three leaders accomplished a great deal. Yet controversy has long surrounded the Yalta conference. Western critics have charged that the concessions made there to Stalin consigned east-central Europe to communist domination and opened the way to the dangerous cold war of the next forty years. At the time, however, the anticipation of victory produced a relatively cooperative spirit among the Allies. Thus, they firmed up plans for military occupation of Germany in separate zones, for joint occupation of Berlin, and for an Allied Control Council, composed of the military

The Big Three at Yalta   With victory over Nazi Germany assured, Churchill, Roosevelt, and Stalin were in reasonably good spirits when they met at Yalta, a Black Sea resort in the Soviet Union, in February 1945. Important sources of friction among them were evident at the meeting, but the differences that led to the cold war did not seem paramount at this point. The Yalta conference proved to be the last meeting of the three leaders. *(F.D.R. Library)*

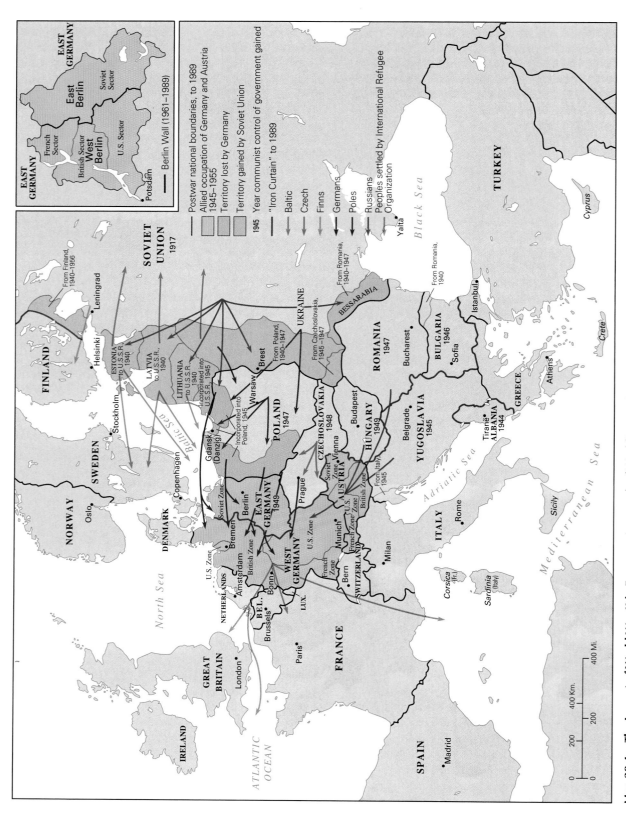

Map 28.4 The Impact of World War II in Europe As a result of World War II the Soviet Union expanded its western borders and Poland shifted westward at the expense of Germany. Territorial changes added to the wartime disruption and produced a flood of refugees. The cold war division of Europe did not depend on immediate territorial changes, but soon Germany itself came to be divided along east-west lines.

Postwar national boundaries, to 1989
Allied occupation of Germany and Austria 1945–1955
Territory lost by Germany
Territory gained by Soviet Union
1945 Year communist control of government gained
"Iron Curtain" to 1989
Baltic
Czech
Finns
Germans
Poles
Russians
Peoples settled by International Refugee Organization

Berlin Wall (1961–1989)

EAST GERMANY
EAST GERMANY
East Berlin
Soviet Sector
French Sector
British Sector
West Berlin
U.S. Sector
Potsdam

SOVIET UNION 1917

FINLAND
From Finland, 1940–1956
Leningrad
Helsinki
ESTONIA to U.S.S.R. 1940
LATVIA to U.S.S.R. 1940
LITHUANIA to U.S.S.R. 1940
Incorporated into U.S.S.R. 1945
Baltic Sea
Stockholm
SWEDEN
NORWAY
Oslo
Copenhagen
DENMARK
North Sea
GREAT BRITAIN
London
IRELAND
ATLANTIC OCEAN

Brest
UKRAINE
From Poland, 1940–1947
Warsaw
Gdańsk (Danzig)
Incorporated into Poland, 1945
POLAND 1947
Soviet Zone
Berlin
EAST GERMANY 1949
Prague
CZECHOSLOVAKIA 1948
Bremen
British Zone
Amsterdam
NETHERLANDS
Bonn
BEL.
Brussels
LUX.
WEST GERMANY
U.S. Zone
Munich
French Zone
SWITZERLAND
Bern
FRANCE
Paris
U.S. Zone

From Czechoslovakia, 1945–1947
From Romania, 1940–1947
BESSARABIA
From Romania, 1940
ROMANIA 1947
Bucharest
BULGARIA 1946
Sofia
HUNGARY 1949
Budapest
Vienna
Soviet Zone
AUSTRIA
British Zone
From Italy, 1945
YUGOSLAVIA 1945
Belgrade
ALBANIA 1944
Tiranë
GREECE
Athens

TURKEY
Istanbul
Black Sea
Yalta
Cyprus
Crete

ITALY
Rome
Milan
Corsica (Fr.)
Sardinia (Italy)
Sicily
Adriatic Sea
Mediterranean Sea

SPAIN
Madrid

400 Mi.
400 Km.
200
200
0
0

commanders-in-chief, which would make policy for all of Germany by unanimous agreement.

Each of the Allies had special concerns, but each got much of what it was seeking at Yalta. Roosevelt was eager for Soviet help against Japan as soon as possible, and he won Soviet commitment to an agreement tentatively worked out earlier. In exchange for territorial concessions in Asia and the Pacific, Stalin agreed to declare war on Japan within three months of the German surrender.

Churchill, meanwhile, worried about the future of Europe in light of the American intention, which Roosevelt announced at Yalta, to maintain occupation troops in Europe for only two years after the war. To help balance Soviet power on the Continent, Churchill felt it essential to restore France as a great power. To this end, he urged that France be granted a share in the occupation of Germany and a permanent seat on the Security Council of the proposed new international organization, the United Nations (see page 975). Roosevelt agreed, even though he had little use for Charles de Gaulle or what he viewed as the pretensions of the French.

It seemed to the Americans that both Britain and the Soviet Union remained too wedded to traditional conceptions of national interest as they sought to shape the postwar world. Hence, one of Roosevelt's major priorities was to secure British and Soviet commitment to the United Nations before the three allies began to disagree over particular issues. He won that commitment at Yalta, but only by giving in to Churchill on the sensitive matter of British colonies.

Because anti-imperial sentiment worked to Japan's advantage in Asia, the United States had pestered Britain on the colonial issue since early in the war. Roosevelt even asked Churchill in 1941 about British intentions in India. So prickly was Churchill that he proclaimed in 1942, "I have not become the King's First Minister in order to preside over the liquidation of the British Empire." The parties agreed at Yalta that the British Empire would be exempt from an anticipated measure to bring former colonies under United Nations trusteeship after the war.

Although it was not the only question on the table, the future of the former Axis territories was central to the seaside deliberations. By the time of the conference, those territories were already being divided into spheres of influence among the Allies, and in light of the location of Allied troops, the eventual alignment was probably inevitable. In Italy, where U.S. and British troops held sway, the two democracies had successfully resisted Stalin's claim for a share in the administration. In east-central Europe, however, the Soviet army was in control. Still, the United States, with its vision of a new world order, objected to spheres of influence and insisted that democratic principles be applied everywhere. At Yalta this American priority led to an awkward compromise over east-central Europe: the new governments in the area were to be both democratic and friendly to the Soviet Union.

Most important to the Soviets was Poland, with its crucial location between Russia and Germany. Although the Soviets insisted that Communists lead the new Polish government at the outset, they compromised by allowing a role for the noncommunist Polish government-in-exile in London and by promising free elections down the road. The Allies agreed that Poland would gain substantial German territory to its west to make up for what it would lose to the USSR to its east (see Map 28.4).

In addition, the United States and Britain were to have a role in committees set up to engineer the transition to democracy in the rest of east-central Europe. However, only the Soviets had troops in the area, and those committees proved essentially powerless. But though the sources of future tension were already at work at Yalta, they generally remained hidden by the high spirits of approaching victory.

■ Victory in Europe

Although the tide had turned in 1943, Germany managed to continue the war by exploiting its conquered territories and by more effectively allocating its domestic resources for war production. Thanks partly to the efforts of armaments minister Albert Speer, war production grew sharply between 1941 and 1944, so Germany had plenty of weapons even as the war was ending. The Germans even proved able to withstand the systematic bombing of cities that the British, especially, had thought might prove decisive.

Beginning in 1942, British-led bombing attacks destroyed an average of half the built-up area of seventy German cities, sometimes producing huge firestorms. (See the box: "Reading Sources: Waiting Out the War in Berlin.") The bombing of the historic city of Dresden in February 1945 killed at least sixty thousand civilians in the most destructive air assault of the war in Europe. But despite this widespread destruction, such bombing did not undermine morale or disrupt production to the extent expected. Even in the face of steady Allied bombing, Germany increased its war production during 1943 and 1944.

But Germany encountered two crucial bottlenecks that finally crippled its military effort: it was running out of both oil and military personnel. Despite making

Waiting Out the War in Berlin

Marie Vassiltchikov (1917–1978) was a member of a noble Russian family that had left Russia in 1919, shortly after the Bolshevik Revolution. Having grown up as a refugee in Germany, France, and Lithuania, she found herself in Germany when the war began in 1939. Though not a German citizen, she was able to find employment in Berlin thanks to her linguistic skills and Germany's labor shortage. She immediately began writing a diary in English, which she had learned as a child. By November 1943, when these excerpts were written, she was working in the information department of the German Foreign Ministry. Her diary is especially vivid in chronicling the later years of the war, as civilians in Germany coped with Allied bombing.

Tuesday, 23 November   Last night the greater part of central Berlin was destroyed.

. . . I was rushing down the stairs to go home when the hall porter interrupted me with the ominous words "Luftgefahr 15" ["air-raid danger 15"]. This meant that large enemy formations were on their way. I took the stairs back two at a time to warn those of my colleagues who lived far away to stay put, since they might otherwise be caught out in the open. . . .

The streets were full of people. Many just stood around, for the visibility was so poor on account of the rain that nobody expected the raid to last long or cause much damage. . . . As one does now in such cases, I . . . packed a few things in a small suitcase. . . .

I had just finished packing when the *flak* opened up. It was immediately very violent. Papa emerged with his pupils and we all hurried down to the half-basement behind the kitchen, where we usually sit out air-raids. We had hardly got there when we heard the first approaching planes. They flew very low and the barking of the *flak* was suddenly drowned by a very different sound—that of exploding bombs, first far away and then closer and closer, until it seemed as if they were falling literally on top of us. At every crash the house shook. The air pressure was dreadful and the noise deafening. . . .

The all-clear came only half an hour after the last planes had departed, but long before that we were called out of the house by an unknown naval officer. The wind, he told us, thus far non-existent, had suddenly risen and the fires, therefore, were spreading. We all went out into our little square and, sure enough, the sky on three sides was blood-red. This, the officer explained, was only the beginning; the greatest danger would come in a few hours' time,

when the fire storm really got going. Maria had already given each of us a wet towel with which to smother our faces before leaving the house—a wise precaution, for our square was already filled with smoke and one could hardly breathe.

. . . [T]he electricity, gas and water no longer worked and we had to grope our way around with electric torches [flashlights] and candles. Luckily we had had time to fill every available bath tub, wash basin, kitchen sink, and pail. By now the wind had increased alarmingly, roaring like a gale at sea. When we looked out of the window we could see a steady shower of sparks raining down on our and the neighbouring houses and all the time the air was getting thicker and hotter, while the smoke billowed in through the gaping window frames. . . .

Wednesday, 24 November . . . At first our Woyrsch-strasse did not look too bad; but one block away, at the corner of Lützowstrasse, all the houses were burnt out. As I continued down Lützowstrasse the devastation grew worse; many buildings were still burning and I had to keep to the middle of the street, which was difficult on account of the numerous wrecked trams. There were many people in the streets, most of them muffled in scarves and coughing, as they threaded their way gingerly through the piles of fallen masonry. At the end of Lützowstrasse, about four blocks away from the office, the houses on both sides of the street had collapsed and I had to climb over mounds of smoking rubble, leaking water pipes and other wreckage to get across to the other side.

Source: Marie Vassiltchikov, *Berlin Diaries, 1940–1945* (New York: Alfred A. Knopf, 1987), pp. 105–110.

The Soviet Victory in Europe
After forcing the Germans back for almost two years, Soviet troops reached Berlin in April 1945. Although it required a day of heavy fighting and bombardment, the Soviets took the Reichstag building, in the heart of the now devastated German capital, on April 30. Here two Soviet sergeants, Yegorov and Kantariya, plant the Soviet flag atop the Reichstag, symbolizing the Soviet victory in the decisive encounter of World War II in Europe.
(ITAR-TAS/Sovfoto)

effective use of synthetics, the Nazi war machine depended heavily on oil from Romania. Late in August 1944, however, Soviet troops crossed into Romania, taking control of the oil fields. And though the terror bombing of cities did not have the anticipated impact, the more precisely targeted bombing favored by U.S. strategists significantly affected the outcome. In May 1944 the United States began bombing oil fields in Romania and refineries and synthetic oil plants in Germany. Soon Germany lacked enough fuel even to train pilots. So serious were the bottlenecks by 1945 that the German air force could not use all the aircraft that German industry was producing.

Soviet troops moving westward finally met U.S. troops moving eastward at the Elbe River in Germany on April 26, 1945. With his regime now thoroughly defeated and much of his country in ruins, Hitler committed suicide in his underground military headquarters in Berlin on April 30, 1945. The war in Europe finally ended with the German surrender to General Dwight D. Eisenhower (1890–1969) at Reims, France, on May 7 and to Marshal Zhukov at Berlin on May 8. The world celebrated the end of the fighting in Europe, but an element of uncertainty surrounded the Allied victory. East-West differences were increasingly coming to the fore within the anti-German alliance.

■ The Potsdam Conference and the Question of Germany

The immediate question for the victorious Allies was the fate of Germany, which they confronted at the last of their notable wartime conferences, at Potsdam, just outside Berlin, from July 17 to August 2, 1945. The circumstances were dramatically different from those at Yalta just months before. With Hitler dead and Germany defeated, no common military aim provided unity. And of the three Allied leaders who had been at Yalta, only Stalin remained. President Roosevelt had died in April, so his successor, Harry Truman (1884–1972), represented the United States. In Britain, Churchill's Conservatives lost the general election during the first days of the conference, so Clement Attlee (1883–1967), the new Labour prime minister, assumed the leadership of the British delegation.

At Potsdam the Allies had to determine how to implement their earlier agreements about Germany, which, devastated by bombing and devoid of a government, depended on the Allied occupying forces even for its day-to-day survival. For a time, U.S. policymakers had even considered destroying Germany's industrial capacity in perpetuity. However, cooler heads understood that the deindustrialization, or "pastoralization," of Germany would not be in anyone's economic interests. Moreover, as the democracies grew increasingly suspicious about Soviet intentions, an economically healthy Germany seemed necessary to help in the balance against the Soviet Union.

For their part, the Soviets had reason to take a much harder line against Germany. Having been ravaged by invading German forces twice within living memory, the Soviet Union wanted to weaken Germany both territorially and economically. And of the three victors, the Soviets had suffered a greatly disproportionate share of the wartime destruction and economic loss, so they also sought to exploit the remaining resources of Germany by exacting heavy reparations. Moreover, the British and the Americans accepted the Soviet proposal that Germany's eastern border with Poland be shifted substantially westward, to the line formed by the Oder and Neisse° Rivers. But just as Poland gained at the expense of Germany, the Soviet Union kept a substantial slice of what had been eastern Poland (see Map 28.4).

Each of the three Allies had responsibility for administering a particular zone of occupation, but they were supposed to coordinate their activities in a common policy toward Germany. This effort was to include de-Nazification, demilitarization, and an assault on concentrations of economic power—to root out what seemed the sources of Germany's antidemocratic and aggressive tendencies. But East-West disagreements over economic policy soon undermined the pretense of joint government.

■ The Atomic Bomb and the Capitulation of Japan

In the Pacific, Japan had been forced onto the defensive by September 1943, and though it mounted two major counterattacks during 1944, the Japanese navy was crippled by shortages of ships and fuel by the end of the year. However, as the situation grew more desperate for Japan, Japanese ground soldiers battled ever more fiercely, often fighting to the death, or taking their own lives, rather than surrendering. Beginning late in 1944, aircraft pilots practiced *kamikaze°*, suicidally crashing planes filled with explosives into U.S. targets. The Japanese used this tactic especially as the Americans sought to take Okinawa in the spring of 1945. The U.S. forces finally prevailed in June, but only after the most bitter combat of the entire Pacific war (see Map 28.3).

In conquering Okinawa, American forces got close enough for air raids on the Japanese home islands. But though the United States was now clearly in control, it seemed likely that an actual invasion of Japan would be necessary to force a Japanese surrender. Some estimated that, because the Japanese could be expected to fight even more desperately to defend their own soil, invasion might well cost the United States 1 million additional casualties. It was especially for this reason that the Americans decided to try to end the war in an altogether different way, by using an atomic bomb.

In 1939 scientists in several countries, including Germany, had started to advise their governments that new, immensely destructive weapons based on thermonuclear fission were theoretically possible. The German economics ministry began seeking uranium as early as 1939, but Hitler promoted jet- and rocket-propelled terror weaponry instead, especially the V-2 rocket bombs that the Germans began showering on England in the fall of 1944. Still, fear that the Nazis were developing atomic weapons lurked behind the Allied effort to produce the ultra-lethal bomb as quickly as possible.

Although the British were the first to initiate an atomic weapons program, by late 1941 the Americans were building on what they knew of British findings to develop their own crash program, known as the Manhattan Project. Constructing an atomic bomb proved far more difficult and costly than most had expected in 1941, and it took a concerted effort by the United States to have atomic weapons ready for use by mid-1945.

The U.S. decision actually to use the atomic bomb on Japanese civilians has been one of the most controversial of modern history. The decision fell to the new president, Harry Truman, who had known nothing of the bomb project when Roosevelt died in April 1945. During the next few months, Truman listened to spirited disagreement among American policymakers. Was it necessary actually to drop the bomb to force the Japanese to surrender? Especially because the ultimate victory of the United States was not in doubt, some argued that it would be enough simply to demonstrate the new weapon to the Japanese in a test firing.

By July, when the Allies met at Potsdam, the United States was prepared to use the bomb. But President Truman first warned Japan that if it did not surrender at once, it would be subjected to destruction immeasurably greater than Germany had just suffered. The Japanese ignored the warning, although the United States had begun area-bombing Japanese cities a few months before. The bombing of Tokyo in March produced a firestorm that gutted one-fourth of the city and killed over 80,000 people. In light of the Japanese refusal to surrender, the use of the atomic bomb could seem the logical next step.

Neisse (NYE-suh)   **kamikaze** (kah-mih-KAH-zee)

At 8:15 on the morning of August 6, 1945, from a height of 32,000 feet above the Japanese city of Hiroshima, an American pilot released the first atomic bomb to be used against an enemy target. The bomb exploded after 45 seconds, 2,000 feet above the ground, killing 80,000 people outright and leaving tens of thousands more to die in the aftermath. Three days later, on August 9, the Americans exploded a second atomic bomb over Nagasaki, killing perhaps 50,000 people. Although sectors of the Japanese military held out for continued resistance, Emperor Hirohito° (1901–1989) finally surrendered on August 15. The bombing of civilians had discredited the Japanese military, which not only had proved unable to defend the country but had systematically misled the Japanese people about their country's prospects.

The war in the Pacific ended more suddenly than had seemed possible just a few months earlier (see Map 28.3). This worked in favor of the various national liberation or decolonization movements that had developed in Asia during the war, for the Europeans had little opportunity to re-establish their dominance in the colonial territories they had earlier lost to the Japanese. In the Dutch East Indies, the Japanese had encouraged anticolonial sentiment, even helping local nationalists create patriotic militias. After the war, the Dutch were never able to reassert their control against this Indonesian nationalist movement. But though the war had severely weakened the old Western imperialism in Asia and the Pacific, what would replace it remained unclear.

■ Death, Disruption, and the Question of Guilt

World War II left as many as 60 million people dead—three times as many as World War I. About that same number were left homeless for some length of time, or found themselves forced onto the mercies of others as refugees. The Soviet Union and Germany suffered by far the highest casualty figures; for each, the figure was considerably higher than in World War I. An appalling 23 million Soviet citizens died, of whom 12 to 13 million were civilians. Germany lost 5 to 6 million, including perhaps 2 million civilians.

In contrast, casualty rates for Italy, Britain, and France were lower than in World War I. Italy suffered 200,000 military and 200,000 civilian deaths. Total British losses, including civilians, numbered 450,000, to which must be added 120,000 from the British Empire. Despite its quick defeat, France lost more lives than Britain because of the ravages of German occupation: the 350,000 deaths among French civilians considerably exceeded the British figure, closer to 100,000.

The United States lost 300,000 servicemen and 5,000 civilians. Figures for Japan are problematic, partly because the Japanese claim that 300,000 of those who surrendered to the Soviets in 1945 have remained unaccounted for. Apart from this number, 1,740,000 Japanese servicemen died from 1941 to 1945, more from hunger and disease than from combat, and 300,000 civilians died in Japan, most from U.S. bombing.

During the war, Jews, Poles, and others deemed undesirable by the Nazis had been rounded up and shipped to ghettos or camps, where the great majority had died. Of those Jews who were still alive when the Nazi camps were liberated, almost half died within a few weeks. Even those who managed to return home sometimes faced pogroms during the difficult months that followed; forty Jews were killed in the worst of them, at Kielce°, Poland, in 1946.

Late in the war, as German forces in the east retreated, ethnic Germans living in Poland, Czechoslovakia, Hungary, and elsewhere in east-central Europe began seeking refuge in Germany. They were fleeing the Soviet advance but also seeking to escape the growing wave of anti-German resentment in those countries. Once the war was over, the Poles began expelling ethnic Germans from the historically German areas that were now to become Polish. These Germans were sometimes sent to detention camps, and when they were shipped out, it was often in cattle cars. According to some estimates, as many as 2 million died in the process. In Czechoslovakia the government expelled 3.5 million Germans from the Sudetenland area by 1947. All tolled, at least 7 million German refugees moved west, into the shrunken territory of the new Germany, by 1947. They were among the 16 million Europeans who were permanently uprooted and transplanted during the war and its immediate wake. And the process continued at a diminished rate thereafter. By 1958 perhaps 10 million Germans had either left or been forced out of the new Poland, leaving only about 1 million Germans still living there.

As the end of the war approached, Europeans began attempting to assess guilt and punish those responsible for the disasters of the era. In the climate of violence, resistance forces in France, Italy, and elsewhere often subjected fascists and collaborators to summary justice, sometimes through quick trials in ad hoc courts. In Italy this process led to 15,000 executions, in France 10,000. French women accused of sleeping with German soldiers were shamed by having their heads shaved.

Hirohito (hee-roh-HEE-toh)

Kielce (KYEL-tsuh)

Reconstruction Begins
Shortly after the end of the war, women in Berlin pass pails of rubble along a line to dump. Wartime bombing had severely damaged cities throughout much of Europe, although destruction was greatest in Germany. *(Hulton Getty/Liaison)*

The most sensitive confrontation with the recent past took place in Germany, where the occupying powers imposed a program of de-Nazification. In the western zones, German citizens were required to attend lectures on the virtues of democracy and to view the corpses of the victims of Nazism. In this context, the Allies determined to identify and bring to justice those responsible for the crimes of Hitler's regime. This effort led to the Nuremberg trials of 1945 to 1946, the most famous of a number of war crimes trials held in Germany and the occupied countries after the war.

Although Hitler, Himmler, and Goebbels had committed suicide, the occupying authorities apprehended for trial twenty-four individuals who had played important but very different roles in Hitler's Third Reich. All but three were convicted of war crimes and "crimes against humanity." Twelve were sentenced to death; of those, two committed suicide, and the other ten were executed.

Questions about their legitimacy dogged the Nuremberg trials from the start. To a considerable extent the accused were being judged according to law made after the fact. The notion of "crimes against humanity" remained vague. Moreover, even insofar as a measure of international law was in force, it was arguably binding only on states, not individuals. But in light of the unprecedented atrocities of the Nazi regime, there was widespread agreement among the victors that the Nazi leaders could not be treated simply as defeated adversaries.

INTO THE POSTWAR WORLD

VEN after the fighting stopped in 1945, remarkable changes continued as the forces unleashed by the war played themselves out. In a number of war-torn countries, the legacies of wartime resistance movements helped shape the political order and priorities for beginning anew. At the same time, differences between the Soviets and the Western democracies began to undermine the wartime alliance, soon producing the division of Germany and a bipolar Europe. Thus the conclusion of World War II led directly to the danger of a third world war, which might involve nuclear weapons and threaten the very survival of human life.

In addition to the dramatic changes in Europe, the wider effects of the war brought to the forefront a whole new set of issues, from anticolonialism to the Arab-Israeli conflict to the spread of communism within the non-Western world. These issues would remain central for decades. By 1949, however, it was already possible to discern the contours of the new postwar world, a world with new sources of hope but also with conflicts and dangers hardly imaginable ten years earlier.

■ Resistance and Renewal

Though the Nazis had found some willing collaborators, the great majority of those living under German occupation came to despise the Nazis as their brutality became ever clearer. Nazi rule meant pillage, forced labor in Germany, and the random killing of hostages in reprisal for resistance activity. In one extreme case, the Germans destroyed the Czech village of Lidice°, killing all its inhabitants, in retaliation for the assassination of SS security chief Reinhard Heydrich in 1942.

Clandestine movements of resistance to the occupying Nazi forces gradually developed all over Europe. In western Europe, resistance was especially prominent in France and, beginning in 1943, northern Italy, which was subjected to German occupation after the Allies defeated Mussolini's regime. But the anti-German resistance was strongest in Yugoslavia, Poland, and the occupied portions of the Soviet Union, where full-scale guerrilla war against the Germans and their collaborators produced the highest civilian casualties of World War II. The Polish resistance achieved some notable successes in sabotaging roads and railroads, although it met disastrous defeat when it sought to tackle the Germans head-on in Warsaw in 1944.

The role of the resistance proved most significant in Yugoslavia, where the Croatian Marxist Josip Broz, taking the pseudonym Tito (1892–1980), forged the opponents of the Axis powers into a broadly based guerrilla army. Its initial foe was the inflated Croatian state that the Germans, early in 1941, carved from Yugoslavia and entrusted to the pro-Axis Croatian separatist movement, the Ustashe°. But Tito's forces soon came up against a rival resistance movement, led by Serb officers, that tended to be pro-Serb, monarchist, and anticommunist. By 1943 Tito led 250,000 men and women in what had become a vicious civil war, one that deepened ethnic divisions and left a legacy of bitterness. Tito's forces prevailed, enabling him to create a communist-led government in Yugoslavia late in the war.

In France and Italy as well, communists played leading roles in the wartime resistance movements. As a result, the Communist Party in each country overcame the disarray that followed from the Nazi-Soviet Pact of 1939, and after the war each enjoyed a level of prestige that would have been unthinkable earlier.

Lidice (LIH-dyit-seh)   Ustashe (oo-STAH-zhiy)

In the French case, the indigenous resistance, with its significant communist component, generally worked well with de Gaulle and the Free French, operating outside France until August 1944. Still, de Gaulle took pains to cement his own leadership in the overall struggle. Among the measures to this end, he decreed women's suffrage for France, partly because women were playing a major role in the resistance. After the liberation of France in 1944, he sought to control a potentially volatile situation by disarming the resistance as quickly as possible.

The western European resistance movements are easily romanticized, their extent and importance overstated. Compared with regular troops, resistance forces were poorly trained, equipped, and disciplined. In France fewer than 30 percent of the nearly 400,000 active resisters had firearms in 1944. But though the Allies never tried to use them in a systematic way, the resistance movements made at least some military contribution, especially through sabotage. And they boosted national self-esteem for the longer term, helping countries humiliated by defeat and occupation make a fresh start after the war.

■ Conflicting Visions and the Coming of the Cold War

Starting with the Atlantic Charter conference of 1941, Roosevelt had sought to ensure that the common effort against the Axis powers would lead to a firmer basis for peace, to be framed through a new international organization after the war. At a conference at Dumbarton Oaks in Washington in September 1944, the United States proposed the structure for a new "United Nations" organization. Meeting in San Francisco from April to June 1945, delegates from almost fifty anti-Axis countries translated that proposal into a charter for the new United Nations. As Roosevelt had envisioned, the major powers were given a privileged position in the organization as permanent members of the Security Council, each with veto power. To dramatize its departure from the Geneva-based League of Nations, which the United States had refused to join, the United Nations was headquartered in New York. In July 1945 the American Senate approved U.S. membership in the international body almost unanimously.

By the end of the war, several international meetings had used the United Nations title. In July 1944 the United Nations Monetary and Financial Conference at Bretton Woods, New Hampshire, brought together delegates from forty-four nations to deal with problems of currency and exchange rates. Although it produced only recommendations subject to ratification by the individual states, the conference indicated a new determination to cooperate on the international level after the failures of the interwar period. And the outcome of the conference, the Bretton Woods Agreement, laid the foundation for international economic exchange in the noncommunist world for the crucial quarter-century of economic recovery after the war. In addition, the conference gave birth to the International Monetary Fund and the International Bank for Reconstruction and Development, which played major roles in the decades that followed.

Whereas the United States envisioned a world order based on the ongoing cooperation of the three victors, the Soviet Union had a different agenda. Its top priority was to create a buffer zone of friendly states in east-central Europe, especially as a bulwark against Germany. While seeking this sphere of influence in east-central Europe, Stalin gave the British a free hand to settle the civil war between communists and anticommunists in Greece, and he did not push for revolution in western Europe. The strong communist parties that had emerged from the resistance movements in Italy and France were directed by Moscow to work within broad-based democratic fronts rather than try to take power. Although no formal deal was made, Stalin saw this moderate position in western and southern Europe as a tacit exchange with the West for a free hand in east-central Europe.

■ The Division of Germany

The site of greatest potential stress between the Soviets and the democracies was Germany. At first, the Western Allies were concerned especially to root out the sources of Germany's antidemocratic, aggressive behavior, but that concern faded as communism, not Nazism, came to seem the immediate menace. And it was especially conflict over Germany that cemented the developing division of Europe. Neither the democracies nor the Soviets lived up to all their agreements concerning Germany, but in light of the fundamental differences in priorities, cooperation between the two sides was bound to be difficult at best.

Disagreements over economic policy proved the major source of the eventual split. At Potsdam, the West had accepted Soviet demands for German reparations, but rather than wait for payment, the Soviets began removing German factories and equipment for reassembly in the Soviet Union. To ensure that they got their due, the Soviets wanted access to the economic resources not simply of the Russian occupation zone but of the whole of Germany. The United States and Britain, in contrast, gave priority to economic reconstruction and quickly began integrating the economies of the Western zones for that purpose.

Friction developed from 1945 to 1948 as the West insisted on reduced reparations and a higher level of industrial production than the Soviets wanted. Finally, as part of their effort to spur economic recovery, the United States and Britain violated inter-Allied agreements by introducing a new currency without Soviet consent. Stalin answered in June 1948 by blockading the city of Berlin, cutting its western sectors off from the main Western occupation zones, almost 200 miles west (see Map 28.4). The Western Allies responded with a massive airlift that kept their sectors of Berlin supplied for almost a year, until May 1949, when the Soviets finally backed down.

By 1948 two separate German states began emerging from the Allied occupation zones. The Western occupying powers had begun restoring local government immediately after the war, to create the administrative framework necessary to provide public utilities and food distribution. Gradually a governing structure was built from the ground up in the Western zones, which were increasingly coordinated.

With Allied support, a "parliamentary council" of West German leaders met during 1948 and 1949 and produced a document that, when ratified in September 1949, became the "Basic Law" of a new Federal Republic of Germany, with its capital at Bonn. This founding document was termed simply the Basic Law, as opposed to the constitution, to emphasize the provisional character of the new West German state. To create a state limited to the west was not to foreclose the future reunification of Germany. But as it became clear that a new state was being created in the Western zones, the Soviets settled for a new state in their zone, in eastern Germany. Thus the Communist-led German Democratic Republic, with its capital in East Berlin, was born in October 1949.

■ The "Iron Curtain" and the Emergence of a Bipolar World

In east-central Europe, only Yugoslavia and Albania had achieved liberation on their own, and the communist leaders of their resistance movements had a plausible claim to political power. Elsewhere, the Soviet army had provided liberation, and the Soviet military presence remained the decisive political fact as the war ended. In much of the region, authoritarianism and collaboration had been the rule for a decade or more, so there was no possibility of returning to a clearly legitimate prewar political order. To be sure, each country had local political groups, some representing former governments in exile, that now claimed a governing role, but their standing in relation to the Soviet army was uncertain.

Discerning the Iron Curtain

Winston Churchill, out of office and touring the United States, sought to explain the postwar international situation in a speech at Westminster College in Fulton, Missouri, on March 5, 1946. To characterize the developing division of Europe, Churchill referred to "an iron curtain," a term that attracted immediate attention and dramatically affected public opinion in both the United States and western Europe. Some have suggested that Churchill was overdramatizing the situation in an effort to keep the United States engaged in Europe.

A shadow has fallen upon the scenes so lately lighted by the Allied victory. Nobody knows what Soviet Russia and its Communist international organization intend to do in the immediate future, or what are the limits, if any, to their expansive and proselytizing tendencies. . . . We understand the Russian need to be secure on her western frontiers by the removal of all possibility of German aggression. We welcome her to her rightful place among the leading nations of the world. . . . It is my duty, however, to place before you certain facts. . . .

From Stettin in the Baltic to Trieste in the Adriatic, an iron curtain has descended across the Continent. Behind that line lie all the capitals of the ancient states of central and eastern Europe. Warsaw, Berlin, Prague, Vienna, Budapest, Belgrade, Bucharest, and Sofia, all these famous cities and the populations around them lie in what I must call the Soviet sphere, and all are subject in one form or another, not only to Soviet influence but to a very high and, in many cases, increasing measure of control from Moscow. Athens alone—Greece with its immortal glories—is free to decide its future at an election under British, American and French observation. The Russian-dominated Polish Government has been encouraged to make enormous and wrongful inroads upon Germany, and mass expulsions of millions of Germans on a scale grievous and undreamed-of are now taking place. The Communist parties, which were very small in all these Eastern States of Europe, have been raised to pre-eminence and power far beyond their numbers and are seeking everywhere to obtain totalitarian control. . . .

If now the Soviet Government tries, by separate action, to build up a pro-Communist Germany in their areas, this will cause new serious difficulties in the British and American zones, and will give the defeated Germans the power of putting themselves up to auction between the Soviets and the Western Democracies. Whatever conclusions may be drawn from these facts—and facts they are—this is certainly not the Liberated Europe we fought to build up. Nor is it one which contains the essentials of permanent peace. . . .

. . . I do not believe that Soviet Russia desires war. What they desire is the fruits of war and the indefinite expansion of their power and doctrines. But what we have to consider here to-day while time remains, is the permanent prevention of war and the establishment of the conditions of freedom and democracy as rapidly as possible in all countries. . . .

From what I have seen of our Russian friends and allies during the war, I am convinced that there is nothing they admire so much as strength, and there is nothing for which they have less respect than for weakness, especially military weakness.

Source: Winston S. Churchill: His Complete Speeches, 1897–1963, vol. VII, *1943–1949,* ed. Robert Rhodes James (New York: Chelsea House, 1974), pp. 7290–7292.

 For additional information on this topic, go to http://college.hmco.com.

Under these circumstances, the Soviets were able to work with local communists to install new communist-led regimes friendly to the Soviet Union in most of east-central Europe. But though Churchill warned as early as 1946 that "an iron curtain" was descending from the Baltic to the Adriatic, the process of Soviet power consolidation was not easy, and it took place gradually, in discrete steps over several years. (See the two boxes "Reading Sources: Discerning the Iron Curtain" and "Reading Sources: Churchill as Warmonger: Stalin's Response to the 'Iron

Churchill as Warmonger: Stalin's Response to the "Iron Curtain" Speech

Soviet leader Joseph Stalin was quick to respond to Churchill's speech. In an interview in the official Soviet newspaper Pravda *eight days later (March 13, 1946), he accused Churchill of calling for war on the Soviet Union. But Stalin also revealed the more subtle concerns that were causing the divergence between the Soviets and their former allies, Britain and the United States. The three countries had joined forces against Hitler, but the Soviets' geographical situation and recent historical experience contrasted sharply with U.S. and British circumstances. These dissimilarities, perhaps even more than ideological differences, led Stalin to his antithetical interpretation of the outcomes and lessons of the recent war.*

Question: How do you appraise Mr. Churchill's latest speech in the United States of America?

Answer: I appraise it as a dangerous act, calculated to sow the seeds of dissension among the Allied states and impede their collaboration. . . .

. . . Mr. Churchill now takes the stand of the warmongers. . . .

. . . The German race theory led Hitler and his friends to the conclusion that the Germans, as the only superior nation, should rule over other nations. The English race theory leads Mr. Churchill and his friends to the conclusion that the English-speaking nations, as the only superior nations, should rule over the rest of the nations of the world. . . .

Question: How do you appraise the part of Mr. Churchill's speech in which he attacks the democratic systems in the European states bordering upon us, and criticizes the good neighborly relations established between these states and the Soviet Union?

Answer: This part of Mr. Churchill's speech is compounded of elements of slander and elements of discourtesy and tactlessness. . . .

. . . [T]he following circumstances should not be forgotten. The Germans made their invasion of the U.S.S.R. through Finland, Poland, Rumania, Bulgaria, and Hungary. The Germans were able to make their invasion through these countries because, at the time, governments hostile to the Soviet Union existed in these countries. As a result of the German invasion the Soviet Union has lost irretrievably in the fighting against the Germans, and also through the German occupation and the deportation of Soviet citizens to German servitude, a total of about seven million people. In other words, the Soviet Union's loss of life has been several times greater than that of Britain and the United States of America put together. Possibly in some quarters an inclination is felt to forget about these colossal sacrifices of the Soviet people which secured the liberation of Europe from the Hitlerite yoke. But the Soviet Union cannot forget about them. And so what can there be surprising about the fact that the Soviet Union, anxious for its future safety, is trying to see to it that governments loyal in their attitude to the Soviet Union should exist in these countries? How can anyone, who has not taken leave of his wits, describe these peaceful aspirations of the Soviet Union as expansionist tendencies on the part of our state? . . .

Mr. Churchill comes somewhere near the truth when he speaks of the increasing influence of the Communist parties in eastern Europe. It must be remarked, however, that he is not quite accurate. The influence of the Communist parties has grown not only in eastern Europe, but in nearly all the countries of Europe which were previously under fascist rule . . . or which experienced German, Italian, or Hungarian occupation. . . .

The increased influence of the Communists cannot be considered fortuitous. It is a perfectly logical thing. The influence of the Communists has grown because, in the years of the rule of fascism in Europe, the Communists showed themselves trusty, fearless, self-sacrificing fighters against the fascist regime for the liberty of the peoples.

Source: Josef Stalin, "Churchill's Speech Is a Call for War on Russia," in Walter LaFeber, ed., *The Origins of the Cold War, 1941–1947* (New York: Weber), pp. 139–143.

Curtain' Speech.") The Communist-led government of Poland held elections in January 1947—but rigged them to guarantee a favorable outcome. In Czechoslovakia the communists anticipated serious losses in upcoming elections and so finally took power outright in 1948. By 1949 communist governments, relying on Soviet support, controlled Poland, Czechoslovakia, East Germany, Hungary, Romania, and Bulgaria, with Yugoslavia and Albania also communist but capable of a more independent line.

Communism might have spread still farther in Europe, and perhaps beyond, but the West drew the line at Greece. There, as in Yugoslavia, an indigenous, communist-led resistance movement had become strong enough to contend for political power by late 1944. But when it sought to oust the monarchical government that had just returned to Greece from exile, the British intervened, helping the monarchy put down the leftist uprising. Although Stalin gave the Greek communists little help, communist guerrilla activity continued, thanks partly to support from Tito's Yugoslavia. In 1946 a renewed communist insurgency escalated into civil war.

As the cold war developed, both the Soviet Union and the United States began taking a more active interest in the Greek conflict, though Soviet intentions remained uncertain. After the financially strapped Labour government in Britain reduced its involvement early in 1947, the United States stepped in to support the Greek monarchy against the communists. American policymakers feared that communism would progress from the Balkans through Greece to the Middle East. Thus, in March 1947, President Truman announced the Truman Doctrine, which committed the United States to the "containment" of communism throughout the world. American advisers now began re-equipping the anticommunist forces in Greece. Faced with this determined opposition from the West, Stalin again pulled back, but the Greek communists, with their strong indigenous support, were not defeated until 1949.

Thus the wartime marriage of expediency between the Soviet Union and the Western democracies gradually fell apart in the war's aftermath. Only in Austria, jointly occupied by the Soviets and the Western democracies, were the former Allies able to arrange the postwar transition in a reasonably amicable way. The Soviets accepted the neutralization of a democratic Austria as the occupying powers left in 1955. Elsewhere, Europe was divided into two antagonistic power blocs.

The antagonism between the two superpowers became more menacing when the Soviets exploded their first atomic bomb in August 1949, intensifying the postwar arms race. By then, in fact, the United States was on its way to the more destructive hydrogen bomb. The split

between these two nations, unmistakable by 1949, established the framework for world affairs for the next forty years.

■ The West and the New World Agenda

At the same time, other dramatic changes around the world suggested that, with or without the cold war, the postwar political scene would be hard to manage. Events in India in 1947, in Israel in 1948, and in China in 1949 epitomized the new hopes and uncertainties that were the offspring of World War II.

Although the British, under U.S. pressure, had reluctantly promised independence for India in order to

Gandhi and Anticolonialism   An apostle of nonviolence, Mohandas Gandhi became one of the most admired individuals of the century as he spearheaded the movement for Indian independence. He is pictured (*center*) in December 1942 with the British statesman Sir Stafford Cripps (*left*), who had come to India to offer a plan for Indian self-government. Despite the good spirit evident here, Cripps's mission failed; Gandhi and his movement held out for full independence. (*Corbis*)

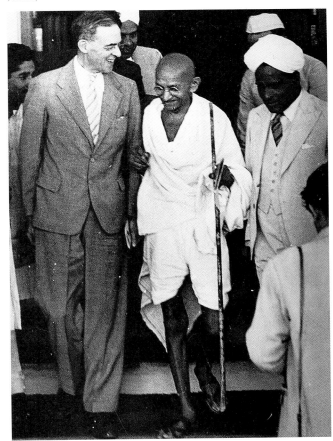

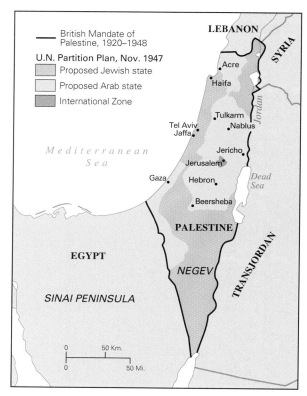

Map 28.5   The Proposed Partition of Palestine and the Birth of the State of Israel   In November 1947 the United Nations offered a plan to partition the British mandate of Palestine, but complications immediately arose. The Jews of the area won their own state, Israel, but the Palestinian Arabs did not. Thus tensions continued in the area.

elicit Indian support during the war, British authorities and Indian leaders had continued to skirmish. Mohandas Gandhi was twice jailed for resisting British demands and threatening a massive program of nonviolent resistance to British rule. But by 1946 the British lacked the will and the financial resources to maintain their control on the subcontinent. Thus Britain acquiesced as the new independent states of India and Pakistan emerged on August 15, 1947. Allowing independence to India, long the jewel of the British Empire, raised questions about Britain's role in the postwar world and portended a wider disintegration of the European colonial system. There would be new countries, many of them poor—and resentful of Western imperialism. What would that mean for the new world order, centering on the United Nations, that Roosevelt had envisioned?

Questions about the fate of the Jews, who had suffered so grievously during World War II, were inevitable as well. Almost two-thirds of the Jews of Europe had been killed, and many of the survivors either had no place to go or had decided that they could never again live as a minority in Europe. Many concluded that the Jews must have a homeland of their own. For decades such Zionist sentiment (see page 824) had centered on the biblical area of Israel, in what had become, after World War I, the British mandate of Palestine. Jewish immigration to the area accelerated during the interwar period, but it caused increasing friction between Jews and the Palestinian Arabs.

Concerned about access to Middle Eastern oil, the British sought to cultivate good relations with the Arab world after the war. Thus they opposed further immigration of Jews to Palestine, as well as proposals to carve an independent Jewish state from the area. The United States, however, was considerably more sympathetic to the Zionist cause. As tensions built, Jewish terrorists blew up the British headquarters in Jerusalem, and the British decided to abandon what seemed a no-win situation. In September 1947 they announced their intention to withdraw from Palestine, leaving its future to the United Nations. In November the UN voted to partition Palestine, creating both a Jewish and a new Arab Palestinian state (see Map 28.5).

Skirmishing between Jews and Arabs became full-scale war in December, and in that context the Jews declared their independence as the new state of Israel on May 14, 1948. When fighting ended in 1949, the Israelis had conquered more territory than had been envisioned in the original partition plan, and the remaining Arab territories fell to Egypt and Jordan, rather than forming an independent Palestinian state. Thus was born the new state of Israel, partly a product of the assault on the Jews during World War II. Yet it was born amid Arab hostility and Western concerns about oil, and so its long-term prospects remained uncertain.

In 1949 the communist insurgency in China under Mao Zedong (Mao Tse-tung) (see page 920) finally triumphed over the Chinese Nationalists under Jiang Jieshi (Chiang Kai-shek), who fled to the island of Taiwan. During the war, the Communists had done better than the Nationalists at identifying themselves with the Chinese cause against both Japanese and Western imperialism. And after their victory, the Chinese Communists enjoyed great prestige among other "national liberation" movements struggling against Western colonialists. To many in the West, however, the outcome in China by 1949 simply intensified fears that communism was poised to infect the unsettled postwar world.

SUMMARY

THE war that began in Europe in 1939 gradually spread to become by far the widest and most destructive in history. Driven by expansionist aims, the aggressors—first Germany and then Japan—won impressive victories at the start. Then a Grand Alliance of Britain, the Soviet Union, and the United States gradually came together and won the war in both Europe and Asia by August 1945. But the war brought unprecedented death and destruction and troubling new forms of violence, from factorylike genocide to the nuclear bombing of civilians.

As a result of the war, the two major fascist powers collapsed and fascist forms of politics, with their hostility to democracy and their tendencies toward violence and war, stood discredited. But it was not clear whether Germany and Italy, and, for that matter, much of the rest of Europe, would be able to develop effective democratic political systems amid defeat and destruction.

The Soviets had borne the brunt of the war in Europe, and the Soviet Union—and its communist system—emerged with enhanced prestige. At the same time, an overseas war had again drawn the United States, which was prepared in the aftermath, as it had not been after World War I, to play an ongoing leadership role in world affairs. The Soviet Union and the United States offered competing visions of the future, and during the decades that followed, their competition helped shape everything from Italian domestic politics to the decolonization struggle in southern Africa.

By 1949 the division of Europe, the advent of nuclear weapons, and the symptomatic events in India, Israel, and China made it clear that the world's agenda had been radically transformed in the ten years since the beginning of World War II. With the Soviet Union and United States emerging from the war as superpowers, and with the once-dominant European countries weakened and chastened, the center of gravity in the West changed dramatically. Thus the relationship between the West and the world was bound to be radically different.

Whereas there had been, for a while, some illusion of a "return to normal" after World War I, it was obvious after World War II that the old Europe was gone forever. Indeed, much of Europe's proud culture, on the basis of which it had claimed to lead the world, lay in the ruins of war, apparently exhausted. What role could Europe play in Western civilization, and in the wider world, after all that had happened? What lessons had been learned, and what foundations for the future could be found, as the experiment continued?

■ Notes

1. From Farrell's full account as related by General Leslie Groves in his "Memorandum to the Secretary of War," dated July 18, 1945, in Philip L. Cantelon, Richard G. Hewlett, and Robert C. Williams, eds., *The American Atom: A Documentary History of Nuclear Policies from the Discovery of Fission to the Present,* 2d ed. (Philadelphia: University of Pennsylvania Press, 1991), pp. 56–57.
2. Quoted in Karl Dietrich Bracher, *The German Dictatorship: The Origins, Structure, and Effects of National Socialism,* trans. Jean Steinberg (New York: Praeger, 1970), p. 423.

■ Suggested Reading

Browning, Christopher R. *Ordinary Men: Reserve Police Battalion 101 and the Final Solution in Poland.* With a new afterword. 1998. A case study approach to the role of ordinary Germans in the Holocaust.

Campbell, John, ed. *The Experience of World War II.* 1989. Focusing on the experience of those touched by the war, this collaborative volume covers everything from prisoners of war to the uses of the arts for propaganda purposes; large format, with superb illustrations and maps.

Gaddis, John Lewis. *We Now Know: Rethinking Cold War History.* 1997. Taking advantage of newly available Russian and Chinese documents, a leading authority reassesses the cold war, from its origins to the Cuban missile crisis of 1962.

Hilberg, Raul. *Perpetrators, Victims, Bystanders: The Jewish Catastrophe, 1933–1945.* 1992. The dean of Holocaust historians offers an accessible, compelling account by weaving capsule portraits delineating the many layers of involvement and responsibility at issue in the Holocaust.

Keegan, John. *The Second World War.* 1989. A detailed but readable study featuring military operations; well illustrated.

Overy, Richard J. *Why the Allies Won.* 1995. Denying that the sheer weight of numbers made the outcome inevitable, this account focuses on the differences in political, economic, and even moral mobilization to explain why the Allies defeated the Axis powers.

Parker, R. A. C. *Struggle for Survival: The History of the Second World War.* 1990. This accessible, comprehensive, and well-balanced survey is especially good on debates over strategy and the wider implications of the strategies chosen.

Trachtenberg, Marc. *A Constructed Peace: The Making of the European Settlement, 1945–1963.* 1999. An original work that pushes beyond the long-standing cold war framework to argue that concerns about Germany and nuclear weapons were central to the postwar settlement.

Weinberg, Gerhard L. *A World at Arms: A Global History of World War II.* 1994. An enlightening global approach by a leading historian of the period that stresses the interrelationship among simultaneous events and decisions in the various theaters of the war around the world.

 For a searchable list of additional readings for this chapter, go to http://college.hmco.com.

Holocaust Testimony

There were loud announcements, but it was all fairly restrained: nobody did anything to us. I followed the crowd: "Men to the right, women and children to the left," we had been told. The women and children disappeared into a barrack further to the left and we were told to undress. One of the SS men—later I knew his name, Küttner—told us in a chatty sort of tone that we were going into a disinfection bath and afterwards would be assigned work. Clothes, he said, could be left in a heap on the floor, and we'd find them again later. . . .

The queue began to move and I suddenly noticed several men fully dressed standing near another barrack further back, and I was wondering who they were. And just then another SS man (Miete was his name) came by me and said, "Come on, you, get back into your clothes, quick, special work." That was the first time I was frightened. Everything was very quiet, you know. And when he said that to me, the others turned around and looked at me—and I thought, my God, why me, why does he pick on me? When I had got back into my clothes, the line had moved on and I noticed that several other young men had also been picked out and were dressing. We were taken through to the "work-barrack," most of which was filled from floor to ceiling with clothes, stacked up in layers. . . . You understand, there was no time, not a moment between the instant we were taken in there and put to work, to talk to anyone, to take stock of what was happening . . . [ellipses in the original] and of course never forget that we had no idea at all what this whole installation was for. One saw these stacks of clothing—I suppose the thought must have entered our minds, where do they come from, what are they? We must have connected them with the clothes all of us had just taken off outside . . . [ellipses in the original] but I cannot remember doing that. I only remember starting work at once making bundles.*

---

*The testimony of Richard Glazar is from Gitta Sereny, *Into That Darkness: An Examination of Conscience* (New York: Random House, Vintage Books, 1983), pp. 176–179, 183.

This is the voice of Richard Glazar, recalling when, as a young Jewish student from Prague, he arrived at the Nazi extermination camp at Treblinka in October 1942. Glazar was telling his story in 1972 to the British journalist Gitta Sereny, who had been covering the trial in Germany of the commandant of the Treblinka camp, Franz Stangl. Seeking to understand Stangl, Sereny tracked down a number of those who had come into contact with him, including survivors like Glazar.

Glazar's recollections are part of a rich body of testimony by Jewish survivors of the Holocaust, testimony that is often moving, gripping, terrifying. Some accounts offer direct personal recollections. Others integrate personal remembrance into literature. Still others use the insights of social psychology in an effort to explain the special features of the camp experience.

Even with all this evidence, we wonder if we can ever really grasp what millions of Jews experienced at the hands of the Nazis in the extermination camps. But listening to witnesses like Glazar, we gain some sense of the uncertainty and fear, the suffering and humiliation, that helped define that experience. And we recognize the determination, the affirmation of life, that marked the Jewish response.

We may be surprised at Glazar's insistence that "we had no idea at all what this whole installation was for." Didn't the Jews understand what the camps held for them? In fact, some Jews had a better idea than others, but in most cases only through rumor, and no one could know the whole story as it was unfolding. Over a year before, Glazar's family had sent him to work in the country, where they assumed he would be safe, so he had been relatively isolated. But what one knew, or could surmise, also depended on what one was prepared to believe was possible, what the world could hold. Some simply could not believe the rumors.

Once they were in the camps, however, the Jews could only come to terms with the unprecedented situation as best they could. Let us listen further to Glazar, whose insights into the minds of the SS overseers help us better to grasp the terrible capriciousness of the situation:

One must not forget their incredible power, their autonomy within their narrow and yet, as far as we were concerned, unlimited field; but also the isolation created by their unique situation and by what they—and hardly anyone else even within the German or Nazi community—had in common. Perhaps if this isolation had been the result of good rather than evil deeds, their own relationship towards each other would have been different. As it was, most of them seemed to hate and despise each other and do anything—almost anything—to "get at" each other. Thus, if one of them selected a man out of a new transport for work, in other words to stay alive at least for a while, it could perfectly easily happen . . . that one of his rivals . . . would come along and kill that man just to spite him. . . . All this created a virtually indescribable atmosphere of fear. The most important thing for a prisoner at Treblinka, you see, was not to make himself conspicuous.

But what, then, can be said about the human attributes that such conditions called forth—and that enabled some, at least, to survive?

Our daily life? It was in a way very directed, very specific. . . . [I]t was essential to fill oneself completely with a determination to survive; it was essential to create in oneself a capacity for

dissociating oneself to some extent from Treblinka; it was important not to adapt completely to it. . . .

It wasn't *ruthlessness* that enabled an individual to survive—it was an intangible quality, not peculiar to educated or sophisticated individuals. Anyone might have it. It is perhaps best described as an overriding thirst—perhaps, too, a talent for life, and a faith in life.

Glazar, of course, was speaking thirty years later, and despite the engaging spontaneity of his testimony, he may have forgotten things, or the experiences of the intervening years may have colored his memory. Moreover, he could only tell what he recalled through the categories of language, which may be inadequate to convey, to those who were not there, what it was like to be sent to Nazi extermination camps. Perhaps survivors called upon, years later, to put their recollections into words are bound to impose too much order, even to romanticize, by using categories their listeners can understand—or want to hear. Glazar was clearly stretching to find the words. Does "talent for life" ring true? We will continue to wonder.

As for Glazar himself, he escaped from Treblinka in an uprising in August 1943, and then made his way to Germany, where he managed to survive the war disguised as a foreign laborer. When Sereny reached him in 1972, he was living in Switzerland, working as an engineer.

Arrival at the Auschwitz Extermination Camp

(Corbis)

CHAPTER 29

T HE atmosphere was festive, euphoric. Those who came to celebrate could hardly believe it was happening, for it had been unthinkable just a few months before. Yet happening it was, one of the defining events of the twentieth century, live on television. This was November 1989, and the Berlin Wall was coming down.

Erected to stop emigration from communist East Germany to the West in 1961, the wall had become an all-too-tangible symbol of the division of Europe, and much of the world, for more than four decades after World War II. The two superpowers that had emerged from the war, the Soviet Union and the United States, had settled into a cold war marked by ideological competition, an arms race, and nuclear stalemate.

As a physical barrier of concrete and barbed wire, the Berlin Wall had divided families and caused much human suffering. Indeed, 191 people died and 5,000 were arrested trying to cross it. But the East German government, by 1989 desperate to preserve its legitimacy, opened the wall on November 9—and began dismantling it within days. However, it proved too late. The communist regime in East Germany collapsed as part of a wider anticommunist revolution that finally enveloped even the Soviet Union in 1991. The anxious cold war era was suddenly over; virtually no one had foreseen its abrupt ending.

Although Berlin had been a particular hot spot, the cold war was global in scope. It seemed that confrontation between the Soviet Union and the United States might take place almost anywhere, sparking the cold war into a hot war threatening nuclear annihilation. And indeed confrontation came closest not over Berlin but over Soviet missiles in Cuba in 1962. That crisis was surmounted, and

East Germans (*backs to camera*) stream through the dismantled Berlin Wall into West Berlin. (Lionel Cironneau/AP/Wide World Photos)

An Anxious Stability: The Age of the Cold War 1949–1989

The Search for Cultural Bearings

Prosperity and Democracy in Western Europe

The Communist Bloc: From Consolidation to Stagnation

Europe, the West, and the World

The Collapse of the Soviet System, 1975–1991

East-West relations alternately warmed and cooled during the quarter century that followed.

Both halves of Europe had to operate within the bipolar framework, but the Western and Soviet blocs confronted different challenges and evolved in different ways. The countries of western Europe adjusted to a diminished international role as they recognized their dependence on U.S. leadership and gradually lost their overseas colonies. The change in scale led many politicians and intellectuals to advocate some form of European union, which might eventually enable the western Europeans to deal with the superpowers on a more equal basis. On the domestic level, the immediate postwar situation was so unsettled that few western European countries could simply return to the prewar norm. Postwar reconstruction rested on a new consensus that government must play a more active role in promoting economic growth and social welfare. By the 1960s the promise of shared prosperity was realized to a remarkable extent. But changing circumstances by the early 1970s threatened the consensus that postwar prosperity had made possible.

Although the Soviet Union had suffered immensely in winning World War II, the communist regime emerged from the war with renewed legitimacy. During the 1950s and 1960s, the Soviet system achieved some significant successes, but its efforts to outgrow its Stalinist framework were halting. By 1980 the system was becoming rigid and stagnant. And thus the dramatic changes in the Soviet bloc that came to a head in 1989, leading to the opening of the Berlin Wall and, by 1991, to the end of communism in Europe. Only as it was ending, more than four decades after World War II, did observers realize that the anxious cold war era had been one of relative stability and peace.

QUESTIONS TO CONSIDER

■ What factors led to the surprisingly rapid restoration of democracy in much of continental western Europe after World War II?

■ How did decolonization and the beginnings of European integration reflect the changing status of western Europe in world affairs during the cold war era?

■ What caused the new sociopolitical discontents evident in western Europe by the end of the 1960s?

■ What led to the collapse of the communist system in the Soviet Union and its satellite states?

TERMS TO KNOW

existentialism	Prague Spring
welfare state	Suez crisis
North Atlantic Treaty Organization (NATO)	European Economic Community (EEC)
Warsaw Pact	Helsinki Accords
Konrad Adenauer	Solidarity
Willy Brandt	Mikhail Gorbachev

THE SEARCH FOR CULTURAL BEARINGS

THE events from World War I to the cold war added up to an unprecedented period of disaster for Europe. Europeans were bound to ask what had gone wrong, and what could be salvaged from the ruins of a culture that had made possible the most destructive wars in history, as well as fascism, totalitarianism, and the Holocaust. With so much discredited or called into question, Europeans faced an unprecedented period of experiment.

The cold war framework crucially shaped responses all over the Western world. Some embraced the Soviet Union or sought a renewed Marxism. Opposition to communism helped stimulate others to return to religious or classical traditions or to embrace new ideas associated with America's recent successes. In western Europe, at least, this effort to take stock led promptly to the renewed determination and fresh ideas that helped produce the dramatically successful reconstruction of the postwar years. But the anxieties stemming from superpower rivalry, and especially the nuclear arms race, were bound to temper any renewed optimism.

■ Absurdity and Commitment in Existentialism

The postwar mood of exhaustion and despair found classic expression in the work of the Irish-born writer Samuel Beckett (1906–1989), especially in his plays *Waiting for Godot* (1952) and *Endgame* (1957). Through Beckett's characters, we see ourselves going through the motions, with nothing worth saying or doing, ludicrously manipulating the husks of a worn-out culture. The only redeeming element is the comic pathos we feel as we watch ourselves.

The same sense of anxiety and despair led to the vogue of existentialism, a movement that marked philosophy, the arts, and popular culture from the later 1940s until well into the 1950s. Existentialism developed from the ideas of the German thinker Martin Heidegger (1889–1976), especially *Being and Time* (1927), one of the most influential philosophical works of the century. Though it was a philosophy of sorts, existentialism was most significant as a broader cultural tendency, finding expression in novels and films. The existentialists explored what it means to be a human being in a world cast adrift from its cultural moorings, with no mutually accepted guideposts, standards, or values.

The most influential postwar existentialists were the Frenchmen Jean-Paul Sartre° (1905–1980) and Albert Camus° (1913–1960), each of whom had been involved in the French resistance, Camus in a particularly central role as editor of an underground newspaper. For both, an authentic human response to a world spinning out of control entailed engagement, commitment, responsibility—even though every action is fraught with risk.

Rather than accept the bleak, ludicrously comic vision of Beckett's plays, Camus sought to show how we might go on living in a positive, affirmative spirit, even in a world that seemed simply absurd in one sense, especially after the recent disasters in Europe. Conventional values like friendship and tolerance could be made usable again, based on the simple fact that we human beings are all caught up in this unmasterable situation together. People suffer and die, but as we come together to help as best we can, we might at least learn to stop killing one another.

Camus split from Sartre in a disagreement over the ongoing value of Marxism and the communist experiment

Sartre (SAH-truh)   **Camus** (kah-MOO)

CHRONOLOGY

1947	India and Pakistan achieve independence Marshall Plan announced
1949	Formation of NATO
1951	Formation of the European Coal and Steel Community
1953	Death of Stalin Workers' revolt in East Germany
1955	West Germany joins NATO Warsaw Pact
1956	Khrushchev de-Stalinization speech Suez crisis Hungarian reform movement crushed
1957	*Sputnik I* launched Common Market established
1958	Beginning of Fifth Republic in France
1959	Bad Godesberg congress: reorientation of German socialism
1961	Berlin Wall erected
1962	Algerian independence from France Cuban missile crisis
1964	Ouster of Khrushchev
1968	Days of May uprising in France Prague Spring reform movement crushed
1969	Brandt becomes West German chancellor
1973	First OPEC oil crisis
1975	North Vietnamese victory and reunification of Vietnam
1979	Election of Pope John Paul II
1980	Formation of Solidarity in Poland Formation of independent Zimbabwe from Southern Rhodesia
1982	Death of Brezhnev
1985	Gorbachev comes to power in the Soviet Union
1986	Chernobyl disaster
1989	Collapse of communism in east-central Europe
1991	Collapse of communism in the Soviet Union Dissolution of the Soviet Union

Sartre and de Beauvoir   Among the most influential intellectual couples of the century, Jean-Paul Sartre and Simone de Beauvoir emerged as leaders of French existentialism by the later 1940s. See the box on page 994.   *(Giansant/Sygma)*

in the Soviet Union. Though never an orthodox communist, Sartre found potential for human liberation in the working class, in communist parties, even in the Soviet Union itself, which he saw as the strongest alternative to U.S. imperialism. By the 1950s he was portraying existentialism as fundamentally a way to revitalize Marxism.

By contrast, Camus, who had started as a communist in the 1930s, had grown disillusioned with communism even before the war, and his major political tract, *The Rebel* (1951), was partly an attack on Marxism and communism. Establishing new bases for human happiness and solidarity meant recognizing limits to what human beings could accomplish, limits even to our demands for freedom and justice. These were precisely the limits that the new political movements of the century had so disastrously overstepped. Communism, like fascism, was part of the problem, not the solution.

■ Marxists and Traditionalists

Sartre was among the many European intellectuals who believed that Marxism had won a new lease on life from the wartime resistance. As they saw it, Marxism could be revamped for the West, without the Stalinist excesses of the Soviet Union. Marxism remained a significant strand in Western political culture throughout the cold war era, but it also attracted periodic waves of denunciation.

In Italy, as in France, the communists' major role in the resistance enhanced their prestige, preparing the way for the extraordinary posthumous influence of Antonio

Gramsci° (1891–1937), a founder of the Italian Communist Party who had spent most of the fascist period in prison. His *Prison Notebooks,* published during the late 1940s, became influential throughout the world and helped make Marxism a powerful force in postwar Italian culture. Seeking to learn the lessons of the fascist triumph in Italy, Gramsci pointed Marxists toward a flexible political strategy, attuned to the special historical circumstances of each country. Thanks partly to Gramsci's legacy, Italy had the most innovative and important communist party outside the communist world for several decades after the war.

Loosely Marxist ideas were central to the renewal of political activism in the West by the later 1960s, although Marxism proved more effective as a critique of capitalism than as a blueprint for change. The best-known spokesman for a renewed radicalism on both sides of the Atlantic during the late 1960s and early 1970s was the German-born social thinker Herbert Marcuse° (1898–1979), who explored the cultural mechanisms through which capitalism perpetuates itself in *One-Dimensional Man* (1964).

Even during the late 1940s, however, others, like Camus, denied that any recasting could overcome the inherent flaws in Marxism. Damaging revelations about the excesses of Stalinism during the 1930s seemed to confirm this view. Such writers as the Hungarian-born Arthur Koestler° (1905–1983) who had believed in communism during the 1930s now denounced it as "the God that failed." Whatever its initial promise, Marxism anywhere would inevitably lead to the kind of tyranny that had developed in the Soviet Union. In his futuristic novel *Nineteen Eighty-Four,* published in 1949, the British intellectual George Orwell, long a partisan of leftist causes, chillingly portrayed the dehumanization that totalitarianism—and by association, communism—conjured up.

By the mid-1970s, the disturbing portrait of the Soviet gulag, or forced-labor-camp system, by the exiled Soviet writer Alexander Solzhenitsyn° (b. 1918) stimulated another wave of anticommunist thinking. And whether or not Marxism was necessarily Stalinist and repressive in implication, its relevance to the increasingly prosperous industrial democracies of western Europe was open to question. By the early 1980s, many had come to believe that the Marxist understanding of capitalism and class relations was simply passé.

Those hostile to Marxism often insisted that the West had to reconnect with older traditions if it was to avoid further horrors like those it had just been through.

Gramsci (GRAHM-she)   **Marcuse** (mar-KOO-zuh)
Koestler (KEST-lur)   **Solzhenitsyn** (soul-zhen-IT-sin)

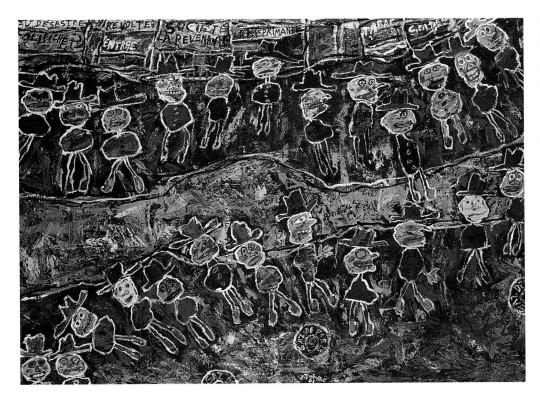

Dubuffet: Spinning Round
Seeking to depart from the European tradition of sophisticated, well-made art, Jean Dubuffet developed imagery that was at once crude and primitive, playful and whimsical. *(Dubuffet, Jean, Spinning Round, 1961. ARS Tate Gallery, London/Art Resource, NY)*

Especially in the first years after the war, many, like the French Catholic thinker Jacques Maritain° (1882–1973), held that only a return to religious traditions would suffice. For the American-born British writer T. S. Eliot (1888–1965), the essential return to tradition had to embrace family and locality, as well as religion. Without a return to tradition, Eliot warned, the West could expect more excesses such as fascism and totalitarianism in the future.

■ The Intellectual Migration and Americanism

The extraordinary migration of European artists and intellectuals to the United States to escape persecution during the 1930s and 1940s profoundly affected the cultural life of the postwar period. An array of luminaries arrived on American shores, from the composer Igor Stravinsky to the theoretical physicist Albert Einstein, from the architect Walter Gropius to the radical social theorist Herbert Marcuse.

Before this cross-fertilization, American culture had remained somewhat provincial, sometimes proudly and self-consciously so. All the direct contact with the Euro-

peans by the 1940s helped propel the United States into the Western cultural mainstream. No longer could "Western" culture be identified primarily with Europe. In some spheres—painting, for example—Americans were now confident enough to claim the leadership for the first time.

With the abstract expressionism of the later 1940s, American painters began creating visual images the likes of which had never been seen in Europe. In comparison with the raw, energetic painting of Jackson Pollock (1912–1956), the work of the Europeans seemed merely "pretty"—and the newly brash Americans were not shy about telling them so. Now New York began to supplant Paris as the art capital of the Western world.

But the American achievement owed something to European existentialism, and it became possible only because so many of the most innovative European painters had come to New York, where the Americans had been able to learn their lessons at first hand. At the same time, European painters such as Jean Dubuffet° (1901–1985) in France and Francis Bacon (1910–1992) in Britain created new forms of their own—sometimes playful, sometimes brutal—as they sought the startling

Maritain (mar-eh-TAHN)

Dubuffet (doo-boo-FAY)

new visual imagery that seemed appropriate to Western culture after the era of fascism and war. Even in the United States, artists began reacting against the deep seriousness of abstract expressionism during the mid-1950s. One new direction led by the early 1960s to "pop art," which was "American" in a different sense, featuring the ordinary objects and mass-produced images of modern consumerist culture. (See the feature "Weighing the Evidence: Pop Art" on pages 1020–1021.)

Some Europeans were eager to embrace what seemed distinctively American because America had remained relatively free of the political ideologies that seemed to have led Europe to totalitarianism and ruin. By the 1950s, there was much talk of "the end of ideology," with America pointing the way to a healthier alternative, combining technology, value-free social science, and scientific management. Whereas the old European way led either to mere theorizing, to political extremism, or to polarization and impasse, the American approach got results by tackling problems one at a time, so that they could be solved by managerial or technical experts.

Such Americanism fed the notion that Europe needed a clean break based on technological values. If such a break was necessary, however, what was to become of the European tradition, for centuries the center of gravity of the West, and until recently dominant in the world? Did anything distinctively European remain, or was Europe doomed to lick its wounds in the shadow of America? These questions lurked in the background as Europeans faced the difficult task of economic and political restoration.

PROSPERITY AND DEMOCRACY IN WESTERN EUROPE

BY 1941 democracy seemed to be dying on the European continent, yet it quickly revived in western Europe after World War II, taking root more easily than most had thought possible. The bipolar international framework helped. The United States actively encouraged democracy, and Europeans nervous about communism and the Soviet Union were happy to follow the American lead. Success at economic reconstruction was important as well. Not only was there greater prosperity, but governments could afford to deliver on promises of enhanced security, social welfare, and equal opportunity. It also mattered that western Europeans learned from past mistakes.

■ Economic Reconstruction and the Atlantic Orientation

It is hard to imagine how desperate the situation in much of western Europe had become by 1945. Major cities like Rotterdam, Hamburg, and Le Havre lay largely in ruins, and normal routines suffered radical disruption. Production had declined to perhaps 25 percent of the prewar level in Italy, to 20 percent in France, and to a mere 5 percent in southern Germany. Cigarettes, often gained through barter from American soldiers, served widely as a medium of exchange.

Although the U.S. commitment to assist European reconstruction was not originally a cold war measure, the developing cold war context made it seem all the more necessary for the United States to help the Europeans get their economies running again. The key was the Marshall Plan, which U.S. secretary of state General George Marshall outlined in 1947, and which channeled $13.5 billion in aid to western Europe by 1951.

Cold war concerns deepened the partnership in April 1949, when the United States spearheaded a military alliance, the North Atlantic Treaty Organization (NATO), that included much of western Europe. The Soviets were tightening their grip on their satellite states in east-central Europe, and the NATO alliance was intended to check any Soviet expansion westward. The Soviets had considerable superiority in conventional forces, which had ready access to western Europe, but U.S. nuclear superiority provided a balance. Indeed, the American nuclear guarantee to western Europe was the cornerstone of the NATO alliance. Thus it seemed crucial for the United States to maintain its superiority in nuclear weapons, a fact that fueled the continuing arms race and nuclear buildup.

On the economic level, the west Europeans quickly proved worthy partners. So impressive was the recovery in continental western Europe by the 1950s that some dubbed it an "economic miracle." West Europeans took advantage of the need to rebuild by adopting up-to-date methods and technologies, though economic strategies differed from one country to the next. The new German government cut state aid to business and limited the long-standing power of cartels—organizations of private businesses that regulate the production, pricing, and marketing of goods. The state was permitted to intervene in the economy only to ensure free competition. In France, by contrast, many were determined to use government to modernize the country, thereby overcoming the weakness that had led to defeat. So France adopted a flexible, pragmatic form of government-led economic planning.

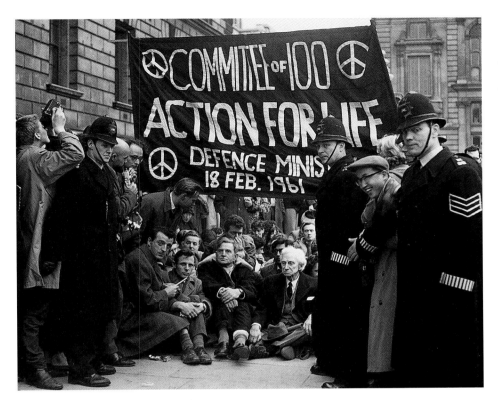

Ban the Bomb   As nuclear tension escalated during the 1950s, some built air-raid shelters; others took to the streets in antinuclear protests. The protest movement was especially prominent in Britain, where the noted philosopher Bertrand Russell (1872–1970) played a central role. Here, seated at right, he awaits arrest during a sit-in demonstration outside the British Defense Ministry.

(Hulton Getty/Liaison)

In 1946 Jean Monnet° (1888–1979) launched the first of the French postwar economic plans, which brought government and business leaders together to agree on production targets. Economic planning enabled France to make especially effective use of the capital that the Marshall Plan provided. French industrial production returned to its prewar peak by 1951, and by 1957 it had risen to twice the level of 1938.

Strong and sustained rates of economic growth were achieved throughout much of western Europe until the later 1960s. From 1953 to 1964, annual rates of growth averaged 6 percent in Germany, 5.6 percent in Italy, and 4.9 percent in France. Britain, however, lagged considerably, averaging only 2.7 percent growth annually during that same period.

As part of the new postwar consensus, labor was supposed to be brought more fully into economic decision making. Thus, for example, the trade unions participated in the planning process in France. In Germany the codetermination law of 1951 provided for labor participation in management decisions in heavy industry, and labor representatives were given access to company books and full voting memberships on boards of direc-

Monnet (moh-NAY)

tors. This measure ultimately made little difference in the functioning of the affected firms, but it helped head off any return to trade-union radicalism.

During the first years of rapid economic growth, the labor movement remained fairly passive in western Europe, even though wages stayed relatively low. After an era of depression, fascist repression, and war, workers were grateful simply to have jobs, free trade unions, and at least the promise of greater prosperity in the future. By the 1960s, however, it seemed time to redeem that promise; labor began demanding—generally with success—to share more fully in the new prosperity. Now, rather abruptly, much of western Europe took on the look of a consumer society, with widespread ownership of automobiles, televisions, and other household appliances.

■ Social Welfare and the Issue of Gender

Western governments began to adopt social welfare measures on a large scale late in the nineteenth century (see page 793), and by the 1940s some degree of governmental responsibility for unemployment insurance, workplace safety, and old-age pensions was widely accepted. Some Europeans, seeking renewal after the war, found attractive models in Sweden and Denmark, where the outlines of a welfare state had emerged by the 1930s. Sweden, especially, drew attention as a "middle way" that avoided the extremes of either Soviet Marxism, with its coercive statism, or American-style capitalism, with its brash commercialism and selfish individualism.

Sweden's economy remained fundamentally capitalist, based on private ownership; even after World War II, its nationalized, or government-run, sector was not large by European standards. But the system of social insurance in Sweden was the most extensive in Europe, and the government worked actively with business to promote full employment and to steer the economy in directions deemed socially desirable. Moreover, the welfare state came to mean a major role for the Swedish trade unions, which won relatively high wages for workers and even enjoyed a quasi-veto power over legislation.

At the same time, the Swedish government began playing a more active role in spheres of life that had formerly been private, from sexuality to child rearing. Thus, for example, drugstores were required to carry contraceptives beginning in 1946. Sweden was the first country to provide sex education in the public schools; optional from 1942, it became compulsory in 1955. By 1979 the Swedes were limiting corporal punishment—the right to spank—and prohibiting the sale of war toys. This depri-vatization of the family stemmed from a sense, especially pronounced in Sweden, that society is collectively responsible for the well-being of its children.

Although the Swedish model was extreme in certain respects, most of western Europe moved in the same direction in an effort to restore consensus and establish the foundations for democratic renewal after the war. Even Britain, one of the war's major victors, quickly began constructing a welfare state, dumping Winston Churchill in the process.

Early in the war most Britons began to take it for granted that major socioeconomic changes would follow from victory. Greater collective responsibility for the well-being of all British citizens seemed appropriate in light of the shared hardships the war had imposed. Moreover, the successes of government planning and control during the wartime emergency suggested that once the war was over, government could assume responsibility for the basic needs of the British people, guaranteeing full employment and providing a national health service. But the Labour Party, led by Clement Attlee (1883–1967), seemed better equipped to deliver on that promise than the Conservatives, whose leader, Churchill, was in fact quite hostile to welfare state notions. So when Britain held its first postwar elections, in July 1945, Churchill's Conservatives suffered a crushing

Social Welfare in Sweden With the state playing a major role, Sweden proved a pioneer in responding to the family and children's issues that became increasingly prominent after World War II. Here children play at a day-care center in Stockholm in 1953. *(Roland Janson/Pressens Bild, Stockholm)*

loss to Labour, which promptly began creating the British welfare state.

Although some expected, and others feared, that the result would be a form of socialism, the new direction did not undermine the capitalist economic system. The Labour government nationalized some key industries, but 80 percent of the British work force remained employed in private firms in 1948. Moreover, even under Labour, the British government did not seek the kind of economic planning role that government was playing in France. Much like the United States, Britain relied on monetary and fiscal policy to coordinate its economy.

The core of the British departure was a set of government-sponsored social welfare measures that significantly affected the lives of ordinary people. These included old-age pensions; insurance against unemployment, sickness, and disability; and allowances for pregnancy, child rearing, widowhood, and burial. The heart of the system was free medical care, to be provided by a National Health Service, created in November 1946 and operating by 1948.

In Britain as elsewhere, gender roles were inevitably at issue as government welfare measures were debated and adopted. Were married women to have access to the welfare system as individual citizens, or as members of a family unit, responsible for child rearing and dependent on their husbands as breadwinners? Should government seek to enable women to be both mothers and workers, or should government help make it possible for mothers not to have to work outside the home? Women themselves did not always agree on priorities, and some instructive differences in accent were evident across national boundaries.

As during the First World War, the percentage of women in the work force had increased significantly during World War II, but both women and men proved eager to embrace the security of traditional domestic patterns once the war was over. So the war did not change gender patterns of work even to the extent that World War I had done. In Britain women made up about 30 percent of the labor force in 1931, 31 percent in 1951. The percentage of women in the U.S. work force increased from 26 to 36 percent during the war years, but by 1947 it had returned to 28 percent. Thus the embrace of welfare measures took place at a time of renewed conservatism in conceptions of gender roles.

British feminists initially welcomed provisions of the British welfare state that recognized the special role of women as mothers. The government was to ease burdens by providing family allowances, to be paid directly to mothers of more than one child to enable them to stay home with their children. This seemed a more progressive step than the perpetual British trade union demand for a "family wage," sufficient to enable the male breadwinner to support a family so that his wife would not have to work. But though women were now to be compensated directly for their role as mothers, the assumptions about gender roles remained essentially the same.

In France, which had refused even to grant women the vote after World War I, the very different situation after 1945 stimulated an especially innovative response to gender and family issues. After the experience of defeat, collaboration, and resistance, the French were determined to pursue both economic dynamism and individual justice. But they also remained concerned with population growth, so they combined incentives to encourage large families with measures to promote equal opportunity and economic independence for women.

As they expanded the role of government after the war, the French tended more than the British to assume that paid employment for women was healthy and desirable. New laws gave French women equal access to civil service jobs and guaranteed equal pay for equal work. However, the French recognized at the same time both that women had special needs as mothers and that husbands shared the responsibility for parenting. So the French system provided benefits for women during and after pregnancy but also family allowances that treated the two parents as equally essential. At the same time, the system viewed women as individual citizens, regardless of marital or economic status. Thus all were equally entitled to pensions, health services, and job-related benefits.

Although female participation in the paid labor force declined just after the war, it began rising throughout the West during the 1950s, then accelerated during the 1960s, reaching new highs in the 1970s and 1980s. Thanks partly to the expansion of government, the greatest job growth was in the service sector—in social work, health care, and education, for example—and many of these new jobs went to women. From about 1960 to 1988, the percentage of women aged 25 to 34 in the labor force rose from 38 to 67 in Britain, from 42 to 75 in France, and from 49 to 87 in Germany.

These statistics reflected significant changes in women's lives, but even as their choices expanded in some respects, women became more deeply aware of enduring limits to their opportunities. Thus a new feminist movement emerged by the early 1970s, drawing intellectual inspiration from *The Second Sex,* a pioneering work published in 1949 by the French existentialist Simone de Beauvoir (1908–1986). (See page 999 and the box "Reading Sources: Human Freedom and the Origins of a New Feminism.")

இ READING SOURCES

Human Freedom and the Origins of a New Feminism

The renewed feminism that emerged during the later 1960s took inspiration from The Second Sex, *a pioneering work by the French existentialist Simone de Beauvoir that was first published in 1949. Even while valuing sexual difference, she showed the scope for opening the full range of human choices to women.*

[T]he nature of things is no more immutably given, once for all, than is historical reality. If woman seems to be the inessential which never becomes the essential, it is because she herself fails to bring about this change. . . .

To decline to be the Other, to refuse to be a party to the deal—this would be for women to renounce all the advantages conferred upon them by their alliance with the superior caste. Man-the-sovereign will provide woman-the-liege with material protection and will undertake the moral justification of her existence; thus she can evade at once both economic risk and the metaphysical risk of a liberty in which ends and aims must be contrived without assistance. Indeed, along with the ethical urge of each individual to affirm his subjective existence, there is also the temptation to forgo liberty and become a thing. . . .

If a caste is kept in a state of inferiority, no doubt it remains inferior; but liberty can break the circle. Let negroes vote, and they become worthy of having the vote; let woman be given responsibilities and she is able to assume them. . . .

. . . [T]here will be some to object that . . . when woman is "the same" as her male, life will lose its salt and spice. . . .

. . . And it is true that the evolution now in progress threatens more than feminine charm alone: in beginning to exist for herself, woman will relinquish the function as double and mediator to which she owes her privileged place in the masculine universe. . . . There is no denying that feminine dependence, inferiority, woe, give women their special character; assuredly woman's autonomy, if it spares men many troubles, will also deny them many conveniences; assuredly there are certain forms of the sexual adventure which will be lost in the world of tomorrow. But this does not mean that love, happiness, poetry, dream, will be banished from it.

. . . New relations of flesh and sentiment of which we have no conception will arise between the sexes; already, indeed, there have appeared between men and women friendships, rivalries, complicities, comradeships—chaste or sensual—which past centuries could not have conceived. . . .

. . . [T]here will always be certain differences between man and woman; her eroticism, and therefore her sexual world, have a special form of their own and therefore cannot fail to engender a sensuality, a sensitivity, of a special nature. . . .

. . . To emancipate women is to refuse to confine her to the relations she bears to man, not to deny them to her; let her have her independent existence and she will continue none the less to exist for him *also:* mutually recognizing each other as subject, each will yet remain for the other an *other.* . . . [W]hen we abolish the slavery of half of humanity, together with the whole system of hypocrisy that it implies, then the "division" of humanity will reveal its genuine significance and the human couple will find its true form.

Source: Simone de Beauvoir, *The Second Sex* (New York: Random House, Vintage, 1989), pp. xxv, xxvii, 728–731.

■ The Restoration of Democracy

Much of continental western Europe faced the challenge of rebuilding democracy after defeat and humiliation. With the developing cold war complicating the situation, the prospects for democracy were by no means certain in the late 1940s. Although the division of Germany weakened communism in the new Federal Republic, in France and Italy strong Communist Parties had emerged from the wartime resistance and claimed to point the way beyond conventional democracy altogether.

The new Federal Republic of Germany held its first election under the Basic Law in August 1949, launching what proved a stable and successful democracy. Partly to counter the Soviet Union, but also to avoid what seemed the disastrous mistake of the harsh peace settlement after World War I, the victors sought to help get West Germany back on its feet as quickly as possible. At the same time, West German political leaders, determined to avoid the mistakes of the Weimar years, now better understood the need to compromise, to take responsibility for governing the whole nation.

To prevent the instability that had plagued the Weimar Republic, the creators of the new government strengthened the chancellor in relation to the Bundestag, the lower house of parliament. In the same way, the Basic Law helped establish a stable party system by discouraging splinter parties and by empowering the courts to outlaw extremist parties. And the courts found reason to outlaw both the Communist Party and a Neo-Nazi Party during the formative years of the new German democracy.

The West German republic proved more stable than the earlier Weimar Republic partly because the political party system was now considerably simpler. Two mass parties, the Christian Democratic Union (CDU) and the Social Democratic Party (SPD), were immediately predominant, although a third, the much smaller Free Democratic Party (FDP), proved important for coalition purposes.

Konrad Adenauer (1876–1967), head of the CDU, the largest party in 1949, immediately emerged as postwar Germany's leading statesman. A Catholic who had been mayor of Cologne under Weimar, he had withdrawn from active politics during the Nazi period, but he reemerged after the war to lead the council that drafted the Basic Law. As chancellor from 1949 until 1963, he oriented the new German democracy toward western Europe and the Atlantic bloc, led by the United States.

The new bipolar world confronted West Germany with a cruel choice. By accepting the bipolar framework, the country could become a full partner within the Atlantic bloc. But by straddling the fence instead, it could keep open the possibility that Germany could be reunified as a neutral and disarmed state. When the outbreak of war in Korea in 1950 intensified the cold war, the United States pressured West Germany to rearm and join the Western bloc. Although some West Germans resisted, Adenauer prevailed, committing the Federal Republic to NATO in 1955. Adenauer was eager to anchor the new Federal Republic to the West, partly to buttress the new democracy in West Germany, but also to cement U.S. support in the face of what seemed an ongoing Soviet threat to German security.

By the late 1950s the West German economy was recovering nicely, and the country was a valued member of the Western alliance. Adenauer's CDU seemed so potent that the other major party, the SPD, appeared to be consigned to permanent—and sterile—opposition. Frustrated with its outsider status, the SPD began to shed its Marxist trappings in an effort to widen its appeal. Prominent among those pushing in this direction was Willy Brandt (1913–1992), who became mayor of West Berlin in 1957, and who would become the party's leader in 1963. At its watershed national congress at Bad Godesberg in 1959, the party officially gave up talk of the class struggle and adopted a more moderate program.

Adenauer stepped down in 1963 at the age of 87, after fourteen years as chancellor. The contrast with Weimar, which had known twenty-one different cabinets in a comparable fourteen-year period, could not be more striking. The Adenauer years proved to Germans that democracy could mean effective government, economic prosperity, and foreign policy success. Still, Adenauer had become somewhat authoritarian by his later years, and it was arguable that West Germany had become overly reliant on him and his party.

During the years from 1963 to 1969, the CDU proved it could govern without Adenauer, and the SPD came to seem ever more respectable, even joining as the junior partner in a government coalition with the CDU in 1966. Finally, in October 1969, new parliamentary elections brought Brandt to the chancellorship, and the SPD became responsible for governing West Germany for the first time since the war.

Brandt sought to provide a genuine alternative to the CDU without undermining the consensus that had developed around the new regime since 1949. He wanted especially to improve relations between West Germany and the Soviet bloc, but this required a more independent foreign policy than Adenauer and his successors had followed. Under Adenauer, the Federal Republic had refused to deal with East Germany at all. So Brandt's opening to the East, or *Ostpolitik*°, was risky for a socialist chancellor seeking to prove his respectability. But he pursued it with skill and success.

In treaties with the Soviet Union, Czechoslovakia, and Poland during the early 1970s, West Germany accepted the main lines of the postwar settlement. This was to abandon any claim to the former German territory east of the Oder-Neisse° line, now in Poland. Brandt also managed to improve relations with East Germany. After the two countries finally agreed to mutual diplomatic recognition, each was admitted to the United Nations in 1973. Brandt's overtures made possible closer economic ties between them, and even broader opportunities for

---

Ostpolitik (OST-po-luh-teek)   **Oder-Neisse** (OH-dur–NYE-suh)

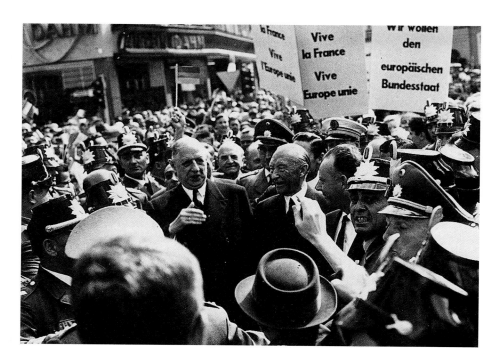

Franco-German Cooperation

French president Charles de Gaulle (*left*) and West German chancellor Konrad Adenauer (*right*) draw an enthusiastic crowd in Bonn in September 1963. De Gaulle was in the West German capital for the first formal meeting after France and West Germany had signed a friendship treaty in January. Each of the two leaders strongly advocated the new cooperation between their countries, and that cooperation proved a cornerstone of the unprecedented peace and prosperity in western Europe after World War II. (*AKG London*)

ordinary citizens to interact across the east-west border. His *Ostpolitik* was widely popular and helped deepen the postwar consensus in West Germany.

In France and Italy, unlike West Germany, communists emerged powerful from major roles in wartime resistance movements. Indeed, in either nation they might conceivably have made a bid for power as the war was ending. But Moscow called for the moderate route of participation in coalitions instead, at least partly because the presence of Western troops in these countries gave the leverage to noncommunists. And the United States intervened persistently to minimize the communists' role as new democracies took root in both nations after 1945. In France support for the communists continued to grow until 1949. Thereafter, the French Communist Party settled into a particularly doctrinaire position, maintaining strict subservience to the Soviet Union—and found itself increasingly marginalized.

As the leader of the French resistance effort, Charles de Gaulle immediately assumed the dominant political role after the liberation of France in August 1944. But he withdrew, disillusioned, from active politics early in 1946, as the new Fourth Republic returned to the unstable multiparty coalitions that had marked the later years of the Third. Still, governmental decision making changed significantly as the nonpolitical, technocratic side of the French state gained power in areas such as economic planning. And government technocrats survived the fall of the Fourth Republic in 1958, when de

Gaulle returned to politics at a moment of crisis, stemming from France's war to maintain control of Algeria (see page 1007).

Although de Gaulle became prime minister within the Fourth Republic, it was clear that his return signified a change of regime. The French legislature promptly gave his government full powers for six months. Taking up the mandate, the regime drafted a new constitution, which was then approved by referendum in the fall of 1958. The result was the new Fifth Republic, which featured a stronger executive—and soon a president elected directly by the people and not dependent on the Chamber of Deputies. It was only in 1958, with the return of de Gaulle and the advent of the Fifth Republic, that government in postwar France began to assume definitive contours.

Italy's political challenge, after more than twenty years of fascism, was even more dramatic than France's. Shortly after the war, the Italians adopted a new democratic constitution and voted to end the monarchy, thereby making modern Italy a republic for the first time. But much depended on the balance of political forces, which quickly crystallized around the Christian Democratic party (DC), oriented toward the Catholic Church, and the strong Communist Party. Many Italian moderates with little attachment to the church supported the Christian Democrats as the chief bulwark against communism. And though they consistently had to work with smaller parties to attain a parliamentary majority, the

Christian Democrats promptly assumed the dominant role, which they maintained until the early 1990s.

The Communists continued to offer the major opposition, typically winning 25–35 percent of the vote in national elections. Taking their cue from Gramsci's writings, they adopted a proactive strategy to make their presence felt in Italian life and to demonstrate the superiority of their diagnoses and prescriptions. And they found considerable success as they organized profit-making cooperatives for sharecroppers, ran local and regional governments, and garnered the support of intellectuals, journalists, and publishers. But though they had proven capable of operating constructively within a democratic framework, their longer-term role remained unclear into the 1970s. What were the Communists trying to accomplish on the national level, and how long was it supposed to take? Could a Communist Party function as part of a majority governing coalition within a democratic political system?

By the 1960s the new democracies in Germany, France, and Italy seemed firmly rooted, and during the 1970s Greece, Spain, and Portugal also established workable democracies after periods of dictatorial rule. Following the death of Francisco Franco in 1975, almost forty years after his triumph in the Spanish civil war, democracy returned to Spain more smoothly than most had dared hope. Franco ordained that a restoration of the monarchy would follow his death, and King Juan Carlos (b. 1938; r. 1975–) served as an effective catalyst in the transition to democracy. The new constitution of 1978 dismantled what was left of the Franco system so that, for example, Catholicism was no longer recognized as the official religion of the Spanish state.

■ New Discontents and New Directions

Even as democracy seemed to be thriving in western Europe, political disaffection began to threaten the consensus in the more established democracies by the late 1960s. Such frustration deepened in the more difficult economic environment of the 1970s, when Britain, for example, began finding it could no longer afford its welfare state. But when disaffection first emerged, in the late 1960s, western Europe was at the height of the new prosperity, and so the discontent did not stem from immediate economic circumstances alone. And it produced a sudden eruption of political radicalism.

The most dramatic instance of radical protest was the "Days of May" uprising of students and workers that shook France during May and June of 1968. The movement's aims were amorphous or utopian, and cooperation between students and workers proved sporadic. But the episode gave vent to growing discontent with the aloofness of the technocratic leaders and the unevenness

Days of May   French students use garbage-can covers as shields just minutes before a violent confrontation with police near the Gare de Lyon in Paris on May 25, 1968. The student-led protest movement revealed a reservoir of resentment that had built up in French society despite the democracy and prosperity of the postwar period.   *(Marc Riboud/Magnum Photos)*

✿ READING SOURCES

Students and Revolution: The "Days of May" in Paris, 1968

As part of the radical demonstrations in Paris in May 1968, the Sorbonne, the most famous university on the European continent, became the focus of student demonstrations. Despite a series of arrests, students took over and occupied the university on May 13. A month later, on June 13, the Occupation Committee of the Sorbonne issued a manifesto reviewing what had happened and specifying the course for the future. The police retook the Sorbonne three days later, but the interplay of frustrations and aspirations evident in this manifesto continued to shape debate and influence policy thereafter.

It was during the evening of 13 May after a week of fighting that we finally reoccupied the Sorbonne. We then realised more than ever that things would never again be as they had been. From that day onwards a new era had begun for the university. During the general strike and factory occupations, hundreds of thousands of students occupied their faculties, transforming them into red centres of support for the workers' struggle and for reflection on the future of the university.

Today, now that the majority of workers have, for the time being, returned to work, where has it all got us? Assemblies and committees have discussed the reforms for the university, the principles of university administration and teaching. We have witnessed the collapse of the academic authorities, the disappearance of rectors. We have heard the professors, the former landlords, shout about their sudden willingness for dialogue! . . .

Everyone knows that in the present circumstances a pure and simple reform of the university structures will by no means suffice. By calling the Sorbonne the "People's University," we have simply said that before changing the internal structures of the university, we must be sure for whom and with what aim it will be used. It took five centuries for the priests and then the bourgeoisie to build their uni-

versity. It is therefore to be expected that in one month we cannot transform their university into one for the workers. . . .

. . . The Sorbonne should be called "the University at the Service of the Revolution":

a. Not only university reform, but also the political atmosphere which conditions it, should be examined during the six-month study programme. All problems concerning society will be examined, studied and discussed. Seminars will be arranged, enquiries carried out. Reports will be prepared. At the Sorbonne, we will talk about social living conditions, about the power of management, about underdevelopment, as well as imperialistic wars, advertising and immigrant workers. . . .

d. It should be an open forum for workers, farm workers, employees, all those wishing to give their opinion on the university of tomorrow. The Sorbonne could be used to help them in their struggle in their factory or profession against capitalism. . . .

THE FORMER REGIME IS DEAD, HELP US TO BUILD A NEW ORDER!

Source: Vladimir Fišera, *Writing on the Wall: May 1968: A Documentary History* (New York: St. Martin's Press, 1979), pp. 245–247.

of the modernization effort in de Gaulle's France. Despite the impressive economic growth, many ordinary people were coming to feel left out as public services were neglected and problems worsened in such areas as housing and education. French universities were a particular tar-

get, drawing protests and even full-scale takeovers by radical students. (See the box "Reading Sources: Students and Revolution: The 'Days of May' in Paris, 1968.")

Enrollment in French universities more than doubled between 1939 and 1960, then more than doubled again between 1960 and 1967. Apart from a few highly selective *grandes écoles,* the institutions of the state-run university system were open to anyone who passed a standard examination. To limit enrollments by restricting access did not seem politically feasible. Instead, the government tried to build to keep up with demand—thereby creating vast, impersonal institutions with professors increasingly inaccessible to students. But overcrowding persisted, and the value of a university degree diminished, leaving graduates with uncertain job prospects.

In Italy frustration with the stagnation of the political system bred radical labor unrest by 1969 and then a major wave of terrorism during the 1970s. By this time many radical young people found the Communists too caught up in the system to be genuinely innovative, yet still too weak to break the Christian Democrats' lock on power. Because the Italian Communists, unlike the German Social Democrats, never established their credibility as a national governing party, the Christian Democrats grew ever more entrenched, becoming increasingly arrogant and corrupt.

In Germany the Green movement formed by peace and environmental activists during the late 1970s took pains to avoid acting like a conventional party. Concerned that Germany, with its central location, would end up the devastated battleground in any superpower confrontation, the Greens opposed deployment of additional U.S. missiles on German soil and called for an alternative to the endless arms race. The SPD, as the governing party in an important NATO state, seemed unable to confront this issue and lost members as a result.

Prominent among the new political currents emerging by the early 1970s was the renewed feminist movement, which recalled the earlier movement for women's suffrage. This movement for "women's liberation" sought equal opportunities for women in education and employment. It was striking, for example, that despite major steps toward equal educational opportunity in postwar France, the country's prestigious engineering schools were still not admitting women in the late 1960s—and would begin doing so only during the 1980s. But feminists also forced new issues onto the political stage as they worked, for example, to liberalize divorce and abortion laws.

At the same time, women faced new questions after a generation of experience with the activist postwar state. In Britain, where government had sought to free mothers from the necessity of employment outside the home, feminists increasingly blamed the welfare state for their ongoing second-class status. But the tradeoffs were complex, and discussion continued, making gender issues central to public policy and personal choice all over the Western world by the last two decades of the century.

THE COMMUNIST BLOC: FROM CONSOLIDATION TO STAGNATION

BY the late 1950s, policymakers in the West were increasingly concerned that the Soviet Union, though rigid and inhumane in important respects, might have significant advantages in the race with the capitalist democracies. Westerners worried especially about producing enough scientists and engineers to match the Soviets. With the Great Depression still in memory, some economists argued that central planning might prove more efficient, and certainly more equitable, than capitalism. The Soviet effort constituted a highly visible chapter in the continuing experiment in the West, and it was not clear what the outcome might be. The sense that the communist system offered formidable competition added to the anxieties in the U.S.-led Atlantic bloc.

Nonetheless, the flawed political and economic order that had emerged under Stalin continued in the Soviet Union. And when it was imposed on the countries within the Soviet orbit after the war, it produced widespread resentment—and new dilemmas for Soviet leaders. Efforts to make communism more flexible after Stalin's death in 1953 proved sporadic at best. The Soviet suppression of the reform movement in Czechoslovakia during the "Prague Spring" of 1968 seemed to prove the inherent rigidity of the Soviet system.

■ Dilemmas of the Soviet System in Postwar Europe, 1949–1955

Even in victory, the Soviet Union had suffered enormously in the war with Nazi Germany. Especially in the more developed western part of the country, thousands of factories and even whole towns lay destroyed, and there were severe shortages of everything from labor to housing. Yet the developing cold war seemed to require that military spending remain high.

At the same time, the Soviet Union faced the challenge of solidifying the new system of satellite states it had put together in east-central Europe. Most of the region had no desirable interwar past to reclaim, and thus there was widespread sentiment for significant change. Even in Czechoslovakia, which had been the most prosperous and democratic state in the region, considerable nationalization of industry was completed even before the communist takeover in 1948. And whatever integration into the new Soviet bloc might mean politically, it was not clear in the late 1940s

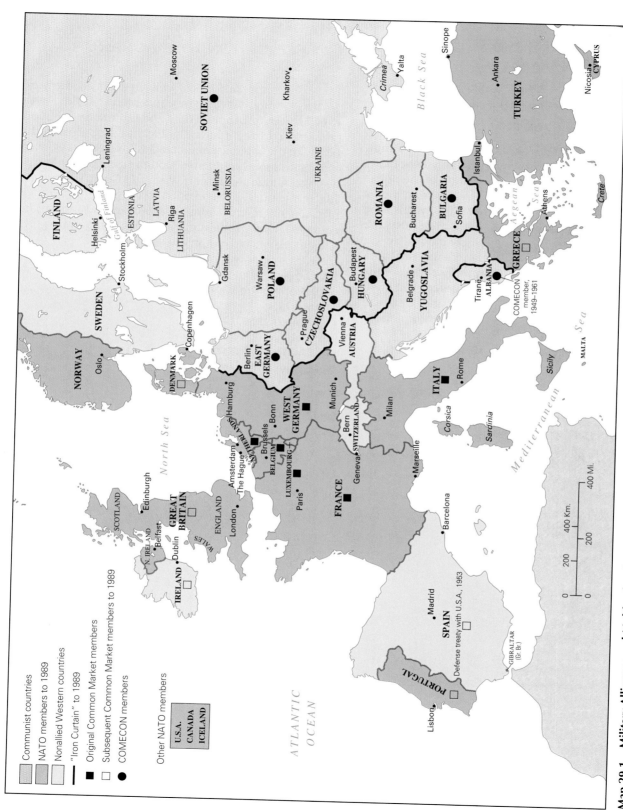

Map 29.1 Military Alliances and Multinational Economic Groupings, 1949–1989 The cold war split was reflected especially in the two military alliances: NATO, formed in 1949, and the Warsaw Pact, formed in 1955. Each side also had its own multinational economic organization, but the membership of the EEC, or Common Market, was not identical to that of NATO. Although communist, Yugoslavia remained outside Soviet-led organizations, as did Albania for part of the period.

that it had to be economically disadvantageous over the long term. The Soviet system seemed to have proved itself in standing up to the Nazis, and many believed that a socialist economic system could be made to work.

Partly in response to U.S. initiatives in western Europe, the Soviets sought to mold the new communist states into a secure, coordinated bloc of allies. In the economic sphere, the Soviets founded a new organization, COMECON, as part of their effort to lead the economies of the satellite states away from their earlier ties to the West and toward the Soviet Union (see Map 29.1). In the military-diplomatic sphere, the Soviets countered NATO in 1955 by bringing the Soviet bloc countries together in a formal alliance, the Warsaw Pact, which provided for a joint military command and mutual military assistance. The Warsaw Pact established a new basis for the continuing presence of Soviet troops in the satellite states, but the tensions within the Soviet-dominated system in east-central Europe soon raised questions about what the pact meant.

From the start, Yugoslavia had been a point of vulnerability for the Soviet system. Communist-led partisans under Josip Tito had liberated Yugoslavia from the Axis on their own, and they had not needed the Red Army to begin constructing a new communist regime (see page 975). Tito was willing to work with the Soviets, but because he had his own legitimacy, he could be considerably more independent than those elsewhere whose power rested on Soviet support. Thus the Soviets deemed it essential to bring Tito to heel, lest his example encourage too much independence in the other communist states. When Soviet demands became intolerably meddlesome from the Yugoslav point of view, Tito broke with the Soviet Union altogether in 1948. Yugoslavia then began developing a more flexible socialist economic system, with greater scope for local initiatives.

Stalin's response to Tito's defection was a crackdown on potential opponents throughout the Soviet bloc. Though the terror did not approach the massive scale of 1937–1938 (see page 922), again the secret police executed those suspected of deviation, inspiring fear even among the top leadership. But as such repression proceeded in the satellite states, opposition strikes and demonstrations developed as well, finally reaching a crisis point in East Germany in 1953.

In East Berlin a workers' protest against a provision to increase output or face wage cuts promptly led to political demands, including free elections and the withdrawal of Soviet troops. Disturbances soon spread to the other East German cities. Though this spontaneous up-

rising was not well coordinated, Soviet military forces had to intervene to save the East German communist regime. But the East German protest helped stimulate strikes and antigovernment demonstrations elsewhere in the Soviet bloc as well, convincing Soviet leaders that something had to be done. However, at this point the leadership of the Soviet Union was again being sorted out, for Stalin had died early in 1953, a few months before the crisis in East Germany came to a head.

■ De-Stalinization Under Khrushchev, 1955–1964

Although a struggle for succession followed Stalin's death, the political infighting involved a reasonable degree of give and take, as opposed to terror and violence. To be sure, the contestants quickly ganged up on the hated secret police chief, who was tried and executed within months, but this stemmed from their prior agreement to limit the role of the secret police. Moreover, although one of the eventual losers was sent to Siberia to run a power station and the other was made ambassador to Outer Mongolia, it was a major departure that the winner, Nikita Khrushchev° (1894–1971), ordered neither of them exiled or executed.

Slightly crude, even something of a buffoon, Khrushchev outmaneuvered his rivals by 1955 partly because they repeatedly underestimated him. Although his period of leadership was brief, it was eventful indeed—and in some ways the Soviet system's best chance for renewal.

At a closed session of the Soviet Communist Party's twentieth national congress in February 1956, Khrushchev made a dramatic late-night speech denouncing the criminal excesses of the Stalinist system and the "cult of personality" that had developed around Stalin himself. (See the box "Reading Sources: Khrushchev Denounces the Crimes of Stalinism.") Khrushchev's immediate aim was to undercut his hard-line rivals, but he also insisted that key features of Stalinism had amounted to an unnecessary deviation from Marxism-Leninism. So the advent of Khrushchev suggested there might be liberalization and reform.

At the same time, however, the growing popular discontent in the satellite states placed the whole system in crisis. In the face of the East German uprising of 1953, the Soviets backed off from hard-line Stalinism, making room for more moderate communists they had previously shunned, such as the Hungarian Imre Nagy° (1896–1958). Khrushchev even sought to patch things up

---

Khrushchev (KROOSH-choff)   **Nagy** (NAHZH)

⋙ READING SOURCES

Khrushchev Denounces the Crimes of Stalinism

In his speech to the Soviet Communist Party's national congress in 1956, Nikita Khrushchev repeatedly contrasted Stalin with Lenin, seeking to show that Stalinism had been an unfortunate and unnecessary deviation, not the logical outcome of the communist revolution. Khrushchev's denunciation of Stalin produced considerable commotion in the hall.

[I]t is impermissible and foreign to the spirit of Marxism-Leninism to elevate one person, to transform him into a superman possessing supernatural characteristics akin to those of a god. . . .

Such a belief about a man, and specifically about Stalin, was cultivated among us for many years. . . .

While ascribing great importance to the role of the leaders and organizers of the masses, Lenin at the same time mercilessly stigmatized every manifestation of the cult of the individual. . . .

Stalin originated the concept "enemy of the people." This term . . . made possible the usage of the most cruel repression, violating all norms of revolutionary legality, against anyone who in any way disagreed with Stalin, against those who were only suspected of hostile intent, against those who had bad reputations. This concept, "enemy of the people," actually eliminated the possibility of any kind of ideological fight or the making of one's views known on this or that issue, even those of a practical character. In the main, and in actuality, the only proof of guilt used, against all norms of current legal science, was the "confession" of the accused himself; and, as subsequent probing proved, "confessions" were acquired through physical torture against the accused. . . .

Arbitrary behavior by one person encouraged and permitted arbitrariness in others. Mass arrests and deportations of many thousands of people, execution without trial and without normal investigation created conditions of insecurity, fear and even desperation. . . .

Lenin used severe methods only in the most necessary cases, when the exploiting classes were still in existence and were vigorously opposing the revolution, when the struggle for survival was decidedly assuming the sharpest forms, even including a civil war. Stalin, on the other hand, used extreme methods and mass repressions at a time when the revolution was already victorious, when the Soviet state was strengthened, when the exploiting classes were already liquidated. . . . It is clear that here Stalin showed in a whole series of cases his intolerance, his brutality and his abuse of power. . . .

Source: The Anti-Stalin Campaign and International Communism: A Selection of Documents, edited by the Russian Institute, Columbia University (New York: Columbia University Press, 1956), pp. 2, 4, 12–14, 17, 20–21.

 For additional information on this topic, go to http://college.hmco.com.

with Tito, exchanging visits with him in 1955 and 1956. In his speech to the party congress in 1956, Khrushchev suggested that different countries might take different routes to communism.

But could liberalization be contained within the larger framework of Soviet leadership, or were openness and innovation bound to threaten the system itself? The test case proved to be Hungary, where reformers led by the moderate communist Nagy had taken advantage of the liberalizing atmosphere by mid-1956 to begin dismantling collective farms and moving toward a multiparty political system. They even called for Soviet troops to withdraw, to enable Hungary to leave the Warsaw Pact and become neutral. These were not changes within the system, but challenges to the system itself. So when a democratic coalition government was set up by November, the Soviets used tanks to crush the Hungarian reform movement. Thousands were killed during the fighting or subsequently executed, and 200,000 Hungarians fled to the West.

Yet even the crackdown in Hungary did not mean a return to the old days of Stalinist rigidity in the Soviet bloc. The Soviets understood that the system had to become more palatable, but liberalization was to be contained within certain limits. Above all, it could not challenge communist monopoly rule and the Warsaw Pact. So after 1956 the satellites were granted greater leeway, and showed greater diversity, than had previously seemed possible. Hungary's new leader, János Kádár, collectivized agriculture more fully than before, but he also engineered a measure of economic decentralization, allowing scope for local initiatives and market mechanisms.

In East Germany, in contrast, Walter Ulbricht (1893–1973) concentrated on central planning and heavy industry in orthodox fashion. But the East German economy became the most successful in the Soviet bloc, primarily because here the new communist regime fell heir to a skilled industrial labor force. Still, that economic growth was built on low wages, so East German workers were tempted to emigrate to West Germany as the West German economic miracle gleamed ever brighter during the 1950s. The special position of Berlin, in the heart of East Germany yet still divided among the occupying powers, made such emigration relatively easy, and 2.6 million East Germans left for the West between 1950 and 1962. With a population of only 17.1 million, East Germany could not afford to let this hemorrhaging continue. Thus, in August 1961 the Ulbricht regime erected the Berlin Wall, an ugly symbol of the cold war division of Europe.

■ From Liberalization to Stagnation

As a domestic leader, Khrushchev proved erratic, but he was an energetic innovator, willing to experiment. He jettisoned the worst features of the police state apparatus, including some of the infamous forced labor camps, and offered several amnesties for prisoners. He also liberalized cultural life and gave workers greater freedom to move from one job to another. The economic planning apparatus was decentralized somewhat, affording more scope for local initiatives and placing greater emphasis on consumer goods. The government expanded medical and educational facilities and, between 1955 and 1964, doubled the nation's housing stock, substantially alleviating a severe housing shortage.

Though living standards remained relatively low, Khrushchev's reforms helped improve the lives of ordinary people. Even his claim in 1961 that the Soviet Union would surpass the Western standard of living within twenty years did not seem an idle boast. The Soviets had launched *Sputnik I* in 1957, assuming the lead in the ensuing space race, and they sent the first human into space in 1961. Such achievements suggested that even ordinary Soviet citizens had reason for optimism. More generally, the communist regimes throughout the Soviet bloc entered the 1960s with confidence after having achieved excellent rates of economic growth during the 1950s.

Yet Khrushchev had made enemies with his erratic reform effort, and this led to his forced retirement in October 1964. After the unending experiment in the economy, his opponents wanted to consolidate, to return to stability and predictability. But not until 1968 did it become clear that the liberalization and innovation of the Khrushchev era were over.

By early 1968 a significant reform movement had developed within the Communist Party in Prague, the capital of Czechoslovakia. Determined to avoid the fate of the Hungarian effort in 1956, the reformers emphasized that Czechoslovakia was to remain a communist state and a full member of the Warsaw Pact. But within that framework, they felt, it should be possible to invite freer cultural expression, democratize the Communist Party's procedures, and broaden participation in public life.

However, efforts to reassure the Soviets alienated some of the movement's supporters, who stepped up their demands. As earlier in Hungary, the demand for change seemed to outstrip the intentions of the movement's organizers. Finally, in August 1968, Soviet leaders decided to crack down, sending Soviet tanks into Prague to crush the reform movement. This end of the "Prague Spring" closed the era of relative flexibility and cautious innovation in the Soviet bloc that had begun in 1953.

A period of relative stagnation followed under Leonid Brezhnev° (1906–1982), a careful, consensus-seeking bureaucrat. In dealing with the United States, Brezhnev helped engineer significant moves toward arms control and easing tensions. But despite this *détente*, the "Brezhnev doctrine" specified in no uncertain terms that the Soviet Union would intervene as necessary to help established communist regimes remain in power. For the Soviet satellite states, there seemed to be no further hope of reform from within. But even as resignation marked the first years after 1968, forces soon emerged that undermined the whole communist system.

Brezhnev (BREZH-nef)

The End of the Prague Spring   Moving tanks into Prague in August 1968, Soviet leaders ended the widely admired reform movement in Czechoslovakia. Though there were protests, as shown here on August 20, the outcome was a foregone conclusion once the Soviets decided to intervene. Although life soon returned to "normal" in the Czechoslovak capital, the ending of the Prague Spring proved a watershed for the fate of communism in Europe.   *(Josef Kondelka/Magnum Photos)*

EUROPE, THE WEST, AND THE WORLD

B Y the early 1950s, the old Europe seemed dwarfed by the two superpowers and, for the foreseeable future, divided by the conflict between them. The colonial networks that had manifested European predominance unraveled rapidly at the same time. One obvious response was some form of European integration. A unified Europe might eventually become a global superpower in its own right. Although the first steps toward European unity did not go so far as visionaries had hoped, a new group of leaders established lasting foundations by the late 1950s. Still, the cold war framework limited the new union's geographical extent and the scope of its activity for decades.

■ The Cold War Framework

The most intense phase of the cold war ended with Stalin's death in 1953. In his speech to the twentieth party congress in 1956, Khrushchev repudiated the previous Soviet tenet that the very existence of Western capitalist imperialism made a military showdown with the communist world inevitable. During a visit to the United States in 1959, he stressed that the ongoing competition between the two sides could be peaceful. However, despite summit conferences and sporadic efforts at better relations, friction between the Soviet Union and the United States continued to define the era.

Indeed, a new peak of tension was reached in October 1962 when the Soviets began placing missiles in

Cuba, just 90 miles from the United States. Cuba had developed close ties with the Soviet Union after a 1959 revolution led by Fidel Castro (b. 1926). With Castro beginning to develop a communist system, a U.S.-supported force of Cuban exiles sought to invade Cuba and foment insurrection against the new regime in April 1961. This particular effort proved a fiasco, but it demonstrated to the Soviets that the new Cuban regime was vulnerable to overthrow from the United States.

Although the United States had placed offensive missiles in NATO-member Turkey, adjacent to the Soviet Union, the Soviet attempt to base missiles in Cuba seemed an intolerable challenge. U.S. president John F. Kennedy (1917–1963) responded with a naval blockade of Cuba, and for several days, the superpowers seemed on the verge of military confrontation. But the Soviets agreed to withdraw their missiles in exchange for a U.S. promise not to seek to overthrow the communist government in Cuba. The Americans also agreed informally to remove their offensive missiles from Turkey. Khrushchev's willingness to retreat antagonized hardliners in the Soviet military and contributed to his ouster from power two years later. Yet Khrushchev himself viewed the outcome in Cuba as a victory. By challenging the United States with missiles, the Soviets had helped secure the survival of the Cuban communist regime, which was now less vulnerable to overthrow by the United States. The long-term significance of the outcome was not clear in 1962, but the Cuban missile crisis produced anxiety on all sides. This was the closest the superpowers came to armed confrontation during the cold war period.

At the same time, it became increasingly clear that international communism was not the monolithic force it had once seemed. The most dramatic indication was the Sino-Soviet split, which developed during the 1950s as the communists under Mao Zedong solidified their regime in China. In the long struggle that led to their victory in 1949, the Chinese communists had often had no choice but to go their own way, and during the 1940s, especially, Stalin had been willing to subordinate any concern for their cause to Soviet national interests. After taking power in 1949, the Chinese communists pursued their own path to development without worrying about the Soviet model. Not without reason, the Soviets feared that the independent, innovative Chinese might be prepared to challenge Soviet leadership in international communism. By the early 1960s, the communist Chinese path had become appealing especially in the non-Western world, though it attracted dissident communists in the West as well.

■ The Varieties of Decolonization

The advent of a new world configuration, with a circumscribed place for Europe, found dramatic expression in the rapid disintegration of the European colonial empires after World War II (see Map 29.2). The war itself had been a major catalyst for independence movements throughout the world. In southeast Asia and the Pacific, quick Japanese conquests revealed the tenuous hold of France, the Netherlands, and Britain on their domains. And it was not colonial reconquest that marked the end of the war, but the atomic bomb and the victory of the United States, which took a dim view of conventional European colonialism.

The effort of the Netherlands to regain control of the Dutch East Indies led to four years of military struggle against the Indonesian nationalist insurgency. Although most independent observers felt they could not win, the Dutch were reluctant to relinquish control of the East Indies, which had been in Dutch hands since the seventeenth century. Especially after the humiliations of defeat and occupation during World War II, many of the Dutch took pride in their imperial role. The struggle lasted from 1945 to 1949, when the Dutch finally had to yield as their former colony became independent Indonesia.

Unlike the Netherlands, Britain was still a great power in the twentieth century, and its empire had long seemed essential to its stature. But the structure of the British Empire had been evolving for decades before World War II. With the Statute of Westminster, passed by the British Parliament in 1931, such dominions as Canada, Australia, New Zealand, and South Africa became truly independent, controlling their own foreign policies and joining the League of Nations. This statute was essentially the founding document of the British Commonwealth of Nations. Though it initially encompassed only former British possessions dominated by people of European origin, the commonwealth provided the basis for relatively orderly decolonization after World War II.

In granting independence to India and Pakistan in 1947, the British understood that traditional colonial arrangements were ending, but they envisioned playing an ongoing leadership role by incorporating their former colonies into the British Commonwealth. However, the commonwealth idea proved to have little appeal for those winning independence, and the British Commonwealth proved little more than a voluntary cooperative association. Still, Britain proved the most realistic of the European colonial powers, grasping the need to compromise and work with emerging national leaders.

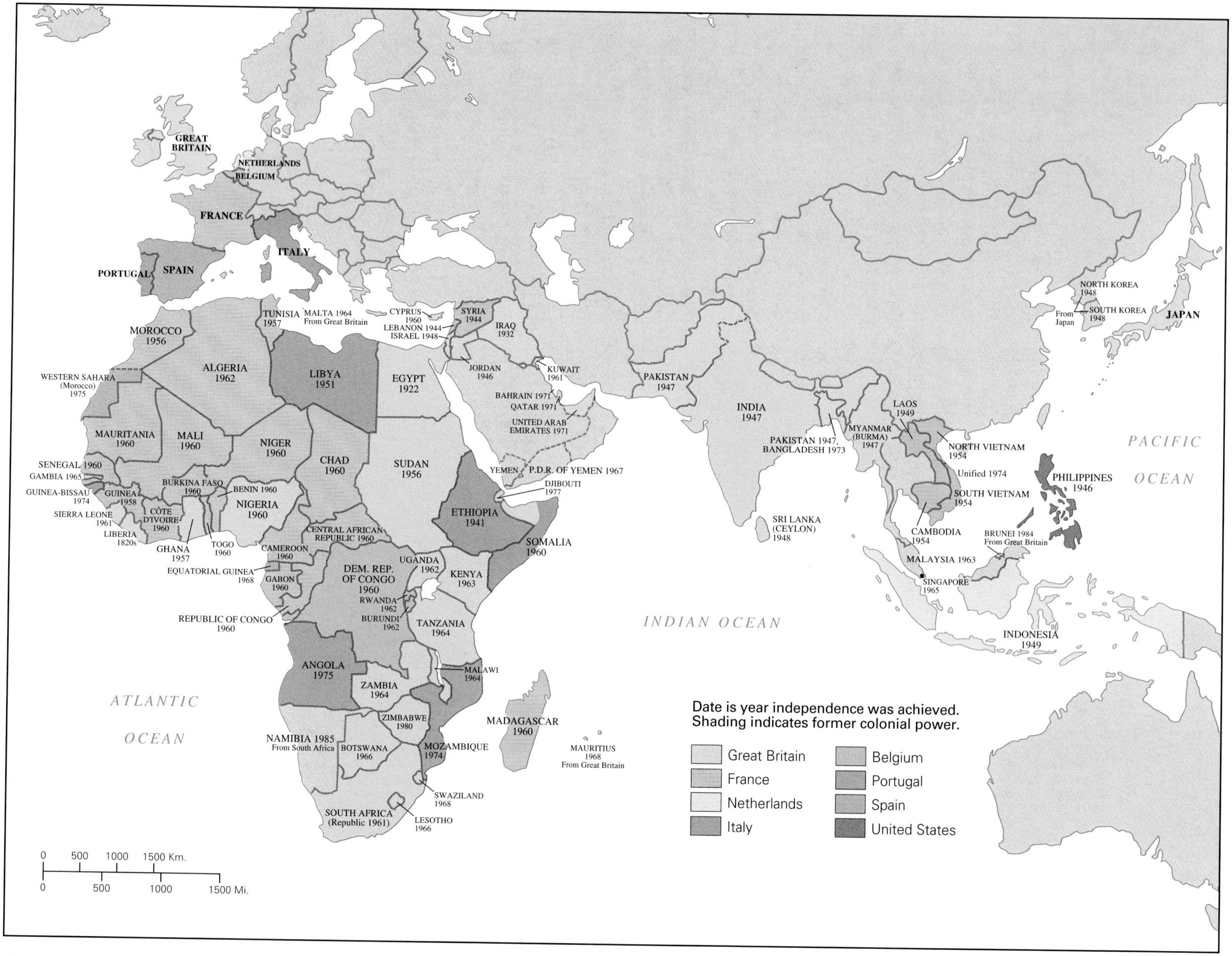
GREAT BRITAIN
NETHERLANDS
BELGIUM
FRANCE
ITALY
PORTUGAL
SPAIN
MOROCCO 1956
WESTERN SAHARA (Morocco) 1975
ALGERIA 1962
TUNISIA 1957
MALTA 1964 From Great Britain
LIBYA 1951
EGYPT 1922
CYPRUS 1960
LEBANON 1944
ISRAEL 1948
SYRIA 1944
IRAQ 1932
JORDAN 1946
KUWAIT 1961
BAHRAIN 1971
QATAR 1971
UNITED ARAB EMIRATES 1971
YEMEN
P.D.R. OF YEMEN 1967
DJIBOUTI 1977
MAURITANIA 1960
MALI 1960
NIGER 1960
CHAD 1960
SUDAN 1956
SENEGAL 1960
GAMBIA 1965
GUINEA-BISSAU 1974
GUINEA 1958
SIERRA LEONE 1961
LIBERIA 1820s
CÔTE D'IVOIRE 1960
BURKINA FASO 1960
BENIN 1960
NIGERIA 1960
GHANA 1957
TOGO 1960
CAMEROON 1960
CENTRAL AFRICAN REPUBLIC 1960
EQUATORIAL GUINEA 1968
GABON 1960
REPUBLIC OF CONGO 1960
DEM. REP. OF CONGO 1960
RWANDA 1962
BURUNDI 1962
UGANDA 1962
KENYA 1963
ETHIOPIA 1941
SOMALIA 1960
TANZANIA 1964
ANGOLA 1975
ZAMBIA 1964
MALAWI 1964
ZIMBABWE 1980
MOZAMBIQUE 1974
NAMIBIA 1985 From South Africa
BOTSWANA 1966
SWAZILAND 1968
LESOTHO 1966
SOUTH AFRICA (Republic 1961)
MADAGASCAR 1960
MAURITIUS 1968 From Great Britain
ATLANTIC OCEAN
INDIAN OCEAN
PACIFIC OCEAN
PAKISTAN 1947
INDIA 1947
PAKISTAN 1947, BANGLADESH 1973
SRI LANKA (CEYLON) 1948
MYANMAR (BURMA) 1947
LAOS 1949
NORTH VIETNAM 1954
Unified 1974
SOUTH VIETNAM 1954
CAMBODIA 1954
MALAYSIA 1963
SINGAPORE 1965
BRUNEI 1984 From Great Britain
PHILIPPINES 1946
INDONESIA 1949
NORTH KOREA 1948
SOUTH KOREA 1948
From Japan
JAPAN
Date is year independence was achieved.
Shading indicates former colonial power.
Great Britain
France
Netherlands
Italy
Belgium
Portugal
Spain
United States
0 500 1000 1500 Km.
0 500 1000 1500 Mi.

Map 29.2 Decolonization, 1945–1980 During a thirty-five-year period after World War II, the European empires in Africa, Asia, and the Pacific gradually came apart as the former colonies became independent nations.

Nevertheless, even Britain decided to resist in 1956, when it provoked an international crisis over the status of the Suez Canal in Egypt (see Map 28.1 on page 950). Once a British protectorate, Egypt had remained under heavy British influence even after nominally becoming sovereign in 1922. But a revolution in 1952 produced a new government of Arab nationalists, led by the charismatic Colonel Gamal Abdel Nasser (1918–1970). In 1954 Britain agreed with Egypt to leave the Suez Canal zone within twenty months, though the zone was to be international, not Egyptian, and Britain was to retain special rights there in the event of war. In 1956, however, Nasser announced the nationalization of the canal, partly so that Egypt could use its revenues to finance public works projects.

Led by the Conservative Anthony Eden (1897–1977), Britain decided on a showdown. Eden won the support of Israel and France, each of which had reason to fear the pan-Arab nationalism that Nasser's Egypt was now spearheading. Israel had remained at odds with its Arab neighbors since its founding in 1948, and Nasser was helping the Arabs who were beginning to take up arms against French rule in Algeria.

Late in 1956 Britain, Israel, and France orchestrated a surprise attack on Egypt. After the Israelis invaded, the British and French bombed military targets, then landed troops to take the canal. But the troops met stubborn Egyptian resistance, and the British and French encountered decisive defeat in the diplomatic maneuvering that accompanied the outbreak of fighting. Both the United States and the Soviet Union opposed the Anglo-French-Israeli move, as did world opinion. The old European powers had sought to act on their own, by the old rules, but the outcome of this Suez crisis demonstrated how limited their reach had become.

Still, the 1956 debacle did not convince France to abandon its struggle to retain Algeria. And that struggle proved the most wrenching experience that any European country was to have with decolonization. For the French the process started not in North Africa but in Indochina, in southeast Asia, during World War II.

Led by the communist Ho Chi Minh (1890–1969), the Indochinese anticolonialist movement gained strength resisting the Japanese during the war. Then, before the French could return, Ho established a political base in northern Vietnam in 1945. Although the French re-established control in the south, negotiations between the French and the Vietnamese nationalists seemed at first to be moving toward some form of self-government for Vietnam. But in 1946 French authorities in Indochina deliberately provoked an incident to undercut negotiations and start hostilities. Eight years of difficult guerrilla war followed, creating a major drain on the French economy.

With its strongly anticolonialist posture, the United States was unsympathetic to the French cause at first. But the communist takeover in China in 1949 and the outbreak of war in Korea in 1950 made the French struggle in Indochina seem a battle in a larger war against communism in Asia. By 1954 the United States was covering 75 percent of the cost of the French effort in Indochina. Nonetheless, when the fall of the fortified area at Dien Bien Phu in May 1954 signaled a decisive French defeat, the United States decided to pull back and accept a negotiated settlement. Partly at the urging of its European allies, the United States had concluded that the Soviet threat in Europe must remain its principal concern.

France worked out the terms of independence for Vietnam in 1955. The solution, however, entailed a north-south partition to separate the communist and anticommunist forces, pending elections to unify the country. The anticommunist regime the United States sponsored in the south resisted holding the elections, so the country remained divided (see Map 29.2). Only in 1975, after defeating the United States, would the communist heirs of those who had fought the French assume the leadership of a unified Vietnam.

In France the defeat in Indochina left a legacy of bitterness, especially among army officers, many of whom felt that French forces could have won had they not been undercut by politicians at home. When the outcome in Indochina emboldened Arab nationalists in North Africa to take up arms against the French colonial power, the French army was anxious for a second chance—and the French government was willing to give it to them. Algeria had been under French control since 1830, and it had a substantial minority of ethnic Europeans, totaling over a million, or 10 percent of the population.

Although France gradually committed 500,000 troops to Algeria, the war bogged down into what threatened to become a lengthy stalemate, with increasing brutality on both sides. As it drained French lives and resources, the war became a highly contentious political issue in France. The situation came to a head during the spring of 1958 when the advent of a new ministry, rumored to favor a compromise settlement, led to violent demonstrations, engineered by the sectors of the French army in Algeria. Military intervention in France itself seemed likely to follow—and with it the danger of civil war.

It was at this moment of genuine emergency that Charles de Gaulle returned to lead the change to the Fifth Republic. Those determined to hold Algeria welcomed him as their savior. But de Gaulle fooled them, working out a compromise with the nationalist rebels that ended the war and made Algeria independent in 1962. Only de Gaulle could have engineered this outcome without provoking still deeper political division in France.

By the end of the 1950s, the colonialist impulse, which had still been significant immediately after World War II, was waning noticeably all over Europe. But resistance remained, through considerable variation, as the colonies of sub-Saharan Africa continued to move toward independence. Outcomes depended on several factors: the number and intransigence of European settlers; the extent to which local elites had emerged; and the confidence of the Europeans that they could retain their influence if they agreed to independence. Of the major imperial powers in the region, Britain had done best at preparing local leaders for self-government and proved the most willing to work with indigenous elites. The two smaller countries, Belgium and Portugal, were less certain they could maintain their influence, and they proved the most reluctant to give up their imperial status.

The transition was smoothest in British West Africa, where the Gold Coast achieved independence as Ghana, first as a commonwealth dominion in 1957, then as a fully independent republic in 1960. Few British settlers lived in that part of Africa, and the small, relatively cohesive African elite favored a moderate transition, not revolution. Where British settlers were relatively numerous, however, the transition to independence proved much more difficult. The very presence of Europeans had impeded the development of cohesive local elites, so movements for independence in those areas tended to become more radical, threatening the expropriation of European-held property. In Southern Rhodesia, unyielding European settlers resisted the British government's effort to promote a compromise. A white supremacist government declared its independence from Britain in 1965, fueling a guerrilla war. The Africans won independence as Zimbabwe only in 1980.

The process of decolonization led to a remarkable transformation in the thirty-five years after World War II. Forms of colonial rule that had been taken for granted before World War I stood discredited, virtually without defenders, by the late twentieth century. Europeans were now accepting the principle of national self-determination for non-Europeans. But decolonization hardly offered a neat and definitive solution. In formerly colonial territories, new political boundaries often stemmed from the way Europeans had carved things up, rather than from indigenous ethnic or national patterns. Moreover, questions remained about the longer-term economic relationships between the Europeans and their former colonies.

The reaction against Eurocentrism that accompanied the turn from colonialism was not confined to those who had been subjected to European imperialism. Westerners themselves were intrigued with the work of Frantz Fanon (1925–1961), a black intellectual from Martinique who became identified especially with the cause of the Algerian rebels. In *The Wretched of the Earth* (1961), Fanon found the West spiritually exhausted and called on the peoples of the non-Western world to go their own way, based on their own values and traditions. (See the box "Global Encounters: The Legacy of European Colonialism.")

■ Economic Integration and the Origins of the European Union

As the old colonialism increasingly fell into disrepute, many found in European unity the best prospect for the future. Although hopes for full-scale political unification were soon frustrated, the movement for European integration achieved significant successes in the economic sphere, especially through the European Economic Community (EEC), or Common Market, established in 1957.

The impetus for economic integration came especially from a new breed of "Eurocrats"—technocrats with a supranational, or pan-European, outlook. A notable example was Robert Schuman (1886–1963), a native of Lorraine, which had passed between France and Germany four times between 1870 and 1945. After serving as a German officer in World War I, he was elected to the French Chamber of Deputies in 1919 just after Lorraine was returned to France. As French foreign minister after World War II, Schuman was responsible for a 1950 plan to coordinate French and German production of coal and steel. The Schuman Plan quickly encompassed Italy, Belgium, the Netherlands, and Luxembourg to become the European Coal and Steel Community (ECSC) in 1951. Working closely with Schuman was Jean Monnet, who served as the ECSC's first president. From this position, he pushed for more thoroughgoing economic integration. The successes of the ECSC led the same six countries to agree to a wider "Common Market," officially known as the European Economic Community (EEC), in 1957.

After the merger of the governing institutions of the several European supranational organizations in 1967, the term *European Community* (EC) and later *European Union* (EU) came to indicate the institutional web that had emerged since the launching of the European Coal

⊕ GLOBAL ENCOUNTERS

The Legacy of European Colonialism

In the following passage from The Wretched of the Earth *(1961), Frantz Fanon probes the negative consequences of colonialism—for both colonizers and colonized— and tries to show why a radical, even violent break from colonialism was necessary.*

The violence which has ruled over the ordering of the colonial world, which has ceaselessly drummed the rhythm for the destruction of native social forms and broken up without reserve the systems of reference of the economy, the customs of dress and external life, that same violence will be claimed and taken over by the native at the moment when, deciding to embody history in his own person, he surges into the forbidden quarters. . . .

. . . In the colonial context the settler only ends his work of breaking in the native when the latter admits loudly and intelligibly the supremacy of the white man's values. In the period of decolonization, the colonized masses mock at these very values, insult them, and vomit them up.

. . . All that the native has seen in his country is that they can freely arrest him, beat him, starve him: and no professor of ethics, no priest has ever come to be beaten in his place, nor to share their bread with him. As far as the native is concerned, morality is very concrete; it is to silence the settler's defiance, to break his flaunting violence—in a word, to put him out of the picture. . . .

. . . The colonialist bourgeoisie, in its narcissistic dialogue, expounded by the members of its universities, had in fact deeply implanted in the minds of the colonized intellectual that the essential qualities remain eternal in spite of all the blunders men may make: the essential qualities of the West, of course. . . . Now it so happens that during the strug-

gle for liberation, at the moment that the native intellectual comes into touch again with his people, . . . [a]ll the Mediterranean values—the triumph of the human individual, of clarity, and of beauty . . . are revealed as worthless, simply because they have nothing to do with the concrete conflict in which the people is engaged.

Individualism is the first to disappear. . . . The colonialist bourgeoisie had hammered into the native's mind the idea of a society of individuals where each person shuts himself up in his own subjectivity, and whose only wealth is individual thought. Now the native who has the opportunity to return to the people during the struggle for freedom will discover the falseness of this theory. The very forms of organization of the struggle will suggest to him a different vocabulary. Brother, sister, friend—these are words outlawed by the colonialist bourgeoisie, because for them my brother is my purse, my friend is part of my scheme for getting on. The native intellectual . . . will . . . discover the substance of village assemblies, the cohesion of people's committees, and the extraordinary fruitfulness of local meetings and groupments. Henceforward, the interests of one will be the interests of all, for in concrete fact *everyone* will be discovered by the troops, *everyone* will be massacred—or *everyone* will be saved.

Source: Frantz Fanon, *The Wretched of the Earth* (New York: Grove, 1968), pp. 40–47.

and Steel Community in 1951. Meanwhile, its membership gradually expanded, encompassing Denmark, Ireland, and Britain in 1973, Greece in 1981, Spain and Portugal in 1986, and Austria, Finland, and Sweden in 1995 (see Map 29.1). For newly democratic countries like Spain, Portugal, and Greece, Common Market membership became a pillar of the solidifying democratic consensus.

The immediate aim of the original EEC was to facilitate trade by eliminating customs duties between its member countries and by establishing common tariffs on imports from the rest of the world. For each member of the EEC, tariff reduction meant access to wider markets abroad, but also the risks of new competition in its own domestic market. So it was hard to be sure who might gain and who might lose from the move. However, the EEC proved advantageous to so many that tariff reduction proceeded well ahead of schedule. By 1968 the last internal tariffs had been eliminated.

With tariffs dropping, trade among the member countries nearly doubled between 1958 and 1962. French exports of automobiles and chemicals to Germany increased more than eightfold. Partly because the increasing competition stimulated initiative and productivity, industrial production within the EEC increased at a robust annual rate of 7.6 percent during those years.

Despite these successes, vigorous debate accompanied the development of the EEC during the 1960s. To enable goods, capital, and labor to move freely among the member countries, some coordination of social and economic policy was required. Thus state sovereignty became an important issue. To what extent was the Common Market to be a new whole, greater than the sum of its parts, as opposed to a mere commercial federation of existing states?

In the mid-1960s French president de Gaulle forced some of the underlying uncertainties to the fore. Though he had willingly turned from the old colonialism, de Gaulle was not prepared to compromise French sovereignty, and he was not persuaded that supranational integration offered the best course for postwar Europe. With the end of the Algerian war in 1962, France began playing an assertively independent role in international affairs. Thus, for example, de Gaulle developed an independent French nuclear force, curtailed the French role in NATO, and recognized the communist People's Republic of China.

This determination to assert France's sovereignty led to friction between de Gaulle and the supranational Eurocrats of the Common Market. Matters came to a head in 1965 when a confrontation developed over agricultural policy. The immediate result was a compromise, but de Gaulle's tough stance served to check the increasing supranationalism evident in the EEC until then. As the economic context became more difficult during the 1970s, it became still harder to maintain the EEC's cohesion. So though the Common Market proved an important departure, it did not overcome traditional national sovereignty or give western Europe a more muscular world role during the first decades after World War II.

■ The Energy Crisis and the Changing Economic Framework

As the political situation in western Europe became more volatile by the early 1970s, events outside Europe made it clear how interdependent the world had become—and that the West did not hold all the trump cards. In the fall of 1973, Egypt and Syria attacked Israel, seeking to recover the losses they had suffered in a brief war in 1967. Although the assault failed, the Arab nations of the oil-rich Middle East came together in the aftermath to retaliate against the Western bloc for supporting Israel. By restricting the output and distribution of the oil its members controlled, the Arab-led Organization of Petroleum Exporting Countries (OPEC) produced a sharp increase in oil prices and a severe economic disruption all over the industrialized world.

Oil, the West, and the World Led by several oil-rich Arab states, OPEC drove up world oil prices by restricting production during the 1970s. The power of the oil cartel made it clear that decisions by non-Westerners could vitally affect the industrialized West. OPEC delegates are shown here in Algiers in 1975. *(Sygma)*

Western Europe, which was heavily dependent on Middle Eastern oil, was especially hard hit. By January 1975 the price of oil was six times what it had been in 1973, before the embargo, and this increase remained a source of inflationary pressure throughout the Western world until the early 1980s.

The 1970s proved to be an unprecedented period of "stagflation"—sharply reduced rates of growth combined with inflation and rising unemployment. The economic miracle was over, partly because the process soon to be known as globalization was now taking off. The European economies were subject to growing competition from non-Western countries, most notably Japan. In light of increasing global competition and rising unemployment, the labor movement was suddenly on the defensive throughout the industrialized West. And the changing circumstances inevitably strained the social compact that had enabled western Europe to make a fresh start after the war.

THE COLLAPSE OF THE SOVIET SYSTEM, 1975–1991

I N the Soviet Union economic stagnation and even crisis were increasingly apparent during the 1970s, finally producing a major reform effort by the mid-1980s. Its leaders actively encouraged liberalization in the satellite states, where new forms of opposition had developed after the crushing of the Prague reform movement in 1968. But the liberalization effort unleashed forces that led to the unraveling of the satellite system in 1989, then even to the collapse of the Soviet Communist regime in 1991.

The disintegration of the communist system stunned Western observers, who had come to take the anxious stability of the cold war framework for granted. But that framework rested on a kind of balance between the superpowers, with their parallel, even competing experiments. By the 1980s those experiments had produced radically different results. Thus the balance was lost, and the framework of anxious stability dissolved.

■ Economic Stagnation in the Soviet Bloc

The impressive rates of economic growth achieved in the Soviet Union and several of the satellite states continued into the 1960s. However, much of that success came from adding labor—women and underemployed peas-ants—to the industrial work force. By the end of the 1960s that process was reaching its limits, so increasingly the challenge for the Soviet bloc was to boost productivity through technological innovation.

By the late 1970s, however, the Soviets were falling seriously behind the West as a new technological revolution gathered force. The state-directed Soviet economy had proven quite capable of technological leadership when marshaling resources for a particular task was required. Thus the Soviets led the way in space travel, for example. But continuing development in high technology demanded the freedom to experiment and exchange ideas and the flexibility to anticipate innovation and shift resources. In these areas, the Soviet system, with its direction from the top, proved too rigid to compete with the free-market systems of the Atlantic bloc. Moreover, as the Soviet system bogged down, the expense of the arms race with the United States dragged ever more seriously on the Soviet economy. Ordinary Soviet citizens grew increasingly frustrated as the communist economy proved erratic in providing the most basic consumer goods. Yet major functionaries enjoyed access to special shops and other privileges.

In satellite countries such as Poland and Hungary, the communist governments managed for a while to win mass support by borrowing from foreign banks to provide meat and other consumer goods at artificially low prices. "Sausage-stuffing," some called it. But as the lending banks came to realize, by the end of the 1970s, that such loans were not being used to foster modernization and productivity, these governments found it much harder to borrow. Thus they began having to impose greater austerity.

Throughout the Soviet bloc, frustration grew especially among women, who seemed to bear a disproportionate share of the burdens. Women were more likely to be employed outside the home in the communist countries than in the West. About 90 percent of adult women in the Soviet Union and East Germany had paid jobs outside the home by 1980. In 1984, 50 percent of the East German work force was female, compared with 39 percent in West Germany. Yet not only were these women concentrated in jobs with low pay and prestige, but they also still bore the major responsibility for child care, housework, and shopping. They had few of the labor-saving devices available in the West, and they often had to spend hours in line to buy ordinary consumer items. Dissatisfaction among women fed a new underground protest movement that began developing in the Soviet bloc in the mid-1970s—an indication of the growing strains in the overall system.

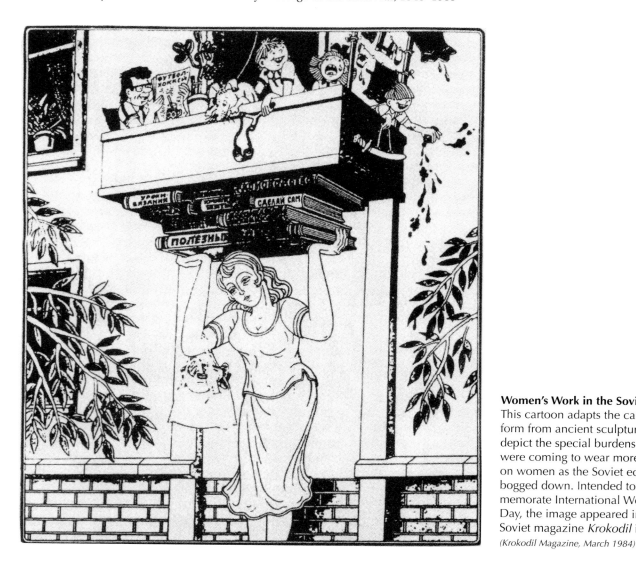

Women's Work in the Soviet Union
This cartoon adapts the caryatid form from ancient sculpture to depict the special burdens that were coming to wear more heavily on women as the Soviet economy bogged down. Intended to commemorate International Women's Day, the image appeared in the Soviet magazine *Krokodil* in 1984.
(Krokodil Magazine, March 1984)

■ The Crisis of Communism in the Satellite States

For many intellectuals in the Soviet bloc, the Soviet suppression of the Prague Spring in 1968 ended any hope that communism could be made to work. The immediate outcome was a sense of hopelessness, but by the mid-1970s a new opposition movement had begun to take shape, especially in Hungary, Poland, and Czechoslovakia. It centered initially on underground (or *samizdat*) publications, secretly produced and privately circulated writings—sometimes mimeographed in as few as five or six copies—that enabled dissidents to share ideas critical of the regime.

In one sense, these dissidents realized, intellectuals and ordinary people alike were powerless in the face of heavy-handed communist government. But they came to believe they could make a difference simply by "living the truth," ceasing to participate in the empty rituals of communist rule. And mere individual honesty could have political potential especially because of the Helsinki Accords on human rights that the Soviet bloc countries had accepted in 1975.

The meeting of thirty-five countries in Helsinki, Finland, in 1975 was one of the most important fruits of the *Ostpolitik,* or opening to the East, that Willy Brandt began pursuing after becoming West Germany's chancellor in 1969 (see page 995). Eager to grasp the chance that

Brandt's policy offered to regularize the status of East Germany and to confirm the western border of Poland, the Soviet bloc found it expedient to accept a detailed agreement on human rights that came to be known as the Helsinki Accords.

Though merely symbolic in one sense, that agreement proved a touchstone for initiatives that would help bring the whole Soviet system crashing down. Through various "Helsinki Watch" groups monitoring civil liberties, anticommunists in the satellite states managed to assume the moral leadership. By demanding that the communist governments live up to their agreements, by noting the gap between idealistic pretense and grim reality, opposition intellectuals began to cast doubts on the very legitimacy of the communist regimes.

The most significant such group was Charter 77, which emerged in Czechoslovakia in response to the arrest of a rock group called "The Plastic People of the Universe." Long-haired and anti-establishment like their counterparts in the West, the Plastic People were deemed filthy, obscene, and disrespectful of society by the repressive Czechoslovak regime. In 1977, protesting the crackdown on the group, 243 individuals signed "Charter 77"—using their own names and addresses, living the truth, acting as if they were free to register such an opinion.

A leader in Charter 77 was the writer Václav Havel° (b. 1936), who noted that after 1968 the notion of reforming the communist system through direct political action was dead. (See the box "Reading Sources: Power from Below: Living the Truth.") Hopes for change depended on people organizing themselves, outside the structures of the party-state, in diverse, independent social groupings. Havel and a number of his associates were in and out of jail as the government sought to stave off this protest movement. And despite their efforts, government remained particularly repressive and ordinary people relatively passive in Czechoslovakia until the late 1980s. For quite different reasons, Hungary and Poland offered greater scope for change.

Even after the failed reform effort of 1956, Hungary proved the most innovative of the European communist countries. Partly because its government allowed small-scale initiatives outside the central planning apparatus, Hungary was able to respond more flexibly to the growing economic stagnation. By the mid-1980s various alternative forms of ownership were responsible for one-third of Hungary's economic output.

This openness to economic experiment enabled reformers within the Hungarian Communist Party to gain the upper hand. Amid growing talk of "socialist pluralism," the Hungarian elections of 1985 introduced an element of genuine democracy. Increasingly open to a variety of viewpoints, the Hungarian communists gradually pulled back from their long-standing claim to a monopoly of power.

The reform effort that built gradually in Hungary stemmed especially from aspirations within the governing elite. More dramatic was the course of change in Poland, where workers and intellectuals, at odds even as recently as 1968, managed to come together during the 1970s. When Polish workers struck in 1976, in response to a cut in food subsidies, intellectuals formed a committee to defend them. This alliance had become possible because dissident intellectuals were coming to emphasize the importance of grass-roots efforts that challenged the logic of the communist system without attacking it directly.

But an extra ingredient from an unexpected quarter also affected the situation in Poland, perhaps in a decisive way. In 1978 the College of Cardinals of the Roman Catholic Church departed from long tradition and, for the first time since 1522, elected a non-Italian pope. But even more startling was the fact that the new pope was from Poland, behind the iron curtain. He was Karol Cardinal Wojtyla° (b. 1920), the archbishop of Kracow, who took the name John Paul II.

After World War II, the Polish Catholic Church had been unique among the major churches of east-central Europe in maintaining and even enhancing its position. It worked just enough with the ruling communists to be allowed to carve out a measure of autonomy. For many Poles, the church thus remained a tangible institutional alternative to communism and the focus of national self-consciousness in the face of Soviet domination. Thus the new pope's visit to Poland in 1979 had an electrifying effect on ordinary Poles, who took to the streets by the millions to greet him—and found they were not alone. This boost in self-confidence provided the catalyst for the founding of a new trade union, Solidarity, in August 1980.

Led by the remarkable shipyard electrician Lech Walesa° (b. 1944), Solidarity emerged from labor discontent in the vast Lenin shipyard in Gdansk, on the Baltic Sea (see Map 29.1). Demanding the right to form their own independent unions, seventy thousand workers took over the shipyards, winning support both from their intellectual allies and from the Catholic Church. Support for Solidarity grew partly because the government, facing the crisis of its "sausage-stuffing" strategy, was cutting

---

Havel (HA-vul)

🙟 READING SOURCES

Power from Below: Living the Truth

Considering the scope for change in the communist world by the late 1970s, Václav Havel imagines a conformist grocer who routinely puts a sign in his window with the slogan "Workers of the world, unite!" simply because it is expected. That same grocer, says Havel, has the power to break the system, which rests on innumerable acts of everyday compliance.

[T]he real meaning of the greengrocer's slogan has nothing to do with what the text of the slogan actually says. Even so, this real meaning is quite clear and generally comprehensible because the code is so familiar: the greengrocer declares his loyalty . . . in the only way the regime is capable of hearing; that is, by accepting the prescribed *ritual,* by accepting appearances as reality, by accepting the given rules of the game. In doing so, however, he has himself become a player in the game, thus making it possible for the game to go on, for it to exist in the first place. . . .

Let us now imagine that one day something in our greengrocer snaps and he stops putting up the slogans merely to ingratiate himself. He stops voting in elections he knows are a farce. He begins to say what he really thinks at political meetings. . . . He rejects the ritual and breaks the rules of the game. He discovers once more his suppressed identity and dignity. . . .

. . . He has shown everyone that it *is* possible to live within the truth. Living within the lie can constitute the system only if it is universal. The principle must embrace and permeate everything. There are no terms whatsoever on which it can coexist with

living within the truth, and therefore everyone who steps out of line *denies it in principle and threatens it in its entirety.* . . .

And since all genuine problems and matters of critical importance are hidden beneath a thick crust of lies, it is never quite clear when the proverbial last straw will fall, or what that straw will be. This . . . is why the regime prosecutes, almost as a reflex action preventively, even the most modest attempts to live within the truth.

. . . [T]he crust presented by the life of lies is made of strange stuff. As long as it seals off hermetically the entire society, it appears to be made of stone. But the moment someone breaks through in one place, when one person cries out, "The emperor is naked!"—when a single person breaks the rules of the game, thus exposing it as a game—everything suddenly appears in another light and the whole crust seems then to be made of a tissue on the point of tearing and disintegrating uncontrollably.

Source: Václav Havel et al., *The Power of the Powerless: Citizens Against the State in Central-Eastern Europe* (Armonk, N.Y.: M. E. Sharpe, 1985), pp. 31, 37, 39–40, 42–43.

---

subsidies and raising food prices. But the new union developed such force because it placed moral demands first—independent labor organizations, the right to strike, and freedom of expression. Reflecting the wider opposition thinking in east-central Europe, Solidarity was not to be bought off with lower meat prices, even had the government been able to deliver them.

After over a year of negotiation, compromise, and broken promises, the tense situation came to a head in December 1981, when the government under General

Wojciech Jaruzelski° (b. 1923) declared martial law and outlawed Solidarity, imprisoning its leaders. Strikes in protest were crushed by military force. So much for that, it seemed: another lost cause, another reform effort colliding with inflexible communist power in east-central Europe, as in 1953, 1956, and 1968. But this time, it was different, thanks especially to developments in the Soviet Union.

Jaruzelski (yah-roo-SHELL-skee)

Lech Walesa and Solidarity   A shipyard electrician, Walesa spearheaded the dissident Polish trade union, Solidarity, formed in 1980, and then emerged from prison to lead the movement that eventually toppled the communist regime in Poland in 1989. Here he addresses a rally during a strike at the Lenin shipyard in Gdansk in August 1988.   *(Sygma)*

■ The Quest for Reform in the Soviet Union

The death of Leonid Brezhnev in 1982 paved the way for a concerted reform effort that began in earnest when Mikhail Gorbachev° (b. 1931) became Soviet Communist Party secretary in 1985. Gorbachev's effort encompassed four intersecting initiatives: arms reduction; liberalization in the satellite states; *glasnost*°, or "openness" to discussion and criticism; and *perestroika*°, or economic "restructuring." This was to be a reform within the Soviet system. There was no thought of giving up the Communist Party's monopoly on power or embracing a free-market economy. The reformers still took it for granted that communism could point the way beyond Western capitalism, with its shallow consumerism, its illegal drugs, its widespread crime. So a measure of idealism guided the reformers' efforts. But they had to make communism work.

Gorbachev understood that "openness" was a prerequisite for "restructuring." The freedom to criticize was essential to check abuses of power, which, in turn, was

necessary to overcome the cynicism of the workers and improve productivity. Openness was also imperative to gain the full participation of the country's most creative people, whose contribution was critical if the Soviet Union was to become competitive in advanced technology.

The main thrust of perestroika was to depart from the rigid economic planning mechanism by giving local managers more autonomy. The alternative did not have to entail privatization or a return to free-market capitalism. It could mean, for example, letting workers elect factory managers. But any restructuring was bound to encounter resistance, especially from those with careers tied to the central planning apparatus. And Gorbachev's program made only partial headway in this crucial sector.

■ The Anticommunist Revolution in East-Central Europe

Meanwhile, in Poland, Walesa remained a powerfully effective leader even from prison. He was able to keep his heterogeneous movement together as the ideas of Solidarity continued to spread underground. Then the advent of Gorbachev in 1985 changed the overall framework, for Gorbachev was convinced that restructuring of the Soviet

Gorbachev (GOR-ba-choff)   **glasnost** (GLAHZ-nost)
perestroika (pair-es-TROY-kah)

system required reform in the satellites as well. So as the Polish economy, already in difficulty by 1980, reached a crisis in 1987, Solidarity began stepping up its efforts.

When proposed price increases were rejected in a referendum, the Polish government imposed them by fiat. Strikes demanding the relegalization of Solidarity followed during the spring of 1988. The government again responded with military force, but Solidarity-led strikes in August forced government leaders to send signals that they might be prepared to negotiate. With the economy nearing collapse, the government recognized that it could no longer govern on its own.

The negotiations that followed early in 1989 proved pivotal. When they began, Walesa and his advisers wanted primarily to regain legal status for Solidarity within the communist-dominated system, still under Jaruzelski. In exchange, they assumed they would have to help legitimate a rigged election to approve painful but necessary economic measures. But as these "Round Table" negotiations proceeded, the government gave ever more in exchange for Solidarity's cooperation. Not only did it consent to legalize Solidarity, but it agreed to make the forthcoming elections free enough for the opposition genuinely to participate.

The elections of June 1989 produced an overwhelming repudiation of Poland's communist government. Even government leaders running unopposed failed to win election as voters crossed out their names. In the aftermath of the elections, President Jaruzelski was forced to give Solidarity a chance to lead. Not all members of the opposition felt it wise to accept government responsibility under such difficult economic circumstances, but finally Tadeusz Mazowiecki° (b. 1927), Walesa's choice and one of the movement's most distinguished intellectuals, agreed to form a government.

The chain of events in Poland culminated in one of the extraordinary events of modern history—the negotiated end of communist rule. That a communist government might give up power voluntarily had been utterly unforeseen. It happened partly because the Soviet Union under Gorbachev was seeking reform and thus had become much less likely to intervene militarily. It also helped that the Polish Catholic Church was available to act as mediator, hosting meetings, reminding both sides of their shared responsibilities in the difficult situation facing their country. By some accounts, General Jaruzelski, who seemed for most of the 1980s to be just another military strongman and Soviet lackey, had proven a national hero for his grace, perhaps even ingenuity, in

yielding power to the opposition. But most important was the courage, the persistence, and the vision of Solidarity itself.

Although the Hungarians were already breaking out of the communist mold, it was especially the Polish example that suggested to others in the Soviet bloc that the whole system was open to challenge. During 1989, demands for reform and, increasingly, for an end to communist rule spread through east-central Europe by means of the domino effect that had preoccupied the Soviets from the start. By the end of that year, the Soviet satellite system was in ruins (see Map 30.1 on page 1026).

A marked increase in illegal emigration from East Germany to the West had been one manifestation that the system was starting to unravel. During 1989 the reform-minded Hungarian communists decided to stop impeding East Germans, many of whom vacationed in Hungary, from emigrating to the West at the Hungarian border with Austria. If the communist reformers in East Germany were to have any chance of turning the situation around, they had to relax restrictions on travel and even grant the right to emigrate. Thus they immediately began preparing legislation to both ends, amid a host of reforms intended to save the system. On November 9, 1989, the East German communist regime did the unthinkable and opened the Berlin Wall, which was promptly dismantled altogether. Germans now traveled freely back and forth between East and West. Although the fate of the Soviet Union itself remained uncertain, the opening of the wall signaled the end of the cold war. It was no longer a bipolar world.

This liberalization effort proved too late, however. By now, discontented East Germans envisioned not simply reforming the communist system but ending it altogether. Within weeks it was clear that the rhythm of events was beyond the control of East Germany's reform communists, who opened the way for German reunification in 1990. Despite some nervousness, the four postwar occupying powers—the United States, Britain, France, and the Soviet Union—gave their blessing as the Federal Republic simply incorporated the five East German states. The communist system in East Germany had simply dissolved.

Although some in West Germany were hesitant about immediate reunification, especially because of the economic costs that seemed likely, West German chancellor Helmut Kohl° (b. 1930) sought to complete the process as quickly as possible. By early 1990 the emigration of East Germans to the West had become a flood.

Mazowiecki (maz-oy-YES-key)

Kohl (KOLE)

West German law treated these Germans as citizens, entitled to social benefits, so their arrival in such numbers presented a considerable financial burden. It seemed imperative for West Germany to regularize the situation as quickly as possible, assuming responsibility for the east and restoring its economy.

The division of Germany, symbolized by the Berlin Wall, had been the central fact of the bipolar cold war world. Now Germany was a unified country for the first time since Nazism and the Second World War. What would it mean?

■ The End of the Soviet Union

Meanwhile, in the Soviet Union, what began as a restructuring of the communist system became a struggle for survival of the system itself. The much-trumpeted glasnost produced greater freedom in Soviet culture and politics, but Gorbachev sought to avoid alienating hard-line communists, so he compromised, watering down the economic reforms essential to perestroika. The result proved a set of half-measures that only made things worse. Because so little was done to force the entrenched Soviet bureaucracy to go along, the pace of economic reform was lethargic. The essential structures of the command economy weakened, but free-market forms of exchange among producers, distributors, and consumers did not emerge to replace them.

In 1986 an accidental explosion at the Soviet nuclear power plant at Chernobyl, in Ukraine (see Map 29.3), released two hundred times as much radiation as the atomic bombs dropped on Hiroshima and Nagasaki combined. The accident contaminated food supplies and forced the abandonment of villages and thousands of square miles of formerly productive land. The radioactivity released would eventually hasten the death of at least 100,000 Soviet citizens. Despite his commitment to openness, Gorbachev reverted to old-fashioned

Map 29.3   The Dissolution of the Soviet Union   As crisis gripped the Soviet system by the late 1980s, the republics of the Soviet Union began declaring first their sovereignty, then their independence. Most of the fifteen republics that had made up the Soviet Union became part of a much looser confederation, the Commonwealth of Independent States, in 1991 and 1992.

Soviet secrecy for several weeks after the accident, in an effort to minimize what had happened. As a result, the eventual toll was far greater than it need have been. The accident and its aftermath seemed stark manifestation of all that was wrong with the Soviet system—its arrogance and secrecy, its premium on cutting corners to achieve targets imposed from above.

By the end of the 1980s, Soviet citizens felt betrayed by their earlier faith that Soviet communism was leading to a better future. A popular slogan spoke sarcastically of "seventy years on the road to nowhere." The economic situation was deteriorating, yet people were free to discuss alternatives as never before. As the discussion came to include once unthinkable possibilities such as privatization and a market economy, it became clear that the whole communist system was in jeopardy.

By mid-1990, moreover, the union of Soviet republics itself tottered on the verge of collapse. Lithuania led the way in calling for outright independence. But the stakes were raised enormously when the Russian republic, the largest and most important in the USSR, followed Lithuania's lead. In June 1990 the newly elected chairman of Russia's parliament, Boris Yeltsin (b. 1931), persuaded the Russian republic to declare its sovereignty. Yeltsin had grown impatient with the slow pace of economic and political change, and by threatening that Russia might go its own way, he hoped to force Gorbachev's reform effort beyond the present impasse. As a further challenge to Gorbachev, Yeltsin dramatically resigned from the Communist Party during its televised national congress in July 1990. When, in June 1991, free elections in the Russian republic offered the first clear contest between communists determined to preserve the system and those seeking to replace it, the anticommunist Yeltsin was elected the republic's president by a surprising margin.

After tilting toward the hard-liners late in 1990, Gorbachev sought a return to reform after Yeltsin's dramatic election as Russia's president in June 1991. He even engineered a new party charter that jettisoned much of the Marxist-Leninist doctrine that had guided communist practice since the revolution. In August the hard-liners struck back with a coup that forced Gorbachev from power—but only for a few days. Yeltsin, supported by ordinary people in Moscow, stood up to the conspirators, while the secret police refused to follow orders to arrest Yeltsin and other opposition leaders. The coup quickly fizzled, but the episode galvanized the anticommunist movement and radically accelerated the pace of change.

Although Gorbachev was restored as head of the Soviet Union, the winner was Yeltsin, who quickly mounted an effort to dismantle the party apparatus before it could regroup. Anticommunist demonstrations across much of the Soviet Union toppled statues of Lenin and dissolved local party networks. In a referendum in December 1991, Ukraine, the second most populous Soviet republic, overwhelmingly voted for independence. Not only the communist system but the Soviet Union itself was simply disintegrating. Late in December, Gorbachev finally resigned, paving the way for the official dissolution of the Soviet Union on January 1, 1992 (see Map 29.3). The European map again included Russia, as well as, in a matter of months, fourteen other sovereign states from what had been the Soviet Union.

One of the notable experiments in the history of the West, nourished by the hopes and ideals of generations, the communist regime in the Soviet Union had proved a resounding failure.

Summary

 N the decades that followed World War II, a bipolar framework, dominated by the United States and the Soviet Union, shaped world affairs. The states of western Europe declined in influence, even losing their remaining colonial possessions. They had to follow the U.S. lead, especially in matters of national security. From within that framework, however, they were able to achieve remarkable prosperity and significant steps toward multinational integration.

In the Soviet bloc, Stalin's death in 1953 brought an end to the most repressive features of the communist system. Under his successor, Nikita Khrushchev, the Soviet Union seemed able to compete with the United States in areas from education to space travel. But the experiment with various forms of central planning in the Soviet bloc proved ever less successful. At the same time, the crushing of a series of opposition and reform efforts, from East Berlin in 1953 to Prague in 1968, made it clear that the Soviets intended to keep their European satellites on a tight leash.

In western Europe, the shared experience of wartime led to a new social compact based on greater government responsibility for economic well-being and social welfare. By 1968, however, strains began to appear in the Western democracies, and the slowdown in economic growth during the 1970s only made them worse. Though the economic improvement remained remarkable, many western Europeans came to feel left out as the key decisions fell to party leaders or technocratic planners. Still, western Europe had come to take for granted a substantial measure of prosperity and political legitimacy, while in the communist countries of eastern Europe, growing economic stagnation fueled a much deeper form of political disaffection during the 1970s and 1980s. The parallel experiments were turning out very differently. Discontent in the Soviet bloc produced forces for change that led the whole communist system to unravel by the end of 1991.

Thus ended the cold war era. The immediate response in the West was euphoria, for the anxieties that had resulted from the rivalries and mutual suspicions of the superpowers seemed to vanish almost overnight. But what would follow remained unclear. Reformers in the former communist countries claimed to want individual freedom, political democracy, and free-market capitalism, but it would be necessary to build these on the ruins of the now-discredited communist system, a task never confronted before. And what sort of international order might replace the dangerous but stable bipolar framework that had stood since World War II?

■ Suggested Reading

Bark, Dennis L., and David R. Gress. *A History of West Germany,* Vol. 1: *From Shadow to Substance, 1945–1963,* and Vol. 2: *Democracy and Its Discontents, 1963–1991.* 2d ed. 1993. A favorable account of West Germany's democracy and its Atlantic and European roles in the face of ongoing suspicion and criticism.

Chamberlain, M. E. *Decolonization: The Fall of the European Empires.* 2d ed. 1999. An updated edition of a highly regarded overview.

Crockatt, Richard. *The Fifty Years' War: The United States and the Soviet Union in World Politics, 1941–1991.* 1995. A balanced history of U.S.-Soviet relations, showing the global impact of their cold war rivalry.

Dedman, Martin J. *The Origins and Development of the European Union, 1945–95: A History of European Integration.* 1996. A concise and accessible introductory work.

Garton Ash, Timothy. *The Magic Lantern: The Revolution of '89 Witnessed in Warsaw, Budapest, Berlin, and Prague.* 1990. Firsthand testimony on the fall of communism by a British intellectual with close contacts among anticommunists in east-central Europe.

Laqueur, Walter. *Europe in Our Time: A History, 1945–1992.* 1992. A comprehensive, well-balanced survey by a leading authority on twentieth-century Europe.

Marwick, Arthur. *The Sixties: Cultural Revolution in Britain, France, Italy, and the United States, c. 1958–c. 1974.* 1998. A lengthy but gripping portrait of a pivotal decade.

Morgan, Kenneth O. *The People's Peace: British History, 1945–1990.* 1992. A thorough survey that seeks to avoid overemphasis on decline and pessimism; accents the relative peace and stability of the period.

Schulze, Max-Stephan, ed., *Western Europe: Economic and Social Change Since 1945.* 1999. A superior collection of essays accenting economic change; some treat individual countries, others overarching topics.

Stokes, Gale. *The Walls Came Tumbling Down: The Collapse of Communism in Eastern Europe.* 1993. Dramatic and comprehensive, the first standard account of the dissolution of communism in east-central Europe.

 For a searchable list of additional readings for this chapter, go to http://college.hmco.com.

Pop Art

Hamburgers, comic strips, soup-can labels, familiar images of entertainment icons—such was the stuff of "pop art," which burst onto the New York art scene in the early 1960s and came to exert a widespread cultural influence. Indeed, with their imaginative renderings of familiar images and whimsical sculptures of everyday objects, artists like Andy Warhol (1928–1987), Roy Lichtenstein (b. 1923), and Claes Oldenburg (b. 1929) helped shape the experience of the later twentieth century. But was this serious art—or simply a joke, a parody, a put-on? Were the pop artists poking fun at the triviality of modern society, or were they deepening our encounter with defining aspects of contemporary culture? Whatever their intent, what does this striking new art form tell us about the direction of Western culture in the decades after World War II?

The term *pop art* was coined in England in the later 1950s, when a group of artists and critics became interested in bridging the cultural gap between "fine art" and the emerging popular culture of mass media and machine-produced images, of advertising and automobiles. Like everyone else, they associated that consumerist mass culture with America—the America of Hollywood, Detroit, and Madison Avenue. And they found it more vital than the conventional fine art of the period. The American pop artists were similarly fascinated by the impersonal, mass-produced, often expendable quality of the objects and images that have come to surround us.

Pop art was part of a wider reaction against the deeply serious abstract expressionist painting that emerged in New York just after the Second World War. By the early 1950s, abstract expressionists like Jackson Pollock and Mark Rothko had created images of unprecedented power, whether seeking to forge an artistic identity in the face of nothingness, or to transcend selfhood in a cosmic wholeness. In the mid-1950s, however, younger artists "tired of the stink of artists' egos" began reacting against the self-importance of abstract expressionism. For these younger artists, art did not have to be a vehicle for the psychological expression of the artist or a quest for "the tragic and timeless." Although the reaction took several forms, pop art proved the most influential. The pop movement emerged especially in the United States, and it interested Europeans as typically American, fresh and fascinating or garish and vulgar, depending on one's point of view.

Whereas the abstract expressionists had sought to rise above the everyday world, Claes Oldenburg's sculptures played with the scale and context of the most ordinary objects—a mixer, a three-pronged plug, a lipstick, a hamburger—to deepen our involvement with the everyday things that surround us. In this sense, the aim of pop art was not simply to parody or satirize, but to affirm our relationship with the trappings of ordinary life. Hollywood, Detroit, and Madison Avenue were all right after all; indeed, they had become the centers of Western culture by the later twentieth century.

Though anonymous and impersonal, the modern world of mass production, mass consumption, and mass media is "popular" because its images and objects are accessible to us all. In fact, they bombard us from all directions, giving shared shape and definition to our everyday lives. This is our world, the pop artists were saying, and they were creating the art appropriate to our time. They invite us to relax and enjoy that world, but they also enhance our experience by making art from it, thereby awakening us to its novelty and vitality.

Oldenburg: Floor Burger, 1962 *(Claes Oldenburg [American, b. 1929], Floor Burger, 1962. Canvas filled with foam rubber and cardboard boxes, painted with acrylic paint. 132.1 × 213.4 cm. Art Gallery of Ontario, Toronto.)*

Warhol: Marilyn Diptych, 1962   (© Copyright ARS, NY. Tate Gallery, London/Art Resource, NY)

But some viewers have found an element of melancholy, nostalgia, even tragedy just beneath pop art's eye-catching surface. In a world of mass media and reproduced images, more of our experience becomes secondhand and literally superficial. Likewise, pop subjects, from fast food to billboards, have no deeper meaning, no expressive personal agenda. With his multiplied image of Marilyn Monroe, Andy Warhol dealt not with the actress herself but with the obsessive familiarity of her image. He cultivated a deadpan, detached style that reflected the machine-made quality of his subject matter—the quality that made the images he started with so familiar in the first place. But even as, on one level, he embraced aspects of the new mass culture, Warhol was exploring precisely the emotional detachment—and the accompanying trivialization of emotion—at work in the culture that had produced the images he adapted. Especially in his paintings treating impersonal newspaper images of disaster and death, Warhol bore witness to our indifference—and perhaps to a cosmic meaninglessness as well. One expert has noted that "in Warhol's pictures of the material objects and other false idols that most of us worship, the pain lies just below the bright surfaces of the images and waits passively to engage us."*

The advent of pop art provoked a series of questions that remain unanswered: Is the embrace of the mass-produced and commercial, at the expense of traditional "fine-art" values, a symptom of exhaustion or a healthy affirmation of contemporary popular culture, so bound up with the commercial world? Or is pop art perhaps a valuable comment on the emptiness of that culture, with its impersonal conformity, garish commercialism, and mechanical repetition? In the final analysis, were the pop artists abandoning the artist's lofty mission and giving in to the ordinary? Or were they the first to show us what "Western civilization" had come to mean by the late twentieth century?

---

*Eric Shanes, *Warhol* (New York: Portland House, 1991), p. 41.

 For additional information on this topic, go to
http://college.hmco.com.

CHAPTER 30

The West and the World Since 1989

DURING the fall of 1989, three teenaged Muslim girls were suspended from a public school near Paris because they insisted on wearing the headscarves traditional for Islamic women. School authorities cited a law barring religious displays in France's secular, state-run school system. The three girls protested that Islamic teaching required women to cover their heads in public as a sign of modesty. Yet in the eyes of some westerners, that practice simply reflected the second-class status of women in Islamic civilization. The leader of France's largest teachers union contended that "this flaunting of a clear symbol of women's subordination negates the teaching of human rights in schools." Thus, when the French minister of education defended the students' right to wear the scarves, he was widely criticized for condoning the oppression of women in Islam.

In fact, the education minister was not seeking to defend Islamic tradition or cultural diversity, let alone the oppression of women. He simply wanted to keep these girls—and the many others like them—in public schools, to expose them to secular influence and to promote their assimilation into French culture.

In 1989 Muslims made up 5 percent of the French population, or 2.7 million people, and this episode prompted many of them to demonstrate for greater pluralism and tolerance in France. Some of France's non-Muslim majority joined in, even wearing scarves in solidarity. Others, in contrast, called for stepped-up efforts to assimilate immigrants and those with foreign backgrounds into the common French civilization.

The Search for a New International Order

Economy and the Political Order in the Mature Democracies

The Postcommunist Experiment

Lifestyles and Identities in the West

The West in a Global Age

Conclusion: Learning from Western Civilization in a Postmodern World

"The hijab [headscarf] is our honor": Muslim women and girls demonstrate in Paris, October 1989. (AP/Wide World Photos)

France's prestigious Council of State soon ruled that the scarves did not violate the constitutional separation of church and state, as long as they were not worn in an effort to flaunt religion or to proselytize. The council left it to local school authorities to decide each case. But the riddles of citizenship, assimilation, and cultural diversity at issue in this "affair of the scarves" kept coming up in France and elsewhere by the early twenty-first century, as contact between the West and other parts of the world took new forms.

Such questions came to center stage partly because of the end of the cold war, which had overshadowed all else for four decades after World War II. With the collapse of communism, "the West" was no longer divided into rival power blocs representing competing experiments. The former communist countries scrambled to institute Western-style democratic capitalism, and several even joined NATO by the end of the 1990s. So there was now a single West, but it was ragged, diverse, and lacking an inner compass. What role would it play in the world? Confronted with post–cold war chaos, NATO proved willing to intervene in Europe to counter massive human rights violations. But whether the West was prepared to act comparably on the wider world stage remained unclear as the new century began.

Largely as the result of unprecedented economic and technological change, even the established Western democracies encountered new questions about immigration, environmental protection, and the role of the state. Such issues intersected to challenge the political consensus that had crystallized since World War II. At the same time, the European Union spread its reach even as new questions arose about Europe's relationship with the United States.

QUESTIONS TO CONSIDER

- Why, and how, did the relationship between western Europe and the United States change with the end of the cold war?

- What can we learn from the experience of post-communist Russia, in light of ongoing questions facing the West and the world?

- Why were issues surrounding immigration, citizenship, assimilation, and cultural diversity increasingly central all over the Western world by the beginning of the twenty-first century?

- What obstacles emerged as the West began playing a more active leadership role in confronting global trouble spots during the 1990s?

TERMS TO KNOW

European Union
Maastricht agreement
euro
"ethnic cleansing"
Kosovo
information technology (IT)

social market economy
Chechnya
digital divide
nongovernmental organizations (NGOs)

THE SEARCH FOR A NEW INTERNATIONAL ORDER

HE disintegration of the Soviet system during 1989–1991 meant the swift, unexpected end of the bipolar cold war framework that had defined the era since World War II. Terrifying, potentially catastrophic though it had been at the time, that framework had provided a measure of order and security for over four decades. What sort of international configuration was to follow? What international roles might the Western democracies be prepared to play now that resisting communism was no longer the central preoccupation? And what place would the former communist countries assume in the new order?

The end of the cold war division of Europe expanded the possibilities for European integration, and the European Union made notable strides during the 1990s. But the capacity of the EU to respond to wider international issues on its own, independently of the United States, remained uncertain. Indeed, the series of wars in what had been Yugoslavia raised questions about the ability of any international body to assure stability in the post–cold war world. At the same time, however, the response of the NATO alliance to the Yugoslav situation by the end of the 1990s suggested the scope for new forms of multinational cooperation—and perhaps a new, more peaceful international order.

■ The West and the Uncertain International Framework

The end of the cold war left the United States "the world's only superpower," but its international role was less certain in a world without the perceived menace of international communism (see Map 30.1). As the potential threat from the Soviet Union dissolved, American support no longer seemed essential for European security. The NATO alliance, formed to check Soviet expansion in Europe, almost inevitably became less cohesive.

With the end of the Soviet Union, it made sense for western Europeans to rethink their security needs and military priorities. This reconsideration led in several directions, not all of them compatible. Some suggested that under the new circumstances, each nation would be well advised to look after its own defense. France even resumed nuclear testing in the South Pacific in 1995, though promptly ceased in light of the resulting international protest. Ten leading members of the European Union began developing a common defense mechanism but it remained tied to NATO. Problems that arose when NATO intervened in the fighting in Yugoslavia (see page 1032) prompted deeper consideration of the scope for an independent European force, but it remained uncertain what role the Europeans might play on their own.

Although its role was less clear with the end of the Soviet threat, NATO remained prominent. It even expanded in 1999 as membership was extended to the former Soviet bloc countries Poland, Hungary, and the Czech Republic. (Czechoslovakia divided peacefully into two nations, the Czech Republic and Slovakia, on January 1, 1993.) Further eastward expansion seemed likely. To these countries, NATO membership meant the definitive repudiation of the cold war division of Europe. But others worried that NATO expansion was a needless provocation to Russia, now, in its postcommunist guise, an especially uncertain player on the international scene.

Whereas the collapse of communism meant renewed pride and independence for the former satellite states, Russia quickly felt humiliated in world affairs. The one-time superpower was now poor, diminished in size,

---

CHRONOLOGY

1979	Thatcher becomes prime minister of Britain
	First direct elections to European parliament
1981	Mitterrand elected president of France
1990	Reunification of Germany
1991	Beginning of fighting in Yugoslavia
	Maastricht agreement expands scope of European Union
1996	Peace in Bosnia
	Yeltsin re-elected as president of Russia
1997	Blair becomes prime minister of Britain
1998	Financial crisis in Russia
	UN establishes international criminal court in The Hague
	Socialist-led coalition under Schröder replaces Kohl's conservative government in Germany
1999	Euro launched as currency of European Union
	NATO bombing of Serbia in response to Serb policies in Kosovo
	Renewal of Russia's war with Chechnya
	Protests at WTO meeting in Seattle
2000	Putin elected president of Russia
	Kostunica defeats Milosevic, becomes president of Yugoslavia

---

apparently ignored. Hard-liners began proposing that the now-collapsed "Soviet Union" be revived as a military alliance. Some even favored selling nuclear technology to such countries as Iran, Iraq, and Algeria—to put pressure on the West, especially the United States, which many Russians blamed for their problems.

The most obvious beneficiary of the end of the cold war was Germany, which promptly reunified as communism collapsed in the East. Some—Germans and non-Germans alike—were eager to have Germany assume a major diplomatic role—and thus the responsibilities commensurate with its economic strength. But reunification also prompted anxiety about the role the new Germany might seek to play. Because 30 percent of the

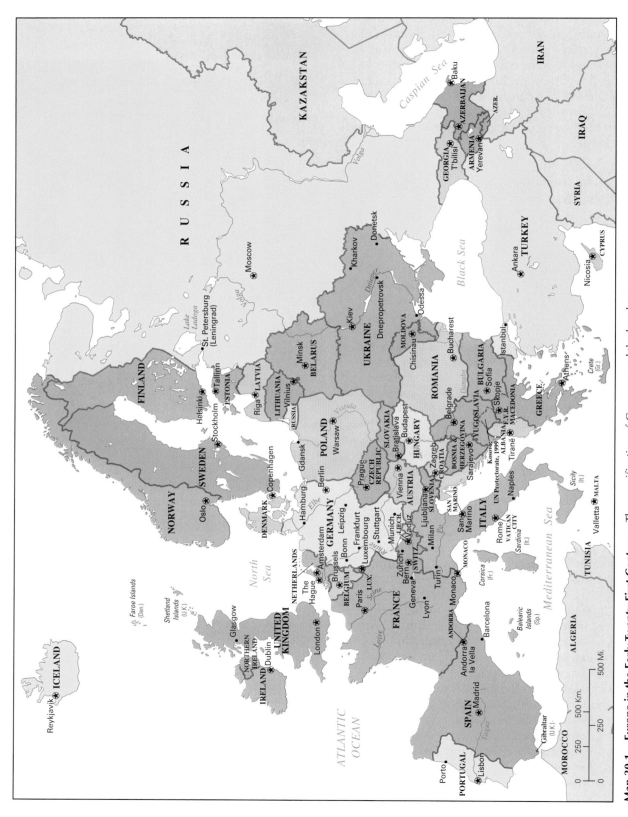

Map 30.1 Europe in the Early Twenty-First Century The reunification of Germany and the breakup of the Soviet Union, Yugoslavia, and Czechoslovakia fundamentally altered the map of Europe during the 1990s.

The Democratic Reichstag, Berlin
The centerpiece of the renovation of the German parliament building, completed in 1999, was the addition of a glass dome, shown here with the sculpture atop the Brandenburg Gate in the foreground. The dome was to manifest the openness of Germany's democracy as its capital moved from Bonn to Berlin.   *(AP/Wide World Photos)*

territory of present-day Poland had been taken from Germany after World War II, the Poles were especially concerned. The German government, however, remained eager to prove its good intentions by pressing for further European integration. Some worried that the European Union would itself become a vehicle for German domination, but the Germans took care to offer reasoned, cautious leadership into the new century.

The Federal Republic officially moved its capital from quiet, provincial Bonn to Berlin in 1999, when the costly makeover of the old parliament (Reichstag) building by a British architect had been completed. (See the box "Reading Sources: Reconstructing Berlin: The New German Capital After the Cold War.") But the return to the traditional German capital, and even the original building, worried some in light of Germany's earlier aggressiveness. As it happened, precisely as the refurbished Reichstag building was opened, German forces were involved in their first combat roles since World War II. This time, however, they were participating in NATO air strikes against a state, Yugoslavia, charged with genocidal aggression. German chancellor Gerhard Schröder, a socialist, insisted that Germany could not turn away but indeed had a particular responsibility to respond, in light of its recent history.

Many Germans still remained reluctant to support an expanded international military role. But as the rich countries of the West seemed expected to respond more widely to an increasingly volatile world, the United States pressured Germany to step up its military spend-

ing, which in 1998 amounted to but 1.5 percent of its economy, compared with 3.2 percent in the United States, and 2.8 percent in both Britain and France. However, German leaders, like those elsewhere in Europe, were reluctant to commit more resources to military spending at a time when budget pressures on the welfare state were already straining the social compact.

■ The European Union

With Europe no longer divided, the scope for European integration was suddenly much wider. The former Soviet bloc countries were eager to join the European club. At the same time, the EU was expanding its scope and developing a still more complex institutional network. Thus new questions accompanied the steps toward fuller integration in the decade after the end of the cold war.

From the start, proponents had envisioned that the Common Market would gradually promote greater uniformity in areas such as tax policy and business law, where national differences constituted barriers to economic activity across national borders. Although a full customs union had been achieved by the late 1960s, national governments continued to compromise the open market, especially by favoring certain companies to give them an advantage in international competition. For domestic political reasons, governments sometimes bought only from national firms or gave subsidies to domestic producers, enabling them to offer artificially lower prices to compete with foreign firms.

✍ READING SOURCES

Reconstructing Berlin:
The New German Capital After the Cold War

Berlin was a city like none other in modern history. Associated with Prussian militarism, then with German nationalism, and finally with the worst features of Nazi aggression, the city ended up divided by the cold war—and the Wall—then restored as capital of reunified Germany in 1999. How could the democratic Federal Republic, modestly headquartered in provincial Bonn since its inception in 1949, best embrace Berlin, with all its historical connotations? Jane Kramer, one of the most authoritative journalistic analysts of contemporary Europe, conveyed what Berlin was like in 1999 as it remade itself to be the capital of an established democracy.

One morning in Berlin this spring, on my way to an interview with a city planner, I stopped at the new Galeries Lafayette, in the east of the city on Friedrichstrasse, to pick up a croissant at the basement supermarket. By then, I had been in Berlin for at least a week. I had tried counting the construction cranes—seven hundred of them, the papers said—dipping over the born-again capital of a united Germany. I had prowled the sites of that construction, tracing the path of a wall and a no man's land that only ten years ago had split the city down its center. I had toured the Chancellery and some of the other new government buildings going up around the Reichstag, itself restored with a new glass dome. I had been through the Potsdamer Platz, where Sony and DaimlerChrysler were hosting a real-estate-development potlatch on twenty-eight acres of what used to be bombed-out desert. And I had seen the Schlossplatz, in East Berlin, where people were still arguing about the fate of an immense and incontestably ugly building called the Palace of the Republic, which until November of 1989, when the Wall came down, had housed the East German parliament. I had dug up the figures: five thousand six hundred and forty architects practicing in Berlin; a hundred and thirty thousand workers officially rebuilding Berlin (and no one knows how many unregistered foreign crews still bunking in converted shipping-container dormitories on the big sites); six thousand bureaucrats drawing salaries to (depending on who's talking) contribute to or complicate the process. I had heard all about "the architecture of the European city," "the architecture of the Berlin Republic," "the architecture of civil society," "the architecture of public space," and "the architecture of democratic transparency." I had spent so much time looking at buildings, thinking about buildings, listening to people whose job it was to try to redeem or redefine or reinvent "Germanness" through the new buildings of the capital, that my trip to the Galeries Lafayette was the first time I had actually used any of those buildings in what for me could be considered a normal way. . . .

. . . [I]t's safe to say that only in Berlin will you hear that a middle-sized, medium-priced department store with seventeen brands of tights and fresh breakfast pastries in the basement is a field of battle for nothing less than the soul of Germany—and not even because of its assault on your pocketbook (Germans call it "consumer terrorism") but because of a cone-shaped glass-and-steel atrium that a planner found "authoritarian," and not the "agora" he had hoped for.

The change in Berlin over the past few years has been astonishing, and, with this sort of architectural anguish (it's endemic now), the most astonishing part may be that anything gets built at all.

. . . Every city creates a market in its own obsessions, and right now in Berlin the obsession is architecture—or, more accurately, how to make a credible Berlin out of a city with no consensual idea of itself, and no common history beyond a negative one. . . .

Source: Jane Kramer, "Living with Berlin," *The New Yorker*, July 5, 1999, pp. 50–52. Reprinted by permission of the author.

After the oil crises of the 1970s, and amid increasing concern about "Eurosclerosis," or lack of innovation and competitiveness, the European Community's twelve members committed themselves in 1985 to creating a true single market with genuinely free competition by the end of 1992. Goods, services, and money would circulate freely among the member countries; manufacturing would conform to uniform product standards; and equal competition for government contracts would apply.

Meeting at Maastricht, in the Netherlands, in 1991, leaders of the member countries agreed to the Treaty on European Union. The treaty provided for a common policy on workers' rights and committed members to a common currency, the *euro,* and a common central banking structure by 1999. The subsequent ratification debates in each country proved more divisive than expected. Some feared German domination; others argued that faceless bureaucrats in foreign cities would now be making the vital decisions for domestic economies. Although the EU's members eventually ratified most of the Maastricht agreements, there were exceptions. Citing the danger of terrorism and drug smuggling, France essentially opted out of a provision for the free movement of people within the Union, a provision Germany found indispensable. And several members, including Britain, remained outside the common currency mechanism.

Moreover, the creation of an internal customs union, benign though it seemed, did not commit the EU to freer trade with nonmember countries such as the United States. Indeed, half the EU budget at the end of the 1990s went to farm subsidies—to protect farmers from outside competition. The possibility that the French government would lower agricultural supports, partly in response to pressures from the United States, led to several massive demonstrations by French farmers during the 1990s. By the late 1990s, EU quotas restricting the import of bananas from Central America produced serious friction with the United States. Such quotas favored former European colonies but thereby hurt American multinational fruit companies. Disputes erupted over the import of American hormone-enhanced beef and over governmental subsidies to the competing aircraft manufacturing giants, Europe's Airbus and America's Boeing.

The most controversial, and potentially most significant, of the Maastricht agreements was the provision for an Economic and Monetary Union (EMU), based on the euro. Especially by eliminating the costs of currency exchange, use of the euro promised to boost trade and economic interaction among the member countries. And it would simplify economic relations with non-EU countries as well. But a common currency required coordina-

tion of fiscal policy, and a number of the countries involved had to reduce their budget deficits substantially by cutting spending or raising taxes. Moreover, any budget deficits thereafter could not exceed a specified, relatively low figure. So whereas this deeper economic integration promised greater prosperity in the long term, it required immediate sacrifices that crashed against the social compact, already under pressure, that had produced high government spending for social welfare measures in the first place.

Although four of the fifteen members of the EU chose to remain outside the mechanism at this point, the euro was launched with much fanfare, and right on schedule, on January 1, 1999. National currencies remained temporarily in use for ordinary transactions, but the euro was used for major governmental and institutional transactions and traded on international currency exchanges. The common currency lived up to its promise, even facilitating a notable increase in supranational mergers and takeovers—a trend that threatened some but promised greater efficiency and international competitiveness for European firms. (See the feature "Weighing the Evidence: The Euro" on pages 1062–1063.)

The EU was more visible than ever. And as countries from Estonia and Poland to Turkey and Cyprus clambered to join, the EU insisted on strict membership criteria, including democratic institutions and alignment with EU laws and procedures in advance. The lure of membership sometimes strengthened democracy in the candidate states. When an apparent drift toward authoritarianism in Slovakia during the mid-1990s prompted EU warnings, Slovak voters ousted their present government in favor of a pro-EU alternative in 1998.

But as the roles and potential geographical reach of EU institutions expanded, long-standing questions about their structure and functioning became more pressing. For though it made democracy a condition for membership, the EU itself was only indirectly democratic in character. With major decisions made by an unelected policy elite, the EU's own "democratic deficit" seemed contradictory, and unacceptable. The issue of openness and accountability was complex, however, because the functioning of each particular EU institution, its relative importance, and the relationships among the institutions were all at issue.

By 2000 the European Union included a network of five interlocking core institutions, variously seated in Brussels, Strasbourg, Luxembourg, and Frankfurt. The executive branch was the Commission in Brussels, consisting of twenty appointed members, but with a professional staff of sixteen thousand. Charged to pursue the

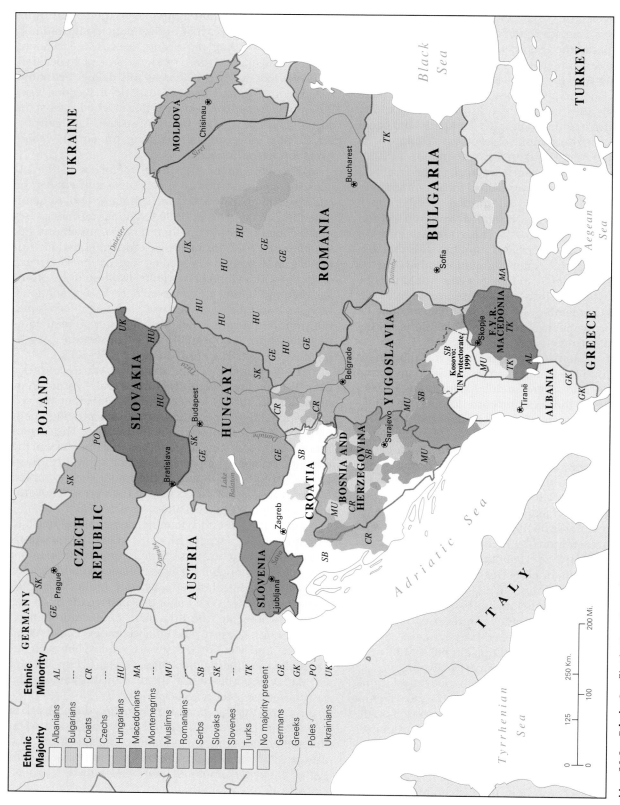

Map 30.2 Ethnic Conflict in East-Central Europe Much of east-central Europe, and particularly the Balkans, has long been an area of complex ethnic mixture. The end of communist rule opened the way to ethnic conflict, most tragically in what had been Yugoslavia. This map shows ethnic distribution in the region in the mid-1990s.

wider interests of the community, not to represent national interests, the commission had considerable power to initiate and enforce EU legislation. The question was whether these unelected Eurocrats had too much power.

The legislative branch of the EU was the Council of Ministers, composed of ministers from the governments of the member countries. On routine matters, the Council voted by majority, weighted by the size of each country's population. But more sensitive issues required unanimity; thus each member country had veto power. Reformers wanted to expand the role of majority rule and minimize the scope for veto. The British, citing concerns about national sovereignty, led resistance to change.

EU membership clearly entailed some loss of sovereignty, thanks especially to the increasingly powerful role of the judicial branch, the European Court of Justice, headquartered in Luxembourg. In a landmark 1988 case, the court struck down a German law on beer purity, which it judged an instance of disguised protectionism. EU agreements took precedence over national legislation, and the court was increasingly willing to interpret EU treaties in ways that had sweeping implications.

In contrast, the power of the European Parliament, which had developed from the assembly of the European Coal and Steel Community, and which divided its time between Strasbourg and Brussels, was more potential than actual. Though it had some oversight over budget and expanding powers to block or amend legislation, the parliament remained much the weakest of the core EU institutions by 2001. So despite the genuinely democratic character of this body, voters in the member countries demonstrated little interest in the elections of its members.

The fifth core institution, the European Central Bank, headquartered in Frankfurt, was born with the commitment to a common monetary policy and currency in 1991. Like central banks everywhere, its chief role was to regulate the money supply. And also like other central banks, this one faced political controversy over priorities. Citing inflation concerns, the bank adopted tight credit policies in the late 1990s, but politicians were quick to blame these policies for Europe's stubbornly high unemployment. Skeptics suggested that the elected politicians appreciated having a scapegoat for policies that were necessary, though not immediately popular.

Through gradual, incremental change over more than fifty years, the EU had become an established and powerful entity by the early twenty-first century, though it was an experiment still very much in progress. By now

"Europe" was a hybrid, at once a genuinely supranational entity and a collection of sovereign states. There had never been anything quite like it before. In such spheres as trade, agriculture, and the environment, the EU was dominant; national governments had little freedom of action. But other spheres, such as defense, taxation, and criminal justice, remained mostly national prerogatives. And though concerns about its "democratic deficit" were widely heard, the EU was successful enough to enjoy broad public support. Many sensed that whereas more democracy was desirable in principle, it would make the EU more beholden to short-sighted, parochially national concerns—and thus less successful.

■ Ethnic Conflict and the Wars of Yugoslav Secession

As the members of the European Union struggled to create a supranational entity, forces in the opposite direction—subnational, religious, ethnic, tribal—grew more powerful in parts of Europe, sometimes producing violent conflict. Beginning in 1969, the British had to use troops in Northern Ireland to keep order in the face of ongoing threats from Irish Catholics seeking the end of British rule and unification with the Republic of Ireland. The result was three decades of conflict between Protestants and Catholics that eluded definitive solution into the twenty-first century. In Czechoslovakia, which had been widely admired for its peaceful, civilized departure from communism in 1989, the Slovak minority broke away to form an independent republic at the beginning of 1993. In Belgium, antagonism between Flemish-speaking Flemings and French-speaking Walloons deepened during the 1990s. And the movement to separate French-speaking Quebec from the rest of Canada almost achieved success in 1995.

Most dramatic was the situation in Yugoslavia, where ethnic and religious conflict led to the disintegration of the country in a series of brutal wars among Serbs, Croats, Bosnian Muslims, and ethnically Albanian Kosovars (see Map 30.2). Defining events of the 1990s, these wars proved a major challenge for the new international order that was emerging, haltingly, after the cold war.

Although much was made of ancient ethnic and religious differences once Yugoslavia began falling apart, the area had long traditions of pluralism and tolerance. But ethnic relations had been poisoned by recent events—especially the civil war during World War II (see page 975). The situation had remained reasonably stable under Josip Tito's independent communist regime, which insisted on Yugoslav unity while affording some

Refugees from Kosovo, 1999 Kosovo, long a potential trouble spot within the Yugoslav Confederation, finally became the focal point of Slobodan Milosevic's Serb nationalism in 1999. The Serb campaign of ethnic cleansing forced many Kosovars to flee, primarily to neighboring Macedonia or Albania, where most had to survive in primitive camps. Here a mass of Kosovar refugees seeks to crowd onto a train to Macedonia. *(Roger Lemoyne/Liaison)*

measure of regional autonomy. But Tito was himself a Croat, and the state structure he devised angered some Serbs. Within a few years of Tito's death in 1980, intellectuals concerned for cultural distinctiveness began demanding cultural autonomy, thereby undermining the Yugoslav identity that Tito had sought to foster. A 1986 manifesto of leading Serb writers and intellectuals charged that Tito had allowed Kosovar genocide against Serbs and had pursued economic policies that favored Slovenes and Croats.

Insofar as this emphasis on ethnic identity pointed simply toward self-determination, it might prove benign, but each region of Yugoslavia harbored minority enclaves. Thus to accent ethnic identity, and grievance, carried the potential for trouble. After the fall of communism, Slovenia and Croatia declared themselves independent of Yugoslavia in May 1991. Led by the nationalist Franjo Tudjman°, Croatia adopted a constitution for a new "state of the Croat people" that left the 600,000 Serbs living in Croatia, most for generations, suddenly a vulnerable minority.

At the same time, the Serb leader of the remaining Yugoslavia, Slobodan Milosevic° (b. 1941), moved to center stage, becoming one of the key figures of the 1990s. A former communist, Milosevic embraced Serb national-

ism at least partly to maintain his own power. His aim was to unite all the Serbs, 2 million of whom lived outside Serbia proper, mostly in Croatia and Bosnia-Herzegovina. He would start by taking over the substantial parts of Croatia with Serb majorities, then divide Bosnia-Herzegovina with Croatia.

Starting in 1991 Milosevic proceeded with extreme brutality, fostering "ethnic cleansing"—forced relocation or mass killing to rid the territory in question of its non-Serb inhabitants. Through his government's control of the media, he encouraged a sense of victimization that incited hatred among the Serbs. And each in the series of wars that followed seemed to open the way to worse atrocity and deeper bitterness.

The Serb assault in Bosnia by 1995 especially brought home to the world the depth of the tragedy at work (see Map 30.2). In the Bosnian capital, Sarajevo, a culturally diverse city long known for its tolerant, cosmopolitan atmosphere, more than 10,000 civilians, including 1,500 children, were killed by shelling and sniper fire during a Serb siege from 1992 to early 1996.

When a Serb mortar killed thirty-seven civilians in a marketplace in Sarajevo in August 1995, NATO forces responded with air strikes that led to peace accords and the end of fighting by early 1996. But though the peace agreement envisioned a unified Bosnian state, the contending Serbs, Croats, and Bosnian Muslims quickly began carving out separate spheres, violating agreements about repatriation and the rights of minorities. By 2001 Bosnia remained an ethnically divided international protectorate, its peace dependent on the foreign troops stationed there.

The next phase of the Yugoslav tragedy centered on the province of Kosovo, which Serbs viewed as the cradle of their nationhood (see Map 30.2). For complex historical reasons, however, Serbs had long constituted only a minority of its population. The majority were ethnically Albanian, and by the late 1980s, they were talking independence—and sometimes mistreating the minority Serbs. As part of his effort to foster Serb nationalism, Milosevic countered by suspending autonomy for Kosovo within the Yugoslav confederation in 1991. The fissuring of Yugoslavia over the next few years emboldened the Kosovars, who counted on Serb intransigence to justify a demand for full independence, as opposed to mere autonomy.

When Milosevic struck against the Kosovars in the spring of 1999, ruthlessly pursuing ethnic cleansing, the Western powers again intervened, first convening a meeting with Serb and Kosovar leaders on Kosovo's future. When the Serb-led remnant of Yugoslavia refused to sign, NATO made good on threats to bomb Serbia in re-

---

Tudjman (TOODCH-mahn)   **Milosevic** (mih-LO-suh-vitch)

taliation. The bombing, concentrated on such economic targets as bridges and power stations, continued for eleven weeks later in 1999.

Critics argued that it set a dubious precedent to attack Serbia for refusing a settlement that would have ceded territory and opened the rest of Serbia to quasi-occupation by NATO. No one could deny that Kosovo was part of Serbia, so the NATO action was an overt interference in the internal affairs of a sovereign state. Under what authority was NATO acting, and according to what criteria? Did it claim the right to bomb any state pursuing policies not to its liking? What about the likely damage to NATO's relations with Russia, long close to Serbia, and now hypersensitive in light of its declining influence in world affairs?

Even the claim that the operation was a humanitarian response to genocide seemed hypocritical to some, who asked why the international community had done nothing in response to the manifestly more systematic genocide in Rwanda in 1994, when 800,000 people had been killed in a hundred days. Defenders countered that it was partly because of the soul-searching in the aftermath of Rwanda that the advanced countries of the West were now changing the rules and taking responsibility for concerted action. But on what basis was NATO the appropriate multinational agent? The response of the Western alliance to Kosovo's plight seemed something of a turning point, but what it would mean for the future remained unclear.

Once the NATO bombing began, the Serbs intensified their ethnic cleansing of Kosovo, burning homes, forcing 800,000 refugees to flee into neighboring Macedonia and Albania. But the bombing finally led both the Serbs and the Kosovars to pull back from their more extreme demands, and Russia agreed to join in the multinational peacekeeping force in Kosovo in the aftermath.

Still, the outcome bore little relationship to the multi-ethnic pluralism NATO had been seeking. The Kosovars clearly dominated the now-ravaged territory. Thirsting for revenge, younger Kosovars engaged in their own ethnic cleansing, targeting not only Serbs but also Roma ("Gypsies") and Bosnian Muslims. The resulting violence sickened even older Kosovars, who remembered years of peaceful coexistence with the Serbs. With many having fled, Serbs constituted only 10 percent of the population, confined to the region adjacent to Serbia proper, by 2000. So in Kosovo, as in Bosnia, fighting resulted in near-complete ethnic separation, with some form of partition likely.

Ethnic cleansing by the Kosovars was but one aspect of the wider anarchy that followed the fighting. Six months after the bombing stopped, the area had no

working government and was essentially run by armed gangs. Beset by domestic political pressures, national rivalries, and problems of coordination, the outside peacekeepers found it difficult to play any meaningful role.

Though he was the first sitting head of state to be indicted for war crimes, Milosevic proved resilient, initially surviving his defeat in Kosovo in 1999, just as he had survived a major protest movement in 1996–1997. In addition to the recent bombing, ongoing economic sanctions hurt ordinary Serbs, arousing a sense of victimization and resentment against the West. But opposition continued as well, and in September 2000, Vojislav Kostunica° defeated Milosevic in Yugoslavia's presidential election. Milosevic was the last of the former communists to continue in power, and some saw his fall as the definitive end of the cold war era. (See the box "Reading Sources: The Fall of Milosevic as the Last Revolution.") In June 2001, under pressure from the international community, the Yugoslav government finally turned Milosevic over to the international war crimes tribunal in The Hague.

ECONOMY AND THE POLITICAL ORDER IN THE MATURE DEMOCRACIES

BY the 1980s democracy had become the unchallenged norm in western Europe, where the radical right remained largely discredited and the left seemed to have been domesticated for good. In important respects, in fact, conservatives and social democrats sounded more and more alike. But at the same time the postwar consensus about governmental responsibility for social and economic well-being began to fade as new questions arose about the reach of the state.

Many of the trends important in western Europe by the 1980s were visible in the United States and Canada as well. All over the Western world, organized labor weakened, more women entered in the work force, and issues from child-care to pension costs moved to center stage. But there were some instructive differences in the ways the various nations of the West dealt with these matters.

■ Rethinking the Welfare State

Government welfare measures had helped establish the new political consensus in western Europe since World War II. Although much publicity surrounded the British welfare state, the percentage of the British economy

Kostunica (kohs-TOO-nih-kah)

The Fall of Milosevic as the Last Revolution

Slobodan Milosevic was the key player in the brutal wars in the former Yugoslavia that produced massive civilian suffering during the 1990s. Despite defeat in Kosovo in 1999, he seemed fully in control of the Serb-dominated remnant of Yugoslavia—until an extraordinary election in September 2000. Milosevic was defeated, but an element of violence was required to oust him during the weeks that followed. In this passage, the noted British historian and journalist Timothy Garton Ash analyzes the chain of events and considers the outcome in light of the end of the cold war.

The last revolution was also the strangest.

On Thursday, October 5, as Serbs stormed the parliament in Belgrade, waving flags from its burning windows, and seized the headquarters of state television, which an opposition leader had once christened "TV Bastille," it looked like a real, old-fashioned European revolution. The storming of the Winter Palace! The fall of the Bastille! . . .

. . . [L]ate on the evening of Friday, October 6, Milosevic appeared on another national television channel to make the kind of gracious speech conceding election defeat that one expects from an American president or a British prime minister. He had just received the information, he said, that Vojislav Kostunica had won the presidential election. (This from the man who had spent the last eleven days trying to deny exactly that, by electoral fraud, intimidation, and manipulation of the courts.)

. . . He stood stiffly beside the Yugoslav flag, with his hands crossed very low in front of him, like a schoolboy who had been caught cheating. Or like a penitent before the priest that his father once aspired to be. Sorry, father, I've cheated in the elections, ruined my country, caused immeasurable bloodshed and misery to our neighbors—but I'll be a good boy now. It was incongruous, surreal, ridiculous in the pretense that this was just an ordinary, democratic change of leader. . . .

. . . What happened between about three and seven o'clock on the afternoon of Thursday, October 5, changed everything. Led by a man in a red shirt, defying police batons and tear gas, a crowd stormed the parliament. Soon thereafter, the nearby state television headquarters was trashed and set alight. A handful of other key media outlets, including the state television studio and transmission center, and Veran Matic's B92 radio, were more peacefully taken over. Kostunica cried, "Good evening, liberated Serbia," to an ecstatic crowd, and they celebrated in the streets.

These events invite a moment's reflection on the relationship between image and reality. Those who stormed the parliament created an unforgettable image of liberation—an image that CNN and the BBC sent around the world. This image then became reality. Taking over the state television was itself another compelling television image: the "TV Bastille" in flames. But it also meant that the opposition now controlled the place that made the images. And that, not the army or police, is the very heart of power in modern politics. . . .

. . . There was . . . a brief moment of 1917: a deliberate yet limited use of revolutionary violence. It is hard to imagine the breakthrough coming without it. But the remarkable thing is how limited it was, and how quickly the country returned to new-style, peaceful revolution. Within a week, Otpor activists were organizing an action to encourage people to return the goods they had looted from the shops. . . .

. . . If the Solidarity revolution in Poland was the beginning of the end of communism, this was the end of the end of communism. It was the last of a twenty-year chain of new-style, Central and East European revolutions, each learning from the previous one but also adding new ingredients and variations. And not just in Europe. There are echoes here of the Philippines or Indonesia. And messages, one hopes, for other countries. In a now globalized politics, we have moved beyond the old 1789 and 1917 models of revolution. If it could happen in Serbia, why not in Burma? Why not in Cuba? . . .

. . . [A]fter the fall of Milosevic there is no longer any external obstacle to our building a liberal community not just of fifteen but of thirty democratic nation-states.

Source: Timothy Garton Ash, "The Last Revolution," *The New York Review of Books*, November 16, 2000, pp. 8, 11–12, 14.

devoted to public expenditure for welfare, housing, and education by the early 1970s—18.2 percent—was about average for the industrialized nations of the West. Sweden had the highest figure at 23.7 percent. But the welfare state began to encounter strains with the more difficult economic circumstances of the 1970s. Globalization and technological change threatened the postwar prosperity, and what government should try to do, could afford to do, became central to the agenda in the West.

Pressures on the welfare state were especially striking in Sweden. By the early 1970s, 40 percent of Sweden's national income was devoted to taxes to finance the system—the highest rate of taxation in the world. At the same time, Sweden found itself less competitive, both because its wages were high and because it was not keeping abreast of technological developments. In Sweden, as elsewhere, opinion-makers grew increasingly doubtful that a welfare state could nurture the initiative and productivity needed for success in the increasingly competitive global economy. By 1980 unemployment and efforts to cut government spending led to the most severe labor unrest the country had experienced since the war. Even on the level of everyday life, more Swedes were coming to believe that the Swedish model entailed excessive governmental intrusion in the private sphere.

In Britain a dramatic assault on the welfare state began developing at the same time, especially because the British economy, having lagged the others of the industrialized West, suffered especially during the 1970s. Between 1968 and 1976, the country lost 1 million manufacturing jobs. By the mid-1970s this economic decline threatened to shatter Britain's postwar consensus around the welfare state as the British people could not agree on how to apportion the pain of the necessary austerity measures.

During the 1970s each of Britain's two major political parties made a serious effort to come to grips with the situation, but neither succeeded, especially because neither could deal effectively with Britain's strong trade unions. But when the militantly conservative Margaret Thatcher (b. 1925) became prime minister in 1979, it was clear that Britain was embarking on a radically different course.

Thatcher insisted that Britain could reverse its economic decline only by fostering a new "enterprise culture," restoring the individual initiative that had been sapped, as she saw it, by decades of dependence on government. Thatcher took it for granted that the free market, undistorted by government intervention, produced optimum economic efficiency and thus, in the long term, the greatest social benefit.

Abandoning its paternalistic tendencies and aristocratic vestiges, the Conservative Party now appealed especially to the upwardly mobile, entrepreneurial

Thatcher's Conservative Revolution   As British prime minister from 1979 to 1990, Margaret Thatcher led an assault on the welfare state and a renewed embrace of free-market economics in Britain. Together with U.S. president Ronald Reagan, who greatly admired her, she came to symbolize the retreat from government that marked the 1980s. Thatcher is shown here at a political rally in London in 1987.   *(D. Hudson/Sygma)*

middle class. But in light of the socioeconomic difficulties Britain faced by the late 1970s, Thatcher's message had broad appeal across the social spectrum. With Labour increasingly isolated, identified with decaying inner cities and old industrial regions, Thatcher easily won re-election in 1983 and 1987.

Three immediate priorities followed directly from Thatcher's overall strategy. First, her government made substantial cuts in taxes and corresponding cuts in spending for education, national health, and public housing. Second, the government fostered privatization, selling off an array of state-owned firms from Rolls Royce to British Airways. The government even sold public housing to tenants, at as much as 50 percent below market value, a measure that helped Thatcher win considerable working-class support. Third, Thatcher curbed the power of Britain's labor unions, which were already on the defensive in this period of high unemployment.

Several new laws curtailed trade-union power, and Thatcher refused to consult with union leaders as her predecessors had done since the war. A showdown was reached with the yearlong coal miners' strike of 1984 and 1985, one of the most bitter and violent European strikes of the twentieth century. The strike's failure in the face of government intransigence further discredited the labor movement and enhanced Thatcher's prestige. Still, the

The Internet

In the late 1960s the U.S. Department of Defense commissioned some bright graduate students to develop a way to share information on computers with university researchers. The program they devised enabled computers to use existing telephone lines to send files from one machine to another. The resulting protocol, or set of rules, included the little-used "at" symbol—@—which soon became the pivot in every electronic mail (e-mail) address in the world.

Thus was born the Internet—not in some Silicon Valley garage but at the U.S. defense department, which made the new program freely available to universities to facilitate research. At first the impact was limited. Computers were big, clunky machines, and only governments, universities, and large businesses could afford them. All of this changed during the 1980s when IBM began marketing the small, affordable personal computer (PC). The potential to share information on computers was now available to individuals—in their professional or working roles, but also as consumers, correspondents, hobbyists, political activists, or simply as human beings curious about their world. Anyone could put information on a computer that others might want to access. The potential magnitude of such sharing became clear only gradually, but by the end of the 1990s the Internet had taken definite form, encompassing an array of possibilities from e-mail to the World Wide Web.

The Internet seemed to overcome physical distance by opening a whole new "cyberspace"—a term derived from *cybernetics*, coined in 1948 to indicate the comparative study of control systems, from the brain to the computer. Since Antiquity people had been able to go to physical places—libraries—to access physical objects containing information. But as the Internet made possible access to all networked computers, and as more people found it advantageous to make more information available, Internet users could find a great deal of information more quickly than ever before. Thus, for example, stock markets became more open and democratic, and interactive learning across physical distance became possible. And though much hype ballyhooed the "new economy," centered around young "high-tech" companies, the Internet revolution offered long-established companies the chance to improve productivity through more efficient procurement and inventory control.

The growth of the Internet was bound up with globalization—or Americanization. By 2000 English was the language of 78.3 percent of webpages worldwide; only 1.7 percent were in Spanish and 1.2 percent in French. However, as Internet access came to seem essential for success in an increasingly competitive world, many worried about the growing "digital divide" between those with and those without such access.

Some suggested that the Internet made possible greater democracy by bypassing the "gatekeepers" in journalism, publishing, or academics, but others grew anxious about quality as the Internet made ever more unedited information available. So much was available that it was easy to get caught up in the technical means; following links threatened to become more important than actually reading content. Moreover, commerce seemed ever more intrusive by the early twenty-first century. With its blinking advertisements, even the website of the once staid Encyclopedia Bri-

---

violent encounters between police and picketing strikers, carried nationwide on television, indicated the cracks in the relative social harmony that Britain had long enjoyed.

In addition, riots by unemployed youths broke out in several major industrial cities in 1981 and again in 1985. On one issue, however, the Thatcher government managed a meeting of the minds with discontented city dwellers. Even before Thatcher took office, increasing immigration from Britain's former colonies was being blamed for a variety of social ills, from unemployment to urban crime. Taking a hard line on the issue, Thatcher's Conservatives sponsored the Nationality Act of 1982, which restricted immigration from the former British colonies.

With her nationalist bent, Thatcher resisted the growing power of the multinational European Union. But her stance on the EU, coupled with what seemed an increasingly arrogant, strident tone, provoked growing opposition even within her own party, which finally ousted her as party leader, and thus as prime minister, in 1990.

Even critics admitted that Thatcher's policies, especially her willingness to curb the unions, had produced a significant change in British attitudes in favor of enterprise and competition. Privatization found increasing approval, while the number of new businesses reflected a revival of entrepreneurship—apparently the basis for better economic performance during the 1990s. But the gap between rich and poor widened, and the old industrial regions of the north were left ever further behind.

Still, even as the welfare state receded in Sweden and Britain, the reach of government expanded elsewhere. In

An Internet Café With the sudden popularity of the Internet by the mid-1990s, "Internet cafés" emerged all over the world. They offered Internet access, along with coffee, to those who did not own personal computers. London's Cyberia café, shown here in 1995, was typical.
(Martyn Hayhow/SIPA Press)

tannica recalled some nineteenth-century carnival. Still, Britannica was not a public service but a profit-making company, which had to be compensated for making its information available.

As a new way of delivering information, the Internet raised complex intellectual property issues, which came dramatically to a head in 2000 over access to recorded music. Through the website of Napster Inc., 10 million people were downloading recorded music from a network of fellow users, bypassing traditional methods of distribution and remuneration. The recording industry filed suit to recover millions in lost compact disk sales, but record companies scrambled to find new ways to distribute music over the Internet at the same time. The Internet was opening new ways for users to compensate the creators of music and other forms of intellectual property.

As they became ever more dependent on the Internet, organizations and individuals also became more vulnerable—and concerned about privacy and security. Third parties could keep track of sites accessed and purchases made

and then develop a profile of interests, buying habits, health concerns—whether for marketing or some less elevated purpose. By the early twenty-first century, critics suggested that tough decisions through the political process were necessary to govern the further development of the Internet. Otherwise, with commercial considerations dominant, the outcome would be less democracy, less free speech, less privacy.

Sheer volume was increasingly a concern as well. By 2000 the number of Internet users reached 300 million people worldwide, and the figure was projected to exceed 1 billion by 2005. The amount of information traveling across the Internet was doubling every three months—prompting concerns that even as high-tech companies devised ever more sophisticated routers and switchers, innovations in hardware could not keep up with mushrooming demand. Some experts predicted gigantic cyber traffic jams, even gridlock. But there was no turning back. The ongoing Internet revolution had become central to the continuing information technology experiment.

Italy reforms during the 1970s made available a wider range of state services than ever before, from kindergarten and medical care to sports and recreational facilities. In France by the mid-1990s, five-week paid vacations were mandatory, with the government sometimes subsidizing the cost of transportation to seaside or mountain resorts. Government subsidies kept the costs of cultural events affordable to ordinary workers. Accustomed to a strong government role in society, Europeans had difficulty understanding how measures such as government-sponsored health care could cause such controversy among Americans. But as global economic competition intensified during the last decades of the century, France and Italy found it more difficult to pay for all the benefits their governments had gradually come to promise.

■ An Uncertain Affluence

As the Soviet bloc economies bogged down during the 1980s, the democratic countries of the West enjoyed renewed affluence. One driving force was the technological change that, during the late twentieth century, produced a "third industrial revolution." Though it encompassed everything from robotics to fiber optics, it was based especially on the computer, or what soon came to be summed up as "information technology" (IT). The advent of these new technologies in a context of increasing global competition affected patterns of employment in ways that damaged some, but also produced new opportunities and new winners. (See the feature "Information Technology: The Internet.")

Some new firms were able to exploit such technologies to start from scratch, without the problems of redundant workers or outmoded plants and equipment that older competitors often faced. A good example was Benetton, an Italian clothing firm founded in 1964 that pioneered the use of computer technology in all aspects of its operation. But Benetton proved a notable success partly because it needed fewer workers. Manufacturing jobs, especially, tended to be lost as competition forced the industrial sector to become more efficient through computers and automation. In the German steel industry, which had spearheaded a remarkable industrial transformation a century before, over half the jobs disappeared during the 1970s and 1980s.

Changing labor patterns reinforced the decline of organized labor, which was decidedly on the defensive throughout western Europe and the United States by the 1980s. In France, for example, the organized labor movement was at once divided and relatively small, encompassing fewer than 10 percent of French workers. The increasing danger of unemployment undercut the leverage of the unions. And as the economy grew more complex, workers were ever less likely to think of themselves as members of a single, unified working class.

So the renewed prosperity of the 1980s was in some ways brittle and uncertain, especially because unemployment reached levels not seen since the Great Depression. Even after solid growth resumed by 1983, unemployment hovered stubbornly at around 10 percent throughout much of western Europe, with 13 percent the norm in some older industrial areas. These figures would have seemed unimaginable fifteen years before and were much higher than the rates of 5 to 7 percent typical in the United States during the same period. Even as unemployment declined to postwar lows in the United States during the 1990s, elevated levels persisted in much of western Europe.

Most attributed the higher European rate to the structure of labor markets and, more generally, to the greater agility and flexibility of the American economy. The relationship was paradoxical because as a result of laws, labor agreements, and the postwar consensus now in place, those European workers who had jobs were more secure than their American counterparts. But, as the other side of the coin, European employers were less able to adapt to changing conditions by laying off workers or hiring new ones with different skills. During the 1980s, American firms were more likely to restructure or downsize in response to technological change and increasing global competition. But thus the American economy proved better at creating new jobs as new opportunities emerged during the 1990s.

In fact, it was increasingly clear that two models of capitalism were at work—and in competition. The U.S. model, increasingly shared by Britain, placed greater emphasis on free enterprise, whereas continental western Europe had evolved a "social market economy," with greater commitment to security, consensus, and communitarian values. (See the box "Reading Sources: The Varieties of Liberal Capitalism.") But was the European model sustainable if it obstructed adaptability and consistently yielded high unemployment, especially among young people?

The continental model was increasingly on the defensive during the 1990s, a period of remarkable prosperity for the United States, which forcefully asserted its leadership in the "new economy" revolving around information technology. Said one executive of Intel, a leading American high tech firm, "If France were a stock, I'd sell it."[1] But the European model provided a more substantial safety net—in health care, for example—as well as a stronger commitment to public goods like transportation and day care. The question by the early twenty-first century was clear. Could Europe maintain and even extend its more socially oriented model while becoming more economically competitive? Or, in light of globalization and the third industrial revolution, was Europe bound to adapt the lean and mean American model?

■ Left, Right, and the Democratic Consensus

Although the timing varied from country to country, the western European democracies tended toward some form of two-party political system after World War II. The domestication of the socialist left was essential to that process. After Willy Brandt became chancellor in 1969, the West German Socialists led the government for thirteen years, finally meeting electoral defeat in 1982. By that point, Socialists and Conservatives agreed on the essentials, squabbling only about degrees. The Socialists had completed the turn to moderation that they began in the late 1950s, leaving Germany with essentially a two-party system.

But the political mainstream seemed to offer fewer choices; the resulting frustration fed the new radicalism evident by the early 1970s. As the established Marxist left seemed unable to deal persuasively with contemporary concerns, new coalitions developed around newly politicized issues like abortion and the environment. The successes of this new left fed hopes for more systematic change in socioeconomic relations. And during the early 1980s, revitalized socialist parties in France, Spain, and Italy marginalized the communists and, for a time, seemed poised to reorient government, even to spearhead that systematic change.

⊱ READING SOURCES

The Varieties of Liberal Capitalism

The collapse of communism during 1989–1991 meant the triumph of capitalism, but it also brought to center stage the choices and tradeoffs at work within the advanced capitalist world. Postwar West Germany had achieved remarkable success with its "social market economy," but as renewed under Ronald Reagan and Margaret Thatcher during the 1980s, the more individualistic, entrepreneurial capitalism of the United States and Britain attracted increasing support. Writing in 1991, the French industrialist and government leader Michel Albert offered a spirited critique of Anglo-American capitalism and advocated that France embrace the German "Rhine model" within a more fully integrated European Union.

The rich need no longer feel ashamed of their wealth. Where they once shunned any hint of ostentation, they now display it with an immodesty that the French used to consider shockingly vulgar when they witnessed it in Americans. And this wealth increasingly rubs shoulders with a new poverty of the kind that is flourishing in the USA. France, too, now has its zones of urban blight, dumping-grounds populated by a growing army of the unemployed, those whose benefit has run out, young people seeking their first job, and immigrants—illegal or otherwise. . . .

The Rhine model . . . embodies, on the one hand, capitalism which can provide social security, and on the other, a system in which the company is seen not just as a heap of capital but a group of people. This is exactly what France badly needs. . . .

. . . If the aim is to harness capitalism without impairing its efficiency, it is no longer to the nation state that we must look, but to Europe. And Europe must produce both powerful financial structures . . . and political institutions. . . .

. . . [A] whole new ideology of capitalism had come to power:

[T]he market is good, the state is bad; social welfare provision, once a sign of progress, is blamed for encouraging laziness; taxation, once an indispensable means for reconciling economic development and social justice, is accused (not without reason) of discouraging talent and initiative. . . . Where the nineteenth century saw capitalism challenge the state, but with no thought of replacing it in such areas as health, education or the media . . . , the late twentieth century now proposes to substitute market forces for the state. . . . [I]n the majority of developed countries, more and more services, from broadcasting to rubbish collection and from the water supply to the post office, are being transferred from the public to the private sector. . . .

We Europeans are, more than anyone else on the planet, faced with the question of which sacrifices we shall make, and for which gains. The European Community is the main battleground on which the conflict of capitalism against capitalism will be fought. . . .

1. Either Europeans will fail to understand what is really at stake, and so will not press their leaders to make the imaginative leap towards true political union: in which case, the Single Market will begin to fray and disintegrate before it has begun; the possibility of unity will recede ever further under a cloud of permanent Euro-pessimism; the slide towards the neo-American model will accelerate as the zones of decay and deprivation already staked out on the periphery of our cities continue to swell. . . .

2. Or we will actually begin to build the United States of Europe: in which case, we will have all the means at our disposal to choose the best possible socioeconomic system, that which has already proven its mettle within one part of the continent and which will become the "European model" of capitalism.

Source: Michel Albert, *Capitalism Against Capitalism* (London: Whurr, 1993), pp. 238–240, 244, 247, 253–254, 260.

 For additional information on this topic, go to http://college.hmco.com.

The pivotal case was France, where François Mitterrand° (1916–1996) was elected president in 1981, promising to create the first genuinely democratic socialism. But despite a vigorous start he gradually abandoned any talk of socialism in the face of economic and political pressures. By the end of the 1980s, he was questioning the relevance of long-standing socialist tenets and playing up the virtues of entrepreneurship, the profit mechanism, and free-market competition. Mitterrand realized that France, like the other industrial democracies, had to operate in an increasingly competitive international economy.

As French socialism seemed to lose its sense of direction, some leading Socialists got caught up in corruption scandals, and the party met massive defeat at the polls in 1993 and 1995. But they had proven they could work within the system, and a socialist-led coalition regained the parliamentary majority in 1997. Much like Germany, France seemed to have settled into a two-party system, which meant stability, but also a narrowing of discussion and choice. Even Italy, long notorious for the surface instability of its government, seemed to settle into a system of alternating left-leaning and right-leaning coalitions after major scandals during the early 1990s undermined the longstanding political establishment.

Although the socialist left had won reforms that were now central to the consensus around democratic capitalism, by the 1990s it had abandoned much of what it had stood for—from class struggle and revolution to state ownership and a centrally planned economy. It could apparently serve only as the mildly left-leaning alternative within the framework of capitalist democracy. When Labour returned to power in Britain in 1997, the popular new prime minister, Tony Blair, did not offer a bold new program or reverse the key Thatcherite measures like privatization.

With the decline of socialism as a political alternative, a new right, associated especially with anti-immigrant sentiment at first, gained prominence by the mid-1990s. Although differing considerably in priorities, respectability, and success, such leaders as Jean-Marie LePen in France, Jörg Haider° in Austria, and Gianfranco Fini° in Italy tapped into political frustration and economic uncertainty.

But what did it mean to be "right wing" or conservative by the late twentieth century? In Italy and Austria, new right politicians criticized the prevailing understanding of the recent past—the era of fascism and the Second World War—playing up the patriotic, anticom-munist thrust of the interwar right. But because Haider seemed to have played down Nazi atrocities, a major international outcry developed when his party was invited to join Austria's governing coalition in 1999.

As far as present priorities were concerned, conservatives sometimes differed sharply among themselves. In Britain the Thatcher government had tamed the labor unions and sold state-owned industries, but conservative critics pointed out that it had expanded centralized control over local government, health care, and education. With its ideological agenda, the Thatcher government had been activist and interventionist, not cautious, gradualist, and pragmatic—not truly conservative. In addressing economic anxieties, the new right sometimes articulated problems that mainstream politicians ignored, but it seemed unable to come up with viable solutions. Its proponents even disagreed over the relative merits of free trade and protectionism. So though some new right politicians could be noisy, they failed to offer a systematic alternative.

Although democratic capitalism rested on broad and solid support by the 1990s, the questions about the quality of democracy that began surfacing in the late 1960s remained on the table. Indeed, as technological change and globalization added up to unprecedented revolution by the 1980s, concerns deepened that key decisions were increasingly being made by multinational corporations or supranational organizations not directly subject to democratic control. As global competition intensified, the logic of capitalism, or the market, seemed increasingly to overwhelm the capacities of democratic politics.

Even on the domestic political level, the increasingly obvious role of money—needed to finance campaigns and win elections—raised doubts about the capability of democratically elected governments to pursue some common interest. In Italy the quest for such political money bred systematic corruption that finally came to light in 1992, discrediting the Christian Democrats and the whole entrenched political class. By the end of the 1990s, even former German chancellor Helmut Kohl, long one of Europe's most respected leaders, stood partly discredited for accepting illegal campaign contributions.

The need for money to finance electioneering and political patronage seemed to keep even a democratic political system on the edge of corruption. And thus, in part, national governments sometimes seemed to lack the muscle or the will to address the pressures following from the third industrial revolution. By the 1990s, declining voter turnout suggested growing political cynicism all over the Western world.

Mitterrand (MEE-tuh-rahn) **Haider** (HY-dur) **Fini** (FEE-nee)

THE POSTCOMMUNIST EXPERIMENT

HATEVER the uncertainties in the capitalist democracies, the former communist countries scrambled to join the Western mainstream after the anticommunist revolutions of 1989–1991. A number of them sought to join NATO and the European Union. But the area had little experience with the give-and-take of democratic politics, and the fragile new political systems found themselves responsible for the difficult transition from a command to a free-market economy. Indeed, political prospects clearly depended in large part on the success of the economic transition. And though several of the countries of east-central Europe made notable progress during the decade that followed, the region lagged dramatically in per capita gross domestic product (GDP). (See Map 30.3.) And Russia, still the major power in the region, experienced wave after wave of difficulty.

With the disintegration of the Soviet bloc, it became clear that the years of communism had produced environmental degradation on an appalling scale. The Stalinist determination to industrialize quickly had combined with the Marxist faith in progress to produce this result, and those who came after were left to clean up as best they could. In many cases, improvement had to wait because jobs or energy sources depended on the old polluting patterns. Ukraine could not afford to replace the remaining nuclear reactors at Chernobyl, despite safety and environmental risks that the 1986 accident had only worsened (see page 1017). International aid finally enabled the country to close the plant in 2000.

■ Success and Uncertainty in East-Central Europe

The economies in the former communist satellite states were close to chaos as the transition began, and their attempts to construct market economies brought on unemployment, inflation, and widespread corruption. No longer could ordinary people count on the subsidized consumer goods or the welfare safety net the communist regimes had provided. While many suffered great hardship, some former communist functionaries quickly got rich by taking over state-owned companies. Still, by the mid-1990s the transition to a market economy seemed to be working, though the pattern of change and the degree of success varied considerably from one country to the next.

Some of the postcommunist governments concentrated on privatizing existing state-owned concerns, while others sought especially to foster entrepreneurship and innovation. In Poland privatization lagged, but a buoyant new private sector emerged as the Poles proved adept at starting new businesses. Privatization was greatest in the Czech Republic under the forceful leadership of Václav Klaus, a passionate partisan of market economics. Each country had a reasonably stable, outward-looking market economy by the mid-1990s. Within a few years, Poland was attracting outside investment at a remarkable rate, and its capital, Warsaw, was emerging as a significant European financial center.

In the political sphere, the former communist countries tended first toward political fragmentation—a multiplicity of parties in a weak, divided parliament—which in turn encouraged reliance on a strong leader. Postcommunist Poland's first parliamentary elections in October 1991 produced a legislature splintered among twenty parties, none commanding more than 12 percent of the vote. This situation seemed to open the way to an ever more authoritarian approach from the president, who, beginning in December 1990, was Lech Walesa, the Solidarity leader who had spearheaded the defeat of communism (see page 1013). Although Walesa, during his five years as president, never became the authoritarian some feared, he was sometimes bullying and intolerant, and his dominant role reinforced concerns about the viability of the new democracies in the face of parliamentary fragmentation.

Throughout the formerly communist part of Europe, most politicians were eager to jettison the communist label at first. But by 1992 those in power in Lithuania, Romania, Bulgaria, and the dominant Serbian part of Yugoslavia were former communists whose long-term commitment to democracy remained suspect. And economic dislocations produced growing support for former communists by the mid-1990s. But some onetime communists were more reformed than others, and their electoral successes did not mean the same thing everywhere.

In Poland and Hungary, maturing politically, the election of former communists during the mid-1990s did not compromise democracy or the market economy. When a charismatic young ex-communist, Alexander Kwasniewski°, defeated Walesa in a watershed presidential election in Poland in 1995, the outcome was not a repudiation of the anticommunist revolution. It was arguable, in fact, that Walesa was no longer a progressive

---

Kwasniewski (kvazh-NEV-skee)

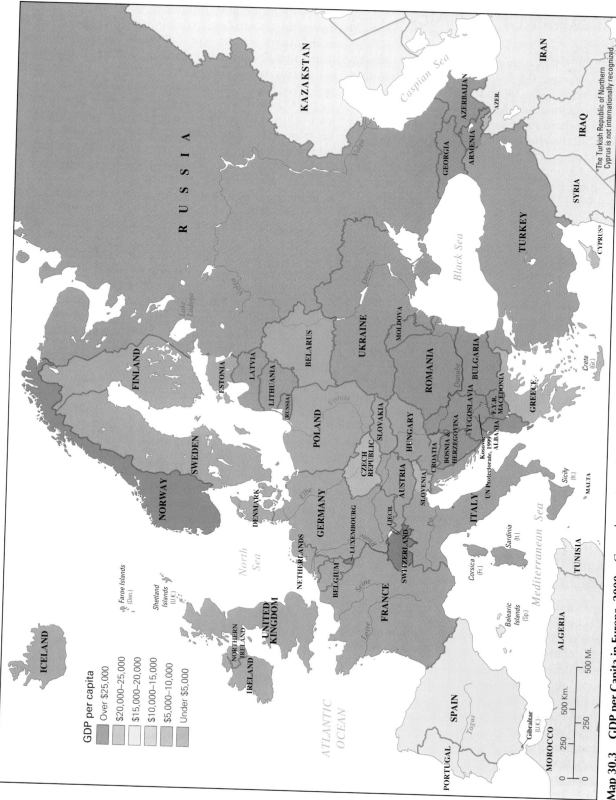

Map 30.3 GDP per Capita in Europe, 2000 Gross domestic product (GDP) per capita is a widely recognized measure of national economic success. By 2000, this measure varied dramatically among the European countries, revealing the wide disparity in economic well-being across the Continent. The former communist countries continued to lag, even as some were growing at impressive rates. The U.S. figure was $33,900, and Canada's was $23,300.

GDP per capita

Over $25,000
$20,000–25,000
$15,000–20,000
$10,000–15,000
$5,000–10,000
Under $5,000

*The Turkish Republic of Northern Cyprus is not internationally recognized.

force. His vote came largely from traditionalist, rural, strongly Catholic parts of Poland, whereas Kwasniewski attracted Poles interested in expanding the market economy and developing closer ties with western Europe.

Although economic reconstruction was paramount, the end of communism opened up divisive new questions across the former Soviet bloc. It quickly became clear that political freedom did not necessarily bring wider rights and liberties. For example, the eclipse of communism in Poland initially promised a major role for the Roman Catholic Church, but angry debate followed when, in 1990, the government ordered that children be taught the Catholic religion in school and the head of the Polish church called for an end to the "communist-inspired" separation of church and state. An effort to pass a strong anti-abortion bill in time for a visit by Pope John Paul II in 1991 caused more heated debate; public opinion polls indicated that a majority of Poles favored abortion rights.

Abortion was similarly a major issue when the former East Germany was incorporated into the Federal Republic of Germany. Abortion law had been more liberal in the communist east than in the west, and East Germany was considerably more generous in providing maternity leaves and day care. Though some East German feminists, by the mid-1980s, were accenting gender differences to enable women to pull back from the workplace, they feared that the transition to capitalism could mean diminished employment opportunities for women. A compromise was worked out on the abortion issue, but as the differences in priorities between West and East German feminists made clear, the end of communism was no panacea.

■ The Yeltsin Years in Russia, 1991–1999

In Russia, communism had far deeper roots than elsewhere in the former Soviet bloc. It had not been imposed by foreigners, and it had been in power far longer. And thus the course that Russia took after the fall of communism was especially uncertain and dramatic.

Boris Yeltsin had emerged from the anticommunist revolution a hero. As Russia's president during the first postcommunist years, he seemed a committed reformer—surely the best hope for an orderly transition to democracy and a market economy. So he enjoyed widespread support from the Western democracies, even when his policies produced a certain messiness in both the political and economic spheres.

In 1993 the elected parliament, which included many communists or former communists opposed to Yeltsin's free-market reforms, challenged the president's authority within the new political system. Yeltsin put down the challenge by force and did much of his governing by presidential decree. His approach seemed especially necessary as the anti-reform backlash by 1995 threatened a return to communism or authoritarianism. At the same time, radical nationalists played provocatively on frustrations with Russia's suddenly diminished stature in world affairs. The danger of anti-Western extremism reinforced the support that Yeltsin enjoyed in the West—even as it increased pressure at home to take an independent foreign policy line.

Although privatization proceeded rapidly in Russia—two-thirds of formerly state-owned industry had been redistributed by 1994—its fairness was disputed from the start. In certain sectors, especially natural resources and energy, the process included much insider dealing. As a result, privatization in Russia, even more than elsewhere, benefited former Communist Party functionaries, some of whom became instant multimillionaires.

By the mid-1990s, Russia had evolved a kind of "crony capitalism," with a small group of economic oligarchs exploiting the nation's resources for their own advantage. They often hid or laundered profits abroad—with Cyprus the favored destination—and they paid no taxes. To be sure, anyone could start a business, but those who did so required the protection of the oligarchs, who manipulated much of the economy through dubious banking practices and outright extortion. With government tax collection lax at best, state employees went many months at a time without being paid. Much of society depended on a barter economy. The combination of economic stringency and governmental weakness also produced a chilling increase in street crime, from mugging to auto theft.

Under the circumstances, disenchantment with reform and nostalgia for the stability of communism grew among ordinary Russians. In 1995, when Russia's second postcommunist parliamentary elections took place, the communists, led by Gennady Zyuganov° (b. 1944), won a plurality of seats, thanks to the support of workers and pensioners. Zyuganov seemed poised to win the presidency the following year. But his economic platform was riddled with contradictions, and it was hardly clear what a communist victory would have meant.

After trailing badly in the polls, Yeltsin defeated Zyuganov to win re-election in July 1996. This highly visible election was Russia's fullest experience of democracy

Zyuganov (zhoo-GAH-noff)

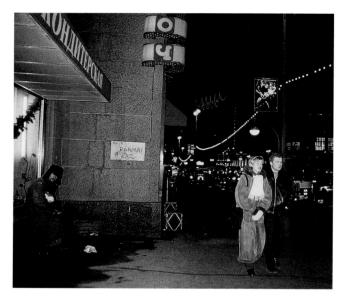

Postcommunist Russia   Images of the new extremes of wealth and poverty became commonplace as postcommunist Russia sought to join the Western mainstream.
(Star-Tass/Sovfoto/Eastfoto)

to date, and optimists saw it as a turning point in the consolidation of a democratic order. But Yeltsin survived because of the heavy financial support of the oligarchs, to whom he was increasingly beholden. Even reform-minded Yeltsinites like Anatoly Chubais° felt that working with the oligarchs was the lesser of evils, the best hope for evolution toward the Western model in light of the "red-brown" menace—the combined danger from communists and nationalists.

However, the imbalances in the economy finally produced a major financial crisis in August 1998, when a collapse of the banking system led the government to default on its domestic debt and deflate the currency. The economy recovered somewhat thereafter, but Yeltsin, in poor health and increasingly erratic, was by now deeply unpopular. Meanwhile, dozens of journalists, politicians, and business leaders were murdered gangland style, with the killers never apprehended. Particularly appalling to Russians was the death of Galina Starovoitova°, a widely admired liberal legislator and potential presidential candidate who was gunned down outside her St. Petersburg apartment in November 1998.

Shrinking every year after the fall of communism, the Russian economy had decreased by perhaps half after ten years. The results inevitably included a sharp decline in living standards and the decay of the infrastructure, in-

cluding roads, schools, and hospitals. But especially sobering were the demographic effects. Russians were dying young and having few children; the population dropped to 143 million—a decline of 6 million people in ten years.

■ Chechnya and the Rise of Vladimir Putin

As it sought to engineer the transition to democratic capitalism, the Yeltsin government had to deal with the attempted defection of Chechnya°, a small, largely Muslim republic located in the Caucasus (see Map 29.3 on page 1017). Long the thorn in Russia's control of the region, the Chechens began demanding independence after the collapse of the Soviet Union in 1991, finally provoking war with Russia in 1994. Yeltsin and Chechen leaders agreed to a compromise settlement in 1996 that was essentially a defeat for Russia, though determination of the precise status of Chechnya was postponed. But in the aftermath Chechen hard-liners oppressed the Russian minority, kidnapping and enslaving some, and even killed journalists and international aid workers. When Islamic militants began spreading the anti-Russian message from Chechnya to adjacent Dagestan, Russia renewed full-scale war with Chechnya in 1999.

This renewed confrontation made possible the rise of Vladimir Putin°, who had been virtually unknown in political circles, though he had been director of Russia's secret police. Calling for a tough stance on Chechnya, Putin was Yeltsin's choice for prime minister in 1999, and he immediately delivered on his promise to clear Dagestan of Chechen terrorists. Whereas most Russians had disliked the earlier confrontation with Chechnya, by now they had had enough—not only of Chechen defiance but also of Russia's weakness. Putin's popularity soared as he talked tough and acted tougher.

In September 1999 a mysterious series of explosions in apartment buildings in several Russian cities killed almost three hundred people. The explosions were immediately blamed on Chechen terrorists, though no conclusive evidence was presented. Some suspected—or took it for granted—that the government had planted the bombs as an excuse for renewing the war against Chechnya. In any case, the explosions inflamed Russian public opinion, buttressing support for the brutal Russian assault that left much of Chechnya, especially the capital, Grozny, in ruins in the months that followed.

Yeltsin resigned at the end of 1999, essentially to make way for Putin, who was elected president early in 2000. Some felt that Putin would prove but a tool of the oligarchical faction that had promoted his rise to power.

Chubais (choo-BYE-eess)   **Starovoitova** (STAH-ro-VOY-to-vah)   **Chechnya** (CHECH-nyah)   **Putin** (POO-tin)

His police background and harsh rhetoric also caused alarm. But for six years during the postcommunist transition, he had worked closely with the reform-oriented democratic mayor of St. Petersburg. Perhaps he had, or could develop, the stature to break the cycle of criminality and corruption that was wrecking Russia's experiment in democracy.

By the early twenty-first century, some noted signs of progress in Russia, including improved tax collection and the emergence of some undeniably well-run companies. But international observers worried that even should Putin engineer the reforms to create legitimate capitalism, his political leadership portended renewed nationalism and authoritarianism, not a more genuinely democratic culture. He represented a new generation coming into positions of power around 2000. He and his cohorts were bold and dynamic, but cynical; they sensed that it was time for postcommunist Russia to start over, without illusions, no longer bound to some Western developmental model.

Putin's inauguration in May 2000 prompted much soul-searching in the West, amid a growing sense that a precious opportunity had been lost, that it was too late to bring Russia into the Western democratic mainstream. Some, including the prominent financier and philanthropist George Soros, began asking, "Who lost Russia?" Recalling the Marshall Plan after World War II (see page 990), Soros suggested that postcommunist Russia could have become not only prosperous and democratic but a true friend of the United States—just like West Germany after Nazism. But it had not happened.

Soros blamed the conservative governments in the United States and Britain for failing to offer Russia sufficient help at the initial stages of the transition, when the scope for Western influence was great. But such influence required a proactive stance, and real money, to help establish the cultural framework, whereas these conservative Western governments, viewing the free market as a panacea, assumed that Russia could simply be turned loose. When the outcome began to entail corruption, crime, and capital flight, Western leaders tended to look the other way. Thus, by the end of the 1990s, the Russians were increasingly resentful of the West, especially the United States, whose free-market gospel was now identified with the graft and greed of the oligarchy. Some came to believe that the United States had simply been seeking to weaken Russia all along.

When Russia's communist experiment ended in failure in 1991, the world had reason to hope for a smooth transition, since Russia was now seeking to embrace the democratic capitalism of the West, not claiming to point the way beyond it. But the effort to move from communism to democratic capitalism was also an unprecedented experiment, the results of which could not be foreseen. And it was hard even to find the words for what had emerged in Russia by the early twenty-first century. Some spoke of "primitive gangster capitalism" or "infantile capitalism run amok," but even these characterizations did not quite get at it, for they still reflected the earlier assumption that Russia was on a predictable course of development.

In fact, the new Russian capitalism was not merely primitive or infantile but often sophisticated. Russia's oligarchs were not babes in the woods doing their best to behave like real capitalists; they could extort and launder money as well as anyone in history. And in doing so they revealed that under certain circumstances, even the experiment with freedom and a market economy could yield something unforeseen and brutal.

But though the juxtaposition of freedom, capitalism, and democracy was no cure-all, it had not always led to these results, so the Russian experience invited a deeper understanding of the institutional and cultural conditions necessary for a happier outcome. If democracy and a market economy were to be socially beneficial, more was required—in particular, a consensus around civic responsibility and the rule of law. People had to be willing to pay taxes. And the state had to be strong enough to collect taxes, to limit corruption, and to sustain genuinely open markets and an orderly banking system. "Negative liberty," getting government out of the way, was not sufficient. Indeed, this second Russian experiment demonstrated that a single-minded accent on negative liberty was no less utopian than Soviet Russia's single-minded insistence on central planning and command from above.

LIFESTYLES AND IDENTITIES IN THE WEST

 OSTWAR economic growth had created a secular, consumerist society throughout much of the West by the mid-1960s, establishing patterns of life that continued into the twenty-first century, when cell phones and personal computers were commonplace. Changing lifestyles brought new sources of identity—but also new challenges, as greater egalitarianism and affluence yielded new choices. Thus conflict was also commonplace, over issues from education to gender roles to the environment.

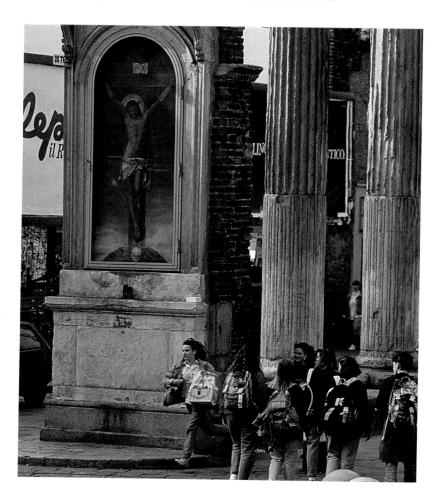

Old and New in Contemporary Europe
Especially with the transformation of Europe since World War II, new styles of life intersect with living artifacts from the past to form sometimes ironic combinations. Here, in a neighborhood in Milan, Italy, teenagers wearing blue jeans and backpacks seem oblivious to the legacies of Roman antiquity and Christianity that are prominent around them. *(© 1993 George Steinmetz)*

By the early twenty-first century, this newly secular, consumerist society had become one of the defining aspects of the West. It was what many nonwesterners hoped to achieve and sought to emulate. Thus, in part, the increased immigration from the non-Western world to the more developed countries of the West. But immigrants often retained aspects of their non-Western cultural identities, prompting new questions about diversity, assimilation, and community in the West. Moreover, important groups of nonwesterners rejected Western secular consumerism altogether. For the various forms of Islamic fundamentalism, it was nothing less than an abomination.

■ The Challenges of Affluence

The impact of rapid economic growth on the European landscape and cityscape provoked ever greater concern by the last third of the twentieth century. The number of automobiles in western Europe increased from 6 million in 1939 to 16 million by 1959 to 42 million by 1969. Almost overnight, traffic and air pollution fundamentally changed the face of Europe's old cities. In 1976 five statues that had supported the Eastern Portico of the Erectheum Temple on the Acropolis in Athens since the fifth century B.C. had to be replaced by replicas and put in a museum to save them from the rapid decay that air pollution was causing. There was talk of the "melancholy of progress" as the dimensions of the conflict between economic prosperity and the tangible monuments of Europe's history became clear.

The natural setting proved just as vulnerable. By the early 1980s acid rain had damaged one-third of the forests of West Germany, including the famous Black Forest of the southwest. Water pollution was a major problem from the Rhine to the Mediterranean to the Black Sea.

A major source of environmental concern was nuclear power, which solved certain environmental problems while posing the risk of still more serious ones. By the 1990s the West's greatest proponent of nuclear energy was France, which was getting 80 percent of its electricity from nuclear plants and was striving for 100 percent. In the United States and Britain the comparable figure was only 20 percent—and shrinking. The French boasted that they had experienced no major safety problems and that by using nuclear power they were avoiding the hazards associated with fossil fuels, from acid rain to global warming.

Much of Europe, however, moved decisively away from nuclear power, even before the Soviet nuclear accident at Chernobyl in 1986. In Germany the environmentalist Greens led demonstrations in 1977 that forced the government drastically to decrease its plans for nuclear power. In 2000, amid growing concerns about nuclear waste disposal, and with the Greens now junior partners in the socialist-led governing coalition, the German government worked out an agreement with the nuclear power industry to phase out all use of atomic energy over a twenty-year period.

Just as it posed unforeseen threats to the environment, the new affluence challenged traditional sources of personal identity in sometimes unexpected ways. Although religion remained a potent force, its reach contracted. In assuming responsibility for social welfare, the state had taken over much of the charitable role that the churches had long played. Regular church attendance dropped steadily, and popular culture revolved less around religious festivals and holy days.

Seeking to change with the times, the Catholic Church undertook a notable modernization effort under the popular Pope John XXIII (r. 1958–1963). But under his more conservative successors, the church became caught up in controversy, especially over issues such as abortion that women had forced to the fore. By the 1990s, its conservative social policy had put the Catholic Church on the defensive.

In traditionally Catholic countries like France, Italy, and Spain, many people considered themselves "cultural Catholics" and ignored church rulings they found inappropriate, especially those concerning sexuality, marriage, and gender roles. The easier availability of contraception—especially the birth control pill, widely obtainable by the late 1960s—fostered a sexual revolution that was central to the new secular lifestyle. In referenda in 1974 and 1981, two-thirds of Italians defied the Vatican by voting to legalize divorce and approve abortion rights. Even in heavily Catholic Ireland, the electorate narrowly approved the legalization of divorce in 1995, after defeating it overwhelmingly in a referendum just nine years before.

In western Europe, as in the United States, a remarkable baby boom had followed the end of the war and carried into the early 1960s. The birthrate declined rapidly thereafter, however, so that family size diminished markedly by 1990. In Italy, where changes in lifestyle accompanying the new prosperity were especially dramatic, the number of births in 1987 was barely half the number in 1964, when the postwar baby boom reached its peak. By 1995 the population was not sustaining itself in a number of European countries (see Map 30.4).

Increasing affluence and egalitarianism led to rising expectations and demands for still wider opportunity. Such pressure focused especially on access to government-supported higher education, the chief vehicle for upward mobility based on merit. In France, university admission required passing the *baccalauréat* exam at the end of secondary school. The percentage of the age group that reached this threshold grew from 1 percent in 1900 to 5 percent in 1949, then rose to 23 percent by 1974. In Italy the number of university students increased sixfold from the late 1930s to the late 1960s, partly the result of an open enrollment policy. In West Germany, higher education was still restrictive, elitist, and authoritarian at the end of the 1960s, but under pressure from the left the university system quadrupled in size by 1975.

The development of a mass-based university system produced new dilemmas. In France, demands for reform of higher education had been central to the uprising of 1968, but subsequent government efforts to decentralize the system produced widespread opposition from students and faculty by the 1980s. The government's proposal to give individual universities the right to choose their own students provoked protests and strikes, the most notable of which, in 1986, involved 400,000 demonstrators and violent clashes with police. Such opposition forced the government to abandon much of its academic reform effort.

The resistance to reform reflected the reverse side of social mobility—the considerable status anxiety among students and faculty, especially those in the humanities and social sciences. As French universities had become institutions of mass education, the market value of the state diploma had declined, as had the prestige of the faculty. For those who opposed reform, fear of loss outweighed the possibility of gain from a more competitive system. The French experience with university reform made it clear that mobility and security, equality and excellence, opportunity and merit meshed uneasily in the democratic societies of the West.

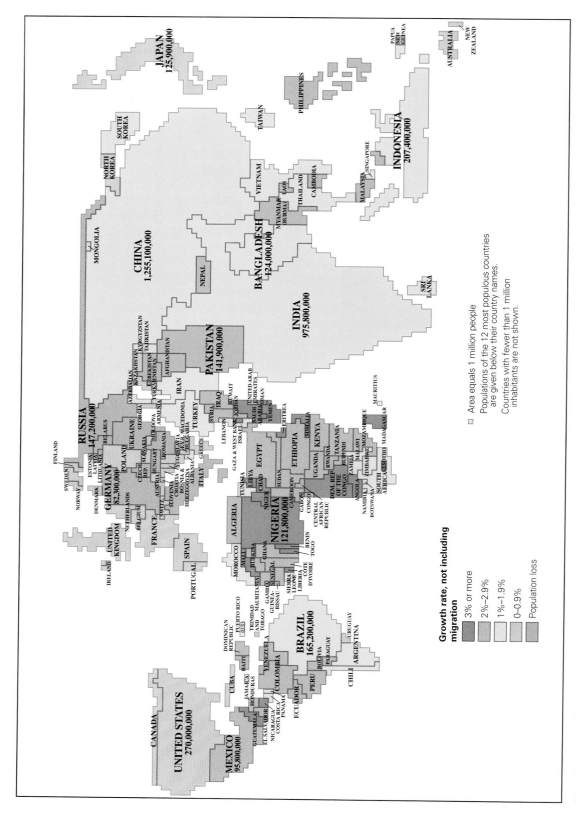

Map 30.4 **World Population Growth** This map shows both current populations and rates of population growth throughout the world. In the developed countries of the West, populations are relatively high but growing slowly, if at all. Most of the world's population growth is occurring in the less developed countries outside the West. *(National Geographic Maps 1998/10 Map Supplement, Population Growth. Used by permission of National Geographic Society.)*

■ The Significance of Gender

The feminist movement that had re-emerged in the late 1960s gradually expanded its focus beyond the quest for formal equality of opportunity. Examining subtle cultural obstacles to equality led feminists to the more general issue of gender—the way societies make sense of sexual difference and allocate social roles. There was much interest in the ideas of the French existentialist Simone de Beauvoir, who had raised in 1949 precisely the issues that came to the fore during the 1980s. (See the box "Reading Sources: Human Freedom and the Origins of a New Feminism" on page 994.) And as debate expanded from "women's issues" to gender roles, the self-understanding of men was inevitably at issue as well.

Insofar as gender roles are "constructed" by particular societies, "gendering" had always been central to the socialization process whereby young people learn how to function in their societies. But the gender roles dictated by society had usually been taken as natural, so gender was only rarely as controversial as it became in the late twentieth century. By the 1990s the gender issue was central not only to public policy but also to private relationships and to decisions about life choices in much of the Western world.

It was increasingly recognized that, at least implicitly, debates about the welfare state had often centered on gender from the beginning. After World War II, concerns about labor shortages in both East and West led to conflicting impulses in policy discussions and decisions. Should women be encouraged to work or to concentrate on rearing the children who would be the workers of the future? In western Europe immigration helped ease the labor shortage, so it was especially in the Soviet bloc that this tension was evident in shifting public policy. In 1981, for example, the Soviet Union reversed course by increasing child-care payments and adopting measures to reduce the hours that mothers worked outside the home.

The dramatic slowdown in population growth in western Europe after the mid-1960s revived fears about shortages of labor. At the same time, the feminist movement, seeking equal opportunity, sought measures such as government-subsidized day care that would enable women to combine paid employment with raising a family. By the 1970s, these impulses had come together in much of western Europe. Seeking to enhance both equality of opportunity and economic vigor, governments sought measures that would combine productive working parents with effective childhood development.

Setting the pace was France, where the government began making quality day care available to all during the 1980s. Government subsidies kept costs within reach for ordinary working families. In addition, 95 percent of French children aged 3 to 6 were enrolled in the free public nursery schools available by the early 1990s. Comparable figures for Italy (85 percent) and Germany (65 to 70 percent) were also high, although Britain lagged at 35 to 40 percent.

As some saw it, the increasing reliance on child-care at once reflected and reinforced a decline in the socializing role of the traditional family. Concerns about "latchkey children," or the decline of "quality time" for families, became prominent in the popular press. But the social changes at work were complex, and their longer-term implications for the well-being of parents, children, and society itself remained unclear. Some studies showed that an early day-care experience enhanced the socialization of children. Others cautioned against romanticizing the traditional nuclear family, which had been less prevalent than widely believed—and not always successful in any case. Moreover, the responsibilities of parenting did not have to fall primarily on mothers. The biological difference in childbearing and nursing remained, however, and even committed feminists disagreed about whether parenting entailed a special role for women and about the implications for public policy. The interrelationship of family, gender, and personal self-realization, never static, was evolving in new ways—a crucial aspect of the ongoing experiment in the West.

Though much remained contested or uncertain, the scope for greater sharing of parental responsibilities and the need for equal career opportunities across gender lines were widely recognized by the 1990s. The French model seemed to work well in combining child support with equal opportunity for paid employment. Moreover, in France social services were delivered with less paperwork and intrusiveness than elsewhere. French family policy was widely popular; the question by 2000 was simply whether France could still afford the costs it required.

The concern with gender equality brought new scrutiny to female political participation during the 1990s. Patterns had come to differ markedly even among the members of the European Union. In 2000, the percentage of women in national legislative bodies ranged from a high of 45 percent in Sweden to under 9 percent in France. Comparable figures included 30 percent in Germany and 17 percent in Britain.

The relative dearth of female officeholders in France prompted much discussion by the mid-1990s.

The outcome was a constitutional amendment in 1999 specifying the right of French women to equal access to public office. On that basis, a law passed in 2000 mandated "parity": political parties had to include women in 50 percent of their slates of nominees to maintain their full share of government campaign funding. This measure did not guarantee that women would be elected, only that voters would have the option of choosing women from among the party nominees.

The issue was discussed elsewhere as well, but by 2000 only Belgium had adopted a comparable quota system—though it mandated not one-half but one-third as the minimal share for women among party nominees. In Germany, Austria, and Spain, individual parties voluntarily established quotas for female representation on their slates of candidates.

It remained to be seen whether these innovative measures would boost the percentage of female office-holders. Moreover, whatever their eventual outcome, such measures offended some who were not otherwise conservative. In France a number of female intellectuals opposed the parity law on what they saw as humanistic and universalist grounds: in their view women had no distinctive way of thinking and did not need special protections. Some pointed out that people of North African origin were not represented at all in the French assembly. Gays objected that the parity law took one basis of human differentiation as privileged at the expense of others. But supporters countered that numerous progressive changes—universal elementary education, for example—would not have occurred without the force of law.

■ Immigration, Assimilation, and Citizenship

With immigration growing sharply in western Europe by the 1980s, questions about citizenship became politically central, giving a new twist to the interaction with the non-Western world that had helped define "the West" from the beginning. The problem grew more complex by the 1990s when refugees from various trouble spots, especially the former Yugoslavia, sought homes in new countries. The claims of immigrants and refugees forced all the Western democracies to wrestle with the meaning of citizenship. And as economic pressures grew during the 1980s and 1990s, the tensions surrounding immigrants and foreigners especially threatened the political consensus in western Europe. For example, increased immigration from disintegrating Yugoslavia

made immigration a central issue in Austria, contributing to the growing popularity, and by 1999 the controversial governmental role, of Jörg Haider's ultra-right Freedom Party.

By 1995, 11 million legal resident immigrants were living in the countries of the European Union—including, as the largest contingent, 2.6 million Turks (see Map 30.5). There were also as many as 4 million illegals. At issue throughout Europe was not only new immigration, but the status of immigrant families already resident, in many cases for several generations since World War II. Some of those raising questions were not seeking simply to preserve economic advantages by limiting access. Rather, they were concerned about community, diversity, and national identity—about what it meant to belong. Because of differences in tradition, individual countries tended to conceive the alternatives differently.

Germany had actively recruited foreign workers during the decades of economic boom and labor shortage that followed the war. By 1973 noncitizens constituted 2.6 million workers, or 11.9 percent of the work force. At first these "guest workers" were viewed not as immigrants but as temporary, almost migrant, workers. But as they remained in Germany, their family patterns came to approximate those of the rest of the country, though their birthrates were considerably higher. By the 1980s, Germany had a large and increasingly settled population of non-Germans, many of them born and educated there.

In addition, the German Federal Republic had adopted a generous asylum law in an effort to atone for the crimes of the Nazi period. With the turmoil surrounding the end of communism in the Soviet bloc, the newly reunified Germany found sixty thousand new arrivals seeking asylum every month by 1993. At that point Germany had a large foreign population of 6.4 million.

The law governing citizenship for immigrants and their descendants had originated in 1913 and reflected a long-standing German assumption that citizenship presupposed German ethnicity—or at least full assimilation. Thus ethnic Germans—over a million of whom moved to Germany from the former Soviet bloc between 1988 and 1991—were immediately accorded German citizenship. But the many Turks, for example, who had been born in Germany could not become citizens. Precisely because citizenship entailed full assimilation, some Germans opposed that status for such "foreigners" out of respect for cultural diversity.

But as the new wave of immigration from the east swelled the "foreign" population in Germany, more mundane motives came to the fore. Germans subject to economic pressures felt that immigrants and asylum-seekers were getting a better deal than ordinary citizens such as themselves. Resentments simmered, and sometimes boiled over. Two thousand attacks on foreigners, some of them fatal, were reported in 1992 alone. As reaction against refugees and foreign workers grew, the German parliament voted in 1993 to restrict the right of asylum.

But questions of immigration and citizenship remained politically central. After Helmut Kohl's conservatives lost the parliamentary elections in 1998, the new governing coalition of Socialists and Greens promptly voted, in 1999, to shelve the 1913 law. Citizenship was now available to almost everyone born in Germany or whose parents who had resided and worked in Germany for at least eight years. Still, controversy and even violence continued. During 2000, right-wing attacks on foreigners and synagogues reached levels not seen since the early 1990s. On November 9, the anniversary of the Crystal Night pogrom of 1938 and several other major events in recent German history, 200,000 Germans marched in Berlin to protest the violence and demand equal rights.

Controversy also raged in France by the 1980s as the country attracted rising numbers of immigrants, especially from Algeria and the other Islamic countries of North Africa. French law accorded citizenship automatically to second-generation immigrants, assuming that these offspring would be readily assimilated. But critics such as Jean-Marie LePen, leader of the right-wing National Front, charged that many recent immigrants did not want to assimilate. Whereas the French left defended cultural diversity and its compatibility with citizenship, the right complained that citizenship was being devalued as a mere convenience, requiring no real commitment to the national community. This difference in perspective helps explain the contentious "affair of the scarves" that gripped France in 1989.

Although some remained nervous about immigrants from outside countries, the fifteen members of the European Union were growing ever more comfortable with the free movements of EU-member peoples across national borders. Indeed, changes in EU rules during the 1990s made dual citizenship easier for the Union's increasingly mobile population. As many began to feel themselves citizens of the European Union itself, even notions of "foreign" began to change.

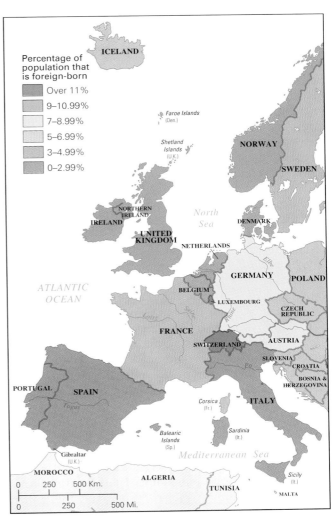

Map 30.5   Foreign-Born Population in Western Europe
Increasing immigration prompted resentment against foreigners and concerns about assimilation in much of western Europe during the 1980s and 1990s. This map indicates the percentage of the population that was foreign-born in each of the countries of western Europe as of 1997.   (*Source:* New York Times, *September 24, 2000. Copyright © 2000 by the New York Times Co. Reprinted by permission.*)

■ Subnational and Supranational Identities

The growing prominence of the supranational EU, and doubts about the import of national politics, nourished a renewed premium on subnational identities in such distinctive European regions as Flanders, Corsica, Scotland, and Catalonia. Flemings and Corsicans, Scots and Catalans actively sought to preserve some measure of their distinct cultures and languages in the face of standardization pressures stemming from globalization, Americanization, or even the EU itself. In Britain the Labour government of Tony Blair fostered the "devolution" of powers from the central government in London to Scottish and Welsh assemblies by 2000. There was a growing recognition that the existing nations were not natural, given, but largely historical constructions. But the resulting weakening of national loyalties could lead to political fragmentation. The breakup of Yugoslavia afforded a particularly tragic example.

Much less dramatic, but also instructive, was the example of Italy, whose movement for national unification had drawn the enthusiasm of the world in the nineteenth century (see pages 745–750). But by the 1990s, disillusionment with national politics made many Italians particularly eager to embrace the EU, while others turned in the other direction, renewing their identification with region or locality. Resentful of the national government's ties to the less prosperous south, a new political movement, the Northern League, pushed for the north to break from Italy and become an independent state. Though some doubted the seriousness of such separatism, the Northern League's persistent strength suggested that "Italian" was becoming less important as a basis of individual identity.

National identities were weakening in much of Europe partly because a generally unspoken, mostly friendly, rivalry with the United States led Europeans increasingly to think of themselves *as* European, rather than some particular nationality. The broadly cultural relationship between western Europe and the United States had been tricky since World War II. For decades the Europeans seemed to have no choice but to follow the U.S. lead. But such subservience was troubling, so a kind of love-hate relationship with the United States had developed in western Europe.

Even after Europe's postwar economic recovery, the United States was clearly setting the pace in high-technology industries, prompting renewed concerns by the 1960s that Europe was becoming a mere economic satellite of the United States. Europe seemed to be caught in a dilemma: to retain its distinctiveness over the long term, it had to become more competitive—which apparently meant becoming more like America in the short term. The French writer Jean-Jacques Servan-Schreiber° (b. 1924) made this case in 1967 in *The American Challenge,* the classic statement of postwar Europe's ambivalent attitude toward Americanization.

Haunted by the decline of earlier civilizations, Servan-Schreiber warned that if Europeans failed to become sufficiently dynamic to compete with the Americans, Europe would gradually sink into decadence without ever understanding why it had happened.

By the 1980s much of western Europe had caught up with the United States in standard of living, and the western Europeans set the pace in confronting some of the new problems that resulted from ongoing socioeconomic change. The French day-care system was one example. The size of the EU economy was about equal to that of the United States by the end of the 1990s, and the Europeans proved quite competitive in certain fields. For example, Europe's Airbus did well in head-to-head competition with American aircraft manufacturer Boeing.

But by the 1990s, as America assumed a decisive lead in the new information technology, and as the American model came to seem better at fostering innovation and competitiveness, the western Europeans again worried about falling behind, even as they also sought to preserve European distinctiveness in the face of Americanization. The dilemma that Servan-Schreiber had noted in the 1960s was still very much at issue.

In light of the countervailing pressures at work, the European relationship with America was bound to remain complex. By the late 1980s consumerism and the widening impact of American popular culture—from blue jeans and American TV to shopping malls and theme parks—suggested a growing homogenization in the capitalist democracies. A Euro-Disneyland opened in France in 1992 and, after a slow start, proved increasingly popular. Though they adopted some European ways, even serving beer and wine, American fast-food chains like McDonald's satisfied hungry locals in cities all over Europe.

But as the fall of communism both ended the division of Europe and removed the common adversary, the ties that had helped bind western Europe to the United States inevitably loosened. In 2000 France charged that the United States was using its satellite surveillance capacity, still in place from the cold war, for industrial espionage to the disadvantage of European firms.

Even what counted as "the West" became more uncertain. Especially when the East Asian economies were booming, America liked to see itself as a Pacific power. Moreover, Americans began stressing the multiple sources of their culture: it was not necessarily superior, but neither was it simply an offshoot of European culture. This reorientation was to place less emphasis on the common "Western heritage." Though they were trading partners, Europe and America were also economic

---

Servan-Schreiber (SAIR-vahn–SHRY-bay)

and cultural rivals, and they might increasingly drift apart. In this continuing experiment, even something so apparently solid as "the Western Alliance" or "the Atlantic orientation" was not cut in stone.

THE WEST IN A GLOBAL AGE

Y the early twenty-first century, the West was part of a world that, in one sense, was dramatically less Eurocentric than it had been a century before, when European imperialism was at its peak. Events in the West competed for attention with the India-Pakistan nuclear rivalry, OPEC oil prices, Chinese trade issues, or the struggle against warlords in parts of Africa. Decisions vitally affecting, or demanding the response of, the industrialized countries of the West might be made anywhere. A planetary culture, a threatened environment, an interdependent economy, and an increasing sense of international responsibility required people to think in global terms as never before.

■ Differentiation and Collaboration in the "Global Village"

By the last decades of the twentieth century, as information and capital flowed instantaneously, a kind of global culture was beginning to emerge for the first time. But as cultural contact increased, it took diverse forms. "Americanization," appealing to some, appalling to others, made products like Coca-Cola and McDonald's burgers and fries familiar worldwide and nourished a common urban youth style. But many spheres, from food to popular music, were marked by fusion, as elements from diverse cultures interpenetrated and enriched each other. At the same time, there was also increasing appreciation of diversity. The British tourist board declared Indian curry to be the official British dish, testimony to the number of Indian restaurants in Britain—itself testimony to the enduring cultural interchange between Britain and its former colony. But even as cultural contact deepened and talk of a single "global village" became commonplace, cultural boundaries loomed larger in some respects—as the controversy in France over the Islamic headscarves makes clear.

Cultural convergence stemmed especially from the process known as modernization, or "Westernization," which entailed, above all, participation in the competitive global market economy that had spread from Europe. Beginning especially in the 1970s, western Europe

and North America encountered formidable economic competition first from Japan, and later from other countries of the East Asian Pacific rim. What increasingly mattered, from this perspective, was the difference between the industrialized, relatively affluent "North" and the less developed "South," including much of Africa, Latin America, southern Asia, and the Middle East.

Indeed, "North-South" tensions, resulting from demographic and economic patterns, quickly moved to center stage to replace the East-West tensions that had ended with the cold war. World population reached 6 billion in 1999, having more than doubled in forty years. This was the fastest rate of world population growth ever, and by the 1990s virtually all of the growth was in Africa, Asia, and Latin America. The population of Europe was growing at only 0.2 percent per year (see Map 30.4).

As the population exploded in the less developed world, the gap between rich and poor nations widened. One aspect, producing much concern by 2000, was the growing "digital divide"—the disparity in access to the computing and Internet technologies that seemed essential to compete in the global economy. New technologies were not bridging but widening the gap between the haves and the have-nots.

At the same time, growing concern with the global environment intensified the sense of world interdependence and pointed to the need for international cooperation. Such problems as global warming, the loss of biodiversity, and the deterioration of the ozone layer were inherently supranational in scope. Yet environmental concerns complicated relations between the industrialized nations and the rest of the world. Countries seeking to industrialize encountered environmental constraints that had not been at issue when the West industrialized. The challenge for the West was to foster protection of the environment in poorer regions of the globe without imposing unfair limitations on economic growth.

■ The Controversy over Economic Globalization

A variety of supranational entities, apart from the European Union, wielded increasing clout by the late twentieth century, making decisions that deeply affected the lives of ordinary people. Most obvious were multinational corporations, but the World Bank and the International Monetary Fund (IMF) also played increasingly visible—and controversial—roles. Developing from the Bretton Woods agreement near the end of World War II (see page 976), these institutions had long drawn praise for helping to keep the world economy stable and growing. Also central, especially in promoting free trade, was the World Trade Organization (WTO), which grew from a multilateral trade agreement in 1947. These organizations were major vehicles for the influence of the wealthy nations, centered in the West, on those from eastern Europe to southern Africa that were trying to catch up. In that role they often swayed domestic policies—by refusing, for example, to lend to countries spending heavily on armaments.

During the 1990s these agencies became the focal points for growing concerns about the new economic globalization—its costs and the distribution of its benefits. Meetings of the WTO in Seattle in 1999 and of the World Bank and IMF in Washington in 2000 drew large demonstrations. Those protesting were often naive about economics and the uses of free trade. But their protests raised genuine questions about wages, working conditions, environmental impact, and international financial arrangements that were not always adequately addressed in the prevailing economic models.

Should a consumer in the United States be free to purchase a cheaper garment made by low-wage workers in Honduras or Bangladesh? Or should that consumer have to pay more to protect the jobs of American workers? Perhaps buying the cheaper product was to support sweatshop conditions and pollution in the interests of multinational corporations and international bankers. But those workers in Honduras or Bangladesh might be eager for such jobs, in light of the even less fortunate alternatives available. It could be argued that it was up to consumers to decide, but even when such choices were

available, consumers rarely had the information to know what they were choosing, how conditions of labor had affected price.

The question was whether it made sense to foster free trade and globalization without greater uniformity in social and environmental policy. In the absence of common standards, free trade was arguably not fair trade. But lines were not easily drawn, and these issues, playing on the North-South divide, promised to remain central—and especially contentious.

Prominent among European critics of globalization by the early twenty-first century was José Bové, the outspoken leader of France's small farmers. When he stood trial in 2000 for vandalizing a McDonald's restaurant, thirty thousand turned up to demonstrate in his support. His book *The World Is Not for Sale* became a bestseller at the same time.

Typically equating globalization with Americanization, Bové articulated a widespread concern for French distinctiveness and identity in the face of U.S. "cultural imperialism." France seemed increasingly overrun with American films, television, music, even novels in French translation. Such uneasiness over diversity and conformity was more pronounced in Latin and southern Europe than in Britain and the North. The Italian film industry, among the most innovative and important in the world for several decades after the war, had largely disappeared by 2000.

Early in 2001, a serious outbreak of foot-and-mouth disease, a highly contagious illness affecting especially

Protesting Globalization at McDonald's
Led by José Bové's association of small farmers, protesters vandalize a McDonald's restaurant in southern France in August 1999. Bové's trial a year later stimulated comparable protests. The American fast-food chain had come to symbolize the two-sided force of globalization and Americanization.
(Frances/Markow/Corbis Sygma)

cows, pigs, and sheep, spread throughout Britain and even to other EU countries. Much of the rest of the world banned livestock imports from the EU. This crisis, too, dramatized the reverse side of the new interconnectedness in a global world. Capital and information flowed more quickly than ever across national borders, but so could epidemic diseases.

■ The West and the Question of Global Responsibility

If people were forced to think in global terms as never before, how far did global responsibility extend in a world that remained divided into sovereign nation-states? The series of brutal, sometimes genocidal conflicts from Yugoslavia to Rwanda to Chechnya to East Timor that helped to define the 1990s fostered a growing sense of collective responsibility in what was increasingly referred to as "the international community." Amorphous though it was, that entity, or community, seemed to take on real existence by the end of the decade. But who or what constituted it, and the conditions under which it should act, remained uncertain.

Of course a prominent international organization was already in place—the United Nations, the fruit of the hopes for a better world in light of World War II. But though it achieved significant successes in such areas as nutrition, health, and education, the UN frequently found difficulty when called on to restore or maintain peace. Its forces were often overburdened as they took on the sometimes incompatible objectives of peacekeeping and humanitarian relief—sometimes in areas where there was no real peace to keep. And its members, especially its leaders on the Security Council, were often divided about what should be done. When Serbs in a UN "safe area" around Srebrenica°, in Bosnia, massacred as many as twenty thousand people in 1995, torturing or burying alive a number of the victims, the Security Council refused the UN secretary-general's pleas for additional troops.

But the UN remained an important, or potentially important, player even as long-standing questions of national sovereignty continued to compromise its ability to act. Ad hoc UN war crimes tribunals dealt with atrocities in the Balkans and in Rwanda, and in 1998 the UN established a permanent international criminal court in The Hague. Its charge was to bring to justice those responsible for war crimes or crimes against humanity. While an overwhelming majority—120 nations—voted in favor of

Diseases and Borders   The outbreak of foot-and-mouth disease early in 2001 raised questions about globalization and strained relations within the European Union. Here a Spanish border official sprays disinfectant on the wheels of a French truck in March 2001, as part of the European effort to keep the disease from spreading.   *(Reuters/STR/Archive Photos)*

the measure, seven opposed it, including the United States, China, Israel, Iraq, and Libya. As efforts to establish the court followed, the United States sought an exemption for itself because it worried that American peacekeepers might be especially tempting targets for false accusations of war crimes. Such concerns were not groundless, and they indicated the unique problems the United States faced as the world's undisputed superpower. But these U.S. reservations also indicated how hard it was to come to meaningful international agreement in light of the different circumstances the nations of the world faced.

An international tribunal, based in The Hague, was already dealing with the crimes against humanity that had marked the Yugoslav wars of the 1990s. Established in 1993, the court proved more aggressive than expected, but it had difficulty apprehending major figures among the accused. The most conspicuous was Slobodon Milo-

---

Srebrenica (shreb-reh-NEET-sah)

The Question of Western Responsibility

As clashes between warlords and peacekeepers became prominent during the 1990s, some called for a more coherent and effective Western role, whereas others worried that the West was becoming overextended. Brian Urquhart, born in Britain in 1919, was long a senior official of the United Nations. Here he offers a pointed analysis of the issues facing the Western-led "international community" by the turn of the century.

What is to be done when hundreds of thousands of people in a hitherto little-known region of the world are hounded from their homes, massacred, or starved to death in a brutal civil war, or even in a deliberate act of genocide? To our credit, we no longer turn away from the face of evil, but we still don't know how to control it. As the new century dawns, one of the biggest problems for international organizations and their member governments is to learn how to react to the great human emergencies that still seem to occur regularly in many parts of the world. . . .

The so-called "international community" is anything but a constitutional system. As far as it is organized at all, it is an institutional arrangement, unpredictable and slow to act. It usually responds only when disaster has already struck and when its members, usually in the UN Security Council, can agree to take action. Even then, since the UN has no standing forces or substantial resources of its own, its action, if it can be agreed upon, is likely to be too little and too late.

In his opening address to the General Assembly on September 20, 1999, Secretary-General Kofi Annan made an impassioned plea for UN intervention in cases of gross violations of human rights. The reactions of governments to Annan's remarks showed very clearly how far the world still has to go before evil can be systematically dealt with internationally. Most comments on Annan's speech were critical and stressed the paramount importance of national sovereignty; some even saw humanitarian intervention as a cloak for American or Western hegemony or neocolonialism. Only a small minority of Western countries supported Sweden's position that the collective conscience of mankind demands action.

A new idea of "human security" has now taken its place alongside the much older concept of "international peace and security." It has emerged as the result of a vaguely defined and fitful international conscience on the part of the liberal democracies, and it has been encouraged both by the prodigious growth of nongovernmental organizations and by the communications revolution. However, the rules and the means for protecting human security are still tentative and controversial, not least because virtually any situation threatening human security is likely to raise questions of national sovereignty. No government wants to set up a system which may, at some point in the future, be invoked against itself.

. . . Humanitarian action as it emerged in the aftermath of World War II was principally concerned with refugee resettlement and the reconstruction of war-shattered countries. In those innocent days, humanitarian relief was seen as a nonpolitical activity, dictated by the needs of the afflicted and by the resources and expertise available to meet them. . . . That relatively nonpolitical concept of humanitarianism has come to a brutal end with the rising importance of warlords and the conflicts within states of the post–cold war world. The international sponsors of humanitarian aid are no longer dealing with more or less responsible governments. . . .

. . . In the new situation of 1990s peacekeeping, humanitarian assistance still saved hundreds of thousands of lives but it could also provide warlords with the means to continue and expand the conflict. . . .

. . . "The whole aid community has been overtaken by a new reality," the IRC [International Rescue Committee] stated. "Humanitarianism has become a resource . . . and people are manipulating it as never before. Sometimes we just shouldn't show up for a disaster." . . .

In the 1990s, humanitarian workers were in the front line as never before and were increasingly dealing with factions, warlords, and thugs who had no respect for international personnel or organizations. For the first time, aid workers were more at risk than military forces, and the death toll rose alarmingly all over the world.

Source: Brian Urquhart, "In the Name of Humanity," *The New York Review of Books,* April 27, 2000, pp. 19–21.

sevic himself, indicted in 1999 while still president of what remained of Yugoslavia. After defeating Milosevic for president in 2000, Vojislav Kostunica insisted that the Yugoslavs would make their own accounting with Milosevic and other top officials. But the tribunal's tireless chief prosecutor, Carla Del Ponte, finally prevailed in June 2001, when Milosevic was extradited to stand trial in The Hague. The major Western powers had forced the Yugoslavs' hand by tying aid for economic reconstruction to cooperation with the tribunal.

Whatever its center of gravity, the international community rested on the commitment and initiative of the rich Western countries, because they had the means to act globally, in response to natural or human-made disasters. Supplementing the efforts of governments was a network of nongovernmental organizations (NGOs), such as the Red Cross, Amnesty International, and Doctors Without Borders, that had gradually emerged to deal with humanitarian relief or human rights issues. Collectively they were a major presence on the international scene by the dawn of the twenty-first century—and central to the international community.

A succession of disasters challenged that community during the 1990s, as ethnic conflict erupted and tyrants terrorized civilian populations in hot spots around the world. Concurrent with the ongoing tragedies in Chechnya and the former Yugoslavia, a series of crises erupted in Africa—natural disasters from famine to flooding, but also civil wars that spawned ethnic massacre, slave trading, and rule by violent warlords. Such horrors spawned an increasing sense by the later 1990s that it was up to the Western-led international community to "do something." But do what—and at what cost? What aims were realistic?

Corruption and theft bedeviled efforts to get even nonpolitical humanitarian aid to the ordinary people who become victims. There was often no responsible government to deal with. Instead, those seeking to provide aid or maintain peace were forced to deal with semi-criminal elements who diverted humanitarian aid to buy weapons and who took peacekeepers and aid workers hostage—or even killed them. In 1994, for the first time, more UN civilian aid workers (twenty-four) than peacekeeping soldiers were killed in the line of duty. And the death toll for aid workers rose rapidly during the decade. In Chechnya a widely admired American relief worker, Fred Cuny, disappeared in 1995.

The rich countries of the West felt a responsibility to deal with such situations, but they were reluctant to supply the means, to take the risks, even to suffer the casualties necessary to do so effectively. Still, how could the leaders of those nations ask for such sacrifice in sit-

uations that perhaps could not be brought under control—at least not without permanent occupation and a return to semi-colonial status? As one crisis followed another, those in the West felt a sense of overload. Some even began to suggest that half-measures only made things worse, so perhaps it was better to stay away altogether. Such was "the new world order" that had emerged in the decade after the end of the cold war. (See the box "Reading Sources: The Question of Western Responsibility.")

■ Old and New, Modern and Beyond

Although the shadow of fascism and war remained, Europe had experienced a radical transformation in the half-century since World War II, a transformation that in some ways had cut Europeans off from their own tradition. Tangible reminders of Europe's distinctive past survived, but the growing "heritage industry" in Britain and elsewhere suggested that they were merely commodities to be packaged like any other. At the same time, Europe's increasingly uncertain, even ironic relationship to its own tradition, including its difficult recent past, found striking expression in architecture and painting by the last decades of the twentieth century.

During the first two decades after World War II, modernist architecture, turning from tradition to embrace the modern industrial age, had triumphed at last, transforming cities throughout the world. By the 1980s, however, architects were turning from modernism to postmodernism, a glitzy way of building with ambiguous or ironic references to a tradition that was still present, even if those living within it were not quite sure what to make of it.

This uneasy contemporary relationship with the past, especially the traumatic past of the earlier twentieth century, took more pointed form in the neoexpressionist painting prominent in Germany and Italy by the 1980s. For a generation after World War II, German artists, especially, had been unsure of their direction—or had settled for following the latest fashion from New York. But by the late 1960s, the new generation that included such artists as the German Anselm Kiefer (b. 1945) and the Italian Sandro Chia (b. 1946) sought to confront the recent past—and thus the meaning of a tradition that now included fascism, total war, and the Holocaust. Through art, they felt, we might deepen our relationship with our own recent history. Kiefer and Chia created striking images, but they offered no clear message. Rather, they conveyed the paradox and ambiguity that we encounter as we engage our multifaceted, seemingly contradictory cultural tradition.

Kiefer: Osiris and Isis   The German artist Anselm Kiefer combined unusual materials to create haunting images that often suggested the horrors of recent history. In this work from 1985–1987, the interpenetrating layers of human culture include images of ruin and death, hope and resurrection.   *(Anselm Kiefer, Osiris und Isis, 1985–87. Mixed media on canvas, 150" × 220½" × 6½". San Francisco Museum of Modern Art. Purchased through a gift of Jean Stein by exchange, the Mrs. Paul L. Wattis Fund, and the Doris and Don Fisher Fund. Photo: Ben Blackwell)*

CONCLUSION: LEARNING FROM WESTERN CIVILIZATION IN A POSTMODERN WORLD

I N what sense was that tradition still to be understood as "Western" by the early twenty-first century, when talk of globalization and cultural fusion was rampant? Was "the West" still a meaningful category at all?

The geographical contours of Western civilization had never been precise, and the center of gravity of "the West" had shifted many times. Moreover, the West had always been involved in dynamic interaction with others, not closed and self-contained. But its contours had become especially uncertain with the dramatic changes that followed World War II. The cold war had split Europe, and western Europe had found itself dependent on the United States. So the United States became, in one sense, the new center of the West, though the Soviet Union offered an alternative, based on different strands of the Western tradition. At the same time, European colonial networks unraveled, leaving "Westernization" as a very mixed legacy in formerly colonial areas.

By the 1990s, Europe was reuniting and the Soviet-style alternative stood discredited. Meanwhile, the United States was considering itself more multicultural and less European. The accelerating sense of globalization bred deeper uncertainty about what was specifically Western. In one sense, to be sure, globalization essentially *meant* Westernization to many advocates and critics alike. But what did that process entail, and what did it say about the meaning of the Western tradition by the early twenty-first century?

Led by businessmen in conservative Western dress, postwar Japan developed the world's second largest economy. Skyscrapers in booming Asian cities proved indistinguishable from skyscrapers in the West. Cultural distinctions remained, bound up with differences in history and memory, in heroes and villains, in art, even in values.

In parts of the non-Western world the successes of "Westernization," especially the global reach of the United States, produced resentment and hostility as well as emulation. Fed partly by such resentments, an unprecedented terrorist attack shook the United States on September 11, 2001. Hijackers seized four large airliners, crashing one into each of the towers of the World Trade Center in New York City and another into the Pentagon, just outside Washington. The World Trade Center crashes collapsed both towers, which had been among the world's most visible landmarks. The concerted attack claimed the lives of 3,300 people, from eighty-two countries.

The United States proclaimed the attack an act of war, and the NATO alliance invoked Article 5 for the first time: the attack on one of its members would be considered an attack against all. German chancellor Schröder called the assault "a declaration of war upon the whole civilized world." But at issue was a new kind of war against a dispersed and barely visible enemy. U.S. leaders promptly assigned responsibility to al Qaeda, an international terrorist network led by the wealthy Saudi Arab Osama bin Laden, who was living in exile in Afghanistan. There he was protected by the Taliban regime, whose extreme, radically fundamentalist version of Islam he shared in certain respects.

When the United States initiated military action against the Taliban regime, bin Laden and his allies claimed it was a war against Islam. But the U.S. effort to root out the terrorist network won support even from much of the Islamic world, and several weeks of U.S. bombing enabled Afghan opposition forces to oust the Taliban and rout al Qaeda. Still, the attack on the U.S. dramatized the fissures in the West's relations with the non-Western world. Whatever its sources, anti-Western and especially anti-American sentiment had given rise to a terroristic mindset that seemed willing to unleash violence and suffering without limit. Terrorist networks often took root under the aegis of warlords in areas torn by civil strife. Unlikely to be eradicated by military force alone, terrorism seemed to pose an ongoing threat to Western security and promised to complicate the West's relations with the non-Western world.

During the last third of the twentieth century, bitter debate erupted in the West over the significance of Western civilization—even its legitimacy as a concept. Some

World Trade Center, New York, September 11, 2001
(Chao Soi Cheong/AP)

critics highlighted the geographical imprecision of "the West" and claimed that the words *Western* and *civilization* had been juxtaposed simply to justify conquest and domination. Even among those who recognized a distinctive Western cultural tradition, some found it elitist and limiting. In their view, Western culture had defined itself around a group of artifacts—writings, paintings, monuments—that reflected the experience of a very restricted circle.

Others countered that imperialism and assumptions of superiority had not been confined to the West. Moreover, they continued, the West had been the source of ideas—the "rights of man," the scope for eliminating exploitation—that were now being eagerly embraced in the non-Western world. Even charges of cultural elitism stemmed from a democratic impulse that had itself grown from within the Western tradition. By the last decades of the twentieth century, that impulse was prompting historians to focus on ordinary people and cultural interpreters to expand the "canon"—the body of works considered worthy of our attention.

Questions about the Western tradition and its contemporary relevance were bound up with the advent of *postmodernism,* a term widely used by the early 1990s for a cultural orientation that had been gathering force for decades. Postmodernists question claims of certainty, objective truth, and intrinsic meaning in language,

⊕ G L O B A L   E N C O U N T E R S

The Case of "Orientalism"

In his influential book Orientalism, *published in 1978, the Palestinian-American scholar Edward Said explored the process through which Westerners had constructed the "Middle East"—as different from the West. Though critical of the West, Said appealed to our common humanity in an effort to overcome the ongoing tendency, which was not confined to the West, to understand oneself as superior by stereotyping others. In the final analysis, he suggested, we all need to learn from one another.*

The Orient is not only adjacent to Europe; it is also the place of Europe's greatest and richest and oldest colonies, the source of its civilizations and languages, its cultural contestant, and one of its deepest and most recurring images of the Other. In addition, the Orient has helped to define Europe (or the West) as its contrasting image, idea, personality, experience. . . .

. . . The relationship between Occident and Orient is a relationship of power, of domination, of varying degrees of a complex hegemony. . . . There is very little consent to be found, for example, in the fact that Flaubert's encounter with an Egyptian courtesan produced a widely influential model of the Oriental woman; she never spoke of herself, she never represented her emotions, presence, or history. *He* spoke for and represented her. He was foreign, comparatively wealthy, male, and these were historical facts of domination that allowed him not only to possess Kuchuk Hanem physically but to speak for her and tell his readers in what way she was "typically Oriental." . . .

. . . [T]here is no avoiding the fact that even if we disregard the Orientalist distinctions between "them" and "us," a powerful series of political and ultimately ideological realities inform scholarship today. No one can escape dealing with, if not the East/West division, then the North/South one, the have/have-not one, the imperialist/anti-imperialist one, the white/colored one. We cannot get around them all by pretending they do not exist; on the contrary, contemporary Orientalism teaches us a great

deal about the intellectual dishonesty of dissembling on that score, the result of which is to intensify the divisions and make them both vicious and permanent. Yet an openly polemical and right-minded "progressive" scholarship can very easily degenerate into dogmatic slumber, a prospect that is not edifying either.

. . . [E]nough is being done today in the human sciences to provide the contemporary scholar with insights, methods, and ideas that could dispense with racial, ideological, and imperialist stereotypes of the sort provided during its historical ascendancy by Orientalism. I consider Orientalism's failure to have been a human as much as an intellectual one; for in having to take up a position of irreducible opposition to a region of the world it considered alien to its own, Orientalism failed to identify with human experience, failed also to see it as human experience. . . . I hope to have shown my reader that the answer to Orientalism is not Occidentalism. No former "Oriental" will be comforted by the thought that having been an Oriental himself he is likely—too likely—to study new "Orientals"—or "Occidentals"—of his own making. If the knowledge of Orientalism has any meaning, it is in being a reminder of the seductive degradation of knowledge, of any knowledge, anywhere, at any time. Now perhaps more than before.

Source: Edward W. Said, *Orientalism* (New York: Random House, Vintage, 1979), pp. 1–2, 4–8, 327–328.

in works of art, and ultimately in all cultural expressions. From their perspective, such claims are assertions of privilege in what is essentially a political struggle for power—the power to set the wider social agenda. Postmodernism reflected a certain conception of what *modernism* had meant, even a sense that modernism had defined an era that was now ending. But what was it that was ending—and how was it bound up with the debate over Western civilization?

Postmodernism emerged partly as confidence in the scope for a neutral, objective social science began to decline during the 1960s. That confidence had reflected the belief in reason that had emerged from the Scientific Revolution and the Enlightenment. Reason had seemed universal, not limited to any particular culture, and it was assumed to be applicable to the human as well as the natural world.

To apply reason seemed "modern," and the West, having progressed by applying reason, had long understood itself to be in the forefront of modernity. Everyone else was scrambling to catch up through the universal process of modernization or Westernization. Such was the "master narrative" through which the West had understood its place in the world as it set the agenda during the modern era. It had indeed been that conception of the world, and the sense of superiority underlying it, that had seemed to justify Western imperialism.

Even as Westernization continued during the later twentieth century, Western thinkers retreated from this long-standing master narrative. There was no question that capitalism had spread from Europe, but the West was not necessarily the model, the standard of development. Indeed, a growing interest in the non-Western world and an increasing respect for its diverse traditions marked Western culture during the last quarter of the twentieth century. At the same time, Edward Said°, a scholar of Palestinian origin teaching in the United States, showed how Western images of the non-Western world had been constructed, and become stereotypes, reinforcing assumptions of Western superiority. (See the box "Global Encounters: The Case of 'Orientalism.'")

Especially in the United States, the postmodernist reaction led by the 1980s to the vogue of the French philosopher and historian Michel Foucault° (1926–1984), who showed that the power to specify what counts as knowledge was the key to social or political power. Since all knowledge was suspect, Foucault's accents invited

mistrust and disruption. An array of equally innovative thinkers, from the German Jürgen Habermas to the American Richard Rorty, sought a more constructive orientation based on a renewed, no longer arrogant understanding of Western traditions, including the place of reason and democracy.

For those embracing this more constructive approach, the point was not to celebrate Western civilization but simply to understand it—as the framework that continued to shape the West and, less directly, the world. That tradition included much that might be criticized, and its present outcome entailed much that might be changed. Habermas, in particular, was a persistent and often radical critic of what he saw as the disparity between Western democratic ideals and contemporary social and political practices. But effective criticism had to rest on free inquiry and rational understanding, as opposed to prejudice or wishful thinking. The invitation to think freely about the Western tradition, to criticize and change it, rested on precisely that tradition; indeed, the scope for such criticism and change had been central to the Western belief in reason. That openness remained perhaps the West's most fundamental legacy. The debate over Western civilization was itself testimony to the openness and freedom of that tradition.

As the twenty-first century began, concerns about diversity and assimilation throughout the West suggested that controversy would continue over the significance of the Western tradition. There seemed ever less agreement about what an educated Westerner should know—about the West, or about the other cultures of the world. Within the framework of globalization, what was best understood as "Westernization," as opposed to cultural fusion, or ongoing diversity? Insofar as the Western element could be pinpointed, was it liberating or did it involve cultural imperialism and renewed exploitation?

The continuing debate made it clear that historical study had become more relevant than ever in this era of rapid cultural cross-fertilization. But, not surprisingly, it had also become more contested, as the ultimate court of appeal. The danger was that historical inquiry would become too politicized to allow us genuinely to learn from it. Such learning is crucial not to enable us to celebrate "who we are," but to deepen our understanding, even to make us more self-critical. As we continue the experiment, we may thereby act more effectively—and possibly create a better future.

Said (sy-EED)   **Foucault** (foo-KOH)

(continued on page 1064)

The Euro

Since ancient times, cities and empires have minted coins to facilitate commerce and trade. Over time, images of gods and symbolic plants and animals gave way to stylized depictions of rulers. The study of coins—numismatics—has long provided insights into how rulers saw themselves and how they displayed their power at home and abroad.

When national banks and governments took over the production of paper money from commercial banks in the nineteenth and twentieth centuries, states gained a much bigger canvas on which to display their national symbols. Monarchies typically featured the current ruler on the face of the note, while republics picked a gallery of national heroes. Take a couple of bills out of your pocket, and you will see this is still the case in North America today: in the United States, the bills honor presidents and the first secretary of the Treasury, Alexander Hamilton. In Canada, Queen Elizabeth II still graces the $20 bill.

In 1991 member countries of the European Union agreed at Maastricht to the creation of a unified currency, to be called the *euro*, to replace their existing currencies (see page 1029). A competition was launched to choose appropriate designs. Two examples of the winning designs, by Robert Kalina of the Austrian National Bank, appear on the right. What can we learn by examining these notes?

First, it would be helpful to know what constraints the European Monetary Institute (the judging body) imposed on the designers. The seven bills (ranging from 5 to 500 euros) were to illustrate the "ages and styles of Europe," specifically Classical, Romanesque, Gothic, Renaissance, Baroque and Rococo, the age of iron and glass architecture, and modern twentieth-century architecture. The European flag was to be included on each bill. The criteria for selecting the winner were "creativity, aesthetics, style, functionality, likely public perception and acceptability (in particular the avoidance of any national bias and the achievement of a proper balance between the number of men and the number of women portrayed)."

You will notice right away that the design avoids the problem of equitably representing men and women by not including any people at all. Featured instead are architectural elements—windows on the front of the bills, bridges on the back. According to the designer, the windows symbolize "the spirit of openness and cooperation

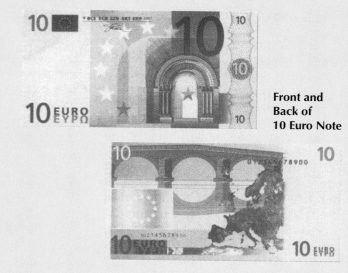

Front and Back of 10 Euro Note

in the European Union," while the bridges are "a metaphor for communication both among the people of Europe, and also between Europe and the rest of the world." Depicted on the back of the bills, with the bridges, is a map of the entire continent of Europe, including not just eastern Europe and western Russia, but parts of Turkey and North Africa. (Notice also how the bills differ: as is customary with European currency, the euro bills are different sizes and colors to help the visually impaired distinguish among them.)

Look first at the 10 euro note, illustrating the Romanesque style. Does the window look familiar? It may, if you have seen pictures of early medieval European churches. What about the bridge? It may remind you of the bridge in the French children's song "On the Bridge of Avignon." But if you were to compare the images with real monuments, you would quickly see that they are not the same. Indeed, unlike the White House on the U.S. $20 bill or countless other buildings shown on currency around the world, the windows and bridges on the euro are not labeled. The reason is simple: the architectural features are supposed to be generic and "European," and not reproduce any real monument. In fact, the initial designs of many of the notes, especially the bridges, were returned to Kalina for modification because they were "too recognizable."

Austrian 2 Euro Coin (Back)
*(Courtesy of the Oesterreichische
Nationalbank [Austrian National Bank],
Vienna, Austria)*

French 5 Eurocent Coin (Back)

Front and Back of 500 Euro Note

There were few such problems with the 500 euro note, illustrating twentieth-century architecture. The modernist style, originating in Europe in the 1920s (see page 908), had spread by the end of the century to virtually every corner of the world. The glass-and-steel buildings on the front of the note could just as well be in Tokyo, Singapore, or Nairobi, and the bridge recalls any number of modern suspension bridges around the world.

Notice how little writing appears on the bills. The word *euro* appears in the bottom corners in both the Latin and Greek alphabets (Greece joined the original eleven participants in the Eurozone on January 1, 2001). By indicating the issuing authority—the European Central Bank (ECB)—only by its initials, the notes have to include only five variants (BCE, ECB, EZB, EKT, EKP) to cover all the languages spoken in the European Union.

The coins were developed in a different way from the bills. Although the "heads" are uniform, each country could choose the design of the "tails" for the coins it produced at its national mint. All euro coins are legal tender in every Eurozone country, regardless where they were minted. Because there are eight coins, ranging in value from one eurocent to two euros, each country has eight opportunities to display its national symbols. The twelve countries took widely varying approaches. France features Marianne, a symbol of the French Republic since the time of the Revolution, on three of its coins. Marianne first appeared on French coins during the Revolution and is a traditional figure of French political art.

The remaining five French coins were divided among just two designs, *La Semeuse* (a woman sowing seeds, another traditional symbol of France) and a tree of life surrounded by the revolutionary motto "Liberty, Equality, Fraternity." None of the nineteenth- and twentieth-century figures currently on French notes—Paul Cézanne or Gustave Eiffel or Marie Curie—were selected. The choice of symbolic figures instead makes clear the continuing centrality of the French Revolution in France's national identity.

Austria, on the other hand, decided on eight different images. The smallest three coins feature different floral motifs; the next three, well-known Austrian buildings. The two largest coins are devoted to individuals whom the designers decided were Austria's most important figures: Mozart—known throughout the world—and Bertha Suttner—barely known anywhere outside Austria. Suttner was a writer and pacifist who is credited with persuading Alfred Nobel to establish the Nobel prizes. She herself was awarded the Nobel Peace Prize in 1905. No one could question the choice of Mozart—but why Suttner? Suttner had been a mainstay of Austrian currency for decades, appearing on the 1,000 schilling note until the mid-1980s. Reviving her somewhat antiquated image on the 2 euro coin may reflect Austria's renewed desire to project itself as a peace-loving, neutral nation that was not a willing partner in Nazi aggression but its first victim.

■ Notes

1. As quoted in Thomas L. Friedman, *The Lexus and the Olive Tree*, as quoted in *Europe*, no. 391 (Nov. 1999): 47.

■ Suggested Reading

Ardagh, John. *France in the New Century: Portrait of a Changing Society.* 1999. An updated edition of a lively, perceptive survey of the remarkable changes in French life since World War II.

Brubaker, Rogers. *Citizenship and Nationhood in France and Germany.* 1992. A lucid comparative study showing how very different conceptions of citizenship emerged in these two countries as a result of their contrasting historical experiences over the past two centuries.

Garton Ash, Timothy. *In Europe's Name: Germany and the Divided Continent.* 1993. A searching essay on Germany's place in Europe and the world, from the years of division, to reunification, to the post–cold war order.

Guttman, Robert J., ed. *Europe in the New Century: Visions of an Emerging Superpower.* 2001. An assessment of Europe's strengths and weaknesses by leading European politicians and journalists, who also seek to envision what the new century will bring.

Ignatieff, Michael. *Virtual War: Kosovo and Beyond.* 2000. An innovative exploration of the 1999 war over Kosovo, arguing that the use of technology to maintain distance transformed the idea of war.

Judah, Tim. *Kosovo: War and Revenge.* 2000. An authoritative account of the origins and unfolding of the Kosovo tragedy of the late 1990s.

Keane, John. *Václav Havel: A Political Tragedy in Six Acts.* 2000. A masterful political biography of the Czech anticommunist who became president of postcommunist Czechoslovakia—and one of the world's most respected moral and political leaders.

McCormick, John. *Understanding the European Union: A Concise Introduction.* 1999. A clear introduction to the history, structure, and functioning of the central institutions of the EU.

Shawcross, William. *Deliver Us from Evil: Peacekeepers, Warlords, and a World of Endless Conflict.* 2000. Accents the limits and contradictions of the Western response to crises in areas lacking an indigenous political class.

Steele, Jonathan. *Eternal Russia: Yeltsin, Gorbachev, and the Mirage of Democracy.* 1994. Places events before and after the fall of communism in useful historical perspective, while criticizing the preoccupation with privatization and the corresponding failure to foster a culture of democracy.

 For a searchable list of additional readings for this chapter, go to http://college.hmco.com.

Glossary

This Glossary covers the complete text, Chapters 1 through 30.

absolutism Extraordinary concentration of power in royal hands, achieved particularly by the kings of France, most notably **Louis XIV,** in the seventeenth century. Proponents argued that hereditary monarchy was the divinely ordained form of government. *(Ch. 16)*

Act of Supremacy (1534) Act of the English Parliament during the Protestant Reformation that finalized the break with the Catholic Church by declaring the king to be head of the Church of England. Henry VIII required a public oath supporting the act, which Sir **Thomas More** refused to take; More was then executed for treason. *(Ch. 14)*

Adenauer, Konrad (1876–1967) Leading statesman of post–World War II Germany. As chancellor (1949–1963), he oriented the country toward western Europe and the United States and proved to Germans that democracy could mean effective government, economic prosperity, and foreign policy success. *(Ch. 29)*

agricultural revolution Dramatic increase in food production from the sixteenth to eighteenth centuries, brought about by changes in agricultural practices, cultivation of new crops, greater availability of animal manure, and introduction of the nutrient-rich potato from the Americas. *(Ch. 18)*

Alexander the Great (356–323 B.C.) King of **Macedon** (r. 336–323) and conqueror of the **Persian Empire.** Son of **Philip II** of Macedon, Alexander was an ingenious warrior who, in the course of his conquests, spread Greek civilization to western Asia, Egypt, and India. His despotism and ruler-worship set a precedent for later monarchs, including many Roman emperors. *(Ch. 4)*

Alexandria Mediterranean seaport in northern Egypt founded by **Alexander the Great** in 332 B.C. It was a thriving Hellenistic city with great harbors, marketplaces, banks, inns, courts, shipbuilding facilities, and a renowned library. *(Ch. 4)*

Amarna reform Term for the ancient Egyptian king Amenhotep IV's seizure of power from temple priests by replacing the god Amun-Re with Aten and renaming himself Akhenaten. After Akhenaten's death, the Amun-Re cult regained power. *(Ch. 1)*

Anabaptists Radical religious reformers in Germany and Switzerland during the Reformation. They rejected the practice of infant baptism, believing that baptism should occur only after confession of sin. They also believed that Christians should live apart in communities of the truly redeemed. Mennonites and Hutterites are their modern descendants. *(Ch. 14)*

Antigonids Dynasty of Macedonian rulers founded in 276 B.C. by Antigonus Gonatas, grandson of Antigonus the One-Eyed, a general of **Alexander the Great.** The Antigonid dynasty lasted about 140 years, until the Roman conquest. *(Ch. 4)*

Antioch Greatest of the cities founded by Seleucus, a general of **Alexander the Great.** Located near the present-day Turkish-Syrian border, it became one of the wealthiest and most luxurious of all eastern Mediterranean cities. *(Ch. 4)*

anti-Semitism Centuries-old prejudice against and demonization of Jews. Anti-Semitism became virulent in Europe in the 1880s with the emergence of the ultranationalist and racist "New Right" ideologies and political movements. An essential part of the Nazi world-view, it led to the Holocaust. *(Ch. 24)*

appeasement The term for the policy employed by Britain's prime minister, Neville Chamberlain, to defuse the 1938 crisis with Germany's **Adolf Hitler.** Chamberlain acquiesced to Hitler's demands to annex the Sudetenland portion of Czechoslovakia, which proved a giant step toward the war that broke out less than a year later. *(Ch. 27)*

Aquinas, Thomas (1225–1274) Dominican friar and theologian. In his two most famous works, *Summa Contra Gentiles* and *Summa Theologiae,* he distinguished between natural truth, or what a person could know by reasoning, and revealed truths, which can be known only through faith in God's revelation. No one before him had so rigorously followed the dialectical method of reasoning through a whole field of knowledge. *(Ch. 10)*

Archaic Greece Period of ancient Greek history from around 700 to 500 B.C. Archaic Greece was characterized by artistic achievement, increased individualism amid communal solidarity, and a moving away from divine and toward abstract, mechanistic explanations. The Western philosophical tradition began during this period. *(Ch. 3)*

Arianism Popular heresy advocated by the priest Arius (ca. 250–336), emphasizing that Jesus was the "first born of all creation." It sought to preserve and purify Christianity's monotheism by making Jesus slightly subordinate to the Father. It was condemned by the **Council of Nicaea.** *(Ch. 7)*

Aristotle (384–322 B.C.) Ancient Greek philosopher, student of **Plato** and tutor of **Alexander the Great.** Aristotle emphasized the goal (*telos* in Greek) of change; in his view the entire cosmos is teleological, and every one of its parts has an essential purpose. Aristotle's scientific writings were the most influential philosophical classics of Greek and Roman civilization and remained so during the Middle Ages. *(Ch. 3)*

Armada (1588) Massive fleet of Spanish warships sent against England by **Philip II** but defeated by the English navy and bad weather. The tactics used by the English helped set the future course of naval warfare. *(Ch. 15)*

Assyrians Warlike people who ruled the ancient Near East during the first millennium B.C. Their innovations included using cavalry as their main striking force and having weapons and armor made of iron. *(Ch. 2)*

Augsburg Confession (1532) Document written by Philip Melanchthon (1497–1560), with the approval of **Martin Luther,** that became the most widely accepted statement of the Lutheran faith. It constitutes part of the creedal basis for today's Lutheran churches. *(Ch. 14)*

Augustine (354–430) North African bishop and one of the most influential Christian thinkers. Augustine wrote that all people were sinners in need of God's redemption, that history is the struggle between those who call on divine grace and those who sin, and that learning was useful only to the extent that it equipped individuals to read and understand the Bible's message of salvation. *(Ch. 7)*

Augustus (63 B.C.–A.D. 14) Honorific title of Gaius Julius Caesar Octavianus, grandnephew of Julius **Caesar** and first Roman emperor. After defeating Mark Antony and Cleopatra at the Battle of Actium (31 B.C.), Augustus ruled the empire for forty-five years. His rule laid the foundations of two hundred years of prosperous Roman peace. See also **Principate.** *(Ch. 6)*

Auschwitz-Birkenau The largest and principal extermination center of Nazi Germany's six death camps, all of which were located in what had been Poland. The Nazis shipped Jews from all over Europe to Auschwitz, which killed about twelve thousand people a day at the height of its operation in 1944. *(Ch. 28)*

avant-garde French for "forefront," the term refers to early-twentieth-century artists who, inspired by novel or unconventional techniques, considered themselves precursors of new styles. Avant-garde movements proclaimed idiosyncratic manifestos and constantly called for the rejection of existing forms of expression and the creation of new ones. *(Ch. 24)*

Aztecs Amerindian people that dominated central Mexico from the fourteenth through the sixteenth centuries from their capital Tenochtitlán (present-day Mexico City). Weakened by exposure to virulent Old World diseases, they were conquered in 1521–1523 by Spanish forces led by **Hernán Cortés.** *(Ch. 13)*

Bacon, Francis (1561–1626) England's lord chancellor during the reign of James I and author of a utopian essay extolling science's benefits for a peaceful society and human happiness. His influential works encouraged the empirical method and inductive reasoning. See also **empirical reasoning.** *(Ch. 17)*

barbarian kingship Central institution in a succession of kingdoms (ca. 300–600) ruled by barbarian (non-Roman) leaders, which evolved from former Roman provinces. Most such kings had been political or military leaders under Roman authority before becoming independent rulers. *(Ch. 7)*

baroque Style of European art and architecture popular from the late sixteenth to early eighteenth century. Baroque artists, such as Peter Paul Rubens, modified Renaissance techniques, adding dynamism and emotional energy. Baroque painting used light to portray dramatic illusion, and baroque churches were both impressively grand and emotionally engaging. *(Ch. 15)*

Bauhaus An influential German art school, founded in 1919, that sought to adopt contemporary materials to develop new forms of architecture, design, and urban planning in response to the cultural uncertainty that followed World War I. Though it arguably failed in its immediate German context, the Bauhaus helped shape the whole idea of "the modern" in the West and throughout the world for decades to come. *(Ch. 26)*

Bernard of Clairvaux (1090–1153) Monk, church reformer, and influential adviser to kings and popes. Bernard believed that faith and divine inspiration were more important than dialectical reasoning. He was instrumental in the success of the Cistercian religious order. *(Ch. 10)*

Bismarck, Otto von (1815–1898) Nineteenth-century German statesman. A Prussian aristocrat, Bismarck was the autocratic architect who, through a series of aggressive wars, united Germany and served as the nation's first chancellor. He administered an emperor-controlled country that became the dominant power in Europe. See also **Realpolitik.** *(Ch. 22)*

Black Death (1348–1351) First of a series of epidemics, probably bubonic plague, that raged in Europe and western Asia for three centuries. The Black Death killed about 60 percent of those infected. The huge population decline fueled the economic and social transformations of the late Middle Ages. *(Ch. 11)*

Bolsheviks Members of a faction of the Russian Socialist Party led by **Vladimir Ilich Lenin** (1870–1924), a zealous Marxist who insisted that a revolutionary cadre could seize power on behalf of the working class. The Bolsheviks gained control of Russia in November 1917. *(Ch. 24)*

Bonaparte, Napoleon. See **Napoleon Bonaparte.**

bourgeois century Characterization of the nineteenth century, especially the latter half. In western Europe, the bourgeois elites (middle classes), which had expanded dramatically in the wake of industrialization, helped fashion much of society. *(Ch. 23)*

Brandenburg-Prussia Group of German territories ruled by the Hohenzollern family that became one of Europe's most powerful states in the seventeenth century. Its military strength was supported by its hereditary landowners, who were granted autonomy in their territories. *(Ch. 16)*

Brandt, Willy (1913–1992) Socialist West German chancellor (r. 1969–1974). Brandt's widely popular policy of opening to the East, or *Ostpolitik*, made possible closer economic ties between West and East Germany and broader opportunities for ordinary citizens to interact across the east-west border. *(Ch. 29)*

Brest-Litovsk, Treaty of (1918) Treaty in which Russia accepted its defeat by Germany and its allies in World War I. The treaty forced the Russians to cede much of European Russia to Germany. After Germany's defeat by the Allies later in the year, the **Bolsheviks** recaptured Ukraine and the Caucasus region. *(Ch. 25)*

British blockade Britain's naval blockade of Germany during World War I. By means of this tactic, which cut off supplies to Germany but which also violated several provisions of international law, the British seriously impeded the German war effort. *(Ch. 25)*

Caesar, Gaius Julius (100–44 B.C.) Roman general gifted at war and politics. Named dictator in 49 B.C., he was assassinated by the members of the **senate** in 44 B.C. He introduced to Europe the calendar of 365¼ days. He was succeeded as ruler by his grandnephew Octavian (**Augustus**). Later Roman emperors were also called *caesar*. *(Ch. 5)*

Caliphate Arab empire established by the successors of **Muhammad**; *caliph* means "successor to the prophet." The Umayyad caliphate, with its capital in Damascus, ruled from 661 to 750; the Abbasid caliphate, based in Baghdad, from 750 to 1258. *(Ch. 8)*

Calvin, John (1509–1564) Franco-Swiss theologian and founder of the Reformed Church in Geneva. Calvin's theological writings, most notably *Institutes of the Christian Religion* (1536), were widely disseminated and hugely influential. Calvin stressed the absolute power of God and the need for moral reform of the Christian community. *(Ch. 14)*

canon law Collection of orderly rules for the government of the Catholic Church, based on papal decrees and decisions of church councils. In 1140 the monk Gratian published the *Decretum*, the first systematic collection of canon law. *(Ch. 10)*

Carlowitz, Treaty of (1699) Treaty imposed by the European allies on a weakening Ottoman Empire. The Habsburgs, Venetians, Russians, and Poles gained territory and power at the Turks' expense. *(Ch. 16)*

Carolingian Renaissance Major revival of learning, combined with reform of religious and political institutions, that occurred under **Charlemagne** and his successors. The revival encompassed the founding of schools in religious institutions, production of textbooks, dissemination of early church teachings and of **canon law,** as well as secular reforms such as regularization of royal estates. *(Ch. 8)*

Catherine the Great (r. 1762–1796) Empress of Russia. Through an astute policy of wars and alliances, Catherine expanded her country's borders south to the Black Sea and west into Europe. An "enlightened despot," she advanced the westernizing reforms begun by **Peter the Great.** *(Ch. 18)*

Cato the Elder (234–149 B.C.) Marcus Portius Cato, Roman general and statesman. Known as Cato the Censor because he denounced luxury goods, he was the first Roman historian to write in Latin. *(Ch. 5)*

Charlemagne Frankish king (r. 768–814), crowned emperor in 800. He carried out a program of legal and ecclesiastical reform, patronized learning, and revitalized the western Roman Empire. See also **Carolingian Renaissance.** *(Ch. 8)*

Charles V (r. 1519–1558) Holy Roman emperor and, as Charles I, king of Spain. His empire included Spain, Italy, the Low Countries, and Germany. Though he vigorously opposed the spread of Protestantism during the Reformation, he was forced to sign the Religious Peace of Augsburg in 1555, which acknowledged the right of German princes to choose the religion to be practiced in their territories, Lutheran or Catholic. Charles abdicated his imperial and royal titles the next year, ceding the empire to his brother Ferdinand and his Spanish possessions to his son **Philip II.** *(Ch. 14)*

Chartism Nineteenth-century British political movement whose goal was to transform Britain from an oligarchy to a democracy. The Chartists' demands were contained in the 1838 "people's charter," which called for universal male suffrage, electoral districts with equal population, salaries and the abolition of property qualifications for Members of Parliament, the secret ballot, and annual general elections. The movement failed, but most of its measures eventually became law. See also **Second Reform Bill.** *(Ch. 21)*

Chechnya Small, largely Muslim republic in the Caucasus region of Russia that attempted to declare independence in 1991. Russia intervened in the resulting civil war in 1994. After the Chechens won a substantial measure of autonomy, fighting resumed in 1999. *(Ch. 30)*

chivalry Initially, a medieval code of conduct for mounted warriors, focusing on military prowess, open-handed generosity, and earning a glorious reputation. Later it evolved into an elaborate set of rules governing relations between men and women. *(Ch. 10)*

Christianity Sect originally rooted in Judaism that emerged as a fully separate religion by around A.D. 200. Emphasizing belief in one God and the mission of his son, **Jesus of Nazareth**, as savior, Christianity offered salvation in the next world and a caring community in the present one. A messianic religion, Christianity emphasized Christ's return, leading to the beginning of a heavenly kingdom on earth. *(Ch. 6)*

Churchill, Winston (1874–1965) British prime minister (1940–1945; 1951–1955). As the leader of his country during World War II, Churchill's courage, decisiveness, memorable words, and boundless energy made him widely seen as one of Britain's greatest leaders of the twentieth century. See also **Yalta conference.**

Cicero, Marcus Tullius (106–43 B.C.) Philosopher, writer, and statesman who was Rome's greatest orator. He was crucial in making the Latin language a vessel for the heritage of Greek thought. *(Ch. 5)*

city-state State consisting of an independent city and the surrounding territory under its control. Early examples were the Sumerian city-states in the third millennium B.C. *(Ch. 1)*

civic humanism An ideology, championed by Florentine writers and public officials during the Renaissance, that emphasized their city's classical republican virtues and history. They argued that a moral and ethical value was intrinsic to public life. *(Ch. 12)*

Civil Code Law code established under Napoleon in 1804 that included limited acceptance of revolutionary gains, such as a guarantee of equality before the law and taxation of all social classes. Also known as the Napoleonic Code, it enshrined modern forms of property ownership and civil contracts, enhanced paternal control of families, outlawed divorce in most circumstances, and placed women under the legal domination of fathers and husbands. *(Ch. 19)*

Classical Greece Period of ancient Greek history from about 480 to 323 B.C. Classical Greek culture emphasized public life as the central theme of art and literature, and its sculpture was the most anatomically precise yet. Classical Greece set many standards for modern Western culture. See also **demokratia**. *(Ch. 3)*

Cluny (Cluniacs) A spiritual reform begun in 910 in central France. The movement emphasized strict adherence to the Benedictine Rule, as well as the ideas that the church should pray for the world without being deeply involved in it and must be free from lay control. *(Ch. 10)*

cold war The hostile standoff between the Soviet Union and the United States that began after World War II, when communist governments, relying on Soviet support, took control of most of east-central Europe. The Soviets' first atomic bomb explosion in 1949 intensified the conflict, which shaped world affairs for the next forty years. *(Ch. 28)*

collectivization The program that reshaped agriculture in the Soviet Union under **Joseph Stalin** during the early 1930s. By forcing peasants into government-controlled collective farms, the Soviet regime sought to take control of agricultural production in order better to finance rapid industrialization. *(Ch. 27)*

Columbian Exchange Historians' term for the blending of cultures between the Old World and the New after Christopher Columbus's arrival in the New World in 1492. The Spanish and other Europeans brought their plants, domesticated animals, and diseases to the Americas. The Americas contributed New World crops, most notably maize (corn) and potatoes, transforming the Old World diet. *(Ch. 13)*

Comintern (Third, or Communist, International) An association founded in March 1919 by the communists (formerly **Bolsheviks**) to translate their success in Russia into leadership of the international socialist movement. Its program of tight organization and discipline under Russian leadership produced a schism between communists and socialists in Europe and throughout the world. *(Ch. 26)*

communes Form of government in Italian towns that rose in the eleventh century. Despite numerous local variations, communes involved common decision making by local notables, including both landed aristocrats and wealthy merchants or industrialists. *(Ch. 9)*

Compromise of 1867 Agreement that divided the Habsburg Empire into Austria in the west and Hungary in the east, a dual monarchy under Emperor Franz Joseph called Austria-Hungary. The compromise confirmed Magyar dominance in Hungary. *(Ch. 22)*

congress system System of European international relations in the first half of the nineteenth century in which the major European states cooperated to preserve the balance of power. This system disappeared as political leaders increasingly used force to pursue their narrow interests. *(Ch. 22)*

Congress of Vienna (1814–1815) Conference called by the victorious powers—Austria, Great Britain, Prussia, and Russia—who defeated Napoleon. Guided by the Austrian foreign minister, Prince Metternich, the Great Powers drew new territorial boundaries advantageous to themselves. They also attempted to provide long-term stability on the European continent and restored some of the rulers who had been overthrown. See also **congress system.** *(Ch. 20)*

conservatism Ideology underlying the order established in Europe in 1815. Conservatives emphasized resistance to change and preservation of the existing order of monarchy, aristocracy, and an established church. *(Ch. 20)*

Copernicus, Nicholas (1473–1543) Polish astronomer who initiated the Scientific Revolution by proposing that the earth and other planets orbit the sun, a theory called the heliocentric, or sun-centered, system. See also **heliocentrism.** *(Ch. 17)*

corporative state, corporativism The system established in fascist Italy beginning in 1926 that sought to involve people in public life not as citizens but as producers, through their roles in the economy. A system based on such occupational groupings eventually replaced parliament as the basis of political representation in fascist Italy. *(Ch. 26)*

Cortés, Hernán (1485–1546) Spanish commander who conquered the **Aztecs** and claimed the Valley of Mexico for Spain. Cortés had only five hundred men but was aided by an outbreak of smallpox and the help of Amerindian peoples eager to end Aztec control. *(Ch. 13)*

Council of Constance (1414–1418) Assembly convened by Holy Roman Emperor Sigismund to heal deep religious and civil divisions. The council declared that its rulings were binding even on the pope. Its selection of Pope Martin V ended the **Great Schism**. *(Ch. 11)*

Council of the Indies Body established by the king of Spain in 1524 to oversee Spain's colonial possessions. Located at court, eventually in Madrid, it supervised all legal, administrative, and commercial activity in the colonies until the early eighteenth century. *(Ch. 13)*

Council of Nicaea (325) History's first ecumenical, or "all-church," council, convened by the emperor Constantine. The council condemned **Arianism** and proclaimed key elements of the Nicene Creed, especially the doctrine that Christ was "one in being with the Father," co-equal and co-eternal. *(Ch. 7)*

Council of Trent (1545–1563) Ecumenical council of the Roman Catholic Church during the Reformation. Though rejecting many Protestant positions, the council reformed and reorganized the church partly in response to Protestant criticisms. Its decrees reaffirmed and defined the basic tenets of Roman Catholicism for the next four hundred years. *(Ch. 14)*

covenant As told in the Hebrew Bible, the pact God made with Abraham, the first patriarch of **Israel**. In return for the land of Canaan and the promise of becoming a great nation, the Israelites agreed to worship no other gods. *(Ch. 2)*

Cromwell, Oliver (1599–1658) English Puritan general and statesman. A military genius and leader in the English Civil War, Cromwell governed as Lord Protector during the Interregnum from 1653 to 1658.*(Ch. 16)*

Crusades (1095–1270) A series of largely unsuccessful wars waged by western European Christians to recapture the Holy Land from the Muslims and ensure the safety of Christian pilgrims to Jerusalem. Later, the term came to designate any military effort by Europeans against non-Christians. *(Ch. 9)*

cuneiform First writing system in Mesopotamia, consisting of wedge-shaped impressions in soft clay. Named from the Latin word for "wedge-shaped," it was developed about 3500–3100 B.C. *(Ch. 1)*

Darwinism Profoundly influential theory of biological evolution, first put forth by Charles Darwin (1809–1882). He proposed that all forms of life continuously develop through natural selection, whereby those that are better adapted to the environment have the advantage and are more likely to survive and pass on their beneficial traits to their offspring. *(Ch. 23)*

D-Day The complex Allied amphibious landings in Normandy, France, on June 6, 1944, that opened a second major European front in World War II. In the aftermath of this invasion, American-led forces in the west began moving toward Germany, completing the Soviet effort, which was already forcing the Germans back on the eastern front. *(Ch. 28)*

Decembrists Group of Russian military officers who led the December 1825 rebellion after the death of Tsar Alexander I, seeking to install a constitutional monarchy with Alexander's eldest brother, Constantine, as tsar. They were defeated and executed by Constantine's younger brother, Nicholas. The Decembrists were seen as martyrs by later Russian revolutionaries. *(Ch. 21)*

Declaration of the Rights of Man and the Citizen (1789) Document issued by the **National Assembly** of France in August 1789. Modeled on the U.S. Constitution, the declaration set forth the basis for the new French government and asserted "the natural, inalienable and sacred rights of man." *(Ch. 19)*

demokratia Term coined in Athens in the fifth century B.C. to describe the city's system of direct government. It means "the power *(kratos)* of the people *(demos)."* Athenian society pioneered today's key democratic principles, including freedom, equality, universal citizenship, and the rule of law. *(Ch. 3)*

Descartes, René (1596–1650) French philosopher, scientist, and mathematician. Descartes emphasized skepticism and deductive reasoning in his most influential treatise, *Discourse on Method*. He offered the first alternative physical explanation of matter after the Copernican revolution. *(Ch. 17)*

digital divide A term for the disparity in access to the computing and Internet technologies that seemed essential to compete in the twenty-first-century global economy. It was one way that new technologies were widening the gap between the world's haves and have-nots. *(Ch. 30)*

Directory French revolutionary government from 1795 to 1799, consisting of an executive council of five men chosen by the upper house of the legislature. It was overthrown in a coup led by **Napoleon Bonaparte.** *(Ch. 19)*

Dominic Dominic de Guzman (1170–1221), Spanish priest and founder of the spiritually influential Dominican mendicant order. The order was known for the irreproachable life of its members, its learning, and its desire to emulate the apostolic life of the early church by poverty and preaching. *(Ch. 10)*

Dutch East India Company Commercially innovative Dutch company formed in 1602 that combined government management of trade with both public and private investment. The formation of the company created a permanent pool of capital to sustain trade and resulted in a dramatic expansion of commerce with Asia. *(Ch. 16)*

Edict of Milan (313) Proclamation issued primarily by Emperor Constantine that made Christianity a legal religion in the Roman Empire. Constantine promoted the Christian church, granting it tax immunities and relieving the clergy of military service. *(Ch. 7)*

Edict of Nantes (1598) Edict of Henry IV granting France's Protestants (**Huguenots**) the right to practice their faith and maintain defensive garrisons. They were also guaranteed access to schools, hospitals, royal appointments, and separate judicial institutions. The edict was revoked by **Louis XIV** in 1685. *(Ch. 15)*

Elizabeth I (r. 1558–1603) First woman to occupy the English throne successfully. Elizabeth's adroit rule brought stability to England after the turmoil of previous reigns. She firmly established Protestantism in England, encouraged English commerce, defended the nation against the Spanish **Armada**, and fostered the English Renaissance in poetry and drama. *(Ch. 15)*

empirical reasoning Philosophical view developed by the seventeenth-century English philosophers **Francis Bacon** and **John Locke**, asserting that all knowledge is based on observation and experimentation and that general principles should be derived from particular facts. *(Ch. 17)*

encomienda A Spanish royal grant of protectorship over a group of Amerindians. The receivers of the grants (*encomenderos*) were obliged to Christianize the people under their charge, but instead most forced the natives to work as virtual slaves in mines and on Spanish lands. See also **Bartolomé de Las Casas**. *(Ch. 13)*

enlightened despotism Term for the reform-oriented rule of eighteenth-century monarchs such as **Frederick the Great**, Joseph II of Austria, and **Catherine the Great**. Enlightened despots applied Enlightenment remedies to economic problems, encouraged education and legal reform, and improved agricultural productivity by enabling some peasants to own the land they worked. *(Ch. 18)*

Epicureans Adherents of the Athenian philosopher Epicurus (341–270 B.C.), who taught that the soul is made up of atoms that do not exist after death. Epicureans emphasized the avoidance of pain and the pursuit of intellectual pleasure. *(Ch. 4)*

Erasmus, Desiderius (1466–1536) Prominent Dutch humanist during the Renaissance, best known for his satire *Praise of Folly*. Erasmus's works reinterpreted Greek and Roman wisdom and emphasized tolerance, reason, and faith in the goodness and educability of the individual. *(Ch. 12)*

"ethnic cleansing" A term describing attempts to remove an unwanted ethnic group from an area, which can include forced relocation and mass killing. Beginning in 1991, this tactic was implemented by Yugoslavian ruler Slobodan Milosevic (b. 1941) to unite all Serbs, many of whom lived in neighboring Croatia, Bosnia-Herzegovina, and **Kosovo**. *(Ch. 30)*

Etruscans Inhabitants of twelve loosely confederated city-states north of Rome in Etruria that flourished in the seventh to sixth centuries B.C. They were conquered by the Romans by the early third century B.C. *(Ch. 5)*

euro The common currency launched by the **European Union** in 1999 to eliminate the cost of currency exchange and boost trade and economic interaction. As of January 1, 2002, it replaced the national currencies of the participating countries (the "Eurozone"). *(Ch. 30)*

European Economic Community (EEC) (1957–1967) Common market formed by Belgium, France, West Germany, Italy, Luxembourg, and the Netherlands to promote free trade. The EEC was replaced by the European Community (EC) in 1967. *(Ch. 29)*

European Union (EU) New name for the European Community after the **Maastricht agreement** of 1991. By 2001 the European Union had nine members in addition to the original six members of the **European Economic Community:** Britain, Denmark, Ireland (joined 1973); Greece (joined 1981); Portugal, Spain (joined 1985); and Austria, Finland, Sweden (joined 1995). See also **euro**. *(Ch. 30)*

"euthanasia" program The Nazi program of systematically killing people, overwhelmingly ethnic Germans, whom the Nazis deemed superfluous or threatening to the German racial health. Victims included chronic mental patients, the incurably ill, and people with severe physical handicaps. Initiated in 1939, the program had claimed 100,000 lives by the time it was discontinued in 1941. *(Ch. 27)*

existentialism A philosophical and cultural movement, influential from the late 1940s into the 1950s, that explored life in a world cast adrift from its cultural moorings. Highly influential were the Frenchmen Jean Paul Sartre (1905–1980) and Albert Camus (1913–1960), for whom an authentic human response to an apparently meaningless universe entailed commitment and responsibility. *(Ch. 29)*

factories Centralized workplaces where a number of people cooperate to mass-produce goods. The first factories of industrializing Europe were made possible by the development of the **steam engine** as a central power source. The mechanized production of factories led to huge productivity increases in the nineteenth century. See also **industrialization, mass production.** *(Ch. 20)*

fascism A violent, antidemocratic movement founded by **Benito Mussolini** in Italy in 1919. The term is widely used to encompass Hitler's Nazi regime in Germany and other movements stressing disciplined national solidarity and hostile to liberal individualism, the parliamentary system, and Marxist socialism. *(Ch. 26)*

February Patent (1861) Enactment issued in February 1861 by the Austrian emperor Franz Joseph (r. 1848–1916) that established a constitutional monarchy in the old Austrian Empire. The patent guaranteed civil liberties and provided for local self-government and an elected parliament. *(Ch. 22)*

feudal revolution The societal change in tenth-century France from prince-dominated territories with loyal, reliable, but few vassals to the advent of many locally powerful magnates with numerous vassals whose fidelity was uncertain and who primarily provided military service. *(Ch. 9)*

Five Pillars of Islam The basic teachings of Islam: (1) the profession of faith, "There is no God but Allah and **Muhammad** is His Prophet"; (2) individual prayer five times daily, plus group prayers at noon on Friday; (3) the sunup-to-sundown fast during the month of Ramadan; (4) giving generous alms to the poor; and (5) pilgrimage to Mecca at least once in a person's lifetime. *(Ch. 8)*

Flavians Dynasty of the Roman emperors Vespasian (r. 69–79), Titus (r. 79–81), and Domitian (r. 81–96), whose rule was a time of relative peace and good government. Unlike the Julio-Claudians, the Flavians descended from Italian landowners, not old Roman nobility. Domitian persecuted the nobility and was assassinated. *(Ch. 6)*

Fourteen Points Proposals by U.S. president Woodrow Wilson (1856–1924) to guide the new international order that would follow an Allied victory in World War I. Specifics included open diplomacy, free trade, reduced armaments, self-determination for nationalities, and a league of nations. *(Ch. 25)*

Francis of Assisi (1181–1226) Italian monk and founder of a new order of friars ("brothers," from the Latin *fratres).* Francis was born wealthy but adopted a life based on the scriptural ideals of poverty, preaching, and service. His apostolate to the urban poor was highly popular. *(Ch. 10)*

Frankfurt Assembly (1848–1849) Popularly elected national assembly that attempted to create a unified German state. The assembly drew up a constitution and offered the German throne to Friedrich Wilhelm IV, king of Prussia, who declined, fearing a war with Austria and not wanting an office offered by representatives of the people. *(Ch. 21)*

Frederick the Great (r. 1740–1786) Autocratic king of Prussia who transformed the country into a major military power, acquired Polish Prussia, and waged three wars against Austria. He participated in and encouraged the study of philosophy, history, poetry, and French literature. *(Ch. 18)*

Freud, Sigmund (1856–1939) Austrian founder of psychoanalysis, a method of treating psychic disorders by exploring the unconscious. Freud believed that people were motivated in part by their unconscious feelings and drives. He helped call attention to the concept that irrational forces play a significant role in human behavior. *(Ch. 24)*

friendly societies Nineteenth-century organizations formed by workers; members pooled their resources to provide mutual aid. Combining business activity with feasts, drinking bouts, and other social functions, friendly societies promoted group solidarity and a sense of working-class identity. *(Ch. 20)*

Galileo Galilei (1564–1642) Italian physicist and astronomer who provided evidence supporting the heliocentric theory of **Nicholas Copernicus** and helped develop the physics of mechanics. His publication of his astronomical observations and his subsequent condemnation by the Catholic Church spurred popular debate and greatly influenced the future of science. *(Ch. 17)*

gentry Class of wealthy, educated, and socially ambitious families in western Europe, especially England, whose political and economic power was greatly enhanced during the sixteenth century. They shared with traditional old-family warrior-aristocrats certain legal privileges, security of landownership, and a cooperative relationship with the monarchy. See also **price revolution**. *(Ch. 15)*

Girondins Political faction during the French Revolution. Republicans and members of the Jacobin Club, the Girondins dominated the French Legislative Assembly when it began to meet in 1791. They favored an activist government but were less radical than other members of the club, called the **Jacobins**. The Girondins were purged from the National Convention in 1793, and many were executed during the **Terror**. *(Ch. 19)*

glasnost Russian term meaning "greater openness." Glasnost was the leading motif in the Great Reforms begun in 1861 by Tsar Alexander II (r. 1855–1881), who sought to strengthen Russia by restructuring its institutions in the wake of defeat in the Crimean War. Glasnost was also part of the reform efforts of **Mikhail Gorbachev** in the Soviet Union during the 1980s. *(Ch. 22)*

Glorious Revolution (1688) Bloodless English revolution in which Parliament replaced the Catholic King James II with William (of Orange) and his wife Mary (James's Protestant daughter). Parliament imposed on the new sovereigns a Bill of Rights that confirmed Parliament's power and protected freedom of speech. *(Ch. 16)*

Golden Bull of 1356 Edict of Holy Roman Emperor Charles IV establishing the method of electing a new emperor. It acknowledged the political autonomy of Germany's seven regional princes. *(Ch. 11)*

Gorbachev, Mikhail (b. 1931) The Soviet Communist Party secretary who, beginning in 1985, attempted to reform the Soviet communist system through arms reduction; liberalization in the satellite states; *glasnost,* or "openness" to discussion and criticism; and *perestroika,* or economic "restructuring." Though widely admired in the West, these measures failed, and Gorbachev ended up presiding over the end of the Soviet communist regime. *(Ch. 29)*

Gothic Period in European architecture, sculpture, and painting from the twelfth to early sixteenth centuries. Gothic architecture was distinguished by the pointed arch, ribbed vault, and point support, which produced a building characterized by verticality and translucency. Examples are the Cathedral of Notre-Dame of Paris and the royal portal at Chartres Cathedral. *(Ch. 10)*

Gracchi Ancient Roman faction led by Tiberius Sempronius Gracchus (163–133 B.C.) and later his brother, Gaius (153–121 B.C.), both of whom were killed by their political opponents. They challenged the conservative **senate** on behalf of the poor. *(Ch. 5)*

Great Northern War (1700–1721) War between Sweden and Russia over control of Baltic territories. **Peter the Great** secured Livonia and Estonia as well as the territory on which he built Russia's new capital, St. Petersburg. Russia became the pre-eminent power on the Baltic. *(Ch. 16)*

"the Great Patriotic War" Term for World War II devised by **Joseph Stalin** to rally Soviet citizens against the German invasion. Stalin appealed to Russian nationalism and recalled past heroic defenses of Russia rather than communist themes. *(Ch. 28)*

Great Reform Bill (1832) British law that broadened the franchise and provided parliamentary seats for new urban areas that had not previously been represented. The bill was a major victory for the government and middle classes over the aristocracy. *(Ch. 21)*

Great Schism (1378–1417) Period during which two, then three, rival popes claimed to rule the Christian Church. The schism ended when the **Council of Constance** deposed all three competing previous popes and elected Martin V as the new pope. *(Ch. 11)*

guilds Merchant groups and associations of crafts and trades established in European cities and towns beginning in the thirteenth century. Guilds expanded greatly during the later

Middle Ages. They provided economic benefits, fostered a sense of community, and served as mutual assistance societies. *(Ch. 9)*

gulag Network of 476 forced labor camps for political prisoners in the Soviet Union. The *gulag* (an acronym for "main camp administration") was first used by Lenin in 1918 but was greatly expanded by **Joseph Stalin** in the 1930s. *(Ch. 27)*

Gutenberg, Johann (ca. 1399–1468) German inventor of movable metal type. His innovations led to the publication of the first printed book in Europe, the Gutenberg Bible, in the 1450s. Printed books and broadsheets played a critical role in disseminating the ideas of the Renaissance and the Reformation. *(Ch. 12)*

Hagia Sophia Largest Christian church ever built, constructed in Constantinople from 532 to 537 for the Roman emperor **Justinian.** The church consists of two intersecting rectangular basilicas that incorporate arches; the whole is surmounted by a huge dome. *(Ch. 7)*

Hanseatic League Late medieval association of over a hundred trading cities, centered on the German city of Lübeck. The league dominated coastal trade in northern Europe from the fourteenth to the fifteenth centuries, until Dutch, English, and south German merchants finally gained shares of the wool, grain, and fur trades. *(Ch. 11)*

heliocentrism Theory advanced by **Nicholas Copernicus** that the earth and other planets orbit the sun. Supported by the scientific and mathematical discoveries of **Johannes Kepler** and **Galileo Galilei,** heliocentrism, which means "sun-centered," won acceptance by the end of the seventeenth century. *(Ch. 17)*

Hellenism Term used to designate ancient Greece's language, culture, and civilization, especially after **Alexander the Great** spread them to other parts of the Mediterranean, western Asia, and North Africa. *(Ch. 4)*

Helsinki Accords (1975) Agreements signed by thirty-five countries in Helsinki, Finland, that committed the signatories to recognize existing borders, to increase economic and environmental cooperation, and to promote freedom of expression, religion, and travel. Dissidents in Soviet bloc countries soon fastened on these provisions to highlight the lack of human rights and to discredit the ruling communist governments. *(Ch. 29)*

Henry IV (r. 1589–1610) First Bourbon king of France, who converted to Catholicism to restore that nation's peace. His **Edict of Nantes** granted rights to the persecuted French Protestants, and he strengthened finance, agriculture, and commerce. *(Ch. 15)*

Henry "the Navigator" (1394–1460) Portuguese prince and director of Portugal's exploration and colonization of Africa's western coast. The Portuguese quickly established trading stations in the region, laying the foundations for their overseas empire. *(Ch. 13)*

Herodotus (ca. 485–425 B.C.) Ancient Greek historian; with **Thucydides,** a founder of history-writing in the West. The word *history* comes from a word used by Herodotus, *historiai,* meaning "inquiries" or "research." In his history of the Persian Wars, Herodotus saw the fall of the Persian Empire as part of a perpetual cycle of the rise and fall of empires. *(Ch. 3)*

Hildegard of Bingen (1098–1179) German abbess who was perhaps the most profound psychological thinker of her age. More than anyone before her, Hildegard opened up for discussion the feminine aspects of divinity. She was also adept in music and biblical studies. *(Ch. 10)*

Hitler, Adolf (1889–1945) The German dictator who, after being legally named chancellor in 1933, militarized Germany and started World War II in 1939, leading the country to defeat in 1945. His enforcement of state-sponsored **anti-Semitism** and racial purity among German people led to the murder of millions of Jews, Gypsies, and Slavic peoples. *(Ch. 27)*

Hobbes, Thomas (1588–1679) English philosopher. In his treatise *Leviathan,* Hobbes asserted that people are made up of mechanistic appetites and so need a strong ruler to hold them in check. However, he also envisioned citizens as potentially equal and constrained neither by morality nor by natural obedience to authority. *(Ch. 17)*

Homer Greatest ancient Greek poet, credited as the author of the epics the *Iliad* and the *Odyssey,* both written during the eighth century B.C. His dramatic stories inspired, moved, and educated the Greeks. *(Ch. 2)*

hominids The primate family *Hominidae,* which includes humans. The modern human being, *Homo sapiens sapiens,* is the only species of this family still in existence. *(Ch. 1)*

hoplite phalanx Battlefield tactic of **Archaic Greece** that relied on a tightly ordered unit of heavily armed, pike-bearing infantrymen. It was the dominant military force in western Asia and the Mediterranean region until 197 B.C. *(Ch. 3)*

Huguenots French Protestants, followers of the teachings of **John Calvin.** Huguenots battled Catholics throughout the sixteenth and seventeenth centuries. Many emigrated to other western European countries and England's American colonies, especially after the revocation of the **Edict of Nantes.** French Protestants gained full religious freedom in the nineteenth century. *(Ch. 15)*

humanism Western European literary and cultural movement of the fourteenth and fifteenth centuries. Humanists emphasized the superiority of ancient Greek and Roman literature, history, and politics, and focused on learning and personal and public duty. See also **Desiderius Erasmus, Francesco Petrarch, Thomas More.** *(Ch. 12)*

Hundred Years' War (1337–1453) Series of conflicts between the ruling families of France and England over territory in France and the succession to the French crown. Sporadic raids and battles devastated the French countryside and checked population growth. The inspirational leadership of **Joan of Arc** contributed to France's eventual success in expelling the English from nearly all of the disputed land. *(Ch. 11)*

hunter-gatherers Food-collecting society in which people live by hunting, fishing, and gathering fruits and nuts, with no crops or livestock being raised for food. During the **Neolithic Revolution,** some hunter-gatherers developed agriculture. *(Ch. 1)*

Hus, Jan (ca. 1370–1415) Czech religious reformer who strongly attacked clerical power and privileges and advocated reform of church practice. His execution for heresy at the **Council of Constance** provoked a civil war in Prague and Bohemia. *(Ch. 11)*

iconoclasm Rejection of, or even the destruction of, religious images in worship. Iconoclasm was the official policy of the Byzantine Empire from 726 to 843 and played a role in the continuing estrangement of Byzantium from the West. *(Ch. 8)*

impressionism Late-nineteenth-century style of painting pioneered by the French artists Degas, Monet, Pissarro,

Renoir, Sisley, and Morisot. Influenced by new theories that images were transmitted to the brain as small light particles, which the brain then reconstituted, the impressionists sought to capture what things looked like before they were "distorted" by the brain. *(Ch. 23)*

Inca A flourishing sixteenth-century empire administered from the mountains of Peru and extending from modern Ecuador and Chile. It was conquered for Spain by Francisco Pizzaro (1470–1541), aided by a smallpox epidemic and native peoples seeking to end Inca domination. *(Ch. 13)*

Index of Prohibited Books A list of books banned by the Roman Catholic Church because of moral or doctrinal error. First announced in 1559, it was only sporadically enforced and had little effect. The Index was suppressed in 1966. *(Ch. 14)*

industrialization Beginning in Britain in the later eighteenth century, a system of **mass production** of goods in which specialization and mechanization made manufacturing efficient and profitable. Early industrialization enabled Britain to become the dominant world power in the nineteenth century. See also **factories.** *(Ch. 20)*

information technology (IT) Term for the revolution in information availability and communications resulting from the late-twentieth-century development of personal computers and the Internet. See also **digital divide**. *(Ch. 30)*

Interregnum (1649–1660) Literally "between reigns," the period in English history from the execution of Charles I to the restoration of Charles II. During these years England was a republic—a Commonwealth—ruled by **Oliver Cromwell**, who became Lord Protector in 1653. *(Ch. 16)*

Israel People who settled on the eastern shore of the Mediterranean around 1200 B.C., or perhaps earlier. Their belief in one God directly influenced the faith of Christians, Muslims, and modern Jews. See also **monotheism**. *(Ch. 2)*

Jacobins In revolutionary France, a political club named for a monastic order. One of the most radical of republican groups, the Jacobins purged the **Girondins**, originally fellow members of the club, from the National Convention in 1793. Leaders of the **Terror**, such as **Maximilien Robespierre**, came from their ranks. *(Ch. 19)*

Jesus of Nazareth (ca. 4 B.C.–A.D. 30) Founder of **Christianity**. A forceful preacher and reformer who, to his followers, was Christ, "the anointed one" (from the Greek *Christos*), foretold in the Hebrew Bible as the redeemer of Israel who would initiate the kingdom of heaven. The dynamism and popularity of his teachings led to a clash with Jewish and Roman authorities in Jerusalem and to his crucifixion by the Romans. *(Ch. 6)*

Joan of Arc (d. 1431) Charismatic French military leader during the **Hundred Years' War.** A late medieval mystic, Joan heard "voices" telling her to assist in driving the English from France. She was captured and burned as a heretic by the English. Later she was canonized as Saint Joan, patron saint of France. *(Ch. 11)*

Julio-Claudians Dynasty of Roman emperors founded by **Augustus** and ruling from A.D. 14 to 68. The succession consisted of Augustus's stepson Tiberius, great-grandson Caligula, grandnephew Claudius, and great-great-grandson Nero. For elite Romans, this era was one of decadence and scandal; for ordinary people, it was a time of stability and peace. *(Ch. 6)*

July Revolution (1830) Uprising in Paris in July 1830 that forced King Charles X to abdicate and signaled a victory for constitutional reform over an absolute monarchy. The liberal Louis Philippe was proclaimed "King of the French," with limited powers, by the chamber of deputies. The revolution sparked democratic uprisings in Belgium, Germany, Italy, and Russian Poland and helped persuade British peers to vote for the **Great Reform Bill.** *(Ch. 21)*

justification by faith Doctrine professed by **Martin Luther** that Christians can be saved (justified) only by faith, a free gift of God, and not by penitential acts or good works. Luther's doctrine directly challenged the authority and fundamental practices of the Roman Catholic Church. *(Ch. 14)*

Justinian (r. 527–565) One of the greatest of all Rome's emperors. His comprehensive collection of Roman law is the most influential legal collection in human history. He built **Hagia Sophia**, reformed the imperial administration, and fought constant wars to expand the empire. *(Ch. 7)*

Kepler, Johannes (1571–1630) German astronomer. Kepler developed the three laws of planetary motion, known as Kepler's Laws, which are still accepted, and mathematically confirmed the Copernican heliocentric hypothesis. *(Ch. 17)*

Kosovo Yugoslav province, viewed by Serbs as the cradle of their nationhood but populated overwhelmingly by ethnic Albanians. After Slobodan Milosevic launched a campaign of **"ethnic cleansing"** there in 1999, NATO bombing forced him to agree to allow a UN peacekeeping force to administer the province. *(Ch. 30)*

Kriegsrohstoffabteilung (KRA) The "War Raw Materials Office" that coordinated Germany's World War I economy. The KRA produced synthetic substitute products and created new mixed (private and government) companies to allocate raw materials. This body served as a model for later economic planning and coordination in Germany and elsewhere. *(Ch. 25)*

laissez faire French term meaning "to leave alone," it was applied to the economic doctrine put forward by **Adam Smith** in 1776. Smith advocated freeing national economies from the fetters of the state and allowing supply and demand to shape the marketplace. Laissez-faire ideas contributed to the drive to lower tariffs in the nineteenth century. See also **liberalism.** *(Ch. 21)*

Las Casas, Bartolomé de (1474–1566) First bishop of Chiapas, in southern Mexico. A former *encomendero*, Las Casas passionately condemned the brutality of the Spanish conquests. In 1542 King Charles accepted Las Casas's criticisms, abolishing Indian slavery and greatly restricting the transfer of **encomiendas**. *(Ch. 13)*

Latin Indo-European language of ancient Rome and its empire, from which today's Romance languages developed. *(Ch. 5)*

laws of motion The natural laws of gravity, planetary motion, and inertia first laid out in the seventeenth century by **Isaac Newton.** Newton demonstrated that these laws apply to the solar system and could be used to predict the existence of an as-yet-unseen planet. *(Ch. 17)*

lay investiture Control of church appointments by laymen. Emperor Henry IV (1066–1106) and Pope Gregory VII (1073–1085) disputed who should have this authority in the Christian world. The 1122 Concordat of Worms stipulated that bishops could be invested by kings only after a free church election. *(Ch. 9)*

League of Nations (1919–1946) An international alliance established at the end of World War I without the membership of the United States. Though its covenant called for the peaceful settlement of disputes among member states and for sanctions against a member that went to war in violation of League provisions, it failed to prevent the escalating violence that culminated in World War II. *(Ch. 25)*

legion Innovative and highly successful ancient Roman battle formation. The legion included many flexible, adaptable, and semi-independent groups that broke their enemies' order with javelins at long range, then charged with sword and shield. *(Ch. 5)*

Lend-Lease Act (1941) Act by the U.S. Congress authorizing President **Franklin Roosevelt** to lend or lease weapons or other aid to countries the president designated. A major declaration of American support for the threatened British, lend-lease was later extended to several other countries. *(Ch. 28)*

Lenin, Vladimir Ilyich (1870–1924) Russian revolutionary. Leader of the **Bolsheviks** since 1903, he launched the November 1917 revolution that overthrew the **provisional government.** He concluded the **Treaty of Brest-Litovsk** with Germany and began the establishment of communism in the Soviet Union. See also **New Economic Policy.** *(Ch. 25)*

liberalism Nineteenth-century economic and political theory that called for reducing government powers to a minimum. Liberals worked to impose constitutional limits on government, establish the rule of law, eliminate state regulation of the economy, and ensure a voice in government for men of property and education. *(Ch. 21)*

linear perspective Revolutionary technique developed by early-fifteenth-century Florentine painters for representing three-dimensional objects on a two-dimensional plane. The technique is based in part on the observation that as parallel lines recede, they appear to converge. *(Ch. 12)*

Livia (58 B.C.–A.D. 29) Wife of **Augustus** and mother of Tiberius, his successor. As one of Augustus's main advisers, she intrigued to secure the succession for Tiberius and was suspected of poisoning several family members, including Augustus himself. *(Ch. 6)*

Locarno, Treaty of (1925) Treaty that introduced a new, more conciliatory spirit in international affairs. France and Germany accepted the postwar border between them, and Germany was again accepted as a diplomatic equal and entered the League of Nations in 1926. *(Ch. 26)*

Locke, John (1632–1704) English philosopher. In his influential *Two Treatises on Government,* Locke asserted that the state arises from a contract that individuals freely endorse. Therefore, because sovereignty resides with the people, rebellion against abuse of power is justified—a revolutionary vision of a political society based on human rights. See also **empirical reasoning.** *(Ch. 17)*

Louis XIV (r. 1643–1715) Longest-reigning ruler in European history, who imposed absolute rule on France and waged several wars attempting to dominate Europe. He was known as the Sun King, and his reign marked a great flowering of French culture. *(Ch. 16)*

Loyola, Ignatius (1491–1556) Spanish nobleman and founder of the Society of Jesus, or Jesuits, which has been called the vanguard of the Catholic reform movement. After papal approval of the order, the Jesuits focused primarily on educating Catholics and reconverting Protestants. *(Ch. 14)*

Luther, Martin (1483–1546) German theologian and religious reformer. Luther began the Protestant Reformation in 1517

with the publication of his *Ninety-Five Theses,* which challenged indulgences and Catholic teachings on penitential acts. His translation of the Bible into German in 1522 standardized the modern German language. See also **Augsburg Confession, justification by faith, sola scriptura.** *(Ch. 14)*

Maastricht agreement (1991) Agreement among twelve European Community countries at Maastricht, the Netherlands, to form the **European Union.** The member states agreed to expand cooperation on social, foreign, judicial, and security matters and adopted a timetable for a common policy on workers' rights, a common currency (the **euro**), and a common central banking structure. *(Ch. 30)*

Maccabees Traditionalist Jews led by the Hasmonean family, who in 168 B.C. revolted against Hellenizing laws and influences. Their success is celebrated today during the Jewish holiday of Hanukkah. *(Ch. 4)*

Macedon Weaker, less culturally advanced state on Greece's northern border. It was unified and led to power by **Philip II** and **Alexander the Great**, who became rulers of Greece. *(Ch. 4)*

Machiavelli, Niccolò (1469–1527) Florentine politician and political theorist. His most famous work, *The Prince,* describes the methods a prince can use to acquire and maintain power. Often misunderstood as a defender of despotism, Machiavelli emphasized that a successful ruler needed to anticipate and consider the consequences of his actions. *(Ch. 12)*

Magellan, Ferdinand (1480?–1521) Portuguese-born Spanish explorer who led the first expedition to sail around the world. After finding the South American passage to the Pacific Ocean, he sailed to the Philippines, where he was killed by natives. Survivors on one of his ships completed the circumnavigation. *(Ch. 13)*

Maginot Line A 200-mile system of elaborate permanent fortifications on France's eastern border, named for war minister André Maginot, and built primarily during the 1930s. It was a defense against German frontal assault; in 1940 the Germans invaded by flanking the line. *(Ch. 26)*

Magna Carta (1215) Momentous document that England's barons forced King John to sign. It required the king to respect the rights of feudal lords, not abuse his judicial powers, and consult the barons—in essence, it put the king under the law, not above it. *(Ch. 9)*

manifest destiny Term coined in 1845 for the belief that the expanding United States was destined to occupy the North American continent from coast to coast. The rhetoric of manifest destiny was invoked to justify war with Mexico in 1846 and the acquisition of California and the southwest from Mexico in 1848. *(Ch. 22)*

manor In western Europe, a type of estate that developed under the Carolingians. One-quarter to one-half of the land was set aside as a reserve (or demesne), to be worked on behalf of the landlord; the remainder was divided into tenancies worked by individual peasants for their own support. *(Ch. 8)*

Maria Theresa (r. 1740–1780) Habsburg archduchess of Austria and queen of Hungary and Bohemia. After successfully defending her right to the Austrian throne against attacks by **Frederick the Great** and others, she reformed and centralized the administration of her Austrian and Bohemian lands. *(Ch. 18)*

Marxism Political and economic theories of the two German philosophers and revolutionaries, Karl Marx (1818–1883) and Friedrich Engels (1820–1895), which they called scientific **socialism** and which gave birth to modern communism. Marxism argued that the oppressed working class should and inevitably would rebel against the capitalist owners and build a communist society. *(Ch. 21)*

mass production System in which great numbers of people work in centralized, mechanized **factories** to produce large quantities of goods; an essential feature of **industrialization**. A series of eighteenth-century inventions, culminating in the **steam engine**, enabled Britain to mass-produce textiles and benefit from the resulting increases in productivity. *(Ch. 20)*

Matteotti murder The 1924 killing by fascist thugs of Italian moderate socialist Giacomo Matteotti after he denounced the fascist violence accompanying national elections. The public outcry following the murder eventually led **Mussolini** to commit to a more radical direction, which included the creation of a new fascist state. *(Ch. 26)*

mechanistic world-view Seventeenth-century philosophical view that saw the world as a machine that functions in strict obedience to physical laws, without purpose or will. Experience and reason were regarded as the standards of truth. *(Ch. 17)*

Mehmed II (r. 1451–1481) Ottoman sultan who completed the conquest of the Byzantine Empire by capturing Constantinople in 1453. Mehmed established Constantinople as the Ottoman capital and repopulated the city with a mix of Greek, Armenian, Jewish, and Muslim communities. *(Ch. 11)*

mercantilism Economic policy pursued by western European states in the seventeenth and eighteenth centuries, stressing self-sufficiency in manufactured goods, tight government control of trade to foster the domestic economy, protectionist policies, and the absolute value of bullion. *(Ch. 16)*

Minoans Society that flourished between 2000 and 1375 B.C. on the Aegean island of Crete, where Greece's first civilization appeared. Their sophisticated culture and economy were administered from their magnificent palaces. See also **Mycenaeans**. *(Ch. 2)*

mir Russian peasant commune. After Tsar Alexander II freed the serfs in 1861, the mir determined land use and paid the government mortgages and taxes. Peasants could leave the land only with the mir's permission. *(Ch. 22)*

monasticism Ascetic way of life. Christian monasticism was founded by an Egyptian layman, Anthony (d. 356), who renounced all worldliness and pursued a life of prayer in the desert. A more communal form of monasticism was created by Pachomius (290–346), who wrote the first monastic Rule—a code for daily living in a monastic community. Monasticism quickly spread throughout the Christian world. *(Ch. 7)*

monophysitism Fifth-century theological doctrine emphasizing the divine nature of **Jesus of Nazareth.** The Council of Chalcedon condemned monophysitism and pronounced that Christ had two authentic natures—he was true God and true man. *(Ch. 7)*

monotheism Belief that there is only one God. The Hebrew Bible places this belief as originating about 2000–1500 B.C., when God commanded Abraham to give up Mesopotamian polytheism for belief in one God. *(Ch. 2)*

More, Thomas (1478–1535) Chancellor of England under Henry VIII. More's best-known work, *Utopia,* was highly critical of contemporary European kingdoms. It describes a fictional land of peace and harmony that has outlawed private property and all forms of wealth. More was executed when he refused to take an oath to support the **Act of Supremacy.** See also **humanism.** *(Ch. 12)*

Muhammad (570–632) Prophet and founder of Islam. In 610 he began to receive revelations commanding him to teach all people a new faith that called for an unquestioned belief in one god, Allah, and a deep commitment to social justice for believers. Before his death, he had converted most of Arabia. See also **Five Pillars of Islam, Quran.** *(Ch. 8)*

Mussolini, Benito (1883–1945) Italian fascist dictator. Mussolini founded the fascist movement in 1919 and took power in 1922. He replaced Italy's parliamentary democracy with a **corporative state** and pursued an expansionist foreign policy. He concluded the Pact of Steel with **Adolf Hitler** in 1939 and took Italy into World War II in 1940. Deposed in 1943, he was killed by partisans in 1945. *(Ch. 26)*

Mycenaeans Militaristic people from the Greek mainland who conquered the **Minoans** around 1550–1375 B.C. Mycenaean civilization was a center of Bronze Age culture until its destruction around 1100 B.C. *(Ch. 2)*

mystery religions Popular Hellenistic cults featuring the initiation of worshipers into secret doctrines. Mystery religions replaced the traditional Greek religion of the Olympian gods. Some ancient Egyptian cults were recast as mystery religions, influencing early Christianity. *(Ch. 4)*

Napoleon Bonaparte (1769–1821) Emperor of the French (r. 1804–1815). A French general who took part in a coup in 1799 against the **Directory**, Napoleon consolidated power as first consul and proclaimed himself emperor with the approval of a national plebiscite in 1804. His military conquests exported French revolutionary reforms to the rest of Europe. He was finally defeated and exiled in 1815. *(Ch. 19)*

National Assembly (1789–1791) Legislative body formed in France in 1789 after the Third Estate insisted on being certified as members of the Estates General as a whole. The National Assembly drafted the **Declaration of the Rights of Man and the Citizen** and a constitution that called for a constitutional (not absolute) monarchy. *(Ch. 19)*

National Socialist (Nazi) Party The political party that grew from the movement that German dictator **Adolf Hitler** made his vehicle to power. Originating from the radical right in Munich in 1919, the Nazi Party won voting support during the early 1930s, paving the way for Hitler to be named German chancellor in 1933. *(Ch. 27)*

nationalism Belief arising in the eighteenth century that people derive their identity from their nation and owe it their primary loyalty. The criteria for nationhood typically included a common language, religion, and political authority, as well as common traditions and shared historical experiences. Nationalism was a major force in most of the revolutions of 1848 and in the subsequent unification of Italy and of Germany. *(Ch. 20)*

Nazi-Soviet Pact (1939) Surprise agreement between the Soviet Union and Nazi Germany in August 1939 that each would remain neutral if either got into a war with some other nation. The pact freed Germany to attack Poland a few days later without fear of Soviet reprisal. *(Ch. 27)*

Neo-Babylonians Rulers of western Asia between 612 and 539 B.C. who elaborately rebuilt Babylon, creating the famous Hanging Gardens. They destroyed Jerusalem, deporting many Judeans in what is known as the Babylonian Captivity. *(Ch. 2)*

Neolithic Revolution Human discovery and spread of agriculture, between about 13,000 and 5000 B.C. People first domesticated dogs and other animals and then learned how to cultivate crops. *(Ch. 1)*

New Economic Policy (NEP) (1921–1928) A Russian economic liberalization measure aimed at reviving an economy in crisis. The NEP restored considerable scope for private enterprise and allowed peasants to sell some of their harvest. After initial economic success, it was eventually considered a threat to the socialist state and was replaced by state-controlled central planning. *(Ch. 26)*

new imperialism Era of European overseas expansion launched in the 1880s. In the following decades, Europeans subjugated 500 million people in Africa and Asia—one half of the world's non-European population. *(Ch. 24)*

Newton, Isaac (1643–1727) English physicist, mathematician, and natural philosopher. Newton's mathematical computation of the laws of gravity and planetary motion, which he combined with a fully developed theory of inertia, completed the explanation for motion initiated by **Nicholas Copernicus.** See also **laws of motion.** *(Ch. 17)*

nongovernmental organizations (NGOs) A network of organizations unaffiliated with governments but central to the international community, such as the Red Cross, Amnesty International, and Doctors Without Borders, that had gradually emerged by the early twenty-first century to deal with humanitarian relief and human rights issues. *(Ch. 30)*

North Atlantic Treaty Organization (NATO) An alliance for regional defense, created in 1949 by the United States, Canada, and western European nations, whose members agree to defend one another from attack by nonmember countries. Its original aim was to contain the Soviet Union. *(Ch. 29)*

Nuremberg trials The war crimes trials conducted in Nuremberg, Germany. Most of the twenty-four defendants were convicted of war crimes and "crimes against humanity." *(Ch. 28)*

On the Donation of Constantine Work by Lorenzo Valla (1407–1457) proving that the *Donation of Constantine* was not written at the time of the emperor Constantine. The forged *Donation* purported to record Constantine's transfer to the pope of jurisdiction over Rome and the western half of the empire. Valla's work undermined the papacy's claim to political rule in central Italy. *(Ch. 12)*

Orthodoxy The Catholic Christian faith of Byzantium. It differed from Roman Catholicism by its use of Greek instead of Latin, the inclusion of icons in worship, an adherence to the Greek church fathers, some differences in basic theology, and many differences in customs and practices. *(Ch. 8)*

papacy Name for the institution ruled by the bishop of Rome who, in Roman Catholic tradition, is the successor to Peter, the most prominent apostle. Since Peter was believed to be the leader of the original followers of Christ, his successors, the popes (from *papa* by the fourth century), were believed to be the leaders of the whole church. *(Ch. 7)*

papal monarchy Period during the twelfth and thirteenth centuries when the power of the Catholic Church was increasingly expanded and centralized in the hands of the popes, as papal policy focused on recovering lost lands and rights in central Italy. *(Ch. 9)*

Papal States Beginning in the eighth century, territories held by the popes in central Italy under the protection of the Frankish kings. *(Ch. 8)*

papyrus Paperlike writing material used by the ancient Egyptians, Greeks, and Romans. Made primarily in Egypt from the papyrus plant, it was durable, flexible, and easy to write on. *(Ch. 1)*

Paris Commune (1871) Parisian workers' uprising intended to establish a workers' government under home rule. Stemming from labor discontent and the radicalization of workers during the siege of Paris in the Franco-Prussian War, the commune was suppressed by the army of the conservative French government. *(Ch. 22)*

Parliament English legislative institution whose ancestors were the royal courts that met in 1265 and 1295. The king considered the courts a device to win support for royal agendas; the barons viewed them as opportunities to play a real policymaking role in government. *(Ch. 9)*

paterfamilias Oldest living male in an ancient Roman family, who had supreme legal power within the household. Only the paterfamilias could own property free and clear. *(Ch. 5)*

Paul of Tarsus (d. ca. 67) Christian apostle and saint. A Jew from Anatolia and a Roman citizen, Paul first persecuted the Christians but became a believer around A.D. 36. Paul taught that the life and resurrection of **Jesus of Nazareth** offered all humanity the hope of salvation through faith. Under Paul, **Christianity** began its complete separation from Judaism. *(Ch. 6)*

pax Romana Latin for "Roman peace," the term refers to the period of peace and prosperity in the Roman Empire from A.D. 69 to 180. During this time the emperors emphasized extending citizenship and spreading prosperity throughout the provinces, and Italy was no longer the tyrant of the Mediterranean. See also **Flavians.** *(Ch. 6)*

Peace of Westphalia (1648) Treaty that ended the **Thirty Years' War.** The principalities within the Holy Roman Empire were recognized as virtually autonomous, severely weakening the power of the emperor. Calvinism joined Catholicism and Lutheranism as tolerated faiths within the empire, and the treaty closed the age of religious wars. *(Ch. 15)*

Pericles Leader of fifth-century-B.C. Athens when **demokratia** became entrenched as the government and way of life. Distinguished for his oratory and honesty, he established Athens as a great center of art and literature as well as a great empire. *(Ch. 3)*

Persian Empire Vast, prosperous, and law-abiding West Asian empire, from about 550 B.C. to its conquest by **Alexander the Great** around 330 B.C. The relatively tolerant rule of the Persian emperors represented the greatest success yet of a universal kingship. The Persians also built the first great navy. *(Ch. 2)*

Peter the Great (r. 1682–1725) Russian tsar. Brilliant, energetic, and tyrannical, Peter revolutionized Russian society by his determined efforts to westernize his nation culturally, economically, and politically. He modernized the army and navy, secured seaports, and made Russia into a great power. See also **Great Northern War.** *(Ch. 16)*

Petrarch, Francesco (1304–1374) Influential Italian poet, biographer, and humanist during the Renaissance. Petrarch advocated imitating the actions, values, and culture of the ancient Romans to reform the excesses of the present world. *(Ch. 12)*

Petrograd Soviet The *soviet* (council) of leaders of strike committees and army regiments elected in March 1917, when Petrograd's workers protested in response to severe wartime food and coal shortages. Central to the Bolshevik Revolution of 1917, the soviet eventually became the ruling power in the Russian capital—but only temporarily. *(Ch. 25)*

pharaoh Ancient Egyptians' title for their king, an absolute, all-powerful, and all-providing ruler. It was believed that the ruler represented the ancestors and guaranteed the fertility of the soil. *(Ch. 1)*

Philip II (382–336 B.C.) King of **Macedon.** A brilliant soldier and statesman, Philip conquered the Greek world. He developed a well-trained, professional year-round army and mastered the technology of siegecraft. He was succeeded by his son, **Alexander the Great.** *(Ch. 4)*

Philip II (r. 1556–1598) King of Spain, son of **Charles V.** An avid Roman Catholic, he ruled Spain at the height of its influence. Philip dispatched the ill-fated **Armada** to invade England and attempted to quash the revolt of the Netherlands. *(Ch. 15)*

philosophes Influential group of eighteenth-century French intellectuals, including **Voltaire** and Diderot, who argued that people have natural rights and that governments exist to guarantee and protect those rights. While not advocating violent revolution, they severely criticized the regime's abuses of power. *(Ch. 18)*

Phoenicians Canaanites whose civilization flourished about 1000–750 B.C. in present-day coastal Syria, where they established major trading ports. Master sailors, they planted colonies around the Mediterranean, many of which, including Carthage, became independent states. The Phoenicians exported the civilization of western Asia—including the Phoenician alphabet, derived from **Ugarit**—to the Mediterranean world. *(Ch. 2)*

plantation system Agricultural practices developed by the fifteenth-century Portuguese to produce sugar on their island colonies in the Atlantic using involuntarily transported slaves from Africa. Portugal's prototype—wealthy absentee landlords and masses of forced labor producing cash crops on vast tracts of land—was the model for the New World plantation system. In seventeenth- and eighteenth-century French and English colonies in the Caribbean, large sugar plantations owned by wealthy, often absentee, landlords replaced smaller-scale independent farming. *(Chs. 13, 16)*

Plato (427–348 B.C.) Ancient Greek philosopher, student of **Socrates.** One of Western philosophy's greatest exponents of idealism, Plato believed that the senses are misleading and that truth can therefore be attained only by training the mind to overcome commonsense evidence. In the *Republic,* Plato describes an ideal state in which philosophers rule as kings, benevolently and unselfishly. *(Ch. 3)*

polis Term for an ancient Greek city-state, a system that reached its height around 700–300 B.C. The ideological and political organization of the polis emphasized equality and a shared community life for all citizens, not just the elite. *(Ch. 3)*

popular front A term for antifascist electoral alliances and governing coalitions that communists promoted from 1934 until 1939 to resist the further spread of fascism. Popular front coalitions won control of government in both Spain and France during 1936. *(Ch. 27)*

positivism Philosophy of the French thinker Auguste Comte (1798–1857). Comte asserted that human history progressed through distinct and irreversible stages, leading inexorably upward to the final and highest stage of development, the positive—or scientific—stage. Positivism and its optimistic outlook for human progress were influential in both Europe and Latin America during the nineteenth century. *(Ch. 23)*

Potsdam conference A July–August 1945 meeting held at Potsdam, Germany, between the USSR, the United States, and Great Britain to implement their earlier agreements concerning the treatment of defeated Germany. Many of the agreements reached were later abandoned amid growing hostility between the USSR and the Western democracies. *(Ch. 28)*

Prague Spring The attempt by Czechoslovakian reformers in 1968 to gain freer cultural expression, democratization of Communist Party procedures, and broader participation in public life within the framework of a communist state. The forcible suppression of the movement by Soviet leaders seemed to signal the end of any hope for flexibility and openness within the Soviet sphere. *(Ch. 29)*

price revolution Steady rise in prices in the sixteenth and seventeenth centuries, resulting from population growth and the influx of precious metals from Spain's New World territories. As wages lost one-tenth to one-fourth of their value, people sought new work, protested against taxes, and attacked scapegoats. The price revolution concentrated wealth in fewer hands and contributed to the rise of a new **gentry** class. *(Ch. 15)*

Principate The constitutional monarchy of the Early Roman Empire, from 31 B.C. to A.D. 192. The term comes from *Princeps,* or "first citizen," an old title of respect used in the **senate.** See also **Augustus, Flavians.** *(Ch. 6)*

professionalization Establishment in the nineteenth century of common standards and requirements, especially in medicine, law, architecture, and engineering. Professionalization brought either government or self-regulation to vocations whose prestige rested on the claim of exclusive expertise in their fields. *(Ch. 23)*

proletariat Term used by Karl Marx to describe the new class of industrial workers who owned none of the means of production and were totally dependent on factory owners for their livelihoods. In Marxist thought, capitalists were destined to be overthrown by the proletariat. See also **Marxism.** *(Ch. 20)*

provisional government The body that ruled Russia from March to November 1917, in the wake of the revolution that overthrew the tsarist regime. Originally intended to be a temporary step to an elected constituent assembly, its policies caused discontents that the **Bolsheviks** were quick to exploit. *(Ch. 25)*

Ptolemies Dynasty of Egyptian kings who ruled from 304 to 30 B.C., founded by Ptolemy I, a Macedonian general of **Alexander the Great.** It was the wealthiest, most sophisticated, and longest lasting of the Hellenistic kingdoms. See also **Alexandria.** *(Ch. 4)*

Punic Wars (264–146 B.C.) Three wars during which the Roman Empire eventually destroyed Carthage. The Romans later adopted the Carthaginians' plantation system using massive numbers of slaves. *(Ch. 5)*

Puritans Radical Protestants in late-sixteenth- and seventeenth-century England. Puritans emphasized Bible reading, preaching, private scrutiny of conscience, and de-emphasized institutional ritual and clerical authority. Puritans became a majority in Parliament during the reign of Charles I and led the campaign against the king during the English Civil War. *(Ch. 15)*

putting-out system The production in country homes of thread and cloth by spinners and weavers for an entrepreneur who bought raw materials and "put them out" to be finished by individual workers. This cottage industry system expanded in eighteenth-century Europe as increased numbers of agricultural laborers needed more nonfarm work in off-seasons. *(Ch. 18)*

Quran Islamic sacred writings, which **Muhammad** communicated in the form of "recitations," insisting that he was transmitting a direct revelation from Allah. After Muhammad's death, his followers arranged the recitations into 114 *Suras*, or chapters, containing legal and wisdom literature and moral teaching. *(Ch. 8)*

rabbinic Judaism Main form of Judaism, which emerged during the first century A.D. under the leadership of the rabbis, the spiritual descendants of the Pharisees. Rabbinic Judaism amplified and interpreted the Hebrew Bible to clarify Jewish practice, elevated the oral law to equal authority with the written **Torah**, and enabled Judaism to evolve flexibly. *(Ch. 6)*

Realpolitik Style of governing that uses all means, including war, to expand the influence and power of a state. The best-known practitioner of Realpolitik was Prussian chancellor **Otto von Bismarck.** *(Ch. 22)*

Reconquista Wars of reconquest in the Iberian Peninsula from the eleventh to fifteenth centuries. Spanish and Portuguese rulers seized territories from the weakening Muslim regime. By awarding reconquered lands to their nobles, Christian kings enhanced their own status and power. *(Ch. 9)*

remilitarization of the Rhineland The reoccupation of Germany's Rhineland territory by German troops in March 1936, in clear violation of the **Treaty of Versailles.** When the French and British did not resist the German move, **Adolf Hitler** was emboldened to additional acts of aggression elsewhere. *(Ch. 27)*

res publica Romans' concept of their republic, which uniquely influenced Western political institutions. *Res publica* is Latin for "public thing," as opposed to *res privata*, "private thing," as the Romans characterized monarchy. *(Ch. 5)*

revisionism Late-nineteenth-century argument that **socialism** could and should come about by gradual, democratic means. This idea was a "revision" of Marx's contention that socialism would require a violent revolution. Most European socialists claimed to reject revisionism while at the same time pursuing revisionist policies. *(Ch. 24)*

risorgimento Italian term, beginning in the late eighteenth century, for the political and cultural renewal of Italy. It later came to describe the political and military events that led to the unification of Italy in 1861. *(Ch. 22)*

Robespierre, Maximilien (1758–1794) French lawyer and revolutionary leader. A **Jacobin** who joined the Committee of Public Safety in 1793, Robespierre called for the **Terror** to suppress internal dissent. *(Ch. 19)*

Romanesque Meaning "in the Roman style," this nineteenth-century term characterized the transitional architecture and painting of the period between the waning of Carolingian art and the full emergence of **Gothic** art in the twelfth century. Distinctive features of Romanesque churches are their exuberant decoration and ornament. *(Ch. 10)*

romanticism Artistic movement, prevalent from the 1760s to 1840s, that rebelled against rationalism. Writers, painters, and composers rejected the Enlightenment and its rationalist values, instead praising emotion and sensitivity, and worshiping nature for its inherent beauty. *(Ch. 20)*

Rome-Berlin Axis Alliance between Hitler's Nazi Germany and Mussolini's fascist Italy. Beginning as an informal understanding by 1936, it was cemented by an anti-Comintern agreement and eventually by an open-ended military alliance, the Pact of Steel, in 1939. *(Ch. 27)*

Roosevelt, Franklin Delano (1882–1945) U.S. president who served from 1933 to 1945, through the Great Depression of the 1930s and World War II. His New Deal program, including large public works projects, was an innovative response to the Depression. *(Ch. 28)*

Rousseau, Jean-Jacques (1712–1778) French writer and philosopher. In his 1762 work, *The Social Contract*, Rousseau depicted a hypothetical state with direct democracy in which citizens have inalienable rights to wide-ranging liberties. He was influential as a critic of an elite society still dominated by status, patronage, and privilege. *(Ch. 18)*

salons Regular gatherings in eighteenth-century Parisian private homes, where **Voltaire** and other **philosophes** read and discussed their works in progress, with the exchange of ideas facilitated by female *salonnières* (salon leaders). Anyone with appropriate manners could participate as an equal, enabling conversation to shift from maintaining the status quo to questioning it. *(Ch. 18)*

sans-culottes Ordinary citizens of revolutionary Paris, whose derisive nickname referred to their inability to afford fashionable knee pants ("culottes"). Because of their effective political organization, they were able to influence the direction of the French Revolution through pressure on the government as well as direct action, such as to overthrow the monarchy in August 1792. *(Ch. 19)*

Sappho (fl. ca. 625 B.C.) Ancient Greek poet from the island of Lesbos. Sappho wrote odes, wedding songs, and hymns expressing intimate feelings, including love for other women. She wrote of female sexuality in a male-dominated culture. *(Ch. 3)*

second industrial revolution Interrelated economic changes that resulted in a significant speedup in production in western Europe after 1850. Key factors were the introduction of new products, new methods of manufacture, and new materials such as mass-produced steel, synthetic dyes, and aluminum. *(Ch. 23)*

Second International International socialist organization founded in 1889 that met yearly to debate issues of broad concern. Beginning in 1907, it called for workers to strike and to refuse military service in case of international conflict. *(Ch. 24)*

Second Reform Bill (1867) British legislation that extended suffrage by lowering property qualifications and set equal population requirements for all parliamentary districts. The legislation bolstered the existing system, as the newly enfranchised clerks, artisans, and other skilled workers felt more a part of society. *(Ch. 22)*

Seleucids Dynasty of rulers of Asia Minor from 312 to 64 B.C. Founded by Seleucus (ca. 358–281 B.C.), a general of **Alexander the Great**, the kingdom spread **Hellenism** by establishing seventy colonies throughout the Near East. *(Ch. 4)*

senate In the ancient Roman Republic and Empire, the powerful council of elders that advised the monarchs (Latin: *senatus*, from *senex*, "old man"). Romans spoke of the senate's *auctoritas*, a quasi-religious prestige. *(Ch. 5)*

separate spheres Notion, especially prevalent in the mid-nineteenth century, of two distinct sets of roles—one male and public, the other female and private. While the man was out in the world advancing his career, the bourgeois woman was to run her home, providing her family with an orderly, comfortable shelter. *(Ch. 23)*

show trials Trials staged for ideological and propaganda reasons in the USSR. In the most famous, orchestrated by **Joseph Stalin** from 1936 to 1938, major communist figures were made to confess to trumped-up charges and executed. These trials helped persuade Soviet citizens that a high-level conspiracy was responsible for the USSR's economic woes. *(Ch. 27)*

Sistine Chapel Chapel at the Vatican Palace commissioned by Pope Sixtus IV in 1475, best known for Michelangelo's magnificent paintings of the Creation and Last Judgment. The monument vividly captures the cultural, religious, and ideological program of the papacy. *(Ch. 12)*

Smith, Adam (1723–1790) Scottish economist who developed the doctrine of **laissez faire.** In his treatise *The Wealth of Nations* (1776), Smith argued that an economy regulates itself better without interference by government and without monopolies and other economic privileges. Smith suggested that people's economic activities are often "led by an invisible hand" to benefit society as a whole. *(Ch. 18)*

social Catholics Catholics in western Europe who believed that society bore responsibility for the well-being of the poor. They were following the ideas set out in 1891 by Pope Leo XIII (r. 1878–1903) in his encyclical *Rerum novarum* ("Of New Things"). *(Ch. 23)*

Social Darwinism Theory of social evolution first articulated by Herbert Spencer (1820–1902). According to Social Darwinists, human societies evolve in the same way as plants and animals, and the weak, poor, and improvident are not worthy of survival. Social Darwinism was used to justify callousness toward the poor at home and imperialist conquest abroad. See also **Darwinism.** *(Ch. 23)*

social market economy The late-twentieth-century socially-oriented model of capitalism practiced in continental western Europe, providing a substantial safety net in health care and a commitment to public services such as transportation and day care. It competed with the U.S. model, shared by Britain, which emphasized free enterprise. *(Ch. 30)*

socialism Nineteenth-century economic and social doctrine and political movement that opposed private ownership and control of the means of production. Socialists believed that the "social" or state ownership of property, unlike private ownership, would benefit society as a whole, creating a more just system. *(Ch. 21)*

Society of Revolutionary Republican Women In revolutionary France, a powerful political club that represented the interests of female **sans-culottes.** The society was included in a general ban on political participation by women that the Committee of Public Safety instituted in October 1793. *(Ch. 19)*

Socrates (469–399 B.C.) Ancient Greek philosopher, a founder of the Western philosophical tradition. Socrates changed the emphasis of philosophy from the natural world to human ethics. He believed that no one who truly understood goodness would ever choose to do evil. Accused of being an atheist and corrupting the young, Socrates was executed in 399. Socrates' teachings were recorded and transmitted by his students, including **Plato**. *(Ch. 3)*

sola scriptura Doctrine put forward by **Martin Luther** in *On the Babylonian Captivity of the Church* (1520) that church authority had to be based on biblical teachings. In particular

he argued that the sacraments of the Catholic Church—other than baptism and communion—were not found in the Bible. *(Ch. 14)*

solidarism Late-nineteenth-century policy of conservative and liberal parties to blunt the appeal of socialism. Solidarism emphasized the mutual responsibility of classes and individuals for one another's well-being and led to the passage of laws and benefits to improve the lot of the working class. *(Ch. 23)*

Solidarity A trade union formed from a movement of shipyard workers in communist Poland in 1980. It became the nucleus of widespread demands for change—including independent labor organizations, the right to strike, and freedom of expression. Though forced underground in 1981, the movement eventually proved crucial to the downfall of the communist regime in Poland. *(Ch. 29)*

Solon (ca. 630–560 B.C.) Statesman of early Athens. Appointed to a one-year term as sole archon in 594 B.C., Solon transformed Greek society through mediation, moderation, respect for law, and measures that liberated the poor and downtrodden. His economic reforms sparked a commercial boom. *(Ch. 3)*

Spanish Inquisition Church court that began in 1478 when King Ferdinand and Queen Isabella obtained papal approval to control the grand inquisitor. The Spanish Inquisition investigated and condemned many former Jews and Muslims who were believed to have insincerely converted to Christianity. It became an important and lucrative instrument to expand state power. *(Ch. 11)*

SS (*Schutzstaffel*) Nazi elite troops, led by Heinrich Himmler. Linked to the Gestapo, the secret political police, the SS specialized in institutionalized terror tactics and were responsible for some of the worst atrocities of the Nazi regime. *(Ch. 27)*

"stab in the back" myth The notion, widely held among Germans after their unexpected loss in World War I, that political intrigue and revolution at home had sabotaged the German military effort. It helped alienate Germans from their new democratic government. *(Ch. 25)*

Stalin, Joseph (1879–1953) Soviet dictator. Secretary of the Communist Party since 1922, Stalin outmaneuvered his rivals after the death of Lenin to take control of the Soviet government by 1929. Stalin jettisoned the **New Economic Policy** and instituted a program of crash industrialization and agricultural **collectivization.** He concluded the **Nazi-Soviet Pact** in 1939 but joined the Allies after the German invasion of the Soviet Union in 1941. Victorious in World War II, Stalin sponsored the takeover of governments in eastern Europe by communist regimes, contributing to the development of the **cold war.** See also **"the Great Patriotic War," gulag, Potsdam conference, show trials, Yalta conference.** *(Ch. 26)*

Stalingrad (1942–1943) Decisive World War II battle. The Soviet Union, at immense cost in lives, launched repeated counterattacks on Germany's Sixth Army, stopping it from advancing farther and finally forcing it to surrender. The battle is often considered the turning point of World War II in Europe. *(Ch. 28)*

steam engine Machine invented in England in its modern form by James Watt in 1777. The steam engine provided mechanized power for manufacturing and made **factories** and **mass production** possible. *(Ch. 20)*

Stoics Believers in a philosophical system begun in Athens by Zeno (335–263 B.C.). Stoicism emphasized the pursuit of wisdom, the reliability of sensory experience, and freedom from all passion. Stoics focused on intentions as well as the results of actions. *(Ch. 4)*

Streseman, Gustav (1878–1929) German statesman of the Weimar Republic. Leader of the conservative German People's Party, Streseman served briefly as chancellor in 1923, then as foreign secretary from 1923 to 1929. He secured a reduction of Germany's reparations payments and negotiated the **Treaty of Locarno,** paving the way for Germany's entry to the League of Nations in 1926. His death in 1929 was a blow to hopes for the development of democracy in Germany and peace in Europe. *(Ch. 26)*

Suez crisis (1956) Crisis prompted by Egypt's nationalization of the British-owned Suez Canal. The effort of Britain, France, and Israel to seize the canal prompted a strong negative reaction in world opinion, forcing them to withdraw. The episode demonstrated the newly limited reach of the western European powers in world affairs. *(Ch. 29)*

suffragists Activists who, beginning in the late nineteenth century, organized to win the vote for women. Adopting increasingly violent tactics, English suffragists (often referred to by contemporaries as "suffragettes") endured attacks by male thugs, were arrested, engaged in hunger strikes, and were force-fed. *(Ch. 24)*

Sumerians Dominant inhabitants of Mesopotamia in the third millennium B.C. They established the world's first civilization, thirty flourishing city-states with a common culture, commerce, and tendency to make war on one another. *(Ch. 1)*

summa An encyclopedic compendium of carefully arrayed knowledge on a particular subject. Examples are the two most famous works of **Thomas Aquinas,** the *Summa Contra Gentiles* and the *Summa Theologiae. (Ch. 10)*

surrealism A movement in literature and the visual arts that emerged in Paris in the early 1920s. Though indebted to dada and its mocking defiance of convention, surrealism sought to find something positive by exploring the realm of the subconscious, partly by following the insights of **Sigmund Freud**'s insights about access to the subconscious. *(Ch. 26)*

Tacitus, Cornelius (ca. A.D. 55–120) Roman historian of the "Silver Age." Tacitus lauded the simple virtues of the German tribes and expressed nostalgia for the Republic. His greatest works were *The Histories,* on the civil wars of A.D. 69, and *The Annals,* chronicling the emperors from Tiberius through Nero. *(Ch. 6)*

Tanzimat Turkish term, meaning "restructuring," for the reform movements in the Ottoman Empire beginning in 1839. Reforms included security of property, equity in taxation, and equality before the law regardless of religion. Government officials were given fixed salaries and subjected to regular inspections. *(Ch. 22)*

Tennis Court Oath (1789) Pledge signed by all but one Third Estate deputy of the Estates General of France on June 20, 1789. The deputies swore to continue to meet until a constitution was drafted. *(Ch. 19)*

Terror (1793–1794) Systematic repression of internal enemies undertaken by revolutionary tribunals across France at the urging of **Maximilien Robespierre.** Approximately fourteen thousand people were executed, including aristocrats, **Girondins,** and **sans-culottes.** The Terror ended with the arrest and execution of Robespierre in July 1794. *(Ch. 19)*

tetrarchy Government ruled by four leaders. Emperor Diocletian established a tetrarchy in about 293 to address the Roman Empire's political instability, huge size, and complexity, as well as to promote experienced men and provide an orderly imperial succession. *(Ch. 7)*

third-century crisis Period from A.D. 235 to 284, when the Roman Empire suffered barbarian invasions, domestic economic problems, plague, assassinations, and urban decline. Attempting to fend off invasions at opposite fronts, the emperors devalued the currency, leading to massive inflation. *(Ch. 6)*

Third Estate In France, the common people, as distinct from the nobles (First Estate) and clergy (Second Estate). In the Estates General in 1789, it was presumed that the votes of the First and Second Estates would overrule those of the Third Estate, although the commoners vastly outnumbered the nobles and clergy. *(Ch. 19)*

Thirty Years' War (1618–1648) Destructive war, involving most European countries but fought in Germany, resulting from sixteenth-century religious tensions, regionalism versus centralizing forces, and dynastic and strategic rivalries between rulers. See also **Peace of Westphalia.** *(Ch. 15)*

Thucydides (ca. 455–397 B.C.) Ancient Greek historian; with **Herodotus,** a founder of history-writing in the West. A failed Athenian general, Thucydides made a careful study of the Peloponnesian War and prided himself on the accuracy of his account of the prolonged conflict. *(Ch. 3)*

Torah First five books of the Bible. Accepted as sacred by the Hebrews around 425 B.C., it relates the working out of God's pact, or **covenant,** with the Hebrews, his chosen people. *(Ch. 2)*

total war The concept, first associated with World War I, that war requires the mobilization of all a nation's resources and energies. The unexpected need to wage total war during World War I accelerated social and economic processes, from technological development to women's suffrage. *(Ch. 25)*

Toussaint-Louverture, François (1743–1803) Former slave who governed the island of Saint Domingue (Haiti) as an independent state after the slave revolt of 1791. In 1802 French forces captured Toussaint-Louverture, who died in prison. *(Ch. 19)*

trading-post empire Commercial system developed by Portugal in the sixteenth century to dominate trade in the Indian Ocean through fortified, strategically placed naval bases. All merchants were expected to acquire export licenses and ship products through Portuguese ports. *(Ch. 13)*

tragedy Serious play with an unhappy ending. Greek tragedy emerged and reached its height in the fifth century B.C. in the works of Aeschylus, Sophocles, and Euripides. The essence of Greek tragedy is the nobility in the spectacle of a great man or woman failing because of a "fatal flaw," but learning from failure. *(Ch. 3)*

trasformismo System of political manipulation used by Count Camillo di Cavour (1810–1861), Piedmont's prime minister, to create majorities in parliament to support his cabinet. The practice of using cajolery and bribery to transform foes into supporters would continue to characterize Italian government in the late nineteenth century. *(Ch. 22)*

Triple Alliance Military alliance established in 1882 among Germany, Austria-Hungary, and Italy to counter the Franco-Russian Alliance (later the **Triple Entente**). The system of rival alliances contributed to the escalation of international tensions. *(Ch. 24)*

Triple Entente Military alliance between Great Britain, France, and Russia, completed in 1907, countering the

Triple Alliance. The system of rival alliances eventually brought all of Europe into World War I. *(Ch. 24)*

triumph Elaborate procession through the streets of ancient Rome. Triumphs were voted by the **senate** to salute a general's victory over a foreign army. *(Ch. 5)*

Truman Doctrine The U.S. policy of containment, or limiting communist expansion, as outlined by President Harry Truman in 1947. Intended most immediately to deter any communist designs on Greece or Turkey, the doctrine was used thereafter to support any country that the United States considered threatened by communism during the **cold war.** *(Ch. 28)*

Ugarit Cosmopolitan port on northern Syria's Mediterranean coast that was a thriving trading center, especially around 1400–1200 B.C. The alphabet invented by Ugaritic scribes is the source of today's widely used Roman alphabet. *(Ch. 1)*

United Nations International organization of nations founded in 1945 to encourage peace, cooperation, and recognition of human rights. The major powers—China, France, Great Britain, the Soviet Union, and the United States—were given a privileged position as permanent members of the Security Council, each with veto power. *(Ch. 28)*

utilitarianism Political theory of Jeremy Bentham (1748–1832). Bentham argued that the purpose of government is to provide "the greatest happiness of the greatest number" and that the test of government is its usefulness. Democracy was implicit in Bentham's philosophy: the greatest number could ensure its own happiness only by voting for its rulers. *(Ch. 21)*

Vasco da Gama (1460?–1524) Pioneering Portuguese explorer and trader whose voyage from 1497 to 1499 around the Cape of Good Hope to Mozambique and India inaugurated a four-hundred-year-long Portuguese presence in the Indian Ocean region. *(Ch. 13)*

vassal Drawing on both Roman and Germanic customs, vassalage linked two men—lord and vassal—in an honorable, reciprocal bond based on loyalty and service. Eventually leading nobles and their vassals formed a social and political elite. *(Ch. 8)*

Versailles, Treaty of (1919) Peace treaty between the victorious Allies and defeated Germany after World War I. The harsh terms of this dictated peace produced a sense of bitterness and betrayal in Germany. *(Ch. 25)*

Vichy France The term for the repressive French government that followed the Third Republic after France's defeat by Nazi Germany in 1940. Headquartered in the resort town of Vichy, the government collaborated with the victorious Germans, who occupied Paris. *(Ch. 28)*

Victorian morality Nineteenth-century ethos wherein the values of the dominant middle class, which emphasized strict moral principles, especially regarding sex and drink, became the social norms. In Queen Victoria, who reigned for two-thirds of the century, the middle classes saw a reflection of their own values. *(Ch. 23)*

Virgil Roman poet whose works contributed to the Augustan renewal. In the *Eclogues,* Virgil (Publius Vergilius Maro, 70–19 B.C.) describes the blessings of peace under **Augustus**; in the *Georgics,* he glorifies Italian agriculture. His *Aeneid* mythologizes Rome and describes both the burden and glory of empire. *(Ch. 6)*

Visigoths Germanic people who served as allied troops for the Romans. When threatened by the Huns, the Visigoths crossed the Danube and settled in the Balkans. Eventually they sacked Rome in 410 and expanded their rule to parts of Spain and southern France. *(Ch. 7)*

Voltaire (François-Marie Arouet, 1694–1778) Prolific French writer, critic, and reformer who believed that literature should bring about social change. His satires and philosophical critiques targeted Christianity, intolerance, and tyranny. He embodied the spirit of eighteenth-century rationalism: its confidence, its increasingly practical bent, its wit and sophistication. *(Ch. 18)*

Vulgate Bible Latin version of new translations of the Hebrew Scriptures and Greek New Testament written by Jerome (331–420) for Pope Damasus. It was called the Vulgate because it was the Bible for the "people" (*vulgus*), whose language was Latin. *(Ch. 7)*

Warsaw Pact (1955–1991) Military-diplomatic alliance of Soviet bloc countries, created to counter NATO. The pact established a joint military command and mutual military assistance, as well as a new basis for the continuing presence of Soviet troops in the satellite states. See also **cold war.** *(Ch. 29)*

welfare state The concept, especially prevalent in western countries after World War II, that government should adopt large-scale social welfare measures, while maintaining a primarily capitalistic economy. Among the welfare measures usually adopted were a national health service, old-age pensions, and insurance against unemployment, sickness, and disability. *(Ch. 29)*

Weltpolitik Meaning "world politics," the term describes the policy pursued by Kaiser **Wilhelm II** (r. 1888–1918) to make Germany a world power, with colonies, a navy, and major influence among the Great Powers. The kaiser implemented his ambitious agenda with nationalistic appeals and bombastic threats. *(Ch. 24)*

Wilhelm II (r. 1888–1918) German kaiser (emperor) whose aggressive diplomatic, commercial, and military policies helped trigger World War I. His pursuit of *Weltpolitik* severely aggravated international tensions. See also *Weltpolitik.* *(Ch. 24)*

Yalta conference The meeting in February 1945 at Yalta, a Soviet Black Sea resort, between Stalin, Roosevelt, and Churchill. With Allied victory assured, they began outlining plans for the postwar order, including the military occupation of Germany. See also **Potsdam conference.** *(Ch. 28)*

Young Turks Term describing the young intellectuals who wanted to transform the Ottoman Empire into a more modern, Westernized state. Self-exiled in the late 1860s in Paris and London, they overthrew the sultan and seized power in 1908. The expression has subsequently come to designate any group of activists pushing for political change. *(Ch. 22)*

Zionism Nationalist Jewish movement. In the late nineteenth century, faced with growing **anti-Semitism**, some Jews argued that they would be safe only in their own nation. Zionism advocated establishing a Jewish state in the Jews' ancient homeland of Palestine, an idea that became reality with the creation of Israel in 1948. *(Ch. 24)*

Zoroastrianism Religion founded about 1000–550 B.C. by the Persian prophet Zarathustra (*Zoroaster* in Greek). Zoroastrians believe in a supreme deity and a cosmic contest between good and evil within each individual. *(Ch. 2)*

CREDITS

Chapter 1: Pages 19, 20, 24, 33: "King Hammurabi Dispenses Justice," "Heroism and Death in Mesopotamia," "Pharaoh the Divine and Invincible," "Prayers of a Hittite Queen," adapted from James B. Pritchard, ed., *Ancient Near Eastern Texts Relating to the Old Testament,* 3rd ed. Copyright © 1969 by Princeton University Press. Reprinted by permission of Princeton University Press. **Page 30:** "Egyptian Attitudes Toward Foreigners" from *Ancient Egyptian Literature, Volume 1,* by Miriam Lichtheim, University of California Press. Copyright © 1973. Reprinted by permission of the University of California Press.

Chapter 2: Pages 43, 46: "The Banquet of Ashurnasirpal II," "Cyrus and His Subjects' Gods" from James B. Pritchard, ed., *Ancient Near Eastern Texts Relating to the Old Testament,* 3rd ed. Copyright © 1969 by Princeton University Press. Reprinted by permission of Princeton University Press. **Page 46:** Ezra 1:1–3 from *Revised English Bible.* © Oxford University Press and Cambridge University Press 1989. **Page 52:** "The Covenant" from Deuteronomy 5:1–2, 6:1–3, 10:12–19, from *Revised English Bible.* © Oxford University Press and Cambridge University Press 1989. **Page 56:** "Ruth" from Ruth 1:1, 3–6, 8–9, 14–18, 2:1–3, 8–12 from *Revised English Bible.* © Oxford University Press and Cambridge University Press 1989. **Page 64:** "Greeks and Trojans" from *The Iliad of Homer,* translated by Richmond Lattimore. Copyright © 1951 by the University of Chicago Press. Reprinted by permission.

Chapter 3: Page 78: "Aristotle Complains" from *Aristotle, The Politics,* translated by Carnes Lord. Copyright © 1984 by the University of Chicago Press. Reprinted by permission. "Plutarch Counters" from *Plutarch on Sparta,* translated by Richard J. A. Talbert (Harmondsworth, England: Penguin Classics, 1988), p. 24. Translation copyright © Richard J. A. Talbert, 1988. Reproduced by permission of Penguin Books Ltd. **Page 82:** Quote by Sappho from *Ancient Greek Literature and Society,* Second Edition, by Charles Rowan Beye. Copyright © 1987 by Cornell University Press. Reprinted by permission. **Page 87:** "The Debate on Democracy" adapted from Euripides, "The Suppliant Women," translated by Frank Jones in *Euripides IV: The Complete Greek Tragedies,* edited by David Grene and Richmond Lattimore. Copyright © 1958 by the University of Chicago Press. Reprinted by permission. **Page 90:** "The Enemy as Barbarian" from *The Histories* by Herodotus, translated by Aubrey de Sélincourt, revised by A. R. Burn (Penguin Classics 1954, revised 1972), pp. 429, 550. Copyright © The Estate of Aubrey de Sélincourt, 1945. Copyright © A. R. Burn, 1972. Reprinted by permission of Penguin Books Ltd. **Page 92:** "Pericles' Funeral Oration" reprinted with the permission of The Free Press, a Division of Simon & Schuster, Inc., from *The Landmark Thucydides: A Comprehensive Guide to the Peloponnesian War* by Robert B. Strassler. Copyright © 1996 by Robert B. Strassler. **Page 97:** "Plato on Philosopher-Kings" from *Plato's Republic,* translated by G.M.A. Grube. Copyright © 1974 by Hackett Publishing Company. Reprinted by permission of Hackett Publishing Company, Inc. All rights reserved.

Chapter 4: Page 118: "Egyptians versus Greeks in a Temple" adapted from M. M. Austin, ed., *The Hellenistic World from Alexander to the Roman Conquest: A Selection of Ancient Sources in Translation.* Cambridge: Cambridge University Press, 1981. Reprinted with the permission of Cambridge University Press.

Chapter 5: Page 137: From *The Aeneid of Virgil,* trans. Allen Mandelbaum. Copyright © 1971 by Allen Mandelbaum. Reprinted by permission of Bantam Books, a division of Bantam, Doubleday, Dell Publishing Group, Inc. **Page 161:** "Tiberius Gracchus on Rome's Plight" from *Roman Civilization,* ed. Naphtali Lewis and Meyer Reinhold. © 1990 by Columbia University Press. Reprinted by permission of the publisher. **Page 165:** "Caesar on the Gauls" from Julius Caesar, *Seven Commentaries on the Gallic War with an Eighth Commentary by Aulus Hirtius,* translated by Carolyn Hammong. Copyright © 1996 Oxford University Press. By permission of Oxford University Press. **Page 167:** "Cicero in Defense of Milo" from *Selected Political Speeches of Cicero* by Cicero, translated by Michael Grant (Harmondsworth, England: Penguin Classics, 1969), pp. 232–234. Copyright © Michael Grant Publications Ltd, 1969. Reproduced by permission of Penguin Books Ltd.

Chapter 6: Page 177: "Augustus: The Official Story" from *Res Gestae Divi Augusti: The Achievements of the Divine Augustus,* edited by P. A. Brunt and J. M. Moore. Copyright © 1967. Reprinted by permission of Oxford University Press. **Page 178:** "Augustus: A Skeptical View" from Tacitus, *The Annals of Imperial Rome,* translated by Michael Grant (Penguin Classics, 1951, revised edition 1971). Copyright © 1956, 1959, 1971 by Michael Grant Publications Ltd. Reprinted by permission of Frederick Warne & Company (Penguin Books UK). **Page 187:** "Slaves With the Right Stuff" from *As the Romans Did: A Source Book in Roman Social History,* Second Edition, by Jo-Ann R. Shelton. Copyright © 1988, 1998 by Oxford University Press, Inc. Used by permission of Oxford University Press, Inc. **Page 190:** "Syria Between Rome and Persia" from *History of Ancient Iran,* translated by Richard N. Frye, Emeritus Professor of Iranian History, Harvard University (Munich: C.H. Beck'sche Verlagsbuchhandlung, 1984). Reprinted by permission of Richard N. Frye. **Page 196:** "Christian Community and Christian Relationships" from The Letter of Paul to the Ephesians 2:11–17, 5:21–6:9 from *Revised English Bible,* © Oxford University Press and Cambridge University Press 1989.

Chapter 7: Page 208: "A Contemporary View of Diocletian's Reforms" from *Roman Civilization,* ed. Naphtali Lewis and Meyer Reinhold. © 1990 by Columbia University Press. Reprinted by permission of the publisher. **Page 228:** "Basic Principles of Roman Law" from *Justinian's Institutes, 1.1–2.* Edited and translated by Peter Birks and Grant McLeod. Cornell University Press, 1987. Reprinted by permission of the publisher. **Page 234:** "The Moment of Augustine's Spiritual Awakening" from *Confessions of St. Augustine,* translated by Rex Warner, copyright © 1963 by Rex Warner, renewed © 1991 by F. C. Warner. Used by permission of Dutton Signet, a division of Penguin Putnam, Inc.

Chapter 8: Page 244: "The Message of the Quran" from *The Meaning of the Holy Qu'ran.* New edition with revised translation, commentary, and newly compiled comprehensive index by Abdullah Yusuf Ali. Amana Publications, 1988. **Page 260:** "A Contemporary Portrait of Charlemagne" from *Vie de Charlemagne*, 4th ed. By Eginhard, edited by Louis Halphen. Copyright © 1967. Reprinted by permission of Société d'Edition Les Belles Lettres. **Page 270:** "The Status of Carolingian Jews" from *Agobardi Lugdunensis Opear Omnia, Opusculum XI,* translated by W.L. North, edited by L. Van Acker, Corpus Christianorum. Copyright © 1981. Permission granted by Brepols Publishers, Turnhout (Belgium).

Chapter 9:   Page 283: "Two Views of Medieval Markets" adapted by Roy C. Cave and Herbert H. Coulson, *A Source Book for Medieval Economic History.* Reprinted by permission of Biblo & Tannen. **Page 299:** "Selections from Magna Carta" from *Magna Carta* by J.C. Holt (Cambridge, England: Cambridge University Press, 1969). Reprinted with the permission of Cambridge University Press. **Page 307:** "William of Rubruck Reports on the Mongols" from *The Mongol Mission* edited by Christopher Dawson. Sheed and Ward, 1953. **Page 310:** "An Arab Perspective on the First Crusade" from *Arab Historians of the Crusades* by Francesco Gabrieli. Selected and translated from the Arabic Sources by E.J. Costello. Copyright © 1969 by the University of California Press. Reprinted by permission of the University of California and the University of California Press.

Chapter 10:   Page 338: "The Making of a Saint and Scholar: Hildegard of Bingen" from *The Life of the Holy Hildegard,* 1.1 by Gottfried and Theodork, translated by James McGrath (Collegeville, Minn.: The Liturgical Press, 1995). Reprinted by permission of the publisher. **Page 343:** "Down there, around Ventadorn" from *The Lyrics of the Troubadour, Trouveres* by Frederick Goldin. Copyright © 1973 by Frederick Goldin. Reprinted by permission of Doubleday, a division of Random House, Inc.; "Friend, if you had shown consideration" from lyrics by Castellozza in *The Women Troubadours* by Meg Bogin (W. W. Norton, 1976). Copyright © 1976 by Magda Bogin. Reprinted by permission of Magda Bogin.

Chapter 11:   Page 366: "The Rising of 1381" from "The Anomialle Chronicle" in R.B. Dobson, *The Peasants' Revolt of 1381.* Reprinted by permission of Macmillan Ltd. Copyright © 1970 by The Macmillan Press Ltd. **Page 368:** "The Inquisition of Joan of Arc" from *The Trial of Jeanne d'Arc,* trans. W. P. Barrett (New York: Gotham House, 1932). **Page 373:** "The Black Death" from *Cronaca fiorentina* by Maarchione di Coppo Stefani, Rerun Italicarum Scriptores, Vol. 30, edited by Niccolo Rodolico. Citta di Castello: 1927. Translation by Duane Osheim. **Page 384:** "A Disputation" from Konstantin Mihailovic, *Memoirs of a Janissary.* Translated by Benjamin Stolz. Commentary and notes by Svat Soucek. Ann Arbor, Mich: Joint Committee on Eastern Europe, American Council of Learned Societies; and the Department of Slavic Languages and Literatures, University of Michigan, 1975. Used by permission.

Chapter 12:   Page 397: "Petrarch Responds to His Critics" from Petrarch, "Oh His Own Ignorance and That of Many Others," in *The Renaissance Philosophy of Man,* edited by Ernst Cassirer, Paul Oskar Kristeller, and John H. Randall. Copyright © 1948 by the University of Chicago Press. Reprinted by permission. **Page 400:** "Cassandra Fedele Defends Liberal Arts for Women" from *Her Immaculate Hand: Selected Works by and about the Women Humanists of Quattrocento Italy* by M. L. King and A. Rabil. Published by Medieval and Renaissance Texts and Studies, Center for Medieval and Early Renaissance Studies, State University of New York, Binghamton, N.Y. Used by permission. **Page 408:** Poem by Michelangelo from *The Italian Renaissance Reader* by Julia Bondanella and Mark Musa. Copyright © 1987 by Julia Conaway Bondanella and Mark Musa. Used by permission of Dutton Signet, a division of Penguin Putnam, Inc. **Page 416:** "A Pilgrimage for Religion's Sake" from Erasmus, *Ten Colloquies,* translated by Craig

R. Thomson. Copyright © 1986. Reprinted by permission of Pearson Education, Inc., Upper Saddle River, NJ 07458. **Page 421:** "Isabella d'Este Orders Art" from "Isabella d'Este, Patron of the Arts" from David S. Chambers, *Patrons and Artists in the Italian Renaissance.* Copyright © 1970 by Macmillan, Ltd. Reprinted by permission of the publisher.

Chapter 13:   Page 440: "Albuquerque Defends the Portuguese Empire" from *Albuquerque: Caesar of the East* edited by T.F. Earle and J. Villiers. Copyright © 1990 by Aris and Phillips. Reprinted by permission of the publisher.

Chapter 14:   Page 467: "Martin Luther's Address to the Christian Nobility of the German Nation" from "Three Treatises" by Martin Luther in *The American Edition of Luther's Works.* Copyright © 1943 Muhlenberg Press. Used by permission of Augsburg Fortress. **Page 484:** "The Conversion of Jeanne d'Albert." Reprinted by permission of the publishers from *Queen of Navarre: Jeanne D'Albert, 1528–1572* by Nancy L. Roelker, Cambridge, Mass.: Harvard University Press, Copyright © 1968 by Nancy L. Roelker.

Chapter 15:   Page 512: "Secret Dispatches from the Venetian Ambassador in Spain" from *Pursuit of Power: Venetian Ambassador's Reports* by James C. Davis, Editor & Translator. English translation copyright © 1970 by James C. Davis. Reprinted by permission of HarperCollins Publishers, Inc. **Page 515:** "A Justification of Rebellion Against the King" from Laski: *A Defense of Liberty Against Tyrants,* Peter Smith Publisher, Inc., Gloucester, Mass., 1963. **Page 530:** "Montaigne Discusses Barbarity in the New World and the Old" from *The Complete Essays of Montaigne* translated by Donald M. Frame, Stanford University Press, 1948. Reprinted by permission of the publisher. **Page 531:** Lines 40–50 from *Richard II,* Act II, Scene I, in *The Riverside Shakespeare,* edited by G. Blakemore Evans. Copyright © 1997 by Houghton Mifflin Company. Reprinted by permission of the publisher.

Chapter 16:   Page 544: "A Courtier Criticizes the King" from Louis, duc de Saint-Simon, *Versailles, the Court and Louis XIV,* ed. Lucy Norton (New York : Harper and Row, 1966), pp 248–251. **Page 550:** "The Putney Debates" from "The Levellers" in *The English Revolution,* edited by G.E. Aylmer (Cornell University Press 1975). Copyright Thames & Hudson Ltd. Reprinted by permission of Doubleday, a division of Random House, Inc. **Page 565:** "Global Encounters: Journal of a Dutch Slave Ship" from *New Netherlands Documents,* v. 17 edited by Charles T. Gehring and J.A. Schiltkamp. Used by permission from the *New Netherland Project,* The New York State Library.

Chapter 17:   Page 581: "Galileo Reassures a Patron" from *Discoveries and Opinions of Galileo* by Galileo Galilei, translated by Stillman Drake, copyright © 1957 by Stillman Drake. Used by permission of Doubleday, a division of Random House, Inc. **Page 595:** "Jesuits and Astronomy in China" from *China in the Sixteenth Century* by Matthew Ricci, translated by Louis J. Gallagher, S.J., copyright 1942, 1953 and renewed 1970 by Louis J. Gallagher, S.J. Used by permission of Random House, Inc.

Chapter 18:   Page 607: "Voltaire on Britain's Commercial Success" from *Philosophical Letters: Voltaire,* edited and translated by Ernest Dilworth. Copyright © 1961. Reprinted by permission of Prentice-Hall, Inc., Upper Saddle River, N.J. **Page 610:** "Rousseau Discusses the Benefits of Submitting to the General Will" from *The Social Contract* by Jean-Jacques Rousseau, translated by Maurice Cranston. Reprinted by permission of PFD on behalf of The Estate of Maurice Cranston. Copyright © 1968 by Maurice Cranston.

Chapter 19:   Pages 649, 655: "Lists of Grievances for the Estates-General" and "Declaration of the Rights of Woman" from *The*

INDEX

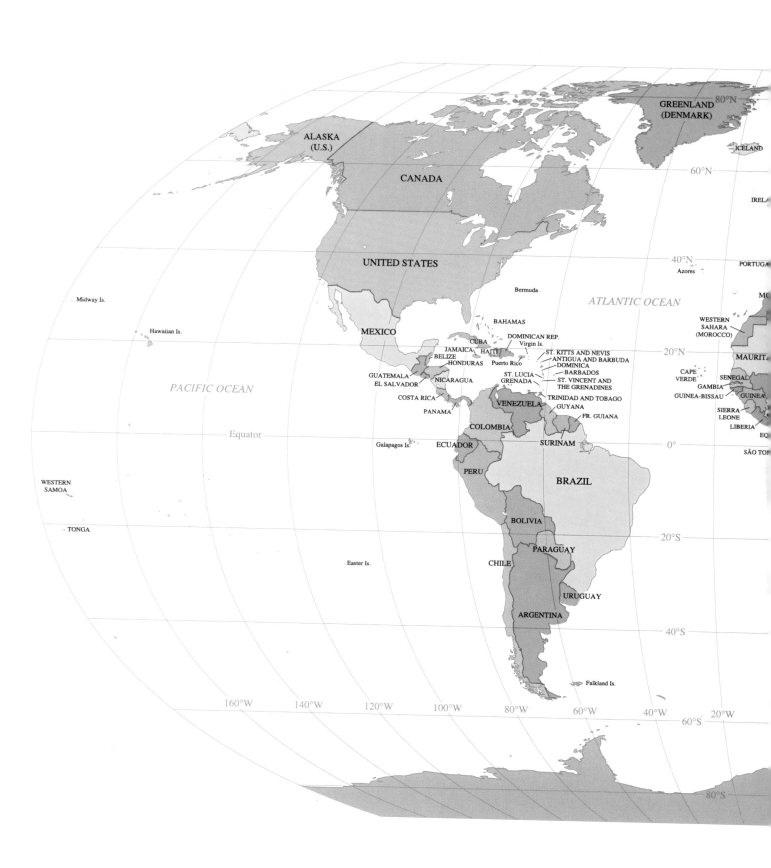